The Icon and the Axe

AN INTERPRETIVE HISTORY
OF RUSSIAN CULTURE

For Marjorie

ATLANTIC
OCEAN

ARCTIC OCEAN

· PETSAMO
Murmansk

· Pustozersk

NORWAY

0   MILES   250

Pechora River

SWEDEN

FINLAND

WHITE SEA
‡ SOLOVETSK

Kuopio

· Archangel
· Kholmogory

· Syktyvkar

*Lake
Vyg*
Vyg Commune
(Old Believers)

Severnaia Dvina River

Tampere

Petrozavodsk
VALAM·

*Lake
Onega*

Uppsala ·
Stockholm

Turku
Helsinki

*Lake
Ladoga*

· Veliky Ustiug

Tallinn
Narva

St. Petersburg

White Lake ST. CYRIL

SAVIOR-IN-
STONE

· Viatka

Tartu

Lake Peipus
*Lake
Pskov*

Novgorod

Lake Ilmen

· Vologda

BALTIC SEA

Riga

Pskov

VALDAI
HILLS

Dvina River

· Kostroma

Danzig ·
Königsberg

Tilsit
Kaunas

Polotsk

Smolensk

Tver·
ST. SERGIUS ‡

Yaroslavl
· Rostov
Suzdal
· Vladimir
Moscow
Murom

Nizhny Novgorod

· Kazan

Vilnius·
Minsk

Neman R.

BORODINO
(1812)

Volga

Riazan

Simbirsk

· Samara

POLAND

Warsaw

Vistula River

Brest-Litovsk

OPTYNA

Tula

Oka River

KULIKOVO
(1380)

· Tambov

Volga River

Cracow

Ostrog

Bug River

Kiev

Chernigov

Dnieper River

· Kursk

· Voronezh

Saratov

CARPATHIAN

Lwow

CZECHO-
SLOVAKIA

HUNGARY

Dniester River

Kharkov

POLTAVA
(1709)

Ekaterinoslav

Donets River

Don River

STALINGRAD (1942-1943)
× · Sarai
Sarepta (Golden Horde)
(German
Pietists)

MTS.

Jassy

Kishinev

Zaporozhian Sech
(Dnieper Cossacks)

Rostov on the Don
Azov·

Astrakhan

RUMANIA

Prut River

Odessa

Kherson

SEA OF
AZOV

CASPIAN
SEA

Belgrade ·

YUGO-
SLAVIA

Bucharest

*Mouth of
Danube*

Danube River

Sevastopol·
SEVASTOPOL
(1854-1855)

Bakhchisarai
(Crimean Tatars)

BULGARIA · Trnovo

BLACK SEA

CAUCASUS

THE EXPANSION OF
MODERN EUROPEAN RUSSIA

Tbilisi
·

Kura River

MTS.

Areas controlled by Moscow about 1300

1945 (after World War II)

1462 (accession of Ivan III)

1598 (accession of Boris Godunov)

Russian boundaries
after World War II

· Erivan

1725 (death of Peter the Great)

× Important battle sites

1815 (after final defeat of Napoleon)

‡ Monasteries

TURKEY

PREFACE

This is an interpretive history of modern Russian thought and culture. It is the product of one man's scholarship, reflection, and special interests. There is no illusion—and I hope no pretense—of offering an encyclopedic inventory of the Russian heritage or any simple key to understanding it. This is a selective account which seeks to provide new information and interpretation and not merely to codify an already established consensus: to open up rather than to "cover" this vast subject.

The period under consideration is the last six hundred years, during which Russia has emerged as a powerful, distinctive, creative civilization. The narrative will deal with some of the anguish and aspiration as well as the achievements of Russian culture; restless dissenters as well as ruling oligarchies; priests and prophets as well as poets and politicians. No attempt will be made to provide a complete picture of any individual cultural medium or personality, or to make the quantity of words devoted to a given subject a necessary index of intrinsic cultural quality. This work will draw on those materials which seem to illustrate best the distinctive central concerns of each era of Russian cultural development.

Two artifacts of enduring meaning to Russians—the icon and the axe—have been chosen for the title. These two objects were traditionally hung together on the wall of the peasant hut in the wooded Russian north. Their meaning for Russian culture will be set forth in the early pages of this book; they serve to suggest both the visionary and the earthy aspects of Russian culture. The eternal split between the saintly and the demonic in all human culture is, however, not provided in the Russian case by any simple contrast between holy pictures and unholy weapons. For icons have been used by charlatans and demagogues, and axes by saints and artists. Thus, the initial focus on these primitive artifacts contains a hint of the ironic perspective with which we shall end our examination of Russian culture. The title also serves to suggest that this is a work which will seek to locate and trace symbols that have played a unique role for the Russian imagination rather than examine Russian reality primarily in terms of the ideas, institutions, and art forms of the West.

The emphasis in this work is on the elusive world of ideas and ideals which Russians refer to as *dukhovnaia kul'tura:* a term far less narrowly religious in suggestion than its English equivalent of "spiritual culture." This work does not purport to relate ideology systematically to economic and social forces, or to prejudge the deeper question of the relative importance of material and ideological forces in history. It seeks only to establish more fully the historical identity of the spiritual and ideological forces which are recognized even by Marxist materialists in the USSR to have been of great importance in the development of their country.

This work does attempt in some measure to balance the frequent concentration on political and economic history by providing a general historical guide for the oft-visited but less charted terrain of thought and culture. The term "culture" is used here in its broad meaning of a "complex of distinctive attainments, beliefs, and traditions,"[1] and not in any of the more specialized senses in which "culture" is sometimes understood: as an early stage in social development that precedes the higher stage of civilization; as a quality of refinement nurtured in museums; or as a distinct type of accomplishment that can be altogether disembodied from its material context.[2] Within the general category of cultural history, which "concentrates upon the social, intellectual and artistic aspects or forces in the life of a people or nation,"[3] this work emphasizes the intellectual and artistic—dealing only incidentally with social history and hardly at all with sociological analyses.

The basic framework for this study is chronological sequence, which is as important in cultural history as in economic or political history. There will be flashbacks and anticipations—particularly in the first, background section; but the main concern is to provide in the sections that follow a chronological account of successive eras of Russian cultural development.

The second section portrays the initial confrontation of primitive Muscovy with the West in the sixteenth and the early seventeenth century. Then follow two long sections covering a century each: the third section dealing with the protracted search for new cultural forms in the rapidly growing empire of the seventeenth and the early eighteenth century; the fourth, with the brilliant if uneasy aristocratic culture that flowered from the mid-eighteenth to the mid-nineteenth century. Two final sections are devoted to the last hundred years, when the problems of industrialization and modernization have been superimposed on earlier patterns and problems of Russian cultural development. The fifth section deals with the richly creative and experimental era that began during the reform period of

Alexander II. The last section considers twentieth-century Russian culture in relation to that of the past.

There has been a kind of unity in most of Russian culture, a feeling that individual Russians and separate artistic forms are all in some sense subordinate participants in a common creative quest, philosophic controversy, or social conflict. To be sure, Mendeleev's chemistry, Lobachevsky's mathematics, Pushkin's poetry, Tolstoy's novels, Kandinsky's paintings, and Stravinsky's music can all be appreciated with relatively little reference to their Russian background or to criteria other than those of the particular scientific or artistic medium. But most of Russian culture—indeed much of that created by these truly European figures—acquires added meaning when set in the Russian context. Some understanding of the national context of individual creative activity is more necessary in the case of Russia than many other national cultures.

As a result of this feeling of common involvement and interdependence, the kind of debate that is usually conducted *between* individuals in the West often rages even more acutely *within* individuals in Russia. For many Russians "to think, feel, suffer, and understand are one and the same thing,"[4] and their creativity often bespeaks "a vast elemental strength combined with a relatively weak sense of form."[5] The exotic contours of St. Basil's Cathedral, the unorthodox harmonies of a Musorgsky opera, the impassioned vernacular of a Dostoevsky novel offend the classical spirit. Yet they speak compellingly to most men, reminding us that the alleged lack of form may be only nonconformity with the traditional categories used to analyze a culture.

As one looks at the history of Russian culture, it may be helpful to think of the forces rather than the forms behind it. Three in particular—the natural surroundings, the Christian heritage, and the Western contacts of Russia—hover bigger than life over the pages that lie ahead. These forces seem capable of weaving their own strange web of crisis and creativity out of the efforts of men. Usually they are working at cross-purposes, though occasionally—as in some fleeting moments in *Dr. Zhivago*—all three forces may seem to be in harmony.

The first force is that of nature itself. It has been said that Russia's thinkers are not formal philosophers but poets; and behind the apparently accidental similarity of the Russian words for "poetry" and "element" (*stikhi, stikhiia*) lie many intimate links between Russian culture and the natural world. Some speak of a "telluric" sense of communion with the earth alternating with a restless impulse to be *skitaltsy* or "wanderers" over the Russian land;[6] others of a peculiarly Russian insight in the poem in which a fetus asks not to be born, because "I am warm enough here."[7] The underground world of the mythological "damp mother earth" has beckoned in many forms from the first monastery in the caves of Kiev to the present-day shrine of the mummified Lenin and the gilded catacombs of the Moscow subway. Not only the earth, but fire, water, the sky—the other "elements" of medieval cosmology—have been important symbols for the Russian imagination; and even today the Russian language retains many earthy overtones that have been filtered out of more sophisticated European tongues.

A second supra-personal force behind modern Russian culture is that of Eastern Christendom. However fascinating pagan survivals, however magnificent earlier Scythian art, Orthodox Christianity created the first distinctively Russian culture and provided the basic forms of artistic expression and the framework of belief for modern Russia. The Orthodox Church also played a key role in infecting Russia with the essentially Byzantine idea that there is a special dignity and destiny for an Orthodox society and but one true answer to controversies arising within it. Thus, religion will play a central role in this narrative—not as an isolated aspect of culture but as an all-permeating force within it.

Along with nature and faith stands a third powerful force: the impact of the West. For the entire period of this chronicle, interaction with Western Europe was a major factor in Russian history. Russians have repeatedly sought to define this relationship, usually seeking a formula by which they could both borrow from and remain distinct from the West. The celebrated controversy between Slavophiles and "Westernizers" in the 1840's is but one episode in a long struggle. Here, as elsewhere, the self-conscious, intellectualized disputes of the nineteenth century will be placed in historical perspective by considering other Westernizing forces that have sought to determine the direction of Russian culture: Latinizers from Italy, pietists from Germany, "Voltairians" from France, and railroad builders from England. Particular attention will also be paid to those centers of Russian life which have provided a Western leaven within Russia: the real and remembered Novgorod and the majestic metropolis of St. Petersburg–Leningrad.

Many of the special emphases of this work are at variance with the general image currently reflected in either the formal interpretations of Soviet ideologists or the informal consensus of most Western intellectual historians. Specialists will be aware (and laymen should be alerted) that my interpretation includes among its unconventional and debatable features: a general stress on earlier (though not on the earliest) periods born of the belief that "all ages are equidistant from eternity" and that formative influences sometimes tell us more about later developments than immediately precedent circumstances; detailed immersion in certain critical and often neglected turning points, such as the onset of the schism under Alexis and of the anti-Enlightenment under Alexander I; a continuing concern for religious as well as secular ideas and trends; and a relative emphasis within the more familiar period since 1825 on the distinctively Russian rather than the more recognizably Western or "modernizing" aspects of Russian development. I have been encouraged both by the volume of the older materials written on these subjects and by the depth of continuing interest in them among many people deeply immersed in Russian culture, both within and outside the USSR, to believe that the special emphases of this study reflect in some degree objective reality about Russia, and not solely the subjective curiosity of an individual historian.

The text is based largely on a fresh reading of primary materials and of detailed Russian monographs—particularly those published during the last great flowering of humanistic scholarship prior to the Bolshevik Revolution. Considerable use has also been made of Western and recent Soviet scholarly writings; but relatively little use has been made of other general histories, and almost none at all of the substantial but repetitive and apocrypha-laden body of popular Western literature about Russia.

The text is written for a broad range of general readers and will, hopefully, be completely intelligible to someone with no previous knowledge of Russian history. The references at the end of the book are designed to provide the more specialized student with the original-language version of key citations and a running bibliographical guide to available materials in major European languages—particularly on subjects that are controversial, unfamiliar, or not adequately treated elsewhere. The length of the documentation is not intended to lend any illusion of completeness or any aura of special authority to my interpretations and emphases. Many good works have not been used or mentioned; many important subjects not discussed.

To both the scholar and the general reader I would offer this work, not as a systematic analysis or thorough coverage, but as an episode in the common, continuing quest for inner understanding of a disturbed but creative nation. The objective is not so much the clinical-sounding quality of "empathy" as what the Germans call *Einfühlung*, or "in-feeling," and the Russians themselves *proniknovenie*—meaning penetration, or permeation, in the sense in which a blotter is filled with ink or an iron with heat. Only some such sense of involvement can take the external observer beyond casual impressions, redeem unavoidable generalizations, and guard against unstable alternation between condescension and glorification, horror and idealization, Genghis Khan and Prester John.

This quest for deeper understanding has long agitated the introspective Russian people themselves. Alexander Blok, perhaps their greatest poet of this century, has likened Russia to a sphinx; and the Soviet experience has added fresh controversy to the unresolved earlier disputes of Russian history. This search for understanding also belongs to the outside world, which has been deeply affected by the two major events in modern Russian culture: the literary explosion of the nineteenth century and the political upheaval of the twentieth. Historians are inclined to believe that study of the past may in some way deepen one's understanding of the present—perhaps even provide fragmentary hints of future possibilities. However, the history of Russian culture is a story worth telling for its own sake; and even those who feel that this earlier culture has little relevance to the urbanized Communist empire of today may still approach it as Dostoevsky did a Western culture which he felt was dead:

> I know that I am only going to a graveyard, but to a most precious graveyard. . . . Precious are the dead that lie buried there, every stone over them speaks of such burning life that once was there, of such passionate faith in their deeds, their truth, their struggle, and their learning, that I know I shall fall on the ground and shall kiss those stones and weep over them.

ACKNOWLEDGMENTS

I am greatly indebted to the libraries in which I have been privileged to work: the Firestone (including the Shoumatoff collection) at Princeton, the Widener and Houghton at Harvard, national libraries at Stockholm, Vienna, and Marburg, the university library at Leiden, the library of the Institut für osteuropäische Geschichte in Vienna, the New York Public Library, the Library of Congress, the Saltykov-Shchedrin Library, the Institute of Russian Literature (Pushkinsky Dom), and the Russian Museum in Leningrad, and the Lenin Library, Tret'iakov Gallery, and Archive of Ancient Acts in Moscow. I am especially grateful to Drs. Valenkoski and Haltsonen and to the excellent national library at Helsinki for a valuable year spent reading in its rich Russian collection. I deeply appreciate the support I received for this work from the John Simon Guggenheim Memorial Foundation, from the Fulbright program in Finland, and from the Council of the Humanities and University Research Funds of Princeton University. I also thank the Center of International Studies at Princeton, the Russian Research Center at Harvard, and the Inter-University Committee on Travel Grants for assistance not directly related to this project, but of real benefit to it. I am grateful to Gregory and Katharine Guroff for, respectively, preparing the index and typing the most difficult sections of this manuscript.

I owe a special debt to Professor Sir Isaiah Berlin of Oxford and the Reverend Professor Georges Florovsky. They are in many ways the spiritual fathers of this book, having generously fortified me with ideas, criticism, and references during and since my years at Oxford and Harvard. I also profited from discussions with Professors Mavrodin and Bialy and Messrs. Malyshev, Gol'dberg, and Volk during my visits to the University of Leningrad as an exchange lecturer in March 1961, and again in January 1965, while on an exchange with Moscow University. On this latter occasion, I had the privilege of lecturing on the substance of this book at both universities. In Moscow, I benefited from discussions with Professors

Klibanov and Novitsky and Mr. A. Sakharov. I am grateful for stimulus as well as courtesies to these and others in the USSR, and only hope that the exchange of often differing views in this area will continue and deepen. I also thank Mme Popova and Director Lebedev for enabling me to study in detail (and obtain reproductions from) the rich collections of P. D. Korin and the Tret'iakov Gallery respectively. I owe a real debt to my colleagues in the History Department at Princeton: Joseph Strayer, Cyril Black, and Jerome Blum, who along with R. Tucker, R. Burgi, G. Alef, N. Berberova, and Professors Berlin and Florovsky were good enough to read and comment upon sections of the book. I owe a special debt to Charles Moser for his reading and comments. None of these people should suffer any measure of guilt by association with the emphases and approach, let alone the imperfections of this work.

Among the many others whom I should properly thank, I can mention only my lively—I might even say *intelligentnye*—students at Harvard and Princeton, and three great, departed teachers who profoundly influenced me and will not be forgotten by any who knew them: Albert M. Friend, Walter P. Hall, and E. Harris Harbison. Finally, I must thank my beloved wife and companion Marjorie, to whom this book is gratefully and affectionately dedicated.

NOTE

For the sake of readability, I have deferred all but the most essential Russian terms to the reference section at the end of the book, and have introduced a few modifications in the usual method of transliterating Russian (principally the use of an initial *Ya* and *Yu* and a terminal *oy* in names, a uniform rendering of all singular adjectives ending in *ii* or *yi* as *y*, and the elimination of terminal soft signs in names like Suzdal and Pestel). I have generally tried to follow familiar usage in determining whether to use the English or transliterated Russian form of a name, but have tended to favor the English version of first names and the transliterated Russian version of last names. Internal soft signs will generally be maintained. Exceptions to general practice in transliteration will be made to conform with accepted English usage in place names (Kharkov, Dnieper), frequently used Russian words (boyar, sobors, Bolshoi Theater), and Russian names rendered differently in English by authors writing themselves in English (Vinogradoff, Gorodetzky).

CONTENTS

ILLUSTRATIONS

I

BACKGROUND

Background

THE COSMOPOLITAN, *Christian culture of Kiev, "the mother of Russian cities," from the conversion of Prince Vladimir in 988 to the Mongol sack of Kiev in 1240. The uncritical adoption by Kievan Rus' of the artistic forms and sense of special destiny of the Byzantine "second golden age." The love of beauty and preoccupation with history; the building of the new city under Yaroslav the Wise (grand-prince of Kiev, 1019–54); the movement north under Andrew Bogoliubsky (grand-prince of Vladimir-Suzdal, 1157–74).*

The rise to dominance of the "forest land," the Volga-Oka heartland of Great Russia, particularly during the Mongol overlordship, 1240–1480. The strengthening of communal ties during a period of weakened central authority. The fears and fascinations of the forest: bears, insects, and, above all, fire. The enduring importance for the Russian imagination of the key artifacts of this primitive frontier region: the icon and the axe within the peasant hut. The cannon and the bell within populated centers: symbols of metallic might in a wooden world.

A culture of concrete sights and sounds rather than abstract words and ideas. The images of sainthood on wooden icons; the image of divine order and hierarchy on the icon screen. The Vladimir Mother of God as the supreme mother figure of Great Russia; Andrew Rublev (1370–1430) as its supreme artist. Bells as "angelic trumpets" and hypnotic cacophony.

I. Kiev

REDUCED TO ITS SIMPLEST OUTLINE, Russian culture is a tale of three cities: Kiev, Moscow, and St. Petersburg. None of them is really old by the standards of world history. The first was probably founded sometime in the eighth century, the second in the twelfth, the last at the beginning of the eighteenth. Each served as the capital of a sprawling Slavic empire on the eastern periphery of Europe; each left a permanent impact on the culture of modern Russia.

The emergence of Moscow and then that of St. Petersburg are decisive events of modern Russian history, and the profound if subtle rivalry between the two cities is one of the recurring themes of its mature cultural development. Yet the cultural context for this drama was provided by Kiev: the first of the three great cities to rise and to fall. However weakened and transformed in later years, however subject to the separate claims of Polish and Ukrainian historians, Kiev remained the "mother of Russian cities" and "joy of the world" to the chroniclers.[1] Memories of its accomplishment lingered on in oral folklore to give the Orthodox Eastern Slavs an enduring sense of the unity and splendor that had been theirs. In the words of the popular proverb, Moscow was the heart of Russia; St. Petersburg, its head; but Kiev, its mother.[2]

The origins of Kiev are still obscure, but its traceable history begins with the establishment by northern warrior-traders of a series of fortified cities along the rivers that led through the rich eastern plains of Europe into the Black and Mediterranean seas.[3] The main artery of this new trade route down from the Baltic region was the Dnieper; and many historic cities of early Russia, such as Chernigov and Smolensk, were founded on strategic spots along its upper tributaries. Kiev, the most exposed and southerly of the fortified cities on this river, became the major point of contact with the Byzantine Empire to the southeast, and the center for the gradual conversion to Orthodox Christianity in the ninth and tenth centuries of both the Scandinavian princes and the Slavic population of this region. By virtue of its protected location on the raised west bank of the Dnieper, Kiev soon became a major bastion of Christendom against the warlike pagan nomads of the southern steppe. Economically, it was an active trading center and probably the largest city in Eastern Europe. Politically, it became the center of a Slavic civilization that was less a distinct territorial state in the modern sense than a string of fortified cities bound by loose religious, economic, and dynastic ties.

Kievan Russia was closely linked with Western Europe—through trade and intermarriages with every important royal family of Western Christendom.[4] Russia is mentioned in such early epics as the Chanson de Roland and the Nibelungenlied.[5] Indeed, the cultural accomplishments of the high medieval West which these works represent might not have been possible without the existence of a militant Christian civilization in Eastern Europe to absorb much of the shock of invasions by less civilized steppe peoples.

These promising early links with the West were, fatefully, never made secure. Increasingly, inexorably, Kievan Russia was drawn eastward into a debilitating struggle for control of the Eurasian steppe.

The political history of this the greatest undivided land mass in the world has been only very partially recorded. Like the Scyths, Sarmatians, and Huns before them (and their Mongol contemporaries and adversaries), the Russians were to acquire a reputation in more stable societies for both ruggedness and cruelty. But unlike all the others who dominated the steppe, the Russians succeeded—not just in conquering but in civilizing the entire region, from the Pripet Marshes and the Carpathian Mountains in the west to the Gobi Desert and the Himalayas in the east.

The inspiration for this accomplishment came from neither Europe nor Asia, but from a Byzantine Empire that lay between the two, Greek in speech but Oriental in magnificence. The Byzantine capital of Constantinople lay on the strait of water separating Europe from Asia and connecting the Mediterranean with the Black Sea and the rivers leading into the heartland of Central and Eastern Europe: the Danube, the Dnieper, and the Don. Known as the "new" or "second" Rome, this city of Constantine continued to rule the Eastern half of the old Roman Empire for almost a thousand years after the Western Roman Empire had crumbled.

Of all the cultural accomplishments of Byzantium, none was more important than the bringing of Christianity to the Slavs. When the Holy Land, North Africa, and Asia Minor fell to Islam in the seventh and eighth centuries, Byzantium was forced to turn north and east to recoup its fortunes. By the ninth century, Constantinople had regained the self-confidence needed for fresh expansion. The long-debated questions of Christian doctrine had been resolved by the seven councils of the Church; Islamic invaders had been repelled from without and puritanical iconoclasts rejected within the capital. Emperors and Patriarchs had both begun to challenge the authority of a West not yet clearly emerging from the Dark Ages.

The rapid extension of Byzantine political and cultural influence into the Balkans during the ninth century dramatized the exuberance of this "second golden age" of Byzantine history. The key moment in this penetration was the mission to the Slavs of two Greek brothers from the borderlands of the Slavic world in Macedonia: Cyril, a widely traveled and renowned scholar, and Methodius, an administrator with experience in Slavic-speaking areas of the Byzantine Empire. In distant Moravia and later in Bulgaria, they helped turn vernacular Slavic into a written language suitable for translating the basic books of Orthodox Christendom. They apparently did their first work with the exotic and specially invented Glagolitic alphabet; but their followers soon concentrated on the Cyrillic alphabet, which had many relatively familiar Greek letters. A rich store of Christian literature was transcribed in both alphabets within a half century of the missionaries' death.[6] Slavonic became the language of worship of all Orthodox Slavs; and Cyrillic, which bore the name of the more scholarly brother, became the alphabet of the Bulgarians and South Slavs.

When the followers of Cyril and Methodius extended these liturgical and literary activities to Kievan Russia in the tenth and the early eleventh century, the Eastern Slavs acquired a language that had become (together with Latin and Greek) one of the three languages of writing and worship in medieval Christendom. Though subjected to many changes and variations, Church Slavonic remained the basic literary language of Russia until late in the seventeenth century.

Among the many Slavic principalities to accept the forms and faith of Byzantium, Kievan Russia—or Rus', as it was then called—occupied a unique place even from the beginning. Unlike the Balkan Slavic kingdoms, the Kievan domain lay entirely beyond the confines of the old Roman empire. It was one of the last distinct national civilizations to accept Byzantine Christianity; the only one never clearly to accept political subordination to Constantinople; and by far the largest—stretching north to the Baltic and almost to the Arctic Ocean.

Culturally, however, Kiev was in many ways even more deeply dependent on Constantinople than many regions within the empire. For the Russian leaders of the late tenth and the early eleventh century accepted Orthodoxy with the uncritical enthusiasm of the new convert, and sought to transfer the splendors of Constantinople to Kiev in the wholesale manner of the *nouveau riche*. Prince Vladimir brought the majestic rituals and services of Byzantium to Kiev shortly after his conversion in 988; and, particularly under his illustrious son Yaroslav the Wise, learned churchmen streamed in from Byzantium bringing with them models for early Russian laws, chronicles, and sermons. Great churches like Santa Sophia and St. George were named for their counterparts in Constantinople, as were the "golden gates" of the city.[7]

Suffused with a "Christian optimism, a joy that Rus' had become worthy of joining Christianity at the 'eleventh hour' just before the end of the world,"[8] Kiev accepted more unreservedly than Byzantium itself the claim that Orthodox Christianity had solved all the basic problems of belief and worship. All that was needed was "right praising" (the literal translation of *pravoslavie,* the Russian version of the Greek *orthodoxos*) through the forms of worship handed down by the Apostolic Church and defined for all time by its seven ecumenical councils. Changes in dogma or even sacred phraseology could not be tolerated, for there was but one answer to any controversy. The Eastern Church first broke with Rome in the late ninth century, when the latter added the phrase "and from the Son" to the assertion in the Nicene Creed that the Holy Spirit proceeds "from God the Father."

Nowhere was the traditional Eastern formula defended with greater zeal than in Russia. As if compensating for the relative lateness of their conversion, Russian Orthodoxy tended to accept unquestioningly Orthodox definitions of truth and Byzantine forms of art; but the complex philosophic traditions and literary conventions of Byzantium (let alone the classical and Hellenic foundations of Byzantine culture) were never properly assimilated. Thus, fatefully, Russia took over "the Byzantine achievement . . . without the Byzantine inquisitiveness."[9]

Working within this ornate and stylized Byzantine heritage, Kievan Russia developed two distinctive attitudes which gave an all-important initial sense of direction to Russian culture. First was a direct sense of beauty, a passion for seeing spiritual truth in concrete forms. The beauty of Constantinople and of its places and forms of worship was responsible for the conversion of Vladimir according to the earliest historical record of the Kievan period. This "Primary Chronicle"—itself a vivid, often beautiful work of literature—tells how Vladimir's emissaries found Moslem worship frenzied and foul-smelling, and "beheld no glory" in the ceremonies of Western Christians. But in Constantinople

the Greeks led us to the buildings where they worship their God, and we knew not whether we were in heaven or on earth. For on earth there is no such splendor or such beauty, and we are at a loss to describe it. We know only that God dwells there among men, and their service is fairer than the ceremonies of other nations. For we cannot forget that beauty. Every man, after tasting something sweet, is afterward unwilling to accept that which is bitter. . . .[10]

The Kievan princes sought to re-create this experience of beauty in the Byzantine-style cathedrals that sprang up in every important city of Eastern Slavdom. The panoply of heaven was represented by the composed central dome; its interior was embellished with the awesome image of the *Pantokrator*, the Divine Creator of both heaven and earth. Prominent among the other mosaic and frescoed figures that beautified the interior walls and domes was the *Theotokos*, the "God-bearing" Virgin. The cathedrals provided a center of beauty and a source of sanctification for the surrounding region. The word *sobor*, used to describe the gatherings in which the authority of God was invoked on all communal activities, also became the word for cathedral;[11] and the life of each "gathering" was built around the liturgy: the ritual, communal re-enactment of Christ's saving sacrifice.

Concrete beauty rather than abstract ideas conveyed the essence of the Christian message to the early Russians, and inspired a fresh flowering of Byzantine art and letters on Russian soil. Man's function was not to analyze that which has been resolved or to explain that which is mysterious, but lovingly and humbly to embellish the inherited forms of praise and worship —and thus, perhaps, gain some imperfect sense of the luminous world to come. Within a few decades of Vladimir's conversion Kiev was transformed into a majestic city. A visiting Western bishop referred to it as "the rival of Constantinople";[12] and its first native metropolitan, Ilarion of Kiev, spoke of it as

> a city glistening with the light of holy icons,
> fragrant with incense,
> ringing with praise and holy, heavenly songs.[13]

In all early Russian writings about a Christian prince "the mention of physical beauty is never lacking. Together with mercy and almsgiving, this is the only constant feature of an ideal prince."[14]

Literacy was more widespread than is generally realized, among those with a practical need for it; but literature was more remarkable for its aesthetic embellishments than for the content of its ideas. The oldest surviving Russian manuscript, the Ostromir Codex of 1056–7, is a richly colored and ornamented collection of readings from the gospels which were prescribed for church services and arranged according to the days of the week. There were no complete versions of the Bible, let alone independent theological syntheses, produced in early Russia. Most of the twenty-two surviving manuscript books from the eleventh century and of the eighty-six from the twelfth[15] were collections of readings and sermons assembled for practical guidance in worship and embellished both verbally and visually by Russian copyists. From the beginning there was a special preference not for the great theologians and lawmakers of Byzantium, but for its preachers, like the "golden-tongued" John Chrysostom. Cascading images of the beauties of resurrection swept away all subtlety of thought in the preaching of the greatest Kievan writers: Ilarion of Kiev and Cyril of Turov.

There was, indeed, no independent critical theology of any sophistication in Old Russia. Even in the later, Muscovite period, "theoretical" was rendered by *zritel'ny,* "visual," and esteemed teachers were known as *smotrelivy,* "those who have seen."[16] Local and contemporary saints assumed a particular importance in Russian theology. They had performed deeds that men had seen in their own time: Theodosius of Kiev, turning his back on wealth and indeed on asceticism to lead the monastery of the caves into a life of active counsel and charity in the city of Kiev; Abraham of Smolensk, painting as well as teaching about the Last Judgment and bringing rain to the parched steppelands with the fervor of his prayers. Above all stood the first Russian saints, Boris and Gleb, the innocent young sons of Vladimir who accepted death gladly in the political turmoil of Kiev in order to redeem their people through innocent, Christ-like suffering.[17]

Theology, "the word of God," was found in the lives of saints. If one could not be or know a saint, one could still have living contact through the visual images of the iconographer and the oral reminders of the hagiographer. The holy picture or icon was the most revered form of theological expression in Russia. Indeed, the popular word for "holy" or "saintly" was *prepodobny,* or "very like" the figures on the icons. But the life of a saint, written to be read aloud "for the good success and utility of those who listen," was also highly valued. The word for monastic novice or apprentice in sainthood was *poslushnik,* "obedient listener"; as one of the greatest Russian hagiographers explained, "seeing is better than hearing"; but later generations unable to see may still "believe even the sound of those who have heard, if they have spoken in truth."[18]

There was a hypnotic quality to the cadences of the church chant; and the hollow, vaselike indentations (*golosniki*) in the early Kievan churches produced a lingering resonance which obscured the meaning but deepened the impact of the sung liturgy. Pictorial beauty was present not only in mosaics, frescoes, and icons but in the vestments worn in stately processions and in the ornate cursive writing (*skoropis'*) with which sermons and chronicles later came to be written. The sanctuary in which the priests celebrated mass was the tabernacle of God among men; and the rich incense by the royal doors, the cloudy pillar through which God came first to Moses, and now to all men through the consecrated bread brought out by the priest at the climax of each liturgy.

The early Russians were drawn to Christianity by the aesthetic appeal of its liturgy, not the rational shape of its theology. Accepting unquestioningly the Orthodox definition of truth, they viewed all forms of expression as equally valid means of communicating and glorifying the faith. Words, sounds, and pictures were all subordinate and interrelated parts of a common religious culture. In Russia—as distinct from the Mediterranean and Western worlds—"Church art was not added to religion from without, but was an emanation from within."[19]

The same desire to see spiritual truth in tangible form accounts for the extraordinary sense of history that is a second distinguishing feature of early Russian culture. As with many simple warrior people, religious truth tended to be verified by the concrete test of ability to inspire victory. The miraculous pretensions of Christianity were not unique among world religions; but Orthodox Christianity offered a particularly close identification of charismatic power with historical tradition: an unbroken succession of patriarchs, prophets, and apostles that stretched from creation to incarnation and on to final judgment. A sense of majesty and destiny was imparted by the Church, which had sprung up around the original sees of Christendom, and by the Empire, which centered on the city of Constantine the Great, the man who converted the Roman Empire to Christianity and took part in the first ecumenical council of the Church at Nicaea. Tales of the great empires of the East and of the holy lands were brought back to Kiev by merchants and pilgrims alike; and these were interwoven into the sacred chronicles with no sense of conflict or incongruity. Whereas Western and Northern Europe had inherited a still primitive and uncodified Christianity from the crumbling Roman Empire of the West, Russia took over a finished creed from the still-unvanquished Eastern Empire. All that remained for a newcomer to accomplish was the last chapter in this pageant of sacred history: "the transformation of the earthly dominion into the ecclesiastical dominion":[20] preparation for the final assembly (*ekklēsia*) of saints before the throne of God.

"Because of the lack of rational or logical elements, ancient Russian theology was entirely historical."[21] The writing of sacred history in the form of chronicles was perhaps the most important and distinguished literary activity of the Kievan period. Chronicles were written in Church Slavonic in Kievan Russia long before any were written in Italian or French, and are at least as artistic as the equally venerable chronicles composed in Latin and German. The vivid narrative of men and events in the original "Primary Chronicle" struck the first Western student of Russian chronicles, August

Schlözer, as far superior to any in the medieval West, and helped inspire him to become the first to introduce both universal history and Russian history into the curriculum of a modern university.

The final form of the Primary Chronicle, compiled early in the twelfth century, was probably based on the work of many hands during the preceding century; and it became, in turn, the starting point for innumerable subsequent chronicles of even greater length and detail. The reverence with which these sacred histories were regarded soon made slight changes in narration or genealogy an effective form of political and ideological warfare among fractious princes and monasteries. Variations in the phraseology of the chronicles remain one of the best guides to the internecine political struggles of medieval Russia for those able to master this esoteric form of communication.[22]

Much more than most monastic chronicles of the medieval West, the Russian chronicles are a valuable source of profane as well as sacred history. A miscellany of non-Christian elements, political and economic information, and even integral folk tales are often presented within the traditional framework of sacred history. In general, Kiev was a relatively cosmopolitan and tolerant cultural center. The chronicles frequently testify to the persistence of older pagan rites. The hallowed walls of the Santa Sophia in Kiev contain a series of purely secular frescoes. The first and most widely copied Russian account of a pilgrimage to the Holy Land includes more dispassionate geographical and ethnographic description than do most contemporary accounts by Western pilgrims and crusaders.[23] The famous epic *The Lay of the Host of Igor* is far more rich in secular allusions and subject matter than epics of the Muscovite period. If one considers it an authentic work of this period, both the worldliness and literary genius of Kievan Russia become even more impressive.[24]

Secular literature no less than theology was infused with a sense of history. As a leading Soviet historian of old Russian literature has written:

> Every narrative subject in Russian medieval literature was looked on as having taken place historically. . . .
> The active figures of old-Russian narrative tales were always historical figures, or figures whose historical existence—even when apocryphal —permitted of no doubt. Even in those cases where a contrived figure was introduced, he was surrounded with a swarm of historical memories, creating the illusion of real existence in the past.
> The action of the narrative always took place in precisely delineated historical circumstances or, more often, in works of old Russian literature, related directly to historical events themselves.
> That is why in medieval Russian literature there were no works in the purely entertaining genres, but the spirit of historicism penetrated it all

from beginning to end. This gave Russian medieval literature the stamp of particular seriousness and particular significance.[25]

The desire to find both roots and vindication in history grew partly out of the insecurity of the Eastern plain. Geography, not history, had traditionally dominated the thinking of the Eurasian steppe. Harsh seasonal cycles, a few, distant rivers, and sparse patterns of rainfall and soil fertility controlled the lives of the ordinary peasant; and the ebb and flow of nomadic conquerors often seemed little more than the senseless movement of surface objects on an unchanging and unfriendly sea.

Any steppe people who felt that time really mattered—and that they as a people had a mission to perform in time—was automatically distinct. Conversion to the profoundly historical creed of Judaism had prolonged the life of the exposed Khazar empire to the south; and to the east, the Volga Bulgars had attained an importance out of all proportion to their numbers by accepting Islam. Christianity had appeared in history midway in time between these two monotheisms, and the Christianity which took root among the Eastern Slavs provided many of the same psychological satisfactions as the prophetic creeds adopted by their neighboring civilizations.

There is a historical cast to the most widely reproduced sermon of the Kievan period, Metropolitan Ilarion's "On Law and Grace." It was apparently first delivered on Easter in 1049, just two days after the feast of the Annunciation of the Virgin in the church of the Annunciation, near the Golden Gate of the city, to celebrate the completion of the walls around Kiev.[26] After contrasting the law of the Old Testament with the grace made possible through the New, Ilarion rushes on to depict something rather like the coming age of glory on Russian soil. He bids Vladimir rise from the dead and look upon Kiev transformed into a kind of New Jerusalem. Vladimir's son, Yaroslav the Wise, has built the Santa Sophia, "the great and holy temple of Divine Wisdom," within the walls of "the city of glory, Kiev," just as David's son Solomon had raised up a temple within Jerusalem in the time of the law.[27] Like the people of Israel, the Kievans were called upon not just to profess the faith but to testify in deeds their devotion to the living God. Thus, churches were built and a city transformed under Yaroslav, not for decorative effect, but for Christian witness. In response to God's gracious gift of His Son, God's people were returning their offering of praise and thanksgiving. The forms of art and worship were those hallowed by the one "right-praising" Church in which His Holy Spirit dwelt.

Conservative adherence to past practices was to serve, ironically, to heighten radical expectations of an approaching end to history. Believing that the forms of art and worship should be preserved intact until the second coming of Christ, Russians tended to explain unavoidable innovations as signs that the promised end was drawing near. Though this "eschatological psychosis" was to be more characteristic of the later Muscovite period, there are already traces of it in the dark prophetic preaching of Abraham of Smolensk.[28]

Kievan Russia received such unity as it attained essentially through waves of conversion—moving north from Kiev and out from the princely court in each city to ever wider sections of the surrounding populace. Conversion was apparently more important than colonization in unifying the region,[29] and each new wave of converts tended to adopt not merely the Byzantine but the Kievan heritage as well. The Slavonic language became the uniform vehicle for writing and worship, slowly driving the Finno-Ugrian tongues which originally dominated much of northern Russia to peripheral regions: Finland and Esthonia to the west and the Mordvin and Cheremis regions to the east along the Volga. The sense of historic destiny grew; and the idea of Christianity as a religion of victorious combat increased as the obstacles—both pagan and natural—grew more formidable.

Everywhere that the new faith went it was dramatically translated into monuments of church architecture: the magnificent Santa Sophia in Novgorod, the second city of early Russia and a point of commercial contact with the Germanic peoples of the Baltic; the lavish Cathedral of the Assumption in Vladimir, the favored northern headquarters for the Kievan princes and a key center on the upper Volga. Both of these twelfth-century masterpieces were modeled on (and named after) counterparts in Kiev; but the building of churches extended beyond the cities, even beyond the records of monastic chroniclers, out to such forbidding spots as the shores of Lake Ladoga. There, in the late 1160's, the church of St. George was built and adorned with beautiful frescoes which illustrate the fidelity to tradition and sense of destiny that were present in the chronicles. The fact that this memorable church is not even mentioned in the chronicles points to the probability that there were many other vanished monuments of this kind. Named after the saintly dragon slayer who became a special hero of the Russian north, St. George's was probably built as a votive offering for victory in battle over the Swedes.[30] Byzantine in its iconography, the surviving frescoes reveal nonetheless a preoccupation with the details of the Last Judgment, which—characteristically in Russian churches—dominated, and even extended beyond, the confines of the inner west wall.

Some of the most memorable figures depicted in the frescoes are the prophets and warrior kings of the Old Testament. The very severity of their stylized, Byzantine presentation makes the compassionate figure of Mary seem a unique and welcome source of relief and deliverance. She was the protectress of Kiev and Novgorod as she had been of Constantinople. Russians were singing hymns to her presanctified state and dedicating churches to her assumption into heaven well before Western Christendom. She alone brought respite from damnation in the famous apocryphal tale of "The Virgin's Visit to Hell," which was brought from Byzantium in the twelfth century to new and enduring popularity in Russia.[31] For the love of departed sinners, she had descended into the Inferno to win them annual release from their suffering during the period from Holy Thursday to Pentecost.

Much of the mythology that had gathered about the holy cities of earlier civilizations was transferred to Kiev and Novgorod; and the lore of ancient shrines and monasteries, to the new ones of the Orthodox Eastern Slavs. The legend that the apostle Andrew had brought Christianity directly to Kiev just as Peter had to Rome was taken over from Constantinople. Legends resembling those about the catacombs at Rome were developed around the caves of Kiev, and the idea subtly grew that Kiev might be a "second Jerusalem."[32]

The unity of Kievan Russia was above all that of a common religious faith. The forms of faith and worship were almost the only uniformities in this loosely structured civilization. Such economic strength and political cohesion as had existed began to break down with the internecine strife of the late twelfth century, the Latin occupation of Contantinople in 1204, and the subsequent assaults almost simultaneously launched against the Eastern Slavs by the Mongols from the east and the Teutonic Knights from the west.

The Mongols, who sacked Kiev in 1240, proved the more formidable foe. They prowled at will across the exposed steppe, interdicted the lucrative river routes to the south, and left the "mother of Russian cities" in a state of continuing insecurity. Cultural independence and local self-government were maintained only by regular payment of tribute to the Mongol khan. Unlike the Islamic Arabs, who had brought Greek science and philosophy with them when they extended their power into the Christian world, the nomadic pagans of Genghis and Batu Khan brought almost nothing of intellectual or artistic worth. The clearest cultural legacy of the Mongols lay in the military and administrative sphere. Mongol terms for money and weapons filtered into the Russian language; and new habits of petitioning rulers through a form of prostration and kowtow known as *chelobitnaia* (literally, "beating the forehead") were also taken over.[33]

The period of Mongol domination—roughly from 1240 until the termination of tribute in 1480—was not so much one of "Oriental despotism"[34] as of decentralized localism among the Orthodox Eastern Slavs. This "appanage period" of Russian history was one of those when, in Spengler's words,

> . . . high history lays itself down weary to sleep. Man becomes a plant again, clinging to the soil, dumb and enduring. The timeless village, the "eternal" peasant reappear, begetting children and burying seed in mother earth—a busy, not inadequate swarm, over which the tempest of soldier-emperors passingly blows. . . . Men live from hand to mouth with petty thrifts and petty fortunes and endure. . . . Masses are trampled on, but the survivors fill up the gaps with a primitive fertility and suffer on.[35]

The "high history" of the period was that of warrior princes from the east whose enervating struggles further fit Spengler's characterization of "a drama noble in its aimlessness . . . like the course of the stars . . . the alternance of land and sea."[36]

Like the Kievan princes before them, the Mongol conquerors adopted a religion (Islam), established a capital on the lower reaches of a great river (Sarai on the Volga), were initially weakened more by a new conqueror from the east (Tamerlane) than by virtually simultaneous assaults from the west (the Muscovite victory at Kulikovo in 1380), and were plagued by inner fragmentation. The khanate of Kypchak, or "Golden Horde," was but one of several dependent states within the far-flung empire of Genghis Khan; it was a racially conglomerate and ideologically permissive realm which gradually disintegrated in the course of the fifteenth century, becoming less important politically than its own "appanages": the separate Tatar khanates in the Crimea, on the upper Volga at Kazan, and at Astrakhan, the Caspian mouth of the Volga. Cunning diplomacy and daring raids enabled the Crimean Tatars and other lesser Tatar groups to maintain militarily menacing positions in the southern parts of European Russia until late in the eighteenth century.

The real importance of the Tatars' protracted presence in the Eastern European steppelands lies not so much in their direct influence on Russian culture as in their indirect role in providing the Orthodox Eastern Slavs with a common enemy against whom they could unite and rediscover a sense of common purpose. Slowly but irresistibly, the Eastern Slavs emerged from the humiliation and fragmentation of the Mongol period to expand their power eastward—beyond the former realm of the Golden Horde, beyond that of the so-called Blue Horde, on the steppes of Central Asia, on to the Pacific. To understand how Russia emerged from its "dark ages" to such triumphant accomplishment, one must not look primarily either to Byzantium or to the Mongols: the Golden Horn or the Golden Horde. One must look rather to the "primitive fertility" which began to bring an agricultural surplus and a measure of prosperity; and, even more important, to "the accumulation of spiritual energies during long silence"[37] in the monasteries and to the accumulation of political power by the new city which rose to dominate this region: Moscow.

2. The Forest

THE MOST IMPORTANT immediate consequence for Russia of the Mongol sweep across the Eurasian steppe in the thirteenth century was that the once-outlying forest regions of the north now became the main center of an independent Orthodox culture. What the change of geographical focus from the central Dnieper to the upper Volga really meant can never be precisely ascertained. Pitifully few documentary or archeological materials have survived the fights, frosts, and fires of the north. Cultural historians are inclined to stress continuities with the Kievan age, pointing out that the principal cities of the northeast—Vladimir, Suzdal, Riazan, Rostov, and Yaroslavl—were almost as old as Kiev; that Vladimir had been the ruling seat of the leading Kievan princes for many years prior to the sack of Kiev; and that Novgorod, the second city of Kievan times, remained free of Mongol invasions and provided continuity with its steadily increasing prosperity. The characters, events, and artistic forms of Kievan times dominated the chronicles and epics "which assumed their final shape in the creative memory of the Russian north."[1] The ritualized forms of art and worship and the peculiar sensitivity to beauty and history—all remained constant features of Russian culture.

Yet profound, if subtle, changes accompanied the transfer of power to the upper Volga: the coldest and most remote frontier region of Byzantine-Slavic civilization. This region was increasingly cut off not just from declining Byzantium but also from a resurgent West, which was just rediscovering Greek philosophy and building its first universities. The mention of Russia that had been so frequent in early medieval French literature vanished altogether in the course of the fourteenth century.[2] Russian no less than Western European writers realized that the Orthodox Eastern Slavs now comprised a congeries of principalities rather than a single political force. The chroniclers in the Russian north sensed that they were somewhat cut off, using the term "Rus'" primarily for the old politico-cultural center on the Dnieper around Kiev.[3]

A sense of separation within the domain of the Eastern Slavs had already been suggested by the tenth-century Byzantine distinction between "near" and "distant" Rus'; and in the thirteenth century the distinction between "great" Russia in the north and "little" Russia in the south was gradually transplanted from Byzantium to Russia. What apparently began as a pure description of size eventually became a favored pseudo-imperial designation in the north. Individual towns like Novgorod and Rostov called themselves "the Great." Details of the life of Alexander the Great—a favorite subject in the epic literature of the East—were blended by the chroniclers of the Russian north into the idealized life of Alexander Nevsky[4]—whose victory over the Swedes in 1240 and the Teutonic Knights two years later was followed by a reign as Great Prince of Vladimir. His victorious exploits helped compensate for the simultaneous humiliation at the hands of the Mongols and made him seem no less "great" than the earlier Alexander. By the late fifteenth century, Ivan III had brought greatness out of legend and into reality, subordinating most of the major cities of the Russian north to Moscow. The first grand duke of Muscovy to call himself tsar (Caesar), he also became the first of several imperial conquerors of modern Russia to be known as "the Great."

There was, however, nothing great, or even impressive, about Great Russia in the thirteenth and the early fourteenth century. It must have seemed highly unlikely that the Eastern Slavs in the bleak Volga-Oka region would in any way recapture—let alone surpass—the glories of the Kievan past. Kiev and the original region of Rus' along the Dnieper had been despoiled by the still-menacing Mongols. The Volga was frozen for much of the year and blocked to the south by Mongol fortresses. Flat terrain and wooden fortifications offered little natural protection from eastern invaders. Slavic co-religionists to the west were preoccupied with other problems. To the northwest, Novgorod had carved out an economic empire of its own and moved increasingly into the orbit of the expanding Hanseatic League. Further north, the rugged Finns were being converted to Christianity, not by the once-active Orthodox missionaries of Novgorod and Ladoga, but by the Westernized Swedes. Directly to the west, the Teutonic and Livonian knights provided a continuing military threat; while Galicia and Volhynia in the southwest were drifting into alignment with the Roman Church. Most of what is now White (or West) Russia was loosely ruled by the Lithuanians, and much of Little Russia (or the Ukraine) by the Poles. These two western neighbors were, moreover, moving toward an alliance that was sealed by marriage and the establishment of the Jagellonian dynasty in 1386.

The surviving centers of Byzantine-Kievan civilization in Great Russia were relatively isolated from these alien forces. As a result, it is difficult to explain the changes in Russian cultural life that accompanied the move from "little" to "great" Russia simply in terms of new contact with other civilizations. There was, to be sure, increased borrowing from the Tatars and from pre-Christian pagan animism in the north. But there are great risks in suggesting that either of these elements provides some simple "key" to the understanding of Russian character. The famed aphorism "Scratch a Russian and you find a Tatar" and the ingenious hypothesis that there was in Russia an enduring *dvoeverie* (or duality of belief between official Christianity and popular paganism) tell us more about the patronizing attitude of Western observers and the romantic imagination of Russian ethnographers respectively than about Russian reality as such.

Of these two theories, that of continuing animistic influences takes us perhaps deeper into the formative processes of Russian thought.[5] The Tatars provided a fairly clear-cut imaginative symbol for the people and an administrative example for the leaders, but were an external force whose contact with the Russian people was largely episodic or indirect. Pre-existent pagan practices, on the other hand, were a continuing force, absorbed from within by broad segments of the populace and reflecting a direct response to inescapable natural forces. If the fragmentary surviving materials cannot prove any coherent, continuing pagan tradition, there can be no doubt that the cold, dark environment of Great Russia played a decisive role in the culture which slowly emerged from these, the silent centuries of Russian history. As in the other wooded regions of Northern Europe—Scandinavia, Prussia, and Lithuania—brooding pagan naturalism seemed to stand in periodic opposition to a Christianity that had been brought in relatively late from more sunlit southerly regions. Far more, however, than her forest neighbors to the west, Great Russia thrust monasteries forth into the wooded wastes during the fourteenth and fifteenth centuries. Thus, in Great Russia, there was not so much a duality of belief as a continuing influx of primitive animism into an ever-expanding Christian culture.

The animistic feeling for nature blended harmoniously with an Orthodox sense of history in the springtime festival of Easter, which acquired a special intensity in the Russian north. The traditional Easter greeting was not the bland "Happy Easter" of the modern West, but a direct affirmation of the central fact of sacred history, "Christ is risen!" The standard answer "In truth, risen!" seemed to apply to nature as well as man;

for the resurrection feast came at the end not just of the long Lenten fast, but of the dark, cold winter. Easter sermons were among the most carefully preserved and frequently recopied documents from the Kievan period. To their Byzantine elegance was added in the north the simple assertion that "the goodness hidden in the hearts of the holy shall be revealed in their risen bodies" just as trees long veiled in snow "put out their leaves in the spring."[6]

The weakening of central authority and the presence of new enemies—both natural and human—forced a deepening of family and communal bonds within the widely scattered communities of the Russian north. Authority in most areas was naturally invested in "elders" and exercised through extended family relationships. Within the Christian name of each Russian is included even today the name of his father. The prevailing Russian words for "country" and "people" have the same root as "birth"; "native land" and "land ownership," the same as "father."[7] The individual had to subordinate himself to group interests to accomplish his daily tasks: the communal clearing of land, building of fortifications and churches, and chanting of group prayers and offices. Later attempts to find in the "Russian soul" an innate striving toward communality (*sobornost'*) and "family happiness" may often represent little more than romantic flights from present realities. But the practical necessity for communal action is hard to deny for the early period; and already in the fourteenth century the word "communal" (*sobornaia*) apparently began to be substituted for the word "catholic" (*kafolicheskaia*) in the Slavic version of the Nicene Creed.[8]

For better or worse, the sense of sharing experience almost as members of a common family was an important element in forming the cultural tradition of modern Russia. Intensified by common suffering and glorified memories of Kievan times, this feeling was perhaps even deeper in the interior than in the more prosperous and cosmopolitan centers of Novgorod, Smolensk, and Polotsk to the west. It was in this inner region that the cult of the Mother of God was developed with the greatest intensity. Feasts like that of the intercession (Pokrov) of the Virgin—unknown to Kiev—were introduced in this region; and a cathedral dedicated to the Assumption of the Virgin (Uspensky Sobor) enjoyed in Vladimir and Moscow the central role played by the more purely Byzantine Santa Sophia in Kiev and Novgorod. Although this cult of the Virgin was also growing concurrently in Byzantium and even in the West, it appears to have generated a special primitive intensity and sense of familial intimacy in the Russian interior.

Within the family the mother seems to have been the binding force. In a society whose rich and imaginative epic literature contains few references to romantic love and no idealized pair of lovers, the mother tended to

become an unusually important focus of reverence and affection.[9] If the
father's role in the family was likened in the household guide of the mid-
sixteenth century (*Domostroy*) to that of the head of a monastery, the
mother's role might well have been compared to that of its saint or spiritual
"elder." She was a kind of living version of the omnipresent icons of the
"Mother of God"—the "joy of all sorrows" and "lady of loving kindness,"
as the Russians were particularly prone to call Mary. Men monopolized the
active conduct of war and affairs, whereas women cultivated the passive
spiritual virtues of endurance and healing love. Women quietly encouraged
the trend in Russian spirituality which glorified non-resistance to evil and
voluntary suffering, as if in compensation for the militant official ethos of
the men. Women played a decisive role in launching and keeping alive the
last passionate effort to preserve the organic religious civilization of medieval
Russia: the famed Old Believer movement of the seventeenth century.[10]

Even in later years great emphasis was placed on the strong mother
figure, who bears up under suffering to hold the family together; and to the
grandmother (*babushka*), who passes on to the next generation the mixture
of faith and folklore, piety and proverb, that comprised Russian popular
culture.[11] Russia itself came to be thought of less as a geographical or
political entity than as a common mother (*matushka*) and its ruler less as
prince or lawmaker than a common father (*batiushka*). The term "Russian
land" was feminine both in gender and allegorical significance, related to
the older pagan cult of a "damp mother earth" among the pre-Christian
Eastern Slavs.

> Earth is the Russian "Eternal Womanhood," not the celestial image
> of it; mother, not virgin; fertile, not pure; and black, for the best Russian
> soil is black.[12]

The river Volga also was referred to as "dear mother" in the first Russian
folk song ever recorded and "natal mother" in one of the most popular: the
ballad of Stenka Razin.[13]

The extension of Kievan civilization on to the headwaters of this the
largest river in Eurasia proved the means of its salvation. The very in-
hospitability of this northern region offered a measure of protection from
both east and west. The Volga provided an inland waterway for future
expansion to the east and south; and its tributaries in northwestern Russia
reached almost to the headwaters of other rivers leading into the Baltic,
Black, and Arctic seas.

But the movement out to the sea and onto the steppe came later in
Russian history. This was essentially a period of retreat into a region where
the dominant natural feature was the forest.

In speaking of the region, Russian chroniclers of the thirteenth and fourteenth centuries depart from their usual tendency to use the name of a dominant city, referring instead to *zaleskaia zemlia,* "the wooded land": a pointed reminder that the virgin forest was the nursery of Great Russian culture.[14] Even in modern times, popular folklore taught that the primeval forest had extended all the way up to heaven.[15] In the formative early period, the forest represented a kind of evergreen curtain for the imagination, shielding it from the increasingly remote worlds of Byzantine and Western urbanity.

It is probably not too much to say that the wooded plain shaped the life of Christian Muscovy as profoundly as the desert plain that of Moslem Arabia. In both areas food and friendship were often hard to find, and the Slavic like the Semitic peoples developed warm compensating traditions of hospitality. At the lowest level, peasants presented the ritual bread and salt to all arrivals; at the highest level, princes welcomed visitors with the elaborate banquets and toasts that have remained characteristic of official Russian hospitality.

If life in the scorching desert was built around the dwelling in the oasis and its source of water, life in the frozen forest was built around the dwelling in the clearing and its source of heat. From the many words used for "dwelling place" in Kievan Russia, only *izba,* meaning "heated building," came into general use in Muscovy.[16] Being permitted to sit on or over the earthenware stove in a Russian dwelling was the ultimate in peasant hospitality—the equivalent of giving a man something to drink in the desert. The hot communal bath had a semi-religious significance, still evident today in some Russian public baths and Finnish saunas and analogous in some ways to the ritual ablutions of desert religions.[17]

Unlike the desert nomad, however, the typical Muscovite was sedentary, for he was surrounded not by barren sand but by rich woods. From the forest he could extract not only logs for his hut but wax for his candles, bark for his shoes and primitive records, fur for his clothing, moss for his floors, and pine boughs for his bed. For those who knew its secret hiding places, the forest could also provide meat, mushrooms, wild berries, and—as its greatest culinary prize—sweet honey.

Man's rival in the pursuit of honey through the forests was the mighty bear, who acquired a special place in the folklore, heraldic symbolism, and decorative wood carvings of Great Russia. Legend had it that the bear was originally a man who had been denied the traditional bread and salt of human friendship, and had in revenge assumed an awesome new shape and retreated to the forest to guard it against the intrusions of his former species. The age-old northern Russian customs of training and wrestling with bears carried in the popular imagination certain overtones of a primeval struggle for the forest and its wealth, and of ultimately re-establishing a lost harmony among the creatures of the forest.[18]

The fears and fascinations of Great Russia during these early years were to a large extent the universal ones of war and famine. The former was made vivid by the internecine warfare of Russian princes as well as periodic combat with Tatars and Teutons. Famine was also never far away in the north where the growing season was short and the soil thin; and where grain could not even be planted until trees were arduously uprooted and soil upturned with fragile wooden plows.

But the forest also gave rise to special fears: of insects and rodents gnawing from below and of fire sweeping in from without. Though common to most societies, fear of these primitive forces was particularly intense in Great Russia. In the military language of our own times, they could be said to represent the guerrilla warriors and thermonuclear weapons of an adversary bent on frustrating the peasants' efforts to combat the cold and dark with the "conventional" defenses of food, clothing, and shelter. Even when he had cleared and planted a field and built a hut, the *muzhik* of the north was plagued by an invisible army of insects and rodents burrowing up through the floorboards and gnawing at his crops. During the brief summer months of warmth and light, he was harassed by swarms of mosquitoes; and when he put on his crude furs and fabrics for the winter, he exposed his body to an even deadlier insect: the omnipresent typhus-bearing louse.

The very process by which the body generated warmth within its clothing attracted the louse to venture forth from the clothing to feast upon its human prey; and the very communal baths by which Russians sought to cleanse themselves provided a unique opportunity for the louse to migrate from one garment to another.[19] The flea and the rat collaborated to bring Russia epidemics of the black plague in the fourteenth and seventeenth centuries that were probably even worse than those of Western Europe.[20] The peasant's wooded hut, which provided rudimentary protection against the larger beasts of the forest, served more as a lure to its insects and rodents. They hungrily sought entrance to his dwelling place, his food supply, and—eventually—his still warm body.

Pagan magicians taught that insects actually begin to eat away at men while they are still alive; and that death comes only when men cease to believe in the occult powers of the sorcerer.[21] The word "underground" (*podpol'e*) literally means "under the floor," and suggests insects and rodents who "creep up" (*podpolzat'*) from beneath. The first official English ambassador in the mid-seventeenth century was advised by Russian officials to sleep together with his servants "lest the Rats run away with them being single."[22]

"The most mischievous enemies of unprotected and primitive man are not the big carnivora," insisted a nineteenth-century student of the Russian peasantry, "but the lower forms of creation—the insects, the mice, rats . . . which overwhelm him by their numbers and omnipresence."[23] No less than the revolutionary who wrote these words, conservative writers like Gogol equated the ever-increasing swarm of inspectors and officials sent out to the countryside with these ubiquitous insects and rodents. Dostoevsky was even more frightened and fascinated by man's links with the insect world from his early *Notes from the Underground* to his apocalyptical images in *The Possessed* of a rat gnawing at an icon and the human community turning into an anthill. Dostoevsky fills his works with haunting references to spiders and flies,[24] which are lifted to the level of the grotesque by his sole surviving imitator in the Stalin era: Leonid Leonov. From his *Badgers* to *The Russian Forest,* Leonov mixes realistic plots with such surrealist creatures as "a new sort of cockroach," a 270-year-old rat, and an unidentified "giant microbe" prowling construction sites.[25]

Even stronger in the forest was the fear of, and fascination with, fire. Fire was "the host" in the house—the source of warmth and light that required cleanliness in its presence and reverent silence when being lit or extinguished. In the monasteries, the lighting of fires for cooking and baking was a religious rite that could be performed only by the sacristan bringing a flame from the lamp in the sanctuary.[26] One of the words for warmth, *bogat'ia,* was synonymous with wealth.

Russians tended to see the heavenly order in terms of the famous writings attributed to the mystic Dionysius, for whom angels are "living creatures of fire, men flashing with lightning, streams of flame . . . thrones are fire and the seraphims . . . blazing with fire."[27] Russians often mention Christ's statement that "I have come to send fire on the earth" and the fact that the Holy Spirit first came down to man through "tongues of fire."[28]

When a church or even an icon was burned in Muscovy it was said to have "gone on high."[29] Red Square in Moscow, the site of ritual processions then as now, was popularly referred to as "the place of fire."[30] The characteristic onion dome of Muscovite churches was likened to "a tongue of fire."[31]

A basic metaphor for explaining the perfect combination of God and man in Christ had long been that of fire infusing itself into iron. Though essentially unchanged, this human "iron" acquires the fiery nature of the Godhead: the ability to enflame everything that touches it. A Byzantine definition of Christian commitment that became popular in Russia explained that "having become all fire in the soul, he transmits the inner radiance gained by him also to the body, just as physical fire transmits its effect to iron."[32] Or again from Dionysius:

> Fire is in all things . . . manifesting its presence only when it can find material on which to work . . . renewing all things with its lifegiving heat . . . changeless always as it lifts that which it gathers to the skies, never held back by servile baseness. . . .[33]

Heat not light, warmth rather than enlightenment, was the way to God.

At the same time, fire was a fearful force in this highly inflammable civilization: an uninvited guest whose sudden appearance came as a reminder of its fragile impermanence. The popular expression for committing arson even today is "let loose the red rooster," and the figure of a red rooster was often painted on wooden buildings to propitiate him and prevent a dreaded visitation. Leonov likens a spreading forest fire to a horde of red spiders consuming everything in its way.[34]

Moscow alone was visited with some seventeen major fires in the period from 1330 to 1453, and was to be gutted by flames many more times between then and the great fire of 1812. The recorded histories of Novgorod mention more than a hundred serious fires.[35] A seventeenth-century visitor remarked that "to make a conflagration remarkable in this country there must be at least seven or eight thousand houses consumed."[36] Small wonder that fire was the dominant symbol of the Last Judgment in Russian iconography. Its red glow at the bottom of church frescoes and icons was recognizable even from afar whenever, in their turn, the flames of the church candles were lit by the faithful.

Perun, the god of thunder and creator of fire, held a pre-eminent place in the pre-Christian galaxy of deities, and the bright-plumed firebird a special place in Russian mythology. Ilya of Murom, perhaps the most popular hero of Christianized epic folklore, was modeled on (and given the Slavic name of) the prophet Elijah, who sent down fire on the enemies of Israel and ascended to heaven in a fiery chariot. The first form of the drama in Russia was the "furnace show," on the Sunday before Christmas, in which the three faithful Israelites—Shadrach, Meshach, and Abednego— were rescued by God from Nebuchadnezzar's fire. Although taken over from Byzantium, this drama received a new richness of staging and musical setting in Russia. Real fire was introduced in the Russian version; and, after their rescue, the three Israelites circulated through church and town to proclaim that Christ was coming to save men, just as the angel of the Lord had rescued them from the furnace.[37] In the first of the critical religious controversies of the seventeenth century, the fundamentalists passionately and successfully defended the rite whereby flaming candles were immersed into the waters that were blessed on Epiphany to remind men that Christ came to "baptise with the Holy Ghost and with fire."[38] In 1618 the head of Russia's largest monastery was beaten by a mob and forced to perform a penance of a thousand prostrations a day for trying to do away with this uncanonical rite. One of the tracts written to denounce him, *On the Enlightening Fire,* accused him of trying to deny Russia "the tongue of fire that had descended upon the apostles."[39] Fire was the weapon of the fundamentalists in the 1640's as they burned musical instruments, foreign-style paintings, and the buildings of the foreign community itself in Moscow. After the fundamentalists had been anathemized in 1667, many of these "Old Believers" sought self-immolation—often with all their family and friends in an oil-soaked wooden church—as a means of anticipating the purgative fires of the imminent Last Judgment.[40]

Apocalyptical fascination with the cleansing power of flames lived on in the traditions of primitive peasant rebellion—and indeed in the subsequent tradition of ideological aristocratic revolution. The atheistic anarchist Michael Bakunin fascinated Europe during the revolutionary crisis of 1848–9 with his prophetic insistence that "tongues of flame" would shortly appear all over Europe to bring down the old gods. After hearing Wagner conduct a performance of Beethoven's Ninth Symphony in Leipzig in 1849, Bakunin rushed forward to assure him that this work deserved to be spared the imminent world conflagration. Fascinated by this man (whom he called the "chief stoker" of revolution), Wagner was haunted by the fact that the opera house did perish in flames shortly thereafter, and may well have been influenced by Bakunin in his characterization of Siegfried, his own fire music, and his over-all conception of "The Downfall of the Gods."[41] When Russia produced its own musical revolution in the early twentieth century, the symbol of fire was equally central: in Scriabin's "Poem of Fire" and the spectacular fusion of music with the dance in Stravinsky and Diaghilev's "Firebird."

Their firebird, like the two-headed imperial eagle, perished in the flames of the 1917 revolution, which the winds of war had fanned out of Lenin's seemingly insignificant *Spark.* Some poets of the old regime felt what one of them called "the attraction of the moth-soul to fiery death,"[42] while one of the first and greatest to be killed by the new regime left behind a posthumous anthology called *Pillar of Fire.*[43] During the terrorized silence that followed under Stalin, the stage production which evoked the greatest emotional response from its audience was probably Musorgsky's "popular music drama" *Khovanshchina,* which ends with the self-destruction of an

Old Believers' community—using real flame on the stage of the Bolshoi Theater. The image recurs in the work of Pasternak; but the question of what arose from the cultural ashes of the Stalin era belongs to the epilogue rather than the prologue of our story. Suffice it here to stress that the sense of spiritual intimacy with natural forces already present in earlier times was intensified in the inflammable forest world of Great Russia, where fire contended with fertility; the masculine force of Perun with the damp mother earth for control of a world in which human beings seemed strangely insignificant.

Why Russians did not sink into complete fatalism and resignation during the dark days of the thirteenth and fourteenth centuries can perhaps be explained in terms of two key pairs of artifacts that stayed with them through all the fires and fighting of the period: the axe and icon in the countryside, and the bell and cannon in the monastery and city. Each element in these pairings bore an intimate relationship to the other—demonstrating the close connection between worship and war, beauty and brutality, in the militant world of Muscovy. These objects were also important in other societies, but they acquired and retained in Russia a special symbolic significance even for the complex culture of modern times.

Axe and Icon

NOTHING BETTER illustrates the combination of material struggle and spiritual exultation in Old Russia than the two objects that were traditionally hung together in a place of honor on the wall of every peasant hut: the axe and the icon. The axe was the basic implement of Great Russia: the indispensable means of subordinating the forest to the purposes of man. The icon, or religious picture, was the omnipresent reminder of the religious faith which gave the beleaguered frontiersman a sense of ultimate security and higher purpose. If the axe was used with delicacy to plane and smooth the wooden surface on which these holy pictures were painted, the icon, in turn, was borne militantly before the peasantry whenever they ventured forth into the forests with axes for the more harsh business of felling trees or warding off assailants.

The axe was as important to the *muzhik* of the north as a machete to the jungle dweller of the tropics. It was the "universal tool" with which a Russian could, according to Tolstoy, "both build a house and shape a spoon."[44] "You can get through all the world with an axe" and "The axe is

the head of all business"[45] were only two of many sayings. As one of the
first and best students of daily life in early Russia has explained:

> In the bleak wild forests and in the fields wherever the axe went, the
> scythe, plow, and whirl-bat of the bee-keeper followed; wherever axes cut
> into them, forests were destroyed and thinned, houses were built and re-
> paired, and villages created within the forests. . . .[46]

Pre-Christian tribes of the region frequently used axes for money and
buried them with their owners. The axe was popularly called the "thunderbolt," and stones found near a tree felled by lightning were revered as part of
the axehead used by the god of thunder.

The baptized Muscovite was no less reverential to the axe. He used it
to cut up, plane, and even carve wood. Not until relatively recent times
were nails—let alone saws and planes—widely used in building.[47] Axes were
used for close-range fighting, neutralizing the advantages that might otherwise be enjoyed by wolves, armored Teutonic swordsmen, or Mongol
cavalry.

One of the very few surviving jeweled works from the twelfth-century
Russian north is, appropriately, the initialed hatchet of the prince most
responsible for the transfer of power from Kiev to the north: Andrew
Bogoliubsky.[48]

The axe played a central role in consolidating the new civilization of
the upper Volga region. With it, Russians eventually cut out the *zasechnaia
cherta*—long clearings lined by sharpened stumps and cross-felled trees—
as a defense against invasion, fire, and plague.[49] The axe was the standard
instrument of summary execution, and became an abiding symbol of the
hard and primitive life on Europe's exposed eastern frontier. There is a
certain suppressed bitterness toward more sheltered peoples in the proverb
"To drink tea is not to hew wood." The Russian version of "The pen is
mightier than the sword" is "What is written with the pen cannot be
hacked away with an axe."[50]

More than the rifles from the west and the daggers from the east, the
axe of the north remained the court weapon of the Russian monarchy.
Even though their name literally meant "shooters," the *streltsy*, Russia's
first permanent infantry force of the sixteenth and seventeenth centuries,
drilled with axes and carried them in processions. The axe was the principal
weapon used by the tsars for putting down the urban rebellions of the
seventeenth century, and by the peasants for terrorizing the provincial
nobility and bureaucracy during their uprisings. Leaders of these revolts
were publicly executed by a great axe in Red Square in the ritual of

quartering. One stroke was used to sever each arm, one for the legs, and a final stroke for the head. Lesser figures merely had their hands, feet, or tongues chopped off.

Though anachronistic as a weapon by the nineteenth century, the axe lived on as a symbol of rebellion. The radical intellectuals were accused by moderate liberals as early as the 1850's of "seeking out lovers of the axe" and inviting Russians "to sharpen their axes."[51] Nicholas Dobroliubov, the radical journalist of the early 1860's, summarized the utopian socialist program of his friend Chernyshevsky's *What Is To Be Done?* as "Calling Russia to Axes." The first call inside Russia for a Jacobin revolution, the proclamation "Young Russia" on Easter Monday of the same 1862, proclaimed prophetically that Russia will become "the first country to realize the great cause of Socialism," and announced "we will cry 'To your axes' and strike the imperial party without sparing blows just as they do not spare theirs against us."[52] By the late 1860's, the notorious Nechaev had set up a secret "society of the axe" and young Russia had begun to develop a conspiratorial tradition of revolutionary organization that was to help inspire Lenin's own *What Is To Be Done?* of 1902: the first manifesto of Bolshevism. The sound of an axe offstage at the end of Chekhov's last play, *The Cherry Orchard,* announced the coming end of Imperial Russia. The terrifying purges of the 1930's, which brought to an end the hopes of the original visionary revolutionaries, finally played themselves out in distant Mexico in 1940 with the sinking of an ice axe into the most fertile and prophetic brain of the Revolution: that of Leon Trotsky. ——

Those who opposed revolution as the answer to Russia's problems often did so by playing back the old theme of the ravished forest eventually triumphing over the axes of men. The felled tree goes to its death more gracefully than dying man in Tolstoy's *Three Deaths;* and a fresh green sapling was planted over his grave by his request. Leonov's powerful novel of the mid-fifties, *The Russian Forest,* indicates that the Soviet regime played a key role in cutting down the forest, which becomes a symbol of Old Russian culture. If Leonov leaves the reader uncertain whether he stands on the side of the axe or the fallen trees, the political custodians of the Revolution made it clear that they stood behind the axe. Khrushchev publicly reminded Leonov that "not all trees are useful . . . from time to time the forest must be thinned." But Khrushchev himself was felled by political fortune in 1964; while Leonov, still standing, reminded his successors in power that "an iron object—that is, an axe—without the application of intelligence can do a great deal of mischief in centralized state use."[53]

Returning to the primitive forest hut of the early Russian peasant, one finds that there was one object which invariably hung next to the axe on the crude interior wall: a religious painting on wood, known to the Russians as a "form" (*obraz*), but better known by the original Greek word for picture or likeness: *eikon*. Icons were found wherever people lived and gathered in Russia—omnipresent reminders of the faith which gave the frontiersman of the east a sense of higher purpose.

The history of icons reveals both the underlying continuity with Byzantium and the originality of Russian cultural development. Though there is probably a continuous history back to the facial death portraits of early Egypt and Syria, holy pictures first became objects of systematic veneration and religious instruction in sixth- and seventh-century Byzantium at the time of a great growth in monasticism.[54] In the eighth century, the original iconoclasts led a movement to reduce the power of monks and destroy all icons. After a long struggle, they were defeated and icon veneration was officially endorsed at the second Council of Nicaea in 787: the last of the seven councils recognized as universally binding by the Orthodox world.

The Slavs were converted in the wake of this "triumph of Orthodoxy" —as the council was popularly called—and inherited the rediscovered Byzantine enthusiasm for religious painting. A sixth-century legend that the first icon was miraculously printed by Christ himself out of compassion for the leper king of Edessa became the basis for a host of Russian tales about icons "not created by hands." The triumphal carrying of this icon from Edessa to Constantinople on August 16, 944, became a feast day in Russia, and provided a model for the many icon-bearing processions which became so important in Russian church ritual.[55]

"If Byzantium was preeminent in giving the world theology expressed in words, theology expressed in images was given preeminently by Russia."[56] Of all the methods of depicting the feasts and mysteries of the faith, the painting of wooden icons soon came to predominate in Muscovy. Mosaic art declined as Russian culture lost its intimate links with Mediterranean craftsmanship. Fresco painting became relatively less important with the increasing dependence on wooden construction. Using the rich tempera paints which had replaced the encaustic wax paints of the pre-iconoclastic era, Russian artists carried on and amplified the tendencies which were already noticeable in eleventh- and twelfth-century Byzantine painting: (1) to dematerialize the figures in icons, presenting each saint in a prescribed and stylized form; and (2) to introduce new richness of detail, coloring, and controlled emotional intensity. The Russian artist stenciled his basic design from an earlier, Byzantine model onto a carefully prepared and seasoned panel, and then painted in color and detail. He gradually substituted pine for the cypress and lime of Byzantine icons, and developed new methods for brightening and layering his colors.

Although it is impossible to apply to icon painting those precise techniques of dating and classification familiar to Western art historians, certain regional characteristics had clearly emerged by the late fourteenth century. Novgorod used vigorous compositions with angular lines and unmixed bright colors. Tver had a characteristic light blue, Novgorod a distinctive bright red. Pskov, the nearby "younger brother" of Novgorod, introduced gold highlighting into robes. Distant Yaroslavl specialized in supple and elongated figures, sharing the general preference of the "northern school" for more simple and stylized design. Between Novgorod and Yaroslavl there gradually emerged in the Vladimir-Suzdal region a new style which surpassed the style of either, and produced some of the finest icons in the long history of the art. The paintings of this Moscow school broke decisively with the severity of the later Byzantine tradition and achieved even richer colors than Novgorod and more graceful figures than Yaroslavl. One recent critic has seen in the luminous colors of Andrew Rublev, the supreme master of the Moscow school, inner links with the beauties of the surrounding northern forest:

> He takes the colors for his palette not from the traditional canons of color, but from Russian nature around him, the beauty of which he acutely sensed. His marvelous deep blue is suggested by the blue of the spring sky; his whites recall the birches so dear to a Russian; his green is close to the color of unripe rye; his golden ochre summons up memories of fallen autumn leaves; in his dark green colors there is something of the twilight shadows of the dense pine forest. He translated the colors of Russian nature into the lofty language of art.[57]

Nowhere is Rublev's artistic language more lofty than in his most famous masterpiece, "The Old Testament Trinity," with its ethereal curvatures and luminous patches of yellow and blue. The subject illustrates how Russian iconography continued to reflect the attitudes and doctrines of the church. Since the Trinity was a mystery beyond man's power to visualize, it was represented only in its symbolic or anticipatory form of the three angels' appearance to Sarah and Abraham in the Old Testament. God the Father was never depicted, for no man had ever seen Him face to face. The Holy Spirit was also not represented in early iconography; and when the symbol of a white dove later entered from the West, pigeons came to be regarded as forbidden food and objects of reverence.

Naturalistic portraiture was even more rigorously rejected in Russia than in late Byzantium; and the break with classical art was even more complete. The suggestive qualities of statuary made this art form virtually unknown in Muscovy; and a promising tradition of bas-relief craftsmanship in Kievan times vanished altogether in the desire to achieve a more spiritualized representation of holy figures.[58] The flat, two-dimensional plane was religiously respected. Not only was there no perspective in an icon, there was often a conscious effort through so-called inverse perspective to keep the viewer from entering into the composition of a holy picture. Imaginative physical imagery of Western Christendom (such as the stigmata or sacred heart) was foreign to Orthodoxy and finds no representation in Russian art. Fanciful figures of classical antiquity were much less common in Russian than in Byzantine painting; and many were expressly excluded from Russian icons.

The extraordinary development of icon painting and veneration in thirteenth- and fourteenth-century Russia—like the original development in seventh-century Byzantium—occurred during a period of weakened political authority. In both cases, iconolatry accompanied a growth in monasticism.[59] The omnipresent holy pictures provided an image of higher authority that helped compensate for the diminished stature of temporal princes. In Russia, the icon often came to represent in effect the supreme communal authority before which one swore oaths, resolved disputes, and marched into battle.

But if the icon gave divine sanction to human authority, it also served to humanize divine authority. The basic icon for the all-important Easter feast is that of a very human Jesus breaking down the gates of hell and emerging from the fires into which he had been plunged since Good Friday —a scene rarely depicted in the Easter iconography of the West, where the emphasis was on the divine mystery of resurrection from an empty tomb. The early church had strenuously opposed the "Apollinarian" attempt to deny the reality of Christ's human nature, beating down this heresy at the Council of Chalcedon in 451. Partly because there had been support for Apollinaris' ideas in the Western Roman Empire, Christians of the Eastern Empire came to equate the fall of Rome with acceptance of this heresy. Byzantium came to view sacred pictures as emblems of a Christendom still resplendent in the "new Rome" of Constantinople at a time when the West had plunged into barbarism and darkness. At the same time, the victory over the iconoclasts represented a triumph over indigenous Eastern inclinations (derived largely from Jewish and Moslem teachings) to view as blasphemous all human images of the divine. Byzantium brought the unifying force of ideology into its multi-national empire by rejecting the idea common to many Oriental religions and Christian heresies that human salvation involved transforming one's humanity into something altogether different.[60]

The humanizing tendency of icon painting is noticeable in the images of the Virgin, which in twelfth-century Byzantium began to turn toward the infant Christ and to suggest maternity as well as divinity. One such icon, in which a large and composed Virgin presses her face down against that of Jesus, became the most revered of all icons in Russia: the Vladimir Mother of God, or Our Lady of Kazan.[61] The migration of this twelfth-century masterpiece from Constantinople to Kiev and thence to Suzdal and Vladimir even before the fall of Kiev symbolizes the northward movement of Russian culture. The cult of the Mother of God was considerably more intense in the North. The transfer of this icon to the Cathedral of the Assumption inside the Moscow Kremlin in the late fourteenth century enabled it to become a symbol of national unity long before such unity became a political fact. She was the supreme mother image of old Russia: at peace with God, yet compassionately inclined toward her infant son. Generation after generation prayed for her intercession within the cathedral dedicated to her entrance into heaven.

The history of this icon demonstrates the close collaboration between faith and fighting, art and armament, in medieval Russia. Brought north by the warrior prince Andrew Bogoliubsky, the icon was transferred to Moscow in 1395 expressly for the purpose of inspiring the defenders of the city against an expected seige by Tamerlane in the late fourteenth century. The name "Kazan" for the icon derives from the popular belief that Ivan the Terrible's later victory over the Tatars at Kazan was the result of its miraculous powers. Victory over the Poles during the "Time of Troubles" in the early seventeenth century was also attributed to it. Many believed that Mary had pleaded with Jesus to spare Russia further humiliation, and that he had promised to do so if Russia would repent and turn again to God. Four separate yearly processions in honor of the icon were established by 1520, moving within a few decades out of the Cathedral of the Assumption in the Kremlin across Red Square to St. Basil's (also called "Kazan") cathedral. This icon was also often used to sanctify troops setting off to battle, and "to meet" other icons or dignitaries coming to Moscow.[62]

In addition to the cult that developed around this icon, new poses of the Madonna began to appear in bewildering profusion. Most models were Byzantine; but there were uniquely Russian variations of this general type of "Our Lady of Tenderness" in some of which the Virgin bends her neck down beyond the point of anatomical possibility to embrace the Christ child. Some four hundred separate styles of representing the Virgin have been counted in Russian icons.[63] Some of the most popular and original resulted from a growing tendency to translate hymns of the church into visual form. The interdependence of sight, sound and smell had long been important in the liturgy of the Eastern Church; and beginning in the twelfth century, there was an increasing tendency to use sacred art as a direct illustration of the sung liturgy and seasonal hymns of the church.[64] Already in the fourteenth-century Russian north, new church murals were becoming, in effect, musical illustrations.[65] The Russian Christmas icon—"The Assembly of the Pre-sanctified Mother of God," illustrating all creation coming in adoration before the Virgin—is a direct transposition of the Christmas hymn. Increasingly popular in Russia also were icons of the Virgin surrounded by a variety of scenes taken from the set of twenty-four Lenten hymns of praise known as *akathistoi*.[66] Individual icons were also drawn from this series, such as the "Virgin of the Indestructible Wall," which perpetuated in almost every Russian city and monastery the Byzantine image of the Virgin strengthening the battlements of Constantinople against infidel assault. So great was the preoccupation with battle that semi-legendary warriors and contemporary battle scenes soon became incorporated into these holy pictures, making them an important source for the history of weaponry as well as piety.[67]

Hardly less dramatic than the broadening of subject matter and refinement of technique was the development of the iconostasis, or icon screen, Russia's most distinctive contribution to the use of icons. In Byzantium and Kiev, illustrated cloths and icons had often been placed on the central or "royal" doors that connected the sanctuary with the nave of the church and on the screen separating the two. Holy pictures had been painted and carved on the beam above the screen.[68] But it is only in Muscovy that one finds the systematic introduction of a continuous screen of icons extending high above the sanctuary screen, representing a kind of pictorial encyclopedia of Christian belief. From at least the end of the fourteenth century, when Rublev and two others designed the beautiful three-tiered iconostasis for the Archangel Cathedral in the Moscow Kremlin—the earliest surviving iconostasis—these illustrated screens began to be a regular feature of Russian churches. Beyond the many icons at eye level on the sanctuary screen were added up to six higher rows of icons, often reaching up to the ceilings of new churches.[69]

The Russian icon screen represented a further extension of the process of humanizing Orthodoxy—offering a multitude of pictorial links between the remote God of the East and the simple hopes of an awakening people. Placed between the sanctuary and the congregation, the icon screen lay "on the boundary between heaven and earth,"[70] and depicted the variety of human forms through which God had come from out of His holy place to redeem His people. Each icon provided an "external expression of the transfigured state of man,"[71] a window through which the believing eye could peer into the beyond. The icon screen as a whole provided a pictorial guide to the sanctification which only the church could give.

The tapers that were lit by the faithful to burn in large candelabras before the icon screen throughout and beyond each service transformed the otherwise dark and cold church into a "candlelight kingdom."[72] These flickering flames reminded the congregation of the forms which God the Father had mysteriously assumed within the "life-giving Trinity": the Son, who appeared to his apostles as pure light at the Transfiguration prior to His death; and the Holy Spirit, which came to them as pure flame at Pentecost after his final ascension.[73]

The iconostasis enabled Russians to combine their love of beauty with their sense of history. Lines became more supple and color richer as icon panels grew larger and the screens more comprehensive. Just as the individual lives of saints were gradually grafted into vast chronicles of sacred history, so icons were soon incorporated into these comprehensive pictorial records of sacred history that moved from Old Testament patriarchs and prophets in the highest row to local saints in the lowest. The panels in the center moved down to man—as had God Himself—through the Virgin to Christ, who sat at the center of the main "prayer row" of panels immediately over the royal doors. Modeled on the *Pantokrator,* who had stared down in lonely splendor from the central dome of Byzantine cathedrals, "Christ enthroned" acquired on the Russian iconostasis a less severe expression. The Lord's hitherto distant entourage of holy figures was brought down from the cupola of earlier Byzantine churches and placed in a row on either side of the traditional images of the Virgin and John the Baptist. These newly visible saints were inclined in adoration toward Christ, who, in turn, seemed to beckon the congregation to join their ranks as He looked straight ahead and held out the gospel, usually opened to the text "Come unto me, all ye that travail and are heavy laden, and I will refresh you."[74] As if in response, the faithful pressed forward during and after services to kiss as brothers in Christ the saints who stood closest to them on the sacred screen. This, like most acts of worship and veneration in Orthodox Russia, was accompanied by the bow or prostration of humility and by a sweeping, two-fingered sign of the cross: the public confession of faith.

The development of the iconostasis and the intensification of icon veneration in fourteenth- and fifteenth-century Russia set off Russian art from that of Western Christendom, where holy pictures were viewed increasingly as optional ornaments without any intrinsic theological significance,[75] and where artists were rediscovering—rather than moving away from—classical models and free inventiveness in depicting sacred subjects. Russia was moving not toward a renaissance, a new release of emancipated creativity and individual self-awareness, but toward a synthetic reaffirmation of tradition. Unlike the earlier "medieval synthesis" of the West, that of Russia was not based on an abstract analysis of the philosophic problems of belief but on the concrete illustration of its glories. The emotional attachment to sacred pictures helps explain why neither the art forms nor the rationalistic philosophy of classical antiquity played any significant role in the culture of early modern Russia. There were no important Russian imitators of the Renaissance art of Italy and Flanders, despite ample contact with both regions; and the rationalistic ideas that were brought into late medieval Russia through Westward-looking Novgorod appealed only to a small, cosmopolitan elite and were consistently banned by the ecclesiastical hierarchy.

It would be hard to overestimate the importance of icons for Muscovite culture. Each icon reminded man of God's continuing involvement in human affairs. Its truth could be immediately apprehended even by those incapable of reading or reflection. It offered not a message for thought but an illustration for reassurance of God's power in and over history for men who might otherwise have been completely mired in adversity and despair.

Amidst this sea of pictures, thought tended to crystallize in images rather than ideas; and the "political theory" that developed in early Russia has been well described as a belief that "the Tsar is, as it were, the living icon of God, just as the whole Orthodox Empire is the icon of the heavenly world."[76] The icon screen provided, moreover, a model for the hierarchical order of Russian society. Each figure occupied a prescribed position in a prescribed way, but all were unified by their common distance from the God of the sanctuary, and by their dependent relationship to the central panel of Christ enthroned. The term *chin* ("rank") was used both for the general order of the icon screen, and for the central *deēsis,* or "prayer row," which was the largest, easiest to see, and the source of many of the most famous large icons now in museums. *Chin* became the general term for prescribed rank in Muscovy, and its verbal form *uchiniti* the main word for command. By the seventeenth century, this concept had become the basis of an entire social order. Tsar Alexis' law code of 1649 was an almost iconographic guide for the behavior of each rank in society; and a few years later he even drafted a *chin* for his hunting falcons.[77]

Russia was fated to maintain hierarchical forms of society while progressively shedding the religious idealism that had originally sanctioned them. Alexis' law code remained in effect until 1833, but the iconographic tradition was shattered and the church split even before the end of his reign in the seventeenth century. Naturalistic figures and theatrical compositions were introduced awkwardly and eclectically from Western models; older icons vanished beneath metal casings and layers of dark varnish; and serpentine rococo frames agitated the icon screen and seemed to constrict the holy figures they surrounded. The traditional *chin* of Muscovy had been replaced by the *chinovnik* ("petty bureaucrat") of Petersburg; and icon painting as a sacred tradition, by icon production as a state concession. The icon is only "good for covering pots," proclaimed Vissarion Belinsky in the 1840's,[78] pointing the way to the new artistic iconoclasm of the Russian revolutionary tradition.

Yet the spell of the icon was never completely broken. Nothing else quite took its place, and Russians remained reluctant to conceive of painting as men did in the West. Russians remained more interested in the ideal represented by a painting than in its artistic texture. To Dostoevsky, Holbein's "Christ in the Tomb" suggested a denial of Christian faith; Claude Lorraine's "Acis and Galatea," a secular utopia. The print of Raphael's Sistine Madonna over his writing desk was the personal icon of his own effort to reconcile faith and creative power.[79] The revolutionaries themselves looked with the eyes of icon venerators on the heroic naturalism of much nineteenth-century Russian secular painting. Many found a call to revolutionary defiance in the proud expression of an unbowed boy in Repin's famous "Haulers on the Volga." Just as the Christian warriors of an earlier age had made vows before icons in church on the eve of battle, so Russian Revolutionaries—in the words of Lenin's personal secretary—"swore vows in the Tret'iakov Gallery on seeing such pictures."[80]

Large-scale cleaning and restoration in the early twentieth century helped Russians rediscover at long last the purely artistic glories of the older icons. Just as the hymns and chants of the church had provided new themes and inspiration for early Russian iconographers, so their rediscovered paintings gave fresh inspiration back to poets and musicians as well as painters in late imperial Russia. Under the former seminarian Stalin, however, the icon lived on not as the inspiration for creative art but as a model for mass indoctrination. The older icons, like the newer experimental paintings, were for the most part locked up in the reserve collections of museums. Pictures of Lenin in the "red corner" of factories and public places replaced icons of Christ and the Virgin. Photographs of Lenin's successors deployed in a prescribed order on either side of Stalin replaced the old "prayer row," in which saints were deployed in fixed order on either side of Christ enthroned. Just as the iconostasis of a cathedral was generally built directly over the grave of a local saint and specially reverenced with processions on a religious festival, so these new Soviet saints appeared in ritual form over the mausoleum of the mummified Lenin on the feast days of Bolshevism to review endless processions through Red Square.

In the context of Russian culture this attempt to capitalize politically on the popular reverence for icons represents only an extension of an established tradition of debasement. The Polish pretender Dmitry, the Swedish warrior Gustavus Adolphus, most of the Romanovs, and many of their generals had themselves painted in semi-iconographic style for the Russian populace.[81] An émigré Old Believer—for whom all modern history represents a foredoomed divergence from the true ways of Old Russia—looked with indifference and even joy upon the transfer of the icon of Our Lady of Kazan from a cathedral to a museum early in the Soviet era:

> The Queen of Heaven, divesting herself of her regal robes, issued forth from her Church to preach Christianity in the streets.[82]

Stalin added an element of the grotesque to the tradition of politically debasing spiritual things. He introduced new icons and relics in the name of science, then proceeded to retouch and desecrate them, before his own image and remains were posthumously defiled. The lesser figures on the Soviet iconostasis had removed the central icon of Stalin enthroned, and largely destroyed the new myth of salvation. But in the uncertain age that followed, lithographs of Lenin and giant cranes continued to hover over prefabricated concrete huts piled on one another much as the icon and the axe had over the wooden huts of a more primitive era.

Bell and Cannon

IF THE ICON AND THE AXE in the peasant hut became abiding symbols for Russian culture, so too did the bell and cannon of the walled city. These were the first large metal objects to be manufactured indigenously in the wooden world of Muscovy: objects that distinguished the city from the surrounding countryside and fortified it against alien invaders.

Just as the icon and the axe were closely linked with one another, so were the bell and cannon. The axe had fashioned and could destroy the wooden board on which the painting was made. Likewise, the primitive foundry which forged the first cannon also made the first bells; and these were always in peril of being melted back into metal for artillery in time of war. The bell, like the icon, was taken from Byzantium to provide aesthetic elaboration for the "right praising" of God; and both media came to be used with even greater intensity and imagination than in Constantinople. The development of the elaborate and many-tiered Russian bell tower—with its profusion of bells and onion-shaped gables—parallels in many ways that of the iconostasis. The rich "mauve" ringing of bells so that "people cannot hear one another in conversation"[83] became the inevitable accompaniment of icon-bearing processions on special feast days. There were almost as many bells and ways to ring them as icons and ways to display them. By the early fifteenth century, Russia had evolved distinctive models that differed from the bells of Byzantium, Western Europe, or the Orient. The Russian emphasis on massive, immovable metal bells sounded by metal gongs and clappers led to a greater sonority and resonance than the generally smaller, frequently swinging, and often wooden bells of the contemporary West. Although Russia never produced carillons comparable to those of the Low Countries, it did develop its own methods and traditions of ringing different-sized bells in series. By the sixteenth century, it has been estimated that there were more than five thousand bells in the four hundred churches of Moscow alone.[84]

Just as the icon was but one element in a pictorial culture that included the fresco, the illuminated holy text, and the illustrated chronicle, so the bell was only part of a torrent of sound provided by interminable chanted church services, popular hymns and ballads, and the secular improvisations of wandering folk singers armed with a variety of stringed instruments. Sights and sounds pointed the way to God, not philosophic speculation or literary subtlety. Services were committed to memory without benefit of missal or prayer book; and the "obedient listeners" in monasteries were subjected to oral instruction. Not only were the saints said to be "very like" the holy forms on the icons, but the very word for education suggested "becoming like the forms" (obrazovanie).

The interaction between sight and sound is also remarkable. If the iconography of fourteenth- and fifteenth-century Russia drew special inspiration from holy singing, and the Russian icon came to be a kind of "abstract musical arabesque . . . purified, like music, of all but its direct appeals to the spirit,"[85] so the new method of musical notation that was simultaneously coming into being in Muscovy had a kind of hieroglyphic quality. The authority of the classical Byzantine chant appears to have waned after the fourteenth century—without giving way to any other method of clearly defining the intervals and correlations of tones. In its place appeared the "signed chant": a new tradition of vocal ornamentation in which "melody not only flowed out of words, but served as the mold on which words were set in bold relief."[86] When written down, the embellished red and black hooked notes offered only a shorthand guide to the direction of melody rather than a precise indication of pitch; but the vivid pictorial impression created by the signs gave rise to descriptive names such as "the great spider," "the thunderbolt," "two in a boat," and so on.[87]

Though even less is known about secular than sacred music in this early period, there were apparently patterns of beauty in it, based on repetition with variation by different voices. The exalted "rejoicing" *(blagovestie)* of the bells used an overlapping series of sounds similar to that which was used in the "many-voiced" church chant—producing an effect that was at the same time cacophonous and hypnotic.

Russians felt the same mixture of joyful religious exultation and animistic superstition in the ringing of the bells as in the veneration of icons. Just as icons were paraded to ward off the evil spirits of plague, drought, and fire, so were bells rung to summon up the power of God against these forces. Just as icons were paraded around the boundaries to sanctify a land claim, so bells were rung to lend solemnity to official gatherings. In both cases, spiritual sanctification was more valued than legal precision. As with the icon, so with the bell, men valued them for their anagogical power to lift men up to God:

> The weak sounds of wood and metal remind us of the unclear, mysterious words of the prophets, but the loud and vigorous play of bells is like the rejoicing of the Gospel, radiating out to all the corners of the universe and lifting one's thoughts to the angelic trumpets of the last day.[88]

The forging and ringing of bells, like the painting and veneration of icons, was a sacramental act in Muscovy: a means of bringing the word of God into the presence of men. This "word" was the *logos* of St. John's gospel: the word which was in the beginning, was revealed perfectly in Christ, and was to be praised and magnified until His Second Coming. There was no need to speculate about this unmerited gift, but only to preserve intact the inherited forms of giving thanks and praise. There was no reason to write discursively about the imperfect world of here and now when one could see—however darkly—through the beauty of sights and sounds a transfigured world beyond.

The importance of bells in lending color and solemnity to church proceedings was heightened by the general prohibition on the use of musical instruments in Orthodox services. Only the human voice and bells were permitted (with an occasional use of trumpet or drum in such rituals as the furnace show or a welcoming procession). The absence from early Muscovy of polyphony or even a systematic scale made the rough but many-shaded harmonies sounded upon the bells seem like the ultimate in earthly music. Just as Muscovy resisted the contemporary Western tendency to introduce perspective and naturalism into religious painting, so it resisted the concurrent Western tendency to use bells to provide orderly musical intervals or to accompany (with fixed tonal values and often in conjunction with an organ) the singing of sacred offices.[89]

The bell played an important part in material as well as spiritual culture through its technological tie-in with the manufacture of cannon. Already by the late fourteenth century—only a few years after the first appearance of cannon in the West—Russians had begun to manufacture cannon along with bells; and, by the sixteenth century, they had produced the largest of each item to be found anywhere in the world. So important were these twin metal products to Muscovy that the largest example of each was given the title "Tsar": the bell, "Tsar Kolokol," weighing nearly half a million pounds; the cannon, "Tsar Pushka," with a barrel nearly a yard wide.

They represent the first example of "overtaking and surpassing" a superior technology. But they illustrate as well the artificiality of the accomplishment. For the bell was too large to hang, the cannon too broad to fire. Technological accomplishments in both fields were, moreover, in good measure the work of foreigners from the time in the early fourteenth century when a certain "Boris the Roman" first came to cast bells for Moscow and Novgorod.[90]

If the bell predated the cannon as an object of technological interest, the cannon soon replaced it as the main object of state concern. Many bells in provincial cities and monasteries were systematically melted down to provide cannon for the swelling Russian armies of the late seventeenth and the eighteenth century; but innumerable bells remained in Moscow, the skyline of which was dominated by the soaring 270-foot Bell Tower of Ivan the Great, which Boris Godunov had erected on a hill inside the Kremlin at the very beginning of this period. This tower was intended (like another massive bell tower built by Patriarch Nikon just outside Moscow in the latter part of the century) to be the crowning glory of a "New Jerusalem" on Russian soil: a center of civilization built in partial imitation of the old Jerusalem, and with enough embellishment to suggest the New. The tower in the Kremlin provided the shelter from which the fundamentalist Old Believers later hurled stones at official church processions.[91] These defenders of the old order resisted the cannon fire of government troops for eight years in their northern monastic redoubt at Solovetsk. After this last, storied bastion fell, they spread out to the provinces to watch for the approach of the Tsar's "legions of Antichrist" from the bell towers of wooden churches, whence they sounded the signal to set fire to the church and the true believers within.[92]

The later Romanov tsars revealed both uneasy consciences and bad taste by filling the ancient monasteries with votive baroque bell towers. By the second quarter of the nineteenth century, the older bell towers had been largely displaced, restrictions placed on the excessive ringing of bells, and their special position in worship services challenged by the intrusion of organs and other instruments into Russian liturgical music.

Yet the echo of bells lingered on. They ring again majestically at the end of the coronation scene in Musorgsky's *Boris Godunov;* and the theological hint of redemption offered by their "ringing through" (*perezvon*) on the eve of festive days is recaptured by the little barking dog of that name that leads Alyosha's youthful comrades to reconciliation at the end of Dostoevsky's *Brothers Karamazov.*

In the world of politics, too, the bell called up memories. Bells had been used in some of the proud, Westward-looking cities of medieval Russia to summon the popular assembly (*veche*). The final silencing of the assembly bell of Novgorod in 1478 ended the tradition of relative freedom from imperial authority and partial popular rule which until then Novgorod had shared with many commercial cities of the West. The ideal of non despotic, representative government impelled the early-nineteenth-century reformer to

take myself in imagination back to Novgorod. I hear the ringing bell of the popular assembly . . . I throw the chains off my feet, and to the "Who goes there?" of the guard, I proudly reply: "a free citizen of Novgorod!"[93]

and the romantic poet to

sound forth like the bell in the assembly tower in the days of the people's celebrations and misfortunes.[94]

When, a few years later, lyricism turned to anguish, Gogol gave a new, more mysterious quality to the image in one of the most famous passages in all Russian literature. Likening Russia to a speeding troika (carriage with three horses) near the end of *Dead Souls,* he asks its destination. But "there was no answer save the bell pouring forth marvellous sound."

A prophetic answer came a few years later in the prefatory poem to the first issue of Russia's first illegal revolutionary journal—appropriately called *Kolokol* (*The Bell*). The long-silent social conscience of Russia will henceforth—promised the editor, Alexander Herzen—sound out like a bell

swinging back and forth with a tone which shall not cease to reverberate until . . . a joyful, orderly, and quietly heroic bell begins to ring in every man.[95]

But Herzen's summoning bell was soon drowned out by the shrill sounds of the *Nabat:* the special alarm bell traditionally used in times of fire or attack and the name of the first Russian periodical urging the formation of a Jacobin recolutionary elite.[96] Tkachev, the editor of *Nabat,* was vindicated by the eventual victory of Lenin's professional revolutionaries. But under Bolshevism, all bells fell silent—their function to some extent taken up by the hypnotic sounding of machines, which announced the coming of an earthly rather than a heavenly paradise.

The enduring Russian fascination with cannon was evidenced in Ivan IV's storied storming of Kazan in 1552; the shooting out of the cannon by a Moscow mob in 1606 of the remains of the False Dmitry, the only foreigner ever to reign in the Kremlin; the determination of Chaikovsky to score real cannon fire into his overture commemorating the defeat of Napoleon in 1812; and in the later tsars' use of a hundred cannon to announce their annointment during a coronation.[97] Stalin was neurotically preoccupied with massed artillery formations throughout the Second World War; and his military pronouncements conferred only on the artillery the adjective *grozny* ("terrible" or "dread") traditionally applied to Ivan IV.[98] Subsequent Soviet success with rockets can be seen as an extension of this long-time interest. There seems a kind of historic justice to the interdependence in the late 1950's between the dazzling effects of cosmic cannoneering and the renewed promises of a classless millennium.

The Communist world that had come into being by then corresponded less to the prophecies of Karl Marx than to those of an almost unknown Russian contemporary, Nicholas Il'in.[99] While the former spent his life as an uprooted intellectual in Berlin, Paris, and London, the latter spent his as a patriotic artillery officer in Russian central Asia. Whereas the former looked to the rational emergence of a new, basically Western European proletariat under German leadership, the latter looked to the messianic arrival of a new Eurasian religious civilization under Russian tutelage. At the very time Marx was writing his *Communist Manifesto* for German revolutionaries refuged in France and Belgium, Il'in was proclaiming his *Tidings of Zion* to Russian sectarians in Siberia. Il'in's strange teachings reflect the childlike love of cannon, the primitive ethical dualism, and the suppressed fear of Europe, which were all present in Russian thinking. His followers marched to such hymns as "The Bomb of the Divine Artillery"; divided the world into men of Jehovah and of Satan (*Iegovisty i Satanisty*), those sitting at the right and left hand of God (*desnye i oshuinye*); and taught that a new empire of complete brotherhood and untold wealth would be formed by the followers of Jehovah along a vast railroad stretching from the Middle East through Russia to south China.

In a similar, but even more visionary vein, Nicholas Fedorov, an ascetic and self-effacing librarian in late nineteenth-century Moscow, prophesied that a new fusion of science and faith would lead even to the physical resuscitation of dead ancestors. Russia was to give birth in concert with China to a new Eurasian civilization, which was to use artillery to regulate totally the climate and surrounding atmosphere of this world, and thrust its citizens into the stratosphere to colonize others. His vision of cosmic revolution fascinated both Dostoevsky and Tolstoy, and influenced a number of Promethean dreamers in the earliest Soviet planning agencies.[100] His most inspired followers fled, however, from Bolshevik Russia to Harbin, Manchuria, to form a quasi-religious commune, which was in turn engulfed when the wave of Leninist, political revolution spread from their native to their adopted land.

Russian history is full of such prophetic anticipations, just as it is of reappearing symbols and fixations. That which has fallen before axe or cannon has often buried itself into the consciousness, if not the conscience, of the executioner. That which is purged from the memory lives on in the subconscious; that which is expunged from written records survives in oral folklore. Indeed, one finds in modern Russian history much of the same recurrence of basic themes that one finds in the unrefined early traditions of bell ringing and popular singing.

It may be, of course, that these echoes from childhood no longer reverberate in the adult Russia of today. Even if real, these sounds may be as enigmatic as the ringing of Gogol's troika; or perhaps only a dying echo: the *perezvon* that remains misleadingly audible after the bell has already fallen silent. To determine how much of Old Russian culture may have survived, one must leave aside these recurring symbols from the remote past and turn to the historical record, which begins in the fourteenth century to provide a rich if bewildering flow of accomplishment that extends without interruption to the present. Having looked at the heritage, environment, and early artifacts of Russian culture, one must now turn to the rise of Muscovy and its dramatic confrontation with a Western world in the throes of the Renaissance and Reformation.

II

THE CONFRONTATION

The Early Fourteenth to the Early Seventeenth Century

THE RISE *of a distinctive civilization under the leadership of Moscow from the establishment of its metropolitan seat in 1326 to the achievement of military hegemony and the first assumption of imperial titles during the reign of Ivan III, "the Great" (1462–1505). Monastic leadership in the colonization of the Russian north (particularly in the century between the founding by St. Sergius of the Monastery of the Holy Trinity in 1337 and the founding of the Solovetsk Monastery on the White Sea in 1436), and in the creation of a sense of national unity and destiny. Increased militance and xenophobia in the face of attacks by knightly orders from the West, continuing conflict with the Mongols, and the Byzantine collapse of 1453. The growth of prophetic passion as an intensification of the historical bias of Russian theology: the fools in Christ, Moscow as the "third Rome."*

The complex, traumatic confrontation of a powerful but primitive Muscovy with a Western Europe in the throes of the Renaissance and the Reformation. The destruction of the rationalistic and republican traditions of cosmopolitan Novgorod; the victory of the Moscow-oriented hierarchy over the Westward-looking heretics. The importance of Catholic ideas in the formation of the authoritarian "Josephite" ideology of the sixteenth century adopted by the Muscovite Tsars even while denouncing "the Latins." The growing military and technological dependence—under Ivan IV, "the Terrible" (1533–84), Boris Godunov (1598–1605), and Michael Romanov (1613–45)—on the North European "Germans" despite ideological opposition to Protestantism.

The reign of Ivan IV as both the culmination and the first breaking point in the Muscovite ideal of building a prophetic, religious civilization. On the one hand, his fixation with genealogical sanctification, his attempt to monasticize all of Russian life, and the similarities of his rule with that of the kings of ancient Israel and of contemporary Spain. On the other, Ivan's breaking of the sacred ruling line (dating back to the legendary summons of Riurik to Novgorod in 862) and preparing the way for the tradition of "false pretenders," and his involvement of Russia in Western politics through his attempt to move west into the Baltic during the costly Livonian Wars of 1558–83. The coming of the Western European religious wars to Russian soil, as Lutheran Sweden and Catholic Poland begin a long, losing struggle with Muscovy for control of northeastern Europe during the Russian interregnum, or "Time of Troubles" (1604–13).

1 . The Muscovite Ideology

THE UNIQUENESS of the new Great Russian culture that gradually emerged after the eclipse of Kiev is exemplified by the tent roof and the onion dome: two striking new shapes, which by the early sixteenth century dominated the skyline of the Russian north.

The lifting up of soaring wooden pyramids from raised octagonal churches throughout this period probably represents the adoption of wooden construction methods which pre-existed Christianity in the Great Russian north. Whatever obscure relationship the Russian tent roof may bear to Scandinavian, Caucasian, or Mongol forms, its development from primitive, horizontal log construction and its translation from wood into stone and brick in the sixteenth century was a development unique to northern Russia. The new onion dome and the pointed onion-shaped gables and arches also have anticipations if not roots in other cultures (particularly those of Islam); but the wholesale replacement of the spherical Byzantine and early Russian dome with this new elongated shape and its florid decorative use—not least atop tent roofs—is also peculiar to Muscovy.[1] The supreme surviving example of the Muscovite style, the wooden Church of the Transfiguration at Kizhi, on Lake Onega, has been likened to a giant fir tree because of the massive, jagged shape produced by superimposing twenty-two onion domes on its sharp, pyramidal roof. The new vertical thrust of the tent and onion shapes is related both to the material need for snow-shedding roofs and to the spiritual intensification of the new Muscovite civilization. These gilded new shapes rising out of the woods and snow of the north seemed to represent something distinct from either Byzantium or the West.

The Byzantine cupola over a church describes the dome of heaven covering earth; the Gothic spire describes the uncontainable striving upward, the lifting up from earth to heaven of the weight of stone. Finally, our fatherland's "onion dome" incarnates the idea of deep prayerful fervor rising towards the heavens. . . . This summit of the Russian church is like a tongue of fire crowned by a cross and reaching up to the cross. When looking from afar in the clear sunlight at an old Russian monastery or town, it seems to be burning with a many-colored flame; and when these flames glimmer from afar amid endless snow-covered fields, they attract us to them like a distant, ethereal vision of the City of God.[2]

Of all the gilded spires and domes that drew Russians in from the countryside to new urban centers of civilization none were more imposing than those of Moscow and its ecclesiastic citadel, the Kremlin. Seated on the high ground at the center of Moscow, the Kremlin had, by the beginning of the seventeenth century, gathered behind its moats and walls a host of objects which seemed to offer the Orthodox some "distant, ethereal vision of the City of God." Here were the largest bells, the most splendid icons (including the Vladimir Mother of God and Rublev's greatest iconostasis), and a cluster of magnificent new churches rising over the graves of princes and saints. Highest of all stood the domes of the bell tower of Ivan the Great. Its more than fifty bells represented the most ambitious single effort to simulate "the angelic trumpets" of the world to come; and the proliferation of lesser bell towers throughout the sprawling city of 100,000[3] attracted to the new capital the enduring designation of "Moscow of the forty forties," or sixteen hundred belfries.

Moscow, the second great city of Russian culture, has remained the largest city of Russia and an enduring symbol for the Russian imagination. The new empire of the Eastern Slavs that slowly emerged out of the divisions and humiliations of the appanage period was known as Muscovy long before it was called Russia. Moscow was the site of the "third Rome" for apocalyptical monks in the sixteenth century, and of the "third international" for apocalyptical revolutionaries in the twentieth. The exotic beauty of the Kremlin—even though partly the work of Italians—came to symbolize the prophetic pretensions of modern Russia and its thirst for some earthly taste of the heavenly kingdom.

Of all the northern Orthodox cities to survive the initial Mongol assault, Moscow must have seemed one of the least likely candidates for future greatness. It was a relatively new wooden settlement built along a tributary of the Volga, with shabby walls not even made of oak. It lacked the cathedrals and historic links with Kiev and Byzantium, of Vladimir and Suzdal; the economic strength and Western contacts of Novgorod and Tver; and the fortified position of Smolensk. It is not even mentioned in the chronicles until the mid-twelfth century, it did not have its own permanent resident prince until the early fourteenth, and none of its original buildings are known to have survived even into the seventeenth.

The rise of the "third Rome," like that of the first, has long tantalized historians. There are almost no surviving records for the critical 140 years

between the fall of Kiev and the turning of the Tatar tide under the leadership of Moscow at Kulikovo field in 1380. Perhaps for this very reason,
there is a certain fascination in weighing and balancing the factors usually
cited to explain the rapid emergence of Muscovy: its favorable central location, the skill of its grand dukes, its special position as collecting agent of the
Mongol tribute, and the disunity of its rivals. Yet these explanations—like
those of Soviet economic determinists in more recent years—seem insuffi-
cient to account fully for the new impetus and sense of purpose that
Muscovy suddenly demonstrated—in the icon workshop as well as on the
battlefield.

To understand the rise of Muscovy, one must consider the religious
stirrings which pre-existed and underlay its political accomplishments. Long
before there was any political or economic homogeneity among the Eastern
Slavs, there was a religious bond, which was tightened during the Mongol
period.

The Orthodox Church brought Russia out of its dark ages, providing a
sense of unity for its scattered people, higher purpose for its princes, and
inspiration for its creative artists. In the course of the fourteenth century,
the prevailing term for a simple Russian peasant became *krest'ianin,* which
was apparently synonymous with "Christian" *(khristianin).*[4] The phrase "of
all Rus'," which later became a key part of the tsar's title, was first invoked
at the very nadir of Russian unity and power at the turn of the thirteenth
century, not by any prince, but by the ranking prelate of the Russian
Church, the Metropolitan of Vladimir.[5] The transfer of the Metropolitan's
seat from Vladimir to Moscow in 1326 was probably an even more important milestone in the emergence of Moscow to national leadership than the
celebrated bestowal by the Tatars in the following year of the title "Great
Prince" on Ivan Kalita, Prince of Moscow. Probably more important than
Kalita or any of the early Muscovite Princes in establishing this leadership
was Alexis, the fourteenth-century Metropolitan of Moscow, and the first
Muscovite ever to occupy such a high ecclesiastical position.

Within the church the monasteries played the key role in the revival of
Russian civilization, just as they had somewhat earlier in the West. Monastic
revival helped to consolidate the special position of Moscow within Russia,
and inspired Russians everywhere with the sense of destiny, militance, and
colonizing zeal on which subsequent successes depended.

The monastic revival of the north took definite form in the 1330's,
when Metropolitan Alexis began to build a large number of churches within
the Moscow Kremlin, providing a new religious aura to the citadel of power
and centers of worship for several new monastic communities. Unlike the
carefully organized and regulated monasteries of Western Christendom,

these communities were loosely structured. Although they subscribed to the ritualized communal rule of St. Theodore Studite, discipline was irregular, the monks often gathering only for common meals and worship services. One reason for this relative laxness was the very centrality of the monasteries in Russian civilization. In contrast to most other monasteries of the Christian East, early Russian monasteries had generally been founded inside the leading princely cities, and monastic vows were often undertaken by figures who continued their previous political, economic, and military activities. Thus, the activities of Alexis as monk and metropolitan were in many ways merely a continuation under more impressive auspices of his earlier military and political exploits as a member of the noble Biakont family in Moscow. Yet Alexis' new-found belief that God was with him brought new strength to the Muscovite cause. His relics were subsequently reverenced along with those of the first metropolitan of Moscow, Peter, who had been canonized at the insistence of Ivan Kalita. The most important of the new monasteries built by Alexis inside the Kremlin was named the Monastery of the Miracles in honor of the wonder-working powers attributed to the saintly lives and relics of these early metropolitans.

The central figure in the monastic revival and in the unification of Russia during the fourteenth century was Sergius of Radonezh. Like his friend Alexis, Sergius was of noble origin; but his conversion to a religious profession was more profound and seminal. Sergius had come to Moscow from Rostov, a vanquished rival city to the east. Disillusioned with Moscow and the lax older traditions of monastic life, he set off into the forest to recapture through prayer and self-denial the holiness of the early Church. His piety and physical bravery attracted others to the new monastery he founded northeast of Moscow in 1337. Dedicated to the Holy Trinity and later named for its founder, this monastery became for Muscovy what the Monastery of the Caves had been for Kiev: a center of civilization, a shrine for pilgrimage, and the second *Lavra,* or large parent monastery, in Russian history.

Certain distinctions between the monastery of St. Sergius and older ones in Kiev and Novgorod point to the new role monasteries were to play in Russian civilization. St. Sergius' monastery was located outside of the political center, and its demands on the individual—in terms of physical labor and ascetic forbearance—were far more severe. This exposed location encouraged the monastery also to assume the roles of fortress and colonizing center.

The monastic revival in Russia depended not only on the heroism and sanctity of men like Sergius but also on important spiritual influences from the crumbling Byzantine Empire. Perplexed by its own misfortunes and embittered by harassment from the Catholic West, Byzantine monasticism in the late thirteenth and the fourteenth century increasingly turned away from the Studite rule in the monasteries and from the growing influence of Western scholasticism to a new mystical movement known as Hesychasm.[6]

This movement contended that there was a direct personal way to God available to man through the "inner calm" (*hēsychia*) which came from ascetic discipline of the flesh and silent prayers of the spirit. Darkness, fasting, and holding the breath were seen as aids to the achievement of this inner calm, and the traditional sacraments of the Church and even the verbal prayer of an individual believer subtly came to be viewed as irrelevant if not positively distracting. The Hesychasts believed that such a process of inner purification would prepare man for divine illumination: for a glimpse of the uncreated light from God which had appeared to the apostles on Mount Tabor at the time of Christ's Transfiguration. The Hesychasts sought to avoid the heretical assertion that man could achieve identity with God by insisting that this illumination placed man only in contact with the "energy" (*energeia*) and not the "essence" (*ousia*) of the divine. This distinction and the belief that man could gain a glimpse of the divine light were upheld as articles of faith by the Eastern Church in 1351.

The triumph of Hesychasm in the late days of the Byzantine Empire further estranged Orthodoxy from the disciplined and ornately sacramental Roman Church of the late Middle Ages. By challenging authority and encouraging men to seek a direct path to God, Hesychasm represented in some ways an Eastern anticipation of Protestantism.

Nowhere was the victory of the new mysticism and the estrangement from Rome more complete than in the newly opened monasteries of the Russian north. The hostility of the surroundings had long required ascetic qualities of resourcefulness and endurance. The political disintegration of Kievan Russia had led some monks like St. Sergius to seek salvation by leaving the cities altogether in imitation of the early desert fathers. Thus, it is not surprising that the new monasteries of these pioneering Russian hermits should prove receptive to the hesychastic teachings which reached the north through pilgrims returning from the Russian monastery on Mt. Athos and through Orthodox Slavs fleeing to Muscovy after the fall of the Balkans to Islam. The separation of Muscovy from classical traditions of rational theology and clear hierarchical discipline rendered the region ripe for a doctrine emphasizing direct contact with God. At the same time, the closeness of the hermit-monks to nature (and to the animistic paganism of non-Christian tribes) led them to dwell in an almost Franciscan manner on the theme of God's involvement in all of creation. Just as the apostles had seen a glimpse of light from God at the Transfiguration of Christ, so could a

true monk in Christ's universal church gain a glimmer of the coming transfiguration of the cosmos. The debilitating bleakness of the environment
created a need to believe not just in human salvation but in a transformation
of the entire natural world.

The theme of transfiguration was sometimes blended with that of the
millennial Second Coming of Christ. Popular "spiritual songs" of the
Muscovite period told of the coming of glory to "the communal church all
transfigured" atop a mountain—a seeming combination of Tabor and
Athos.[7] The hermit-monks who founded new monasteries on the northeastern frontier of Europe thought of their new houses not so much as institutions designed to revivify the established Church as transitory places in
man's pilgrimage toward the Second Coming. The icons showing St. Sergius
calming the wild beasts and preaching to animals and plants[8] emphasized
the fact that the promised end was not just the resurrection of the dead but
the transfiguration of all creation.

In the century following the establishment of St. Sergius' new monastery at Zagorsk, some 150 new monasteries were founded in one of the most
remarkable missionary movements in Christian history.[9] Most of the founders were strongly influenced by Hesychasm, but they were also, like the
Cistercians of the medieval West, hard-working pioneers opening up new
and forbidding lands for cultivation and colonization. The outward reach of
the monasteries had extended some three hundred miles north of Moscow
by 1397, with the founding of the monastery of St. Cyril on the White Lake.
By 1436, just a century after the founding of St. Sergius' monastery, the
movement had reached yet another three hundred miles north into the
islands of the White Sea with the founding of the Solovetsk Monastery by
Savva and Zosima. There were more saints from this period of Russian
history than any other; and prominent among them were Sergius, Cyril,
Savva, and Zosima, whose monasteries became leading shrines because of
the miraculous powers accredited to their relics and remains.

Another widely venerated local saint of the fourteenth century was
Stephen of Perm, whose career illustrates the civilizing and colonizing function of Russian monasticism. This learned and ascetic figure carried Christian teachings 750 miles east of Moscow to the most distant tributary of the
Volga, at the foot of the Ural Mountains. There he evangelized the pagan
Komi peoples, inventing an alphabet for their language and translating Holy
Scripture into it. Stephen left an enduring impact on the distant region as its
cultural leader and first bishop. He returned to Moscow to be buried in a
church appropriately called Savior in the Forest. Thanks largely to Moscow
chroniclers the story of his heroic battles with natural elements and pagan
sorcerers kindled the awakening imagination of Russian Christians. The

"Life of Stephen of Perm" by the greatest hagiographer of the age, Epi-phanius the Wise, set a new standard for flowery eulogy and became perhaps the most popular of the many new lives of local saints.[10]

The most influential of Epiphanius' *Lives,* however, was that of St. Sergius of Radonezh, which he wrote shortly before his death in 1420. Richer than his earlier works in factual material and the use of vernacular terms, Epiphanius' life of Sergius reads like a history of Russia in the fourteenth century and helps explain how this lonely ascetic has come to be known as the "builder of Russia."[11] Respect for his selflessness and sanctity enabled Sergius to become a counselor and arbiter among the warring princes of the Volga-Oka region. The links that developed with nearby Zagorsk helped Moscow assume leadership of the region during the prepara-tions for battle with the Mongols in the 1370's. St. Sergius prayed for victory over the Tatars, mobilized the resources of his monastery to support the fighting, and sent two monks to lead the troops in the famous victory at Kulikovo. Because his aid and intercession were widely credited with this decisive turn in the fortunes of Muscovy, his monastery soon became—almost in the modern sense—a national shrine. It was connected not with any purely local event or holy man, but with the common victory over a pagan enemy of a united army of Orthodox Russians.

The new monasteries were full-time centers of work and prayer, con-trolling rather than controlled by the ecclesiastical hierarchy. Often modeled on the monasteries of Mount Athos, they were organized communally and strongly influenced by the new Athonite tradition of Hesychasm. The "eld-ers" who had attained mastery of their passions and spiritual clairvoyance through long years of prayer and vigilance often commanded greater au-thority within the monastery than did the hegumen or archimandrite (the nominal head of a small and a large monastery respectively). These elders played a leading role in the "accumulation of spiritual energies," which was the main work of Muscovite monasticism.

Like a magnetic field, this spiritual energy attracted loose elements and filled the surrounding area with invisible powers. This energizing effect has already been noted in the field of icon painting, which received much of its stimulus from the need to decorate new monasteries. Rublev's "Old Testa-ment Trinity" was painted by a monk for the monastery of St. Sergius, depicting the subject to which that key monastery had been dedicated.

Literary culture was stimulated by the monastic revival. About twic as many manuscript books have survived from the fourteenth century a from the three previous centuries combined.[12] These manuscripts were embellished with a new type of decoration known as belt weaving, and the style adorned with a new technique known as word weaving.[13] Both of these

skills were brought to Russia by many of the same monastic emigrants from
Athos, who were bearers of Hesychasm. Both of these "weaving" techniques
represented in some ways an extension to literature of principles common to
both Hesychasm and the new iconography: the subordination of verbal
inventiveness and pictorial naturalism to the balanced and rhythmic repetition of a few simple patterns and phrases designed to facilitate direct links
with God.

Even more striking in the new literary activity was the intensification
of the previous historical bias of Russian theology. In sacred history as in
iconography, Muscovite monks succeeded in "transforming an imitative
craft into a conscious national art."[14] Increasingly, lives of saints and sacred
chronicles tended to identify the religious truth of Orthodoxy with the
political fate of Muscovy. This trend was already evidenced in the late
thirteenth century in the extraordinarily popular "Life of Alexander
Nevsky." The story of the prince who vanquished the Teutonic knights is
filled with comparisons to Old Testament figures, military images drawn
from Josephus Flavius' *Tale of the Destruction of Jerusalem,* and details of
heroism transferred from legends about Alexander the Great to Alexander
Nevsky. This work was also infused with a militant anti-Catholic spirit that
was absent from epics of the Kievan period (and probably from the outlook
of Alexander himself) and was almost certainly introduced by the Monk
Cyril, who had fled his native Galicia after it had entered the Roman orbit,
and deepened his anti-Catholicism with a stay in Nicaea just as the Latin
crusaders were overrunning nearby Constantinople, in the early thirteenth
century.[15]

Even more exalted than this story of victory over "the Romans" were
the tales of combat with the Tatars that became particularly popular after
the victory at Kulikovo in 1380, under Dmitry Donskoy. The life of this lay
prince was written in purely hagiographic style. He is repeatedly referred to
as a saint, and is placed higher in the firmament of heaven than many biblical
figures. The cause of Dmitry in the most famous epic of this period, "The
Tale from Beyond the Don" (*Zadonshchina*), is that of "the Christian faith"
and "the holy churches"; just as the icon commissioned for Dmitry's grave
by his widow was that of the Archangel Michael, the bearer of heavenly
victory over the armies of Satan.[16] Whereas epics of the Kievan era were
relatively hospitable to naturalistic and even pagan detail, the *Zadonshchina*
imparts a new spirit of fanaticism in a new idiom of eulogy and epithet.[17]

The extraordinary emphasis in the chronicles on the battle of Kulikovo
(which was not in itself particularly decisive in turning back the tide of Tatar
domination) represents in good measure the echoing by Muscovite chron-

iclers of the call—first sounded in Latin Christendom at the time of its great awakening several centuries earlier—for a Christian crusade against the infidel East. Once again, a people struggling out of darkness and division were invited to unite behind their faith to fight a common foe. The ideological accompaniment for the gradual subordination of all other major Russian princes to Moscow in the course of the fifteenth century was provided by a series of chronicles beginning with that of the St. Sergius Monastery in 1408, and by supporting songs and legends that stressed (in contrast to those of Novgorod, Pskov, and Tver) the importance of the holy war against the Tatars and the need for Muscovite leadership in reuniting "the Russian land."[18]

The monastic literature of the late fourteenth and the fifteenth century moved increasingly into the world of prophecy—developing two interrelated beliefs that lay at the heart of the Moscow ideology: (1) that Russian Christendom represents a special culminating chapter in an unbroken chain of sacred history; and (2) that Moscow and its rulers are the chosen bearers of this destiny.

The belief in a special destiny for Orthodox Christianity was not new. Orthodoxy was heir to the earliest sees of Christendom, including all the regions in which Christ himself had lived. Chiliastic teachings from the East entered early into Byzantine thinking. When Jerusalem was falling to the Moslems in 638 the true cross and other sacred relics were transferred to Constantinople, and the thought arose—particularly under the Macedonian dynasty at the time when Russia was being converted—that Constantinople might in some sense be the New Jerusalem as well as the New Rome.[19]

Just as the Eastern Church claimed to be the only truly apostolic church, so too the Eastern Empire claimed a specially sanctified genealogy through Babylonia, Persia, and Rome. From the end of the fourth century, Constantinople began to be thought of as the New Rome: capital of an empire with a destiny unlike that of any other on earth. Byzantium was not *a* but *the* Christian Empire, specially chosen to guide men along the path marked out by the chroniclers that led from Christ's incarnation to His Second Coming.

Following Clement and Origen rather than Augustine, Orthodox theology spoke less about the drama of personal salvation than about that of cosmic redemption.[20] Whereas Augustine willed to Latin Christendom a brooding sense of original sin and of pessimism about the earthly city, these Eastern fathers willed to Orthodox Christendom a penchant for believing that the Christian Empire of the East might yet be transformed into the final, heavenly kingdom. Hesychast mysticism encouraged the Orthodox to believe that such a transformation was an imminent possibility through a spiritual intensification of their own lives—and ultimately of the entire Christian *imperium*.

In times of change and dislocation, the historical imagination tended to look for signs of the coming end of history and of approaching deliverance. Thus, the growing sense of destiny in Muscovy was directly related to the anguish among Orthodox monks at the final decline and fall of Byzantium.

The flight into apocalyptical prophecy began in the late fourteenth century in the late-blooming Slavic kingdoms of the Balkans, and spread to Muscovy via a migration of men and ideas from the Southern Slavs. Unlike the Southern Slav influx of the tenth century, which brought the confident faith of a united Byzantium, this second wave in the fifteenth infected Russia with the bombastic rhetoric and eschatological forebodings that had developed in Serbia and Bulgaria as they disintegrated before the advancing Turks.

The Serbian kingdom, during its golden age under Stephen Dushan, 1331–55, represented in many ways a dress rehearsal for the pattern of rule that was to emerge in Muscovy. Sudden military expansion was accompanied by a rapid inflation of princely pretensions. With speed and audacity Dushan assumed the titles of Tsar, Autocrat, and Emperor of the Romans; styled himself a successor to Constantine and Justinian; and summoned a council to set up a separate Serbian patriarchate. He sought, in brief, to supplant the old Byzantine Empire with a new Slavic-Greek empire. To sustain his claim he leaned heavily on the support of Mt. Athos and other monasteries that he had enriched and patronized.

The Bulgarian kingdom developed during its much longer period of independence from Byzantium a prophetic tradition which was to be taken over directly by Muscovy. Seeking to glorify the Bulgarian capital of Trnovo, the chroniclers referred to it as the New Rome, which had supplanted both the Rome of classical antiquity and the declining "second Rome" of Constantinople.

When the infidel Turks swept into the Balkans, crushing the Serbs at Kossovo in 1389 and overrunning the flaming Bulgarian capital four years later, the messianic hopes of Orthodox Slavdom had only one direction in which to turn: to the unvanquished prince and expanding church of Muscovy. In 1390 a Bulgarian monk from Trnovo, Cyprian, became Metropolitan of Moscow, and in the course of the fifteenth century men and ideas moved north to Muscovy and helped infect it with a new sense of historical calling.[21] The Balkan monks had tended to sympathize politically with the anti-Latin zealots in Byzantium and theologically with the anti-scholastic Hesychasts. They brought with them a fondness for the close alliance between monks and princes which had prevailed in the Southern Slav kingdoms and a deep hatred of Roman Catholicism, which in their view had surrounded the Orthodox Slavs with hostile principalities in the Balkans and had seduced the Church of Constantinople into humiliating reunion. The Southern Slavs also brought with them Balkan traditions of compiling synthetic genealogies to support the claims of the Serbian and Bulgarian kingdoms against Byzantium, and a penchant for ornate and pompous language heavily laden with archaic Church Slavonic forms. Particularly noteworthy and influential was the *Tale of the Great Princes of Vladimir of Great Russia,* by a Serbian émigré who solemnly connected the Muscovite princes not only with those of Kiev and the legendary Riurik but with the even more fanciful figure of Prussus, ruler of an imaginary ancient kingdom on the Vistula and a relative of Augustus Caesar, who was in turn related through Antony and Cleopatra to the Egyptian descendants of Noah and Shem. This widely copied work also encouraged Russians to think of themselves as successors of Byzantium by advancing the extraordinary fiction that the imperial regalia had been transferred from Constantinople to Kiev by Vladimir Monomachus, who was said to be the first tsar of all Russia.[22]

Meanwhile, a sense of having superseded Byzantium was subtly encouraged by one of the very few ideological conditions of Tatar overlordship: the requirement to pray for only one tsar: the Tatar khan. Though not uniformly observed or enforced among the tribute-paying Eastern Slavs, this restriction tended to remove from view in Muscovy the names of the later Byzantine Emperors. Muscovy found it only too easy to view the collapse of this increasingly remote empire in the mid-fifteenth century as God's chastisement of an unfaithful people.

In the Muscovite view—which was developed retrospectively in the late fifteenth century—the Byzantine Church betrayed its heritage by accepting union with Rome at Lyons, at Rome, and finally at the Council of Florence in 1437–9.

Ill-equipped to evaluate the theological issues, Muscovy equated Rome with the hostile knightly orders of the eastern Baltic and the growing power of the Polish-Lithuanian kingdom. The Muscovite church refused to accept the decisions of the council, driving into exile the Russian representative who had approved them, Metropolitan Isidore. This Greek prelate became a Catholic in exile, and was replaced as metropolitan by a native Russian at the Russian Church council of 1448.[23] The Turkish capture of Constantinople five years later came to be viewed as God's revenge on Byzantium and prophetic confirmation that the Russian church had acted wisely in repudiating the Florentine union. Yet the sense of Russian involvement in the Byzantine tragedy was far greater than nationalistic historians have often been willing to admit. From the late fourteenth century on, Muscovy was sending financial support as well as expressions of sympathetic concern to Constantinople.[24] Those fleeing the Turks brought with them the fear that the whole Orthodox world might succumb. When the Khan Akhmet attacked Moscow in 1480, a Serbian monk issued a passionate plea to the populace not to follow

> the Bulgars, Serbs, Greeks . . . Albanians, Croatians and Bosnians . . . and the many other lands which did not struggle manfully, whose fatherlands perished, whose lands and governments were destroyed, and whose people scattered in foreign lands.

Then, almost in the form of a prayer:

> May your eyes never see the bondage and ravaging of your holy churches and homes, the murder of your children and the defiling of your wives and daughters—sufferings such as the Turks have brought to other great and revered lands.[25]

In such an atmosphere, the psychological pressures were great for the comforting belief that the Christian Empire had not died with the fall of Byzantium and the other "great and revered" Orthodox kingdoms of the Balkans. The site of empire had merely moved from Constantinople to the "new Rome" of Trnovo, which became, by simple substitution, the "third Rome" of Moscow. This famous image originated with Philotheus of the Eleazer Monastery in Pskov, who probably first propounded it to Ivan III, though the earliest surviving statement is in a letter to Vasily III of 1511:

> The church of ancient Rome fell because of the Apollinarian heresy, as to the second Rome—the Church of Constantinople—it has been hewn by the axes of the Hagarenes. But this third, new Rome, the Universal Apostolic Church under thy mighty rule radiates forth the Orthodox Christian faith to the ends of the earth more brightly than the sun. . . . In all the universe thou art the only Tsar of Christians. . . . Hear me, pious Tsar, all Christian kingdoms have converged in thine alone. Two Romes have fallen, a third stands, a fourth there shall not be. . . .[26]

The transfer of Orthodox hopes to Muscovy had already been dramatized by the elaborately staged marriage in 1472 of Ivan III to Sophia Paleologus, niece of the last Byzantine emperor, and by the introduction into Russia a few years later of the former imperial seal of the two-headed eagle.[27]

Russians were encouraged to view change in apocalyptical terms by the purely fortuitous fact that the old Orthodox Church calendar extended only to the year 1492. The 7,000 years that began with the creation in 5508 B.C. was drawing to a close, and learned monks tended to look for signs of the approaching end of history. The close advisers of the Tsar who showed sympathy at the Church council of 1490 with the rationalistic "Judaizing" heresy were denounced as "vessels of the devil, forerunners of the Antichrist."[28] An important issue in the subsequent persecution of the Judaizers was their sponsorship of an astrological table for computing the years, "The Six Wings" (*Shestokryl'*), which seemed to suggest that "the years of the Christian Chronicle have expired but ours lives on."[29] In combating the Judaizers, the Russian Church unwittingly kept historical expectations alive by translating into readable Russian for the first time much of the apocalyptical literature of the Old Testament, including such apocrypha as the apocalypse of Ezra.[30]

By the turn of the century, expectations were raised that God was about to bring history to a close; but there was uncertainty as to whether one should look immediately for good or evil signs: for Christ's Second Coming and thousand-year reign on earth or for the coming reign of the Antichrist. Philotheus believed that "Russian Tsardom is the last earthly kingdom, after which comes the eternal kingdom of Christ," but another Pskovian saw the conquering Tsar as a harbinger of the Antichrist.[31] This uncertainty as to whether disaster or deliverance was at hand became characteristic of Russian prophetic writings. In later years too, there was an unstable alternation between anticipation and fear, exultation and depression, among those who shared the recurring feeling that great things were about to happen in Russia.

The rise of prophecy in fifteenth- and early sixteenth-century Muscovy is evidenced in the growth of extreme forms of Christian spirituality, such as "pillar-like immobility" (*stolpnichestvo*) and the perpetual wandering of "folly for Christ's sake" (*iurodstvo*). Though both traditions have Eastern and Byzantine origins, they acquired new intensity and importance in the Muscovite north.

Pillar-like immobility came to be regarded in the non-communal monasteries as a means of gaining special sanctity and clairvoyance. This tradition received popular sanction through the fabulous tales of Ilya of Murom, who allegedly sat immobile for thirty years before rising to carry out deeds of heroism.

The holy fools became revered for their asceticism and prophetic utterances as "men of God" (*bozhie liudi*). Whereas there had never been more than four saint's days dedicated to holy fools in all of Orthodox Christendom from the sixth to the tenth century, at least ten such days were

celebrated in Muscovy from the fourteenth to the sixteenth centuries.[32]
Churches and shrines were dedicated to them in great numbers, particularly
in the sixteenth and the early seventeenth century, when this form of piety
was at its height.[33]

Holy fools often became the norm, if not the normal, in human life.
Renunciation of the flesh "for Christ's sake" purified them for the gift of
prophecy. The role of the holy fool at the court of the princes of Muscovy
was a combination of the court confessor of the Christian West and the
royal soothsayer of the pagan East. They warned of doom and spoke darkly
of the need for new crusades or penitential exercises, reinforcing the already
marked tendency of Slavic Orthodoxy toward passion and prophecy rather
than reason and discipline.

Those who became holy fools were often widely traveled and well
read. It was, after all, the learned figure Tertullian who had first asked the
Church, "What has Athens to do with Jerusalem?" and asserted that "I
believe because it is absurd." Erasmus of Rotterdam, one of the most
learned of Renaissance humanists, also sang "in praise of folly"; and his
essay of that name became appropriately widely read by Russian thinkers.[34]
Troubled Russian thinkers in later periods—Dostoevsky, Musorgsky, and
Berdiaev—would feel tempted to find the true identity of their nation in
this undisciplined tradition of holy "wanderers over the Russian land."[35]
But the prophetic fools provided a source of anarchistic and masochistic
impulses as well as strength and sanctification.

The holy fools bore many points of resemblance to the prophetic
hermit-saints that became common in Muscovy during the fourteenth and
fifteenth centuries. Indeed, the term for holy wanderer (*skitalets*) is related
to the one used to describe the isolated hermit communities: *skity*. The most
famous ascetic hermit and defender of these small communities was Nil
Sorsky, through whom the spiritual intensity of the Hesychasts was brought
from Greek to Russian soil.[36] A monk from St. Cyril's monastery on the
White Lake, Nil traveled to the Holy Land and to Constantinople in the
years just after its fall and thence to the "holy Mountain" of Athos. There
he acquired the deep devotion to an inner spiritual life free from external
discipline and constraint, which he brought back to Russia and used as the
basis of his model *skit* in the wilderness along the Sora River beyond the
White Lake. In his devotional writings there is a kind of primitive Franciscan love of nature and indifference to things of this world. There were to
be no more than twelve "brothers" in any *skit,* all living in apostolic poverty
and close communion with the natural world. The gospels and a few other
"divine writings" were to be the only sources of authority.

Nil saw the *skit* as the golden mean of monastic life, combining the communal type of monastery with the cellular type. Within the individual cell there was to be a kind of apprentice system with an experienced "elder" tutoring one or two apprentice monks in spiritual prayer and holy writings. All the various cells were to gather together for Sundays and other feast days, and each *skit* was to support itself economically but resist all temptations of wealth and luxury. Externals were irrelevant to this apostle of the inner spiritual life. He was not deeply concerned with the observance of fasts or the persecution of heretics. Nil preached rather the power of spiritual example, and sought to find the means of producing such examples in monasteries. Spiritual prayer was in Nil's metaphorical language the running wind that could lead man across the turbulent seas of sin to the haven of salvation. All externals—even spoken prayer—were only tillers, means of steering men back into this wind of the spirit which had first blown on the apostles at Pentecost.

Nil's life and doctrine had a profound effect in the new monasteries of the expanding northeastern frontier. His followers, known as trans-Volga elders, came chiefly from the dependent cloisters of St. Sergius and from the lesser-known "Savior in Stone" monastery and its nine monastic colonies in the Yaroslavl-Vologda region. When this monastery came under the direction of a Greek Hesychast in 1380, it became a center of training for "inner spirituality," offering counsel not only to monastic apprentices but to a variety of tradesmen, colonizers, and lay pilgrims.[37]

Nil's teachings had the disturbing effect of leading men to think that direct links with God were possible—indeed preferable—to the ornately externalized services of Orthodoxy. The belief that God had sent inspired intermediaries directly to His chosen people outside the formal channels of the Church lent a kind of nervous religious character to life.

Muscovy at the time of its rise to greatness resembled an expectant revivalist camp. Russia was a primitive but powerful religious civilization, fatefully lacking in critical sense or clear division of authority. It had, of course, always been incorrect to speak even in Byzantium of "church" and "state" rather than of two types of sanctified authority (*sacerdotium* and *imperium*) within the universal Christian commonwealth.[38] In Muscovy the two were even more closely intertwined without any clear commitment to the theoretical definitions and practical limitations that had evolved in the long history of Byzantium.

In the civil sphere there were no permanent administrative chanceries (even of the crude *prikaz* variety) until the early sixteenth century.[39] In the ecclesiastical sphere, the lack of any clear diocesan structure or episcopal hierarchy made it difficult for leading prelates to provide an effective substitute for political authority during the long period of political division. Nor was there even a clear line of precedence among the monasteries. In contrast to the medieval West, where compendia of Roman law were waiting to be discovered and where the Moslem invader brought the texts of Aristotle with him, distant Muscovy had almost no exposure to the political and legal teachings of classical antiquity. At best they read some version of Plato's arguments for the closed rule of a philosopher-king—but only to fortify their conclusion that a good and holy leader was necessary, never as an exercise in Socratic method.

Lacking any knowledge of political systems in the past or much experience with them in the present, the Muscovite vaguely sought a leader on the model of the divinized sun-kings of the East and the princes and saints of popular folklore. The victory in the Christian East of Platonic idealism, which was exemplified by the veneration of ideal forms in the icons, led Russians to look for an ideal prince who would be in effect "the living icon of God."[40]

Unlike the Platonic ideal, however, the ideal Russian prince was to be not a philosopher but a guardian of tradition. The highest good in Muscovy was not knowledge but memory, *pamiat'*. Where one would now say, "I know," one then said, "I remember." Descriptions, inventories, and administrative records in the *prikazes* were all known as *pamiati;* epic tales were written down "for the old to hear and the young to remember." There was no higher appeal in a dispute than the "important, good and firm memory" of the oldest available authority.[41]

Thus, Muscovy was bound together not primarily by formal codes and definitions or rational procedures, but by an uncritical and unreflective collective memory. Special authority tended to devolve on those local "elders" whose memory went back furthest toward the apostolic age and whose experience made them most knowledgeable in Christian tradition: the ascetic *starets* in the monastery, the respected *starosta* in the city, and the epic *stariny* (tales of old) for the popular imagination. Rarely has a society been more attached to antiquity, but Muscovy looked to the past for tales of heroism rather than forms of thought, rhetoric rather than dialectic, the "golden-tongued" sermons of St. John Chrysostom rather than the "cursed logic" of Aristotle.[42] Even the princes had to trace their genealogies and heraldic seals back to a sacred past in order to gain respect in the patriarchal atmosphere of Muscovy.[43]

An essential element in making Muscovite authority effective throughout Russia was monastic support. The monasteries had reunified Russia by lifting men's eyes above the petty quarrels of the appanage period to a higher ideal. The Muscovite grand dukes made innumerable pilgrimages to the leading cloisters; corresponded with monks; sought their material aid and spiritual intercession before undertaking any important military or political action; and were quick to bestow on them a large share of newly gained land and wealth. In return, the monasteries provided an all-important aura of sanctity for the Grand Duke of Muscovy. He was the protector of monasteries, the figure in whom "the opposition between the principle of Caesar and the will of God was overcome."[44]

The ideology of Muscovite tsardom, which took shape in the early sixteenth century, was a purely monastic creation. Its main author was the last and most articulate of the great monastic pioneers, Joseph Sanin, founder and hegumen of Volokolamsk. Like the others, Joseph established his monastery out of nothing in the forest, whence he had fled in despair of existing cloisters and in the hope of creating the ideal Christian community. A man of striking appearance and ascetic personal habits, Joseph insisted on absolute obedience to detailed regulations covering dress, seating precedence, and even bodily movements. His central conviction that acquired, external habits have internal, spiritual effects placed him in diametric opposition to his contemporary and rival, Nil Sorsky; and their fundamental philosophic conflict came to a head in the famous controversy over monastic property. Against Nil's doctrine of apostolic poverty, Joseph defended the tremendous wealth which had accrued to his growing chain of cloisters through the bequests of the brother of Ivan III and other wealthy patrons and novices. Joseph was neither an advocate nor a practitioner of luxurious living. He insisted that monastic possessions were not personal wealth but a kind of sacred trust given in thanks for the sanctity and intercession of the monks, and in the hope that their holiness would radiate out into society.[45]

The controversy between the "possessors" and "non-possessors" was essentially a conflict between two conceptions of monastic life. All major participants were monks who conceived of Muscovy as a religious civilization with the grand duke its absolute sovereign. The real issue was the nature of authority in this patriarchal monastic civilization: the physical authority of the hegumen against the spiritual authority of the elder; centralized organization and regular discipline against loosely bound communities of prophetic piety.

Although Ivan III—like other ambitious state builders of the early modern period—wanted to secularize church holdings, the church council of 1503 decided in favor of the possessors. The successive deaths of Ivan III and Nil shortly thereafter and a series of persecutions against Nil's followers cemented the alliance between the Josephite party and the grand dukes of Muscovy. The monk Philotheus' idea of Moscow as the Third Rome may have been addressed to the Tsar's vanity in an effort to divert him from any action against the church hierarchy.[46] He addressed the Grand Duke not only as Tsar, but as "holder of the reins of the divine holy throne of the universal apostolic Church."[47] As the influence of the Josephite party grew at court, the conception of tsardom itself was given a monastic flavor. All of Muscovy came to be viewed as a kind of vast monastery under the discipline of a Tsar-Archimandrite. The beginning in the sixteenth century of the tradition of "the Tsar's words"—the obligation of all Russians to report immediately under threat of execution any serious criticism of the sovereign—probably represents an extension to the public at large of the rigid obligations to report fully any wavering of loyalties inside Josephite monasteries.

The close alliance that developed between monks and tsars in the first half of the sixteenth century can, of course, be analyzed as a venal, Machiavellian compact: the monks keeping their wealth, gaining freedom from the ecclesiastical hierarchy, and receiving as prisoners prophetic advocates of monastic poverty; the tsar receiving ecclesiastical permission for divorce and propagandistic support for the position that "though he be in body like all others, yet in power of office he is like God."[48] Yet it is important to realize that the victory of the Josephites and the extension of their influence in sixteenth-century Russia was a direct result of popular reverence for monasteries and the monastic ideal. Men strove for the new wealth but still sought to dedicate it to God. They wanted power, but also monastic sanction for its exercise. If even Cosimo de Medici amidst the worldly splendors of fifteenth-century Florence felt the need of periodic retreats to his monastic cell, it is hardly surprising that the princes and leaders of the primitive religious civilization of Muscovy should at the same time give so much of their worldly goods and services to Russian monasteries.

The victorious monastic party brought new confusion of authority into Muscovy by blurring the division between the monastery and the outside world. The tsar became a kind of archimandrite-in-chief of all the monasteries, and the monasteries in turn began to serve as prisons for the tsar's political opponents. The asceticism and discipline of the Josephite monasteries began to be applied to civil society; and the corruption and vulgarity of a crude frontier people made ever deeper inroads into the cloisters.

Although monastic corruption has often been the subject of lurid exaggeration, there is little doubt that the increasing wealth and power of Russian monasteries provided strong temptations to worldliness. The increasing number of monastic recruits brought with them two of the most widespread moral irregularities of Muscovite society: alcoholism and sexual perversion. The latter was a particular problem in a civilization that had been curiously unable to produce in its epic poetry a classic pair of ideal lovers and had accepted—in the teachings of the Josephites—an almost masochistic doctrine of ascetic discipline.

The high incidence of sexual irregularity shocked and fascinated foreign visitors to Muscovy. Nothing better indicates the intertwining of sacred and profane motifs within Muscovy than the fact that the monastic epistle to Vasily III first setting forth the exalted "third Rome" theory also included a long appeal for help in combating sodomy within the monasteries. Continued monastic concern over this practice helped reinforce the prophetic strain in Muscovite thought, convincing Silvester, one of Ivan the Terrible's closest clerical confidants, that God's wrath was about to be visited on the new Sodom and Gomorrah of the Russian plain.[49]

Less familiar than the growing worldliness of the monasteries in the sixteenth century is the increasing monasticism of the outside world. The "white," or married, parish priests were often more zealous than the "black," or celibate, monastic clergy in the performance of religious duties. Simple laymen were often the most conscientious of all in keeping the four long and rigorous fasts (for Advent, Easter, the apostles Peter and Paul, and the Assumption); observing weekly days of abstinence not only on Friday, the day of the Crucifixion, but also on Wednesday, the day on which Judas agreed to betray Christ; keeping vigil before the twelve universal feast days of Orthodoxy; and observing private devotions and local feasts. The simple Christian often came from considerable distances to go to a church which offered him neither heat nor a seat. Each visit was something of a pilgrimage, with the worshipper often spending as much time kneeling or prostrate upon the cold floor as standing. Religious processions were frequent and lengthy—the daily services of matins and vespers often lasting a total of seven or eight hours.[50]

Behind the elaborate rituals of Russian Orthodoxy there often lay a deeper popular spirituality that was only slightly touched by the new tsarist ideology of the Josephites. Ordinary believers were dazzled by imperial claims and excited by its prophetic pronouncements. But they had no real interest in polemics which were conducted in a language that they could not understand and written in a script that they could not read.

Thus, along with the militant prophetic ideology of Muscovy went the cult of humility and self-abnegation: the attempt to be "very like" the Lord in the outpouring of love and the acceptance of suffering in the kenotic manner of Russia's first national saints: Boris and Gleb.[51] The persecuted followers of Nil Sorsky "beyond the Volga" were closer to this tradition than the victorious Josephites and enjoyed greater popular veneration to-

gether with all those willing to suffer voluntarily in the manner of Christ: as
a propitiation for the sins of others and a means of purifying God's sinful
people.

The contrast between active militarism and passive kenoticism is more
apparent than real. Hatred to those outside a group with a sense of destiny
is often combined with love to those within it: and both the compulsion
and the compassion of early Russian spirituality resulted from the over-all
prophetic, historical bias of its theology. Soldiers followed images of the
saints into combat, while dedicated figures at home followed the image of
Christ into the battle with sin. Each was performing a *podvig* (glorious deed)
in history and earning a small place in the great chronicle which would be
read back at the Last Judgment. *Podvizhnik,* a word which more secular
subsequent ages have tended to use pejoratively in the sense of "fanatic,"
still carries with it the meaning of "champion"—whether in sports, war, or
prayer.[52] Ephrem the Syrian, the very same fourth-century saint from
whom Russian iconographers derived their graphic and terrifying image of
the coming apocalypse and judgment, provided the ordinary believer with
his most familiar call to repentance and humility in a prayer recited with
prostrations at every Lenten service:

> O Lord and Master of my life! the spirit of vanity, of idleness, of
> domination, of idle speech, give me not. But the spirit of chastity,
> of humility, of patience, of love, do Thou grant to me, thy servant.

> Yes, O Lord and King, grant me that I may perceive my transgressions
> and not condemn my brother, for Thou art blessed forever and ever,
> Amen.

Muscovite soldiers were not primarily mercenaries nor were Muscovite
saints basically moralists. The Russian ideal of kenotic sainthood does not
correspond exactly with the "imitation of Christ" advocated by Thomas à
Kempis and the "new devotion" of late medieval Europe. Muscovites spoke
of "following" or "serving" rather than "imitating" Christ, and put greater
stress on the suffering and martyrdom which such service entailed. They
dwelt on Christ's mission rather than his teachings, which were in any
case not widely known in the absence of a complete Slavonic New Testament. Man's function was to enlist in that mission: to serve God by beating
off his enemies and by following Christ in those features of his earthly life
that were fully understood—his personal compassion and willingness to
suffer.

In general practice, however, the monastic civilization of Muscovy was
dominated more by fanaticism than kenoticism, more by compulsion than

compassion. This emphasis is illustrated vividly by Ivan the Terrible, the first ideologist to rule Muscovy, the first ruler to be formally crowned tsar, and the man who ruled Russia longer than any other figure in its history. Ascending the throne in 1533 at the age of three, Ivan reigned for just over a half century and became even in his lifetime the subject of fearful fascination and confused controversy that he has remained till this day.[53]

In some ways Ivan can be seen as a kind of fundamentalist survival of Byzantium. Following his Josephite teachers, he used Byzantine texts to justify his absolutism and Byzantine rituals in having himself crowned in 1547 with the Russian form of the old imperial title. His sense of imperial pretense, formalistic traditionalism, and elaborate court intrigue all seem reminiscent of the vanished world of Constantinople. Yet his passion for absolute dominance over the ecclesiastical as well as the civil sphere represented caesoropapism in excess of anything in Byzantium, and has together with his cruelty and caprice led many to compare him with the Tatar khans, with whom he grappled so successfully in the early years of his reign. The leading contemporary apologist for Ivan's ruthlessness, Ivan Peresvetov, may have infected the tsar with some of his own admiration for the Turkish sultan and his Janissaries.[54] Some of Ivan's more famous acts of cruelty seem lifted from the legends of Dracula, which were popular in early sixteenth-century Russia, with their tales of a cruel yet gallant fifteenth-century governor of Wallachia, an exposed Balkan principality between the Turkish and Catholic worlds.[55]

Worldly Western contemporaries often expressed admiration for his forceful rule. Many entered his service, and one visitor from Renaissance Italy used terms reminiscent of Machiavelli's *Prince* in hailing Ivan for *le singulare suoi virtù*.[56] Then as now, there has been a tendency to see in Ivan merely another example of the strong ruler struggling to centralize power and build a modern nation at the expense of a traditional, landholding aristocracy. From this perspective the men of his famed *oprichnina,* or "separate estate," appear not so much as oriental Janissaries but as builders of the modern service state. They were the first group to swear allegiance not just to the sovereign *(gosudar')* or the "sovereign's business" *(gosudarevo delo)* but to the sovereign state *(gosudarstvo).*[57]

There are, however, far too many differences between Ivan and his Tudor or Bourbon contemporaries to permit his name to be quietly buried in some anonymous list of modernizing state builders. His cruelty and pretension were regarded by almost every contemporary Western observer as more extreme than anything they had ever seen.[58] His very innovations, moreover, appear on closer examination to stem not from some new secular perspective but from his very desire to preserve tradition. The man who

placed Russia irrevocably on the path toward European statehood was at
the same time the supreme codifier of the Muscovite ideology. Much of the
confused ambivalence that Russians came to feel toward modernization and
Europeanization resulted from this unresolved tension between the highly
experimental policies and the fanatically traditional explanations of Ivan IV.

Ivan was steeped in Muscovite traditionalism by his monastic tutors,
corresponded extensively with monastic leaders, and made frequent pilgrimages to monastic shrines—including at least one 38-mile penitential
procession in bare feet from Moscow to the monastery of St. Sergius. He
sometimes spoke of himself as a monk, and personally defended Orthodoxy
in theological debates with Western thinkers who ranged from the left wing
of Protestantism (the Czech Brethren) to the new right wing of Catholicism
(the Society of Jesus).

Under Ivan the monastic conception of the prince as leader of an
organic Christian civilization was translated into reality. Rival centers of
potential political power—traditional landholding boyars, proud cities like
Novgorod, and even those friends who sought to formalize conciliar limitations on autocracy—all were subjected to humiliations. The power and
potential independence of the Church hierarchy was checked by the imprisonment and murder of the ranking metropolitan: Philip of Moscow.
Dissident religious views were expunged by anti-Jewish pogroms in western
Russia and by the trial and execution of early Protestant leaders from
the same region.

The justification for his rule was rooted in the historical theology of
Muscovy. The massive *Book of Degrees of the Imperial Genealogy,* drawn
up by his monastic advisers, carried to new extremes the blending of sacred
and secular history. Hagiography was applied wholesale to the descriptions
of tsars, and imperial ancestries were traced to miracle-working saints as
well as emperors of antiquity. Ivan was as diligent in gathering in for Moscow the historical legends and monastic ideologists of Novgorod and other
principalities as he was in crushing their independent political pretensions.

In all of his activities, Ivan conceived of himself as head of a monolithic religious civilization, never simply as a military or political leader.
His campaign against the Tatars at Kazan in 1552 was a kind of religious
procession, a storming of Jericho. The great Kazan Cathedral was built
in Red Square, and came to be named for the holy fool, Vasily the
Blessed, to whom the victory was credited. Its nine asymmetrical tent
roofs, exotically gilded and capped by onion cupolas, represent in many
ways the climax of Muscovite architecture, and form a striking contrast
with the balanced Italo-Byzantine cathedrals built in the Kremlin under Ivan

III. Many other churches arose in this high Muscovite style, and more than ten were named for holy fools under Ivan.[59]

Ivan's legislative council of 1549–50—which provided some precedent for later parliamentary "councils of the land" *(zemskie sobory)*—was conceived as a religious gathering.[60] The Church code enacted in 1551 known as the hundred chapters was designed only to "confirm former tradition," and prescribed rules for everything from icon painting to shaving and drinking. Every day of the calendar was covered and almost every saint depicted in the 27,000 large pages of the encyclopedia of holy readings, *Cheti Mnei*.[61] Every aspect of domestic activity was ritualized with semi-monastic rules of conduct in the "Household Book" *(Domostroy)*. Even the *oprichnina* was bound together with the vows, rules, and dress of a monastic order.

The consequence of this radical monasticization of society was the virtual elimination of secular culture in the course of the sixteenth century. Whereas Russia had previously reproduced a substantial number of secular tales and fables—drawn both from Byzantium and the West through the Southern and Western Slavs respectively—"there did not appear in Russian literature of the sixteenth century a single work of belles lettres similar to those already known in the fifteenth. . . . There cannot be found in Russian manuscripts of the sixteenth even those literary works which were known in fifteenth century Russia and were subsequently widely disseminated in the seventeenth."[62] The chronicles and the newly embellished genealogies, hagiographies, military tales, and polemics of the age were purged of "useless stories." Nil Sorsky, no less than Joseph of Volokolamsk, favored this form of censorship; and the "hundred chapters" of 1551 extended these prohibitions on secular culture to music and art as well. By the time of Ivan the Terrible, Muscovy had set itself off even from other Orthodox Slavs by the totality of its historical pretensions and the religious character of its entire culture.

The peculiarities of Muscovite civilization as it took finished shape under Ivan IV invite comparisons not only with Eastern despots and Western state builders but also with two seemingly remote civilizations: imperial Spain and ancient Israel.

Like Spain, Muscovy absorbed for Christendom the shock of alien invaders and found its national identity in the fight to expel them. As with Spain, the military cause became a religious one for Russia. Political and religious authority were intertwined; and the resultant fanaticism led both countries to become particularly intense spokesmen for their respective divisions of Christianity. The introduction into the creed of the phrase "and from the Son," which first split East and West, took place at a council in Toledo, and nowhere was it more bitterly opposed than in Russia. The Russian and Spanish hierarchies were the most adamant within the Eastern and Western churches respectively in opposing the reconciliation of the churches at Florence in 1437-9. The leading Spanish spokesman at Florence was, in fact, a relative of the famed inquisitor, Torquemada.

Amidst the rapid expansion of Russian power under Ivan III, the Russian hierarchy appears to have found both a challenge to its authority—and an answer to that challenge—coming from distant Spain. Whether or not the search for "Judaizers" in the late fifteenth century was prompted by a confusion between the early Russian word for "Jew" *(Evreianin)* and that for "Spaniard" *(Iverianin),* as has been recently suggested,[63] there seems little doubt that many of the proscribed texts used by these alleged heretics (such as the *Logic* of Moses Maimonides) did in fact come from Spain. Looking for a way of dealing with this influx of foreign rationalism, the Archbishop of Novgorod wrote admiringly to the Metropolitan of Moscow in 1490 about Ferdinand of Spain: "Look at the firmness which the Latins display. The ambassador of Caesar has told me about the way in which the king of Spain cleansed *(ochistil)* his land. I have sent you a memorandum of these conversations."[64] Thus began the Russian fascination with, and partial imitation of, the Spanish Inquisition—and the use of the word "cleansing" for ideological purges.[65] There seems little doubt that the subsequent purge of "Judaizers" was undertaken "not on the model of the Second Rome, but of the First."[66] The techniques of ritual investigation, flagellation, and burning of heretics were previously unknown to the Russian Church and vigorously opposed by the traditionalist trans-Volga elders. Although the Muscovite purges were directed against Roman Catholics, often with special fury, the weapons used were those of the Inquisition that had flourished within that church.

A strange love-hate relationship continued to exist between these two proud, passionate, and superstitious peoples—each ruled by an improbable folklore of military heroism; each animated by strong traditions of veneration for local saints; each preserving down to modern times a rich musical tradition of primitive atonal folk lament; each destined to be a breeding ground for revolutionary anarchism and the site of a civil war with profound international implications in the twentieth century.

As national self-consciousness was stimulated by the Napoleonic invasion, Russians came to feel a new sense of community with Spain. The leader of Russian partisan activities against Napoleon in 1812 drew inspiration from the Spanish resistance of 1808-9: the original *guerrilla,* or "little war."[67] The Decembrist reformers of the post-war period also drew inspiration from the patriotic catechisms and constitutional proposals of their Spanish counterparts.[68]

Ortega y Gasset, one of the most perceptive of modern Spaniards, saw a strange affinity between "Russia and Spain, the two extremities of the great diagonal of Europe . . . alike in being the two 'pueblo' races, races where the common people predominate." In Spain no less than in Russia the "cultivated minority . . . trembles" before the people, and "has never been able to saturate the gigantic popular plasma with its organizing influence. Hence the protoplasmic, amorphous, persistently primitive aspect of Russian existence."[69] If less "protoplasmic," Spain was equally frustrated in its quest for political liberty; and "the two extremities" of Europe developed dreams of total liberation, which drove the cultivated minority to poetry, anarchy, and revolution.

Modern Russians felt a certain fascination with Spanish passion and spontaneity as a spiritual alternative to the dehumanized formality of Western Europe. They idealized the picaresque roguery of Lazarillo de Tormes, and the implausible gallantry of Don Quixote, in the book Dostoevsky considered "the last and greatest word of human thought."[70] One Russian critic attributed his preference for Spanish over Italian literature to the Spaniards' greater freedom from the confinements of classical antiquity.[71] Even Turgenev, the most classical of the great Russian novelists, preferred Calderón's dramas to those of Shakespeare.[72] Russians loved not just the world-weary beauty and sense of honor that pervaded the works of Calderón, but also the fantastic settings and ironic perspectives provided by a man for whom "life is a dream" and history "is all foreshadowings." The malaise of the Russian intelligentsia in the twilight of Imperial Russia is not unlike that of the great dramatist who lived in the afterglow of the golden age of Imperial Spain:

> The cause lies within my breast
> Where the heart is so large
> That it fears—not without reason—
> To find the world too narrow for it.[73]

Spain was the only foreign country in which Glinka, the father of Russian national music, felt at home. He gathered musical themes on his Spanish travels, and considered Russian and Spanish music "the only instinctive musics" in Europe, with their integration of Oriental motifs and ability to portray suffering.[74] The first Western operatic performance in Russia had been the work of a Spaniard with a suitably passionate title— *Force of Love and Hate*—in 1736.[75] The setting was Spanish for the only important Western opera to have its premier in Russia (Verdi's *Force of Destiny*), the one that subsequently became perhaps the most popular (Bizet's *Carmen*), and one of the most consistently popular Western plays (Schiller's *Don Carlos*)—even though these works were written in Italian, French, and German respectively. The most famous scene of Dostoevsky's greatest novel, "The Legend of the Grand Inquisitor" in *The Brothers Karamazov*, was set in Seville at the time of the Inquisition. Fascination turned to repulsion in the twentieth century, as the Spanish and Russian revolutions took opposite turns. Participation in the Spanish Civil War became almost a guarantee of liquidation in the Stalinist purges of the late thirties and the forties. But Communist incursions in Latin America in the late fifties and the sixties brought not only political pleasure to the Soviet leaders, but also a curious popular undertone of envious admiration for the naive idealism of the Cuban Revolution—perhaps reflecting in some ways the older but equally distant and romantic appeal of the Hispanic world.

One of the most fascinating points of resemblance between Russia and Spain is the obscure but important role played by Jews in the development of each culture. Although Jewish influence is more difficult to trace in Russia than in Spain, there are repeated hints of a shadowy Jewish presence in Russian history—from the first formation of a Slavonic alphabet with its Hebrew-derived letters "ts" and "sh" to the philo-Semitism of dissident intellectuals in the post-Stalin era.[76]

From the point of view of Jewish history, there is a certain continuity in the fact that the Russian attack on "Judaizing" followed closely the expulsion of the Jews from Spain, and accompanied the transfer of the cultural center of world Jewry from the southwestern to the northeastern periphery of Europe: from Spain to Poland and Western Russia.

The anti-Jewish fervor that was built into the Muscovite ideology in the sixteenth century represents in part the eastward migration of a Western attitude and in part classical peasant antipathy to the intellectual and commercial activities of the city. However, this attitude bespeaks an inner similarity between the ancient claims of Israel and the new pretensions of Muscovy. A newly proclaimed chosen people felt hostility toward an older pretender to this title. The failures and frustrations which might logically have caused the Muscovites to question their special status led them psychologically to project inner uncertainty into external fury against those with a rival claim to divine favor.

Like ancient Israel, medieval Muscovy gave a prophetic interpretation to bondage and humiliation, believing in God's special concern for their destiny and developing messianic expectations of deliverance as the basis of national solidarity. Like Israel, Muscovy was more a religious civilization than a political order. All of life was hedged with religious regulations and rituals. Like Old Testament prophets, ascetic monks and wandering fools saw Russia as the suffering servant of God and called its people to repentance. Philotheus of Pskov addressed the Tsar as "Noah in the ark, saved from the flood."[77] Moscow was referred to as "Jerusalem" and "the New Israel"[78] as well as the "third Rome." Its savior, Dmitry Donskoy, was likened to Moses and Gideon; its princes, to Saul and David.[79] Like the early Jews, the Muscovites dated their calendar from creation, celebrated their New Year's Day in September,[80] wore beards, and had elaborate regulations about the preparation and eating of meat. The Muscovites no less than the Jews looked for the righteous remnant that would survive both persecution and temptation to bring deliverance to God's chosen people.

Some of this prophetic passion and Old Testament terminology was a continuation of Byzantine tradition and a reasonable facsimile of medieval Western practice. However, there also appear to have been direct and indirect Jewish influences, even though they have never been systematically assessed. There had been much contact during the Kievan period with the Jewish Khazar kingdom of the Caucasus, and even where Judaism was decried—as in Ilarion of Kiev's sermon "On Law and Grace"—the prince of Kiev was given the Khazar title *kagan*.[81] Early Russian literature shows extensive borrowing not only from the Old Testament and Apocrypha but also from works of later Jewish history, such as the *History of the Judaic War*. Direct translations were made from the Hebrew as well as the Greek in eleventh-century Kiev;[82] and by the twelfth century, Kiev had become—in the words of one meticulous student of Jewish history—"a center of Jewish studies."[83] It seems likely that some Jewish elements were absorbed by Muscovy after the sudden and still mysterious disappearance of the Khazars in the twelfth century.[84] There are traces of influence in surviving place names and clear indications of it in the thirteenth century, when there suddenly appeared Russian compilations of Jewish chronicles and a Russian glossary of Hebrew words.[85] The elusive and neglected area of early Russian music also offer some hints of Jewish influence. As in Spain, the Jews in Russia appear to have been important intermediaries in bringing Oriental motifs into folk music.[86] Some of the divergences of Russian from Byzantine church cantillation may also be attributable to Jewish influence.[87]

Whatever the early impact of Karaite Jews from the south,[88] there can be no doubt about the importance of the later influx of Talmudic Jews fleeing from persecution in the high medieval West. The growing influence of the large Jewish community may be reflected in the Muscovite use of Talmudic terms, such as *randar* for rent and *kabala* for service contract.[89]

Anti-Jewish measures were based in part on a realization that contemporary Jews were bearers of a more rationalistic, cosmopolitan culture than that of Muscovy. Indeed, the Jews did perform this stimulative function when they finally emerged from their ghetto confinement in the twenty-five regions known as the Pale of Settlement to contribute significantly to the ideological ferment, artistic creativity, and scientific activity of the late imperial period.[90] But fear and hatred did not abate; and there is an eerie similarity between the rooting out of "Judaizers" and hanging of Jewish doctors in the Moscow Kremlin for allegedly poisoning the son of the Grand Duke in the early sixteenth century and the lashing out against "homeless cosmopolitans" and the "doctor-poisoners" in Stalin's last years.[91]

The most important aspect of Jewish influence in Russia lies, however, not in the sophisticated world of art and science, but in the primitive world of messianic expectation. The two great periods of apocalyptical excitation in Muscovy—at the beginning of the sixteenth century and the middle of the seventeenth—coincide exactly with times of disaster and renewed apocalypticism in the Jewish community and with violent anti-Jewish measures in Muscovy. What began as a crude imitation of Spanish persecution in the purge of "Judaizers" by believers in the messianic theory of the Third Rome led eventually to a massacre of Jews in 1648 that was unequaled anywhere prior to the twentieth century. By this time, however, the Russians were sufferers as well as persecutors; and one finds both the Muscovite Old Believers and Jewish Sabbataians expecting the end of the world in 1666. The subsequent history of Russian schismatic and sectarian movements is filled with apocalyptical, Judaizing elements which indicate far more interaction than either Russian or Jewish historians seem generally willing to admit.[92] In some small part, at least, one could apply to Russia the statement that "it is not a paradox, but an elemental truth that Spanish society grew more and more fanatical in its Christianity as more and more Jews disappeared or were Christianized."[93]

Messianic expectations found parallel expressions among Jews and Russians of the late imperial period through populism and Zionism respectively; and when revolution finally convulsed Russia in 1917, gifted Russian Jews, like Zinov'ev, Kamenev, Sverdlov, and above all Trotsky, helped give the Bolshevik cause the compelling voice of prophecy and a contagious conviction that messianic deliverance was about to occur on Russian soil.[94] But the Jews who lent apocalyptical passion to the Revolution became victims rather than beneficiaries of the new order. Driven by a strange ideological compulsion of which he himself seemed unaware, Stalin accompanied his own mounting promises of millennial accomplishment with increasing persecution of the Jews. They were hounded out of the Third International as they had been from the Third Rome: scapegoats for the xenophobia that was to prove an enduring legacy of the Muscovite ideology.

The figure of Ivan the Terrible calls for both Spanish and Jewish comparisons. His crusading zeal, ideological fanaticism, and hatred of deviation make him closer in spirit to Philip II of Spain than to any other contemporary. His conviction that God had called him to lead His chosen people into battle made Ivan resemble the Old Testament kings, to whom he was repeatedly likened by chroniclers. One of the key points of the Josephites or "possessors," who were Ivan's teachers, was precisely their insistence on the crucial importance of the Old Testament and their rejection of the "non-possessors' " exclusive reliance on the New Testament and the "Jesus prayer." Ivan's favorite reading was the Book of Kings.[95] He appears to have viewed the Tatars as the Canaanites and the Poles as the Philistines during his campaigns against Kazan and Livonia respectively. This Old Testament perspective is well illustrated in Ivan's famous letters to Prince Kurbsky after this former military leader had left Russia to live in Polish Lithuania. Writing in the alternately bombastic and profane Josephite style, Ivan defends his right to cruelty and absolutism as the leader of a chosen people locked in battle with "Hagarenes" and "Ishmaelites."

"Did God," asks Ivan rhetorically, "having led Israel out of bondage, place a priest to rule over men, or a multitude of ordinary officials? No, Moses alone, like a Tsar, he made lord over them."[96] Israel was weak under priests, strong under kings and judges. David, in particular, was a just ruler "even though he committed murder."[97] Having gone over to the enemies of Israel, Kurbsky can only be described as a "dog" who even befouled the waters in his baptismal font. Kurbsky deserves nothing but contempt; for, unlike his messenger Shibanev, whom Ivan tormented by nailing his feet to the ground with a spear, Kurbsky lacked the courage to return to face in person the judgment of God and of His earthly regent, the Tsar.[98] God's intercession and not man's arguments can alone vindicate one who has betrayed God's cause.

Kurbsky, no less than Ivan, is dazzled by the Muscovite ideology. Although he adduces a wide variety of examples and ideas from classical scholarship, his main desire is clearly to find a place once more within Muscovy and not to challenge its basic ideology. Indeed, Kurbsky's letters seem at times little more than an anguished repetition of the question with which he opened the correspondence: "Why, O Tsar, have you destroyed the strong in Israel and driven to death the generals given to you by God?"[99] Far from aligning himself with the Poles and Lithuanians, Kurbsky considers his foreign residence as temporary and seeks to justify himself in terms of Ivan's favorite Old Testament figures: "Consider, O Tsar, how even David was compelled by Saul's persecution to wage war on the land of Israel together with a pagan king."[100] But eloquent pleadings from abroad only served to convince the leader in the Kremlin that his former lieutenant was secretly unsure of his position. Ivan's campaign of vilification —like those of his great admirer, Stalin—served the purpose of hardening his own convictions and warning potential defectors in his realm.

If Kurbsky as the defender of traditional boyar rights found himself unconsciously accepting the pretentious claims of the Muscovite ideology, defenders of independence for the church hierarchy and the city communities went ever further. Metropolitan Philip argued for an independent church establishment using a Byzantine text, which undermined his position by including the classic argument for unrestricted imperial power.[101] The *Discourse of Valaam,* written by monks from the ancient monastery in Lake Ladoga to advocate some return to the old town assembly principle in Muscovy, argued at the same time for an increase in imperial power and the recognition of its absolute and divinely ordained nature.[102] Thus, for all the discontent with Ivan's rule, there was never any effective program for opposing him. Generally ignorant of any but Byzantine political teachings, the anguished pamphleteers of the day included in their programs for reform Byzantine texts advocating unlimited power for the Tsar—often "to an even greater extent than did the apologists and theoreticians of the Muscovite imperial claims."[103] Perhaps the leading apologist for Ivan's rule was the widely traveled and essentially secular figure of Ivan Peresvetov, who argued on grounds of expediency that

> A Tsar that is meek and humble in his reign will see his realm empoverished and his glory diminished. A Tsar that is feared and wise [*grozen i mudr*] will see his realm enlarged and his name praised in all the corners of the earth. . . . A realm without dread [*bez grozy*] is like a horse beneath a Tsar without a bridle.[104]

For the second half of his reign, Muscovy was indeed a realm of fear, terrorized by the *oprichnina,* the hooded order of vigilantes which was then often designated by the Tatar-derived word for military district, *t'ma,* which was also the Russian word for darkness. The coming of this "darkness" to Russia and the flight of Kurbsky coincided with the fateful turn of Ivan's military interests from east to west. The unsuccessful twenty-five-year Livonian War that Ivan launched in 1558 was probably more responsible than any sudden madness or change of character in Ivan for the crisis of his last years. By moving for the Baltic, Ivan involved the pretentious Muscovite civilization in military and ideological conflict with the West, and in costly campaigns which shattered economic and political stability, and ultimately led to the building of a new, Western type of capital on the shores of the Baltic. The dramatic confrontation of the closely knit religious civilization of Muscovy with the diffuse and worldly West produced chaos and conflict that lasted from Ivan to Peter the Great and subsequently left its imprint on Russian culture.

2. The Coming of the West

FEW PROBLEMS have disturbed Russians more than the nature of their relationship to the West. Concern about this question did not begin either in the salons of the imperial period or in the mists of Slavic antiquity, but in Muscovy from the fifteenth to the early seventeenth century. This account will attempt to suggest both that there was an over-all psychological significance for Muscovy in the rediscovery of the West during this early modern period, and that there were a number of different "Wests" with which important contact was successively established. A consideration of how the West came to Russia may throw some light not only on Russian but on general European history.

The general psychological problem posed by confrontation with the West was in many ways more important than any particular political or economic problem. It was rather like the trauma of adolescence. Muscovy had become a kind of raw youth: too big to remain in childhood surroundings yet unable to adjust to the complex world outside. Propelled by the very momentum of growth, Muscovy suddenly found itself thrust into a world it was not equipped to understand. Western Europe in the fifteenth century was far more aggressive and articulate than it had been in Kievan times, and Russia far more self-conscious and provincial. The Muscovite reaction of irritability and self-assertion was in many ways that of a typical adolescent; the Western attitude of patronizing contempt, that of the unsympathetic adult. Unable to gain understanding either from others or from its own resources, Muscovy prolonged its sullen adolescence for more than a century. The conflicts that convulsed Russia throughout the seventeenth century were part of an awkward, compulsive search for identity in an essentially European world. The Russian response to the inescapable challenge of Western Europe was split—almost schizophrenic—and this division has to some extent lasted down to the present.

Novgorod

MUCH OF THE COMPLEX modern Russian feeling about the West begins with the conquest and humiliation of Novgorod by Moscow in the late fifteenth century. The destruction of the city's traditions and repopulation of most of its people shattered the most important natural link with the West to have survived in the Russian north since Kievan times. At the same time, the absorption of Novgorod brought into Muscovy new ecclesiastical apologists for autocracy who had come to rely partly on Western Catholic ideas and techniques in an effort to combat the growth of Western secularism in that city. Here we see the faint beginnings of the psychologically disturbing pattern whereby even the xenophobic party is forced to rely on one "West" in order to combat another. The ever more shrill and apocalyptical Muscovite insistence on the uniqueness and destiny of Russia thus flows to some extent from the psychological need to disguise from oneself the increasingly derivative and dependent nature of Russian culture.

Other contacts with the West besides those in Novgorod had, of course, survived the fall of Kiev, and might have helped make the rediscovery of the West less upsetting. Travelers to the Orient during the Mongol period like Marco Polo and the Franciscan missionaries to China passed through southern Russia; western Russian cities, such as Smolensk and Chernigov, remained channels of cultural and economic contact; and even in Great Russia, Western influence can be detected in the ecclesiastical art of Vladimir and Suzdal.[1] The division between East and West was, moreover, far from precise. Techniques and ideas filtering in from Paleologian Byzantium and from the more advanced Southern and Western Slavs were often similar to those of the early Italian Renaissance with which these "Eastern" regions were in such intimate contact.[2]

Nevertheless, there was a decisive cultural and political break between Latin Europe and the Orthodox Eastern Slavs in the thirteenth and fourteenth centuries. Catholic Europe concentrated its interest on the Western Slavs, and displayed more interest in the Mongol and Chinese empires to the east than in Great Russia. Muscovy, in turn, became preoccupied with the geopolitics of the Eurasian steppe, and lost sight of the Latin West except as a harassing force that had occupied Constantinople and encouraged Teutonic forays against Russia.

Novgorod, however, retained and increased the many-sided Western links that had generally prevailed in the major cities of Kievan Rus'. "Lord

Great Novgorod," as it was called, was the "father," just as Kiev was the "mother," of Russian cities.[3] The peaceful coexistence of Eastern and Western culture within this proud and wealthy metropolis is dramatized by one of its most famous and imposing landmarks: the twelfth-century bronze doors of the Santa Sophia cathedral. One door came from Byzantium, the other from Magdeburg; one from the seat of Eastern empire, the other from the North German city that had received the model charter of urban self-government from the Western Empire.[4] Novgorod had older traditions of independence and more extensive economic holdings than Magdeburg or any other Baltic German city. But Novgorod faced in the rising grand dukes of Muscovy a far more ambitious central power than the Holy Roman Emperors had become by the fifteenth century.

The cultural split between Moscow and Novgorod was far more formidable than the geographical divide which the wooded Valdai Hills defined between the upper tributaries of the Volga and the river-lake approaches to the Baltic. Novgorod had completely escaped the Muscovite subjection to the Mongols, and had developed extensive independent links with the Hanseatic League. Novgorodian chronicles reflected the commercial preoccupations of the city by including far more precise factual information on municipal building and socioeconomic activity than those of any other region.[5] When Moscow launched its military assault against Novgorod in the 1470's, it was still paying tribute to the Tatars and using Mongol terms in finance and administration, whereas Novgorod was trading on favorable terms with a host of Western powers and using a German monetary system.[6] Literacy was, moreover, almost certainly decreasing in Moscow because of the increasingly ornate language and script of its predominately monastic culture; whereas literacy had risen steadily in Novgorod to perhaps 80 per cent of the landholding classes through the increasing use of birch-bark commercial records.[7]

The Muscovite assault on Novgorod was, thus, in many ways, the first internal conflict between Eastward- and Westward-looking Russia—foreshadowing that which was later to develop between Moscow and St. Petersburg. In subjugating Novgorod, the Moscow of Ivan III was aided not just by superiority of numbers but also by a split between East and West within Novgorod itself. This split became a built-in feature of Westward-looking Russian gateways to the Baltic. Sometimes the split was clearcut, as between the purely Swedish town of Narva and the Russian fortress of Ivangorod, built by Ivan III across the river on the Baltic coast. The split ran directly through the great port of Riga, when Russia took it over and surrounded a picturesque Hanseatic port with a Russian provincial city. One Riga centered on a towering late Gothic cathedral containing the largest organ in the world; the other Riga was dominated by a xenophobic Old Believer community that forbade any use of musical instruments. The split became more subtle and psychological in St. Petersburg, where completely Western externals conflicted with the apocalyptical fears of a superstitious populace.

The split in Novgorod was all of these things. There was, to begin with, a clear division marked by the Volkhov River between the merchant quarter on the right and the ecclesiastical-administrative section on the left. There was an architectural contrast between the utilitarian, wooden structures of the former and the more permanent and stately Byzantine structures of the latter. Most important and subtle, however, was the ideological split between republican and autocratic, cosmopolitan and xenophobic tendencies. By the fourteenth century, Novgorod had both the purest republican government and the wealthiest ecclesiastical establishment in Eastern Slavdom.[8] The latter acted, for the most part, as a kind of ideological fifth column for Moscow: exalting the messianic-imperial claims of its grand prince in order to check the Westward drift of the city.

As early as 1348 the Novgorod hierarchy haughtily referred the king of Sweden to the Byzantine emperor when the Western monarch proposed discussion of a religious rapprochement.[9] Conscious of its unique role of independence from the Tatars and unbroken continuity with Kievan times, articulate and imaginative Novgorodian writers cultivated a sense of special destiny. They argued that Novgorod received Christianity not from Byzantium, but directly from the apostle Andrew; that Japheth, the third son of Noah, had founded their city; and that holy objects—the white monastic hood allegedly given by the Emperor Constantine to Pope Silvester and the Tikhvin icon of the Virgin—had been miraculously brought by God from sinful Byzantium to Novgorod for the uncorrupted people of "shining Russia."[10]

As political and economic pressures on Novgorod increased in the fifteenth century, the Novgorodian church frequently interpreted negotiations with the West as signs that the end of the church calendar in 1492 would bring an end to history.[11] Archbishop Gennadius of Novgorod and Pskov took the initiative shortly after his installation in 1485 in imploring a still-reluctant Moscow to prepare for this moment of destiny by cleansing its realm of heretics just as he had in the see of Novgorod.[12] Subsequently, of course, the leaders of two key monasteries within the see of Novgorod, Joseph of Volokolamsk and Philotheus of Pskov, became the architects of the Muscovite ideology. Some of its nervous, apocalyptical quality almost certainly came from the fear that secularization of both intellectual life and church property was imminent in this westerly region, and that the Tsar himself might emulate the new state builders of the West (or indeed the iconoclastic emperors of Byzantium) by presiding over such a revolution. The holy fools, who did so much to charge the atmosphere of Muscovy with prophetic expectation, trace their Russian beginnings to the confrontation of Byzantine Christianity and Western commercialism in Novgorod. Procopius, the thirteenth-century itinerant holy man who was the first of this genre to be canonized in Russia (and whose widely read sixteenth-century biography made him the model for many others), was in fact a German who had been converted after years of residence in Novgorod.[13]

Both economic and ideological factors tended to check any far-reaching Westernization of Novgorod. Unlike Tver, the other important westerly rival of Moscow subdued by Ivan III, Novgorod was firmly anchored against political drift toward Poland-Lithuania.[14] Novgorod had its most important Western economic links with German cities far to the west of Poland, and was linked with the northern and eastern frontiers of Great Russia through a vast, independent economic empire. Psychologically, too, the "father" of Russian cities felt a special obligation to defend the memory and honor of Rus' after the Kievan "mother" had been defiled by the Mongols. Riurik was, after all, said to have established the ruling dynasty in Novgorod even before his heirs moved to Kiev; and the fact that Novgorod was spared the Mongol "scourge of God" was seen by many as a sign that Novgorod enjoyed special favor and merited special authority within Orthodox Slavdom.

The political subordination of Novgorod to Moscow intensified Muscovite fanaticism while crushing out three distinctive traditions which Novgorod and Pskov had shared with the advanced cities of the high medieval West: commercial cosmopolitanism, representative government, and philosophic rationalism.

Cosmopolitanism was shattered by Ivan III's and Vasily III's destruction of the enclave of the Hanseatic League in Novgorod, and by subsequent restrictions on the independent trade and treaty relations that Novgorod and Pskov had enjoyed with the West since even before association with the Hanse. Representative government was destroyed by ripping out the bells which had summoned the popular assembly *(veche)* in Novgorod, Pskov, and the Novgorodian dependency of Viatka to elect magistrates and concur on major policy questions. Though neither a democratic forum nor a fully representative legislature, the *veche* assembly did give propertied interests an effective means of checking princely authority. The Novgorod *veche* had gradually introduced property qualifications for participation, and had also spawned smaller, more workable models of the central assembly in its largely autonomous municipal subsections. Like the

druzhina (or consultative war band of the prince), the *veche* represented a
survival from Kievan times that was alien to the tradition of Byzantine
autocracy. The *veche* was a far more serious obstacle to the Josephite program for establishing pure autocracy, for it had established solid roots in
the political traditions of a particular region and in the economic self-
interest of a vigorous merchant class.

The activity of the critical secular intellectuals was even more feared
by the monastic establishment than that of republican political leaders. For
the monks were more interested in lending mythologized sanctity to a Christian emperor than in defining concrete forms of rule. Their fascination with
Byzantine models led them to conclude that ideological schisms and heresies
had done far more to tear apart the empire than differences in political and
administrative traditions. Accompanying the extraordinary reverence for
whatever "is written" within the monastic tradition was an inordinate fear
of anything written outside. In the early modern period, the phrase "he
has gone into books" was used to mean "he has gone out of his mind"; and
"opinion is the mother to all suffering, opinion is the second fall" became
a popular proverb.[15] As Gennadius of Novgorod wrote during the ideological ferment prior to the church council of 1490:

> Our people are simple, they are unable to talk in the manner of
> books. Thus, it is better not to engage in debates about the faith. A council
> is needed not for debates on the faith, but in order that heretics be judged,
> hanged and burned.[16]

The ecclesiastical hierarchy sought—and gradually obtained the help of
princes in stamping out the rationalistic tendencies of the "Judaizers"
through procedures strangely reminiscent of the show trials of a later era.
Though little can be known for certain about the "heretics," their ideas
clearly came in through the trade routes into Novgorod as had those of the
anti-ecclesiastical "shorn heads" of the previous century. The "Judaizers"
were anti-trinitarian, iconoclastic, and apparently opposed to both monasticism and fasting. Linked in some ways with the European-wide phenomenon of late medieval heresy, they nevertheless differed from the Lollards
and Hussites of the West by appealing not to popular sentiments with emotional revivalism, but rather to the intellectual elite with radical rationalism.
Revulsion at the anti-rational historical theology of the xenophobic masses
thus led cosmopolitan intellectuals into the diametrically opposite thought
world of rational, anti-historical philosophy. Whether or not the Judaizers
were as interested in "the cursed logic" of Jewish and Moslem thinkers as
their persecutors insisted,[17] that very accusation served to suggest that the
logical alternative to Muscovite Orthodoxy was Western rationalism. This

became the alternative when St. Petersburg succeeded Novgorod as the cosmopolitan adversary of Moscow, and gradually gave birth to a revolution in the name of universal rationalism.

The initial crippling of Novgorod under Ivan III was accompanied by some of the same obsessive fear of the West that was to recur under Ivan IV and Stalin. The ideological purge of cosmopolitan intellectuals was accompanied by massive deportations east—the first of the periodic depopulations of the more advanced Baltic provinces by the vindictive force of Muscovy.[18] The pretext for this first fateful move on Novgorod was that Novgorod had gone over to the "Latins." Although probably untrue in any formal political or ecclesiastical sense, the accusation does highlight the unsettling effect produced by the first of the "Wests" to confront Muscovy in the early modern period: the Latin West of the high Renaissance.

"The Latins"

ITALIAN INFLUENCES in Russia may have been far more substantial than is generally realized even in the early period of the Renaissance. Italian products and ideas came to Russia indirectly through Baltic ports and directly through the Genoese trading communities in the Crimea in the late thirteenth and the fourteenth century. By the mid-fourteenth century there was a permanent colony of Italian tradesmen in Moscow, and Italian paper had come into widespread usage in Russia.[19] The only example of Russian church architecture from the mid-fourteenth century to survive down to modern times contains frescoes that were closer to the style of the early Renaissance than to that of traditional Byzantine iconography— including animation and realism that would have been advanced even in Italy and purely Western compositions, such as a pietà.[20] How far this Italian influence might have persisted in the decor of churches is one of the many no doubt insoluble mysteries of early Russian history. Subsequent Russian iconography does not appear to have been affected by these frescoes, however; and the next clear point of Italian cultural impact occurred nearly a century later, at the Council of Florence.

About a hundred representatives from various parts of Russia accompanied Metropolitan Isidore on his Italian journey. Some had previous contact, and some may have sympathized with Isidore's ill-fated endorsement of union with Rome. Though the Russians recoiled from the secular art and culture of the high Renaissance—two monks from Suzdal left a rather unflattering description of an Italian mystery play which they saw in

1438 in the Cathedral of San Marco[21]—contact with Italy increased thereafter. Gian-Battista della Volpe was put in charge of coinage in Muscovy. Through his intermediacy, the Italian influx reached a climax in the 1470's, with the arrival of a large number of Venetian and Florentine craftsmen in the retinue of Sophia Paleologus, Ivan III's second wife. These Italians rebuilt the fortifications of the Moscow Kremlin and constructed the oldest and most beautiful of the churches still to be found there and in the monastery of St. Sergius.[22]

Sophia came to Russia after long residence in Italy as the personal ward of the Roman pontiff and a vehicle for bringing the "widowed" Russian Church into communion with Rome. The persecution of the Judaizers was a cooperative effort on the part of Sophia (and the court supporters of her son Vasily's claim to the succession)[23] and the leaders of the Novgorod hierarchy. Both parties were acquainted with the stern methods of dealing with heretics that had been adopted by the Latin Church in the high Middle Ages. Joseph of Volokolamsk, whose grandfather was a Lithuanian, leaned heavily on the writings of a Croatian Dominican living in Novgorod to defend his position on monastic landholding, just as Gennadius of Novgorod had set up a kind of Latin academy in Novgorod to combat the heretics. Gennadius' leading consultants were two Latin-educated figures whom he brought to Russia for what proved to be long and influential years of service at the imperial court: Nicholas of Lübeck and Dmitry Gerasimov. Gennadius' entourage produced the first Russian translations of a number of books from the Old Testament and Apocrypha; and the model for the "Bible of Gennadius," which later became the first printed bible in Russia, was, significantly, the Latin Vulgate.[24] In the early sixteenth century, moreover, the Josephites supported ecclesiastical claims to vast temporal wealth with the spurious document that had long been used by Western apologists for papal power: the *Donation of Constantine.*[25]

If the apprentice inquisitors of Muscovy can be said to have borrowed from the Latin West, the same is even more clear in the case of their victims. "The trouble began when Kuritsyn [the diplomat and adviser of Ivan III] arrived from Hungarian lands," Gennadius wrote.[26] The rationalistic heresy which he sponsored and protected in Moscow was only part of a many-sided importation of ideas and habits from the secular culture of the high Renaissance. Indeed, the Josephites—like Dostoevsky's Grand Inquisitor—conceived of their mission as a service to the people. Like the original inquisitors of the medieval West, the Russian clergy was faced with appalling ignorance and debauchery in the society they were attempting to hold together. If the ignorance was part of the Russian heritage, the debauchery was at least partly Western in origin. For vodka and venereal disease, two of the major curses of Russia in the late fifteenth and the early sixteenth century, appear as part of the ambiguous legacy of the Italian Renaissance to early modern Russia.

Venereal disease first came to Moscow along the trade routes from Italy, apparently by way of Cracow in the 1490's, and a second wave of infection was to come in the mid-seventeenth century (along with the black plague) by way of mercenaries from the Thirty Years' War.[27] The designation of the disease as "the Latin sickness" is one of the first signs of growing anti-Latin sentiment.[28]

Vodka came to Russia about a century earlier, and its history illustrates several key features of the Renaissance impact on Muscovy. This clear but powerful national drink was one of several direct descendants of aqua vitae, a liquid apparently first distilled for medicinal purposes in Western Europe at the end of the thirteenth century. It appears to have reached Russia by way of a Genoese settlement on the Black Sea, whence it was brought north a century later by refugees fleeing the Mongol conquest of the Crimea.[29]

It was fateful for Russian morals that this deceptively innocuous-looking beverage gradually replaced the crude forms of mead and beer which had previously been the principal alcoholic fare of Muscovy. The tax on vodka became a major source of princely income and gave the civil authority a vested interest in the intoxication of its citizens. It is both sad and comical to find the transposed English phrase *Gimi drenki okoviten* ("Give me drink aqua vitae": that is, vodka) in one of the early manuscript dictionaries of Russian. A Dutch traveler at the beginning of the seventeenth century saw in the Muscovite penchant for drunkenness and debauchery proof that Russians "better support slavery than freedom, for in freedom they would give themselves over to license, whereas in slavery they spend their time in work and labor."[30]

The fact that vodka apparently came into Russia by way of the medical profession points to the importance of Western-educated court doctors as channels for the early influx of Western ideas and techniques.[31] The fact that vodka was popularly believed to be a kind of elixir of life with occult healing qualities provides a pathetic early illustration of the way in which the Russian *muzhik* was to gild his addictions and idealize his bondage. This naive belief also indicates that the initial appeal of Western thought to the primitive Muscovite mind lay in the belief that it offered some simple key to understanding the universe and curing its ills. If one were to resist the overwhelmingly traditionalist Muscovite ideology it could best be in the name of another way to truth outside of tradition: some panacea or "philosopher's stone."

Together with the works of Galen and Hippocrates, which began to appear in Russian translation in the fifteenth century, doctors in Muscovy—and throughout Eastern Europe—began to incorporate into their compendia of herbs and cures extracts from the *Secreta Secretorum.* This work purported to be the secret revelation of Aristotle to Alexander the Great about the true nature of the world, contending that biology was the key to all the arts and sciences, and that this "science of life" was ruled by the harmonies and confluences of occult forces within the body.[32] This book held a key place among the works translated by the Judaizers and was destroyed during the Josephite persecution of heretics in the early sixteenth century, along with the Jewish doctors who presumably either translated or possessed the work.

The interest in alchemistic texts continued, however, and became a major preoccupation of the translators in the foreign office, who soon replaced the doctors as the major conveyor of Western ideas. Fedor Kuritsyn, the first man effectively to fill the role of foreign minister in Russia, was accused of bringing back the Judaizing heresy from the West. One of the earliest surviving documents from the foreign office was a memorandum written by a Dutch translator at the beginning of the seventeenth century, "On the Higher Philosophical Alchemy."[33] Later in the century Raymond Lully's 350-year-old effort to find a "universal science," his *Ars magna generalis et ultima,* was translated and made the basis of an influential alchemistic compilation by a western Russian translator in the same office.[34]

Hardly less remarkable was the Russian interest in astrology. Almost every writer of the late fifteenth and the early sixteenth century was taken at one time or another with "delight in the laws of the stars" (*zvezdozakonnaia prelest'*). Archbishop Gennadius was himself fascinated with the astrology he felt called on to destroy;[35] and after his death, Nicholas of Lübeck, his original protégé, became an active propagandist for astrological lore in Muscovy. Known as a "professor of medicine and astrology," he had come to Moscow by way of Rome to help draw up the new church calendar. He stayed on as a physician, translating for the imperial court in 1534 a treatise written in Lübeck on herbs and medicine, *The Pleasant Garden of Health,* and campaigning actively for unification of the Catholic and Orthodox churches. He produced astrological computations which lent urgency to his pleas for reunion by purporting to show that the end of the world had been merely postponed from 1492 to 1524.[36] Maxim the Greek devoted

most of his early writings to a refutation of Nicholas' arguments but revealed in the process that he too had been fascinated by astrology while in
Italy. Maxim's follower, the urbane diplomat Fedor Karpov, confessed that
he found astrology "necessary and useful to Christians," calling it "the art
of arts."[37] The first Russians sent to study in England at the turn of the
sixteenth century were particularly interested in the famous Cambridge
student of astrology, magic, and spiritism, John Dee.[38] The rapid spread of
fortune-telling, divination, and even gambling in the sixteenth and seventeenth centuries reveals in part a popularization of astrological ideas current
throughout Renaissance Europe.[39]

Thus, during this early period of Western contact, Russians were fatefully conditioned to look to the West not for piecemeal ideas and techniques
but for a key to the inner secrets of the universe. Early diplomats were
interested not in the details of economic and political developments abroad
but in astrological and alchemistic systems. These Renaissance sciences
held out the promise of finding either the celestial patterns controlling the
movements of history or the philosopher's stone that would turn the dross
of the northern forests into gold. Thus, secular science in Russia tended to
be Gnostic rather than agnostic. There is, indeed, a kind of continuity of
tradition in the all-encompassing metaphysical systems from the West that
fascinated successive generations of Russian thinkers: from the early
alchemists and astrologers to Boehme's occult theosophy (literally, "divine
knowledge") and the sweeping totalistic philosophies of Schelling, Hegel,
and Marx.[40]

The most consistent opponents of astrology and alchemy in Muscovy
were the official Josephite ideologists. In a formulation which, again, seems
closer to Roman Catholic than Orthodox theology, Joseph's principal
disciple, Metropolitan Daniel of Moscow, argued that "man is almost
divine in wisdom and reason, and is created with his own free power"; and
again "God created the soul free and with its own powers."[41] The individual was, thus, responsible for working out his salvation without reference to the humors of the body or the movements of the stars. The good
works evidenced in the disciplined and dedicated life were as important to
the Josephites as to the Jesuits. But this emphasis on human freedom and
responsibility was a lonely voice in the Christian East—never fully
developed by the Josephites and totally rejected by others as threatening the
social order.[42]

Not all early Russian writings about the heavenly bodies can be
dismissed as occult astrology. *The Six Wing*s of the late-fifteenth-century
Judaizers provided an elaborate guide to solar and lunar eclipses and was,
in effect, "the first document of mathematical astronomy to appear in

Russia."[43] Such a document was, however, deeply suspect to Josephite ideologists; for it was the translated work of a fourteenth-century Spanish Jew based on Jewish and Islamic authorities who seemed to propose that a logic of the stars replace that of God. Throughout the Muscovite period there was an enduring fear that "number wisdom" was a challenge to divine wisdom—although mathematics was—as a practical matter—widely used and even taught in monasteries.[44]

The Josephites feared that Russian thinkers would make a religion of science if left free of strict ecclesiastical control. To what extent the Judaizers and other early dissenters actually intended to do so will probably never be known. But it is clear that the fear of the Russian Church gradually became the hope of those who resented its authority—and the supreme reality for the revolutionary forces that eventually overthrew that authority.

A final aspect of the early Latin impact was the muffled echo of Renaissance humanism that was heard in Muscovy. Early-sixteenth-century Russia produced a small band of isolated yet influential individuals that shared in part the critical spirit, interest in classical antiquity, and search for a less dogmatic faith which were characteristic of Renaissance Italy. It is, of course, more correct to speak of random influences and partial reflections than of any coherent humanist movement in Russia; but it is also true that this is generally characteristic of humanism outside the narrow region stretching up from Italy through Paris and the Low Countries into southern England.

A critical attitude toward religion became widespread among the civilians in the tsar's entourage who traveled abroad on diplomatic missions in the late fifteenth and the early sixteenth century. Both Fedor Kuritsyn, who headed the foreign office under Ivan III, and Fedor Karpov, who headed the much larger one under Ivan IV, became thoroughgoing sceptics; and the perspectives of Ivan IV's most trusted clerk, Ivan Viskovaty, and his leading apologist for absolutism, Ivan Peresvetov, appear to have been predominately secular.[45] Sacramental worship—and even the unique truth of Christianity—was implicitly questioned in the mid-fifteenth century by a literate and sophisticated Tver merchant, Afanasy Nikitin. In the course of wide travels throughout the Near East and South Asia, he appears to have concluded that all men were "Sons of Adam" who believed in the same God; and, although he continued to observe Orthodox practices in foreign lands, he pointedly wrote the word "God" in Arabic, Persian, and Turkish as well as Russian in his *Journey over Three Seas*.[46]

The search for a more rational and universal form of faith appears to have attracted considerable interest in cosmopolitan western Russia, where a syncretic, unitarian offshoot of the Protestant Reformation had to be anathemized by a special church council of 1553–4. Like the Judaizers who were condemned by a council just a half century before, this movement is shrouded in obscurity. Once again, some connection with Judaism seems probable in view of the importance that the leader, Fedor Kosoy, attached to the teaching of the Pentateuch and his later marriage to a Lithuanian Jewess.[47] Kosoy insisted eloquently at the council of 1553–4 that "all people are as one in God: Tatars, Germans and simple barbarians."[48] It seems reasonable to assume that this movement like that of the Judaizers continued to have sympathizers after official condemnation; and that the rapid subsequent flowering of anti-trinitarian Socinianism in Poland continued to attract attention in western Russia.

Four influential Russians of the mid-sixteenth century, Andrew Kurbsky, Fedor Karpov, Ermolai-Erazm, and Maxim the Greek, reproduced on Russian soil the philosophic opposition to both superstition and scholasticism that was characteristic of Western humanism. Each of them had a vital interest in classical antiquity—particularly Ciceronian moralism and Platonic idealism.

Despite his traditional, Muscovite view of politics and history, Kurbsky was the most deeply enamored with the classical past and was the only one to leave Russia to soak up the Latinized culture of the Polish-Lithuanian kingdom. Having acquired a direct knowledge of Platonic and early Greek thought from Maxim the Greek, he added an even more extensive knowledge of the Latin classics during his long stay abroad. Informally associated with a coterie of Latinized White Russian noblemen, Kurbsky visited the easternmost Latin university of medieval Europe at Cracow and sent his nephew to Italy. In the later stages of his correspondence with Ivan the Terrible, he included a long translation from Cicero as a means of proving that forced flight cannot be considered treason.[49]

An even deeper absorption of classical culture is evident in the writings of Karpov, a Latin interpreter and leading official for more than thirty years in the Russian foreign office. He consciously strove to write with "Homeric eloquence" in a pleasing, grammatical "non-barbaric" way.[50] His few surviving compositions reveal subtlety of intellect as well as considerable style and a sense of irony and concern for moral order.[51] This latter quality bordered on the subversive in Muscovy, for it led him to conclude that moral laws were higher than the will of the sovereign. Almost alone in his day he contended that civil and ecclesiastical affairs should be separated, and that justice is both a moral imperative and a practical necessity for human society. The monastic virtue of "long suffering" is not sufficient for civil society, which will be ruined if law and order are absent. Law is, however, not bracketed with terror as it was in the writings of Peresvetov. Together with justice must go mercy, because "mercy without justice is faint-heartedness, but justice without mercy is tyranny."[52]

In keeping with the spirit of the time, Karpov invokes a providential theory of history; but his style is ironic and his conclusion pessimistic. Man has progressed from a primitive law of nature through the Mosaic law to the Christian law of grace; but the men who live under this law do not live by it. Greed and lust prevail, so that even the first of the apostles would be denied a hearing in contemporary Muscovy without money for bribery.

An equally pessimistic view of Muscovite life is propounded in the writings of the monk Ermolai-Erazm, who echoes another favorite theme of Western reformers: the dream of a pastoral utopia, of a return to a natural economy and true Christian love. The source of all the world's ills is pride and estrangement from the land; peasants should be freed of all duties save a single donation of a fifth of each harvest to the tsar and nobility. Other exactions should be taken from parasitic merchants and tradesmen; gold and silver exchange should be eliminated; knives should be made unpointed to discourage assassins—such are some of the often naive ideas contained in his handbook of the 1540's: *On Administration and Land-measurement*.[53] The number mysticism and cosmic neo-Platonic theologizing of the high Renaissance is also apparent in Ermolai's efforts to vindicate the doctrine of the trinity by finding triadic patterns hidden in almost every natural phenomenon.[54]

The finest representative of Renaissance culture in early-fifteenth-century Russia and the teacher of Kurbsky, Karpov, and Ermolai-Erazm, was the remarkable figure of Maxim the Greek. Through him humanism acquired an Orthodox Christian coloration and made its strongest efforts to modify the uncritical fanaticism of the Muscovite ideology.[55] An Orthodox Greek brought up in Albania and Corfu, he spent long years studying in Renaissance Italy before becoming a monk and moving to Mount Athos. From there, he was called in 1518 to Russia, where he remained—at times against his will—for the thirty-eight remaining years of his life. Summoned by the Tsar to help translate holy texts from the Greek and Latin, Maxim proceeded to write more than 150 surviving compositions of his own, and attracted a large number of monastic and lay students. He was the first to bring news to Russia of Columbus' discovery of America, and he called attention as well to undiscovered areas of classical antiquity.[56]

Maxim illustrates the humanist temperament not only in his knowledge of the classics and interest in textual criticism, but also in his concern for style and his inclusion of poetry and a grammar among his works. He delighted in the favorite humanist pastime of refuting Aristotle[57] (even though this hero of the medieval scholastics was barely known in Russia), and had a typical Renaissance preference for Plato. He frequently wrote in dialogue form, and identified reason closely with goodness and beauty:

> True Godly reason not only beautifies the inner man with wisdom, humility and all manner of truth; but also harmonizes the outer parts of the body: eyes, ears, tongue and hands.[58]

Florence, the home of the Platonic Academy of the *cinquecento,* infected Maxim not only with neo-Platonic idealism, but also with the authoritarian and puritanical passion of Savonarola, whose sermons he admired as a young student.[59] His admiration for this famed prophet may hold a key to his fate in Russia. Like Savonarola, Maxim commanded attention for his passionate opposition to the immorality and secularism of his day, and was lionized by prophetic and apocalyptical elements. Like the Florentine, Maxim suffered martyrdom—though both his ordeal and his influence lasted longer than Savonarola's.

Unlike Savonarola, Maxim retained the style and temperament of the humanist, even in prophecy. There is a poetic quality to his denunciation of the three evil passions: "love of sweets, praise and silver" (*slastoliubie, slavoliubie, srebroliubie*).[60] He defends his efforts to correct faulty translations in Russian churchbooks, and pleads with those who have placed him in monastic imprisonment at least to let him return quietly to his library: "If I am wrong, subject me not to contempt, but to correction, and let me return to Athos."[61] Maxim always felt close to this center of the contemplative life and of Hesychast spirituality. Opposition to clerical wealth and dogmatism forged a link between his early humanist teachers from Italy and his later monastic followers from the upper Volga.

Maxim opposed the Josephite defense of monastic wealth not only for bringing "a blasphemous, servile, Jewish love of silver"[62] into holy places, but also for tampering with sacred texts for calculating, political purposes. In the course of his sustained debate with the Josephite Metropolitan Daniel of Moscow, Maxim voices the fear that the church is coming under the authority of "devious rules" (*krivila*) rather than "just rules" (*pravila*) —thus anticipating the opposition between "crookedness" and "truth" (*krivda-pravda*) which was to become so important in Russian moral philosophy.[63] In a skillful dialogue, Maxim likens the Josephite argument that monastic property is a common trust to a group of sensualists' justifying their relations with a prostitute on the grounds that she "belongs to us all in common."[64]

Maxim gradually turned to political writings denouncing Tsar Vasily III's divorce, and unsuccessfully attempting to make young Ivan IV "the just" rather than "the terrible." Maxim's political philosophy was moralistic and conservative: a kind of moral rearmament program designed by a sympathetic foreigner for the less-educated leader of an underdeveloped area. All conflict can be resolved without changing the social order. The first task is to infuse the prince with moral fervor. "Nothing is so necessary to those ruling on earth as justice";[65] but no prince can ultimately be just without the accompanying virtues of personal purity and humility.[66]

The fall of Byzantium was a moral warning to Muscovy against pride and complacence in high places rather than an assurance that Moscow was now the "third Rome." In a letter to young Ivan IV Maxim implies that adherence to the true faith will not in itself guarantee God's favor to an unjust prince, because evil Christian kings have often been struck down, and a just pagan like Cyrus of Persia enjoyed God's favor "for his great justice, humility, and compassion."[67] Maxim juxtaposed the classical Byzantine idea of a symphony of power between imperial and priestly authority to the Muscovite arguments for unlimited tsarist power. Like his friend Karpov, Maxim explicitly said that the tsar should not interfere in the ecclesiastical sphere, and implied that he was bound even in the civil sphere by a higher moral law.

This foreign teacher was revered, however, not for the logic of his arguments or the beauty of his style but for the depth of his piety. In his early years he argued for a crusade to liberate Constantinople and for a preventive war against the Crimean khan;[68] but as time went on, the simple Pauline ideals of good cheer, humility, and compassion dominate his writings. In and out of monastic prisons, confronted with false accusations, torture, and near starvation, Maxim underscored with his own life his doctrine of love through long-suffering. Far from showing bitterness toward the ungrateful land to which he had come, he developed a love of Russia, and an image of it different from that of the bombastic Josephite monks in the Tsar's entourage.

Maxim shows almost no interest in the mechanics of rule or the possibilities of practical reform, but he feels compassion for the oppressed and sorrow for the wealthy in Muscovy. He is convinced that "the heart of a mother grieving for her children deprived of the necessities of life is not so full as the soul of a faithful Tsar grieving for the protection and peaceful well-being of his beloved subjects."[69] Whatever its faults, Russia is not a tyranny like that of the Tatars. She bears the holy mission of Christian rule in the East, through all her harassment from without and corruption from within.

Toward the end of his life and during the early years of Ivan the Terrible's reign, Maxim transposes the image of the fallen church in Savonarola's *De ruina ecclesiae* into that of a ruined Russian empire.

Maxim describes how in the midst of his travels he noticed a woman in black weeping by a deserted path and surrounded by wild animals. He begs to learn her name, but she refuses, insisting that he is powerless to relieve her sorrow and would be happier to pass on in ignorance. Finally, she says that her real name is Vasiliia (from the Greek *Basileia,* "Empire"), and that she has been defiled by tyrants "unworthy of the title of Tsar" and abandoned by her own children for the love of silver and sensual pleasure. Prophets have ceased to speak of her, and saints to protect her. "And thus I sit here like a widow by a desolate road in a cursed age."[70]

Here, in essence, is the idea of "Holy Rus' ": humiliated and suffering, yet always compassionate: a wife and mother faithful to her "husband" and "children," the ruler and subjects of Russia, even when mistreated and deserted by them. Although the idea has been traced to Maxim's pupil Kurbsky,[71] and shown to have first acquired broad popularity during the troubles of the early seventeenth century,[72] the concept of "Holy Rus' " as an ideal opposed to the mechanical and unfeeling state finds its first expression in Maxim.

At the same time, Maxim linked the Hesychast ideal of continual prayer outside established worship services to the humanist ideal of a universal truth outside the historical truths of Christianity. He implored his readers to pray without ceasing that Russia would "put away all evil, all untruth, and embrace the truth."[73] "Truth" (*pravda*) already carried for Maxim some of that dual meaning of philosophic certainty and social justice which the word carried for later Russian reformers. Like many of these figures, Maxim was frequently accused of sedition, and died a virtual prisoner.

After his death, Maxim (like Nil Sorsky before him) gradually came to be officially revered for the very pious intensity which the official church had feared and sought to discipline during his lifetime.[74] But his efforts to leaven the Muscovite ideology with humanistic ideals failed. Archimandrite Artemius of the monastery of St. Sergius, who had been a learned follower of Nil and a devoted patron of Maxim, was banished to Solovetsk for heresy by the council of 1553–4. Artemius later fled to Poland like Maxim's pupil, Kurbsky—both of them remaining faithful to Orthodoxy, but despairing of any further attempt to blend humanist ideals with the Muscovite ideology.

Maxim had refused to participate in the church council of 1553–4, just as Nil had opposed the condemnation and execution of the Judaizers. When Maxim expired in 1556 in the monastery of St. Sergius, the last influential advocate of a tolerant Christian humanism vanished from the Muscovite scene. A many-sided assault against foreign cultural influence was under way. A severe penance was imposed on the Tsar's closest lay adviser, Ivan Viskovaty, for opposing a strict prohibition on alien influences in iconography. The brief flicker of interest in Renaissance art shown by Ivan's priestly confidant, Silvester (who had ordered Pskovian artists to provide Moscow with copies of paintings by Cimabue and Perugino), was also extinguished.[75] Interest in the ornate polyphonic music of Palestrina (which had been awakened by Maxim's friend and collaborator in Latin translations Dmitry Gerasimov, during his diplomatic visit to Rome in 1524–5) was also snuffed out by Ivan's decision to codify the prevailing system of church chant as the sole form of musical "right praising" for Russian churches.[76] Finally, and most important, the work of reproducing sacred texts was taken away from critical and linguistically gifted figures like Maxim and put in the hands of more ignorant but dependable imperial servants. The Josephite monks around Ivan preferred vast compendia to a rational ordering of ideas. The objection to textual criticism extended even to the use of printing as a means for propagating the faith and reproducing holy books. The brief and unproductive effort to set up a state printing shop in Moscow under the White Russian Ivan Fedorov ended in disaster in 1565, when the press was destroyed by a mob and the printers fled to Lithuania.[77] This was the year of Kurbsky's flight and the establishment of the *oprichnina*. A new xenophobia was in the air, and the period of relatively harmonious small-scale contact with the many-sided culture of Renaissance Italy was giving way to the broader and more disturbing confrontation which began in the late years of Ivan's reign.

The main result of a century of fitful Italian influences was to arouse suspicion of the West. These feelings were strongest among the monks whose influence was on the rise, and were increasingly channeled into animosity toward the Latin church. This anti-Catholicism of official Muscovy is puzzling, since the aspects of Renaissance culture most feared by the Josephite—astrology, alchemy, utopian social ideas, philosophical scepticism, and anti-trinitarian, anti-sacramental theology—were also opposed by the Roman Church. In part, of course, anti-Catholicism was merely an extension of the earlier Hesychast protest against the inroads of scholasticism within the late Byzantine empire. Maxim the Greek was faithful to his Athonite teachers in telling the Russians that "the Latins have let themselves be seduced not only by Hellenic and Roman doctrines, but even by Hebrew and Arab books . . . attempts to reconcile the irreconcilable cause trouble for all the world."[78]

To understand fully, however, why resentment was particularly focused on the Roman Church, one must keep in mind both the nature of Muscovite culture and the perennial tendency to conceive of other cultures in one's own image. Since Muscovy was an organic religious civilization, Western

Europe must be one. Since all culture in eastern Russia was expressive of
the Orthodox Church, the bewildering cultural variety of the West must be
expressions of the Roman Church, whatever that Church's formal position
on the matter. *Latinstvo,* "the Latin world," became a general term for the
West, and the phrase "Go to *Latinstvo*" acquired some of the overtones of
"Go to the devil." By the mid-sixteenth century prayers were being offered
for the Tsar to deliver Russia from *Latinstvo i Besermanstvo:* the Latin and
the Moslem worlds; and the terms used to contrast Russians and Westerners
were "Christian" (*krest'ianin*) and "Latin" (*latinian*).[79] Since political rule
in the Christian East was now concentrated in the tsar of the "third Rome,"
it was assumed that such rule in the West was concentrated in the hands of
the Holy Roman Emperor (*Tsezar'*). Other princely authorities in the West
were equated with the lesser appanage princes of Russia. Their diplomatic
communications were translated into the new vernacular "chancery language," which provided the basis for modern Russian, while the predominantly Latin communications from the Emperor were translated into
Church Slavonic.[80]

It would be a mistake to read back into this early period the systematically cultivated anti-Catholicism that developed in the following
century of struggle with Poland. During this earlier century, relations were
relatively cordial with the Vatican despite the Muscovite rejection of union.
There was a Catholic church in Moscow in the late fifteenth century,[81]
numerous Catholic residents throughout the sixteenth, and several occasions
when dynastic marriages nearly enabled Rome to parallel in Great Russia
the proselyting success it was enjoying in White and Little Russia. Nevertheless, the basis for Russian anti-Catholicism was already being established in
the need for a lightning rod to channel off popular opposition to the
changes which the triumphant Josephite party was imposing on Russian
society. One did not dare challenge the newly exalted figure of the tsar and
his ecclesiastical entourage; but many conservative elements in Russian
society felt a profound if inarticulate repugnance at the increase in hierarchical discipline and dogmatic rigidity which the Josephites had brought
to Russia. Accordingly, there was a growing tendency to attack ever more
bitterly the distant Roman Catholic Church for the very things one secretly
hated in oneself.

Thus, even while borrowing ideas and techniques from the Roman
Catholic Church, the Josephite hierarchy found criticism of that Church a
useful escape valve for domestic resentments. A Western scapegoat was also
sought for the inarticulate opposition to the concentration of power in the
hands of the Muscovite tsars. At precisely the time when autocracy was
crushing out all opposition in Muscovy a new genre of anti-monarchical

pantomime appeared in Russian popular culture. The name of the play—and of the proud, cruel king who is eventually smitten down—was *Tsar Maximilian,* the first Holy Roman Emperor with whom the Muscovites had extensive relations.[82]

Distrust of Rome thus had from the beginning in Russia a psychological as well as an ideological basis. During this first formative century of contact from the mid-fifteenth to the mid-sixteenth century "the West" was for Russia the urbane Latin Church and Empire of the high Renaissance. Fascination mixed with fear, however; for the Russian Church had begun its fateful series of partial borrowings from the West, and the small literate elite, its gradual turn from Greek to Latin as the main language of cultural expression.

"The Germans"

MUSCOVITE CONTACT with the West changed decisively during Ivan IV's reign from indirect and episodic dealings with the Catholic "Latins" to a direct and sustained confrontation with the Protestant "Germans." It is doubly ironic that the point of no return in opening up Russia to Western influences occurred under this most ostensibly xenophobic and traditionalist of tsars, and that the "West" into whose hands he unconsciously committed Russia was that of the Protestant innovators whom he professed to hate even more than Catholics. It was Ivan who suggested that Luther's name was related to the word *liuty* ("ferocious"); and that the Russian word for Protestant preacher (*kaznodei*) was really a form of *koznodei* ("intriguer").[83] Yet it was Ivan who began the large-scale contacts with the North European Protestant nations, which profoundly influenced Russian thought from the mid-sixteenth to the mid-eighteenth century.

Even as Ivan swept the icons and banners of Muscovy past Kazan down the Volga to the Caspian Sea in the early 1550's, he granted extensive extra-territorial rights and economic concessions to England in the White Sea port of Archangel far to the north. The English became Ivan's most eager collaborator in opening up the lucrative Volga trade route to the Orient. The Danes simultaneously supplied technologists ranging from key artillerists in the battle for Kazan to the first typographer to appear in Muscovy (who was in fact a disguised Lutheran missionary). The best mercenaries for Ivan's rapidly expanding army came largely from the Baltic German regions that were among the first to go over to Protestantism.

Other Germans gained places in the new service nobility through membership in the *oprichnina;* and the entire idea of a uniformed order of warrior-monks may well have been borrowed from the Teutonic and Livonian orders with which Muscovy had such long and intimate contact. In any event, Ivan's organization of this anti-traditional order of hooded vigilantes followed his turn from east to west, and coincided with his decision to increase the intensity of the Livonian War. Baltic Germans had already moved in large numbers to Muscovy during the early, victorious years of the war, as prisoners or as dispossessed men in search of employment. In the 1560's and 1570's began the first systematic organization four miles southeast of Moscow of the foreign quarter—then called the "lower city commune," but soon to be known as the "German suburb": *nemetskaia sloboda.* The term *nemtsy,* which was applied to the new influx of foreigners, had been used as early as the tenth century[84] and carried the pejorative meaning of "dumb ones." Although usage often varied in Muscovy, *nemtsy* became generally used as a blanket term for all the Germanic, Protestant peoples of Northern Europe—in short, for any Western European who was not a "Latin." Other "German" settlements soon appeared (often complete with "Saxon" or "officers'" churches) in key settlements along the fast-growing Volga trade route: Nizhny Novgorod, Vologda, and Kostroma. By the early 1590's, Western Protestants had settled as far east as Tobol'sk in Siberia, and the Orthodox Metropolitan of Kazan was complaining that Tatars as well as Russians were going over to Lutheranism.[85]

The pressures for conformity with local customs were, however, strong in Muscovy; and few enduring traces remained of these early Protestant penetrations. More important than direct conversions to foreign ways and beliefs at the hands of assimilated Baltic and Saxon Germans was the increasing Russian dependence on the more distant "Germans" from England, Denmark, Holland, and the westerly German ports of Lübeck and Hamburg. By invading Livonia and involving Russia in a protracted struggle with neighboring Poland and Sweden, Ivan IV compelled Russia to look for allies on the other side of its immediate enemies; and these industrious and enterprising Protestant powers were able to provide trained personnel and military equipment in return for raw materials and rights for transit and trade. Although Russian alliances shifted frequently in line with the complex diplomacy of the age, friendship with these vigorous Protestant principalities of Northwest Europe remained relatively constant from the late sixteenth to the mid-eighteenth century. This alignment was a function of the same "law of opposite boundaries" (*Gesetz der Gegengrenzlichkeit*) which had earlier caused Ivan III (and Ivan IV) to look with a friendly eye at the Holy Roman Empire for support against Poland-Lithuania, and was later to transfer Russian attention from the Germans to the French in the mid-eighteenth century, when the Germans had replaced the Poles and Swedes as the principal rivals to Russia in Eastern Europe.

The mounting fury of Ivan IV's last years seems less a product of his paranoia than of a kind of schizophrenia. Ivan was, in effect, two people: a true believer in an exclusivist, traditional ideology and a successful practitioner of experimental modern statecraft. Because the two roles were frequently in conflict, his reign became a tissue of contradictions. His personality was increasingly ravaged by those alternations of violent outburst and total withdrawal that occur in those who are divided against themselves.

The Livonian War provides the background of contradiction and irony. Launched for astute economic and political reasons, the war was portrayed as a Christian crusade in much the same manner that the Livonian order had once spoken of its forays with Russia. To aid in fighting, this zealot of Orthodoxy participated in a mixed Lutheran-Orthodox church service, marrying his niece to a Lutheran Danish prince whom he also proclaimed king of Livonia. At the same time, Ivan made strenuous, if pathetic, efforts to arrange for himself an English marriage.[86] To aid in making peace, Ivan turned first to a Czech Protestant in the service of the Poles and then to an Italian Jesuit in the service of the Pope.[87] Though antagonistic to both, Ivan found a measure of agreement with each by joining in the damnation of the other. He was, characteristically, hardest on the Protestants on whom he was most dependent—calling the Czech negotiator "not so much a heretic [as] a servant of the satanic council of the Antichrists."[88]

Meanwhile, this defender of total autocracy had become the first ruler in Russian history to summon a representative national assembly: the *zemsky sobor* of 1566. This was an act of pure political improvisation on the part of this avowed traditionalist. In an effort to support an extension of the war into Lithuania, Ivan sought to attract wandering western Russian noblemen accustomed to the aristocratic assemblies (*sejmiki*) of Lithuania, while simultaneously enlisting the new wealth of the cities by adopting the more inclusive European system of three-estate representation.[89] As constitutional seduction gave way to military assault, Lithuania hastened to consummate its hitherto Platonic political link with Poland. The purely aristocratic diet (*sejm*) that pronounced this union at Lublin in 1569 was far less broadly representative than Ivan's *sobor* of 1566; but it acquired the important role of electing the king of the new multi-national republic (*Rzeczpospolita*) when the Jagellonian dynasty became extinct in 1572.

Ivan and his successors (like almost every other European house) participated vigorously in the parliamentary intrigues of this body, particularly during the Polish succession crisis of 1586. Then, in 1598, when the line of succession came to an end in Russia also, they turned to the Polish procedure of electing a ruler—the ill-fated Boris Godunov—in a specially convened *zemsky sobor:* the first since 1566. For a quarter of a century thereafter these *sobors* became even more broadly representative, and were in many ways the supreme political authority in the nation. Not only in 1598 but in 1606, 1610, 1611, and 1613 roughly similar representative bodies made the crucial decisions on the choice of succession to the throne.[90] Despite many differences in composition and function, these councils all shared the original aim of Ivan's council of 1566: to attract western Russians away from the Polish-Lithuanian *sejm* and to create a more effective fund-raising body by imitating the multi-state assemblies of the North European Protestant nations.[91]

Thus, ironically, this most serious of all proto-parliamentary challenges to Muscovite autocracy originated in the statecraft of its seemingly most adamant apologist. Increasingly torn by contradiction, Ivan brought the first printing press to Moscow and sponsored the first printed Russian book, *The Acts of the Apostles,* in 1564. Then, the following year, he let a mob burn the press and drive the printers away to Lithuania. He increased the imperial subsidies and the numbers of pilgrimages to monasteries, then sponsored irreverent parodies of Orthodox worship at the *oprichnik* retreat in Alexandrovsk. Unable to account for the complexities of a rapidly changing world, Ivan intensified his terror against Westernizing elements in the years just before abolishing the *oprichnina* in 1572. In 1570, he razed and depopulated Novgorod once again, and summarily executed Viskovaty, one of his closest and most worldly confidants. One year later, Moscow was sacked and burned by a sudden Tatar invasion. In 1575, Ivan—the first man ever to be crowned tsar in Russia—retired to Alexandrovsk and abdicated the title in favor of a converted Tatar khan. Though he soon resumed his rule, he used the imperial title much less after this strange episode.

Ivan's denigration of princely authority provided a shock that terror by itself could not have produced on the toughened Muscovite mentality. The image of the tsar as leader of Christian empire, which Ivan had done so much to encourage, was severely damaged. The divinized prince—the focal point of all loyalties and "national" sentiment in this paternalistic society— had renounced his divinity. The image was impaired not so much by the fact that Ivan was a murderer many times over as by the identity of two of his victims. In murdering Metropolitan Philip of Moscow in 1568, Ivan sought primarily to rid himself of a leading member of a boyar family suspected of disloyalty. But by murdering a revered First Prelate of the Church, Ivan passed on to Philip something of the halo of Russia's first national saints, Boris and Gleb, who had voluntarily accepted a guiltless death in order to redeem the Russian people from their sin. Philip's remains were venerated in the distant monastery of Solovetsk, which began to rival St. Sergius at nearby Zagorsk as a center for pilgrimage. The close ties between the great monasteries and the grand dukes of Muscovy were beginning to loosen.

An even more serious shock to the Muscovite ideology was Ivan's murder of his son, heir, and namesake: Ivan, the tsarevich. The Tsar's claim to absolute kingship was based on an unbroken succession from the distant apostolic and imperial past. Having spelled this genealogy out more fully and fancifully than ever before, Ivan now broke the sacred chain with his own hands. In so doing he lost some of the aura of a God-chosen Christian warrior and Old Testament king, which had surrounded him since his victory at Kazan.

The martyred Philip and Ivan became new heroes of Russian folklore; and the Tsar's enemies thus became in many eyes the true servants of "holy Russia." In the religious crisis of the seventeenth century both contending factions traced their ancestry to Philip: Patriarch Nikon, who theatrically transplanted his remains to Moscow, and the Old Believers, who revered him as a saint. In the political crises of the seventeenth century the idea was born that Ivan the tsarevich had survived after all, that there still existed a "true tsar" with unbroken links to apostolic times. Ivan himself had helped launch the legend by donating the unprecedented sum of five thousand rubles to the Monastery of St. Sergius to subsidize memorial services for his son.[92]

The struggle between the two became one of the most recurrent of all themes in the popular songs of early modern Russia.[93] The most dramatic of all nineteenth-century Russian historical paintings is probably Repin's crimson-soaked canvas of Ivan's murder of his son, and Dostoevsky entitled the key chapter in *The Possessed,* his prophetic novel of revolution, "Ivan the Tsarevich."

Ivan the Terrible was succeeded by a feeble-minded son Fedor, whose death in 1598 (following the mysterious murder of Ivan's only other son, the young prince Dmitry, in 1591) brought to an end the old line of imperial succession. The accession to the throne of the regent Boris Godunov represented a further affront to the Muscovite mentality. Boris, who had a non-boyar, partly Tatar genealogy, was elected amidst venal political controversy by a *zemsky sobor,* and with the connivance of the Patriarch of Russia (whose position had been created only recently, in 1589, and by the somewhat suspect authority of foreign Orthodox leaders). Kurbsky's anti-autocratic insistence that the Tsar seek council "from men of all the people" was seemingly gratified by the official proclamation that Boris was chosen by representatives of "all the popular multitude."[94]

Once in power, Boris became an active and systematic Westernizer. He encouraged the European practice of shaving. Economic contacts were greatly expanded at terms favorable to foreign entrepreneurs; thirty selected future leaders of Russia were sent abroad to study; important positions were assigned to foreigners; imperial protection was afforded the foreign community; Lutheran churches were tolerated not only in Moscow but as far afield as Nizhny Novgorod; and the crown prince of Denmark was brought to Moscow to marry Boris' daughter Xenia, after an unsuccessful bid by a rival Swedish prince.

Any chance that Russia might have had under Boris for peaceful evolution toward the form of limited monarchy prevalent in the countries he most admired, England and Denmark, was, however, a fleeting one at best. For he was soon overtaken with a series of crises even more profound than those brought on Russia by Ivan. In the last three years of Boris' reign, his realm was struck with a famine that may have killed as much as one third of his subjects and with a wild growth of brigandage and peasant unrest. At the same time his daughter's prospective Danish bridegroom suddenly died in Moscow, and all but two of his thirty selected student-leaders elected to remain in the West.[95]

Death must have come almost as a relief to Boris in 1605; but it only intensified the suffering of a shaken nation which proved unable to unite behind a successor for fifteen years. This chaotic interregnum produced such a profound crisis in Muscovy that the name long given to it, "Time of Troubles," has become a general historical term for a period of decisive trial and partial disintegration that precedes and precipitates the building of great empires.[96] This original "Time of Troubles" (*Smutnoe vremia*) was just such an ordeal for insular Muscovy. A rapid series of blows stunned it and then propelled it half-unwittingly into a three-cornered struggle with Poland and Sweden for control of Eastern Europe. As it summoned up the strength to defeat Poland in the First Northern War of 1654–67 and Sweden in the Second or Great Northern War of 1701–21, Russia was transformed into a continental empire and the dominant power in Eastern Europe.

The Religious Wars

ONE OF THE GREAT MISFORTUNES of Russian history is that Russia entered the mainstream of European development at a time of unprecedented division and degradation in Western Christendom. Having missed out on the more positive and creative stages of European culture—the rediscovery of classical logic in the twelfth and thirteenth centuries, of classical beauty in the fourteenth and fifteenth, and the religious reforms of the sixteenth—Russia was suddenly drawn into the destructive final stages of the European religious wars in the early seventeenth.

By the late sixteenth century, the genuine concern for religious reform and renewal which had precipitated the many-sided debates between Protestant and Catholic Europe had been largely sublimated into a continent-wide civil war. All of Europe was succumbing to the dynamics of a "military revolution" that weighed down each state with vast, self-perpetuating armies subject to ever-tightening discipline, more deadly weapons, and more fluid tactics. By harnessing ideological propaganda and psychological warfare to military objectives and by silencing in the name of *raison d'état* "the last remaining qualms as to the religious and ethical legitimacy of war,"[97] Europe in the early seventeenth century was savoring its first anticipatory taste of total war. The religious wars were late in coming to Eastern Europe. But the form they assumed at the turn of the sixteenth century was that of a particularly bitter contest between Catholic Poland and Lutheran Sweden. When both parties moved into Russia during the Time of Troubles, Orthodox Muscovy was also drawn in under conditions which permanently darkened the Russian image of the West.

Muscovy had been living in political uncertainty and ideological confusion ever since the late years of Ivan the Terrible's reign. He had done much to break the sense of continuity with a sacred past and the internal solidarity between sovereign, church, and family on which Muscovite civilization was based. The early seventeenth century brought the deeper shock of military defeat and economic spoliation. Twice—in 1605 and 1610—the Poles overran and dominated Moscow; as late as 1618 they lay siege to it and held lands far to the east. To combat the powerful Poles, Muscovy deepened its dependence on the Swedes, who in turn helped themselves to Novgorod and other Russian regions. To lessen dependence on the Swedes, Russia turned to the more distant "Germans," particularly the English and the Dutch, who extracted their reward in lucrative economic concessions.

The confrontation with Poland represented the first frontal conflict of ideas with the West. This powerful Western neighbor represented almost the complete cultural antithesis of Muscovy. The Polish-Lithuanian union was a loose republic rather than a monolithic autocracy. Its cosmopolitan population included not only Polish Catholics but Orthodox believers from Moldavia and White Russia and large, self-contained communities of Calvinists, Socinians, and Jews. In striking contrast to the mystical piety and formless folklore of Muscovy, Poland was dominated by Latin rationalism and a stylized Renaissance literature. Poland not only contradicted Russian Orthodox practice by using painting and music for profane purposes but was actually a pioneer in the use of pictures for propaganda and the composition of instrumental and polyphonic music.

Most important, however, the Poland of Sigismund III represented the European vanguard of the Counter Reformation. Sigismund was newly enflamed by the Jesuits with the same kind of messianic fanaticism that the Josephites had imparted to Ivan the Terrible a half century earlier. Obsessed like Ivan with fears of heresy and sedition, Sigismund used a translation of Ivan's reply to the Czech brethren as an aid in his own anti-Protestant campaign in White Russia.[98] Because his realm was more diffuse and Protestantism far more established, Sigismund became in many ways even more fanatical than Ivan. If Ivan resembled Philip II of Spain, Sigismund became a close friend and Latin correspondent of the Spanish royal family.[99] If the Josephites borrowed some ideas from the Inquisition, Sigismund virtually turned his kingdom over to a later monument to Spanish crusading zeal: Ignatius Loyola's Jesuit Order.

The wandering monks and holy men that traditionally accompanied the Muscovite armies and lent prophetic fervor to their cause were now confronted by a rival set of clerical aides-de-camp: the Jesuits in Sigismund's court. It is precisely because the Jesuits gave an ideological cast to the war with Muscovy that the order became a subject of such pathological hatred— and secret fascination—for subsequent Russian thinkers.

The Jesuit order had long tried to interest the Vatican in the idea that losses to Protestantism in Western and Northern Europe might be at least partially recouped in the east by combining missionary zeal with more flexible and imaginative tactics. They had encouraged the formation in the Lithuanian and White Russian Orthodox community of the new Uniat Church—which preserved Eastern rites and the Slavonic language while accepting the supremacy of the Pope and the Latin formulation of the creed—and helped secure its formal recognition by the Vatican in 1596.

In the late years of Ivan the Terrible's reign, the Jesuit statesman Antonio Possevino had entertained the idea that Russia might be brought into union with Rome; and this suggestion was frequently echoed throughout the seventeenth century, particularly by uprooted Eastern European Catholics and leaders of the newly formed Society for the Propagation of the Faith. But by the beginning of the century, the Jesuits had succeeded in committing Vatican policy in Eastern Europe to a close working partnership with Sigismund III of Poland. Since Sigismund exercised full control over Lithuania and had a strong claim on Sweden, he seemed the logical bearer of the Catholic cause in Northeast Europe; and he sealed his allegiance to the cause of Rome with two successive Hapsburg marriages.

One of the most eloquent and strategy-minded Jesuits, Peter Skarga, was responsible for capturing the imagination of Sigismund and his court in his "Sermons to the Diet" of the late 1590's.[100] Capitalizing on the knightly and apocalyptical cast of Christian thought in the still-embattled East, Skarga inspired Sigismund's entourage with that mixture of gloomy premonition and crusading romanticism which was to become an essential part of the Polish national consciousness. Capitalizing on the confused Muscovite hopes that a "true Tsar" was still somewhere to be found, the Jesuits helped the Poles ride to power in the retinue of the pretender, Dmitry. Capitalizing on the rising power of the press in the West, the aged Possevino, under a pseudonym, printed pamphlets in support of Dmitry in a variety of European capitals.[101] Capitalizing on the religious reverence accorded icons in Muscovy, pictures of Dmitry were printed for circulation to the superstitious masses. Anxious to secure the claims of the new dynasty, a Catholic marriage for Dmitry was staged within the Kremlin.

The combination within the Polish camp of proselyting Jesuit zeal at the highest level and crude sacrilege at the lowest led to the defenestration and murder of Dmitry by a Moscow mob in 1606. The pretender who had entered Moscow triumphantly amidst the deafening peal of bells on midsummer day of 1605 was dragged through the streets and his remains shot from a cannon less than a year later. However, the Polish sense of mission was in no way diminished. A Polish court poet spoke of Cracow in 1610 as "the New Rome more wondrous than the old,"[102] and Sigismund described his cause in a letter to the Catholic king of Hungary as that of "the Universal Christian republic."[103] Despite the coronation in Moscow of Michael, the first Romanov, in 1613, there was no clear central authority in Muscovy until at least 1619, when Michael's father, Patriarch Philaret Nikitich, returned from Polish captivity. Pro-Polish factions continued to be influential inside Muscovy until the 1630's, and Polish claimants to the Muscovite throne continued to command widespread recognition in Catholic Europe until the 1650's.

The identification of the Catholic cause with Polish arms weakened whatever chance the Roman church might have had to establish its authority peacefully over the Russian Church. The military defeat of Poland became the defeat of Roman Catholicism among the Eastern Slavs— though not of Latin culture. For in rolling back the Polish armies in the course of the seventeenth century, and slowly wresting from them control of the Latinized Ukraine and White Russia, Muscovy absorbed much of their literary and artistic culture.[104]

Forms of
the Virgin

PLATES I–II

Russia brought new tenderness and imagination to the depiction of the Virgin Mary in Christian art. The famed early-twelfth-century "Vladimir Mother of God" (Plate I) has long been the most revered of Russian icons: and the restoration of the original composition (completed in 1918) revealed it to be one of the most beautiful as well. Originally painted in Constantinople, the icon was believed to have brought the Virgin's special protective power from the "new Rome" to Kiev, thence to Vladimir, and finally to Moscow, the "third Rome," where it has remained uninterruptedly since 1480.

This icon was one of a relatively new Byzantine type emphasizing the relationship between mother and child; it was known and revered in Russia as "Our Lady of Tenderness." Characteristic of this general type was the "Virgin and Child Rejoicing" (Plate II), a mid-sixteenth-century painting from the upper Volga region. The downward sweep of the Virgin's form conveys in visual terms the spiritual temper of the icon's place of origin: combining physical exaggeration with a compassionate spirit. The liberation and semi-naturalistic portrayal of the infant's arms are designed to heighten the rhythmic flow of sinuous lines into an increasingly abstract, almost musical composition.

PLATE I

PLATE II

PLATE III

PLATE IV

Hardly less revered than the omnipresent individual icons of the Virgin and Child were the various representations of the Virgin on the icon screens of Muscovy. The third picture in this series shows the Virgin as she appears to the right of Christ on the central tryptich (deēsis) of a sixteenth-century screen. The richly embossed metal surface, inlaid with jewels, that surrounds the painted figure is typical of the increasingly lavish icon-veneration of the period. This icon, presently in the personal collection of the Soviet painter P. D. Korin, bears the seal of Boris Godunov, who presumably used it for private devotions.

The picture to the left illustrates the survival of the theme of Virgin and Child amidst the forced preoccupation with socialist themes and realistic portraiture of the Soviet era. This painting of 1920 (popularly known as "Our Lady of Petersburg" despite its official designation of "Petersburg, 1918"), with its unmistakable suggestion of the Virgin and Child standing in humble garb above the city of Revolution, continues to attract reverent attention in the Tret'iakov Gallery of Moscow. It is the work of Kuzma Petrov-Vodkin, who had studied under Leonid Pasternak, illustrator of Tolstoy and father of Boris Pasternak. Petrov-Vodkin turned from painting to teaching for the same reason that the poet Pasternak turned to translating—to keep his integrity during the oppressive period of Stalinist rule; both men attracted talented young followers and quietly passed on to later generations some sense of the older artistic traditions and spiritual concerns of Russian culture.

The Vatican-supported Polish offensive against Orthodox Slavdom served mainly to stimulate an ideological and national rising in Muscovy which drove out the Poles and gradually united Russia behind the new Romanov dynasty. For more than three hundred years the Romanovs reigned—even if they did not always rule or ever fully escape the shadows cast by the dark times in which they came to power. From early ballads through early histories into the plays and operas of the late imperial period, the Time of Troubles came to be thought of as a period of suffering for the sins of previous tsars and of foreboding for tsars yet to come. The name of Marina Mnishek, Dmitry's Polish wife, became a synonym for "witch" and "crow": the Polish mazurka—allegedly danced at their wedding reception in the Kremlin—became a leitmotiv for "decadent foreigner" in Glinka's *Life for the Tsar* and later musical compositions. The anti-Polish and anti-Catholic tone of almost all subsequent Russian writing about this period faithfully reflects a central, fateful fact: that Muscovy achieved unity after the troubles of the early seventeenth century primarily through xenophobia, particularly toward the Poles.

Operatic romanticism about the national *levée en masse* against the Polish invader has, however, too long obscured the fact that the price of Russian victory was increased dependence on Protestant Europe. The subtle stream of Protestant influence flowed in from three different sources: beleaguered Protestants in nearby Catholic countries, militant Sweden, and the more distant and commercially oriented "Germans" (England, Holland, Denmark, Hamburg, and so on).

The diaspora of the once-flourishing Protestants of Poland (and of many in Hungary, Bohemia, and Transylvania) remains a relatively obscure chapter in the complex confessional politics of Eastern Europe. It is fairly clear that the Counter Reformation zeal of the Jesuits combined with princely fears of political disintegration and social change to permit an aggressive reassertion of Catholic power throughout East Central Europe in the late sixteenth and the early seventeenth century. But it seems implausible to assume that these relatively extreme communities of Calvinists, Czech brethren, and Socinians simply vanished after military defeat and passively accepted Catholicism. To be sure, many regions were totally exhausted by the end of the fighting, and had no alternative to capitulation. But in eastern Poland, where Protestantism had some of its strongest supporters and the power of the Counter Reformation had come relatively late, the anti-Catholic cause was strengthened by the Orthodox community of White Russia and the proximity of Orthodox Muscovy. Forced Catholicization tended to make defensive allies of the large Protestant and Orthodox minorities under Polish rule. It seems probable that the Orthodox community absorbed some of the personnel as well as the organizational and polemic techniques of the Protestants as they were hounded into oblivion. Thus, when the anti-Catholic Orthodox clergy of White Russia and the Ukraine eventually turned to Muscovy for protection against the onrushing Counter Reformation, they brought with them elements of a fading Polish Protestantism as well as a resurgent Slavic Orthodoxy.

The formation of the Uniat Church accelerated this chain of developments by securing the allegiance to Rome of most of the Orthodox hierarchy in the Polish kingdom. The union with Rome was not accepted so readily at the lower levels of the hierarchy or among local lay leaders anxious to maintain their historic liberties and autonomy. In organizing for their resistance to Catholicization, Orthodox communities leaned increasingly on regional brotherhoods, which took on a Protestant tinge. Their origins, though still obscure, appear to lie in contact with the neighboring Czech dissenters who had also helped steer Polish Protestants into the closely knit "brotherhood" form of organization.[105] The initial strength of the Orthodox brotherhoods was concentrated in many of the same semi-independent cities in eastern Poland, where Polish Protestants had made their most spectacular gains a half century earlier. The anti-hierarchical bias, close communal discipline, and emphasis on a program of religious printing and education in the vernacular among the Orthodox brotherhoods are reminiscent of both Hussite and Calvinist practice.

Sigismund helped further the sense of identification between non-Uniat Orthodox and Protestants by lumping them together as "heretical," and thus denying the Orthodox the somewhat preferred status of "schismatic" traditionally accorded in Roman Catholic teaching. Protestants and Orthodox began the search for a measure of common action against Sigismund's policies at a meeting of leaders from both communities in Lithuania in the summer of 1595.[106] During the decade preceding this meeting, the Orthodox had formed at least fourteen brotherhood organizations and a large number of schools and printing shops.[107] During the years that followed, Protestant communities were often forced into the protective embrace of the more established Orthodox communities as Sigismund's persecution of religious dissenters increased. At the same time, the Orthodox opponents of Catholicism adopted many of the apocalyptically anti-Catholic ideas of Protestant polemic writings and absorbed into their schools harassed but well-educated Polish Protestants as well as Slavic defectors from Jesuit academies.

The brotherhood schools and presses of White Russia were the first broad media of instruction to appear among the Orthodox Eastern Slavs. The first two brotherhood presses—those of Vilnius and Lwow—made particularly great contributions to enlightenment. The former published the

first two Church Slavonic grammars (in 1596 and 1619), and the latter
published more than thirty-three thousand copies of basic alphabet books
(*bukvar'*) between 1585 and 1722.[108] The school at Ostrog taught Latin as
well as Greek, and sponsored the printing in 1576–80 of the first complete
Slavonic bible.[109] The brotherhood schools continued to multiply in the
early seventeenth century, and spread to the east and south as the Orthodox
communities in those regions sought to combat the spread of Catholic influence. The Kiev brotherhood played a particularly important role, setting
up (while still under Polish control in 1632) the first Orthodox institution
of higher education ever to appear among the Eastern Slavs: the Kiev
Academy.

   Two leading Orthodox personalities of the late sixteenth and the early
seventeenth century illustrate the Protestant influence on the beleaguered
Russian Orthodox community during this period. Stephan Zizanius, the
White Russian author of the first Slavonic grammar in 1596, followed the
Lutheran practice of inserting catechistic homilies and anti-Catholic comments into his instructional material. His *Book of Cyril*, a gloomy, anti-
Uniat compilation of prophetic texts, incorporated many of the polemic
arguments used against the Roman Church by Protestant propagandists.
Just as the Kiev Academy became the model for the monastic schools and
academies that began to appear in Muscovy in the late seventeenth century,
so Zizanius' arguments that the reign of Antichrist was at hand became
the basis for the xenophobic and apocalyptical writings of the seventeenth-
century Muscovite Church.[110]

   Even more deeply influenced by Protestantism was Cyril Lukaris, the
early-seventeenth-century Greek Patriarch of Constantinople, who had
served as a parish priest and teacher in the brotherhood schools of Vilnius
and Lwow during the 1590's. Deeply influenced by their anti-Catholicism,
he was one of the two representatives of the Orthodox hierarchy to vote
against the final acceptance of the union at Brest in 1596. In the course
of his subsequent career, Lukaris became a close friend of various Anglicans
as well as Polish and Hungarian Calvinists, and became doctrinally a virtual
Calvinist. After his elevation to the Patriarchate of Constantinople in 1620,
he "attached himself to the Protestant powers,"[111] and was called by the
Hapsburg ambassador to the Porte "the archfiend of the Catholic Church."[112]
Through his close links with Patriarch Philaret, Lukaris was instrumental
in bringing Russia into the anti-Hapsburg coalition in the second half of
the Thirty Years' War.

   A final link between the Orthodox and Protestant worlds that was
forged by a common Slavic and anti-Catholic association may be found in
the great seventeenth-century Czech writer and educator, Jan Comenius.

Though distressed at the low educational level of the Eastern Slavs, Comenius wrote, after the destruction of the Czech Protestant community in 1620, that Muscovy offered the only hope of defeating the Catholic cause in Europe.[113] Subsequently, as an émigré among the Protestant communities of Poland, Comenius became interested in the Orthodox brotherhoods and was probably influenced by their curricula and pedagogical theories while drawing up his own famous theories of education and public enlightenment.[114]

Hardly less important than the influx of Protestant influences by way of the anti-Uniat movement in western and southern Russia was the direct impact of Sweden, the powerful Protestant rival and northern neighbor of Muscovy.

The Swedish presence began to be felt in the 1590's with the Swedish sack and occupation of the northernmost Russian monastery, at Petsamo on the Arctic Ocean,[115] and the movement of Swedish colonists and evangelists into the region of Lake Ladoga. The real influx began, however, with the Swedish efforts to curb the Polish advance into Russia during the Time of Troubles. Sigismund's Protestant uncle, Charles IX of Sweden, launched a campaign to stiffen the resistance of the new tsar Shuisky to Catholic Poland in the name of "all Christianity."[116] In 1607 Charles sent the Russians the first treatise to appear in Russia on the burgeoning new European art of war;[117] and in the following year addressed the first of three unprecedented propaganda appeals directly to "all ranks of Russia" to rise up against "the Polish and Lithuanian dogs."[118] In the ensuing months, the Swedes began a large-scale intervention that extended from Novgorod through Yaroslavl and involved the occupation of the venerable Orthodox monastery of Valaam on islands within Lake Ladoga and the issuance of anti-Catholic propaganda to the Solovetsk monastery and other centers in the Russian north.

The Swedes were, indeed, the unsung heroes of the liberation of Moscow from Polish occupation. Intervention against Poland in 1609 was followed by the dispatch to Muscovy of money and of a Dutch-trained general in the Swedish service, Christernus Some, who helped organize the army of Skopin-Shuisky for the critical campaigns of 1609–10, which expelled Sigismund from without and suppressed Cossack insurrection within.[119] The non-noble militia of Minin and Pozharsky which drove the aristocratic Polish legions from Moscow for the second and final time in 1612–13 was in some respects a rudimentary version of the revolutionary new citizen type of army with which the Swedes were shortly to crush the aristocratic Hapsburg armies in the Thirty Years' War. At the high point of the Polish penetration in 1612, a *zemsky sobor* convened at Yaroslavl entered into negotiations with Sweden for the Swedish crown prince to take over the vacant throne of Russia.[120] At the same time, the English extended Russia an offer of protectorate status.[121] The Dutch, who rivaled and soon supplanted the English as the main foreign commercial power in Russia, helped launch the first organ of systematic news dissemination inside Russia in 1621, the hand-written *kuranty,* and provided much of the material and personnel for the rapidly growing Russian army.[122] Twice—in 1621–2 and 1643–5— the Danes nearly succeeded in foreclosing royal marriages with the insecure new house of Romanov.[123]

The extent of Swedish influence in the early years of the Romanov dynasty is still insufficiently appreciated. Not only did Sweden take away Russia's limited access to the eastern Baltic by the terms of the Treaty of Stolbovo in 1617, but Swedish hegemony was gradually extended down the coast beyond Riga and Swedish trading prerogatives maintained in Novgorod and other important Russian commercial centers. The Swedes were granted fishing rights on the White Lake, deep inside Russia, by the Monastery of St. Cyril in 1621, and there was considerable intercourse between Sweden and Solovetsk on the White Sea until a general crackdown on relations with Lutherans was decreed in 1629 by the Metropolitan of Novgorod, for the entirety of northern Russia.

The reason for his concern was the energetic proselyting that was being conducted by the Swedes, who had founded a Slavic printing press in Stockholm in 1625. Orthodox priests living under Swedish rule were required to attend a Lutheran service at least once a month, and a Lutheran catechism was printed in Russian in 1625 in the first of two editions. Another catechism was later printed in a Cyrillic version of the Finnish language for evangelizing the Finns and Karelians. In 1631 the energetic new governor general of Livonia, Johannes Skytte, founded a school on the future site of St. Petersburg that included the Russian language in its curriculum. In 1632 a Lutheran University was founded at Tartu (Dorpat, Derpt, Yur'ev) in Esthonia, in the place of a former Jesuit academy.[124] In 1640 a higher academy was founded in Turku (Åbo), the chief port and capital of Swedish Finland (whose name may derive from the Russian "trade," *torg*). During 1633–4 a Lutheran over-consistory was established in Livonia with six under-consistories and a substantial program of public instruction. The university at Tartu and the academy at Kiev—both founded in 1632 by non-Russians with an essentially Latin curriculum— were, in a sense, the first Russian institutions of higher education, founded more than a century before the University of Moscow in 1755. The conquest of Kiev from the Poles in 1667 and Tartu from the Swedes in 1704 were, thus, events of cultural as well as political importance.

Nor were the reformed Protestant churches inactive. By the late 1620's there was at least one Calvinist church in Moscow supported mainly by Dutch residents as well as three Lutheran Churches;[125] and the existence of a Russian-language Calvinist catechism of the 1620's or 1630's for which no known Western model has been found indicates that there may have been some attempts to adopt Calvinist literature for Russian audiences.[126]

With such a variety of Protestant forces operating inside Muscovy in the early seventeenth century, it is hardly surprising that anti-Catholicism grew apace. One of the first acts of Patriarch Philaret, after becoming in 1619 co-ruler of Russia with his son Tsar Michael, was to require the re-baptism of all Catholics; and discriminatory regulations were enacted in the 1630's to exclude Roman Catholics from the growing number of mercenaries recruited for Russia in Western Europe.[127] The continued expansion of Jesuit schools in western Russia and the Polish Ukraine, the establishment of a new Catholic diocese of Smolensk, and Sigismund's proclamation of a "Universal Union" of Orthodoxy with Catholicism had intensified anti-Catholic feeling in the 1620's.[128] The Swedes supported and encouraged the Russian attack on Poland in 1632; and the Swedish victory over the Catholic emperor at Breitenfeld in the same year was celebrated by special church services and the festive ringing of bells in Moscow. Orthodox merchants in Novgorod placed pictures of the victorious Gustavus Adolphus in places of veneration usually reserved for icons.[129]

Indeed, it was not until the crown prince of Denmark arrived in Moscow in 1644 to arrange for a Protestant marriage to the daughter of Tsar Michael that Russian society became aware of the extent that the young dynasty had identified itself with the Protestant powers. The successful campaign of leading clerical figures to block this marriage on religious grounds combined with the intensified campaign of native merchants against economic concessions to foreigners to turn Muscovy in the 1640's away from any gradual drift toward Protestantism. But by the time Russia began to restrict the activities of Protestant elements and prepare for battle with the Swedes, it had established a deepening technological and administrative dependence on the more distant "Germans"—and particularly the Dutch. This dependence was hardest of all to throw off, because it arose out of the military necessities of the struggle against the Poles and Swedes.

Beginning in the 1550's, Russia had plunged into its "military revolution," as Ivan the Terrible mobilized the first full-time, paid Russian infantry (the *streltsy*) and began the large-scale recruitment of foreign mercenaries.[130] The number of both *streltsy* and mercenaries increased; and in the first three decades of the seventeenth century, the total number of traditional, non-noble elements fell from one half to about one fourth of the Russian army.[131] Swedish and Dutch influences became evident in the introduction of longer lances, more mobile formations, stricter drill methods, and the first use of military maps. Polish foes begrudgingly—and not inaccurately—referred to the "Dutch cleverness" of the Russian troops.[132]

As the Dutch joined the Swedes in the building of the Russian army for its inconclusive war with Poland in 1632–4, the Muscovite army began the most dramatic expansion of its entire history, increasing from its more or less standard size of about 100,000 to a figure in the vicinity of 300,000 in the last stages of the victorious campaign against Poland in the 1660's.[133] Most of the officers and many of the ordinary soldiers were imported from North European Protestant countries, so that a good fourth of this swollen army was foreign.[134]

Those Western arrivals (like many newly assimilated Tatars, Southern Slavs, and so on) were uprooted figures, completely dependent on the state. They became a major component in the new service nobility, or *dvorianstvo,* which gradually replaced the older and more traditional landed aristocracy. Other developments which accompanied and supported the "military revolution" in early-seventeenth-century Russia were the growth of governmental bureaucracy, the expanded power of regional military commanders (*voevodas*), and the formalization of peasant serfdom as a means of guaranteeing the state a supply of food and service manpower.

Typical of the new military-administrative leaders that helped transform Russian society during the weak reign of Michael Romanov was Ivan Cherkasky.[135] His father was a converted Moslem from the Caucasus who had entered the service of Ivan the Terrible and served as the first military *voevoda* of Novgorod, where he married the sister of the future Patriarch Philaret and befriended the brilliant Swedish mercenary general de la Gardie. Young Ivan was brought up as a soldier with his loyalty to the Tsar uncomplicated by local attachments. He studied the military methods of the nearby Swedes and collaborated with them in mobilizing Russian opinion against the Poles during the Time of Troubles. His military activity earned for him (along with the co-liberator of Moscow, Dmitry Pozharsky) elevation to boyar rank on the day of the Tsar's coronation in 1613. By amassing personal control over a number of Moscow chanceries, including a new, semi-terrorist organization known as the "bureau for investigative affairs," he became probably the most powerful single person in the Muscovite government until his death in 1642.[136] Throughout his career, his use of (and friendship with) Swedish and Dutch military and administrative personnel was indispensable to his success. He hailed the Swedes and the alliance "of the great tsar and the great king" against "the Roman faith of heretics, papists, Jesuits."[137] He insisted that the Russians, like the

Swedes, should defend their "sovereign nature" against new Roman pretensions to universal Empire. He emulated the Swedes and Dutch (who showered him with gifts often more lavish than those given the Tsar) by introducing secret writing into Russian diplomatic communications.[138]

In 1632 the Dutch built the first modern Russian arms plant and arsenal at Tula; and in 1647, printed in the Netherlands the first military manual and drill book for Russian foot soldiers, which was also the first Russian-language book ever to use copper engravings.[139] French Huguenot fortification specialists were put to work, and the building of the first fortified line of defense in the south spelled the end to the traditional vulnerability to pillaging raids from that direction.[140]

A final by-product of the Russian links with their more distant "German" allies was the turning of Russian eyes at last toward the sea. The eastern Baltic (and indeed some of the lakes and rivers of the north) had become areas of contention in which the Swedes had exercised humiliating advantages over the landlocked Muscovites; and the southward movement of Russian power down the Volga and Don confronted Russia with Persian and Turkish naval power at the point where these rivers entered the Caspian and Black seas respectively. Thus, the period from the late sixteenth to the late seventeenth century—which also saw the opening of Siberia and the Russian drive to the Pacific—witnessed a series of efforts to build a Russian navy. The Russians received aid and encouragement in this endeavor from the Danes (who were anxious to strengthen Russia against the Swedes) and even more from the English and Dutch (who were anxious to protect trade routes from their respective ports of Archangel and Kholmogory on the White Sea through Russian rivers to the Orient). Ivan IV was the first to think about a navy; Boris Godunov, the first to buy ships for sailing under the Russian flag; Michael Romanov, the first to build a river fleet; and Alexis, the first to build an ocean-going Russian warship.[141]

The fateful feature of this Russian orientation toward the North European Protestant countries was that it was so completely military and administrative in nature. Muscovy took none of the religious, artistic, or educational ideas of these advanced nations. Symptomatic of Muscovy's purely practical and military interest in secular enlightenment is the fact that the word *nauka,* later used for "science" and "learning" in Russia, was introduced in the military manual of 1647 as a synonym for "military skill."[142] The scientific revolution came to Russia after the military revolution: and natural science was for many years to be thought of basically as a servant of the military establishment.

The long military struggle which led to the defeat of Poland in the war of 1654–67, and of Sweden a half century later, produced a greater cultural change in the Russian victor than in either of the defeated nations. Poland and Sweden both clung to the forms and ideals of a past age, whereas Russia underwent a far-reaching transformation that pointed toward the future. What had been a monolithic, monastic civilization became a multi-national, secular state. Under Alexis Mikhailovich and his son Peter the Great, Russia in effect adopted the aesthetic and philosophic culture of Poland even while rejecting its Catholic faith, and the administrative and technological culture of Sweden and Holland without either the Lutheran or the Calvinist form of Protestantism.

Symbol of the Polish impact was the incorporation into the expanding Muscovite state in 1667 of the long-lost "mother of Russian cities," the culturally advanced and partially Latinized city of Kiev. The acquisition of Kiev (along with Smolensk, Chernigov, and other cities) inspired the imagination but upset the tranquillity of Muscovy, marking a return to the half-forgotten unity of pre-Mongol times and the incorporation of far higher levels of culture and enlightenment.

Symbol of the Swedish impact was the last of the three great centers of Russian culture: St. Petersburg, the window which Peter forced open on Northern Europe in the early eighteenth century and transformed into the new capital of Russia. Built with ruthless symmetry on the site of an old Swedish fortress and given a Dutch name, Petersburg symbolized the coming to Muscovy of the bleak Baltic ethos of administrative efficiency and military discipline which had dominated much of Germanic Protestantism. The greatest territorial gains at the expense of Poland and Sweden were to follow the acquisition of these key cities by a century in each case —the absorption of eastern Poland and most of the Ukraine occurring in the late eighteenth century and the acquisition of Finland and the Baltic provinces in the early nineteenth. But the decisive psychological change was accomplished by the return of Kiev and the building of St. Petersburg.

Bringing these two Westernized cities together with Moscow into one political unit had disturbing cultural effects. The struggle for Eastern Europe had produced profound social dislocations while increasing popular involvement in ideological and spiritual controversy. As the stream of Western influences grew to a flood in the course of the seventeenth century, Russians seemed to thrash about with increasing desperation. Indeed, the entire seventeenth and the early eighteenth century can be viewed as an extension of the Time of Troubles: a period of continuous violence, of increasing borrowing from, yet rebelling against, the West. The deep split finally came to the surface in this last stage of the confrontation between Muscovy and the West.

III

THE CENTURY OF SCHISM

The Mid-Seventeenth to the Mid-Eighteenth Century

THE PROFOUND CONFLICT *in the seventeenth and the early eighteenth century between the practical need to master the skill and cleverness* (khitrost') *of foreigners and the emotional need to continue the ardent devotion* (blagochestie) *to the religious traditions of Old Muscovy.*

Religious leadership in the national revival that resulted from the political humiliation of the Time of Troubles and continued economic and military dependence on the West. The growth in monastic prestige and wealth and the resultant schism (raskol) *between two reforming parties within the Church during the reign of Tsar Alexis (1645–76). The effort of the "black," or celibate, monastic clergy to maintain the centrality of religion in Russian culture through expanding the power of the Patriarch of Moscow, a position first created in 1589; invested with special authority under the patriarchate of Philaret (1619–33), father of Tsar Michael; and raised to theocratic pretensions under Patriarch Nikon (1652–8, formally deposed in 1667). The concurrent campaign of the "white," or married, parish clergy to maintain the centrality of traditional religion through popular evangelism, puritanical exhortation, and fundamentalist adherence to established forms of worship. The mutual destruction of the theocrats led by Nikon and the fundamentalists led by the Archpriest Avvakum (1621–82); condemnation of both by the Church Council of 1667; points of similarity with the earlier conflict between Catholicism and Protestantism in the West, which also led to the exhaustion of both religious approaches and the triumph of the new secular state.*

The advent of Western-type drama, painting, music, and philosophy during the later years of Alexis' reign. Efforts to find religious answers from the West, especially during the regency of Sophia (1682–9); the beginnings of the flagellant, sectarian tradition. The consolidation of a Westernized, secular state under Peter the Great (1682–1725), particularly after his first visit to Western Europe in 1697–8. The foundation of St. Petersburg in 1703; the Dutch-type naval base on the Baltic which became an enduring symbol of the geometric uniformities, Westward-looking vistas, and underlying cruelty and artificiality of rule by the Romanov dynasty. The found-

*ing of the Academy of Sciences in 1726, and the discovery of the human
body in portraiture and ballet. Various attempts in the eighteenth century
to defend and reassert the old Muscovite order amidst the general trend
toward centralized and secularized aristocratic rule; the communalism of
the Old Believers; recurrent, Cossack-led peasant rebellions; and the monastic revival by the "elders" of the late eighteenth century.*

THE PRICE of Russian involvement in Europe was participation in the
almost continuous fighting out of which emerged the new monarchical absolutism of the late seventeenth and the early eighteenth century. Russian
involvement was part of a deeper interrelationship that was developing between Eastern and Western Europe. Gustavus Adolphus, who made
Sweden a model for much of Europe, sensed the interconnection in the late
1620's, explaining—even before his alliance with Russia—that "all European wars are being interwoven into one knot, are becoming one universal war."[1]

Universal war seems, indeed, a good designation for a combat which
moved rapidly from super-celestial ideals to subterranean behavior, and
swept back and forth across the continent with a certain rhythm and logic
of its own. The Catholic-Protestant war between Swedes and Poles at the
beginning of the century abated just as the conflict spread West via Imperial Bohemia in 1618. Then, in 1648, the very year that the complex and
savage Thirty Years' War drew to a close in Western Europe, fighting
erupted again in the east with the greatest single massacre of Jews prior to
Hitler.[2] For most of the next seventy-five years Eastern Europe was a battlefield. Veterans of the Thirty Years' War and English Civil War hired on
as mercenaries for the highest bidder, bringing with them plague, disease,
bayonets, and the resigned belief that "the very state of mankind is nothing
else but *status belli*."[3] Gradually, though by no means decisively, Russia
emerged victorious in fighting that was animated by the passion for total
victory (and the unwillingness to grant more than a temporary truce) previously confined to frontier warfare between Moslems and Christians.[4]
Confessional lines disintegrated altogether in the fighting of the 1650's and
1660's. Russians fought Russians and used Scottish Catholic royalists to
humiliate the Catholic king of Poland. Simultaneously, Catholic France
fought Catholic Spain; Lutheran Denmark, Lutheran Sweden; Protestant
Holland, Protestant England. As exhaustion set in and fighting spread out
to such distant places as New York, Brazil, and Indonesia, forces of stabili-
zation began to bring order back to continental Europe. By the end of the

War of the Spanish Succession in 1713, and of the Great Northern War in 1721, Europe was relatively secure. The Turks had been contained, and peace attained under monarchs uniformly dedicated to maintaining a monopoly of power at home and a balance of power abroad.

It is a final irony that the Swedes, who initially encouraged the Russians to enter "the universal war," were defeated by the same Russians in the last great battle of the war, at Poltava, in 1709. This effort of Charles XII to defeat a vastly superior Russian force in the distant Ukraine and to conspire with the even more remote Cossacks and Turks seems strangely in keeping with the heroic unreality of the age. The strategic vistas of the "universal war" in Eastern Europe were animated throughout by a kind of baroque splendor and thirst for the infinite: from Possevino's vision of a renewed Catholicism moving through Russia to India and linking up with a Jesuit-controlled China to the fantastic Russo-Saxon project late in the century for an alliance between Moscow and Abyssinia to join with Persia for a crusade against the Turks and then, presumably, with Protestant Europe to vanquish Rome.[5]

As in so much baroque art, the vista was based on illusion: on a nervous desire to see things that cannot be. The realities of the universal war in Eastern Europe were, if anything, even more harsh and terrible than in the Civil War in England or the Thirty Years' War in Germany. Historians of these eastern regions have never been able to settle on neutral descriptive labels for the periods of particular horror and devastation which successively visited their various peoples. Russians still speak in anguish and confusion of a "Time of Troubles"; Poles and Ukrainians of a "Deluge"; Eastern European Jews of "The Deep Mire"; and Swedes and Finns of "the great hate."[6]

Military blows from without were accompanied by political and economic contractions within as the tsars extended centralized bureaucratic power throughout their domain and imposed crushing burdens on the peasantry. After seeming to be at the height of their authority, the loose representative assemblies of Eastern Europe (the Russian *zemsky sobor*, the Swedish *riksdag*, the Polish *sejm*, the Jewish *Council of the Four Lands*, and the Prussian *Stände*)—all suddenly collapsed or lost effective power in the late seventeenth century. New quasi-military forms of discipline were imposed on the agrarian society of Eastern Europe, as "economic dualism" split early modern Europe into an increasingly entrepreneurial and dynamic West and an enserfed and static East.[7]

Nowhere were the convulsions more harrowing than in seventeenth-century Russia. Massive shifts in population and changes in the texture of society took place with bewildering speed.[8] Thousands of foreigners flooded into Russia; Russians themselves pushed on to the Pacific; cities staged flash rebellions; the peasantry exploded in violence; Cossack and mercenary soldiers drifted away from battle into disorganized raids and massacres. It seems not excessive to estimate that twice during the seventeenth century —in the early years of the Time of Troubles and of the First Northern War respectively—a third of the population of Great Russia perished from the interrelated ravages of war, plague, and famine.[9] By the 1660's, an English doctor resident at the tsar's court wrote that the ratio of women to men was 10:1 in the region around Moscow; and Russian sources spoke of cannibalism at the front and wolves at the rear—4,000 of them allegedly invading Smolensk in the bitter winter of 1660.[10]

Unable to understand, let alone deal with, the changes taking place about them, Russians resorted to violence and clung desperately to forms and distinctions that had already lost their meaning. Russia's first printed law code, the *Ulozhenie* of 1649, was elaborately and rigidly hierarchical and gave legal sanction to violence by explicitly denying the peasantry any escape from their serfdom and by prescribing corporal—even capital— punishment for a wide variety of minor offenses. The knout alone is mentioned 141 times.[11] The seventeenth century was a period when old answers were inadequate, but new ones had not yet been found to take their place. The inevitable waning of old Muscovy could well be described under the first three chapter headings of Johann Huizenga's classic *Waning of the Middle Ages:* "The Violent Tenor of Life," "Pessimism and the Ideal of the Sublime Life," and "The Hierarchical Conception of Society."

Nor did the West gain much in understanding despite the increasing numbers of its soldiers, doctors, and technicians in Moscow—and of Russian emissaries abroad. The latter insulted everyone by repeatedly demanding complete and exact recitation of the Tsar's lengthy title, while omnipresent and odoriferous bodyguards cut the leather out of palace chairs for shoes and left excremental deposits on walls and floors. Western visitors outdid one another with tales of Russian filth, servility, and disorder; and there were enough genuinely comic scenes to enshrine fatefully among Western observers an anecdotal rather than an analytic approach to Russia. A Dutch doctor who brought a flute and skeleton with him to Moscow was nearly lynched by a passing mob for attempting to conjure up the dead;[12] and an English doctor was executed during the First Northern War when a mealtime request for Cream of Tartar was thought to indicate sympathy for the Crimean Tatars.[13] Most Western writers continued to identify Russians with Tatars rather than other Slavs throughout the seventeenth century. Even in Slavic Prague, a book published in 1622 grouped Russia with Peru and Arabia in a list of particularly bizarre and exotic civilizations;[14] and the year before in relatively nearby and well-informed Uppsala a thesis was defended on the subject "Are the Russians Christians?"[15]

The irony, of course, is that Russia in the seventeenth century was far more intensely Christian than most of the increasingly secular West. Indeed, whatever the ultimate causes of the crisis that overtook Muscovy in this turbulent century, its outer form was religious. The *raskol,* or schism, which fatally divided and weakened Russian Orthodoxy under Tsar Alexis, had repercussions in every area of this organic religious civilization. The administrative consolidation and building of a new Western capital by Alexis' son, Peter the Great, did not bridge the ideological cleavages that the schism had opened in Russia, but only made them deeper and more complex. Religious dissent continued to haunt modern Russia.

1. The Split Within

THE DECISIVE MOMENT of the century—what Russians call the *perelom* (divide in the stairs, breaking point of a fever)—was the formal, ecclesiastical pronouncement of the schism in 1667. It represented a kind of *coup d'église,* which in religious Muscovy was as far-reaching in its implications as the Bolshevik *coup d'état* exactly 250 years later in secularized St. Petersburg. The decisions of the Moscow Church Council of 1667, like those of the St. Petersburg Soviet in 1917, were a point of no return in Russian history. Even more than in 1917, the significance of 1667 was not fully appreciated at the time and was challenged from many different directions by various defenders of the old order. But change had taken place at the center of power, and the divided opposition was unable to prevent the arrival of a new age and new ideas.

The *raskol* (like the Revolution) came as the culmination and climax of nearly a century of bitter ideological controversy which involved politics and aesthetics as well as personal metaphysical beliefs. Seventeenth-century Muscovy was in many ways torn by a single, continuing struggle of "medieval and modern," "Muscovite and Western," forces. Such terms, however, apply better to the self-conscious and intellectualized conflicts of the eighteenth and nineteenth centuries. The issue in seventeenth-century Russia might be better described with two conflicting terms that recur in the chronicles and polemic literature of the time: *khitrost'* and *blagochestie.*

These terms—like the controversies in which they were used—are difficult to translate into the Western idiom. *Khitrost'* is the Slavic word for cleverness and skill. Though derived from the Greek *technikos,* it acquired overtones of sophistication and even cunning in Muscovy. For the most part, this term was used to describe proficiency in those activities that lay outside religious ritual. "Cleverness from beyond the seas" (*zamorskaia khitrost'*) came to be applied to the many unfamiliar new skills and techniques which foreigners brought with them in the sixteenth and seventeenth centuries.¹ When Boris Godunov became Russia's first elected Tsar in 1598, he had to quiet popular misgivings about the procedure by publicly proclaiming that he had been chosen "in faith and truth without any kind of guile" (*bezo vsiakie khitrosti*).² The revolt of the Old Believers was based on the belief that the Russian Church, like those in the West, was now seeking to know God only through "external guile" (*vneshneiu khitrostiiu*).³ Subsequent Russian traditions of peasant revolt and populist reform were deeply infused with the primitive and anarchistic belief that even the use and exchange of money was a "deceitful mechanism" (*khitraia mekhanika*).⁴ The post-Stalinist generation of rebellious writers was also to cry out against the "deceitful (*khitry*) scalpel" of bureaucratic censors and "retouchers."⁵

In his famous troika passage Gogol insists that Russia be "not guileful" (*ne khitry*) but like a "straightforward *muzhik* from Yaroslavl." Precisely such types organized in Yaroslavl in 1612 the "council of all the land," which mobilized Russian resources for the final expulsion of the Poles from Moscow, and served as the model for the council which installed Michael Romanov as tsar in 1613. The primitive frontier forces that had descended on Moscow from the cities of the Volga brought with them a deep distrust of all "cleverness from beyond the seas." Brutal directness was characteristic of the military men who liberated Moscow and stayed on for the councils which acted as a kind of collective regent for the young tsar. Like Gogol's "straightforward *muzhiks* of Yaroslavl" who moved "not through the turn of a screw" but "with the clean stroke of axe and chisel," the provincial ruffians decapitated Polish prisoners in Red Square with scythes, and pulled out the ribs of suspected traitors with hot irons. The seal of Yaroslavl—a bear carrying an axe—seemed for awhile to have become a symbol of the new regime.

Along with their violence, these provincials brought the raw strength which transformed Muscovy into a great modern state. They also brought from their harsh environment a new religious intensity and a special reverence for the quality known as *blagochestie*. Usually translated as "piety," this term has a fuller, and thus more accurate, sound to the modern ear when translated as "ardent loyalty." *Blago* was the Church Slavonic word for "good," carrying with it the meaning of both "blessing" and "welfare"; *chestie* was the word for "honor," "respect," "directness," and "celebration." All of these many-shaded meanings entered into the ardent devotion of the average Muscovite. *Blagochestie* meant both faith and faithfulness, and the adjectival form was inseparably attached to the word "tsar" in Muscovy. Ivan's main accusation against Kurbsky was that, for the sake of "self-love and temporal glory," Kurbsky had "trampled down *blagochestie*" and "cast *blagochestie* out of his soul."[6] The chroniclers saw in the sufferings of the seventeenth century the vengeful hand of God calling his people to repentance. Like Old Testament prophets, Muscovite revivalists repeatedly called not just for belief in a dogma or membership in a church but for a life of renewed dedication. This was a society ruled by custom rather than calculation. As social and economic changes made life more complex, Muscovites increasingly sought refuge in the simple call for devotion to that which had been. If men did not cling to old forms, they tended to become uncritical imitators of foreign ways. There was no real middle ground between the calculating worldliness of *khitrost'* and the complete traditionalism of *blagochestie*.

Khitrost' was clearly the wave of the future; and its development, the legitimate preoccupation of military and political historians. Western measurement slowly imposed itself on the dreamlike imprecision of the Eastern Slavs. A gigantic, English-built clock was placed over the "gate of the Savior" (*Spasskaia vorota*) of the rebuilt Moscow Kremlin in 1625; and shortly thereafter weathervanes began to appear atop the crosses of Muscovite churches. Reasonably accurate military maps and plans were first drawn up in Muscovy in the course of preparing for the 1632–4 war with Poland; and the first large-scale native production of armaments began at about the same time within the rebuilt armory of the Kremlin and the new, Dutch-built foundry at Tula.[7] Clearly, Russia was to be dependent for national greatness on "The Skill [*Khitrost'*] of Armed Men"—to cite the title of its first military manual of 1647. The reign of Peter the Great represents the culmination of the slow transformation of Russia through Northern European technology into a disciplined, secular state.

For the historian of culture, however, the real drama of the seventeenth century follows from the determination of many Russians to remain— through all the changes and challenges of the age—*blagochestivye*: ardently loyal to a sacred past. The heroism and the violence of their effort drove schism deep into Russian society and helped prevent Russia from harmoniously adjusting to modernization. The childhood of Russian culture had been too stern and the first contacts with the West too disturbing to permit the peaceful acceptance of the sophisticated adult world of Western Europe.

To seventeenth-century Russia the humiliation of the Time of Troubles demonstrated not the backwardness of its institutions but the jealousy of its God. The overt and massive Westernization of Boris Godunov and Dmitry was discarded and the belief in God's special concern for Russia intensified. While Western techniques continued to pour into Russia throughout the seventeenth century, Western ideas and beliefs were bitterly resisted. Ordinary Russians saw Muscovy as the suffering servant of God and looked to the monasteries for the righteous remnant.

The historical writings of the early seventeenth century were filled with introspective lamentations and revivalist exhortations, which shattered the dignity of the chronicling tradition without pointing the way toward serious social analysis. Abraham Palitsyn of the Monastery of St. Sergius bemoaned the "senseless silence of all the world"[8] in the face of Russian humiliation; Ivan Timofeev of Novgorod decried the tendency to "tear ourselves away from our bonds of love toward one another . . . some looking to the East, others to the West":[9] and the semi-official "new chronicler" of the Romanovs bequeathed to Pushkin and Musorgsky their moralistic view that the troubles of Russia were divine retribution for Boris' alleged murder of the infant Dmitry.[10]

The deliverance of Russia was uniformly seen as an act of God. The subsequent growth in Russian wealth provided new resources for discharging the debt Russians felt to God, but at the same time new temptations to turn away altogether. Ivan Khvorostinin, courtier of two tsars, became a convert to Socinianism, ceased to keep fasts or revere icons, and wrote elegant syllabic verse well before anyone else in Muscovy. Andrew Palitsyn, cousin of the monastic chronicler and governor of a newly colonized Siberian province, introduced smoking, studied sorcery, and preached the irrelevance of the clergy within his realm.[11] Far more common, however, was the widespread reassertion of traditional faith which predominated in the early seventeenth century and caught the imagination of later Russian poets and historians. Even the tolerant, pre-Revolutionary historian who saw in Khvorostinin "the first swallow of a cultural springtime" felt obliged to add that, in general, "there was nothing principled or ideological (*ideiny*)" in the impulse to look West.[12] The defenders of the old beliefs were nothing if not "principled and ideological," with their implausible but psychologically compelling loyalty to "true Tsars" and "old rituals." Paradoxical as it may seem, the determination of later radical intellectuals to take "principled and ideological" positions may originate in this early dedication of conservative anti-intellectuals to a very different set of principles.

The most dramatic event of the seventeenth century was not any direct confrontation of East and West, nor indeed the action of any tsar, reformer, or writer—though there were remarkable examples of each. The central event was rather the dramatic confrontation of two "straightforward *muzhiks*" from the upper Volga region: Patriarch Nikon and Archpriest Avvakum. These two rough-hewn priests were the key antagonists in the schism within the Russian Church. Each viewed himself as unalterably opposed to *khitrost'*: to all forms of corruption, guile, and foreign innovation. Each began his rise to fame through membership in a circle known as the "lovers of God" (*Bogoliubtsy*) and the "zealots of the old devotion" (*revniteli drevnego blagochestiia*). They fell from grace simultaneously in 1667, returning as prisoners to the frozen northlands whence they had come. Their disappearance was the decisive moment in the waning of Old Muscovy and marked the beginning of the slow and progressive banishment of the "old devotion" and the "love of God" from the new civilization of Imperial Russia.

To understand the rise and fall of these two powerful personalities one must consider first the general resurgence of religious concern in early-seventeenth-century Russia. Hand in hand with the political success of the new dynasty and the "formation of a national market" went the unifying power of a religious revival. At the center of it stood the monastic community, which—unlike merchants, boyars, and even tsars—had actually gained stature during the Time of Troubles. Almost alone of the major fortresses near Moscow, the Monastery of St. Sergius never fell to foreign hands. From behind its walls, moreover, came ringing appeals to rise up against the foreign invaders. The monastic community as a whole withheld from both Wladyslaw of Poland and Charles Philip of Sweden the aura of sanctification that would have been needed to sustain their claims to the Russian throne. All the surviving Russian contenders for power had fled to monasteries by the late years of the interregnum; and they were joined by increasing numbers of military deserters and dispossessed people seeking alms and shelter around these great national shrines.[13] The two best and most famous short stories to appear in the primitive, moralistic literature of the seventeenth century (the tales of *Savva Grudtsyn* and *Gore-Zlochastie*) both end with the spiritual purgation of the hero and his entry into a monastery.[14] A popular woodcut of the period shows a monk being crucified in monastic garb by figures representing the various evils of the day.[15]

Bequests and pilgrimages to monasteries increased steadily; and new cloisters, retreats, and churches were built in large numbers. Particularly remarkable were the "one-day churches" (*obydennye tserkvi*) fashioned out of the virgin forests as a penitential offering in times of suffering. A chronicle of the Vologda region tells a typical story of how people reacted to the plague in 1654 with neither blasphemous anger nor medical prudence, but rather gathered together at sunset to build "a temple to our God even as King David commanded." Working by candlelight through the night while women held icons and chanted *akathistoi* to the Mother of God, they completed the church in time to celebrate the Eucharist inside before sundown of the following day. They prayed, "Take, O Lord, the plague from

Israel," and asked for the strength not to curse their "man-loving and long-tolerant God."[16]

There were, however, unreal and unhealthy aspects to the rapid growth of religious institutions. The monasteries were burdened with far greater wealth than at the time of the controversy over monastic property— without having acquired the strict discipline on which the original "possessors" had based their case. The monasteries were becoming preoccupied with their role of feudal landowner at precisely the time when serfdom was becoming most oppressive. Bequests were, moreover, increasingly tainted by the institution of "pledging" (*zakladnichestvo*): a form of tax evasion in which property was nominally donated to a monastery, but the old owner continued to use and profit from it in return for a nominal service charge.

There was so much activity in and around churches that one might have had the impression of an unprecedented blossoming of religious ardor. In truth, however, it represented more the sagging overgrowth of Indian Summer than the freshness of springtime. The ornate brick churches with Dutch and Persian features, which sprang up at the rate of better than one every two years in Yaroslavl,[17] appear today as a kind of unreal interlude between the Byzantine and baroque styles: heavy fruit languishing in the hazy warmth of October, unaware that the stem linking them with the earth had withered and that the killing frost was about to descend. Innumerable icons of local prophets and saints clustered on the lower tier of the iconostases, rather like overripe grapes begging to be picked; and the rapid simultaneous singing of paid memorial services (of which the *sorokoust* or forty successive services for the dead are the best-known survival) resembled the agitated murmur of autumn flies just before their death.

The crowds that built and worshipped in the brick and wooden churches of the late Muscovite period were animated by a curious mixture of spirituality and xenophobia. Holy Russia was viewed not simply as suffering purity, but as the ravished victim of "wolf-like Poles" and their accomplices the "pagan Lithuanians" and "unclean Jews." Thus, the political revival and physical expansion of Russia were made possible not only by a common faith, but by an oppressive sense of common enemies. Mounting violence and suppressed self-hatred fed the traditional Byzantine impulse toward apocalypticism. Some of the new wooden churches beyond the Volga became funeral pyres for entire congregations, who sought to greet the purifying flames of the Last Judgment with many of the same hymns that their parents had sung while building these churches. To understand both the tragic end of Russia's "second religiousness" and its subtle links with the religious controversies of the West, one must turn to the two principal factions within the Russian religious revival: the theocratic and the fundamentalist. Each faction answered in a different way one common, central question: How can religion be kept at the center of Russian life in the radically changing conditions of the seventeenth century?

The Theocratic Answer

A THEOCRATIC SOLUTION was favored by many of the "black," or celibate, monastic clergy from which the episcopal hierarchy of the Russian Church was drawn. Partisans of this position sought to strengthen the ecclesiastical hierarchy, increase central control of Russian monasteries, and increase both the discipline and educational level of the clergy by editing and printing systematic catechistic and devotional manuals. In fact, though not in theory, they sought to elevate the spiritual estate over the temporal by greatly increasing the power of the Moscow Patriarch. They continued to speak in Byzantine terms of a "symphony of powers" between the ecclesiastical and temporal realms, but the increased strength of the clergy and continued weakness of the new dynasty offered temptations for establishing virtual clerical rule.

Although the Metropolitan of Moscow had been elevated to the title of Patriarch only in 1589, the position had almost immediately assumed political as well as ecclesiastical significance. The post was created during a period of weakened tsarist authority—indeed, the first patriarch had been largely responsible for securing Boris Godunov's elevation to the throne. During the troubles of the interregnum, patriarchal authority increased dramatically, largely because Patriarch Hermogenes refused to deal with foreign factions and accepted a martyr's death within the Polish-occupied Kremlin. When, in 1619, the father of the tsar and former Metropolitan of Rostov, Philaret Nikitich, finally returned from Polish imprisonment to become the new patriarch, the stage was set for a great increase in the power of the ecclesiastical hierarchy. Until his death in 1633 he was co-ruler with Tsar Michael, using the title "Great Sovereign" and presiding over more important affairs of state than the Tsar. At the same time he created new sees in the east, increased central control of canonization and ecclesiastical discipline, and determined the form that the first printed versions of some church service books should take.[18]

If Philaret created the precedent for a strong patriarchate and a disciplined hierarchy, the theological arming of the Orthodox clergy was largely the work of Peter Mogila, the most influential ecclesiastical leader in Orthodox Slavdom for the period between Philaret's death in 1633 and his own in 1647. Mogila's career illustrates the way in which non-Muscovite elements were beginning to control the development of the Russian Church. He was the well-educated progeny of a Moldavian noble family and had fought with the Poles against the Turks in the storied battle of Khotin in 1620. Moved by the five pilgrimages he had made to the Monastery of the Caves in Kiev, Mogila settled in that Polish-controlled city. He became a monk, then archimandrite of the monastery, Metropolitan of Kiev, and founder of the Kievan academy "for the teaching of free sciences in the Greek, Slavonic, and Latin languages."[19]

Under Mogila the theological struggle of the Orthodox brotherhoods with the Catholic Uniats acquired new sophistication and organizational skill. He wrote for his co-religionists a concise *Bible of Instruction,* a *Confession,* and a *Catechism,* which were reprinted after receiving the endorsement of Orthodox synods that he organized in Kiev in 1640 and in Jassy in 1642. Even more important was Mogila's leadership in checking the drift toward a theological rapprochement with Protestantism that had been aided by Cyril Lukaris' patriarchate in Constantinople. He prevented attempts by Calvinists to spread their ideas in the Ukraine in the 1630's. His *Confession* begins with a direct contradiction of the Protestant position on justification by faith. Although he remained firm in rejecting the authority of Rome, his writings were so deeply influenced by Jesuit theology that his *Catechism* (originally written in Latin) was approved at the synod of Jassy only after substantial revisions had been made by a Greek prelate.[20] Mogila also introduced into the Orthodoxy of the Eastern Slavs a Western element of scorn for superstitious accretions and irrationalism. He particularly challenged the charitable—even indulgent—attitude of the Russian Church toward those possessed, drawing up a purely Western guide for exorcising unclean spirits and preparing believers for proper instruction.[21]

Although Mogila was a Moldavian who spent his entire life under the political authority of Poland and the ecclesiastical authority of Constantinople, he properly belongs to Russian history. Most of his pupils either moved to Moscow or accepted its authority in the course of the victorious Muscovite struggle with Poland that began shortly after his death. To the Russian Church he gave priests capable of holding their own in theological discourse with Westerners, and infected the Russian hierarchy with some of his own passion for order and rationality. As early as April, 1640, Mogila had written Tsar Michael to urge the establishment of a special school in a Moscow monastery where his pupils could teach Orthodox theology and classical languages to the Muscovite nobility. Though such an institution did not formally come into being until the creation of the Slavonic-Greek-Latin Academy in 1689, considerable informal instruction was conducted in Moscow in the 1640's by Mogila's pupils.

With the accession to the patriarchate of the energetic Joseph in 1642 (and of the pious Alexis to the throne in 1645) a large-scale program of religious instruction began. The central weapon in this campaign was the patriarchal printing press—the only one in Moscow—which turned out in the first seven years of Alexis' reign (the last seven of Joseph's patriarchate) nearly ten thousand copies of the basic alphabet book in three editions, eight printings of the book of hours, and nine of the psalter.[22]

The key figure in this printing program was Ivan Nasedka, a well-educated and widely traveled priest whose *Deposition against the Lutherans,* written in 1644, was influential in blocking the proposed marriage of Tsar Michael's daughter to the Danish crown prince.[23] Nasedka, whose anxiety about the growth of Protestant influences in Russia dated from his first trip as informal emissary to Denmark in 1621, found ready support for his theological position from the pupils of Mogila, who had taken the lead in combating the drift toward Protestantism elsewhere in the Orthodox world.

Thus, in the mid-forties there began a steady and increasing flow of Ukrainian priests to Moscow. These priests brought with them an emotional opposition to Catholicism and a doctrinal antipathy to Protestantism. Before the end of Joseph's patriarchate in 1652, the Ukrainian priests trained by Mogila had set up in Moscow two centers of translation and theological instruction: that of Fedor Rtishchev in the Monastery of St. Andrew and that of Epiphanius Slavinetsky in the Monastery of the Miracles.[24]

The times, however, were hardly favorable for tranquil intellectual activity. In 1648 war and revolution broke out in the east with unprecedented fury. Anti-Polish and anti-Jewish violence in the Ukraine and White Russia was accompanied by an uprising in Moscow itself. The foreign quarter was sacked and leading government administrators literally torn to pieces. Like the plague epidemic that accompanied a second wave of bloodshed in 1653–4, urban violence spread contagiously from city to city. The restive commercial centers of Novgorod and Pskov predictably sought to canalize the general violence into specific demands for greater freedom from central control in the last wave of uprisings in 1650. Basically, however, it was a formless series of rebellions. Bewildered Western observers noted only the blood-lust of the mob combined with a certain hatred of foreigners and reverence for the Church. When one prisoner of the mob in

Kursk rebuked a hooded cleric who had joined his tormentors by crying "Off with your hood!" the horde screamed back with redoubled fury, "Off with your head!"[25]

The fear of a new "Time of Troubles" loomed up before the young Tsar. His own infant son had just died; he was afraid of a new Tatar invasion, and he initially hesitated to support the Cossack insurrectionists, apparently fearing that "the rebellion of the Cossacks and peasants of Russia might spill over into his own country, where sparks had already appeared from the fire sweeping over Poland."[26] There was even a pretender waiting in the wings: a thief, arsonist, and sexual pervert, Timothy Ankudinov, who had attracted some interest in both Poland and Rome for his claim to be the son of Shuisky and true heir to the Russian throne.[27]

Faced with this threat of disintegration, Alexis rallied support by summoning one *zemsky sobor* of 1648-9 to draw up, approve, and print a uniform national law code, and another in 1650 to assure the pacification and reabsorption of rebellious Novgorod and Pskov. For all its deference to hierarchy and tradition, the law code of 1649 represented an important stage in the rationalization and secularization of Russian culture. The power of the annointed sovereign was fully invested in his appointed bureaucrats to punish "without any mercy" almost anyone challenging the "sovereign honor" of the "Muscovite state." The monasteries were hurt economically by the outlawing of any new tax-exempt pledging of wealth and property, and politically by the creation of a government bureau to administer their affairs.

The monopoly of Church Slavonic as the written language of Muscovite culture was also broken by the large-scale reprinting and dissemination of a law code written in a language close to the contemporary vernacular. This *Ulozhenie* remained the basic code of the land until 1833, and played a role in the development of the modern Russian language that has been compared with that of Luther's Bible in the making of modern German. Indeed, the language of the *Ulozhenie* was in some ways "closer to the contemporary Russian literary and conversational language than the language not only of Karamzin, but of Pushkin."[28]

Alexis, however, was not prepared to build his rule on laws rather than autocratic authority, or to speak in the language of the chanceries rather than the chronicles. Having conceded a code to the rebellious city dwellers, he turned to a program of xenophobic distraction—discriminating against foreign merchants and convening in 1651 and 1653 *zemsky sobors* to sanction mobilization against Poland, then the protectorate over the Ukraine, which made war inevitable. At the same time, Alexis turned in desperation for administrative support and spiritual guidance to a monk named Nikon, in whom the theocratic answer to Russian disorder found its last and greatest exponent.

Nikon was an ascetic from the trans-Volga region who awed his contemporaries with both spiritual intensity and physical presence. Shortly after arriving in Moscow as head of the New Monastery of the Savior (*Novospassky*), this six-foot six-inch monk cast his spell over young Tsar Alexis, who began to have regular Friday meetings with him. The decisive event in Nikon's career appears to have been the arrival in Moscow in January, 1649, of Patriarch Paissius of Jerusalem. He was impressed by Nikon and helped secure his appointment as Metropolitan of Novgorod, the second highest position in the Russian hierarchy. Nikon for his part appears to have been dazzled by Paissius' retinue of priests and scholars, who brought with them tales of the Holy Land and of the lost splendors of the Greek Church.

Paissius told of the horrors he had seen in the Balkans and the Ukraine, pleading for "a new Moses" who would "liberate pious Orthodox Christians from unclean hands, from wild beasts—and shine like a sun amidst the stars."[29] The call for deliverance was addressed to the Tsar, but he—like his father before him—felt the need amidst widespread social unrest and intrigue to lean upon the Patriarch. Thus, in November, 1651, the Tsar began pairing his own name with that of Patriarch Joseph in official charters, while commencing a theatrical transfer of the remains of past patriarchs to the Moscow Kremlin for reburial. The remains of Patriarch Hermogenes were exhumed and venerated; and Alexis sent Nikon to Solovetsk to bring back to the Cathedral of the Assumption the remains of Metropolitan Philip, whose murder by Ivan the Terrible had given an aura of holy martyrdom to the ecclesiastical hierarchy. While Nikon was still gone, Patriarch Joseph died; and within a few weeks Alexis wrote Nikon a long, half-confessional letter of grief addressed to "the great sun" from "your earthly tsar."[30] Clearly Nikon was some kind of higher, heavenly tsar, and it is hardly surprising that he was appointed Joseph's successor as Patriarch in July. For six years, Nikon became the virtual ruler of Russia, using the ecclesiastical hierarchy and the printing press to extend the program of ecclesiastical discipline he had developed at Novgorod.

In the far-flung see of Novgorod, Nikon dealt not only with a rebellious, Westward-looking city, but also with the chaotic and primitive northern regions, where he had previously served as a monastic administrator. There Nikon became attached to ecclesiastical splendor and magnificence as a kind of compensation for the bleakness of the region and the asceticism of his personal life. As Metropolitan of Novgorod, he was able to extend and even tighten central control over the monasteries of the north by securing from the Tsar complete exemption from subordination to the new governmental department created by the law code of 1649 to regulate monasteries.

As patriarch, Nikon not only shared with the Tsar the title "Great Sovereign," as had Philaret, but in fact exercised sole sovereignty when the Tsar went off to lead the battle against Poland. Nikon used this position to set up a virtual theocracy in Moscow with the aid of visiting Greek and transplanted Ukrainian and White Russian prelates. Not just the Patriarch, but the entire episcopal hierarchy was given a new aura of majesty. Theatrical rituals were introduced, more elaborate vestments and miters required, and elaborate church councils held with foreign Orthodox prelates participating. The traditional Palm Sunday procession, in which the Tsar led the Patriarch on a donkey through Red Square in imitation of Christ's entry into Jerusalem, was instituted in the provinces, where local civil authorities were encouraged also to humble themselves in this way before local metropolitans and bishops.[31]

Most important was Nikon's effort to bring order and uniformity to Russian worship through a new series of printed service books. The printing program in the last years of Joseph's patriarchate had already contributed to the sense of special dignity and destiny that Nikon felt about the Russian Church. Publication of a *Book of the One True and Orthodox Faith* in 1648, an edited version of Mogila's *Catechism* in 1649, and the *Pilot Book* (*Kormchaia Kniga*) in 1650 provided Muscovy with, respectively, an encyclopedia of polemic materials directed largely against Uniats and Jews; "its first manual for popular religious instruction";[32] and its first systematic corpus of canon law. The first two works (and the apocalyptical *Book of Cyril,* which was also enjoying new popularity in Moscow of the late forties) came to Moscow from Kiev, the *Pilot Book* from Serbia. Moscow was rapidly becoming the focal point for all the hopes of the Orthodox East. As Muscovy launched its successful attack on Poland in the early years of Nikon's patriarchate, its sense of holy mission and special calling grew apace. Even non-Slavic Orthodox principalities, such as Moldavia and Georgia, began to explore the possibilities of a protectorate status under Moscow similar to that which Khmelnitsky's Cossacks accepted in 1653. Meanwhile the Greek-speaking monk Arsenius Sukhanov, who had accompanied Paissius back to Jerusalem on the first of two lengthy trips to gather books and information from the rest of the Orthodox world, reported that Orthodoxy had been corrupted in the Mediterranean area by Latin errors. He revived the long quiescent theme of Moscow as the third and last Rome, and added that "all Christendom" awaited the liberation of Constantinople by Russian force.[33] While Alexis led Russian troops into battle against foreign enemies of the faith, Nikon led his miscellaneous array of editors into combat against alleged corruptions within.

Between his deletions from a new psalter in October, 1652, and the appearance of new service books in 1655–6, Nikon sponsored an extensive and detailed series of reforms.[34] He changed time-honored forms of worship: substituting three fingers for two in the sign of the cross; three hallelujahs for two; five consecrated loaves for seven at the offertory; one loaf rather than many on the altar; processions against rather than with the direction of the sun. Nikon eliminated some practices altogether (the twelve prostrations accompanying the prayer of Ephrem the Syrian during Lent, the blessing of the waters on Epiphany eve); introduced textual changes affecting all three persons of the Holy Trinity. He altered the form of addressing God in the Lord's prayer, the description of the Holy Spirit in the creed, and the spelling of Jesus' name (from *Isus* to *Iisus*) in all sacred writings.

At the same time, Nikon tried to impose a new, more austere artistic style, ordering the elimination of florid, northern motifs from Russian architecture (tent roofs, onion domes, seven- and eight-pointed crosses, and so on). In their place he introduced a neo-Byzantine emphasis on spherical domes, classical lines, and the use of the plain, four-pointed Greek cross. Two buildings that he constructed in the first years of his patriarchate launched this effort to transplant the imagined glories of the Greek East to Russia: the patriarchal church of the Twelve Apostles, within the Moscow Kremlin, and the ensemble of buildings for the new Iversky Monastery on Valdai Island.

All of this was accompanied by a determined effort to heighten the personal authority of the patriarch and that of the ecclesiastical hierarchy. Prior to accepting the patriarchate, Nikon had exacted an unprecedented pledge from the Tsar to obey Nikon "as your first shepherd and father in all that I shall teach on dogma, discipline, and custom."[35] This promise was taken from a ninth-century Byzantine defense of separate but equally absolute temporal and ecclesiastical authority. Like matter and form, body and soul, the two realms were supposed to co-exist harmoniously within the Christian commonwealth. Such a strong assertion of patriarchal authority was altogether unheard of in Muscovy. It seemed to challenge not only the Tsar, but the new law code, which had made the monasteries (and thus the church hierarchy) subject to secular jurisdiction. Nor was Nikon's program very securely based in Byzantine tradition. The reforms were rapidly and secretly drawn up, and based on the selective use of Western compilations of Byzantine texts by an inadequately equipped research team.[36]

To counter the power of the civil estate, Nikon issued a revised edition of the *Pilot Book* in 1653, and in the following year persuaded the Tsar to instruct provincial *voevodas* to make more general use of canon law in criminal matters.[37] Nikon brought in a steady stream of foreign patriarchs to approve his reforms and foreign relics and icons to sanctify them (beginning with the Georgian Mother of God, which Nikon had procured from Mt. Athos as early as 1648). He set up an academy in the Zaikonospassky Monastery for translating Greek and Latin texts and instructing priests in useful secular knowledge as well as theology. During the plague of 1653–4, for instance, the best of his imported Kievan translators, Epiphanius Slavinetsky, was diverted from a proposed translation of the Bible to a translation of Vesalius' work on human anatomy; and Nikon's book purchaser in the Greek East spent much of his time seeking out savants and manuscripts that would offer additional medical guidance.[38]

Nikon had the profound misfortune of introducing his program into Russia at a time of great suffering through plague and war. He soon became a focal point of resentment for those who were anxious for a scapegoat and jealous of his closeness to the Tsar. His position was made untenable by the opposition of influential boyars, bureaucrats, and monastic leaders (often one and the same person) and by his own mixing of political and religious considerations. In his campaign against new trends in icon painting, for instance, Nikon ordered the *streltsy* to confiscate icons forcibly, to gouge out the eyes of the painted figures, and parade them through Moscow—warning that anyone henceforth painting similar icons would be treated in the same way. Nikon himself publicly shattered each of the mutilated pictures—naming just before each "burial" the high state official from whom it had been taken. This action terrified the bureaucracy and led the confused and superstitious Moscow mob to conclude that Nikon was a complete iconoclast responsible for the plague. In his campaign to gain acceptance for the new rituals, Nikon censured uncooperative boyars and anathemized priests during regular church services. He aroused opposition to his program among the proud and conservative monks of Solovetsk by trying to establish patriarchal control even over such sensitive disciplinary matters as drinking habits. He solidified popular feeling in the north behind the monks of Solovetsk by trying to found a rival monastery in the area and giving it a Greek name (*Stavros,* "cross").

Solovetsk was thus emboldened to begin the organized resistance to Nikon, refusing to accept his new service books in 1657. A few months later three appointed heads of newly created provincial dioceses refused to leave their Moscow sinecures for the distant posts to which Nikon had assigned them. In the following summer the head of the Tsar's imperial household beat Nikon's chief official assistant as the latter was in the official act of arranging the order of religious procedure for a dinner in honor of the Orthodox crown prince of Georgia. When the Tsar failed to rebuke his official and subsequently the Tsar himself failed to appear at several worship services, Nikon reacted with a characteristic sense of drama.

Following a special liturgy in the Cathedral of the Assumption, Nikon announced that he was retiring to his new monastery, the New Jerusalem, outside Moscow until the Tsar reaffirmed confidence in him and his program. Not for eight years, however, did Nikon receive the Tsar's summons; and then it was to appear before a church council to be formally deposed as Patriarch and sentenced to life exile in a distant northern monastery. Most of his modifications of church worship were formally approved by this council of 1667; but the heart of his program—the attempt to establish a theocratic state under a powerful and disciplined hierarchy—was rejected definitively. It is a tribute to the power and magnetism of Nikon that it took the *prikaz* of secret affairs and other servants of the new secular state nearly a decade to depose him formally.[39] But never again was the church hierarchy to exercise or even claim comparable political power in Russia. The abolition of the patriarchate and the thorough subordination of church to state was to follow in a few decades under Peter the Great.

The Fundamentalist Answer

AT THE SAME TIME that Nikon was heading off to exile and oblivion, another clerical figure was secretly taken even farther north to an even more grisly fate. Superficially, the Archpriest Avvakum was very similar to Nikon. He was a dedicated priest from northeast Russia, passionately opposed to Western influence and deeply determined to keep the Orthodox faith and ritual as the controlling force in Russian life. Avvakum had, indeed, been a friend of Nikon in Moscow during the late 1640's, when both were "zealots of the old devotion." They agreed that the Russian Church must be kept free of Western contamination and secularization. They both supported the first important church reform of the 1650's: the elimination of the "forty-mouthed" simultaneous readings of different offices within the churches.[40]

However, in the years that followed, Avvakum came to view the need for reform in totally different terms, and indeed to consider Nikon his deepest foe. Avvakum made himself the spokesman and martyr for the fundamentalist position. Like the theocratic view of Nikon, Avvakum's fundamentalism summarized and brought into focus attitudes that had been developing for more than a century.

The fundamentalist position was mainly advanced by the "white" or parish priests in the provinces and was a faithful reflection of the conservatism, superstition, and vitality of the Eastern frontier. It was less a clearly articulated position than a simple equation of trouble with innovation, innovation with foreigners, and foreigners with the devil. The past that the fundamentalists sought to maintain was the organic religious civilization that had prevailed in Russia prior to the coming of "guile from beyond the seas." To do this, they began to urge strict puritanical decrees against such Western innovations as tobacco ("bewitched grass," "the devil's incense") and hops ("bewitched Lithuanian grapes"). Instrumental music and representational art were particularly suspect. The burning of six carriages full of musical instruments in Moscow in 1649 was a graphic illustration of the anti-foreign and puritanical activities of the early years of Alexis' reign.[41]

Specially hated by the fundamentalists were the "Frankish icons" that had worked their way into Russian churches in imitation of representational art of Holland in the early seventeenth century. "They paint the image of Our Savior," cried Avvakum, "with a puffy face, red lips, curly hair, fat arms and muscles, and stout legs and thighs. All this is done for carnal reasons."[42] Although Nikon formally shared their views on icons,[43] he had permitted churches near the Kremlin to be decorated with frescoes based on German models, and he was shortly to follow the unprecedented course of posing for a portrait by a Dutch painter.[44]

Morbid excess, masochism, and heretical dualism often lay just below the surface of puritanical extremism. The numerous though still obscure communities founded north of Yaroslavl in the 1630's by a strange figure known only as Kapiton appear to have discarded Christian doctrine along with ecclesiastical authority. The leader wore heavy chains held down by two huge weights, practiced extreme fasting and mortification of the flesh as well as certain Jewish rites, such as circumcision and abstention from pork. He enjoyed a sufficient following to escape repeatedly from the imprisonment which local officials imposed on him.[45]

Puritanical and xenophobic discontent was given focus by a revival of prophecy within the established church. Leadership came primarily from a group of the married white clergy who held the title of "archpriest" (*protopop*), the highest open to the non-monastic clergy. The first of the archpriests, Ivan Neronov, championed a revival of the old trans-Volga tradition of piety, poverty, and prophecy. As a young preacher in Nizhny Novgorod on the upper Volga he was known as "the second Chrysostom." He attracted attention by opposing the war against Poland in 1632 and by adding special buildings for feeding and housing the poor to the new cathedral which he took over in Moscow. Neronov began the grass roots opposition of the parish priesthood to Nikon's reforms early in 1653 by speaking in defense of another archpriest whom Nikon had deposed for insolence to civil authority. Though Neronov was also punished for his defiance, he rallied a number of other archpriests to his defense, including Avvakum, who rapidly became Nikon's most violent critic. The diaspora of the protesting archpriests began in September with the banishment of Avvakum to distant Tobol'sk in Siberia, and was continued the following year by a Church council which anathemized and exiled Neronov. Neronov set the pattern for the future Old Believers by rejecting the authority either of the Church council (which he likened to the Jewish court that had tried Christ) or of Nikon (who was unworthy to hold office because of his "voevodish tricks" and "lack of respect to the priestly class").[46]

Intertwined with their objections to Nikon's authoritarianism was the archpriests' profound opposition to any change in the familiar forms of worship. Changing the two-fingered sign of the cross (the form used on Russian icons and in all the reverences of the Russian peasant) and the double hallelujah meant to them destroying symbols of Christ's divine-human nature. Changing the spelling of Jesus (one of the few words that all could read in old Muscovy) implied a change in God Himself. Changing the form of address in the Lord's Prayer from "our Father" to "our God" seemed to remove God from the intimate relationship most easily understood in a patriarchal society.

Many of the changes seemed to shorten and simplify the worship service at a time when the puritanical archpriests felt there should be more rather than less demands. Changes in the creed seemed to weaken the relevance and immediacy of God to human history. Nikon changed the traditional Russian reading in the creed that Christ's kingdom "has no end" to "shall have no end." From representing Christ as "sitting" at the right hand of God, the new creed read "was seated"; and from affirming belief in the "true and life-giving Holy Spirit," the new creed substituted "life-giving Holy Spirit." Though these changes were intended merely to rid the Russian church of uncanonical accretions, their effect to the fundamentalists was to imply that Christ was now sometimes on and sometimes off his throne (like a seventeenth-century monarch) and that the Holy Spirit merely participates in truth (like any student of the worldly sciences).

The most passionate and irrational defenders of fundamentalism were women. Indeed, without the initial support of influential noblewomen, no coherent movement of schismatics would probably have emerged from the religious crisis. The attachment of women to the old ways was more deep and purely spiritual than that of the men; for they shared none of the earthly rewards and glory that Muscovy had to offer. Left to the isolation of the upper chamber (*terem*) and relegated to an inferior position in every aspect of Muscovite life, many of them nonetheless developed a passionate attachment to the religious ritual which gave meaning and sanctity to their world. The most tender and saintly devotional passages in all of Old Believer literature are found in the letters of Avvakum's feminine supporters in Moscow, such as the Boyarina Morozova, widowed scion of the wealthy Morozov family. Avvakum was indebted to his own mother for his religious upbringing; and the most moving figure in his *Autobiography* is, in many ways, his long-suffering wife, who accompanied him on all his arduous missions. The greatest retrospective artistic study of an Old Believer theme is, appropriately, Surikov's large canvas of the black figure of Morozova on a sledge taking her to martyrdom, with her hand extended upward in a defiant, two-fingered sign of the cross.[47]

If the women simply clung to the old ways, the restless men required some kind of explanation, or program for resistance. As the archpriests' despair deepened over securing repeal of the reforms, they began to turn to the belief that Russia was entering the last stage of earthly history.

The natural connection between Byzantine fundamentalism and apocalypticism provides a key to understanding the formation of the schismatic tradition in Russia. However animistic their identification of faith with form, however confused their understanding of tradition, the fundamentalists stood on solid Byzantine ground in insisting that inherited church traditions were begun by Christ, sanctified by the Holy Spirit at the early church councils, and must be preserved inviolably until His coming again. Jesus' last assurance to the apostles that "I am with you always, even to the end of time" applied to the ideas and forms of His Holy Church. If these were to be changed on a large scale by human decree, it must necessarily mean that the "end of time" is at hand.

Unlike Protestant fundamentalists these fundamentalists of Russian Orthodoxy identified God not with the words of scripture but with the forms of worship. Indeed, the only parts of scripture they knew were the psalms and those passages from the prophets and New Testament which were read orally in regular worship services. Some extremists among the Russian fundamentalists even took the position that the Bible itself was a secular book, since it contained many worldly and even pornographic stories and had first come to Russia by means of the "guileful" printing presses of corrupted Western Slavs.[48]

When Avvakum cried "Give us back our Christ!" he was not speaking figuratively; nor was he rhetorically addressing those who had changed the spelling of Jesus' name. He was praying directly to God for the only Christ he had ever known: the Christ of the Russian frontier. This Christ was not a teacher like the pagan Greek philosophers, nor the bearer of a sacred book like the Tatar Mohammed, but the original suffering hero, or *podvizhnik,* in whose name and image Muscovites had taken the rudiments of civilization far out into a cold and forbidding wilderness. If the Holy Spirit was no longer to be described as "true and life-giving" in the creed, then its sanctifying presence must be cut off from the Church. But the tongues of fire with which the Spirit first came upon the apostles at Pentecost cannot be extinguished by the hand of man. They will, on the contrary, come again in the purifying fire that prepares man for the final judgment of God.

Thus, changes in church practices led directly to the "eschatological psychosis" of the mid-seventeenth century. This psychosis arose directly out of the emphasis on the concrete and historical in the Muscovite ideology. The intensified spirituality of monastic asceticism and holy folly was directed not primarily toward establishing private, ecstatic union with God but rather toward receiving the concrete guidance and reassurance which God was believed to be continually offering his chosen people through voices and visions. Amidst the confusion and upheaval of the First Northern War, God's seeming silence led the overpopulated monastic estate into a "sensual hallucinatory cast of mind."[49] The exhumation and canonization of St. Cyril of the White Lake late in 1649 set off a veritable panic of efforts to possess relics from the uncorrupted bodies of saints. The officially sponsored austerity and asceticism of Alexis' early years intensified the psychological pressure to find spiritual compensation for material privation. Meanwhile, historical memory, or *pamiat'*, the supreme source of authority and wisdom in Muscovy, was becoming an increasingly confused "nervous reservoir"[50] of sensual impressions and wish projections. In mid-seventeenth-century Europe Muscovy had come to resemble the house of a stubborn but powerful eccentric in a fast-changing city. Rooms were cluttered with vast quantities of unsorted memorabilia which were, strictly speaking, neither antique nor modern. The more insistently that apostles of change and rationalization came knocking at the door, the more fanatically the unkempt inhabitants burrowed back into their congenial world of illusion.

At the end, there is, of course, nothing but chaos suitable for rodents or combustion. Everyone noticed the rats in congested and plague-ridden Muscovy; and fire continued to be a menace in the wooden city. As the city slowly came to the conclusion that the living God was no longer present in the agitated voices and visions of its holy men, the most fanatical of its fundamentalists pressed on to a conclusion which—however shocking to modern rationalism—was entirely consistent with its emphasis on a concrete and historical Christianity. In the popular imagination as well as the monastic chronicles, all history was permeated with God's presence. God's silence and withdrawal from present history, therefore, could mean only that history was at or near its end. Those who looked desperately for some final, tangible way to fulfill His will in this unprecedented situation could find but one act left to perform: the committing of oneself to the purgative flames which, according to tradition, must precede the Last Judgment.

Before turning to this final, desperate expedient of self-immolation, however, the fundamentalists sought an explanation in the ancient idea that adversity heralded the reign of the Antichrist and was to precede the true Christ's Second Coming and final, thousand-year reign on earth. Already at the time of Alexis' coronation, a lonely hermit in Suzdal contended that the new Tsar was a "horn of the Antichrist."[51] Russian prophets found many more signs that this terrifying last stage of history was about to begin in the reforms, plagues, and wars of the following decade. Ukrainians and White Russians brought with them prophetic ideas that had been developed in the course of the long Orthodox struggle with Catholicism in those regions. The learned Deacon Fedor, of the Cathedral of the Annunciation in the Moscow Kremlin, wrote that "a dark and impenetrable pagan god" which had "taken Lithuania captive" had now come to Russia to "devour the condemned within the churches."[52] The original anti-Uniat treatise from White Russia, *The Book of Cyril,* with a long epilogue on the coming reign of Antichrist, was published in a Moscow edition of six thousand copies. *The Book of the One True and Orthodox Faith,* a later anti-Uniat compilation from Kiev, was also published in a large edition. It blamed Roman Catholicism not only for attacking Orthodoxy but for letting loose in the West the spectre of "evil-cunning (*zlokhitrykh*) and many-headed heresies."[53]

Even further afield, from the anti-scholastic Hesychasts on Mt. Athos, came reinforcement for the anti-intellectualism of the fundamentalists. As early as 1621, Ivan Vyshensky, a Ukrainian elder, had returned to lead the fight against union with Rome and had urged the "Russian, Lithuanian, and Polish people" to leave their "different faiths and sects" for a revived Orthodoxy. In his *Council on Devotion* (*Blagochestie*), this "Savonarola of the Ukrainian renaissance" juxtaposed the Roman "Church of Jezebel" with an idealized Orthodoxy in apocalyptical terms:

> I say to you that the land under your feet weeps and cries aloud before the Lord God, begging the creator to send down his sickle as of old in Sodom, preferring that it stand empty and pure rather than populated and corrupt with your ungodliness and illicit activity. Where now in the Polish land can faith be found?[54]

There were two opposing forces in his world: the devil, who dispenses "all worldly graces, glory, luxury and wealth," and "the poor pilgrim," who renounces the temptations offered by "a wife, a house, and an ephemeral piece of land."[55] The Latin academies of the Jesuits and even of Mogila were part of the devil's campaign to destroy the true Eastern Church and lead men away from the world of the early fathers and hermits. "Thou, simple, ignorant, and humble Russia, stay faithful to the plain, naive gospel wherein eternal life is found," rather than the "phrase-mongering Aristotle" and "the obscurity of pagan sciences." "Why set up Latin and Polish schools?" he asked. "We have not had them up to now and that has not kept us from being saved."[56] The introduction of Aristotelian concepts into the discussion of divine mysteries was a form of "masquerade before the portals of our God Christ." Following Vyshensky's line of thought (and quoting many of the same patristic sources), Avvakum inveighed also against "philosophical swaggering" and "almanac mongers" (*almanashniki*) with his statement "I am untutored in rhetoric, dialectic and philosophy, but the mind of Christ guides me from within."[57]

One of the original Muscovite correctors of books, Ivan Nasedka, suggested that the turn of the Greek Church to Latin philosophizing indicated the approach of Antichrist. "We have no time now to hear your philosophy," he proclaimed to the learned Lutheran theologians who accompanied the Danish crown prince to Moscow in 1644. "Don't you know that the end of this world is coming and the judgment of God is at the door?"[58] Reinforcement for these ideas was also found in the prophetic sermons of Ephrem the Syrian, who had fought the saturation of the Byzantine Church with pagan philosophy in the fourth century, warning the Syrian church in his *Seven Words on the Second Coming of Christ* that impending doom awaits those who stray from the simplicity of Christ. Never before printed in any Slavic language, Ephrem's sermons suddenly appeared in four different editions in Moscow between 1647 and 1652. Part of his impact upon the fundamentalists came from the fact that his work had been the basic patristic source for the pictorial representation of the Last Judgment in Russian icons and frescoes. The sudden discovery of his text, therefore, seemed to offer the unlearned Russian priests "confirmation" of their traditional image of coming judgment—and led them to believe that the hour itself might be approaching. Renewed reverence was also attached to Ephrem's prophecies because of the fact that Nikon was believed to have "insulted" this early ascetic by eliminating the prostrations that had traditionally accompanied his famed Lenten prayer of humility.[59]

The fundamentalists were also stirred by the writings of Arsenius Sukhanov. Sent by three successive patriarchs to examine the practices and procure the writings of other Orthodox Churches, Arsenius returned with a lurid picture of corruption and of craven submission before Latin authority and Turkish power. In all of the East, Arsenius seemed to find but two sources of hope: Muscovy, the third and final Rome, in which alone "there is no heresy,"[60] and Jerusalem, the original font of truth.

Influenced by his friendship with Patriarch Paissius and deeply impressed by such rites as the lighting of candles on Easter Eve from the "heavenly flame" in the church at the Holy Sepulcher, Arsenius sought in his writings to link Muscovy with the pre-Hellenistic church. Christ had lived and died and the Apostolic Church grown up around Jerusalem. The first gospels were not written for the Greeks; Russia was converted not by Byzantium but by the apostle Andrew; and, in any case, "from Zion came forth the law and the word of the Lord from Jerusalem." The "word of the Lord" had been muffled in Byzantium since the seventh ecumenical council of the church; and it was not accidental that the white cowl given by Pope Silvester to Constantine the Great was now in Moscow, or that the icon of first the Tikhvin and then the Georgian Mother of God had been miraculously transferred from Athos to Moscow.[61]

Jerusalem became—both literally and figuratively—a kind of alternative to Constantinople and Athos for the excited Muscovite imagination. Nikon, who had first sent Arsenius to the Holy Land, sent him back to Jerusalem to make a model of the Church of the Resurrection that sheltered the Holy Sepulcher; and sent a visiting Serbian metropolitan to Jerusalem to provide additional details on the rites and services of the Church. The new Muscovite theocracy was to be nothing less than the New Jerusalem. With this lofty vision in mind, Nikon set about building his "holy kingdom," the Monastery of the New Jerusalem, on a spot of great beauty by the Istra River outside Moscow. Giant bells, gilded gates, and a central cathedral modeled on the church over the Holy Sepulcher—all were part of Nikon's plan for bringing heaven to earth in Muscovy.[62]

For the puritanical fundamentalists, however, this New Jerusalem suggested the kingdom of the Antichrist, who was to establish his universal reign in Jerusalem. Rumors spread that Nikon's translators and editors were secret Moslems, Catholics, and Jews. Given the large numbers of refugees employed and the fluidity of confessional lines in the East, there were enough recent converts and mysterious personalities to lend some credence to this charge. Meanwhile, two well-educated brothers, the Potemkins, came to Muscovy from Smolensk, the advanced base for Uniat efforts to win the Eastern Slavs to Catholicism, warning that Latinization of the Greek Church indicated the imminent coming of the Antichrist. Spyridon Potemkin was hailed as a friend and prophet by the fundamentalists for his ten treatises about the coming end; and his own death in 1664 was seen as a sign that history itself was drawing to a close. His brother Ephrem immediately set out for the woods north of Kostroma to await the end with fasting, prayer, and reading of the church fathers. Bearing the monastic name of the apocalyptical Syrian, this Ephrem proved no less gloomy and prophetic. He gathered a substantial following in the northern Volga region—partly by preaching doom at the famous summer fairs in the major trading cities.

Ephrem taught that Patriarch Nikon was the Antichrist, that the Second Coming was shortly to take place, and that men should gather provisions, because the seven years without bread prophesied in the Book of Daniel had already begun.[63] Early in 1666 the government sent a special expedition to the trans-Volga region to burn the cells of his followers, imprisoned most of them, and brought Ephrem to Moscow. He was forced to recant and go on a humiliating public tour to demonstrate his acceptance of the new forms; but Ephrem's recantation and the simultaneous anathemization of Avvakum only deepened the apocalyptical gloom of the fundamentalists and sent them looking for more precise guidance on the expected end of the world.

Once again they turned to prophetic anti-Uniat writings. As early as 1620, one Kievan monk had prophesied that the spread of Catholicism would lead to the coming of the Antichrist in 1666.[64] Spyridon Potemkin developed this idea by computing that it had taken Rome a thousand years after the birth of Christ to break with Orthodoxy; six hundred more years for the White and Little Russian hierarchies; sixty years after that for the Great Russians; and six more years for the end of the world.[65]

The date 1666 became fixed in the popular imagination, because it contained the number 666—which held the key to the identity of the apocalyptical beast. The Book of Revelation had promised that

. . . anyone who has intelligence may work out the number of the beast. The number represents a man's name, and the numerical value of its letters is 666.[66]

Since numbers were still written by letters in seventeenth-century Russia, the Russians found it easy to apply the ancient practice of *gematria:* adding together the numerical value of the letters in a man's name to find his "number." The early Christians had found that the Greek form of Nero's name written in Hebrew characters added up to 666; and Zizanius at the time of the forming of the Uniat Church in 1596 had started the Orthodox community speculating about the possible meaning for their plight of the figure 666. In the course of the theological crisis of the sixties, Russians found that this magic number could be reached by adding together the numbers for the Tsar (Alexis = 104), the Patriarch (Nikon = 198), and one of Nikon's suspect foreign editors (Arsenius the Greek = 364). Later computations showed that the letters in the word for "free thinker" (vol'nodum) also added up to 666.[67]

Signs of the coming Antichrist were found in the natural world by Theoktist, former hegumen of the Chrysostom monastery in Moscow, who had moved to distant Solovetsk and used his erudition and association in prison with Neronov to provide ideological support for that monastery's resistance to the new forms of worship. In his *On the Antichrist and His Secret Reign,* Theoktist contended that the reign of the Antichrist had already begun and appended a catalogue of signs to watch for: a kind of program guide for the last days.[68] Another shadowy figure, Abraham, Avvakum's "spiritual son" and constant companion in his last days of prison, saw signs of the Antichrist not only in the name "New Jerusalem" but also in the fact that Nikon called the river Istra "Jordan," a nearby mountain "Golgotha," and young monks his "seraphims." Frontier superstition was blended unconsciously with apocalyptical symbolism as Nikon was variously said to be the child of a water sprite (rusalka) or of the pagan Mordvin or Cheremis tribes.[69] The atmosphere was charged with expectation that 1666–7 was to bring portentous new events. The expectations were justified, for 1667, the first year in the expected reign of the Antichrist, was in many ways the beginning of a new order in Russia.

The Great Change

THE DECISIVE TURNING POINT in the religious crisis of seventeenth-century Russia was the church council of 1667, which excommunicated the fundamentalists en bloc. It was, superficially, a victory for Nikon, because the council upheld the central authority of the hierarchy and all of Nikon's reforms except his "our God" form of address in the Lord's prayer and his elimination of a dual blessing of the waters on Epiphany. Moreover, the ecclesiastical administration was greatly enlarged by the addition of twenty new dioceses to the already existing fourteen, and by the addition of four metropolitans, five archbishops, and nine bishops to the hierarchy.[70]

Yet defeat for the fundamentalists did not mean victory for the theocrats. On the contrary, the council devoted most of its attention to the final deposition and exile of Nikon. Its main result was to establish the clear subordination of church to state by flooding the church bureaucracy with

new priests who were, in effect, state appointed. One new Ukrainian metropolitan admitted with remarkable candor in sentencing Avvakum that "we
have to justify the Tsar, and that is why we stand for these innovations—in
order to please him."[71] Joachim, the new patriarch, was blunt in addressing
the Tsar: "Sovereign, I know neither the old nor the new faith, but whatever
the Sovereign orders I am prepared to follow and obey in all respects."[72]

A cosmopolitan, primarily Ukrainian and western Russian hierarchy
was replacing the older Great Russian Church administration, just as
Muscovy, having wrested from Poland key sections of these regions, was
rapidly being transformed into a multi-national empire. The ideal of an
organic religious civilization—whether fundamentalist or theocratic in
structure—was becoming as anachronistic as the ill-defined economic and
administrative procedures of patriarchal rule.

The defenders of the Muscovite ideal of an organic, religious civilization were being confronted in their own land with a sovereign secular state
similar to those of Western Europe. The year 1667 accelerated this trend
through the formal transfer of Kiev from long years of Polish overlordship
to Muscovite control and the promulgation of a new decree to insure national control over all foreign trade.[73] The process of freeing autocratic
authority from any effective restraint by local or conciliar bodies had
already been accomplished in the early years of Alexis' reign by the crushing
of town revolts and the abolition of the *zemsky sobors.*

A new polyglot caste of tsarist officials was being assembled by the new
head of the Tsar's royal household, Bogdan Khitrovo, a previously obscure
war hero and court intriguer who bore within his name the label "guileful"
(*khitry*). Two important new appointments of 1667 illustrate the growth of
a state servitor class *plus royaliste que le roi*. Metropolitan Theodosius, a
displaced Serb who had formerly been custodian of the Tsar's burial places
in the Archangel Cathedral of the Kremlin, was named as the administrator
of Nikon's patriarchal properties. Afanasy Ordyn-Nashchokin, a Westernized professional diplomat from Pskov, was made head of the ambassadorial
chancery, which at last acquired the character of a full-fledged foreign
ministry.[74]

The subservient nature of the new Church hierarchy is well illustrated
by the two figures who drew up the agenda of the 1666–7 councils: Paissius
Ligarides and Simeon Polotsky. The former was a Catholic-educated Greek
priest who had corresponded secretly for some years with the Roman
Congregation for the Propagation of the Faith and had come to Russia as
the disputed metropolitan of the meaningless Orthodox see of Gaza.
Ligarides' tangled history is so full of deceit and intrigue that it is hard to
ascribe anything but opportunistic motives to him. He had passionately

defended Greek ways in Rumania, where he had gone in the late forties to set up a Greek school at Jassy and help produce a Rumanian edition of the basic Byzantine digest of canon law. Now, however, he appeared as a savage attacker of the Grecophile Nikon; and his efforts after the council were principally devoted to advancing Alexis' claim to the vacant throne of Poland.[75]

Polotsky is a more serious figure: an articulate White Russian priest who wrote the *Sceptre of Rule,* a stern guide to ecclesiastical discipline which received the formal endorsement of the 1667 council. Later in the same year he became court preacher and tutor to the Tsar's children. For the secular occasion of New Year's Day, 1667, Polotsky published *The Eagle of the Russias,* an elaborate secular panegyric to his imperial bene-factor, replete with baroque decorations, anagrams on the Tsar's name, and praise above that given to Hercules, Alexander the Great, and Titus. All this adulation merely echoes his earlier poem, which called Alexis the sun and his wife the moon and ended:

> May thou be victorious over all the world
> And may the world find faith by means of thee.[76]

Polotsky's knowledge of classical political philosophy enabled him to give a sophisticated secular defense of tsarist absolutism. The scholastic method acquired in his Kievan education rapidly became a fashionable idiom of the new church hierarchy in Moscow, thanks to such works of the late sixties as *The Key of Reason* by Rector Goliatovsky of the Kiev Academy and *Peace with God for Man* by "the Russian Aristotle," Archimandrite Gizel of the Monastery of the Caves.

Gizel's *Sinopsis,* an officially commissioned history of Russia that underwent five editions by the end of the century, flatly attributed the victory of Muscovy over Poland to God's preference for absolute autocracy over the divided sovereignty of a republic. "Hetmans" and "senators" had led Poland "from tsardom to princedom, and from princedom to voevodism." But the Tsar of Muscovy has now delivered "the mother of Russian cities" from its bondage to Catholic Poland, and emerged as "the strongest of monarchs." True Christian Empire has thus returned to the East for the first time since the fall of Byzantium "as if the eagle had recaptured its youth."[77]

Polotsky also popularized in Moscow this new sense of imperial destiny and the new language of scholastic disputation which the Kiev academy had introduced. He was, moreover, an aggressive spokesman for new, Western art forms. His ornate syllabic verse and decorative book illustrations establish him as a master of the baroque. In 1667 Polotsky wrote a memorandum to the Tsar, setting forth a new and more permissive theory of iconography, which was upheld during the following two years in a series of pronouncements by visiting patriarchs, by the leading practitioner of the new methods of painting, Simon Ushakov, and by the Tsar himself.[78] Citing classical as well as Christian authorities, Polotsky contended that creative talent was a gift of God and must be used inventively; that icons could convey the physical realities and inner feeling of a given subject along with its traditional, stylized form. In the same year, 1667, Alexis went even further, hiring Nikon's former portrait painter as the official painter of the royal family. Within a few months illustrations from the German Piscator Bible were adorning the walls of his son Alexis' apartment, and a new illustrated manuscript even depicted the long-proscribed figure of God the Father—as a fat and prosperous figure reclining on a divan.[79]

Polyphonic baroque music also rushed in to challenge the older Russian forms of chant; and original secular dramas were produced for the first time. The first two were written and produced in rapid succession in the autumn of 1672 by the pastor of one of the German churches in Moscow, Johann Gregory. Four other plays and two ballets followed, with Gregory's original cast of sixty from the foreign suburb of Moscow soon augmented by recruits from the Baltic regions. Performances were given in both German and Russian in settings that ranged from private homes and the Kremlin to a specially built wooden theater. Ukrainians and White Russians also wrote and staged a number of the "school dramas" that had been popular in those Latinized regions. Music accompanied most of these performances, so that Russia "first became acquainted with secular singing and secular instrumental music not in life, but in spectacles."[80]

The overlapping of old and new sounds at the court of Alexis was likened by his English doctor to "a flight of screech owls, a nest of Jackdaws, a pack of hungry Wolves, seven Hogs on a windy day, and as many cats. . . ."[81] Nowhere was the cacophony greater than at Alexis' second wedding reception in the Kremlin, an affair which lasted most of the night and contrasted with his first puritanical wedding of 1645, in which no music was permitted. There was a kind of restoration atmosphere about Moscow in these last years of Alexis' reign. In the instructions of 1660 to his first ambassador to the restored English monarchy Alexis requested that "masters in the art of presenting comedies" be brought back to Russia.[82] The first ambassador from Restoration England staged "a handsome Comedie in Prose" with musical accompaniment on arrival in Moscow four years later.[83] Gregory's plays were of the "English comedy" variety; and Alexis' second wife (whom he married early in 1671, two years after the death of his first) was from the Marx Maryshkin family which was close to foreigners including Scottish royalists who had fled the Puritan Protectorate in England.

In many ways 1672 marked "the end of the secular isolation of Russia."[84] The Tsar's new wife produced a son, the future Peter the Great, and the exultant Alexis dispatched to all the major countries of Europe a "great embassy"[85] which both announced the birth and prefigured the trip that Peter himself was to take West at the end of the century. Another indication in 1672 of the coming of age of Russia as a full member of the European state system was the appearance of a sumptuously colored and officially sponsored *Book of Titled Figures,* with 65 portraits of foreign as well as Russian rulers. These relatively lifelike pictures of European statesmen were identified as the work of individual artists in sharp contrast to the idealized, anonymous images of purely Orthodox saints that had previously dominated Russian painting.[86]

Already under Alexis the semi-sanctified title of tsar was giving way to the Western title of emperor. Although the title was not formally adopted until the time of Peter, Alexis' new Polish-designed and Persian-built throne of the 1660's carried the Latin inscription *Potentissimo et Invictissimo. Moscovitarium Imperatori Alexio.*[87] Subtly, the distinctively modern idea was being implanted of unlimited sovereignty responsible only to the national ruler. The "great crown" that arrived in June, 1655, from Constantinople contained a picture of the Tsar and Tsarina where symbols of God's higher sovereignty used to be; and pictures of Alexis began to replace those of St. George on the seal of the two-headed eagle.[88] To the large group of dependent foreigners in Muscovy, Alexis was no longer the leader of a unique religious civilization but a model European monarch. As Pastor Gregory wrote in a poem of 1667:

> . . . how can I praise enough
> the incomparable tsar, the great prince of the Russians?
> Who loves our German people more than Russians
> Dispensing posts, distinctions, grants and riches.
> O most praiseworthy Tsar, may God reward you.
> Who would not be glad to live in this land?[89]

Secular curiosity was reaching out in every direction. Russians acquired their first regular postal contact with the West[90] and, in 1667, made their first use of astronomical calculations for navigation[91] and sent their first trade caravan to Peking, empowered to negotiate with the Chinese emperor. The head of the delegation was to bring back a favorable report on the literacy and civic spirit engendered by the Confucian tradition.[92] Within Russia itself, Alexis transferred artistic talent from sacred to secular activities. Icon painting in the Kremlin was placed under the administrative supervision of the armory; and the most important new construction inside the Kremlin in the late years of Alexis' reign was undertaken not for the church but for the foreign ministry, whose director surrounded himself not with icons but with clocks and calendars.[93]

Whereas Muscovy had thought of Russia as a "vineyard planted by God" for ultimate harvest in the life to come, Alexis seemed now to think of it as a place in which man could create his own "many-flowered garden." These were the titles respectively of the most famous Old Believer protest against the reforms and the most famous collection of poems by the new court poet Simeon Polotsky. Just as Simeon's "garden" of verse was full of tributes to such non-Muscovite subjects as "citizenship" and "philosophy,"[94] so Alexis' new Izmailovo gardens outside Moscow were full of Western innovations. Behind the baroque entrance gate there were windmills, herb and flower gardens, irrigation canals, caged animals, and small pavilions for rest and relaxation.[95]

An even greater symbol of secular elegance was the palace built by Alexis between 1666 and 1668 at Kolomenskoe, outside Moscow.[96] There was, to be sure, the superficial traditionalism so characteristic of Alexis' reign, as onion domes and tent roofs dominated the basically wooden construction. But light streamed in as it never had before in Muscovite buildings, through three thousand mica windows, revealing a vast fresco depicting the universe as heliocentric and an equally unfamiliar world of mirrors, opulent furniture, and imported mechanical devices. Pictures of Julius Caesar, Alexander the Great, and Darius stared down from walls where icons might have been, and Alexis received visitors on a throne flanked by two giant mechanical lions whose eyes rolled and jaws opened and roared on prearranged signals. Polotsky considered Kolomenskoe the eighth wonder of the world. It would perhaps be more correct to speak of it as the first wonder of a new world in which Western technology began to dominate the monuments of a new empire. Retaining the garish and ostentatious features of native tradition, Alexis had built the first of the palatial pleasure domes that came to symbolize Romanov Russia. He had taken over the pretentious building program of Nikon and the xenophobic arrogance of Avvakum; but he had left behind the religious convictions of both. The path was to be long and agonizing—but in some ways direct and inescapable—from seventeenth-century Kolomenskoe and Izmailovo to twentieth-century parks of culture and rest.

The Westernizing changes of Alexis' late years were profoundly revolutionary in the modern sense of the word. But in the seventeenth-century meaning of revolution—the restoration of a violated natural order, based on the image of a sphere revolving back to its original position—the defeated religious reformers were the true revolutionaries.[97] Both the theocrats and the fundamentalists were trying to return Russia to its presumed original Christian calling after an unnatural capitulation to foreign ways. Each put his faith in the Tsar to lead Russian Christendom back to its former purity; yet each instinctively understood that his cause was hopeless. They sorrowfully concluded that Alexis was either another Julian the Apostate who had secretly deserted the faith, or that Moscow had become the "fourth Rome," which they had previously thought would never be.[98]

Everywhere that the religious reformers looked in the new secularized court culture they found signs that the reign of the Antichrist had begun. Not only had the church council been summoned in a year containing the number of the beast, but the new doctrinal work *Peace with God for Man* presented to the Tsar in that very year by Gizel had 666 pages in it.[99] The frontispiece of another Kievan work of the same year showed King David and St. Paul pointing swords toward a globe on top of which rode the tsar of Russia into battle accompanied by a citation from the Book of Revelation —one of the most frequently quoted biblical books of the period.[100] The first painting done for the Tsar by his newly commissioned Dutch court painter (and presented to him on New Year's Day of 1667) further intensified the feeling of foreboding by depicting the fall of Jerusalem.[101]

The apocalypticism of the schismatics was the logical outgrowth of their extreme fidelity to the prophetic Muscovite ideology. But any full understanding of the schism requires not only Russian but Byzantine and Western perspectives as well. Indeed, this seemingly exotic and uniquely Russian schism can, in many ways, be described as "Byzantine in form, Western in content."

Of the Byzantine form, there can be little question. The concern over minute points of ritual and procedure, the elaborate court intrigue involving both emperor and patriarch, the constant appeal to Greek fathers on both sides, and the polemic invocation of apocalyptical and prophetic passages— all is reminiscent of earlier religious controversies in the Eastern Christian Empire. Church councils, which included foreign patriarchs along with Russian clergy, were the arenas in which the decisive steps were taken: the initial approval of the Nikonian reforms in 1654 and the condemnation of the fundamentalists and deposition of Nikon in 1667. The destructive internecine warfare between the intellectually sophisticated patriarchal party and the prophetic Old Believers during a century of continuing peril to the Muscovite state recalls in some respects the fateful struggle between the pro-scholastic and the Hesychast party during the embattled later days of Byzantium.

Nonetheless, in reading the detailed argumentation of the ecclesiastical debates, one feels that the essence of the controversy lies deeper than the verbal rationalizations of either party. Avvakum turned to patristic sources for the same reason that Nikon turned to Byzantine precedents: as a means of justifying and defending a position that had already been taken. Indeed, both men violated basic traditions of the Orthodoxy that they claimed to be defending. Avvakum's dualism led him in prison to defend the heretical position that the Christ of the Trinity was not completely identical with the historical Jesus. Nikon's ambition led him to claim—in fact if not in theory —greater power for the patriarchate than it had ever tried to assume in Constantinople.

Nothing would have shocked either Avvakum or Nikon more than the suggestion that his position resembled anything in the West. Neither had any appreciable knowledge of the West; and compulsive anti-Westernism was in many ways the driving force behind both of them. This very sensitivity, however, points to certain deeper links; for Russia in the time of Alexis was no longer a hermetically sealed culture. Inescapably if half-unconsciously, it was becoming involved in broader European trends— ideologically as well as economically and militarily. Indeed, the schism in the Russian Church can in some ways be said to represent the last returns from the rural precincts on the European Reformation: a burning out on the periphery of Europe of fires first kindled in the West a century before.

In broad outline, the schism in the Russian Church—like the schism in the West—grew out of renewed concern for the vitality and relevance of religion amidst the disturbing economic and political changes of early modern times. This "second religiousness" occurred later in Russia than in the West, primarily because economic change and secular ideas came later. It was more extreme in Russia than in many parts of the West largely because it followed rather than preceded the great wars of the late sixteenth and the early seventeenth century. The revival of Russian religious concern followed a course broadly similar to the preceding Western pattern. Contending forces within the Church became embroiled in bitter strife, which soon led to physical violence and doctrinal rigidity. The two major parties to the dispute burned themselves out fighting one another and thus cleared the way for the new secular culture of modern times.

If one bears in mind that no precise parallel is intended or direct borrowing implied, one may speak of the fundamentalist faction as a Protestant-like and the theocratic party a Catholic-like force within Russian Orthodoxy.

Neronov's opposition to the wars against Poland, his love of simple parables, his desire to preach to the forgotten, uprooted figures who hauled barges on the Volga or mined salt in Siberia—all were reminiscent of radical Protestant evangelism. The fundamentalists represented, moreover, the married parish clergy's opposition to the power of the celibate episcopacy. Like the Protestants, the fundamentalists found themselves fragmented into further divisions after breaking with the established Church hierarchy. As with Protestantism, however, there were two principal subdivisions: those with and without priests: the *popovtsy* and *bespopovtsy*. The "priestists" roughly correspond to those Western Protestants (Lutherans and Anglicans) who rejected Roman authority while continuing the old episcopal system and forms of worship; the "priestless," to those (Calvinists and Anabaptists) who rejected the old hierarchical and sacramental system as well.

The possibility of Protestant influence on some of the early Old Believers cannot be excluded, though there is an absence of direct evidence and an obvious theological gulf between the fundamentalists' fanatical dedication to ritual and icon veneration and the outlook of Protestantism. The already noted saturation of Muscovy with Protestant merchants and soldiers in the seventeenth century may nonetheless have had an impact on attitudes and practices, if not on the actual beliefs, of the fundamentalists. Some of the White Russian Protestants decimated by the Poles in the mid-seventeenth century must have resettled in Russia and may well have retained elements of their former faith even while formally accepting Orthodoxy. Throughout the seventeenth century the Swedes pursued an active program of Lutheran evangelism in the Baltic and Karelian regions, which later became centers of Old Believer colonization. One converted Russian priest wrote a Russian language tract in the late fifties or early sixties seeking to convince Russians that Lutheranism was the way to check the corrupted practices of Orthodoxy.[102] The banishment of the once-favored Protestants from Moscow in the late forties was partly justified by accusations of Protestant proselytizing. There were still some eighteen thousand Protestants resident in Russia and five Protestant churches in the Moscow area during the late years of Alexis' reign,[103] and the provincial regions in which the Old Belief took root were precisely those where Protestant presence had been the greatest: in the Baltic region, White Russia, and along the Volga trade routes.

Like the first Protestant circles around Luther, the original Old Believers came largely from a bleak but pious region of Northern Europe. For all their anti-intellectualism, many of the early Old Believers (such as Deacon Fedor and the Solovetsk monks) were—like Luther—learned students of sacred texts. They juxtaposed an idealized original Christianity to the recent creations of the ecclesiastical hierarchy, reviled the decadence and complacency of a distant Mediterranean civilization, and sought to bring monastic piety into everyday life. Neronov, like Luther, was particularly versed in the epistles of St. Paul and was often compared to him by contemporaries.[104]

The backing of local political leaders was as indispensable in turning the theological concerns of Neronov and Avvakum into a social movement as was the backing of German princes to Luther. Indeed, the amorphous, newly expanded empire of the Romanovs was no less vulnerable to the pressure of divisive forces than the empire of Charles V a century before. If Lutheranism proved more successful than Neronovism, it was only because it accepted the institution of the secular state more unreservedly. But this distinction only serves to identify the Russian schismatic tradition more with the radical, "non-magisterial" reformation: the tradition of Anabaptists, Hutterites, and the like, whose strength had in any case been greatest in Central and Eastern Europe.[105] In their relentless opposition to war and *raison d'état* and their tendency to speak of "houses of prayer" rather than consecrated churches, the Russian schismatics resemble Quakers and other radical Protestant sects.[106] In their apocalyptical expectations and ingrown communal traditions, the Old Believer colonizers on the distant eastern frontier of Christendom were close in spirit to some of the sectarian pioneers of colonial America on its far-western periphery.

Other minority religions of the expanding Russian empire may have melted into the schismatic tradition, for the new secular state tended to produce a sense of community among persecuted dissenters. One of the earliest and most influential defenders of the Old Belief in Siberia was an Armenian convert to Orthodoxy, who had been conditioned by his previous Nestorianism to make the sign of the cross with two fingers rather than three.[107] Nor can the possibility of some interaction with the Jewish community be excluded. The year 1666, in which the Antichrist was expected by the fundamentalists, was the same year in which Sabbatai Zevi claimed to have become the long-expected Messiah of the Jews. Using many of the same prophetic passages and computations as the Old Believers and influenced perhaps by a wife who was a Ukrainian survivor of the Khmelnitsky massacres, Sabbatai attracted a greater following for his claim than any Jew since Jesus, particularly within the decimated Jewish community of Poland and Russia. The Ukrainian hierarchy which was dominating the new Russian Church denounced Jews along with Old Believers. One Ukrainian priest wrote the first major Christian refutation anywhere of the claims of Sabbatai, *The True Messiah*, in terms that indicated that Sabbataian ideas were finding some response within the Orthodox community.[108] Since Sabbatai himself became an apostate to Islam and the entire movement was resolutely condemned by Orthodox Jewry, absorption into other creeds became the norm rather than the exception. Sabbataian ideas influenced Polish thought; and it must have infected the substantial numbers of Jews who sought anonymity and shelter in Muscovy amidst the confusion and massive repopulation of the mid-seventeenth century.[109] At the very least, there is a striking similarity between the Sabbataians and the Old Believers in their apocalypticism, fascination with occult numerical computations, ecstatic sense of election, and semi-masochistic acceptance of suffering.

If the Old Believers show a certain kinship with radical Protestantism and Sabbataian Judaism, the theocratic party bears a curious resemblance to Counter Reformation Catholicism. Although Patriarch Philaret was a prisoner and then a diplomatic foe of Catholic Poland, he nonetheless adopted many Catholic ideas—just as Peter was later to borrow heavily from his Swedish adversary. In establishing centralized control over ecclesiastical publication and the canonization of saints, in expanding the bureaucracy, jurisdiction, and landholding power of the hierarchy, Philaret was following Catholic rather than Russian precedents. The same was frequently true of Mogila, whose opposition to Catholicism was purely external and political, but whose conflict with Protestantism was profoundly ideological.

A Swede in Moscow in the early fifties described Vonifatiev, the Tsar's confessor and heir apparent to the patriarchate, as "a cardinal under a different name";[110] and an Austrian likened Nikon, who was chosen over Vonifatiev, to the Pope himself.[111] Nikon's attempt to provide rigid dogmatic definition in matters of phraseology is more reminiscent of the Council of Trent than of the seven ecumenical councils. Many of the Greek texts he used for models came from Venice or Paris, with Catholic accretions. His sense of the theatrical in court and ecclesiastical ceremony, his calculated reburials and canonizations, his orders to bring back secular classics along with church books from Greece, his opposition to any council which challenged the authority of the first primate—all have more the ring of a Renaissance pope than of a return to Byzantine purity. His program for building and embellishing new monasteries in spots of great natural beauty climaxed by the creation of his monastery of the New Jerusalem seems strangely reminiscent of Julian II and the building of St. Peter's just before the great split in Western Christendom.

In defending the ecclesiastical realm from civil authority, Nikon used traditional Byzantine texts. But his actual policies as patriarch went beyond established Orthodox practice. An Orthodox visitor who accompanied the Patriarch of Antioch to Russia in 1654–5 complained that Nikon had in fact become "a great tyrant over . . . every order of the priesthood and even over the men in power and in the offices of the Government."[112] Nikon, he complained, had arrogated to himself the Tsar's traditional right to name the archimandrites of Russia's leading monasteries and had increased the number of serfs bonded directly to the patriarchate by 250 per cent. Although Nikon was careful not to claim pre-eminence of the patriarch over the Tsar, he did at times argue that the spiritual power was higher than the temporal. In his new edition of the canon law in 1653, he cites the Donation of Constantine, the forged document that had been used to sustain extreme papal claims in the late Middle Ages. Although Nikon at no time suggested the establishment of a Russian papacy, he claimed that the authority of the Muscovite patriarchate derives from its replacement of the lapsed see of Rome, seeming to imply that some of the pretensions of the latter have been transferred to the former.[113] His quasi-papal ideal is revealed in a vision he claimed to have had of Metropolitan Peter, the founder of the Muscovite hierarchy, appearing to him through the imperial crown on a throne with his hand on the holy gospel.[114] In the long and adamant defense of his position throughout the early sixties, Nikon insisted that the patriarch possessed a kind of papal infallibility. "The first primate is the image of Christ and all the others pupils and apostles, and a slave is not entitled to the seat of a sovereign."[115]

A final indication of catholicizing tendencies in Nikon lies in the area of foreign policy. Whereas the fundamentalists particularly hated Rome and the Poles, Nikon appears to have been more fearful of Protestantism and the Swedes. He opposed the war against Poland of 1653 and the rebaptism of Catholics. Some of his assistants in the correction of books were former Uniats from White Russia and the Ukraine; and the decision of the council in 1667 to confirm his abolition of the requirement of 1620 for rebaptising Catholics was one of many concessions to these non-Great Russian priests. Nikon compared the situation in Russia to that produced by the "Latin heresies" in the West, lamenting that "we have come to those times when we [priests] are fighting one another like lay people."[116] He called Nikita Odoevsky, the principal author of the Law Code of 1649 and leading apologist for the subordination of church to state, "a new Luther."[117]

The multiple ironies as well as the confessional confusions of the age are demonstrated by the fact that the principal collaborator of this "new Luther" in the trial of Nikon was Ligarides, a former Vatican agent wearing the robes of an Orthodox metropolitan. It seems only fitting that this erstwhile Grecophile from distant Gaza ended up destroying Nikon's Greek revival and posing as the defender of Muscovite tradition. Ligarides summoned up the distinctively Russian symbol of the icon screen as the model for an ordered hierarchical society to challenge Nikon's concept of a symphony of powers between civil and ecclesiastical authority. Recognizing the patriarch as in any way equal to the Tsar would, Ligarides warned, place two icons in the center of the *chin,* where only the "Christ enthroned" is traditionally found; and man "cannot serve two masters . . . pray through two icons."[118]

In contrast to Ligarides, both Nikon and Avvakum devoted much of their lives to such prayer and were constant in their loyalties. They were both profoundly Muscovite in temperament and training, "unlearned in speech, yet not in thought; untaught in rhetoric, dialectic and philosophy, but with the mind of Christ our guide within us."[119] Thus, it would be misleading to end a consideration of the original schism between them on any note of comparability with the West. The conflict between Nikon and Avvakum was not a theological debate, but a death struggle between two towering frontiersmen in a world of one truth. Only after they had destroyed one another did Russia become a safe place for Ligarides' doctrine of state service and many, shifting truths.

The idea that there is but one truth in any controversy was Byzantine; and both Nikon and Avvakum thought of themselves as defending its apostolic heritage from either foreign corruption or domestic debasement. Each sought to make that truth relevant to Russian society through the force of his own prophetic personality. Each underwent severe physical suffering and spent his last years in lonely isolation from Muscovy. Each was ascetically indifferent to the bourgeois virtues of cleanliness and moderation. Neither of them was ever outside of Russia.

The essential similarity of these two Muscovite prophets becomes particularly striking in their years of tribulation and exile. Each viewed himself as the suffering servant of God. Each was fortified in his convictions by visions. Each continued to seek vindication in history, appealing to the Tsar and other authorities for restitution of the True Church rather than engaging in disputations with the new hierarchy. Each sought to prove the rightness and sanctity of his own cause by deeds rather than words. Denied access to the councils of the great, they sought to prove themselves by working miraculous cures on the humble believers who came to their distant retreats.

Of the two, Avvakum has become better known to posterity because of the magnificent autobiography he wrote in the early years of his exile. In it, the old hagiographic style is fully adopted to the vernacular idiom, and the prophetic Muscovite ideology is transformed into a deeply personal profession of faith. Named for the Old Testament prophet Habakkuk, whose name means "strong fighter," Avvakum reacts like a true prophet to persecution, asking for God's help rather than men's mercy. Even while being beaten with the knout in Siberia by the leader of a military expedition,

> I kept saying, "O Lord Jesus Christ, Son of God! Help me!" And this I kept repeating without pause, so that it was bitter to him in that I did not say, "Have mercy!"[120]

Inveighing tirelessly against "lovers of new things who have fallen away from truth," Avvakum calls for active witness to the truth rather than talk about it:

> What matter that they talk vanity of me; in the day of judgment they shall all know of my deeds, whether they be good or evil.[121]

Avvakum represents in many ways a culminating expression of the Muscovite ideology: a passionate prophet seeking to fill his life with "deeds of devotion" (*podvigi blagochestiia*). He combines within himself both the kenotic and the fanatic strains of early Russian spirituality. His polemic style is as pungent and polemic as that of Ivan IV, yet his message is conservative and his counsel compassionate. He bids men simply to preserve the old faith and accept suffering gladly in imitation of Christ, rather than fight back with the sword as do followers of "the Tatar God Mohammad," or with the "fire, knout and gallows" of the new faithless state.[122] His own martyrdom gave his writings a special crown of authority, which tended to perpetuate among Russian religious dissenters Avvakum's semi-Manichean view of the world. Avvakum called himself not an Old but a "True Believer," insisting (in objection to a Nikonian deletion from the creed) that

> It were better in the Creed not to pronounce the word Lord, which is an accidental name, than to cut out "True," for in that name is contained the essence of God.[123]

Avvakum places light first among the "essential names" of God and sees Christianity as "the first light of truth" now darkened by Western heresy. In advocating self-immolation he develops a dualistic dissociation of the body from the soul. "Burning your body, you commend your soul into the hands of God,"[124] he wrote to one martyr. Shortly before he was burned at the stake, his attitude became almost masochistic: ". . . run and jump into the flames. Here is my body, Devil, take and eat it; my soul you cannot take!"[125] Avvakum was rebuked for his heretical views by his more learned prison mate, Deacon Fedor;[126] but the archpriest's fanaticism and dualism were to exercise great influence on native Russian traditions of religious dissent.

Nikon also left an admiring life written in the hagiographical style by a seventeenth-century follower,[127] and he too emerges as a deeply Muscovite figure. A Dutch visitor at his Monastery of the New Jerusalem in 1664 found nothing but Slavic and Russian books in his personal library.[128] Everywhere he went Nikon had special retreats from the world for meditation and prayer. Like Avvakum, he disciplined himself with strenuous physical labor. During his final monastic exile he actually built a small island retreat in the lake by hauling huge stones down through the water and building a synthetic island. He was fascinated with bells and had a large number cast with mysterious inscriptions at the New Jerusalem monastery. Almost the only question about the outside world that he asked his Dutch visitor pertained to the size and nature of bells in Amsterdam.[129] Nikon was as opposed as Avvakum to new icons, and had visions in which Christ appeared to him as He did in the icons. Nikon was said to have achieved in his last years even more miraculous cures of the sick than Avvakum: 132 in one three-year period.[130]

Nikon was, of course, less decisively rejected by the new church than was Avvakum. In contrast to the fiery martyrdom of the archpriest, the dethroned patriarch died peacefully on his way back to Moscow in 1681 with a partial pardon from the imperial court. Nonetheless, Nikon used prophetic terminology similar to that of Avvakum in denouncing the principal author of the resolutions of the Church council as a "precursor of the Antichrist." He saw in the new "Babylonian captivity" of the Russian Church to state authority a worse bondage than the Mongol yoke.[131] A pamphlet supporting him in 1664 divided the world into those who sing "praises to the holy patriarch" and those who serve in the regiments of Antichrist.[132]

Rebels against the new secular state looked on Nikon no less than on Avvakum as a potential deliverer: the defender of an older and better way of life. Just as the rioting *streltsy* were to glorify the rejected Old Believers, so did the Cossack leaders of the Stenka Razin uprising of 1667–71 glorify the rejected patriarch as a possible deliverer from the "reign of the voevodas."[133]

The points of similarity between these two figures serve as a reminder that the basic schism in Christian Russia was not the formal one between those who accepted and those who rejected the Nikonian reforms. The real schism was, rather, the basic split between the Muscovite ideal of an organic religious civilization shared by both Avvakum and Nikon and the post-1667 reality—equally offensive to both of them—of the church as a subordinate institution of a secularized state.[134]

The real loser amidst all this religious conflict in Russia was—as it had been in the West—the vitality of surviving Christian commitment. The two main forces within the Church spent their time and energy combating and discrediting each other rather than the secular forces undermining them both. The Russian Church after 1667 tended to borrow secular ideas rather than spiritual ideals from each of the old positions. The official Church became neither a prophetic community as the fundamentalists had wished nor a self-governing sacramental institution as the theocrats had desired. From the fundamentalists modern Russia took not fervid piety so much as xenophobic fanaticism; from the theocrats, not so much Christian rule as ecclesiastical discipline.

This ideological protest against modernization left a corrosive legacy of xenophobia. Internal schism in the wake of widespread violence engraved the anti-Jewish attitude implicit in the Muscovite ideology deep into the popular imagination. The Old Believers accused Nikon of permitting Jews to translate sacred books; and the Nikonians accused the Old Believers of letting Jews lead sacred services. Both parties considered the council of 1666–7 a "Jewish mob," and an official publication of the council blamed its opponents for falling victim to "the lying words of Jews." Throughout the society rumors spread that state power had been turned over to "cursed Jewish governors" and the Tsar lured into a corrupting Western marriage by the aphrodysiacs of Jewish doctors.[135] Anti-Catholicism also became more widespread if not more intense than during the Time of Troubles. One Orthodox historian has pointed out that "until the sixties of the seventeenth century, aside from the name itself, the simple people could in no way distinguish Uniat from Orthodox."[136] Henceforth, the general antagonism vaguely felt toward the Pope of Rome and "the Latins" was also directed at the Uniat Church as a tool for the "guileful politics of the Polish republic."[137]

To say who was responsible for the schism in the Eastern Church of Christ would be no easier than to determine who was responsible for the crucifixion of its founder. In both cases, the main historical arena of the immediate future belonged to men of state: the "great" Peter and Catherine and the "august" Caesar. Yet the "third Rome" was to be haunted by schismatics almost as much as the first Rome had been by the early Christians.

The year 1667, which brought a formal end to religious controversy, saw the beginning of two powerful social protest movements against the new order. From the north the monks and traders of Solovetsk began their active resistance to tsarist troops, which was to inspire the Old Believer communities that soon formed along the Russian frontier. At the same time Stenka Razin (who had made two pilgrimages to Solovetsk) began the Cossack-led peasant rebellion which provided the precedent for a new tradition of anarchistic rural revolt. The subsequent history of Russia was to be, in many ways, the history of two Russias: that of the predominantly Baltic German nobility and the predominantly White and Little Russian priesthood, which ran the Romanov empire; and that of the simple peasants, tradesmen, and prophets from whom its strength was derived.

The original fundamentalists and theocrats made an impressive final exit from the stage of history in the late seventeenth century. Even after both positions had been rejected and Avvakum and Nikon were dead, each camp managed to give one last witness to its old ideals: one final ringing vote of no confidence in the new order.

The fundamentalist protest was that of communal withdrawal from the world. In the very year after the council in 1667, peasants in Nizhny Novgorod began to leave the fields and dress in white for all-night prayer vigils in anticipation of the coming end. Further north along the Volga, the unkempt Vasily Volosaty ("the hairy one") was attracting interest in his program for the destruction of all books and the launching of a penitential fast unto death. Others taught that the reign of Antichrist had begun in 1666, or that the end of the world would come in 1674 or 1691 (which was thought to be 1666 years after the entrance of Christ into hell). The death of Tsar Alexis in 1676 just a few days after the final fall of the fundamentalist redoubt at Solovetsk was seen as a sign of God's disfavor and an assurance of His intention to vindicate soon the defenders of the old faith.

Some sought to anticipate the purgative fires of the Last Judgment through self-immolation; others withdrew to form new puritanical communities in the virgin forests. The formation of these communities permitted the fundamentalist tradition to survive into modern times; but their creative activities belong more to the eighteenth than the seventeenth century. The final years of the seventeenth century were dominated by more negative protests against the new order, reaching a climax in the movement to abjure all worldly speech save repetition of the word "no"—the famous *netovsh-china* of a peasant from Yaroslavl named Kozma Andreev.[138]

Only a few miles from the spot where Kozma was trying to exercise his veto power against the modern world, there arose at the same time the last great monument to the rival, theocratic protest against secularism: the new Kremlin of Rostov the Great. Built by the Metropolitan Ion Sysoevich during the 1670's and 1680's as part of a deliberate effort to perpetuate the cause of his friend Nikon, the Rostov Kremlin is one of the most magnificent architectural ensembles in all of Russia. The majesty of its symmetry and relative simplicity of its brick and stone construction represent a direct effort to perpetuate the Nikonian style in architecture, and they constitute a massive, silent rebuke to the exotic pretentiousness of the new state architecture. There could hardly be a more striking contrast than that of this massive yet white and austere ecclesiastical ensemble with the garish colors and chaotic appearance of the new architectural ensembles concurrently built in wood by Tsar Alexis: the palace at Kolomenskoe and the foreign office building within the Moscow Kremlin.

More important, however, the ecclesiastical construction at Great Rostov represented an effort to vindicate Nikon's theocratic ideas by dramatizing the majesty of the ecclesiastical estate and its pre-eminence over the civil. Sysoevich borrowed many of the ideas and technicians that Nikon had used in his own building program. Like Nikon's new monasteries, the ensemble of churches and ecclesiastical buildings at Rostov was built in a spot of beauty by a lake and was richly endowed. As in Nikon's monasteries, Sysoevich established a kind of theocratic rule over the village of Rostov, which even today is totally dominated by its Kremlin.[139] Like Nikon, Sysoevich had become preoccupied with the need for discipline and order while serving in the hierarchy of Novgorod. He went so far as to declare once in public that "the Jews were right to crucify Christ for his revolt"—which became regarded by the Old Believers as one of the outstanding blasphemies of the new church even though Sysoevich was severely punished for it.[140]

Sysoevich's Kremlin in Rostov was the headquarters for a metropolitan who controlled the rich and powerful Yaroslavl-Kostroma region of the upper Volga, where the most lavish churches of the century were built. The elaborate frescoes of the 1670's and 1680's that filled every nook and arcade of the new churches in this diocese represented a final effort of Muscovy to produce an all-encompassing hieroglyphic encyclopedia of the faith. But the intrusion of secular subject matter—a harvest scene, women looking in a mirror, a nude being seduced by a devil—destroyed the spiritual integrity of these vast new compositions.[141] In Yaroslavl and Rostov as elsewhere in late-seventeenth-century Russia, scenes of Christ's passion and crucifixion borrowed from the West began crowding out the more exalted images of transfiguration and resurrection that had traditionally dominated the iconography of the Savior in the East. Christ no longer seemed altogether comfortable on His throne at the center of the new icon screens in the cathedrals of Yaroslavl.[142] There was no longer any sanctuary, no place for God to be present on earth, behind the icon screens of the Old Believer temples that were springing up in the nearby woods along the Volga. But there was still the hope that God's presence might be maintained within the great Kremlin of the metropolitan at Rostov; and the legend had begun that "one must see Rostov the great before dying."

Many of its churches rose up directly and majestically over the walls of the Kremlin. Within them, classical columns framed the approach to the royal doors and a throne behind the altar provided the metropolitan with a suitably Nikonian place of authority. The main church of the Savior on the Walls must have been the scene of marvelous singing in view of its unparalleled acoustics and a choir area nearly as big as the nave. Even today its bells are among the most sonorous in Russia. Faithful to both the xenophobia and the love of pictorial beauty of Old Muscovy, the Last Judgment scene on the west wall of the Church of the Savior is a magnificent monolith that depicts an unprecedented three rows of foreigners among the ranks of the condemned.[143]

But history was about to condemn this mighty monument of Muscovy rather than the foreigners in its frescoes. In 1691, the year of Metropolitan Ion's death, young Tsar Peter began the humiliation of Rostov, making the first of many forced exactions from its rich store of silver. He was soon to complete the process of subordinating the church by abolishing the patriarchate and establishing a state-controlled synod as its ruling body. There were to be no more "Great Sovereigns" from the clergy like Philaret and Nikon, no more Great Rostovs in the world of Peter the Great, Catherine the Great—and the Great Revolution.

2. The Westward Turn

THE REJECTION of both fundamentalists and theocrats meant the end of any serious efforts to maintain a civilization completely distinct from that of the West. The religious ideology of Muscovy was rejected as unworkable for a modern state, and the rigid barriers against Western influence which both Nikon and Avvakum had sought to shore up were largely removed after 1667.

It was not yet clear how much and what kind of Western influence was to prevail in the ungainly new empire. Only gradually and fitfully was Russia able to fashion a creative culture and an administrative system which harmonized with those in the rest of Europe. The celebrated reforms of Peter the Great pointed the way to the future. But the fresh religious gropings that preceded these reforms and the exotic resistance movements that developed in reaction to them indicate that the triumph of secular modernization was far from complete.

New Religious Answers

THE LAST QUARTER of the seventeenth century—from the death of Alexis to the assumption of real power by Peter the Great—was a kind of interregnum. The continued progression toward Western ways was dramatized by the emancipation of women from the *terem* (the special upstairs chamber to which they had previously been largely confined) under the regent Sophia, daughter of Alexis, who became the first woman to rule Russia. Her principal minister, V. V. Golitsyn, provided an important link between the Westernizing work of Alexis and that of Peter. Golitsyn helped reorganize the military establishment, abolish the antiquated system of social precedence (*mestnichestvo*), and modify many of the more cruel forms of legal investigation and punishment.

However, Golitsyn was more successful in changing old ways than in establishing anything in their place. He was eventually rejected and exiled —as were most other innovators of the period. Russia was not yet willing to commit itself to new ways of doing things. The continuing search for new answers was concentrated in the overgrown wooden metropolis of Moscow, where every shade of opinion was represented from the xenophobic fundamentalism of the *streltsy* quarter to the transplanted Germanic efficiency of the foreign suburb. The young Peter the Great derived many of his new ideas and tastes from a carefree boyhood spent largely in this Western enclave of Moscow. But the preoccupation of the uneasy ruling elite with combating religious-tinged rebellions against innovation—by Razin, Solovetsk, and the *streltsy*—naturally conditioned them to look for religious answers of their own: for a viable religious alternative to that of Old Muscovy. Thus, although the ruling elite had nowhere to look for guidance after 1667 but to the West, it still looked for religious answers: solutions of the old sort from the new font of wisdom.

The late years of the seventeenth century saw the consideration in Moscow of four religious answers—all of them brought in from the outside. Only after rejecting these last efforts to find religious answers for Russia's problems did Russia turn to the West for the secular and political solutions of Peter the Great.

Each of the four religious answers proposed in Moscow represented an effort to come to grips with the reality of the schism and the irreversible changes in Russian life. None of these solutions was proposed by Great Russians steeped in the Muscovite ideology, like Nikon and Avvakum. Two of the solutions—those of the Latinizers and Grecophiles—were group movements sponsored by new elements within the Russian Orthodox Church anxious to give it solid new foundations. Two other, more radical proposals—direct conversion to Roman Catholicism and Protestant sectarianism—were offered from without by lonely prophets coming to Moscow from the West. This proliferation of conflicting solutions bears testimony to the state of confusion and uncertainty into which the schism had plunged Russian Christendom.

The Latinizing and Grecophile solutions arose because of the belated acceptance within the Russian Church of the need to develop a systematic educational system. Such a need had not been keenly felt by prophetic partisans of the Muscovite ideology. Neither Nikon nor Avvakum had attached any importance to systematic education of the clergy, though both advocated careful study of the holy texts of which they approved. The question that divided the two parties in the post-1667 church was simply whether Latin or Greek language and culture should dominate the religious education of the new polyglot hierarchy.

The continued influx of Ukrainian and White Russian priests and the banishment of the Grecophile Nikon gave a considerable initial advantage to the Latinizing party. Polotsky set up in Moscow during the 1660's an informal school for instructing state servants in Latin culture; and one of Polotsky's first students, Silvester Medvedev, became the champion of the Latinizing party in the 1670's. Medvedev was a widely traveled diplomat who had helped negotiate the treaty with Poland in 1667 and had taken monastic vows only in 1674. In 1677 he was given important new responsibilities in Moscow as chief corrector of books and head of the Zaikonospassky Monastery, which became the center of an expanding program of Latin instruction in the capital. In 1685 he petitioned the regent Sophia (who had also studied under Polotsky) for permission to convert his school into a semi-official academy.

Medvedev's efforts to extend his already great authority rendered him vulnerable to the savage intrigues that were characteristic of Moscow during this period of upheaval and suspicion. He met much of the same resistance that Nikon had encountered; but Medvedev lacked the personality, the patriarchal power, and the authority of Byzantine precedent to carry out his reforms. He was soon attacked by a rival faction supported by the Patriarch Joachim and by a rival Greek school attached to the Moscow Printing Office.

The Grecophile faction acquired new strength with the arrival from Constantinople in 1685 of two well-traveled and educated Greeks, the Likhudy brothers. They undermined Medvedev's position with doctrinal attacks and wrested away, for the use of their Greek school, stone buildings originally designed for Medvedev's Latin academy. Rapidly stripped of his various positions, Medvedev was soon arrested for alleged treason and, after two years of torture and mistreatment, burned for heresy in 1691. As in the Nikon-Avvakum controversy, however, the Medvedev-Likhudy affair resulted in mutual defeat rather than clear victory for either side. The Likhudies themselves soon became suspect as foreign intriguers, and their influence declined precipitously in the early 1690's.[1]

There were two important issues with long-term implications for Russian culture lying beneath the sordid external details of the controversy. Each side was vindicated on one issue: the Latinizers on that of the basic language and style of theological education and discourse, the Grecophiles on fundamental matters of dogma.

The Latin bias in theological education represented the final victory of the new clergy over the traditional Greek-oriented monastic establishment of Muscovy. Henceforth, Russian theological education—almost the only form of education in eighteenth-century Russia—was far more Western in content than before. Latin replaced Greek forever as the main language of philosophic and scientific discourse; and Russia adopted through its church schools a more sympathetic attitude toward secular learning and scholastic theology than the more patristically inclined Grecophiles would have tolerated. It is not accidental that the late seventeenth and the early eighteenth century saw a flood of learned treatises on the Russian Church by Western theologians, and that most of the important theological writing and teaching in the Russian Church during this period was the work of Russian priests originally trained in the Latin-speaking theological academies of Western Europe.[2]

The vindication of the Greeks in matters of dogma was in many ways more surprising than the victory of Latins in matters of form. The scholastic theology of Roman Catholicism has always attracted those in search of rational order and synthesis. Moreover, for the Orthodox, Catholicism was doctrinally far closer than Protestantism. A number of Catholic positions had been endorsed by the Orthodox Church generally at the synod of Bethlehem in 1672;[3] and others were quietly accepted by the post-1667 Russian Church without any sense of contradiction or betrayal. The Catholic definition of the Immaculate Conception of the Virgin Mary was widely accepted. Leaders of the new Church even proposed that the long-proscribed Catholic phraseology on the procession of the Holy Spirit be reinserted in the Russian creed and that the Russian Church appoint a pope and elevate its four metropolitans to patriarchal rank.[4] But the critical doctrinal issue over which the Latinizers came to grief was the nature of the eucharist, or holy communion.

Behind the seemingly technical debate over this sacrament, this commemorative re-enactment of the Last Supper, lay the deeper question of man's relationship to God in a changing world. The nature of God's presence in the bread and wine had deeply bothered the reformers of the West, most of whom had retained this rite while changing its form or redefining its nature. The Hussites had sought to make the "common service" (the literal meaning of "liturgy") truly common by making the elements readily available to all. Luther spoke of con- rather than trans-substantiation, in an effort to reconcile the concurrent fact of Christ's real presence and of essentially unchanged bread and wine. The Roman Catholic doctrine of the eucharist was systematically drawn up only when the need came to deal with the varying challenges of the reformers. It contended (1) that Christ was really, and not merely symbolically, present in the sacrament; (2) that a total change in the substance of the elements (transubstantiation) took place at the time the priest repeated Christ's original words of institution: "This is my body . . . This is my blood"; and (3) that only the purely "accidental" aspects of the bread and wine remain unchanged.[5]

In the course of the seventeenth century the Orthodox Church also felt the challenge of the reformers and adopted the Catholic term "transubstantiation" as "the only possible word to deny Protestant heresy and at the same time affirm the Orthodox belief."[6] The Russian church hierarchy, which was especially fearful of divisive heresies, played a leading role in the general hardening of doctrinal positions and the increased use of dialectic method and scholastic casuistry in dogmatic writing. Catholic, and more specifically Jesuit, theological technique and terminology is evident in the two small efforts of the Orthodox Church of the Eastern Slavs to provide a systematic catechism for its communicants: Mogila's catechism of 1640 and the catechism of 1670 of Simeon Polotsky, *Crown of the Catholic (Kafolicheskaia) Faith*. Medvedev was, thus, only continuing the tradition begun by his teacher Polotsky in speaking of transubstantiation and echoing other aspects of Roman Catholic teachings about the eucharist in his long dogmatic dialogue *Bread of Life* and in a second more polemic work, *Manna of the Bread of Life*.

Medvedev's exposition of the Catholic position offended Russian Orthodox sensibilities in two important ways. First of all, the distinction between accidents and substances introduced a kind of terminological hair splitting into something which the Orthodox considered a holy mystery (literally, "secret," *tainstvo*). It was celebrated behind the closed doors of the sanctuary during the third, most hallowed part of the Orthodox mass, the *liturgiia vernykh*, or "service of the believers." Second, it specified the exact time at which God comes down to man through the transformed elements.

On this latter point Medvedev was challenged and eventually anathemized; for it related to an issue that had been at the heart of the original split between the churches: the Eastern refusal to accept the Western version of the Nicene Creed, in which the Holy Spirit was said to descend from the Father *and Son*. A certain awesome if mysterious primacy within the unity of the Trinity was reserved for the Father in the East, and this primacy seemed once more jeopardized by Medvedev's position. Insofar as one can define the precise moment at which God becomes present in the elements, Medvedev's critics insisted that it came after the priest's call for the descent of the Holy Spirit, following the repetition of Christ's words of institution. In other words, the miracle of God's presence in the sacrament was not assured by a priest's re-enactment of Christ's sacrifice, but rather by the "common work of the believers" in supplicating God for the descent of His Holy Spirit.[7]

Thus, behind all the venality of intrigue which eventually doomed Medvedev lay the reluctance of the Russian Church to accept fully the detailed doctrinal formulations of post-Reformation Roman Catholicism, however much they were to borrow from its language and methods of instruction. The Russian Church displayed a stubborn determination to reassert the uniqueness of its doctrinal position even at a time when it was losing its independence from the state and rejecting its original orientation toward Greek culture.

On one point the Latinizers and Grecophiles had been in agreement: their opposition to the Western churches. Medvedev had inveighed against the heretical ideas he had found among foreign book correctors in Moscow; the Likhudies had written a series of tracts against Catholics, Lutherans, and Calvinists.[8]

The xenophobia of the Russian Church, which they helped thus to fortify, was to claim two foreign victims in the waning years of the seventeenth century: Quirinus Kuhlmann and Yury Krizhanich. Each came from the western borderlands of European Slavdom to Moscow with high expectations of the role Russia could play in the religious regeneration of Europe. Each was a prophet without honor in his own country, who was to be rejected as well in Russia. From a purely Western point of view they represent only curious distant echoes of the Reformation and Counter Reformation respectively. Yet in Russia they stand as harbingers of important new ideas and developments. Each bears witness to the extent to which "uniquely Russian" movements and ideas can be traced to Western, or at least non-Russian, origins.

The Croatian Catholic priest, Yury Krizhanich, was the first to come to Russia, arriving with a Polish diplomatic mission in 1647 and returning in the guise of a Ukrainian war refugee in 1659.[9] Throughout his long second stay in Russia, which lasted two decades, Krizhanich sought to advance both an old and a new idea. The old idea was the conversion of Russia to Catholicism; the new was the development of Russia as the center of a new united Slavdom. Only such unity could, in Krizhanich's view, counter the growing strength of the Protestant Germans on the one side and the infidel Turks on the other. The ideal that Russia rather than Poland should serve as the anchor of Catholic hopes in Eastern Europe had been favored in Vatican circles during periods of demonstrated Muscovite strength under the two Ivans. The idea was particularly popular with certain Croatian Catholics who had participated in the Vatican-sponsored Illyrian movement and whose strategic imagination may have been captured by the idea of Slavic unity,[10] which had already been set forth in 1601 by an Italian priest, Mauro Orbini, in his *Il regno degli Slavi, hoggi corrottamente detti Schiavoni:* the first over-all history of the Slavic peoples ever written.[11] The official recognition of the Romanov dynasty by the Holy Roman Empire in 1654 cleared the way for the resumption of close ties with Russia and the dispatching of embassies which regularly included Catholic clergy.

Special interest in Russia was also shown by the Sacred Congregation for the Propagation of the Faith, which was founded in 1622 largely to open lines of communication with Eastern Christians. The Congregation was a useful vehicle for Catholic activities inside Russia, because it was not identified with Polish expansion, as was the Society of Jesus. However, the Congregation also lacked the Jesuits' semi-military structure and could not exercise binding authority over those who went to Russia in its name. Ligarides, for instance, was educated by, and loosely affiliated with, the Congregation, but soon discarded his allegiance as he began to carve out a career for himself in the Orthodox world.[12] Krizhanich, however, appears to have remained a dedicated Catholic throughout his much longer stay in Russia. Because of the incomplete records surviving, the extent of his proselytizing activities in Russia cannot be determined. But it is clear that he became a librarian and cataloguer within the Kremlin shortly after his second arrival and refused to collaborate in the formation of the new state church. Probably for this reason, he was sent early in 1661 to distant Tobol'sk, in Siberia, where he remained until after Alexis' death. During this exile Krizhanich wrote some of the most perceptive and profound essays in pre-Petrine Russia, returning to Moscow only in 1677 in an unsuccessful bid to gain the support of the new tsar.

Of his many works on different subjects—all written in a strange mélange of Croatian, Latin, and Russian—much the most interesting is his "Political Thoughts," or "Conversations on Power," an argument for absolute monarchy based largely on classical and Renaissance authorities.[13] Even though Krizhanich is the first writer in Russia to quote extensively from Machiavelli, his argument is essentially moralistic. The monarch derives his authority from God, who has decreed objective natural laws for all the world. The Russian people, who are still superstitious and lacking in moderation, are in particular need of a strong monarchy. All of Eastern Europe is, in turn, dependent on Russian leadership. The Ukraine should cease its political intrigues and subordinate itself to Russia. The Russian monarch must not permit his authority to be diluted either by a Polish type of aristocratic diet or by the German merchants who cover the land "like a swarm of locusts devouring all the fruit of the earth."[14] Russia has unique advantages for effective absolute rule because neither of the two classic sources of palace intrigue (women and traditional noblemen) are of any real importance in Muscovy.

To realize its destiny, however, Russia had to rid itself of many of its myths, and of its subservience to the Greeks in theology and the Germans in practical affairs. The idea that Kievan Russia was dependent on Varangian princes for political order was rejected by Krizhanich more than a century before native Russian historians began to question the predominant role of the Normans in early Russian history. Krizhanich also rejected the mythical descent of Russian imperial authority from Prus and the anti-Catholic idea of a Third Rome. Krizhanich's political recommendations were embellished with detailed commentaries on the language, history, economy, and geography of Russia. The cumulative effect of his prolific writings was to suggest that a great destiny lay before the Russian nation. To realize it, however, Russia would have to unify the oppressed Slavs, accept Roman Catholicism, and be the bearer of its mission to heathen lands east and south.

Krizhanich anticipated a number of different movements in modern Russian thought. He was one of the first to appeal on moralistic grounds for enlightened despotism as the best means of civilizing Eastern Europe. Indeed, it is interesting to note that the status and intellectual influence of Catholic priests in Russia was at its highest precisely during those periods when reforming despots were on the throne: Peter I, Catherine II, and Alexander I. Even Krizhanich, despite his exile, was not nearly so badly treated under Alexis as most other religious dissenters. Technically, he was not even under compulsion, having been officially sent on "government business." He was given a pension and freedom to write, and devoted much of his time to tasks that might conceivably have been assigned him by the central government: the gathering of historical and geographic material on Siberia and the refutation of the schismatics.

Krizhanich is most important, however, as the forerunner of two widely contrasting currents of thought that would reappear in nineteenth-century Russia with far greater strength: Catholic proselytism and militant Pan-Slavism. The fate which eventually met Krizhanich after his last sad departure from Russia was one worthy of veneration by either movement —and suitably heroic for the romantic temperament of the nineteenth century. Krizhanich remained in the Slavic East, drifting about Poland, taking monastic vows, and finally dying outside Vienna in 1683 with the army of Jan Sobieski as it turned back the last great Turkish assault on European Christendom.

If the visionaries of the Counter Reformation were to be rejected in late-seventeenth-century Russia, extreme prophets of the Reformation were to fare no better. Just as Krizhanich sought to have Russia revitalize for Europe the strategic hopes of a revived Catholicism, so Quirinus Kuhlmann sought to realize through "the unknown people of the north" the fading messianic expectations of the radical Reformation.

Kuhlmann was born in Silesia, the heartland of European mysticism which lies along the ill-defined border between the Slavic and German worlds. His mother was Polish, his father German; the city in which he was brought up bears the dual names of Wrocław and Breslau; and his own strange life was equally divided between East and West.

He was less interested in his formal studies at Breslau and Jena than in a personal quest for religious understanding. He set forth his ideas in mystical poems with that "alchemy of speech" based on hypnotic repetition which was so characteristic of the German baroque. Coming from a part of Europe particularly devastated by the Thirty Years' War, he sought to further a "cooling down" of passions, considering his own name an indication of divine selection for this *Verkühlung*. He wrote a "cooling psalter" (*Kühlpsalter*) and was briefly associated with a literary-patriotic fraternal order, "The Fruit-bearing Society," in which each member took a new name from the vegetable kingdom and swore to defend the florid peculiarities of German vernacular culture.[15]

Kuhlmann soon drifted to Amsterdam, where he became fascinated by the theosophical treatises of an earlier Silesian mystic, Jacob Boehme. Standing at the end of the Reformation, Boehme had rehabilitated the ancient Gnostic belief that esoteric inner secrets of the universe could be discovered both within and beyond the traditional source of revelation for older Protestantism: the Holy Bible. Boehme's gnosticism was particularly appealing to those who shared both the religious concerns of the age and the new taste for intellectual speculation freed from traditional authority. There was, after all, no higher goal for the mind to aspire to than "the wisdom of God"—the literal meaning of the word "theosophy," which Boehme used to describe his system of truth.

Boehme's speculations had been used by his followers as the basis for prophetic predictions about the coming of a new order. Just as man was to recapture the lost perfection of Adam before the fall, so was the whole world on the eve of a new millennium, according to many prophetic Protestants in the mid-seventeenth century. Jan Comenius, the brilliant educator and long-suffering leader of Czech Protestantism, had died in Amsterdam in 1671, predicting that the millennium would come in 1672. In his last great work, *Lux e Tenebris,* Comenius gathered together the writings of a number of recently martyred East European Protestants and spoke in a Manichean manner of the coming struggle of light and darkness. Kuhlmann was much influenced by this work, which was published and widely discussed in Amsterdam (and perhaps also by Jewish Sabbataianism, which claimed Amsterdam as one of its centers). In his treatise of 1674, *Boehme Resurrected*, Kuhlmann announces his own expectation that the thousand-year reign of righteousness is about to begin on earth:

> Jesus Christ, the King of all Kings and Lord of all Lords is coming with his Lily and Rose to bring back Adam's forgotten life of paradise on Earth.[16]

Kuhlmann sought to recruit various rulers of Europe as leaders of the righteous remnant, instruments of the New Jerusalem. His preaching took him progressively farther East: to Lübeck and Rostock on the Baltic in the mid-seventies, to Constantinople and the court of the Sultan in the late seventies. By the 1680's he had become a political extremist, urging the rulers of Europe to abdicate from power in preparation for the coming "Jesuelite" kingdom, implying at times that they should hand over power during the interim to the custody of the inspired prophet himself. Kuhlmann provided his own devotional literature of mystical songs and hymns. In his *Kühlpsalter* the word "triumph" occurs several hundred times. His works circulated together with those of Boehme throughout the Baltic region and became known among German merchants as far afield as Archangel and Moscow. Sympathizers among the foreign colony in Moscow urged Kuhlmann to come to discover for himself the spiritual potential of this new land, and when Kuhlmann arrived in Moscow by way of Riga and Pskov in April, 1689, there was already a nucleus of sympathizers quick to respond to his preachings.

The purpose of Kuhlmann's visit was to prepare Russia for transformation into the apocalyptical fifth monarchy: the place on earth where Christ would come again and launch a thousand-year reign on earth together with his chosen saints. Before leaving England for Moscow, Kuhlmann had set forth such a program in a collection of writings addressed jointly to the young Peter the Great and his ill-fated co-ruler, Ivan V. It was similar to appeals that he had unsuccessfully addressed to the rulers of France, Sweden, and Brandenburg Prussia, and reflected an attempt to carry over to the continent the ideas he had picked up from yet another prophetic group: the rejected "Fifth Monarchy men" of the English Revolution.

Kuhlmann quickly established a following within the German suburb of Moscow. He appears also to have won supporters at the imperial court and to have written a memorandum for his Russian followers.[17] He taught that the Jesuits had taken over the world and that Lutheranism had betrayed the true Reformation, which was provided by the teaching of Boehme and the witness of the persecuted East European Protestants whom Comenius had praised. Such views frightened the leading Lutheran pastor of the German community, who pleaded for help from the Tsar in silencing this disruptive prophet. Translators in the Russian foreign office advised that his teachings were, indeed, "similar to those of the schismatics."[18] Probably fearing that he might gain influence over the impressionable young Tsar Peter, who was an habitué of the German quarter, Sophia designated Kuhlmann and his followers as bearers of "schism, heresy, and false prophecy." In October, 1689, just six months after his arrival, Kuhlmann was burned in a specially built thatched hut in Red Square together with his writings and his principal local collaborator. The English mercenary colonel in the Tsar's service, whose family had sponsored Kuhlmann's trip to Moscow, was placed in prison, where he committed suicide. Orders were distributed to provincial *voevodas* for the suppression of his ideas and destruction of his writings.[19]

Like the Catholic Krizhanich, this lonely Protestant prophet had little direct impact on the Russian scene. Russia in the late seventeenth century was in the process of rejecting all purely religious answers to its problems.[20] The West to which Russia had turned was not moving from one religion to another but from all religions to none at all. This was the time of the "crisis of the European consciousness," when faith suddenly became nominal and scepticism fashionable.[21] Russia was deeply affected. Grecophiles and Latinizers within the Orthodox Church were rejected as decisively as theocrats and fundamentalists had been earlier; and Russia refused to accept either a purely Catholic or radical Protestant solution to its problems. Thus, from one point of view Krizhanich and Kuhlmann represent two final, foredoomed efforts to provide a religious solution for Russia. From another point of view, however, they represent early examples of an important future phenomenon: the Western prophet who looks to Russia for the realization of ideas not given a proper hearing in the West. Though unreceptive to such prophets in the late seventeenth century, the rulers of Russia were to lend increasingly sympathetic ears to prophetic voices from the West: Peter the Great to Leibniz, Catherine the Great to Diderot, Alexander I to De Maistre. But these were a new breed of prophets; and they brought their messages not to the chaotic religiosity of a city on the upper Volga but to the geometric new secular capital on the Baltic. It was not to Moscow but to St. Petersburg that the new Western prophets were to bring their ideas.

The Sectarian Tradition

MORE THAN KRIZHANICH—or any other foreign religious voice in seventeenth-century Russia—Kuhlmann was a harbinger of things to come in Russia. For the rejected radical Protestantism of Central Europe was to find roots in eighteenth-century Russia second in importance only to those it found in America.

Kuhlmann was, of course, only one of many prophetic influences that helped launch the vigorous Russian sectarian tradition. There is no firm evidence for the contention that Kuhlmann's teachings provided the original doctrine for either of the two sects that he is sometimes alleged to have founded: the *khlysty,* or "flagellants" (the sect that first appeared in the late seventeenth century) or the *Dukhobortsy* (the "spirit wrestlers" who date from the eighteenth century). But the teachings of these and other Russian sects bear greater over-all similarities to the teaching of Boehme, Kuhlmann, and other sectarian Protestant extremists than to that of the Russian schismatics with whom they are often loosely identified.[22]

In practice, of course, sectarians (*sektanty*) and schismatics (*raskol'-niki*) were equally persecuted and equally fractious forms of religious dissent. They often merged or interacted with one another (and at times also with Jewish and even Oriental religious traditions). Moreover, Russian sectarians generally shared with schismatics a hatred of bureaucrats and "Jesuits" as well as a general expectation that providential changes in history were about to take place. Nonetheless, the two traditions are fundamentally different. For the sectarians represent totally new religious confessions rather than attempts to defend an older interpretation of Orthodoxy. This distinction separated the heirs of Kuhlmann from the heirs of Avvakum in two important ways. First, the sectarians built their devotional life around an extra-ecclesiastical calisthenic of self-perfection and inner illumination. Russian sectarians disregarded church ritual—old or new—and paid little attention to the celebration of sacraments in any form—or even to the building of churches.

A second difference between schismatics and sectarians lay in the contrasting nature of their historical expectations. Although both traditions were prophetic, the schismatics were basically pessimists, and the sectarians optimists. The followers of Avvakum dwelled on the coming reign of Antichrist and the need to prepare for judgment. They believed that earthly corruption had gone so far that God's final, wrathful judgment was all that could be expected from history. The followers of Kuhlmann, on the other hand, generally believed that the promised thousand-year reign of right-eousness on earth was about to begin. However sectarians differed as to the nature and location of this millennium, these self-proclaimed "men of God" generally believed that they could help bring it about.

> The Old Believers believed that heaven had moved irretrievably be-yond reach; the men of God, on the contrary, believed themselves ca-pable of bringing heaven back within man's reach.[23]

The sectarians were in many ways modern religious thinkers, begin-ning with the assumption that man was essentially an isolated being, sepa-rated from God in an unfriendly universe. The aim was to recapture lost links with God by uniting oneself with divine wisdom. Following the pan-theistic tendencies of Central European mysticism, they saw all of creation as an expression of divine wisdom, for which Boehme used the hallowed Greek word "sophia," giving to it for Russian mystical and sectarian thought a different meaning from what it had traditionally possessed in Eastern Orthodoxy. "Sophia" was understood as a physical—sometimes even sex-ual—force as well as a merely intellectual form of "divine wisdom." New paths to salvation were provided by a host of sectarian writers, some em-phasizing the physical and ecstatic, some the rationalistic and moralistic, path to God. Occult and kabbalistic tracts were translated, revised, and plagiarized by a series of religious popularizers. Boehme's claim to have unraveled the "great mystery" of creation and read the divine "signature of things" inspired other prophets—as it had Kuhlmann—to draw up their own "new revelation" or "key to the universe."[24]

Each sect tended to regard the teachings of its particular prophet as the revealed word of God, which was meant to supplement if not supplant all previous tradition and scripture. The emphasis on simplifying ritual and introducing new beliefs gave sectarianism many points of contact with the emerging secular culture of the new aristocracy. In contrast, the schismatics remained suspicious of, and isolated from, this new and Westernized world. Only when the aristocratic dominance of Russian culture came to an end in the mid-nineteenth century did the schismatics become an important force in the main stream of Russian culture.

The Russian sectarian tradition can be traced not only to the proph-ecies of Kuhlmann but also to transplanted White Russian Protestants who filtered into Muscovy in the late seventeenth century: the persecuted sur-vivors of a once-rich Polish Protestant tradition. Typical of these was the gifted Jan Belobodsky, against whom Medvedev wrote his doctrinal trea-tises. Belobodsky was formally converted to Orthodoxy apparently to qualify as a diplomat and official translator in Moscow. His main interest, however, lay in converting the new academy in Moscow into a kind of *revanchist* theological bastion for the struggle with the Jesuits: the "Pelagians" of the modern world.[25] The Jesuits offended Belobodsky's Calvinism by placing too much emphasis on what man can accomplish through his own works and on the saving power of the sacraments and too little on God's awesome remoteness. Although Belobodsky was soon condemned for heresy, his anti-traditional approach became fashionable in Petrine Russia, where even native Russians were found substituting a placard of the first two commandments for the traditional icon in the reception hall.[26]

Under Peter one finds the first mention of a new Russian sect: a curious group who called themselves "God's people" (*Bozhie liudi*). Their more familiar name, "flagellants" (*khlysty*), points to the ecstatic, Eastern strain that was incorporated into Russian sectarianism.[27]

The first documentary reference to this sect occurred in 1716, at the time of its founder Ivan Suslov's death; but it allegedly originated in the weird proclamation of a runaway soldier, Daniel Filippov, on a hillside near Viazma in 1645. Daniel claimed that he was God Sabaoth himself, come to give men twelve commandments in place of the ten originally given on Mount Sinai. He spent the disturbed early years of Alexis' reign prophetically exhorting Russians to leave the existing church in order to live as "God's people," throwing all books of secular learning into the Volga, and abstaining from alcohol, honey, and sexual relations. In 1649 Daniel apparently declared that Suslov (a peasant formerly bonded to the Westernized Naryshkin family, from which Peter the Great was descended) was his son, and thus a Son of God. Suslov's followers referred to Jesus as "the old Christ" and Suslov as the new. As he moved from Nizhny Novgorod to Moscow and thence (apparently in 1658) to prison, fanciful pseudo-Christian legends were attached to his name. The building in Moscow where his followers met was said to be "the House of God" or the "New Jerusalem." Suslov was said to have been born of a barren 100-year-old woman, crucified in the Kremlin (with Patriarch Nikon as Caiaphas and the author of the law code of 1649 as Pontius Pilate), and then resurrected from a tomb which was watched over by a faithful group of virgins dressed in white.

Actually, Suslov appears to have lived on in Moscow until his death at the age of nearly 100, and the Suslov legend may well have been embellished by the new "Christs" that succeeded him.[28] The first of these was a former leader of the *streltsy,* who entered a monastery and began systematically recruiting harassed monks for the new sect in the early eighteenth century.[29] His wife also entered a convent and began winning over feminine followers. The growing strength of the sect led to a heresy trial of seventy-eight in 1733, the exhumation and complete destruction of all remains of the two "Christs" in 1739, and a further trial involving 416 of "God's people" that lasted from 1745 to 1752. But the sect flourished under conditions of increased publicity and martyrdom. New "Christs" began appearing in various sections of Russia, often accompanied by twelve apostles and by feminine "angels" who were in turn headed by a prophetess known as the "Mother of God."

The forms of devotion practiced by "God's people" link them with the classic dualistic heresies of Christendom with their demands for self-mortification and their claim to constitute a secret elect. "God's people" met not in a church but in a secret meeting place usually known as "Jerusalem" or "Mt. Zion." They conducted not a service but a "rejoicing" (*radenie*) or "spiritual bath." They comprised not a congregation but a "boat," and were led not by a consecrated priest but by a "pilot" for the voyage from the material to the spiritual world—into the seventh heaven where men could in fact become gods. The means of ascent lay partly in the "alchemy of speech"—spiritual songs were sung and incantations uttered in semi-hypnotic repetition, such as "Oh Spirit, Oh God, Tsar God, Tsar Spirit." Soon, however, rhythmic physical exercises began; and the one most certain to produce spiritual ecstasy, a sense of liberation from the material world, was the "circle procession." As the pace of circular motion increased, these whirling dervishes of Russian Christendom began their process of mutual- and self-flagellation accompanied by the rhythmic incantation: *"Khlyshchu, khlyshchu, Khrista ishchu"* (I flagellate, flagellate, seeking Christ).[30]

If the flagellants represent the frenzied aspect of Russian sectarianism, the second important sect to arise, that of the "spirit wrestlers," illustrates a more moralistic, Western element. Characteristically, this sect arose as a reform movement among "God's people" rather than as a completely separate movement. The sectarians, like the schismatics, split up into many subgroups, but all sectarians shared key characteristics derived from the first sect, just as all schismatics derived their main characteristics from the original, fundamentalist martyrs.

The spirit wrestlers first appeared in the 1730's or 1740's in the region of Tambov. They accepted the flagellant idea of the need to combat earthly things while seeking the world of spirit; and they produced as many "Christs" for leaders as had their forebear. But the new sect appears to have been largely founded by military personnel seeking refuge from tsarist service. Their main interest was in finding a faith more simple than that of the alien Orthodox Church and in securing relative freedom from the authority of the state-controlled hierarchy. Within their own communities they became increasingly concerned with moral questions—leading a highly puritanical, communal life that minimized prophetic revivalism in favor of homely readings from their "revealed" book: *The Living Life*.[31]

Only a little later than the "spirit wrestlers" a similar sect arose in the Tambov region: the "milk drinkers" (*molokane*). The spirit wrestlers received their name from a Church official who had meant to imply that they were fighting with the Holy Spirit; and they accepted it as an indication of their intention to combat matter with spirit. The milk drinkers had been so named because of their practice of continuing to drink milk during the Lenten fast, but they too accepted the name, insisting that it meant they were already drinking the milk of paradise, or dwelling by milky waters. They insisted more than any of the other sects on equality of wealth, and their efforts to produce a simplified, syncretic religion led them to incorporate certain Jewish practices into their essentially Christian forms of worship. One of the most interesting of the many splits that developed within the sectarian movement is the one that occurred between the "Saturday" and "Sunday" milk drinkers.[32] The very fact that Jewish elements participated in the life of the sects provides testimony to the fact that the sectarian communities tended to be cosmopolitan in composition. Unlike the Great Russian schismatics, the sectarians tended to welcome all comers as "brothers" (the usual term for member) in a common effort to attain the true spiritual life. The growing number of foreign settlers—particularly Germans and Central Europeans with Mennonite and Anabaptist backgrounds who began streaming into southern Russia after it was opened to foreign colonization in 1762—reinforced the trend toward austere egalitarianism. But this was already implied in Kuhlmann's teaching that in the coming millennium "there will be no Tsars, kings, princes, but all will be equal, all things will be communal, and no one will call anything his own. . . ."[33]

In addition to this tendency toward communal and egalitarian living, Russian sectarians shared a common belief that man was capable of attaining direct links (if not actual identity) with God outside all established churches. Behind all the sects stands the symbol which Kuhlmann (following Boehme) had used as the frontispiece for his new book of spiritual psalms: the figure of a cross melded into a latticework leading men up through the symbolic lily and rose to a new heaven and a new earth.

For each new sect, the ascent to higher truth lay in fleeing the material world outside for the spiritual world within. In place of the old liturgy and ritual, the sectarians worshipped with "spiritual songs," which became a rich and many-sided form of popular verse. The word "spirit" (*dukh*) itself was to be found in the name or credo of each of the early sects. The flagellants considered the most important of their new commandments to be "Believe in the Holy Spirit," and intoned their prayers and incantations to "Tsar spirit." The spirit wrestlers carried the dualistic denial of the material world even farther than the flagellants, viewing all of world history as a struggle between the flesh-bound sons of Cain and the "fighters for the spirit" who were descended from Abel. The name the milk drinkers gave themselves was "spiritual Christians."

As with other dualists, there was a kind of totalitarian fanaticism about the sectarians. In rejecting the "tyranny" of the established churches for the "freedom" of spiritual Christianity, the sectarians tended to set up even more rigorous tyrannies of their own. Contending that earthly perfection was possible within their community led them to assume that such perfection was possible only within their community. New forms of "higher" baptism and new sources of infallible truth were introduced; and the quest for perfection often drove them on to acts of self-mortification. It is characteristic that the popular names assigned to all the major sects of the eighteenth century designated some action which was thought to expedite their flight from the material to the spiritual world: flagellation, wrestling, drinking, and finally—in the last and most eerie of all the eighteenth-century sects—self-castration.

As time went on and Russian sectarianism became influenced by pietistic sectarians from the West, the masochistic and dualistic qualities of the tradition tended to be less dominant. Nonetheless, sectarianism kept alive its pretensions at offering a utopian, communal alternative to the official Church; and it played an increasingly important role in the depressed agrarian regions of southern and western Russia. Sectarianism exercised considerable influence as well on the intellectual community. Its greatest periods of subsequent growth at the grass roots level coincided with the periods of increased political ferment and ideological Westernization at the intellectual level: under Catherine, Alexander I, during the sixties and nineties of the nineteenth century—and perhaps even the fifties and sixties of the twentieth.

Thus, contact with the West brought sectarian Protestant ideas into Russia along with secular rationalism. The centers of this strange sectarian tradition were the relatively new, western cities of Russia: St. Petersburg and the cities that had arisen on the southern plain of Russia during the Tatar and Ottoman recession: Voronezh, Kharkov, Ekaterinoslav, and Tambov. This latter city played such an extraordinary role in producing prophetic sectarians that it was often popularly called *Tambog* ("God is there").[34] It seems darkly fitting that Tambov should prove a center of utopian anarchism during the Civil War, one of the last to capitulate to

Bolshevik rule, and the one to which anxious Soviet academicians flocked in the late 1950's seeking to discover why sectarian sentiment continued to exist after forty years of atheistic rule.[35] Perhaps it is also appropriate that the leading defender of an ascetic and utopian reading of Communist doctrine amidst the waning of ideological fervor in post-Stalinist Russia was Michael Suslov, who was brought up in a family of religious dissenters and bore the name of the founder of Russian sectarianism.

The New World of St. Petersburg

THE EIGHTEENTH CENTURY was greeted in Moscow with parades, festivities, and bonfires that lasted for an entire week. Like almost everything else in the official culture of the century to follow, these activities were ordered from above for reasons of state. Author of the decree—and of the change in New Year's Day from September to January—was, of course, Peter the Great, who has remained in the eyes of historians as towering a figure as his six feet eight inches rendered him to contemporaries. Having finished his tour of Western Europe and crushed the unruly *streltsy*, Peter was to turn in the first quarter of the new century to the administrative reforms and military campaigns that were to consolidate the position of Russia as a great and indisputably European power. In 1700 he took the first decisive step: he decreed that beards should henceforth be shaved off and short, German style of coats worn for "the glory and beauty of the government."[36]

Yet the suddenness of such reforms and the ruthlessness of their enforcement generated a passionate reaction. From many directions men rose up to defend the greater "glory and beauty" of the old ways. In the same year, 1700, an educated Muscovite publicly proclaimed that Peter was in fact the Antichrist, and a violent Cossack uprising on the lower Volga had to be crushed by long and bloody fighting.[37] Such protest movements continued to plague the "new" Russia and to influence its cultural development. A history of that culture must, therefore, include not only the relatively familiar tale of Peter's modernizing reforms but also the counterattack launched by Old Muscovy.

The soldiers of the new order, Peter's glittering new guards regiments, were, after the total destruction of the *streltsy*, opposed only by a disorganized guerrilla band of Muscovite loyalists. The guards regiments had all the weapons of a modern, centralized state at their command, but the guerrilla warriors had the advantage of vast terrain, ideological passion, and grass roots support. Although the ultimate victory of the new order was perhaps inevitable, the defenders of the old were able to wage a more protracted and crippling warfare against modernization than in most other European countries. Within the amorphous army of those opposed to the Petrine solution were three groups of particular importance for the subsequent development of Russian culture: merchant Old Believers, peasant insurrectionaries, and monastic ascetics. Even in defeat these voices of Old Muscovy were able to force the new state to adopt many of their ideas as it sought to extend and deepen its authority.

Before looking at the counterattack of Moscow, however, one must consider the new legions which Peter called into being and their new cultural citadel, St. Petersburg. This city was the most impressive creation of his turbulent reign: the third and last of Russia's great historic cities and an abiding symbol of its new Westernized culture.

In 1703 Peter began building this new city at the point where the Neva River disgorges the muddy water of Lake Ladoga out through swamps and islands into the eastern Baltic. The way had been cleared for Russian activity in the area by the capture in 1702 of the Swedish fortress city of Noteborg at the other end of the Neva. This was the first turning of the tide of military fortune from Sweden to Russia in northeast Europe, and the vanquished city was appropriately renamed Schlüsselburg: "key city." The key made possible the opening of what an Italian visitor soon called Russia's "window to Europe."[38] In February, 1704, the first of a long line of foreign architects arrived to direct all construction on the new site—assuring thereby that the "window" would be European in style as well as in the direction it faced. Within a decade, St. Petersburg was a city of nearly 35,000 buildings and the capital of all Russia—though it was not fully recognized as such until the Empress Anna permanently transferred her residence from Moscow to St. Petersburg in 1732 and a fire gutted Moscow five years later.

Almost no buildings have survived from the original city, whose bleak appearance bore little resemblance to the elegant city of later periods. The utilitarian structure of early Petersburg reflects the taste and preoccupations of its founder. Originally known by the Dutch name of Sankt Piter Bourkh (the abbreviation Piter remaining a familiar term for the city), St. Petersburg was conceived as a kind of Dutch-style naval base and trading center. In partial imitation of Amsterdam, the new city was systematically laid out along canals and islands. The pattern of construction was geometric and the pace rapid. The human cost of building in such a damp, cold climate was probably greater than that involved in building any other major city of Europe. Even more illustrative of Peter's military preoccupations was a

second city founded in 1703 and bearing his name: Petrozavodsk, or
"Peter's factory." Built to provide an arms manufacturing center near the
metal resources of the north, this distant city on Lake Onega was thrust
into an even more cold and inhuman location than Petersburg.

Military expediency and *raison d'état* were the abiding considerations
of Peter. The practical-minded, shipbuilding countries of the Protestant
North were the source of most of his reformatorial ideas and techniques.
Sweden (and to a lesser extent Prussia) provided him with quasi-military
administrative ideas: a utilitarian "table of ranks" requiring state service on
a systematic basis and a new synodal pattern of church administration subject to state control. Holland provided him with the models (and much of
the nautical terminology) for the new Russian navy. Saxony and the Baltic
German provinces provided most of the teachers for his military training
schools and the staff for the new academy of sciences that was set up immediately after his death.[39] His efforts to advance Russian learning were almost completely concentrated on scientific, technical, or linguistic matters
of direct military or diplomatic value. "To Peter's mind, 'education' and
'vocational training' seem to have been synonymous concepts."[40]

This practical, technological emphasis is evidenced in the first periodical and the first secular book in Russian history—both of which appeared
in 1703, the year of the founding of St. Petersburg. The printed journal,
Vedomosti, was largely devoted to technical and order-of-battle information.
The book, Leonty Magnitsky's *Arithmetic,* was more a general handbook of
useful knowledge than a systematic arithmetic.[41] Though often labeled the
first scientific publication in Russian history, the term "science" (*nauka*),
as used in its subtitle, carries the established seventeenth-century Russian
meaning of "skilled technique" rather than the more general European
meaning of theoretical knowledge.[42] Far more general and abstract than
Peter's "science" was the lexicon of political and philosophical terms that
Peter took over from the Poles. This process of borrowing also continued a
seventeenth-century Russian trend, whereby new labels were adopted
piecemeal as the practical need for them arose.[43]

Thus, although Peter met and corresponded with the doctors of the
Sorbonne while in Paris, and made the first purchase while in Holland for
what was to become a magnificent imperial Rembrandt collection,[44] his
reign was not one of philosophic or artistic culture. Indeed, from this point
of view, Peter's reign was in many ways a regression from that of Alexis or
even Sophia. There was no painting equal to that of Ushakov, no poetry
equal to that of Polotsky, no historical writing equal to that of Gizel. The
perfunctory dramatic efforts of Peter's reign represent an aesthetic decline
from those of Alexis'; and even the theological disputes between Yavorsky

and Prokopovich came as an anticlimax after the intense controversies that had raged about Nikon, Medvedev, and Kuhlmann.

Peter's celebrated new departures in statecraft also moved along lines laid out by his predecessors. The drive to the Baltic was anticipated by Ivan III's establishment of Ivangorod, Ivan IV's attempt to capture Livonia, and Alexis's attempt to capture Riga and build a Baltic fleet. His reliance on Northern European ideas, technicians, and mercenaries continued a trend begun by Ivan IV and expanded by Michael. His ruthless expansion of state control over traditional ecclesiastical and feudal interests was in the spirit of Ivan and Alexis, and his secret chancellery in the spirit of their *oprichnina* and *prikaz* of secret affairs, respectively. His program of modernization and reform was anticipated in almost all its major respects by the long series of seventeenth-century proposals for Westernization, extending from Boris Godunov and the False Dmitry to Ordyn-Nashchokin and Golitsyn.

But if Peter's reign represents the culmination of processes long at work, it was nonetheless new in spirit and far-reaching in consequences. For Peter sought not just to make use of Western personnel and ideas but to be made over by them. A century before Peter's important victory over the Swedes, Skopin-Shuisky had begun the process of adopting Western military techniques to defeat a Western rival. Alexis' decisive victory over the Poles had removed a far greater potential threat to Russian dominance of Eastern Europe than Sweden. But all of these earlier victories were won in the name of a religious civilization; Peter's victories were won in the name of a sovereign secular state. Peter was the first Russian ruler to go abroad, to meet foreigners as an apprentice seeking to learn from them. He formally called himself not "tsar" but "emperor"; and insofar as he provided any ideological justification for his relentless statecraft of expediency, he spoke of the "universal national service," the "fortress of justice," or the "common good." He used "interests of the state" almost synonymously with "utility of the sovereign."[45] The official court *apologia* for Peter's rule, *The Justice of the Monarch's Will,* echoed the pessimistic, secular arguments of Hobbes about the practical need of a debased humanity for absolute monarchy. Its author, Feofan Prokopovich, was the first in a long line of Russian churchmen willing to serve as "an ideologist of state power using Christianity as its instrument."[46]

In plays and sermons Prokopovich exalted the glories of the people whom he designated by the new term *Rossianin,* "imperial Russian." Russian self-confidence was strengthened by Peter's defeat of the Swedes, whom Prokopovich called "our great and terrible foe . . . the strongest warriors among the German peoples and, until now, the terror of all the others."[47] The new secular nationalism was, however, more limited in its ambitions than the religious nationalism of the Muscovite era. Peter, no less than other European monarchs of the early eighteenth century, spoke of "proportion" and the need to "maintain a balance in Europe."[48]

His courtiers adopted not only the manners and terminology of the Polish aristocracy but also the self-gratifying feeling of being culturally superior "Europeans." Court poets began to speak patronizingly of other "uncivilized" peoples in much the same manner that Western Europeans had written about pre-Petrine Russia.

> America is wilfully rapacious,
> Her people savage in morals and rule . . .
> Knowing no God, evil in thought
> No one can accomplish anything
> Where such stupidity, vileness and sin prevail.[49]

If one uses the essentially organic term *perelom* ("rupture") to describe the changes under Alexis, one may use the more mechanistic term *perevorot* ("turnabout of direction") to describe those of Peter.[50] Political expediency based on impersonal calculation replaced a world where ideal ends and personal attachments had been all-important. The traditional orders of precedence under Alexis were far less binding and rigid than Peter's new hierarchical *Table of Ranks* but lacked the special new authority of the modern state. Moscow under Alexis had welcomed more, and more cultured, Western residents than St. Petersburg in the first half of the eighteenth century, but was not itself a living monument to Western order and technology. This new city was, for the pictorial imagination of Old Russia, the icon of a new world in which, as the corrector of books in the early years of Peter's reign put it,

> geometry has appeared,
> land surveying encompasses everything.
> Nothing on earth lies beyond measurement.[51]

There was a kind of forbidding impersonality about a world in which the often-used word for "soul" (*dusha*) was now regularly invoked to describe the individual in his function as the basic unit for taxation and conscription by the new service state; in which the traditional familiar form of address (*ty*) was rapidly being supplanted by the more formal and officially endorsed *vy*.

Nothing better indicates Peter's preoccupation with state problems and underlying secularism than his complex religious policy. He extended an unprecedented measure of toleration to Catholics (permitting at last the building of a Catholic Church inside Russia), but at the same time expressed approval of the stand taken by Galileo against the Church hierarchy and reorganized the Russian Church on primarily Protestant lines. Peter persecuted not only the fanatical Old Believers who sought to preserve the old forms of worship, but also those thoroughgoing freethinkers who sought more drastic and permissive ecclesiastical reforms. Peter curtailed and harassed the established Orthodox Church at home, but simultaneously supported its politically helpful activities in Poland.[52] He vaguely discussed the unification of all churches with German Protestants and French Catholics.[53] Yet the church he created was more than ever before the subordinate instrument of a particular national state. He recreated the state bureau for supervising monasteries, severely restricted the authority of the "idle" monastic estate, melted down their bells for cannon, and substituted a synod under state control for the independent patriarchate.

Yet Peter also built the last of the four major monastic complexes of Russia: the Alexander Nevsky Lavra in St. Petersburg. It was a practical necessity for his new capital to be linked—like Kiev and Moscow—with a great monastery; just as it was essential to stability to have an established church. Thus, Peter built his monastery, naming it for Alexander Nevsky, patron saint of St. Petersburg and the entire Neva region. The saint's remains were duly transferred from Vladimir for public exhibition, not in Moscow, but in Novgorod, and then floated down river and lake for final reburial in St. Petersburg, the new gateway to the West. The Tsar decreed that henceforth the saint was to be portrayed not as a monk but as a warrior, and that the saint's festival be held on July 30, the day of Peter's treaty with Sweden.[54] The architectural style of the monastery and the theology later taught in its seminary were to be in many ways more Western than Russian.

The beginnings of rationalistic, secular thought can be seen in the works of three native Russians of the Petrine era—each of whom approached intellectual problems from an earthy background of practical activity of the type encouraged by Peter.

The apothecary Dmitry Tveritinov was one of the many men with medical knowledge who were brought to Moscow prior to the foundation of the first Russian hospital in 1709. As a native Russian from nearby Tver, he was more trusted than foreign doctors and soon had many influential friends at court. His rationalistic and sceptical approach to miracles and relics appears to have been an outgrowth both of his scientific training and of his sympathy for Protestantism. Church leaders feared that he was connected with a like-minded group, known as "the new philosophers," within the Slavonic-Greek-Latin Academy in Moscow, and he was imprisoned and forced to recant in 1717.[55]

The manufacturer Ivan Pososhkov was one of a number of self-made men who arose from relatively humble origins to positions of influence during the reign of Peter. By accumulating land and developing state-supported economic enterprises (including a vodka-distilling plant), he acquired great wealth and considerable experience in trade and commerce. Amidst the general reformatorial atmosphere of the Petrine period, he felt encouraged to write in the early 1720's *On Poverty and Wealth,* the first original theoretical treatise on economics ever written by a Russian. He argued that economic prosperity was the key to national welfare rather than the actual wealth in possession of the monarch at any given time. Trade and commerce should be stimulated even more than agriculture. A rationalized rule of law and an expanded educational program are necessary for economic growth, and both the superstitions of the Old Believers and the Western love of luxury are to be avoided. Pososhkov's tract was evidently designed to appeal to Peter as a logical extension in the economic realm of his political reforms, just as Tveritinov's ideas were designed to represent such an extension in philosophy. But Pososhkov like Tveritinov never gained imperial favor for his ideas. He finished his book only in 1724, was imprisoned shortly after Peter's death the following year, and died in 1726.[56]

Tatishchev, the third of these Petrine harbingers of new secular thought patterns, lived longest and attained his greatest influence after Peter's death. He formed, together with Prokopovich and the learned poet-diplomat Antioch Kantemir, a group known as the "learned guard," which was in many ways the first in the long line of self-conscious intellectual circles devoted to the propagation of secular knowledge. Tatishchev's career illustrates particularly well how Peter's interest in war and technology led Russian thought half-unconsciously to broader cultural vistas.

Tatishchev was first of all a military officer—trained in Peter's new engineering and artillery schools and tested by almost continuous fighting during the last fifteen years of the Northern War. He spent the last, peaceful years of Peter's reign supervising work in the newly opened metallurgical industries of the Urals (later to become his major vocation) and journeying to Sweden to continue his engineering training at a higher level. The combination of geographic explorations in the East and archival explorations in the West turned this officer-engineer toward the study of history. In 1739 he presented to the Academy of Sciences the first fruit of a long and panoramic *History of Russia:* the first example of critical scientific history by a native Russian.

Tatishchev's history was not published until thirty years after it was written and twenty years after his death. Even then, it produced a remarkable effect, for it was still decades ahead of its time. Unlike the *Sinopsis* of Gizel, which remained the basic history of Russia throughout the early eighteenth century, Tatishchev's *History* was a scientific work, seeking to combine his knowledge of geographical and military problems with a critical, comparative examination of the manuscript sources. Its aim was, moreover, the frankly secular one of proving useful background reading for those engaged in war and statecraft. Not only was its framework free of the traditional preoccupation with sacred history and genealogy, but it was even free of a narrowly Russian focus, making an effort to include the history of the non-Russian peoples of the empire. It introduced a descriptive scheme of periodization, defended unrestricted autocracy as the only form of government suited to a country of Russia's size and complexity, and generally served as a model for many of the subsequent synthetic histories of Russia.[57]

There is a kind of continuity between the reign of Peter and that of the Empress Anna, the most important of his immediate successors. During her rule throughout the 1730's, the influence of Baltic Germans continued to predominate. Bartolomeo Rastrelli, the son of a metal forger and sculptor brought to Russia by Peter, built a new Winter Palace—the first permanent imperial residence in the new capital—but he devoted more of his talent to building a new palace for her favorite, Biron, miles to the west at Mitau (Jelgava) in Courland. St. Petersburg was still looked on as a kind of hardship post for mercenary officers. Court life in the new capital was marked by continued crudeness and vulgarity. Like Peter, Anna relied on dwarfs and freaks for entertainment and enjoyed mocking traditional ceremonies and court personalities. Probably the most remarkable new building of her reign was the great ice palace she built on the Neva during the severe winter of 1739–40. Eighty feet long and thirty-three feet high, the palace was equipped with furniture, clocks, and even chandeliers—all molded from ice. It was built largely as a mock gesture to an unfaithful courtier, who was forced to marry an old and ugly Kalmyk and spend his wedding night naked in the icy "bedroom" of the palace, with his "bride" the only conceivable source of warmth.[58]

Like Peter, Anna was suspicious of intellectual activity that had no practical value and might conceivably lead men to question the imperial authority. She conducted a personal vendetta against the most cultured Russian of the age, the new scion of the Westernized Golitsyn family, Dmitry. Even more than his first cousin once removed, Vasily, who had been exiled by Peter, Dmitry Golitsyn was a man of ranging cultural interests. As an ambassador to Constantinople and *voevoda* of Kiev from 1707–18, he had amassed a six-thousand-volume library and launched an extensive personal project for translating such Western political theorists as Grotius, Pufendorf, and John Locke. Under their influence, Golitsyn became, in effect, Russia's first secular political theorist. He was the first native Russian to popularize the familiar Western idea of objective natural law.[59] At the same time, Golitsyn became the spokesman for the new service nobility by drawing up the constitutional project of 1730 in an effort to limit autocratic authority by a council of the higher nobility. This project represented a genuine innovation rather than a traditionalist protest movement. The models were Swedish, and the objective was to extend the Petrine reforms further in the same Westward direction which the original reforms pointed.[60] The Senate, which Peter had created in 1711, was not basically a legislative or even a consultative body, but an executive organ of the emperor for transmitting his commands to the provinces and to the administrative colleges, which were created subordinate to it in 1717. Like Peter, Anna was inhospitable to any limitation on her power; and Golitsyn suffered an even crueler fate than had befallen Tveritinov and Pososhkov in the preceding decades. His library was taken, and he was imprisoned in the Schlüsselburg fortress. In 1737 he became the first in a long line of reformers to die within its walls.

Nonetheless, Anna was forced to concede a few new privileges to the service nobility. The founding in 1731 of a school for the Corps of Nobility accelerated the trend begun by Peter of providing a veneer of Western manners to his crude new ruling class. The name of the corps, *shliakhetsky korpus,* was derived from the Polish word for nobility, *szlachta,* and reveals the source of inspiration for this effort to civilize the ruling classes. But the teachers and the language of instruction were—as in the Academy of Sciences—primarily German. This school, like that founded for the Corps of Pages in 1759, provided the non-technical curriculum of an aristocratic finishing school.[61] Graduates of these schools (and of the somewhat more rigorous gymnasium of the Academy of Sciences) provided the nucleus of a Western-educated minority. A new secular culture slowly began to emerge under Anna as the first orchestra was assembled and the first opera was performed on Russian soil. Certain emphases of this new culture were already apparent by the end of her reign.

First of all this new world rejoiced in the discovery of the human body. The cutting off of the beard destroyed man's sense of community with the idealized likenesses of the icons. The introduction of secular portraiture, of heroic statuary, and of new, more suggestive styles of dress—all aided in the discovery of the human form. The beginnings of court ballet and of stylized imperial balls under Anna placed a premium on elegance of form and movement that had never been evident in Muscovy.

Gradually, the individual was being discovered as an earthly being with personal attributes, private interests, and responsibilities. The word *persona* was used to describe the new portraits which were painted of men in their actual, human state rather than in the spiritualized saintly manner of the icons. By the late seventeenth century, this word had begun to acquire the more general meaning of an important or strong individual. Even he who was not important enough to become a *persona* in his own right was now considered an individual "soul" by the all-powerful state, which began to exact taxes and services directly from the individual rather than from the region or household.

Prokopovich introduced the word "personal" (*personal'ny*) in its modern sense early in the eighteenth century; and the first precise terms for "private" and "particular" also entered the Russian language at this time. Words that are now used for "law" and "crime" had long existed in Slavic, but "they did not penetrate into the language of Russian jurisprudence with their modern meaning until the eighteenth century."[62]

There was also a new love of decorative effects, of embellishment for its own sake. The lavish ornamentation and illusionism of the European baroque quickly imposed itself on the new capital. Guided by the bold hand of Rastrelli, the first original style for Russian secular architecture emerged under Anna's successor: the so-called Elizabethan rococo. At Peterhof and in the rebuilding of Tsarskoe Selo and the Winter Palace, this style superimposed decorative effects drawn from Muscovite church architecture on the giant façades, theatrical interiors, and monumental staircases of the European baroque. A similar ornateness soon became evident in furniture, hair styles, and porcelain.

Finally, a cult of classical antiquity began to emerge on Russian soil. Taken over first from Poland and then from Italian and French visitors was the idea that classical forms of art and life might serve as a supplement (if not an alternative) to Christian forms. The belief subtly grew that classical antiquity could—unaided by Christian revelation—answer many of the pressing problems of life. The first work of classical antiquity translated into Russian in the eighteenth century was Aesop's Fables; and the first ensemble in the new medium of sculpture to be displayed in St. Petersburg was a series of statues by the older Rastrelli, illustrating the morals of these fables. The new poets and writers that emerged under Elizabeth's reign in the 1740's all used classical forms of exposition: odes, elegies, and tonic verse rather than the syllabic verse of the late seventeenth century. The new operas, plays, and ballets of the Elizabethan era were built around classical more often than scriptural subjects—in marked contrast to the theater of Alexis' time. Peter the Great had himself sculpted in the guise of a Roman emperor; and Latin became the scholarly language of the new Academy of Sciences.

This summoning up of classical images in a land so remote from the classical world points to the underlying unreality of early post-Petrine culture. The turquoise blue with which buildings were painted lent an unreal coloration to the great edifices of the new capital. The endless proliferation of three-dimensional decorative effects—artificial pilasters, statuary, and garden pavilions—reflects the general desire of baroque art to achieve mastery over its material and, in the last analysis, over nature itself.[63] This effort seemed particularly presumptuous and unreal for such an untutored people in such an inhospitable natural environment.

Perhaps there was an unconscious realization of this unreality in Elizabeth's almost compulsive fondness for masquerades. Things were not what they seemed to be in either the decor or the dances of the Elizabethan court. Cryptic maxims, fables, and acrostics had already established themselves at the Tsar's court;[64] and ever since 1735 there had been a special chair of allegory in the Academy of Sciences. Elizabeth's coronation in 1740 had been celebrated by two examples of allegorical ballet, her favorite form of theatrical entertainment. Increasingly during her reign, she sponsored not only masked balls of various sorts but a particular type known as a "metamorphosis," wherein men came disguised as women and vice versa. A laboratory for making artificial fireworks and a wooden "theatre of illuminations" jutting out into the Neva across from the Academy of Sciences were other forms of artifice initiated by Elizabeth. The greatest Russian scientist of the day, Michael Lomonosov, seems to have relished his assignment as official chronicler of these illuminations. He describes one in which a giant colossus looks toward the sea, holding up a torch and the initials of Elizabeth.

> Far o'er the restless sea its beam would pour
> And lead the periled vessels safe to shore . . .[65]

St. Petersburg, at the eastern extremity of the Baltic, was such a colossus, but it did not rest on firm foundations. It had been built over a swampy region which the Finns and Swedes had used only for forts and fisheries. It was constantly menaced by floods. Pushkin, Gogol, and other writers of the late imperial period were fascinated with the defiance of nature inherent in the creation of the new capital. The history of European culture in this city is rather like that of the extraordinary palm tree in a story by Vsevelod Garshin. Artificially transplanted from more sunlit southern regions to the greenhouse of a northern city, the plant restlessly seeks to bring the expansive freedom of its former habitat to all the docile native plants confined in the greenhouse. Its brilliant growth upward toward the elusive sun attracts the fascinated attention of all, but leads ultimately to a shattering of the enclosure and a killing exposure to the real climate of the surrounding region.[66]

By the end of Elizabeth's reign St. Petersburg had a population about equal to that of Moscow and a culture similar to that of the leading capitals of Europe. It was already

> . . . one of the strangest, loveliest, most terrible, and most dramatic of the world's great urban centers. The high northern latitude, the extreme slant of the sun's rays, the flatness of the terrain, the frequent breaking of the landscape by wide, shimmering expanses of water: all these combine to accent the horizontal at the expense of the vertical and to create every-where the sense of immense space, distance, and power. . . . Cleaving the city down the center, the cold waters of the Neva move silently and swiftly, like a slab of smooth grey metal . . . bringing with them the tang of the lonely wastes of forests and swamp from which they have emerged. At every hand one feels the proximity of the great wilderness of the Russian north—silent, somber, infinitely patient.[67]

The soaring and exotic motifs of Muscovite architecture had been rejected, and the only vertical uplift was provided by the Admiralty and the Peter and Paul Fortress, reminders of the military preoccupations of its founder. The setting was completed by the bleak seasons of the north: the dark winters, the long, damp springs, the "white nights" of June, with their poetic iridescence,

> and, finally, the brief, pathetic summers, suggestive rather than explicit . . . passionately cherished by the inhabitants for their very rareness and brevity.
>
> In such a city the attention of man is forced inward upon himself. . . . Human relationships attain a strange vividness and intensity, with a touch of premonition. . . .
>
> The city is, and always has been, a tragic city, artificially created . . . geographically misplaced, yet endowed with a haunting beauty, as though an ironic deity had meant to provide some redemption for all the cruelties and all the mistakes.[68]

Such was St. Petersburg, symbol of the new Russia and a city which was to dominate the quickening intellectual and administrative life of the empire. Yet the victory of St. Petersburg and of its new secular culture was not complete. The thought patterns of Old Muscovy continued to dominate the old capital and much of the Russian countryside. Indeed, its tradi-tionalist, religious culture made a number of powerful—if uncoordinated and ultimately unsuccessful—counterattacks against the culture of St. Petersburg. These protest movements commanded widespread popular followings and helped turn the ideological split between old and new into a deep social cleavage between popular and elite culture.

The Defense of Muscovy

ALREADY in Peter's lifetime two of the main forms of Muscovite protest reached a fever pitch of intensity: Old Believer communalism and Cossack-led peasant insurrectionism. Each of these movements first appeared under Alexis; but it was only under Peter that each became a distinct tradition with a broad social base and a deep ideology. The two movements often overlapped and reinforced one another—sharing as they did a common idealization of the Muscovite past and a hatred of the new secular bureaucracy. They did much to shape the character of all opposition movements under the Romanovs, not excepting those which brought about the end of the dynasty in 1917.

The Old Believers consolidated their hold over many Great Russians under Peter. The gathering strength of the amorphous Old Believer movement represented not so much increased support for their doctrinal position as resentment at the increased authority of foreigners in the new empire. The transition from Muscovite tsardom to multi-national empire was a particularly painful one for the Great Russian traditionalists. It involved the growth of a government bureaucracy dominated by more technically skilled Baltic Germans and the absorption from former Polish territories of better-educated Catholics and Jews. The confusions of war and social change gave a certain appeal to the simple Old Believer hypothesis that the reign of Antichrist was at hand, that Peter had been corrupted in foreign lands, and that the flood at the time of Peter's death was but a foretaste of God's wrathful judgment on this new world.

The Old Belief became particularly embedded in the psychology of the merchant classes, not only because of its fear of foreign competition, but also because of its special resentment of central bureaucracy. The Great Russian merchants, whose wealth had been amassed in the Russian north and protected by the traditional liberties of its cities, were hard hit by the new policies of increased central control. They tended to find solace in the Old Belief—identifying their own lost economic privileges with the idealized Christian civilization of Old Muscovy. They often preferred to move on to new areas rather than surrender old liberties or change old business practices. Gradually a pattern developed of internal colonization by disaffected Great Russians who practiced puritanical, communal living along with the old forms of worship. Belief in the coming end of the world was not abandoned in these new communities, but the expectation of judgment was increasingly invoked to provide a sense of urgency about the work of the new community rather than a sense of imminent apocalypse. Salvation was no longer to be found through the sacraments of the Church or the activities of the state after the reforms of Nikon and Peter respectively. One sought salvation now in the grim and isolated communities in which alone the organic religious civilization of the Muscovite past was preserved.

The parallel between the Calvinists of Western Europe and the Old Believers of the East is striking. Both movements were puritanical, replacing a sacramental church with a new, this-worldly asceticism; an established hierarchical authority with local communal rule. Both movements stimulated new economic enterprise with their bleak insistence on the need for hard work as the only means of demonstrating one's election by a wrathful God. Both movements played leading roles in colonizing previously unsettled lands. The Old Believer communities pushing on into Siberia were, like the pilgrims sailing to North America, driven on both by the persecution of established churches and by their own restless hope of finding some unspoiled region in which God's ever-imminent kingdom might come into earthly being.[69]

Perhaps the most extraordinary of these new communities were those that spread out along the frozen lakes and rivers of northern Russia. Inspired by the heroic resistance to central authority of the Solovetsk monastery,[70] these new communities continued their old communal business practices and traditional forms of worship in surroundings where the imperial authority was less likely to pursue them. The model community for the entire region was that which developed in the 1690's along the Vyg River between Lake Onega and the White Sea. By 1720 there were more than 1,500 Old Believers in this community, and a rich hagiographical and polemic literature was developing in the Old Muscovy style. An impoverished princely family of the Russian north, the Denisovs, became the administrative and ideological leaders of the new community: in effect, lay elders of a new monastic civilization. The older brother, Andrew Denisov, provided the first systematic defense of the Old Belief in his *Answers from Beside the Sea,* drawn up in response to theological interrogation by the Holy Synod in 1722. His younger brother Semen developed and codified the martyrology of the schismatics with his *History of the Fathers and Sufferers of Solovetsk* and his *Vineyard of Russia.*[71]

The settlements that developed in the Vyg region were virtually divorced from the new Petrine empire. Recognizing the value of their commercial activities to the Russian economy, Peter granted them freedoms which continued into the nineteenth century. The "fathers" and "brothers" of Vyg amassed considerable wealth and set up in their central commune one of the largest educational centers in eighteenth-century Russia—teaching the literature, music, and iconography of Old Muscovy. There were no professors in this informal center of instruction, just as there were no priests in their temples and monasteries. Yet there was higher literacy and deeper devotion to church forms in these "priestless" communes of Old Believers than in most parishes of the synodal church. Their entrepreneurial economic activity constitutes, moreover, a remarkable chapter of pioneering heroism. Because of their strong sense of solidarity they set up trading networks which were often able to produce and ship goods to Moscow and St. Petersburg more cheaply than they could be made on the spot. Their ascetic sense of discipline enabled them to establish settlements in some of the bleakest arctic regions of Russia and to send fishing expeditions as far afield as Novaia Zemlia to the east and Spitzbergen to the west. Their own fanciful chroniclers even speak of Old Believer expeditions reaching North America.[72]

Much less peaceful (and thus somewhat more typical) is the early history of the Old Believers in the Volga region. The Old Beliefs were zealously defended in these newly converted and newly colonized regions, "not for ourselves . . . but for our fathers and grandfathers." Long-suffering faithfulness was the supreme virtue of the region where "to change faith would be a hell beneath hell."[73] Cossacks had recently brought their own traditions of violence to this already embattled region. These Cossack settlers and merchants who controlled the flourishing Volga trade were equally opposed to centralized authority and to Western ways. When representatives of Peter the Great arrived in the Volga town of Dmitrievsk in 1700 to shave, uniform, and mobilize Cossack troops for the forthcoming battles with the Swedes, the Cossacks rebelled. Aided and abetted by the local populace, Cossacks swarmed into the city at night and massacred officials from the capital. Heads without beards were cut off and mutilated, local collaborators were drowned in the Volga, and the *voevoda* was able to survive only by hiding out long enough to grow a beard and returning as a convert to the Old Belief.[74]

Whether from conviction or necessity, officials in eastern Russia often had to follow the *voevoda* of Dmitrievsk and make their peace with the Old Belief. Outside of the main towns in forward areas of colonization, communes of Old Believers were often more numerous than parishes of the official church. There were relatively few orthodox Orthodox in the lower

Volga region and in many other key trading and colonizing areas of eastern Russia. As with the Calvinists, the "this-worldly asceticism" of the Old Believer communities soon made them wealthy and, by the late eighteenth century, politically as well as theologically conservative. The prophetic priestless sects began to be challenged by the more sedentary communities of "priested" Old Believers (*popovtsy*), such as the one which developed in the wilds at Irgiz, beyond the Volga, or at Belaia Krinitsa, in the Carpathian mountains near the border between Russia and the Hapsburg empire. The voice of prophecy was kept fresh, however, by the repeated splitting off of messianic groups and wandering prophets from the Old Believer communities—and also by increasingly frequent contact and interaction with the sectarians.

The historical importance of the Old Believers in the development of Russian culture is out of all proportion to the relative smallness of their numbers. By effectively seceding from the political and intellectual life of the empire, this important nucleus of the Great Russian merchant community helped turn the main centers of Russian life over to foreigners and to the Westernized service nobility. The Old Believers' unique qualities of industry and abstemiousness were never integrated into the building of a genuinely national and synthetic culture. Instead, they withdrew petulantly into their own world, defying the march of history in the belief that history itself was coming to an end. Their communities represented a continuing rebuke to the luxurious life of the Westernized cities and the aristocratic estates. Their intense religious convictions and communal pattern of life represented a voice from the Muscovite past that was to become a siren song for the Russian populists in the nineteenth century.

Equally important for the fate of Russian culture was the fact that much of the native entrepreneurial class became wedded not to a practical world outlook or rationalistic form of religious belief but rather to a most irrational and superstitious form of fanaticism. However ingenious and experimental in their business habits, the Old Believers rebelled at any change or modernization of their beliefs. Thus, whereas the development of an entrepreneurial bourgeoisie in the late medieval West tended to encourage the growth of rationalism in twelfth-century Paris and of sceptical humanism in fifteenth-century Florence and Rotterdam, the emergent merchant class of early modern Russia played no such role. In reality, no Russian bourgeoisie analogous to that of the West survived the transformations wrought by Alexis and Peter. Shorn of their ancient privileges and immunities after the urban riots of the mid-seventeenth century, the entrepreneurial leaders of Old Muscovy had only two choices. They could melt into the medium and upper level of officialdom of the new state along with various foreign and mercenary elements. Or they could cling to their former ways and ideals by moving on to newly opening areas of the empire and blending their xenophobic complaints with those of other dispossessed elements. One could choose bureaucracy or *raskol*,[75] the "homeless cosmopolitanism" of the new urban centers or the narrow chauvinism of the Russian interior.

Those who chose the latter course, the native Russian bourgeoisie, were spiritual relatives not of the secularized entrepreneurs of early modern Europe but of its messianic urban preachers: Waldo, Savonarola, and Winstanley. But unlike these Western preachers, the Old Believers were able to survive and flourish into modern times. They were sheltered by vast spaces and fortified by the belief that they were defending the true tradition which would yet prevail rather than synthetically re-creating early Christian piety. By appealing to instinct rather than intellect, to communal honor rather than individual reason, the Old Believers achieved a popular following that proved more enduring than that of most revivalist prophets in the West.

Old Believers rejected the name *raskol'nik*, or schismatic, which they applied rather to the new, synodal church. Nonetheless, the word *raskol*, with its physiological suggestions of cracking open as well as its theological meaning of schism, indicates the historical effect of this movement on Russian life. The wounds which it opened in the body politic would never be entirely healed. It weakened Russia politically and lent a utopian and apocalyptical flavor to its internal debates which frustrated the harmonious development of a stable national culture.

Here are but a few of the divisions opened up by the *raskol'niki*. There was, first of all, their own separation from the civil as well as the religious life of Russia. The Old Believers went so far as to use secret codes, nets of informers, and at least two private languages for their internal communications.[76] They were, moreover, split off from history—believing that earthly history was nearing an end and that all talk of historical greatness in the empire represented only the predictable delusions of the Antichrist. Among themselves the *raskol'niki* were soon split into endless divisive groups: the Theodosians, Philipists, wanderers, runners, and so on—each pretending to be the True Church of the original Old Believer martyrs. There was, finally, a schizophrenia in the attitude of all these Old Believers toward the world about them. Extremely stern, puritanical, and practical in everyday life, they were nonetheless ornate, bombastic, and ritualistic in art and religion. Indeed, one may say that the simultaneous allegiance of Old Muscovy to both icon and axe, to both formalized idealism and earthy harshness, was kept alive by the Old

Believers. With the passing of time their influence grew and deepened. Some of the oppressive restrictions of the early eighteenth century were removed in the 1760's. Important settlements of both "priested" and "priestless" Old Believers were established shortly thereafter, significantly in Moscow rather than St. Petersburg.[77] They became pioneers in providing care for the sick in destitute sections of Moscow. Gradually, the Old Believers began to attract sympathizers and sentimental admirers and to become, in spite of themselves, an influential force in the formation of a new national culture.

The second tradition of conservative protest against the new world of St. Petersburg, that of Cossack-led peasant insurrection, bears many points of similarity to that of the fundamentalist Old Believers. Both traditions have their origin in the religious revival of the Time of Troubles and produced their greatest martyrs during the great change under Alexis. Stenka Razin was for southern Russia the same semi-legendary hero that Avvakum and the monks of Solovetsk were for the north. Yet, just as the Old Believers' tradition did not become fully formed except in reaction to Peter, so the tradition of peasant insurrection was in many ways established only with the Bulavin uprising against Peter's rule in 1707–8.[78] If the merchants who led the Old Believer movement were protesting against the destruction of the old urban liberties by the central government, the Cossacks who led the insurrectionists were also protesting the extension of burdensome state obligations to their once free way of life. Just as the Old Believers were able to survive because of the remoteness of their settlements and the value of their commercial activities, so were the Cossacks able to sustain their traditions because of the distance of their southern settlements from the centers of imperial power and the importance of their fighting forces to the military power of the empire.

At times the tradition of insurrection merged with that of the Old Believers—particularly in the lower Volga region. However, their methods of opposing absolutism and their social ideals were quite different. The Old Believers were essentially passive in their resistance to the new regime, believing in the imminence of God's intervention and the redemptive value of unmerited suffering. The peasant insurrectionaries were violent, almost compulsive activists, anxious to wreak suffering on the nearest available symbols of bureaucratic authority. The Old Believers' ideal order was an organic religious civilization of Great Russian Christians united by traditional forms of ritual worship and communal activity. The insurrectionaries were animated by a purely negative impulse to destroy the existent order, an impulse which they sought to share with Moslem and pagan as well as Christian groups, along the multi-racial southeastern frontier of Russia.

The peasant insurrectionaries were, of course, protesting a far more degrading and debilitating form of bondage than that which faced the traditional merchants of the north. With the final sealing of all escape routes from lifetime peasant servitude in the mid-seventeenth century and the extension of military service obligation to twenty-five years in the early eighteenth, the lot of the ordinary peasant was, in effect, slavery. The violence of the peasant rebellions must also be placed against the background of continuing Tatar raids and military mobilizations along the exposed southern steppe. The final wresting of the southern Ukraine and Crimea from Tatar and Ottoman hands did not occur until the late years of the reign of Catherine the Great, well after the last great rebellions had been suppressed.

For all their disorganized violence, however, the peasant rebellions were animated by one recurring political ideal: belief in a "true tsar." From one point of view this was a revolutionary idea, a call for a *coup d'état* based on a claim that a *samozvanets,* or "self-proclaimed" insurrectionary leader, was the rightful heir to the throne. But fundamentally this ideal was profoundly conservative—even more so than that of the Old Believers. For the concept of a true tsar implied that the ultimate ruler of the system was its only possible redeemer. The political and administrative system of the new empire was simply to be destroyed so that Russia could return to the congenial paternalism of Muscovite days. The "true tsar" of peasant and Cossack folklore was thus a combination of benign grandfather and messianic deliverer: *batiushka* and *spasitel'*. He was a "real, rustic man" (*muzhitsky*), the true benefactor of his children, who would come to their aid if only the intervening wall of administrators and bureaucrats could be torn down. At the same time, the "true tsar" was given divine sanction in the eyes of the peasant masses by providing him with a genealogy extending in unbroken line back to Vladimir, Constantine the Great, and even to Riurik and Prus.

The first popular rumors of a "true tsar" appear to have started during the reign of Ivan IV, who was largely responsible for both establishing and breaking this mythical line of succession.[79] The False Dmitry, the first of the "self-proclaimed" in Russian history, and the only one ever to gain the throne, drew skillfully on the people's longing to believe that there had been a miraculous survivor of the Old Muscovite line. Although soon disenchanted because of Dmitry's Catholicism, many Russians came to believe during the Time of Troubles that only a tsar from the old line favored by God could deliver Russia from intrigue and anarchy. The idea that a true tsar existed somewhere spilled over into the peasant masses who participated in the chaotic uprisings that followed the murder of Dmitry. Some attached themselves to a second Polish-sponsored pretender, but more followed the leadership of a former serf, Cossack, and Turkish prisoner, Bolotnikov, who was rumored to be the nephew of the true Dmitry and the son of Fedor. The chaotic and violent uprising led by Bolotnikov in 1606–7 came close to capturing Moscow and is properly considered the first of the great nationwide peasant rebellions.[80] The peasant insurrectionaries appear thus as a throwback to the old Muscovite ideology: their true tsar was to be the leader of an organic religious civilization. At first the idea was also maintained that such a tsar must be descended from the old line through Ivan the Terrible; but it soon became enough merely to show that the pretender's claim was more ancient and honorable than that of the incumbent. Much emphasis was laid on the fact that the self-proclaimed leader of rebellion and claimant to the throne was to be a holy tsar (of which there could be but one) rather than just another king or emperor, such as abounded in the corrupted West. The peasant rebels often echoed themes sounded by the Old Believers: that the title "emperor" came from the "satanic" pope, that passports were an invention of Antichrist, that the emblem of the two-headed eagle was that of the devil himself (because "only the devil has two heads"), and that the special identifying cross mark placed on the left hand of runaway soldiers was an abomination of the holy cross and the seal of Antichrist.[81]

There were fourteen serious pretenders in the seventeenth century, and the tradition developed so vigorously in the following century that there were thirteen in the final third of it alone. There were some even in the early nineteenth century—the legends about Constantine Pavlovich as the true tsar rather than Nicholas I providing a kind of uncoordinated popular echo of the aristocratic Decembrist program.[82] One reason for the boost which the tradition received in the eighteenth century was the sudden development of the belief in a "substitute tsar." Properly sensing that Peter's reforming zeal was intensified by his trip abroad, partisans of the old ways began a series of apocryphal legends purporting to explain how someone else (usually the son of Lefort) had been substituted for the Tsar. As a result, the claims of Bulavin, the leader of peasant insurrection under Peter, to be rightful heir to the throne were more widely accepted than those of earlier rebel leaders. The Tsar's cruel treatment of his son Alexis a decade later enabled even the weak Alexis to appear to many as the rightful heir. Special opportunities were created for a belief in a true tsar after Peter's death by the fact that women ruled Russia almost continuously until 1796. The peasants tended to equate the worsening of their lot with the advent of feminine rule. "Grain does not grow, because the feminine sex is ruling"[83] was the popular saying; but by the time of the Pugachev rebellion

Theme and Variations in Iconography

PLATES V–VII

So perfect was the blending of aesthetic and spiritual values in the monk Andrew Rublev's "Old Testament Trinity" (Plate V) that the Church Council of 1551 prescribed it as the model for all future icons on the subject. Painted in about 1425 for the monastery founded by St. Sergius on the religious subject to which that monastery was dedicated, Rublev's celebrated masterpiece is a fitting product of the intensified spirituality and historical theology of Muscovy. It depicts the concrete Old Testament event that foreshadowed the divulgence of God's triune nature rather than the ineffable mystery itself. Three pilgrims come to Abraham (Genesis 18: 1–15) in accordance with the sung commentary of the Orthodox liturgy ("Blessed Abraham, thou who hast seen them, thou who hast received the divine one-in-three").

The spiritualized curvilinear harmony of Rublev's three angels gathered about the eucharistic elements contrasts sharply with the cluttered composition and gourmet spirit of a mid-fifteenth-century icon on the same theme (Plate VI). Based on a Byzantine-Balkan model, this painting of the Pskov school subtly betrays the more worldly preoccupations of that westerly commercial center.

The third representation of the theme of the Trinity (Plate VII), an icon by the court painter Simon Ushakov in 1670, illustrates the decline of Russian iconography under Western influences in the late years of the reign of Alexis Mikhailovich. The outline form of Rublev's three figures is maintained, but the spirit has drastically changed. The symbolic tree of life, which gave aesthetic balance to both the Rublev and the Pskovian icon has become a spreading oak, balanced now by a classical portico with Corinthian columns. The semi-naturalistic, faintly self-conscious figures and sumptuous furnishings suggest the imminent arrival of an altogether new and secular art.

PLATE V

PLATE VI

PLATE VII

PLATE VIII

Typical of the new secular portraiture that replaced icon-painting in the eighteenth century as the most vital form of the visual arts is the picture (Plate VIII) of the merchant-aristocrat F. Demidov. Completed in 1773 by the court painter of Catherine the Great, D. Levitsky, this painting is done full figure in the manner of the so-called "parade portraits," amidst pseudo-classical surroundings. The old obraza, or "forms," through which God was thought to have intervened in history were replaced by persony, or "persons," of importance who were thought to be making history in their own right. Demidov is pointing, not like the central figure in the "Old Testament Trinity" to God's mysterious gifts to man, but to his own eminently tangible benefactions to humanity as an "enlightened" patron of agriculture in the countryside and of botanical beautification in the new cities. The virtue of the painting lies in the faint note of caricature which Levitsky has injected into his portrayal of this rather vain and venal scion of a famous aristocratic family.

The New Portraiture

PLATE VIII

under Catherine it was unclear what the relationship of the true tsar was to be toward the woman on the throne. For many of his followers, Pugachev was simply the miraculously returned figure of Peter III, the slain husband and imperial predecessor of Catherine. A few thought he should replace Catherine, but many thought he should marry her, and he himself seems to have looked on Catherine as a mother being ravished by her courtiers.[84]

The fundamentally conservative nature of the belief in a true tsar may be seen from the fact that each of the major pretenders gained national support not through any positive program but through his ability to serve as the focus for a variety of forces resisting change. In each case the tsar most immediately threatened was attempting to extend central authority and cultural Westernization: Boris Godunov (the False Dmitry), Shuisky (Bolotnikov), Alexis (Stenka Razin), Peter the Great (Bulavin), and Catherine (Pugachev). The effect of the heroic rebellions was to strengthen rather than weaken the bureaucratic centralization they were opposing. Peasant animosities were in effect directed into periodic bloodbaths of local officials, who were relatively expendable for the central government, while peasant loyalty to the autocrat, the pivot and heart of the system, was intensified. Even in rebellion the peasants could not conceive of an alternative political system. They refused to believe that the reigning tsar was responsible for the evils of the time and the bureaucrats and foreign elements around him.

As in the case of the Old Believers, the conservative peasant insurrectionaries bear certain resemblances to other European protest movements against modernization. In social composition and messianic utopianism the Russian peasant rebellions resemble those of sixteenth-century Germany. In their conservative longing for a more godly ruling line, they resemble the Jacobites of late-seventeenth- and eighteenth-century England. Just as the Jacobite myth lived on in agrarian Scotland and northern England long after it had failed as an insurrectionary force, so the myth of peasant rebellion lived on in the mentality of southern Russia long after the last great insurrection under Pugachev.

Thus, although the state bureaucracy and army grew steadily and the service aristocracy gained in wealth and local authority throughout the eighteenth and the early nineteenth century, many Russians continued to believe in the superiority of the small schismatic communities or to dream of a new Stenka Razin who would lead them to a tsar-deliverer.

Less dramatic than either the schismatics or the peasant insurrectionaries was a third form of religious protest against the new world of St. Petersburg: the monastic revival within the official Church. This movement was the slowest to develop and the most restricted in terms of popular participation. But it was perhaps the deepest of all and the one most faithful to the culture of Old Muscovy. The central institution of that culture had always been the monasteries; and their ability to recover even in part from the crippling blows of the early eighteenth century is perhaps the surest indication of the continued importance of this "old" culture in the "new" period of Russian history.

The possibility of any such revival must have seemed extremely remote in the early eighteenth century. The efforts of Peter and Anna to bring the Russian Church closer organizationally to the Lutheran state churches of the Baltic regions had resulted in a great weakening of the monastic estate. Whereas there had been about twenty-five thousand in monastic orders at the beginning of the eighteenth century, there were less than fifteen thousand by the end of Anna's reign; and the number was to decline still further after Catherine the Great formally confiscated monastic property in 1763. The listing of 1764 showed that only 318 monasteries remained out of more than two thousand in the late seventeenth century.[85]

The initial reactions of many monasteries had been to lash out in defense of their former privileges, allying themselves at times with those who advanced the claims of another "true" line of tsars. Typical was a monk of Tambov who fled his cloister convinced that the Antichrist had taken the place of the real Peter and was responsible for the murder of Peter's son. Although his prediction proved ill-founded that the end of the world would come early in 1723, he continued to gain monastic followers in the excitable Tambov region and went to Moscow at the time of Peter's death with high hopes of turning Russia back to the true path. Instead, he was arrested and executed, his followers rounded up and mutilated, and his head exhibited in the streets of Tambov by troops from one of the new guards regiments.[86]

Only after the impossibility of a full return to the old ways had been clearly realized, perhaps, was the way clear for fresh approaches in Russian monasticism. Once all hope was lost of recovering their lost wealth and independence, the Russian monasteries began to return to the long-submerged tradition of the original fourteenth-century monastic pioneers and evangelists. This spiritual revival began quietly in the late eighteenth century and continued throughout the nineteenth, producing a gradual increase in the size of the monastic establishment[87] and a deepening of its spiritual life.

The heart of the revival was, once again, the "holy mountain" of Athos and the rediscovery of its still-vigorous traditions of patristic theology and inner spirituality. The man who brought the spirit of Mt. Athos a second time to Russia was Paissius Velichkovsky, the son of a Poltavan priest and a converted Jewess. Although descended from one of the greatest Ukrainian baroque poets, Paissius was repelled by the "pagan mythology" that he found in this Westernized heritage. Like Maxim the Greek in the sixteenth and Ivan Vyshensky in the seventeenth century, Paissius came to Russia from Athos in the eighteenth century with a simple message: turn back from secularism to the simple ways of the early desert fathers. Like these earlier elders, Paissius was deeply opposed to worldly learning, yet was himself a learned and articulate figure. He began a series of Russian translations of the works of the early fathers—the best and longest collection of patristic writings yet to appear in Russia—and translated the popular Greek collection of ascetic spirituality, the *Philokalia*.[88]

Unlike Maxim or Vyshensky, however, Paissius was the initiator of a movement within the church rather than a prophetic voice crying in the wilderness. He founded a number of new cloisters in Moldavia and southern Russia, and provided them with a series of "Letters of Spiritual Direction" as guides for the purification of the monastic estate. The key to monastic life for Paissius was common obedience to the spiritual elder within a community of ascetic hermits dedicated to the practice of unceasing prayer. The spiritual life was thus seen in hesychastic terms as one of internal prayer and self-discipline; and the "rule" adopted was modeled on that of the early desert fathers. The term *pustyn'*, or desert, increasingly replaced other designations for a monastery as the austere rule of Paissius became more widely accepted.

Even more influential and original was Tikhon Zadonsky, an anguished seeker for a new religious calling in a new kind of world. Born and brought up near St. Petersburg and educated in Novgorod, Tikhon was fully exposed to the new secularizing influences of the capital and also to the new wave of German pietistic thought. Influenced perhaps by the pietistic idea of inward renewal and rededication. Tikhon moved from his high post as suffragan bishop of Novgorod, by way of the bishopric of Voronezh, to a new monastery in a frontier region of the Don. The title of Arndt's influential pietistic tract *On True Christianity* became the title of Tikhon's own *magnum opus* on the holy life. In it and in his other writings and sermons Tikhon emphasizes the joys of Christ-like living. At Zadonsk, Tikhon took the role of the spiritual elder out of the narrow confines of the monastery into the world of affairs, becoming the friend and counselor of lay people as well as monastic apprentices.[89]

The man who carried this revival into the nineteenth century, Seraphim of Sarov, combined Paissius' ascetic and patristic emphases with Tikhon's insistence on self-renunciation and ministering to the people. Seraphim gave up all his worldly goods and even his monastic habit to don a white peasant costume and spend fifteen years as a hermit in the woods near his new monastery at Sarov. A devoted Hesychast, he believed that "silence is the sacrament of the world to come, words are the weapons of this world."[90] After returning from his forest retreat, Seraphim traveled widely in and out of cloisters, urging men to rededicate themselves to Christ. "Boredom," he taught, "is cured by prayer, by abstaining from vain speech, by working with the hands. . . ."[91] Virginity he regarded as particularly desirable, and he was a frequent visitor to women's convents, the rapid growth of which was an important sign of the revived interest in religious callings.

The spiritual intensity generated by the new monastic communities which Seraphim set up began to attract a new kind of pilgrim—secularized intellectuals—back for visits if not pilgrimages. The famous Optyna Pustyn, to the south of Moscow, became a center of counseling and of spiritual retreats for many of Russia's most famous nineteenth-century thinkers: beginning with the Slavophile Ivan Kireevsky, who spent much of his later life there, and extending on through Dostoevsky, Tolstoy, and Vladimir Solov'ev. The figure of Father Zossima in Dostoevsky's *Brothers Karamazov* presents a fairly accurate composite picture of Father Ambrose, the monastic elder at Optyna Pustyn, whom Dostoevsky frequently visited, and of Tikhon Zadonsky, whose writings Dostoevsky reverently studied.[92]

The problems of the new monasticism were those of any religious calling in a primarily secular society. The new monks were bothered by self-doubt, harassed by demands that they prove themselves useful to the state like everyone else. Shorn of their role as court ideologists and great landlords, they were not yet sure what the role of the monastery could be in the new society. The monastic revival tended to be strongest outside the traditional monasteries.

On the one hand, there was a tendency to withdraw to ever more remote hermitages, where the saintly ideal was removed from ordinary social life and related to individual ascetic exercises. In this strange, semi-Oriental world the attainment of physical incorruptibility after death was thought to be the ultimate fruit of ascetic self-mastery; and proof of some degree of this incorruptibility became a pre-requisite for canonization in the eighteenth-century Russian Church.[93] The ascetic emphases of the new monasticism took it outside of the history and politics in which Muscovite monasticism had been continually involved. In its emphasis on repentance and reversion to the silent asceticism of the early Church, the new Russian monasticism was similar to the Trappist movement in post-Reformation Catholicism. Tikhon was typical not only in fleeing from ecclesiastical authority and civilization in general but also in his attempt to compile a "spiritual thesaurus gathered from the world." Only scattered fragments of insight and experience were worth finding and preserving in the contemporary world.

> As a merchant gathers varied wares from different countries, brings them into his house and hides them, so the Christian can gather from this world thoughts that are useful for the soul, lock them in the prison of his heart, and build up his soul with them.[94]

At the same time, there was a new desire within the monasteries to communicate more directly with people in all walks of life. The emphasis on ascetic piety tended to break down the older ritual and formality of the communal monasteries, just as the confiscation of monastic lands had taken away the former preoccupation with economic affairs. The influence of Protestant pietism tended to turn monastic elders like Tikhon into part-time popular evangelists. Elements of self-doubt may lie behind the almost masochistic desire of the new monks to humble themselves. Tikhon requested that he be buried under the entrance stone of a simple church so that he could be literally trampled underfoot by the humblest believer. When hit by a freethinker in the course of an argument, Tikhon replied by throwing himself at the feet of his astonished assailant to ask forgiveness for driving him to such a loss of self-control.[95] It is perhaps fitting that Tikhon was canonized and his works studied anew in the 1860's, when Russian thinkers were turning again to the problem of moral purification and humbling themselves before the simple people. The principal ideological movement of that age, the famous "movement (literally 'procession' or 'pilgrimage': *khozhdenie*) to the people," was in many ways only an extension and secularization of the effort to take the monastic ideal out to a bonded but still believing peasantry. Indeed, the complex populist movement—the most genuinely original social movement of modern Russian history—appears in many ways as a continuation of all three post-Petrine forms of conservative protest to the Westernization and secularization of the Russian empire. Like all of them, populism was a loose tradition rather than an organized movement. Like most Old Believers, the populists believed in preserving the old communal forms of economic life and in the imminent possibility of sudden historical change. Like the peasant insurrectionaries, the populists believed in violent action against police and bureaucrats and in the ultimate benevolence of the "true tsar." Even after killing Alexander II in 1881, the populists could conceive of no other program than to address utopian appeals to his successor.[96] Like the monastic revivalists, the populists believed in ascetic self-denial and in humbling oneself before the innocently suffering Russian people.

But before considering this and other movements of the late imperial period one must turn to the new and distinctive culture that took shape under Elizabeth and Catherine and lasted for a century. During this period the schisms and tensions that had been opened in Russian society by the reforms of Alexis and Peter were plastered over with the decorative effects of aristocratic culture. It is to the brilliant and self-confident culture of the aristocratic century—and to its lingering inner concerns—that attention must now be turned.

IV

THE CENTURY OF
ARISTOCRATIC CULTURE

The Mid-Eighteenth to the Mid-Nineteenth Century

THE UNCHALLENGED REIGN *of a distinctive, if disturbed aristocratic culture during the century from 1755–6 (the date of the Russian alliance with the France of Louis XIV and the founding of the first Russian university and permanent theater) to 1855–6 (the year of decisive military defeat in the Crimea and the advent of the reforming tsar, Alexander II). The constant struggle between French and German influences, between rationalistic and romantic impulses; the adoption of the French language and the importation of French ideas as an aristocratic badge of class beginning in the reign of Elizabeth (1741–62); the emphasis on Prussian discipline under Peter III (1762) and Paul I (1796–1801) immediately before and after the long Francophile reign of Catherine the Great. The Russian Enlightenment: the breadth and scientific achievement of Michael Lomonosov (1711–65), the neo-classical art forms and the new cities that accompanied Catherine's age of conquest.*

The recurrent dilemma, first met by Catherine, between the desire for rational rule based on natural laws and the concurrent determination to maintain an unlimited autocracy based on rigid class distinctions. The crucial change in the character of opposition to tsarist rule under Catherine, from the last of the great peasant revolts under Pugachev (1773–5) to the first manifesto of the "Pugachevs from the universities": The Journey from Petersburg to Moscow *(1790) by the alienated aristocratic intellectual Alexander Radishchev (1749–1802). The struggle against frivolous "Voltairianism," the journalistic activities of Nicholas Novikov (1744–1818), and the seminal importance of Russian Freemasonry in the deepening communal life of the reforming aristocracy.*

The great expectations during the reign of Alexander I (1801–25); the national revival in resisting the Napoleonic invasion (1812–14); the frustration of political reform and the suppression of the aristocratic Decembrist uprising of 1825. Russia as the focal point of the European-wide reaction to the Enlightenment and the French Revolution; Catholic, pietistic, Orthodox, and occult, Eastward-looking elements in the wave of reactionary thinking that culminated in the pronouncement in 1833 of "Orthodoxy, autocracy, and nationality" as the official ideology of the Russian Empire.

The immersion of aristocratic thinkers in German romantic philosophy during the authoritarian, Prussophile rule of Nicholas I (1825–55). The intense desire to discover within the fraternity of small discussion groups and to set forth on the pages of "thick journals" the answers to certain "cursed questions" about the meaning of history, art, and life itself. The transition from the aristocratic poetry of Alexander Pushkin (1799–1837) to the anguished prose of Nicholas Gogol (1809–52); from neo-classical architecture to the ideological paintings of Alexander Ivanov (1806–58); from the visionary romanticism of Schelling and the Slavophiles of the 1830's to the revolutionary rationalism of the young Hegelians and "Westernizers" of the 1840's. The legacy of metaphysical anguish left by the aristocratic search for Truth; the symbolic importance of Shakespeare's Hamlet *and Raphael's "Sistine Madonna" in the unresolved search for cultural identity.*

For all its tribulations and divisions, Russia had become by the mid-eighteenth century a great European power. Frontier ruggedness and Tatar ruthlessness had been harnessed by Prussian discipline and Swedish administrative technique. The officer class, newly swollen with Northern European mercenaries, had led Russia in conquest abroad and defended its autocrat from unrest within. It was now being rewarded by grants of land and civil authority. The culture of old Russia was rejected by the new aristocracy, but nothing had as yet taken its place except a patina of Latin culture acquired from the newly absorbed Polish territories.

Under Peter and his immediate successors, the aristocracy stood suspended between many worlds. They generally had to speak at least three languages: German, Russian, and Polish; and their semi-official handbook of instruction advised them to learn three different numerical systems: the Arabic (needed for military and technical purposes), the Roman (used in classical and modern Western culture), and the Church Slavonic lettered numerals still used in Russia itself.[1]

The name first assigned to the new service nobility, *shliakhetstvo,* symbolized the polyglot derivation of the class; for this was the Russified form of the Polish *szlachta,* which was itself derived from the German word for hereditary lineage *Geschlecht.* In the course of the century, the nobility came to be known by the term *dvorianstvo,* "men of the court," which suggested the growing interdependence of the tsar and the aristocracy. In return for the services to the state prescribed in Peter's *Table of Ranks* (1722), the aristocracy received almost unlimited local power in a series of grants climaxed in 1785 by the Charter to the Nobility. Just as the new nobility shed its Germano-Polish name, so it soon shed the shell of Latin culture that had been the vehicle for rejecting the traditional Greco-Byzantine heritage. Latin remained the principal language of seminaries and academies; but it did not—and in the eighteenth century could not—provide the common language for the new Russian ruling class.

Only late in the reign of Peter's youngest daughter, Elizabeth, did this rootless but triumphant class begin to find a sense of identity through the language and culture of France. Elizabeth's reign began a period of creativity that can justly be called the golden age of the Russian aristocracy, and roughly identified with the century between 1755–6 and 1855–6.

In 1755–6 Russia witnessed the first performance of a Russian opera by Russians, the founding of the first permanent Russian theater, and the establishment of the first Russian university. A century later, Alexander II ascended the throne to free the serfs, open up Russia to accelerated industrialization, and thus end forever the special position of the aristocracy. In terms of foreign influence this frame of dates is equally significant: 1756 marking the "diplomatic revolution" that aligned Russia with the *ancien régime* in France; 1856 bringing an end to the Crimean War, which, as the first great setback for the old order in Russia, prepared the way for an influx of liberalizing ideas from the victorious English and French.

The new turn in Russian diplomacy helped French become the common language of the aristocracy. Although the Russian aristocracy was also to create modern literary Russian, they continued to speak to one another and even to think largely in French. This new language brought Russian noblemen into the main stream of European culture, and also helped isolate them more than before from their own countrymen. Much of the drama of the aristocratic century lies in the struggle of a refined but essentially foreign culture to strike roots in Russian soil.

In its attempt to take hold in this chilly northern climate, the rationalism of the French Enlightenment was opposed not just by the dogged piety and superstition of the masses but also by a fresh surge of pietistic thought within the aristocracy itself. However one divides the aristocratic century, one finds a struggle going on beneath a seemingly tranquil surface: between rationalism and romanticism, French and German influence, universalism and nationalism, St. Petersburg and Moscow.

One can speak impressionistically of an enlightened eighteenth and a romantic nineteenth century; of the cult of Voltaire and Diderot giving way to that of Schelling and Hegel; of an alternation between Francophile reform under Catherine and Alexander I and Prussian discipline under their successors Paul and Nicholas; or of a general attraction toward France that was weakened first by the revolutionary terror and then by the Napoleonic invasion of 1812 In any case, the struggle throughout this century was essentially between French and German approaches to political, personal, and aesthetic problems.

The controversies occurred within an uneasy aristocratic minority which also felt pressures from below and harassment from above. Yet, viewed in the broad context of Russian history, there has probably never been a century in which the controlling elite has had the liberty to discuss problems and ideas free from the disruptions of major social and political change. During this period, the aristocratic elite produced a culture that was both national and European, and created poetry, ballet, and architecture equal to the finest of the age.

Yet it was just in the realm of ideas that the aristocratic century left its most fateful legacy. The very security and freedom from practical responsibilities of the aristocracy permitted it to become involved in the controversies of a disturbed century in European philosophy. Partly from idle curiosity, partly from deeper concern, the Russian aristocrats generated a sense of philosophic anguish which gradually focused on certain nagging questions about the meaning of history, of culture, and of life itself.

A special kind of fraternity emerged within the aristocracy of those who felt alienated from official Russia and concerned about these "cursed questions." Out of debates that began innocuously among bored officers in masonic lodges, fraternal societies, and philosophic "circles" came a sense of solidarity and spiritual purpose. To be sure, the aristocratic philosophers agreed on almost nothing and generated great confusion in the society around them. In their unreal efforts to bring to life on Russian soil the heroics of Byron's poems and Schiller's plays, they often lost themselves in the indecisive melancholy of their favorite dramatic character, Hamlet, and created the literary type known as "the superfluous man." Yet, at the same time, they created an aura of heroism about their own implausible dedication to high ideals. They created an enduring dissatisfaction with compromise, philistinism, and partial answers.

Frustrated in matters of practical political and social reform, thinking aristocrats increasingly poured their passion into artistic creativity and historical prophecy. They harrowed the soil and sowed the seeds for a rich harvest. Their restless pursuit of truth enabled succeeding ages to produce the most profoundly realistic literature and the most profoundly revolutionary political upheaval of modern times.

1. The Troubled Enlightenment

As DISTINCT from the pattern that developed in the early modern West, secular enlightenment in Russia began late, proceeded fitfully, and was largely the work of monks or foreign technicians—always in response to imperial commands and patronage.

Even Soviet scholars who minimize the importance of religion and generally maximize Great Russian influences now tend to date the beginning of the Russian Enlightenment from the influx of learned White Russian and Ukrainian monks into Moscow at the time of schism in the Russian Church.[1] Monks and seminarians indeed continued to play a large role in the Russian Enlightenment down into the twentieth century, and are responsible for some of the religious intensity of much Russian secular thought. At the same time, the Westernized regions of the empire played a key role in opening up the Russian mind to the speculative philosophy and classical art forms which soon dominated aristocratic culture. While under Polish dominance, Kiev had been transformed into an eastern bastion of scholastic education and baroque architecture. For nearly a century after its return to Russian control, Kiev was the most literate city in the empire. The Kiev-Mogila Academy (which was not made a theological academy until the nineteenth century) was the closest approximation to a Western-style liberal arts university. Between 1721 and 1765, twenty-eight seminaries were founded—all on the Kievan model; and it is probably not too much to say that Kiev taught Russia not only to read and write in the eighteenth century, but also to think in the abstract, metaphysical terms which were to prove so attractive to the aristocratic intellectuals.[2]

Foreign technicians were also bearers of literary and secular ideas in the early modern period of Russian history. Yet the various military, commercial, and medical specialists that flooded into Russia in increasing numbers from the fifteenth to the early seventeenth century were, for the most part, kept in hermetically sealed settlements in the major ports and administrative centers. The price of extensive residence or broad Russian contact was almost invariably complete assimilation: change of name, religion, and dress. Those willing to pay this price did not generally have very much intellectual or cultural vitality to contribute to their adopted land.

Peter the Great was important not for introducing foreign technical ideas into Russia, but for making them the basis of a new state-sponsored type of education. By making a measure of elementary education obligatory for much of his service aristocracy and by introducing an official civil script, a reformed alphabet, and innumerable Western words and concepts into the language, Peter prepared the way for a more purely secular enlightenment. Shortly after his death, the first institute of secular scientific learning, the Academy of Sciences, was established in St. Petersburg along lines that he had prescribed. By entrusting the organization and staffing of the Academy to the German mathematician and natural philosopher Christian Wolff, Peter recognized the dependence on foreigners that would continue under his successors but willed to them his own bias in favor of secular learning. Whereas the school system set up early in Peter's reign in key Russian cities by Pietist evangelists from Halle soon collapsed, the academy organized by Wolff (who had been forced to leave Halle by fearful Pietists) survived and gradually became the center of a new educational system.[3]

Only, however, under Elizabeth in the 1750's did the work of the Academy begin to have a broader impact on Russian culture. By then the many-sided effects of Peter's opening to the West had begun to reach a fruition that can properly be called a Russian Enlightenment. Within the space of a few years in the mid-fifties the Academy issued a number of ethnographic and geographic publications that broadly stimulated aristocratic society with fresh information about other cultures; and Russia acquired a university, permanent theater, academy of arts, decorative porcelain factory, and so on.

The early years of Catherine's reign were perhaps the most decisive of all, for the new sovereign virtually commanded the literate public to consider a new spectrum of problems—problems ranging from politics to architecture to agriculture. Whereas the number of books printed annually in the Russian empire had risen from a low of seven in the year after Peter the Great's death to twenty-three by the end of the fifties, the average in the 1760's leaped to 105 a year: the first in a series of geometric increases. Whereas almost all of the few books printed in the first half of the eighteenth century were religious, 40 per cent of the eight thousand books printed in the second half of the century (almost all of them during Catherine's reign) were purely secular.[4] The number of new books put in circulation in Russia in the 1760's and 1770's was more than seven times the number for the 1740's and 1750's.[5]

Accompanying this sudden growth in the number of books printed (and also imported) went an extraordinary spread of secular learning to the provinces. Outlying regions that had been bastions of religious conservatism and xenophobia began to make important contributions to secular enlightenment. The poet Tred'iakovsky came from Astrakhan; Lomonosov from Kholmogory; and the personnel for the first permanent Russian theater from Yaroslavl. The director and principal playwright of the theater, Sumarokov, came from Finland—as did most of the granite used for rebuilding St. Petersburg. The first provincial journals in Russian history appeared late in the eighties in Yaroslavl and in Tobol'sk in distant Siberia.[6] Voltaire's best translator (and most eloquent defender even after Catherine had become disillusioned with the Russian Enlightenment) came from the Siberian city of Orenburg.[7]

The sudden influx of private foreign tutors, and the efforts to transform provincial cities into imperial cultural and administrative centers, increased provincial involvement in the new secular culture. Also important were the sudden rash of scientific expeditions to the north and east in the sixties and seventies led by the great biologist, mineralogist, and linguist Peter Simon Pallas. Sponsored by the Academy of Sciences, these large-scale attempts to gather and collate scientific information of all sorts necessarily drew into their activities many provincial figures with first-hand knowledge of local conditions and problems.

The arrival of the Academy of Sciences as a serious institution for the higher scientific education of native Russians can be dated from the beginnings of group research by the Russian apprentices of Pallas and of the great mathematician Leonhard Euler. Despite blindness which overtook Euler shortly after he returned permanently to Russia in 1766, Euler wrote almost half of the eight hundred papers in his completed works during the years that remained in his life, which were eminently productive ones. His very infirmity forced him to rely on young Russian apprentices; and his previous experience as head of the Berlin academy fortified him with an ability to organize as well as inspire his fellow scientists. When he died in 1783, he left Russia with a significant number of Russian-speaking scientists capable of introducing advanced mathematics into the curricula of other educational institutions.[8]

Having taken away from Catherine the Great her personal cook, who provided his aging physique with richer food than it could digest, Euler repaid her by providing Russia with more food for thought than its youthful intellect could yet assimilate. But after his death three of his sons remained in Russia, at least for a time, to help begin the process; and Nicholas Fuss, the man who pronounced the eulogy at Euler's burial in St. Petersburg, married his granddaughter and helped found an indigenous tradition of higher mathematical study in early-nineteenth-century Russia.

Even more important than this development of a native scientific tradition was the prior emergence of scientific self-confidence in the person of Michael Lomonosov, the best-known figure of the Russian Enlightenment. He was a scientist in both the Renaissance and the modern sense of the word: a universal man, symbolizing the arrival of Russia as a contributor to, rather than a mere dependency of, the secular scientific culture of Europe.[9] The decisive moment in Lomonosov's life came in the mid-thirties, when a new director of the Academy of Sciences requested that a number of well-trained Russian students be transferred from theological academies for scientific training at the gymnasium of the academy. As one of the small group chosen, Lomonosov arrived in St. Petersburg on New Year's Day of 1736—a milestone in the cultural rise of the new capital, no less important than the arrival of Empress Anna for permanent residence just four years before.

From St. Petersburg, Lomonosov went to study with Christian Wolff, who had left the domain of Prussian pietism at Halle for the University of Marburg. There Lomonosov acquired not only the scientific training which enabled him to become a pioneer in the field of physical chemistry, but also a fascination with the institution of a university hitherto nonexistent in Russia. Upon his return, he immersed himself in the scientific activities of the St. Petersburg Academy, and also helped found Moscow University and give it an initial Germanic bias in favor of developing a library and research institutes.

Lomonosov was not only a scientist and educator but a poet, essayist, orator, and historian. He gathered the material which was sent to Voltaire for his biography of Peter the Great; questioned the then dominant "Norman" emphasis on the Germanic elements in early Russian civilization; and wrote a Russian grammar which served as the basic text on this subject from its appearance in 1755 until the 1830's. By praising vernacular Russian and providing guidance for its use, Lomonosov helped clear the way for truly national forms of expression—even though he wrote most of his literary production in a more bombastic language replete with Church Slavonic forms.

Lomonosov was in no sense a revolutionary. He rejected sloth and superstition wherever he found it. But he admired royalty no less than most other leaders of the European Enlightenment, and his religious beliefs were considerably more fervent. His new methods of rhetoric and panegyric were invoked for the commemoration of coronations and Christian holidays; his new chemical techniques for glass manufacture were used for church mosaics. His curiosity extended up into the sky (where he and a colleague duplicated Benjamin Franklin's experiments with electricity and fascinated St. Petersburg society by producing "thunder machines" that brought electrical charges into bottles during thunderstorms), and far out to sea (where he proposed the founding of an international academy to develop more scientific methods of navigation and championed an expedition to find a northern passage to the Orient).

Lomonosov is, together with Pushkin, one of those rare figures admired by almost all factions in subsequent Russian thought. Those who came after him have looked back longingly, not only at the breadth of his accomplishment, but at his practical-minded attitude toward life. The passion of their nostalgia no less than the uniqueness of Lomonosov himself serves as a reminder that the Enlightenment in Russia was a relatively frail and insecure phenomenon compared to that of the West. Indeed, much of Lomonosov's scientific work was not fully uncovered and understood by his countrymen until the early twentieth century.

After Lomonosov's death in 1765, the Enlightenment seemed to be moving toward its greatest triumphs under the new empress, Catherine the Great. If Peter had opened a window to Europe and Elizabeth had decorated it with rococo frills, Catherine threw open the doors and began to rebuild the house itself. She looked beyond the technological accomplishments of the North European Protestant nations to the cultural glories of France and Italy and the political traditions of England. But this early optimism was soon to fade. The all-pervading sun of the Enlightenment found the Eastern skies more cloudy than they at first appeared.

The Dilemma of the Reforming Despot

THE REIGN of Catherine illustrates dramatically the conflict between theoretical enlightenment and practical despotism that bothered so many eighteenth-century European monarchs. Few other rulers of her time had such sweeping plans for reform and attracted so much adulation from the *philosophes,* yet few others were so poor in practical accomplishment. In her failure, however, she created the conditions for future change—posing vexing questions for the aristocracy while creating intolerable conditions for the peasantry. As the only articulate ideologist to rule Russia between Ivan IV and Lenin, she changed the terms of reference for Russian thought by linking Russian culture with that of France, and by attempting to base imperial authority on philosophic principles rather than hereditary right or religious sanction.

The attractions of France had, of course, been noticed earlier. Peter had visited the Sorbonne and sent three students to Paris for study in 1717. Kantemir and Tred'iakovsky both spent most of the thirties absorbing French culture in Paris. The former translated Molière and wrote independently in the manner of French satire; the latter, as secretary of the Academy of Sciences and court poet, began the wholesale introduction of Gallicisms into Russian speech. From the beginning, the uneasy aristocracy looked to French thought for philosophic guidance as well as forms of expression; and this philosophic thirst brought them into conflict with the guardians of Orthodoxy in the new state Church. Throughout Elizabeth's reign the Holy Synod made repeated efforts to suppress Fontenelle's *Discourse on the Plurality of Worlds,* with its popularized image of an infinite universe.[10]

Under Catherine, however, the stream became a flood. Fontenelle was freely published but hardly noticed. New books and ideas flowed in from France and were soon superseded by more daring and fashionable ones. The previous book was discarded before it had been used, like an unworn but suddenly outmoded hat. The first French thinker to enjoy popular vogue under Catherine was "the immortal Fénelon," whose poem *Télémaque* provided an exciting image of a utopian society and whose *Education of Girls* partly inspired Catherine's experiments in educating noble women.[11] Fénelon was succeeded by Montesquieu, and Montesquieu by Voltaire—with each infatuation more intense than the last.

Francomania had an artificial and programmatic quality that did much to determine the character—or lack thereof—of aristocratic culture. Contact with France took place frequently through intermediaries. Catherine herself acquired her own taste for things French during her education in Germany; the first systematic Russian translations of French works were by the German "Normanist" Gerhard Friedrich Miller, in a Russian journal which was an imitation of German imitations of Addison and Steele; Molière reached Russia largely through Baltic intermediaries, and his influence on Russian satire of Catherine's day was mixed in with that of Ludvig Holberg, "the Danish Molière." The Russian word for "French" is derived from German, and the word for "Paris" from Italian.[12]

If French culture often reached Russia through intermediaries, it was nonetheless generally viewed as a single, finished product to be rejected or accepted en bloc. Even more than in the original confrontation with the Byzantine, Russians sought to transplant French achievement without the critical spirit which had accompanied it. Catherine saw in the French Enlightenment the means of placing her rule on firm philosophic foundations and providing a national guide for the moral leadership of Europe. The Russian aristocracy used French culture to establish a common identity. The French tongue set them off from both the Russian- or Ukrainian-speaking peasantry and the German-, Swedish-, or Yiddish-speaking mercantile elements of the empire. Chateaux, parks, and theatrical productions provided a congenial and elegant place for leisured gatherings and communal functions and a relief from the austerities of long years of warfare.

Catherine described the purpose of her reign in one of her many philosophical parables: "the thornless rose that does not sting."[13] The rose represents virtue which can be attained only by following the guide, reason, and avoiding the irrational temptations that try to impede this secular pilgrim's progress. Catherine saw no element of pain or unhappiness in true virtue which must naturally lead to "the heavenly city of the eighteenth century philosophers": the rule of justice and right reason.

Her self-confident optimism helped her to create, and forced her to confront, the dilemma of the reforming despot. This dilemma was also to haunt her grandson Alexander I and his grandson Alexander II, while his grandson Nicholas II was to flee in terror from even facing it. How can one retain absolute power and a hierarchical social system while at the same time introducing reforms and encouraging education? How can an absolute ruler hold out hope for improvement without confronting a "revolution of rising expectations"? The two Alexanders, like Catherine, were to find it necessary to check the liberality of their earlier years with despotic measures later. Each of them was to be succeeded by a despot who would seek to block all reform. But the Prussian methods of these successors—Paul, Nicholas I, and Alexander III—could not solve essential problems of state, and thus rendered the need for reform even more imperative. By frustrating moderate reformers, moreover, Paul, Nicholas I, and Alexander III strengthened the hand of extremists in the reformist camp and saddled their imperial successors with artificially pent-up and exaggerated expectations.

The scent of violence hovered about all these imperial reformers. Catherine and Alexander I had each come to power by encouraging the assassination of their predecessors and next of kin; Alexander II, whose reforms were the most far-reaching of all, was rewarded not with gratitude but assassination.

It was almost certainly fear which drove Catherine first to confront the dilemma of reforming despotism. Her position on the throne was initially little more secure than that of her recently murdered husband, Peter III. Threatened in particular by the plan of Nikita Panin to limit severely imperial authority by an aristocratic Imperial Council, Catherine turned in 1763 to the drawing up of a comprehensive defense of absolute monarchy. After three separate drafts, she submitted it to a specially convened legislative commission of 1766–7 which had a majority of non-aristocratic elements subject to her bidding. The commission unanimously awarded Catherine the title "Catherine the Great, Wise, Mother of the Fatherland" and arranged for the publication in Russian, German, French, and Latin of the final draft of her flowery philosophic defense of monarchy, generally known as the Instruction, or Nakaz.[14]

Catherine and her successors paid a severe price, however, for this curious method of legitimizing usurpation. By undercutting the Panin proposals for bringing the aristocracy into the business of government, Catherine added to the already substantial sense of rootlessness which beset this class. The fact that she subsequently granted the aristocracy vast compensatory economic authority over their serfs and exemptions from government service only increased their capacity for idleness without increasing their sense of participation in affairs of state.

Even more important was the unsettling effect of justifying one's right to power on the totally new grounds of natural philosophy. Though the legislative commission did not in fact codify any laws, its detailed discussion and formal approval of Catherine's treatise helped put a large number of new and potentially subversive political ideas in circulation. According to the Nakaz, Russia was a European state, its subjects "citizens," and its proper laws those of the rational, natural order rather than the traditional historical one. Although the Nakaz was not widely distributed within Russia, the legislative commission was broad enough in its representation to carry its ideas to every social group in Russia except the bonded peasantry. With four out of 18 million Russians represented by the 564 deputies, the commission was the first crude attempt at a genuinely national assembly since the zemsky sobors of the early seventeenth century;[15] but it was strikingly different from all previous assemblies ever held on Russian soil in that it was totally secular. There was one deputy from the Synod, but none at all from the clerical estate.

Catherine's basic idea of the "good" and "natural" encouraged scepticism not only toward revealed religion but toward traditional natural philosophy as well. Her "Instruction" directed men's thinking not to ultimate truths or ideal prototypes but to a new relativistic and utilitarian perspective. It seems altogether appropriate that Jeremy Bentham, the father of English utilitarianism, was one of the most honored of foreign visitors to Catherine's Russia; and that translated books of and about Bentham in Russia soon began to outsell the original editions in England.[16]

Like a true utilitarian, Catherine defined legislation as "the Art of conducting People to the greatest Good," which is "whatever may be useful to mankind" in a given tradition and environment. Autocracy must rule through intermediary powers and clear laws, which require that the individual "be fully convinced that it was his Interest, as well as Duty, to preserve those Laws inviolable." The French monarchy rightly appraised the subversive implications of such an approach to the justification of authority, confiscating some two thousand copies en route to France in 1771, and preventing any of the twenty-four foreign versions of the work from being printed there.[17]

Catherine admired not only Bentham but his adversary, Blackstone, whose *Commentaries* she carefully studied and had translated in three volumes. She was widely admired not only in England but also in Italy, where a vast treatise was dedicated to her in 1778, celebrating the victorious alliance of power and reason in the eighteenth century.[18] Nearly one sixth of the articles in Catherine's *Nakaz* were taken directly from the work of another Italian, Beccaria's *On Crimes and Punishment,* which armed Catherine with her conviction that crime comes from ignorance and poor laws, and punishment should be precise and pedagogic rather than arbitrary and vindictive.[19]

But it was always with the French that Catherine felt the greatest kinship. Commenting on the new alliance with France in 1756 just after it was concluded and well before her own accession to the throne, Catherine wrote that "if the gain is not great in commerce, we shall compensate ourselves with bales of intelligence."[20]

The bales had already begun to arrive with the first appearance of a French-language journal on Russian soil in 1755, and with the unprecedented sale of three thousand copies of Voltaire's *Philosophy of History* in St. Petersburg alone within a few days of its appearance in 1756.[21]

Voltaire soon became the official historian of the Russian Empire and a kind of patron saint for the secular aristocracy. The many-sided French Enlightenment was thought to be all of a piece, with Voltaire at its center. Friend and foe alike spoke of *Vol'ter'ianstvo* ("Voltairianism") as the ruling force in Western culture, just as they had spoken of *Latinstvo* ("Latinism") in the fifteenth century. With Catherine's active encouragement, much of the Russian aristocracy became enamored with Voltairianism, which had the general meaning of rationalism, scepticism, and a vague passion for reform. In the first year of her reign, at the age of 34, she opened a correspondence with Voltaire, who was nearly 70. Almost all of the sixty-odd separate works of Voltaire translated into Russian in the last third of the eighteenth century appeared during Catherine's reign. At least 140 printed

translations of Voltaire's works were published in the course of the aristocratic century; numerous abstracts and handwritten copies were made; and
no aristocratic library was thought complete if it did not contain a substantial collection of his works in the original French. The name of Voltaire
was enthroned literally as well as figuratively; for the new high-backed,
thin-armed easy chair in which Russian aristocrats seated themselves for
after-dinner conversation was modeled on that on which Voltaire was often
depicted sitting, and is known even today as a *Vol'terovskoe kreslo* or
"Voltaire chair."[22]

If Voltaire was the symbol, the Gallicized German Friedrich Grimm
was the major source of information for Catherine's court. He supplemented
his famed literary newsletter on the intellectual life of the salons with a
voluminous correspondence with the Empress, who showered him with
many favors, including eventual appointment as her minister in Hamburg.
Grimm became a kind of public relations man for Catherine, and was
probably only partly jesting when he rephrased the Lord's prayer to read
"Our mother, who art in Russia . . ."; changed the Creed into "I believe in
one Catherine . . ."; and set a "Te Catherinam Laudamus" to the music
of Paisiello.[23] Voltaire avoided distinctively Christian terminology, addressing Catherine as "a priest in your temple," confessing that "there is no God
but Allah, and Catherine is the prophet of Allah."[24] Only a more systematic materialist like Helvetius was able to refrain from theistic references
altogether, dedicating his last great work, *On Man, His Intellectual Faculties and His Education,* to her as a "bulwark against 'Asiatic despotism,'
worthy by her intelligence of judging old nations as she is worthy of governing her own."[25]

On this all-important question of government, Catherine was most
indebted to Montesquieu. His mighty *Spirit of the Laws* was both the final
product of a lifetime of urbane reflection and the opening salvo in the "war
of ideas" against the old order in France.[26] Within eighteen months of its
first appearance in 1748, Montesquieu's work had gone through twenty-two
editions, and infected previously untouched segments of society with its
ranging curiosity about politics, its descriptive and comparative approach,
and its underlying determination to prevent arbitrary and despotic rule.

All these features of Montesquieu's work appealed to the young empress as she sought to fortify herself for combat against the political chaos
and religious mystique of Old Russia. Her attitude upon assuming power
was that of one of her generals, who satirically remarked that the government of Russia must indeed be directed "by God himself—otherwise it is
impossible to explain how it is even able to exist."[27] Her *Nakaz* sought to
introduce rational order into the political life of the Empire, and Montes-

quieu was her major source of inspiration. She set aside three hours each day for reading the master, referred to his *Spirit of the Laws* as her "prayer book,"[28] and derived nearly half of the articles in the *Nakaz* from his works.[29]

To be sure, Catherine's entire effort went against Montesquieu's own assumption that Russia was foredoomed by its size and heritage to despotic rule; and she distorted or neglected some of his most celebrated ideas. Montesquieu's aristocratic "intermediary bodies" between the monarch and his subjects served not, in Catherine's proposal, to separate power between executive, legislative, and judicial functions but rather to consolidate government functions and create new lines of transmission for imperial authority.

Nevertheless, Catherine was closer to the spirit of Montesquieu's politics than many who followed him more literally on specific points. Her effort to make monarchy unlimited yet fully rational; her sense of adjusting political forms to environmental necessities; her increasing recognition of the need for active aristocratic support so that the spirit of honor could be enlisted to support the rule of reason—all of this was clearly in the spirit of the man who did so much to turn men's eyes away from the letter to the spirit of law.

If the *Spirit of the Laws* provided Catherine with the image of rationally ordered politics, the *Encyclopedia* of Diderot and D'Alembert, which began to appear three years later in 1751, provided the image of rationally ordered knowledge. Her enthusiasm for this work soon rivaled her passion for Montesquieu. D'Alembert declined Catherine's invitation to serve as tutor to her son; but Diderot considered transferring the editorial side of his work to Riga, and eventually sold his library to Catherine and came to St. Petersburg.[30] Three volumes of the *Encyclopedia* had been translated almost immediately into Russian under the supervision of the director of Moscow University. A private translation was concurrently being made by the future historian Ivan Boltin, and many articles and sections were translated individually.

For the rational ordering of economic life, Catherine turned first (at Diderot's suggestion) to the French physiocrat, Lemercier de la Rivière; then, following his unhappy visit to Russia,[31] she sent two professors from Moscow to study under Adam Smith in Glasgow. Her most original approach was the founding in 1765 of a Free Economic Society for the Encouragement in Russia of Agriculture and Household Management: a kind of extra-governmental advisory body. Two years later she offered one thousand gold pieces for the best set of recommendations on how to organize an agricultural economy "for the common good." The society received

164 entries in this remarkable Europe-wide contest, with the greatest response and the prize-winning essay coming from France.[32]

In practice, however, there was no reorganization of agriculture, just as there was no new law code or synthesis of knowledge. The shock caused by the Pugachev uprising put an end to the languishing legislative commission and to the various efforts to make the *Encyclopedia* the basis for widespread public enlightenment. Boltin's translation died at the letter "K"— the first of the host of uncompleted reference books with which Russian history is so tragically full.[33]

Yet even while Cathering was preparing Pugachev for quartering, she continued to correspond with the Corsican revolutionary Paoli (and another restless Corsican, the then obscure Napoleon Bonaparte considered entering her service).[34]

Only after the French Revolution did Catherine's thoughts turn away from reform altogether to a final assertion of unleavened despotism. Even then she bequeathed the dilemma to Alexander I by assigning to him the Swiss republican La Harpe as a tutor and by surrounding him with an aristocratic entourage of Anglophile liberals. Alexander I in turn willed to Alexander II some of this dangerous taste for partial reform when a friend from his own liberal days, Michael Speransky, became one of the tutors.

At the end of her long trail of literary and literal seductions, Catherine left aristocratic Russia stimulated, but in no way satisfied. By sending most of the aristocratic elite abroad for education, she imparted a vague sense of possibility, a determination to "overtake and surpass" the Enlightenment of the West. Yet the actual reforms accomplished in her reign were too meager even to provide clear guidance toward this goal. From Catherine, aristocratic thinkers received only their inclination to look Westward for answers. They learned to think in terms of sweeping reforms on abstract, rationalistic grounds rather than piecemeal changes rooted in concrete conditions and traditions.

Particularly popular under Catherine was the vague idea that newly conquered regions to the south could provide virgin soil on which to raise out of nothing a new civilization. Voltaire told Catherine that he would come to Russia if Kiev were made the capital rather than St. Petersburg. Herder's earliest dream of earthly glory was to be "a new Luther and Solon" for the Ukraine: to make this unspoiled and fertile region into "a new Greece."[35] Bernardin de Saint-Pierre believed that an egalitarian agricultural community, possibly even a new Pennsylvania, might be created in the region around the Aral Sea.[36] Catherine herself dreamed of making her new city below Kiev on the Dnieper, Ekaterinoslav ("Praise Catherine"), a monumental center for world culture and her newly conquered port on the Black Sea, Kherson, a new St. Petersburg.[37]

Rather than come to grips with the concrete problems of her realm, Catherine became infatuated in her declining years with her "grand design" for taking Constantinople and dividing the Balkans with the Hapsburg emperor. She named her second grandson Constantine, placed the image of the Santa Sophia on her coins, and wrote a dramatic extravaganza, *The First Government of Oleg,* which ends with this early Russian conqueror-prince leaving his shield behind in Constantinople for future generations to reclaim.[38]

Having subdued at last the entire northern coast of the Black Sea, Catherine adorned it with a string of new cities—often on the site of old Greek settlements—Azov, Taganrog, Nikolaev, Odessa, and Sevastopol. The latter, built as a fortress on the southwest corner of the Crimean peninsula, was given the Greek version of the Roman imperial title *Augusta.* Built by an English naval engineer, Samuel Bentham, the "august city" (*sevastē polis*) inspired nothing original except for the eerie plan of Samuel's famous brother Jeremy for a panopticon: a prison in which a central observer could peer into all cells.[39] Sevastopol is remembered not for the awe it inspired but for the humiliation it brought to Russia when captured by British and French invaders during the Crimean War. More than any other single event, the fall of the "august city" in 1855 dispelled illusion and forced Russia to turn from external glory to internal reform.

But external glory preoccupied Catherine during the latter part of her reign. Her world of illusion is symbolized by the famed legend that portable "Potemkin villages" were devised by her most famous courtier to camouflage the misery of the people from her eyes during triumphal tours. She spent her last years (and almost her last rubles) building pretentious palaces for her favorites, foreign advisers and relatives: Tauride in St. Petersburg and nearby Gatchina and Tsarskoe Selo (which she intended to name Constantingorod). The costumes and sets were more impressive than the actual plays in Catherine's theater. She expressed a preference for extended *divertissements,* and insisted that serious operas be cut from three acts to two. It seems strangely appropriate that four different versions of the Pygmalion story were staged during the reign of Catherine. This minor German princess had been transformed into a northern goddess by the sages of the eighteenth century; but in this case the reality was less impressive than the figure on the pedestal. Even today the monument to her in front of the former imperial (now Saltykov-Shchedrin) library in Leningrad still is usually seen rising up from a sea of mud. Her every movement was surrounded with cosmetic camouflage and rococo frills. In an age when cutout

silhouettes and surface flourishes were in vogue throughout Europe, Catherine brought the silhouette without the substance of reform to Russia.[40]
As a final monument to her vanity, she left behind five feast days consecrated to her alone on the church calendar: her birthday, day of succession
to the throne, day of coronation, name day, and the day of her smallpox
vaccination, November 21.[41]

Catherine's turn from inner reform to external aggrandizement is
dramatically illustrated by the three-sided and three-staged dismemberment
of Poland. Having helped place her youthful friend and lover, Stanisław
Poniatowski, on the Polish throne in 1764, Catherine participated in the
first partition of Poland in 1772; then took the lead in the last two, which
followed Stanisław's adoption in 1791 of a reform constitution not dissimilar
to those which Catherine had considered in earlier days.[42] The absorption
of Poland had, however, the ironic effect of helping to perpetuate the very
tradition that Catherine was rejecting. For Stanisław promptly moved to St.
Petersburg along with his relatives, the Czartoryski family, and many other
reform-minded survivors of the old Polish republic.

Catherine's first grandson, Alexander, resembled less the Macedonian
conqueror for whom he was named than the Polish visionaries whom he
met in his youth. Her second grandson, Constantine, became the rallying
point for the reformist elements in the guards regiments who assembled in
Senate Square in St. Petersburg on December 14, 1825, after Alexander's
death. But these "Decembrists" related the name Constantine not to Constantinople but to constitution—some of their illiterate followers even believing that the Russian word *konstitutsiia* was the name of his wife. The
Decembrists were calling not for an imperial commander but for a man
who had become the governor of Poland and was thought to provide some
kind of link with its more moderate reformist traditions. To understand
why these moderate constitutionalists were crushed, and the dilemma
of the reforming despot firmly resolved in favor of despotism under Nicholas
I, one must turn from symbols and omens to the crucial substantive changes
which were effected in the direction of Russian thought under Catherine.

The Fruits of the Enlightenment

THE CONCRETE ACHIEVEMENTS of Catherine's domestic program seem
strangely insignificant: the introduction of vaccination, paper money, and
an improved system of regional administration. Yet her impact on Russian
history went far deeper than the superficial statecraft and foreign conquest

for which she is justly renowned. More than any other single person prior to the Leninist revolution, Catherine cut official culture loose from its religious roots, and changed both its physical setting and its philosophical preoccupations. Important changes in architecture and ideas must thus be analyzed if one is to understand the revolutionary nature and fateful consequences of Catherine's Enlightenment.

Catherine substituted the city for the monastery as the main center of Russian culture. She, and not Peter, closed down monasteries on a massive scale and tore down wooden symbols of Muscovy, such as the old summer palace of the tsars at Kolomenskoe. In some of the monasteries that remained open she placed pseudo-classical bell towers that clashed with everything else and demonstrated her inability to make even token gestures to the old religious culture of Muscovy.

Convinced that men have always honored "the memory of the founders of cities equally with the memory of lawmakers,"[43] she appointed a commission at the beginning of her reign to plan a systematic rebuilding of Moscow and St. Petersburg, and encouraged it to draw up plans for building or renovating some 416 other cities. St. Petersburg was soon transformed from an imitation Dutch naval base into a stately granite capital. New cities were built, and the over-all urban population, which had increased only slightly since the time of Peter the Great, nearly doubled between 1769 and 1782. In many of her rebuilt cities, from Tver to Tobol'sk, Catherine was able to realize her ideal of rational uniformity. Yaroslavl, second in size only to Moscow among cities of the interior, was beautifully transformed by superimposing a radiocentric grid of broad streets onto the jumbled city, and by subtly converting its ornate late-Muscovite churches into decorative terminal points for streets and promenades. The perfection and large-scale manufacture of uniform-sized bricks created new practical possibilities for rebuilding wooden provincial cities. Throughout the realm, architectural mass began to replace the florid decorative effects of both the high Muscovite style and the Elizabethan rococo. Simple, neo-classical shapes—semi-circular arches and domes and Doric columns—dominated the new urban architecture, where the design of the ensemble generally determined the proportions of the individual structure.

Of course, many of Catherine's plans for cities were completely impractical; many more were never acted on; and the percentage of total population in the cities remained minute and to a large extent seasonal. Those cities which were built conformed only to a prescribed pattern of roads and squares, and of design on important facing surfaces. Lesser streets and all block interiors were completely uncontrolled—testifying in their squalor to the superficiality of Catherine's accomplishment. Behind all the façades and profiles lay an enserfed peasantry and a swollen, disease-ridden army distracted from their collective misfortunes by a running tide of military conquest. Thousands of provincial figures—including many who were neither aristocratic nor literate—participated in building the new cities; and architecture proved in many ways as important as literature in spreading the new ideal of rational order and classical style.

Nevertheless, the majestic, artificial city of Catherine's era provided a new center and symbol for Russian culture. Catherine's new cities were not basically commercial centers, the traditional arenas for the development of a practical-minded bourgeois culture, but rather aristocratic cities: provincial showplaces for the newly acquired elegance and pro-consular power of the aristocracy. Town planners were more concerned with providing plazas for military reviews than places for trade and industry; architects devoted their ingenuity to convertible theater-ballrooms rather than convenient facilities for ordinary goods and services.

Because so many of her new cities were administrative centers for her newly created provincial governments, the city center was dominated by political rather than religious buildings. Horizontal lines replaced vertical ones as the narrow streets, tent roofs, and onion domes of the wooden cities were swept away. The required ratio of 2:1 between the width of major streets and the height of facing buildings became 4:1 in many cases. Such artificially broadened promenades and the sprawling squares visible from pseudo-classical porches and exedras gave the ruling aristocracy an imposing sense of space.

Having just conquered the southern steppe and settled on a provincial estate, the officer-aristocrat in the late years of Catherine's reign was newly conscious of the land; and its vastness seemed both to mock and to menace his pretensions. In the new cities to which he repaired for the long winter, he could feel physically secure in a way that was never before possible in Russian cities. The danger of fire was greatly reduced by the progressive elimination of wooden buildings and narrow streets; the last great peasant uprising had been quelled; and the key bases of Tatar raiders in the south were finally captured.

Yet gone also was the psychological security of the old Muscovite cities with their outer walls and inner kremlins capped by the domes and spires that lifted eyes upward. The city was now dominated by the horizontal stretch of roads leading from a central space at the heart of the city to the greater spaces that lay all around. Into such cities, the ruling aristocrats brought an inner malaise not unrelated to the limitlessness and monotony of the steppe and to the artificiality of their own position on it.

A belief in the liberating and ennobling power of education was perhaps the central article of faith in the European Enlightenment. But the practical problem of providing secular education for the relatively rootless and insecure Russian aristocracy proved profoundly vexing. Both the limited accomplishments and the deeper problems are illustrated in the career of Ivan Betskoy, Catherine's principal court adviser on educational matters. His long life spanned ninety-two years of the eighteenth century; and most of his many-sided reformist activities were dedicated to the central concern of that century, the spread of education and public enlightenment.

The ideal of an expanded, Western type of school system had been present for several decades in the more advanced Western sections of the Russian Empire. German-educated Ukrainian seminarians like Gregory Teplov drew up elaborate plans; Herder, while a young pastor in Riga, dreamed of installing a system of instruction modeled on Rousseau's *Émile*. Baltic German graduates of Tartu, in Esthonia, brought with them the ideas of the Enlightenment that had begun to permeate that institution. Officers like Andrew Bolotov returned from the Seven Years' War with plans for streamlining Russian aristocratic instruction along lines set down by the victorious Frederick the Great.[44]

At first glance, Catherine's educational projects appear to be nothing more than another example of high hopes and minimal accomplishment. Encouraged by Locke's *On the Education of Children* (translated into Russian in 1761) and his *Essay Concerning Human Understanding* to think of man as a *tabula rasa* on which education is free to print any message, Catherine discussed plans for education with everyone from the encyclopedists to the Jesuits (to whom she offered shelter after the Pope abolished the Society in 1773). However, the statute for public schools in the empire, drawn up with the aid of Jankovich de Mirievo, a Serb who had reorganized public education within the Hapsburg empire, remained largely a paper proclamation. While she talked of sowing seeds of knowledge throughout the empire, she let the St. Petersburg Academy of Sciences lapse into a relatively fallow period in which little serious work was published.[45]

Yet certain important developments did take place in education; and almost all of them were connected with Betskoy, who, like most eighteenth-century Russian aristocrats, was widely traveled, trained to think in abstract, universal terms, and almost totally without deep roots in his Russian homeland. Estrangement was built into his very name, for Betskoy was a contraction of the old aristocratic name of Trubetskoy, of the sort frequently assumed by the illegitimate children of noble families. The Vorontsovs gave birth to more than a few Rantsovs; Golitsyns, Litsyns; Rumiantsevs, Miantsovs; Griboedovs, Gribovs, and so on. Betskoy was not alone in bearing this constant reminder of aristocratic profligacy. Ivan Pnin, whose

1804 treatise, *On Enlightenment in Russia,* went even further in proposing education for the peasantry, was also the bastard offspring of an old aristocratic line. His father, Prince Nicholas Repnin, was a friend of Betskoy known as the "Russian Aristides" for his enlightened administrative activities in western Russia.[46] Herzen, whose publications abroad later helped revive interest in the reformist currents of Catherine's time, also bore the stamp of illegitimate aristocratic birth.

Betskoy was born in Stockholm, educated in Copenhagen, spent most of his early life in Paris, and had close if not intimate relations with a host of minor German princesses, including the mother of Catherine the Great. Thus, when Catherine ascended to the throne, Betskoy commended himself to the young empress as a man with excellent intellectual and physiological qualifications for the court. Like Catherine's special favorites, Orlov and Potemkin, Betskoy was drawn to the Empress and her projects for reform partly because of antagonism to the more established aristocracy. Whereas most older aristocrats sympathized with Panin's efforts to have an aristocratic council limit tsarist authority, Betskoy and his allies sought to expand that authority as a means of furthering their own relative position in the hierarchy. Whereas the older aristocrats tended to adopt the measured rationalism of Voltaire and Diderot, Catherine's less secure courtiers tended to prefer the visionary ideas of Rousseau. There was perhaps a certain sense of identity between these relative outsiders to the Russian aristocracy and the Genevan outsider to the aristocratic Paris of the *philosophes.* Basically, however, the Russian turn from Voltaire to Rousseau reflected a general turn in intellectual fashion among European reformist circles of the 1770's and 1780's. Orlov invited Rousseau to come to Russia and take up permanent residence on his estate; one of the Potemkins became Rousseau's principal Russian translator; Catherine retreated increasingly to her own Rousseauian "Hermitage"; and the "general plan of education" which Betskoy presented to her was partly based on Rousseau's *Émile.*[47]

Betskoy sought to create in Russia "a new breed of man" freed from the artificiality of contemporary society for a more natural way of life. The government was to assume responsibility for this new type of education, seeking to develop the heart as well as the mind, to encourage physical as well as mental development, and to place the teaching of morality at the head of the curriculum. In his search for elements suitable for remolding through pedagogical experiment he had to look no further than his own origins. Bastards and orphans—the rejected material of society—were to become the cornerstones of his new temple of humanity. On the basis of a close study of secular philanthropic activities in England and France, Betskoy set up in Moscow and Petersburg foundling homes which were to become major centers of initiation into the new Russian Enlightenment. Foundling homes are even now called "educational" (*vospitatel'nye*) homes in Russia, and these first ones were set up

> ... to overcome the superstition of centuries, to give the people their new education and, so to speak, their new birth (*porozhdenie*).[48]

They were to remain totally removed from the outside world in these secular monasteries from age five or six to eighteen or twenty; but, in fact, many entered at two or three, and were neither bastards nor orphans.

Betskoy was Russia's first de facto minister of education, serving as president of the Academy of Arts, organizing planner for the Smolny Monastery for women (the only one of these "monastic" schools to outlive him), and reorganizer of the curriculum for the infantry corps of cadets—as well as head of the foundling homes and an influential adviser to the Academy of Sciences and many private tutors. He was also a resourceful fund raiser, promoting special theatrical benefits and a lucrative tax for education on another favorite aristocratic recreation: playing cards. He died in 1795, just a year before his sovereign benefactor, and willed his substantial private fortune of 400,000 rubles to his educational projects. As he was lowered into the grave, the most honored poet of the age, Gabriel Derzhavin, read a specially written "On the End of the Philanthropist" to this "ray of goodness." The poem was, as it were, the secular substitute for the "Eternal Memory" of the Orthodox burial service. Now "heaven, truth, saintliness" were made to "cry out above the grave" that their "light" was immortal even if their lives were only "smoke." "Without good deeds," Derzhavin concludes, "there is no blessedness."[49]

One can, of course, question what the real number of "good deeds" or extent of civic "blessedness" was under Catherine. She never shared her courtiers' fondness for Rousseau, and forbade—long before the Pugachev uprising—the circulation of many of his key works, including *Émile*. She viewed Rousseau as "a new St. Bernard," who was arming France and all of Europe for "a spiritual crusade against me."[50] Nevertheless, the all-important fourth part of *Émile,* the "Profession of Faith of the Savoyard Vicar," readily slipped through the hands of the censors when it appeared in Russian translation in 1770 under the "Aesopian" title "Meditations on the Majesty of God, on His Providence and on Man."

The historical importance of the Russian Enlightenment under Catherine cannot be denied. Russians had been introduced to a new world of thought that was neither theological nor technological, but involved the remaking of the whole man in accordance with a new secular ideal of ethical activism. Moreover, the idea was established that this moral education was properly the responsibility of the government. Betskoy was thoroughly devoted to autocracy, and sought to enlist government support for his educational program on the grounds that it would serve to produce a select elite uniquely loyal to the imperial cause.

Like Montesquieu in politics, Betskoy in education set the tone for much subsequent discussion in Russia, without seeing many of his practical prescriptions adopted. Betskoy's interest in using the Russian language was disregarded by academies and tutors alike, who were expected to familiarize aristocratic youth with Western European rather than Russian or Byzantine tradition. His interest in a measure of practical training in trades was never able to modify the pronounced emphasis on non-technical and broadly philosophical subjects. Time spent in higher educational institutions generally counted as state service for noblemen or for those aspiring to a title. A leisurely and dilettantish education was better preparation for life among the aristocracy than industrious specialization.[51] Betskoy's more earnest boarding schools were remembered mainly as the object of humorous barbs, usually aimed at the "child-like Betskoy" (*detskoy-Betskoy*).

Betskoy's last important service to Catherine was supervising the embellishment of St. Petersburg. With characteristic thoroughness he organized expeditions to Siberia to bring back rare and decorative stones, arranged for importation of stone from Finland and the manufacture of bricks in St. Petersburg, and helped put in their final place a variety of statues, including Falconet's long-labored equestrian statue of Peter the Great in the Senate Square.[52] This imposing memorial to Peter became, through Pushkin's famous poem "The Bronze Horseman," an enduring symbol of both the majestic power and the impersonal coldness of the new capital. Catherine's pretense in placing a monumental façade over widespread suffering seems in some ways anticipatory of the *dostoprimechatel'nosti* ("imposing sights") in the midst of terror in the Stalin era. Her city below Kiev on the Dnieper (Ekaterinoslav, now Dniepropetrovsk) became the site of the first and most celebrated mammoth construction project of the Soviet era: the hydroelectric dam of the 1920's.

The most important link between the Russia of Catherine and that of the revolutionary era lies, however, in the creation of a new class of secular intellectuals vaguely inclined toward sweeping reform. Betskoy had spoken of developing through education a "third rank" of citizens along with the aristocracy and the peasantry.[53] The educated intellectuals did indeed come to constitute a new rank in society outside the table of ranks created by Peter. They found their solidarity, however, not as a class of enlightened state servitors, as Betskoy had hoped, but as an "intelligentsia" estranged from the state machine. This was the "new race of men" to come out of

Catherine's cultural upheaval: the unofficial "third rank" between the ruling aristocracy and the servile peasantry.

For Catherine's reign saw a profound and permanent change in the source of internal opposition to imperial authority. Whereas the first half was plagued by violent protest movements among the lower classes, climaxing in the Pugachev uprising, the latter half of her reign saw the first appearance of "Pugachevs from the academies": a new kind of opposition from within the educated aristocracy. The estrangement of these intellectuals from their aristocratic background resulted not so much from any changes in the sovereign's attitude toward reform as from an inner ripening of ideas within the thinking community itself. Since this intellectual ferment was to play a vital role in subsequent Russian history, it is important to consider the first steps on the path of critical questioning that was to lead Russia to form an intelligentsia, a "new Soviet intelligentsia," and perhaps something even beyond that in the post-Stalin era.

The Alienation of the Intellectuals

THE ALIENATION of the intellectuals in modern Russia was, from the beginning, not so much a matter of conflict between different classes and factions as of conflicting feelings and impulses at work within the same groups and even the same individuals. The conflicts inside these disturbed groups and individuals were, in a sense, minor compared with the great sense of distance that was felt between those who participated in the conflicts and those who did not; between what came to be called *intelligentsiia* and *meshchanstvo,* "intelligence" and "philistinism."

The inner conflict that first created the modern Russian intelligentsia was a personal and moral one within the ruling aristocracy. This fact created a peculiar psychological compulsion for passionate personal engagement in ethical questions, which was to become a key characteristic of the alienated intellectuals.

The personal moral crisis for the ruling aristocrat of Catherine's era was not, in the first instance, created by economic and political privilege but rather by the new style of life within the aristocracy itself: by the vulgar hedonism and imitative Gallomania of their own increasingly profligate lives. Much of this self-hate was sublimated into biting denunciations of foreign forms and customs, which led in turn to an increased, if hyper-sensitive national self-consciousness by the late years of Catherine's reign.

But there was also much introspection and self-criticism. Russians expressed distress that "the worship of Minerva was so often followed by the feasts of Bacchus," and sought to discover how the wisdom of Minerva might be applied to problems of practical conduct. Still, however, the need was felt for some external source of their perversion; and one was soon found in the symbolic figure of Voltaire, who was said to have "made animal life the sole aim of man."[54] Voltairianism came to be viewed as a force leading into self-indulgent immorality.

As was so often to be the case subsequently, thoughtful Russians tended to unite around what they rejected rather than what they accepted. A convenient object for this collective hatred was provided by Theodore Henri Chudi, the principal foreign agent of the Francophile Shuvalov family and a major vehicle for the importation of French culture into Russia.

Chudi was one of the more odious sycophants in the Russian imperial entourage. He was a Swiss actor who had first come to Russia as a minor figure in the new imperial theater. After adopting a more impressive name (Chevalier de Lussy) and a synthetic French noble ancestry, he made a successful career at court as a gigolo and glorified gossip columnist—editing the first French-language journal on Russian soil, *Le Caméléon littéraire.* On its pages, he frankly admitted that he would be "lost without frivolity."

> I am French, one would expect it, the frivolity of my work announces a man of my nation. To this first quality, I could add the title of Cosmopolitan.[55]

Under such unfortunate auspices was introduced the term "cosmopolitan," which became a classic term of invective in Imperial and Soviet Russia alike. Sensuality, superficiality, and cosmopolitanism were interrelated sins —all equated with the virus of Voltaire and with bearers of the infection like Chudi.

The first dim outlines of a deeper moral reaction to Voltairianism was evidenced in the theater: the central ideological arena of Catherine's era. The importance of the emerging Russian theater derived not solely from the sheer numbers of the plays, operas, ballets, and pantomimes that were written and performed—including those of the imperial playwright and patron herself. Its importance lay in the fact that in a world where the court life of the aristocracy had become stylized and theatrical, the impersonal, formal theater tended to become by ironic transposition the only public arena in which the deeper concerns of the aristocracy could be dealt with in polite society.

The alienation of the intellectuals in many ways begins with the growing antagonism of serious playwrights toward the increasingly frivolous, largely musical theater of Catherine's later years. A typical comic opera of the 1780's, *Love Is Cleverer than Eloquence,* made fun of professors, philosophers, and enlightenment generally, ending with the chorus:

> However people deceive,
> However reason jokes,
>   Truth proclaims to everyone:
>   Love will out-deceive you all.

Catherine forced the entire Holy Synod to sit through another, *Le Philosophe ridicule;* and her own profligacy was extolled in *The New Family Group,* which ended with a chorus to happiness at last freed from "either longing or monotony":

> As you wish, so shall you live
> We will never interfere . . .[56]

One sees the beginning of the reaction in Alexander Sumarokov, the director of the St. Petersburg theater, whose tragedies, comedies, and opera libretti provided the mainstay of the repertoire throughout the eighteenth century. Though always operating within the framework of secular enlightenment, Sumarokov tried to lead Russian taste back from hedonistic Voltairianism to Fénelon, Racine, and the Stoic philosophers of antiquity.

He gave Russian tragedy a disciplined fidelity to the classical unities of time and place and at the same time a bias for instructive moralistic themes. The aim of tragedy was "to lead men to good deeds," "to cleanse passion through reason."[57] His short sketches and fables also sought to edify, and his writings did more than those of any other single figure of the age to provide Russian aristocratic thinkers with a new lexicon of abstract moral terminology. Far less religious than a natural scientist like Lomonosov, this natural philosopher attached the supreme value to reason, duty, and the common good. Even when writing "spiritual odes," he was calling for a new secular morality of aristocratic self-discipline.

To some extent, Sumarokov's ideal was that of "the immortal Fénelon" in *Télémaque: vaincre les passions.* This pseudo-classical poem was the first French work to become a smash literary hit in Russia. It was translated several times, and inspired a Russian continuation: the *Tilemakhida* of Tred'iakovsky—just as the *Télémaque* had been offered by Fénelon as a kind of continuation of Homer's *Odyssey.*

The search for links with the classical world led Sumarokov and other philosophically inclined Russian aristocrats to Stoic philosophy. The play that had been staged in Kiev in 1744 on the occasion of Elizabeth's pilgrimage to the Monastery of the Caves was *The Piety of Marcus*

Aurelius.[58] The vanquished villain in the play was Anger, just as it was invariably passions like self-seeking and carnal love in the plays of Sumarokov. Falconet's statue of Peter was originally modeled on the statue of Marcus Aurelius in Rome, and was popularly referred to as Marcus Aurelius; Fonvizin's translation of the contemporary *Elegy of Marcus Aurelius* appeared in 1771; and La Harpe cited Marcus Aurelius as a model for all kings in his memorandum to Catherine on the education of Alexander I.[59] The Stoic calm of the Roman emperor was seen as a model for the Russian aristocrat's efforts to master passion with reason. As Sumarokov put it:

> The man of reason
> Moves on through time with tolerance,
> The happiness of true wisdom is not moved to rapture
> And does not groan with sorrows.[60]

The stoicism of Seneca also gained a following through such books as *The Moral Cures of the Christianized Seneca,* which promised to "correct human morals and instill true health" with the "true wisdom" of Stoic philosophy.[61]

This concept of "true wisdom" (*premudrost'*) was at variance with the ethos of Catherine's court even when advanced by scrupulously loyal monarchists like Sumarokov. Like the concept of natural law that was simultaneously being introduced into the philosophy curriculum of Moscow University, "true wisdom" seemed to propose a standard of truth above that of the monarch's will. Unsystematic Voltairianism, with its ideal of a cultivated earthly life and urbane scepticism, was more to Catherine's liking. Rather than Marcus Aurelius' *Meditations,* she wanted her courtiers to read Tatishchev's *Honorable Mirror of Youth.* By 1767 this manual had undergone five editions, with its homely reminders (often reinforced with proverbs) not to repeat the same story incessantly, pick teeth with a knife, or keep spurs on while dancing. In such a world, morality tended to be Epicurean rather than Stoic. The starting point was self-interest rather than higher reality:

> Rational egoism necessarily includes in itself love toward God and one's neighbor. Man will love independently because one needs the love of others for one's own happiness.[62]

Earthy satire was even more important than Stoic uplift in giving dramatic expression to aristocratic discontent with Voltairianism. Catherine wrote a number of plays satirizing the aristocracy, and helped give birth to a new and potentially subversive genre which was first mastered by Denis

Fonvizin. If Catherine's pretensions as a writer far exceeded her accomplishments, exactly the opposite is true of Fonvizin. He was a diffident, self-effacing aristocrat who became incurably ill in his late thirties, yet lived to complete in *The Adolescent* one of Russia's first original masterpieces of secular literature and "first drama of social satire."

The Adolescent challenged the prevailing pseudo-classical literary style and gave an altogether new direction to Russian writing. It anticipates in some ways the distinctively Russian theatrical tradition of "laughter through tears" which was to lead through Gogol to Chekhov. Nearly twenty years in the making, it also stands as the first of those life projects which were to drain away the talents of so many sensitive artists of the late imperial period.

The Adolescent is a short, deceptively simple prose comedy on a contemporary theme—exactly the opposite of the ponderous rhymed tragedies in mythological settings then in favor. It is one of the ironies of Catherine's reign that Fonvizin, who developed to perfection the satirical form which Catherine introduced, was the secretary to Count Panin, the man who had originally led the fight to limit her autocratic power. Frustrated in their efforts to curb imperial absolutism, her opponents now turned to satire. It was an indication of things to come; for Catherine's successors were to be limited more by ideological disaffection than political restraint. Dramatic satire became in the nineteenth—and indeed in the post-Stalin twentieth century—the vehicle for a distinctively Russian form of passionate, if seemingly passive, communal protest against tyranny. As an acute German observer of the 1860's noted: "Political opposition in Russia takes the form of satire."[63] *The Adolescent* was the first Russian drama to be translated and performed in the West; and it has remained the only eighteenth-century Russian drama still regularly performed in the USSR.

Fonvizin was a cosmopolitan eighteenth-century figure. His German ancestry is revealed in his name (derived from von Wiesen), and his plays betray the influence of the Danish social satirist, Ludvig Holberg (whose plays he read and translated from the German), and of the Italian *commedia dell'arte* (whose traditions were filtering in through the Italian personnel imported for the operatic theater). His real model was, however, France, and its pre-Revolutionary satirical theater in which—as he put it in a letter from Paris—"you forget that a comedy is being played and it seems that you are seeing direct history."[64]

The Adolescent comes close to being "direct history" and thus anticipates much of nineteenth-century Russian literature. The play deals with the key problem of the Russian Enlightenment itself: the education of the aristocracy. Part of it depicts the conventional education for virtue and responsibility of an aristocratic couple preparing for marriage. But most of the play and all of its interest centers on the education of "the adolescent," a brutish, sixteen-year-old provincial aristocrat, Mitrofan, by an unforgettable galaxy of characters "in the village of the Prostakovs" (literally, "Simpletons"). Three fraudulent teachers, a worthless father, a pig-loving uncle, and a gross, doting mother, all hover around the sulking Mitrofan and contribute to his mis-education. Those who preach the gospel of aristocratic virtue are made to appear boring and faintly ludicrous in a world where unvarnished barbarism is still the norm.

Thus, Fonvizin turns Catherine's world upside down in a way he never had as part of Panin's political opposition—and in a way he may not entirely have intended. Western education does not lead to the grail of enlightenment in adolescent Russia. At the end of the adventure, there is no "thornless rose that does not sting," but only a sea of brambles. The last line of the play is: "Here are the worthy fruits of an evil nature." Perhaps human nature is not perfectible after all. Perhaps there is no point in cultivating one's garden, as Voltaire advised, because nothing but poisoned fruit will grow.

But such splenetic thoughts were to come later. Fonvizin's perspective is still one of life-affirming laughter. He shared the breadth of interests that was typical of the Russian Enlightenment, and the sense of confidence and pride that comes from being a privileged member of a rising power. For deeper disaffection one must look to three other figures who deliberately set out to find radically new answers to the problems of the day: Gregory Skovoroda, Alexander Radishchev, and Nicholas Novikov. They were probably the most brilliant men of the late eighteenth century in Russia; and the depth and variety of their searchings illustrate the true seriousness of the alienation of the intellectuals under Catherine. The only common feature of their divergent careers is the intensity with which they all rejected the dilettantism and imitativeness of court culture and the finality with which their own new ideas and activities were, in turn, rejected by Catherine.

Skovoroda represented the most complete rejection of Catherine's ethos with his ascetic indifference to things of this world and his search for the hidden mysteries of "true wisdom." Of Cossack descent, Skovoroda studied at the Kiev Academy and attracted imperial attention in the 1740's as a vocalist in the baroque choirs of Kiev. A brilliant teacher at the Academy, he soon turned to seminary teaching and then left for a life of lonely wandering and reading, relieved only by endless philosophical dialogues and a few close friendships.

He taught for brief periods in all of the great centers of theological education in eighteenth-century Russia: Kiev, St. Petersburg, Kharkov, and the Moscow Academy in the Monastery of St. Sergius. He concluded that happiness lay only in full inner knowledge of oneself, which in turn required a highly personal and mystical link with God. He wandered throughout Russia for most of his last thirty years, with no possessions except a knapsack containing a Hebrew Bible and books in many languages. He wrote haunting poems, letters, and philosophic dialogues rather in the style of Blake, rejecting the high culture of the Enlightenment for the "primordial world which delights my heart's abyss."[65] Influenced by Stoicism and Neo-Platonism, he taught, in his *Dialogue of the Archangel Michael with Satan,* that there was a fundamental conflict between the spiritual and material worlds. Carnal lust and worldly ambition are the principal lures of the devil; he inveighed against the one in his *Israelite Snake* and the other in his *Icon of Alcibiades.* He died in 1794, leaving behind as his epitaph: "The world hunted me but it did not catch me."[66]

Skovoroda called himself the Russian Socrates, and he was one of Russia's first original speculative philosophers. He shared, moreover, the Platonic qualities of dedication and perhaps also homosexuality. His songs of praise to "father freedom"[67] reflect the anarchistic sentiments of his Cossack forebears. His mysticism and dualism made him feel more at home with religious sectarians than with the official Orthodox Church, which was particularly infused with scholasticism in the Latinized Ukraine. Skovoroda helped compose a declaration of faith for the "spirit wrestlers" and music for the psalm-singing ceremonies of the "milk drinkers."[68]

Skovoroda never joined any sect, however, and is properly described as "a lonely mountain on the steppe."[69] He foreshadowed the romantic, metaphysical *Auswanderung* of the Russian intelligentsia. For he was discontent not so much with the Russia of his day as with the entire earthly world. He was driven on by Faustian discontent with all formal and external knowledge. Favored with positions in all the leading theological centers, he never took holy orders, and he eventually left the Church altogether. He sought to teach religion through poetry and a symbolic study of the Bible. He described himself as "not a beggar but an elder"[70] and became a kind of secular version of the medieval mendicant pilgrim.

The sincerity and intensity of his quest—like that of many Russian thinkers to follow—commanded respect even among those unable to understand his ideas or language. In his native Ukraine he became a legendary figure, whose manuscripts were passed about like sacred writings and whose picture was often displayed as an icon. Not least among those who stood in awe of him was the tsarist government, which refused to permit any collected edition of his voluminous (and largely unpublished) works to appear until a century after his death. Even then, the edition was incomplete and heavily censored; and subsequent editors have drawn only very selectively from this profound—and profoundly disturbing—thinker. Many of his writings he called "conversations," and they were apparently the out-growth of his many oral disputations on metaphysical matters which helped launch the seemingly interminable discussion of cosmic questions by modern Russian thinkers. Skovoroda sought a kind of syncretic higher religion, the essence of which is revealed in this characteristic "conversation" between Man and Wisdom (*Mudrost'*):

> Man: Tell me thy name, tell it thyself;
>   For all our thoughts are corrupt without thee.
> Wisdom: I was called sophia by the Greeks in ancient days,
>   And wisdom I am called by every Russian.
>   But the Roman called me Minerva,
>   And the good Christian gave me the name of Christ.[71]

Radishchev's alienation from Catherine's Russia assumed the more familiar form of social and political criticism. The first of Russia's "repent-ing noblemen" to propose a thoroughgoing reform of Russia's aristocratic absolutism, Radishchev was a pure creation of Catherine's Enlightenment. While a boy of thirteen, he was chosen at Catherine's coronation to be one of forty members of her exclusive new corps of pages and was later one of twelve sent to study abroad at Leipzig. He returned to occupy a series of favored positions in the imperial service, culminating in the lucrative post of chief of customs in St. Petersburg.

Almost from the beginning of his career, Radishchev sought to temper despotism with enlightenment. His early satirical writings were critical of the institution of serfdom; and he soon began arguing for some form of responsible popular sovereignty: particularly in the introduction to his translation of Mably's *Reflections on Greek History* in 1773, in his *Ode to Liberty* of 1781–3, in praise of the American Revolution, and in his essays on legislation in the 1780's.

His famous *Journey from St. Petersburg to Moscow,* which he printed at his own expense in 1790, was the first in a long series of literary bomb-shells which the privileged aristocracy was to set off against the established order. Yet it was in many ways a typical product of Catherine's time: moralistic in tone and pretentious in style. Imitating Sterne and Volney, Radishchev couches his social criticism in the philosophic language of the European Enlightenment. Evil comes "from man himself, and often only from the fact that he has not yet seen surrounding places in the right light." Artificial divisions and restrictions rather than inherent limitations keep man from realizing his "inviolable worth."[72]

Even his criticism of serfdom, which was the most novel and daring feature of the book, was in some ways only a kind of delayed response to the demand for social and economic criticism which Catherine herself had made to the Free Economic Society a few years before. The basis for Radishchev's objections to serfdom were, moreover, in conformity with those of Catherine's Enlightenment. His protest was based not on practical or even compassionate grounds but rather on the high philosophic plane that the system prevented serfs from using their own rational faculties to conceive of any alternative to their degrading lot.

Appearing as it did without official approval in the first year of the French Revolution, Radishchev's book alarmed Catherine. She arrested him for treason and sentenced him to decapitation, which was commuted to exile in Siberia. In distant Tobol'sk he reaffirmed his faith in human dignity with verse written in the inelegant singsong style that was to become fashionable among the radical "civic" poets of the nineteenth century:

> I am what I have always been, and shall be evermore
> Neither cow, nor tree, nor slave, but a man.[73]

When he returned from Siberia after Catherine's death, his last years were spent in drafting a republican constitution for Russia which he hoped young Alexander I would put into effect. Radishchev committed suicide in 1802, leaving behind unfulfilled hopes for social and political reform which continued to agitate the aristocracy throughout Alexander's reign. Interest in his ideas was revived again only during the reform period of Alexander II's reign, when Herzen brought out a new edition of his *Journey* in 1858, on the eve of peasant emancipation.

Skovoroda and Radishchev stand at the headwaters of two mighty streams of thought that swept through modern Russian thought. Skovoroda was the precursor of Russia's alienated metaphysical poets, from Tiutchev to Pasternak, and of a host of brooding literary figures from Lermontov's Hero of our Time to Dostoevsky's Idiot. Skovoroda is the untitled outsider in aristocratic Russia, the homeless romantic, the passionate believer unable to live within the confines of any established system of belief. He stands suspended somewhere between sainthood and total egoism, relatively indifferent to the social and political evils of this world, thirsting rather for the hidden wellsprings and forbidden fruits of the richer world beyond.

Radishchev was the privileged nobleman with a European education, conscious of the artificiality of his position; he was conscience-stricken by the suffering of others and anxious to create a better social order. His preoccupation with social problems foreshadows the civic poetry of the Decembrists and Nekrasov, the literary heroes of Turgenev, and even the search for family happiness and social adjustment from Eugene Onegin to Anna Karenina. At the same time, there is in Radishchev a heroic Prometheanism that anticipates the ecstatic, secular belief in the future of Lunacharsky and Trotsky. In his last book, *On Man, His Mortality and Immortality*, Radishchev rejects the prosaic materialism of the French Encyclopedists and sees man attaining perfection—even immortality— through heroic effort and a creative evolution that includes a regeneration (*palingenesis*) of the dead. His conviction was that "if people feared death less they would never become slaves of superstition. Truth would find for itself more zealous defenders."[74]

Radishchev and Skovoroda were precursors rather than decisive influences in their own right; and it is dangerous to lift their ideas out of the complex context of their own life and times. Nevertheless, they stand as pioneers if not prophets: they were the first to set out on the argosy of alienation that would lead to revolution. Almost all Russian revolutionaries have seen in Radishchev the founding father of their tradition; and it has now been revealed that Skovoroda was one of the very few religious thinkers who was read and admired by Lenin himself. There are many memorials to Radishchev in the USSR, and Lenin planned also to erect a monument to Skovoroda.[75]

Novikov and Masonry

FAR MORE INFLUENTIAL than either Radishchev or Skovoroda in Catherine's time was Nicholas Novikov, who shared both the philanthropic reformism of the former and the religious anguish of the latter. Novikov was a serious thinker and, at the same time, a prodigious organizer who opened up new paths of practical activity for the aristocracy. A member of the exclusive Izmailovsky regiment and of Catherine's legislative commission, Novikov imitated Catherine in the sixties by founding his own weekly satirical journal, *The Drone,* named after the dull pedant in a play then popular at court. In this journal—and even more in its successors of the early seventies, *The Painter* and *The Purse*—Novikov voiced the increasing dissatisfaction of the native Russian nobility with Catherine's imitation of French ways and toleration of social injustice. Novikov's journals became the first organs of independent social criticism in Russian history. Like later "thick journals," each of these was shut down by imperial authority. Novikov then linked his publishing energies to two other institutions which were to play a key role in the cultural development of the alienated intellectuals: the university and the small discussion group, or "circle."

The university was, of course, Moscow University, which, prior to the arrival of Novikov and his circle in the late seventies, had been a moribund institution with a total enrollment of some one hundred students listening to uninspired lectures in Latin and German. When, however, the poet Kheraskov became curator of the university in 1778, it was rapidly transformed into a center of intellectual ferment. Novikov took over the Moscow University Press in 1779 and organized a public library connected with the university. From 1781 to 1784 he printed more books at the university press than had appeared in the entire previous twenty-four years of its existence, and within a decade the number of readers of the official *University Gazette* increased from six hundred to four thousand.[76]

In 1783 he set up Russia's first two private printing presses, capitalizing one of them the following year as Russia's first joint-stock printing company. He also took the lead in organizing Russia's first private insurance company and, in 1787, a remarkable nationwide system for famine relief. His *Morning Light*, begun in the late seventies, was the first journal in Russian history to seek to impart a systematic knowledge of the great philosophers of classical antiquity, beginning with translations of Plato and Seneca. He edited a series of journals and collections in the eighties, ranging from children's books to voluminous documents on early Russian history. His "Library of Russian Antiquity" underwent two large editions during the eighties. Together with the *History of Russia* and *Decline of Ancient Morals* by his friend, Prince Shcherbatov, Novikov's works tended to glorify the moral fiber of old Muscovy, and implicitly challenged Catherine's cavalier dismissal of traditional elements in Russian life. The publication in the seventies and eighties of Chulkov's encyclopedic collections of Russian folk tales, songs, and popular legends pointed to a wealth of neglected native material for literary development: sources of popular wisdom neglected by the Voltairians of St. Petersburg. Even Ivan Boltin, an admirer of Voltaire and translator of Diderot, rose up to extol Russian tradition in his *Notes on the History of Ancient and Modern Russia by Le Clerc* in 1789: a vigorous refutation of the unflattering six-volume history of Russia published in 1782 by a Russophobic French surgeon.[77]

The return of Moscow to intellectual prominence in the second half of Catherine's reign was closely connected with the upsurge of Great Russian nationalist feeling that followed the first partition of Poland, the first Turkish war, the final crushing of Pugachev, and the subordination of the Zaporozhian Cossacks in the mid-seventies. Kheraskov was totally educated in Moscow and had always been a partisan of using Russian rather than foreign languages in Moscow University. Novikov was also less traveled and less versed in foreign languages than most other aristocrats. Aided by the presence of these two figures, Moscow became a center for the glorification of Russian antiquity and a cultural Mecca for those opposed to the Gallic cosmopolitanism of the capital. The intellectuals opposed to Catherine's Enlightenment had found a spiritual home.

Moscow alone was powerful enough to resist the neo-classical culture that was being superimposed on Russian cities by Catherine. Catherine made many efforts to transform the city—even placing the European style of government buildings and reception rooms inside the Kremlin. But the former capital retained its exotic and chaotic character. Wooden buildings were still clustered around bulbous and tent-rooved churches; and the city still centered on its ancient Kremlin rather than its newer municipal buildings and open squares. A city of more than 400,000, Moscow was more than twice the size of St. Petersburg, and was perhaps the only city large enough to cherish the illusion of centralized control and a uniform national culture for the entire disparate empire. Foreigners generally found Moscow an uncongenial city. Falconet in the course of his long stay in Russia visited almost every city in Russia (including those in Siberia), but never Moscow. Only late in Catherine's reign did Moscow come to possess a theater comparable to that of St. Petersburg; but many performers preferred not to play before its spitting, belching, nut-cracking audiences. Sumarokov was not alone in his complaint:

> Moscow trusts the petty clerk more than Monsieur Voltaire and me; and the taste of inhabitants of Moscow is rather like that of the petty clerk![78]

Absorbed in its narrow ways and self-contained suburbs, closer both historically and geographically to the heart of Russia, and forever suspicious of new ideas, Moscow was the natural center for opposition to the ideals of the European Enlightenment. The features of Catherine's court which most deeply infected Moscow were the venal and self-indulgent ones. Moscow, not St. Petersburg society was to be the butt of Griboedov's celebrated satirical comedy *Woe from Wit,* in which the hero, Chatsky, is at war with Moscow society and all its vulgarity and monotony. This world, in which forty to fifty aristocratic dances were held each night of the winter season,[79] was held up to iambic scorn by Chatsky:

> What novelty can Moscow show to me?
> Today a ball, tomorrow two or three.[80]

The venality and ennui of Moscow society added an element of vindictiveness to attacks on the Voltairianism and cosmopolitanism of St. Petersburg.

The struggle between Enlightenment and anti-Enlightenment went on within both cities—and in others as well. However, St. Petersburg remained the symbol and center of the former, and Moscow of the latter, trend.

To understand the roots of the anti-Enlightenment tradition among the Russian aristocracy one must look at the activities of Novikov's Moscow period. To understand these activities, one must appreciate not only the special atmosphere of Moscow, but also the history of Russian Freemasonry: the first ideological class movement of the Russian aristocracy and the one through which Novikov channeled almost all his varied activities. The split in Novikov's career and in Russian Masonry between a St. Petersburg and a Moscow phase illustrates the deep division in Russian aristocratic thought between rationalism and mysticism—which was later to reappear in the famous controversy between Westernizers and Slavophiles.

Freemasonry was the fraternal order of the eighteenth-century European aristocracy.[81] Within its lodges, the landholding officer class of Europe acquired a sense of belonging; and new arrivals gained access to aristocratic society more easily than through the more rigid social system prevailing outside. But Masonry was also a kind of supra-confessional deist church. It provided its members with a sense of higher calling and sacramental mystery which they no longer found in traditional churches. It gave new symbolic elaboration to the basic eighteenth-century idea that there was a natural, moral order to the universe; it offered secret rites of initiation and confession to those who recognized this central truth; and it prescribed philanthropic and educational activities which reassured them of their belief in human perfectibility.

The oft-alleged medieval origins of Freemasonry belong to the category of legend,[82] although there does appear to have been some connection with the stone mason guilds, particularly in the period of the rebuilding of London after the fire of 1666. Masonic lodges of the modern type made their first appearance in England in the late seventeenth and the early eighteenth century. Members were led through three stages or initiation similar to those of medieval trade guilds: apprentice, journeyman, and master. English tradesmen set up the first lodges in Russia no later than the 1730's, and thereafter, Russian Masonry, like the Russian aristocratic culture which it helped form, was deeply influenced by foreigners.

All of the flamboyant qualities of a medieval knight in search of a cause are personified in James Keith, the man who brought Masonry from England to Russia. Descended from a Scottish noble family, Keith had been banished from England for his support of the rebellion on behalf of the Stuart Pretender in 1715 and had served in the Spanish army before setting off to Russia in 1728. There he became a leading general, a military governor of the Ukraine, and—in the early 1740's—Provincial Grand Master of Russian Masonry.

Keith was a beloved and cultivated figure, "an image of the dawn," who attracted Russians to the new aristocratic fraternity. As a Masonic song of the time put it:

> After him [Peter the Great], Keith, full of light, came to the Russians; and, exalted by zeal, lit up the sacred fire. He erected the temple of wisdom, corrected our thoughts and hearts, and confirmed us in brotherhood.[83]

Keith left Russia to enter the service of Frederick the Great in 1747; but Masonry continued to grow in Russia. By the late 1750's lodges had appeared in almost every country of Europe, in North America, in some sections of the Middle East, and—on a large scale—in Russia. In 1756 a lodge including many men of letters was formally established in St. Petersburg under the Anglophile Count Vorontsov; and the first official police investigation of "the Masonic sect" was conducted in response to hostile rumors about its foreign and seditious plans. Masonry was exonerated, however; and during his brief reign, Peter III appears to have joined the movement, founding lodges near his residences in both St. Petersburg and Oranienbaum.

The existence of an organized command structure within the Masonic lodges dates from the installation of a wealthy courtier, Ivan Elagin, as Provincial Grand Master in the Russian Empire. Elagin was a figure of extraordinary influence in the early years of Catherine's reign. She sometimes jocularly signed letters to him "Mr. Elagin's chancellor,"[84] and he stands as the organizer and apologist for the first phase of Russian Masonry; the practical-oriented, St. Petersburg-based English form of Masonry which Catherine found relatively acceptable.

English Masonry partook, indeed, of the dilettantish atmosphere of Catherine's court. Elagin admitted that he turned to the movement originally out of boredom; and his main addition to the standard practices of English Masonry lay in the addition of exotic initiation rituals, which he justified on practical grounds as needed substitutes for the rites of the Church. His definition of a Mason differed little from the description of any enlightened member of Catherine's entourage: "a free man able to master his inclinations . . . to subordinate his will to the laws of reason."[85] Elagin's lodges had a base membership in 1774 of some two hundred Russian and foreign aristocrats, almost all occupying leading positions in the civil or military service.[86]

Novikov first joined the Masonic order in 1775 through Elagin's lodge in St. Petersburg. But he refused to submit to the usual initiation rituals and was dissatisfied with the way they "played 'mason' like a child's game."[87] Within a year he had broken away to form a new lodge and to send Russian Masonry into a second, more intense phase, which was mystical-Germanic rather than English in origin, and had Moscow rather than St. Petersburg as its spiritual center. Novikov took the lead in turning Russian Masonry from the casual fraternal activities of Elagin to the inner groups and esoteric higher orders which were characteristic of this second, Moscow phase of Russian Masonic history and were to have such an important impact on the subsequent development of Russian culture.

This new trend in Russian Masonry was part of a general European movement away from English toward "Scottish" Masonry, which taught that there were higher levels of membership beyond the original three: anywhere from one to ninety-nine additional stages. This "higher order" Masonry[88] introduced closer bonds of secrecy and mutual obligation, special catechisms and vows, and new quasi-Oriental costumes and rituals. Their lodges claimed origins in the sacred past through the Knights Templars or Knights of Jerusalem back to the Gnostics and the Essenes. In Russian these higher orders were generally known as the "Orders of Andrew," the apostle who allegedly brought Christianity to Russia even before Peter took it to Rome.

The turn to "true Masonry" had rather the effect of religious conversion for many members of the aristocracy. Chudi, the "literary chameleon" who had been a leading symbol of frivolity and sensuality, became a passionate apologist for the movement as the only bulwark against the moral disintegration of Europe. From writing pornographic literature, Chudi turned to the writing of Masonic sermons and catechisms, and the founding of his own system of higher lodges of "The Flaming Star."[89]

The Russian aristocracy was a fertile field for such conversions in the 1770's and 1780's. Increasing numbers were anxious to dissociate themselves from the immorality, agnosticism, and superficiality of court life, and the higher aristocracy was bound together by a new sense of insecurity in the wake of the Pugachev uprising. They felt cut off from the religion of the people they were now empowered to rule, yet not content with the Voltairianism of Catherine's court. "Finding myself at the crossroads between Voltairianism and religion," Novikov writes of his own conversion,

"I had no basis on which to work, no cornerstone on which to build spiritual tranquility, and therefore I unexpectedly fell into the society."[90] His philosophic journal of the late seventies, *Morning Light,* was explicitly designed to "struggle with that sect which prides itself on the title 'philosophical' "[91] by publishing the great classical and medieval philosophers.

The turn to occult, "higher order" Masonry in Eastern Europe was part of the general reaction against French rationalism and secularism that was gathering momentum in the fifteen years prior to the French Revolution. The model was the so-called Swedish system, which had nine grades and a tenth secret group of nine members known as the "Commanders of the Red Cross," who met Fridays at midnight and conducted special prayers, fasts, and other forms of self-discipline. This idea of a new mystical-military order attracted wide attention in Germany, where the Swedish system became known as the "strict observance." Members of these new brotherhoods generally adopted new names as a sign of their inner regeneration and participated in communal efforts to discover through reading and meditation the inner truth and lost unity of the early Christian Church. The theosophic treatises of Jacob Boehme were supplemented in these circles by the works of the Swedish mystic Emanuel Swedenborg, who from 1747 to his death in 1772 had written a long series of occult works, such as *Secrets of the Universe* and *The Apocalypse Revealed.* By 1770 there were at least twelve major lodges in eastern Germany and the Baltic region; and the next decade was to see a wild proliferation of these higher orders within the two great powers of the region: Prussia and Russia.[92]

Higher order Masonry appealed to the princes and aristocrats of Eastern Europe as a vehicle for fortifying their realms against the reformist ideas of the French Enlightenment. Two such princes, King Gustav III of Sweden and Crown Prince Frederick William of Prussia, played a major role in bringing the movement into Russia. Gustav gave Swedish Masonry a special stamp of respectability when he flaunted his Masonic ties during his visit to St. Petersburg in 1776 and won over Crown Prince Paul to friendly association if not full membership.[93] He entered into negotiations for a royal marriage and sought to link Russian and Swedish Masonry in one system of lodges under the direction of his brother.

Even more important was the influx from Germany, where the idea of higher orders on the Swedish model was enjoying great vogue. In 1776 Prince Gagarin, a close friend of Paul and leader of the main Swedish type of lodge in St. Petersburg, journeyed to Germany to accept the authority of the Berlin lodge Minerva ("of the strict observance") and to bring back with him both an aristocratic German leader for the Russian "province" and a dynamic young teacher of occult lore, Johann Georg Schwarz.

A twenty-five-year-old, German-educated Transylvanian, Schwarz was given a position at Moscow University and rapidly threw himself into the business of transforming Russian Masonry in collaboration with the two key Russian admirers: Kheraskov and Novikov. Schwarz's lectures at Moscow University on philology, mystical philosophy, and the philosophy of history attracted the attention of a host of admirers, including two prominent visitors of 1780: Joseph II of Austria and Prince Frederick William of Prussia.

In 1781 Schwarz, Novikov, Kheraskov, and others combined to organize "the gathering of University foster children," the first secret student society in Russian history. The following year Schwarz was made inspector of a new "pedagogical seminary" to train teachers for the expected expansion of Russia's educational system and to reorganize the preparatory curriculum for the university. From this position, Schwarz tried in effect to integrate Russian higher education with higher Masonry. With Novikov organizing a supporting program of publication, Schwarz gradually gained the interest of a number of wealthy patrons who joined the two of them in the new "secret scientific [*sientificheskaia*] lodge, Harmony," of 1780.[94]

Like the tenth order in Swedish Masonry, this secret lodge had nine members and was dedicated to "returning the society to Christianity." The pursuit and dissemination of knowledge was to be intensified but placed under Christian auspices, for "science without Christianity becomes evil and deadly poison."[95] In 1782 the Moscow group formed a "fraternal learned society" with an affiliated "translator's seminary" for publishing foreign books and an "all-supreme philosophic seminary" of thirty-five learned figures, twenty-one of whom had been chosen from the seminaries.

The final form of "higher order" which the leading Moscow Masons adopted was Prussian Rosicrucianism, into which Schwarz was initiated on a trip abroad in 1781–2. He had set out as the Russian delegate to the Wilhelmsbad Convention of 1781–2, which had been summoned to try to bring order out of chaos in the higher Masonic orders. Disillusioned with the charlatanism of so much of higher order Masonry, Schwarz fell under the sway of the Prussian Rosicrucian leader, Johann Christoph Wöllner, who had also converted Crown Prince Frederick William and was shortly to preside over a purge of rationalistic teachings in the Prussian schools.[96] Schwarz was initiated into the Rosicrucian order and empowered to set up his own independent province in Russia, which he called the society of the "Golden-rosed Cross." The central conviction of the "Harmony" group was that science and religion were but two aspects of one truth. As Novikov put it in 1781 in the first issue of his new series of publications for the university press:

> Between faith and reason . . . philosophy and theology there should
> be no conflict . . . faith does not go against reason . . . does not take from
> us the savor of life, it demands only the denial of superfluousness.[97]

For Schwarz's Rosicrucians the world itself was the "supreme temple"
of Masonry and their brotherhood the final "theoretical level" for which all
other grades of Masonry were mere preliminaries. The attainment of this
level involved a flight from the rationalism of the Russian Enlightenment
as Novikov clearly indicated in the opening number of his new journal,
Twilight Glow, in 1782:

> comparing our present position with that of our forefather before the fall
> who glistened in the noon-day light of wisdom, the light of our reason can
> hardly be compared even to the twilight glow. . . .[98]

The "light of Adam" is, nonetheless, "still within us, only hidden."[99] The
task is to find it through inner purification, and a dedicated study of the
"hieroglyphics" of nature—and of the most ancient history, which still contained some reflections of this lost light. In a series of lectures given in both
the university and the lodges, Schwarz sought to provide a guide. Reason,
he explained, was only the first and weakest path to the light; feeling (the
aesthetic sense of the rose) the second; and revelation (the mystery of the
cross) the third. Each led man to the progressively higher stage of knowledge: the curious, the pleasant, and the useful. Following Boehme, Schwarz
contended that all of the cosmos was moving in triads toward perfection.
Both the triune God (for whom the world was "created out of his own inner
essence," as an "endless wish of his unfathomable will") and God's image,
man (who also contained a "trinity" of body, mind, and spirit), were moving toward reunion in the ultimate trinity: "the good, the true, and the
beautiful."[100] In order to help bring "unripe minds" back from Voltairianism, Schwarz and Novikov published a series of mystical tracts in large
editions in the early eighties, ranging from Boehme's *Path to Christ* and
Arndt's *On True Christianity* to such anonymous compilations as *The Errors
of Reason* and *The Secrets of the Cross.*

The death of Schwarz early in 1784 was caused largely by an excess
of ascetic self-discipline in his quest for inner perfection and knowledge. A
large crowd of mourners gathered at his funeral even though it was held
in a remote village; and a memorial service was also spontaneously organized by his students in Moscow. He played an important innovating role
in the development of Russian thought even though he spent less than
five of his thirty-three years in Russia and never formally enjoyed noble
status. He was in many ways the father of Russian romanticism, with

his deprecation of natural reason, his belief that art was closer to the inner harmony of nature, and his love of twilight, mystery, and chivalric ideals. At the same time he was the first of a long line of German idealistic philosophers to impart to Russia a thirst for philosophic absolutes, insisting that perfection could be realized through the special knowledge and dedication of a select brotherhood. The Moscow Rosicrucians of the eighties began the tradition of semi-secret philosophic circles which became so important in the intellectual life of Russia. They introduced practices which were to become characteristic in varying forms of such circles: assumed names, bonds of friendship and mutual aid, secret discussion and mutual criticism, and an obligatory system of quarterly confession to the grand master of the order.

The casual moralism and philanthropy that had dominated early Masonry was, under Schwarz, transformed into a seductive belief in the realizability of heaven on earth through the concentrated effort of consecrated thinkers. It seems fitting that Schwarz was apparently the first to use the term *intelligentsiia.* Though using it in the sense of the Latin term *intelligentia* ("intelligence"), Schwarz gave the term its distinctive Russian spelling, *intelligentsiia,* and the sense of special power which would eventually come to be applied to the class of people who went by its name. *"Chto takoe intelligentsiia?"* "What is intelligence?" asks Schwarz in a phrase that was to be much repeated in subsequent Russian history. It is, he says,

that higher state of man, as a mental essence, free from all base, earthly perishable matter; eternally and imperceptibly capable of influencing and acting on all things.[101]

Intelligentsia was the magical force for which Catherine had prayed at the beginning of her *Nakaz:* "Domine Deus . . . da mihi intelligentiam . . ." But it was given a different, mystical meaning by Schwarz. The first comprehensive history of Russian Masonry claimed with some justice that Russian Masonry first gave the aristocracy "a sense of mission as an intellectual class" (*kak intelligentnoe soslovie*).[102]

After Schwarz's death, a new grand master arrived from Germany convinced that "true Rosicrucians are the true restorers of order in Europe," and that a leading role in this restoration would be played by Russia ("a camel that does not realize it is laden with precious goods").[103] Numerous young Russians flocked to Berlin for fuller study of the order, some hoping to unravel there the secret of eternal life. The movement received new encouragement in 1786 when a practicing Rosicrucian, Prince Frederick William, became king of Prussia. A bewildering profusion of occult fraternities flooded into Russia in the late eighties: the "New Israelites," or "people of God," who called themselves true Masons but seemed more like religious sectarians; the "children of the New Jerusalem" who were followers of Swedenborg; and an aristocratic group formed in Avignon by Admiral Pleshcheev and Prince N. Repnin, which was transferred to St. Petersburg under the ideological guidance of Dom Pernety, a former Benedictine and librarian of Frederick the Great, who had taken up occult studies.[104]

Novikov became uneasy about the new occult turn that Masonry had taken, and proposed forming a more purely Christian and philanthropic order in the late eighties. His harsh criticism of the Jesuits in 1784 as being a political order and thus a betrayal of the monastic ideal had brought a sharp rebuke from their benefactress, Catherine. Increasingly she stepped up her harassment of all Masons, wrote three satirical anti-Masonic plays, closed down Masonic printing presses, and finally arrested Novikov in his village home in 1792.

Catherine's persecution of Novikov is usually bracketed with her treatment of Radishchev as illustrating her general disillusionment with the Enlightenment in France in the wake of the French Revolution. Actually, her opposition to Masonry was of many years standing and appeared in her writings even before her accession to the throne. It was based not on a sudden disillusionment with a former ideological infatuation, but on a deep antagonism to all forms of obscurity and secretiveness. Catherine was suspicious of anything mystical which "inclines the mind away from participation in the affairs of this world,"[105] and was also politically apprehensive of Swedish and Prussian influence over these higher orders.

There may, moreover, have been real acuteness in her premonitions of special danger lurking within this movement. She knew that the occult orders had influence over her son Paul and sensed that they might establish broader links with other disaffected elements of the population. Having defeated religion in the countryside, Catherine was now seeing it stage a comeback in the drawing rooms. The literature of urban nostalgia was beginning. Chulkov, Shcherbatov, Novikov, and others were leading men's gaze back to the idealized rural and religious culture of Muscovy. Novikov's increasing interest in the religious traditions of Old Russia was giving his publications a new kind of quasi-religious appeal. Novikov adopted the Old Believer habit of counting dates from creation rather than the birth of Christ and published a number of Old Believer documents. Indeed, his publication of an apologia for the rebellious monks of Solovetsk was the immediate cause of his arrest and deportation.

In the late years of Catherine's reign there was a general turn toward desperation within the religious community. Monks fled from monasteries to the ascetic "desert" settlements (*pustyni*) during this period. Within the schismatic community arose the prophetic "wanderers" led by a man who deserted first from the army and then from the sedentary Old Believer settlement itself. He refused even to touch coins or anything else that bore the imperial "seal of Antichrist." The entire government apparatus was the work of the Antichrist, whose sign was "the division of men into different ranks and the measurement of the forests, seas, and land."[106] Among the sectarians a new leader of the Dukhobors gave a flagellant cast to his sect that they have retained ever since by proclaiming himself Christ and setting out as an itinerant preacher with twelve apostles.

But the most extreme and ghoulish new form of religious protest to Catherine's rule appeared within the flagellant movement: the sect of *skoptsy,* or self-castrators. As with the "runner" movement among the schismatics, the self-castrators among the sectarians were founded by a deserter from the army. Driven apparently at one of the ecstatic flagellant "rejoicings" to the point of self-castration, he began persuading others to follow his example in the course of the 1770's. For more than a half century he continued to preach the need for this form of purification to interested listeners, which included many of his civil and monastic jailors, General Suvorov, and even Alexander I.

As with the self-burners of the late seventeenth century, the self-castrated of the late eighteenth should not be looked at solely as a masochistic curiosity. Both groups viewed their act as a "new baptism" into the elect of the world to come and as a kind of sacrificial atonement for the redemption of a fallen society. The self-burners appeared at the time of maximum violence and cruelty among the ruling class; the self-castrators, at the time of greatest profligacy. The sacrifice that they each chose to make was thus, in some degree, determined by the character of the society they were protesting against.

The self-castrators, however, had curious political pretensions which provide the first hint of the revolutionary social doctrines that were later to come from the sectarian tradition. They worshipped before icons of Peter III; many believed God had created him impotent in order to lead them.[107] The attempt of their leader Selivanov to characterize himself as a castrated Peter III was based on the old myth of the "true tsar." What was new was the contention that the *skoptsy* as a whole were a kind of "true aristocracy" destined to replace the false, promiscuous aristocracy of Catherine's court. Selivanov's expressed purpose was to set up a world-wide rule of the castrated. The first stage of admission to this elite (castration) was referred to as "the small seal"; and the second stage (total removal of the sexual organs), "the imperial seal" (*Tsarskaia pechat'*). Selivanov had remarkable success in gaining converts—particularly in Moscow among wealthy merchants and military leaders who had been denied access to the inner circles of Catherine's court. One of his converts was the former chamberlain to the king of Poland, who came to Moscow after the final partition of Poland and spoke of the *skoptsy* leadership as a "divine chancery."[108]

Like the other sectarians the *skoptsy* considered themselves the true "spiritual" Christians, referring to one another as "doves."

Among the schismatics, the wanderers devised a loose chain of communication and command centered on a village near Yaroslavl, and the new and more radical Dukhobors in the sectarian community came to view Tambov as the region in which God was coming to gather his true servants for the millennial reign of saints. Thus, all of the new forms of religious dissent under Catherine contained an element of radical if essentially passive protest. They were all determined—as the leader of the wanderers put it in his prophetic book *The Garden* (*Tsvetnik*)—not to go on "with one eye on earth and one eye in heaven."[109] Both eyes were to be lifted above; and the true capital of Russia for these dissonant elements was not St. Petersburg or any of the cities built or rebuilt by Catherine, but the villages or mountains where the leader of the new spiritual army lived—be it the *pustyn'* of St. Seraphim, the wanderer center near Yaroslavl, or the perennial sectarian center of Tambov.

Catherine viewed all of this with a mixture of disgust and patronizing sympathy. Her attitude toward religion was the typically modern one of toleration-through-indifference. She had been born a Lutheran, educated by Calvinists and Catholics, and welcomed into the Orthodox fold. She was deeply suspicious of Jews and sectarian extremists; but was otherwise ruled by considerations of *raison d'état* in matters of religion. She welcomed Jesuits for their intellectual and pedagogic abilities, encouraged the immigration of agriculturally skilled German pietists, and started the "one faith" (*edinoverie*) movement whereby Old Believers were permitted to rejoin the official Church, preserving most of their old rites so long as they recognized the authority of the established hierarchy.

But she correctly sensed that popular religious sentiment was deeply offended by her rule; and she may have felt that the secret groups meeting under Novikov in Moscow were, or would become, a focal point of opposition. Beginning with her edict of 1785, ordering supervision of the Masonic presses and interrogation of Novikov, she repeatedly expressed the fear that "Martinists" were fostering some concealed schism (*raskol*) in Russian society. In January, 1786, she referred to the Masons as "that crowd of the notorious new schism" and in a special note to the Metropolitan of Moscow, she suggested that there lay "hidden in their reasonings incompatibilities with the simple and pure rules of faith of our Orthodox and civil duty."[110] Although briefly reassured by the Metropolitan's vote of confidence in Novikov, she must have been disturbed by his statement that he could not pass judgment on Novikov's occult books, because he could not understand them. Her steady war on Masonry continued through both satiric writings and increased administrative pressure, particularly after the appointment of a new chief commandant for Moscow in February, 1790. A measure of her special concern about Novikov is the fact that his arrest in April, 1792, was carefully staged at a time when he was outside of Moscow, and carried out by an entire squadron of hussars. "A poor old man plagued with piles," said Count Razumovsky of Novikov, "was besieged as if he were a city!"[111] He was sent under guard to Yaroslavl; and then, apparently realizing that this metropolis on the Volga was a center both of Masonic activity and of sectarian agitation, transferred to a more distant and secluded place of confinement.

The term "Martinist," which Catherine repeatedly used for Novikov's circles, was well chosen, for it highlights the central importance within higher order Masonry of the mystical teachings of Henri de Saint-Martin, the last of the long line of French thinkers to establish an overpowering influence on Russian thought in the eighteenth century. Saint-Martin was the anti-Voltaire of French thought, and his first and greatest work, *On Errors and Truth,* was a kind of Bible for the mystical counterattack against the French Enlightenment. Published in 1775, it became known almost immediately in Russia and was translated, copied, and widely extracted within higher Masonic circles.

Saint-Martin was in many ways a caricature of the alienated intellectual: a small, sickly bachelor with an oversized head, no real occupation, and few friends. As a wealthy aristocrat he had ample time to read and travel; but he appears to have found a sense of purpose and identity only when he met Martinez de Pasqually, said to be a Portuguese Jew, who introduced him to spiritualism through his own secret order of "elected Cohens (priests)." It was under the spell of this order that he wrote his *On Errors,* signing it mysteriously "the unknown philosopher."[112]

The meaning of the book is deliberately obscure, heavily draped with portentous talk of spiritual forces and sweeping attacks on the alleged sensualism and materialism of the age. "I was less the friend of God than the enemy of his enemies, and it was this indignation that impelled me to write my first book."[113] The opposite of the animal man is the man of intelligence, whom he later also calls the "man of desire," the "man of spirit." Thus Saint-Martin gives to the term "intelligence" an even broader meaning than Schwarz. Intelligence can alone save the world, for it is impelled by desire and spirit and its object is a return to God. Following the Neo-Platonists,

Saint-Martin insists that all beings are emanations from God. The original perfection of man has been lost only because his spiritual nature has been diluted with matter; but "the reintegration of beings in their primal wholeness"[114] is now possible through the use of "intelligence" within the new spiritualist fraternities.

Saint-Martin attracted many Russian followers through his promise to lead men to this reintegrating principal, or—as he also called it—"the thing" (la chose). Nobody knew exactly what "the thing" was; but the place to look for it was in occult writings and the higher Masonic lodges. More than any other single man, Saint-Martin established the idea among Russian thinkers that the real world was the world of spirit, and that the key to truth lay in establishing some kind of contact with, or understanding of, that world. This introduction of spiritualism within the intellectual community gave it a potential community of interest with sectarian "spiritual Christianity." Catherine seems to have sensed instinctively that some such unified opposition to her might develop on a religious basis under the "Martinists," and that firm action was necessary to defend the strength of the state.

Whatever her reasoning, Catherine's arrest of Novikov and dispersal of the Moscow Martinists also brought an end to her program of enlightenment. For Novikov had combined within himself both aspects of the Russian Enlightenment: the St. Petersburg and Moscow, practical philanthropy and theoretical mysticism. His early career shows the predominance of satire, moralism, and Anglo-French influences. All of this was typical of the early, casual forms of English Masonry and of the cosmopolitan and activistic capital.

With his move to Moscow, he became preoccupied with religious themes. From the world of Addison and Steele, he moved to that of Bunyan and Milton. Novikov encouraged the translation of Paradise Lost and Pilgrim's Progress, and began his own Selected Library of Christian Readings in 1784 with the first Russian translation of à Kempis' Imitation of Christ. He involved himself less in practical activities than in the search for a new esoteric religion through studying the theosophy of Boehme and the older religious traditions of the Russian people.

The later struggle between "Westernizers" and "Slavophiles" is anticipated in the difference of perspective between lower and higher order Masonry. In both cases the Westernized activism of St. Petersburg contrasts with the more contemplative Eastern preoccupations of Moscow. But in both cases, there was a close bond between the parties. Herzen said of the Westernizers' relationship with the Slavophiles: "Like Janus or like a two-headed eagle we looked in different directions while the same heart throbbed within us."[115] In like manner the rationalist Radishchev dedicated his *Journey from St. Petersburg to Moscow* to the mystic Kutuzov a half century earlier: "My opinion differs from thine . . . but thy heart beats as one with mine."[116]

Thus, the real sense of solidarity among the alienated, aristocratic intellectuals lay not so much in the mind as in the "heart": in their common sense of caring. The word "intelligence" included "desire" and "spirit" for Saint-Martin, and these qualities were important to men whose heirs were to call themselves collectively the *intelligentsiia*. It was Catherine's lack of concern, rather than her lack of intelligence, that alienated the intellectuals.

The quality most highly valued by these dedicated aristocratic circles in the late years of Catherine's reign was "love of truth" (*pravda-liubov'*). This was the pen name of Novikov and a favorite inscription on gravestones. The aristocratic intellectuals believed that there was such a thing as Truth; in search of it they joined higher Masonic orders, set off on travels, and read new books from the West with special intensity. Following Boehme and Saint-Martin, they attributed their failure to read the "hieroglyphics" of truth to their own fallen sinfulness. Reading came to be regarded not as a casual form of leisure activity but as part of an over-all program of spiritual and moral regeneration. Foreign books became sacred objects that were thought to possess redeeming powers; key sections were often read in an intoned, semi-liturgical manner. Yet behind all these mystical activities of the "circle" stood the supreme Enlightenment belief in an "inner reason," an "ultimate harmony" behind all the seeming incongruity and misfortune in the world. Thus there was a logical connection between the "rational" and the "mystical" side of the Enlightenment, as well as a psychological connection through the personality of Novikov.

Of course, the flight into occult methods of exegesis was partly the result of virginal enthusiasm. Holy chants of the Church were replaced by new declaratory hymns consecrated to abstract virtues and mythological deities. Icons were replaced by statues—above all busts of great philosophers. The pseudo-science of physiognomy was flourishing in Russia thanks to the extraordinary influence of the Swiss mystic Johann Caspar Lavater; and the belief was widespread that one could divine the inner characteristics of a man (and by extension the essence of his ideas) from a careful study of his facial contour and features. Gardens and rooms full of realistic busts or portraits were increasingly common; and Catherine's famous smashing of her bust of Voltaire as a result of the French Revolution was almost a totemistic act.

But what did the "lovers of truth" expect to find inside their circles and behind the sculptured masks of philosophers? The answer may be partly revealed by the Russian word for "truth," *pravda*. As one nineteenth-century aristocratic intellectual said:

> Every time that the word *pravda* comes into my head I cannot help but be enraptured by its wonderful inner beauty. Such a word does not, it seems, exist in any other European language. It seems that only in Russia verity (*istina*) and justice (*spravedlivost'*) are designated by one and the same word and are fused, as it were, into one great whole. . . . Truth in this wide meaning of the word has been the aim of my searching.[117]

Truth thus meant both knowledge of the nature of things and a higher form of justice. Some indication that it had both meanings for the aristocrats of the Russian Enlightenment can be found by looking at the classical divinities they substituted for the saints of old as revered intermediaries between ultimate truth and the world of men. Two goddesses stand out in the pseudo-classical pantheon of the Russian enlightenment: Astrea and Athena, the goddesses of justice and of wisdom; of *pravda-spravedlivost'* and *pravda-istina*. Elizabeth had a large statue of Astrea built for her coronation and a temple to Minerva (the Latin form of Athena) placed in front of the Winter Palace shortly thereafter. Catherine had a masquerade, "Minerva Triumphant," performed for her coronation and had herself depicted as Astrea when she drew up her legislative proposal. The first higher order Masonic lodge to establish a chain of dependencies in Russia was the Berlin lodge Minerva; and the last and most influential chain of higher order lodges was that of the Russian lodge Astrea.

The influence of higher order Masonry on the development of Russian intellectual life can hardly be exaggerated. The concept of small circles meeting regularly, the idea of a corporate search for true knowledge and higher justice, the love of esoteric ritual and readings, the tendency to see moral, spiritual, and aesthetic concerns as part of one higher concern—all this became characteristic of Russian aristocratic thought and was to leave a permanent if ambiguous legacy of chaos and intensity. These circles—rather than the government chanceries or the new universities—were the main channels for creative thought in early-nineteenth-century Russia. Martinism had charged the air with expectation and created a sense of solidarity among those searching for truth, even if they differed as to what it was. Most important, ideas were creating a thirst for action. As one speaker put it at a "creative gathering" of a new "fraternal literary society" at the turn of the century:

> . . . The good lies in the order which we bring into our meetings; the beautiful in the union of friendship. . . . What is to be done? . . . how and

who will open this rich treasury which sometimes lies too deeply hidden in the invisible future? Activity. Activity is the guardian and mother of all success. It gives us the key and shows us the path to the sanctuary of nature. Labor, unhappiness, and the crown of victory unite us closer than all our speeches.[118]

The Frustration of Political Reform

THE LAST DECADE of the eighteenth century was a bleak period for Russian culture. Catherine was frustrated physically by the increasing difference in age between herself and her courtiers and ideologically by the increasing difference between her old ideals of enlightenment and the reality of revolution. Only a few days after the fall of the Bastille she received prophetic warnings from her ambassador in Paris about the new "political enthusiasms" of the revolutionaries. Slowly she turned her back on France. By 1791 she had recalled all Russian students from Paris and Strasbourg and declared ideological war on the revolutionary "constitution of Antichrist." The assassination of Gustav III of Sweden at a masked ball in 1792, followed closely by the execution of Louis XVI and of Catherine's close friend Marie Antoinette in 1793, deepened Catherine's gloom and precipitated an almost farcical witch hunt in St. Petersburg. A French royalist general wearing a red hat was mistakenly arrested by an official anxious to find a Jacobin; illiterate police officials ordered to destroy suspect books ended up destroying books adjacent to them in the library for fear they had been contaminated.

Poetic transcriptions of psalms were censored, and all copies burned of an innocuous melodrama, *Vadim of Novgorod,* by one of Catherine's former favorites. The play depicted the love of Vadim for the daughter of Riurik, who had come to rule over them. Realizing that his attachment to the old ways in Novgorod makes him bad building material for the new order, Vadim commits suicide together with his beloved. Everything is done with stoic dignity in the interest of good government and to the glory of Russian rule; but Vadim's occasional nostalgic soliloquies in praise of the lost liberties of Novgorod sounded too much like revolutionary oratory to Catherine.[119]

Catherine had, however, let out the leash too far to be an effective dictator. She was unable to gain the cooperation of university professors and other educated groups for tightening the censorship; and only her son and successor Paul was willing to institute a real purge and establish a blanket censorship. Under his brief rule it became a crime to use the word "citizen" or to possess a copy of his mother's legislative proposal. In 1797, his first complete year of rule, the number of regular periodicals published in Russia declined to 5 (from 16 in 1789), the number of books printed during the year to 240 (from 572 in 1788).[120] But Paul lacked the authority to stake out a new course for Russia. His reign made the need for reform more urgent than ever and affected the course of Russian thought under Alexander I in two important ways. First of all, Paul's overt admiration of Prussian ideas had the negative effect of driving much of the nobility back to the French Enlightenment. Whereas there had been a strong wave of reaction against all things French in the early stages of the Revolution, Russian aristocrats now tended to look again to France for political guidance in preventing a recurrence of Paul's arbitrary rule. Thus Paul unintentionally stimulated the renewed discussion of political reform during the first half of Alexander's reign.

At the same time, however, Paul's methods for combating revolutionary thought anticipated in many respects the pattern which prevailed in the second half of Alexander's reign. For Paul sought to enlist mystical religion in the counter-revolutionary cause. He formally assumed the title "Head of the Church" at his coronation (administering communion to himself) and became an enthusiastic patron of both higher order Masonry and the Roman Catholic Church. Shortly after his coronation he released Novikov and promoted Repnin, head of the "New Israel" sect, to the post of field marshal and special adviser. In 1798 he made himself the new commander of the Maltese Order of the Knights of Jerusalem (who had been evicted from Malta by the advancing tide of the French Revolution), and appointed the higher Masonic leader Labzin as its official historian. He also offered shelter to the Pope from the Revolution and approved the establishment of a Catholic parish in St. Petersburg and of a Catholic academy in Vilnius under a former general of the Jesuit Order.[121]

Thus the "spiritual mobilization" against revolution during the second half of Alexander's reign was in some respects a development of ideas and techniques first crudely tried out by Paul. This frail yet Draconian ruler often complained that there were ghosts in the castle at Gatchina, before he was strangled by reform-minded guards officers in 1801. But it was his ghost that returned a quarter of a century later to strangle at the gallows five Decembrist officers who had led the aristocratic counterattack against autocratic discipline. In the intervening Alexandrian age, expectations of thoroughgoing political reform were raised as they had never been before.

Rarely have the vague hopes of so many different groups converged so clearly on one man as on the handsome young prince who became tsar in 1801. Alexander's loosely worded promises of reform at his coronation encouraged the hopes of everyone. The peasant hailed him as "blessed Alexander" after the harsh reigns of Catherine and Paul. Dissenting religious groups were heartened by his promises of tolerance. The venerable historian, Professor Schlözer, who had spent many years in Russia and attracted many Russian students to Göttingen, hailed the nineteenth century as "the Alexandrian century."[122] Optimism was everywhere as Russia prepared to send its first round-the-world naval expedition under a flagship appropriately named Hope.

Hope ran perhaps highest of all among the liberal reformers. Radishchev hailed Alexander as a "guardian angel";[123] and reformers were encouraged by his long association with La Harpe, his repeal of the ban on secret societies, and his decision to charter four new universities. Liberated from the harsh reign of Paul and exhilarated by Russia's growing importance in Europe, they were anxious to aid Alexander in his professed intention to modernize the political system of Russia. As he introduced modern ministries and gathered about himself a liberal-minded entourage of advisers known by the French revolutionary designation "Committee of Public Safety," Alexander placed political reform squarely on the agenda.

In response, the aristocracy produced a bewildering array of political ideas during Alexander's reign. Three major currents of thought predominated: constitutional monarchism, autocratic conservatism, and federal republicanism. The first current dominated the first or "liberal" period of Alexander's reign; the second predominated in the second half; and the third was an undercurrent which came to the surface only briefly after his death. Each of these three positions was defended in the measured manner of the Enlightenment as the best rational alternative for Russia. Each of the positions was drawn up without much consideration of economic and social problems; each was deeply aristocratic in its assumption that only a few were qualified either to discuss or to implement political change.

Constitutional monarchy was the predominant ideal for the first decade of Alexander's reign, the dominant figure of which was Michael Speransky. Like most other leading thinkers of the Alexandrian age, Speransky divided his time between political theorics and religious concerns. He began his career as a student and teacher at the St. Petersburg Theological Academy and ended it as a mystical student of the occult. His most lasting accomplishment lay in law and administration: as a reforming governor-general of Siberia in the 1820's and the principal editor of the new law code of 1833.[124] But in the first decade of Alexander's rule he advanced more sweeping programs for transforming Russia into a constitutional monarchy of a Western type. As the son of a priest and a relative outsider to the higher levels of Russian society, Speransky was far more interested in

The Evolution of Old Russian Architecture

PLATES IX–X

The late-twelfth-century Cathedral of St. Dmitry in Vladimir (Plate IX) illustrates the creative development of Byzantine architecture which began in the Kievan period and which was particularly characteristic in this wooded heartland of Great Russia. The storied "white stone" (limestone and mortar) here replaced the Byzantine brick and cement still in use in both Kiev and Novgorod—encouraging massive and simple structural forms while providing surfaces suitable for sculptured relief of a kind previously confined to impermanent wooden surfaces. Traces of Armenian and Romanesque influences in the structural forms and a profusion of unfamiliar flora and fauna in the lavish reliefs, all reveal the relative cosmopolitanism of pre-Mongol Russo-Byzantine culture.

Later architecture in the same region reflected the growing Muscovite intolerance not only of secular subject matter in sacred art, but of sculptured forms as such. New traditions of inventiveness in church construction nevertheless accompanied the great growth of monasticism. The early-sixteenth-century Church of the Annunciation over the entrance to the women's monastery of the Protection of the Virgin in Suzdal (Plate X) illustrates one of the many places in which churches were built and special services held in this increasingly ritualized and intensely ecclesiastical society. The cult of the Virgin was particularly intense in the Russian North (where indeed the feast of the Protection of the Virgin was introduced); and the three asymmetric cupolas—a special feature of Suzdalian architecture—illustrate the transposition into stone of the decorative, onion-shaped gables previously used in wooden architecture.

PLATE X

PLATE IX

PLATE XI

PLATE XII

By the late Muscovite period, the composed, semi-circular Byzantine dome had given way altogether to the soaring, pointed forms of tent roof and onion dome, first developed in the wooden architecture of the North. At the top (Plate XI) is depicted the relatively simple Church of the Epiphany, built in 1605 in Chelmuzhi, Karelia. The increasing importance attached to bells in Muscovite worship accounts for the large bell tower, which is characteristically joined to the church itself. The sharp slope of the roofs and towers shed snow and protected the heavy horizontal log structures beneath, which were often raised to permit entrance atop snowdrifts. Fire and frost have destroyed all but a few of these older churches in the relatively unsettled regions of Karelia and further north and east from Archangel, where Soviet expeditions have recently discovered wooden churches and chapels dating back as far as the fourteenth century.

The wild proliferation of onion-shaped gables and domes during the century that followed the building of this church represented an increasing preoccupation with external silhouette; and a rustic, Muscovite defiance of both the neo-Byzantine style introduced by Patriarch Nikon and the purely Western architecture of Peter the Great. At the very time when Peter was building the totally Westernized city of St. Petersburg on the spot where the Neva River flows into the Baltic Sea, defenders of the old order were raising up the magnificent Church of the Transfiguration (Plate XII) on one of the Karelian lakes from which the Neva ultimately drew its water. The silhouette of this church at Kizhi on Lake Onega has been likened to the jagged fir tree from which its wooden substance was largely hewn.

heightening the position of the state servant than most of the independently wealthy aristocracy. As the husband of an Englishwoman and an admirer of Bentham, he was particularly interested in the English tradition of public service.[125]

Thus, while Speransky edited Radishchev's last contribution to Russian thought, the "Charter of the Russian People," he had little sympathy with the latter's abstract, rhetorical approach.[126] He spent his early years in practical administrative activity: reforming Russia's chaotic financial system and attempting to establish clear responsibility and delineation of authority within the newly created ministries. Recognizing the need for a better-educated civil service, he helped organize two new schools for training them: the polytechnic institute and the *lycée* at Tsarskoe Selo. The latter in particular became a major channel through which reformist ideas were to penetrate the Russian aristocracy.[127]

After Alexander's rapprochement with Napoleon at Tilsit in 1807, the idea of a thoroughgoing reform of the Russian government on French models gained favor. Asked to prepare a secret plan for the reform, Speransky proposed a constitutional monarchy with a separation of powers, transformation of the senate into a supreme judiciary, and a system of regional representative bodies under a central legislature. The executive was to be responsible to the central legislature; but ultimate control remained with the tsar and an imperial council responsible solely to him.[128]

This ingenious, somewhat eclectic proposal of 1809 was never taken any further than the creation of the imperial council with Speransky himself as secretary. Speransky's determination to tax the aristocracy more effectively and to require systematic examinations for the civil service was resented by the aristocracy. As a man of humble origins popularly identified with the French alliance, Speransky was vulnerable to attack when Napoleon invaded Russia. Thus, although Alexander had assured La Harpe only the year before that "liberal ideas are moving ahead"[129] in Russia, he dismissed Speransky and exiled him to the East in 1812. With him went the most serious plan for the introduction of representative and constitutional forms into the Russian monarchy that was to appear for nearly a century.

Nicholas Karamzin, the spokesman for autocratic conservatism, entered the political arena dramatically with his *Note on Old and New Russia:* a frontal attack on Speransky written at the request of the Tsar's sister in 1811. The Tsar was delighted by the piece and invited Karamzin to take up residence at the Anichkov palace, where he secured his position as the new court favorite by writing his famous multi-volume *History of the Russian State*.

Karamzin was a widely traveled aristocrat whose journalistic and literary activities had already established him as a champion of Westernization and linguistic modernization. Like others who became politically conservative after the French Revolution, Karamzin preferred the wisdom of history to that of abstract laws: the rule of "people" to that of "forms." He had been abroad in 1789, during the Revolution, and had a real aversion to revolutionary slogans. In an ode to Alexander at the time of his coronation he wrote pointedly:

> Freedom is where there are regulations,
> Wise freedom is holy;
> But equality is a dream.[130]

With verve and erudition he hammered away at the need to return to the absolutism of the past. The simplicity of his message appealed to an age perplexed by the profusion of new proposals for reform and by the fact that the reformer-in-chief of Europe, Napoleon, had suddenly become the foe of Russia. The sophistication of his arguments also made conservatism appear intellectually respectable. His examination of possible political alternatives was typical of the Enlightenment and similar to that of Speransky. Anarchy is the worst solution of the political problem, and despotism almost as bad. Republicanism is theoretically the best but requires a small country to be effective. Aristocratic rule can lead only to fragmentation and political domination by foreigners. Therefore, autocratic monarchy is the best form of rule for Russia.[131]

For all its elegance, however, Karamzin's position remains little more than an attack on innovation fortified with sentimentality and casuistry. He attacks Speransky unfairly as a "translator of Napoleon," makes the questionable contention that the aristocracy is a more faithful servant of the crown than civil servants, and plays on the anti-intellectualism of the petty nobility by ridiculing Speransky's educational requirements for state service. His *History*, too, for all its style and erudition, is propagandistic in intent. All history is that of the triumphant state, which is a patrimony of the tsar, whose moral qualities determine success or failure. For decades histories of Russia were merely paraphrases of this work, which at times seems closer to the historical romances of Walter Scott than to analytic history.

Karamzin was a kind of monastic chronicler in modern dress. He rehabilitated for the intellectuals of St. Petersburg many of the old Muscovite beliefs about history: the belief that everything depended on the tsar, that Providence was on the side of Russia if it remained faithful to tradition, that foreign innovation was the source of Russia's difficulties. He echoed the Old Believer and Cossack defenders of Old Muscovy by professing hatred for bureaucracy and compromise; but he gave these attitudes a totally new appeal in St. Petersburg by suggesting that the true ally of the tsar was not the isolated defenders of the old rites or the old liberties but rather the aristocracy. Any dilution of the powers that Catherine had wisely given it would be dangerous for Russia. Karamzin criticizes Ivan the Terrible and Peter the Great for their indifference to established authority, praising the holy fools and prophets who warned against headstrong innovation and Westernization. Karamzin seems to have viewed himself as a latter-day version of these court prophets, warning Alexander against liberalization.

Karamzin's hero in Russian history is Ivan III, in whom tsarist authority was undiluted and under whose all-conquering banners the chivalric aristocracy of that time spontaneously rallied and marched off to heroic battle. In his story "Martha the City-leader or the Subjugation of Novgorod," Karamzin glorifies the conquest of that city by Ivan III. "They should have foreseen," one of the characters asserts, "that resistance would lead to the destruction of Novgorod, and sound reasoning demanded from them a voluntary sacrifice."[132] In another speech, one of the conquering princes notes that "savage people love independence, wise people love order, and there is no order without autocratic power." Or again, in lines that could have been taken from any dictator of modern times, one of the characters notes that "not freedom, which is often destructive, but public welfare, justice, and security are the three pillars of civil happiness."[133] It is curiously fitting to see Soviet editors defending the "progressiveness" of Ivan's conquest and of Karamzin's interpretation against the glorification of Martha and of Novgorod's freedom by the revolutionary Decembrists.[134]

The gradual triumph of Karamzin's conservatism at court forced proponents of reform in the second half of Alexander's reign to assume more extreme positions than those taken by Speransky. The exposure of the officer class to the West after the pursuit of Napoleon gave them new ideas. Alexander kept alive the old hope of "reform from above" by vaguely promising to make the constitution granted Poland a pattern for his entire empire and by appointing a commission under Novosiltsov to draft a federal constitution for Russia.

The political reformers that history has come to call the Decembrists can be thought of as returning war veterans, hoping to make Russia worthy of the high calling it had assumed through victory over Napoleon. They were unified mainly by certain things they opposed: the military colonies of Arakcheev, the irrational cruelties of petty officialdom, and the succession of Nicholas I to the throne. They were, in part, simply bored with Russia, determined to "awake it from its slumber," to prove themselves the heroes at home that they had been abroad. They spoke of themselves initially as "Russian knights" and "free gardeners" and considered vaguely everything from building a web of canals between Russia's great rivers to annexing Serbia, Hungary, and even Norway.[135] The Decembrist movement had its origins in the formation by guards officers early in 1817 of a "Union of Salvation or of Sincere and Loyal Sons of the Fatherland," and patriotic journals, such as *Son of the Fatherland,* were important media for the publication of their initial proposals for political reform.[136]

A romantic interest in the history and destiny of their own country was as important to these new radicals as it was to the new conservatives like Karamzin. "History leads us," wrote the Decembrist Lunin, "into the realm of high politics."[137] He called himself "the False Dmitry," whose Westernizing policies he glorified in defiance of Karamzin, and he started the general Decembrist chorus in praise of the traditions of Novgorod.[138]

The parliament (*sejm*) of early Poland and Lithuania was glorified along with the assembly (*veche*) of Novgorod. The aristocratic reformers had many links with Poland and Lithuania.[139] Some of the more radical officers sublimated nationality altogether in such new brotherhoods as the Society of the United Slavs. Poland was a model for the hoped-for transformation of the entire empire, because it had been allowed to keep its *sejm* by Alexander I, who had appeared before it.[140] From Lithuania came one of the first and most far-reaching plans for an all-Russian constitution, Timothy Bok's *Note to Be Presented and Read to an Assembly of the Lithuanian Nobility.* Bok was arrested shortly after sending it to Alexander I in 1818, but his work helped put in circulation the romantic idea that genuine popular rule had existed throughout Eastern Europe prior to the German *Drang nach Osten* of late medieval times. The spontaneous and communal qualities of the Baltic peoples and their deep opposition to Germanic autocracy was a theme in the writings of the gifted Esthonian poet-Decembrist Wilhelm Küchelbecker, which was echoed by the Decembrist poet Bestuzhev-Marlinsky and by the great Polish writer and friend of the Decembrists Adam Mickiewicz.[141] There was also a tendency to glorify the Cossacks for their methods of "gathering the 'eldest ones' from all tribes for the promulgation of laws in accordance with the spirit of the people."[142]

Aside from their general bias in favor of increased constitutional liberties and some form of representative government, the Decembrist reformers were most concerned with turning the Russian empire into a federation. The United States was generally the model, Nikita Murav'ev actually proposing that Russia be divided into thirteen original states with the Moscow and Don district serving as an oversized version of the District of Columbia.[143] The change of the "Union of Salvation" into the "Union of Commonweal" in 1818 involved the adoption of a new decentralized organizational system among the reformers. The Moscow congress of the various regional councils of the Union early in 1821 was the first nation-wide, secret political meeting in Russian history, and it called itself a "constituent duma."

But in the early 1820's Alexander began to take alarm. The model for the "Union of Commonweal" had been the radical German "Union of Virtue." In the face of unrest among these German students and a confused mutiny in 1820 within his own favored Semenovsky regiment, Alexander took drastic measures to cut Russia off from the Western Enlightenment: he purged professors and burned books, expelled the Jesuit order, and finally, in the summer of 1822, abolished all Masonic and secret societies.

Secret societies nevertheless continued to exist and to discuss the political questions that Alexander had himself once raised. Still faithful to the concept of reform from above, these groups focused their hopes for a constitutional monarchy on the heir apparent to the throne, the Grand Duke Constantine. A former Mason and long-time resident of Poland, Constantine was thought to be sympathetic with constitutional forms of rule; but when it became apparent after Alexander's death late in 1825 that Constantine's Prussian-trained brother Nicholas was to be the successor, the St. Petersburg reformers staged a large, confused demonstration on December 14 in the Senate Square, which was followed a few days later by an equally fore-doomed if somewhat more protracted rising in the Kiev district.

Although the Decembrist movement is often regarded as the starting point of the Russian revolutionary tradition, it is perhaps more properly considered the end of aristocratic reformism: the last episode in the sixty-year period of political discussions that had begun when Catherine first convened her legislative assembly. The majority of Decembrists sought no more than to realize the original aspirations of Catherine and Alexander, to prod their nation into political and moral greatness commensurate with the military greatness assured by Suvorov and Kutuzov.

Most of these loosely affiliated reformers sought only some kind of constitutional monarchy with a federated distribution of power without any major changes in the economic or social order. One of the Decembrist leaders, however, did advocate a more radical course of action for Russia in the 1820's. In so doing, Paul Pestel, leader of the southern wing of the movement, identified himself less with the romantic age in which he lived than with the age of blood and iron which was to follow. He is the most original and prophetic of the Decembrists; a kind of lonely, halfway house between the Russia of Peter and Catherine and that of Lenin and Stalin.

Pestel gave more consideration to the problem of power than any of his reform-minded associates. He believed that a homogeneous, highly centralized state was necessary in the modern world. Nationalities that will not assimilate (the Jews and Poles) are to be excluded from it; and all other nationalities are to be completely absorbed and Russified. He looked for guidance not to the romantic past traditions of Novgorod and the Cossacks, still less to what he considered the "opiate" of an English- or French-style constitution. Rather he looked to Russia's first national law code, the Kievan *Russkaia Pravda,* which he made the title of his own major political treatise. Only uniform, rational laws could bring order out of chaos in Russia; and under current Russian conditions, this required radical social and political change: agrarian redistribution and the transfer of sovereign power to a unicameral republican legislature.

All of this was to be brought about by force if necessary and would require a kind of Jacobin network of organized plotters as well as an interim military dictatorship between the seizure of power and the full realization of "Russian justice."[144] Pestel devoted great attention to matters of military reform and reorganization and made the most serious effort of any Decembrist to utilize the forms of Masonry for the purposes of revolutionary organization.[145] He recognized the value of maintaining the Orthodox Church as an official unifying force in Russia, although he himself was a freethinker, with a partly Protestant background.

His extremism and preoccupation with power link Pestel with Lenin more than with his fellow Decembrists. His vague belief in the peasant commune as a model for social reorganization and his willingness to consider assassination as a weapon of political struggle form a link with the future populists and Social Revolutionaries. His program for resettling the Jews in Israel (though partly anticipated by Potemkin) represents a curious anticipation of Zionism by an unsympathetic outsider.

Yet for all his extremism Pestel bears certain similarities to the two other leading political theorists of the Alexandrian age: Speransky and Karamzin. Taken together, the three of them illustrate the diversity within unity of Enlightenment political thought in Russia. All three were patriotic former Masons who based their arguments on rationalistic grounds. Even if Karamzin was driven by a purely sentimental and conservative impulse and Pestel by a purely ambitious and revolutionary one (as their detractors contended), both wrapped themselves in the mantle of dispassionate, rational analysis and seemed to wear it with at least moderate distinction. All believed that sovereignty in Russia must be undivided, that government should impose order and harmony on the nation rather than wait for a chaotic play of conflicting interests. If Karamzin and Speransky advocated a monarchy, they nonetheless recognized a certain attractiveness in republicanism, which they considered far better than tyranny or anarchy and inapplicable to Russia only because of its size.

With the ascent to the throne of Nicholas I, despotism lost its links with the Enlightenment. Reason gave way to rationalization as Nicholas borrowed eclectically from various enlightened thinkers while disregarding the basic spirit of their ideas. Nicholas executed Pestel along with other leading Decembrists, and Karamzin's death in the same year enabled Nicholas to claim that the historian's writings provided a carte blanche for autocratic rule. He used Speransky to draw up a new law code in 1833 but not to complete any of the more basic constitutional reforms which had interested Speransky. He assimilated Poland in accordance with Catherine's previous practice, and worked for a unified, Russified state as Pestel had urged—but never even considered the proposals for reform that had interested Catherine and Pestel. Nicholas destroyed the sense of fluid political possibility which had lent excitement to the Alexandrian age. The frustration of political reform turned the thinking classes away from any sense of involvement in the tsarist political system and encouraged them to look outside the political arena altogether for new vision.

2. The Anti-Enlightenment

A CENTRAL QUESTION haunts any consideration of Russian thought in the aristocratic century: Why was political reform, so much discussed under Catherine and Alexander I, so decisively removed from the intellectual agenda under Nicholas I? This waning of political interest among the upper class proved not just a temporary change of fashion but an enduring malady of the late imperial period. The aristocratic passion for political discussion all but died with the Decembrists. Lonely survivors of the movement, like Nicholas Turgenev, could not arouse interest in political questions even among fellow exiles. The reforms which were eventually enacted by Alexander II in the 1860's touched on administrative and legal procedure rather than political authority. Reformers were preoccupied with the legal and economic bondage of the peasantry, not the political servitude of the entire country. There was no important modification of autocracy until the flood tide of twentieth-century war and revolution swept across Russia in 1905 and 1917. By then interest in political reform had lost all its connections with aristocratic culture, and was largely the province of harassed nationality groups within the empire, full-time revolutionaries, and the demimonde of urban and professional workers.

The narrow fears and insular perspectives of court life may explain why the imperial family and most of its immediate entourage proved incapable of creative involvement in domestic politics after the reign of Alexander I. But the general abdication of interest by the educated and well-traveled aristocracy seems difficult to understand, particularly when so little had been accomplished of what they had been led to expect from the Tsar. Nicholas I frankly confessed his dependence on the landed aristocracy serving as "unsleeping watchdogs guarding the state." Why then did the aristocrats remain content in their kennels and not extract in return at least some of the political concessions they had long demanded?

Some of the explanation lies in the absence of external stimulus, a perennially important factor in initiating movements for reform inside the amorphous Russian realm. Under Nicholas no discussion was launched from above by the Tsar as under Catherine and Alexander I. Nor was Nicholas' reign shaken from without by a sudden invasion either of foreign reformers (as under Catherine) or of military conquerors (as under Alexander). Yet the landed aristocracy would seem to have had enough contact with the outside world and enough domestic stimulus from peasant unrest and economic insolvency to sustain the pressure for political reform.

To understand why this pressure was not sustained—and why the reactionary rule of Nicholas I was in fact idolized by most educated aristocrats —one must look beyond the usual psychological and economic arguments for conservatism, and behind the predictably Prussian figure of Nicholas. He merely formalized developments which he had neither the ability to initiate nor the imagination to understand. The foundations of his reactionary rule were laid during the late years of Alexander I's reign. This turn to obscurantism under Nicholas' mystical and visionary predecessor is one of the most fateful developments in modern Russian history: it coincided with the increase in national self-consciousness that followed the Napoleonic wars to produce in Russia an identification of nationalism with social conservatism which did not become widespread in the rest of Europe until the late nineteenth century.

Many figures and interests were involved in Alexander's reactionary turn: Arakcheev, the new military leader and author of plans for the military colonies; Photius, the spokesman for the xenophobic Church hierarchy; and Rostopchin, the vulgar, anti-intellectual spokesman for much of the higher civil service. But to understand more fully this decisive turn of events, one must consider the dominant ideological current of the age: the powerful surge of religiously tinged reaction against the rationalism and scepticism of the French Enlightenment.

The main force behind this anti-Enlightenment was higher order Masonry. The Moscow "Martinists" had created higher fraternities dedicated to combating scepticism and license, but had not provided any clear idea of where new belief and authority were to be found. They had left Russians with only a vague belief in spiritual rather than material forces, in esoteric symbols rather than rational propositions. These occult, quasi-religious circles led the aristocratic retreat from the rationalism of the Enlightenment. The retreat was not to be sudden and precipitous, as Paul had hoped, into a kind of garrison state ruled by a knightly order of mystical obscurantists. It was, rather, a gradual progression under Alexander I from the high noon of the Enlightenment into the gathering dusk of morbid romanticism.

Three figures can be said to have led this retreat: Joseph De Maistre, Ivan Lopukhin, and Michael Magnitsky. Each had roots in higher order Masonry. Each illustrates the basically rootless nature of reactionary political thought and the desperate quality of the search for some new principle of authority. De Maistre looked to Catholicism, Lopukhin to Protestant pietism, Magnitsky to Orthodoxy. Yet the churches to which they looked were not the historical churches of their respective communions but rather the private creations of their own disturbed minds. All three thinkers were haunted by memories of the French Revolution and fear that revolution was the inevitable by-product of secular enlightenment. Against the real and imagined dangers of Jacobins, "illuminists," and revolutionaries, this reactionary trio created some of the first ideological blueprints in modern Europe for what may be fairly called "the radical right."

De Maistre and Lopukhin, who were essentially transmitters of Western counter-revolutionary ideas onto Russian soil, are key figures in the ideological ferment of the early years of Alexander I's reign. Magnitsky, who was more extreme than either of them, was almost unknown during their period of influence. His sudden rise to prominence in the second half of Alexander's reign was a dramatic indication of the extent to which the anti-Enlightenment had struck roots in Russian soil. Through Magnitsky, Russia produced an original "Orthodox" species of counter-revolutionary theory, which was then refined and codified by Count Uvarov as the official ideology of the Russian Empire.

Catholics

OF ALL the counter-revolutionaries, De Maistre was the most philosophically profound in his denial of the possibility of human enlightenment. He rejected not just the light of reason but also Rousseau's "inner light" and Pascal's "reasons of the heart." There are, he warns, "shadows within the heart"[1]—and even darker shadows lengthening across the path of history. His famous philosophical dialogue *Evenings of St. Petersburg* is suffused with the metaphor of gathering darkness; and his elliptical imagery and polemic intensity represents a further setting of the sun of enlightened discourse. This process had begun in Russia with Novikov's *Twilight Glow* and would culminate in another lengthy and obscure philosophic dialogue of the 1840's: Prince Odoevsky's *Russian Nights*. As the work of a Western émigré in Russia, de Maistre's *Evenings* also stands as a kind of eastward extension of the romantic revolt against optimistic rationalism which had begun with Young's *Night Thoughts* and culminated in Novalis' *Hymns to the Night*.

De Maistre's first contact with Russia came in 1797. As the dispossessed son of the former president of the senate of Savoy, he was fleeing the advancing legions of the French Revolution when he accidentally met and was taken aboard a boat on the Po River by the Russian ambassador.[2] After many subsequent wanderings, De Maistre joined his brother Xavier and many other Savoyards and Piedmontese who had already taken refuge in St. Petersburg. He brought with him a passionate opposition to the French Revolution and the entire philosophy of the Enlightenment: "the destructive fanaticism of the eighteenth century."[3] Unlike most other émigrés, he did not formally enter the Russian service but came rather in the capacity of ambassador of Sardinia. As such he moved into a position of independent authority and began fifteen years of influential activity in and around the imperial court. De Maistre arrived during a high period of Catholic favor in Russia. Paul had obtained from Pius VII permission to restore the disbanded Society of Jesus in Russia. The Jesuits' educational zeal endeared them to Alexander as it had earlier to Catherine. The head of the Society lived in Russia, and it continued to flourish throughout the early years of Alexander's reign independently of the Catholic hierarchy.[4]

De Maistre argued that the Revolution of 1789 and the Terror of 1793 followed inevitably from the real revolution that had taken place in the European mind some years before, "the insurrection against God."[5] In his denunciation of "theophobia"[6] and contemporary nihilism (*rienisme*),[7] he became a favorité figure in the drawing rooms of St. Petersburg and by 1805 was already a confidant of the young emperor, advocating Roman Catholicism as the only antidote to revolution.

Yet De Maistre was no ordinary Catholic. His ideological background lay not in Thomist philosophy and Roman Catholic academies but in occult mysticism and secret societies. In the seventies and eighties he had been a leading theorist and organizer of higher order Masonry—a background which prepared him well for the disturbed atmosphere of aristocratic Russia. Like the Russian intellectuals, De Maistre had a kind of unstable ideological convertibility. "I owe to the Jesuits," he wrote, "not having become an orator of the constituent assembly."[8] He often seems more fascinated than outraged by the mystical and destructive side of the Revolution. Morbid themes weave in and out of his provocative writings, creating an impression that terrifying forces are loose in the world and that only total surrender to the Roman priesthood can stave off disaster. He picks up essentially where Schwarz and Novikov had left off in their attacks on "the pale light of reason." While still a Mason he had written an ambitious project for the congress of higher orders at Wilhelmsbad in 1782. His espousal of the Roman priesthood came not on rational or traditional grounds but as an answer to the need which he felt for a new society dedicated to combating scepticism and recapturing the "true divine magic" of the early Christian Church.[9]

Essential to De Maistre's war on the Enlightenment was his conviction that man was incurably and irrevocably corrupt. He is harshly critical of

the banal hypothesis that man has lifted himself gradually from barbarism to science and civilization. It is the favorite dream, the mother-error . . . of our century.[10]

"We must not let ourselves be seduced by what we perceive of order in the universe,"[11] he warns in an italicized passage. The ecclesiastical optimism of Bishop Berkeley is no less wrong than the scientific optimism of Bacon. Man has triumphed in the natural world not because he is more reasonable, as the eighteenth century contended, but because he is more barbaric. Man is a "terrible and superb king," the supreme killer who takes perfume "from the heads of sharks and whales," tramples triumphantly on the skins of tigers and bears, "kills for the sake of killing."

Man demands everything at once: the entrails of the lamb to play on his harp, the bones of the whale to stiffen the virgin's corset, the most murderous tooth of the wolf to polish light works of art, the defences of the elephant to fashion a child's toy: his tables are covered with corpses.[12]

Man will finish by destroying himself in accordance with an "occult and terrible law" which permeates nature. It was far harder for Peter the Great to abolish beards than to get his people to go to war—even when they were losing. There is an irresistible fascination with bloody violence, which is attested to even in man's highest religions. Lofty prophetic monotheisms, such as Islam and Judaism, require bloodletting in circumcision, and the loftiest of all, Christianity, required crucifixion. Salvation is a mysterious gift gained only through bloody sacrifice and requiring a special priestly caste to keep the secrets and disperse authority.[13] Political authority likewise is based on fear of the hangman and requires the right of summary execution by the sovereign to be effective.[14] He hails the Jesuits as "the Janissaries of St. Peter," who "alone could have prevented the Revolution."[15] But he feels that Europe is disintegrating and will give way to some savage tribe, such as the natives of New Holland, who have a word for forced abortion but not for God.[16] His last words were: "the earth is trembling, yet you want to build."[17]

A hint of premonition is introduced at the beginning of his most famous work dealing with Russia. The setting for the *Evenings* is the "fleeting twilight" of the northern summer, where the sun "rolls like a flaming chariot over the somber forests which crown the horizon, and its rays reflected by the windows of the palaces give the spectator the impression of an immense conflagration."[18] De Maistre believed that the flames were already reaching St. Petersburg; but, like the Old Believers, he considered fire a purifying rather than a destructive force. He saw the flame of poetry mixed in with the flame of revolution, and he betrays the same mixture of horror and fascination with which many Russian intellectuals were to look on their country. De Maistre was appalled in 1799 at the arrival in Italy of Suvorov's army, "Scyths and Tatars from the north pole coming to slit the throats of the French,"[19] yet he soon became convinced that Russia was an instrument chosen by Providence for the salvation of Europe. He spoke contemptuously about Russia's tendency toward violence and assassination, yet was fascinated with the potentialities for sudden political and ideological change with which this "Asiatic remedy" provided Russia.[20] He loved to visit the supposedly haunted regions of Gatchina and the room in the Mikhailovsky Palace in which Paul was killed.

Almost immediately upon arrival he wrote of the danger to Russia of "minds fashioned by La Harpe"[21] in the Tsar's entourage and soon gathered about himself a constellation of older noblemen who also had reason to be apprehensive of the Tsar's new advisers and liberal inclinations: the Stroganovs, Tolstoys, Kochubeis, and the Viazemskies. The leader of the latter family, Catherine's former procurator general, provided the salons which, along with the new Jesuit headquarters in St. Petersburg, became the centers for De Maistre's activities.

Like Possevino in the sixteenth century and Krizhanich in the seventeenth, De Maistre became fascinated by the possibility of converting this vast land to Catholicism. He launched a program for the conversion of "one dozen women of quality" and helped gain for the Jesuits increasing authority within the empire.[22] As the euphoria of the summit meeting of 1807 between Napoleon and Alexander receded and the possibility of war with France grew, De Maistre's influence increased proportionately. He became a leader in the ideological mobilization of the Russian aristocracy, portraying their struggle as that of Christian civilization against the new Caesar.

He began his public attack on the liberalism of Alexander's earlier years in 1810 with *Five Letters on Public Education in Russia,* an indictment of Speransky's proposed educational reforms.[23] The following year he began his correspondence with Count Uvarov, the future minister of education and theoretician of reaction. He also delivered a long memorandum to

Alexander Golitsyn, later printed as *Four Chapters on Russia*,[24] and participated with Admiral Shishkov and other reactionary leaders in the newly
formed patriotic society Lovers of Russian Speech. At the time of Speransky's dismissal in the spring of 1812, De Maistre reached the height of his
influence. He held a number of long private conversations with the Tsar
and was offered the position of official editor of documents published in the
Tsar's name.

Catholicism generally was at a high point of favor. The Jesuit order,
which had been permitted to extend its activities to Siberia in 1809 and the
Crimea in 1811, changed its collegium at Polotsk into a seminary in 1812
with university status and wide supervisory rights over secondary education
in White Russia. In 1813 Alexander even expressed sympathy for the Roman
Catholic position on the classical ecclesiastical controversy over the origin
of the Holy Spirit. The appointment of Catholic émigrés as governors of
exposed western provinces, Paulucci in Riga and Richelieu in Odessa, was
also a boon to Catholic activity.

However, the *levée-en-masse* against Napoleon in 1812 raised passions
that were to sweep both De Maistre and the Jesuits out of Russia within a
few years. Increased national pride and anti-foreign feeling made Roman
Catholicism a particularly suspect faith; but Russia was in any case suddenly captured by a new religious infatuation that was anathema to De
Maistre and Catholicism: ecumenical pietism. This syncretic and emotional
offshoot of Protestantism was even more hostile to the secular rationalism
of the Enlightenment than the ultramontanism of De Maistre. It was to be
far more important in consolidating the anti-Enlightenment in Russia.

De Maistre had seen the new movement coming; and in his critique of
the Pietist-influenced course of study for the new St. Petersburg Theological
Academy in 1810, he had tried to counter what he called the "German sickness" of vagueness with "the Parisian mercury otherwise known as ridicule."[25] He remained in Russia long enough to voice his objections to the
two main by-products of the new pietism: the Russian Bible Society and
the Holy Alliance. He objected to the idea of distributing Bibles to the
people without any guide for reading and interpretation, and to the subordination of religious activities to a state official. General discussions of
scripture and intra-confessional prayer meetings merely "accommodate
human pride by freeing it from all authority." Like the Bible Society, the
Holy Alliance reduced Catholicism to the status of a subordinate cult,
represented only by the Catholic Austrian Emperor who was one of its three
signers. The Pope refused to sign or approve the text of the Alliance, and
De Maistre denounced it as a "Socinian plot" and "mask for revolution."[26]

Nonetheless, De Maistre felt that the idea of inter-confessional tolerance would eventually benefit Catholicism, as the only participant certain to remain intolerant and proselytizing. The vague movements sponsored by Alexander were "a blind instrument of providence" preparing the world for "I don't know what kind of great unity" which will "drive out all doubt from the city of God."[27] Thus, even after Alexander had turned to pietism and expelled the Jesuits from Moscow and St. Petersburg in 1815, De Maistre lingered on in hopes of playing some role in the mysterious march of providence. He wrote a valedictory appeal for tightened censorship and discipline, *Five Letters to a Russian Gentleman on the Spanish Inquisition.*[28] He may have been encouraged by a long interview with the Tsar in February, 1816, when Alexander assured him that the Society and the Alliance were but the first stages in the establishment of a universal church. Later in the year Alexander succeeded in enlisting the ranking Catholic prelate in the empire as a member of the Society and the following year sent a Catholic deputy to Rome to discuss a peace of the churches to accompany the peace of the nations. In moments of crisis, even after the departure of De Maistre in May, 1817, and the banishment of the Jesuits from Russia in 1820, Alexander turned periodically to Rome, coordinating his ban on secret societies in Poland in September, 1821, with the concurrent Papal bull, *Ecclesia Iesu Christo.* In 1825, the last year of his life, Alexander sent an old friend of De Maistre and fellow Catholic from Savoy on a secret mission to Rome apparently to procure a high Church official for instruction in the Catholic faith. Thus he may have been contemplating conversion on the eve of his death.[29]

Pietists

FAR MORE IMPORTANT than the Catholic reactionaries in the mobilization of Russia against revolutionary and Enlightenment thought were the religious thinkers that held sway over Alexander in the fateful second half of his reign: the Pietistic prophets of a universal, "inner" church. More amorphous than the Catholic party, the ecumenical party drew its strength from both higher order Masonry and mystical Protestantism. Indeed, this party represents the final forging of an alliance between aristocratic mysticism and popular sectarianism that Catherine had feared. This party left a complicated legacy; its truest spiritual heirs were anti-authoritarian moralists like Leo Tolstoy; but its immediate legacy to Russia lay, ironically, in the intensification and deepening of counter-revolutionary thought in Russia. Vaguely seeking a universal church, the proponents of a new church helped lay the groundwork for the new restrictiveness and exclusiveness of Russia under Nicholas I.

The new ingredient in this movement was Protestant Pietism, an ideological force that had been filtering into Russia ever since it began to dominate ecclesiastical life in Germany in the early eighteenth century. Pietism was the main rival to secular rationalism in the Age of the Enlightenment and the spiritual forebear of the romantic counterattack of the early nineteenth century. Like Methodism, its most familiar offshoot, Pietism first received its name as an epithet and was for a time little more than an impulse toward a more emotional, personal religious commitment within the established Church. Pietists generally sought to do away with dogma in favor of what they called "true Christianity," a phrase from the title of a book written at the beginning of the seventeenth century by Johann Arndt. Pietism first acquired identity through the movement to create a new interconfessional and international brotherhood of Christians largely in response to two writings of the late seventeenth century: Philipp Spener's *On True Evangelical Churches* and Gottfried Arnold's *Non-Party History of Church and Heresy*. The Pietists' main base of operations became Halle University, where they set up a special program of devotional instruction and an institute for the study and evangelization of Eastern peoples. They paid special attention to Russia and exerted an ever-increasing influence within Russian theological academies of the early eighteenth century, still the major educational institutions of the time. Particularly in White and Little Russia, where there had been much crossing of confessional lines, Pietism seemed to offer a new approach free of traditional doctrinal bitterness. The most learned Russian Orthodox theologian of the early eighteenth century, Simeon Todorsky, was the Ukrainian son of a converted Jew who was educated by Jesuits but found his spiritual calling among the Pietists, translating Arndt into Russian along with the most complete version of the Bible yet to appear in Russia: the so-called Elizabeth Bible of 1751.[30]

Pietism was the first international missionary movement of Protestantism to accept the obligation of evangelizing the heathen as a primary duty of the church independent of state support. Even under Peter the Great, the Pietists had found Russia a fruitful field for evangelization. They set up small and short-lived schools in Moscow, St. Petersburg, Narva, Astrakhan, and Tobol'sk—all of them teaching at least one Oriental language for purposes of future evangelization.[31]

Of more lasting importance for Russia was the colonization that began soon after the founding of a central base for Pietism on the estate of Count Zinzendorf in Saxony in the 1720's. Known as Herrnhut ("Watch of the Lord"), this community attracted survivors of the old Czech Protestant movement from Moravia, along with Lutherans, Calvinists, and even some Catholics. Zinzendorf's community became the germ of the religious fraternity known as the Moravian Brethren, or more properly, the United Brethren. Almost from the beginning, the Brethren were anxious to transplant to foreign soils not just Pietist ideas but the entire experience of the Herrnhut community. Settling everywhere from colonial Georgia to Greenland and India, they began in the 1730's their most natural and extensive colonizing movement: into Eastern Europe. Moving partly through Latvia and Esthonia, partly through Poland and Hungary, they took advantage of Catherine's toleration decrees of 1762 and 1763 to enter Russia in large numbers.

The Moravian Brethren soon became the dominant force within a steadily expanding community of non-conformist German Protestants (Mennonites, Hutterites, and so on) in the rapidly opening regions of the Russian south and east.[32] Seeking at first the remnants of the original Moravian Church which they believed had settled in the Caucasus, they soon settled down in the desolate region of Sarepta, on the lower Volga, rapidly transforming it into a model agricultural community.

By the 1790's German Pietists were immensely popular with the Russian aristocracy. The Free Economic Society studied their efficient agricultural methods with interest; aristocrats flocked to Sarepta to patronize its fashionable mineral baths;[33] and after the beginning of the French Revolution, Russians began to see in these pious and industrious people a kind of antidote to the abstract rationalism of the French Enlightenment. Zhukovsky, who turned Russian poetry from classical to romantic patterns, was (like the great German romantic poet Novalis) largely educated by German Pietists. Tikhon Zadonsky, who founded his own "true Christian" community along the Don, emphasized the Pietistic idea that God's truth was to be found in reading the Bible and in acts of devotion and charity.[34]

The tolerance, industry, and devotional intensity of the Herrnhut communities made a profound impact on the budding romantic imagination of Europe. Novalis' education with the brethren probably influenced his only superficially Catholic vision of a reunited Christendom in *Europe or Christianity*. Mme de Staël devoted the fourth part of her *On Germany* to praise of the Moravian Brethren; and the Slavophile Kireevsky later called the movement the true germ of Christian unity.[35]

Pietism encouraged education and had been seen as an ally of enlightenment in Eastern Europe; but after the French Revolution it became increasingly mystical and traditionalist. Pietists found themselves increasingly close in spirit to the mystics within the higher Masonic orders, who had long spoken of a Europe-wide conservative alliance of "true Christians."

Both groups tended to speak of the Revolution in apocalyptical terms, blaming it on the rationalism of the Enlightenment. There was a tendency in Central and Eastern Europe to blame everything on "the plot against altars and thrones" of a small group of rationalistic Masons: the "illuminists of Bavaria."[36] Lavater, who was equally influential in Masonic and Pietist circles, felt that the only answer to universal revolution was a universal, inner church teaching "universal speech, universal monarchy, universal religion, universal medicine."[37] Lavater almost certainly had a decisive influence on the turn to conservatism of Karamzin, who called him a "true Christ" and visited him in Zurich in 1789.[38] Lavater and Saint-Martin both implored their followers beyond the Rhine to produce a new Christianity that would vanquish the apocalyptical beast of the Revolution. The response was extraordinary: the German "society of Christ" called for a universal biblical Christianity free of dogma; others advocated a link between higher Masonry and all Christian confessions; an influential Rosicrucian introduced a program of attending Catholic mass in the morning, Lutheran services in the afternoon, and "visiting in the evening either the community of the Moravian Brethren, the lodge, or the synagogue."[39]

The most widely read prophets of a mystical, counter-revolutionary union were Jung-Stilling and Karl Eckartshausen. In his widely read *Victorious History of the Christian Religion* of 1799, Jung said that humanity must either continue in endless revolution or subordinate itself to a higher form of Christianity. Jung's work helped influence De Maistre's concept of counter-revolutionary Catholicism;[40] but Jung wrote that the new church would come from the East. The Moravian Brethren, among whom Jung had lived for many years, are to be its nucleus, and it will have new quasi-Oriental initiation rites in the manner of a Masonic temple. Jung took a new name in the manner of the higher orders, choosing one to dramatize his belief in the Pietist ideal of inner peace (*Stille*).

The prolific Eckartshausen was even more influential in propagating the idea of a new mystical church in his writings of the eighties and nineties: *A History of Knighthood, God Is True Love, Religious Writings on Light and Darkness*, and *The Key to Occult Science and the Mystical Night*. In his last and most influential book, *The Cloud over the Sanctuary* of 1802, he took pains to point out that the new church would be above all presently existing ones. It was to be the primal religion (*Urreligion*) that lay behind all other religions: a "new world" known "to the hidden saints of all religions" in which "Christian, Jew, and barbarian go hand in hand."[41]

Eckartshausen's writings were probably the most important single vehicle for popularizing the idea of a new counter-revolutionary Christian alliance inside Russia. As a former leader of the government commission which investigated and uprooted the rationalistic "Illuminists" of Bavaria even before the French Revolution, he was looked to as an experienced and erudite veteran of the counter-revolutionary camp. During the reign of Alexander I almost all of his works were published inside Russia—most of them in several different editions.[42] Alexander was reading his *Cloud over the Sanctuary* while drawing up his draft of the Holy Alliance; and Eckartshausen's fame encouraged Russian authorities to seek out other ecumenically oriented Bavarian mystics during the latter part of Alexander's reign.

The man responsible for popularizing this undistinguished (and elsewhere almost totally unknown) German was the second key figure in the Russian anti-Enlightenment: Ivan Lopukhin. In Lopukhin's career, sectarian Pietism and higher order Masonry were fused and given a clear counter-revolutionary bias.

Lopukhin had been, like De Maistre, an active Mason who slowly turned first against revolution and then against rationalism altogether. The first crisis in his life came in the early eighties when he was asked to translate Holbach's *Code of Nature* as part of his Masonic duties. When he realized that its materialistic philosophy was alien to Christian teaching, he burned his translation and immersed himself in the occult pursuits of the Rosicrucians. In 1789 he experienced a second crisis. Having just recovered miraculously from a life-long illness and shortly after hearing of the outbreak of revolution in France, he experienced a kind of mystic conversion while walking in the garden of Count Razumovsky. Henceforth he was to be —to cite the title of a tract he wrote in 1791—"A Spiritual Knight, or Searcher for True Wisdom." He resolved to write a great new treatise for the times, which he published after nearly a decade of labor in 1798: *Several Characteristics of the Inner Church, or the One Path to Truth and the Different Paths to Error and Damnation.*[43] The work created an instant sensation in higher Masonic circles—and throughout Europe. In 1799 a French edition was published in Russia; in 1801 there was published another French edition in Paris and a second Russian edition; and, shortly thereafter, two German editions and several other Russian editions. The aged Eckartshausen particularly admired the work, established close relations with Lopukhin, and arranged for the translation into Russian of his own writings and those of other German members of the "inner church."

Meanwhile Lopukhin was sent by the new Tsar Alexander to southern Russia to investigate the growth of sectarian religion in the region. He discovered and lived among the spirit wrestlers, whom he proclaimed to be hidden saints of his new church in his essay "Voice of Sincerity." The foes of his mystical church were the secular learning and self-indulgence which kept man from following Christ and gaining "true wisdom." In an essay of 1794, "The Baneful Fruits of Idle Dreams, of Equality, and of Tumultuous Freedom," he had seen the acquisitive instincts of the French revolutionaries as the cause of all Europe's ills; and in his church he expressed his ire at the equally materialistic response of the churches. He proposed that the inner church excommunicate believers in "the kingdom of property [*tsarstvo sobstvennosti*], who bear on them the image of Antichrists."[44] In 1809 he became the guiding spirit behind the journal *Friend of Youth,* publishing such anti-rationalistic tracts as "Fruits of the Heart in Love with Truth" and "Paths of the Praying Heart." He was joined by another protégé of Schwarz, Labzin, whose mystical journal *Herald of Zion* made its first appearance on January 1, 1806. Labzin had been "converted" to the new mystical Christianity after an initial infatuation with the Encyclopedists, whom he then denounced in a poem, "The French Shop."

The Pietistic reactionaries fell briefly out of favor in the years immediately after the alliance with Napoleon in 1807. Labzin's journal was shut; Lopukhin was forced to leave Moscow for his country estate; and Grabianka's "New Jerusalem" sect, which had taken to ecstatic prophecy in the manner of the flagellants, was shut down. But at the same time, the proponents of a counter-revolutionary "inner church" gained a key disciple within the Tsar's immediate entourage. Prince Alexander Golitsyn, a former lover of the Encyclopedists and a descendant of one of the most learned and Francophile of Russian noble families, also underwent a kind of conversion. As Alexander's civilian procurator of the Holy Synod, Golitsyn decided to read (for the first time in his life) the New Testament. He found in Christ's life and teaching a wealth of inspiration that he had never found in Orthodoxy. As he looked about his empire, he began to feel that the Christian sectarians—particularly the Protestant Pietists—were better practitioners of New Testament Christianity than the Orthodox. He had particular regard for the Moravian Brethren's community at Sarepta, which he had often visited for mineral baths.[45] Accordingly, in 1810, he resigned as procurator of the Synod to become supervisor of foreign confessions in Russia. What was ostensibly a demotion was to this new believer in interconfessional Christianity a fresh opportunity.

Golitsyn brought Ignatius Fesler, a defrocked Trappist monk who had become an historian of German Masonry and leader of the Berlin "Society of the Friends of Humanity," to St. Petersburg in 1810 to teach philosophy at the St. Petersburg Theological Seminary.[46] Nominally a Protestant, this Silesian pamphleteer was mainly interested in promoting a new interconfessional "Society of Brotherly Love" (*Philadelphia*). Bitterly attacked by De Maistre, Fesler received full support from Golitsyn, who encouraged him to pay a long visit to Sarepta and eventually made him superintendent of the special consistory created for the seventy-three evangelical colonies of South Russia.

Most important of all, Golitsyn persuaded the Tsar himself to read the Bible (also for the first time) and make it a kind of manual for the "spiritual mobilization" of Russia to combat Napoleon. Golitsyn lent his own Bible to Alexander, who read it on a voyage through newly conquered Finland in the summer of 1812. Especially moved by the prophetic books of the Old Testament and the Apocalypse in the New, Alexander attended Protestant churches in Finland and confessed that "a new world is opening up before me."[47] The impressionable Tsar began to interpret contemporary events in Biblical terms, to attend prayer meetings and Bible readings in Golitsyn's inter-confessional chapel. He adopted as his own the idea of a new inner Christianity, an inter-confessional brotherhood of "Biblical" Christians who would heal the wounds of Christian division and revolutionary strife.

The key organization in this "spiritual mobilization" was the Bible Society, an organization which came to Russia through Protestant Finland from Pietism and its English version, the Methodist Church. It is interesting that this church, which played such an important role in steering English popular enthusiasm away from revolutionary paths,[48] should play a similar role in Russia. Alexander delayed his departure from St. Petersburg to Moscow to pursue the retreating Napoleon late in 1812 in order to meet with the English leader of the society, who had just arrived by way of Turku in Finland to help set up a Russian chapter. The Tsar and his two brothers became patrons of the society, and Golitsyn its president.

At the founding meeting of the society in January, 1813, there were representatives of a variety of domestic and foreign Protestant churches, with the Moravians playing the key role. Under Golitsyn's leadership the original plan to print Bibles only in foreign languages was expanded during the next two years to include Russian-language New Testaments and Bibles; its primarily Protestant clerical leadership was expanded to include Orthodox and even Catholic clergy; and chapters spread out all over Russia for dissemination and discussion of Holy Scripture.[49]

As Alexander moved slowly into Europe behind the advancing Russian army, his movements at times resembled more an inter-confessional religious pilgrimage than a military campaign. He read the Bible daily, interpreting events about him in Biblical terms. As he explained to a Lutheran bishop from Prussia:

> The burning of Moscow brought light to my soul, and the judgment of God on the icy fields filled my heart with the warmth of faith which I had not felt till then. I then recognized God as He was described in holy

scripture. I owe my own redemption to [God's] redemption of Europe from destruction.[50]

En route to the final showdown with Napoleon he stopped off to see the flourishing communities of Moravian Brethren in Livonia and the pilot community of Herrnhut in Saxony, attended Quaker meetings at London, and celebrated an outdoor Easter liturgy with his entire officer corps at the very spot in the Place de la Concorde in Paris where the Catholic King Louis XVI had been beheaded.[51]

One witness to this scene wrote ecstatically that "the smoke of incense mounts to the sky in order to reconcile heaven and earth. Religion and liberty have triumphed."[52] Russian officers were encouraged to fraternize with French Masons; European romantics from the libertarian Mme de Staël to the restorationist Chateaubriand hailed the redeeming piety of the Russian monarch; while Lopukhin on his Baltic estate staged a symbolic burial of Napoleon at midnight by the light of five hundred burning crosses.[53]

Between Alexander's first entrance into Paris in 1814 and the final defeat of Napoleon at Waterloo the following year, there was a veritable chorus of voices prophesying a great destiny for Alexander. The aged Jung-Stilling professed occult knowledge that the end of the world would occur in 1819 or 1836; the millennium would begin in the East, with Alexander as the elected instrument of God. Alexander visited him and heard him preach in 1814, sent special grants to him thereafter, and remained in close touch until his death in 1817.[54] During the same period the Baroness Krüdener, who had close links with Herrnhut and Jung-Stilling, conducted Pietistic devotion services with the Tsar and impressed him with his sense of mission to save Christendom.[55] Other important associates of the period were the French mesmerist Nicholas Bergasse and the Bavarian mystic Franz von Baader, who early in 1814 had sent a memorandum to the rulers of Russia, Austria, and Prussia: *On the Need Created by the French Revolution for a New and Closer Union of Religion with Politics.*[56] The following summer he resubmitted it to the Tsar alone, dedicating the memorandum to Golitsyn. All education and political rule must, in Baader's view, be suffused with Christian teachings; and Christianity itself must assimilate vital elements from other religions and mythologies.

Whether Mme Krüdener, Baader, or Alexander was its principal author, the Holy Alliance that was promulgated in September, 1815, and presented to the Russian people on Christmas day was the culmination of the effort to find a "Christian answer to the French Revolution." A Protestant, Catholic, and Orthodox monarch publicly pledged themselves to base their entire rule "upon the sublime truths which the holy religion of our savior teaches." The name of the alliance was taken from a prophetic passage in the Book of Daniel; the dedication is to "the Most Holy and Indivisible Trinity"; and the monarchs pledge aid to one another rather in the manner of a higher Masonic order. They speak of themselves as "three branches of the one family" pledged to aid one another in unfolding "the treasures of love, science, and infinite wisdom."[57]

It was, of course, mainly in Russia that the religious nature of the Alliance was taken seriously. In the first two years of its existence an extraordinary effort was made to transform Russian society in accordance with the spirit of the Alliance. Golitsyn was given a new portfolio without parallel in nineteenth-century Europe: as "minister of education and spiritual affairs." He maintained contact with Baader, who recruited for him a number of anti-scholastic and anti-papal Catholic mystics from Bavaria in order "to provide good priests for all the cults." Alexander commissioned Baader to write a manual of instruction for the Russian clergy, and Golitsyn enlisted him as his "literary correspondent" late in 1817. Baader and the other Bavarian mystics hoped to reunite Christendom with an esoteric neo-Platonic theology that would bypass both "Protestant rationalism" and "Roman dictatorship." Ignatius Lindl, a great preacher and leader of the Bavarian Bible Society, came to Russia in 1819; Johann Gosner came from Bavaria by way of Switzerland and Silesia the following year. They all played a leading role in the effort under Golitsyn to devise a system of instruction in which "simple unlearned people" could be "tutored by the Holy Ghost."[58]

Spiritual regeneration was to be accomplished not only through the Bible Society and a new system of spiritual instruction but also through such philanthropic societies as the nationwide "Lovers of Humanity," which was founded by Alexander for "the fulfillment of the divine commandments that the Bible Society teaches us."[59] Most important of all was the florid expansion of higher order Masonry, which Alexander encouraged by visiting lodges both in Prussia and in Russia. His birthday became one of the two special holidays of Russian Masonry, and regional lodges began to spring up in the provinces as a counterpart to the regional chapters of the Bible Society and the "Lovers of Humanity." In 1815 higher Masonry was subordinated to the Grand Lodge Astrea, named for the Goddess of Justice, who had been the last to leave the earth at the end of the Golden Age. New Masonic hymns, inspired by the Holy Alliance, spoke of restoring the golden age "when love illuminated all with its beauty and men lived in brotherhood." Lutheran and Catholic priests joined, and prayers of invocation were addressed to "God, Odin, Zeus, Jehovah, Thor, and the White God."[60] Pietists were particularly active in the rapidly expanding chain of provincial lodges, and German became the main language within the lodges.[61]

Quirinus Kuhlmann was venerated as a prophet of the new religion. Lopukhin included a statue of Kuhlmann in his garden of heroes, a kind of outdoor pantheon of the inner church. Labzin, in his introduction to an edition of *The Path to Christ* in 1815 by "our father among the saints, Jacob Boehme," suggested that Kuhlmann's teachings had been well received by "some of the boyars closest to the Tsar."[62] Certainly, Labzin's mystical writings gained such favor. He published nine books on Boehme, and in 1816 was decorated by the Tsar and asked to revive his *Herald of Zion*. He became a kind of coordinator-in-chief for publications of the new supra-confessional church. In addition to the *Herald,* twenty-four books of a new devotional manual entitled "The Spiritual Year in the Life of a Christian" appeared in 1816. Other "spiritual journals," like *Christian Reading* and *Friend of Youth* (to which had been added *and of All Ages*), flourished as part of a general program to "bring thinking people back to faith."[63] Previously proscribed prophetic works by Jung-Stilling were published. His famous *Homesickness,* which was serialized by the Moscow University Press throughout 1817–18, included among its subscribers twenty-four from Irkutsk alone.[64] The *Herald of Zion* had among its sponsoring subscribers the Tsar, the Grand Duke Constantine, and all the theological academies of the empire.

In 1817 the *Herald* added a special section, *The Rainbow,* purporting to reveal new symbols and prophecies pertaining to the unification of the churches and of all humanity. Rainbows were a key symbol for higher order Masonry, because they combined sunlight (the light of the past) with rain (the sins of the present) to give men a hint of the future transformation of the world.[65] The spectrum of colors in the rainbow was likened to the various churches and nationalities that were all formed from the One True Light.

For the optimistic, romantic imagination,

> The One remains, the many change and pass;
>   Heaven's light forever shines, Earth's shadows fly;
>   Life, like a dome of many-colored glass,
> Stains the white radiance of Eternity.[66]

As supervisor of heraldic symbols, Golitsyn sought to invest the official iconography of the state with the portentous symbols of occult Masonry. Classical mythology and esoteric, pseudo-Oriental motifs were incorporated into the coinage, architecture, and embellishments of the period.

The principal coin struck to commemorate the victory over Napoleon bore the legend "Not ours, not ours, but thine be the praise, oh Lord."[67] Alexander participated in prayer meetings with Quakers and Methodists; and the Moravians were gaining followers among the Kalmyks to the east and the Latvians to the west. The curator of the university at Tartu was converted, and the Moravians grew from about three thousand to forty thousand in the Baltic provinces under Alexander.[68]

By the late years of Alexander's reign, the pietistic idea of a universal church and an inner spiritual regeneration seemed to be endangering the stability of the established order. The hierarchy complained that Labzin's *Herald of Zion* had supplanted the patristic writers in the seminaries, and sectarian preachers the Orthodox clergy. Selivanov, the prophet of the self-castrated sects, was given opulent quarters in St. Petersburg by Golitsyn and continued to proselytize freely until 1820. In that year the ubiquitous Fesler returned from the Protestant consistories that he was supervising in southern Russia to deliver prophetic sermons in St. Michael's Church in Moscow, while Gosner arrived from Bavaria to begin his preaching career in St. Petersburg. Mme Krüdener came to St. Petersburg in 1821; but by then, another German noblewoman had eclipsed "the lady of the Holy Alliance" with an even more exotic form of supra-confessional revivalism. Mme Tatarinova, the German widow of a Russian colonel, was sponsoring devotional meetings which were climaxed by her own inspired prophecies, recited in a semi-trance in the manner of the flagellants. She held frequent meetings with the Tsar and, like the native Russian sectarians, claimed mysterious links with extinguished branches of the royal family.

This wave of emotional Pietism receded in the mid-twenties with the same sudden finality that the Catholic wave had ebbed a decade before. The fall from grace of Golitsyn and the dissipation of the Pietistic euphoria in 1824 followed the realization by the Orthodox clergy that a new syncretic church was in effect becoming the established church of the empire. Baader had spoken in his dispatches to Golitsyn about the "invisible church" coming into being on Russian soil and was formulating the idea of establishing a new type of Christian academy in St. Petersburg.[69] Gosner had lived at Sarepta and published a manual for the new faith in St. Petersburg, *The Spirit of the Life and Teaching of Christ*. Fesler had published a new liturgy in St. Petersburg, supplementing it with his *Christian Sermons* of 1822 and his *Liturgical Handbook* of 1823.[70]

The campaign to oust the German mystics was fought largely over two other texts that they introduced in the early twenties. One was a government-sponsored translation of Mme Guyon's earlier quietistic tract *Call to People on the Following of the Inner Path to Christ*, which was denounced for rendering the Orthodox Church completely irrelevant. Even stronger was the opposition that developed to Gosner's essay on the gospel of St. Matthew. By juxtaposing the spiritual kingdom of Christ with the material kingdom of Herod, Gosner was thought to be attacking tsardom. His talk of a church without a hierarchy was disturbing to fellow Catholic as well as Orthodox priests. His books were confiscated and burned along with Mme Guyon's work. The witch hunt for subversive preachers was under way, and both Golitsyn and the Bible Society were bound to suffer. Fesler became a "well-known Jesuit-Jacobin,"[71] "worse than Pugachev,"[72] and all Methodists (the leaders of the Bible Society) "deceptive intriguers."[73]

When Golitsyn tried to bring Franz Baader himself to St. Petersburg, Baader never got beyond Riga and was forced to return to Bavaria late in 1823. He was a victim both of the general campaign against foreign influences and of the fear in official circles that a new religion was coming into being on Russian soil. Baader vainly pleaded directly to the Tsar in December, 1822, protesting that he was not in touch with "a certain Pietist sect in Russia" and had "no links of principle with Pietism in general, separatism or raskolnikism."[74] The charge was being made with increasing frequency against Golitsyn and his associates. The military governor of Riga was faced with a particularly acute increase in the strength of the Moravian Brethren within his province. As an émigré friend of De Maistre, he must have been glad to block Baader's efforts to proceed beyond Latvia. De Maistre was, in effect, wreaking a kind of belated revenge on the Pietists who had supplanted him at the Imperial Court. The Russian court seemed to be accepting at last his judgment that

in truth Martinism and Pietism penetrate one another such that it would be very difficult to find a sectarian of one of these systems who did not adhere to the other.[75]

The mystical teachings of higher order Masonry were indeed spilling out into mass sectarian religious movements. The most dramatic illustration was that of the new sect of "spirit bearers" (*dukhonostsy*) that suddenly sprang up among the traditionally rebellious Cossacks of the Don. The Cossack leader Evlampy Kotel'nikov had been profoundly influenced by Lopukhin's idea of a new "inner church" of "spiritual knights."[76] Kotel'nikov recognized Lopukhin's *Characteristics of the Inner Church* as the inspired word of God; and his followers considered it to be co-equal in authority with the Bible itself. Following Lopukhin's teachings, the spirit bearers claimed to be the true spiritual church of Jung-Stilling's prophecies. They insisted that the reign of the Antichrist had already begun through the official Church hierarchy, but that Alexander I was a reincarnation of Christ, who would destroy this many-headed serpent and establish spiritual rule on Russian soil.

The spirit bearers caused apprehension not only by their doctrine but even more because of the support felt for them in court circles. Their prophetic teachings bore many points of resemblance with occult Masonry and Mme Tatarinova's circle. A long series of interrogations of Kotel'nikov throughout 1823–4 revealed considerable indecision about how to deal with such a figure.

A second illustration of links between the mystical aristocracy and the sectarian masses may be found in the remarkable preacher Theodosius Levitsky, who arrived in St. Petersburg in 1823, and began prophesying the imminent end of the world.[77] He had been an active evangelist among Old Believers in White Russia and had found Jung-Stilling's prophetic writings an invaluable asset. His works had made an impression on Golitsyn, for he proposed to bring the Jews into the new inner church. Levitsky had preached among Jews in White Russia and sought to remind Christians that the Jews were to re-enter the Church just prior to the millennium. Baader had attached importance to the fact that Martinez de Pasqually, the founder of higher order Masonry, claimed to be "at the same time a Jew and a Christian" and had revived for humanity "the ancient alliance not only in its forms, but in its magical powers."[78] Martinez's "elected Cohens" and other higher orders of Masonry frequently invoked Jewish words and symbols and sometimes even the Jewish Kabbala as aids for their spiritual quest—particularly in White Russia, where there was a large Jewish population and some Jewish participation in Masonic activities.[79]

The idea of a new church unifying Christians and Jews was gaining grass roots support in the Orel-Voronezh region with the sudden appearance of the sabbatarian (subbotniki) sect. They added to the usual rejection of Orthodox forms of worship opposition to the doctrine of the trinity, celebration of Saturday as the sabbath, and the rite of circumcision. The sect made its first appearance in the second half of Alexander's reign. Though the added increase in strength from the Synod's estimate of fifteen hundred in 1819 to the Council of Ministers' estimate of twenty thousand the following year probably reflects less an increase in real strength than a desire of the latter body to undercut Golitsyn, the sect was gaining strength. A new secret census confirmed the importance of the sect, which apparently included Karaite as well as Talmudic Jews. It taught that all men could be rabbis and that the coming Messiah would be an occult philosopher who would unlock the secrets of the universe.[80]

As it became evident in the last years of Alexander's life that there would be no universal church on Russian soil, those who continued to believe in it became darkly apocalyptical. In St. Petersburg Levitsky preached the need for repentance in a famous sermon, "The Catastrophic Flood"; Kotel'nikov began to practice daily communion with his followers in imitation of the early apostles and in expectation of the coming end of the world. He addressed two meditations on the apocalypse, *The Cruel Sickle,* to the Tsar and his wife, likening St. Petersburg to Sodom and beseeching him to join the fellowship of the spirit bearers who alone would be spared in the coming judgment.

By 1824 many of the Tsar's key advisers had concluded that a subversive plot against the established order lay behind all this ferment; and that Jung-Stilling's prophetic writings contained the "hidden plan of revolution."[81] Beginning in 1824 Levitsky was incarcerated in a monastery on Lake Ladoga; Kotel'nikov sent first to Schlüsselburg prison, then to distant Solovetsk; Gosner and Fesler expelled from the country; Golitsyn relieved of all his positions of ecclesiastical authority; and harsh measures enacted to suppress the sabbatarians. The Bible Society was weakened and soon shut altogether "in order not to produce schism in the church."[82]

The idea of a "universal church" as a counter to revolution, rationalism, and all forms of external coercion had been dealt a blow from which it could not recover. Its only point of reference had been the "internal life" of each member, and all its hopes had been focused on "the blessed Alexander" whom all of the "spiritual knights" felt to be their patron if not their messiah.

The main unifying concept among all the heretical prophets of a new universal church was the idea that occult spiritual forces ruled the world. Saint-Martin had led the intellectuals into spiritualism with his last two major works: *On the Spirit of Things* and *The Ministry of the Man-Spirit,* the titles of which dramatized his opposition to two works of the Enlightenment: Montesquieu's *Spirit of the Laws* and La Mettrie's *The Man-Machine.* Following him, Lopukhin had written his books on "spiritual knighthood" and "the inner church of the spirit." These in turn had forged a link with the Russian sectarian and the German pietist traditions, both of which had tended to view the world of spirit as the supreme reality. The spirit bearers, who recognized Lopukhin's works as holy scripture, were the heirs of a sectarian tradition that included spirit wrestlers and "spiritual Christians."

The last years of Alexander's reign saw the degeneracy of this fashionable belief in disembodied spirits. Tatarinova's circle became a center for séances; Labzin's presses turned out vulgarized pocket guides for the understanding of the spirit world. Levitsky began referring to all his activities as "spiritual deeds"; and great attention was devoted to Jung-Stilling's treatise on the functioning of the spirit world: *The Science of Spirits*. Matter was seen as an imperfect form of reality in which Christ had only seemed to exist. Christ himself became a disembodied spirit, "the representation of the wisdom of a thinking God."[83]

If all of this was shocking to rationalistic minds of the Enlightenment, it was equally abhorrent to the Orthodox Church, which saw in all of this romantic occultism the reappearance of the dualistic heresies that had periodically plagued Eastern Christendom. Well might the clergy complain that Golitsyn had substituted belief in spirit (*dukh*) for belief in the soul (*dusha*), and that Fesler was in effect "a new Manichean."[84] They looked almost imploringly to the government to re-establish Orthodox Christianity in their land. Thus the Orthodox clergy played the last and most decisive role in the "reactionary uprising" against the Enlightenment. Orthodoxy supplanted Pietism; but the flight from rationalism continued just as it had when Pietism supplanted Catholicism at court a decade earlier.

Orthodox

IN TERMS of sheer size and growth, the expansion of the educational system of the Orthodox Church ranks among the most remarkable accomplishments of the late eighteenth century. Whereas there had been but twenty-six "spiritual schools" in 1764, there were 150 by 1808.[85] Administered by the state-controlled Synod, these schools imparted the rudiments of a pious and patriotic education to the majority of those civil servants and professional people who made the empire run. Teachers and alumni provided the grass roots support for the reactionary counterattack against the secularism and rationalism of the more cosmopolitan universities and lyceums, and of the more urbane teachers in the Church, such as Platon Levshin, who markedly improved the quality of the teaching in Church schools during his long tenure as Metropolitan of Moscow from 1775 to 1812, and fought to retain Latin rather than Russian as the basic language of instruction.

The generation of Orthodox leaders that rose to power after Platon's death resented the prominence of foreigners in the church school system, and shared the nationalistic enthusiasm that swept through Russia during the resistance to Napoleon. They were stung by the searching critique of De Maistre, who characterized the Orthodox Church as "an object of pity" incapable of understanding, let alone defending Christianity.

Take away the Catholicizing and the Protestantizing groups: the illuminists who are the raskolniks of the salons and the raskolniks who are the illuminists of the people, what is there left to it?[86]

There was growing agreement that Orthodox tradition needed more aggressive spokesmen if it was to survive in an age of ideological upheaval and
confusion. The first important plan for a distinctively Orthodox battle
against impiety, heresy, and revolution was provided by Alexander Sturdza,
a gifted Moldavian nobleman who had become fascinated with occult orders
when commissioned by the Russian court to write a history of Russian
relations with the Maltese order. His *Considerations on the Doctrine and
Spirit of the Orthodox Church,* written in 1816 for the benefit of the Lovers
of Humanity Society, proposed in effect that the Orthodox Church be transformed into a kind of spiritual overseer for the Holy Alliance. Two years
later, he wrote his widely discussed *Memoir on the Present State of
Germany,* which dealt mainly with the problem of education.[87]

In Sturdza's view, Germany's unrest was a direct result of undisciplined student activities. The Western Church had mistakenly granted the
universities autonomy from the guiding discipline of the Church. Germany
should revoke the medieval liberties of its universities. Orthodox Russia
should not permit any such liberties to be granted in its new universities
and should limit the numbers and regulate the curriculum of the German
professors who were flooding into Russia's universities and seminaries.

If Sturdza sounded the warning, it was the remarkable figure of Michael
Magnitsky who produced the call to battle stations and the detailed blueprints for an Orthodox Christian assault against the armies of godless
rationalism. Magnitsky illustrates the new blend of bureaucratic opportunism and philosophical obscurantism that was frequently to reappear in court
circles during the remaining century of tsarist rule. In the early years of
Alexander's rule, Magnitsky had done all the proper things for a member
of the lesser nobility anxious to get ahead. He had served in the Preobrazhensky Regiment and in Russian embassies in Paris and Vienna. He had
composed sentimental verses and participated in masonic and philanthropic societies. Indeed, so liberal had his posture been that he was identified with Speransky's reformist ideas and forced to share his downfall
in 1812.

Exiled to Vologda, Magnitsky's talents were soon put to use (like
those of Speransky) in the provincial civil service. He became vice-governor
of Voronezh on the upper Don, then governor of Simbirsk on the Volga.
This city had a long record of extremism; it was the former center of peasant
rebellion and was to be the birthplace of Lenin. It was in Simbirsk that

Repin and Russian Realism

PLATES XIII–XIV

Ilya Repin, the most famous and influential of all Russian realist painters, is a rarity among modern Russian artists in that he had a relatively long life (1844–1930) and enjoyed the favor of both official and radical circles. His career began with successful prize paintings in the Imperial Academy of Arts in the 1860's and imperial commissions in the 1870's, and he flourished during the brief liberal democratic era, when he painted portraits of leading politicians, and lived on in the U.S.S.R. (although he spent his last years abroad as an émigré), where he was hailed as a founder of the monumentalism and exhortative realism of Soviet art.

Repin capitalized on the peculiar fascination with historical themes that has animated Russian culture since the early illustrated chronicles. His famous representation of Ivan the Terrible with his murdered son (1885; Plate XIII) used the new realistic medium melodramatically to convey the horror and fascination with which Russians had always regarded this decisive act in the severing of the sacred line of succession from Riurik. The real-life model for Repin's picture of the tsarevich was the prophetic writer Vsevolod Garshin, who died three years later at 33, the same age as Christ, whom friends thought he resembled.

Many of Repin's portraits (such as his Tolstoy standing barefoot in peasant dress) provided the images by which a famous personality came to be remembered. Particularly revered by fellow Russian artists was Repin's painting of Musorgsky (Plate XIV), completed during four days of visits to the psychiatric hospital just a few days before the composer died in March 1881. Repin's rendering of his suffering friend caused many figures of the populist era to contend that Musorgsky had—almost literally —"survived" death through this vindication of Repin's own search for a natural "people's" art.

PLATE XIII

PLATE XIV

PLATE XV

Repin also brought to the centuries-old tradition of genre painting a new populist passion for identification with the simple, suffering people. His "Haulers on the Volga" (1870–3; Plate XV) became a monumental icon of populist revolutionaries (even though it had been commissioned by the Grand Duke Vladimir) and vaulted Repin to the symbolic leadership of the new quest for a realistic "art of the people" which the "wanderers" had launched a decade earlier. Partly inspired by the famed song of the Volga boatmen, the painting in turn inspired Musorgsky to seek a new music of redemption from the spontaneous sounds of his native Volga region. Revolutionaries saw a call to defiance and a plea for help in the proud bearing and searching gaze of the unbowed young boy. The ship provided a hint of other, distant lands to the East to which the river led; perhaps even of romantic deliverance by some future Stenka Razin from the toil and bondage of the landlocked empire.

The substantial amount of time that Repin spent planning this composition and traveling about in search of real-life models represented a continuation of the obsessive preoccupation of Russian painters with some single redemptive masterpiece—a tradition that began with Ivanov's "Appearance of Christ" and which has continued to the present with a painting like "Requiem of Old Russia, the Uspensky Sobor," which P. D. Korin, a principal designer of the monumental historical frescoes in the Moscow subway, has worked on for more than twenty-five years. Repin's greatest obsession (from 1878 to 1891) was his "Zaporozhian Cossacks Write a Letter to the Turkish Sultan," in which a historical theme was successfully blended with the genre style. Revolutionaries took heart at the rustic glorification of Cossack liberties, while conservative Pan-slavs took equal pleasure in the anti-Turkish subject.

Magnitsky began in 1818 his extraordinary war on the educational system of the Russian empire. In an anonymous letter to the Simbirsk branch of the Bible Society he urged the establishment of a Russian Inquisition to extirpate heresy from all published works. He then began public attacks on the influential new Masonic lodge, "Key to Virtue," in Simbirsk, as a center of subversion.[88] Early in 1819 he was empowered to investigate the University of Kazan, where Lopukhin's ideas had found particular receptivity;[89] and in April he became famous overnight with his lurid exposé.

Twenty of twenty-five professors are "hopeless," Magnitsky reported as a result of his inspection tour. Heretical German philosophy has replaced Orthodox theology in the curriculum, but "fortunately the lectures are so badly delivered that no one can understand them."[90] Like an outraged taxpayer, Magnitsky rhetorically demands to know why two million rubles have been spent on a den of heresy and subversion in which lectures are mainly given in languages unintelligible to Russians.

His proposed remedy administered a real shock to the vague euphoria of tolerance then prevalent in the empire. He recommended to Golitsyn that the university be not reformed, but closed, formally sentenced like a criminal, and then razed. In its place should be established a controlled gymnasium, a medical institute, and a school for indoctrinating Tatars and teaching the Orthodox about the East.[91] These measures were not adopted, but he was made head of the university in June and proceeded with reforms that were almost as drastic.

The university was henceforth to base its entire curriculum on the Bible and "on piety, in accordance with the decrees of the Holy Alliance."[92] Each student was required to own a Bible, and scriptural passages were written all over the walls and corridors often in ornate gold letters. Geology was outlawed as hostile to Biblical teachings, and mathematicians were instructed to point out that the hypotenuse of a right triangle represented the mercy of God descending to man through Christ.[93] Books were removed from the library, professors forced to write long spiritual autobiographies, and puritanical discipline and communal scripture readings instituted. Three grades of punishment were instituted for student infractions, the highest involving solitary confinement in a barred room containing only a wooden table and bench, a large crucifix, and a picture of the Last Judgment. Students were ordered to pray for offenders in this category, who were in some cases forcibly transferred to military service.[94]

The supreme danger of modern universities was, in Magnitsky's view, their teaching of philosophy, which was bound to raise doubts about revealed religion. He found an invaluable ally in Runich, the first curator of the new university in St. Petersburg, who was called "Magnitsky's echo" and "a corpse stimulated to life by Magnitsky." A German professor had been dismissed at Kharkov in 1816 for teaching that Napoleon's crimes lay in overthrowing the natural rights of the people rather than the traditional rights of monarchs. In 1820 Runich and Magnitsky broadened the assault with a combined attack on a professor of the Imperial Lyceum at Tsarskoe Selo who had just presented a copy of his book, *Natural Law,* to the Emperor. In the following year they succeeded in obtaining the dismissal of three key professors from St. Petersburg University.

Early in 1823 Magnitsky launched an expanded campaign against the "Hellish Alliance" which he claimed was now at war with the Holy Alliance. He claimed to find the "doctrines of Marat" in one professor's book and the secret plans of "illuminists" in another. In February he proposed the outlawing of philosophy, warning that "from one line of a professor can come 200,000 bayonets and 1,000 ships of the line."[95] In May he denounced the "bloody cap of freedom" which "used to be called only *philosophy* and *literature* and is now already called *liberalism*."[96]

"Down with altars, down with sovereigns, long live death and hell." They are already howling forth in several countries in Europe. How can one fail to recognize who is speaking? The Prince of Darkness himself is coming visibly closer to us; the veil covering him is becoming more and more transparent and soon, no doubt, will fall altogether. This assault, the last perhaps that he will lead against us, is the most terrible, for it is spiritual. The word is being spread from one end of the world to the other invisibly and rapidly like an electric shock, and suddenly culminates in a shattering of the earth. The human word, that is what transmits this diabolical force; the printing press is its arm. *Godless university professors are distilling the atrocious poison of disbelief and of hate towards legitimate power for our unhappy youth. . . .*[97]

Russia should simply

separate herself from Europe so that not even a rumor about the horrible events taking place there could reach her. The present war of the spirit of evil cannot be arrested by the force of arms, for against a spiritual assault an equally spiritual defense is needed. A clairvoyant censorship united with a system of popular education founded on the unshakable base of faith is the only dike against the flood of disbelief and depravity engulfing Europe.[98]

There was little support within the ministry of education and spiritual affairs for such an extreme position. One member pointed out that countries like Spain and Portugal in which revolutions had occurred were precisely the ones in which enlightenment was least far advanced;[99] another wrote that a successful state could not function in this manner even "if we could surround our fatherland with a Chinese Wall . . . transplant to Russian soil the Spanish Inquisition . . . and blot out everything that has ever been written about philosophy."[100] But Magnitsky found more powerful allies in Archimandrite Photius, a young ascetic influential with the Tsar who had recently turned from long friendship with Golitsyn to violent denunciation of the Bible Society. "It is the cleverness of Hell itself that the ancient faith is being destroyed by pious foreigners," echoed an anonymous informant of Admiral Shishkov.[101] Runich wrote that it was essential "to pluck even one quill from the dark wing of the foe of Christ."[102]

Magnitsky followed the new Metropolitan of St. Petersburg, Seraphim, to the Winter Palace in the spring of 1824, when the latter went to request Golitsyn's dismissal. He waited outside on Admiralty Boulevard in order to tell immediately from the expression on Seraphim's face whether or not the Tsar had acceded to the request. The news was, of course, good for the Orthodox reactionaries: Golitsyn was dismissed from all posts: replaced as head of the Bible Society by Seraphim, as minister of education by Shishkov. "Foreign cults" were placed in a separate category, subordinate at last to the Orthodox Synod and to the Draconian Arakcheev. Thus, Golitsyn's unique concentration of spiritual and pedagogical authority was broken up; and the dream of a new universal church destroyed.

The Orthodoxy which Magnitsky opposed to syncretism made use of the same supra-confessional terminology from higher order Masonry that Lopukhin had used before him. He described life as "passing through the Great Temple . . . in holy darkness" in order to reach "the all-seeing eye of holiness . . . the Church of the first centuries."[103]

Like De Maistre, Magnitsky's main concern was the mobilization of Russia to combat the infection of Russia with the rationalism that had been spawned by the Protestant Reformation in religion and by the French Revolution in politics. But there were critical differences between the absolutist remedies proposed by the two men. Whereas De Maistre had sought the rule of an international church hierarchy subordinate to the pope, Magnitsky looked rather to the Russian tsar as supreme authority and to his civil and ecclesiastical bureaucracy as the "hierarchy." Whereas De Maistre assumed that the new Christian civilization would be suffused with the classical culture of the Latin world, Magnitsky insisted that Russian civilization must deepen its sense of identification with the East.

Magnitsky's fascination with the East was in part a reflection of occult Masonry and the related vision of a new church coming from the East. Masonic temples were always built facing the East, and the term "Orient" was used as a synonym for a city in which Masons were active.[104] Pietist missionaries and the vernacular translators of the Russian Bible Society had spoken excitedly of the rich "harvest" they hoped to reap in the Russian East; and Lopukhin had insisted that Russia's "most sincere collaborators" in combating revolution and secularism were to be found among "Asians [*Aziattsy*] from Peking to Constantinople."[105] Magnitsky criticized Karamzin for saying that the Mongol period was one of decline for Russia, since the Tatars saved it from Europe and enabled it to preserve the purity of its Christian faith at a time when all others were falling into heresy. Beginning with his proposal of 1819 for evangelizing the Tatars, Magnitsky displayed a romantic fascination with the idea that the cultivation of Eastern links would help qualify Russia for the role of redeeming the fallen West.

Orientalism received a new boost with the establishment of a chair in Arabic at St. Petersburg in the same year; and in 1822 Magnitsky drew up a plan for an "Institute of the East" to be established in Astrakhan to train future Russian civil servants and place them "in touch with the learned circles of India." He cherished the belief that an unspoiled apostolic Church still flourished in India and claimed to see Biblical influences in Hindu sacred writings. The wife of Brahma, Sara-Veda, was thought to be Sarah, the wife of Abraham in the Old Testament. He organized the search for lost treasures in the monasteries of Armenia and sought to sponsor cultural safaris to Siberia and Samarkand.[106]

The career of Magnitsky illustrates the vulnerability of the Russian body politic to extremist pressures. The very extremity of his denunciations exercised a certain fascination and made some of his victims almost anxious to believe that they were as powerful and purposeful as Magnitsky alleged them to be. In a confused intellectual atmosphere he offered a simple explanation for all difficulties: an enemy to replace Napoleon as a stimulus to national unity. All difficulties came from the "illuminists." Revolutions in Spain, Naples, and Greece were interrelated parts of their eastward-moving plot. Students in Germany had already been infected; but Orthodox Russia, the anchor of the Holy Alliance, was its principal target. In denouncing a Masonic leader in Simbirsk, Magnitsky added the accusation of secret links with the Carbonari; in denouncing Fesler, he hinted at Jewish and Socinian connections.

In the absence of dispassionate investigation, the confused impression grew that some kind of spiritual invasion was indeed underway. Concealment and suspicion grew apace and helped encourage nervous displays of loyalty to the Tsar. With relentless logic, the denunciations and purges ran their course until Magnitsky himself fell a victim. An accusation that Magnitsky was a secret illuminist was among Alexander's papers at the time of his death. Shortly thereafter his administration of Kazan University was investigated and his foes treated to the revelation that he had employed a Jew as supervisor of studies, had spent as much in seven years as his predecessor had been accused of spending in twelve, and so on. In vain Magnitsky argued that the apostles themselves were converted Jews and that his accusers were repeating the arguments of Voltaire. He journeyed to St. Petersburg to plead his case and wrote two eleventh-hour detailed analyses of the "world-wide illuminist plot" for the new Tsar from his exile in Esthonia early in 1831.

The illuminists were attacking at four levels: academic, political, ecclesiastical, and popular. "Levelers," "millennarians," "methodists," and "schismatics" were bracketed together as part of a giant conspiracy to substitute a "Tsar-Comrade" for the "Tsar-Father" of simple Russians. Even conservative Austria was alleged to be sending in agents to subvert Russian institutions.[107]

But Magnitsky had made too many enemies, and his main friend, Arakcheev, had fallen from power. Having ridden the wave of obscurantism, he was now swept aside into the stagnant backwaters of the provincial civil service from which he was to witness the success of the policies he advocated without benefiting from them. He wrote briefly for a journal bearing a title from the symbolism of higher Masonic orders: *The Rainbow*. But his last writings represent only a broken-spirited endorsement of his long-standing anti-rationalism: a treatise on astrology and a series called "simple thinker," which defended the unquestioning faith of "muzhik Christianity."[108]

The Legacy

UNDER CATHERINE and Alexander, Russia had moved deep into Europe physically and spiritually but had not equipped itself to share in the political and institutional development of the West. Russian cities had been rebuilt on neo-classical models, but Russian thought had remained largely untouched by classical form and discipline. An experiment that had begun with Catherine's promise to provide the most tolerant and rational rule in Europe had ended with Magnitsky's intolerance and glorification of the Mongols. Imprecise hopes had given way to equally vague fears without the major problems being defined, let alone solved. The debate was cut off before Russia had achieved either a rationalized political system or a rational theology; and the imperial government committed itself to the difficult reactionary position of simply preventing the questions from being asked.

The religious purge of 1824 ended all broad discussion of belief within the official Church, just as the repression of the Decembrists the following year ended all discussion of basic political questions within the government. But expectations once raised are not easily dispelled. Denied a hearing in official circles, the problems continued to agitate Russia unofficially.

Indeed, the leading agitators of the Alexandrian age acquired in martyrdom an historical significance they had been unable to gain in action. The trial and humiliation of the Decembrists left a keen impact on the newly awakened moral sensibilities of the aristocracy. Having been unable to agree on their own political program, the aristocratic thinkers were united by their opposition to the spectacle of a "generation on trial" and by their revulsion at the execution of the leaders and the sanctioning of odes in praise of those throwing mud at others en route to Siberian exile. The "Hannibalic oath" of Herzen and Ogarev to avenge the fallen Decembrists is the real starting point of Russia's modern revolutionary tradition.

Equally remarkable was the continued appeal throughout Nicholas' reign of the new religious answers that had been offered under his predecessor. The Catholic Church attracted many Russian aristocrats—particularly after the official anti-Catholicism that accompanied the crushing of the Polish rebellion. The beautiful Zinaida Volkonsky, a close friend of Alexander I and former maid of honor to the dowager empress, became a leading figure in Catholic charity work in Rome and an apostle of reunification of the churches and conversion of the Jews.[109] Sophia Svechin, the daughter of one of Catherine's leading advisers, became a leading benefactress of the Jesuit order in Paris. She set up a chapel and Slavic library and helped induce a young diplomat, Ivan Gagarin, to join the order.[110] The Decembrist Lunin became a Catholic and the freethinker Pecherin a Redemptorist friar ministering to the poor of Dublin. Most remarkable of all was the conversion of a large part of the Golitsyn family, which had pioneered since the seventeenth century in the secular Westernization of Russia. Dmitry Golitsyn, son of Diderot's main Russian contact, joined the Church and went to Baltimore, Maryland, where he became the first Catholic priest to receive all his orders in the United States. Ordained in 1795, he led a Sulpician mission to western Pennsylvania, administering a vast area stretching from Harrisburg to Erie, Pennsylvania, from a log church near the present town of Loretto.[111]

Prophetic sectarianism continued also to exercise an appeal. The various "spiritual Christians" in the south continued to flourish: the "milk drinkers" in the Caucasus, whence they were deported in 1823 and began establishing new contacts extending into Persia; the "spirit bearers" in the

Cossack center of Novocherkassk, where various followers of Kotel'nikov told of his martyrdom in Solovetsk and predicted the end of the world in 1832, 1843, and 1844.[112]

For better or worse the unorthodox religious ideas of the Alexandrian era were to have far greater impact on subsequent Russian history than the reformatorial political ideas of the age. Speculative religious thinkers of the late nineteenth century tended to pick up where men of Alexander's time left off. Faithful to the main line of Alexandrian spirituality, they tended to oppose both revolution and rationalism. They also tended to vacillate between De Maistre's idea of a disciplined inquisitorial church and Lopukhin's idea of a spiritual "inner" church.

The two ideals confront one another in Dostoevsky's "Legend of the Grand Inquisitor." The returning Christ figure is Lopukhin's ideal spiritual knight who opposes the dedicated and articulate Inquisitor with the spiritual weapons of silent suffering and freely given love. The two ideals are also present in Vladimir Solov'ev, whose personal rapprochement with Roman Catholicism and with De Maistre's views on war conflicted with his vision of churches reunited in a "free theocracy."[113] Even Constantine Pobedonostsev, the semi-Inquisitorial procurator of the Synod, felt the contrary appeal of the "inner church," and translated Thomas à Kempis' *Imitation of Christ*.

It seems appropriate that the most famous convert to the ideal of a new inner church in nineteenth-century Russia, Leo Tolstoy, spent several key years of his life studying the history of the Alexandrian era. The fruit of his study was, of course, Russia's greatest historical novel, *War and Peace*, which began as a study of the Decembrists and ended as a panoramic epic of the war with Napoleon and of the spiritual strivings which accompanied it.

Tolstoy subsequently became an archetype of Lopukhin's "spiritual knight" with his "conversion" to a new non-doctrinal Christianity that abjured violence and taught that "the kingdom of God is within you." Tolstoy's idea that man could rid the world of evil by reading the secret message on a little green stick represents a perhaps unconscious borrowing from higher order Masonry for which a green stick was the symbol of eternal life. Even his celebrated parody of the externals of Masonic rituals in *War and Peace* reflects the contempt for mere ritual which was central to Novikov's and Lopukhin's ideal of higher spiritual orders. Tolstoy's first youthful vision of a new fraternity "of all the people of the world under the wide dome of heaven" went by the name of "Ant Brotherhood" (*muraveinoe bratstvo*), which was apparently a mutation of the idealized Moravian Brotherhood (*Moravskoe Bratstvo*).[114] Tolstoy's tendency to keep himself surrounded with Bibles or Gospels in all languages[115] and his general sympathy for pietistic Protestant teachings was reminiscent of the Bible Society. In his old age he devoted great energy to aiding the original persecuted sect of "spiritual Christians," the Dukhobors.[116] Tolstoy opposed De Maistre's ideal of an inquisitorial Church, though Solov'ev implied that he secretly wished to set up one of his own.[117] De Maistre's historical scepticism and pessimism also profoundly influenced *War and Peace*.[118]

However rich in speculative ideas, the Alexandrian age tended to discredit religion in the eyes of many thinking people. Alexander's personal vacillation encouraged a jockeying for imperial favor among the various religious confessions, which soon degenerated into inter-confessional polemic and intrigue. Terms like "Jesuit" and "Methodist" were used as epithets almost as often as "Jacobin" and "illuminist." Thus, ironically, Alexander's efforts to encourage tolerance only intensified sectarian bitterness.

To compound the irony, Alexander's manifest failure to provide leadership strengthened rather than weakened the adulation that he personally received. All the partisans of reform idealized the tolerant Alexander and cherished the thought that the benign and enigmatic emperor really subscribed to their particular views. Alexander was indeed until his death the one concrete focal point for all the vague hopes of the age. He remained Alexander the Great to a host of would-be Aristotles throughout Europe and a near god to the peasantry, who launched no great insurrection against him. Catholics cherished the thought that Alexander had contemplated conversion at the time of his death; and the popular religious imagination clung to the idea that Alexander was not dead at all but lived on as the wandering holy man, Fedor Kuzmich.[119]

The hopes for a transformation of Russia through Alexander were too vague and romantic, too unchastened by experience in the real world. Yet Alexander—like other well-meaning political leaders who have been looked to as saviors—appears to have become hypnotized by the adulation he received. In his late years he became even more incapable than before of sober statesmanship. "Moving from cult to cult and religion to religion," complained Metternich, "he has upset everything and built nothing."[120] He died in a distant Southern retreat from reality, after visiting various churches, mosques, and a synagogue and rejecting medical treatment.[121] The champion of tolerance had permitted Russia to become the scene of ideological interrogation, anonymous denunciation, and arbitrary exile. The most beloved tsar in modern Russian history had let Russia drift into policies that were in some respects even more reactionary than those of Paul.

Most of the leading theorists of the age—whether Russians like

Radishchev, Novikov, Karamzin, Speransky, Pestel, Lopukhin, and Magnitsky, or foreign teachers like Schwarz, De Maistre, Baader, and Fesler—had been active in the Masonic movement. Though Masonry was formally neither a political nor a religious movement, it had profound influence in both of these areas. Higher order Masonry excited Russians to believe that self-perfection was possible and that the new temple of Solomon to be built by "true Masons" was nothing short of the world itself. But there was no way of knowing exactly how or where this rebuilding was to take place. "One can have knowledge about Masonry," one leader was fond of saying, "but Masonry itself is a secret."[122]

The lodges filled for the culture of aristocratic Russia something of the role that had been played by the monasteries in the culture of Muscovy. They provided islands of spiritual intensity and cultural activity within a still bleak and hostile autocratic environment. Like the monasteries of old, the Masonic lodges represented both a challenge and an opportunity to the ruling authorities. But Catherine and eventually Alexander chose to view Masonry as a challenge, just as Peter had regarded monasticism. If the various protest movements of the seventeenth and eighteenth centuries represent a kind of counterattack against the autocratic destruction of the old monastic culture, so the ideological rebellion of the nineteenth-century intellectuals appears in some ways as a form of protest against the autocratic destruction of the new Masonic culture.

The sacred chants of this Masonic culture were the declamatory hymns consecrated to abstract virtues and mythological deities. Initiation into the lodge was a kind of second, adult baptism. Sacred texts were those of Boehme, Saint-Martin, Jung-Stilling, and other mystical thinkers who were regarded as equal to the evangelists and early Church fathers. The Masons, however, sought no salvation in the next world, which was the goal of the monks, but truth in this world: *pravda,* the "two-sided truth" of wisdom and justice.

The icons of the Masonic culture were statues and busts of great figures of the past. It was only under Catherine that statuary had first assumed importance in Russian art.[123] The bronze statue of Peter the Great was her monumental icon to Westernization, her statue of Voltaire her icon for private veneration. Lopukhin had a private garden full of symbolic sculpture and busts of the "spiritual knights" of his "inner church."[124] Magnitsky made statuary crucifixes a key part of his decor for the reformed university at Kazan; and Runich kept a private bust of Christ with a crown of thorns.[125]

The extraordinary attention paid to physical characteristics of the face was partly the new enthusiasm of a people just discovering the naturalistic art that had been present in the West for several centuries but partly also a

new version of the iconographer's old belief that a painting was a means of
communing with the saints. The private gallery of busts and paintings in
the castle that Rastrelli built for the Stroganovs in St. Petersburg became
a kind of hall of icons; and the Decembrist Bestuzhev's painting portraits
in exile of all those who had participated in the uprising marked the beginnings of a new martyrological portraiture.[126]

Herzen, who launched the secular revolutionary tradition in an effort
to avenge the fallen Decembrists, was also influenced by the culture of
higher order Masonry: in his youthful oath-taking, his early talk of
palingenesis ("rebirth");[127] in the title of his first journal, *Polar Star* (which
was taken from a Decembrist paper named after a key Masonic lodge and
symbol); and in his decision to edit, even amidst the exciting early years
of Alexander II's reign, the works of the original "spiritual knight," Lopukhin. Many symbols of higher order Masonry seem, indeed, strangely applicable to the Russian revolutionary tradition: the basic slogan "Victory
or Death"; the supreme symbol of the sword (representing the need to fight
for an idea); the lower symbol of the knife (representing the need to punish
traitors); the idea of inscribing messages on a cross; and the candles within
the temple symbolizing the light of Adam within man and the perfection of
the starry firmament which they would soon bring down to earth. In ex-
tinguishing these candles, the Romanovs did not succeed in snuffing out the
spark that had lit them; and the journal in which Lenin first developed
his revolutionary ideas was to bear the name of this key Masonic symbol,
The Spark—again through the intermediacy of Decembrist usage.

The Masonic culture of the Alexandrian age was, of course, a far different thing from the revolutionary movements that were to make use of its
symbols and techniques. All Masons were pledged to belief in God, but he
had many names and faces. One could find him equally well in the world
(macrocosm), in oneself (microcosm), or in books of revelation (mesocosm).
God's very name had symbolic and allegorical meaning for the Russian
occultists. The letters BOG stood for *blago* ("good"), *otets* ("father"), and
glagol' ("the word"), which were the three essential characteristics of the
"God above God" of Russian mysticism. The letter "O" stood in the middle
—a self-contained circle of perfection signifying that there was neither beginning nor end to God's fatherhood.[128] The birth of Christ was said to have
occurred in all three forms: as the moral incarnation of the good and the
scientific incarnation of the true word. Thus the "imitation of Christ" meant
in higher order Masonry the attainment by man of the "two-sided truth" of
knowledge and justice.

But how did such a God relate to Russia? Beneath the anguish and
frustrations of the Alexandrian age lies the pathos of intoxicated mystics

trying to apply their insights to the real world, and the deeper drama of an awakening nation in search of a national creed. De Maistre offered Russia the Catechism of the Council of Trent. Pietistic sectarians looked to Lopukhin's *Moral Catechism of the True Free Mason* to lead them away from "dreams born of smoke from the dull light of false wisdom."[129] Conservative military leaders looked admiringly to the pietistic and patriotic *Short Catechism for German Soldiers* written in 1812 by Ernst Arndt for German soldiers fighting Napoleon in Russia.[130] Rationalistic sceptics turned to Voltaire's *Catechism of an Honest Man.*[131] Patriotic reformers admired the Russian translation of a Spanish *Citizen's Catechism* drawn up during the Peninsular War, and tended toward the view set forth in the *Catechism* of the Decembrist Murav'ev-Apostol that Russians should "rise up all together against tyranny and establish faith and freedom in Russia. Whoever rejects this path will, like the traitor, Judas, be cursed with anathema. Amen."[132]

The creed which Russia adopted under Nicholas I was far closer to that described by Catherine's courtier, the conservative historian M. Shcherbatov, in his "utopian" novel of 1783–4, *A Voyage to the Land of Ofir,* than to anything outlined in Alexander's time. Shcherbatov, for all his erudition and his unexcelled fifteen-thousand-volume library, was deeply suspicious of undisciplined intellectual activity. He proposed an absolute monarchy with a rigid class structure and an educational system that would be totally oriented toward practical problems. Religion was to be completely rational and authoritarian. In place of all other reading matter (even the Bible), the ordinary citizen was to be given two new catechisms: a moral and legal catechism. Both the priests who taught the former and the police who taught the latter should have as their object the maintenance of order and the inculcation of respect for morality and law.[133]

Under Nicholas I, Russia acquired both its "moral" and its "legal" catechism: the former in Metropolitan Philaret's *Orthodox Catechism,* the latter in Uvarov's famous circular outlining the doctrine of "official nationality." At the same time, social and economic policies followed the rigid lines set forth in Shcherbatov's novel. Class distinctions were strictly maintained; the peasantry remained in bondage; and commerce and industry were kept subordinate to agriculture, which Shcherbatov had considered the source of all wealth.

This represented in some ways a return to order and rationality after the confusions of Alexander's time. Nicholas discarded the most extreme figures in the "reactionary uprising" of the mid-twenties: Arakcheev for Benckendorff in the army, Magnitsky for Uvarov in education, Photius for Philaret in the Church, the archaic Slavicisms of Shishkov for the Europeanized prose of Karamzin. Yet Nicholas' policies were more resented because of their finality, their refusal to leave room for further discussion of religion and politics by the aristocracy. His ideal society was the army, in which, "there is order . . . no impertinent claims to know all the answers . . . no one commands before he himself has learned to obey."[134] God was the supreme commander and Nicholas "a subordinate officer determined to execute his orders well and to occupy an honorable place in the great military review to be held in the next world."[135] Never again, except for a few brief years under Alexander II, were the Romanovs to encourage the discussion of political reform. Never again, except in the last decadent days under Rasputin, was the court to encourage the extra-ecclesiastical pursuit of religious truth.

Thus, the suspicions of rational enlightenment engendered during Alexander's lifetime had a debilitating effect on the subsequent development of Russian culture. It was particularly fateful that the high tide of anti-Enlightenment feeling should occur at the very time when Russia was becoming fully conscious of its national power and identity. Anti-rationalism was given special sanction within Russia because rationalism was identified with revolution, revolution with Napoleon, and Napoleon with the invasion of Russia and burning of Moscow.

The new Moscow that arose on the ruins of the old soon began to eclipse St. Petersburg and to think of itself as distinct from European culture. Following the burning of Moscow, Michael Zagoskin, one of the most widely read writers of the era, began a lifetime of gathering material for sketches on "Moscow and Muscovites," which enjoyed great popularity when they finally appeared in the 1840's. As he said in his introduction:

> I have studied Moscow too much for thirty years and can say emphatically that it is not a city, not a capital, but an entire world that is profoundly Russian. . . . Just as thousands of rays of sunshine come to a focus at one point in passing through a magnifying glass, in precisely the same way in Moscow the different characteristics of our Russian popular physiognomy are unified in one national countenance . . . you will find in Moscow a treasure house of all the elements in the worldly and civil life of Russia, that great colossus for which Petersburg acts as the head, and Moscow the heart.[136]

The "heart" was more important than the "head" for the mystical romantics of the new Muscovite culture. Their attempts to find truths hidden in the physiognomy of a city was an extension of the occult fascination with statuary and phrenology under Alexander. The very uniqueness and asymmetry of Moscow appealed to their imagination. Marvelous meaning was discovered in the strange shapes of the old capital, whereas fear and foreboding were found on the face of the new—in the contemporaneous *Physiology of Petersburg* and a number of literary works.[137] This was no longer the Moscow which had appeared on Latin-inscribed medals struck in honor of the founding of Russia's first university, showing the Kremlin towers illumined by the rising sun,[138] but a Moscow of mysterious moonlight:

> How clear and brilliant is the moon
> Contemplating sleeping Moscow.
> Can it have ever seen in all its journeys through the vault of heaven
> A city so magnificent? Can it have seen a second Kremlin?[139]

The remarkable cultural activity of Moscow under Nicholas I was, however, no mere return to the Muscovy of old. Catherine and Alexander I had wrought an irrevocable change in Russian thought. The aristocracy had undergone a stimulating exposure to the West, and to books that were hitherto inaccessible in the vernacular—from the complete New Testament to Diderot's *Encyclopedia*. They had acquired a taste for the fraternal and intellectual activity of small circles. Secular journalism and art, organized education and philanthropy, had all become part of the life of many Russian aristocrats.

The changes that had already taken place in the intellectual atmosphere are illustrated by the figure who finally set down the official state philosophy of Nicholas I, Sergius Uvarov. From the time he first propounded his sacred trilogy of "Orthodoxy, Autocracy and Nationality" as the newly installed minister of education in 1833 until he died just a few months after Nicholas in 1855, Uvarov was an urbane and effective apologist for the anti-Enlightenment. Just as Speransky's new law code of 1833 spelled an end to the hopes of the Russian Enlightenment for political-constitutional reform, so Uvarov's circular of the same year brought to a close hopes for educational reform. But in contrast to the law code, Uvarov's writings helped open up new avenues for Russian thought by keeping alive some of the ideological passion of the preceding era.

Superficially, Uvarov appears as yet another epigon of occult Masonry —arguing that some supra-rational basis must be found for truth and authority and that one must look to the ancient East for surviving reflections of the "lost light of Adam." Russia should treasure its links with Asia and conduct extensive "metaphysical archeology" into its Eastern heritage, Uvarov argued, in his blueprint of 1810 for an Asian Academy.[140] Two years later, his *Essay on the Eleusinian Mysteries* idealized the authority of mystery in a primitive Greek civilization still thought to be linked to its Oriental heritage. The implication was that the democracy and critical philosophy for which Greece had generally been praised in the Age of the Enlightenment were, in fact, corrosive forces that had destroyed the "intellectual solidarity"[141] of an earlier, proto-Oriental society.

This early statement of pro-Asian sentiment attracted increased attention as Napoleon's invasion of Russia fanned anti-European and anti-Enlightenment sentiment. Uvarov's reiteration of this position in the 1830's benefited from a second wave of anti-Western feeling that followed the Polish uprising of 1830. Pletnev, Uvarov's leading lieutenant and popularizer, insisted that Western classicism was incompatible with autocracy; Osip Senkovsky, professor of Oriental languages at St. Petersburg, became a propagandist for Uvarov's views; and Count Rostopchin, the reactionary pamphleteer who had defended Moscow from Napoleon, was posthumously assigned a genealogy from Genghis Khan.

"We must Easternize ourselves [*ovostochit'sia*]," proclaimed one leading critic,[142] and, as if in response, Asians suddenly became heroes in a number of new and distinctly second-rate historical plays and novels—such as those of the prolific Raphael Zotov, which ranged from the embellished saga of his Tatar father's battles against Napoleon, *The Last Descendant of Genghis Khan,* to the picture of enlightened Chinese struggling with corrupt Western intruders in *Tsin-Kin-Tong, or the Three Good Deeds of the Spirit of Darkness.* A play of 1823, *The Youth of Ivan III, or the Attack of Tamerlane on Russia,* even goes so far as to have the Mongol invader tutor the Russian tsar. An almanac of 1828 completed the picture by offering an anthology of Mongolian proverbs to a people always responsive to this type of folk wisdom.[143]

Pan-Asianism did not become part of Uvarov's doctrine of "official nationality"; but his fascination with the Orient illustrates his own remoteness from any simple doctrine of returning to primitive, purely Russian practices. Instead, he appears as an uncertain seeker for some new form of authoritarianism. He speaks of "complete societies . . . where the philosophic element triumphs,"[144] and where shallow *philosophes* are confounded by "complete thought" which integrates intelligence, imagination, and sentiment.[145]

Uvarov fully shared the general aristocratic contempt for the commercially oriented West and its periodical press which has "dethroned the word."[146] But he places on his ideological throne not the Word that was in the beginning but slogans that never were before. Orthodoxy comprised only one third of his formula; and his critical writings reveal a general indifference to Christianity—if not actual atheism.[147] He is the voice not of faith but of inner uncertainty and romantic longing. He seems to be looking not for a philosopher-king or Christian emperor, but for the grand master of some occult order. His image of the "complete society" is not one in which each individual has perfected his rational faculties and remade the social order in accordance with moral law. Rather it is a rigidly hierarchical society ruled by an "intelligence" that is unintelligible to all but the inner initiates.

Uvarov fought Cartesianism and scepticism not with tradition but with a new ideology that often seems to anticipate modern totalitarianism. In the process, however, he helped create other problems. By introducing *narodnost'* ("nationality") as one of the three pillars of official ideology, he gave increased authority to a vague term which radicals later interpreted to mean "spirit of the people." By founding in 1834 and presenting his views regularly in a monthly "thick journal," *The Journal of the Ministry of Public Education,* Uvarov moved the government into the risky terrain of ideological journalism. By idealizing the "effervescence of ideas"[148] in the ancient Orient, he helped encourage the new effervescence of exotic thought that became characteristic of the age of Nicholas. By setting forth an all-encompassing state ideology, Uvarov helped turn Russian thinkers to broad questions of personal and national belief, which increasingly interested Russians as the possibility of political and pedagogic reform faded.

New vistas had been opened to the imagination in the Age of Alexander I. Despite Uvarov's efforts to hold them in check, the aristocrats were to enjoy a last period of creative exploration under Nicholas before the stage became filled with the new social classes and material concerns of a more open and industrialized society under Alexander II.

3. The "Cursed Questions"

Under Nicholas I, the imperial pendulum swung back from French Enlightenment to German discipline far more decisively than it had done during the brief reigns of Peter III and Paul. The various contacts and associations with the German-speaking world that had been growing fitfully but steadily in importance were climaxed during the long and superficially glittering reign of Nicholas by new bonds of princely and aristocratic brotherhood. Russian and German rulers stood together as guardians of the conservative restoration sealed at the Congress of Vienna. Far closer to his Germanophile mother than to his much older and more cosmopolitan brothers, Constantine and Alexander I, Nicholas married a Prussian princess and leaned constantly throughout his own thirty-year reign on his father-in-law and brother-in-law, who successively ruled Prussia as Frederick William III and IV. The addition to the Russian Empire of the Baltic provinces with their German baronial overseers further flooded the Russian aristocracy with Germans, and led to the famous incident whereby an aristocrat given his choice of new rank by the Tsar asked to be redesignated "a German."[1] Survivors of the Alexandrian era complained in exile that Russia's movement into Central Europe had been its undoing:

> The Germans have conquered Russia in the very process of letting themselves be conquered. This is what happened in China with the Mongols, in Italy with the Barbarians, in Greece with the Romans.[2]

Extending the Prussian ideal of military discipline to all corners of society, Nicholas became the *bête noire* of liberals and nationalists throughout Europe. Leaning for civil order on the investigative activities of his newly created "Third Section," Nicholas was said to have meant by the phrase *le bien-être général en Russie*, "it is well to be a general in Russia."[3]

Nicholas' reign occupies in some respects a place in Russian history similar to that of Peter the Great, of whom Nicholas' official apologists were

such great admirers.[4] Like Peter, Nicholas came to power at the end of a
period of religious and political ferment in which allegiances and institutions
all seemed subject to change. Like Peter, Nicholas was primarily a soldier,
fascinated from boyhood with military weapons and technology; and sought
to re-establish order on military lines with the aid of a Lutheran-style
church clearly subordinate to the state. Just as Peter came into power by
curbing rebellion within the palace guard in Moscow, so Nicholas ascended
to the throne while crushing the Decembrist uprising within the new elite
regiments in St. Petersburg.

Peter, of course, was opening, while Nicholas was shutting, windows
to the West. But the century between the end of Peter's reign and the beginning of Nicholas' had brought too much cultural exposure to the West
ever to be blocked off; ideas from the West could not be stopped as Magnitsky would have wished. Like a swollen river suddenly confronted with a
major obstacle, the flow was merely diverted into channels that had hitherto
carried only a small trickle of ideas. Philosophy, history, and literary criticism replaced politics and religion in the mainstreams of Russian culture.

For awhile it seemed that Russian intellectual life was to be diverted
from practical concerns altogether. Many leading figures went abroad for
visits that slowly lengthened into semi-exile. Many of Russia's finest minds
moved into the realm of the distant or theoretical. In Kazan in the aftermath
of the Magnitsky era, a young mathematician, Nicholas Lobachevsky,
sought to supplant Euclid with a new "pan-geometry." His modern geometry, perhaps the greatest Russian contribution to scientific thought during
the reign of Nicholas, earned him an unprecedented six terms as rector of
Russia's easternmost university.[5] Another area of scientific accomplishment
lay in astronomy, which had been since the days of Kepler an area of active
inquiry in the navigation-minded Baltic world. The long nights and northern
lights stimulated interest, and as early as 1725 there was an observatory in
St. Petersburg. Russia later fell heir to a larger observatory at Tartu, and
in the 1830's Russia turned to the building of an observatory at Pulkovo,
outside St. Petersburg, which became the largest in the world upon its
completion in 1839. Its director, F. G. W. Struve, had turned from literary
to astronomical studies during the late years of Alexander's reign, and his
life's work at Pulkovo was a long study of a relatively nebulous astronomical
subject: the Milky Way. Another fascination of the age was comets, which
were a lively topic of speculative discussion, particularly before and after
the rare appearance of Halley's comet in 1835.[6] The most important philosophic journal of the Nicholaevan period called itself *The Telescope*.

There was also a romantic interest in exotic portions of the Russian
Empire itself. One scientific explorer, who was forced to make a long dis-

claimer of any association with Masonic or secret societies upon returning from abroad in 1830, even idealized the frozen northern region of *Novaia Zemlia* (New Land).

> Novaia Zemlia is a real land of freedom, where each man may act and live as he wishes. It is the only land where there is no police force or other ruling force besides hospitality. . . . In Novaia Zemlia each man who arrives is greeted as an honest man.[7]

The most important flight from harsh realities was, however, the flight to German romantic philosophy. On soil that was thoroughly prepared by the occult theosophic pursuits of higher order Masonry, the seeds of Schelling's and Hegel's great philosophic systems were now sown. The harvest was to be rich indeed, for these cosmic systems provided the thinking aristocracy not only with consolation from the frustrations of the Nicholaevan age but also with a vocabulary to discuss certain deep philosophical questions that troubled them.

Thus, far from turning to new problems, the aristocratic intellectuals resolved to make one last heroic effort to answer the old ones. The material world, which was increasingly preoccupying a Western world in the throes of the Industrial Revolution, was simply not yet on the agenda of Russian thought. Occult spiritual forces were still thought to rule the world; and small circles of dedicated truth seekers were believed capable of understanding and serving these forces. As the optimism and reformist enthusiasm of the Alexandrian era waned, Russian thinkers turned from the outer to the inner world: from practical affairs to problematic philosophy. Beneath the tranquil surface of Nicholaevan Russia, disturbing questions were asked as never before about the meaning of history, art, and life itself. In their increasingly desperate effort to answer these so-called "cursed questions," they turned to Germany no less enthusiastically than Nicholas himself—but to its universities rather than its drill fields. The answers they found in the philosophy taught at these outwardly conservative institutions were new, and in many cases potentially revolutionary.

The Flight to Philosophy

OLD RUSSIA had repeatedly and consistently rejected the need for any systematic secular philosophy. "The Russians are philosophers not in words, but in deeds,"[8] Krizhanich wrote sadly after his unsuccessful efforts to introduce Western philosophic ideas into seventeenth-century Russia. Philosophy was rejected not only because it was irrelevant to salvation but because it can lead men—in the words of an early nineteenth-century Old Believer—"to contemplate the overthrow of kingdoms."[9]

Thus, from the beginning of the Enlightenment, philosophy held for the Russian mind some of the exotic fascination of soaring comets and distant lands. Almost from the first introduction of philosophy into the curriculum of Moscow University, it acquired the subversive reputation of being a rival and potential substitute for revealed religion. Even during the early years of Catherine's reign, a follower of Hume was forced to resign from the university and a dissertation on natural religion publicly burned. With the founding of new universities early in Alexander's reign and the influx of German-trained professors, German philosophic idealism gained such a foothold that Magnitsky could with some justice speak of "substituting Kant for John the Baptist and Schelling for Christ." So heavily censored were lectures on philosophy by the end of Alexander's reign that the most serious discussion of broad philosophic issues often took place in faculties like medicine and jurisprudence. In the wake of the revolution of 1848, Nicholas I abolished philosophy altogether as a legitimate subject of study. This extraordinary ban was lifted in 1863, but other crippling restrictions on academic philosophy remained in effect until 1889.[10]

The effect of such harassment was not to prevent the study of philosophy but rather to force it out of the classroom into the secret society: away from an atmosphere of critical discipline into one of uncritical enthusiasm. The philosophy that was popularized by Schwarz was similar to that with which the ancient Gnostics had opposed the worldliness of late Hellenistic culture. Schwarz believed in a supra-rational knowledge (*gnosis* or *mudrost'*, *premudrost'*) which could harmonize reason with revelation. To the clinical study of the natural world, they opposed the mystical "light of Adam," which man could recapture only through inner purification and illumination.

The most important single influence on the formation of a Russian philosophical tradition was Jacob Boehme, of whom Schwarz, Saint-Martin, and the other heroes of higher order masonry were little more than popularizers. In Boehme's richly metaphorical writings, all of the universe—even evil—became expressions of the wisdom of God. It was this "wisdom of God" (theosophy) rather than any "love of wisdom" (philosophy) that Boehme held out to his followers as an attainable ideal. Boehme's God was not the finite clockmaker and repairman of the deists, but an infinitely transcendent and, at the same time, omnipresent force. God created the world not out of nothing but out of his own essence. All of man's intellectual pursuits, sexual longings, and social impulses were expressions of what Jung-Stilling called "homesickness" (*Heimweh*) for the lost unity between

God and man. This thirst for reunion is present in God's own longing for Sophia, which meant for Boehme and Saint-Martin not merely the Holy Wisdom of the ancient East but also the principle of "eternal femininity." In his original state of perfect union with God, Adam had been spiritually perfect without sex; and part of man's return to God would be the attainment of perfect androgyny: union of male and female characteristics.

Sophia, the mystical principle of true wisdom and lost femininity, was the common object of the strivings of both God and man.[11] Saint-Martin and Baader followed Boehme in making Sophia a fourth person within the Trinity; and Baader related this concept to the old Pythagorean idea of the world being composed of four parts. He saw "in the number 4 the symbol of creation and the formula which provides the key to the mysteries of nature";[12] the cross itself was a hidden symbol of the figure four.

Sophia was, to cite the title of one occult manuscript of the Alexandrian period, "the auspicious eternal virgin of Divine Wisdom."[13] Labzin, Boehme's principal translator and popularizer, gave himself the pen name Student of Wisdom (*Uchenik Mudrosti*), which he often abbreviated as *UM*, or "mind."[14] It is not too much to say that Russian thinkers turned to German idealistic philosophy, not for keys to a better critical understanding of the natural world, but rather—to cite the title of a typical occult handbook of the age—for "the key to understanding the divine secrets." The key appeared as the second volume of "selected readings for lovers of true philosophy,"[15] and the most influential philosophic circle to develop late in the reign of Alexander called itself Lovers of Wisdom (*liubomudrye*). Thus, philosophy, as the term came to be understood in the Nicholaevan era, was closer to the occult idea of "divine wisdom" than to the understanding of philosophy as rational and analytical investigation in the manner of Descartes, Hume, or Kant.

The lovers of wisdom circle appears in many ways as a continuation of the last great system of higher order Masonry, that of the lodge Astrea, which defined truth as "that original cause which gives movement to the whole of the universe." Those seeking admission to the lodge were forced to wait in a dark room in the presence of a Bible and a skull, which bore the ominous inscription *memento mori:* Remember Death.[16] The lovers of wisdom also met in secret, with an inscribed skull greeting them at the door. The language was still Latin, but the message was different: "Dare to Know" (*Sapere Aude*),[17] and the book on the table was not the Bible but Schelling's *Naturphilosophie*. As one of the members explained: "Christian doctrine seemed to us to be good only for the popular masses, but unacceptable for us, lovers of wisdom."[18]

Schelling's pantheistic teachings about the organic unity of all nature and the presence therein of a dynamic "world soul" commended itself to the Russian imagination. Characteristically ignoring the complexities of Schelling's later writings and relying partly on vulgarized digests of his ideas,[19] Russians were thrilled by the appearance of a doctrine that purported to account for phenomena which they felt had been artificially excluded from the mechanistic world view of the eighteenth century: the beauty and variety of the organic world, telepathy and mesmerism. They also derived some satisfaction from the doubts of scientists themselves in the early nineteenth century that magnetism and electricity had been adequately accounted for by Newtonian mechanics. The long residence in St. Petersburg from 1757 to 1798 of the German authority on magnetism and electricity, Franz Aepinus, stimulated a dilettantish interest in these phenomena (particularly after he rather than D'Alembert became tutor to the future tsar, Paul) without bringing real understanding (outside of the Academy where he worked and Tartu where he retired and died in 1802) of scientific problems and method.

Schelling appears as a kind of absentee grand master of a new higher order. The most popular university lecturer of the period, Professor Pavlov, was master of initiations, greeting students at the door of his lecture hall with his famous question: "You want to know about nature, but what is nature and what is knowledge?"[20] The leading speculative philosopher of the age, Ivan Kireevsky, was iconographer and master of ceremonies, bringing back a bust of Schelling to Russia, after hearing him lecture, presiding over discussions of his philosophy, and insisting that the very word "philosophy" has "something magical about it."[21] A philosophic popularizer of the time independently described the creation of a Russian philosophy as "the problem of our time," professing to find three ascending levels of meaning within the maxim "Know thyself." The first, or "Delphic," was knowledge of oneself as an individual person; the second, or "Solonic" level was knowledge of self as a "social-national" being; the third and highest—the Socratic level—was knowledge of oneself as a form of divinity.[22] Nadezhdin, the Schellingian professor of art and archeology at Moscow during the 1830's, captivated his students by treating artifacts of past civilizations as occult symbols, finding "the secret of the ages in an elegant piece of archeology."[23] He was the first Russian to use the term "nihilist"—in describing the materialism which was the opposite of his own idealism.[24] Perhaps he acutely sensed that a world view which finds ideal purposes everywhere in general might end up finding them nowhere in particular. Odoevsky attempted to draw up a "Russian system of theosophic physics" designed to study "the inner substance of physical objects as the basis for studying their external forms."[25] Schelling's philosophy inspired this and other fanciful ideas. As Odoevsky wrote:

> You cannot imagine what an impact it produced in its time, what a jolt it gave to people slumbering before the monotonous humming of Locke's rhapsody. . . . He opened to man an unknown part of the world, about which there had previously existed only legendary tales: *his soul.* Like Christopher Columbus, he did not find what he sought and raised unfulfilled hopes, but he gave new direction to the activity of man. All threw themselves into this miraculous, luxuriant land.[26]

In this "miraculous land" ideal ends rather than material causes determined life and history. The universe was a work of art, and man, its supreme creation, was uniquely capable of understanding its hidden harmony and advancing its higher purposes.

Practically speaking, the philosophy of Schelling had a double effect in Russia. On the one hand many aristocrats rediscovered through philosophy something they had ceased to find in religion: assurance that there was an ideal, unifying purpose to life and history. In that sense Schelling's philosophy was one of reassurance and consolation, tending to encourage social and political conservatism. Thus, it is not surprising that a reactionary writer like Pogodin should try to enlist Schelling's aid in formulating the ideology of "official nationalism"; or that a future radical like Belinsky should find himself reconciled to reality and writing odes to tsardom under the impact of Schelling (and later, of Hegel) in the 1830's.

At the same time, Schelling's philosophy was the starting point for revolutionary thought in Russia. Under Schelling's influence the greatest biologist of Nicholaevan Russia, Karl von Baer, developed an idealistic theory of purposeful evolution which was to influence subsequent radical thinkers like Kropotkin and Mikhailovsky. More important, however, was the intoxicating effect Schelling's ideas produced on large numbers of thinkers who never acquired more than a confused third-hand knowledge of them. Frustration was drowned in philosophy as men saw themselves promised cosmic redemption, without being tied down to any predetermined scheme of how it would take place. Schelling encouraged men to think that profound changes might be forthcoming from the process of becoming, which was the essence of life itself. The belief grew that the previous generation's search for hidden keys to the universe, far from being chimerical, was merely immature and unrefined. The search for all-encompassing answers continued; and Schelling stands as a transitional figure from the crude occultism of Boehme and Eckartshausen to the ideological systems of Hegel, Saint-Simon, and Marx.

The Meaning of History

THE MOST WIDELY DEBATED of all the "cursed questions" during Nicholas' reign was the meaning of history. In the wake of the Napoleonic war, Russians were more than ever anxious to know their place in history. The anti-Enlightenment had insisted that irregular, traditional patterns in history had meanings of their own; and Russians were not less determined to find out what these patterns were than romantic thinkers elsewhere. Their theology had been historically oriented, and their flight to philosophy led them naturally on to the philosophy of history.

The development in the romantic age of a broad, philosophical interest in history was to some extent the work of Baltic Germans who had been stimulated by contact with the Slavic world. Herder's broodings in Riga helped crystallize his idea that truth lay within history rather than beyond it; and that each culture was destined to grow and flower in its own way in the garden of humanity. Schlözer's long years of teaching and study in Uppsala and St. Petersburg helped him formulate his original plan for a "universal history." He pioneered in the use of Old Russian manuscripts for historical purposes, challenging the "Norman school" of Russian history and exciting his many Russian students at Göttingen with the idea that Russia had a unique role to play in the next stage of history. Throughout the Germanophile reign of Nicholas I, Baltic German writers continued to play a leading role in investing the distinctive popular institutions of Russia with a romantic aura of "higher truth": Haxthausen in his writings about the peasant commune (*obshchina*) and Hilferding in his "discovery" of the oral epics (*byliny*) of the Russian north.[27]

Meanwhile, the Russian interest in history grew rapidly. In 1804, the Society of History and Russian Antiquities was founded under the president of Moscow University. The defeat of Napoleon and the reconstruction of Moscow created a broad, popular interest in history, and Nicholas I contributed to it by encouraging the activities of a large number of patriotic lecturers and historians: Ustrialov, Pogodin, and others.[28] Between Pushkin's *Boris Godunov* (1825) and Glinka's *Life for the Tsar* (1836), historical plays and operas dominated the Russian stage. Even in the underdeveloped cultural area of painting there was an abortive tendency toward monumental, patriotic canvases: climaxing in Briullov's "Fall of Pskov" and in his unfulfilled commission of the late thirties to provide Russian historical frescoes for the Winter Palace.[29] Historical novels dominated the literary scene, as vulgar imitators of Walter Scott appeared even in the provinces.

M. Zagoskin started the long line of chauvinistic "Russians-and-Poles" novels with his *Yury Miloslavsky* of 1829, and his subsequent patriotic novels and plays enjoyed a spectacular vogue during the thirties. One scholar has counted 150 long poems on historical themes in the style of Byron and Pushkin written in Russia between 1834 and 1848.[30]

Schelling's philosophy lent special intensity to the interest in history, with its insistence that the world was in a perpetual state of "becoming" and that peculiar national patterns were part of its ever-unfolding divine plan. As one "lover of wisdom" put it, Schelling provided "consolation" and kept him from being "stupefied by the atmosphere around me" by "summoning up to me my sacred fatherland."[31] Schelling was sought out personally by many Russians, and he assured them that "Russia is fated to have a great destiny; never, until now, has it realized the fullness of its strength."[32]

The man who focused all of this interest of history on the problem of Russia's destiny was Peter Chaadaev. Chaadaev had gone off to fight Napoleon at the impressionable age of eighteen and had subsequently been subjected to most of the disquieting intellectual influences of the second half of Alexander's reign. He had known De Maistre, participated in higher order Masonry, and was a leading intellectual light in the restive Semenovsky regiment. As a specially favored adjutant, he carried news of that regiment's rebellion in 1820 to the Tsar, who was then meeting with the other leaders of the Holy Alliance at Laibach. Shortly thereafter, he resigned his commission and set off for Switzerland to begin a long period of romantic wandering and philosophic introspection, which kept him abroad until after the Decembrist uprising and brought him into contact with Schelling.

Returning for the coronation of Nicholas I in 1826, he began writing eight "philosophical letters" about Russia's historical development, which were largely completed by 1831. Though widely discussed in the early thirties, the first letter was not published until 1836. It echoed "like a pistol shot in the night,"[53] bringing the wrath of official Russia on him and his editor, Nadezhdin, but serving to open up the unofficial debate over Russia's destiny that has come to be known as the Slavophile-Westernizer controversy.

Chaadaev's letter stands as a kind of signpost, pointing toward the radical, Westernizing path that was soon to be advocated for Russia. Written in polemic French and calling Moscow "Necropolis" (the city of the dead), Chaadaev insisted that Russia had so far been a part of geography rather than history, totally dependent on ideas and institutions imposed from without.

Chaadaev's extreme rejection of the Russian heritage is partly the result of De Maistre's influence—evident both in his tendency toward bold statement and in his sympathy for Roman Catholicism. More profoundly, however, Chaadaev's dark portrayal of Russia's past and present serves to dramatize the brightness of the future. He emphasizes that Russia's absence from the stage of history may actually be an advantage for its future development. Chaadaev was, in effect, restating in philosophical terms what had been said by Leibniz to Peter the Great, the Encyclopedists to Catherine the Great, and the Pietists to Alexander the Blessed: that Russia was fortunate in being uncommitted to the follies of Europe and was still capable of serving as the savior of European civilization. Unlike all these predecessors, however, Chaadaev was a Russian speaking to Russians inside Russia. Moreover, at a time when tsarist pretensions were at their highest, he was not addressing himself primarily to the Tsar. To the guardians of "official nationality" there was a faintly subversive quality to his contempt for the cultural barrenness and excessive humility of Orthodoxy and to his blunt assertion that "political Christianity . . . has no more sense in our times," and must "give way to a purely spiritual Christianity [which will] illuminate the world."[34]

Chaadaev's suggestion that Russia overleap the materialistic West in the interest of all Christian civilization was typical of the Russian Schellingians. Odoevsky had written that there would have to be "a Russian conquest of Europe, but a spiritual conquest, because only Russian thought can unify the chaos of European science. . . ."[35] Thus, belief in a special destiny for Russia did not, to the Russian idealists, imply a lack of interest in Western Europe. Just as the autocratic Karamzin had entitled his journal the *Herald of Europe,* so did the leaders of early Slavophilism, the Kireevsky brothers, entitle their new journal of 1832 *The European.* Yet interest in the West did not imply sympathy with secularism or rationalism. Chaadaev, for all his sympathy with Catholicism, was hostile to scholastic philosophy and felt that Russian thought had been corrupted with the intrusion of "the categories of Aristotle." His editor, Nadezhdin, entertained the idea throughout the thirties of visiting all of the shrines of the Orthodox East in order to write a great history of the Eastern Church.

The idealists of early Nicholaevan Russia agreed that their land must play a significant role in the solution of the common problems of Christian civilization. But what are the real problems? they began to ask. What is the nature of Russia vis-à-vis the West? and what should its role in history be? In response to such questions Russian thinkers produced a remarkable rash of analyses and prophecies in the twenties and thirties.

There was general agreement that the absence of a classical heritage was responsible for much of the difference between Russia and the West. The extravagant praise of Pushkin's poetry and Glinka's music was partly produced by the desire to overcome this deficiency. There was deep resentment of Nicholas' policy of downgrading the classical emphases that Alexander had introduced into Russian education. Chaadaev's editor, Nadezhdin, was expelled from theological seminary in 1826 for his interests in classical writers, and his widely hailed Latin thesis of 1830, *De Poesi Romantica*, argued that Russia should fuse classicism and romanticism in order to play a role in "the great drama of the fate of man."[36]

Nadezhdin's conception of the classical age was itself romantic. Schelling was the new Plotinus, Napoleon the new Caesar, Schiller the new Virgil; and the implication was clear that the Russians were the new Christians. Nadezhdin had read Gibbon's *Decline and Fall of the Roman Empire;* and, in his lectures at Moscow University in the early thirties, he likened Russia to a new band of barbaric hordes swarming over the collapsing West. Gogol wrote a historical essay on the barbarian conquest of Rome and lectured on the fall of Rome during his brief period as history lecturer at St. Petersburg University. Briullov's "The Last Days of Pompeii" was thought to be fraught with contemporary meaning by Russian critics after its first showing in 1836.

The young idealists also agreed that the woes of contemporary Europe followed from the materialism and scepticism of the eighteenth century which led to the French Revolution. Though influenced by De Maistre, Saint-Martin, and the entire anti-Enlightenment tradition, they were particularly indebted to German romantic thought for their conception of the deeper, historical causes of Western decline. Kireevsky argued that the defeat of Pascal and Fénelon by the Jesuits was a critical turning point in the loss of Western spirituality; Khomiakov blamed it on the annexation of the Western church by lawyers and logicians in the twelfth century; Odoevsky on Richelieu's philosophy of *raison d'état,* which made war between nations inevitable by "taking away the thin lining of paper which had kept the porcelain vases apart."[37]

The young idealists all viewed Russia's suffering and humiliation by Europe during the early modern period as a purifying process guaranteeing Russia a redemptive role in the new era that is coming into being. German pietist preachers and their philosophic heirs, Baader and Schelling, encouraged Russians to believe that the evangelical ideal of the Holy Alliance must be kept alive; that Russia must remain a new supra-political force dedicated to healing the spiritual wounds of Europe. An even more vivid conception of the nation as suffering messiah was developed by the leaders of suppressed nationalist movements within the Russian empire: Poles like Mickiewicz and the Ukrainians of the Brotherhood of Sts. Cyril and Methodius.[38]

The idealists generally agreed that (in the words of Pogodin's inaugural lecture as professor of history at Moscow in 1832) a "grandiose and almost infinite future"[39] lies before Russia, and with the literary critic Shevyrev's declaration in the same year: "We all have one task: to set forth thought that is all-encompassing, universal, all-human, and Christian in the Russian vernacular of today."[40]

Yet the idealists rejected the social and political conservatism of Pogodin and Shevyrev as well as the example of the bourgeois West. Their despair over all existing alternatives gave an increasingly prophetic and revolutionary cast to their writings. Much attention was paid to a pessimistic look into the future cast in 1840 by Philarète Chasles, a relatively obscure French journalist. Even more emphatically than Tocqueville, Chasles wrote that the future belonged to Russia and America, "two young actors seeking to be applauded, both ardently patriotic and expansive." He spoke of a coming time when men will "discover twelve thousand new acids . . . direct aerial machines by electricity . . . imagine ways of killing sixty thousand men in one second."[41] He could well have been describing his admirer, Chaadaev, as he depicts the prophetic philosopher looking down at this picture of destruction,

> . . . from the heights of his solitary observatory, gliding over the obscure expanse and howling waves of the future and past . . . burdened down with sounding the hours of history . . . forced to repeat the lugubrious cry: Europe is dying.[42]

The most remarkable and original historical prophecy of the age may well be that of Prince Odoevsky, the original "lover of wisdom" and one of the leading musical and literary critics of the period. In a series of dialogues written during the thirties and published together in 1844 as *Russian Nights,* Odoevsky wrote that "the West is perishing," that "the nineteenth century belongs to Russia," and that "the sixth part of the world designated by Providence for a great deed (*podvig*) . . . will save not only the body but the soul of Europe as well."[43] He was well aware of the West and its accomplishments, writing learnedly on Bach and Shakespeare as well as contemporary figures; but he felt that "in Russia many things are bad, but everything together is good; in Europe many things are good, but everything together is bad."[44] He was particularly haunted by the writings of Malthus and wrote a sketch, "The Last Suicide," showing humanity lighting a fire to relieve overpopulation, then trying in vain to check it in order to save some vestige of life on earth.[45]

Much of his thought was devoted in the thirties to an historical trilogy designed to set forth the nature and destiny of Russia. He thought of writing on the impact of Asia on Russia but soon decided on a more ambitious conception. He planned to write one volume on the past, one on the present, and one on the future of Russia; and his attention was soon focused on the tantalizing third volume.

He published first in 1835 and then, more fully, in 1839 his picture of the future in a remarkable fantasy, *The Year 4338*. Appearing under the pseudonym "the voiceless one," the story purports to be a series of letters written from Russia by a visiting Chinese student from "the chief school in Peking" in "the year 4338." The world has been divided between Russia and China. The historical calendar is now divided into three parts: from the creation of the world to the birth of Christ, from thence to the division of the world between these two powers, and from that time till the present. Little is even remembered of other countries or of history preceding the Russo-Chinese era. No one can read the few surviving lines of Goethe. The English long ago went bankrupt, and saw their island sold to Russia at a public auction.

Russia is the cultural center of the world. Great new cities have been built, the weather transformed throughout the north, special aerial platforms, aerial hotels, and balloons fill the sky. The supreme sovereign of Russia is now a poet, who is aided by a "minister of reconciliation" and "philosophers of the first and second rank." Artificial lights are made from electricity; hostile impulses are deadened by "magnetic baths," in the course of which all secrets are revealed; communication is by magnetic telegraph; and marvelous, pliable synthetic products have been devised to provide every possible form of physical comfort. Love of humanity has become so great that all tragedy has been eliminated from literature. A month is set aside for rest and relaxation at the beginning and middle of each year. There is a "continuous congress of the learned" to aid artists and scientists, and the capital is full of museums and gardens containing extinct curiosities, such as paper and animals. China is not quite so advanced but is busy learning from Russia and has progressed rapidly in the five hundred years since "the great Khun-Gin awoke China at last from its long slumber, or rather, deathly stagnation." Without his leadership, China

would have been made over by now in the likeness of those unsociable Americans, who for the lack of other speculative ventures, sell their cities on the public market, then come to us to expropriate. [They are] the only people in the whole world against whom we must maintain troops.[46]

The only drawback to the picture as presented is that the subsidized scientists of this super-state have calculated that Halley's comet is about to hit the earth; and although people have already begun to move to the moon to help relieve overpopulation, no one seems able to devise a means of preventing this catastrophe.

This blend of science fiction with utopian prophecies of future comfort and Russian pre-eminence went largely unnoticed in pre-Revolutionary Russia. Far more attention was paid to the famous historical debate of the 1840's between Slavophiles and Westernizers. Each of these grew out of the romantic idealism of the day; each was opposed to both Nicholaevan bureaucrats and Western entrepreneurs; each sought to borrow Western ideas without Western practices, so that Russia could assume leadership in the revival of European civilization.

The Slavophile view of history was tinged with the dualism of German romanticism. All of history was a contest between spiritual and carnal forces. The poet Tiutchev saw it as a struggle between *cosmos,* the organic unity of all nature, and *chaos,* the basic principle of the material world. Russia was, of course, on the side of cosmos; and in his famous verse he warned that

> With the mind alone Russia cannot be understood,
>   No ordinary yardstick spans her greatness:
> She stands alone, unique—
>   In Russia one can only believe.[47]

Tiutchev's fellow poet and Schellingian, Alexis Khomiakov, set forth an even more ingenious dualism in his ambitious but never-finished *Sketches of Universal History.*[48] The opposing forces throughout all history became for Khomiakov the spirit of Kush and of Iran. The former comes from the oppressive Ethiopians in the Old Testament who believed in material force and worshipped either stone (physical construction) or the serpent (sensual desire). The Iranian spirit was one of belief in God, inner freedom, and love of music and speech. The victory of the Roman legions over Greek philosophy had been a triumph of Kush, as was the more recent imposition of Byzantine formalism on happy Slavic spontaneity. The Jews had been the original bearers of the Iranian spirit, which had now passed on to the unspoiled Slavs. The spirit of Iran had penetrated particularly deeply into the life and art of the Russian people, whose strong family sense, communal institutions, and oral folklore had kept alive the principle of harmony and unity. Khomiakov assumes that the Iranian spirit will triumph, thus assuring a glorious future to Russia once it throws off the Kushite shackles of Byzantine formalism and Prussian militarism.

Khomiakov is best understood as a perpetuator of the pietistic ideal of a universal, inner church. He was widely traveled in the West and viewed his Lutheran, Anglican, and Bavarian Catholic friends as allies in the

"Iranian" camp. His two contending principles are reminiscent of Schlegel's "spirit of Seth" and "spirit of Cain."[49] But Khomiakov is less romantic in his attitude toward the East than Schlegel and many other Western romantics. He decisively rejects the glorification of Asian ways which Magnitsky had made fashionable. The major Kushite worshippers of "the stone" were those who built pyramids in Egypt and temples in Asia; the worst followers of "the serpent" are the Indian disciples of Shiva.

Khomiakov illustrates his theory in two plays of the 1830's, *Dmitry the Self-Proclaimed* and *Ermak*. The first play pictures the False Dmitry being first welcomed by the Russian people, then rejected when he is converted to the Latin ideal of earthly power. The later work shows the Cossack conqueror of Siberia struggling with the power-worshiping philosophies of his pagan domain. Ermak refuses to accept the Kushite beliefs of the Siberians and, indeed, renounces power altogether to seek forgiveness for earlier misdeeds from his father and his original home community.[50]

Quite different from the Slavophile view, with its pietistic glorification of inner regeneration, family harmony, and a new universal church, was the view of the radical Westernizers. They looked to French more than German thought, Catholic more than Protestant sources for ideas.

De Maistre was generally the starting point for Russians who took a more jaded view of the Russian past and Russian institutions. But he was soon supplanted by Lamennais, the real point of transition in French thought between Catholicism and socialism. Beginning as a standard counter-revolutionary Catholic with his famous call for a revival of faith in his *Essay on Indifference* in 1817, Lamennais had dreamt of a new "congregation of St. Peter" to replace the Jesuit Order and lead Europe into a glorious new era. Shortly after founding a journal, *The Future*, in 1830, Lamennais despaired of the Catholic Church and turned to Christian socialism and a passionate belief in the spirituality of the downtrodden masses. His writings, like those of De Maistre, were permeated with a kind of prophetic pessimism. As he wrote to the Savoyard:

. . . Everything in the world is being readied for the great and final catastrophe . . . all now is extreme; there is no longer any middle position.[51]

Russian converts to Catholicism during the Nicholaevan era were generally converted à la Lamennais, to a life of mendicant communion with the suffering masses. Pecherin, who served as Catholic chaplain in a Dublin hospital, saw in Lamennais "the new faith" for our times and felt convinced that the oppressed outer regions of Europe were the only hope for the decaying center. "Russia together with the United States is beginning a new cycle in history."[52] Chaadaev was also influenced by Lamennais; and he generally served Russians as a guide in moving from an early infatuation with Catholicism to a later interest in socialism. From a Russian point of view, Catholicism and socialism did not seem as incompatible as they did in the West. Both forces seemed to offer the possibility of introducing social discipline and sense of purpose into a passive and unorganized Russia.

Saint-Simon, whose theory of history eventually became the credo of the young Westernizers, had himself been influenced by De Maistre's deep fear of anarchy and revolution and admired the ordering function which the Catholic Church had fulfilled in medieval society. In his call for a "new Christianity" that was to be purely ethical and a new hierarchy that was to be purely managerial, Saint-Simon and his disciple Auguste Comte were proponents of what has been called "Catholicism without Christianity." Whereas Saint-Simon's theories of industrial organization and class tensions interested his Western followers, it was "the breadth and grandioseness of his historical-philosophical views" which excited the Russians.[53]

Saint-Simon's first Russian disciple was the Decembrist Lunin, who actively propagated Saint-Simon's ideas from exile after 1825 and was silenced only by imprisonment in 1841. Paralleling his career as a prophet of socialism was a religious life that brought him eventually into the Roman Catholic fold. A romantic student-soldier during the Napoleonic wars, Lunin felt alienated from his native land after becoming acquainted with Paris and Saint-Simon in 1814–16. Like Saint-Simon, Lunin was neither an advocate of revolution nor an admirer of the West as it actually was. "In your superficiality," he told a French friend, "you need only the light and playful. But we, inhabitants of the north, love all that which moves the soul and forces us to plunge into thought."[54]

Saint-Simon made one of his infrequent visits to a fashionable Parisian soirée expressly for the purpose of bidding Lunin farewell in 1816.

> Through you, I would like to establish links with a young people not yet withered up with scepticism. The soil is fertile there for the reception of the new teaching. . . .
>
> Superstition considers that the golden age was some time in the distant past, whereas it is still to come. Then again giants will be born; but they will be great not in body but in spirit. Machines will work then in place of people . . . another Napoleon will stand at the head of an army of workers. . . .
>
> If you forget me, do not at least forget the proverb: "by running for two hares, one catches neither." From the time of Peter the Great you have been ever widening your borders; do not become lost in endless space. Rome was destroyed by its victories; the teaching of Christ entered

into a soil fertilized with blood. War supports slavery; peaceful work prepares the basis for freedom which is the inalienable right of each.[55]

Saint-Simon did not see his ideas take hold during his lifetime. His pleas to Alexander I for the adoption of his new Christianity by the Holy Alliance were no more heeded than his disciple Comte's later appeal to Nicholas I to adopt his new "system of positive politics."[56] But these theologians of progress were perceptive in addressing their grandiose theories to a nation "not yet withered up with scepticism" or (in Comte's words) "retrograde empiricism." Neglected by the tsars, their new theories of history were taken up by the Westernizing aristocracy. "Spiritually we lived in France," explained one of the Westernizers of Nicholas' reign. "We in studying turned to France. Not, of course, to the France of Louis Philippe and Guizot, but to the France of Saint-Simon, Cabet, Fourier, Louis Blanc, and particularly George Sand. From there, came to us a belief in humanity; from there, certainty burst upon us that 'the golden age' lay not behind, but before us."[57] Pecherin heard in Saint-Simon "the giant steps of the approaching future."[58] Most important of all, the young figure of Alexander Herzen, who had sworn to avenge the Decembrists and continue their Westernizing traditions, carried around Saint-Simon's works "like the Koran." His Moscow circle of the 1830's began to lead the opposition to Schellingian philosophy and the turn to social problems which became characteristic of the new radical Westernizers.

After Saint-Simon's death in 1825, Prospère Enfantin, one of his French followers who had begun his study of philosophy and economics in Russia, established a new Saint-Simonian religion. One of its adepts linked himself with Moses, Zoroaster, and Mohammed and darkly hinted that he might even be a reincarnation of Christ in modern dress. The Russians were fascinated by this strange, semi-sectarian movement and read its journal, *The Globe,* with great interest. Herzen's early followers can be considered a kind of splinter group within this "new Christianity"; for, although they were neither industrialists nor cultists in the manner of Enfantin's group, they were inspired by the Saint-Simonian view of history. By 1833 Herzen subscribed to the view that history moves in a three-stage progression from medieval Catholicism to philosophic Protestantism to the "new Christianity." This last phase was the "truly human" phase, a "renovation" rather than a revolution of society, designed to abolish poverty and war by the systematic application of scientific method to social and economic problems.[59] A new elite of social managers and organizers must give man a modern, practical form of Christianity. The three-stage theory of history of Saint-Simon's protégé Auguste Comte enjoyed even greater popularity among the radical Westernizers in Russia after being introduced by Valerian Maikov in the forties. Comte's idea that everything must progress from a theological through a metaphysical into a "positive" or scientific stage became the reigning theory of history among populist intellectuals.[60]

At first the difference between Westernizers and Slavophiles was not great. Both believed in some new form of Christianized society and were opposed to revolution and egalitarian excess. The tendency to idealize the peasant commune and *narodnost'*, or "spirit of the people," as a regenerative life force in history was particularly characteristic of Slavophilism but also to be found among Polish revolutionaries and radical Westernizers. *Narodnost'* for all of these visionary reformers meant neither nationality as it did for Uvarov nor popularity in the Western electoral sense. It meant the unspoiled wisdom of the noble savage as revealed in the newly collected popular proverbs of Vladimir Dal or the folk songs and poems of Alexis Kol'tsov. Almost all the great social theorists had philological or ethnographic interests and rejoiced that a writer of their generation had written a *History of the Russian People* in answer to Karamzin's *History of the Russian State*.[61]

The man who dispelled the euphoria of friendly agreement and romantic fancy from Russian historical thinking was Georg Hegel, the last of the German idealistic philosophers to cast his spell over Russia. More than any other single man, he changed the course of Russian intellectual history during the "remarkable decade" from 1838 to 1848. He offered the Russians a seemingly rational and all-encompassing philosophy of history and led the restless Westernizers—for the first time—to entertain serious thoughts of revolution.

The introduction of Hegelian thought into Russia followed a pattern that had become virtually institutionalized. The seed was planted in a new philosophic circle formed around a suitably handsome and brooding figure (Stankevich) with some intense younger members (Belinsky and Bakunin) and a new foreign center for pilgrimage and study (Berlin). The new prophet was hailed as "the Columbus of philosophy and humanity" and became identified with a new intellectual generation. Stankevich, Belinsky, Bakunin, and Herzen—unlike Chaadaev, Odoevsky, and Khomiakov—had no memories of the war against Napoleon and the mystical hopes of the Alexandrian era. They were nurtured on the frustrations of Nicholas' reign, and Hegelian philosophy became their weapon of revenge.

As with the preceding Schellingian generation, the young Hegelians were inspired by a series of new professors: Redkin in law with his constant reminder that "you are priests of truth"; Rul'e in zoology, tracing Hegel's dialectic in the animal world; and above all, Granovsky in history. Like earlier circles, Stankevich's followers called one another "brother" and engaged in group readings and group confessions.

As with previous Western thinkers, Hegel was known as much through Western discussions of his work as through original texts—Stankevich discovering him through a French translation, Herzen through a Polish disciple. But Hegel's basic conviction that history makes sense shone through even the most superficial reading of Hegel and appealed to the young generation. Hegel's famous declaration that "the real is rational and the rational is real" offered reassurance to a generation overcome by a feeling of isolation and subjective depression. Stankevich wrote from Berlin that "there is only one salvation from madness—history."[62] Hegel made it possible to find meaning in history—even in the oppressive chapter being written under Nicholas. "Reality, thou art wise and all-wise,"[63] Belinsky exclaimed, applying the adjectives of higher order Masonry, *mudra i premudra,* to the real world. One need no longer run away to find truth in a lodge or circle. Objective truth can be found in the everyday world by the "critically thinking" individual who is informed by Hegelian teachings, "As a result of them," said Belinsky in the condescending tone of the converted Hegelian, "I am able to get along with practical people. In each of them I study with interest the species and type, not the individual. . . . Every day I notice something. . . ."[64] Coming at a time when depression, wanderings, and even suicide were taking an increasing toll among the romantic idealists, Hegel seemed to say that all purely personal and subjective feelings are irrelevant. Everything depends on objective necessity. "My *personal I* has been killed for ever," wrote Bakunin after his conversion; "it no longer seeks anything for itself; its life will henceforth be life in the Absolute; but in essence my *personal I* has gained more than it has lost. . . . My life is now a truthful life."[65]

Whether Slavophile or Westernizer, the older generation found this philosophy repellent. In comparison with Schelling, Hegel stood in the tradition of those who "placed the root of intimate human convictions . . . outside the sphere of aesthetic and moral sense."[66]

Many of the Hegelians who contributed to building the modern German state were excited by the Hegelian idea that the state was the supreme expression of the World Spirit in history. In Russia, too, Hegel found some disciples principally concerned with increasing rationality and civic discipline through the state; but they tended to be (like Hegel himself) relatively moderate figures mainly concerned with political reform: the so-called *Rechtsstaat* liberals like the historian Granovsky and Chicherin, the mayor of Moscow.

However, Hegel convinced many more Russians that the dialectic requires not the apotheosis of the present state but its total destruction. Seemingly impossible changes suddenly became possible by considering the fact that history proceeded through contradictions. Even more than the Hegelian left in Germany, the Russian Hegelians found in his theory of history a call to revolution: to the destruction of "God and the State," "the Knouto-Germanic Empire."[67]

Ostensibly, Belinsky turned revolutionary by rejecting Hegel:

> All the talk in Hegel about morality is pure nonsense, for in the kingdom of objective thought there is no morality any more than in objective religion. . . . The fate of the subject, the individual, the personality is more important than the fate of the whole world and the health of the Emperor of China (i.e. the Hegelian *Allgemeinheit*). . . . All my respects, Igor Fedorovich, I bow before your philosophic nightcap, but . . . even if I should succeed in lifting myself to the highest rung on the ladder of development I should demand an accounting for all the victims of circumstance in life and history . . . of the inquisition, of Philip II. . . .[68]

This passage was often cited by radical reformers (and provided the inspiration for Ivan Karamazov's famous rejection of his "ticket of admission" to heaven). But it did not mark the end of Hegel's influence on Belinsky or on Russian radicalism. Although Belinsky came to look to French socialists for leadership in the coming transformation of European society, he still expected the change to occur in a Hegelian manner. History remained "a necessary and reasonable development of ideas" moving toward a realization of the world spirit on earth, when "Father-Reason shall reign" and the criminal "will pray for his own punishment and none will punish him."[69] The final "synthesis" on earth will be a time in which the realm of necessity gives way to the realm of freedom. The present, seemingly victorious, "thesis," the rule of kings and businessmen in Europe, will be destroyed by its radical "antithesis." This "negation of negation" will make room for the new millennium.

Bakunin was the most truly "possessed" and revolutionary of all the Hegelians with his ideological commitment to destruction. He spent almost all of the "remarkable decade" in Western Europe and was a major catalyst in the "revolution of the intellectuals" in 1848. Only the hint of final liberation contained in Schiller's "Ode to Joy" in the choral movement of Beethoven's Ninth Symphony was to be saved from the coming conflagration. Bakunin's Hegelian conviction that total destruction must precede total freedom had an immense influence on European revolutionary thought—particularly in Southern Europe—and had only just begun to wane at the time of his death in 1876. Even his ideological rival for influence within the populist movement, the evolutionary Peter Lavrov, used Hegelian appeals in his famous "Historical Letters" of the late sixties by urging men to renounce their purely personal lives in order to be "conscious knowing agents" of the historical process.[70]

It is perhaps more correct to speak of the vulgarization of Hegelian concepts than the influence of Hegel's ideas in Russia. In either case, the impact was great—and, on the whole, disastrous. The strident presentation of Hegelian philosophy as an antidote to occult mysticism was rather like offering typhoid-infected water to a man thirsty with fever. Koyré provocatively says of Belinsky's rejection of Hegel that it did not represent a real change of philosophy but "the cry of revolt of a sick man whom the Hegelian medicine has not cured."[71] One might almost say that the Hegelian medicine turned the Russian taste for all-encompassing philosophic systems into an addiction. Those who managed to recover from the intoxication with Hegel were left with a kind of philosophic hangover. They tended to reject philosophy altogether but were left with a permanent sense of dissatisfaction with moderate positions and tentative compromises. The "ex-Hegelians" Belinsky and Herzen were no less extreme than the permanently intoxicated Bakunin in their hatred of *posredstvennost'* ("mediocrity"), *meshchanstvo* ("bourgeois philistinism"), and *juste-milieu*.

The Hegelian idea that history proceeds through necessary contradictions also lent a new quality of acrimony to the previously mild debate between Slavophiles and Westernizers. Hegelianism seemed to demonstrate the "power of negative thinking." It is difficult to find any positive statement of belief in the late writings of the "furious" Belinsky. Yet, because of the passionate sincerity of his personality, negative thinking was made to appear a virtue and became a kind of tradition in the new literary criticism which he largely introduced into Russia. Herzen too—for all his literacy and concern for individual liberties—was at his best in attacking the attackers of freedom. He became convinced that revolutionary change was coming and left Russia forever in 1847 to greet the coming stage of history in Paris. After the failure of 1848, he decided—along with Bakunin—that revolutionary change was to come from Russia after all. Suddenly in 1849–50 Herzen and Bakunin both turned to the ideal of the peasant commune and a free federation of Slavic peoples[72]—not primarily because they were morally or spiritually desirable as they had been for the Slavophiles and were soon to be for the populists, but because they represented the "negation of negation": an historical battering ram for upsetting the philistinism of bourgeois Europe.

The necessity of a coming final synthesis in history, a revolutionary deliverance from oppression and mediocrity, was a belief common to all Hegelians of the left from Marx to Proudhon, the most influential Western revolutionaries after 1848. Herzen and Bakunin shared the conviction and sided more with their common friend Proudhon than with Marx in looking for revolution through an heroic elite rather than economic forces. Bakunin embraced the coming revolution unreservedly, Herzen with deep reservations; but both believed it to be inevitable.

Hegel had given them an "algebra of revolution" without any equivalents for the formula. Thus, the Russian disciples differed widely in their understanding of who was the agent of the absolute at the present stage of history. Bakunin looked by turns to Western urban revolutionaries, East European peasants, Nicholas I, the anarchist movement in Switzerland and Latin Europe, and finally to conspiratorial terrorists in Russia. Herzen looked to Paris, to the Russian countryside, and to Alexander II before losing both his influence and his faith in the 1860's. Although Herzen never participated in revolutionary activity in the Bakunin manner, he was hypnotized by it. "Better to perish with the revolution than live on in the alms house of reaction,"[73] he had advised his son in 1849; and in his late years one detects a certain elegant nostalgia for the days when it was possible to believe in absolute liberation as he wrote his pessimistic "letters to an old comrade," Bakunin.[74]

There were perhaps only two constant elements in the troubled careers of these, the two most interesting figures of the "remarkable decade." First was their romantic attachment to the image of a better society probably derived not so much from socialist blueprints as from nostalgic reminiscences of childhood and literary portrayals of fraternal heroism and happiness. Second was their essentially Hegelian conviction that a revolutionary repudiation of the existing order of things was historically inevitable.

The fascination with Hegel led many Russians to believe in a coming liberation without deepening their understanding of liberty. Hegelianism revived in a secular form the prophetic hopes of the Muscovite ideology and provided a philosophy of history that was no less absolute and metaphysical (though considerably less clear). The idea that negation was merely a stage in the preparation for the final realization of the absolute was a kind of depersonalized, philosophical version of the Christian conception that the reign of the Antichrist would precede the second coming of Christ. It is a tribute to the depth of Hegel's influence on Russian thought that even those who subsequently rejected his philosophy still felt the need for a philosophy of history: Comte's positivism, social Darwinism, or Marxist materialism. Hegel encouraged Russian secular thinkers to base their ideas on a prophetic philosophy of history rather than a practical program of reform, to urge action in the name of historical necessity rather than moral imperatives.

The Prophetic Role of Art

IF THERE WAS ANY supreme authority for the emancipated men of the "remarkable decade," it was not a philosopher or historian but a literary critic like Belinsky or a creative artist like Gogol. The extraordinary prestige of those connected with art followed logically from romantic philosophy. For the creative artist was in many ways the prophet; and the critic, the priest, of romanticism.

The Enlightenment had found truth in objective laws, physical and moral, which were assumed to be uniformly valid throughout the natural world. They could be discovered by study and explained rationally by the natural philosopher. In romantic thought, however, truth was organic and aesthetic; its hidden meaning was best perceived intuitively and communicated poetically. Since different cultures were an important expression of the variety and hidden patterns of history, the romantic artist bore a special responsibility to find the meaning of national identity.

The contrast between pure and propagandistic art, which became so important to a subsequent generation, did not concern the idealistic romantics of Nicholaevan Russia. All art was pure in the sense that it expressed little direct concern over social and political problems, yet strongly propagandistic in the sense that it conceived of artistic ideas as a force capable of transforming the world. It was called "monastic" by Khomiakov;[75] Saint-Martin, "the unknown philosopher" of the anti-Enlightenment, spoke of it as "prophetic." It was indeed infused with prophecy in the Biblical sense of purporting to represent the word of God to man. It can also be characterized with the less familiar Greek term *theurgic* used by Saint-Martin to describe the spiritualist's act of establishing contact with other worlds, and by Berdiaev to suggest that art was viewed as divine work and not merely divine words.[76]

The idea that art was divine activity was particularly rooted for Russians in Schelling's philosophy. He defined philosophy as "higher poetry" and sought to relate philosophic speculation to artistic rather than scientific pursuits. Inspired by Schelling, the Russians were quick to conclude that new progress in philosophy required the development of new art forms. The Schellingian Nadezhdin accordingly drew up the first of many calls for new prophetic art beyond either classicism or romanticism in his writings and lectures as professor of art and archeology at Moscow. As early as 1818 he defined the poet's calling:

To teach people the good is the duty of the poet.
He is the true herald, the dread teacher of the world,
His task is to strike down and unmask vice,
To teach and guide people onto the true path.
A Christian poet is the organ of eternal truths.[77]

Belinsky served his journalistic apprenticeship under Nadezhdin in the thirties, and, for all his philosophic convolutions, remained faithful to his teacher's belief in the high calling of the artist: "Art is the direct intuition of truth, i.e. thought in the form of images."[78] These images of truth had—for the awakening imagination of Nicholaevan Russia—a uniquely national configuration. As Glinka was reputed to have said, "nations create music, composers only arrange it." The artist thus became "the nerve end of the great people," who "like a priest or judge should not belong to any party" and must never substitute "earthly reason for the heavenly mind."[79] Literary criticism became a kind of exegesis of sacred texts, the chief critic of any major "thick journal" a high priest, and his desk "the altar on which he performs his holy rites."[80] Through Kireevsky, Nadezhdin, and Belinsky literary criticism became the major medium for discussing philosophical and social questions. Far from being mere reviewers, the critics of this period acquired a key place in the development of intellectual life. Belinsky, in particular, acquired a unique moral authority through his uncompromising moral fanaticism. His mantle was passed on in a kind of apostolic succession to Chernyshevsky in the sixties and Mikhailovsky in the seventies. Problems and ideas raised in his writings found their way back into the literary milieu from which they had come and reached a new level of intensity in the ideological novels of Dostoevsky.

The first proclamation of the new exalted conception of the artist was made by the Schellingian Prince Odoevsky in a new journal he founded in 1824 (with the Decembrist poet Küchelbecker) to help create "a truly Russian poetry." Enjoying the collaboration of Pushkin and many of the leading poets of the age, the journal was appropriately called *Mnemosyne* (the mother of the muses). "Sculpture, Painting, and Music," a story by the young poet Venevitinov, illustrates the general feeling that the arts were all divinely inspired. The three arts are depicted as three celestial virgins with a common mother, Poetry, of whom the whole world is an expressive creation. In a similar vein stands Odoevsky's idea that "poetry is the number, music the measure and painting the weight" of a common truth.[81] Similarly, the story "Three Artists" by Stankevich, the philosopher-artist who dominated the philosophical life of the thirties as much as Odoevsky had the twenties, told of three brothers trying to capture "the eternal beauty of mother nature" in different media, each inspiring the other until at last "the three lives flowed into one life, the three arts into beauty . . . and an invisible force was in their midst."[82]

This sense of divine interdependence of all art media was of great importance for the creative artists of Nicholaevan Russia. Artists in one medium generally knew those working in others. It was customary for poets to draw pictures and for artists to write poems in the notebooks that they kept and exchanged. The Ukrainian poet Taras Shevchenko began his career as a painter, and Lermontov left behind almost as many paintings and sketches as poems.[83] His *Demon* later inspired Rubinstein's opera of the same name (one of the most popular of the many Russian operas that remain virtually unknown abroad), and many of the best canvases of Vrubel (one of the best of the many painters who also remain little known outside of Russia). Briullov's painting, "The Last Days of Pompeii," was inspired by an opera, and in turn inspired the novel of Bulwer-Lytton. Odoevsky as a music critic and Botkin as an art critic acquired positions of general influence almost as great as those of the literary critics (and were themselves creative writers).

Poetry was viewed, at least until the late thirties, as the first and greatest of the art forms: "the first-born daughter of the deathless spirit, the holy hand-maiden of eternal elegance, nothing less than the most perfect harmony."[84] Such flowery tributes seem not altogether inappropriate; for the 1820's and 1830's were the golden age of Russian verse. In the quantity of good poetry and the quality of its best, Russia drew equal to any other nation of Europe and far ahead of anything in its own past. The greatest of all, Alexander Pushkin, represents in poetry what his ill-fated Decembrist friends represented in politics: the final flowering of eighteenth-century aristocratic aspiration. But, whereas the Decembrists came to an inglorious end and had little impact on subsequent political thought, Pushkin was lionized even in his lifetime, and sounded forth many of the themes that were to dominate a rich literary culture in the late imperial period. His extraordinary success helped attract gifted Russians to art as a kind of alternative to politics during the reactionary period that followed the crushing of the Decembrists.

From a background of privilege and a largely French, neo-classical education at the newly founded imperial lyceum at Tsarskoe Selo, Pushkin grew continually in the range and depth of his interests. Within his relatively brief life of thirty-eight years, he wrote plays, stories, and poems with equal facility about a wide variety of times and places. His most influential work was the "novel in verse" *Eugene Onegin*. Its portrayal of provincial aristocratic life and its muted tale of unfulfillment made it "the real ancestor of the main line of Russian fiction," while "superfluous" Onegin and the lovely Tatiana became "the authentic Adam and Eve of the Mankind that inhabits Russian fiction."[85] One of his last poems, *The Bronze Horseman,* is probably the greatest ever written in the Russian language. A much shorter and more intense work than *Onegin, The Bronze Horseman* struck a resonant chord in the Russian apocalyptical mentality with its central image of a flood descending on St. Petersburg without any ark of salvation. Drawing on his own memories of the flood in 1824, Pushkin transforms Falconet's bronze statue of Peter the Great into an ambiguous symbol of imperial majesty and inhuman power. The clerk Eugene, in whose final delirium the statue comes to life, became the model for the suffering little man of subsequent Russian fiction—pursued by natural and historical forces beyond his comprehension, let alone control.

Pushkin remains the outstanding illustration of Russian aristocratic culture. In his hands, Russian poetry came close to Nadezhdin's ideal synthesis of classical and romantic elements; the Russian language attained an elegance and precision that was at last devoid of affectation; and the famous "broad Russian nature" was combined with the classical virtues of clarity and disciplined moderation. For all his breadth of interest and subject matter, Pushkin was a different temperament from the Shakespeare with whom Russians often compare him. His was not the "golden uncontrolled enfranchisement" of the Elizabethans but rather the fulfillment of the oft-maligned aristocratic ideal: disinterested curiosity freed from dilettantism; ranging sympathies freed from condescension; and honest self-awareness freed from morbid introspection.

For a poet with natural musicality, it seems appropriate that Pushkin wrote about music and musicians and had so much of his own work adapted for the musical stage.[86] There is a kind of compatibility between the grace of his verse and that of the imperial ballet, which by the 1820's had surpassed all others in Europe. During thirty of Pushkin's thirty-eight years the ballet was directed by Charles Didelot, the first of the great Russian impresario-choreographers. He admired Pushkin's work, and Pushkin found fresh inspiration for his poetry in one of Didelot's greatest ballerinas, Istomina.[87] The verses of Pushkin and the movements of Istomina gave Russians a new confidence that they were capable of surpassing the West not only in primitive combat but also in sophisticated cultural accomplishment.

For all his genius and symbolic importance, however, Pushkin did not affect the path of Russian cultural development as much as many lesser writers.

> He exerted, it is true, a vast influence on Russian literature, but almost none on the history of Russian thought, of Russian spiritual cul-

ture. In the nineteenth century and generally into our own times, Russian thought and spiritual culture has followed another, non-Pushkinian path.[88]

Pushkin was a relatively unpolemical writer, a man of shifting interests, tantalizing fragments, and elusive opinions. Yet he gradually developed an outlook that can be characterized as conservative in social and political matters and liberal in the realm of spiritual and creative culture. After a youth of many love affairs and close contact with Decembrists and other romantic reformers, he became a supporter of autocracy in the 1820's and a half-domesticated *paterfamilias* in the 1830's. He had always shared the aristocratic distaste for the vulgarity and capriciousness of the common horde. He was skeptical about the possibilities of democracy in America, and tended to praise great men—Peter the Great, Lomonosov, and even at times Napoleon—who had disregarded majority opinion in order to lift standards and advance culture. Always a monarchist, he hailed Nicholas I in more cordial terms than he had Alexander I; praised Peter and derided his Ukrainian foe Mazeppa in his *Poltava* of 1829; and endorsed the crushing of the Polish insurrection of 1830. Increasingly, he felt reverence for continuity and tradition. Violent change of any sort, he came to feel, would bring forth an inescapable revenge of fate—just as uncontrolled excess in poetry produces an imbalance that destroys true art. Pushkin was horrified by the terror of the French Revolution, and inveighed against the unleashed fury of the mob in his own major historical work of the early 1830's, *The History of the Pugachev Rebellion.*

Yet insofar as revolutionary figures become distinct personalities rather than mere weapons of the impersonal war on tradition, Pushkin treats them with the same relative detachment that is accorded to princes, gypsies, and all humanity in his work. Pugachev as an individual is sympathetic and understandable in Pushkin's *History* and an idealized figure in his fictional *Captain's Daughter.* Poles are portrayed objectively in *Boris Godunov,* as are Crimean Tatars in "The Fountain of Bakhchisarai." The crushing of the Decembrists saddened him not because of his sympathy for their programs but because of the foreshortening of imaginative vistas implied in the loss to Russia of gifted poets like Ryleev and Küchelbecker. In the very year of the Decembrist rebellion, Pushkin identified himself with the neo-classical French poet André Chenier, who was guillotined during the terror of the French Revolution. Pushkin's Chenier "sings to freedom at the habitual popular festival of execution, unchanging to the end," and exclaims just before his death:

> thou, sacred Freedom,
> Immaculate Goddess, thou art not guilty.[89]

Individual creative freedom must be preserved if human life is to have any dignity. "Pushkin defends the viewpoint of a true conservatism, based on the primacy of culture and the spiritual independence of the individual personality and society."[90] Even in the relative security from mob rule and commercial pressures provided by Nicholas I, Pushkin felt "the primacy of culture" challenged by petty bureaucrats and stifling censorship. The flood and madness which engulfs the poor clerk in "The Bronze Horseman" are the revenge of fate for the precipitous reforms of Peter, just as the calamities and death which overtake Boris Godunov are revenge for the presumed crimes of an otherwise sympathetic Boris. The optimism of Pushkin's early lyrics becomes more obscured in his later works by a deepening sense of human loneliness amidst an essentially unfeeling nature, and a growing consciousness of the irrational chaotic depths within man himself. His late years were characterized by attempts to deepen his hitherto perfunctory understanding of Christianity, a nostalgia for his youth, and a general movement away from poetry to prose. "I am," he said, "an atheist of happiness. I do not belive in it."[91] He died early in 1837 as a result of wounds incurred in a senseless duel.

The posthumous veneration for Pushkin was, and has remained, extraordinary. His papers were immediately impounded as state property; and Lermontov wrote a poem which vigorously attacked Pushkin's censors and critics, signalizing the transfer of the mantle of poetic pre-eminence to another who was to die unnecessarily and prematurely just four years later. Lermontov was a more brooding and introspective figure than Pushkin. With him, the floodgates of emotionalism were opened and the heroes of European romanticism—Byron, Chateaubriand, and Goethe—came to dominate a poetic culture they had previously only influenced. Goethe's *Faust* was particularly influential. It was translated by Venevitinov, the original poetic *Wunderkind* of the twenties, and again in the thirties by Eugene Guber, a Saratov pietist who was a friend both of Pushkin and of Fesler, the occultist of the Alexandrian era.[92] Odoevsky calls the hero of his highly romantic and widely read *Russian Nights* "the Russian Faust." The romantic longings and metaphysical preoccupations that were already marked in Lermontov are even further developed in the work of Fedor Tiutchev, who outlived Lermontov by many years, to become the last great survivor of the golden age of Russian poetry. Beginning with translations from Goethe's *Faust* in a deliberately archaic Russian, Tiutchev turned to a world of private fantasy and nocturnal themes that is reminiscent of early, world-weary romantics like Novalis and Tieck.[93]

This drift toward emotionalism, metaphysics, and obscurity signified the waning of the Pushkinian tradition and a general decline in the popu-

larity of poetry. Growing impatience with the more disciplined and classical
art forms of poetry and architecture did not diminish the enthusiasm for art
itself, which was still believed to contain the answers to the great questions
of life. The idea of art as prophecy can again be traced to Pushkin, whose
magnificent poem of 1826, "The Prophet," describes how the angel of the
Lord came to him when he was weary and lost in the wilderness "and my
prophetic eyes were awakened like those of a startled eagle." The angel took
away his idle inclinations, placed a living coal of fire where once his
"trembling heart" had been, and bade him arise and speak the word of God
to burn "the hearts of people."[94]

The generation of artists that succeeded Pushkin tried to do just that.
The way in which philosophic concerns created a new prophetic art is
illustrated in the interlocked careers of two towering personalities of the
"marvelous decade": the writer Nicholas Gogol and the painter Alexander
Ivanov. The former dramatizes the transition from poetry to prose in
Russian letters; the latter the change from architecture to painting in the
visual arts. Though they labored in different art forms and Gogol was far
more successful, they shared deep common concerns, and forged the first of
the many close links that were to develop between prose writers and painters:
Tolstoy and Ge, Garshin and Vereshchagin, Chekhov and Levitan.[95]

The active lives of Gogol and Ivanov cover almost exactly the same
space of time—roughly the reign of Nicholas I—and illustrate in many ways
the inner discontent of that age. Both left St. Petersburg dissatisfied in the
1830's to seek a new source of inspiration for their art and to spend most of
their remaining years abroad.

Pilgrimages to foreign shrines were typical of the Nicholaevan era. A
steady stream of Russians was visiting the residences of Schiller and Goethe.
Zhukovsky, the father of Russian romantic poetry, spent many of his last
years in Germany; the Munich of Schelling attracted Kireevsky, Shevyrev,
and Tiutchev; the Berlin of the Hegelians drew Bakunin and Stankevich.
Glinka and Botkin went to Spain, Khomiakov to Oxford, Herzen to Paris.
The exotic regions of the Caucasus beckoned to Russians through the
poetry of Baratynsky, Pushkin, and above all Lermontov. Romantic
Auswanderung was so characteristic of the day that Stankevich suggested—
in a caricature of Pushkin's *Prisoner of the Caucasus*—that the Russian
intellectual secretly wished to become "a prisoner of the Kalmyks."[96]

Behind some of this travel lay the homesickness of the romantic
imagination for the lost beauty of classical antiquity: "the glory that was
Greece and the grandeur that was Rome." The search for links with this
world was particularly anguished in Russia, which had no roots in classical
tradition and little familiarity with the forms of art and life that had grown

out of it in the Mediterranean world. The best that Russia could do was to "discover" the Crimea: the exotically beautiful peninsula in the Black Sea, which had been the site of a former Greek colony where Iphigenia had found asylum, and Mithradates, exile and death.

The Crimea had increasingly attracted aristocratic visitors in the years since Catherine incorporated it into the empire in 1783 and compared the region to "a fairy tale from the 1001 nights" after a visit four years later.[97] The embellished account of a journey through the Crimea in 1820 by the tutor in classical languages to the future Tsar Nicholas I and the Grand Duke Constantine lent a glow of classical and pseudo-classical glory to what Pushkin was moved to call the "enchanted periphery" of the Russian empire.[98] Though known in this period by the classical name of Taurida (Tauris), the more familiar, Tatar-derived name of Crimea also came into use—a reminder that this was the land of a recently vanquished Moslem people. Legends of Moslem magnificence began to mingle with memories of classical antiquity in the Russian romantic imagination. Pushkin's glittering pseudo-historical poem "The Fountain of Bakhchisarai" became one of his most popular works and immortalized the Tatar capital.

Pushkin's "Fountain," as distinct from Mickiewicz's *Crimean Sonnets* (or Lermontov's *Hero of Our Time*), has a balanced structure and a plot free from morbidity or melodrama. His picture of the captive Polish maiden at the court of the Tatar khan in Bakhchisarai inspired one of the most popular ballets of the Stalin era, and became, through the magic of Galina Ulanova's characterization, a suggestive symbol of a European heritage in bondage to despotic, quasi-Oriental rule.

Pushkin remained essentially a classical European even while staying inside Russia and visiting no more than the periphery of the classical world. Gogol and Ivanov, on the other hand, became profoundly and self-consciously Russian even while leaving their native land and journeying to the very heart of classical culture: to Rome, the artistic and religious capital of the Western world. A Russian colony had assembled there around Zinaida Volkonsky. She had brought with her a rich art collection and memories of her intimate friendship with Alexander I and the poet Venevitinov. She seems to have viewed herself as a kind of Russian Joan of Arc—having written, and sung the title role in, an opera of that name.[99] It was in Rome, in the shadow of the Volkonsky villa, that Gogol and Ivanov were to create their greatest masterpieces.

The two artists brought to their new home a profound conviction that their work must in some way exemplify Russia's redemptive spiritual mission in the world. They sought, as it were, to provide the artistic guides and weapons for the "spiritual conquest of Europe" that the prophets of the thirties were predicting for Russia. Gogol had a special sense of responsibility born of the feeling that he had succeeded Pushkin as the first man of Russian letters. Ivanov felt a similar sense of special responsibility as the son of the director of the St. Petersburg Academy of Arts.

Each man devoted his life to one great work which was never really completed. Each became more politically conservative toward the end of his life (as did many of the Slavophiles), believing that Nicholas I and the existing powers could alone bring about a new order. Most important—and fateful for the subsequent history of Russian creative art—each came to believe that aesthetic problems should be subordinated to moral and religious ones. Each remained unmarried and apparently unmoved by women. Each life ended in strange wanderings, partial mental derangement, and a death that was unnecessary and—like that of Venevitinov, Pushkin, and Lermontov before them—brought on by their own actions. Unlike these earlier poets, however, the new prophetic artists included in their wanderings the idea of pilgrimage to the Holy Land and ascetic self-mortification.

Their work was—as they had wished it to be—uniquely Russian and quite unlike anything else in the world of art. By commanding the fascinated attention of Russia in their last years, they helped excite others with their blend of stark realism and aesthetic moralism. They swept aside not only the conventions of classicism but the sentimentality of romanticism as well. Despite their final conservatism, these two figures were idolized by radical and disaffected intellectuals who helped invest their anguish with an aura of holiness that had previously been confined to saints and princes.

> The main point about Gogol's advent into Russia is that Russia was, or at least appeared to be, a "monumental," "majestic," "great power," yet Gogol walked over these real or imaginary "monuments" with his thin weak feet and crushed them all, so that not a trace of them remained.[100]

Gogol was the first of those original Russian prose writers whose work requires analysis from a religious and psychological as well as a literary point of view. He shared the sense of loneliness and introspection that had been characteristic of many fellow Ukrainians from Skovoroda to Shevchenko. Yet both the form and content of his work is deeply Russian. His early career is at least superficially typical of the romanticism of the twenties and thirties: beginning with weak, sentimental poetry on German pastoral themes, followed by an abortive attempt to flee to America, vivid stories about his native Ukraine (*Mirgorod*), Hoffmannesque sketches about St. Petersburg and the meaning of art (*Arabesques*), and a brief career as teacher and writer of history. His early career culminated in 1836 in the satirical play the *Inspector General;* and his last great work, *Dead Souls,* appeared six years later in the familiar romantic form of observations during a voyage through the countryside.

The triumphal appearance of the *Inspector General* in the same year as that of Glinka's *Life for the Tsar* and Briullov's "Last Days of Pompeii" marks a kind of watershed in the history of Russian art. The three works were hailed as harbingers of a new national art capable of engaging dramatically a broader audience than that of any previous Russian art. Yet Gogol's work with its "laughter through invisible tears" at the bureaucratic pretense of Nicholaevan Russia was far different in tone from the heroic theatricality of the other two. The contrast is made even more striking by the divergent pattern of Gogol's subsequent personal career. For, whereas Briullov accepted imperial patronage and Glinka became *Kappelmeister* to Nicholas I, Gogol left Russia altogether in the wake of his great success. He was driven by a strange inner compulsion to pronounce through art what others were expressing through philosophy and history: a new word of redemptive hope for Russia and all humanity.

After visiting Paris, which he found even more vulgar and venal than St. Petersburg, Gogol settled in Rome and set forth on his effort to rise above the negativism of the *Inspector General* with a trilogy to serve as a Russian *Divine Comedy*. His sense of mission was intensified by the death of Pushkin in 1837, and his fame increased by the successful appearance in 1842 of *The Adventures of Chichikov, or Dead Souls,* the first part of his great work. Yet in the remaining ten years of his life, Gogol was unable to make further progress on his project. *Dead Souls* remains, like Dostoevsky's *Brothers Karamazov* and Musorgsky's *Khovanshchina,* the glorious first part of an uncompleted trilogy. Other Slavic exiles in Italy were also trying to write a new *Divine Comedy*. Juliusz Słowacki's *Poem of Piast Dantyszek about Hell* was a Polish *Inferno;* but whereas Słowacki went on to provide a *Paradiso* in a poetic "rhapsody" *King Spirit,* and Krasiński finished his *Undivine Comedy,* Gogol's terrifying honesty never permitted him to go beyond the *Inferno* of *Dead Souls*. Unlike his Polish contemporaries—and indeed most popular patriotic literature of the day—Gogol was not seduced by idealistic and nationalistic appeals. He could only sweep the stage clean without providing any positive answers.

In *Dead Souls* (as in another of his unforgettable pictures of provincial pettiness, "How the Two Ivans Quarreled") Gogol borrowed in part from an earlier picaresque writer from the same section of the Ukraine, Vasily Narezhny. The satirical style and vivid tableaux of *Dead Souls* are often reminiscent of Narezhny's *Russian Gil Blas*. But just as Gogol distorts the name of Narezhny's hero (Chistiakov) in the direction of caricature (Chichikov), so he transforms the image of a picaresque hero from a boisterous adventurer to an enigmatic wanderer, moving through the distorted world of the living in search of his claims on the dead. Narezhny was able to move on to provide Russia with a valedictory message in his posthumously published *Dark Year, or the Mountain Princes,*[101] which criticized Russian rule in Transcaucasia and anticipated in some ways both the novel of social reform and the separatist propaganda of the late imperial period. Gogol, on the other hand, could offer no simple message or hopeful conclusions; he could find no guiding road except one which led to destruction—first of his later works and then of the frail body that had linked him with the world.

The caricatured figures of *Dead Souls,* the surviving first part of his trilogy, reveal Gogol's fascination with human disfigurement together with an unvoiced, but passionate concern for wholeness and perfection. But there is no bearer of salvation, nothing as compelling as the images of evil and blight. He concluded that one had to be perfect in order to write about perfection. He failed to create positive heroes because

> you cannot invent them out of your head. Until you become like them yourself, until you acquire a few good qualities by your perseverance and strength of character, everything you produce by your pen will be nothing but carrion, and you will be as far from the truth as earth is from heaven.[102]

Driven by this quest for moral perfection, Gogol felt impelled to burn most of the second part of *Dead Souls,* his *Purgatorio,* and turn away from art altogether at the end, dying at the age of forty-three. From the artistic perfection of the *Inspector General* (perhaps the greatest play in the Russian language)[103] Gogol moved within a decade to a plea for a total subservience to the established Church in his *Selected Passages from Correspondence with Friends.* His voluntary renunciation of art was to have echoes in the careers of Leo Tolstoy and others. The call of morality was beginning to claim precedence over that of art, and Belinsky, who rejected Gogol's religious appeal, nonetheless contrasted Gogol's moral concern with the "idea-lessness" of Griboedov's work. The prophet of the sixties, Nicholas Chernyshevsky, was to draw an even more extreme contrast between "Pushkinian" disciples of pure art and "Gogolian" concern for the injustice of humanity.

It was not until the Orthodox revival of the early twentieth century that Gogol's final plea for a return to the Church would receive serious attention; but other enigmatic hints at a way out of the inferno acquired a haunting symbolism for subsequent nineteenth-century thinkers. The final image in *Dead Souls,* Chichikov's troika heading off across the steppe to an unknown destination, came to epitomize the enigma of Russia's future. The ending of *The Greatcoat,* his most famous short story, written between the *Inspector General* and *Dead Souls,* left an even more spectral message. In it Gogol transforms a drawing-room story that others had found humorous concerning a man's excessive grief over the loss of his rifle into a tale of great pathos and meaning. The hero is a poor and insignificant clerk in St. Petersburg, a passive figure whose pitiable life finds focus only in saving money for a new greatcoat. He finally gets it, but is robbed of it in a dark street and dies. Then, in a strange final sequence, he returns to reclaim his coat and cause his superiors to fear for their own. The clerk is not at all noble or heroic in Gogol's story. Thus, his final victory over Nicholaevan St. Petersburg seems all the more fantastic. By making it seem, however, both unavoidable and convincing, Gogol creates not only one of his greatest artistic effects but perhaps also the positive prophecy he was unable to offer in *Dead Souls.* For not only does the strange victory of the little man represent the best example of Gogol's "thin, weak feet" crushing the "real or imaginary monuments" of Nicholaevan Russia; it may also—as one close student of Soviet literature has contended—provide some hope to those who must live with the greater monumentalism of the Soviet era.[104]

Gogol's imagination was so vivid and pictorial that it sometimes requires the language of painting to discuss it. His writings lent themselves readily to pictorial representation, just as Pushkin's lent themselves to music in the same period. Gogol was, indeed, as interested in pictorial art as Pushkin was in music; the subject matter of Gogol's *Portrait* came as naturally to him as did that of *Mozart and Salieri* to Pushkin. Painting held for Gogol not only a special interest but a unique advantage over sculpture and all other forms of plastic art:

> It deals not just with one man, its borders are wider: it includes in itself the whole world; all the beautiful phenomena surrounding man are within its power; all the secret harmony and the linking of man with nature are found in it alone.[105]

Thus, it is not surprising that, when Gogol's own faith in the possibility of pronouncing words of artistic deliverance to Russia weakened, he focused many of his last hopes on the work of a painter, for whose labors he arduously solicited support during the last years of his life. The painter was, of course, Alexander Ivanov, a friend of many years standing, who had often painted Gogol in Rome and who kept pasted within his album for new sketches a letter Gogol had sent him:

> God grant you His aid in your labours, do not lose heart, be of good courage, God's blessing be on your brush and may your picture be glori-

ously completed. That at any rate is what I wish you from the bottom of my heart.[106]

The painting of which Gogol spoke was Ivanov's "Appearance of Christ to the People," on which he worked for twenty-five years, drawing up more than six hundred sketches amidst one of the most extraordinary and anguished artistic searches of modern times. Ivanov's work illustrates far better than that of the more successful and uniquely gifted Gogol the profoundly disquieting effects of this search for a new prophetic message on accepted forms of art and thought.

Ivanov was born into the artistic world with every possible advantage as the gifted aristocratic son of the leading academic painter in St. Petersburg. Despite his privileged position, excellent training and prize-winning early compositions in the prevailing classical style, the young Ivanov became infected with the restlessness of the times. In 1830 he left St. Petersburg proclaiming: "A Russian artist cannot remain in a city like Petersburg which has no character. The academy of fine arts is a survival of a past century."[107] In Rome he embarked on a vigorous search for a new, more meaningful style. He began a lifelong, first-hand study of classical and Renaissance art. In his own work he moved from mythological subjects in oil to somber sketches and chiaroscuro water colors of Roman street scenes and the semi-impressionistic color studies of the Italian countryside. His quest for authenticity in rendering the human form took him away from Rome to Perugia and other cities where the nude body could be studied at length in the public baths.

Throughout this early period of experimentation, Ivanov was driven by the conviction that he was living on the threshold of a new era. The solemn coronation of Nicholas I had made a profound religious and aesthetic impression on him as a youth of twenty, and he felt that a new "golden age of Russian art" was dawning.[108] The responsibility of the artist was in a sense even greater than that of the political leader; for "all the aesthetic life of humanity, and, as a result, the very happiness of its future" depends on "the development of the artist's capabilities."[109]

After this initial period of intensive technical preparation, Ivanov turned his attention to the creation of a canvas which would serve as a kind of monumental icon for the new age: a transposition into painting of the heroic sculptural and architectural style of the early nineteenth century. The subject matter that he chose for his first efforts in this direction was invariably Biblical: Samson and Delilah, David before Saul, Joseph's brothers, and—much the best—"Christ with Mary Magdalen." Finally, in the late thirties he began to turn all his attention to the preparation of his "Appearance of Christ to the People." In contrast to Briullov's canvas of 1836, which conveyed the negative message of the fall of Rome in an artistically sloppy and sentimental manner, Ivanov's painting was to carry a positive message in a technically perfect manner. The subject was to be the decisive moment in history when the agitated and uncertain followers of John the Baptist first caught sight of Christ. The style was to be that of Raphael, with the composition based partly on Leonardo's "Last Supper" and Michelangelo's ceiling in the Sistine Chapel.

Throughout his long labors on this painting, he was driven by a concern for authenticity that astonished all who came in contact with him. He spent long hours in synagogues studying Jewish faces, made trips to the courtrooms of Rome to study the expressions of despair on the face of condemned criminals, and invited peasants into his otherwise impenetrable study to tell them jokes and then sketch their spontaneous expressions of happiness and enjoyment. He was particularly haunted by the problem of depicting Christ in art. He sought, up until the very eve of his death, to find the oldest and most authentic representation of Christ's earthly form—studying in museums, Byzantine frescoes, and finally embarking on a trip to Jerusalem and the Near East. At the same time, his sketches for the Christ of his painting reveal a desire to incorporate the beauty of classical statuary into the representation of Christ's visage.

Slowly but inexorably, driven by some dark inner force which bears the mark either of sainthood or demonic pride, Ivanov became obsessed with the idea that he must in fact *be* Christ in order to be worthy of depicting him. The "golden age of all-humanity" which his canvas was to announce now required "perfection in morality as well as art." He immersed himself in reading the Bible and the *Imitation of Christ*. When Turgenev tried to show him some humorous drawings in the early forties, Ivanov suppressed his mirth and stared at them for a long time before suddenly lowering his head and repeating softly, "Christ never smiled."[110]

The course of Ivanov's subsequent religious quest brought a frenzied climax to the century-long search for direct new links with God. At the same time it gives a hint of the new paths into which prophetic impulses and messianic longings were shortly to be channeled. For, although he spoke longingly in 1845 of a need for links with a Christian Church linked to the apostolic age "when religion was not a corpse,"[111] he turned neither to the Orthodox Church that had attracted Gogol nor to the Roman Catholic Church that had won the allegiance of other Russians in Rome. Nor did he seek solace in some new form of inner devotion following the sectarian or pietistic tradition, as one might think from the title of his 1846 manuscript, *Thoughts upon Reading the Bible*. He turned instead to messianic patriotism, a position that had been implied in the general assumption that Russia was to provide spiritual salvation for all mankind. Ivanov was profoundly moved by a visit to the artist's studio in December, 1845, which was made by Nicholas I during his trip to Rome. Ivanov became lost in a kind of fantastic eschatological chauvinism. Russia became "the last of the peoples of the planet. . . . The Messiah whom the Jews await and in whose second coming symbolic Christians believe is the Russian Tsar, the Tsar of the last people."[112]

He borrows the language of occult masonry in speaking of "symbolic Christians," the "elect (*élu*) of providence" and "all-wise rule" (*premudroe tsarstvovanie*). Humanity is about to enjoy "the eternal peace, which will be given to it by the great and final people." Truth is to be "the basis of everything"; the artist, who is "the priest (*zhrets*) of the future of humanity," will soon be superfluous, because there will be no conflict—or even any difference between the sexes. The Tsar will become "entirely equal to Christ in his high authority and belief in God" and will establish his authority "over the Slavic races" and

> . . . then shall the prophecy be fulfilled that there shall be one kingdom and one pastor, for all surviving kings will ask his counsel in order to bring order to their governments in a manner befitting each separate nationality.

The Russian artist of today must speak

> . . . in the Asian spirit, in the spirit of prophecy . . . like musicians going before a regiment all aflame, lifting men up and away from worry and grief to the finest moments of life through marvelous sounds.[113]

Thus, the theme of consecrated combat, so central to later militant Pan-Slavism, was given an early and exalted formulation. Like his friend, the poet Tiutchev, who had also seen messianic portents in Nicholas' visit to Rome, Ivanov saw apocalyptical implications in the revolution of 1848 and hailed Nicholas' stern repressive moves.

Deeply impressed that "the parabola of the bombs has missed my studio," Ivanov set forth on a frenzied secret project to found a new academy for a consecrated army of "public artists." Their shrine was to be a temple to "the golden age of all humanity," which was to be built in Moscow "on that very spot where the fate of Russia was resolved by the speech of Abraham Palitsyn."[114] The temple, in turn, was to be dominated by a vast fresco, one half of which was to show the Holy Lands as they appeared in Christ's lifetime, the other to show the Holy Lands as they now appeared, with Nicholas I in the center as the form taken by the Messiah in His second coming.[115] Apparently believing that his project would gain the approval of the Tsar, he made some 250 sketches for murals and icons, including events from secular history and mythology along with sacred subjects.

If the idea of the temple represents a final flight of fantasy, the murals themselves show a deep relation to the problem that had haunted him since beginning his "Appearance of Christ to the People": how can one depict the perfection of Christ in the world of imperfect men? All the murals were to be built around a monumental series portraying the earthly life of Christ. Under the influence of David Strauss' *Life of Christ,* which he first read in French translation in 1851, he began to conceive of Christ primarily as a human being, whose story of heroism and suffering had been needlessly complicated and etherealized by the historic churches. Abjuring all traditional models for representing the life of Christ, Ivanov's starkly original sketches show a lonely figure passing through real suffering, cruelty, and indifference. There is no trace of sentimentality or artificial adornment. Christ emerges as an almost totally passive figure surrounded by mobs of people and phalanxes of pharisees, with the scourging and crucifixion treated in particular detail. In only two of the 120 scenes in the published version of the series is there any real animation on the face of Christ. In the wilderness, when he is being tempted by the devil, Christ is seated facing straight ahead in the manner of Christ enthroned on the icons, but he is looking nervously at Satan out of the corner of his eye. In the last picture, which shows Christ on the cross, he is looking straight ahead at the viewer with a weird and piercing look that bespeaks less physical suffering than some terrible unspoken doubt about himself.[116]

Ivanov recognized that he was plunging on to something entirely new. He insisted that the murals did not belong in any existing church and disavowed all links with the pre-Raphaelites, with whom he is often erroneously compared. He was, he insisted in 1857, the year of his visit to Strauss in Tübingen, attempting to "unite the techniques of Raphael with the ideas of the new civilization."[117] He wrote to Herzen (who like Gogol before him and Chernyshevsky after him was attempting to enlist support for his efforts) that he was "trying to create a new path for my art in the sketches," and later confessed that "I am, as it were, leaving the old mode of art without having any bedrock for the new."[118] In 1858 he set off, after twenty-eight years of absence, for St. Petersburg to exhibit at last his "Appearance of Christ to the People" and to solicit the support of the new Tsar for his temple. Disappointed by public indifference upon arrival and exhausted morally and physically by his strange quest, Ivanov died only a few days after the first showing of his work in St. Petersburg.

Ivanov's "Appearance of the Messiah" must be judged as a failure by almost any standard. The corrupt figures in the foreground dominate the picture and seem totally indifferent to the distant figure of Christ, who seems strangely insignificant and almost unrelated to the picture. The much-labored face of Christ lacks any clearly defined characteristics and conveys an expression of weakness and even embarrassment.

It is perhaps fitting that this final artistic legacy of a monumental and prophetic age should be dominated by the figure of John the Baptist, who stands at the center of the canvas as its most majestic personality. The day of John the Baptist had been the most elaborate official holiday of Russian higher masonry. Chaadaev had encouraged Russians to believe that "great things have come from the desert" and had written on the title page of Kant's *Critique of Pure Reason* that "I am not the savior, but he who announces his coming."[119] Ivanov had tried first to create and then to become Christ, but he had left behind only sketches of human suffering and a noble failure dominated by the ascetic prophet who can do no more than announce that someone mightier is coming.

John the Baptist was known in Russia as "the forerunner" (*predtecha*), a designation that seems particularly appropriate for Ivanov. His vision of universal Russian rule aided by "public artists" and adorned with "temples of humanity" seems at times like an anticipation of Soviet ideology. His initial stylistic experimentation anticipates the emancipated search for new art forms in the late nineteenth and the early twentieth century. His final realism and preoccupation with suffering helped usher in the bleak, semi-photographic style that was to dominate painting until the 1890's. Nonetheless, for all his qualities as a prophet and precursor, Ivanov stands at the end rather than the beginning of an age. His life and work represent a final heroic effort to attain a kind of moralistic self-transformation into the likeness of Christ.

Ivanov's failure to find a new religious philosophy—or a philosophical religion—represents the frustration of a pursuit that had begun in higher order Masonry. Higher order Masonry was known to its adepts as the "royal art";[120] and the prophetic artists of the Nicholaevan era had sought to find the art forms for the new kingdom. But no one was yet sure what kind of a kingdom it would be, and artists tended to become either haunted by the God they had lost or driven to madness in pursuit of His inner secrets. Ivanov's failure only posed in more dramatic terms the nagging question that Herzen had asked as early as 1835:

Where is *our* Christ? Are we students without a teacher, apostles without a Messiah? [121]

In their anguish, thinkers of the late Nicholaevan era looked for a messiah almost everywhere: in the person of Nicholas I (Ivanov), the holy wanderer Fedor Kuzmich, suffering Poland (Mickiewicz), the Ukrainian peasantry (Shevchenko), or among the ascetic elders of the Optyna Pustyn (Kireevsky). The religious works of Gogol and Ivanov made Christ no longer appear to be a source of deliverance or tenderness. Ivanov's picture of Christ as a lonely, suffering, and uncertain man was reflected and magnified in subsequent nineteenth century paintings: suffering predominating in the work of Ge, brooding loneliness in that of Kramskoy. The seductive thought that the aristocratic reformer himself might prove to be the messiah was suggested by Pleshcheev, the prophetic "first poet" of the Petrashevsky circle in the late forties, who exhorted that confused circle of reformers to "believe that thou shalt meet, like the Savior, disciples along the way."[122]

As if to clear the stage for new and less narrowly aristocratic movements, the brief period from 1852 to 1858 claimed the lives of a host of gifted figures of the Nicholaevan age: Nadezhdin, Chaadaev, Granovsky, Gogol, Ivanov, Aksakov, and Kireevsky. None of these were old men; but they had burnt themselves out like those who had died even earlier and at much younger ages: Venevitinov, Pushkin, Stankevich, Lermontov, and Belinsky. Out of their collective effort had come an art that was truly national and rich in prophetic overtones. Khomiakov, who was himself to die in 1860, wrote the epitaph for this chapter of Russian culture in a letter of 1858 on the occasion of Ivanov's death:

> He was in painting what Gogol was in writing and Kireevsky in philosophy. Such people do not live long, and that is not accidental. To explain their death it is not enough to say that the air of the Neva hangs heavy or that cholera enjoys honorary citizenship in Petersburg . . . another cause leads these laborers prematurely to the grave. Their work is not mere personal labor. . . . These are powerful and rich personalities who lie ill not just for themselves; but in whom we Russians, all of us, are compressed by the burden of our strange historical development.[123]

The Missing Madonna

THE WANING of classical form in art and life was one of the many fateful results of the reign of Nicholas I. His official ideologists—Uvarov and Pletnev—had found the literary heritage of classical antiquity largely incompatible with the new doctrine of official nationality. The continued loyalty of the aristocratic intellectuals to the distant world of classical antiquity and the neo-classical Renaissance became a sign of their estrangement from official ideology.

The most gifted creative figures of the late Nicholaevan period—Gogol, Ivanov, and Tiutchev—had gone to Rome in hopes of forging some kind of link between the awakening culture of Russia and classical antiquity. Slavophiles sought these links no less than Westernizers; Shevyrev's lectures did much to introduce Russia to the wonders of classical literature. Herzen called his oath to avenge the Decembrists "Hanniballic." Catherine was the "Semiramis" and St. Petersburg the "Palmyra of the North." Most masonic lodges bore names from classical mythology, and there was an abundance of classical statuary, Latin and Greek anthologies, and classical captions and titles. A century of aristocratic poetry was in a sense framed by the figure of Homer. The first poem to enjoy real popularity was Fénelon's continuation of the *Odyssey, Télémaque,* and the first important Russian epic poet, Kheraskov, was known as "the Russian Homer." The most eagerly awaited poetic accomplishment in the late years of Nicholas' reign (after the death of Pushkin and Lermontov) was Zhukovsky's translation of the *Odyssey.* Both Skovoroda and Kireevsky were called "the Russian Socrates" by their followers.

Closely identified with classical antiquity in Russian eyes was the neoclassical Renaissance, which Russians also idealized. Belinsky's sobriquet "furious Vissarion" was a conscious adoption of Ariosto's *Orlando Furioso.* Batiushkov built up a cult of the Italian Renaissance. Many lyric poets compared themselves to Petrarch, and "universal men" like Venevitinov likened themselves to Pico della Mirandola. The literary circles of the age looked for inspiration to the Neoplatonic mysticism of Ficino's Academy.

The nostalgia which Russians began to feel even during this period for the measured form of Pushkin's poetry and the broader vistas of Russian life under Catherine and Alexander bears tribute to the sense of lost opportunity which Russians were later to feel about this age. This was to remain the golden age of Russian letters, in which classical forms and Renaissance exuberance first struck real roots in Russian soil.

Perhaps the finest legacy of this vanishing neo-classicism was the rich supply of palaces, parks, and public buildings that had been built in most of the cities and many of the estates of Russia. There was a last flurry of building in this grand ensemble manner during the early years of Nicholas' reign: the triumphal gate over the Tver entrance to Moscow from the St. Petersburg road; the Bolshoi Theater and Square in Moscow; the imposing complex around the Synod and senate building in one part of St. Petersburg (and around the library, theater, and university buildings in another); and the stately ring of library, cathedral, and government buildings around the great square in Helsinki, the new capital of Russian-occupied Finland. The building of St. Isaac's Cathedral and the refashioning of the surrounding square in St. Petersburg were the last of these monumental efforts. Henceforth the style was to be more eclectic and utilitarian, the architectural development of the great cities more piecemeal and haphazard.

The forty years of work on St. Isaac's finally came to an end in 1858, the year in which Ivanov returned to die in St. Petersburg with his long-labored canvas. Ivanov's painting and sketches failed to inspire painters to remain faithful to the "technique of Raphael" just as decisively as St. Isaac's failed to encourage continued architectural allegiance to the neo-classical style of the past.[124]

The highest symbol of the classical culture that the Russians longed to share and the quintessence of ideal beauty to their romantic imagination was Raphael's Sistine Madonna. On exhibit in Dresden—an accustomed stopover point for Russians traveling by land to Western Europe—the painting inspired Russians to sigh for a world of "beauty and freedom! . . . the madonna of Raphael and the primitive chaos of mountain heights."[125] Zhukovsky made frequent pilgrimages to the painting and wrote of it in the true romantic spirit:

> Ah, not in our world dwells
> The genius of pure beauty:
> Only for a time it visits us
> From the heights of heaven.[126]

The painting became a kind of icon of Russian romanticism. A Russian visitor of the fifties wrote that after looking at the painting he was "deprived of all capability for thinking or talking about anything else."[127] By that time, the painting had become an object of heated controversy as well as extreme veneration. Lunin cited it as a principal factor in his conversion to Catholicism;[128] Belinsky, moving in the opposite direction, felt obliged to condemn it as a mere aristocratic portrait:

> She looks at us, the distant plebeians, with cold benevolence, fearful at one and the same time either of being dirtied by our looks or of bringing grief to us.[129]

Herzen contended that the face of Mary revealed an inner realization that the child she held was not her own. Uvarov spoke of "the Virgin of Dresden" as if Dresden itself had been the site of new miracles.[130] Dostoevsky kept a large print of the painting over his writing desk as a symbol of the combination of faith and beauty which he hoped would save the world.

But the feeling was growing in the fifties that beauty in truth "dwells not in our world." If men of Gogol's and Ivanov's talent could succeed only in depicting earthly suffering, perhaps there were no other worlds—or at least no .other worlds that could be reached through art. Chernyshevsky, whose admiration for Gogol and Ivanov had helped lead him out of the seminary, began to cast doubt on the intrinsic merit of art in his *Aesthetic Relations of Art to Reality* in 1855. It was only a short stride to Pisarev's declaration that a cook in St. Petersburg had done more for humanity than Raphael; to the slogan "boots rather than Raphael" (or in some versions, Shakespeare); and to the popular revolutionary legend that Bakunin had urged that the Sistine Madonna be pitched onto the barricades to keep the slavish soldiers of the old order from firing on his revolutionary uprising in Dresden in 1849.

The passion for ideas and the development of psychological complexes about certain names and concepts, though generally characteristic of European romanticism, was carried to extremes in Russia. Bakunin's alleged fury at Raphael—like Belinsky's earlier rage at Hegel—is more understandable in terms of passion than of intellect. There was an unhealthy compulsion about some of the Russian attachment to classical antiquity and an element of sublimated sexuality in the creative activity of the period. The prodigious and original careers of Bakunin and Gogol both seem to have been developed partially as a compensation for sexual impotence. There is, in general, little room for women in the egocentric world of Russian romanticism. Lonely brooding was relieved primarily by exclusively masculine companionship in the lodge or circle. From Skovoroda to Bakunin there are strong hints of homosexuality, though apparently of the sublimated, Platonic variety. This passion appears closer to the surface in Ivanov's predilection for painting naked boys, and finds philosophic expression in the fashionable belief that spiritual perfection required androgyny, or a return to the original union of male and female characteristics. Ivanov in his preliminary sketches of the all-important head of Christ in his "Appearance" used as many feminine as masculine models. Gogol in his strange essay *Woman* compared the artist's effort to "transform his immortal idea into crude matter" with the effort to "embody woman in man."[131]

Women in romantic literature were often distant, idealized creatures, such as Schiller's *Maid of Orleans* or his Queen in *Don Carlos*. In the relatively rare cases in Russian literature of this period where a woman was simple and believable—like Tatiana in Pushkin's *Eugene Onegin*—she tended to be venerated almost as a saint. Zinaida Volkonsky was a kind of mother figure to Gogol and Ivanov in Rome; and the suffering, faithful wives of the exiled Decembrists became a favorite subject for fanciful and idealized poems.

The aristocratic intellectual whose outlook was still primarily heterosexual was often just as deeply unhappy in his personal life. Just as he tended to be experimental and inconstant in his attachment to ideas, so he was in his relations with the opposite sex. Indeed, frustration in love was at times relieved by infatuation with an idea (and vice versa). Always the egocentric lover, he embraced both women and ideas with a mixture of passion and fantasy that made a sustained relationship almost impossible. Whether the object was a woman or an idea, the embrace tended to be total and intercourse almost immediate. Then came a fleeting period of euphoria after which the aristocratic intellectual resumed his restless search to find somewhere else the ecstasy that eluded him. His dreamy idealism was transferred en bloc to some new object of ravishment; and all that was venal or ungratifying was associated with the former partner. Thus, ideological attachments were often an extension of personal ones, and neither area of life can be fully understood without some understanding of the other.

But it would be irreverent and inaccurate to concentrate too narrowly on physiological factors. The Russian romantics of the period liked to express their plight in terms of Schiller's *Resignation*. There were, according to the story, two flowers in the garden of life, the flower of hope and that of pleasure; and one cannot hope to pluck them both.[132] The Russian aristocrats had no hesitation in choosing hope. Inconstant in faith and love—the other qualities that St. Paul had commended to the young church of Corinth —the anguished Russians held fast to hope. An implausible, impassioned sense of expectation was the most important single legacy of the aristocratic century to the century that lay ahead. Frustrated both personally and ideologically, the thinking elite of Russia sought with increasing intensity to find a prophetic message in history and art.

At the base of their plight lay not just a world-weary desire to "return to the womb" but also perhaps a subconscious nostalgia for the "other Russia" on which the aristocracy as a class had turned its back. They seemed almost to be feeling their way back to the dimly perceived, half-remembered world of Muscovy where belief was unquestioning and where truth was pronounced by the original prophetic historian and artist: the monastic chronicler and iconographer.

The missing Madonna was perhaps not that of Raphael, which they had never really known, but rather the Orthodox icon of the Mother of God. This icon stands at the center of a prophetic dream for which Tolstoy later sought an explanation from the elders of Optyna Pustyn. In the dream a single candle is burning in a dark cave before a solitary icon of the Mother of God. The cave is full of faceless people praying with lamentation that the time of the Antichrist has come; while Metropolitan Philaret and Gogol's fanatical spiritual guide, Father Matthew Konstantinovsky, stand trembling outside, unable to enter. The "fear and trembling" which Kierkegaard found missing from the complacent Christendom of nineteenth-century Europe is literally present in this dream—as it is in the ugly, shivering, naked old men that John the Baptist is trying to lead into the river Jordan in one of Ivanov's best sketches,[133] and in the trembling, skeletal figure of Gogol being forcibly bled by leeches as he lay uncovered and trembling on his deathbed underneath an icon of the Virgin.

Father Ambrose explained to Tolstoy that the dream illustrates the plight of Christian Russia which "looks with lively feeling, sadness, and even fear on the sad state of our present faith and morality, but will not approach the queen of heaven and pray to her for intercession like those in the cave."

When a trickle of intellectuals began to return to the Church in the late imperial period, one of the converts likened the process to an exchange of the Sistine Madonna for the icon of Our Lady of Vladimir.[134] In both cases the missing God was feminine—linked not only to the Christian image of the Virgin but also perhaps to the "damp mother earth" of pre-Christian Russia and La Belle Dame Sans Merci of European romanticism.

The "Hamlet Question"

ALTHOUGH none of the "cursed questions" were fully answered in the "remarkable decade," the debate now tended to take place within the framework of certain basic assumptions. Truth was to be found within rather than beyond history. Russia had some special destiny to realize in the coming redemption of humanity. A new, prophetic art was to announce and guide men to this destiny. The golden age "lay not behind us but ahead": in a time when man's Promethean labors will end and he will come to rest both physically and spiritually in eternal and ecstatic union with the elusive feminine principles of truth and beauty.

Within this vague romantic cosmology, however, the Russians pressed on relentlessly, seeking more complete answers. What was this truth, this destiny? Where was this feminine principle to be found? And, above all, what specific message does prophetic art bring to us?

Thus, however impractical their ideas may seem to the Western mind, the driving force behind Russian thought during this period was an essentially practical impulse to find more specific answers to these psychologically compelling questions. They were not interested in form or logic, which were part of the artificial "pseudo-classicism" of the eighteenth century. They were not afraid to seek truth in fantasies and symbols, though they were no longer fascinated with the occult for its own sake as in the Alexandrian age. The men of the "marvelous decade" wanted answers to the questions that arose inescapably, existentially, along the new path they had chosen. Any kind of inconsistency or idiosyncrasy was permissible as long as a thinker remained dedicated to "intelligence" in the prophetic spiritual sense in which Saint-Martin and Schwarz had understood the word; as long as they remained what their Schellingian and Hegelian professors had commended them to be: "priests of truth."

In their heated desire to find answers for the "cursed questions," the aristocratic intellectuals mixed fact, fantasy, and prophecy at every turn. They created a unique fusion of intense sincerity and ideological contradiction, which has been the fascination and despair of almost every serious chronicler of Russian thought. Though not an aristocrat, Belinsky, "the furious Vissarion," epitomized this combination. The special authority which he—and his chosen ideological medium of literary criticism—came to occupy in the culture of the late imperial period is not understandable without appreciating the sense of human urgency that lay behind the Russian quest for answers. In a famous scene that became part of the developing folklore of the Russian intelligentsia, Belinsky refused to interrupt one particularly heated all-night discussion, professing amazement that his friends could consider stopping for breakfast when they had not yet decided about the question of God's existence.

Belinsky was not at all embarrassed by his own contradictions and convolutions. He was not trying to transplant the clean, but remote categories of classical thought to the Russian scene—let alone the tidy, confining categories of timid bourgeois thinkers. "For me," he wrote, "to think, feel, understand, and suffer are one and the same thing."[135] Books casually received in the West drove him and his contemporaries into intense personal and spiritual crises. They were pored over by Belinsky and other literary and bibliographical critics for hints of the "new revelation" and prophecy that Schelling and Saint-Martin had taught them to look for in literature.

Belinsky was particularly concerned with discovering among his Russian contemporaries examples of the new prophetic art his teacher Nadezhdin had insisted lay beyond both classicism and romanticism. The great Russian novels of the sixties and seventies can be considered examples of such art, and it is impossible fully to understand the genius of those works without considering how it was influenced by, and responsive to, the traditions of philosophic and critical intensity pioneered by Belinsky.

The Russians looked to literature for prophecy rather than entertainment. There is almost no end to the number of Western literary influences on Russian thought. They range from inescapable ones like Schiller, Hoffmann and George Sand[136] to all-but-forgotten second-rate figures like Victor-Joseph Jouy, whose depiction of Parisian life was transposed to St. Petersburg and given new intensity by Gogol.[137] Perhaps the most important of all was Sir Walter Scott, whom Gogol called "the Scottish sorcerer," and whose works inspired the writing of history as well as of historical novels.[138] Pseudo-medieval romances helped give an active, historical cast to the "spiritual knighthood" of higher order Masonry. Russians dreamed of being "a knight for an hour," to cite the title of a famous Nekrasov poem; or of recreating the masculine friendship and implausible heroism of Posa and Don Carlos in opposing the authoritarianism of the Grand Inquisitor and Philip II in Schiller's *Don Carlos*. They also identified themselves with the metaphysical quest of such favorite romantic heroes as Byron's Cain and Don Juan, Goethe's Faust and Wilhelm Meister.

But there was one literary character who seemed particularly close to the soul of the aristocratic century. He was the favorite stage figure of the "marvelous decade," the subject of one of Belinsky's longest articles, and a source of unique fascination for modern Russian thought: Shakespeare's Hamlet.

The romantic interest in the melancholy prince began in the eastern Baltic, on the gloomy marshes that divide the German and Slavic worlds. It was in Königsberg (now Kaliningrad) that the *"magus* of the North," Johann Hamann, first taught the young Herder to regard the works of Shakespeare as a form of revelation equal to the Bible and to use *Hamlet* as his basic textbook for this new form of symbolic exegesis.[139] Hamann was an influential pietist preacher, a student of the occult, and a bitter foe of what he felt to be the excessive rationalism of his neighbor and contemporary, Immanual Kant. If Kant's influence was great, indeed decisive, on the subsequent development of Western philosophy, the immediate influence on ordinary thinking of men like Hamann was far greater, particularly in Eastern Europe. For better or worse, Kant's critical philosophy never gained a serious hearing in Russia until the late nineteenth century, whereas Hamann's quasi-theosophic idea of finding symbolic philosophic messages in literary texts became a commonplace of Russian thought.

By the time Herder moved east from Königsberg to Riga, Russia had already welcomed *Hamlet* as one of the first plays to be regularly performed on the Russian stage. Sumarokov started the Russian critical discussion of the tragedy with his immodest claim to have improved on the original by his garbled translation of 1747.[140] Whether or not Herder first imparted his fascination with the original version directly while in Russian-held Riga or only indirectly through his later impact on German romantic thought, *Hamlet* became a kind of testing ground for the Russian critical imagination.

The extraordinary popularity of *Hamlet* in Russia may have come in part from certain similarities to the popular drama about the evil Tsar Maximilian confronted by his virtuous son. But the principal reason for the sustained interest of the aristocracy lay in the romantic fascination with the character of Hamlet himself. Russian aristocrats felt a strange kinship with this privileged court figure torn between the mission he was called on to perform and his own private world of indecision and poetic brooding. By the early nineteenth century there seemed nothing surprising in a Russian aristocrat's leaving his boat to make a special pilgrimage to "the Hamlet castle" at Elsinore. Standing on the Danish coast in the straits where the Baltic Sea moves out into the Altantic, this castle loomed up before Russian ships en route to Western Europe like a darkened and deserted lighthouse. Lunin paid a nocturnal visit to it at the beginning of his trip to Western Europe in 1816 that led him onto the path of revolution.[141]

Particular attention was always paid to the famous monologue "To be or not to be," which posed for Russia the one "cursed question" that was —quite literally—a matter of life or death. The famous opening phrase was translated in 1775 as "to live or not to live";[142] and the question of whether or not to take one's own life subsequently became known in Russian thought as "the Hamlet question." It was the most deeply personal and metaphysical of all the "cursed questions"; and for many Russians it superseded all the others.

In the spring of 1789, when Europe was standing on the brink of the French Revolution, the restless young aristocrat Nicholas Karamzin was writing the Swiss phrenologist Lavater in search of an answer to the question of why one should go on living. There is, he complained, no real joy in living, no satisfaction in the knowledge of one's own being. "I am—even my *I* is for me a riddle which I cannot resolve."[143] Three years later, after extended wandering through Europe (including visits to Lavater and to a performance of *Hamlet* in Drury Lane Theatre),[144] he returned to write a story—not about the social and political turmoil that was convulsing the continent but about "Poor Liza," who solves the riddle of being by ending her own life. The suicide of sensitivity—in protest to an unfeeling world— became a favorite subject of conversation and contemplation. Visits were frequently made by young aristocrats to the pond where Liza's Ophelia-like drowning was alleged to have taken place. The lugubrious institution of Russian roulette was apparently created out of sheer boredom by aristocratic guards officers.

Radishchev was perhaps the first to turn special attention to Hamlet's monologue in his own last work: *On Man, His Mortality and Immortality,* and resolved the question by taking his own life thereafter, in 1802. The last decade of the eighteenth century had already seen a marked rise in aristocratic suicides. Heroic suicide had been commended by the Roman Stoics, who were in many ways the heroes of classical antiquity for the eighteenth-century aristocrats. Although this "world weariness" was a Europe-wide phenomena and the Russian *mirovaia skorb'* is an exact translation of *Weltschmerz,* the term *skorb'* has a more final and unsentimental sound than the German word *Schmerz.* By the late years of the reign of Alexander I the high incidence of aristocratic suicide was causing the state grave concern and was used as an important argument for tightening censorship and increasing state discipline.[145]

The rigid rule of Nicholas I did not, however, relieve Russian thinkers of their compulsive preoccupation with "the Hamlet question." Indeed, it was this search for the meaning of life—more than ethnographic curiosity or reformist conviction—that inspired the turn to "the people" by Belinsky (and the radical populists after him). Belinsky felt that preoccupation with the cursed questions set his own time apart from that of Lomonosov and the confident, cosmopolitan Enlightenment:

> In the time of Lomonosov we did not need people's poetry; then the great question—*to be or not to be*—was solved for us not in the spirit of the people (*narodnost'*), but in Europeanism.[146]

To the men of the "remarkable decade"—many of whom courted or committed suicide—Hamlet stood as a kind of mirror of their generation. As with so many attitudes of the period, Hegel was their indirect and unacknowledged guide. Hegel had associated the melancholy and indecision of Hamlet with his subjectivism and individualism—his "absence of any formed view of the world" or "vigorous feeling for life"[147]—problems besetting any modern man who stands outside the rational flow of history as a proud and isolated *individuum.* This pejorative Hegelian term for "individual" was precisely the label that Belinsky adopted in his famous letter to Botkin rejecting Hegel. It is in the context of this strange struggle that Belinsky waged with Hegel—always accepting Hegel's basic terminology, definitions, and agenda—that one must read Belinsky's extended portrayal of Hamlet in 1838 as a true idealist dragged down by the venal world about him.[148]

Belinsky was captivated not only by the quality of frustrated idealism in Hamlet but also by the intense way in which the part was played by Paul Mochalov. This extraordinary actor played the role of Hamlet repeatedly until his death in 1848, the last year of the "remarkable decade." So popular did the play become that simplified versions began to be given in the informal theatricals presented by serfs seeking to entertain their landowners; and the term "quaking Hamlet" became a synonym for coward in popular speech.[149]

Mochalov was the first in a series of great stage personalities that was to make the Russian theater of the late imperial period unforgettable. The remarkable feature of Mochalov's acting—like that of Nizhinsky's dancing and Chaliapin's singing—was his ability to *be* the part. Just as later generations found it difficult to conceive of *Boris Godunov* without Chaliapin, or of *The Specter of the Rose* without Nizhinsky, so Russians of the forties could not think of Hamlet without Mochalov. The simple peasant, of course, always thought of Christ as he appeared on icons. Popular saints were "very like" the figures on icons, and the aristocratic hero felt impelled to become "very like" the figures on the stage. Stankevich confessed that he came to regard the theater as a "temple" and was deeply influenced in his personal patterns of behavior by watching Mochalov.[150]

Turgenev used *Hamlet* as a symbol of the late-Nicholaevan generation of intellectuals in his famous essay "Hamlet and Don Quixote." Having just created one of the most famous Hamlet figures in Russian literature in his first novel, *Rudin,* Turgenev now spoke of the contrasting but also typical Quixotic type: the uncomplicated enthusiast who loses himself in the service of an ideal, unafraid of the laughter of his contemporaries. Such figures were to become prominent in the Quixotic social movement of subsequent decades, but "Hamletism" remained typical of much of Russian thought. Indeed, many of Turgenev's subsequent literary creations were to end in suicide.

The conflict of these two types is mirrored in the career of one of the most interesting thinkers of late Nicholaevan Russia: V. S. Pecherin. There seems a kind of poetic justice in the similarity of his name to that of Pechorin, Lermontov's wandering and brooding "hero of our time." For this real-life Pecherin was an even more peripatetic and romantic figure. He moved from philology to poetry, from socialism to Catholicism, to an English monastery, and finally to an Irish hospital, where he died in 1885 as a chaplain to the sick—a distant admirer and faint echo of the populist movement in Russia. Yet he was tortured throughout—not so much by the fear that his ideas were utopian as by gnawing uncertainty whether life itself was worth living. He had in his student days been driven to "the Hamlet question" by Max Stirner, whose lectures at Berlin inspired him to embark on one of the many unfinished trilogies of the Russian nineteenth century. The first part of this untitled drama is a weird apotheosis of Stirner's idea that man can achieve divinity through his own uncaused act of self-assertion: suicide. The leading character (with the heroic Germanic name of Woldemar) not only kills himself but convinces his lover (with the spiritualized name of Sophia) to do likewise. "Sophia," he tells her, "thy name means Wisdom, Divine Wisdom. . . . There is but one question: To be or not to be."[151]

The second part of the trilogy, entitled *The Triumph of Death,* elaborates this theme with ghoulish delight, as King Nemesis watches the destruction of the entire world—announced by a storm, a musical chorus, and five falling stars representing the slain Decembrist leaders. The chorus in praise of death echoes some of the dark thoughts of Pushkin's "Hymn in Praise of the Plague" and draws freely from both apocalyptical and romantic symbolism. Death appears as a youth on a white horse and is hailed as "the God of freedom, the God of striving." Then the stage is cleared for one last monologue, which ends this second (and last) part of the trilogy. It is a song of the dying poet. "The poet," says Pecherin, "is Don Quixote . . . (who) will save the fatherland . . . find the new world for us." Then, in an ending that runs off into dots to indicate its incompleteness, the "dying poet" speaks of Russia as the land of "the brightening dawn" and says: "I shall pour forth abundant strength on Russia, and the steeled Russian knife . . ."[152]

If "the Hamlet question" was never resolved by the aristocratic intellectuals, preoccupation with it nonetheless served to clear away secondary concerns. Indeed, the oft-ridiculed generation of "the fathers," the romantic, "superfluous" aristocrats of the forties, in some ways did even more to tear Russian thought away from past Russian practices and traditions than the iconoclastic "sons," the self-proclaimed "new men" of the sixties. The fantasy-laden romanticism of the Nicholaevan age swept away petty thoughts with the same decisiveness with which actors were swept off the stage in the last act of *Hamlet* or the final scene of *The Triumph of Death.* The passion for destruction which burst onto Europe in the late forties in the person of Bakunin was only the most extreme illustration of the philosophic desperation produced by the interaction of German ideas, Slavic enthusiasm, and the personal frustrations and boredom of a provincial aristocracy. Bakunin illustrates as well the transfer of the vision of a "brightening dawn," of "abundant strength," and "steeled knives" from the lips of a "dying poet" to the life of a living revolutionary. His volcanic career anticipated, and in some degree influenced, the proliferation of quixotic causes and crusades which swept through Russia during the eventful reign of Alexander II. All of these movements—Jacobinism, populism, Pan-Slavism, and variants thereof—elude the usual categories of social and political analysis and can be seen as parts of an implausible yet heroic effort to realize in life that which had been anticipated in prophecy but could not be realized in art: the final act of Pecherin's play, the *Paradiso* of Gogol's *Poemà,* the new icons for Ivanov's temple.

One of the powerful if invisible forces driving Russian aristocrats to the "cursed questions" was the oppressive, inescapable boredom of Russian life. To Francophile or Germanophile aristocrats, Russia appeared as the immense and final province of Europe. Life was an unrelieved series of petty incidents in one of those indeterminate towns "in N province," in which the stories of Gogol generally take place. Pent-up hysteria was released in prophetic utterance. Even in their travels Russians complained with Belinsky: "Boredom is my inseparable companion."[153] They were impelled onward to question the value of life itself by the feeling expressed in the world-weary last lines of Gogol's tragicomic "How the Two Ivans Quarreled": "Life is boring on this earth, gentlemen."

When a revolutionary social transformation finally came to Russia in the twentieth century, Stalin's "new Soviet intelligentsia" sought to ridicule Hamlet as a symbol of the brooding and indecisive old intelligentsia. A production of *Hamlet* during the period of the first five-year plan portrayed the Danish prince as a fat and decadent coward who recites "To be or not to be" half-drunk in a bar.[154] A critic of that period went so far as to claim that the real hero of the play was Fortinbras. He alone had a positive goal; and the fact that he came from victory in battle to pronounce the final words of the play symbolized rational, militant modernity triumphing over the "feudal morality" of pointless bloodletting that had dominated the last act prior to his arrival.[155]

Modernization under Stalin was to be far from a rational process, however; and the Russian stage was not to be dominated entirely by faceless Fortinbras figures. The aristocratic century left a legacy of unresolved anguish and unanswered questions that continued to agitate the more complex culture that emerged in the following century of economic growth and social upheaval.

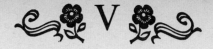

ON TO NEW SHORES

The Second Half of the Nineteenth Century

THE SEARCH *for new forms of art and life in the midst of social dis-location, industrial development, and urbanization during the second half of the nineteenth century. The symbol of a ship at sea in search of another shore. The gradual turn to social thought during the late years of Nicholas I's reign; the influence of moralistic French socialism; the Petrashevsky circle of the 1840's; the transfer of hopes to Russia by Alexander Herzen (1812–70) and Michael Bakunin (1814–76) after the failure of the revolutions of 1848 in the West. Railroads as a bearer of change and symbol of apocalypse in the countryside.*

The ironic growth of revolutionary radicalism during the relatively liberal reign of Alexander II (1855–81). The spread of iconoclastic materialism among the younger generation, or "new men," during the early 1860's—the very period in which Alexander liberated the serfs and instituted trial by jury and a measure of provincial self-government. The turn toward prophetic extremism in the 1870's: the rise in Moscow of reactionary Pan-Slavism based on Darwinistic ideas of struggle for survival; and in St. Petersburg the rise of revolutionary populism based on a Proudhonist idealization of "the people" and a Comtian religion of humanity.

The peculiar genius of art in the age of Alexander II, seeking both the remorseless realism of the materialistic sixties and the idealization of the Russian people of the visionary seventies. The painting of "the wanderers," the short stories of Vsevolod Garshin (1855–88); the music of the Russian national school, particularly the great historical operas of Modest Musorgsky (1839–81); and the psychological novels of Fedor Dostoevsky (1821–81) with their dramatic penetration "from the real to the more real" and their ideological efforts to overcome the schisms in Russian life and consciousness.

Chekhovian despair of the period of "small deeds" during the reign of Alexander III (1881–94). The inability of either the reactionary Orthodoxy of Alexander's tutor, Constantine Pobedonostsev (1827–1907), or of the unorthodox anarchism of Leo Tolstoy (1828–1910) to provide effective leadership in late imperial Russia. The emergence amidst the accelerating tempo of life in the 1890's of three new perspectives that broke with the prevailing atmosphere of subjectivism and despondency as well as with the parochialism of previous ideologies. Constitutional liberalism at last took root in Russia, producing an articulate spokesman in Paul Miliukov (1859–1943) and a Constitutional Democratic Party. Dialectical materialism commanded attention through the writings of George Plekhanov (1856–1918), the increased intellectual interest in problems of economic development, and the formation of a Marxist, Social Democratic Party. Mystical idealism received from Vladimir Solov'ev (1853–1900) a brilliant new apologia, which provided the basis for a revival of Russian poetry and a long-delayed development of formal philosophical study within Russia.

WITH THE DEATH of Nicholas I, defeat in the Crimean War, and the preparations for peasant emancipation, the realization rapidly grew in the late 1850's that Russia was heading for profound changes. The English and French ships which brought troops to Russian soil during the Crimean War did not disrupt Russian culture nearly so much as the new techniques and ideas that streamed in peacefully after the Treaty of Paris. For the reign of Alexander II saw not just another case of cautious contact with "guile from beyond the seas" but the beginnings of a massive, irreversible process of modernization. With the freeing of the serfs, the new incentives for foreign investment, and the beginnings of industrialization, Alexander II cut Russia off forever from its static, agrarian past. But neither he nor anyone else was able to determine exactly what form of society and culture the modernizing empire would adopt.

The dividing line that falls across Russian history in the mid-nineteenth century is distinct from all the many others which set off periods of insularity from those of Westernization in Russian history. For the innovations that began seriously in Alexander's reign involved the entire nation and not merely selected regions and groups. Industrialization and urbanization —however fitful and uneven in development—altered the physical surroundings and social relations of the Russian people in a profoundly disturbing manner. Up until this, the last century of Russian history, all developments in thought and culture were concentrated in a small minority. The peasant masses had suffered on in silence and been heard from only in military campaigns, peasant insurrections, and sectarian movements.

The final conquest and colonization of all of southern Russia in the late eighteenth and the early nineteenth century had swollen the ranks of the peasant population; and the image of the steppe began to replace the more northerly image of the forest in the Russian imagination. There were two major forms that life took on the steppe; and both forms were reflected in the brutalized earthbound life of the average peasant. There was vegetable life, free from striving, passively accepting whatever nature sends. There was also the life of the predators—the insects, rodents, ponies from Mongolia, and grain collectors from the cities. Passive, vegetable existence was in many ways the peasant ideal; but many of the Russian peasants transformed themselves into predators through one of those metamorphoses in which peasant folklore abounds. Nothing was more brutal than the peasant who had become a landowner or state official. For he was a new and particularly hungry predator who knew the secrets of the vegetable kingdom: where the deep roots of the plants were kept, and how the silent vegetables managed to survive endless attacks from avaricious nomads. Many peasants secretly aspired to join the ranks of the predators; and when authority weakened or a prophet appeared, many seemingly happy vegetables suddenly turned into rabid animals. Many peasants went through the more peaceful form of metamorphosis which changed him into a wealthy peasant who came to be designated by the Russian word for "fist," *kulak*.

The century since emancipation has seen this long-silent class slowly and reluctantly stream into the cities, and be transformed by modern culture. Behind this seething human drama looms, however, a nagging question which can again be expressed in terms of the older peasant folklore. Have the masses been lifted up from their previous animal and vegetable state? Or have these lower forms of life simply come to prevail over a higher, human culture that was, or might have been?

As more and more Russians became infected with the aristocratic spirit of inquiry, they turned to the question of how Russia might lift itself from the animal and vegetable life of the steppe to some loftier type of reality. In their anguished discussion, Russians of all persuasions tended to turn their metaphorical imagination to the image of a ship at sea. Just as the very coldness of the north had created a fascination with heat and fire; so the vastness and monotony of their land created a certain fascination with the water and those who voyage upon it.

Unlike Gogol's enigmatic image of Russia as a flying troika, the popular image of Russia as a ship had clear roots in early Christian symbolism. The overwhelming majority of Russians in the mid-nineteenth century still felt secure in the "second ark" of the Russian Church, which reminded them that

> just as a boat under the guidance of a pilot leads man across the stormy sea to the safe harbor, so does the Church guided by Christ save man from drowning in the depths of sin, and leads him to the heavenly kingdom.[1]

The book of law and direction for the Church was known as the "Pilot Book"; and most major monasteries were located on islands or peninsulas, like Athos, best reached by boat. Most pilgrimages ended with sailor-priests piloting the faithful across bodies of water separating them from their shrine. The journey was sometimes dangerous—particularly the increasingly popular route on the pilot ships Faith and Hope across the stormy and ice-clogged White Sea to Solovetsk. In the years after the Crimean War, pilots on these ships were fond of telling pilgrims how the English warships had been unable to harm the monastery with artillery fire because God had miraculously sent flocks of seagulls into the path of their shells.[2] Old Believers derived new hope from Russian explorations across the northern Pacific, contending that a surviving remnant of Christ's uncorrupted Church might be found on some island beyond the reach of Antichrist in the Pacific.[3] Just as Avvakum's first religious calling came to him in a youthful dream that God offered him a ship to pilot,[4] so the flagellant sectarians spoke of their itinerant prophetic groups as "boats" led by "pilots" in search of converts whose robes of initiation were known as "white sails."

Secular images of ships as symbols of hope blended with, and sometimes replaced, the religious image of the Church as ark of salvation. In the Russian north, legends arose about the mythical origins and special personalities of ships, which were often launched with songs of invocation:

> Water-maiden
> All-providing river!
> . . . Here is thy gift:
> A white-sailed bark![5]

In the south, ships along the Volga were associated with the free life of the Cossacks; and the favorite form of popular variety show was known as *lodka,* or the bark. Many of its songs and traditions were absorbed into popular folklore about the Volga, and the popular productions of the naval theater.[6]

For the troubled aristocracy the image of Russia as a ship had long ceased to be a comforting one. Magnitsky likened the Russia of Alexander I to "a ship without a rudder, moved about by every gust of wind";[7] and Alexander's former tutor, La Harpe, darkly warned that "we are passengers in the boat of revolution. We must either reach the shore or sink."[8] Not long before committing suicide, Radishchev likened the old order to "a ship hurled on the reef," and helped turn the aristocratic imagination away from the image of the ship to that of the sea itself. History, he declared, is moving into "a wild watery abyss . . . into an ocean where neither boundaries nor banks can be seen."[9] Lunin later likened his thoughts to "storms at sea";[10] and Turgenev compared the romantic flight abroad under Nicholas to the original search of the Eastern Slavs "for leaders among the Varangians from across the seas." Alienated from Russian soil, "I flung myself head first into the 'German sea' which was destined to cleanse and renew me."[11]

With the revolution of 1848, the "German sea" became a "maddening tumult of waves" for the poet Tiutchev, whose haunted counter-revolutionary writings likened Russia to "a giant granite cliff" providing Europe with its last "solitary rock of refuge" against engulfment by revolution.[12] At the other end of the political spectrum, Herzen looked not back to this rock but on to "the other shore" that lay beyond the tides of 1848. His famous post-mortem on the events of that year, "From the Other Shore," began with a plea to his son not to remain "on this shore":

> Modern man, that melancholy Pontifex Maximus, only builds a bridge—it will be for the unknown man of the future to pass over it.[13]

Herzen hoped with his friend Proudhon that a new world might be found in which all past suffering would "appear like a magic bridge cast in the river of forgetfulness";[14] but he was haunted by the fear that any bridge to the future could only be built—like those of St. Petersburg itself—out of human suffering.

Only in the next student generation after Herzen's, among the "new men" of the early years of Alexander II's reign, were Russians willing to cut themselves loose from traditional moorings and familiar landmarks. Modest Musorgsky, the greatest musician of the age, sounded the call:

> To unknown shores, must be our cry, fearless through the storms, on, past all the shallows. . . . On to new shores, there is no turning back.[15]

Populist revolutionaries journeyed "down by mother Volga" hoping to summon up the insurrectionary tradition of Razin with such chants as:

> Our bark has run aground.
> The Tsar, our white helmsman, is drunk.
> He has led us straight upon the shoals.
> . . . Let us speed it on its way,
> And throw the masters into the water.[16]

At its purest, the quest of young Russia was that of Dante, who had used the same metaphor at the beginning of his *Purgatorio:*

> The frail bark of my ingenuity lifts its sail
> In order to course over better waters
> And leave behind so cruel a sea.[17]

The Russians plunged on oblivious of the prophetic warning that Dante placed at the beginning of his *Paradiso:*

> O you, who sit within a frail bark . . .
> Turn back to gaze upon your native shores:
> Do not set out upon the deep:
> Lest, in losing me, you should be altogether lost.
> The waters that I take were never sailed before.[18]

At its simplest, the image of plunging out into the deep was only a reflection of the fact that Russia had at last become in the early nineteenth century a thoroughly sea-conscious empire. The Pacific Ocean and the Black Sea offered a host of new outlets for oceanic trade and travel; regular steamship service was opened into St. Petersburg in the 1830's; and Goncharov's famous account of a sea voyage to Japan in the 1850's, *Frigate Pallada,* opened up a new genre of sea adventures to the Russian reader.[19]

Uncertain of where they were going, anxious to find out who they really were, the increasingly uprooted intellectuals of the late imperial period came to discover many levels of meaning in the sea. It was for some a symbol of purity and renewal: Keats' "moving waters at their priest-like task of pure ablution round earth's human shores." For others, the ocean was the symbol of romantic liberation: Byron's "glad waters of the dark blue sea" in which thoughts were "boundless" and souls were "free."[20]

An increasingly important symbolic meaning for the sea in late-nineteenth-century Russia was that of the "silent stranger," the faceless peasant masses: the *narod.* The relatively privileged intellectuals looked fearfully upon the peasantry as a "churned-up sea," the title of Pisemsky's widely read novel of 1863; and upon themselves in the way Herzen had described the Winter Palace, as

> a ship floating on the surface of the ocean [having] no real connection with the inhabitants of the deep, beyond that of eating them.[21]

The populist movement represented a self-denying, penitential effort to establish some other connection. Aristocratic leaders of the movement cried forth their desire to reject "the Divine Raphael" and "immerse themselves in the ocean of real life,"[22] "to drown in that grey, rough mass of the people, to dissolve irrevocably. . . ."[23] Young activists went almost eagerly to prison or death for the futile populist cause, less in the manner of modern revolutionary technicians than of brooding romantic heroes.

Imperceptibly the image of the sea became that of self-annihilation: the death wish for the "German sea," the harmony beyond death in Wagner's *Tristan;* the beckoning abyss of Novalis' *Hymns to the Night,* in which

"Memory dissolves in the cool shadow-waves."[24] This romantic longing for self-annihilation was related to an older, Oriental ideal of finding the peace of Nirvana by the annihilation of will, by losing oneself like a drop in the ocean. Schopenhauer, the most profound apostle of the futility of striving and the wisdom of suicide, drew inspiration from the Orient, as did Tolstoy, one of his many Russian admirers. Russia's other novelists of the Alexandrian period also give many literary reflections of Schopenhauer's gloomy teaching. There is the death-wish figure of Svidrigailov in Dostoevsky's *Crime and Punishment,* the heroic, ideological suicide of Kirillov in *The Possessed.* There is the suicidal double drowning which ends Leskov's powerful novella of 1865: *Lady Macbeth of the Mtsensk District.* Turgenev's works abound in suicides;[25] and the influence of Schopenhauer is woven in with the image of the sea in such passages as the darkly prophetic dream of his revolutionary heroine, Elena, just before the hero dies in *On the Eve.* This novel, which was finished in the same year as Wagner's *Tristan* and its strange, symbolic *Liebestod,* begins with Elena imagining herself drifting across a lake

> in a boat with some people that she did not know. They were silent and sat quite still. No one was rowing the boat, which moved of its own accord. Elena was not feeling frightened, but she was bored; she wanted to know who these people were and why she was with them.

Out of this boredom and confusion comes a revolutionary upheaval:

> She looked around and as she did so, the lake grew wider, the banks disappeared; and now it was no longer a lake, but a heaving sea; Elena's unknown companions jumped up, shouting and waving their arms. . . . Elena recognized their faces now; her father was among them. Then a sort of white hurricane burst upon the waters.

Thus, the aristocracy itself was being consumed. In an effort to chart the course that lay beyond, Turgenev turns the water into "endless snow," moves Elena from a boat to a sleigh, and gives her a new companion: "Katya, the little beggar-girl she had known years ago." Katya is, of course, a prototype of the new populist saint: a "humiliated and insulted" figure who retains nonetheless inherent nobility and imparts to the aristocratic Elena the ideal of running away from established society to "live in God's free world."

"Katya, where are we going?" Elena asks; but Katya, like Gogol's troika and Pushkin's bronze horseman, does not answer. Instead, traditional symbols of messianic deliverance race before her eyes in the last sequence of the dream:

She looked along the road and saw in the distance, through the blown snow, the outlines of a city with tall white towers and silver-gleaming cupolas. "Katya, Katya, is that Moscow? But no," she thought, "that's not Moscow, that is the Solovetsk monastery"; and she knew that in there, in one of its innumerable narrow cells, stuffy and crowded together like the cells of a beehive—in there Dmitry was locked up. "I must free him."

Liberation comes, however, only in death; and, at this very moment, "a yawning, grey abyss suddenly opened up in front of her." The sleigh plunged into it, and Katya's last distant cry of "Elena" proved in reality the voice of her Bulgarian lover, Insarov, the "true Tsar" of the new Russia, its would-be revolutionary deliverer, saying "Elena, I am dying."[26]

In the metaphysics of late romanticism, death offers a kind of liberation; and the sea appears more as a place for obliteration than purification. Suggestions of such thinking are present even in Christian thinking. The Spanish martyr and mystic Raymond Lully (one of the most popular of medieval Western writers among Russians) had proclaimed "I want to die in an ocean of love";[27] and Dante's *Paradiso* had likened the peace of God to "that sea toward which all things move."[28]

In Chekhov's "Lights," the night lights of a half-finished railroad by the sea are likened to "the thoughts of man . . . scattered in disorder, stretching in a straight line toward some goal in the midst of darkness" leading the narrator to look down from a cliff at the "majestic, infinite, and forbidding" sea:

Far below me, behind a veil of thick darkness, the sea kept up a low angry growl. . . . And it seemed to me that the whole world consisted only of the thoughts straying through my head . . . and of an unseen power murmuring monotonously somewhere below. Afterwards, as I sank into a doze, it began to seem that it was not the sea murmuring, but my thoughts, and that the whole world consisted in nothing but me. Concentrating the whole world in myself in this way, I . . . abandoned myself to the sensation I was so fond of: the sensation of fearful isolation, when you feel that in the whole universe, dark and formless, you alone exist. It is a proud, demonic sensation, only possible to Russians, whose thoughts and sensations are as large, boundless, and gloomy as their plains, their forests, and their snow.[29]

An artist rather than a metaphysician, Chekhov looks in the end to "the expression on the face" of the thinker rather than to the logical conclusion of his thoughts. The hero of "Lights" contemplates rather than commits suicide; just as Chekhov himself moves from the melodramatic suicide at the end of his first great play, *The Sea Gull,* through an unsuccessful suicide in *Uncle Vanya,* to the elegiac beauty of his last play, *The Cherry Orchard,* in which there is no attempt at suicide—or any other form of escape from the lingering sadness of late Imperial Russia. Nonetheless, Chekhov's fascination with what he was the first to call "the Hamlet question" helped keep thoughts of suicide before his audiences.

To some extent drowning was a romantic imitation of Ophelia in *Hamlet* or of the real-life Byron. But drowning had also been an important form of ritual execution in Old Russia. Pre-Christian beliefs had survived about the need to propitiate jealous water spirits. Perhaps the missing madonna was really a *rusalka,* one of those transformed figures of drowned women who became a kind of enchanted Rhine maiden in the florid pagan mythology of Russian romanticism. Perhaps also somewhere at the bottom of a lake lay a purer existence than existed on land—perhaps the "shining city of Kitezh" which was said to have descended uncorrupted to the bottom of a trans-Volga lake at the time of the first Mongol invasion.

A final symbol increasingly connected with the sea in the late imperial period was that of the coming apocalypse. Belief in a past or coming flood is one of the oldest and most universal ways in which man's poetic imagination has expressed his fear of divine judgment and retribution.[30] There may be traces of the Eastern myth of "an insatiable sea" seeking to inundate all humanity in the belief among Old Believers in the Urals that a great flood was coming and that God's people must flee to the mountains, where alone they could be rescued by God.[31]

Fear of the sea was perhaps to be expected among an earthbound people whose discovery of the sea coincided with their traumatic discovery of the outside world. The fact that the westward-looking capital of St. Petersburg was built on land reclaimed from—and periodically threatened by—the sea gave special vividness to the Biblical imagery of the flood. The occurrence of the first important flood of the city in 1725, the very year of Peter's death, encouraged those who had resisted Peter's innovations to speak of a "second flood" and the coming end of the world. Belief that these calamities represented the wrathful judgment of God was encouraged by the curious fact that two of the greatest subsequent floods of the city occurred almost exactly one hundred and two hundred years later, at the very times when two other imperial innovators had just died: Alexander I and Lenin respectively. In both subsequent cases, the death and flood occurred at the end of periods of hopeful expectation and brought more prosaic, repressive forces into power: Nicholas I and Stalin. Thus, the rich historical imagination of Russia found portentous omens lurking behind these strange coincidences.

Particularly after Pushkin's "Bronze Horseman," the image of a flood consuming St. Petersburg recurs frequently in the literature of the late imperial period. Whereas fire was the enduring fear and symbol of judgment in the wooden world of Moscow, the sea provided such a symbol for the city on the Neva.

The man who perhaps did most to bring Russia both visually and imaginatively in contact with the sea in the late nineteenth century was the gifted and prolific painter Ivan Aivazovsky. Born by the sea in the Crimea in 1817, Aivazovsky was fascinated by the sea and ships throughout the eighty-three years of his life. As a favored painter for the St. Petersburg academy, he traveled widely during the Nicholaevan era, and became a personal friend of its most gifted creative figures: Glinka and Briullov, Ivanov and Gogol. While visiting the latter two in Rome during the early 1840's, he sold one of his early canvases to the Vatican—on the appropriately romantic subject "Primitive Chaos." He followed one of Ivanov's early leads by painting numerous scenes of the idealized Italian sea coast and has been credited with introducing sea painting to Italy and influencing the work of Joseph Turner.

Almost all of his more than five thousand paintings were scenes of the sea, and, particularly after his return to Russia, the majority showed either violent storms or battles. Following the tradition of Briullov and Ivanov, Aivazovsky painted his major works on a gigantic scale, many of them well over fifty feet in width. The sheer size of the sea in his canvases creates a sense of human insignificance both for the figures tossed upon it in the picture and for those looking at it in the gallery. His most influential paintings were his largest and most dramatic: "The Storm," which shows a ship sinking and a lifeboat bobbing in the midst of a vast panorama of contrasting light and darkness; and "The Ninth Wave," which lends a kind of incandescent glory to the last wave of the final flood predicted in the Book of Revelation.

Despite continuing success and popularity Aivazovsky remained consumed by romantic wanderlust throughout his life. In his last months he was contemplating another sea journey in search of new inspiration; but he died in 1900 while working on his last canvas, "Destruction of a Turkish Warship." Just as poets had often sought to express themselves in painting during the age of Lermontov, so did this last leaf on the tree of Russian romanticism sometimes turn to poetry to express his feelings:

> The great ocean heaves beneath me.
> I see the distant shore,
> The magic regions of a sunlit land:
> With agitation and longing, thither do I strive.[32]

In his later years Aivazovsky, like so many romantics, became intensely nationalistic. He dreamed of a glorious series of Russian naval victories, which he hoped to record on canvas—just as Briullov had once envisaged designing murals of Russian military victories. Russian victories in the new century were, of course, to lie in other directions; and Soviet strategists were to transform the Russian navy from a somewhat futile surface fleet to a somber submarine flotilla within half a century of Aivazovsky's death. Yet in the folklore of the new regime, two surface ships lived on as symbols of the revolutionary hopes of the new order: the battleship *Potemkin,* which mutinied briefly against tsarist authority during the Revolution of 1905, and the Cruiser *Aurora,* which provided perfunctory support fire for the Bolshevik insurrection of 1917. Thus, two ships became symbols of deliverance in the new Soviet ideology.[33] The symbol of creative culture in the Soviet period was, however, provided by a persecuted poet, Osip Mandel'shtam, who likened his verse to a message cast out in a bottle on the high seas by a drowning man in the hope of reaching some unknown distant reader.[34] Before setting out on those waters and scanning the new horizons of Soviet Russia, one must chart the course which Russian creativity followed across the troubled seas of the late imperial period.

1. The Turn to Social Thought

A DISTINCTIVE FEATURE of Russian culture from the 1840's to the early 1880's was its extraordinary preoccupation with what the Russians call "social thought" (*obshchestvennaia mysl'*). There is no exact equivalent for this category of thought in Western culture. It is too undisciplined and literary to be discussed fairly in the language of traditional moral philosophy or of modern sociology. Its concerns were not primarily political, and may be best understood in terms of psychology or religion.

In any event, Russian social thought is a phenomenon of the late imperial period. It represents in many ways an artificially delayed, and characteristically passionate, Russian response to the rich ferment of reformist ideas in France between the revolutions of 1830 and 1848. Social thought provided a kind of intellectual bridge between aristocratic and proletarian Russia. It reflects the impracticality and utopianism of the aristocracy, yet shows a new awareness that the time had come to move from philosophical to social questions—or, in Belinsky's words, "from the blue skies into the kitchen."[1] So morally pure was this tradition that almost all subsequent radical reformers felt constrained to represent themselves as heirs to its aspirations. Soviet ideologists have constructed for their citizens a kind of hagiographical guide that places Herzen and Belinsky, Chernyshevsky and Dobroliubov, Pisarev, and (with some reservations) Lavrov and Plekhanov in the prophetic line that allegedly reached its fulfillment in Lenin.

But social thought in the middle and late nineteenth century was far more than a mere anticipation of Bolshevism or a mere critique of tsarism. It involved a free play of the mind and heart: an uncompromising earnestness that reflects the projection out into the broader arena of society of many of the deeper questions that had long been disturbing the aristocracy. The longing for a better world so evident in Russian social thought became subversive once more in the Stalin era; "social thought" in the profound, searching sense ceased to be tolerated in the public culture of the USSR; and

even canonized prophets like Herzen and Chernyshevsky were expurgated
or reinterpreted.

In a general sense the distinctively Russian tradition of social thought
began with the economic and political discussions of Catherine's time, with
Radishchev's anguished critique of serfdom, with the various proposals of
Bentham, Owen, and Saint-Simon for including social reform in the program
of Alexander's Holy Alliance, with Pestel's proposals for agrarian redistribution in the 1820's, and with the Russian interest in Saint-Simon in the
thirties.[2] But these were all subordinate or episodic concerns of an aristocracy still dominated by religious and aesthetic questions. Indeed, the only
important socialist-style experiments on Russian soil during this period were
the non-aristocratic communities of foreign sectarians, such as the Hutterites of southern Russia, who practiced a form of egalitarian communal living
that has yet to be approached in the USSR.

A trend toward communalism among native sectarians was evidenced,
however, in the 1830's with the appearance of a new group called "the sect
sharing all in common" (*sekta obshchykh*). This sect adopted the old
flagellant idea of forming groups of twelve apostles, with the emphasis on
Communist forms of organization rather than prophetic activities. Interpreting St. Paul literally, this sect insisted that each member was actually
and literally but one part of a common body. All things were shared in
common by the nine men and three women in each commune; public confessions were conducted in order to excoriate infection from any part of the
body; and each person in the community was given a function corresponding
to some bodily organ. Abstract thought was the exclusive province of the
thinker (*myslennik*); physical work, of "the hands"; and so on. In this way,
no one was complete in and of himself; each one depended on the community. The "tidings of Zion" sect of the 1840's reveals the same preoccupation with a new ideal conception of society, insisting that the coming
millennial kingdom should be divided into twelve inseparable parts and that
each member of each kingdom should live in total equality. This form of
social organization was to be accompanied by the divinization of man, the
rearrangement where necessary of his physical organs, and the physical
enlargement of the earth in order to accommodate his expanding physical
needs.

In this same period one finds the first serious interest in social analysis
and socialism among the aristocratic intellectuals. They turned to social
thought because of deepening disillusionment in the possibility of peaceful
political change. Russian thinkers of the late Nicholaevan period, seeking to
develop a program of reform for the real world, gradually concluded that
the Decembrists had chosen the wrong field of battle. Political programs,

constitutions, projects, and so on, were merely an elegant form of deception that the bourgeoisie of England and France had devised for deceiving and enslaving their people. The most magnetic figures of the decade all tended to reject political reform as a subject worthy of consideration. Herzen, Belinsky, and Bakunin all thought in terms of a social rather than a political transformation. All had brief periods of idealizing the ruling tsar as a possible instrument for effecting social reform; but none of them ever idealized the forms of political organization to be found in the liberal democracies of Western Europe. Whether one's vision of social transformation began with liberating Slavs abroad or serfs at home, the ultimate objective remained that which a Serb explained to a radical itinerant Russian in the 1840's: the creation of a new type of human society in which men can live simply and communicate with one another spontaneously "without any politics" (*bez vsiakoi politiki*).[3]

To be sure, there were some voices raised in behalf of the old Decembrist ideal of political reform and representative government. Nicholas Turgenev in his *Russia and the Russians* in 1847 eloquently restated the classical enlightened arguments for constitutional monarchy; but this was the voice of an old man writing in Paris. His tone is already that of the innumerable memoirists of the late imperial period: semi-fatalistic and elegiac regret combined with a scholarly desire to set the record straight. Turgenev's work is a masterpiece of this genre, with his praise of the civilizing effects of pietism and Masonry under Alexander, his criticism of the "Adonises in uniform" who prevailed over right reason at the court, and his indictment of "the fatalism which seems to weigh on Russia as much as despotism."[4]

One interesting new feature of Turgenev's book is his admiration for the more advanced portions of the Russian Empire: Poland and Finland. Sympathy for subjugated Poland was to become a mark of the new radical social thinkers in Russia; and interest in Finland was to become in some respects even more important. Finland was, first of all, a Protestant state; and Turgenev was not alone in suggesting that Protestantism provided a more favorable atmosphere for free social development than Catholicism. One of the leading new journals devoted to the discussion of social questions in St. Petersburg was entitled *The Finnish Herald*, and there was a steady increase in Finnish settlement in the St. Petersburg region as well as increased contact through the Helsinki–St. Petersburg steamboat line.

Of particular interest to Russians was the fact that the Finnish diet included not only the standard three estates but also—following the model of the Swedish *riksdag*—representatives of a fourth estate: the peasantry. For it was the aristocratic discovery of the peasantry that was principally responsible for the turn to social reform in the 1840's. Interest in the peasantry was stimulated by the gradual increase in peasant disorders under Nicholas I and by the attendant activities of the various commissions appointed to analyze and make recommendations on the peasant problem. At the same time, the peasantry appears as a kind of final object of romantic fascination for the alienated intellectuals. Having traveled in vain to foreign lands and studied at the feet of foreign sages, the Russian Faust now heard happy murmurs from the peasant masses calling him back to the provincial surroundings of his youth.

Although synthetic pastoral themes were sounded much earlier in Russian culture, they tended to become dominant for the first time in the 1840's. Harbinger of the new trend was the posthumous critical praise heaped on the poems and folksongs of Alexis Kol'tsov by Belinsky, who found in the unaffected and unperfected art of the rough-hewn Kol'tsov a "new simplicity" that seemed to satisfy the "longing for normalcy" that was characteristic of his last years.[5] "Sociality or death" had been Belinsky's valedictory slogan to the aristocratic intellectuals just before his death in 1848. They were to find this "sociality" (or "social life," *sotsial'nost'*) in the real or imagined company of the noble savages in the Russian countryside. With the appearance in 1846 of Dmitry Grigorovich's *The Village* and of the first of Ivan Turgenev's *Sportsman's Sketches* the following year, the peasant emerged as a new heroic type for Russian literature. In part, this new interest was just another Russian reflection of a Western trend noticeable in the sudden popularity of Berthold Auerbach's *Village Tales of the Black Forest* and George Sand's *François de Champi*. But there was a peculiar intensity to the Eastern European interest in the peasantry that resulted from the survival there of the brutalizing institution of serfdom, and is exemplified in such writers of the forties as the Pole Kraszewski and the Ukrainian Shevchenko.[6]

It is a measure of the Russian aristocrats' alienation from their own peoples that they discovered the peasants not on their own estates but in books—above all in the three-volume study of Russian life by Baron Haxthausen, a German who had made a long trip through Russia in 1843. On the basis of his study, Russian aristocrats suddenly professed to find in the peasant commune (*obshchina*) the nucleus of a better society. Although the peasant commune had been idealized before—as an organic religious community by the Slavophiles and as a force for revolution by Polish extremists—Haxthausen's praise was based on a detailed study of its social functions of regulating land redistribution and dispensing local justice. He saw in the commune a model for "free productive associations like those of the Saint-Simonians"; and the idea was born among Russians that a renovation of society on the model of the commune might be possible even if a political revolution were not.[7]

The belief in a coming transformation of social relationships was propagated actively by two influential social analysts of the late Nicholaevan era: Valerian Maikov and Vladimir Miliutin. Each was a highly pedigreed aristocrat (and one of three well-known brothers). Each was a teacher of law and a popularizer of Auguste Comte's plea for a new non-metaphysical science of society; each enjoyed great influence in his day and died an early and unnatural death.

Maikov was the son of a famous painter, the grandson of a director of the imperial theater, and a descendant of the most famous masonic poet of the eighteenth century. Had he not died in a mysterious drowning in 1847, it is likely that this extraordinary child prodigy would have been the most famous of all the Maikovs, including his distinguished brother, the poet Apollon. He received a *kandidat* degree at the age of nineteen, founded a journal for the study of society, *The Finnish Herald,* at twenty-two, was the principal author of the first volume of the *Pocket Dictionary of Foreign Words Used in Russian,* and wrote two thick volumes of essays (and many others that remained unpublished) on every subject from chemistry to agriculture. He was hailed by many as the leading literary critic in Russia before dying shortly after his twenty-fourth birthday.

Maikov's most important essay was his long and never completed "Social Sciences in Russia" of 1845, in which he called for a new "Philosophy of Society" to provide the basis for a regeneration of Russian life. This "philosophy of society" was to be a combination of the historical ideas of Auguste Comte and the moralistic socialism of Blanc and Proudhon. Only such a philosophy can provide the basis for an "organic" culture that will avoid the "disembodied" metaphysical speculations of German culture ("the Hindus of today") and the "one-sided" and "soulless" English preoccupation with economic production. The preoccupation of Adam Smith and English liberal economists with wealth as something separable from the quality of social development he finds "false in theory and disastrous in practice."[8]

Miliutin picked up where Maikov left off with his long study, "The Proletariat and Pauperism in England and France," which was serialized in the first four issues of *The Annals of the Fatherland* (the journal on which Maikov had just succeeded Belinsky as chief literary critic) in 1847. Miliutin contrasts the vigor of French social thought with the degeneracy of bourgeois society. Both his articles and his lectures at Moscow University reflect a Comtian optimism about the possibility of resolving "the struggle of interests" characteristic of a growing economy like that of France and

England through the "future development of science." Miliutin was a friend
of many Decembrists and a leading court advocate of reform in the institution of serfdom; and his two brothers were to become important court
figures under Alexander II. But Miliutin succumbed to the melancholia of
late Nicholaevan Russia and shot himself in 1855.

The translation of the new interest in social questions into socialist
activity was the work of the last of the key circles of the Nicholaevan era:
that of Michael Petrashevsky. In conscious imitation of the French Encyclopedists, Petrashevsky sought to gather a group that would lead the intellectual development of the Russian people. *The Pocket Dictionary* was
drawn up by Petrashevsky and Maikov to serve as its *Encyclopedia* and also
as a kind of ideological guidebook for combating German idealism. Young
writers and civil servants largely from the petty nobility gathered to discuss
the renovation of society as discussed by various French social thinkers.
Lamennais' *Words of a Believer* was read in a Church Slavonic translation
at one meeting, and friends of the group scheduled a dinner to honor the
birthday of Fourier on April 7, 1849.[9]

Though the various programs discussed by the Petrashevsky group
came to nothing, its determination to find a program of action was a
decided sign of change. Indeed, the *Petrashevtsy* developed the first network
of affiliated provincial circles to appear since the time of the Decembrists—
stretching thinly from Reval in Esthonia to Kazan on the middle Volga. A
recent returnee from the revolutionary world of Western Europe, Speshnev,
called himself a Communist rather than a socialist and urged the creation of
a "central committee" of nine to eleven with two of its members to be
associated with each affiliated group. A military officer from the East,
Chernosvitov, suggested that eastern Siberia be separate from Russia and
joined through revolution to a great Pacific empire that was to include
Mexico, California, and Alaska.[10] Others favored peaceful agitation designed to transform the peasant commune into the nucleus of a new socialist
society.

Some of the most imaginative minds of the late nineteenth century
served their intellectual apprenticeship in this stimulating atmosphere: the
biologist and ideologist of militant Pan-Slavism, Nicholas Danilevsky, the
satirist, Michael Saltykov-Shchedrin. Above all, in future importance,
stands Fedor Dostoevsky, a young writer interested in the idea of propaganda among the Old Believers and socialism built on the village commune
and artel forms of organization.[11] He was the one who read to the Petrashevsky group Belinsky's famous letter rebuking Gogol for his reconciliation
with official Russia. Belinsky's contrasting of Christ's example with that of
official Christendom was to find an echo not only in Dostoevsky's *Brothers*

Karamazov, but in much of the tortured thinking of Russian radicalism. The theme of Christ as a revolutionary social reformer of his day was, of course, a commonplace of early socialist thought, particularly in France. But Russian intellectuals also derived this idea from Russian traditions of religious dissent of which they were becoming increasingly aware through common persecution and imprisonment. Thus, the new "philosophy of society" which Maikov had called for tended from the first to be a kind of Christian socialism: a dedication to Christ without God—in opposition, as it were, to the God without Christ of Nicholaevan Russia.

Although the *Petrashevtsy* were not explicitly Christian (unlike the contemporaneous Ukrainian circle, the Brotherhood of Cyril and Methodius), they did claim to be rediscovering "the teaching of Christ in its original purity," which "had as its basic doctrine charity and its aim the *realization of freedom and the destruction of private ownership.*"[12] Following Saint-Simon and Comte, they spoke of a "new Christianity"; a new "normal" and "natural" society of social harmony that was evolving peacefully from history.

Essential to the idea of a "new Christianity" among Russian social thinkers was the need to avoid the pattern of social and political life that was developing in the bourgeois West. Thus, the *Petrashevtsy* were sceptical (as the Decembrists had never been) of both the institution of private property and the value of constitutions.

> Defenders of constitutions forget that the human character is contained not in personal property but in personality, and that in recognizing the political power of the rich over the poor, they are defending the most terrible despotism.[13]

The early social thinkers followed Belinsky in regarding socialism as "the idea of ideas" which "has absorbed history, religion, and philosophy."[14] Maikov used "socialism" as a synonym for his "philosophy of society" and specifically advocated the sharing of profits with all workers. The *Pocket Dictionary* guardedly uses the synonym "Owenism"; and Petrashevsky described Fourier as "my only God," attempting rather pitifully to set up a communal house for seven peasant families on his estate near Novgorod. The peasants burned down his model phalanstery; but the detailed Fourierist blueprint for harmonizing passions and solving all the conflicts of man with nature, himself, and his fellow men had a profound impact on the formation of Russian social thought. Fourier's plan was the most sensually appealing of all images of the coming golden age with its ideal of a free "play of passions." The phalansteries were, moreover, to be built around agricultural and craft manufacturing activities and thus seemed peculiarly suited to Russian conditions. However passing the infatuation with Fourier, the belief in a kind of Christianized socialism remained a constant of Russian social thought. Those like Speshnev who advocated more violent and conspiratorial methods in the forties were careful to call themselves "Communists," and Herzen went to some pains to distinguish ethical and aristocratic socialism from authoritarian and metaphysical communism, "the socialism of revenge."[15]

Along with "socialism," the social thinkers of the forties tended to believe in "democracy." The *Pocket Dictionary* defined it as the form of government where "each citizen takes part in the review and decisions of the affairs of the whole nation." It was destined to prevail everywhere, assuming different forms "in accordance with the stage of development of the moral forces in a people and the consciousness of true, rational freedom."[16] The political goal for Russia is never spelled out, but the *Pocket Dictionary* also includes entries under "opposition" and "national gatherings"; and some kind of a representative body permitting a free play of opposing political forces was clearly assumed.

"Democracy" in Russian social thought was, however, juxtaposed from the beginning to constitutionalism or liberalism as understood in the West. Democrats and liberals were in fact often contrasted, the former being portrayed as egalitarian socialists, the latter as English businessmen interested in purely formal liberties for the middle class. One article of the fifties insisted that Siberia was a more congenial land for true democrats than liberal England. A dictionary of foreign terms prepared in the early sixties in imitation of the Petrashevsky dictionary defines a liberal as

> a man loving freedom, usually a boyar [who enjoys] freedom to look through a window without doing anything, then to go for a walk, to the theatre, or a ball—that is what is known as a liberal man.[17]

Democracy was something to be found in remote places like America, Switzerland, or ancient Greece. It involved the weakening of man's authority over his fellow man and not the "new despotism" of a liberal "aristocracy of wealth" or "kingdom of property."

The new concern with social questions in the forties coincided with a dramatic increase in the size of the reading public. Of 130 periodical journals in Russia in 1851, 106 had been founded since 1836. The university population had increased by more than 50 per cent from the early forties to 1848, and the secondary-school population was increasing even faster. The annual volume of mail, which had risen only three million items in the first fifteen years of Nicholas' reign, increased by fifteen million from

1840 to 1845. In the following three years more than two million foreign publications were imported into Russia.[18]

At the same time, the center of intellectual gravity quietly moved back from Moscow to St. Petersburg in the 1840's. St. Petersburg had dominated Russian cultural life under Catherine until the movement of Novikov and Schwarz to Moscow and the final disillusioned years of her reign. Peter's city had also dominated the optimistic early years of Alexander's reign until the burning and reconstruction of Moscow made that city the focus of the nationalist revival. But the gradual triumph of the Westernizers (or the "Europeans" and "Cosmopolitans" as they were more often called during the "remarkable decade") was to a large extent a victory of St. Petersburg over Moscow, Chaadaev's "city of the dead." Belinsky's move from Moscow to St. Petersburg in 1839 was accompanied by the ostentatious declaration: "To Petersburg, to Petersburg, therein lies my salvation."[19] St. Petersburg was the largest and most commercially active of Russian cities. The journals to which Belinsky contributed there, *The Annals of the Fatherland* and *The Contemporary,* attained by 1847 an unprecedented number of subscriptions (4,000 and 3,000, respectively)[20] and were to become the leading vehicles for the populism of the seventies and the radical iconoclasm of the sixties, respectively. By 1851, more than half of the privately operated journals in Russia were in St. Petersburg, and more of the remaining private journals were printed in Westward-looking Riga and Tartu than in Moscow. Pogodin's *Muscovite* was the last effort of the romantic nationalists to found a major "thick journal" (that is, a journal with ideological pretensions supported by comprehensive bibliographical and critical sections) in Moscow. Despite (or perhaps because of) official support, it enjoyed nothing like the success of the new journals of social criticism in St. Petersburg. When it collapsed in 1856, most of its personnel moved to St. Petersburg, where the most important new anti-Westernizing journals were also to be published: ranging from Katkov's *Russian Herald* to Aksakov's *Day.*

The optimistic hope that a new social order might come into being in the West on the basis of advanced French social theories was dealt a profound blow by the failure of the revolutionary uprisings of 1848–9 in Western and Central Europe. Russia did not participate in this wave of revolutions and thus did not feel discredited by their failure. Indeed, the Russians were influenced by the impassioned writings of Herzen, who witnessed these events, and Bakunin, who participated in them, to conclude that the torch of leadership in the coming transformation of society had simply been passed from the defeated workers of the West to the slumbering peasants of the East.

The furious reaction of Nicholas I to the revolutionary events of 1848–9 further crystallized the sense of identification that Russian social thinkers came to feel with the frustrated Western hopes for social reform. The arrest of fifty-two *Petrashevtsy* (of whom twenty-three were convicted and exiled) and the dispatching of Russian troops to help put down the Kossuth rebellion in Hungary—both in late April of 1849—were followed by a crude effort to kill off the intellectual ferment of the "remarkable decade." No more than three hundred students were to be enrolled in a university at one time. Philosophy was banned from the curriculum, and all public mention of Belinsky's name was prohibited. Letters signed "all my love" were censored for the implied denial of affection to God and the Tsar, and the musical compositions of an astonished Rubinstein were confiscated as he returned from the West by border officials who feared that musical notes might be a secret revolutionary code.

Lacking as yet the "escape valve" of large-scale emigration to America that was draining off so many of the revolutionary intellectuals of Central Europe, the Russian intellectuals compensated themselves with the vague and appealing idea that Russia—or perhaps all of Slavdom—was in fact a kind of America in the making. Glorification of the communal peasant forms of organization among the Slavs was thus combined with the political ideal of a loose, democratic federalism. Bakunin proposed after the Slav Congress of 1848 in Prague the ideal of a revolutionary federation of Slavic peoples opposed to the "knouto-Germanic" rule of central authority. A friend of Herzen wrote a verse play praising the "socialist" William Penn, and spoke of America as the "natural ally" of a regenerated Russia.[21] Herzen believed that the Pacific Ocean would become the "Mediterranean Sea of the future," which Russia and America would jointly build.[22] Russian radicals followed with romantic fascination the half-understood developments in the distant, continent-wide civilization, whose westward advance resembled the Russian eastward advance in so many respects; and the semi-anarchistic criticism of all existing political authorities which was to become commonplace in Russian radical social thought was rarely extended to America.

Saltykov spoke retrospectively of the *Petrashevtsy* as a group which wanted "to read without knowing the alphabet, to walk without knowing how to stand upright."[23] Yet its strivings inside Russia and the prophetic reflections of Herzen and Bakunin outside reflect the turn in mid-century Russian thinking from philosophic to social thought: from Hamlet to Don Quixote, to use the terminology of Turgenev's famous essay of the late fifties. In order for the brooding Hamlet to become the chivalric Don Quixote—to leave his castle and set forth into the countryside—there had to be an ideal to serve. This ideal was the vision of a coming golden age in which there would be no more serfdom, bureaucracy, private property, or oppressive central authority. In its place men would adopt a new, ethical Christianity, build socialism on the model of the peasant commune, and live under a loose federal system vaguely like that of distant America. These themes were to be developed more explicitly and fully during the reign of Alexander II, and particularly in the populist movement; but all of them are already present in this initial turn to social thought in the late Nicholaevan period.

More than any other single event, the Crimean War opened Russia up for a more serious and widespread discussion of social issues. Indeed, of all the leitmotivs of modern Russian history, few are more striking than the unsettling influence of great wars on Russian thought and culture. Just as the schism in the Church was an outgrowth of the first northern war and Peter's reforms of the second, just as the agitation of the late years of Alexander I's reign and the Decembrist uprising grew out of the Napoleonic invasion, so did the great wars of the late nineteenth and the twentieth century have a profound and unsettling impact on Russian cultural development. The Turkish war of the mid-seventies was followed by the movements of revolutionary populism inside Russia; the Japanese war of 1904–5, by the Revolution of 1905; and the First World War, by the revolutions of 1917. War invariably put new strains on the outmoded social and economic system and at the same time exposed Russian thinkers to the methods and ideas of the outside world.

The Crimean War appears as a watershed in Russian history. Resounding defeat on Russian soil shattered the pretentious complacency of Nicholaevan Russia and left a legacy of national bitterness as well as an incentive for innovation and reform. The failure of Russia's traditional allies, Austria and Prussia, to come to her aid discredited these continental monarchies and forced Russia to look to the victorious liberal nations of the West, France and England, for techniques and ideas. Russia embarked hesitantly but irreversibly on the path toward industrialization and the redefinition of its social structure. No one realized better than the admirers of Nicholas' rule what defeat in the Crimea meant for Russia. Even before the war was irrevocably lost, Tiutchev saw in it "the birthpangs of a new world."[24] Pogodin summoned up the fire symbol with a strange mixture of apocalypticism and masochism that was to become characteristic of the new nationalism:

> Burn with your burning fire which the English have lighted in hell, burn . . . all our political relations with Europe! Let everything be burned with fire! Qui perd gagne![25]

Of all the material signs of change in post-Crimean Russia, none was more tangible and inescapable than the building of railroads. Nothing spread to the provinces so directly and dramatically the news that a new world was in the making as the forward movement of iron roads from the northwest corner of Russia into the deep interior of Russia in the sixties and seventies. The old, winding, dirt roads of Russia had been in 1812 (as they were still to be in 1941) a form of defense against heavily equipped invaders from the West and a source of picturesque appeal to the romantic imagination. Radishchev, for all his reforming zeal, had been charmed by the old road used on his famous trip from St. Petersburg to Moscow; and Gogol had made them symbols of the beauty and mystery of Old Russia.

The new railroads were to become symbols of modern Russia with its interrelated process of spiritual destruction and material progress. At first some Russian nationalists dreamed of integrating railroads harmoniously into Russian culture. Fedor Chizhov, the son of a priest and a close friend of Gogol, Ivanov, and Khomiakov, lectured in physics and mathematics at St. Petersburg and published in 1837, at the age of 26, an anthology giving a history and description of steam machines. He wrote that "the railroad is for me the slogan of our time," and his resolve to lead Russia into the railroad age was undampened by a long period of arrest for allegedly fostering discontent among the Slavs of the Hapsburg empire during the late years of Nicholas' reign. When railroad building began in earnest under Alexander II, Chizhov became consumed with a passionate desire to prevent foreigners from controlling the development of Russian railroads. He sought to harness this new form of power to spiritual ends and in 1860 formed a company which had as its first project the penitential building of a railroad from Moscow to the Monastery of the Holy Trinity and St. Sergius. But he was soon outstripped by his Anglo-French rivals and died disillusioned in 1877, to be buried near Gogol.[26] The sense of confusion and bitterness toward the railroads is reflected in the speech which the rector of the Riga Theological Seminary made in December, 1872, when asked to bless a new railroad bridge:

> Conflicting thoughts rise up in the soul when looking on a new route like this. What is it going to bring us? . . . Will it not be in part the expeditor of that would-be civilization, which under the guise of a false all-humanity and a common brotherhood of all . . . destroys . . . true humanity, true brotherhood?[27]

Not only traditionalists but Westernizing reformers found themselves brooding over these harbingers of a new iron age. Although Belinsky professed admiration for railroads and loved to watch them being built, the "reality" from which he rebelled assumed the shape of a steam engine: an "iron" monster with "jaws of steel" that belched forth "smoke and tongues of fire." The more moderate Westernizer, Prince Viazemsky, had written in 1847 in his "Review of Our Literature in the Decade since Pushkin":

> Railroads have already annihilated, and in time shall completely annihilate, all previous means of transportation. Other powers, other steams have already long ago put out the fire of the winged horse, whose weighted hoof has cut off the life-giving flow that has quenched the thirst of so many gracious and poetic generations.[28]

In the novels of the age of Alexander II, the earth-bound Pegasus of Russian realism found itself repeatedly crossing railroad tracks. It is in a railroad coach that Dostoevsky's Christ figure, Prince Myshkin, returns to Russia at the beginning of the *Idiot* and first meets the dark and venal figure with whom his fate becomes so strangely intermixed. Just as the peasants likened the railroads to the spinning of a giant spider web over the Russian land, so Dostoevsky's *Idiot* sees in them the fallen star Wormwood spoken of in the Book of Revelation (8:11). Turgenev's *Smoke* sees in the billows of the steam engines transporting Russians back and forth to the West an image of their confused state of mind and the obscurity surrounding Russia's future. The early leader and guiding force in the movement toward programmatic realism in music, Mily Balakirev, worked as a porter in a railroad station in St. Petersburg in the 1870's as his form of penitential "movement to the people." Tolstoy died in an obscure railroad station, and his great novel *Anna Karenina* begins and ends with a human being crushed under a train. The poet Nekrasov coined the term "King Hunger" (*Tsar Golod*) in a poem he wrote in 1865, "The Railroad."

At the same time, railroads became a symbol of light and hope to those who dreamed primarily of dramatic material transformations. The "Tidings of Zion" sect of the 1840's had seen the millennium in terms of a new civilization to be built along a vast Eurasian railway whose stations were to serve as giant distribution centers of material benefits. Il'in, the founder of the sect, died in Solovetsk in 1890, just a year before his vision began to be realized through the building of the Trans-Siberian railway, which was to become and remain the longest in the world. Lenin's arrival at the Finland station of St. Petersburg in a sealed train in April of 1917 was a key moment of *charisma* in the development of Bolshevism. Trotsky's impassioned forensic forays into the countryside in his famed armored train played an important and dramatic role in rallying armed support for the Revolution, and the vast and pretentiously adorned stations of the Moscow subway became symbols of the new civic religion of the Stalin era.

The first Russian railroad had been a short line from St. Petersburg to Tsarskoe Selo in 1835. Sixteen years later, Moscow was joined by rail with St. Petersburg, thanks largely to the American engineer George Washington Whistler (the husband of James Whistler's famous mother), who helped standardize in Russia a track gauge broader than the accepted European norm. By 1856, the first year of Alexander's reign, construction was under way on two new stations in St. Petersburg for lines leading to the west and east; construction accelerated rapidly under the new tsar. French Saint-Simonians, who financed much of this program, were fascinated by the parallel extension of railroads across America and Russia ("these two Hercules in their cradles"), considering the Russian expansion less impressive technically, but far more important historically in its linking of Europe with Asia. The Russian program was "an operation without parallel on our continent," destined to replace political divisions with a new "economic community" that will unite Eastern and Western Europe, and become "like Russia itself . . . half European, half Asiatic."[29]

For Russia, the new railroads brought the first massive intrusion of mechanical force into the timeless, vegetating world of rural Russia, and a great increase in social and thus class mobility throughout the empire. The first train ride of the "liberated" peasant represented the traumatic moment of departure from native surroundings—probably for a lifetime in the army or the urban work force. The ride was long and cold; and he was denied the use of toilet facilities during brief station stops and then beaten for "offensive conduct" if caught relieving himself on or near the tracks.

Railroads nevertheless became a symbol of progress to the new materialistic and egalitarian students of the sixties, who generally enjoyed more comfortable initial rides. One of the most gifted young technologists of this generation, Nicholas Kibalchich, came eagerly to St. Petersburg in order to study the engineering subjects that would equip him to participate in the railroad-building program, declaring:

> For Russia railroads are everything. This is the most necessary, most vital problem of our time. Covering Russia by sections with an interconnected network of railroads such as exists for example in England, we shall prosper and blossom forth [with] unheard-of progress . . . numberless factories.
> Civilization will go rapidly forward, and we—true, not all at once—will overtake the rich and advanced nations of Western Europe.[30]

Yet within a few years this apostle of progress and railroad building had become a full-time revolutionary, whose talents were completely absorbed in designing explosives to blow up the trains of Russian officials and—in 1881

—the body of Tsar Alexander II himself. This sense of lost opportunity was given added poignancy by the fact that he devoted his last days in prison prior to his hanging to designing a flying machine, which he felt was destined to supplant the railroad as a bearer of material progress. To understand why this gifted youth became an apostle and technician of assassination, one must turn to the disturbed reign of Alexander II and the psychology of the new revolutionary generation.

Under Alexander the dilemma of the reforming despot was lifted to the level of high irony as the virus of social thought began to infect wider circles of the population.

Like the reign of Alexander I, that of Alexander II lasted almost exactly a quarter of a century and can be roughly divided into two halves: a period of reform and one of reaction. The period of expectation and reform is generally referred to as "the sixties" even though it ran from 1856 to 1866. The period of reaction followed the first attempt on the life of the Tsar in 1866 and lasted until the successful assassination of 1881. Unlike Alexander I, Alexander II actually promulgated a series of profound reforms: freeing the serfs, instituting trial by jury, and creating zemstvos for limited local self-government. Yet Alexander II was far less popular. The most important cultural and intellectual development of the age was done outside of, and in opposition to, him and his court. Moreover, the period of most passionate rejection of official ideology occurred during the "sixties," the period of greatest liberalization; whereas the most optimistic affirmations of the alienated intellectuals occurred during the period of governmental reaction in the seventies.

Clearly the concerns of the thinking class were developing their own independent dynamic. To understand it one must consider the psychology of the self-conscious, "new men of the sixties." This iconoclastic student generation effected in a few short years one of the most thorough and far-reaching rejections of past tradition in the history of modern Europe. Out of this ferment Russia produced in the later years of Alexander's reign a number of disturbing new ideologies of which the most important and original was the populist movement. So central was this movement to the cultural accomplishments and aspirations of the period that it is more correct to speak of it as the populist age than the age of Alexander II.

This new generation had been brought up in the harsh last years of Nicholas' reign and had come to study in St. Petersburg amidst the great expectations for reform that prevailed under Alexander. They looked to the new regime with some of the optimism with which the reform-minded aristocracy a half century earlier had greeted the coming of Alexander I after the death of Paul. But the new reformers lacked the broad aristocratic perspectives of earlier reformers. They included "men of various ranks" (*raznochintsy*): children of minor officials, priests, professional men, and various minority groups. They included many provincial figures, who brought with them the pent-up frustrations and sectarian religious ideas of the less developed regions of rural Russia. The new student generation was, in short, a motley group with social aspirations as well as reforming ideas, arriving on the stage of history at a time when the old regime—and not merely the tsar himself—was in disrepute because of defeat in battle.

The new student generation included an unusually large number of former seminarians, who brought with them a certain passion for absolute answers to the "cursed questions" which hypnotized and seduced many of their uprooted and impressionable fellow students. The most important among these were the "two Saint Nicholases," Chernyshevsky and Dobroliubov, two former seminarians who dominated an editorial staff known as "the consistory" of the journal with which Belinsky had ended his career, *The Contemporary*.

Taking the materialism of Feuerbach and the rationalism of the English utilitarians as their starting point, these influential critics helped lead the young generation into a systematic rejection of all past tradition and of the entire idealistic framework within which the discussions of the aristocratic century had been conducted. They championed a new system of ethics based on "rational egoism" and a strict application of the utilitarian calculus of maximizing material pleasure. They imitated Belinsky's iconoclasm and glorified at the same time the art of the "Gogolian period" of Russian literature with its concerns for suffering humanity over that of the more composed "Pushkinians," for whom art did not basically serve a social purpose. They preached the equality of sexes, the sanctity of the natural sciences, and the need for recognizing that material self-interest lay behind every ideological pose. They—and even more, their imitators—dramatized their complete sense of separation from the past by adopting bizarre forms of dress, practicing free love, and attempting to live and work communally. Medallions of Rousseau were worn in place of Orthodox medals; the staccato cry "Man is a worm" (*chelovek-cherviak*) was shouted out at theology lectures; insulting remarks were made about Shakespeare, Raphael, Pushkin, and other artists especially revered by the older generation.

The war of the generations was dramatized by Turgenev in his famous novel *Father and Sons,* which he published in 1862 just after he, as a representative of the "fathers' " generation, had left *The Contemporary*, denouncing Chernyshevsky and Dobroliubov as "literary Robespierres" "trying to wipe from the face of the earth poetry, the fine arts, all aesthetic pleasures, and to impose in their place mere seminarian principles."[31] The hero of the novel is Bazarov, the leader of the "sons" and a young medical student who rejects all established aesthetic, moral, or religious ideals and spends his time dissecting frogs. His credo is that "two and two is four and everything else is rubbish." The term Turgenev used to describe Bazarov's philosophy was "nihilism," which accurately suggests the almost totally negative attitude of the "men of the sixties" to all traditional ideas and practices. Chernyshevsky's associates considered Bazarov a caricature, but Pisarev, another rising young iconoclast, hailed Bazarov as a worthy model for the "new men" of the sixties. When Dobroliubov died in 1861 and Chernyshevsky was arrested the following year, Pisarev became the leading apostle of nihilistic materialism and remained so until 1868, when he—like Dobroliubov and so many others—went to an early death.

The importance of this spasm of negation would be hard to over-emphasize. Although it was almost entirely confined to the young generation, it affected precisely those talented figures who were to provide the leadership in almost every field of cultural endeavor for the remainder of the century. Pisarev was correct in saying that "if Bazarovism is a malady, it is the malady of our time."[32] No one was ever quite the same again, because the young generation had deliberately broken with the broader humanistic culture of the aristocracy as well as the official Orthodox culture of the tsarist regime. The first and perhaps most important result of the iconoclastic revolution was the opening of a decisive split between the new nihilists and the original moderate Westernizers of the forties. Chernyshevsky took the lead in breaking with Herzen for his friendliness with liberals like Kavelin and Chicherin and his "naive" hope for "reform from above" through Alexander II. "Let your 'bell' sound not for prayer but for the charge," he wrote shortly after breaking with Herzen in 1859.[33] The lesson to be learned from the revolution of 1848 was that radicals must avoid ceding leadership of revolutionary movements to timid liberals. The imperfect and hesitant nature of the Alexandrian reforms—above all their purely formal emancipation of the peasantry, whose actual lot may in fact have worsened—seemed a perfect illustration to the extremist generation of what to expect from liberal reformers.

In addition to encouraging political extremism, the nihilism of the sixties virtually promoted to the level of a new orthodoxy the new analytic and realistic approach in science and literature. Prose replaced poetry as the main vehicle of literary expression (a change which Petrashevsky had called indispensable for human progress at the last meeting of his ill-fated circle in 1849). There was a sudden passion for meticulously realistic presentations of scenes and problems from everyday life. A decade of strident insistence on the social responsibility of the artist—from Chernyshevsky's

Aesthetic Relations of Art to Reality in 1855 to Pisarev's *Destruction of Aesthetics* in 1865—resulted in the establishment of a kind of "censorship of the left" alongside that of the tsarist regime. Subtly but effectively the realistic story and the ideological novel replaced the poems and plays of the aristocratic century as the major literary milieu of the new culture in St. Petersburg. Buckle's *History of Civilization in England,* with its attempts to explain cultures by climate, geography, and diet, was extraordinarily popular; and the beginnings of a purely materialist Russian school of physiology can be traced to the publication in 1863 of Ivan Sechenov's *Reflexes of the Brain.* Following the lead of Claude Bernard (whose detailed descriptive study of the human heart was written while Sechenov was studying under him in Paris), Sechenov attempted to make a purely physiological study of the brain. He provided the basis for the famed Pavlovian theory of conditioned reflexes with his contention that all movements traditionally described as voluntary in physiology are in fact material reflexes in the strictest sense of the word.[34]

But perhaps the most fateful result of the sixties was the emergence of the intelligentsia as a self-conscious and distinct social group and its creation of the new doctrine of populism (*narodnichestvo*). The idea that a half-hidden higher intelligence rules the world was, as we have seen, a commonplace of higher order Masonry; and Schwarz had actually introduced various forms of the Latin *intelligentia* and *intellectus* into the Russian language in this exalted sense in the early 1780's. The *Pocket Dictionary* of the *Petrashevtsy* added the word "intellectual" (*intellektual'ny*) to the Russian vocabulary, suggesting that it had the all-embracing meaning of the Russian word for "spiritual" (*dukhovny*). This lofty conception of the ruling force of intelligence and the intellect was given a distinctly historical cast by Pisarev in his insistence that "the moving force of history is intelligentsia, the path of history is marked out by the level of theoretical development of intelligentsia."[35]

But the striking new feature about the use of the term "intelligentsia" in the sixties is that it meant not just "intelligence" but also a specific group of people. This group was essentially those who felt a certain sense of unity-through-alienation because of their participation in the iconoclasm of the sixties. The Russian term *intelligent* (pronounced with a hard "g," accented on the last syllable, and conceived as a member of this *intelligentsiia*) was used by the novelist Boborykin to describe his own sense of estrangement from the petty concerns of provincial life after returning to Nizhny Novgorod from Tartu, the freest university in the Russian empire in the 1850's. One of the reasons for the alienation of the intelligentsia from the ordinary folk of Russia was revealed in the verb that was derived from the name of this prolific writer: *boborykat'* ("to talk endlessly"). But the ever-prophetic Herzen provided the best characterization of both the alienation and the eventual fate of the intelligentsia in the pages of the *Bell* in July, 1864. Having been long since rejected by the young generation, Herzen characterizes them as

> . . . non-people (*ne-narod*) . . . intelligentsia . . . democratic lords (*shliakhta*), commanders, and teachers . . . you bear nothing. . . . You have not yet thought about what Holstein-Arakcheev, Petersburg-Tsarist democracy means, soon you will feel that it means a red cap on a Petrine cudgel. You shall be destroyed in the abyss . . . and upon your grave . . . there will look on, facing each other: from above a bodyguard the Emperor dressed in all his powers and all the self-willed arrogance in the world, and from below the boiling, ferocious ocean of the people in which you shall vanish without a trace.[36]

Thus the intelligentsia are the leaders of the coming democracy who are destined to be devoured by it. They are alienated both from the ordinary people and from all the "self-willed" political authorities of the present, transitory world of repression.

The intelligentsia are not self-willed because they are dedicated men, as Shelgunov—a leading participant in the ferment of the sixties—stresses in his almost simultaneous article of May, 1864.

> The intelligentsia of the XVIII century was purely bourgeois. . . . Only the intelligentsia of the XIX century, schooled in generalization, has posed as the aim of all its efforts the happiness of all   equality.[37]

That which deepened and intensified the sense of common dedication within this alienated intelligentsia was its growing belief that progress was an inevitable historical law. Following Pisarev's articles in 1865 on "The Historical Ideas of Auguste Comte" and several serialized works of the late sixties, such as Mikhailovsky's "What is Progress?" and Lavrov's *Historical Letters,* the nascent intelligentsia can be said to have found new encouragement and unity in the broad vision of progress presented by Auguste Comte. Comte's idea that all of human activity moved from theology through metaphysics to a positive or scientific stage encouraged them to believe that all social problems would soon be resolved by the last and most promising of the positive sciences—the science of society. Thus, the appeal which Comte had addressed in vain to Nicholas I to overleap the West by adopting his new "religion of humanity" elicited, in effect, a belated response a decade later from the alienated intelligentsia. They were excited by his appeal for a new aristocracy of talent rather than privilege, which would hasten the inevitable transformation of society by pledging themselves to the service of humanity and a socialism that was "practical" and "positive" rather than "metaphysical" and revolutionary.

Newly infused with historical optimism, the intelligentsia required a further sense of identity through its common revulsion at the repressive policies that predominated in the late years of Alexander's reign. They felt obliged to carry on the tradition of uncompromising protest and striving for social betterment that had been championed by the imprisoned Chernyshevsky; to carry on the critical traditions of the dead Dobroliubov and Pisarev and the journalistic traditions of the newly abolished *Sovremennik*. Ironically enough, the introduction of trial by jury in no way pacified the intelligentsia's thirst for justice. On the contrary, it helped fortify their sense of unity-in-martyrdom by providing them with ample opportunities for self-defense through impassioned oration.

Thus, in the late sixties, the iconoclasts became the *intelligents*. The radicals had converted their youthful attachment to science into an optimistic theory of history and had developed a strong sense of identity with those like Chernyshevsky who had suffered for their beliefs. They viewed themselves as a dedicated elite of *intelligentnye, kul'turnye, tsivilizovannye*, though they were not necessarily "intelligent," "cultured," or even "civilized" in the usual Western sense of these terms. They thought of themselves as practical rather than "superfluous" people: students of science and servants of history. However much they debated over what the scientific "formula for progress" might be and what the coming "third age" of humanity might bring, they all viewed themselves as members of a common group which Pisarev and Shelgunov called the "thinking proletariat," Lavrov "critically thinking personalities," and others "cultural pioneers."

In the summer of 1868, the group can be said to have been formally baptized as "the Russian intelligentsia." For at that time Mikhailovsky entitled his critical column for the new "thick journal," *The Contemporary Review*, "Letters on the Russian Intelligentsia." This column was the central one in a journal designed to perpetuate the traditions of Chernyshevsky and Dobroliubov (its title being deliberately chosen for its resemblance to that of their *Contemporary*). Although this journal did not last long, Mikhailovsky soon joined the revived *Annals of the Fatherland*, the old journal of Maikov and Belinsky in the forties, which now became the medium for propagating the belief that Russian social thought was providing a new elite who were the elect of history and the builders of a new world. From 1867 to 1870, the *Annals* increased its circulation from 2,000 to 8,000—the largest monthly circulation attained up to that time by any radical journal. Mikhailovsky, as chief critic of the journal, kept a bust of Belinsky over his writing desk. Other critics on it were Eliseev, a former associate of Chernyshevsky, and Skabichevsky, a former leader of the Sunday-school movement; and the belles-lettres department was dominated by the great satirist and former *Petrashevets,* Saltykov, and the "civic poet" and former editor of *The Contemporary,* Nekrasov. The *Annals* became "the bible of the Russian intelligentsia," not only because of its self-conscious pose as heir to the radical traditions of Russian social thought, but also because of its propagation of the new optimistic theory of history. Another former associate of Chernyshevsky pointed independently in the summer of 1868 to the importance of the optimistic historical faith for the nascent intelligentsia:

> the union of the heights and depths, of intelligentsia with the people is not an empty dream. This union is an inevitable historical law. It is the path of our progress. . . .[38]

Intelligence must flow into people, just as the intelligentsia must go out among the people. This was the imperative that Herzen had first presented the young generation on the pages of the *Bell* late in 1861, when the University of St. Petersburg was closed because of student riots:

> Whither should you go, youth from whom science has been taken away? . . . Listen—from all corners of the vast fatherland: from the Don and Urals, from the Volga and Dnieper the groans are increasing, the murmur is rising—It is the gathering roar of an ocean wave. . . . Into the people, to the people (*v narod! k narodu*)—there is your destination, banished men of science. . . .[39]

Herzen's plea had already been answered to a considerable extent by the extraordinary Sunday-school movement which flourished in Russia between 1859–62 and may properly be described as the first of the large-scale penitential efforts of the urban intellectuals to take the fruits of learning to the ordinary people. P. Pavlov, the professor of Russian history at Kiev, was the pioneer of this movement to provide free part-time instruction for the indigent.[40] He was but one of a large number of provincial historians to build an aura of heroic dignity about Russian popular institutions and stimulate the desire of urban intellectuals to rediscover the richness and spontaneity of rural Russia. A. Shchapov and G. Eliseev, two of the most influential populist journalists of the seventies, both began their careers as students of the *raskol* at the Kazan theological seminary. Kostomarov, a veteran of Ukrainian radical activities and professor of Russian history at St. Petersburg, lent a new glamor to the tradition of peasant revolution and was perhaps the most popular of all lecturers among the radical new men of the sixties. Ivan Pryzhov wrote a *History of Taverns,* contending that the true communal feelings and revolutionary spirit of the simple people can only be appreciated in their taverns. Herzen paid great attention to the Old Believers and printed up a special supplement for them. Even the rationalistic and utilitarian-minded Chernyshevsky began his journalistic career with an article in praise of the "fools for Christ's sake" and ended it with a defense of the Old Believers. This extraordinary interest in the peculiarities of Russian rural life—and particularly in the unique traditions of popular religious dissent—helped convince the urban intellectuals that Russia had a special destiny to fulfill and untapped popular resources for realizing it.

Populism was a pure creation of intellectuals, who had become convinced by the late sixties that history was on their side whatever the Tsar and his ministers did or said; and that a direct reconstitution of society was morally necessary, logically implied by the progress of science, and uniquely possible among the Russian people. Following social themes that had been developing in Russia since the 1840's, the populists believed that a special path for Russian social development lay in extending the principles of profit sharing and communal endeavor still prevailing in the peasant commune. This peaceful transformation of society could be accomplished only by dedicated servants of humanity who had no desire to aggrandize wealth in the English manner or power in the German fashion. They saw little hope in working through political media for reform, since European politics was dominated by the meaningless parliaments and constitutions of Anglo-French liberalism or the brutally centralizing tendencies of German militarism. They vaguely hoped for some kind of loose, decentralized federation on the American pattern—the Ukrainian populist group actually calling themselves "the Americans." But their basic conviction was that of Shelgunov's original *Proclamation to the Young Generation* of 1861 that "we not only can, but we must . . . arrive at some new order unknown even to America."[41]

The major source of foreign inspiration was French socialist thought. Louis Blanc, who had attempted to set up actual socialist experiments among the people of Paris in the belief that a new age of brotherhood was dawning, replaced the "purely theoretical" Fourier and Owen as the socialist saint most revered by the populists. But the principal prophet of the new order for the populists was the passionate figure of Pierre-Joseph Proudhon, who dominated French socialist thought from the failure of the revolution of 1848 until his death in 1865. Proudhon introduced an element of passionate egalitarianism and heroic, semi-anarchistic opposition to political authority which made him a particularly sympathetic figure for survivors of the iconoclastic revolution in Russia. Proudhon was, like Rousseau, a French provincial who brought with him to Paris a certain plebeian indignation against aristocratic elites and centralized authority. He opposed a proposed constitution during the revolution of 1848, "not because it is bad, but because it is a constitution"; flatly labeled private property "theft"; and in his famous journals *The People, The Representative of the People,* and *The Voice of the People,* he developed a kind of mystical belief in "the people" as a mighty force capable of rejuvenating Europe.

All of this appealed to the alienated intellectuals of the Alexandrian era, who were also provincial outsiders in many cases with an iconoclastic attitude toward authority, an incisive and disjointed polemic style, and an anguished desire to establish or re-establish links with "the people." Proudhon viewed himself, moreover, as a kind of Christian socialist, working intermittently all his adult life on a never-completed study of Christ as a social reformer and frequently introducing apocalyptical language—all tending to increase his appeal to the Russians, who tended to view socialism as an outgrowth of suppressed traditions within heretical Christianity. Both of the prophetic forerunners of the populist movement, Herzen and Bakunin, were friends and admirers of Proudhon, fellow provincials, so to speak, who had come to Paris, the Mecca of revolution in the late forties. They accepted Proudhon's explanation that the debacle of 1848-9 resulted from the failure of the revolutionaries to link themselves unreservedly with the elemental power of the people. They, and Russian radical thought generally, had continued to hope that socialist transformation might yet be accomplished on French soil through a working-class movement led by Proudhon; but they gradually began to place their hopes for change in the unspoiled Russian people.

This transfer of hopes from West to East became complete in 1871 after Bismarck's Germany defeated France in the Franco-Prussian War and "a republic without ideals" came into being over the ruins of the Paris Commune. France was now a center of fashions rather than "the lighthouse of the world"; it had become, in the title of Mikhailovsky's famous essay of October, 1871, the land of "Darwinism and the Operettas of Offenbach." All of Europe is now ruled by jungle laws of the survival of the fittest and a culture whose highest symbol is the cancan; and Mikhailovsky pointedly ends his piece with the phrase *novus rerum mihi nascitur ordo.*

The new order of things as envisaged by the main line of populist thought as it developed from Herzen and Chernyshevsky through to Lavrov, Mikhailovsky, and Shelgunov was a unique Russian variant of the general European phenomenon of moralistic, "utopian" socialism. The populists believed in "subjective socialism" to be brought about by moral ideals rather than "objective socialism" that is created irrespective of human wishes by economic forces. Friends of the populist movement abroad were closer to the French than the German tradition of socialism. Thus, Marx's theories about revolutionary organization and economic determinism gained almost no support among Russians during the populist era, though the moral outrage of his denunciation of capitalism was warmly applauded.

Populist socialism did not involve just a reconstitution of society on the communal model of the peasant *obshchina,* but a creative development of the *obshchina* form itself in order to guarantee the full development of the human personality. Herzen stressed the need for assuring individual rights within the new socialist society, Chernyshevsky the need for maintaining individual incentives, and Mikhailovsky the need for preventing dehumanizing overspecialization. For all of them the full development of human personality was, in Belinsky's words, "more important than the fate of the whole world." Mikhailovsky described all of history as an endless "struggle for individuality" and described the coming golden age as one of "subjective anthropocentrism." Nicholas Chaikovsky, whose circle in St. Petersburg was the real center of the populist movement, thought that he was founding a "religion of humanity" and included in his group several members of a "God-manhood sect" which taught that each individual was literally destined to become a god.[42]

The populists professed to accept industrial development but wished to preserve the more moral *type* of society found in the commune while moving to the higher *stage* of civilization which scientific progress was bringing into being. Indeed, the first of the mass "movements to the people" in 1871–3 was directed by the *Chaikovtsy* at the urban workers of St. Petersburg, who were thought to hold the key to the future and be particularly capable of "mental and moral development." This movement to the people appealed to intellectuals in other cities, who formed groups loosely affiliated with the *Chaikovtsy* in many major cities of the empire. This initial effort to educate urban workers and evangelize them with the new belief in the inevitability of progress involved many of the Russian radicals who were to become well known in the West through prolific later writings in exile: Peter Kropotkin and Serge Kravchinsky (Stepniak). Disillusioned with the lack of response to their teachings among the working class, the *Chaikovtsy* concluded that they must go instead to the peasantry, which still dominated the thinking of the Russian masses. Accordingly, they suddenly found themselves caught up in the "mad summer" of 1874, one of the most fantastic and unprecedented social movements of the entire nineteenth century.

Suddenly, without any central leadership or direction, more than two thousand students and a number of older people and aristocrats were swept away by a spirit of self-renunciation. In almost every province of European Russia, young intellectuals dressed as peasants and set out from the cities to live among them, join in their daily life, and bring to them the good news that a new age was dawning. Rich landowners gave away their possessions or agreed to let students use their estates for social propaganda and experiment; agnostic Jews had themselves baptised as Orthodox in order to be more at one with the peasantry; women joined in the exodus in order to share equally in the hopes and suffering.[43]

The regime was perplexed and terrified by this "movement to the people," arresting 770 and molesting many more in its effort to crush the movement. This harsh repression of a non-violent movement only pushed populism into more violent and extreme paths. Mikhailovsky, the leading popularizer of evolutionary populism in the seventies, always described populism as a middle way for Russia between the Scylla of reaction and the Charybdis of revolution. It was the fate of populism in the late seventies to be first dashed against the rock to the right and then sucked into the whirlpool to the left. To understand the fate of populism and the climactic events of the late seventies and early eighties, one must consider the peculiar nature of the reactionary and revolutionary traditions that had concurrently developed in Russia.

The Scylla of reaction was expressed not so much in the ruthless arrests of late 1874 as in the subsequent war with Turkey. This war was the direct result of the new imperialistic doctrine of messianic Pan-Slavism. It was a large-scale deliberate war of aggrandizement, brutally fought against a brutal foe by a citizen's army that Russia had assembled through the introduction of a more systematic and universal conscription in 1874. This war gave Russian society and Russian social thought a feeling for violence and ideological fanaticism that made any return to the optimistic, evolutionary ideals of early populism extraordinarily difficult.

Reactionary Pan-Slavism began in the second half of Alexander's reign to replace in many minds official nationality as the ideology of tsarist Russia. Faced with a many-sided ideological assault in the course of the sixties, the tsarist regime had turned from its initial policy of pragmatic liberal concessions to a new militant nationalism. Great Russian chauvinism first proved its worth as an antidote to revolutionary enthusiasm during the Polish uprising of 1863. The semi-official yellow press skillfully sought to discredit the revolutionaries as traitors because of their sympathy with the Poles and to glorify a series of Russian military leaders as popular folk heroes. A former radical, Michael Katkov, championed this approach in his new newspaper, *Moscow News,* which he proudly designated "the organ of a party which may be called Russian, ultra-Russian, exclusively Russian."[44]

To compete in the idealistic atmosphere of the sixties, however, a party bidding for public favor had to offer some noble, altruistic goal to the public. Thus, the "exclusively Russian party" of Katkov resurrected the old romantic ideal of Slavic union and presented it to the Russian public as a kind of latter-day crusade against both the "Romano-German" West and the heathen Turks.

The center of this new reactionary Pan-Slavism was Moscow, in which the Jacobin extremists of the left were concurrently gathering strength in the late sixties. The decisive event in the emergence of reactionary Pan-Slavism was the Moscow Slavic Congress of 1867, which was largely supported by the city of Moscow and loudly hailed by Aksakov's journal *Moscow* as well as Katkov's *Moscow News*. The only previous congress of Slavs had taken place in Prague in 1848, with the only Russian representatives being two outcasts: the revolutionary Bakunin and an Old Believer bishop. But the new congress was given lavish support and sponsorship by official Russia. It became, in effect, the first of those now-familiar "cultural" festivals whose main practical result is to advance Russian political objectives. The writing that most perfectly expressed the views of reactionary Pan-Slavs in Russia was a hitherto unpublished treatise by an obscure Slovakian called *Slavdom and the World of the Future,* which was suddenly vaulted to prominence in the closing days of the congress. It called for the unification of the Slavs under Russian leadership, with Moscow to be the capital, Russian to be the language, and Orthodoxy to be the religion.[45] The idea of a violent, irreconcilable conflict between the Slavic and the Romano-German worlds was given a kind of pseudo-scientific formulation by a biologist and former *Petrashevets,* Nicholas Danilevsky, in his *Russia and Europe,* published serially in 1868, and as a book in 1871.

Pan-Slavism became a kind of imperialist ideology through such works as the shorter and more blunt memorandum of General Rostislav Fadeev, *Opinion on the Eastern Question,* which was also published serially in the late sixties and then as a book in 1870. During the Russo-Turkish War of 1877-8, this frankly expansionist ideology proved strikingly effective in rallying mass support for a successful war effort. This autocratic, imperialistic Pan-Slavism bore little resemblance to the mellow and idealistic Slavophilism of an earlier generation, or even to the earlier Pan-Slav proclamations of men like Aksakov and Bakunin, who had linked Pan-Slavism with the federative principle and with support for the Polish efforts to break loose from the Tsarist yoke.

It was a brutal, but at the same time popular, doctrine. It provided a simple, dramatic picture of the world that glorified tsarist autocracy and channeled off domestic feuds and resentments into hatred of foreigners. It played on classic Russian prejudices by denouncing not only the Turks and Germans but also the Poles as Western traitors and the Hungarians as "Asian interlopers" in Eastern Europe.

Pan-Slavism can be described as Moscow's prophetic alternative to the prophetic, St. Petersburg–based doctrine of populism. Like populism, Pan-Slavism challenged the earlier tendency of Russian intellectuals to flee to Berlin, Paris, or Rome in search of inspiration, holding out the promise of a new destiny and deliverance in the East. But, whereas the populists pointed prophetically to the Russian countryside, the Pan-Slavs harked back to the old imperial dream of reconquering Constantinople. Like the populists, the Pan-Slavs offered a theory of history based on the application of allegedly scientific principles to social problems; but they appealed to the Darwinistic principle of inevitable struggle and survival of the fittest, which the populists steadfastly refused to recognize as scientifically applicable to humanity. The violent repression of the movement to the people and the violence and fanaticism of the Turkish war seems to have subtly convinced many radicals that perhaps the Darwinistic image was right. In their desire to swerve away from the Scylla of reaction in the post-war years, they found themselves increasingly drawn into the Charybdis of Jacobin revolution, the opposite extremism of the Alexandrian period. The whirlpool of professional revolutionary activity had frequently beckoned to confused participants in the populist movement. But prior to the formation of a nationwide, populist revolutionary organization (the second organization to bear the title "Land and Liberty") late in 1878 and the more explicitly terrorist People's Will organization that supplanted it the following year, populism had been identified principally with evolutionary rather than revolutionary approaches.

The revolutionary Jacobinism of the left was, like the reactionary Pan-Slavism of the right, a Muscovite outgrowth of the restless iconoclasm of the sixties. The first call for secret revolutionary organization and direct action was contained in the pamphlet "Young Russia," published in 1862 by a nineteen-year-old mathematics student at Moscow University, P. Zaichnevsky. He was one of a group of about twenty Moscow students who called themselves "The Society of Communists" and devoted themselves almost entirely to the reading and publishing of Western revolutionary literature. The most thoroughgoing program for nationwide revolutionary organization was provided, curiously enough, by Herzen's old friend and collaborator, Nicholas Ogarev, in connection with the efforts to make a nationwide movement out of the Land and Liberty group of the early sixties. The first Land and Liberty group was based in St. Petersburg and accommodated a wide range of radical views; but Ogarev sought to transform it into a conspiratorial revolutionary organization run by a secret central committee with regional organization, veiled front groups as a mask for revolutionary organization, and a publication center abroad to provide ideological support and theoretical direction.[46] The first Land and Liberty group went out of existence in 1863 and never seems to have adopted a fully revolutionary program or organization. The next stage in the development of a professional revolutionary tradition occurred once more in Moscow, with the formation of two new extremist circles in 1865, those of N. Ishutin and N. Nefedov, respectively. The first group, known as "The Organization," commissioned a young student, Dmitry Karakozov, to attempt an assassination of Tsar Alexander II the following year, thus launching the tradition of active revolutionary terrorism. It also formed a secret circle within the revolutionary group known as Hell (*Ad*) to combat police provocateurs and conduct terrorist activities. Members of the Hell group were expected to give up all family ties, assume new names, and be prepared to sacrifice their lives. The counter-revolutionary white terror that followed the Karakozov attempt drove the leading protégé of N. Nefedov, young Sergius Nechaev, to further extremes in outlining a course for professional revolutionaries.

Like the Ishutin group, Nechaev had visions of founding a professional revolutionary cadre that was to be linked with a vast, Europe-wide conspiratorial organization. He journeyed abroad, received a measure of approval from a fascinated Bakunin and Ogarev, and returned to Moscow in 1869 to put his fantastic plans into practice. He brought with him as a guide for his revolutionary organization the famous *Revolutionary Catechism,* with its doctrine of a revolutionary association (*tovarishchestvo*) that has "not just in words, but in deed, broken every tie with the civil order, with the educated world and all laws, conventions . . . ethics."[47] The professional revolutionary was to be an ascetic, totally dedicated to overthrowing the civil order through a coldly rational campaign of terror, blackmail, manipulation, and deception. To implement his program Nechaev set up a series of "revolutionary fives," each secret from the other and connected only by a hierarchy that exercised absolute discipline over all. Nechaev evolved the extraordinary technique of seeking to guarantee obedience by deliberately involving his fellow revolutionaries in a common crime. In a famous incident on November 21, 1869, he and the three other members of a Moscow "five" killed a young student and fellow conspirator because of incriminating information that Nechaev told them he had received from a (nonexistent) "central committee." The Nechaev affair became a *cause célèbre* that did not leave the public eye for nearly five years. It took the Tsarist government two years to catch him and much of 1871 to try him. The courtroom revelations about his activities and the literary representation given them in Dostoevsky's *The Possessed* precipitated a vigorous journalistic discussion that lasted throughout the early seventies.

The populists who dominated this period deliberately sought to represent themselves as an alternative to the Nechaevism which they considered a "monstrosity," a survival of the bygone "eccentric" or "metaphysical" stage of history. They believed in Comte's and Chaikovsky's "religion of humanity" rather than Nechaev's religion of revolution.

With, however, the general turn to violence and the triumph of reactionary Pan-Slavism, populists were no longer able to scoff at the cynical contention of Nechaev that "to love the people means to lead it by grapeshot."[48] In order to sustain its all-important vision of a dramatic social transformation in Russia, the populists were forced to consider the long-neglected question of a political alternative to autocracy. The lack of any parliamentary or legal opposition bodies through which to work and the enduring superstition of "idea-less" liberal reformers left them no anchor to prevent drifting into the whirlpool of revolution.

The siren song which lured them was that of the last great theorist of Russian Jacobinism, Peter Tkachev. He was a veteran of almost every important conspiratorial organization of the sixties, a confirmed materialist and egalitarian who had led the war of the sons against the fathers by helping write "Young Russia" and urging at one point that mercy killing be administered to everyone over the age of twenty-five.

True to the tradition of professional revolutionaries, Tkachev was deeply opposed to the vagueness and optimism of the populist tradition; but unlike previous theoreticians of revolutionary organization, he saw in the intelligentsia that had created populism the logical social grouping from which to recruit revolutionary leadership. In a correspondence with Engels in 1874–5, he foresaw the emergence of an *"intelligentnaia* revolutionary party" in Russia. In his Russian-language journal *Nabat* (*The Alarm Bell*) published from 1875–81 and aimed only at the intelligent, elite audience, he urged the rootless intellectuals of Russia to form a disciplined, military revolutionary organization out of their own ranks. He opposed relying on the populist illusion of peasant support or waiting for the emergence of an urban proletariat to provide material for a Marxist type of revolution. The important thing was to develop a militant organization capable of overthrowing the existing regime through revolution. The *nabat* provided the signal to rally for emergency combat in Old Russia: and that was precisely what Tkachev intended that his journal should provide for Young Russia.

Tkachev did not exercise major influence on either the ideology or the tactics which the second Land and Liberty and the People's Will adopted. These organizations were true to their populist heritage in continuing to believe in the possibilities of support from peasants, workers, sectarians, and other groups; in being reluctant revolutionaries and poor organizers whose principal technique of political struggle was random assassination; and in seeking to represent themselves as expressions of "the people's will." Nevertheless, the People's Will organization represents a fulfillment of (if not a response to) Tkachev's basic idea that Russia could and should produce out of its uprooted intellectual community a revolutionary organization with the conscious political objective of overthrowing tsarism.

With the formation of the People's Will organization in the summer of 1879, revolutionary extremism obtained a dramatic program and a nationwide organization to parallel the program and organization that reactionary extremism had gained earlier through the Pan-Slav movement. Just as Muscovite Pan-Slavism had become the policy of the once-liberal government in St. Petersburg, so Muscovite Jacobinism had become the policy of the once-moderate populist counter-government in St. Petersburg. Peaceful, reformatorial optimism in both the government and the anti-government camps had given way to extremism. Moderate populists like Mikhailovsky and Shelgunov were carried along by the new extremist enthusiasm of the left just as moderate liberals had been by the Pan-Slav enthusiasms of the right. The terrorist campaigns and clandestine meetings and proclamations of the Executive Committee of the People's Will provided the anti-government forces with a form of conflict as colorful and dramatic as the Turkish war. The People's Will organization was a prophetic anticipation of and (to a greater extent than is generally realized) model for the next nationwide organization of professional revolutionaries seeking to overthrow tsardom, Lenin's Bolshevik Party. At the same time, populist journalists were institutionalizing certain practices that anticipated those of Lenin: ritual denunciations of "enemies of the people," "careerism," and "lack of ideology" (*bezideinost'*), and a rigid editorial and critical insistence that art must have a realistic style and a clear social message.

But the People's Will was still far more deeply rooted in the romantic, compassionate thought-world of populism than in the calculating Jacobinism of Tkachev and Lenin. As the Tsar lay dying by a canal in St. Petersburg on March 1, 1881, his legs shattered by a terrorist's bomb, another terrorist forfeited his chance for escape by rushing in to prop up Alexander's head with his own packaged bomb. The terrorists who were brought to trial were true to the populist courtroom tradition of confessing guilt but seeking to vindicate the ideals for which they had acted. Zheliabov insisted that "the essence of the teachings of Jesus Christ . . . was my primary moral incentive" and was at pains to point out how reluctant all the populists were to turn to terror and violence.[49] The executive committee of the People's Will addressed its first action after the assassination, not to its own revolutionary affiliates or any potentially revolutionary segment of the populace, but to the new Tsar himself, urging him to summon a national assembly to initiate reforms and end the "sad necessity" of bloodshed.

The acceleration of the terrorist campaign which climaxed in the assassination of Alexander presents, however, one last piece of high irony. For this turn to extremism among the populists occurred at precisely the time that Alexander had begun to turn away from extremism. Serious discussions of social and political reform were once more being conducted among the Tsar's inner circle of advisers. On March 1, the very day of his assassination, Alexander had tentatively approved a year-old project to include part of the intelligentsia and bourgeoisie in the machinery of government. The renewed interest and encouragement which the Tsar had shown the zemstvo movement (in an effort to enlist its support in combating terrorism) had led to a rapid increase in the vitality and political ambitions of this nationwide chain of provincial administrative groups. Journalistic friends of populism, such as Mikhailovsky in St. Petersburg and Zaitsev and Sokolov in Geneva, were actively working to encourage some kind of populist-liberal rapprochement. The objective possibilities for a broadly based moderate reform movement seem to have been bright in retrospect. Populism and liberalism were both St. Petersburg–based movements inherently opposed to extremism.

But the People's Will knew nothing about the secret constitutional project that the Tsar had approved; and the Tsar's liberal advisers had no knowledge of the more moderate trends that were still present within the populist movement. The differences between a populist *intelligent* and a pragmatic liberal were in many ways even deeper than those between populism and either of the Moscow-based extremist ideologies. Revolutionary Jacobinism, evolutionary populism, and reactionary Pan-Slav imperialism all developed out of the iconoclastic revolution. Each position contended that dramatic changes were about to take place in human history; and it was easier for proponents of one such ideology to drift into another than to leave ideology altogether for a more mundane liberal approach. Once begun, the search for truth could not be abandoned for the pursuit of pleasure or the consolation of half-truths. Fragmentary ideas of aristocratic intellectuals were becoming programs for action and articles of faith in the hands of the new intelligentsia. Whatever it might have been, the intelligentsia was to become what Katkov feared and Tkachev hoped it would be: the herald of revolution. The intelligentsia was a class above classes that in the populist age helped translate the cursed questions of the aristocratic century into the cursed movements of modern Russia.

2. The Agony of Populist Art

THE CENTRAL FACT of the populist era, which haunted the imagination of its creative artists, was that all of Russian life was being materially transformed by modernizing forces from the West. Even in its initial stages under Alexander II, this process had gone far deeper than the massive Westernization of aristocratic thought under Catherine and the extensive administrative and technological changes under Peter. The only previous confrontation comparable in psychological effect was that of the seventeenth century. Like that century, the populist era was distinguished by profound schism and search that affected all of society and culture. Just as the most dynamic and original movement of the seventeenth century was that of the schismatics and other defenders of the old ways, so the most arresting movement of the Alexandrian age was the heroic populist effort to defend the old patterns of life and culture. This similarity helps explain the peculiar fascination of the Russian populists with the Old Believers and the period of Russian history that stretched from the Time of Troubles to the advent of Peter the Great.

Both the Old Believers and the populists were defending a partially imagined and idealized past along with very real forms and practices of Old Russian life. Each was basically a peaceful, non-revolutionary movement which was, however, sometimes allied with violent insurrectionaries: the peasant rebels and student terrorists respectively. But there was a critical difference between the late seventeenth and the late nineteenth century. For the Old Believers and peasant rebels who defended Old Muscovy all had a clear religious faith and a clear idea of the enemy—whether it was the rituals and priests of the new church or the administrators and bureaucrats of the new state. The St. Petersburg populists, on the other hand, had no such clear faith and no agreed conception of what or who was the enemy. They were, for the most part, "repentant noblemen" projecting the anguish of earlier aristocratic thought onto Russian society as a whole. They were determined to overcome their own "superfluousness" by becoming active agents of a new communal form of social life, anxious to overcome their alienation from the real world by establishing direct personal contact with Russia as it really was.

The desire for realism, for the remorseless honesty of the natural scientist, produced a sense of despair among the young intelligentsia as they went forth to discover the long-forgotten masses. But the certainty that Russia was somehow destined to produce a new kind of society, perhaps even a "new Christianity," rescued most of them from the total *Weltschmerz* of the aristocratic century. Indeed, whereas suicide was the besetting moral illness of creative thinkers in the "romantic" first half of the nineteenth century, insanity tended to be the curse of the "realistic" second half. Many of the most original and imaginative figures of the populist age —revolutionaries like Khudiakov and Tkachev, writers like Garshin and Uspensky—went completely insane long before they died. The "mad summer" of the mid-seventies seems at times like part of a confused dream sequence in which the main characters suffer from nervous tics, alcoholic addictions, aimless wanderings, epileptic fits, or neurotic oscillations between extreme exaltation and bleak depression. All of these disorders were widespread among the "cultural pioneers" of the populist age.

One disturbing factor was the fact that the urban intellectuals were looking to the simple people at precisely the time when they were losing their sense of purpose and identity. The peasantry had been confused by the emancipation and was tending to lose confidence, not just in the Church, but in the entire animistic cosmology of Russian rural life. For the primitive peasant imagination of pre-industrial Russia, the world was saturated with religious meaning. God came to man not just through the icons and holy men of the Church but also through the spirit-hosts of mountains, rivers, and, above all, the forests. Each animal, each tree had religious significance like the details in a medieval painting. Belief in the magic power of words and names persisted; the fear of *naklikanie,* or bringing something upon oneself merely by mentioning its name, was widespread, and one always referred to the devil by such euphemisms as "he," "the unclean," or "not ours."

Christianity had melted into and enriched this world of primitive nature worship without supplanting it. Religious rites, particularly the ever-repeated sign of the cross and the "Christ have mercy" prayer in the orthodox liturgy, were often little more than an animistic effort at *naklikanie*—at summoning up God's power and force by endless repetitions of His name. Trees and birds were thought to have derived their present characteristics from their imagined relationship to the events of Christ's life and death. And the revered intermediaries of the gods of nature—swans or mountain birds—were often brought in for the cure of a dying man when a "wonder-working icon" had failed.

As the mentality of the Russian intelligentsia sought to enter into the plight of the masses, it tended to feel even more keenly than the peasants themselves the waning of these naive and superstitious but beautiful and ennobling beliefs. The vague pantheism of the peasantry was easier to accept than the doctrines of the Church, and it appealed to the romantic imagination of the populists. But they were forced to recognize at the same time that these beliefs were powerless to relieve the dislocations and suffering of peasant life.

The basic cause of the madness and near madness of the populist age was the unresolved (and largely unacknowledged) conflict that existed within the intelligentsia between its relentless determination to see things as they really are and its passionate desire to have them better. It was the old conflict between harsh facts and high ideals—lifted, however, to a new level of intensity by the conviction that facts and ideals were but two aspects of one Truth. The populists followed Mikhailovsky in contending that both objective and subjective truth were contained in the Russian word *pravda* and that both must be realized by those "servants of truth," the Russian intelligentsia. The optimistic Comtian belief that there was no contradiction between the truths of science and those of morality was particularly hard to sustain in Russia, where analysis tended to lead to revulsion and ideals to utopianism.

The agony of populist art resulted essentially from its unique sense of tension between things as they are and as they should be. The tension between the limpid realism of Tolstoy's novels and the muddled moralism of his religious tracts is a classic illustration. But this conflict is illustrated even more dramatically in the brief career of Vsevolod Garshin, one of the greatest short-story writers of modern Russia.

Garshin was born in the first year of Alexander's reign, and he had an early brush with the "new men of the sixties" when his mother eloped with a revolutionary, taking the four-year-old Garshin with her. He read Chernyshevsky's *What Is To Be Done?* at the age of eight and developed a life-long interest in the natural sciences while at the gymnasium. With his first short story, "Four Days," in 1877, he proved himself a master of clipped realism. It is a compelling, semi-autobiographical account of a Russian volunteer lying wounded for four days on the battlefield, driven almost to madness not so much by his own suffering as by his inability to explain why he killed a poor Egyptian peasant fighting for the Turks.

When a Pole made an unsuccessful attempt on the life of a Tsarist minister in February, 1880, Garshin suddenly became possessed with the idea that he must save the life of the young would-be assassin. Garshin wrote and visited the minister, but all to no avail, as the Pole was led through the streets, humiliated, and publicly hanged, in an obvious effort to discourage further terrorism. Garshin had never been a terrorist, but this action and the general reaction that set in in the 1880's demonstrated to him the illusion of the populist belief that there could ever be an alternative to the horror and cruelty of the real world. Uspensky had already reached that conclusion in his mammoth study of the Russian countryside, *The Power of the Earth,* which proved the prelude to insanity. Garshin, just before he too went insane, suggested in the manner of Dostoevsky's *Idiot* that perhaps insanity was the form that sainthood must now assume in the world. His masterpiece of 1883, "The Red Flower," tells of a man committed to an insane asylum because of his neurotic preoccupation with ridding the world of evil. Removed from the real world, he clearly does go mad—imagining that all the evil in the world is concentrated in one red flower in the courtyard. Plucking the red flower becomes in a sense the dying gesture of the modern Don Quixote, for whom there is no longer any place in the real world. He is found dead in the garden.

> When they placed him on the stretcher, they tried to loosen his hand and take out the red flower. But the hand stiffened, and he took his trophy down into the grave.[1]

The dark thought that those within asylums are more complete human beings than those who commit them became a recurrent theme of Russian literature—from Chekhov's uncharacteristically terrifying tale *Ward No. 6* to the *cri de coeur* of the 1960's by the dissident writer whom Soviet authorities had sent to a mental institution: *Ward 7* by Valery Tarsis.

By the narrow standards of physiological realism painting was bound to be the most successful art medium, and the painters of the populist era felt generally less deeply perplexed than writers or composers. Yet the history of painting and, even more, of its impact during this period illustrates the same movement from realism to moral agony and madness that was characteristic of much populist art. The story is told succinctly in one of Garshin's short stories, "The Artists," in which an innocuous painter of idealized landscapes is contrasted with another artist, Riabinin, who seeks to render realistically the expressions of suffering on the face of workmen and finally abandons painting to become a village schoolmaster.[2]

The real-life counterpart of Garshin's hero was the new school of painters known as the "wanderers" (*peredvizhniki*). They were a kind of artistic by-product of the iconoclastic revolution. Rebelling in 1862 at the proposed subject for the painting competition in the St. Petersburg academy,

"The Entrance of Odin into Valhalla," they resolved to paint henceforth
only live Russian subjects and to use a remorselessly realistic style. They accepted ostracism from the academies with populist eagerness and proved
true "wanderers" in their search both for subject matter and places of
exhibition.

The leader of this new school of painting was Ilya Repin, whose famous canvas of 1870-3, "Haulers on the Volga," may be regarded as the
icon of populism. It presented a realistic portrayal of popular suffering in
such a way as to arouse in the sensitive viewer's mind the hint of a better
alternative. For behind the dark and beaten-down figures of the haulers
there looms the distant, brightly colored boat itself; and, in the middle of
the picture, a good-looking young boy has lifted up his head and is staring
off out of the picture. To the young students who saw this picture, its meaning was clear: the boy was raising his head up in a first, subconscious act
of defiance and was looking inarticulately to *them,* the student generation of
Russia, to come and lead the suffering people to deliverance.

Recognizing the popularity of the new realistic style, the government
enlisted the talents of one of Russia's best painters, Vasily Vereshchagin, to
serve as official artistic chronicler of the Russo-Turkish War. But some of
Vereshchagin's paintings were awesomely realistic in portraying the horrors
of war and inspired emotions other than the intended one of patriotic
exultation. His three-part study, "All Quiet on the Shipka," which showed
a soldier gradually freezing to death, inspired Garshin to write a poem, "The
Exhibition of Vereshchagin," contrasting the horror of the scene in the
painting with the blasé, well-dressed viewers walking past it.[3]

Another creative genius of the populist era, Modest Musorgsky, also
tried to describe people at an art exhibition with a total realism that described the viewers as well as the paintings in his "Pictures at an Exhibition." Like Garshin's poem, Musorgsky's tone poem was part of a strange
artistic quest for both realism and redemption which led to brilliant and
original results.

Musorgsky was the most distinguished member of a group of musical
iconoclasts known as the "mighty handful" (*moguchaia kuchka*), or "The
Five," whose rebellion from established musical conventions almost exactly
parallels that of the "wanderers" in art. This group sought to lead Russian
music on a special path that would avoid sterile imitation of the West and
also sought to "wander" in search of new forms of musical construction.
The organizer of the group and founder of the Free Music School, which
became the populist rival to the conservatory, was Mily Balakirev, a native
of Nizhny Novgorod, who gathered about him a group of talented musicians influenced by the new materialism and realism of the sixties: a

chemist, Borodin; a military engineer, Cui; a naval officer, Rimsky-Korsakov; and Musorgsky, a young military officer who had been devouring the works of Darwin and living in a typical student commune of the sixties. The mighty handful sought a new popular style of music; and Musorgsky went far toward creating one.

Musorgsky was the consummate "man of the sixties" in his passion for realism and novelty, his rejection of sentimentality, melodrama, and classical art forms. He was convinced that "nothing that is natural can be either wrong or inartistic,"[4] and that art must "plow up the black earth . . . the virgin soil . . . that no man has touched" rather than "reclaim tracts already fertilized"; it must "penetrate unexplored regions and conquer them . . . past all the shadows, *to unknown shores* . . ."[5]

His means of plunging on into the deep were those of the populist age carried to new extremes. He sought to derive all his music from the hidden sounds and cadences of human speech. Beginning with the texts of Gogol, whom he felt to be the closest of all writers to Russian popular culture, he moved on to try to reproduce in music the themes and hypnotic repetitions of Russian oral folklore, the babble in the market place at Nizhny Novgorod, and the mysterious murmurs of nature itself. In a manner reminiscent of Ivanov's quest in painting, Musorgsky insisted that he sought "not beauty for its own sake, but truth wherever it be."[6] But unlike Ivanov, Musorgsky was a true populist, priding himself on his lack of formal musical training and insisting that "art is a means of conversation with the people, and not a goal." He sought "not merely to get to know the people but to be *admitted to their brotherhood*," and stated his populist credo in a letter to Repin, whose "Haulers on the Volga" had been a major source of inspiration for his music:

> It is *the people* I want to depict; sleeping or waking, eating or drinking, I have them constantly in my mind's eye—again and again they rise before me, in all their reality, huge, unvarnished, with no tinsel trappings! How rich a treasure awaits the composer in the speech of the people—so long that is, as any corner of the land remains to which the railway has not penetrated. . . .[7]

In his effort to reproduce and bring forth the true national music that he felt lay within the Russian people, he moved slowly toward the musical stage. Since Gogol ceased writing for the theater there had been little of true value written for the stage, which was dominated in the third quarter of the nineteenth century by Ostrovsky's colorful but ideologically insipid *théâtre de moeurs*.[8] On the musical stage, however, there had been a steady development since Glinka of a body of native Russian operas rich in choral music and based on thematic material from Russian history and folklore. More impressive than any plays produced before Chekhov's great successes in the 1890's was the rich body of operatic literature that appeared during that period and included not only comfortably lyrical works, such as *Sadko* and *Eugene Onegin,* but certain important, idiosyncratic operas that are less familiar outside, such as Rubinstein's *Demon,* Dargomyzhsky's *Rusalka,* and Rimsky-Korsakov's *Maid of Pskov.*

Music, the universal language, was a means of communicating with the new, more polyglot audiences of the late imperial period; and the serious musical drama was a way of effectively conducting that "conversation with the people" which was Musorgsky's conception of art. The subjects which he chose to talk about with his audience in his later years were drawn entirely from Russian history. The various scenes of his operas were viewed not as constituent parts of a drama so much as "illustrations to a chronicle," which dealt with the destiny of the Russian people. A simultaneous drift toward historical subject matter was also noticeable in the paintings of the "wanderers."

> One of the peculiar traits of Russian realism was that the boldest and most resolute followers of an art based on the study of the surrounding world very willingly abandoned this reality and turned to history, that is, to a domain where the immediate connection with actuality is, naturally, lost.[9]

The domain of history held out the promise of prophetic insight. Moscow, the great repository of Russian tradition, was specially revered by Musorgsky's circle, who gave it the name of Jericho, the city which had brought the Jews into the promised land of Canaan. The heartland of Russia was the new Canaan for the restless artists of the populist age. They wandered through it like holy fools of old, and turned to the ever-expanding volume of writing about its history rather in the way monastic artists had previously studied sacred chronicles in search both of worthy subject matter and of personal reassurance and inspiration. Their attention gravitated toward the late Muscovite period: a time similar to their own in spiritual crisis and social upheaval. The same fascination that produced Repin's image of Ivan the Terrible with his murdered son and Surikov's picture of Morozova dragged into exile (as well as some of the most popular plays of Ostrovsky and A. K. Tolstoy) also led Musorgsky to devote most of his last thirteen years to two great historical operas dealing with the late Muscovite period.

The first of these operas, *Boris Godunov,* deals with the beginnings of the century of schism; the second, *Khovanshchina,* with the end. Taken together, they begin on the eve of the Time of Troubles and end with the self-immolation of the Old Believers and the coming of Peter the Great. They are permeated with the desire for artistic fidelity to the musical laws of speech and emotion; historical fidelity to the known desires and habits of the leading characters; and theatrical fidelity to such traditions as there were in Russian opera since Glinka. But the real triumph of these operas—that which gives them a unique place even in this century of rich operatic accomplishment—is that they tell with artistic integrity much about the aspirations of the populist age itself. A key to understanding his music—and perhaps the populist movement itself—lies in the confession that he made to Balakirev just a year after resigning his army commission:

> I was oppressed by a terrible disease which came on very badly while I was in the country. It was mysticism, mixed up with cynical thoughts about God. It developed terribly when I returned to Petersburg. I succeeded in concealing it from you, but you must have noticed traces of it in my music. . . .[10]

This is as close as we are ever brought to the origins of the strange nervous disorder which framed his career and led him to drink himself into derangement and death. It is probably not accidental that he was occupied at the beginning of his career with translating Lavater, the spiritualist and physiognomist who had fascinated Russian mystics of the aristocratic century with his claim to be able to read the nature of men from the shape and expression of their faces; or that the greatest aria in *Khovanshchina* should be Marfa's strange aria of prophecy and divination. Musorgsky himself was endowed with a strange genius for penetrating through the outer veil of speech and action to the inner desires of his fellow men. There are traces of prophecy in *Boris*, though they are often concealed from view by the distracting addition of the Polish scene (demanded by Musorgsky's original theatrical producers); by the melodic and melodramatic additions of the Rimsky-Korsakov and other revisions used in present-day productions; and above all by the dramatic and critical overemphasis on the role of Boris, which has become conventional since Chaliapin.

If Boris is the sole—or even the main—focus of interest, the opera becomes little more than another of the many historical melodramas on themes that were characteristic of national theaters in the late nineteenth century. It is, indeed, rather lacking in subtlety and moral sensitivity when compared with the accounts of Karamzin and Pushkin, from which Musorgsky derived his story. Only when the opera is placed in the context of populism does the uniqueness and power of Musorgsky's version become fully apparent. For, just as his friend the populist historian Kostomarov insisted that the simple people rather than tsars were the proper subject of the true historian, so does Musorgsky make the Russian people rather than the figure of Boris the hero of his opera.

The Russian people frame the entire drama. It begins and ends with them. Boris is guilty before them from his first words, "My soul is heavy," to his last cry, "Forgive"; and the only alibi he ever offers comes at the height of his maddened clock monologue, when he claims that it was not he who killed the infant Dmitry but "the will of the people." It is the people's plight that is the focus of Musorgsky's attention; the climax of the opera comes in the last scene, which shows the people in the Kromy Forest after Boris is dead. This is a pure addition to the Pushkin version and to Musorgsky's own first version. But unlike the addition of the Polish scene, the forest scene was Musorgsky's own idea—one that drew from a variety of impressions he had gathered throughout the 1868–72 period. He discussed its contents with numerous historians and critics and wrote it in a state of enthusiasm at his "novelty and novelty—novelty out of novelty!"[11]

The "revolutionary scene," as Stasov called it, reflects with astonishing insight the revolutionary longings of the age in which Musorgsky lived, whatever it may or may not tell us about the original Time of Troubles. The scene was banned from public performances during the Revolution of 1905. The activities of the mob in the forest reflect in microcosm the search for a new basis for authority in late Imperial Russia. The people in the forest—like the populists who were headed there—have lost confidence in the Tsar and have a new and heady belief in the elemental strength and wisdom of the people. As the curtain opens, they are rejecting and deriding the first of five figures that come before the people as a possible alternative to the authority of the dead Tsar. They are mocking and torturing the boyars, the hereditary aristocracy that has gained its authority through an unholy alliance with the Tsar: "Boris stole a throne and he stole from Boris," they chant as they give the Boyar Khrushchev (sic) a whip for a scepter and a 100-year-old peasant woman for a "queen." The scene of mockery swells to a crescendo, with the magnificent chorus based on an old popular rhythm: "Slava boyarinu, Slava Borisovu," which becomes a kind of leitmotiv for the entire scene. Enthusiastic students left the theater singing this anarchistic chorus through the streets of St. Petersburg as Boris made its spectacular entry into the repertoire early in 1874 on the eve of the mad summer that took them off into Kromy forests of their own.

The second alternative to appear before the mob is the prophetic holy fool, or yurodivy, who had told Boris in a preceding confrontation before St. Basil's Cathedral that the "Tsar-Herod" had lost the right to pray for intercession from the Mother of God. He represented the quixotic longing to follow Christ, the half-heretical voice of Christian prophecy which was so deeply enmeshed in the populist mystique. But his fate in Kromy Forest, like that of the fools who "went to the people," is to be robbed and humiliated by an ungrateful mob. His last coin is taken from him; and he retreats to the back of the stage to make room for the next suitors for the affections of the uprooted masses.

They are the vagabond, pseudo-holy men, Varlaam and Missail, who come out of the depths with bass voices and baser motives to fan the flame of revolution. It is these forest monsters who advise the mob that the Tsar is "a monster eating human flesh"; and they trigger a swelling chorus singing the praises of "power, beautiful power," "terrible and capricious power." The orgiastic climax comes with the women's cry of *smert'!* ("death"), and then the music swirls and degenerates into a kind of chaotic anticlimax. It is all a kind of uncanny picture of the populist revolutionary movement that was to come: inspired by vagabond conspirators from outside, finding climactic release only in a tsaricide in which women played a prominent part, and dissolving shortly thereafter.

Just at this moment of revolutionary excitement a fourth alternative leadership for the mob is heard offstage: the sound of two Polish Jesuits from the entourage of the False Dmitry chanting a Latin prayer in measured tenor notes. Varlaam and Missail's booming bass voices incite the mob to haul off these "ravens and vampires," even though they themselves are committed to the support of Dmitry. The Jesuits are hauled off to be lynched. They represent *Latinstvo,* the oldest and most enduring symbol of Western ideology, which is rejected with particular violence by proponents of a special path for the Russian people, whether presented in an old Catholic or in a new liberal form. It was the unfortunate fate of the two Jesuits to arrive on the scene—like the constitutional proposals of Alexander II's last years—at the precise moment when revolutionary passions were aroused and their fate foredoomed. These two Jesuits are disciples of the sinister and diabolic Rangoni, who is not present in Pushkin's play but dominates the Polish act in Musorgsky's final version of the opera: a kind of reminder that Musorgsky's age was more profoundly anti-Western than Pushkin's.

Finally, the fifth and last external force to come before "the people" appears: the False Dmitry himself, who is hailed as the new Tsar by the gullible mob. The masses in Kromy Forest, like those of Alexander's time, thus end up no better off than they were to begin with. They have a new tsar, who—we have been repeatedly led to believe—will probably be worse than the one he replaced, which was indeed the case with Alexander III.

This is the final message that comes at the end as the mob leaves the stage, trailing blindly behind the False Dmitry. Bells ring; a red glow from a distant fire lights the background; and the humiliated fool steps forth. He, like Boris before him, can no longer pray; and as the orchestra clears away the echoes of praise for God and Dmitry with a few lacerating chords of grief, the fool brings the opera to an end:

> bitter tears
> tears of blood
> weep, weep, Orthodox soul
> soon the enemy will come
> and the darkness fall
> the dark darkness
> impenetrable . . .
> weep, weep, Russian people,
> hungry people.[12]

Musorgsky had plunged out into the deep but had not found "the other shore." The bark is lost at sea, a helpless prey for alien currents. We are left only with the cry of the man in the boat, in all its honest, agonizing simplicity.

He had written to Repin that "a true artist who should dig deep enough would have cause to dance for joy at the results";[13] but fathoming the depths further led him only to "songs and dances of death," his most famous song cycle. The melancholia which overcame him—and which Repin has preserved in the haunting portrait of him painted two weeks before his death —is amplified in *Khovanshchina,* the chaotic and unfinished first part of a trilogy which occupied much of the last eight years of Musorgsky's life. The ostensible theme is the end of Old Russia in an orgy of wild excess, *Khovanshchina,* that ends in the self-immolation of the Old Believers in the last act; and the coming victory of "new" Russia that is foreshadowed by the offstage sounds of the coming Preobrazhensky regiment at the end. Yet there is no clear message; people no longer seem capable of affecting or even understanding what is going on. The mob at Kromy was at least able to look for answers and follow leaders, whereas the *streltsy* can only drink, dance, and give way to another mob which murders their leader, Khovansky. The arias of Boris involve a recognition of sin and a search for expiation; but those of Shaklovity, Marfa, and Dosifei are only lamentations and divinations, obscure in meaning and charged with foreboding. Gradually one senses that Russia is only superficially the subject of the opera, even though Musorgsky spent endless months studying Russian history before writing it. Russia is rather the background against which two deeper forces are contending for the destiny of men: the God-saturated world of nature and pride-saturated world of material force. *Khovanshchina* stands as a kind of mammoth naturalistic tone poem that begins at sunrise and ends in moonlight, that begins by the river in Moscow and ends with a fire in the forest.

The Christian substratum of *Boris Godunov* (and of early populism?) has been eliminated. The two scenes devoted to the *streltsy* show them as—to cite the phrase of the scribe in the opera—"beasts in human shape." In the carousing scene, they become, in effect, a mob of dancing bears exiled from humanity in the manner of peasant folklore. They are reminiscent of an extreme and debauched revolutionary circle of Musorgsky's time which mystified the police by referring to itself as "the Bear Academy."[14] Their leader, Ivan Khovansky, is a "white swan" who is first hailed and then mocked after his assassination with the hushed and beautiful line "Glory and honor to the white swan."

If the defenders of Old Russia are corrupt, the advocates of innovation are also: the venal Prince Golitsyn and the self-satisfied Emma from the German suburb.

Meanwhile, with increasing frequency, the dark figures of Old Believers move in and out, singing choruses and muttering semi-intelligible prayers. Hovering over all this strange, disconnected activity like a druid priest watching the senseless struggles of animals in the forest stands Dosifei, the leader of the Old Believers. At the end he beckons his followers to join him in mounting the great funeral pyre which will return them to the elements through fire. The contrast between the long and beautiful aria with which he bids farewell to earth and the shrill, banal chords used to announce the approach of Peter the Great's army suggests that the bleak world of the elements brings man closer to truth than the dazzling world of artificial invention.

The real conflict in *Khovanshchina* is between these two primal forces: the real world of nature and the artificial world of human striving. Both old and new Russia have succumbed to the latter, Musorgsky seems to be saying through the figure of Marfa, the leader of the sisterhood of feminine Old Believers. Marfa seeks to expiate her sin of having loved Andrew Khovansky, the symbol of Old Russia, and is thus led to join Dosifei in the final scene of immolation. The venal Khovansky does not understand her and elopes with the German girl, Emma; and the *streltsy* are spared at the last minute. Thus physical life survives while spiritual life seeks release in death. Both Old and New Russia tried to kill Marfa: Golitsyn by drowning her, Khovansky by seducing her. But Marfa survives so that she may voluntarily free herself of the world and its chains; and music from the divination scene returns in reprise in a particularly beautiful fashion as Golitsyn sets off for exile.

In the course of successive drafts of *Khovanshchina*, Marfa became the main character. She was, together with the great contralto Daria Leonova —for whom Musorgsky was a touring accompanist in his last years—the "missing madonna" of his lonely life, the "damp mother earth" of his naturalistic cosmology. He gave to Marfa—and to Leonova who sang the part—his most beautiful love music and his most haunting music of foreboding and prophecy. One evening shortly before he died—apparently from epileptic alcoholism—he was accompanying Leonova on the piano as she was singing selections from the still-incomplete *Khovanshchina* for a small group of friends. When she came to the line "Glory and honor to the white swan," Musorgsky suddenly stopped at the piano. A strange shudder ran through the whole group, and neither Leonova nor Musorgsky could go on. It was the moment of truth—or perhaps a decisive instant in his own final turn to insanity. A shudder was the last stage direction he had written in for the fool after his last lament in *Boris Godunov,* and now the full impact of the shudder had come back to him.

Wagner alone in the nineteenth century had a conception as vast as that of Musorgsky. He too sought to transcend the conventions of the operatic stage with a new type of music drama to be constructed out of a new musical idiom and rediscovered pagan folklore. It was largely fear of succumbing to the influence of Wagner (who had come to St. Petersburg in 1862–3) that the "mighty handful" came together in the sixties. If Musorgsky's rival musical culture was less successful in terms of formal perfection and subsequent influence than that of Wagner, the difference between their two independent and simultaneous careers tells us something about the inner aspirations of the Germanic and Slavic worlds respectively in an age of awakening national self-consciousness. Unlike Wagner, for whom the *Downfall of the Gods* was seen as the prelude to a new heroic age, there is no hint of redemption as Musorgsky's Brünnehilde mounts her final funeral pyre. Whereas Wagner had sought to uncover the music of the future, Musorgsky had sought to recapture the music of the past—actually writing some of *Khovanshchina* in the hook note style of the Old Believers. There is no Siegfried in Musorgsky's "popular music drama"; no prize songs in his sunless song cycles; no tinsel of religion or nationalism. Instead, there is a kind of Eastern resignation of willful striving, a strange mixture of clairvoyant insight and realism with no way out.

Similar to Musorgsky in many respects is the figure of Fedor Dostoevsky: another epileptic artistic genius who died just a few weeks before the musician early in 1881 and was laid to rest near him in the graveyard of the Alexander Nevsky monastery. Like Musorgsky, Dostoevsky illustrates the agony of art in the populist age: the tension between relentless realism and the search for a positive message in the people. Like Musorgsky's operas, Dostoevsky's novels offer a tragic depth and dramatic power that was not present in the fashionable plays of the time, let alone the newly popular operettas of Offenbach and Strauss. Like Musorgsky, Dostoevsky had a special reverence for Gogol and considered himself a child of the sixties. The epilepsy that affected Dostoevsky was more intense but less debilitating than the creeping madness of Gogol and Musorgsky. Dostoevsky was able to bring his work to a greater measure of fruition than either of these two figures.

His cosmology of characters and ideas belongs, in many ways, more to the twentieth than to the nineteenth century. One Soviet writer at the end of the Russian Civil War was hardly exaggerating when he said that "all contemporary literature is following in Dostoevsky's footsteps . . . to talk of Dostoevsky still means to talk of the most painful, profound issues of our current life."[15] Ilya Ehrenburg, writing during the period of forced industrialization in the thirties, called Dostoevsky's novels "not books, but letters from someone close" which alone tell "the whole truth" about human nature.

> It is a truth which is undeniable and deadly. One cannot live with it. It can be given to the dying as formerly they gave last rites. If one is to sit down at a table and eat, one must forget about it. If one is to raise a child, one must first of all remove [it] from the house. . . . If one is to build a state, one must forbid even the mention of that name.[16]

The Soviet Union came close to such a prohibition during the era of high Stalinism; for truth was to Dostoevsky both Christian and anti-authoritarian. Dostoevsky fused, if he did not altogether harmonize, Gogol's search for religious faith with Belinsky's passionate anti-authoritarian moralism to provide a new type of positive answer designed for those who had experienced the iconoclasm of the sixties.

Dostoevsky's positive answer did not bypass or even transcend the real world but rather penetrated into it. From the time of his first bleak novel of urban life, *Poor People* in 1845–6, Dostoevsky was unwilling to gloss over unpleasant facts or offer romantic flights to far-off lands or distant history—even Russian history. He is relatively indifferent to scenery or even beauty of language; his subject matter is prosaic and contemporary— much of it taken directly from the newspapers. His focus is on people, and on the most real thing about them: their inner drives, desires, and aspirations. Amidst all the crime and sensualism of his novels the focus is always on psychological development, never on physiological details. He was a "realist in the higher sense of the word." As he wrote at the end of the sixties:

> If one could but tell categorically all that we Russians have gone through during the last ten years in the way of spiritual development, all

the realists would shriek that it was pure fantasy! And yet it would be pure realism! It is the one true, deep realism; theirs is altogether too superficial.[17]

Thus Dostoevsky takes us "from the real to the more real."[18] A veteran of the Petrashevsky circle—the first expressly devoted to "social thought"—of arrest, mock execution, and Siberian exile, Dostoevsky resolved in the late sixties to find that which was most real in the confused experience of the intelligentsia. His method is that of "deep penetration," *proniknovenie,* a term of which he was particularly fond. He was prompted to fathom these depths not only by his own traumatic experience in prison but also by his association upon return with the so-called *pochvenniki,* or "men of the soil." This group, led by the remarkable Muscovite critic Apollon Grigor'ev, sought to oppose both the romantic idealism of the older generation and the materialism of the younger generation with a kind of Christian naturalism, which they felt could be the basis of an original and independent Russian culture. They sought to penetrate through life's artificial exterior for a "restoration in the soul of a new, or rather a renewed, faith in the foundation [*grunt*], the soil [*pochva*], the people—*a restoration in the mind and heart of everything immediate* [*neposredstvenny*]."[19] Criticism, Grigor'ev felt, must be "organic"—taking account of the historical, social, and spiritual forces as well as the physiological forms of life and art. Ostrovsky's dramatic portrayal of Muscovite and provincial life was thought to have prepared the way for a new popular literature by moving back into the soil and away from aristocratic convention.

Dostoevsky moves beneath the surface in the first remarkable literary creation of his period of post-exilic prophecy: *Notes from the Underground* of 1864. Then, having presented the dark recesses of malice in human nature, he plunges on from the real to the more real: to the deeper reality of human nature as a divided complex of feeling and intellect.

The problem of division within man had fascinated Dostoevsky since the time he wrote his *Double* in 1846 and called his divided hero "the greatest and most important type which I was the first to discover and proclaim."[20] In *Crime and Punishment* of 1866, the first of his great novels, he presents us with a hero, Raskolnikov, whose very name has the word for "schism" within it. Already in this work we see the beginning of his more grandiose conception of bringing the divided inner impulses of men into open confrontation and attempting to overcome the sense of separation and division in modern man. In this as in his other great novels he presents ordinary Russians not in any epic, descriptive sense but in a dynamic state of development. His characters become actors in a broader human drama where all are involved in the fate of each. The scene is the city, primarily St. Petersburg: "the most abstract and contrived city on the entire earthly sphere."[21] There are no happy pastorales to relieve the tension. The stage is filled with the babel of intellectualized chatter and a sense of continued expectation and suspense. The scenario is that of the detective stories and melodramas that were currently popular all over Europe. But all of these ingredients are lifted to the level of a modern passion play, for the drama is, in truth, played out on a stage which has salvation at one end and damnation at the other. Through Dostoevsky, the novel form became invested with the dimensions of religious drama; and the ideas of salon thinkers were developed to their extreme and brought into conflict before the largest single audience available in Russia: the subscribers to Katkov's *Russian Herald*.

The unique importance of Dostoevsky for Russian cultural history—as distinct from the world-wide development of psychology, literature, and religious thought—lay in his attempt to uncover some new positive answer for humanity in the depths of Russian popular experience. At about the same time in the late sixties that Musorgsky was beginning the first of his epochal "popular music dramas," Dostoevsky turned his attention toward the composition of a novel that would deal not with underground men, crime and punishment, but with redemption and renewal. Like Gogol, he turned to his Russian "divine comedy" after going abroad; and his first effort, *The Idiot*, of 1867–8, reveals some of the incipient madness of the late Gogol in its agonizing incapacity to create a credible image of pure goodness. Dostoevsky brought with him the faith of the *pochvenniki* that ultimately all men were in harmony and that there were no unbridgeable barriers between one man and another, or between the world of men and that of the insects below and the angels above. The division between the actual and the ideal—the real and the more real—is ultimately artificial; but it can be overcome only by penetrating deeply into the entire problem of division.

Schism had been a deep and abiding theme of Russian history in the Romanov period. The seventeenth century saw the separation of the government from the people; the eighteenth, the aristocracy from the peasantry; the early nineteenth, the intellectual from the non-intellectual aristocracy; and the mid-century, the "sons" from the "fathers" within the thinking elite. In writing *The Idiot* Dostoevsky proved that the mere injection of a Christ-figure into this situation is not enough. Dostoevsky's would-be redeemer is incomplete in the novel without his alter ego, the sensualist Rogozhin, with whose life and fate that of "the Prince-Christ" Myshkin is completely intertwined. The helpless idiocy of Dostoevsky's holy fool at the end of the novel is in many ways reminiscent of the final cries of anguish by the fool at the end of Musorgsky's *Boris Godunov*.

To overcome the separation in Russian life, it is necessary to fathom that separation which lies at the base of all others: the separation from God. Thus, while still in the last stages of writing *The Idiot*, Dostoevsky first conceived of a new novel to be called "The Atheist" or "The Life of a Great Sinner." In it a man was to lose his faith and embark on a search for positive answers that would lead him eventually to a Russian monastery and the recovery of faith at a higher level. It was to be "a gigantic novel," after the writing of which "I shall be ready to die, for I shall have uttered therein my whole heart's burden."[22]

Thus, whereas Musorgsky in the Kromy scene of *Boris* ends his search for new answers with a cry of total despair, Dostoevsky's cry at the end of *The Idiot* is only the beginning of his search. But whereas Musorgsky was closer to the populists of the seventies in looking for sociopolitical leadership in the Kromy Forest, Dostoevsky was closer to the realists of the sixties in looking for metaphysical truth in the real St. Petersburg. Whereas Musorgsky looked to the Russian past, Dostoevsky looked to its present and future. The realism of historical lament in the one gives way to the realism of religious prophecy in the other.

In his first outline of "The Atheist" late in 1868, Dostoevsky indicated his intention to spend at least two years in preparatory reading of "a whole library of atheistic works by Catholic and Orthodox writers." From atheism his hero is to move on to become a Slavophile, Westernizer, Catholic, flagellant sectarian, and "finds at last salvation in the Russian soil, the Russian Saviour, and the Russian God."[23] He attaches repeated importance to the need he feels to be in Russia to write such a work. The two great novels which he wrote during his fascination with this never fully realized idea both take the problem of separation out of the individual into a broader and more distinctively Russian context. *The Possessed* of 1870–2 anatomizes the ideological divisions in Russian society as a whole. *The Brothers Karamazov* of 1878–80, which is the closest Dostoevsky came to giving finished form to "The Atheist," illustrates the separation within individuals, society, and the family itself. *The Brothers* focuses on the ultimate form of human separation: that which leads man to murder his own progenitor. If *The Possessed* depicts "Turgenev's heroes in their old age,"[24] the social dénouement as it were of the philosophic nihilism of *Fathers and Sons, The Brothers* lifts the conflict of fathers and sons to the metaphysical plane, on which alone it could be overcome.

The scene of *The Possessed* is Skvoreshniki, the provincial estate which bears the name of an outdoor house for feeding starlings and migratory birds. It is in truth a feeding place for the noisy black birds of revolution, a way station through which the unsettling ideas of the aristocracy are migrating out from St. Petersburg to the Russian countryside. All the characters are interconnected in a hallucinatory forty-eight hours of activity, most of which is a compressed and intensified version of real-life events. In a series of strange and only partially explained scenes we see the movement of Russian thought from the dilettantish aristocratic romanticism of Stepan Trofimovich, with whom the novel begins, to the activity of a host of young extremists. Conversation leads directly to murder and suicide; the "literary quadrille" of intellectuals to a strange fire. "It's all incendiarism," cries out one perplexed local official, adding prophetically that "the fire is in the minds of men and not in the roofs of houses." But he and others not caught up in the hot stream of ideas are powerless to understand, let alone check, the conflagration of events. This is a novel of ideas in action, and those who are not *intelligentnye* (whether they be babbling bureaucrats or garrulous liberals) are foreigners to it.

At the center of the drama stands Stavrogin, the magnetic yet empty aristocrat around whom the other characters, in Dostoevsky's words, "revolve as in a kaleidoscope." "Everything is contained in the character of Stavrogin—Stavrogin is EVERYTHING," Dostoevsky wrote in his notebooks.[25] An air of mystery hangs over his entrance onto the scene. His face is likened to a mask; and his first activities—grabbing one man by the nose and biting another one's ear—are seen as offenses against society by a "wild beast showing his claws." Like the beast of the apocalypse, this human beast has many heads. He is the progenitor of all the "devils" in the novel ("Devils" being a more accurate translation of the Russian title, *Besy*, than "Possessed").

Superficially he is "a paragon of beauty," surrounded by women, yet unable to have a complete relationship with any of them. Dasha is only a nurse to him, Lisa an unsatisfactory sex partner, and Maria Lebiadkin a maimed and estranged wife. There is a hint of illicit relationship with a small girl in his confession; but whether or not the novel includes this section, the story is still dominated by his ideological relationships with other men. Three of his disciples are among the most original creations in Russian literature: Shigalev, Kirillov, and Shatov. Each is inspired by Stavrogin with an idea that drives him to destruction. Each incarnates one aspect of the revolutionary trinity, liberty, equality, fraternity. Their collective epitaph is provided by the words of Babeuf, which Kirillov writes just before killing himself: *Liberté, égalité, fraternité ou la mort.* Shigalev represents absolute equality with his demand that mountains be leveled and human anthills raised in their place. Kirillov preaches absolute freedom, which he asserts by committing an heroic and purely ideological suicide. Shatov's ideal is absolute fraternity, which he associates with the peasant life of the Russian people.

Shigalev is modeled on Bartholomew Zaitsev, one of the most extreme iconoclasts of the sixties, who had been a close journalistic associate of Pisarev and then had fled abroad to join Bakunin in active revolutionary agitation. Kirillov offers a majestic distillation of the Schopenhauerian argument for suicide and is one of Dostoevsky's greatest creations. The only ultimate way to prove one's freedom is freely to will one's own destruction. Any other act merely serves some earthly purpose and is subject to the various determining factors of the material world. But uncaused suicide is a supreme vote of confidence in man's freedom from, and triumph over, the natural world. By this one heroic stroke man can become a kind of God.

Shatov is, together with Kirillov, the figure with whom Dostoevsky demonstrates greatest sympathy. They are both brought back from America to Russia by Stavrogin to live on Bogoiavlensky (Epiphany) street. They are both looking for a new epiphany, the appearance of the lost God: Kirillov in himself, Shatov in the Russian people. Shatov was originally modeled on an Old Believer whom Dostoevsky met in 1868; but he becomes a kind of God-seeking spokesman of Dostoevsky's own curious brand of populism. Stavrogin has taken away his belief in God and his roots with his peasant past. Unlike Kirillov, whose name is derived from one of the founding saints of Russia and whose dedication to an idea is saintly in intensity, Shatov is plagued by doubts, as his name (derived from *shatanie,* or "wavering") indicates. Whereas Kirillov's moment of truth comes in self-destruction, Shatov's comes in hitting Stavrogin. "I can't tear you out of my heart, Nicholas Stavrogin," he cries, as he—like populism itself—slowly drifts into alliance with the revolutionary forces around him. "I believe in Russia . . . in Orthodoxy . . . I believe that the new advent will take place on Russian soil. . . . In God. I, I will believe in God."

Stavrogin is the dark, malignant force in Russian intellectual life which kept Dostoevsky, like Shatov, from making a confident affirmation of belief in God and of harmonious communion with his creation. Dostoevsky is very explicit in stating what the nature of that evil force is, when he compares Stavrogin to the radical Decembrist Lunin and the brooding poet Lermontov:

> There was perhaps more malice in Stavrogin than in these two put together, but this malice was cold, calm, and if one may put it that way *rational,* which means that it was the most abominable and terrible kind of malice.

Stavrogin's evil is reason without faith: cold intellect born in aristocratic boredom, nurtured during a scientific expedition to Iceland, confirmed by study in a German university, and brought by way of St. Petersburg to the Russian people. It is because he is rational, because he is "a wise serpent" that his power is so truly terrifying.

Yet Stavrogin is also a symbol of the Russian intelligentsia, a bearer of its prophetic hopes, which Dostoevsky himself partially shared. Stavrogin was tutored by Stepan Trofimovich, the incarnation of the romantic aristocratic intellectual; he is compared to figures like Lunin and Lermontov and represents a kind of fulfillment of both of their quests. He was created by Dostoevsky in the midst of his search for a new positive hero. He bears the Greek word for cross (*stavros*) within his name, has been to Jerusalem, and is called "Prince Harry," Shakespeare's future king Henry V who was destined to save England after sowing his wild oats. In his notebooks Dostoevsky referred to Stavrogin as "Prince" and, in a key chapter heading, as "Ivan the Tsarevich": the murdered son of Ivan the Terrible whom Russian folklore taught would return to deliver Russia. In some sense, Dostoevsky is saying that the future of Russia belongs to Stavrogin: to the aristocratic intelligentsia. The intelligentsia—the alienated and elect of history—cannot be bypassed because it is possessed by ideas; and without "a great idea," "the people cannot live and will not die."

The drama of the novel results largely from the struggle of two very special personalities for the raw power that Stavrogin generates and the dark fire that he bears within him. Traditional and revolutionary ideals are struggling for the mind—and thus the future—of Russia. The old is represented by a woman, Maria Lebiadkin, the new by a man, Peter Verkhovensky. The names immediately dramatize the contrasting forces. Maria suggests, of course, the mother of God, the missing Madonna; Peter suggests Peter the Great and the arrogant march of technology and irreverent innovation. Lebiadkin is derived from "swan" (*lebed'*), the popular symbol of purity, grace, and redemption; Verkhovensky from "height," the classic symbol of pride and arrogance.

The old never has a chance. Just as Musorgsky's "white swan" is killed early in *Khovanshchina,* so is Dostoevsky's afflicted with some strange, deep wound even before we meet her. Yet she never blames Stavrogin, who has spurned and humiliated her. Feeling that "I must have done him some wrong," she accepts suffering gladly in the spirit of the Old Believers and denounces Stavrogin as the False Dmitry before dying with her infant baby.

The new and victorious force is that of Verkhovensky, who is, of course, modeled on the conspiratorial Nechaev. Unlike Nechaev, however, who rejoiced in the total nihilism of his revolutionary ethos, Verkhovensky feels the need of links with the prophetic intelligentsia. Without Stavrogin, he considers himself only "Columbus without America, a bottled fly." Verkhovensky's revolutionary party gives us a kind of anticipatory glimpse at the conspiratorial confusion of the Bolsheviks awaiting the arrival of Lenin at the Finland Station. The scene in which Verkhovensky inspires a thug to desecrate an icon by putting a mouse inside its container is an anticipation of the organized sacrilege by the league of the militant godless. The Shpigulin scene, in which Verkhovensky appears in the streets actively agitating among striking workers, illustrates Dostoevsky's unique ability for depicting where events were going rather than merely where they had already been. Based on the first real industrial strike in Russia (which occurred in St. Petersburg in May–June, 1870, while Dostoevsky was completing the novel), the scene is treated not as an isolated, economically motivated demonstration of confused protest but rather as part of the fire in the minds of men. The professional revolutionary organizers who were not to move in among the urban workers for some years are already there in Dostoevsky's novel.[26]

The future, we are led to believe, belongs to Verkhovensky; for, although his immediate plan came to nought, he escapes at the end and is the only major figure who still seems to have a future ahead of him. There is, to be sure, the hope voiced by Stepan Trofimovich in his last wanderings that the devils will be driven out of Russia, which will then sit repentant at the feet of Christ in the manner of the passage in Luke (8:32–7), which introduces the novel. But compared to most of the rest of the action, this is an unconvincing, almost comic scene—prophetic in some ways of the shortly forthcoming "movement to the people" by the "repentant nobility" and by the other great novelist of the age, Leo Tolstoy.

However repelled by the idea of a coming rational social utopia, Dostoevsky was fascinated by it. This was the "Geneva idea," so called perhaps because it represented a mélange of the ideas of two famous Genevans: Calvin's moral puritanism and Rousseau's boundless faith in human perfectibility and equality. Dostoevsky's own image of the new social order was in part drawn from impressions of Switzerland and tales of Bakunin; and it is to Jura, Switzerland, center of Bakunin's revolutionary socialist activities at that time, that Stavrogin makes his final flight abroad. He becomes "like Herzen a naturalized citizen of the Canton of Jura" just before he returns by railroad to commit suicide; just as Kirillov's last self-applied name before his suicide was *"citoyen du monde civilisé."*

The "Geneva idea," with its emphasis on the bourgeois ideal of citizenship, is less attractive to Dostoevsky than the "dream of the golden age," which we first meet in Stavrogin's confession and which is presented much more sympathetically in *A Raw Youth,* the otherwise less successful novel that he wrote in the mid-seventies, between *The Possessed* and *The Brothers Karamazov. A Raw Youth* was published in the populist journal *Annals of the Fatherland,* and presents a generally more complimentary picture of radical aspirations than *The Possessed.* An older figure dreams of the golden age of perfect harmony after seeing Claude Lorraine's painting "Acis and Galatea" in Dresden; Dostoevsky interjects:

> Marvelous dream, lofty error of mankind. The golden age is the most implausible of all the dreams that ever have been, but for it men have given up their life and all their strength, for the sake of it prophets have died and been slain, without it the people will not live and cannot die. . . .

But Rousseauism becomes merged with Christianity in this new, more positive image of the golden age. For the old man concludes:

> . . . I always complete my picture with Heine's vision of "Christ on the Baltic Sea." I could not get along without Him. He comes to them, holds out His hands, and asks them, "How could they forget Him?" And then, as it were, the scales would fall from their eyes and there would break forth the great rapturous hymn of the new and last resurrection.

In *The Brothers Karamazov* Dostoevsky anatomizes this myth of a Christianized utopia. His famed "Legend of the Grand Inquisitor" depicts the fundamental split within this very dream between social and material well-being and the freely given love of Christ. The Inquisitor defends his authoritarianism as a form of philanthropy which keeps ordinary people from being weighed down by the "unbearable burden" of freedom. The people, he points out, are grateful for the assurance of daily bread and are dependent on—even attached to—his despotic leadership.

Dostoevsky's Inquisitor represents all political authority which recognizes no higher principle than the effectiveness of its own exercise. He is a dedicated, rational man; and it is these qualities that make authoritarianism, whether Catholic or socialist, so seductive.

The Inquisitor claims to have improved on Christ's work, to have remedied the mistakes Christ made in not succumbing to the temptations in the wilderness. He incarnates the principle of "truth without Christ," the cold certainty of the crystal palace, of Euclid's geometry and Claude Bernard's physiology, which Dostoevsky felt must inevitably be extended to a society not carrying within itself the image and ideal of Christ.

But Dostoevsky had written long ago that

> I am a child of the age, a child of unbelief and scepticism; I have been so far, and shall be I know to the grave . . . if anyone proved to me that Christ was not the truth, and it really was a fact that the truth was not in Christ, I would rather be with Christ than with the truth.[27]

Alyosha Karamazov reacts to the legend which his brother Ivan relates by saying: "Your inquisitor does not believe in God, that is his secret." But his real secret seems to be that he believes in God without Christ. Dostoevsky, following Belinsky, seems to believe in Christ even without God. Ivan Karamazov's recitation of human cruelties and atrocities just before reciting the legend leads him to "return his ticket of admission" to heaven and, in effect, accuse God of being the author of human suffering. The only explicit answer given to the Inquisitor is the final kiss of the silent Christ: an implausible, almost desperate call for freely given love as the only Christlike answer to human pride.

In his last journalistic writings—and particularly his speech dedicating the Pushkin memorial in the last year of his life—Dostoevsky plays anew with the seductive idea that the Russian people carry within themselves a unique consciousness of the reconciling qualities of Christianity. He speaks of the "Russian idea" of universal reconciliation through love and suffering as an antidote to the "Geneva idea" of organized theocracy. In the West generally "all is now strife and logic," driven on by "the dream of Rothschild," the thirst for wealth and power.

The idea that Russia was the bearer of some new Christ-like harmony among the nations is often extrapolated from his works as the essence of Dostoevsky's "message." Yet it would be more accurate to speak of it as his private version of the myth—common to populists and Pan-Slavs alike—of a special path of Russian development that would redeem the errors of recent Western history. He loved the idea, but his belief in it—like that of Shatov, its most articulate fictional exponent—was hypothetical, even "wavering." Sometimes—particularly in his *Diary of a Writer*—Dostoevsky's position seems chauvinistic, and he is usually characterized as an extreme conservative. But he is not at all interested in preserving the status quo, let alone returning to some idealized past. He is merely opposed to the "less real" ideals of the political and industrial revolutionaries. He is a counter-revolutionary in De Maistre's sense that a *"contre-révolution ne sera point une révolution contraire* mais le *contraire de la révolution."*[28] But Dostoevsky was not primarily a social theorist or philosopher but a master of suspense, a novelist of dramatic temperament. Thus, it is best to look to his novels—and above all to *The Brothers Karamazov,* his last one —for such "answers" as Dostoevsky may have sought to provide in this age of agonized agitation and social messages.

In *The Possessed* we are led to believe that the entire intelligentsia is possessed, that Verkhovensky and Stavrogin are the true and logical heirs of Stepan Trofimovich. There is no way out, and Stepan Trofimovich's last repentant wanderings are even less convincing than Raskolnikov's final "conversion" in *Crime and Punishment.* In *The Brothers,* however, Dostoevsky, unlike Musorgsky, is able to end on a note of hope, without either the melodramatic *deus ex machina* of eleventh-hour repentance and conversion or the romantic blending of religion with nationalism. Dostoevsky had experimented earlier with both answers, and there is both a melodramatic murder and a romantic image of the "Russian monk" at the center of *The Brothers.* But both the "repentance" and the "conversion" of the Karamazovs is incomplete and unconventional.

Yet Dostoevsky does conclude that man can eliminate the need for salvation by raising himself to the level of a superman for whom "all is permissible" since there is no God. The idea of a new breed of men "beyond good and evil" motivated the ideological murder by Raskolnikov and ideological suicide by Kirillov and lies behind much of Ivan Karamazov's thinking about the central crime in *The Brothers.* Yet Ivan is a tortured figure who comes close to the madness that was so characteristic of the age. Ivan wants to believe in God but is visited only by the devil; and there is, seemingly, no way out.

But Ivan is only one of three brothers, all of whom share in the common crime of patricide. The name of Smerdiakov, the illegitimate fourth brother who actually commits the crime, suggests the word for "stink" (*smerdet'*); and the word Karamazov is a compound of words meaning "black" (Tatar *kara*) and "grease" (*maz'*). Like Sophocles in *Oedipus Rex* and Shakespeare in *King Lear,* Dostoevsky's drama deals with injustice to one's father. Yet unlike these, *The Brothers Karamazov* is not a tragedy. None of the three brothers dies; and the story sounds a final message of redemption.

Essential to any understanding of this "message" is the fact that it is conveyed dramatically and not didactically. The "Legend" in itself solves nothing for Dostoevsky—although it may for those who read it and take sides between the protagonists. It occurs relatively early in the novel and is itself an episode in the confrontation of the two extremes among the brothers: the humble Alyosha and the proud, intellectual Ivan. The movement toward resolution of this familiar Dostoevskian antinomy proceeds through the third brother, Dmitry, the most original creation of the novel. Dmitry is closest to the crime and is put on trial for it—thereby becoming the focus for most of the drama.

Dostoevsky's allusions to dramatists help us to understand Dmitry's curious nature. Shakespeare was to Dostoevsky not merely a writer but "a prophet sent by God to proclaim to us the mystery of man and of the human soul"; and much of that mystery was for Dostoevsky contained in *Hamlet*, to which there are many allusions in *The Brothers*. One of the most important of these occurs at the climax of the prosecutor's summary at the trial of Dmitry, where he contrasts "Hamlets" to "Karamazovs." The immediate usage is ironic; but in the "echo" of this contrast which is sounded in the courtroom discussions, it becomes clear that Dostoevsky was contrasting intellectualized "liberal" Europe with spontaneous, earthy Russia. For the former, life itself is problematic and all questions are "sicklied o'er with the pale cast of thought"; for the latter there is a passionate love of life that lives for and fathoms each immediate experience. Dmitry is related to Demeter, the goddess of the earth; he is the *pochvennik* incarnate, a lover of the immediate and spontaneous. Dmitry and the peasants in the audience "stand firm" not only against the half-lies of witnesses and judges but against the whole artificial, casuistic procedure of human trial itself.

Dmitry's vibrance and honesty at the trial is not just a reflection of his "broad Russian nature" but also of the half-hidden influence on Dostoevsky of the dramatist who made perhaps the greatest impact on him of any single literary figure: Friedrich Schiller.[29] *The Brothers* is saturated with borrowings and citations from Schiller—particularly from those hymns to human freedom and perfectibility: *The Robbers* and the "Ode to Joy." For his last and loftiest work, Dostoevsky returns, involuntarily perhaps, to this influence of early youth and subsequent source of inspiration "for my finest dreams." Dostoevsky's Grand Inquisitor is essentially a projection of the inquisitor in *Don Carlos;* and just as the inquisitor's opposite in Carlos is the spontaneous brotherhood of Posa and Don Carlos, so the brothers Karamazov as a whole provide the alternative to the closed world of Dostoevsky's Inquisitor. The Karamazov alternative to both Hamlet and the Grand Inquisitor unfolds in terms of an aesthetic theory which Schiller propounded as his alternative to the arid rationalism of the French Revolution but which he himself was never able to incorporate fully into any of his own dramas.

In his *Letters on the Aesthetic Education of Mankind* of 1794–5 Schiller contended that both the rational and sensual faculties were necessary attributes of the fully developed man; but that they were incomplete and even conflicting forms of good. In seeking to harmonize them one cannot use any abstract philosophic formulas which would automatically lead to a one-sided dominance by rationalism. One must rather undergo an aesthetic education (*Erziehung*) through developing the instinct for play (*Spieltrieb*). Children, who make up their rules of play as they go along and spontaneously reconcile their conflicts without formal regulations and imposed rules, provide the key to harmony for the perplexed adult world. Man was born not to repress but to fulfill his sensual self through play which is the fruit of love, "the ladder on which man climbs to the likeness of God."[30]

Dmitry's love of life and his exuberant spontaneity (as well as his numerous citations from Schiller) all suggest that he is a kind of incarnation of this spirit of play. He startles people with sudden outbursts of laughter. The play instinct gives him a special attraction to beauty, which is "not just a terrible, but a mysterious thing. There God and the devil strive for mastery, and the battleground is the heart of men."

The battleground is also inside the Karamazovs; and the passionate Dmitry alone transcends and thus resolves the dialectic between the feeling faith of Alyosha and the rational brilliance of Ivan, between one brother visited by God and another visited by the devil. Dmitry teaches the Karamazovs to "love life more than the meaning of life." Love of life is part of the love of all created things. Man was for Schiller the supreme participant in an endless festival of creation; and Dostoevsky seems to be beckoning us to join it. The sin of social utopias is that they cut off the spontaneity of this creative process; they "deny not God, but the meaning of his creation." Dostoevsky seems to be saying that even if man cannot believe in God he must love and rejoice in the created universe. Man must enjoy "the game for the sake of the game," as Dostoevsky explained his own passionate love of gambling. As distinct from the ordered and rational habits of ants,

> man is a frivolous, improbable creature, and like a chess player, loves only the process of attaining goals, not the goal itself.

In defiance of Bazarov's contention that "two times two is four and the rest is nonsense," Dostoevsky's man from the underground even suggests that "the formula two times two is five is not without its attractions."[31]

Dmitry is resigned to his fate not by any exercise of logic but by a dream of a cold and hungry baby and a sudden, supra-rational desire "to do something for them all, so that the babe shall weep no more." Dostoevsky heavily underlined these lines in the original sketch for this chapter. Dmitry's "something" is to accept imprisonment and even blame. Though he did not commit the crime, he recognizes that "we are all responsible for all" and gladly goes with the convicts—and with God:

> If they drive God from the earth, then we shall shelter him under-
> neath the earth! . . . singing from the bowels of the earth our tragic hymn
> to God, in whom there is joy! All hail to God and his joy!

Dmitry's own "Ode to Joy" reaches a feverish, Schilleresque climax in his
cry:

> . . . There is so much of strength in me that I shall overcome all things,
> all sufferings, just in order to say with every breath: I am! In a thousand
> agonies—I am! I writhe on the rack—but am! I sit in prison, but still I
> exist; I see the sun, and—even when I don't—I know that it is. And to
> know that the sun is—is already the whole of life.

After the trial Dmitry's joy is dampened with illness and second
thoughts; but he is cured and his faith in life restored through the sudden
irrational desire of the once-proud Katya to accompany him in suffering and
exile. "For a Moment the Lie Becomes Truth" is the title of this section.
Two times two has, for a moment, become five, for the underground man
has suddenly discovered the sun and decided to reach for it with an act of
implausible moral heroism. Katya helps win Dmitry—and through him the
Karamazovs—back to life.

> ". . . Now let what might have been come true for one minute. . . . You
> loved another woman, and I love another man, and yet I shall love you
> forever, and you will love me; do you know? Do you hear? . . ."
> "I shall love you, . . . Katya," Mitya began, drawing a deep breath
> at each word, ". . . All my life! So it will be, so it will be forever. . . ."

But how does this Schilleresque play of instinct and pantheistic love
of life acquire any specific link with Christianity? Perhaps in substituting
Christ for Posa and Carlos as the ideological adversary of the Grand
Inquisitor Dostoevsky is saying that Christ alone can fulfill their romantic
longing for some new brotherhood of freedom and nobility. Yet there is no
conversion of Dmitry; and in the Schilleresque moment of irrational truth
between Katya and Dmitry, Alyosha, the man of faith, "stood speechless
and confounded; he had never expected what he was seeing." Alyosha's
teacher, and the major Christ figure in the novel, the monk Zosima, had
already bowed down before Dmitry as if to say that God himself has need
of such men.

Zosima does, of course, bear a Christian message. He is a composite
of the most holy traditions of Russian monasticism: he bears the name of
the co-founder of Solovetsk and the attributes both of Tikhon Zadonsky and
Father Ambrose of Optyna Pustyn. But he does not bring salvation in the
conventional monastic way. Old Karamazov says that Zosima is in reality a

sensualist; and the lecherous old man is proven partly right by the smell of corruption that emanated from Zosima's body after death and destroyed his claim to sainthood. The one key conversion that Zosima effects, that of Alyosha, takes place after the latter, too, has experienced his "breath of corruption" by visiting Grushenka ("the juicy pear"). His conversion over the putrefying body of Zosima is completely devoid of the miracle and authority which the Inquisitor glorified. Like the murder, which it parallels, Alyosha's conversion occurs at night in a manner that is not clinically disclosed. It takes place amidst tears and under an open sky and leads immediately not to a state of beatified withdrawal but to falling on the ground and embracing the earth and then to Alyosha's decision to leave the monastery and go out into the world.

We do not know what the future of Alyosha—let alone Dmitry and Ivan—might have been, for in *The Brothers* we have only the first part of a projected longer work of which he was to be the ultimate hero. The name is again significant, for it is the diminutive of Alexis, calling to mind the idealized figure of Alexis Mikhailovich and the popular folk hero, Alexis the man of God. Yet *The Brothers* stands complete in itself; and within it there comes at the end a beautiful subplot which ties together dramatically and ideologically the Schilleresque themes and Christian elements in Dostoevsky's cosmology.

The story of "the boys" gives us our only image of Alyosha in action after his conversion. For the most part it is pure Schiller. The setting is boys at play, free of all restraining influences, rejoicing in their spontaneity of expression, their sense of daring, their playful rejection of all that impedes the game of life. Then, into this scene comes something that Schiller and the romantics had viewed as foreign to "the aesthetic education of man": uncaused and irreversible suffering. The very exuberance of children makes their capacity to wound one another's spirit terrifyingly great; and the slow death of the frail little boy Iliusha is clearly related to the mockery of his playmates.

The seemingly disconnected story is related to the novel as a whole in a number of important ways. The principal ringleader of the gang, Kolya Krasotkin, is an echo of Ivan: a detached intellectual who attempts to repress emotion and dreams up the crime which others act upon. Just as Ivan's hypothesis that "all things are permissible" provides the basis for a patricide which others commit and are punished for, so Kolya rigs up the trap which causes a peasant inadvertently to kill a goose and be punished for it. Dostoevsky tells us that there was no trace of corruption about little Iliusha's body (in contrast to that of Zosima) after death. In his death Iliusha atones, as it were, for the crime of the Karamazovs by embracing his own father and nobly defending him from the taunts of the doctor, who mocks his poverty. Even more important, over his grave Kolya and the other boys suddenly feel reconciled to the world and to one another. Alyosha, who has been with them as friend and observer, is able to build on this moment of friendship and harmony; and we suddenly find him solving with Kolya the problem he was never able to solve with Ivan:

> "We shall remember his face and his clothes and his poor little boots, and his coffin and his unhappy sinful father, and how boldly he stood up for him alone against the whole class."
> "We will, we will remember," cried the boys. "He was brave, he was good!"
> "Ah, how I loved him!" exclaimed Kolya.
> "Ah, children, ah, dear friends, don't be afraid of life! . . ."

Love and bravery, the qualities of adventure, are more important than morality, let alone logic, in the festival of life. The boys suddenly find themselves with a new faith in life, a life that must go on for Iliusha's sake.

> "Hurrah for Karamazov," Kolya shouted ecstatically.
> "And may the dead boy's memory live for ever!" Alyosha added again with feeling.

Their last gathering by Iliusha's little stone recalls the Biblical parable about the stone that was rejected becoming the cornerstone of the new building and also the incident where Iliusha was stoned and humiliated. The scene seems to illustrate the central message that Ivan and all other proud men of intellect have yet to digest: that "except ye . . . become as little children ye shall not enter into the kingdom of heaven." The "Hamlet question" about the meaning of life is not answered but transcended by a naive and animated leap of faith.

> "Karamazov," cried Kolya, "is it really true what religion says that we shall all rise from the dead and live and see one another again, all of us and little Iliusha too?"
> "Surely we shall rise, surely we shall see and gaily, gladly tell one another about everything that has happened," Alyosha answered, half laughing, half in enthusiasm.

The meaning of this reconciliation over the dead body of Iliusha is that of the passage from St. John which Dostoevsky placed at the beginning of *The Brothers:* "Except a grain of wheat fall into the ground and die, it abideth alone; but if it die, it bringeth forth much fruit." New life comes out of death: old Karamazov's, Zosima's, and above all that of the innocent little boy. The one essential miracle is that of resurrection: the recurring wonder of nature and the central miracle of Orthodox Christianity. One rediscovers God not by studying dogma but by believing in His creation. Christ's first miracle—turning water into wine at the marriage festival in Cana of Galilee—is the biblical text which leads to Alyosha's conversion; and his first impulse is to embrace the earth. Christianity is the religion not of the ascetics and puritans but of the "dark" Karamazovs who rejoice in God's creation and seek to enjoy it. It is the fulfillment of the law and the prophets, not of the Old Testament, but of the romantic apostles of creative freedom; a religion of adventure. Its only dogma is that freely given love in the imitation of Christ will ultimately triumph over everything, for in the words of à Kempis "love pleads no excuse of impossibility."[32]

In his final Christian affirmation as in his focus on man's inner nature Dostoevsky was not typical of his age. The trend had been to move away from religion, whether toward the nihilism of the Stavrogins or toward the preoccupied agnosticism of the modern world. One then found a kind of consolation in quasi-religious social ideology, whether of a radical populist or a reactionary Pan-Slav nature. Dostoevsky was too deeply affected by these trends to attempt with any confidence a full reaffirmation of traditional Christianity. His faith is rather that of a realist in search of "the more real." There are, perhaps, two icons for this deeply personal and precarious faith.

The first is the image of the Sistine Madonna, which he always kept over his writing desk as if in defiance of Bakunin and the revolutionaries who would have thrown it on the barricades at Dresden. (Dostoevsky himself caused a minor uproar in Dresden when he defied the guards in the museum to climb onto a chair for a closer look at the painting.)[33] The Madonna depicted the source of all creation, the supreme mother, with the consummate technique of European art in which his own novels are steeped. This painting was a reminder of the "marvelous dead" that lay buried in the "strife and logic" of post-Christian Europe and which he hoped to resurrect through the rejuvenated Christian commitment of the Russian people and the prophetic power of his own art.

The second icon of Dostoevsky's anguished faith is a picture of hands. *The Brothers* is filled with hands and feet. They are the implements for doing things in this world, symbols of the "harsh and terrible thing" of love in action as opposed to love in dreams. "What have I come for?" asks Katya rhetorically in the last scene with Dmitry, "to embrace your feet, to press your hands like this, till it hurts." Hands have been a symbol of laceration throughout the novel. In the fable of the onion we are told of a peasant woman who lost her last chance for salvation from the fiery lake of hell by trying to beat off the hands of others who sought to grasp the onion which the peasant woman once gave in charity and which God in his compassion had extended to her. The hands of innocent children beckon Ivan to rebellion against God. He tells Alyosha about the murderer who held out a pistol to a baby and waited to blow its brains out until the precise moment that the baby extended its little, trusting hand to touch it. Then he is driven to insanity by the image of a five-year-old girl tortured by her parents and left in an outhouse with her face smeared in excrement by a sadistic mother who sleeps calmly in the warm house while the little girl prays without any resentment to "dear kind God" and "beats her little aching heart with her tiny fist in the dark and cold." Ivan rebels against God because of the need to avenge the tears of the little girl; and even Alyosha admits that he would be unwilling to accept any ideal harmony that tolerated the sight of "that baby beating its breast with its fist." Yet Dmitry is led to accept his fate by the dream in which "a little babe cried and cried, and held out its little fists blue from cold."

The final message of redemption occurs at the end of the story of "the boys," which is also the end of the novel. Just before, we are given a last pathetic image of the suffering of Iliusha's bereaved father. Last seen sobbing incoherently by his dying son "with his fists pressed against his head," he returns to dominate the early part of the funeral scene. He is all hands: grasping at the flowers from the bier, embracing the coffin, crumbling the bread and throwing it in the grave. In a masterly inversion of the scene in which Dmitry is forced to take off his boots and expose his ugly feet in court, Dostoevsky leaves Iliusha's father kissing the boots of his buried boy and asking, "Iliusha, dear little man, where are thy little feet?"

When they leave the old man's room and go back into the open air, the boys are suddenly impelled to sound a final joyful chorus. There was a hint of it in the mysterious metamorphosis of Iliusha's dog "Beetle" (*Zhuchka*), whom Iliusha had tortured and driven away (in a way prescribed by Smerdiakov) into Kolya's dog, "Ringing of Bells" (*Perezvon*), who turned the last visit of the boys to Iliusha almost into a time of joy. The ringing of church bells provides the transition from Katya's scene with Dmitry to the funeral of Iliusha. But the sound of bells soon gives way to one last "Ode to Joy." It is almost as if the choral movement of Beethoven's Ninth Symphony, which Bakunin had exempted from destruction by revolutionaries, were suddenly being acted out; as if each "beautiful daughter of the divine spark" (as Bakunin used to address his anarchistic followers) had suddenly reached the moment in the Schiller-Beethoven text when "all men shall be brothers" and the "aesthetic education of mankind" shall be completed by the realization that "above the vault of stars there must live a loving father."[34]

In this joyous final moment of *The Brothers* the image is again that of hands. They are not joined in prayer as Dürer would have them or making the sign of the cross in the manner of either the Orthodox or the Old Believers. Least of all is the image one of hands raised to salute Caesar or register votes in some parliamentary body. Rather it is the picture of the hands of children joined near a grave in an unexpected moment of warmth which overcomes all sense of schism and separation, even between this world and the next. A shared newness of life has mysteriously come out of the death of their little comrade. "Let us be going," says Alyosha. "For now we go hand in hand." "Forever so, hand in hand through all of life!" echoes Kolya "rapturously."

The image of reconciliation is profoundly Christian. It is very different from the late Ibsen's pagan picture of hands joylessly joined by shadow people on an icy mountaintop over the dead body of John Gabriel Borkman. Yet Dostoevsky's novel ends not with the traditional heavenly hallelujah but with an earthly cry of joy. As they go off hand in hand to enjoy the funeral banquet and life thereafter, Kolya calls out, and the boys echo, one of the last and best hurrahs in modern literature: "Hurrah for Karamazov!"

3. New Perspectives of the Waning Century

THE EARLY MONTHS of 1881 brought the death of Musorgsky and Dostoevsky and the end of the populist period in the history of Russian culture. It seems strangely appropriate that Surikov's "Morning of the Execution of the *Streltsy*," one of the "wanderers'" most famous historical canvases, was first exhibited in St. Petersburg on March 1, 1881, the very day of Alexander II's assassination.[1] This murder precipitated a program of execution and purge that was as decisive, if not quite as bloody, as that to which Surikov's canvas alluded. The wave of reaction and repression that followed the death of the "tsar-liberator" did not recede significantly until the revolutionary crisis of 1905, nearly a quarter of a century later.

The artists of the populist age had combined remorseless realism with a compulsive conviction that "the people" contained in some way the hidden key to the regeneration of Russian society. Artists and agitators alike—many of whom had been educated in seminaries—frequently subscribed to the vague but passionate belief that some new, primarily ethical form of Christianity was about to be realized on Russian soil. It was not uncommon for "liberty, equality, and fraternity" to be written on crosses; or for radicals to affirm their belief in "Christ, St. Paul, and Chernyshevsky." The ideal of a new Christian form of society drew strength from the indigenous schismatic and sectarian traditions, from the Comtian idea of a religion of humanity, from the quasi-religious socialism of Proudhon, and even from official insistence that Christian Russia had a unique spiritual heritage to defend against the heathen Turks and the corrupt West.

It is hard to recapture the great sense of expectation that pervaded the atmosphere of Alexander's last years. There was a general feeling that dramatic changes were inevitable precisely because of Russia's increasing importance in the world and the need to be worthy of its calling. Dostoevsky's famous speech in Moscow on June 8, 1880, extolling Pushkin as a uniquely Russian prophet of universal reconciliation, was the scene of a public demonstration typical of the age. For half an hour he was cheered as scores of people wept, and he was publicly embraced by everyone from the old Slavophile Aksakov to the old Westernizer (and his long-time antagonist) Turgenev. Voices in the crowd called out "prophet" just as they had burst forth in the court scenes of the late seventies to call out their approval for the pleas of political prisoners to fight "in the name of Christ" for "the humiliated and the weak." The raised section in which the accused sat was referred to as Golgotha, and the revolutionaries frequently spoke of themselves as "true Christians" or a "Christian brotherhood." Even the most positivistic of populists, Mikhailovsky and Lavrov, claimed Christ on occasion as the source of their moral ideas; and most "men of the seventies" believed that moral ideals—not political or economic forces—would ultimately determine the course of history.

The assassins of Alexander II seemed to believe that this act was a kind of spiritual duty which would in itself bring about the new age of brotherhood. The moral fervor and selflessness of the conspirators appealed to the intellectuals, many of whom (in the manner of the Karamazov brothers) felt responsible in some way for the assassination and involved in the trial and punishment. Prominent intellectuals like Tolstoy and Solov'ev appealed to the new Tsar for clemency—often precipitating emotional demonstrations of student support. Though few outside of the leadership of the People's Will organization favored terroristic assassination, many believed that the Tsar now had a unique opportunity to perform an act of Christian forgiveness that could resolve the disharmonies in society. It seemed as if the thirty thousand who had flocked to Dostoevsky's grave in January of 1881 were looking to Alexander III to be the "true Tsar," the long-lost Ivan the Tsarevich who would realize the hopes of his suffering people.

Alexander, however, followed the path that Nicholas I had taken after the Decembrist uprising, hanging the killers and initiating a reign of reaction. In a series of manifestoes and decrees he attempted to suppress once and for all both the activity of the revolutionaries and the intellectual ferment that lay behind it. The steady expansion of the educational system (and the unusually liberal range of higher educational opportunities for women) under Alexander II was curtailed by a return to Uvarov's idea of education as a form of civic discipline. By the end of 1884 all ministers even faintly interested in constitutional or federal rights had been dismissed, all publications of the People's Will curtailed, and the leading journal of legal populism, *The Annals of the Fatherland,* outlawed forever. This determined dash of cold water produced a stunned silence among those who had shared in the great expectations of the populist period. From a cultural point of view the reign of Alexander III (1881–94) was a period of profound depression. The populist mythos continued to dominate Russian social thought, but gone were the old utopian expectations and excitement. The period was referred to as one of "small deeds" and "cultural populism" as distinct from the great deeds and socially revolutionary populism of the seventies.

Two long-labored masterpieces of populist art were completed during this period: Repin's painting "The Zaporozhian Cossacks Write a Letter to the Turkish Sultan" and Borodin's opera *Prince Igor*. They stand as final monuments of the new national art promised by the "wanderers" and the "mighty handful" respectively. Repin's canvas, which occupied him from 1878 to 1891, depicts the idealized exuberance of the rough-hewn "people," spontaneously and communally defying a would-be alien oppressor. Borodin's opera, on which he worked from 1869 till his death in 1887, elaborates the epic tale of Igor's ill-fated battle with the *Polovtsy* into a colorful stage pageant that harmoniously combined equal measures of earthy comedy, exotic dancing, and vocal lyricism.

Igor was Borodin's only mature opera, and came close to being a collective enterprise of the Russian national school even before Rimsky-Korsakov and Glazunov were called on to finish the work after his death. Borodin often composed in the company of his friends. He used his knowledge as one of the outstanding chemists of his age to devise a special gelatin for preserving his crudely penciled scores and also to help develop Russian medical education. Despite his cosmopolitan education and mastery of many languages and disciplines, Borodin looked to Russian popular culture for his dramatic subject matter. He died in Russian national costume at a benefit ball, and was laid to rest near Musorgsky and Dostoevsky in the Alexander Nevsky cemetery. If subsequent generations were to remember Borodin's opera primarily for the famed dances in the camp of the *Polovtsy,* those who first saw the opera in the melancholy Russia of the early 1890's must have felt a special sense of identification with an earlier scene in the same act. The lonely figure of Igor, defeated in his great campaign and frustrated by his captivity, seeks private consolation by summoning up—in some of the most ecstatic music ever written for the bass voice—the image of his faithful wife; and by stepping forward to sing a line that is echoed by the surging orchestra and might well stand as the unanswered lyric prayer of the populist age: "O, give, give me freedom."[2]

Left with "small deeds" and unfulfilled hopes, idealists in the age of Alexander III fled from the broad arena of history to private worlds of lyric lament. The failure of the populist age and its prophetic artists to find any new redemptive message for Russia was accepted as final. The only consolation was to find beauty in the very sadness of life. The fairy-tale beauty of Chaikovsky's ballets, *Swan Lake, The Nutcracker,* and *The Sleeping Beauty,* began during this period their long service to Russia of providing childlike interludes of graceful fancy for a harassed people. The talent that was to produce in 1890 the powerful, at times hallucinatory operatic masterpiece, *The Queen of Spades,* had already fashioned from another famous text of Pushkin, *Eugene Onegin,* the most popular opera of the 1880's (thanks partly to Alexander III's special passion for it). The preoccupation of this opera with unideological problems of personal relations and its mood of lush musical melancholy corresponded in many ways to the spirit of the times. Lensky's tenor lament for his wasted youth and Onegin's own farewell to his lost love amidst falling leaves in the last act seemed to drown sadness in a gush of melody. The composer who had entered the Russian musical scene with a buoyant cantata of 1865 based on Schiller's "Ode to Joy" died in 1893, just nine days after conducting the first performance of his grief-laden Sixth Symphony, appropriately known as the "Pathétique."

The leading painter of this period, Isaac Levitan, retreated altogether from the world of people to become perhaps the greatest of all Russian landscape painters. Not a single human figure appears in the paintings of the last twenty-one years of his life.[3] Yet Levitan, like Chaikovsky, projects a deeply human sense of sadness into the beauty of his work. Many of his best compositions—"Evening on the Volga," "Evening Bells," and "The Golden Autumn"—depict the afterglow of nature rather than daylight or the promise of springtime.

An even sadder mood is set in the work of Levitan's lifelong friend, Anton Chekhov. Nowhere more than in Chekhov's plays does one find the pathos-in-comedy of human futility portrayed with more beauty and feeling. Although his greatest plays were written early in the reign of Nicholas II, they reflect the mood that had developed under Alexander III, the period of Chekhov's development as a writer. "I am in mourning for my life," explains the leading character at the beginning of Chekhov's first great play, *The Sea Gull.* The idea of a dead sea gull as a symbol of pathos had been suggested to him by Levitan; but through Chekhov's plays the symbol became equated with the slow and graceful gliding out to sea of old aristocratic Russia.

Characters wander across the stage unable to communicate with one another, let alone with the world about them. "There is nothing for it," says Sonya at the end of *Uncle Vanya.* "We shall live through a long chain of days and weary evenings; we shall patiently bear the trials which fate sends us . . . and when our time comes we shall die without a murmur." Consis-

tently, Chekhov glorifies those who suffer and succumb, still believing in
the ideals of populism, but no longer expecting to see them realized on
earth. Sonya suggests that "beyond the grave we shall see all our sufferings
drowned in mercy that will fill the world." But this is only a lovely lyric
moment like the melody from the "Pathétique Symphony." Progressively in
his dramas, Chekhov moves away from all hope and consolation—even
those found in the familiar conventions of melodrama, such as the escape-
through-suicide which he invoked in *The Sea Gull* and *Three Sisters*.
Seeking perhaps the tranquil twilight of Levitan's landscapes, Chekhov fled
to a cherry orchard for his last play and went to the Black Forest to die.
But he knew that the forces of material change were prevailing, and the
offstage sound of the axe in the orchard brings down the final curtain in his
last play.

Lyric lament was replacing the harsh but inclusive realism of the
populist age. Short stories and sketches replaced the great works of the
populist age. There is nothing in the late nineteenth century to compare
in scope and realistic intensity with Nekrasov's poem "Who Then Is Happy
in Russia?" (1863–76) or Saltykov's *Golovlev Family* (1872–6), let alone
with *Khovanshchina* or *The Brothers Karamazov*. The golden age of the
realistic novel came to an end in the eighties just as the golden age of
Russian poetry had ended in the forties. Turgenev wrote his last novel (and
Tolstoy his last great one) in the late seventies. Pisemsky, another pioneer of
the realistic novel, died within a few weeks of Dostoevsky and Musorgsky in
1881. By the end of the decade Saltykov, Shelgunov, Eliseev, and Chernyshevsky had died, thus severing the last living links with the critical journalistic traditions of the sixties. Of the leading populist writers, only
Uspensky and Mikhailovsky remained active in Russia and uncompromised
in their fidelity to populist ideals throughout the eighties. But the former was
going slowly insane after completing his bleak masterpiece *The Power of the
Land* (1882) and such prophetic fragments as *Man and the Machine* (1884).
Mikhailovsky had developed a marked nervous tic and was increasingly
preoccupied with publishing the memoirs of himself and his friends.

It was, in general, a time for memoir writing and commemorative
meetings in imitation of the Pushkin fete of 1880. Some former revolutionaries like Tikhomirov publicly renounced their previous beliefs and
achieved notoriety inside Russia; others like Kravchinsky (Stepniak) and
Kropotkin fled abroad and earned reputations in Western radical circles
as martyred heroes and revolutionary theorists. The pathetic conspiratorial
effort to kill Alexander III in 1887 (in which such unlikely bedfellows as
Pilsudski and Lenin's older brother were involved) reflected the futility and

addiction to old patterns that prevailed among the few who continued as active revolutionaries inside Russia.

More typical of the age than this isolated act of terroristic heroism was the emotional but essentially apolitical student demonstration of 1886 on the twenty-fifth anniversary of Dobroliubov's death. With the death of Ostrovsky in the same year and of Garshin and Saltykov in 1888 and 1889 respectively, the age of realism in Russian literature can be said to have ended.

In its place a new popular culture appeared that sought neither to depict reality nor to answer vexing questions but to distract the masses with sex, sensationalism, and crude chauvinism. Illustrated weeklies captured the attention of those who might previously have turned to the thick monthly journals for ideas and inspiration. One of these journals, *Niva,* grew rapidly from its relatively obscure origins in 1869 to gain, by the end of the reign of Alexander III, the totally unprecedented circulation of 200,000. It and other journals offered a new literature of faded romantic escapism. Exotic travel literature, sentimentalized love stories, and stereotyped historical novels rushed in to fill a void created both by the tightened censorship and by general exhaustion at the no-exit realism of the previous era.

Amidst the lassitude and *bezideinost'* ("lack of ideology") of the era, two powerful figures struggled, as it were, for the soul of Russia: Constantine Pobedonostsev and Leo Tolstoy. They had both opposed and outlived the revolutionaries of the sixties and were already relatively old men by the eighties, yet both were destined to live on into the twentieth century. Neither of them founded a movement, yet each contributed to the climate of fanaticism that made revolution rather than reform the path through which modernization was accomplished in twentieth-century Russia.

These two figures helped define the unresolved and often unacknowledged conflict of political ideas within the thought of the populist age: between irrational adherence to authoritarian tradition and rationalistic insistence on a direct transformation of society. Pobedonostsev, the lawyer and lay head of the Church Synod, was the symbol and author of Alexander III's program of reaction. Tolstoy, the novelist turned barefoot religious teacher, was the enduring symbol and example of anarchistic populist protest. However bitterly they were opposed to one another, each was in a sense true to the populist age in which he was nurtured. For each of them was uniquely willing in the succeeding age of small deeds and great compromises to sacrifice his personal happiness and well-being to the ideal in which he believed. The ideal of each was, moreover, that of a totally renovated Christian society rather than of partial improvement through practical economic or political reforms.

Their paths first crossed in 1881, when Pobedonostsev withheld from Alexander III Tolstoy's letter urging clemency for the assassins of the Tsar's father. "As wax before the fire, every revolutionary struggle will melt away before the man-tsar who fulfills the law of Christ," Tolstoy wrote; but Pobedonostsev correctly retorted that "our Christ is not your Christ."[4] They met again in 1899, when Tolstoy included in his last novel *Resurrection* a thinly veiled caricature of Pobedonostsev. The latter responded in 1902 by excommunicating Tolstoy, whose followers countered with the defiant statement that "your anathemas will far more surely open to us the doors of the Kingdom of Heaven than could your prayers."

Like Dostoevsky's Grand Inquisitor, Pobedonostsev favored theocratic rule through mystery and authority. He was opposed to all freedom of expression and favored the systematic subordination of sectarian and minority cultures to a monolithic Russian Orthodox culture. Access to pernicious foreign ideas was to be confined to an intellectual elite; but otherwise education was to be limited to catechistic indoctrination in Russian traditions and moral values.

In some respects Pobedonostsev's social doctrine resembles the theory of "freezing up Russia to avoid rotting" contemporaneously being advanced by Constantine Leont'ev. He detested the tendency toward uniformity in "the Europe of railroads and banks . . . of increasing material indulgence, and prosaic dreams about the common good."[5] Reminiscent of Nietzsche is his aesthetic antagonism to bourgeois mediocrity, which amplifies a sentiment already found in Herzen as well as Pisemsky and other anti-nihilist novelists of the populist era:

> Is it not dreadful and humiliating to think that Moses went up upon Sinai, the Greeks built their lovely temples, the Romans waged their Punic Wars, Alexander, that handsome genius in a plumed helmet, fought his battles, apostles preached, martyrs suffered, poets sang, artists painted, knights shone at tournaments—only that some French, German or Russian bourgeois garbed in unsightly and absurd clothes should enjoy life "individually" or "collectively" on the ruins of all this vanished splendor?[6]

There will be no beauty in life without inequality and violence. To pluck the rose, man must be willing to pierce his fingers on the thorns. Even before the outbreak of the first Balkan War in the mid-seventies Leont'ev insisted that "liberal nihilism" has produced such "decrepitude of mind and heart" that what is needed for rejuvenation may well be "a whole period of external wars analogous to the Thirty Years' War or at least to the epoch of Napoleon I."[7]

For aristocratic and aesthetic reasons, Leont'ev rebelled at all reforms, proposing a total return to the ritual and discipline of Byzantine rule. He died as a monk in the monastery of the Holy Trinity, bemoaning the end of the age of poetry and human variety. Pobedonostsev, on the contrary, was a thoroughly prosaic lay figure, whose ideal was the gray efficiency and uniformity of the modern organization man. He was the prophet of duty, work, and order—shifting his bishops around periodically to prevent any distracting local attachments from impeding the smooth functioning of the ecclesiastical machine. He was unemotional, even cynical, about his methods. But they were generally effective and earn him a deserved place as one of the builders of the centralized bureaucratic state. Like the modern totalitarian regimes which his own rule often seems to anticipate, he has a low view of human nature and insists that regimes based on a more optimistic reading of the masses will collapse. "The state must show in itself a living faith. The popular mind is suspicious and may not be seduced . . . by compromise,"[8] he insists in criticizing advocates of constitutional processes for Russia. Any efforts to transplant democratic institutions to Russia will merely lead to revolution.

> Organization and bribery are the two mighty instruments used with such success for the manipulation of the masses. . . . In our time a new means has been found of working the masses for political ends . . . this is the art of rapid and dexterous generalization of ideas disseminated with the confidence of burning conviction as the last word of science.[9]

In a sense Pobedonostsev foresaw the program of revolution that would prevail in Russia even before the revolutionaries themselves. He sought to combat it with his own forms of organization, indoctrination, and forced conformity.

The most consistent opponent of his policies was Tolstoy, who after completing *Anna Karenina* in 1876 had given up his brilliant career as a novelist to preach his own form of Christian living to the Russian masses. The extraordinary spectacle of a magnificent writer and exuberant aristocrat wandering in peasant garb among the peasants of his estate and writing elementary primers on Christian morality attracted world-wide attention and deprived Tsarist absolutism of its moral authority among many thinking people. By the end of his long life many Russians spoke of their "two Tsars": the crowned Tsar in St. Petersburg and the uncrowned Tsar in Yasnaya Polyana.

Tolstoy was such a formidable figure that he transcends the environment in which he lived, yet he was deeply rooted in it. His greatest novel,

War and Peace, is a panoramic, epic tale of Russian history. His other monumental work, *Anna Karenina,* is an effort to solve the problem of family happiness and social adjustment that had plagued Russian aristocratic literature from Pushkin through Turgenev. In the character of Platon Karataev in the first work and Levin in the second, Tolstoy begins to develop his new ethical philosophy of returning to the harmony of the natural world. In contrast to the Karamazovs' love of the elemental and sensuous, of "life more than the meaning of life," Tolstoy's Levin insists that life without meaning is unbearable, that life "has the positive meaning of goodness, which I have the power to put into it." The last thirty years of Tolstoy's own life were spent in trying to define "the meaning of goodness" and to saddle his own earthy personality to the task of bringing good into the corrupted life of late Imperial Russia.

During this long and baffling period of religious teaching, Tolstoy develops a number of concepts that had become important in the Russian intellectual tradition. His moral puritanism and rejection of sexual lust and artistic creativity are in the tradition of the sixties; his personal passion for identity with the peasants and the unspoiled natural world is a reflection of the populist ethos of the seventies. His belief in human perfectibility puts him in the main stream of Russian radical thought, as does his anarchistic rejection of institutional coercion and constitutional processes. Most important of all, Tolstoy avidly defended and was deeply influenced by the Russian sectarians. He viewed his own ethical teaching as the "true Christianity" of morals rather than metaphysics, a rational syncretic religion that required no church or dogma.

What is unique in Tolstoy is the relentlessness with which he developed lines of thought that his predecessors had never carried to their logical conclusions. Implicitly throughout *War and Peace* and explicitly in the second epilogue he extends belief in the power of the people to the point where he denies any significance to the individual. In his religious writings he develops the populist faith in the power of moral ideals to the point where he renounces all use of coercion in support of such ideals. The populist belief that the search for justice must be accompanied by the search for truth led him to renounce his art and finally his family: to go off like Stepan Trofimovich at the end of *The Possessed* on a last pathetic pilgrimage into the countryside, which led to death in 1910 in a lonely provincial railroad station.

The contrast is frequently made between Tolstoy and Dostoevsky, two of Russia's greatest thinkers and of the world's greatest novelists. The epic, pastoral world of Tolstoy, the high aristocrat and rationalistic "seer of the flesh" is in many ways the very antithesis of the dramatic, urban world of

Dostoevsky, the low aristocrat and often irrational "seer of the spirit."[10] One image perhaps goes to the heart of the difference. In contrast to Dostoevsky's early love of Schiller and final apotheosis of the play instinct in *The Brothers* stands Tolstoy's early statement that "life is not a game but a serious matter"—which is repeated almost verbatim in his last letter to his wife. As he put it in his *What Is To Be Done?* of the mid-eighties:

> Human life . . . has no other object than to elucidate moral truths . . . and this elucidation is not only the chief but ought to be the sole business of man.

Life was a serious matter for Tolstoy because it was the arena in which man's quest for moral perfection and universal happiness had to be realized. Unlike Dostoevsky, for whom evil and death were part of the greater drama of suffering and redemption, they were for Tolstoy unaccountable intrusions into his world of Promethean perfectibility.

Tolstoy was terrified by death—an event which he portrayed in his works with the vividness and psychological insight of one who had obviously dwelt deeply on the problem. He was fascinated in his late years by Nicholas Fedorov, the librarian of the Rumiantsev museum (now Lenin Library) in Moscow, who taught that the advance of science would make possible the perpetuation of life and even the resurrection of those already dead. He also returned periodically to the idea that the assertive, artificial world of men contains less wisdom than that of animals, and that of animals less than that of the composed and earth-bound vegetable world.

In all these interests, the naturalistic mind of Tolstoy seems to be pointing toward the areas in which Russian scientists of the 1880's and 1890's were to make some of their most distinctive theoretical innovations. The idea of prolonging life through dietary means and the establishment of new moral and biological harmonies within the body was an *idée fixe* of Russia's greatest biologist of the period, Elie Mechnikov. He subsequently became Pasteur's assistant in Paris and Nobel Prize winner in 1908. But his predominant interest in his later years lay in the science of geriatrics, or the prolongation of life—a field that was to continue to fascinate scientists of the Soviet period.

The idea that many secrets of the universe are contained in the natural harmonies that exist between the earth and the vegetable world was the point of departure for Russia's greatest geologist of this period, Vladimir Dokuchaev. This imaginative figure from Nizhny Novgorod believed that all of Russia was divided into five "natural historical zones," each of which determined the forms of life and activity that developed on it. He was the founder of the untranslatable Russian science of "soil learning" (*pochvove-*

denie), which is a kind of combination of soil genetics and soil mechanics. Like Mechnikov in biology, Dokuchaev in geology tended to be progressively more interested in the philosophic implications of his work, though Soviet hagiographers prefer to concentrate exclusively on the detailed investigations and practical discoveries of their earlier periods. Dokuchaev sought to study

> those eternal, genetic, and invariably regular links which exist between forces, bodies, and events; between living and dead nature; between the plant, animal, and mineral kingdoms on the one side and man, his life, and even the spiritual world on the other.[11]

Dokuchaev was extremely critical of Western geology, which studied the soil only for utilitarian reasons. *Pochvovedenie,* in contrast, sought to gain an inner understanding not just of the soil but of the life that comes from it. Dokuchaev believed that there were "extremely close and everlasting interrelationships between water, air, land, plant and animal organisms" as well as the growth and changes in human society.[12] Dokuchaev's science —together with the idealistic polemics of a former populist writer on village life for *The Annals of the Fatherland,* Alexander Engel'gardt—began the first serious interest in forest conservation in Russia as well as a vast reorganization and improvement in higher agricultural education. He compared water in the soil to blood in the body and inspired his followers to establish a science of "phyto-sociology," the study of forests as "social organisms."[13] Raised in a clerical family and partly educated in a seminary, Dokuchaev freely acknowledged his debt to Schellingian *Naturphilosophie.* Most Western geologists still consider him an eccentric. But Dokuchaev's combination of detailed regional investigations and general idealistic enthusiasm was largely responsible for placing Russia at the beginning of the twentieth century at the forefront of scientific discovery in many fields of soil mechanics, permafrost research, and so on.

Dokuchaev and Fedorov died a few years before Tolstoy and Mechnikov. None of these idealistic naturalists found the secrets of the tangible, physical world for which they all searched. Tolstoy lived longest, dying at the age of eighty-two. In accordance with the decrees of Pobedonostsev (who had preceded him to the grave by three years) Tolstoy was denied any religious rites at his burial. He was laid to rest on his estate at Yasnaya Polyana by the green stick on which, he had thought as a youth, could be found the secret by which all men could live in happiness and brotherhood.

It was primarily this secret—the secret of a rational moral society— that Tolstoy had sought in vain to find. The passionate sincerity of his quest had kept alive, however, the populist tradition of moral dedication and

utopian hope. In contrast to the traditionalism and coerciveness of Pobedonostsev, Tolstoy presented the ideal of a non-violent moral revolution. In
his religious teachings there is a curious blend of sectarian Protestant
puritanism and Oriental resignation before the mysteries of nature. He has
always been admired (and was to some extent influenced by) the more
syncretic and anti-traditional forms of Protestantism.[14] As a student at
Kazan he had originally studied Oriental languages; he had a life-long
admiration for Buddhism; and his own religious search brought him to
admire Confucianism as the model for a religion of morality rather than
metaphysics. It seems appropriate that his religious ideas were to have by
far their greatest impact in the Orient—above all through Gandhi's adoption
of Tolstoy's doctrine of non-violent resistance.[15] Whereas Europeans have
tended to view his later religious writings as a marked decline from the
glories of *War and Peace* and *Anna Karenina,* non-Europeans often tend to
view the latter as the minor youthful works of a man on the path toward
rediscovering in the fullness of years the abiding truths of the agrarian East.

Within Russia Tolstoy had only a handful of real followers. Neither he
nor his foe Pobedonostsev was able to address himself to new problems
and concerns. They were old men defending established traditions of the
imperial bureaucracy and the truth-seeking aristocratic intelligentsia respectively. The power exercised by Pobedonostsev and the spell cast by
Tolstoy helped weaken the effectiveness of more moderate reformers. Yet
neither Pobedonostsev nor Tolstoy was able to dispel the prevailing
melancholia of the eighties, let alone point the way to any new approaches
to the problems of the day.

Both looked on the major new trends in the surrounding world with
fear and antagonism. The intellectual and political agitation of contemporary
Europe seemed to them irrelevant, corrupting, and self-serving. In exasperation more than exultation, they both fled to a Christianity of their own
devising: linked in Pobedonostsev's case to Oriental despotism and in
Tolstoy's to Oriental mysticism.

Yet it would be unjust to link the protean Tolstoy with the narrow
Pobedonostsev. Tolstoy was, in many ways, the last true giant of the
reformist aristocratic intelligentsia. He sought to find both their lost links
with the soil and, at the same time, the answers to "the cursed questions"
about the meaning of art, history, and life itself. The greatest novelist of his
age, Tolstoy died wandering far from home muttering the words: "Truth . . .
I love much . . . how they."[16]

Here, truly, was a case of Gulliver held down by the Lilliputians: that
fallen giant in one of Goya's last drawings over whose body an antlike army
of little people swarms, planting their banner atop his sleeping head. Yet

Tolstoy, like so much of the aristocratic intelligentsia, volunteered for his bondage to the people. Indeed, he identified the people with Gulliver in a characteristic entry in the diary of his later years:

> I went through the village and looked into windows. Poverty and ignorance were everywhere, and I reflected on the slavery of earlier days. Formely, the cause was visible, and the chain which bound the peasants easily perceived. Now there is no chain. In Europe there are threads —as many as bound Gulliver. With us one can still see ropes, or at least strings; there, threads—but they all still hold down that giant, the people, so firmly that it cannot move. There is only one salvation: not to lie down, not to fall asleep.[17]

This restless ethical passion was to dominate the new and sleepless century. Indeed, the new bondage of the Soviet era was to be built in part out of attitudes of humorless puritanism and ethical fanaticism that the later Tolstoy shared with the revolutionary tradition. Tolstoy, however, rejected revolution,[18] and died like a lonely sectarian pilgrim in search of truth. The admonition "life is not a joke"[19] in his last letter to his wife is strikingly similar to the last entry in Ivanov's notebooks: "It is not permissible to joke with God."[20] The icon for his peculiar faith was the famous canvas "What Is Truth?" in which his friend Nicholas Ge portrayed a harried Christ before an imposing and imperious Pilate. The paintings and drawings by Ilya Repin of the aging Tolstoy in peasant garb on his estate served as the last icons of a dying faith that inspired awe but not imitation. There was no desire to be "very like" the late Tolstoy. His links were with the past, and his ideas developed in a world largely out of touch with the urban and industrial Russia that was coming into being.

During Tolstoy's last years, which were the early years of Nicholas II's reign, a number of fresh ideas took root among the more cosmopolitan and better-educated populace.[21] The 1890's began the richly creative final period of imperial culture known variously as "the Russian Renaissance" and "the silver age." There was a kind of renaissance quality to the variety and virtuosity of new accomplishment. If silver is less precious than gold, it nonetheless enjoys wider circulation. Never before had the high culture of art and theater, of politics and ideology, involved so many people.

Reduced to its essence, the silver age may be said to have presented Russia of the 1890's with three new and very different perspectives: constitutional liberalism, dialectical materialism, and transcendental idealism. Each of these schools of thought sought to relieve the general air of Chekhovian despondency that was settling over much of Russia; each sought to break sharply with the confining reactionary rule of Pobedonostsev and the atmosphere of Russian particularism that had been characteristic of populist and Pan-Slav alike. Each school of thought benefited from renewed cultural and diplomatic contact with Western Europe and related its ideas to those of Europe as a whole. The leading figure in each new movement of ideas—the liberal Miliukov, the Marxist Plekhanov, and the idealist Solov'ev—was born in the fifties and nurtured on the optimistic Comtian view of history. Each had participated in the radical unrest of the populist era, but had found the populist ideology inadequate and sought to provide a new antidote for the confusion and pessimism of the late imperial period.

Constitutional Liberalism

THE FIRST broadly based liberal movement in Russia dates from the 1890's. Only then did proponents of moderate reform, constitutional rule, and increased civil liberties acquire a nationwide platform and an intellectual respectability comparable to that which had long been enjoyed by more extreme positions to the right and left. Suddenly in the new atmosphere of the late 1890's a number of forces rapidly came together and coalesced under the banners of "liberation" and "zemstvo constitutionalism" into a nationwide political movement that found expression in the formation of the Constitutional Democratic (Cadet) party in 1905.

The interesting question for those brought up in the liberal democratic tradition of the West is: Why was constitutional liberalism so late in coming to Russia? Basically, of course, the reason lies in the different pattern followed in Russian social and economic development. Russia remained until the very end of the nineteenth century a relatively backward society still dominated by religious habit and a traditional agricultural economy. The intelligentsia had fused elements of religious utopianism and of aristocratic snobbery into an attitude of contempt for such partial measures as constitutional reform and representative government. The very term "liberalism" was in disrepute throughout the nineteenth century; and the genuinely liberal movement of the late century carefully avoided using the label "liberal" in its official titles.

The Russian bourgeoisie had not developed the same interest in political and civil liberties as the bourgeoisie of Western Europe. As late as 1895, the liberal *Herald of Europe* explained the absence of bourgeois liberalism in Russia by the lack of "a bourgeoisie in the West European sense of the word." Much of the native Russian business class was more interested in commerce than manufacture, and thus was attached to an essentially conservative, agrarian way of life. Russian entrepreneurs seemed generally more anxious to gain government support for their developmental projects than to limit governmental interference. The involvement of Jews, Germans, and Armenians in Russian trade and the growing influx of foreign capital made laissez-faire liberalism seem synonymous with turning Russia over to foreign masters. Finally—and in many ways most important—there was an enduring contempt for the bourgeoisie within the intellectual community. Rooted in the traditional distaste of the intelligentsia for *meshchanstvo* and nourished by aristocratic aestheticism, this prejudice against the bourgeois form of life was confirmed in the late nineteenth century by a tendency to equate the bleak world of Ibsen's plays with bourgeois society as a whole.[22]

Despite these practical and psychological difficulties, liberalism (both political and economic) had attracted articulate and at times influential spokesmen inside Russia throughout the nineteenth century. Liberalism in the sense of a constitutional rule of law rather than of men dates back to the time of Catherine. The Decembrists had sought constitutional rule, as had many influential advisers to both Alexander I and Alexander II. The idea of a national assembly on the model of the old *zemsky sobors* had found many advocates, including Herzen and numerous Slavophiles. Liberalism in the Manchesterian sense of freeing the economy from government interference and restraint had also found advocates—particularly in the Free Economic Society which had been founded by Catherine the Great. Adam Smith was known and studied earlier in Russia than in many other countries; a period of almost complete economic *laissez faire* was enjoyed during the finance ministry of Count Reutern in the early 1860's; and Manchesterian liberalism gained the support of an influential journal, *The Herald of Europe,* and an articulate pressure group, The Society for the Promotion of Trade with the Fatherland.

A coherent Russian liberal tradition began not with aristocratic plans for constitutional rule under Alexander II or arguments advanced for *laissez faire* under Alexander II, but with the social and economic changes of the 1890's: the beginning of the Trans-Siberian railway in 1891; the famine and accelerated flight to the cities of 1891–2; the expansion of mining and industry in the Donets Basin; the growth of the Baku oil complex into the largest in the world; and the tremendous general expansion of transportation and communication facilities under the ministry of Count Witte from 1892 to 1903.[23]

The logic of modernization created the need for uniform laws, of greater rights for suppressed minorities and nationalities—particularly those with badly needed technical and administrative skills, such as Finns, Baltic Germans, and Jews. Efficiency in economic development required that large numbers of people be consulted before embarking on any course of action; and some form of consultative if not legislative body seemed clearly desirable.

Arguments for rational laws and increased popular participation in government were advanced mainly by two very different groups in late-nineteenth-century Russia. The first group were those connected with the provincial zémstvos, the organs of local administration that Alexander II had created in 1864 without ever clearly defining their purpose and authority. Through their involvement in such problems as the supervision of local road-building and conservation projects, the zemstvos almost immediately became involved in broad matters of public policy. Already in the sixties, the aristocratic leaders of several of the zemstvos in relatively Westernized regions like Tver and Chernigov sought to convert the zemstvos into organs of self-government as a kind of federative counter to the authoritarianism and bureaucratic sloth of the central government. The Tsar placed new restrictions and checks on the zemstvos during the general reaction of the late sixties, but called them back to life in the seventies to help in the mobilization of local resources and opinion first against the Turks and then against terrorism and revolution.

The zemstvos aided the central government in both enterprises but sought to exact a price for their aid in the form of a constitution that would protect them from "terrorism from above" as well as "terrorism from below." Many joined the informal organization of zemstvo constitutionalists organized by Ivan Petrunkevich in 1878–9 and seconded his call for a constitutional assembly. When the new Tsar once more restricted zemstvo activities during the reaction of the early eighties, zemstvo liberals acquired a voice abroad in the journal *Free Word,* published by the "Society of Zemstvo Union and Self-Government." Although this society proved short-lived and nationwide political agitation by the zemstvos was drastically curtailed after the assassination of Alexander II, the zemstvos continued to grow in importance because of the great increase in their non-aristocratic, professional staffs (the so-called third element, after the government-appointed and locally elected elements). There were nearly 70,000 zemstvo employees by the late nineties. The zemstvo ceased being an exclusively aristocratic preserve, and the two key organizations of constitutional liberalism at the turn of the century each included professional along with aristocratic "elements": the Moscow discussion group, "the Symposium," and the émigré journal *Liberation.*

The new generation of educated professional men in the cities provided the real cement for the emerging liberal movement. The growth of professional competence in an increasingly educated and diversified society created a growing fund of exasperation with what seemed to them an outmoded and irrational legal system. Prophet of this new no-nonsense professionalism was Vladimir Bezobrazov, an imaginative follower of Saint-Simon, who organized a series of "economic dinners" to discuss various hypothetical patterns of future development for Russia. Following his French teacher, he urged the replacement of the old aristocracy of privilege by a new aristocracy of talent. He believed that the hope for Russia lay in the development of a practical, professional attitude toward the solution of its economic problems and attached particular importance to his own Saint-Simonian plan for a network of canals inside Russia. As early as 1867 he argued that the zemstvos were the natural organ for developing in Russia this thirst for "practical results" (*prakticheskie rezul'taty*), and that the growing professionalism of the zemstvos must be protected both from the traditionalism of the local aristocracy and the "bureaucratism" of the central government.[24]

Increased confidence in the "practical results" being achieved by the various professions in Russia led to an increased desire for political and social recognition. The static political and social system of Imperial Russia offered little place for the new professional groups that formed in the late nineteenth century: student unions, committees on illiteracy, doctors and lawyers associations, and so on. These associations tended to be second only to the zemstvos as a recruiting ground for the future Constitutional Democratic Party.

Russian liberalism was—more than any other current of ideas in nineteenth-century Russia—the work of college professors. The most influential university professors tended to sympathize with liberalism from the time when Professor Granovsky first tried to present some of its salient ideas in his lectures at Moscow University in the 1840's. Granovsky, the spiritual father of the original Westernizers, was the first to lecture in detail to Russians on the historical development of laws and liberties in the democratic West.[25] He suggested that this pattern of development was preferable to that of Russia—without raising utopian hopes that it could be duplicated overnight on Russian soil. Although the radicals of the sixties soon overshadowed and disregarded their more moderate liberal professors, the latter were largely responsible for some of the most important liberalizing reforms of the sixties: the introduction of trial by jury and the extension of higher educational rights to women (well before such rights were recognized in the liberal democratic United States).

Chicherin, who became mayor of Moscow and outlived his friend Granovsky by nearly half a century, was the prototype of the moderate *Rechtsstaat* liberal.[26] In his lectures as professor of law at Moscow, he stressed the importance of rational laws rather than of parliamentary bodies as an effective limitation on arbitrary autocratic power.

By the 1890's, however, a new generation of reform-minded intellectuals was once more viewing Chicherin as a timid conservative, just as Herzen had forty years earlier. The major spokesman for this new, more radical liberalism was another professor, Paul Miliukov, the learned and encyclopedic historian of Russian thought and culture. Miliukov's interpretation of Russian culture generally followed the line sketched out by Alexander Pypin, an Anglophile and positivist whose learned articles in *The Herald of Europe* had really begun the dispassionate, analytical study of the development of Russian thought. In the unfriendly atmosphere of the populist age, he took refuge in exhaustive studies of Russian thought and culture—a path which Miliukov was to follow on several occasions. Though a cousin of Chernyshevsky, Pypin opposed all extremism and sought to continue the tradition of the liberal Westernizers of the forties.

Miliukov translated this wish into practical political activity at the turn of the century. He fortified his liberal, constitutional convictions with extensive travel in France, England, and America and was influential in steering the amorphous liberal movement into a clear-cut program for "the political liberation of Russia." The older aristocratic idea of increased local autonomy and personal liberty was subordinated in the program of the Union of Liberation to the abolition of autocracy. Miliukov urged the immediate convention of a legislative assembly during the war and upheaval of 1904–5; and the Cadet party, of which he was a leading spokesman, consistently sought to extend the authority of the consultative dumas which technically acquired legislative rights in August of 1905.

By identifying themselves psychologically with a still distant and idealized America even more than with England and France, the new Russian liberals were able to think of themselves as apostles of progress rather than apologists for bourgeois self-interest. Miliukov was only the first of a series of Russians to lecture widely in America and write for American journals; and the writings of Woodrow Wilson were known in Russia even before he entered the political arena in the United States. The introduction to a 1905 Russian translation of Wilson's *The State,* by Maxim Kovalevsky, a long-time government official from one of Russia's most learned families, is as urbanely insistent on the rational rule of law (whether through constitutional monarchy or representative republicanism) as any contemporary Western essay. Two years earlier, Paul Vinogradoff, an émigré Russian veteran of the zemstvo constitutional movement, had climaxed his career as an authority on English constitutional law by his appointment to the Corpus chair of Jurisprudence at Oxford. Miliukov, however, went beyond their moderate demand for a state of laws rather than men, insisting that the constitution of 1905 did not go far enough.

In addition to demanding popular sovereignty as the prerequisite for any reform, the Miliukov brand of liberals also contended that social reform and partial agrarian redistribution were necessary concomitants of political reform. The radicalism of the Cadet party led in 1906 to the introduction of new restrictions on the activities of the second duma: the most representative national political forum that had existed in Russia since the *zemsky sobors* of the early seventeenth century. The Cadets had dominated the first duma, seeking in effect to turn it into a legislative body. They protested its dissolution and stated their program in even more radical terms in the Vyborg manifesto of 1906. These radical liberals continued to try to bring Russian political practices into line with those of the Western democracies with which Russia was now allied diplomatically through the triple entente. Miliukov, because of his extensive knowledge of Western practice as well as Russian history, became an increasingly important spokesman for the tradition of constitutional democracy. He was one of the few to accept—indeed claim—the title of liberal; and he was the leading figure in the agitation of the so-called progressive bloc in the last duma of 1915–16: the eleventh-hour effort of liberal reformism to seize the reins of power from the corrupt and inefficient monarchy of the last Romanov.[27]

The fact that the constitutional liberals were inundated by the revolutionary upheaval of March, 1917, and outlawed by the Bolshevik coup of November should not be taken as indication of any inherent Russian antipathy to liberalism. These events occurred during a war which Russia was technically ill-equipped to continue. Considering the obstacles under which liberals had been laboring in Russia, their progress had been rapid and their programs intelligently conceived. Indeed, the Bolsheviks were in many ways more fearful of the liberals than of any other group during their initial efforts to seize and consolidate power. The Cadets were among the first to be imprisoned; and the appeal of the liberal democratic idea of a constituent assembly had become so great even among the revolutionaries that the Bolsheviks were forced to permit the elections for it to take place in November, 1917. Thirty-six million Russians cast ballots; and when only one fourth voted for the Bolsheviks, the dissolution of the assembly became almost a foregone conclusion. The liberal tradition had come to Russia with too little too late. It was denounced by Lenin as "parliamentary cretinism." Miliukov and other Cadet leaders had sought to overcome the uncertainty and political inexperience of Russian liberals. But it is doubtful if even a more confident and experienced liberal party could have established constitutional and parliamentary frameworks for evolutionary change amidst conditions of war, revolution, and social disintegration.

Through the more radical program of Miliukov, the constitutional democrats had succeeded in gaining new appeal among the intellectuals and in overcoming the indifference to political reform that had been characteristic of the populists. The liberals were aided in this task by chastened, non-revolutionary elements in the populist camp. Mikhailovsky pointed the way for this more moderate populism. After refusing to collaborate with the zemstvo constitutionalists in 1878, he began to argue—on the very pages of the People's Will journal of the late seventies—that socialists should reconsider their traditional hostility toward Russian liberals. His "Political Letters of a Socialist" recognized that political reforms and constitutional liberties might facilitate the non-violent transformation of society envisaged by the evolutionary populists. A number of influential populists also assigned increased priority to political reform in the émigré journal of the late eighties, *Self-Government.* The "People's Justice" organization of 1893-4 committed Mikhailovsky and some three thousand other populist sympathizers inside Russia to the proposition that abolition of autocratic government in Russia was—in the words of one of their pamphlets—"the pressing question" of present-day Russian life. The liberal movement adopted many of the folk rites of populism in order to broaden their intellectual appeal. Banquets, circle discussion meetings, commemorative gatherings, and illegal publications abroad were all utilized by the new generation of liberals as they had been by earlier radicals. Many populists and Marxists, who sought to advance their socialist objectives through practical political activity rather than illegal revolutionary agitation, formed tactical alliances with the constitutional liberals in the late imperial period.

Nevertheless, the constitutional democratic cause in Russia was handicapped by the split among non-revolutionary reformers between radical and conservative impulses. In order to gain the support of many intellectuals, minority groups, and populist sympathizers it was necessary to combine socialist and egalitarian proposals with constitutional reforms. Such proposals, however, alienated many provincial aristocrats and entrepreneurs. Many of those who had originally joined in the cry for constitutional reform and representative government at the turn of the century were willing to settle for the extension of civil liberties, the approval of a consultative national duma and the constitution of October, 1905. These "Octobrists" dominated the third and fourth dumas with an essentially conservative emphasis on historical continuity and the danger of revolution. Even this cautious group showed signs of vitality, however. Octobrists, aristocratic zemstvo elements, and members of various splinter groups between the

Cadets and the Octobrists played the leading role in forming the remarkable "village city" (*zemgor*) committees which helped finance the Russian war effort in 1915. The very divisions within the liberal camp in the early years of the twentieth century indicated, moreover, a certain vigor. Men of differing philosophic and economic outlooks sought to ally themselves with the traditions of constitutional democracy. Although the Cadets were unable to make their party the forum for all this diversified liberal sentiment, they were not nearly as timid and confused in the face of mounting chaos during the war as many other elements in Russian society. The Cadets were, indeed, the only major political group with a counter-program to that of the Bolsheviks in the critical years of revolution and civil war. The Cadets were both determined reformers and clear foes of totalitarian elements within the reforming camp.

In his elaborate post-mortems on the Revolution, Miliukov suggested that the abstract utopianism of the intelligentsia was a contributory factor to the success of Bolshevism. Criticism of the intelligentsia had been a constant theme in the writings of the ill-fated constitutional liberals of imperial Russia. In contrast to populists on the left and Pan-Slavs on the right, liberals stressed the importance of learning from the West and recognizing the rights and sanctity of the individual. But they generally favored a creative adaptation of Western liberal values to Russian conditions, not merely a slavish imitation. Kavelin, one of the original Westernizers of the forties and an articulate aristocratic liberal throughout the rest of the century, was typical in his insistence that Russians avoid taking over "outmoded forms in which Europe itself no longer believes."[28] He was as prophetically perceptive as Dostoevsky in his memorandum of 1866, depicting the revolutionary paths into which the intelligentsia was drifting; yet he also had the courage to challenge the confusion between universal values and Russian national characteristics in Dostoevsky's Pushkin speech of 1880.

One of the many neglected liberal critics of the intelligentsia in the nineteenth century was Eugene Markov, the widely traveled editor of the journal *Russian Speech*. He accused Russian intellectuals of being responsible for a new fanaticism that was the very antithesis of the pragmatism and empiricism of the positivists whom they were forever quoting.

The "intellectual layer" of Russia has withdrawn from participation in the activity of this essentially "practical" century. It has plunged Russia into a needless "turmoil of thought" (*smuta umov*) that is far more dangerous than the turmoil (*smuta*) of the seventeenth century, because the intelligentsia bears within itself the "sickness of narrow party-mindedness" (*bolezn' parteinosti*).[29] Russia needs responsible citizens not "ideologues," deep criticism not "talmudism in journalism" and "judgment by shrieking."[30] He rejects the "Muscovite school in literature" for its "zoological" chauvinism. In an article of the late seventies called "Books and Life," Markov relates the revolutionary crisis in Russia not just to the worsening of material conditions but to the continuing refusal of the intellectuals to apply anything but "bookish theories" to Russian problems. In a perceptive passage that applies to the seventeenth as well as the nineteenth century, Markov notes:

> Books, in the general course of Russian spiritual growth, have played a remarkably unimportant role, in any case considerably less than in other European countries. But, in Russia, books have produced something which they have not produced anywhere else—they have produced schism (*raskol*).[31]

The greatest need in Russia is to overcome schism, the separation between books and life. The future for Russia is almost unlimited, if its writers can "open for Russian thought the broad path to practical activity."[32]

Russian intellectuals are "good-for-nothings" (*nikchemnye*), "hypochondriacs," who prefer to be "ideologues rather than citizens or even people." His model for imitation is English political life, which teaches one "how to live, struggle, and accomplish things."[33] Everyone, Markov insists, has spiritual doubts and problems; but only the English have learned to separate these concerns from political life. Unfortunately in Russia

> none of us know or want to know anything about local interests or local facts. Every schoolboy seeks first of all final ends, first causes, the fate of governments, questions of the world and all humanity.[34]

Markov issues an almost plaintive plea for an experimental approach to Russian problems and an end to sectarian intolerance:

> Let us recognize honorably and clearly the existing world . . . cease the despotic system of proscriptions and intolerance. . . . Let us be, in a word, men, enlightened citizens of Russia and not of a party or a journal. Let us be grown men of experience and strength, and not children all excited about some little book.[35]

His hero is Alexander II. As Markov wrote immediately after the Tsar's assassination (and shortly before his own journal was shut down by Pobedonostsev):

> This Tsar-liberator suffered like Christ at Golgotha for the sins of others. May his sufferings, like those of Christ, point the way to salvation for his true people.[36]

But the path of liberalization was not the way taken by Russia. The sufferings of Alexander II were commemorated not by continuing his work of reform but by building on the spot where he died a large brick church in the artificially revived Muscovite style of the late imperial period. The intrusion of this pseudo-Muscovite style into the classical architectural milieu of St. Petersburg was a kind of symbol of the return to reactionary nationalism under Alexander III and Nicholas II. Constitutional democracy was given only a brief and troubled moment on the stage of history. Its temperate ideology was lost between the frozen Russia of Pobedonostsev and the flaming Russia of social revolution. However telling the critiques advanced by Markov, Miliukov, and other liberals, the more extreme traditions of the intelligentsia prevailed over the forces calling for more moderate and experimental approaches. Two new philosophies of the late imperial period—dialectical materialism and transcendental idealism—encouraged the very tendency toward doctrinal and metaphysical thought which the liberals had tried to challenge.

Dialectical Materialism

OF THE TWO NEW philosophic currents that emerged in the silver age, dialectical materialism and transcendental idealism, one was more radical and one more conservative than constitutional liberalism. Unlike liberalism, these two traditions shared a common resolve to build on the previous experience of the intelligentsia. Each of them sought to fortify Russia through ideology rather than reform it with a political program. Each sought to answer the philosophic concerns of the intelligentsia rather than challenge the relevance of these concerns to Russian problems. Whereas the constitutional liberals tended to be sharp critics of the abstract traditions of the radical intelligentsia, both the new materialists and the new idealists were solidly rooted in these traditions. The materialists claimed to be the heirs to the traditions of the iconoclastic sixties; the idealists claimed to be developing the traditions of Dostoevsky's aesthetic and religious reaction to iconoclasm.

A major reason for the simultaneous appeal of these two ideologies in the nineties was the exasperation of a new student generation with the subjectivism, pessimism, and introspection of the age of small deeds. This new generation no longer hoped to find a positive message among the oppressed Slavs of the Ottoman Empire or the oppressed peasants of the Russian Empire. The new generation felt the need to check the preoccupation with personal salvation and the self-defeating drift toward an anarchistic rejection of all authority that was characteristic of reformers of the seventies and eighties. Evolutionary populists, such as Mikhailovsky, spoke of history as a "struggle for individuality" against all forms of collective authority and all "books of fate, however learned." Revolutionary populists drifted into the indiscriminate terrorism of the People's Will and its anarchistic "disorganization section."

The passionately anti-authoritarian and semi-anarchistic Proudhon was the most important single teacher of Russian radicals during the populist age. The violent anarchism of Bakunin, the non-violent moralistic anarchism of Tolstoy, and the optimistic evolutionary anarchism of Kropotkin —all represented creative developments of Proudhon's widely studied social teachings.[37] Tolstoy probably took the title *War and Peace* from Proudhon's tract of the same name. The tradition of courtroom oratory by radicals tried under the new jury system first caught the public eye in 1866, with Nicholas Sokolov's impassioned defense of Proudhon's anarchistic socialism as the true Christian answer to the problems of society. Sokolov had talked with Proudhon in Brussels in 1860 and, in his book *The Heretics,* designated Proudhon as "the model heretic" and last in a long line of "true Christian" revolutionaries. Proudhon's insistence on a Christianity of ethics rather than metaphysics and his opposition to all forms of political authority (including that which is "made respectable by having it proceed from the people") made him the leading prophet of the moralistic anarchism which dominated much of the thinking of the populist era.[38] Following Proudhon, Russian populism was a highly emotional and moralistic doctrine that appealed to men through idealistic exhortations, which are difficult to sustain in the face of prolonged adversity. Its passionate plea for simplicity and morality in human relationships seemed inadequate to a generation that was entering the more complex world of industrialized modernity; its philosophic thinness and frequent anti-intellectualism made it repellant to the better-educated and more widely read student generation of the nineties.

Thus, the spirit of protest led the new radicals of both right and left to seek some new philosophic bedrock on which to stand. The lonely anarchistic dreamer was beginning to feel out of place in the busy society of the nineties. The subjective depression, the disjointed memoirs and sketches of the era of small deeds began to give way to the ideologies of two new prophetic figures: the Marxist George Plekhanov and the idealist Vladimir Solov'ev. Subjectivity and a sense of isolation were challenged by these two influential prophets of objective truth. Plekhanov and Solov'ev were both real philosophers rather than publicists or journalists. Each had been active in the agitation of the populist age; each went abroad in the

eighties to discover a new faith for the Russian intelligentsia. Each looked
to the West—but to different Wests. Solov'ev, the partial model for
Alyosha Karamazov in *The Brothers Karamazov,* was interested in religious
and philosophic ideas. He went to the Catholic West in search of spiritual
union and the regeneration of society through a new mystical and aesthetic
attitude toward life. Plekhanov, who had led the first major demonstration
of revolutionary populism in front of the Kazan Cathedral in St. Petersburg
in 1878, was interested in economic and social problems. He went to the
West of the international working class movement and became the father
of Russian Marxism.

Prior to Plekhanov's conversion Russians had known and venerated
Marx, but had either neglected or misunderstood the main tenets of Marxism. Engels' *Situation of the Working Class in England* and Marx's *Critique
of Political Economy* and *Capital* had been widely studied in Russia during
the populist era. But populists tended to view Marx's works as an eloquent
argument for bypassing capitalism altogether. The populists insisted that
the way to socialism in Russia lay in preventing rather than undergoing a
capitalist stage of development; in relying on the moral idealism of the educated classes rather than the material forces of historical inevitability. Russian radicals remained close to Proudhon—Marx's original ideological foe
in the European socialist movement—in their suspicion of the centralized
state and of all dogma, and in their ideal of peasant simplicity and a "conservative revolution." Russian revolutionaries abroad sympathized almost
to a man with the revolutionary anarchist Bakunin in his struggles with
Marx in the First Socialist International (1864–76). Populist writers inside
Russia looked on Marx's philosophy as a complicated Germanic theory
with little application to Russian reality.

Marx himself disliked most Russians that he met, generally favored
the extension of German over Russian influence in Europe, and consistently
viewed Russian developments as a minor sideshow in a historical drama
centered on the industrialized West. Nonetheless, he was flattered by the
attention his writings received in Russia. Particularly after the failure of the
French Commune in 1871, he became interested in the possibility that unrest in Russia might serve as a catalyst for a new wave of revolutionary
risings in the West. He also began to study the economic development of
Russia, suggesting that many Russian peasants would have to become urban
workers but that the economic analysis of "capital is neither for nor against
the peasant commune," which might well serve as a "point of support for
social regeneration."[39] Marx died in 1883 without leaving any clear analysis
of Russian developments and possibilities. Engels, who was less interested
in Russia than Marx, never took the time to make any detailed study of

Russian developments prior to his death in 1895; but he recognized that populism was related to the idealistic forms of socialism which he and Marx had long opposed within the international socialist movement. Shortly before his death he wrote one of his Russian correspondents that "it is necessary to fight populism everywhere—be it German, French, English, or Russian."[40]

It fell on the shoulders of Plekhanov to conduct the Russian phase of the international struggle between authoritarian and libertarian socialism. It is curious that Marxism, which theoretically down-graded the role of the individual in history, was in practice extraordinarily dependent on the leadership of individuals. Plekhanov almost single-handedly introduced Marxism into Russia as a serious alternative to the populist ideology; just as the "three who made a revolution"—Lenin, Trotsky, and Stalin—were responsible for enthroning it as a new state ideology after the unrest of 1917–21.

The essence of Plekhanov's Marxist position is contained in "Socialism and the Political Struggle" of 1883, his first major work published after his flight abroad in 1880. Plekhanov had strongly opposed the political terrorism of the People's Will while in Russia, forming his own splinter group, Black Redistribution, which attached priority to redistributing land among the dispossessed "black" elements of the population. After the failure of terrorism to produce anything but a swing to reaction, Plekhanov was in a position to claim vindication. Instead, he sought to conciliate the rival camp, to discard his own previous ultra-populist attachment to peasant ways and to federal dilution of power, and to provide a new outlook altogether for Russian radicalism.

Plekhanov begins his pamphlet of 1883 by praising the populist tradition for its "practical" orientation in going "among the people" and leading them into a "conscious political struggle."[41] However, he insists that such a struggle will fail unless based on "scientific socialism" and above all on the repudiation of the anarchistic romanticism and abstract moralism of Proudhon, "the French Kant."[42] A rational understanding of economic development is indispensable for those who seek revolutionary political change. He returns regularly to this theme, most effectively in his long essay "Socialism and Anarchism," where he challenges the implicit populist idea that these two social philosophies are in some sense complementary. Socialism is the necessary form which social life must take in a modern society where the means of production have been socialized. Anarchism is an irrational form of protest against these processes. Plekhanov and his "liberation of labor" organization were the first important group of Russians to become familiar with the German Social Democratic tradition, with its emphasis on ordered progress; and they shared some of the German contempt for anarchism, which was at best a "bourgeois sport" and at worst an invitation to irrationalism of all kinds:

> In the name of revolution anarchists serve the cause of reaction; in the name of morality they encourage the most immoral actions; in the name of individual freedom they trample underfoot the rights of their neighbors.[43]

Marxism provides the theoretical basis for the revolutionary movement in Russia as elsewhere by providing an objective science of society and history. In contrast to the dualism of the populists, which was unable to "build a bridge across this seemingly bottomless abyss"[44] between noble ideals and harsh realities, Plekhanov's philosophy is totally monistic. The material world alone is real, he proclaims repeatedly in a series of studies on materialism that was climaxed by his most influential book (and the only one published in Russia prior to the revolution), *On the Question of the Development of the Monistic View of History: In Defence of Materialism*. Absolute objectivity is possible, because "the criterion of truth lies not in me, but in the relations which exist outside of me."[45]

Plekhanov thus offered to a new generation of radical thinkers a monistic, objective philosophy that would liberate them from schism and subjectivity. As distinct from classical materialism of France in the eighteenth century (and Russia in the 1860's), Plekhanov's materialism contained a built-in guarantee of revolutionary change, for it is "historical" or "dialectic" materialism. Following Marx, it contends that the material world is in a state of motion and conflict and that the liberation of all humanity will inevitably come out of the clash of opposing forces in the material world. The driving forces in human society are social classes; and the social class to whom the future ultimately belongs is the proletariat.

As early as his 1884 pamphlet, "Our Differences," Plekhanov bluntly insisted that Russia was already in a capitalist stage of development. It was irrelevant to him whether private or state capitalism was controlling the economy; the practical result was that a new urban proletariat was coming into being. This class—rather than the demagogic and self-important intelligentsia or the confused and primitive peasantry—was the true bearer of progress in Russia. The proletariat had a practical familiarity with the tools of material progress and would not be so easily misled by demagogic talk of a "people's will." The growth of a proletariat was historically inevitable, and the old communal forms of organization no longer had any realistic potential for serving as socialist alternatives to the pattern of economic development which Marx had outlined in *Capital*. In his consistent attempt to "appeal to reason, not feelings," Plekhanov insisted that the

Russian revolutionary movement must effect an "unconditional break with its present theories" by accepting "a revolutionary theory" rather than "theories of revolutionaries."[46] The program of the Liberation of Labor group urges not the dissolution of other radical groups but rather that the revolutionary struggle be fortified by a group recognizing the importance of "organizing a Russian workers' *socialist party*" and acknowledging the "international character of the present-day working-class movement."[47]

Plekhanov brought into the light of day many of the inconsistencies and presumptions of populist thought: the romantic attachment to the idea of a special path for Russia, the exaggerated belief in the ability of individuals to change the course of history, and the palpably unscientific theories of history and "formulas of progress" advanced by populist writers. The rational cosmopolitanism of Plekhanov's Marxism had a particular appeal to leaders of some of the minority cultures within the Russian empire, whose peoples were subjected to new indignities by the Russification campaigns of the late imperial period. Even before the first Marxist circle was formed inside Russia proper in 1885, a Marxist circle and journal had appeared in Russian-occupied Latvia; and the rapidly growing Social Democratic movement of the nineties had particular strength among the more advanced and Westernized peoples of the Russian empire: Poles, Finns, and Georgians. Plekhanov's chief lieutenant, Paul Axelrod, was a Jew, and the Jewish Bund was one of the most important catalysts in bringing together the Social Democrats of the Russian Empire for their first national congress in 1898.

Plekhanov's Marxism also had a more general appeal for the increasing number of thinking Russians who were becoming preoccupied with problems of material growth and economic analysis. Economic analysis became in the last two decades of the century a major subject of intellectual interest in Russia. There were sophisticated populist economists like Nicholas Danielson (Marx's most regular Russian correspondent), liberal economists like Alexander Chuprov (a lecturer on political economy at the University of Moscow and a regular economic analyst for the daily newspaper *Russkie Vedomosti—Russian Reports*), and an increasing number of professional economists in the service of the central government and local zemstvos. The predominant influence on Witte and most government economists was Friedrich List's national system urging protective tariffs and state investment in order to develop a balanced and self-sufficient national economy.[48] Also influenced by List was the great chemist Dmitry Mendeleev, who devoted much of his energy to devising the regional and industrial patterns and the necessary tariff structure for the development of a Russian national economy. He visited and admired America, but not the "politic-mongering" (*politikanstvo*) of democratic politicians. As early as 1882 he advocated separating the ministry of industry from that of finance in order to stimulate economic growth; and he was active in the agitation that led to the founding in 1903 at the St. Petersburg Polytechnical Institute of the first separate faculty of economics in a Russian institution of higher learning.[49]

Amidst all this interest in economic problems, Marxism with its unique and unequivocal insistence on the primacy of the economic factor to all of life and history was bound to have a strong intellectual appeal. So great was the infatuation with Marxist ideas in Russian intellectual circles of the nineties that Marxism rapidly became caught up in the factional debates that were simultaneously raging in the liberal camp. Some Russian Marxists, the so-called economists, accepted a Marxist analysis of economic development but wished to concentrate on improving the economic lot of the workers rather than working for a political revolution. Somewhat more radical were the "legal" Marxists, who built on Marxist economic analysis and accepted the need for a political struggle against autocracy but favored a merging of the socialist and liberal causes in a common struggle for the democratic liberties that were prerequisite for social democracy.[50]

The leading spokesman for the "legal" or "revisionist" Marxists was Peter Struve, one of the most ranging minds of the late imperial period, who also participated in the new currents of liberalism and idealism. Grandson of the Danish-German first director of the Pulkovo Observatory, Struve spent much of his early life in Stuttgart, and brought to the study of Russian reality a deep grounding in the philosophical and economic thinking of the German universities and the German Social Democratic movement. His *Critical Comments on the Economic Development of Russia,* written in 1894 at the age of twenty-four, was the first full-length original Marxist work to be published in Russia, and it provided the guidelines for the general assault of economists in the late nineties on the populist contention that the capitalist phase of development might be avoided or bypassed in Russia. He also wrote a seminal philosophic critique of the shallow progressivist ideology of Mikhailovsky and other populists in his long introduction, in 1901, to Nicholas Berdiaev's first book, *Subjectivism and Individualism in Social Philosophy.* This work also reflected his critical attitude toward rigid philosophical orthodoxy and revolutionary "Jacobinism" within Russian Marxism. His *Marxist Theory of Social Evolution* of 1899 had denied that there was a fundamental, dialectical opposition between capitalism and socialism, and foresaw a natural, continuing progression toward socialism along lines proclaimed in Eduard Bernstein's famous work of the same year, *Evolutionary Socialism.*[51]

All three of the new perspectives of the late imperial period came to play a role in Struve's protean intellectual development. Although retaining an essentially Marxist approach to social and economic analysis, Struve became an active leader in the movement for constitutional liberalism, beginning with his founding of the semi-monthly journal *Liberation* in Stuttgart in June, 1902. His continuing interest in the Russian cultural and intellectual tradition brought him into increasingly sympathetic contact with philosophic idealists and neo-Orthodox thinkers. In his incisive contribution to their famous symposium, *Landmarks,* Struve blamed Bakunin and the modern tradition of "irreligious alienation from government" for the lack of constructive evolution in contemporary Russian social and political life.[52]

Plekhanov resented Struve's blurring of the revolutionary element in Marxism, and insisted on fidelity to the ideology of dialectical materialism and on the development of a working-class movement distinct from those of bourgeois liberals. The main body of Russian Social Democrats (who became known as Mensheviks after the split with Lenin's Bolsheviks at the Second Congress of the Social Democrats in 1903) remained faithful to Plekhanov's doctrine, looking to him for intellectual guidance and a continuing link with the Second Socialist International, which had come into being in 1889.

Plekhanov and the Mensheviks represented the rationalistic middle way in Russian Marxism. They rejected any accommodation with political liberalism or philosophic idealism. But at the same time they rejected as a reversion to the discredited tactics of earlier Russian Jacobins Lenin's call for a professional revolutionary elite in his *What Is To Be Done?* of 1902 and his speculations on the possibility of a proletarian alliance with the revolutionary peasantry in his *Two Tactics* of 1906. Only amidst the turmoil of the revolutionary period would these Bolshevik ideas gain widespread popularity in Russia—along with the even more un-Marxist idea advanced during the Revolution of 1905 by Trotsky that the bourgeois and proletarian revolutions might be compressed into one uninterrupted revolutionary transformation.

Plekhanov was unable to return to Russia until the collapse of tsardom in 1917, at which time he urged continuing the war and avoiding any premature proletarian bids for power. Ill and increasingly unnoticed amidst the rushing tide of events in the late summer of 1917, the father of Russian Marxism went, together with Vera Zasulich, his old friend and associate through the long years of emigration, on one last nostalgic climb up the Sparrow Hills, which were shortly to be renamed for Lenin. It was a melancholy reprise of the excited youthful climb of Herzen and Ogarev more than a century before, when they had sworn their oath to avenge the fallen Decembrists on the same spot. After the October Revolution, his house was ransacked by the victorious Bolsheviks, and he was deliberately called "citizen" rather than "comrade" in view of his "pedantic" insistence that a democratic revolution must precede a proletarian one. An old and lonely man now in disgrace with left and right alike, Plekhanov left Russia shortly thereafter for newly independent Finland, where he died of tuberculosis early in 1918.[53] With him perished Marxism as an extension of Western radical humanism into Russia and a rational doctrine of economic progress and cultural enrichment. Plekhanov had hoped to overcome the conspiratorial attitudes and peasant-bred, utopian fanaticism of the Russian revolutionary tradition on which Lenin with his greater opportunism—and perhaps deeper roots in Russian popular thinking—was building.

Plekhanov dying in Finland while Russia was in flames in 1918 resembled in many ways Miliukov dying in France while Russia was again in flames in 1943. Both men were intellectuals, men of European culture who were at the same time profound analysts of Russian thought. Both wished to correct the errors and irrationalities of past Russian traditions by introducing rational methods of analysis and encouraging greater familiarity with the reformist traditions of the West. Both maintained concern for their native country even in defeat and oblivion, Plekhanov calling for resistance to White as well as Red terror in his last lonely days, just as Miliukov called for support of Russia against Hitler's invasion.

Both were rejected in the early twentieth century partly because of the primitiveness of Russian thought and the unfamiliarity and complexity of their proposals. Even more decisive, however, in the defeat of both liberal and social democracy was the failure of the West either to prevent the great war which crushed and disintegrated Russian society, or to support fully in the aftermath of that war those forces that still clamored for a chance to relate Russian development to the patterns of Western democracy.

Mystical Idealism

IF DIALECTICAL MATERIALISM provided a method for a new generation of radicals to rise above the isolation and pessimism of the age of small deeds, mystical idealism provided the way out of subjectivism for more conservative thinkers. If Plekhanov, the prophet of Marxism, was a critic of populist particularism, Solov'ev, the spokesman for the new mysticism, was a trenchant critic of Pan-Slav and Orthodox parochialism. No less than Miliukov and Plekhanov, Solov'ev was a man of broad European interests who was steeped in Comtian philosophy and widely traveled in the West.

But his preoccupations were religious and aesthetic rather than political. He was concerned for spiritual rather than political reasons with the fate of the Poles and the Jews within the Russian empire, and was anxious to affect a rapprochement with Roman Catholicism in the interests of a re-united and totally renovated "universal church": a "free theocracy" that would include Jews as well as Christians and would harmonize science and religion with a "free and scientific theosophy."

Like Plekhanov and Miliukov, Solov'ev was born in the fifties and deeply affected by the ideological trends of the sixties. He was the second son and fourth child of Sergius Solov'ev, author of a history of Russia which has never been equaled either in size or in encyclopedic command of sources. From his early years young Vladimir seems to have dreamed of accomplishing something equally remarkable. As a boy, however, he was less close to his stern, humorless father than to his part-Polish mother and his grandfather, who was a priest. His youth was enlivened by a vivid imagination and a Schilleresque love of play. Known as "the pecheneg" (the most feared and adventuresome of the early steppe people), he was fascinated by tales of Spanish knights in his youth. At the age of nine he had the first of his visions of the divine feminine principle which would inspire both his poetry and his social theories. The image of the divine woman, whom he later called sophia, came to him holding a flower in the midst of shining light and is typical of the occult mystical tradition which he did much to revive and make respectable in Russia. A second vision of sophia came to him in the British Museum, where on a traveling scholarship in the mid-seventies he was studying Gnostic philosophy. He set off immediately for Egypt, where he had a third vision of sophia, before returning to Russia to present his new theories to a large and excited audience. The major philosophic rival in late Imperial Russia to the materialistic doctrine which Marx had drawn up from the economic treatises and revolutionary reflections in the British Museum proved to be the new idealism that Solov'ev conceived from religious writings and mystical visions in another part of the same great library.

Solov'ev's conception of renovation was, in many respects, even more revolutionary and utopian than that of the Marxists. No less than the materialist Plekhanov, the idealist Solov'ev offered an absolute, monistic philosophy to the new generation. "Not only do I believe in everything supernatural," he wrote, "but strictly speaking I believe in nothing else."[54] The material world was "a kind of nightmare of sleeping humanity."[55] But just as Plekhanov's materialism appealed to the younger generation because it was a dynamic, historical form of materialism, so does Solov'ev's ideal-istic supernaturalism have a dynamic, historical cast. It is based on the belief that all things in the world are in search of a unity that is bound to be realized in the concrete world through sophia. The sophia of his visions is the feminine principle of Jacob Boehme's theosophy as well as the "divine wisdom" of the Greek East. In seeking a kind of mystical erotic union with sophia, man puts himself in communion with the ideal "all-unity" (*vseedinstvo*) which pervades God's cosmos. Solov'ev does not, however, advocate a contemplative retreat from the world. On the contrary, the striving for "all-unity" impels one into the world of the concrete. God himself seeks "all-unity" through his creation, which is an intimate form of God's own self-expression. Man must seek this same unity and self-expression through art, personal relations, and all other areas of creative experience.

Solov'ev's *bête noire* in the Russian intelligentsia is Tolstoy, whose later philosophy sought to deny man's sensual and creative nature. Like Dostoevsky, Solov'ev was haunted by the problems of division and separation; but the Tolstoyan idea that human striving was itself the cause of evil was deeply repellent. Whereas Tolstoy, the exuberant lover of family life, ended up denying the validity of sexual desire, Solov'ev, the lonely bachelor, saw in it one of the positive impulses through which the sense of division in humanity was overcome. Tolstoy's morality is shallow because it seeks to repress rather than engage the passions of men; because it is general and abstract rather than concrete and specific. Solov'ev pointedly entitled his long philosophic treatise of 1880 *A Criticism of Abstract Principles*. Abstraction followed from the separation from God, which had produced "The Crisis of Western Philosophy" (the title of his first major philosophic treatise of 1874).

A new integral philosophy was still possible in the East, Solov'ev felt, if Russia were willing to be "the East of Christ" rather than "the East of Xerxes." God demonstrated His own approval of the urge toward the concrete and sensual by taking on human form through Christ; and this act was only the first in the divinization of the world and the transfiguration of the cosmos. His famous lectures on God-manhood, which were delivered in the first half of 1878, affirm bluntly that "Christianity has a content of its own, and that content is solely and exclusively Christ."[56] The important thing is not Christ's teachings—as Tolstoy might have said—for these, Solov'ev agrees, are all contained in the higher ethical pronouncements of other great religious teachers. The important thing about Christ was the concrete, integral fact of his life and mission in overcoming the separation between man and God. Men are drawn to Christ—and thus to the possibility of overcoming their own separation from God—not by the abstract thought that He is the word (*logos*) incarnate but by concrete attraction to the goodness and beauty of Christ's life. Man is attracted thus to the quality of sophia in Christ Himself; for sophia is "the idea which God has before him as Creator and which He realizes" in his creation.[57]

But how is one concretely to find sophia, to help attain God's "all-unity" on earth? Solov'ev offered a variety of programs and ideas for overcoming conflict in the course of the late seventies. He began by donating the substantial amount of money that he received for his twelve lectures on God-manhood to the Red Cross on the one hand and to the fund for restoring the Santa Sophia Cathedral in Constantinople on the other. Practical steps to alleviate immediate suffering and renewed reverence for the older spiritual unity of Christendom—these were the main points in his program. In May, 1878, he joined Dostoevsky (who had attended his lectures) on a pilgrimage to visit the elders of the Optyna Pustyn. The death of his father in October, 1879, further intensified his sense of spiritual calling.

The split between science and faith could be overcome by less dogmatic philosophies in both fields. He proposed a "free and scientific theosophy" which—following Boehme—would recognize as equally valid and ultimately complementary three methods of knowledge: the mystical, the intellectual, and the empirical. The split between East and West could be overcome if each recognized that it had something to learn from the other. The East believes in God but not humanity; the West believes in humanity without God. Each needs to believe in both. Secular humanism cannot survive on a philosophic base which contends in effect that "man is a hairless monkey and *therefore* must lay down his life for his friends.[58] But the Orthodox East is equally doomed with its contention that man is made in the image of God and must therefore be ruled with the knout. Russia must learn from the West, and particularly from Auguste Comte's humanistic positivism. In Comte's religion of humanity and his identification of humanity as *le Grand Être,* or as a kind of feminine goddess, Solov'ev detected an idea strikingly akin to that of sophia. The Comtian idea that history moved from a theological to a metaphysical to a final "positive" stage and a rational, altruistic society seemed entirely compatible with Solov'ev's concept of God Himself moving toward self-realization in the concrete world of men. The good society is for Solov'ev, as for Comte, that of "normal" man; and the divisions in humanity are only passing and irrational holdovers from the senseless doctrinal quarrels of the past.[59]

In the late seventies Solov'ev began to speak out sharply against excessive chauvinism, denouncing, for instance, the proposal made by some Pan-Slavs for using chemical warfare against the Turks. His famous lecture after the assassination of Alexander II, in which he urged the new Tsar to forgive the assassins and thus usher in a new era of Christian love in Rus-

sia, was received with tears of joy by a large audience, including Dostoevsky's widow, who assured Solov'ev that her husband would have approved.

As a result of this experience, Solov'ev was publicly reprimanded and
temporarily prohibited from giving public lectures. He decided to resign
from his teaching position and also from a post in the ministry of public
education. Like Miliukov and Plekhanov, Solov'ev used the period of reaction in the eighties as one of "withdrawal and return": of intellectual
reassessment in order to provide new answers for Russia's problems. Like
Miliukov and Plekhanov, Solov'ev acquired a new appreciation for the importance of change in the social and political sphere; but he advocated
neither liberal democracy nor proletarian socialism but "free theocracy."

This highly original conception, which Solov'ev sought to perfect
throughout his writings and travels of the eighties and early nineties, was
designed to reconcile total freedom with a recognition of the authority of
God. God was to have three earthly vicars: the Tsar, the Pope, and the
Prophet. The Tsar would bring into the new age the ideal of a Christian
ruler, the Pope of a unified church, and the prophet would speak in the
poetic language of the higher unity yet to come. Free theocracy would come
about not through coercion but through man's free impulse toward "all-
unity" through sophia, "to whom our ancestors with wonderful prophetic
feeling built temples and altars without yet knowing who she was."[60]

He urged Alexander III to become "the new Charlemagne," who
would unite Christendom politically; and he was blessed by the Pope and
leading Western Catholic officials, many of whom were deeply impressed
by his project for reunification. Solov'ev was perhaps the most profound and
searching apostle of Christian unity in the nineteenth-century world. For,
although he was in his later years more sympathetic with Catholicism than
with Orthodoxy or Protestantism, he had (almost alone in nineteenth-
century Russia) a sympathetic understanding of all three branches of
Christendom. Moreover, he conceived of the problem of unification not
in terms of conversion but in terms of leading all the churches to a higher
form of unity that none of them had yet found. The Catholic Church was
admired as the germ of a social order that transcended nationalism. The
isolation and persecution of the Jews in Russia was condemned not only
for humane reasons but also because the coming theocracy needed the
prophetic spirit and interest in social justice that the Jews had kept alive:

> Their only fault perhaps is that they remain Jews and preserve their
> isolationism. Then show them visible and *tangible* Christianity so that they
> should have something to adhere to. They are practical people—show
> them Christianity in practice. . . . The Jews are certainly not going to
> accept Christianity so long as it is rejected by Christians themselves. . . .[61]

Solov'ev seems to have regarded himself as the prophet of this new theocracy; and the poems, fables, and essays on art that he wrote in his last years are in many ways an effort to give concrete form to this prophetic spirit. But pessimism began to replace his earlier hopeful expectation of a "free theocracy." A new and violent paganism was rising to challenge the Judaeo-Christian world; and the symbol of this new force was Asia, which was just being discovered by the Russian popular mind, thanks to the completion of the Trans-Siberian railroad and the beginnings of Russian imperialistic adventures in the Far East.[62] Solov'ev was both repulsed and fascinated by the rising East. Even before the first Sino-Japanese War in the mid-nineties, Solov'ev wrote a poem, "Pan-Mongolism," which depicted the conquest of Russia by a horde of Mongolians. In his *Three Conversations with a Short Story of the Antichrist,* written in 1900, the year of his death, Solov'ev portrays Japan as having unified the Orient and overrun the world. This anticipation of the surprising triumph that Japan was shortly to register over Russia is only one of the many prophetic elements in the work. The Antichrist has come to rule over this new world empire —claiming like Dostoevsky's Inquisitor to be carrying on and perfecting Christ's work. The Antichrist is rather uncharitably given many of the opinions and attributes of Solov'ev's ideological opponent, Tolstoy. All three Christian churches have declined in strength with the growth of material prosperity and new forms of entertainment. They are easily subordinated to his rule. But a few from each communion have the strength to resist and retire to the desert, including an Orthodox community under the leadership of an elder.

> Russian Orthodoxy had lost millions of its nominal members when political events changed the official position of the Church, but it had the joy of being united to the best elements among the Old Believers and even among many sectarians. . . . The regenerated Church, while not increasing in numbers, grew in spiritual power.[63]

These Orthodox are reunited with all other Christians when the Jews, who had helped build the rule of Antichrist, suddenly realize that he is not the Messiah and begin a rebellion against him. Thus, the Jews are reunited in solidarity with Christians, the pagan cities are swallowed up by rivers of fire, the dead are resurrected, and Christ comes again to launch his millennial rule on earth together with his saints and "the Jews and Christians executed by Antichrist."[64]

Solov'ev's prophetic writings and magnetic personality helped inspire a variety of new developments of the silver age. First of all, he played a leading role in the revival of idealism as an intellectually respectable philosophy. He attempted to show that philosophic idealism was logically implied by the moral idealism of the populist tradition. Whereas Plekhanov cited this same fact to criticize the populists, Solov'ev cited it in order to beckon the moral idealists on to idealism and his own brand of dynamic mysticism. Many who started out as Marxists in the nineties soon went over to the new idealism under Solov'ev's influence: Berdiaev, Struve, and others. His *Justification of the Good,* which began to appear serially in 1894 (and was republished as a book in 1897 and 1899), vigorously contended that idealism was the only possible basis on which moral imperatives could be elevated above material self-interest and defended from philosophic scepticism.

Related to his rehabilitation of idealism is Solov'ev's more general role in helping launch a tradition of serious critical philosophy in Russia. Only with the lifting of curricular restrictions on the teaching of philosophy in 1889 did such a tradition become possible in Russia. With the founding of the journal *Questions of Philosophy and Psychology* in the same year, Russia at last acquired its first professional journal of technical philosophy. At last there was a medium for critical absorption of Western ideas rather than voracious consumption in the manner of earlier thick journals. The bracketing together of philosophy and psychology in the new journal indicates an immediate willingness for fresh approaches. Solov'ev contributed not only to this journal but also to an even more widely read medium for philosophic education in the 1890's, the Brockhaus-Efron encyclopedia. This eighty-six-volume collection remains even to this day the greatest single treasure chest of published information in the Russian language; and Solov'ev, as the director of its philosophy section and author of many individual articles, contributed richly both to its literacy and to its sophistication.

Solov'ev also had an influence on the small but significant return to the Russian Orthodox Church that began to take place after his death in the early twentieth century. Dostoevsky's late works and Solov'ev's writings combined to enable a number of former radicals suddenly to discover in the Orthodox Church something more than the organ of state discipline that it appeared to be for Pobedonostsev. Men like Bulgakov, Frank, and Berdiaev were willing to brave ridicule by their intellectual associates in order to reaffirm allegiance to the Church in *Landmarks* of 1909 and several other collections. These intellectuals professed to believe in the new rather than the old Christianity, insisting that true Christianity taught freedom rather than coercion and was not in conflict with social change but was rather necessary to fulfill and sanctify it. The movement for renewal in the Russian Orthodox Church was part of the general movement toward religious modernism that was noticeable in most Christian communities in the early twentieth century. Although the Russian Orthodox Church was remarkably slow in acknowledging the need for new approaches, it did demonstrate an element of independent vitality amidst the disintegration of authority in 1917, convening a church council in August of 1917, which re-established the long-abolished Patriarchate and launched a belated but nonetheless important claim to be an institution with a destiny and mission that should continue even though the old dream of an Eastern Christian empire should be shattered.

Finally, and perhaps most important, Solov'ev had a profound impact on the remarkable artistic revival of the silver age. Solov'ev was one of the pioneers in the rediscovery of the joys of poetry. Although his own poems are, for the most part, not masterpieces, his idea that the world is but a symbolic reflection of a more vital ideal world all around us gave poets a new impulse to discover and proclaim these higher beauties and harmonies. Solov'ev's cosmological theories revived the old idea of prophetic poetry common to Schelling and Saint-Martin. His philosophy was as important in calling forth the poetry of the silver age as had the philosophy of these earlier romantic figures been in inspiring the poetry of the golden age a half century earlier. The rediscovery of poetic beauty, of viewing the sensual world as an avenue to a higher spiritual world, came as a welcome relief from the increasingly dry prose of realism in decline. The art of social utility and photographic naturalism had held the stage for several decades; but with the decline of the thick journals, whose critics had consistently shouted down all believers in art for art's sake, the way was being opened for fresh artistic approaches. With the acquisition of *The Northern Herald* by Solov'ev and several other religiously oriented poets in 1891, the idea that beauty has a meaning of its own gained a new mouthpiece. The publication of Dmitry Merezhkovsky's "Symbols" in 1892 and his "On the Present Condition of Russian Literature and the Causes of Its Decline" the following year gave new popularity to the idea that the real world is only a shadow of the ideal and that the artist is uniquely able to penetrate through the former to the latter.

Solov'ev's poetic references to a mysterious "beautiful lady" were both a symptom and a cause of the new turn toward mystical idealism. The beautiful lady was in part Comte's goddess (*vièrge positive*) of humanity, in part the missing madonna of a revived romanticism, and in part the divine wisdom (*sophia*) of Orthodox theology and occult theosophy. Although Solov'ev died earlier than either Plekhanov or Miliukov, his immediate posthumous influence in early-twentieth-century Russia was probably as great as the living impact of these other figures. Solov'ev appealed to visionary impulses which were still very much alive in Russia. He offered Russia, so to speak, one last chance to transcend the world of the ordinary and immediate, the "conglomerated mediocrity" (*posredstvennost'*) that so repelled the intelligentsia. The political and economic thought of Plekhanov and Miliukov influenced those who contended for power in an age of revolutionary change; but the extraordinary cultural revival of the early twentieth century was born under the brilliant if evanescent star of Solov'ev.

The change in artistic styles from populist realism to the idealism of the silver age may be likened to the change in drinking tastes from the harsh and colorless vodka of the earlier agitators and reformers to the sweet, ruby-colored *mesimarja,* which became popular among the new aristocratic aesthetes. *Mesimarja* was a rare, exotic drink, extremely costly and best appreciated at the end of a large and leisurely meal. Like the art of the silver age, *mesimarja* was the product of an unnatural, half-foreign environment. *Mesimarja* came from Finnish Lapland, where it was distilled from a rare berry that was ripened by the midnight sun during the brief Arctic summer. The culture of early-twentieth-century Russia was equally exotic and superlative. It was a feast of delicacies tinged with foreboding. As with the *mesimarja* berry, premature ripeness carried with it the promise of rapid decay. Sunlight at midnight in one season led to darkness at noon in the next.

VI

THE UNCERTAIN COLOSSUS

The Twentieth Century

THE CULTURAL EXPLOSION *amidst war and revolution during the first quarter of the twentieth century. Music as the dominant art form in an age of passionate liberation and liberated passion. The Prometheanism of the revolutionary "God-builders" and of the attempt by Alexander Scriabin (1872–1915) to transform the world by synthesizing the arts. The ascent into outer space through the rockets of Constantine Tsiolkovsky (1857–1935) and the "suprematist" art of Casimir Malevich (1878–1934). The concurrent descent into sensualism and diabolism. Apocalypticism in art and life: the poetry of Alexander Blok (1880–1921); the prose of Eugene Zamiatin (1884–1937); the politics of Leon Trotsky (1879–1940).*

The March and November revolutions of 1917, and the debt of Lenin (1870–1924) to the traditions of the Russian intelligentsia. A quarter century of catechistic totalitarianism under Stalin (1879–1953) from the beginning of the first Five-Year Plan in 1928 to his death in 1953. The complex roots of Stalinism in both the tsarist and the revolutionary traditions, in the Leninist conception of an authoritarian party, but, above all, in the need to provide an appealing mass culture for a primitive peasant people. The revenge of Muscovy on St. Petersburg, the site of the Revolution and the symbol of cosmopolitanism during the psychotic purges of the Stalin era. The Stakhanovites as "flagellants" and party apparatchiki *as "Old Believers" of Muscovite Bolshevism. The metamorphosis of luminous icons, ringing bells, and consoling incense into lithographs of Lenin, humming machines, and cheap perfume.*

Boris Pasternak (1890–1960) and Dr. Zhivago (1958) as both a last echo of the mystical, poetic culture of late Imperial Russia and a prophetic interpretation of the Russian revolution and the Russian future. Old and new themes in the cultural ferment of the Khrushchev era (1953–64). The restless new generation "of the sixties." The recurring ironies and future possibilities of Russian culture.

1. Crescendo

THE REVOLUTIONS of 1917 occurred in the midst of a profound cultural upheaval which Bolshevism had not initiated and did not immediately curtail. Between the late 1890's and the "great change" (*perelom*) effected by Stalin during the first Five-Year Plan (1928–32), Russian culture continued to sputter and whir through what might be called its electric age.

Like electricity—which spread through Russia during this period— new currents of culture brought new energy and illumination into everyday life. The leading revolutionary rival of Lenin and Trotsky later complained of the "electric charges of will power" that they imparted in 1917; and those leaders in turn sought to move from power to paradise by defining Communism as "Soviet power plus electrification." Many assumed that the bringing of light and energy to the intellect was equally compatible with Soviet power. Just as amber, long thought to be merely decorative, had revealed the power of electricity to mankind, so the theater was "destined to play the part of amber in revealing to us new secrets of nature."[1] Just as raw electricity often ran wildly through new metal construction in the rapidly growing cities of early-twentieth-century Russia, so these new artistic currents broke through the insulation of tradition to jolt and shock the growing numbers of those able to read and think. As with electricity, so in culture it was a case of old sources for new power. Man had simply found new ways of unlocking the latent energy within the moving waters and combustible elements of tradition. Thus, the new, dynamic culture of this electric age was, in many ways, more solidly rooted in Russian tradition than the culture of the preceding, aristocratic era.

In poetry, the new symbolism soon gave way to futurism, acmeism, imaginism, and a host of unclassifiable styles. On the stage, the spirited ensemble work of Stanislavsky's Moscow Art Theater, the fiery impressionism of Diaghilev's Ballet Russe, the "conditionalism" and "biomechanical" expressionism of Meierhold's theater—all demonstrated an accelerating pace of life and exuberance of expression. In music, Stravinsky sounded the death knell of romantic melodic cliché with his cacophonous "Rite of Spring"; and Russia produced a host of new musical forms along with two of the relatively few figures whose pre-eminence in a given area of the musical stage has remained undisputed: the bass Chaliapin and the dancer Nizhinsky. In all phases of creativity there was an exhilarating new concern for form and a concurrent revulsion against the moralistic messages and prosaic styles that had dominated Russian culture for half a century.

Of all the art media, music was perhaps the determining one. Alexander Blok, the greatest poet of the age, spoke of escaping from calendar time to "musical time."[2] Vasily Kandinsky, its greatest painter, considered music the most comprehensive of the arts and a model for the others. Chiurlionis, another influential pioneer of abstract painting, called his works "sonatas" and his exhibitions "auditions."[3] The "futurist" Khlebnikov, the most revolutionary of poets and self-proclaimed "chairman of the world," broke up familiar words just as cubist painters broke up familiar shapes, seeking to create a new and essentially musical "language beyond the mind" (*zaumny iazyk*). Words, he contended, "are but ghosts hiding the alphabet's strings."[4] The Moscow home of David Burliuk, where futurist poets and painters met, was referred to as "the Nest of Music."

In prose, a new musical style was evolved and a new form of lyrical tale, "the symphony," developed by the seminal figure of Andrew Bely.[5] In the theater Meierhold's fresh emphasis on the use of gesture and the grotesque was born of his belief that "the body, its lines, its harmonic movements, sings as much as do sounds themselves."[6]

Even among the most puritanical and visionary of Marxist revolutionaries there was a curious fascination with music. Alexander Bogdanov, theoretician and leader of the remarkable effort to produce an integral "proletarian culture" during the Civil War, believed that oral singing was the first and model form of cultural expression, because it arose from man's three most basic social relationships: sexual love, physical labor, and tribal combat.[7] Bogdanov's friend, Maxim Gorky—the proletarian realist among the aristocratic nightingales—dedicated his anti-religious *Confession* of 1908 to Chaliapin; and Lenin confided to Gorky that music provided a profoundly disturbing force even in his monolithic world of revolutionary calculation:

> I know nothing more beautiful than the "Appassionata," I could hear it every day. It is marvellous, unearthly music. Every time I hear these notes, I think with pride and perhaps childlike naïveté, that it is wonderful what man can accomplish. But I cannot listen to music often, it affects my nerves. I want to say amiable stupidities and stroke the heads of the people who can create such beauty in a filthy hell. But today is not the

time to stroke people's heads; today hands descend to split skulls open, split them open ruthlessly, although opposition to all violence is our ultimate ideal—it is a hellishly hard task. . . .[8]

The revolutionary events of 1917–18 in which Lenin played such a crucial role have a kind of musical quality about them. Mercier's characterization of the French Revolution, "Tout est optique,"[9] might be changed for the Russian Revolution into "Tout est musique." In France there was a certain "demonic picturesqueness" in the semi-theatrical public execution of the King (on which Mercier was commenting) and in the aristocratic, neo-classical poet, André Chenier, stoically writing his greatest poetry in prison while awaiting execution. In Russia, however, there was no "Latin perfection of form"[10] to the Revolution. The Tsar was brutally shot with his entire family in a provincial basement and their bodies mutilated in a forest, while poets from the old order, like Blok and Bely, wrote half-mystical, half-musical hymns to the Revolution in the capital, seeing in it, to cite Blok, "the spirit of music."

Symbolic of these chaotic revolutionary years was the extraordinary institution of the *Persimfans,* an orchestra freed from the authoritarian presence of a conductor.[11] In the emigration, there sprung up the so-called "Eurasian movement," which saw in the Bolshevik Revolution "the subconscious revolt of the Russian masses against the domination of an Europeanized and renegade upper class." Leading Eurasians hailed the new Soviet order for recognizing that the individual man fulfilled himself only as part of the "higher symphonic personality" of the group; and that "group personalities" could alone build a new "symphonic society."[12] A kind of icon was provided for artists of this period by the pre-revolutionary painting of the "suprematist" Casimir Malevich, "The Cow and the Violin," which symbolized the vague hope that the agitated creativity of the violin might somehow replace the bovine contentment of bourgeois Russia.[13] Even a future fighter for the old order like Nicholas Gumilev wrote a pre-Revolutionary poem bidding the artists of his age "look into the eyes of the monster and seize the magic violin."[14]

Stringed instruments provide, indeed, the background music for this period of violent change: the gypsy violins of Rasputin's sectarian orgies in imperial palaces, the massed guitars of fashionable aristocratic nightclubs, the unparalleled profusion of virtuoso violinists in Odessa, and the balalaikas which accompanied the popular melodies sung around campfires by both sides throughout the Civil War. The consolidation of Bolshevik power between the coup of November, 1917, and the peace of 1921 provides a kind of feverish crescendo to the music of runaway violins. The sound of "harps and violins" (the title of one of Blok's collections of poems) began to fade soon thereafter, so that the later, Stalinist, revolution brought silence to the cultural scene from exhaustion as well as repression. The silence was broken only by prescribed ritual, communal chants and the grotesque merriment of collective farmers dancing at pre-arranged state festivals. The role of music in the Stalin era is typified by Alexis Tolstoy's paean to Shostakovich's Fifth Symphony as the "Symphony of Socialism."

> It begins with the Largo of the masses working underground, an accelerando corresponds to the subway system; the Allegro in its turn symbolizes gigantic factory machinery and its victory over nature. The Adagio represents the synthesis of Soviet culture, science, and art. The Scherzo reflects the athletic life of the happy inhabitants of the Union. As for the Finale, it is the image of the gratitude and enthusiasm of the masses.[15]

The pendulum of history had swung back from the freedom and experimentalism of the electric age to the authoritarianism of the candle-lit past. Indeed, "the silence of Soviet culture"[16] was all the more terrifying for its simulacra of sound.

The remarkable brief interlude of freedom that preceded a quarter century of Stalinist totalitarianism was dominated by three general attitudes: Prometheanism, sensualism, apocalypticism. These were preoccupations rather than fixed ideologies: recurring leitmotivs amidst the cacophony of the age, helping to distinguish it from the period immediately before or after. Each of these three concerns had been central to the thought of Solov'ev; each was developed to excess in the years following his death in 1900; each became suspect as Russia plunged back into a new "iron age" under Stalin.

Prometheanism

PARTICULARLY PERVASIVE was Prometheanism: the belief that man—when fully aware of his true powers—is capable of totally transforming the world in which he lives. The figure of Prometheus, the Greek Titan chained to a mountain by Zeus for giving fire and the arts to mankind, had long held a certain fascination for radical romantics. Marx had idealized this legendary figure; and Goethe, Byron, and Shelley had elaborated the legend in their writings. Now the Russians, as they plunged more deeply into the mythological world of antiquity, also turned admiring eyes to Prometheus.

Merezhkovsky translated Aeschylus' *Prometheus Bound;* others read *Prometheus und Epimetheus* of the Swiss Nietzschean, Carl Spitteler, or *La scommessa di Prometeo* of Leopardi. Ivanov wrote a *Prometheus* of his own in 1918, and objects as far afield as a leading publishing house and a key musical composition of Scriabin bore the name Prometheus. Revolutionary admirers of Beethoven in Russia as elsewhere saw themselves as "creatures of Prometheus" and hailed the Prometheus theme in the last movement of their hero's Eroica Symphony, in which Beethoven was thought to defy Christian doctrine about man by shouting "in a voice of thunder: 'No, thou art not dust, but indeed the Master of the Earth.' "[17]

Russians of this period sought like Prometheus to bring fire and the arts to humanity. Thus, their interest in questions of form and technique did not, for the most part, create indifference to social questions, but rather excitement over the possibility of solving them with the alchemy of art. Moreover, increased interest in contemporary European culture did not imply indifference to Russian tradition. On the contrary, the amassing in Russia of unparalleled collections of contemporary French art and the popularization of a wide variety of contemporary Western art on the shimmering pages of *The World of Art* (*Mir iskusstva*) coincided with the rediscovery, restoration, and reproduction of icons and the development of a new, more spiritualized form of religious art by figures like Michael Nestorov.

The diversity of Russian culture in the late imperial period is exemplified by the three most widely discussed events in Russian culture during the last year before the outbreak of World War I: the first performance of Stravinsky's ultra-modern, neo-pagan "Rite of Spring," the opening of the first large exhibit of fully restored ancient icons and the "futurist tour" of a group of avant-garde poets and painters. The first event took place in Paris, the second in Moscow, and the third in seventeen provincial cities. But there was little sense of conflict. As in the golden age of Pushkin, Russians of the silver age sought answers that would be equally applicable for all mankind. The preceding age of Alexander II and III and the succeeding age of Stalin were far more parochial. Populists and Pan-Slavs under the Alexanders were interested mainly in the peculiar possibilities of Russia: just as Stalinists concentrated on "socialism in one country." Populists, Pan-Slavs, and Stalinists all looked to the West primarily to learn from its natural scientists and social theorists. But Russian thinkers in this period looked at the full spectrum of Western artistic and spiritual experience.

With the enthusiasm of fresh converts, Russian artists saw in the newly discovered world of art something to be enjoyed for its own sake and exalted for the sake of all mankind. The term "Russian Renaissance,"

which is sometimes used to describe the cultural activity of the early twentieth century, is appropriate in suggesting a similarity with the love of art
and exaltation of human creative powers of the Italian Renaissance. Art
offered Promethean possibilities for linking Russia with the West, man with
man, and even this world with the next.

The exciting possibilities of creative art tended to lure many away
from democratic socialism or liberalism which should perhaps have commanded the allegiance of the educated anti-authoritarian intellectuals.
Nicholas Berdiaev, who had been interested in social democracy in the
1890's, reflected the new indifference to piecemeal reformism when he said
almost derisively of the representative Duma of 1906: "These Russian
Girondists will not save Russia, for something great and important is necessary to accomplish such a salvation."[18] Creativity, he argued, was the only
way in which the human spirit can free itself from "the prison" of ordinary life:

> The idea behind every creative art is the creation of another way of
> life . . . the breaking through from "this world" . . . the chaos laden, dis-
> torted world to the free and beautiful cosmos.[19]

The "free and beautiful cosmos" of art seemed to offer new possibilities
for harmonizing the discords of an increasingly disturbed world. The romantic idea so prevalent in the age of Pushkin that different art forms were
all expressive of a common spiritual truth was revived and intensified.

The Ballet Russe represented a harmonious fusion of the scenic
designs of Benois, Bakst, and Roerich, the music of Stravinsky, the dancing
of Nizhinsky, the choreography of Fokin, and the guiding genius of
Diaghilev. One artistic medium tended to flow into another. Futurism, the
most bold and revolutionary of the new artistic schools, began in painting
before moving into poetry.[20] The painter Vrubel drew much of his inspiration from poets; and his florid colors, in turn, inspired other poets. Briusov
praised the "peacock sheen of outstretched wings" that Vrubel raised over
the "desert" of contemporary life;[21] and Blok, at Vrubel's funeral, waxed
lyrical over the color of his sunset:

> As through a broken dam, the blue-lilac twilight of the world bursts
> in, to the lacerating accompaniment of violins and tunes reminiscent of
> gypsy songs.[22]

Poetry in turn burst into song, most notably in the work of Blok.
Before the Revolution, he had written a cycle of poems to tell "What the
Wind Sings About"; and just after the coup of November he suggested in his

famous "Twelve" that it was singing about the Revolution. Powerful, gust-like lines bring a Revolutionary band of twelve into wintry St. Petersburg. Then, the poet introduces the Revolutionary song traditionally played to the accompaniment of throbbing balalaikas:

> No sound is heard from the city,
>   There is silence in the Nevsky tower,
> And on the bayonet of the sentry
>   Glistens the midnight moon.[23]

In Blok's version, the last two lines are changed to suggest liberation rather than confinement:

> And there are no more policemen—
> Rejoice, lads, without need of wine![24]

Yet the unheard melody is still that of lamenting strings; and Blok came to look on his own poetic tribute to revolution with irony before his early death in 1921.

Blok loved painting and music, wrote plays, studied philology, discoursed with philosophers, and married the daughter of Russia's greatest scientist, Mendeleev. As the greatest poet of a poetic age, he is, ex officio, one of its key cultural figures. But because Blok himself felt that music was closer than poetry to the spirit of the age, it is perhaps appropriate to use Alexander Scriabin, one of the greatest pianists and the most original composer of the age, as the main illustration of Russian Prometheanism.

Scriabin's creative activity was inspired by Solov'ev's mystical faith in divine wisdom and also by the international theosophic movement which had been launched by Mme Blavatsky, the teacher of Solov'ev's elder brother and self-styled bearer of the hidden secrets of universal brotherhood and communion with the dead. The anniversary of her death, May 8, 1891, became known to her followers as White Lotus Day; and it was—among the intellectuals of the silver age—at least as well known as the socialist festival of May Day, which had been established by the Second International exactly a week before her passing.

Solov'ev and the symbolists saw in sophia a mystic union of the divine wisdom and the eternal feminine; and Scriabin sought to possess sophia in both senses through his art. "Would that I could possess the world as I possess a woman,"[25] he wrote, reverting to the obscure, but seductive language of Boehme so familiar to Russian mystics:

> The world is in impulse toward God. . . . I am the world, I am the search for God, because I am only that which I seek.[26]

Christ
Dethroned

PLATES XVI–XVII

The nineteenth century's increasing preoccupation with the purely human aspects of Christ's personality manifested itself in Russian art in a particularly dramatic fashion.

Traditional iconography had displayed a serene but powerful Christ enthroned in triumph—resolving, as it were, the trace of anguish still noticeable in the face of his "precursor," John the Baptist, who is reverently inclined toward him from the left-hand side of the central tryptich of the icon screen. In Ivanov's long-labored "Appearance of Christ to the People" (Plate XVI), John the Baptist is the dominant, central figure; and the timid Christ is less noticeable than the worldly figures in the foreground.

By the end of the century, the somewhat artificial links that Ivanov and aristocratic Russia had sought to forge with the classical world of Rome (where he painted) and Raphael (whom he emulated) had given way to harsh, plebeian realism. Thus, the crucifixion of 1891 by Nicholas Ge (Plate XVII) is a bleak, purely human scene. This painting, which moved Ge's friend Leo Tolstoy to tears, shows a wretched, wasted Christ, no longer capable of resurrection, let alone enthronement. To the left is no longer the iconographic John the Baptist pointing to the coming glory of God's world, but only a thief whose frightened look suggests the self-centered pathos of a new, godless world.

Worse was yet to come in the twentieth century. Repin, in exile from Bolshevism in 1922, painted a crucifixion which showed only the two thieves, with Christ's cross lowered and a wolf-like dog licking the blood of an altogether vanished saviour.

PLATE XVI

PLATE XVII

PLATE XVIII

PLATE XIX

The influence of Michael Vrubel (1856–1910) in late imperial Russia was almost as great on poets and composers as on experimental painters, for whom he had an impact that Naum Gabo likens to that of Cézanne on modern Western artists. Apprenticed in the restoration of church frescoes and mosaics, he soon turned from traditional religious subjects to the mystery of earthly beauty. From his early painting of "Hamlet and Ophelia" to his powerful illustration of Pushkin's "Prophet," Vrubel displayed his greatest power in portraying those figures from the pantheon of romanticism who in some way incarnated the proud beauty of his ultimate hero: the devil.

Beginning with a first sketch in 1885 and stimulated by a commission to illustrate a commemorative edition of Lermontov's "The Demon" in 1890–1, Vrubel painted the devil in a variety of forms, and increasingly referred to "seances" with Satan himself. The two illustrations on the left show his first and last major efforts to depict Satan through a monumental oil canvas. "The Demon Seated" (1890; Plate XVIII) broke sharply with the prevailing artistic realism and provided the Silver Age with a brooding hero: the newly seated prince of this world replacing, as it were, the traditional "Christ enthroned" of the next. "The Demon Prostrate" (1902; Plate XIX, central part only) was completed in the year of Vrubel's mental breakdown. The artist succeeds in suggesting the devil's own mental anguish by distending the figure in a manner somewhat reminiscent of some Russian variants of icons of "Our Lady of Tenderness." The swirling background reveals the influence of art nouveau and expressionism, and contrasts with the more controlled, semi-cubist backgrounds of the earlier "Demon."

Scriabin appears as the consummate romantic, a kind of cosmic Novalis, conceiving of his art as "the last great act of fulfillment, the act of union between the male creator-spirit and the woman-world."[27] His mysticism of endless desire flows, thus, with a certain logic out of the lush Chopin- and Liszt-like melodies of his early piano works. Yet the complex orchestral works to which he soon turned show both technical inventiveness and a unique ability to express the inner aspirations of the age. There were essentially four musical stages in his late artistic-spiritual development: "The Divine Poem" of 1903, his third and last symphony; "The Poem of Ecstasy" of 1908; "Prometheus: The Poem of Fire" of 1909–10; and his "Mystery," which he had only begun at the time of his sudden death in 1915.

The "Divine Poem" depicted the ascent of humanity to divinity: the first movement represented the struggles, the second the sensual delights, and the last the "divine play" of the spirit liberating itself from matter. While composing the "Poem of Ecstasy" abroad, he met many socialists and proposed at one point to use the famous line from *The International* ("Arise ye wretched of the earth") as the epigraph to his work.[28] Deliverance was to come, however, not from a revolutionary leader, but from a messiah who would unify the arts and provide mankind with a "new gospel" to replace the outmoded New Testament. Scriabin apparently viewed himself as a new Christ preaching from a boat in Lake Geneva and establishing close links with a radical Swiss fisherman named Otto: his St. Peter.[29]

The language of his new gospel was to be even more unconventional than the iridescent "Poem of Ecstasy," which still bore some musical resemblance to the tonal sheen of *Tristan and Isolde*. Wagner's "music of the future" was enjoying great popularity in Russia at the turn of the century; and the new musical world of Scriabin's "Prometheus: The Poem of Fire" has been described by one leading Russian critic as

a continuation and development of the grandiose, inspiring finale of Wagner's *Götterdämmerung*. . . . But . . . Wagner's fire brings destruction. Scriabin's, rebirth . . . the creation of that new world which opens up in the presence of man's spiritual ecstasy. . . . His fundamental condition is ecstasy, flight. His element is fire. . . . Fire, fire, fire; everywhere fire. And accompanying it, the sounding of alarm bells and the ringing of invisible chimes. Awesome expectation grows. Before the eyes rises up a mountain breathing fire. "The Magic Fire" of the Wagnerian Valkyries is childish amusement, a cluster of glow-worms in comparison with the "consecrating flame" of Scriabin. . . .[30]

The "consecrating flame" of Prometheus is provided by a totally new harmonic system. Among other features, Scriabin introduced the mystic chords of the flagellants into his music, just as Blok had ended his "Twelve" with the flagellant image of a returning "Christ" at the head of a "boat" of twelve apostolic followers. He also devised a correlation between the musical scale and the color spectrum, writing into the score chords of color to be projected through the symphony hall by a "keyboard of light," a giant reflecting machine to be played like a toneless piano. Fascination with color was a particular feature of an age anxious to compensate for the grayness of early industrialization. Rimsky-Korsakov had independently conceived of correlating sound and color; and the rediscovery of the pure colors of the newly restored icons encouraged a new generation of painters to see in color itself many of the miraculous powers originally attributed to the icons. Vasily Kandinsky, who exhibited the first of his pioneering, non-representational paintings in 1910, the year of Scriabin's "Prometheus," insisted that "color is in a painting what enthusiasm is in life,"[31] and that each color should start a "corresponding vibration of the human soul,"[32] ranging from the total restfulness of heavenly blue to the "harsh trumpet blast" of earthly yellow.[33]

In the last year of his life, Scriabin turned to the great work he hoped would unify the arts and lift man to the level of the gods. In the score for "Prometheus," he had already insisted that the chorus wear white robes to emphasize the sacramental nature of the occasion. Now he began sketching out plans for a "Mystery" that was to involve two thousand performers in a fantastic fusion of mystery play, music, dance, and oratory. It was to be a "ritual" rather than music, with no spectators, only performers; the emission of perfumes was written into the score, along with sounds and colors, to provide a kind of multi-sensory polyphony; and the action was to begin in Tibet and end in England.[34] The fact that this "Mystery" could not be staged—or even clearly written out by Scriabin—was not held against him by artists of the silver age, most of whom agreed with Kandinsky that art is "the expression of mystery in terms of mystery."[35] Humanity was not yet spiritually prepared for anything but mystery. A great cataclysm was needed to prepare humanity for the sublime ritual that would unify the good, true, and beautiful. The cataclysm came with the beginning of World War I, shortly after Scriabin had set forth the first plan ("initial act" he called it) for his "Mystery." Scriabin died just a few months later.

The purpose of art was not to depict but to transform the real world for most artists of the age. In their desire to bring the most advanced art directly into life, they staged innumerable exhibits, concerts, and cultural tours throughout provincial Russia. A highlight perhaps occurred in the summer of 1910, when Scriabin's complex tonal patterns were played on a boat floating down the Volga under the direction of young Serge Kousse-

vitzky, wafting music out across the unresponsive and uncomprehending
countryside.

This Promethean aristocratic art helped spur on a simultaneous revival
of popular art, which in turn provided fresh stimulus for the restless avant-
garde. The aristocracy developed fresh interest in ceramics, woodcarving,
weaving, and embroidery as industrialization began to threaten them. Cottage industries and peasant crafts were given new encouragement by the
provincial zemstvos; and a totally new form of musical folk poem, the
harmonically complex *chastushka,* arose as a kind of grass roots equivalent
to the new and more musical poetry of the symbolists.[36]

Thus, it seems appropriate that much of the initial impulse toward
creating a new experimental Russian art in Russia should come from the
collective attempt of a small circle of artists to rediscover and recreate the
artistic forms and craft techniques of Old Russia near Moscow on the estate
of a wealthy railroad baron, Savva Mamontov.[37] In 1882 they began by
designing, building, and decorating a small church in the early Novgorod
style, and then turned to fashioning stagings for the first private opera
company in Russian history, which Mamontov established in Moscow the
following year.

Mamontov's activities helped move the center of artistic gravity from
St. Petersburg back to Moscow in the 1890's. Even painters like Surikov
and Repin, who had been trained in the dominant St. Petersburg traditions
of realism and social significance drifted to Moscow and the Mamontov
estate, portraying in their masterpieces of the late eighties and nineties
early Russian historical subjects on a vast fresco scale and with a richness of
color that became characteristic of Muscovite painting. In 1892 a wealthy
merchant, P. M. Tret'iakov, donated his vast collection of Russian art to the
city of Moscow, where a gallery bearing his name was established—the first
ever devoted exclusively to Russian painting. Two other Moscow merchants,
Serge Shchukin and Ivan Morozov, subsequently brought to Russia more
than 350 French impressionist and postimpressionist paintings: the greatest
collection of Western art since Catherine the Great's massive importation of
Rembrandts. Moscow became the major center inside Russia for experimental modern artists like Kandinsky, who made the city the subject of a
number of his paintings.

Among the young painters in Moscow stimulated to fresh experimentation by the Shchukin and Morozov collections was Casimir Malevich, an
artist in many respects even more revolutionary than Kandinsky. Like so
many of the avant-garde, Malevich was influenced by a curious combination
of primitive Russian art and the newest, most sophisticated art of the West.
His development through a bewildering variety of approaches in search of

the basic elements of painting illustrates the peculiar Promethean passion that became characteristic of experimental modern art in Russia. Like Kandinsky, Malevich soon left the world of recognizable people and objects for the fresh start of his "black square on a white ground" followed by his famous "white on white" series of 1918.

As Malevich's art became more radical in form, it became more Promethean in purpose; for he sought to free the visual arts from "the tyranny of easel painting" and impose his new ideal forms on the wall-paper, the buildings, the plates—even the coffins—of the future. In what he called "my desperate attempt to free art from the ballast of the objective world," he and his followers attempted to found in the year of Scriabin's death, 1915, an "art of pure sensation,"[38] which he called Suprematism and later "the art of the fifth dimension."[39] The latter phrase, used at a time when Einstein's fourth dimension was still known only to specialists, was no mere figure of speech. As he put it in one typical passage:

> . . . man's path lies through space. Suprematism is the semaphore of color. . . . The blue color of clouds is overcome in the Suprematist system, is ruptured and enters white, as the true, real representation of infinity, and. is therefore freed from the colored background of the sky.[40]

Thus even line and color, the last links which Kandinsky's art enjoyed with the real world, are severed in Malevich's doctrine. A reviewer described him as "a rocket sent by the human spirit into non-existence";[41] and he himself insisted in a manifesto of 1922 that man

> is preparing on the earth to throw his body into infinity—from legs to aeroplanes, further and further into the limits of the atmosphere, and then further to his new orbit, joining up with the rings of movement towards the absolute.[42]

Malevich stands as a kind of artistic prophet of the space age, practical preparations for which were already being undertaken by Constantine Tsiolkovsky, a sickly, self-taught genius from the Russian interior. As early as 1892, he had written about the scientific feasibility of a journey to the moon, and in 1903 he began a long series of amateur cosmic probes with his own small-scale, jet-propelled ballistic appliances. "This planet," he wrote, "is the cradle of the human mind, but one cannot spend all one's life in a cradle."[43]

Space tended to replace for twentieth-century Russia the symbol of the sea with all its symbolic overtones of purification, deliverance from the ordinary, and annihilation of self. The Russian Prometheans spoke no more of an ark of faith or a ship at sea, but of a new craft that would take them into outer space. After his "white on white" series of 1918, Malevich did not paint again for nearly a decade, producing instead a series of sketches for what he called an "idealized architecture": future dwelling places for humanity bearing the name *planity,* from the Russian word for "airplane." Malevich's only serious rival for dominance of the artistic avant-garde in the 1920's, Vladimir Tatlin, was ostensibly far more down to earth with his doctrine of utilitarian "constructivism" and his demand for a new living art of "real materials in real space." But he too reflected this Promethean urge to move out and master that space. Increasingly, his three-dimensional constructions acquired an upward, winged thrust that seems to be tugging at the wires connecting them to earth. Tatlin spent most of the last thirty years of his life designing a bizarre new glider that looked like a giant insect and was called a *Letatlin*—a fusion of the Russian word "to fly" and his own name.[44]

The first thirty years of the twentieth century in Russia was a period in which traditional terms of reference seemed largely irrelevant. As Leo Shestov, the philosopher and future Russian popularizer of Kierkegaard, proclaimed in his *Apotheosis of Groundlessness* in 1905: "Only one assertion has or can have objective reality: that nothing on earth is impossible."[45] Men believed in an earthly "world without end," to cite the title of a Futurist anthology of 1912.[46] Followers of Fedorov continued to believe that the resurrection of the dead was now scientifically possible; Mechnikov argued that life could be prolonged indefinitely by a diet centered on yoghurt; and a strange novel of 1933, *Youth Restored,* by the most popular writer of the 1920's, Michael Zoshchenko, offered a final Promethean reprise on the Faust legend by portraying an old professor who believes that he can restore his youth merely through the exercise of his will.[47]

Beyond the five dimensions of Malevich's art lay the seven dimensions offered by the philosopher, psychologist, and Oriental traveler P. D. Uspensky. Beginning with his *Fourth Dimension* of 1909, he provided new vistas for self-transformation: a completely internal "fourth way" which lies beyond the three past ways to godliness of the fakir, the monk, and the yogi. He offered—in the words of two of his later book titles—"a key to the enigmas of the world" and "a new model for the universe."[48] He insisted that man was capable of a higher inner knowledge that would take him into "six-dimensional space." There are three dimensions in time, which are a continuation of the three dimensions of space, and which lead in turn to a "seventh dimension" of the pure imagination.[49]

In St. Petersburg, Prometheanism found its most extreme—and historically important—expression in the movement known as "God-building" (*Bogostroitel'stvo*). St. Petersburg intellectuals were, predictably, more concerned with social questions than their Moscow counterparts; and, amidst the agitation of the first decade of the new century, a group of Marxist intellectuals struck upon the Promethean idea of simply transferring to the urban proletariat the attributes of God. "God-building" developed partly in reaction to "God-seeking," an earlier movement of St. Petersburg intellectuals who followed Merezhkovsky in turning from aesthetic to religious questions. Their return to philosophic idealism (and in many cases Orthodox Christianity) was celebrated in a variety of publications from the periodicals *New Road* (1903–4) and *Questions of Life* (1905–6) to the famous symposium of 1909, *Landmarks* (*Vekhi*), which offered an impressive philosophic challenge to the positivist and Marxist categories which had long dominated the philosophic thinking of the urban intelligentsia. A musical landmark in this return to religious mysticism was the primarily choral opera *The Tale of the Invisible City of Kitezh*, which was finished amidst the revolutionary turmoil of 1905–6 and first produced early in 1907 by the last survivor of the "mighty handful," Rimsky-Korsakov.

God-building developed somewhat later than God-seeking, and sought to harness the religious anguish of the intellectuals not to traditional faith but to the coming revolution. During the dark days of reaction that followed the failure of the Revolution of 1905, a group of intellectuals sought to supplement Marx with a more inclusive and inspiring vision of the coming revolution. Led by Maxim Gorky, the rough-hewn writer and future high priest of Soviet literature, and Anatol Lunacharsky, the widely traveled critic who became the first commissar of education in the new Soviet state, the God-builders considered themselves to be merely elaborating the famous Marxist statement that philosophers should change rather than merely explain the world. Traditional religion was always linked with intellectual confusion and social conservatism, and the "God-seekers" were only rebuilding the tower of Babel rather than moving on to the New Jerusalem.[50] Nevertheless, religious conviction had been the greatest force for change in history, Lunacharsky contended, and Marxists should, therefore, conceive of physical labor as their form of devotion, the proletariat as their congregation of true believers, and the spirit of the collective as God. Gorky concluded his long *Confession* of 1908 with a prayer to "the almighty, immortal people!"

> Thou art my God and the creator of all gods, which thou hast fashioned from the beauties of the spirit in the toil and struggle of thy searchings!
> And there shall be no other gods in the world but thee, for thou art the one God that creates miracles!
> Thus do I believe and confess![51]

Some contemporary critics referred to Gorky's position as "demotheism" or "people-worship,"[52] and there are many resemblances to the more extreme forms of populism. But Gorky spoke in the more universal language of the silver age. He referred to all men, not merely Russians; to the conquest of death, not merely of hunger. In the final sentence of the *Confession,* Gorky holds out the image of "the fusion of all peoples for the sake of the great task of universal God-creation."[53]

An anonymous Marxist pamphlet published in 1906 and subsequently reissued by the Soviet regime bluntly declared that man is destined to "take possession of the universe and extend his species into distant cosmic regions, taking over the whole solar system. Human beings will be immortal."[54]

Death is only a temporary setback, Lunacharsky affirmed as early as 1903:

> Man moves toward the radiant sun; he stumbles and falls into the grave. But . . . in the ringing clatter of the grave-diggers' spades he hears creative labor, the great technology of man whose beginning and symbol is fire. *Mankind* will carry out his plans . . . realize his desired ideal.[55]

His *Faust and the City* declares that the idea of an immortal God is only an anticipatory "vision of what the might of men shall be,"[56] and ends ecstatically with the people crying over the dead body of Faust "he lives in us! . . . Our sovereign city roused in might."[57]

After the Revolution, Lunacharsky turned to an undertaking that had attracted many past Russian artists: the composition of a trilogy which would provide a new redemptive message for mankind. Like Gogol's *Dead Souls,* Dostoevsky's *Brothers,* and Musorgsky's *Khovanshchina,* Lunacharsky's trilogy was never finished. In keeping with the spirit of the silver age, the first part, *Vasilisa the Wise,* was fantastic in form and cosmic in pretensions. The second part, "a dramatic poem," *Mitra the Saviour,* was never published, and the final part, *The Last Hero,* was apparently never written. The last lines we have of the trilogy is the paean at the end of the mythological *Vasilisa* to the coming of "man's divinity on earth."[58] Such talk was clearly dangerous in a society bent on camouflaging its own myths and absolutes with scientific terminology.

The figure who best portrayed the Promethean vision of the early God-builders was Alexander Malinovsky, a brilliant theorist who has suffered the relative oblivion of those who neither joined the emigration nor rose to high authority in the new Soviet state. Shortly after taking his first regular position as a journalistic critic in 1895 at the age of twenty-two, Malinovsky assumed a new name which remained with him and accurately conveys the image he had of his own high calling: Bogdanov, or "God-gifted." He soon became active in the Social Democratic movement, siding immediately with the Bolsheviks after the split of 1903, and helping edit their theoretical journal *New Life,* where he began his friendship with Gorky.

Bogdanov believed that the ultimate key to the future lay not in the economic relationships and class struggles that were characteristic of past history, but in the technological and ideological culture of the future that was already being created by the proletariat. Marx's fascination with dialectical struggle was an unfortunate holdover from his youthful Hegelianism. In the manner of Saint-Simon rather than Marx, Bogdanov argued that the destructive conflicts of the past would never be resolved without a positive new religion: that the unifying role once played in society by a central temple of worship and religious faith must now be played by the living temple of the proletariat and a pragmatic, socially oriented philosophy of "empiriomonism."

In a long series of studies, beginning with his *Basic Elements of a Historical View of Nature* in 1899, Bogdanov developed the idea that the revolutionary movement would lift man beyond the level of economics, and nature beyond all previous laws of material determinism. The key to this program of cultural regeneration within the revolutionary movement was presented in a long work published in installments throughout the decade 1913–22 under the title *The Universal Organizational Science (Tectology).* This new super-science of "tectology" was designed to provide a harmonious unity between the spiritual culture and the physical experience of the "working collective," in whose interest all science and activity were to be organized and all past culture reworked.[59]

Bogdanov felt that the creation of a new proletarian culture should precede the political annexation of power by the Bolsheviks. His concept of God-building through tectology was designed—like Sorel's concurrent call for a new heroic myth—to kindle enthusiasm and assure the revolutionary movement of success not only in gaining power but also in transforming society. Like Sorel, Bogdanov was enthusiastic over the initial Bolshevik annexation of power; and he rushed into print with a series of writings designed to spell out the God-building possibilities of the new society: the second part of his *Tectology* (1917) and two utopian novels, *Red Star* (1918) and *Engineer Menni* (1919). Though originally published in 1908, *Red Star* produced its greatest impact when it appeared in the second, 1918 edition.[60] Its image of an earth dweller suddenly transported to another planet which was in a feverish ecstasy of socialist construction seemed to many the image of a new socialist society into which Russia might suddenly leap. The novel was reprinted several times; and Bogdanov's organization for the creation of Proletarian Culture (*Proletkult*) enjoyed nationwide popularity throughout the period of Civil War and "war communism"—publishing about twenty journals throughout Russia during those difficult days.

Late in 1920 Lenin forced the subordination of the hitherto free-wheeling Proletkult to the Commissariat for Education. Bogdanov's organization was censured for its claim to have brought about "immediate socialism" in the cultural sphere, a proletarian culture totally emancipated from the bourgeois past. Bogdanov, for his part, in a suppressed pamphlet of 1919, had already expressed the fear that the new rulers were merely a parasitic class of managerial organizers.[61] Proletkult was soon abolished altogether; he and his followers, the so-called Workers' Truth group, denounced; and his prestige undercut by the time *Tectology* was completed in 1922. Bogdanov spent his last days in the relatively obscure but appropriately visionary post of director of an institute for "the Struggle for Vital Capacity" (*Zhiznesposobnost'*). He died in 1928, apparently from a dangerous experiment involving transfusions of his own blood—a front-line casualty, as it were, in his undaunted efforts to take harmony and immortality away from imaginary gods and put them into the real life of men.

The most extreme Prometheanism of the age was found in the so-called Cosmist movement, an offshoot of the God-building movement that flourished in St. Petersburg during the Civil War years of 1918–21. The Cosmists and the closely related Blacksmith (*Kuznitsa*) group of Moscow poets spoke with a kind of frenzied hyperbole about the imminent transformation of the entire cosmos. Under the leadership of Alexis Kuz'min, who took the appropriate pen name Extreme (Kraisky) and entitled his first fantastic book of poems *The Smiles of the Sun*,[62] the Cosmists burst forth with expletives: "We shall arrange the stars in rows and put reins on the moon" and "We shall erect upon the canals of Mars the palace of World Freedom."[63]

One important feature of Revolutionary Prometheanism was its attractiveness to long-submerged minority groups of the Russian Empire. At a time when a groping and desperate Tsar was increasingly relying on repression and Russification, minority peoples looked increasingly to the new worlds being opened up in the cosmopolitan culture of the silver age. Jewish painters like Marc Chagall and Lazar Lissitzky played a key role in the experimental painting of the day; and the Lithuanian painter-musician-writer, Michael Chiurlionis, anticipated much of the most revolutionary art of the day and exerted a shadowy influence over much of the Russian avant-garde. Among the Revolutionaries the role of minority people was no less conspicuous; and it seems appropriate to conclude with two of the most visionary, brilliant, and universal-minded of all Russian Revolutionaries: the

Pole, Wacław Machajski, and the Jew, Leon Trotsky. The silencing of their voices in the course of the twenties was a measure of the retreat of the new regime from the great expectations of the earlier period.

Machajski, who wrote under the pseudonym A. Vol'sky, believed even more passionately than Bogdanov in the need for a totally new type of culture. One must move beyond the culture not only of the aristocracy and the bourgeoisie but also of the newest and most insidiously oppressive social class, the intellectuals. Beginning with his *Evolution of Social Democracy* in 1898, the illegally published first part of his magnum opus, *The Intellectual Worker,* Machajski warned that articulate intellectuals will inevitably find their way to the head of the revolutionary movement and become the controlling oligarchy within any future revolutionary regime. In order to protect the interests of the inarticulate manual workers he called for a world-wide "workers' conspiracy" dedicated to gaining enough economic improvement to permit the workers to raise their level of literacy and culture. Only in this manner could the advantage that the intellectual enjoyed over the worker be neutralized, and the working class assured that a genuine proletarian culture rather than a mythic culture of the intellectuals be built after the revolutionary attainment of power.

Machajski's position resembles the revolutionary syndicalism of Sorel, with its belief in "direct action" in the economic sphere and the development prior to any bid for power of an autonomous, anti-authoritarian working class culture. His form of social analysis is also reminiscent of Pareto's theory of the "circulation of elites," Michels' "iron law of oligarchy," and Burnham's subsequent theory of a purely "managerial revolution." But unlike all these figures Machajski remained an unreconstructed optimist, confident that the workers' conspiracy could save the Revolution and develop fully the Promethean possibilities of the proletariat. Machajski's ideas, which were particularly popular in Siberia, were anathemized by the Bolshevik leadership with particular venom long before his death in 1926.[64]

Even more dramatic was the gradual fall from grace in the 1920's of Leib Bronstein, known as Trotsky, the passionate and prophetic co-author of the Bolshevik coup. From his early days as a populist and a renegade Jew, Trotsky had seen in the coming revolution the possibilities for a total reshaping of human life. Change was to come about not so much through the staged, dialectical progressions that Marx had outlined as through an uninterrupted or "permanent" revolution, through a "growing over" (*pererastanie*) of the bourgeois into the proletarian revolution, of the Russian Revolution into an international revolution, and of a social revolution into a cultural transformation of mankind.

Thus, although Trotsky professed dissatisfaction with the mysticism of the God-builders and Cosmists, he leaves no doubt in his abundant writings on cultural matters about his own "limitless creative faith in the future." In the last lines of his famous collection, *Literature and Revolution,* written in 1925, when his own authority was already on the wane, he expresses confidence in man's ability

> to raise himself to a new plane, to create a higher social biological type, or, if you please, a superman.
> . . . Man will become immeasurably stronger, wiser and subtler; his body will become more harmonized, his movements more rhythmic, his voice more musical. The forms of life will become dynamically dramatic. The average human type will rise to the heights of an Aristotle, a Goethe, or a Marx. And above this ridge new peaks will rise.[65]

Even above these peaks rose the sky-borne hope of transforming the cosmos expressed in "The Chains of Blue," the longest poem ever written by Khlebnikov in his "alphabet of stars." But at the end of a long "blue chain" of images, the poet gives us a prophetic glimpse into a future that was to devour its futurists. He suddenly introduces the familiar figure of Prometheus. But it is a distorted image in which we see only his liver being devoured by eagles.[66]

Sensualism

ALONG WITH THE EFFORT to storm the heavens went a simultaneous impulse to plunge into the depths. Cosmic Prometheanism was accompanied by a counter-current of personal sensualism; boundless public optimism, by morbid private pessimism. Indeed, the early years of the twentieth century brought about a preoccupation with sex that is quite without parallel in earlier Russian culture.

In part, the new sensualism was a reaction against the long-dominant moralism and ascetic puritanism of the radical tradition which had been carried to extremes in the late Tolstoy. The new generation of writers delighted in the knowledge that their main source of inspiration, Vladimir Solov'ev, had used the sage of Yasnaya Polyana as the model for his portrayal of the Antichrist. They longed to rediscover the delights of sex and artistic indulgence which Tolstoy had denied himself no less systematically than had Pobedonostsev.

Exaltation of the flesh was to some extent caused by the rapid advent of a mass, urban culture. The lonely, atomized man of the city found in sex one of his few surviving links with the vital, natural world dimly remembered from his rural boyhood. The provincial, rural elements that increasingly flooded the ranks of art and literature also tended to bring with them elements of earthy folklore, of a popular culture previously suppressed by the official, Orthodox culture of the Empire. The novels of bleak realism that had previously concentrated on characteristic sufferings of the countryside—starvation and exploitation—now turned in the first decade of the new century to the peculiar shame of the cities—sexual degradation. From Leonid Andreev's picture of syphilis and suicide in *The Abyss* and *In the Fog* to Alexander Kuprin's panorama of urban prostitution in *The Pit,* the Russian reading public was subjected to vivid portrayals of sordid sexuality.

To a large extent, however, the increasing preoccupation with sexual matters was a logical development of the romantic preoccupation with the will that had become characteristic of the emancipated aristocratic intelligentsia. Having tried to discover the will of the historical process in the early nineteenth century and the will of the people in the late century, the intellectuals now turned to discovering the inner recesses of their own wills. They now sought to discover not just "the other shore," the new society dreamed of in the nineteenth century, but also "the other side" of human personality. It is significant that both phrases came from German—the language of romantic longing. The original title of Herzen's call for Russia to fulfill the revolutionary hopes that had been betrayed in the West by the failure of 1848 was *Vom andern Ufer;* and *Die andere Seite* was the title of a widely studied German treatise in psychology calling for a new "psychographic" art.[67]

In part, the new sensualism was a Nietzschean effort to find "bloody truths" capable of supplanting the lifeless truisms of a society just entering into a phase of bourgeoisation and national delusions, such as that which Germany had experienced in Nietzsche's lifetime. But Russian sensualism was more than an aristocratic program for replacing Christ with Dionysus in the manner of Nietzsche or Stefan George. It was also at times a confused plebeian effort to revitalize the image of Christ with the flesh that had been taken away from him by the official churchmen in the nineteenth century. Dostoevsky's Schilleresque praise of the earthy and spontaneous, his allusion to "the indecent thoughts in the minds of decent people . . . which a man is afraid to tell even to himself"[68] was taken as a signpost pointing to a new world of experience. Ivan Karamazov's dictum that, in the absence of God, "all things are permissible" became a kind of invitation to sexual adventure for a new generation.

The final repeal of the censorship in the wake of the Revolution of 1905 led to an increasingly candid public discussion of sex. A feverish climax was reached in 1907 with the appearance of Viacheslav Ivanov's semi-mystical exaltation of sex in his collection of poems, *Eros;* his celebration of the varieties of the sexual act in *Veneris Figurae;* and an apologia for homosexuality in the story *Wings,* by Michael Kuzmin, who suddenly became one of the favorite authors of the age.[69] The most remarkable literary events of this time of titillation were the two best-selling novels of 1907, *Sanine* by Michael Artsybashev and *The Petty Demon* by Fedor Sologub.[70]

Sanine, read today, appears as a bad imitation—even a caricature—of the cheap sexual novel. The scene is continually being prepared for seductions in stereotyped nocturnal surroundings to the accompaniment of pretentious monologues on the artificiality of everything but sex, with names like Lida used for added metaphorical suggestion. The reason for the extraordinary impact of *Sanine* was simply that Russian readers saw in it a new philosophy of life. Its philosophical asides (sometimes referred to as "mental ejaculations") ridicule Tolstoy and other moralists, urging men to be true to their sensual desires in the realization that life is senseless and death the only ultimate reality. The novel reaches a climax with three suicides; and self-inflicted death becomes the main theme of many of Artsybashev's subsequent works, such as *At the Brink* in 1911–12. But the preoccupation with sex as the only source of meaning in life was all the public remembered about Artsybashev.

Turgenev's novels had offered to the tired liberals of the 1840's the Schopenhauerian consolation that sexual love provided man with a "focus for willing," "the kernel of the will to live," and suicide a means of overcoming the meaningless monotony of life.[71] In like manner, *Artsybashev-shchina*—the most tongue-twisting of all isms of the late imperial period—rehabilitated for a large segment of the disillusioned and apolitical aristocracy the cult of sex and suicide.

Far greater than *Sanine* was *The Petty Demon,* on which a little-known St. Petersburg schoolteacher, Fedor Teternikov (Sologub), had been quietly working for ten years. The book puts on display a Freudian treasure chest of perversions with subtlety and credibility. The name of the novel's hero, Peredonov, became a symbol of calculating concupiscence for an entire generation. The name literally means "a Don done over," and may refer to the hero of *Don Quixote,* Sologub's favorite book from childhood.[72] His Don, however, seeks not the ideal world but the world of petty venality and sensualism, *poshlost'.* He torments his students, derives erotic satisfaction from watching them kneel to pray, and systematically befouls his apartment before leaving it as part of his generalized spite against the universe. The sexual perversion that underlies his hallucinations and paranoia is underscored by a secondary plot featuring a love affair between the youthful Sasha and Ludmilla, which has undertones of voyeurism, transvestism, and—above all—homosexuality.

The theme of voluptuous corruption even in "innocent youth" is a constant feature of Sologub's eerie short stories—and of many written in imitation of him. It seems appropriate that this theme should be presented to the mass audience of the West most dramatically and effectively through the work of a transplanted Russian, in Vladimir Nabokov's *Lolita.* Yet Sologub's world of perversion is far more subtle and profound, suggesting more universal involvement in the all-consuming world of *poshlost'.* Peredonov, far from being the source of vulgar depravity in the novel, is merely the heightened expression of the general condition of man. The petty demons are everywhere; and no one can be sure where fantasies end and perversions begin, because one man's dream is another man's act and men and women are involved even in one another's gender.

After the extraordinary success of his *Petty Demon,* Sologub turned to the writing of a trilogy designed to satisfy his own Quixotic desire to redeem man from the world of sensuality and mediocrity. Unlike Gogol, Sologub was able to finish his attempt at a *Divina Commedia;* but the *Purgatorio* and *Paradiso* of his poetic imagination tend to offer only more subtle forms of the same preoccupation with sex that had characterized the *Petty Demon.*

Written between 1907 and 1911, the trilogy bears the title *Legend in the Making,* although its original title was *Charms of the Dead.* It begins with the famous declaration that although life is "vulgar . . . stagnant in darkness, dull and ordinary," the poet "creates from it a sweet legend . . . my legend of the enchanting and beautiful."[73]

In the first part, *Drops of Blood,* we are in the same town that provided the site for *The Petty Demon;* but attention is now focused on the mysterious poet Trirodov, who has taken up residence there. Perversion is projected onto the phallic towers and subterranean passageways of his country estate, where he presides over a weird colony of "silent children" but ventures forth to take part in revolutionary agitation. The second part of the trilogy, *Queen Ortruda,* takes one to an imaginary kingdom of lithesome virgins and naked boys on a Mediterranean island, where a volcano is continually preparing for a final eruption, which kills the queen and serves as a mixed symbol of sexual orgasm, political revolution, and death. In the last section, *Smoke and Ash,* Trirodov leaves Russia to take over the vacant throne of the burned-out Mediterranean kingdom. Thus, the poet-magician reaches a kind of Nirvana by fleeing the real world of the Peredonovs and petty demons to the non-being of an imaginary kingdom—beyond good and evil, beyond male and female (as his name "three genders" suggests), beyond the different reincarnations of his personality (also suggested by the variant reading of his name as "three types"), perhaps beyond life itself.

In one of his late stories, "The Future," Sologub speaks of "a place where the future gleams through an azure veil of desire . . . where those as yet unborn rest in peace."[74] Four souls in this happy place suddenly conceive the desire to be born into the world, each expressing a special fondness for one of the primal elements: earth, water, fire, and air. Sologub goes on to tell how the first became a miner and was buried alive, the second was drowned, the third burned alive, and the fourth hanged. He concludes by asking:

Oh, why did Will lead them forth from the happy place of non-existence![75]

In one of his late short stories, "The Kiss of the Unborn," he lends a certain lyric beauty to this gloomy view of the world. The story begins with the suicide of a fifteen-year-old boy, who had become discouraged by reading in the works of Tolstoy and other Russian intellectuals that truth could not be found in life. The boy's unmarried aunt sets off to console her sister, the boy's mother, but soon turns to thinking about her own unborn son: the purely imaginary fruit of an unrequited early love. Suddenly, in the midst of her lonely weeping before the door of her sister, the unborn son appears to her, gives her a kiss, and thanks her for sparing him the agony of being born into the world. She goes in then to see her sister "full of calm and happiness," suddenly armed with "power to strengthen and console."[76]

The happiness of those who are never born was preached most eloquently by Vasily Rozanov, the high priest of the new cult of sex who likened himself to a fetus in the womb asking not to be born "because I am warm enough here."[77] Through Rozanov, the Dostoevskian origins of the new sensualism can be most dramatically traced. Rozanov gave a kind of physical immediacy to this link by seeking out and marrying Dostoevsky's former mistress, Apollinaria Suslova, and launched the new philosophic interest in Dostoevsky with his lengthy essay of 1890, *The Legend of the Grand Inquisitor.*

For Rozanov, Dostoevsky appeared as the harbinger of a new suprarational freedom: a liberation first hinted at in the *Notes from the Underground* and finally developed in the *Legend.* Rozanov insists that Lobachevsky's non-Euclidian mathematics (which were being reproduced in a variety of new editions in the 1880's) demonstrated the tentativeness of scientific truths,[78] and that Dostoevsky's works showed the falsity of any scientific attempt to organize society. Neither God nor reality can be apprehended by reason alone. The only way to rediscover both is through sexual experience.

The cult of the immediate, which had been a precarious way back to traditional Christianity in Dostoevsky, became for Rozanov the way back to a God who is not Christ but Dionysius. Rozanov's "sexual transcendentalism"[79] exalts the religion of the early Hebrews and primitive fertility cults over the ascetic and unnatural traditions of Christianity, which by sterilizing the idea of God have prepared the way for atheism: the inevitable attitude of thought devoid of sex.

Rozanov agreed with the general preference for the earthy, anguished Dostoevsky over the aristocratic, moralistic Tolstoy expressed in Merezhkovsky's famous series on *Tolstoy and Dostoevsky*. But he dissented from Merezhkovsky's view that Dostoevsky was a kind of Christian seer. This tendency to view Dostoevsky as the prophet of a renovated Christianity and *The Brothers Karamazov* as (to cite Gorky's phrase) "a fifth gospel," predominated in the Religio-Philosophical Society of St. Petersburg from the time of its dedication "to the memory of Vladimir Solov'ev" in 1907 until its dissolution in 1912. The view was perpetuated in the brilliant critical works on Dostoevsky written by two of the society's most famous members: Viacheslav Ivanov and Nicholas Berdiaev.

Although Berdiaev has subsequently become better known in the West, Ivanov was in many ways the more seminal thinker. A student of Mommsen in Berlin who had become converted to the Nietzschean idea that "a new organic era" was at hand, Ivanov bade his associates join him in plunging "from the real to the more real"; to leave behind the prosaic realities of the present for a future that will bring with it a new tragic sense. Ivanov insisted that he longed not for the unattainable but simply "for that which has not yet been attained."[80] "Viacheslav the Magnificent" was the crown prince and *chef de salon* of the new society, which met in his seventh-floor apartment "The Tower," overlooking the gardens of the Tauride Palace in St. Petersburg. Walls and partitions were torn down to accommodate the increasing numbers of talented and disputatious people who flocked to the Wednesday soirees, which were rarely in full swing until after supper had been served at 2 A.M.

Nietzsche was in a sense the guiding spirit, for Ivanov looked nostalgically to the lost world of classical antiquity through the eyes of Nietzsche's own academic discipline—philology—and worshipped at the shrine of the vitalistic Dionysus: the god of fertility and wine and patron of drama and choral song. But from the time of his early studies of 1904–5, "Nietzsche and Dionysus," "The Religion of Dionysus," and "The Hellenic Religion of the Suffering God," to his scholarly dissertation on Dionysus defended at Baku in 1921,[81] Ivanov tended to see in the Dionysian cult a prefiguration of Christianity; and he became after his exile in 1925 a resident of Rome and convert to Catholicism. Berdiaev, who later became an émigré apologist for Christianity within the Orthodox fold, was in pre-Revolutionary days closer to Nietzsche in such books as *The Meaning of the Creative Act* of 1916.

Rozanov went much further, insisting that there was a basic conflict between Dionysus and Christ. In a famous speech to the Religio-Philosophical Society, Rozanov attacked Jesus as a figure who never laughed or married, and pleaded for a new religion of uninhibited creativity and sensuality.[82] Rozanov's proposal was given support by Nietzsche's suggestion that all morality is rationalization and that a new type of superman is needed with the courage to live beyond the stultifying categories of good and evil. Shestov's *Dostoevsky and Nietzsche: The Philosophy of Tragedy* saw these two figures as the twin prophets of a new world in which the tragic spirit was to be freed from the shackles of morality for a new life of sensual and aesthetic adventure.[83] Shestov later sought to contrast the German with Tolstoy, the *bête noire* of silver age aestheticism, in his *The Good in the Teaching of Tolstoy and Nietzsche*.[84] The tendency to identify Dostoevsky with Nietzsche rather than Christ was particularly marked among those of Jewish origins like Shestov and A. Shteinberg, who tended to see in Dostoevsky a revolutionary new "system of freedom," to cite the title of a lecture series he gave in St. Petersburg in 1921.[85]

Another important source of the new sensualism was the return to primitivism in the arts. Kandinsky had turned to the *lubki,* or popular wood cuts, of Old Russia for inspiration, and published in 1904 his *Poems without Words,* a portfolio of his own cuts, en route to his more abstract and experimental compositions. Malevich also went through a primitivist period; as did Michael Larionov, who turned to folk themes, simple figures, and distorted anatomies in a desperate effort to find a truly original Russian style of art. He eventually created a purely abstract style of "rayonism," which sought to base painting on "rays of color" rather than lines and fields of color. But in the experimental, interim period that followed the Revolution of 1905, Larionov championed the introduction of pornographic material into painting: salacious slogans in his "Soldier" series and ingenious improvisations on sexual shapes in his subsequent "Prostitute" series.[86] These and other primitive and suggestive paintings were exhibited in Moscow early in 1912 by a group with the deliberately shocking name "The Donkey's Tail," which represented "the first conscious breakaway from Europe"[87] within the artistic avant-garde. A similar movement through primitivism to modernistic innovation can be traced in music. Stravinsky's revolutionary "Rite of Spring" was suggested to him by an unexpected and erotic vision of a solemn pagan rite in which a circle of elders watched a young girl dance herself to death to propitiate the god of spring and fertility.[88]

The bawdiness of Larionov endeared him to the literary futurists, who used him and his friends as illustrators for their works. The use of erotic motifs, infantile forms of expression, and vulgar epigrams became common to painters and poets alike of the "futurist" persuasion, who were in pre-war Russia generally more preoccupied with the sensuous and personal than the original Franco-Italian futurist Marinetti, who had been more interested in "the aesthetics of the machine." Russian futurism represented, in the title of its most famous manifesto, "a slap in the face of public taste." Rather in the manner of Oscar Wilde and the aesthetes and dandies of Edwardian England, the Russian futurists delighted in bizarre attire—appearing on the street with abstract signs painted on their cheeks and radishes in their buttonholes. The painter-poet Burliuk brothers, who organized the futurist tour of 1913–14, typified the egocentric exuberance of the movement. Vladimir, a professional wrestler, carried mammoth weights with him everywhere he went, and his equally gigantic older brother, David, appeared with the legend "I am Burliuk" painted on his forehead

If one can speak of a synthetic proclamation of liberated sensualism comparable to Scriabin's Promethean proclamation, it would probably be the futuristic movie "Drama in Cabaret No. 13," which was filmed late in 1913. In contrast to the melodramas set in remote times and places which were the standard fare of the infant Russian movie industry, this film was simply an average bawdy day in the life of the futurists. Its actors were the artists themselves—the Burliuk brothers, Maiakovsky, and Larionov—behaving in particularly shocking ways as they satirized the movie industry, the society that patronized it, the world itself, and the entire subject of sex, through which one senseless generation leads on to another.

By late 1913, sensualism was giving way to Prometheanism, and the subjective side of futurism ("ego-futurism") to a more dispassionate and formal "cubo-futurism." Malevich was the harbinger of the new, designing cubistic sets and costumes in December, 1913, for the futurist opera with the appropriately Promethean title, *Victory over the Sun*. People were transformed into "moving machines" by costumes of cardboard and wire. Some actors spoke only with vowels, others only with consonants, while blinding lights and ear-splitting sounds rocked through the theater in an effort to give man "victory over the sun": freedom from all dependence on the traditional order of the world.[89] Freud, too, make his impact on the new art; and plays were written in which the various roles did not represent different people but different levels and aspects of one person.[90]

In the manifesto that accompanied his first Suprematist exhibition in December, 1915, Malevich insisted:

> Only when the habit of one's consciousness to see in paintings bits of nature, madonnas and shameless nudes has disappeared, shall we see a pure-painting composition.[91]

Shameless nudes had, however, not altogether vanished from Russian culture. They dominated the literary debut late in 1916 of one of Russia's great storytellers of this century, Isaac Babel.[92] His description of a seduction in the manner of the French naturalists, whom he admired, attracted the wrath of the government authorities, who transferred to the inventive young writer from Odessa the puritanical denunciations and threats that could no longer be visited upon the absent Larionov. Yet nowhere was sensualism more in evidence than in the inner circles of the imperial government itself. The imperial family was under the sway of the notorious Rasputin, and the rival court figures who succeeded in killing this "holy devil" in December of 1916 were if anything even more corrupt than the remarkable peasant holy man from Siberia. Protopopov, the minister of the interior who was Rasputin's friend and protégé, was a sensualist thought by many to be a practitioner of necrophilia. Prince Yusupov and the Grand Duke Dmitry (the high aristocrats who carried out the poisoning, shooting, and drowning of the rugged Rasputin) were widely renowned for their sexual exploits and intrigues.[93]

Within a year, however, all these figures had been swept aside by the winds of change. First came the gust from the progressive bloc of liberal reformers in the Duma, then the unexpected hurricane of March, 1917, which ended the autocracy, and finally the swirling winds of civil war set in motion by the Bolshevik coup of November.

Revolution and civil war turned the attention of Russian writers from the private to the public arena, and made apocalypticism, the third ideological current of the age, suddenly seem the most relevant of all. Blok, who had already felt himself "drawn into the whirlpool" by "the lilac world of the first revolution," now tended to see in the erotic and mystical "unknown lady" of his earlier poems only the mother of harlots spoken of in the Book of Revelation.[94] Sensual desire was cauterized with the fire of revolution and civil war, and zealously repressed by the puritanical Bolsheviks once power was consolidated.

Nonetheless, sensualism—like other attitudes of the late imperial period—did not vanish immediately under the new regime. One writer likened the experience of revolution to that of a "voluptuous shudder."[95] A remarkable Soviet novel of the early twenties tells of an aristocratic girl who, by becoming head of a local secret police, converts her sexual appetite into state-sanctioned sadism, proudly proclaiming that "the revolution is all permeated with sex for me."[96] Another tale tells of a deacon who leaves his religious calling ostensibly to join the Revolutionary forces, but actually to live freely with the prostitute Marfa. "Underneath all his Marxism rank Marfism was hidden," the author wryly observes.[97] Most memorable of all is the picaresque sensuality and ironic spirit in Babel's tales of the revolutionary era, *Red Cavalry,* of 1926, and in his *Odessa Tales* of the following year dealing with the Odessa underworld.

There was an engagingly straightforward irrationalism about the bohemian sensualism of the "Imaginist" school of poetry, which was formed in 1919. Seeking to "smash" grammar and return to primitive roots and suggestive images, they produced such remarkable works as Vadim Shershenevich's $2 \times 2 = 5$ and Anatoly Marienhof's *I Fornicate with Inspiration.*[98] Before the group collapsed in 1924 and Shershenevich settled down to the prosaic task of becoming Upton Sinclair's Russian translator, this leader of the group wrote a number of poems exalting the anti-progressive sensualism that was still widespread among the intelligentsia:

> Women, make haste to love us,
> For we sing of wonders still,
> And we are the last thin cracks
> That progress has yet to fill![99]

Sensualism was, however, not entirely without its official patrons in the early years of Bolshevik rule. Indeed, the Revolution was in a very real sense "permeated with sex" for Alexandra Kollontai, the gifted daughter of a Ukrainian general and first commissar of public welfare in the new Bolshevik regime. Between the publication of her *New Morality and the Working Class* in 1919 and her collection *Free Love* in 1925, she campaigned incessantly for free love in the new society. She argued, however, for sublimating the physical side of love ("wingless eros") to a socially creative love, with wings, which seeks a kind of spiritual union with the new proletarian society.[100] Thus, just as Bogdanov saw the proletariat as God, Kollontai saw it as a kind of cosmic sex partner. She favored (to cite the title of one of her stories) "the love of worker bees," with women as queen bees, producing children from semi-anonymous fathers whose true love lies in productive labor. In a famous metaphor one of her fictional female creations insisted that sexual intercourse in itself had no greater significance than the simple act of drinking a glass of water.[101]

Although she favored monogamy for purely practical reasons, she was an ardent apologist for the liberalized divorce laws that were promulgated early in the Soviet era. Both she and her wealthy Finnish mother were divorcees. Her own supreme love affair was clearly the one she enjoyed with the working class. A wealthy intellectual, she identified herself with the most ruggedly proletarian faction of Bolshevism, the so-called Workers' Opposition, which vainly sought to combat the growing power of the new state bureaucracy with a system of decentralized trade union control. Unlike others in the movement, she was not disbarred from further positions of authority after its repudiation in 1921. She spent the entire period from 1923–45 in high diplomatic posts, most of them in the Scandinavian regions that she knew so well (involving herself in such colorful episodes as her attempt to negotiate an end to the Russo-Finnish War together with another militant Bolshevik feminist, the Estonian-born playwright Hella Wuolijoki, whose most famous work, the Loretta Young movie *The Farmer's Daughter,* deals with that enduring popular symbol of promiscuity).[102] Kollontai's advocacy of sexual liberation can be said to represent in some ways a curious and short-lived introduction of Scandinavian perspectives into the gloomy puritanical picture of Russian Bolshevism. The fact that she was the only important opposition leader within the Bolshevik Party to survive the purges of the thirties could testify to some vestigial nostalgia among old Revolutionaries for her image of the Revolution as "eros with wings."

There was little room for eros in the Bolshevik ethos, however. The last great festival of public passion may well have been the remarkable production of the play *Carmencita and the Soldier,* at the Moscow Art Theater in 1923. This "lyric tragedy" was an original reworking of Bizet's *Carmen* designed to focus attention exclusively on the savage, love-hate relationship between man and woman. The chorus of older tragedies was reintroduced, and the frivolities of the opera eliminated in an effort to depict that which Nietzsche had written in the margin of his score of Bizet's *Carmen* at the "Habanera": "Eros as the Greeks imagined him, bitterly demonic and untamed."[103]

The sensualism of the age was in a very intimate sense demonic. Solov'ev, the author of the turn to sensualism, had begun in his last years to have visions of the devil rather than of sophia, and seems to have felt himself strangely drawn toward the Antichrist of his last writings.[104] Within a few years of Solov'ev's death, his follower Alexander Blok moved from his earlier mystical reverence for "the beautiful lady" who brought harmony to the universe to his poetic preoccupation with "the unknown woman," an enigmatic prostitute from the nether world of the city taverns. The less well remembered figure of Alexander Dobroliubov actually championed the worship of Satan, and wrote poems and tracts extolling "the beauty of death" before turning to a life of ascetic self-mortification and radical sectarian preaching.[105] Demons are everywhere in the literary world of Sologub, where the lure of the flesh is almost invariably related to the power of Satan.

Alexis Remizov, one of the most popular storytellers of the late imperial period, believed that the world was ruled by the devil. His portrayal of Satan in the vernacular language and fantastic metaphor of the Russian countryside made him seem almost a congenial figure. Remizov's popular marionette production *The Devil's Show* was a kind of satanic mystery play; and his *Flaming Russia* of 1921 paid tribute to Dostoevsky as the author of the strange dualism and "theomachism" (*bogoborchestvo,* or "struggle with God") that underlay his own exotic writings. Chiurlionis suggested that the sun was really black; and in *Satan's Diary,* the last work of Leonid Andreev, the author identifies with Satan, who—in the shape of an American millionaire—records his deceptions and triumphs in a deeply corrupted world.[106]

Diabolism also found expression in music, where Scriabin professed to find a kind of exaltation of the devil in the music of Liszt and in his own celebration of sensual delights. The devil found his most notable conquest in the field of painting, where the gifted figure of Vrubel moved from early religious paintings to experimentalism to anguish and insanity in the course of an artistic quest centered on representing Lermontov's *Demon* in painting.[107]

From his early representation of the demon as a seated figure similar in form to his earlier Pan, Vrubel proceeded to a final picture which showed the demon stretched out horizontally, as if on a rack, with his head cocked up at an unnatural angle, staring out in horror at the viewer. It is as if the devil were conducting a kind of final satanic review of his lesser servants: those "pillars of society" who always lined up in ignorant admiration before any work of a widely acclaimed artist. Vrubel both shocked and fascinated society by returning periodically to retouch and further distend his devil even after it was placed on public exhibit. The only refuge left on earth was to be found in an insane asylum, where Vrubel spent the last years before his death in 1910. The devil which haunted Vrubel had, of course, fascinated thinkers of the romantic age throughout Europe. Faust was, after all, inconceivable without Mephistopheles; and in their brooding about paradises lost or regained, the romantics found Milton's Satan somehow more credible and interesting than his God. In their determination to revitalize the mechanistic universe of the eighteenth-century philosophers, romantic philosophers often preferred to equate vitality with Satan rather than attempt to redefine or rehabilitate the discredited idea of God.

Yet there is something strange and uniquely Russian about Vrubel's effort to encase Satan in a painting. It was a kind of inversion of the quest launched in Russian painting by Alexander Ivanov a half century earlier.[108] As in the case of Ivanov, Vrubel's effort became a kind of focal point of the communal interests and expectations of the entire intellectual elite. Just as Ivanov had attempted to portray "The Appearance of Christ to the People," Vrubel was trying to have the devil make his appearance to the people. But whereas Ivanov's Christ was an artistic failure, Vrubel's Demon was a relative success. Romanticism had found its icon; and the sensualists of late imperial Russia, their patron saint.

Apocalypticism

THIS SENSE of the satanic presence led to a brooding and apocalyptic mentality. Apocalypticism, the third key characteristic of the era, was in many ways the by-product of the unresolved psychological tension between the other two: Prometheanism and sensualism. How, after all, can one reconcile great expectations with petty preoccupations? an intellectual belief in a coming utopia and a simultaneous personal involvement in debauchery? One way of holding on to both commitments was to convince oneself with a certain amount of *Schadenfreude* that apocalyptical change was in the offing, that the sensualism of today forebodes the transformation of tomorrow. As Diaghilev put it during the revolutionary year of 1905 (in a toast delivered in connection with the exhibit of three thousand Russian historical portraits which he organized at the Tauride Palace):

> We are witnesses of the greatest moment of summing-up in history, in the name of a new and unknown culture, which will be created by us, and which will also sweep us away. That is why, with fear or misgiving, I raise my glass to the ruined walls of the beautiful palaces, as well as to the new commandments of a new aesthetic. The only wish that I, an incorrigible sensualist, can express, is that the forthcoming struggle should not damage the amenities of life, and that the death should be as beautiful and as illuminating as the resurrection.[109]

The second and more obvious source of apocalypticism was the popular religious mentality which tended to influence even many of the openly irreligious contributors to the emerging mass culture of the early twentieth century. Reading and writing were now becoming regular activities of many with a primitive, peasant background for whom it seemed natural to talk of change in apocalyptical terms.

The stridently secular manifestos of the futurists were filled with images of prophecy and martyrdom. The poet Maiakovsky, who rapidly became their leader, called himself "the thirteenth apostle" and "an uncrowned king of souls," whose body will someday be "lifted to heaven like the communion wafer by prostitutes to cleanse them of their sins." His sonorous verse captures, like the *zaumny iazyk,* the language of pure sound of Khlebnikov, some of the musical cascading quality of the original *zaumny iazyk* of the church: the *blagovestie* of church bells. If the bells of "rejoicing" are harsh ones, jangled out of tune by the iconoclastic poet, his ultimate assurance of salvation is phrased in the language of apocalypse, which is, after all, a kind of "theology beyond reason." He alone, the ultimate romantic, "will come through the buildings on fire" to see "the second tidal flood."[110] If futurist poets were led into a kind of masochistic apocalypticism in their effort to reach beyond the ordinary world, abstract artists tended to follow a similar path in their quest for a new art of pure form and color. Kandinsky in the critical period of his development, during 1912–14, repeatedly returned to the theme of apocalyptical horsemen and the Last Judgment in the canvases with which he slowly rode altogether out of the world of objective art.[111]

In the feverish literature of this decade of war and revolution, apocalypticism became an increasingly central theme. Solov'ev's posthumously published short story of the Antichrist heralded a host of imitators who were, for the most part, less interested in his positive vision of ultimate Christian unification than in his negative vision of the coming Asian domination of Europe.

Merezhkovsky's trilogy, *Christ and Antichrist,* presented a vast historical panoply of the death of gods under Julian the Apostate, their resurrection under Leonardo da Vinci, and a final struggle between Christ and Antichrist that had begun under Peter and was to be resolved on Russian soil.[112] Far more interesting and original was the apocalyptical work of Boris Bugaev, the brooding son of a famous Moscow mathematician who became a leading symbolist writer and moved from Buddhism to theosophy to anthroposophy: the attempt to create a new humanistic culture by the Austrian philosopher Rudolph Steiner.[113] Early in his religious and philosophic studies Bugaev became fascinated with the inner links that he felt existed between the intelligentsia and the popular religious mentality. He chose the pen name Andrew Bely—combining that of the "first chosen" saint who allegedly brought Christianity to Russia with the word for "white," the apocalyptical color. Bely thus rebaptized himself with a name which symbolized his own sense of mission in bringing tidings of apocalypse to the Russian people. Like Solov'ev he saw the problem in terms of the confrontation of Europe and Asia with Russia as the critical arena of conflict. Like Briusov, who wrote apocalyptically about "the coming Huns" during the Japanese defeat of Russia in 1904–5,[114] Bely was haunted by this unexpected Asian victory and soon embarked on a great novelistic trilogy *East or West*. The first part appeared in two large volumes in 1910 under the title *Silver Dove*, telling the story of a Moscow student who gives away all his earthly goods in order to follow a mad flagellant "Mother of God." He is in search of a world-wide resurrection: a union of West and East through a conflagration out of which will come the bird that can rise to heaven: the "dove" of the sectarian tradition, the firebird of Russian mythology. The practice of self-immolation by the Old Believers is represented as a kind of prophetic anticipation of what the entire world is about to experience on the way to salvation.

The outbreak of World War I and the enormous casualties on the eastern front seemed to provide further evidence to Bely that the end was indeed coming; and the second part of the trilogy which appeared in 1916, under the title *Petersburg,* is even more haunted by the distortion of traditional shapes and the sense of approaching catastrophe. He sees the calamity being brought on by "both father and son, both reactionary and revolutionary," who are equally nihilistic at heart, secret collaborators in bringing on "the kingdom of the beast, . . . of the Antichrist, of Satan."[115]

The outbreak of revolution seemed to Bely and many others to be the beginning of the last great earthly struggle that would deliver men from the reign of Antichrist to that of the returned Messiah. "Christ is Risen," Bely wrote in a famous hymn to the Revolution just a few months after Blok's *Twelve*.[116] At almost the same moment Russia was called the "new Nazareth" by the most authentically earthy and rural of all the great poets of the age, Serge Esenin.[117] Another peasant poet, Nicholas Kliuev, hailed the Revolution as a sign of messianic deliverance, in his remarkable works of the early twenties: "Song of a Bearer of the Sun," "The Fourth Rome," and "Lenin," in which he compared the Bolshevik leader to Avvakum.[118]

It was not long before the new revolutionary regime became equated with Antichrist rather than Christ. The identification of the Revolutionary leader with the returning Christ in Blok's "Twelve" had been only tentative and symbolic, and Blok died disillusioned in 1921. Berdiaev, Merezhkovsky, Kandinsky, Remizov, and many others had emigrated abroad permanently by 1922, and begun writing about the new order in tones of Spenglerian gloom.[119] Even Gorky, a man of lower-class origin, who was close to Lenin, went abroad late in 1922 for a long stay. His departure was but one sign of the revulsion that passed through precisely those writers who were closest to the simple people and to the great hopes they had originally had for the Revolution.

The city joined the railroad train as the symbol of apocalypse. An apocalyptical poem of 1903 by Briusov, "The Pale Horse," inspired Blok to write in 1904 "The Last Day," the first in a gloomy series called *The City*.[120] The modern city was "a curse of the beast," to cite the title of Andreev's famous story of 1908: "the final curse of man," a labyrinth with "many doors and no exits," populated by people with "small compressed, cubic souls."[121] Bolshevism was only the last and most extreme product of the "steel fever" of the cities, of an "electrical uprising"[122] which was leading men to Armageddon and the final struggle between "iron and the land."[123] People were only minor actors in this Manichean battle between factory chimneys and the cupolas of churches. Chimneys became "red fingers" of the beast threatening to rip out of the soil the onion domes of the faithful, or trumpets reaching above the city to announce the Last Judgment.[124]

Within the accursed cities "earth no longer resembles earth. . . . Satan has beaten and trampled it down with iron hoofs . . . riding over it like a foaming horse across a meadow."[125] The image of an apocalyptical horseman is blended into that of an armored train carrying the curse of the city out into the countryside and provinces by means of "dragon trains," "the iron serpent in the clean field," "the forty-mouthed creature":

> Did you see
> Racing over the steppe,
> On cast-iron paws
> Knifing through lakes of mist
> Snorting with iron nostrils
>
> —the train?
> And after him
> Across the great lawn
> As in some festival of desperate races
> Pitching his thin legs forward
> The galloping red-maned foal?[126]

The train symbol was given new suggestiveness by the Bolshevik use of brightly ornamented propaganda trains and Trotsky's repeated forays to the front in an armored command train during the Civil War. Among the most powerful early prose accounts of this period are Vsevelod Ivanov's *Armoured Train No. 14–69,* the chapter "Train No. 58" in Pil'niak's panoramic *Naked Year,* and Nikitin's memorable story "Night," in which the Civil War is portrayed as a nocturnal collision between two armored trains, red and white, moving from East and West to a fated collision in the heart of Russia.[127]

Almost alone among the visionary writers of the silver age, Bely returned permanently to the USSR in 1923, professing to see signs of deliverance rather than apocalypse in the new order. Yet the second part of his trilogy, *Petersburg,* written between 1913 and 1916, had already presented an apocalyptical picture of men and women in a half-mad city paralyzed by a box containing a bomb, which no one can either disarm or discard. His literary efforts of the twenties—such as the *Baptized Chinamen* and *Moscow*—are less successful; and his attempt to invest older religious symbols with new Bolshevik content are even more inept than in his "Christ is Risen." His most successful work after *Petersburg* was *Kotik Letaev,* depicting the coming into awareness of a small child by journeying imaginatively back into the child's infant and even pre-natal experience. This world had already been discovered by the greatest of all literary apocalypticists of the period—Vasily Rozanov, who had variously fancied himself as a fetus longing to remain in the womb and as "the baby Rozanov lost somewhere on the breast of the earth."[128]

Shortly before his death in 1919, this prince of sensualism retreated altogether from the Revolutionary chaos around him to the Monastery of St. Sergius and the Holy Trinity, where he wrote his *Apocalypse of Our Time.* The Russian Revolution was, he declared, a catastrophe of apocalyptical proportions for all human civilization. It was the result not of Revolutionary agitation but of the total failure of Christianity to deal with the social and physical spheres of life. Believing that the original apocalypse of St. John was written as an indictment of the early Christian Church, Rozanov designed his new apocalypse as an indictment of the modern church, which has stood by helplessly amidst war, famine, and revolution, making the flight to Bolshevism all but inevitable. Rozanov seemed to be longing for the church to reassert in this Time of Troubles the leadership that it had assumed during the *Smuta* three centuries earlier, which had led to the national revival of the seventeenth century under the new Romanov dynasty. Appropriately enough, Rozanov wrote his *Apocalypse* in the Monastery of St. Sergius, which alone had not fallen under foreign domination during this earlier Time of Troubles. He received the sacrament shortly before his death, which took place (to cite the title of one of his best works) "in the shadow of church walls."[129]

In Rozanov's religion, the flesh was made word, rather than the word flesh, as Berdiaev noted. His views represented the fulfillment of the cult of earthy immediacy (*pochvennost'*) that his idol Dostoevsky had launched. He called for a "return to the passions and to fire" near the end of the *Apocalypse,* insisting that there is more theology "in a bull mounting a cow" than in the ecclesiastical academies, and citing Dostoevsky in support of the view that "God has taken the seeds of other universes and sowed them in the earth."[130]

Apocalypse and judgment were immediate sensuous realities for Rozanov just as the physical world had been. He could not believe in "the immortality of the soul" (he invariably put such abstract phrases in quotation marks) but could not bring himself to believe that "the little red beard" of his best friend would ever perish. He envisaged himself as standing before God on Judgment Day saying nothing, only sobbing and smiling.

Rozanov died early in 1919 before finishing his *Apocalypse;* but in the following year there was written an even more remarkable description of the coming end, in the prophetic novel *We* by Eugene Zamiatin. A former naval engineer and Bolshevik, Zamiatin portrays the coming totalitarianism with such penetrating acuteness that *We* has never yet been published in the USSR. The scene of the novel is "the United State," a horrendous utopia of the future, which has subordinated the earth to a mysterious "Well-Doer" and a uniform "Table of Hours." The latter is a kind of cosmic extension of the railroad timetable: "that greatest of all monuments of ancient literature." Election Day is the Day of Unanimity, and order is maintained by electric whips, with death by evaporation the ultimate sanction.

The narrator and hero—like everyone in the United State—is known by a number (D–503) rather than a name. D–503 is still, however, a recognizable human being—indeed, in some ways, a distilled representation of the silver age. He combines Prometheanism and sensualism, the two abiding attitudes of that period; and the tension in the novel arises from the inherent conflict between the two. On the one hand he is the ultimate Prometheus: a mathematician who has built "the glass, electric, fire-breathing Integral," an object that is about to "integrate the indefinite equation of the Cosmos" by sending to all other planets "the grateful yoke of reason . . . a mathematically faultless happiness." At the same time, however, D–503 suffers from an irrational attachment to a woman, I–330, who is associated with the music of the past, which, unlike the mathematical harmony of the present, is the product of purely individual inspiration ("an extinct form of epilepsy").

I–330 leads D–503 out beyond the Green Wall of the United State to a wilderness in which live the Mephi: semi-bestial survivors of the Two Hundred Years' War which preceded the founding of the United State. The Mephi are, of course, the ultimate sensualists, children of Mephistopheles, as their name suggests. In their world the breasts of women break through the uniforms of the state like the shoots of plants in spring; fire is worshipped; and insanity advocated as the only form of deliverance. Only the Mephi have not succumbed to "the mistake of Galileo" in believing that there is "a final number."

In a series of surrealistic scenes, D–503 almost succumbs to their world of energy, which is contrasted with the entropy of the United State. Insisting on the infinite and Dionysian in face of the need for rationality is, however, ominously likened early in the novel to placing one's hand over the barrel of a rifle. As D–503 begins to succumb, this image becomes magnified to apocalyptical proportions. With the "forces of unreason" on the loose, Doomsday is at hand. D–503 prepares for suicide, but, at the very end, he is mysteriously brought back to daylight. His faith in finitude and the power of reason is restored by an operation which removes his soul.

We is not only a brilliant forerunner of the anti-utopian *Brave New World* and *1984,* it is also a culmination of the essentially anti-Christian preoccupation with Prometheanism and sensualism in the late imperial period. It might even be called a kind of black scripture for the satanists. Black masses had, after all, become a fashionable form of diversion in certain aristocratic circles; and Khlebnikov had not been alone in seeing "the world upside down" and life itself as little more than "a game in Hell."[131]

We is divided into forty "records" (rather than chapters), a number almost certainly suggested by the length of Christ's temptation and of the flood. It is related in the chronicle form of the Gospels, beginning with a black parody of the first chapter of St. John ("I am only copying—word by word . . . Before taking up arms, we shall try out the word") and a kind of annunciation ("The great historic hour is near, when the first INTEGRAL will rise into limitless space"). It ends with a surrealistic mock passion, crucifixion, descent, and resurrection of a hero whose age is that of Christ at the time of his passion. These events occur in the final "records," which correspond to the last days of Christ. The wall is shattered like the temple of Jerusalem; his descent into hell is portrayed through the image of the latrine in the underground railway, where he meets the Anti-God of the sensualists in a satanic parody on the image of Christ seated in glory at the right hand of God the father. Amidst the "unseen transparent music" of the waters in the latrine, Satan approaches D–503 from a toilet seat to the left. He introduces himself with an affectionate pat, and soon proves to be nothing more than a gigantic phallus: the true God of this neo-primitive and unnaturally erotic age. His "neighbor" is nothing but "a forehead—an enormous bald parabola" with "indefinable yellow lines of wrinkles" that suddenly seemed to be "all about me." This strange shape assures D–503 that he is capable of orgasm and not the "discarded cigarette butt" (which D–503 had assumed himself to be after an unsuccessful attempt at sexual union with I–330).

I understand you, I understand completely—he said—but just the same you must calm down: it is not necessary. All of that will return, it will inevitably return.[132]

He then tries to get D–503 to believe that "there is no infinity." Comforted by this thought, D–503 hastens to finish his chronicle on toilet paper and "put down a period just as the ancients placed a cross over the pits into which they threw their dead." In the last record, the fortieth, he is mysteriously resurrected and shown the path to salvation. This is again a kind of parody of the final vision of glory in the New Testament. The walls of the New Jerusalem are "a temporary wall of high voltage waves"; its bells are one giant Bell (*Kolokol*), which is the name given a torture chamber. Into it is led a mysterious person with sharp white teeth and dark eyes, a final satanic metamorphosis of the missing Madonna into the sensuous "unknown lady" of the silver age. As she is placed under "the Bell" she stares out at D–503 rather like the Queen of Spades in Pushkin's story and Chaikovsky's opera and the Demon of Vrubel's painting. However, for D–503, from whom the soul has now been removed, she is a creature from another world. He turns instead to look on "the Numbers who have betrayed reason" as they enter into the purgatory of the Gas Chamber, which will reintegrate them in preparation for "the ascent up the stairs to the machine of the Well-Doer."

This new heaven was a hell to Zamiatin, for whom Christian imagery was primarily a device for heightening man's sense of the grotesque. Thus, in the comatose aftermath of the Civil War, the author of *We* turns away from Christian symbols to those of the primordial, pre-Christian world in an effort to depict the unprecedented events that had just taken place. Pil'niak wrote an apostrophe to "damp mother earth"; and in 1924, the year when Leonov presented a collection of dinosaur fossils consumed by fire as the symbol of the end of the old order, Zamiatin turned from the future depicted in *We* to suggestions of the primordial past in his famous story "The Cave." His eerie picture of man's reversion to stone-age conditions during the Civil War begins with a verbless vignette:

Glaciers, mammoths, wastelands. Nocturnal, black rocks somehow like houses; in the rocks—caves.[133]

Within the caves, men forage around in search of food and fuel, furtively hiding from "the icy roar of some super-mammothish mammoth" which "roamed at night among the rocks where ages ago Petersburg had stood." In one of the caves, amidst such symbolic artifacts as an axe and a copy of Scriabin's *Opus 74,* a cultured hero sits half-hypnotized by "the greedy

A Satirical View of Russian Liberalism

PLATE XX

The suspicion and enmity with which the iconoclastic "new men" during the reign of Alexander II viewed the rising power of the entrepreneurial bourgeoisie is reflected in the masthead (Plate XX) of the satirical journal Iskra ("The Spark"). This short-lived journal, by borrowing from the radical press of England and France the weapon of political caricature, paved the way for future Soviet propagandists. The masthead depicted here was first introduced early in 1861.

The coiling serpent is labeled "disrespect for law, for the rights of personality and property . . . self-assumed power and fist-justice . . ." The human parade moves from money through gambling, alcohol, and "speculators" to a scene that shows a mounted, villainous "monopoly" triumphant over a cringing and obese caricature of Justice, whose scales show money far outweighing "truth." At the far right emerge the final fruits of the depraved system: the cannon-bearing zealots of the new post-Crimean chauvinism, a woman trumpeting "publicity," and a man pushing the locomotive that was spreading the new industrial order throughout the empire. It seems appropriate that Lenin later chose the same title, Iskra (derived in both cases from earlier usage by the Decembrists), for the seminal weekly publication of revolutionary Bolshevism, which he founded in 1900.

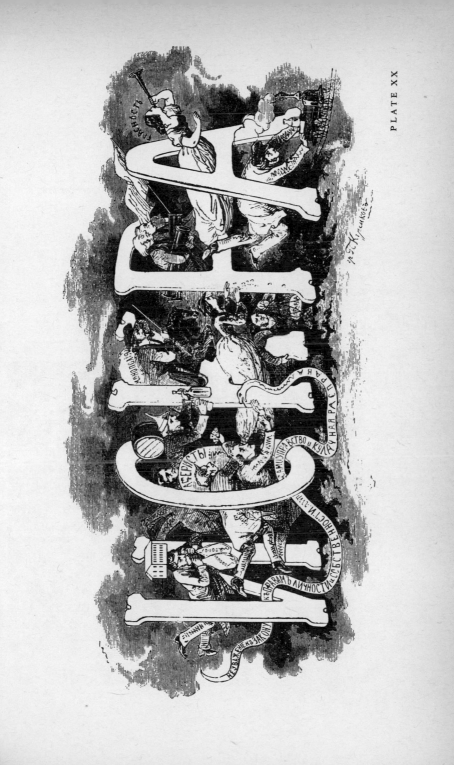

PLATE XX

PLATE XXI

PLATE XXII

The experimental spirit of Russian art in the late imperial period is well illustrated by Malevich's "Dynamic Suprematism" (Plate XXI): a typical product of the revolutionary style of non-objective art which he conceived in 1913, proclaimed in a manifesto of 1915, and exemplified in a variety of such paintings during the period of war and revolution.

The cultural richness and stylistic variety of this age was obliterated by the canonization under Stalin of "socialist realism," a two-dimensional poster art devoted largely to the glorification of socialist construction and, increasingly, Great Russian historical successes.

There were, however, more imaginative efforts to portray the ideal of the new proletarian culture; and Malevich (unlike most of the best experimental artists from the pre-revolutionary era) stayed on in the U.S.S.R. until his death in 1935, seeking to introduce the leaven of art into the dough of a new mass culture. The sturdy but faceless form of his simple, semi-abstract "Woman with a Rake (Plate XXII) offers a cleaner artistic statement of the idealized "heroine of socialist labor" than official Soviet art, and a secular icon to replace the semi-abstract religious image of a woman with child with which the illustrations for this book (and in many ways the story of Russian culture) begin. It is perhaps a fitting, final irony that the Byzantine Vladimir "Mother of God" is still on public view in the Tret'iakov Gallery in Moscow, whereas this thoroughly contemporary Russian painting of a working woman is consigned to the reserve collection of the same museum.

Malevich's "Art of Outer Space"

PLATES XXI–XXII

cave-god: a cast-iron stove." In a weird sequence of scenes, the Christian
symbols he mentions initially fade away and he becomes in effect a stone
age man—robbing his neighbor and burning all available written work in
order to feed his new God. At the end of the story

> . . . everything is one gigantic, silent cave. Narrow endless passageways . . .
> dark, ice-encrusted rocks; and in the rocks are deep holes glowing crimson;
> there, in the holes by the fire are people squatting . . . and heard by no
> one, . . . over the boulders, over the caves, over the squatting people comes
> the huge, measured tread of some super-mammothish mammoth.

In his "On Literature, Revolution and Entropy," written in 1923,
Zamiatin made explicit his opposition to the "measured tread of the mammoth" that was taking over Russia:

> Revolution is everywhere, in everything; it is endless, there is no last
> revolution, no last number. Social revolution is only one of innumerable
> numbers: the law of revolution is not social, but infinitely greater—a
> cosmic and universal law. . . .[134]

He invokes Nietzsche to show that dialectical materialism has become the
ideological "crutch" for a "weak-nerved" generation unable to face "the
fact that today's truths become tomorrow's mistakes. . . . This (the only)
truth is only for the strong. . . ." Realism was the literary language appropriate only for the outmoded "flat coordinates of a Euclidian world." True
realism now requires a feeling for

> The absurd. Yes. The meeting of parallel lines is also absurd. But it is
> absurd only in the canonical, flat geometry of Euclid: in non-Euclidian
> geometry it is an axiom. . . . For today's literature the flat surface of life
> is what the earth is for an airplane: a take-off path for the climb from
> ordinary life to true being [ot byta k bytiiu] to philosophy to the fantastic.

Into the world of the fantastic, Zamiatin plunged along with others of the
"Serapion Brotherhood," the brilliant new literary group named for a story
of Ernst Hoffmann about a hermit in a cave who believed in the reality of
his own visions. Primitive images of apocalypse continued to populate the
visions of Zamiatin, as can be seen simply from the titles of his later works:
Attila and *The Flood*.[135] Zamiatin's work stands as a kind of valedictory
not only for the imaginative Silver Age but for the century of cultural ferment that had led up to it. He was gloomily convinced that "the only future
for Russian literature is its past";[136] and he left behind one last image of the
writer's task, an elegiac reprise on the symbol of the sea as apocalypse.[137]
In times such as these, Zamiatin contends, the writer is like a lonely lookout

on the mast of a storm-tossed ship. He still stands high above the din of the ordinary deckhands, and is better able to survey dispassionately the dangers that lie ahead. Yet he too stands to sink with the ship of humanity, which is already listing at a forty-five-degree angle and may soon be confronted with the all-consuming ninth wave of the apocalypse.

Silence soon fell on this anti-authoritarian modernist. *We* and many of Zamiatin's other writings could only be published abroad, where he too went in 1931, dying six years later in Paris at the very time when Babel, Pil'niak, Gorky, and others were going to their death within the USSR. Zamiatin's belief in infinite numbers and unending Revolutionary aspiration was giving way to Stalin's world of fixed quotas and five-year plans; crescendo, to silence; electrification, to liquidation.

In summarizing the cultural upheaval during the first three decades of the twentieth century, one may say that all three major currents—Prometheanism, sensualism, and apocalypticism—helped sweep Russia further away from its moorings in tradition. Intellectuals drifted from one of these rushing currents to another—unable to chart a stable course, but unwilling to look back for familiar landmarks. Each of the three attitudes of the age was an extension of an idea already present among the anguished aristocratic philosophers of the nineteenth century: Prometheanism made explicit the transfer from God to man of the title to dominion over the external world; sensualism brought to the surface their secret fascination with the world of immediate physiological satisfaction and with its demonic patron; apocalypticism represented an agonizing, often masochistic clinging to the Judeo-Christian idea of retribution by those unable to believe in salvation.

The first two emphases in Russian thought can be considered an Eastern intensification of a general European trend. Russian Prometheanism reflected the faith of many Europeans in the new creative vistas opened up by the growth of science, industry, and human inventiveness. This faith was particularly vivid in Eastern Europe, where the rapidly growing, increasingly cosmopolitan cities seemed to offer new possibilities to hitherto static peasant empires.

Sensualism tended to be the creed of the aging aristocrat rather than the prodding parvenu—of those who saw in industrial development the multiplication rather than the solution of the world's problems. Russian sensualism was closely related to the contemporary turn toward sex and irrationalism in men like Swinburne, Wilde, Lawrence, and Rimbaud. Nevertheless, with a few exceptions which properly merit the overused designation of decadence, Russian sensualism was generally less pictorially lurid and programmatically anti-moral than that of the Anglo-French sen-

sualists of this period. Russian sensualism was tinged with aesthetic melancholy, rooted in the German philosophic tradition of Novalis, Schopenhauer, and Wagner's *Tristan:* a world of insatiable metaphysical longing in
which life was a "disease of the spirit"; sexual experience, the means
through which the foredoomed human will best expresses itself; and the
"Death and Transfiguration" of the body, the only "cure" for the flesh-
contaminated spirit.[138]

Apocalypticism was, however, an attitude that was in many ways more
uniquely confined to Russia in the still-optimistic pre-war European world.
To be sure, some Western writers like Verhaeren had seen apocalyptical
meaning in the rise of the modern "tentacular city," and there was an undercurrent of biblical-tinged pessimism even in such a triumphant spokesman
of the European imperial age as Rudyard Kipling. But nowhere else in
Europe was the volume and intensity of apocalyptical literature comparable
to that found in Russia during the reign of Nicholas II. The stunning defeat
by Japan in 1904–5 and the ensuing revolution left an extraordinarily
large number of Russians with the feeling that life as they had known it
was irrevocably coming to an end. There was a tendency to see apocalyptical significance in everything, from the rise of Asia to the reappearance
of Halley's Comet in 1910.[139] Unable to find joy or consolation in religion,
the Russian creative artist nonetheless looked with fascination at the apocalyptical literature of the Bible and Russian folklore. These writings commended themselves to the brooding psychological condition of Russian
writers, and also provided a model for the art they hoped to produce; for
tales of apocalypse were both uniquely familiar to the new mass audience
that they hoped to reach and, at the same time, rich in the esoteric symbolic
language that they themselves admired.

In its apocalypticism as in other ways, the culture of this disturbed
age seems at times to represent a throwback to the distant past: more a
finale to the Old than a prelude to the New Russia. Artists seemed more to
be looking back to the secrets of the seven days that created the world than
forward to the slogans of the ten days which shook it. They sought the
sources, not the benefits, of electricity; the lost lines and colors of the old
icons, rather than the photographic heroism of the new movies.

Russian Prometheanism thus had elements of utopian compulsion and
poetic fantasy that resemble less the optimistic and utilitarian scientism of
contemporary Europe than the religious intoxication of earlier Russian
heresy—the Judaizers with their pseudo-scientific "Secret of Secrets"; the
Boehmist mystics with their esoteric paths to androgyny and divinity; and
the recurrent sectarian prophets who sought to supplant traditional Chris-

tendom with a new group that would immediately realize the kingdom of heaven on earth.

Sensualism and apocalypticism were attitudes more reminiscent of the time of Ivan III and IV than of Alexander II and III. Philotheus of Pskov had seen a prophetic connection between the present reality of Sodom and the coming victory of the "third Rome," just as many in the Silver Age were prone to see their own decadence as the harbinger of final deliverance. But what precisely was to come out of Sologub's "dust and ashes"? Was it to be the enigmatic Christ of Blok's poem? Boris Savinkov's or Briusov's "Pale Horse," the fourth and most mysterious of the horsemen of the apocalypse? Stravinsky's and Balmont's "Firebird," the spectacular phoenix of pre-Christian Slavic mythology? or perhaps only the prehistoric dinosaurs of Zamiatin's "Cave"?

The more Russia's experimental intellectuals tried to plunge into the future, the more they tended to drift back into the past. Old themes and metaphors kept returning in new dress—such as the Hamlet symbol. Blok wrote a great deal about the character and even courted his future wife by acting out the scenes between Hamlet and Ophelia.[140] In the early twenties the play provided the framework for a new Revolutionary parable which was acted out with great éclat by Michael Chekhov, nephew of the playwright. The new *Hamlet* portrayed a kind of Manichean struggle between the passionate and heroic Hamlet (and his allies, Horatio and Ophelia) and the haughty and repressive figure of the King (and his allies Polonius and the courtiers).[141] Gothic sets were used to emphasize that this drama took place in the Middle Ages, prior to the coming of light; and the King's forces wear dark costumes and repellent expressions, whereas those of Hamlet are light. The Ghost—as the unalloyed voice of revolutionary conscience—is represented by a pure shaft of light.

From a variety of perspectives Russians seemed to be feeling their way back to the shrine of light, the mythological, pre-Christian sun gods of the East. "Let us be like unto the sun," Balmont had written in one of the most widely quoted of the early symbolist poems. Remizov's *Following the Sun* of 1907 was but one of many hymns of praise to the real and imagined sun gods of Eastern mythology. Gorky's *Confession* of the following year hailed "the people" as "the master of the Sun."[142] In 1909 Blok found his symbolic harbor for the long-lost ship at sea in the all-consuming, coldly impersonal Sun:

> Set forth your boat, plunge to the distant pole
> through walls of ice . . .
> And midst the shudders of the slow-moving cold

Acclimate your tired soul
So that *here* on earth it will nothing need
When *from there* the rays come streaming through.[143]

The same sun symbol becomes one of intoxicating neo-pagan life affirmation in early post-Revolutionary poetry: Khlebnikov's "Chains of Blue," Kliuev's *Song of the Sunbearer,* and Maiakovsky's "Extraordinary Adventure," where the poet plays host to the sun at tea, and is told:

Let us sing
In a world of dull trash.
I shall pour forth my sun
And you—your own
In verse.

Together the "double-barreled suns" break through "a wall of shadows and jail of nights" and pledge themselves

To shine always
To shine everywhere
To the depth of the last days
To shine
And nothing else.[144]

Maiakovsky invokes the Sun God of antiquity in the final ecstatic hymn of his *Mystery Bouffe,* the famed dramatic apotheosis of the new order, which he presented on the steps of the St. Petersburg stock exchange building in the early days of the Soviet regime:

Over us sun, sun and sun . . .
The sun—our sun!
Enough! . . .
Play a new game!
In a circle!
Play with the sun. Roll the sun. Play in the sun![145]

"Mystery" had, of course, also been the title of Scriabin's unfinished revolutionary symphony of sound, speech, and smell—which seems strangely reminiscent of the Church liturgy. There, too, drama, speech, and music were fused with the color of the icons and the smell of incense. Scriabin and Maiakovsky were, each in his own idiom, writing mystery plays for a new organic society in which all participated in the common ritual the aim of which was not entertainment but redemption. But if they were Christian in form, they were in many ways mystical and semi-Oriental in content. Meierhold insisted that there were no mystery plays in modern times and that "the author of 'Prometheus' is longing for the Banks of the Ganges."[146] Khlebnikov was preoccupied with mystical, Asian themes and called himself "A dervish, a yogi, a Martian . . ."[147] adopting the ancient Slavonic version of Vladimir, "Velimir," as his pen name. His search for a language of pure sounds as a prerequisite for the utopian society to be created by his "society for the presidents of the world" also bears some resemblance to the quest of earlier, Slavic Christendom. There, too, the liturgy, the "common work" of salvation, proceeded through the rhythmic incantations of the human voice to the joyous and climactic ringing of bells: a pure "language beyond reason," a *zaumny iazyk* prefiguring the celestial rejoicing of the world to come.

The entire emphasis on the non-literary, supra-rational arts is a throwback to the culture of Old Muscovy, with its emphasis on sights, sounds, and smells. Yet in Old Russia there had been a unifying faith to give each of the art media a common focus and a willingness to accept its limitations. In modern Russia the poetry of Blok and Khlebnikov was straining to burst into music. The music of Scriabin was seeking to unravel the language of color; and the colors of Kandinsky, the language of music.

Kandinsky, the pioneer of abstract art, was in some ways the most deeply rooted of all in the aesthetics of Muscovy. He sought not art for its own sake but "the spiritual in art," and sought to end idle spectatorism by re-creating the intimacy between man and art that existed in earlier religious art. His painting was based on pure line and color—the two primary ingredients of icon painting. Kandinsky's art was—like that of the ancient icons—not concerned with the visual aspects of the external world, but was rather a kind of "abstract musical arabesque . . . purified like music of all but its direct appeals to the spirit."[148]

Yet the most abstract and purified of all sound, the language farthest "beyond reason," is that of silence. The most inclusive of all colors is the all-containing womb of white: the "white on white" of Malevich's painting, the *bely* which the "symphonic" novelist chose for his very name. An unleashed fantasy of line leads men into the infinity of space. A mystical longing for annihilation often followed the frenzied assertion of Promethean power. Whiteness, space, and infinity had replaced the sea as the symbol of this fulfillment-in-obliteration.

Moving within a generation from authoritarian traditionalism to ego-futurism, Russian culture had produced an extraordinary "commotion of verse and light."[149] But everything had been taken to excess; and it seems strangely symbolic that the awesome decimation of the artistic community in the mid-thirties began with Andrew Bely's death in 1934 from over-exposure to the sun.

Russia was not yet a fully self-sustaining industrial power, and had not yet evolved social and political institutions capable of combining the philosophy of its new leaders and the traditions of its people. By the late twenties the awesome decision was made to build socialism with "the methods employed by the Pharaohs for building the pyramids."[150] The thirties witnessed the merciless herding of workers into new industrial complexes and of peasants into new collectives. The "commotion of verse and light" gave way to the coercion of prose and darkness. It is to the fate of Russian culture in the wake of Stalin's "second revolution" that attention must now be turned.

2. The Soviet Era

For a long time after 1917, it was not entirely clear how profound a break in cultural tradition was implied in the founding of a new social order. The various proposals for bringing about a total break with past culture—whether through the God-building intoxication of Proletkult or the masochistic Eurasianism of the Scythians—were rejected along with the visionary social and economic programs of "war communism." Following the end of the Civil War and beginning of the New Economic Policy in 1921, a more permissive atmosphere was established; and some came to think in the course of the twenties that considerable cultural variety was to be tolerated within the new Revolutionary state.[1]

Perhaps the dominant literary group of the early twenties, the so-called fellow travelers (*poputchiki*), accepted the new Soviet state while professing reservations about its ideology. The even more heterodox "Serapion Brotherhood" took shape in 1921, and a number of leading pre-revolutionary literary figures soon returned to resume their writing careers. Two gifted young novelists, Alexis Tolstoy and Ilya Ehrenburg, came back from the emigration in 1923 to produce works that showed little hint of the servility to Stalin that became characteristic of their later works. Tolstoy incorporated into his prose writings many of the anti-urban, anti-utopian ideas of the peasant poets, notably in his "Sky-blue Cities," in which an anarchistic intellectual sets fire to a newly constructed Soviet town.[2] Ehrenburg introduced Jewish themes into his writings of the twenties. The founding of the Yiddish magazine *Shtrom* (*Stream*) in Moscow in 1922 helped Russia retain its central role in vernacular Yiddish culture despite Jewish population losses to newly independent Poland and to the emigration. A more ancient Hebrew culture also spoke forth through the newly formed Moscow Habima Theater, which was soon taken over by the prestigious advocate of "fantastic realism," Eugene Vakhtangov. Until his death in 1924, this Hebrew theater exerted a strange fascination on its Russian audiences. Ancient chants mixed with modern gestures in humorous yet haunting scenes showing the soul—the famed *Dybbuk*—coming back from the dead to take possession of the living.

> . . . all of Moscow, ravaged, reduced to rags, weary from hunger, fear, and revolution without regard to race or religion . . . rushed every evening to assault the 125 seats of the minute and improvised Habima amphitheater. . . . Subjugated, gasping for breath in this suburb—cemetery of the vanities of a condemned nobility—men who had just lived through the most modern, the most implacably mechanical of revolutions crowded around words that they did not understand. . . . The theater was returning to its origins and they were submitting to its religious spell. The mysticism, the ancient chaos, the animal divinity of the crowd—all that makes up the secret and powerful depth of revolutions was expressed by the *Dybbuk* and imposed on Moscow.[3]

It may seem surprising that a Hebrew troupe was able to provide such a vital leaven for Russian culture, particularly at a time when the native stage was itself in full flower. But

> In certain liturgical hymns each verse is preceded with a word in Hebrew. The faithful do not understand it; but by modulating it strangely and mysteriously, the clear Christian hymn is impregnated, the unknown word strikes against the faithful and confers an unsuspected profundity. Thus did the Hebraic soul of the Habima act upon the Russian soul.[4]

At the same time, the futurists provided a more secular form of cultural stimulus, continuing to clamor for public attention on the pages of *Lef* ("Left Front in Literature"), which began to appear in 1923 with the collaboration of Maiakovsky and Meierhold. Older traditions of satirizing contemporary life were revived by promising new writers, such as the Odessa team of Ilf and Petrov and Michael Zoshchenko. The latter, the son of a Russian actress and a Ukrainian painter, became probably the most widely read contemporary Soviet writer in the twenties, with more than a million copies of his works sold from 1922 to 1927.[5] In the field of history, non-Marxist and pre-Revolutionary figures like Tarlé and Platonov continued to work inside Russia, though some of their works (and many in the literary world) were published in Berlin. Serge Prokof'ev, one of the greatest Russian composers, returned to take up permanent residence in the USSR in 1927, and was followed within a year by Maxim Gorky, its most renowned prose writer.

Even religion seemed to be receiving a new lease on life in the USSR of the mid-twenties. In 1926 the newly chosen Patriarch of the Russian Church was released from prison. In the following year, both he and the patriarchal church were grudgingly recognized by the regime and the puppet "Living Church" allowed to die. The various sects—and particularly the locally organized and administered communities of the newly consolidated Protestant community (the "Evangelical Christians-Baptists")—grew rapidly in strength. Lenin's secretary, V. D. Bonch-Bruevich, was an historian of Russian sectarianism who argued with some success that the industriousness, productivity, and communal methods of the sects might have something to contribute to the construction of a socialist society.[6]

The relatively permissive cultural atmosphere of the twenties was, in part, the result of Bolshevik preoccupation with political consolidation and economic reconstruction in the aftermath of seven years of international and internal war. In part also it was the result of the relatively optimistic and humanistic reading of Marx's theories of culture that were advanced by the reigning ideologists of the early Soviet period: Deborin in philosophy and Voronsky in literature.[7] These men insisted that a new culture must follow rather than precede a new proletarian society. Following Marx and his most brilliant interpreter among the Bolsheviks, Nicholas Bukharin, they considered literature and art part of the superstructure rather than the base of human culture. Art could, thus, be transformed only in the wake of profound social and economic change. In the meantime, the arts had a duty to absorb the best from past culture and provide an independent reflection of reality in a complex era of transition. The practical consequences of this position were to discredit the earlier hopes for "immediate socialism." One could no longer speak seriously of replacing the traditional university with a new "fraternity of teachers, students and janitors"; nor of replacing the family system with "the new family of the working collective."[8]

Gradually, however, it became apparent that this relaxation of control and return to old ways was only temporary. Whereas about two fifths of all publishing was outside of government hands at the time of Lenin's death early in 1924, only one tenth had survived three years later.[9] The beginnings of tightening ideological control can be traced to the founding of the official theoretical journal of the Communist Party, *Bolshevik,* in 1924,[10] and to a series of party discussions on the role of literature in the new society held in 1924 and 1925. Although the party resolutions rejected the demand of the extremist "on guard" faction for detailed party regulation of literature, they did assert the right of party control over "literature as a whole" and call for a centralized "All-Union Association of Proletarian Writers" (VAPP): the first in an apostolic succession of increasingly powerful organs for tight regulation. In the same 1925 a comparable group was formed on what was soon to be called "the musical front," "The

Association of Young Professional Composers"; and a new shock army was constituted in the "struggle for scientific atheism," the notorious "League of the Militant Godless." The suicide of Esenin and the collapse of Maiakovsky's LEF movement within a few months of each other in 1925 provided testimony to the growing gulf between the new regime and some of the very intellectuals who had initially supported the Revolution.

The destruction of a living Russian culture was made complete in 1930 with the suicide of Maiakovsky, the formal abolition of all private printing, and Stalin's sweeping demand at the Sixteenth Party Congress that the first five-year plan be expanded into a massive "socialist offensive along the entire front."[11] Not a single delegate abstained, let alone dissented, as Stalin began to introduce his techniques of therapeutic purges and prescriptive uncertainty. The classical Leninist opposition to relying on "spontaneity" (*stikhiinost'*) rather than strict party guidance in preparing a political revolution was expanded into a new Stalinist opposition to tolerating "drift" (*samotek*) on the "cultural front" while preparing a social and economic revolution.

Moderate planners who argued that there were unavoidable limitations on the productive possibilities of the Soviet economy were denounced as "mechanists" and "geneticists," devoid of Revolutionary spirit and "dialectical" understanding. The purge of Bukharin, the apostle of relative freedom in the agricultural sphere and of balanced development of heavy and light industry, was accompanied by the purge of advocates of relative freedom and balance in the cultural sphere. Thus, Voronsky in literary theory and Deborin in philosophy were denounced for "Menshevizing idealism" and forced to recant publicly. Marxist philosophical ideas were not to be permitted to interfere with the development of the new authoritarian state; and Deborin and his followers were swept from the direction of *Under the Banner of Marxism* in 1930. The dominant idea in the twenties, that state law was a "fetish" of the bourgeoisie and "the juridical world view . . . the last refuge of the remnants and traditions of the old world," was replaced by the new concept of "socialist legality."[12] The dictatorship of the proletariat would not wither away in the foreseeable future, and the authority of the Soviet state and Soviet law would have to be strengthened, Stalin told the Party Congress in 1930. This contradiction of one of Lenin's fondest beliefs was pronounced "a living, vital contradiction" which "completely reflects Marxist dialectics."[13] Freud, whose doctrines of psychic determinism had been hailed in the twenties as "the best antidote to the entire doctrine of free will,"[14] was denounced at the first All-Union Congress of Human Behavior in 1930 for denying the possibility of "a socially 'open' man, who is easily collectivized, and quickly and profoundly transformed in his behaviour."[15]

A collective shock treatment paralleling that being given to the reluctant peasantry was being administered to the intellectual elite. Figures like Averbach in literary theory and Pokrovsky in history were used in this first "proletarian" phase of Stalinist terror to discredit others before being rejected themselves. Stalin emerged from it all as the benign father, the voice of moderation and protector of the little man from the "dizziness from success" of his less humane lieutenants.[16] This "proletarian episode" in Russian culture, which lasted roughly from the first party decree on literature in December, 1928, to the abolition of the distinctively proletarian organs of culture in April, 1932, was coterminous with the period of the first Five-Year Plan; part of the unprecedented effort to transform Russian society by forced-draft industrialization and agricultural collectivization.

The cultural transformations of the age, no less than the social and economic changes, bear little relationship to anything that went before in Russian history —not even to the garrison atmosphere and fierce proletarian emphases of the Civil War period. Proletarian origins and Marxist convictions were losing all importance. Indeed, the Marxist intellectuals who had played a key part in refining Communist ideology and building the new Soviet state became increasingly prime victims in the new purges of the thirties, and fanatical proletarian advocates of Revolutionary egalitarianism were denounced as "levelers" and left deviationists. There was no serious threat to the Soviet state in the late twenties; and by 1930 the depression in the West had made the danger of "capitalist encirclement" even more remote and contrived. The purpose of this "second revolution" was—as Stalin made clear in a famous speech in 1931—to create a "new Soviet intelligentsia"[17] dedicated to acquiring the technological skills needed for Soviet construction. The demand for a new intelligentsia required the destruction, or drastic remaking, of the old, including those whose emotional dedication to radical humanism might also stand in the way of building the new authoritarian state. Technological skill alone was not enough. Rigid obedience to party leaders was required. As Stalin put it bluntly in 1935: "Cadres decide everything,"[18] and the ideal cadre is the tempered, "castiron" servant of the dictator. To understand how such a drastic conclusion was reached one must look back to the legacy left by Vladimir Il'ich Lenin, the founder and patron saint of Bolshevism, the man in whose name Stalin tightened his totalitarian grip on all of Russian society. One must consider as well the relationship which both Lenin and Stalin bear to the complex cultural heritage of the land they ruled.

The Leninist Legacy

AT FIRST GLANCE, the powerful and arresting figure of Lenin seems to be only a particularly intense example of the alienated Russian intellectual of the nineteenth century. Born and educated in the Volga region, classic center of Russian revolutionary sentiment, brought up as a member of the petty, provincial nobility in a bookish home where he was closer to his mother than his father, Lenin was an educated and qualified lawyer, but never really had any other profession than that of an illegal publicist turned revolutionary. One is tempted to see in Lenin's sudden vault to power the vindication of the intelligentsia's long-frustrated hopes for a new order in which they would play a key part.

Yet Lenin was different from almost all his intellectual predecessors in nineteenth-century Russia; and it was his profound alienation from the dominant intellectual trends of the late imperial period which enabled him to appear as the bearer of a genuinely new order of things.

First of all, Lenin was uniquely single-minded in an age of diffusion. In the midst of the soaring visionaries, Lenin focused his attention on one all-consuming objective that had not traditionally been uppermost in the thinking of the intelligentsia: the attainment of power. His dedication to this objective enabled him to establish a puritanical discipline over his own emotions and those of his associates. By never giving himself over to the enervating enthusiasms of the late imperial period, he avoided its unsettling alternations between Promethean optimism and morbid sensualism. He was able to capitalize on the sense of expectation generated by the intelligentsia without becoming involved in the ebb and flow of its inner feelings.

Sentiment of all sorts was suppressed in Lenin, whose icy and ascetic manner sets him off strikingly from the traditional loose camaraderie of the intelligentsia and its conviction that feelings were inextricable parts of the thought process. His beloved mother was German, and most of his foreign travel was in Northern Europe: the advanced areas of industrialization and urbanization. Southern Europe with its sunlight, wine, and song played— with one exception—little role in his bleak life.[19] Even before he turned to Marxism in the early nineties, Lenin seems to have acquired a hatred for the vagueness, sentimentality, and—above all—futility of the aristocratic intelligentsia. He was embittered by the execution of his elder brother, a revolutionist, in 1887, and soon acquainted himself with revolutionary circles in Kazan. He introduced himself to his future wife, the stolid revolutionary Nadezhda Krupskaia, in 1894, as the younger brother of the martyred revolutionary, and identified himself in this fashion in a short autobiographical sketch. There are few traces of tenderness in his childless, ideological marriage.[20]

Lenin's vituperation provides a striking contrast with the accustomed form of discourse even among revolutionary intellectuals. There is some precedent in Marx for his language of denunciation. But his acerbic style and constant imputation of deformity to his opponents often seems closer to the rough-hewn fanaticism of peasant insurrectionists, schismatics, and sectarians—all of whom flourished in the Simbirsk-Samara-Kazan regions of Lenin's youth. His style seems more a throwback to the powerful inter-mixture of prophecy and epithet in Ivan the Terrible and Avvakum than a continuation of the traditional debates of the nineteenth century.

When earlier revolutionary leaders spoke of "them and us," they were contrasting power with truth, the ruling bureaucracy with the rulers in the world of ideas. For Lenin, however, "purity of ideas" was equated with "impotence."[21] Potency requires power, which in turn, demands not truth, "but a true slogan of the struggle."[22] Morality was not to be based on "idealistic" standards or inner feelings, but on the ever-changing dictates of revolutionary expediency. Thus, Lenin was not fundamentally concerned with truth (*pravda*) in either of its two meanings of scientific fact (*pravda-istina*) or moral principle (*pravda-spravedlivost'*). *Pravda* became, instead, the title of his newspaper, with its daily directives for action. "Cursed questions" were replaced by cursory commands.

These commands were binding because of a second basic and novel feature of Lenin's teaching: his emphasis on organization. The tradition of secret, disciplined, hierarchical organization had never struck deep roots in the Russian revolutionary tradition—though there was a substantial the-oretical literature of Jacobin proposals from such figures as Pestel, Ogarev, Nechaev, and Tkachev. Even the full-time revolutionaries within the People's Will were undisciplined, politically naive, and visionary—their most professional members being members not of an organization but of a "disorganization group." Lenin's new conception was partly dictated by the techniques needed for self-protection against the vastly improved methods of police espionage and enforcement; in part also it followed from the re-examination of revolutionary methods that had gone on steadily since the failure of the People's Will. Increasingly, the idea of consolidation under a more military type of organization had been mooted. The term "cadre," which became such a key concept in Bolshevik organizational thinking, was introduced in the late eighties, along with the idea of the manipulative use of "front" groups.[23] The leading theoretician of refurbished revolutionary populism, Victor Chernov, head of the new Social Revolutionary Party, also insisted in 1901 that unity would have to be superimposed on the revolutionary movement so that "we will not have social democrats and social revolutionaries, but one indivisible party."[24]

Lenin's final formula for organizational discipline was that of "democratic centralism," whereby decisions were reached on the basis of free discussion among party members, moving from the bottom to the top. Ultimate decisions were reached in the central committee of the party, of which the first secretary was the absolute center. Once made, a decision became totally binding. Such a system logically lent itself to the "substitutism" foreseen from the very beginning by Trotsky, whereby "the party organization supersedes the party as a whole; then the central committee supersedes the organization; and finally a single dictator supplants the central committee."[25]

Elaborating Marx's theory of a coming dictatorship of the proletariat, Lenin insisted that such a form of rule would emerge only after the total destruction of the bourgeois state machine; that the dictatorship would then "wither away" with the imminent transformation to full communism;[26] but that it would, in the interim, exert power "that is unrestricted by any laws."[27]

What Lenin actually brought to Russia was the dictatorship of the Bolshevik Party: his own "party of a new type" which, once in power, was renamed "Communist" to set it off from the more familiar European label of "socialist" or "social democratic."[28]

Within this party, relationships were to be animated not just by the mechanical laws of democratic centralism but by the untranslatable principle of *partiinost'*. This "party-mindedness" or "sacrificial party spirit" appealed to the sectarian impulse to find new life in some dedicated, secret group. Lenin sought to preserve and develop the sacrificial revolutionary tradition of Chernyshevsky and of his own elder brother to develop "complete comradely confidence among revolutionaries."[29] He refused to call himself a materialist (even a dialectical one) unless it be recognized—as he wrote in 1894—that "materialism contains within itself, so to speak, *partiinost'*."[30]

Even more appealing to intellectuals than the new spirit within Lenin's party was its promise to overcome their classic separation from "the people." Lenin insisted that "all distinctions between workers and intellectuals" be "utterly eliminated"[31] within his party; but that, at the same time, it must act as a "vanguard" within, rather than a "Blanquist" clique outside, other mass movements of the age. In fleeing from "Blanquism," the party must not fall into "tail-endism": the renunciation of Revolutionary goals in favor of "gazing with awe upon the 'posteriors' of the Russian proletariat."[32] Indeed, no "spontaneous" movement will produce the all-important political changes for which strategic organization and discipline are required. Lenin's party offered the intellectuals an intoxicating sense of identification with the true interests of the masses, a program for involvement in their activities, and the promise of union with them in the coming liberation.

Lenin's manifesto and proposal of 1902, *What Is To Be Done?*, had given Russia a new answer to that classic question, which induced Lenin's Bolsheviks to split from the Mensheviks at the Second Congress of the Russian Social Democratic Party in 1903. Unlike Chernyshevsky's *What Is To Be Done?* of 1863, Lenin's did not present the picture of a new social order; unlike Tolstoy's *What Is To Be Done?* of 1883, Lenin's does not call for a regeneration of individual moral responsibility. Lenin called rather for a new organization dedicated to the attainment of power by an ethic of expediency.

In the wake of the Revolution of 1905 Lenin introduced a series of opportunistic modifications of traditional Marxist doctrine: the neo-populist idea of a fusion (*smychka*) of poor peasants with workers in the revolutionary party;[33] the conception of a "growing over" (*pererastanie*) of the bourgeois into the proletarian revolution without the long interim which Marx had foreseen; and the idea that imperialism was the "highest stage" of a new cannibalistic finance capitalism, that was inevitably leading to world war and world-wide revolution.[34]

Liberal democracy rather than autocracy was Lenin's principal foe as he steered his party along the road to power in the chaotic and fateful year of 1917. He was aided in exile and in his return from Switzerland in April by autocratic Germany; he overthrew not a tsarist, but a provisional democratic Russian government. Constitutional Democrats were the first political rivals he arrested after the *coup d'état* of November 7; and the Constituent Assembly was forcibly dismissed in January after only one meeting. Lenin rejected not just the "parliamentary cretins" of liberalism, but also those more orthodox Marxists like the Mensheviks and Plekhanov, who believed that socialist forms of ownership could only be superimposed on an advanced industrial society that had developed democratic political institutions.

The one indispensable pre-condition for Bolshevik success in gaining and holding power was the First World War. It put intolerable strains on the old Russian Empire and on Russia's brief experiment with democracy in 1917. Wartime divisions among the European powers and post-war lassitude enabled Lenin to consolidate power in the critical 1918–21 period. Yet Lenin's ability to capitalize on such conditions stemmed from his realization that crisis was part of the nature of things, and that the job of a revolutionary party was not to create revolutionary situations, but to provide organized leadership for them.

His prophetic opposition to the war placed him in a strong position for appealing to the war-weary Russian populace. Lenin arrived at the Finland Station surrounded by the aura of a genuine alternative coming from another world to demand an end to war, and promising the beginning of a new era to all who would follow him "with icons against cannon."[35] The establishment and consolidation of his dictatorship represents a masterful case study of the opportunism and daring of a gifted strategist clearly focused on the realities of power. Details of the Bolshevik rise to power belong properly to political and military history; but inextricably involved in this story are a number of profound, if only partly conscious, Bolshevik borrowings from the radical traditions of the Russian intelligentsia. In at least four important ways, Bolshevism benefited from these traditions in threading its way from a relatively obscure revolutionary party of twenty-five thousand on the eve of the March revolution of 1917 to the unchallenged ruling force of an empire of 150,000,000 by the end of the Civil War four years later.

The first and most important debt to the Russian intellectual tradition was the conviction that any alternative to tsarist authority must be cemented together by an all-embracing ideology. From the time of the early Boehmists, Martinists, Schellingians, Hegelians, and Fourierists, Russian reformers had tended to gravitate toward Western thinkers who offered a new view of the world rather than mere piecemeal proposals for reform. The turn in the late nineteenth century from romantic ideologists to sweeping pseudo-scientific theorists, such as Comte and Spencer, prepared the way for the Bolsheviks' turn to Marx. Tkachev, the lonely Jacobin theorist who anticipated many of Lenin's elitist ideas, had written to Engels in 1874 that Russia, in contrast to the West, required "an intelligentsia-dominated revolutionary party."[36] Lenin provided such a party far more adequately than the Mensheviks, for whom Marx provided a rational guide for practical social and economic changes rather than a prophetic invocation for the coming millennium. Lenin was truer to the tradition of *ideinost'*, of being "possessed with an idea," than most rival groups, who in the turbulence of 1917 still seemed immersed in the world of *meshchanstvo:* of philistinism and "small deeds." The *ideiny,* or ideological quality, of Lenin's party helped attract a much-needed increment of gifted intellectuals to its ranks in 1917: the so-called *mezhraiontsy,* or "interregional" group, of Trotsky, Lunacharsky, Bogdanov, and others.

In the second place, Lenin benefited from the Russian predilection for theories of history that promise universal redemption but attach special importance to Russian leadership. The appeal of such philosophies of history had been a constant feature of the Russian intellectual tradition, and was rooted in the subconscious hold of an historically oriented theology. The old belief in a coming millennium had been secularized by a century of preaching that "the golden age lies ahead and not behind us"; and a people steeped in utopian thought patterns were attracted by Lenin's claim that the transition to classless communism was imminent, and that all human problems were about to be solved in the manner that friendly crowds arbitrate occasional squabbles on the street.[37]

The belief that Russia was destined to provide ideological regeneration for the decaying West had been propagandized by conservative as well as radical theorists. And the radical belief in a coming earthly utopia had often fascinated even those who rejected it. Dostoevsky, as he moved from radicalism to conservatism, still felt the seductive power of this "marvellous dream, lofty error of mankind":

> The Golden Age is the most implausible of all the dreams that ever have been. But for it men have given up their life and all their strength, for the sake of it prophets have died and been slain, without it the peoples will not live and cannot die. . . .[38]

For this dream people proved willing to die resisting the counterattacks of the old order during the Civil War. In times of chaos and disruption the most utopian visions may provide the most practical banner for rallying popular support.

A third area of indebtedness to the indigenous traditions of Russian radical thought lay in the Bolshevik expropriation of the populist myth of "the people" as a new source of moral sanction. Shortly after the Bolshevik coup, enemies of the new regime were denounced as "enemies of the people," and ministries of state were rebaptized as "people's commissariats."[39] Summary executions soon came to be glorified as "people's justice"; and Bolshevik dictatorships dressed up for export as "people's democracies."[40] The vaguely appealing populist belief that "the people" carried within themselves the innate goodness for building a new social order provided the Bolsheviks with the opportunity of camouflaging instruments of state control with the lexicon of popular liberation. Without this widespread belief in "the people" as a regenerative life force, the Bolsheviks would have had far more difficulty convincing the Russian people and themselves that their own coercive measures were morally justified.

A final borrowing from earlier tradition was the subtle Bolshevik adoption of the concept of the "circle" as a new type of dedicated community in which all distinctions of class and nationality were eliminated. Such Bolshevik concepts as sacrificial "party spirit" and internal "self-criticism" had been in many ways characteristic of Russian intellectual circles from the first secret gatherings of Novikov and Schwarz in the eighteenth century. The idea that diverse social groupings could find common unity and purpose in a circle dedicated to radical change had been present in some of the early masonic groups, and had become dominant with the entrance of non-aristocratic and national minority elements into the main stream of Russian intellectual life in the late nineteenth century. Lenin accepted in practice, if not in theory, the populists' highly un-Marxian idea that the instrument of radical social change would be an alliance of "workers, peasants, and the intelligentsia." "Poor" and "poor middle" peasants were said to be the proletariat of the countryside; and "progressive" intellectuals and "oppressed" nationalities were invited to join the revolutionary movement.[41] During the brief period between the end of the Civil War and his physical deterioration and death, Lenin's attitude toward culture was more that of a nineteenth-century Russian radical fervently committed to Westernization and secularization than that of a twentieth-century totalitarian despot. He had been generally unsympathetic with Bogdanov's wartime effort to build a monolithic new "proletarian culture," and permitted a variety of new artistic schools to flourish after the initiation of the more relaxed New Economic Policy in 1921. Lenin disliked the artistic avant-garde, but viewed their work as incomprehensible rather than dangerous, irrelevant rather than subversive. His main cultural preoccupations were with the spread of basic education and the inexpensive mass publication of older literary classics. It was in essence a neo-populist program tempered with a Victorian emphasis on general utility.

Elements of populist evangelism had already appeared in Lenin's call for a new elite to raise the historical "consciousness" of the working class, and in his insistence on beginning with a new journal. Elements of Victorianism were already evident in his patronizing, pedagogic manner, his humorless moral puritanism, and his matter-of-fact distaste for either primitive, popular superstition or sophisticated, intellectual metaphysics. Once in power, Lenin did not forbid further flights of fancy; but he did seek to bring Russian culture back to earth. He was interested in the technical task of spreading literacy rather than the imaginative art of creating literature.[42]

For all the benefits which he received from the radical intellectual tradition and all of his inner links with it, Lenin paved the way for its destruction. It is not just that he severed the ties that Russia had been developing with Westward-looking political and cultural experimentation.

Periods of repression and forced isolation were not new in Russian culture, and democracy was a relatively recent and unfamiliar concept for many Russians. What was profoundly revolutionary in Lenin was his deliberate break with a belief that underlay almost all previous Russian radical thought: belief in the existence of objective moral laws for human behavior.

With only a few, peripheral exceptions in the nineteenth century, Russian intellectuals had resisted all efforts to find a totally new basis for morality whether in a calculus of social utility in the manner of Bentham or in the manufacture of mythic goals for the self-realizing ego in the manner of Fichte. Russian radicals had continued to use religious terminology, juxtaposing the ethical teachings of Christ to the corrupt practices of a supposedly Christian society; or the language of idealism in relating their ethical passion to the nature of goodness, or to the absolute dictates of conscience.

With Lenin, however, morality was made relentlessly relative, dictated by party expediency. He reviled not just traditional religion and philosophical idealism but also the practical idealism implicit in traditional secular humanism. His movement was to be based on a scientific theory that would free his cause from the charge of myth and purify his ethic of expediency from any trace of caprice and sentimentality. The moralistic exhortations that populists like Lavrov and Mikhailovsky had mixed in with their pseudo-scientific theories of progress were only "bourgeois phrasemongering." Modern revolutionaries needed the resilient armor of science, not the ceremonial uniforms of tradition.

Of course, the open inductive thinking of the modern scientific spirit was totally unfamiliar to Lenin, whose relentlessly political mind tended to equate it with anarchism. His longest philosophic treatise was devoted to refuting the "empirio-criticism" of those most intimately concerned with the philosophical implications of contemporary science.[43] In Lenin's activist ideology, morality was deduced from scientific Marxism, of which he, the son of a schoolmaster, was the leading teacher, and he, the student of jurisprudence, the final judge. In the last analysis, arguments were not to be resolved but cut off, because the chief justice was also chief of the Revolutionary army. And this was no ordinary army, but a messianic band scientifically certain of utopia, ruthlessly fighting for peace.

The full-blown totalitarianism that emerged under Stalin thus had organic roots in Leninist theory. There were no external criteria by which the actions of the Leninist party could be judged and criticized; no limitations established on the types of questions it was entitled to resolve. Nothing could better illustrate the depth of his break with the critical tradition of

Russian letters than his 1905 article insisting that *partiinost'* in literature
requires that literature for the proletariat not only

> not be an instrument of gain for individuals or groups, but not be an in-
> dividual matter at all, independent of the common proletarian cause.
> Down with non-party writers! Down with literary supermen! Literature
> must become *a part* of the common proletarian cause: a "wheel and
> screw" of the one and only great social-democratic mechanism which is
> driven by the entire conscious avant-garde of the entire working class.
> Literature must become a component part of organized, planned, unified
> social-democratic party-work.[44]

The fact that there was genuine intra-party dissent and debate in
Lenin's lifetime, that he never intended the party to regulate all of human
life, and that he was personally fond of simple living and sincerely convinced that a new age was about to dawn—all is of primarily biographical
interest. Far more important to the historian is the fact that the totalitarianism of Soviet society under Stalin followed logically (even if it may not have
followed necessarily) from the Leninist doctrine of the party.

The Revenge of Muscovy

FOR THE HISTORIAN of culture, Lenin's brief rule was still something of
a chaotic interregnum; and it is the age of blood and iron under Stalin that
marks the real watershed. Once his dictatorial power was securely established in the late twenties, Stalin systematically imposed on Russia a new
monolithic culture that represented the antithesis of the varied, cosmopolitan, and experimental culture that had continued on into the twenties from
pre-Revolutionary days. During the quarter of a century that stretched
from the beginning of his first five-year plan in 1928 to his death in 1953,
Stalin sought to convert all creative thinkers into "engineers of the human
soul." They were to be cheerleaders along his assembly lines—deliberately
kept uncertain of what cheer was required of them and denied that last
refuge of human integrity in most earlier tyrannies: the freedom to be silent.

It is hard to know how Lenin would have reacted to all of this. He
suffered his first stroke in 1922, just a little more than a year after the end
of the Civil War, and was virtually incapacitated for nearly a year before his
death in January, 1924. He never had time clearly to indicate how fully he
would have applied to a society at peace the totalitarian principles advocated
earlier for a revolutionary party in times of war and crisis. Cultural problems had always been peripheral to his interests. Despite his party-centered

perspective, he had many friends among non-party intellectuals, many years of exposure to Western society, and a fairly rich grounding in the nineteenth-century Russian classics. There was, to be sure, a foreshortening of intellectual vistas from Marx, who knew his Aeschylus, Dante, Shakespeare, and Goethe, to a Lenin steeped largely in the civic poetry and realistic prose of his native land. But Lenin's vistas were still ranging compared with those of Stalin; and Lenin must at least be given credit for belatedly warning against the "rudeness" of his successor in his long-suppressed political testament.[45]

Born into an obscure cobbler's family in the mountains of the Caucasus, educated in the seminaries and tribal traditions of his native Georgia, Stalin shared none of the broader European perspectives of Lenin and most other Bolshevik leaders. This small, pock-marked figure never knew the life of the Russian *intelligent,* did not even write in Russian until late in his twenties, and spent only four months outside Russian-occupied territory—during brief trips to Party congresses in Sweden and England in 1906 and 1907, and to study the national question in the Austro-Hungarian empire in 1912 and 1913.

The qualities that Stalin professed to admire in Lenin—"hatred for snivelling intellectuals, confidence in one's own strength, confidence in victory"—were those which he attempted to instill in himself. To these were added the compulsive chauvinism of the provincial parvenu, the scholastic dogmatism of the half-educated seminarian, and a preoccupation with organizational intrigue already noticeable during his revolutionary apprenticeship in the world's largest oil fields in Baku.

Stalin's only god was Lenin; yet in Stalin's depiction the god acquires a bestial if not satanic form. Stalin compared Lenin's arguments to "a mighty tentacle which twines all around you and holds you as a vice"; Lenin was said to have been obsessively concerned that the enemy "has been beaten but by no means crushed" and to have rebuked his friends "bitingly through clenched teeth: 'Don't whine, comrades. . . .' "[46]

Stalin's formula for authoritarian rule was experimental and eclectic. It might be described as Bolshevism with teeth or Leninism minus Lenin's broad Russian nature and ranging mind. Lenin, for all his preoccupation with power and organization, had remained, in part, a child of the Volga. He had a revolutionary mission thrust upon him and took his revolutionary name from one of the great rivers of the Russian interior: the Lena.

Stalin, by contrast, was an outsider from the hills, devoid of all personal magnetism, who properly derived his revolutionary name from *stal',* the Russian word for "steel." His closest comrade—and the man he picked to succeed him as formal head of state throughout the 1930's went even further—shed his family name of Scriabin, so rich in cultural association, for Molotov, a name derived from the Russian word for "hammer." No figure better illustrates the unfeeling bluntness and technological preoccupations of the new Soviet culture than this expressionless bureaucratic hammer of the Stalin era, who was generally known as "stone bottom" (from "the stone backside of the hammer"—*kamenny zad molotova*).

Yet for all the grotesqueness, gigantomania, and Caucasian intrigue of the Stalin era, it may in some way have had roots in Russian culture deeper than those of the brief age of Lenin. Lenin benefited from the St. Petersburg tradition of the radical intelligentsia, studied briefly in St. Petersburg, began his Revolution there, and was to give his name to the city. When Lenin moved the capital from St. Petersburg and entered the Moscow Kremlin for the first time on March 12, 1918, he was uncharacteristically agitated, remarking to his secretary and companion that "worker-peasant power should be completely consolidated here."[47] Little did he imagine how permanent the change of capital was to prove and how extensive the consolidation of power in the Kremlin. The year of Lenin's death brought a flood to the former capital, newly rebaptized as Leningrad. It was an omen perhaps of the traditionalist flood that was about to sweep the revolutionary spirit out of the Leninist party. With Stalin in the Kremlin, Moscow at last wreaked its revenge on St. Petersburg, seeking to wipe out the restless reformism and critical cosmopolitanism which this "window to the West" had always symbolized.

Stalin had many roots in the Russian past. His addiction to mass armies overbalanced with artillery follows a long tradition leading back to Ivan the Terrible; his xenophobic and disciplinarian conception of education is reminiscent of Magnitsky, Nicholas I, and Pobedonostsev; his passion for material innovation and war-supporting technology echoes Peter the Great and a number of nineteenth-century Russian industrialists. But Stalinism in the full sense of the word seems to have its deepest roots in two earlier periods of Russian history: the nihilistic 1860's and the pre-Petrine era.

First of all, Stalinism appears as a conscious throwback to the militant materialism of the 1860's. Insofar as there was a positive content to Stalinist culture, it was rooted in the ascetic dedication to progress of the materialistic sixties rather than the idealistic spirit of the populist age. Stalin and some of his close associates—Molotov, Khrushchev, and Mikoyan—were like Chernyshevsky and so many other men of the sixties largely educated by priests, and had merely changed catechisms in midstream. Stalin's belief in physiological and environmental determinism—evidenced in his canonization of Pavlov and Lysenko—reflects the polemic prejudices of Pisarev more than the complex theories of Engels, let alone the thoughts of practicing scientists. His suspicion of all artistic activity without immediate social utility reflects the crude aesthetic theory of the sixties more than that of Marx.

All of the enforced artistic styles of the Stalin era—the photographic posters, the symphonies of socialism, the propagandistic novels, and the staccato civic poetry—appear as distorted vulgarizations of the predominant styles of the 1860's: the realism of the "wanderers," the programmatic music of the "mighty handful," the novels of social criticism, and the poems of Nekrasov. This artificial resurrection of long-absent styles brought a forced end to the innovations in form so characteristic of art in the silver age. Whole areas of expression were blighted: lyric poetry, satirical prose, experimental theater, and modern painting and music.

Art was, henceforth, to be subject not just to party censorship but to the mysterious requirements of "socialist realism." This doctrine called for two mutually exclusive qualities: revolutionary enthusiasm and objective depiction of reality. It was, in fact, a formula for keeping writers in a state of continuing uncertainty as to what was required of them: an invaluable device for humiliating the intellectuals by encouraging the debilitating phenomena of anticipatory self-censorship. It seems appropriate that the phrase was first used by a leading figure in the secret police rather than a literary personality.[48] Publicly pronounced in 1934 at the first congress of the Union of Writers by Andrew Zhdanov, Stalin's aide-de-camp on the cultural front, the doctrine was given a measure of respectability by the presence of Maxim Gorky as presiding figurehead at the congress. Gorky was one of the few figures of stature who could be held up as an exemplar of the new doctrine. He had a simple background, genuine socialist convictions, and a natural realistic style developed in a series of epic novels and short stories about Russian society of the late imperial period.

Socialist realism no less than the Revolution itself was to "dispose of its children."[49] Gorky died under still-mysterious circumstances two years later in the midst of the terror which swept away imaginative storytellers like Pil'niak and Babel, lyric poets like Mandel'shtam, theatrical innovators like Meierhold, as well as the inclination toward experimentalism in such gifted young artists as Shostakovich.

The often chromatic and grotesque extension of *verismo* opera, *Lady Macbeth of Mtsensk,* which Shostakovich fashioned from Leskov's bleak novella, was denounced after two years of performances and forcibly shut in 1936. Thenceforth, after nearly two years of silence, he turned almost exclusively to instrumental music, breaking the promise of distinctive national music drama that was implicit in his first opera, *The Nose* of 1930, which (like the preparatory work of Musorgsky) was based on a text by

Gogol. The unfinished fragment of a later, wartime effort to make an opera of Gogol's *Gamblers* and the post-Stalin revival of *Lady Macbeth* (revised and retitled *Katerina Izmailova*) offer tantalizing hints of what might have been. Nor was the full promise of Prokof'ev ever realized, perhaps the most technically gifted and versatile of all modern Russian composers. As a nine-year-old boy in the first year of the new century he roughed out his first complete opera score, *The Giants;* and his rapid development of a clean, "cubist" style combined with a love of rugged, often satirical themes seemed to herald the arrival of a creative giant whose return from emigration might in some way compensate for the permanent flight from the new order of Stravinsky, Rachmaninoff, and so many others. His protean powers shine through even the confining forms of expression forced on artists in the Stalin era: infant pedagogy (*Peter and the Wolf*) and heroic movie scores (*Alexander Nevsky*), and the reshaping of "safe" literary classics for the musical stage (the ballet *Romeo and Juliet* and the opera *War and Peace*). Denounced by Zhdanov and harassed by his lieutenants, this giant of Russian music died on March 4, 1953, just one day before Stalin, the man who had so crippled its development.

Zhdanov died under mysterious circumstances in 1948 after launching the purge of "homeless cosmopolitans" in the post-war era. Michael Zoshchenko, the last of the great satirists of the twenties, was silenced; the patriotic poet and widow of Gumilev, Anna Akhmatova, was called "half-nun, half-harlot" for her apolitical lyricism; and a bewildered Communist historian of philosophy was reviled as a "toothless vegetarian" for paraphrasing Western thinkers without sufficient polemic ridicule.[50] The search for distinctive proletarian art forms had, of course, been suppressed no less than the aristocratic experimentalism of the silver age. Stalin consistently favored a melodramatic art glorifying "heroes of socialist labor" and a pretentious architectural style variously characterized as *sovnovrok* ("new Soviet rococo") and—in a play on a line of Pushkin—"the empire style from the time of the plague."[51]

The peculiarities of Stalinist architecture lead us into a world very different from anything imagined by Lenin, let alone the materialists of the 1860's. The mammoth mosaics in the Moscow subway, the unnecessary spires and fantastic frills of civic buildings, the leaden chandeliers and dark foyers of reception chambers—all send the historical imagination back to the somber world of Ivan the Terrible. Indeed, the culture of the Stalin era seems more closely linked with ancient Muscovy than with even the rawest stages of St. Petersburg–based radicalism. One can, to be sure, find a certain bias in favor of bigness in the earlier period of rapid industrial development in the 1890's—evidenced in the preponderance of large factory complexes and in the building of the Trans-Siberian railway. There are also hints of classical Oriental despotism in the spectacle of giant canals and ostentatious public buildings thrown up by forced labor. Plans for a canal strikingly similar to Stalin's famous White Sea Canal of the early thirties had been mooted late in the Muscovite era at the court of Alexis Mikhailovich.[52] If this, the first major forced labor project of the Soviet era, had in some ways been anticipated in the Muscovite era, the site chosen in the twenties for the first of the new prison camp complexes of the USSR was one of the enduring symbols of Old Muscovy: the Solovetsk monastery. Ivan IV had been the first to use this bleak island monastery near the Arctic circle as a prison for ideological opponents, and the Soviet government—by evacuating the monks—was able to accommodate large numbers.

Quietly heroic testimony to some survival of Old Russian culture into the twenties is provided in the works published with the apparent consent of camp authorities by intellectuals incarcerated on the archipelago. In the monthly journal *Solovetsk Islands,* "an organ of the directorate of the Solovetsk Camps of ordinary designation OGPU," we read during the twenties of new discoveries of flora, fauna, and historical remains; of the founding of new museums; of 234 theatrical performances in a single year; and of a nineteen-kilometer ski race between inmates, Red Army guards, and the camp directorate. One article writes with obvious sympathy about Artemius, the first prisoner in Solovetsk under Ivan IV, as "a great seeker of truth and an agitator for freedom of thought."[53]

The camps of the Stalin era seemed at times to contain more scholars than the universities; but the relative freedom of Solovetsk in the early days was not to be maintained in the thirties; and only the terrible northern cold was to remain a constant feature of Stalin's concentration-camp empire. It seems eerily appropriate that the last publications to appear from Solovetsk (in 1934–5, long after the monthly journal had ceased to appear) tell of discovering prehistoric relics on the archipelago and exploring the vast, uncharted labyrinths that had long fascinated visitors to the monastery.[54]

At the very time when the emaciated prisoners of Solovetsk were plunging down to chart its frozen catacombs, thousands of laborers under various forms of compulsion were plunging even deeper beneath Moscow itself to build the greatest of all monuments of the Stalin era: the Moscow subway. From all over the empire party officials flocked to the capital like the faceless priests of some prehistoric religion to place ornate stalactites and stalagmites from the local republics into this giant communal labyrinth. The cult of the underground party also began in earnest at this time. Traditional idealistic leaders of foreign Communist parties began to be replaced by serpentine Stalinists: a cold-blooded species capable of fast, lizard-like movements in dark places and sudden chameleon-like changes of color.

Silenced prisoners in Solovetsk and authoritarian power in the Moscow Kremlin present a picture strangely reminiscent of ancient Muscovy. In some ways, the Stalin era calls to mind the compulsive Byzantine ritualism of those pre-Petrine times which had remained "contemporary" for so many Russians throughout the Romanov era. Icons, incense, and ringing bells were replaced by lithographs of Lenin, cheap perfume, and humming machines. The omnipresent prayers and calls to worship of Orthodoxy were replaced by the inescapable loudspeaker or radio with its hypnotic statistics and invocations to labor. The liturgy or "common work" of believers was replaced by the communal construction of scientific atheists. The role once played by the sending of priests and missionaries along with colonizing soldiers into the heathen interior of Russia was now assumed by "soldiers of the cultural army," who departed from mass rallies for "cultural relay races" into the countryside to see who could win the most converts for communism and collectivization in the shortest possible time.[55]

Something like the role of the holy fools and flagellants of Muscovy was played by frenzied "heroes of Socialist labor" ascetically dedicated to "overfulfilling their norms." Just as Ivan the Terrible canonized his favorite holy fool and built a cathedral later named for him, so Stalin canonized and built a national movement around Nicholas Stakhanov, a coal miner who in a fit of heroic masochism cut out 102 tons of coal (fourteen times his quota) in one shift. "Voluntary subscriptions to the state loan" replaced earlier tithes as a token of devotion to the new church; the "shock quarter" of the year replaced Lent as the periodic time of self-denial in the name of a higher cause. Like the zealous Old Believers, who sought to storm the gates of heaven by outdoing the Orthodox in their fanatical adherence to the letter of the old liturgy, the Stakhanovites sought to hasten the millennium by their "storming" (*shturmovshchina*) of production quotas. These were looked at in the way the Old Believers looked at sacred texts: as something not to be tampered with by bureaucratic innovators or scoffed at by Western sceptics, as a program of salvation if acted upon with urgency.

The Third Rome had been succeeded by a new Third International; and the ideal cultural expression in the latter as in the former was the believer's cry of hallelujah in response to the revealed word from Moscow. The term *alliluishchik* ("hallelujah singer") was in fact widely used in the Stalin era. Russia, which had overthrown a discredited monarchy, suddenly fell back on the most primitive aspect of the original tsarist mystique: the idea that the *batiushka,* the father-deliverer in the Kremlin, would rescue his suffering children from malevolent local officials and lead them into the promised land.

Thus, Stalin was able to succeed Lenin as supreme dictator not only because he was a deft intriguer and organizer but also because he was closer than his rivals to the crude mentality of the average Russian. Unlike most other Bolshevik leaders—many of whom were of Jewish, Polish, or Baltic origin—Stalin had been educated only in the catechistic theology of Orthodoxy. At Lenin's funeral, when the other Bolshevik leaders were speaking in the involved rhetoric and glowing generalities of the intellectual community, Stalin spoke in terms more familiar to the masses with his litany-like exhortations:

> Departing from us, Comrade Lenin adjured us to hold high and keep pure the great title of member of the Party. We swear to thee, Comrade Lenin, that we will fulfill thy bequest with honor! ...
> Departing from us, Comrade Lenin adjured us to guard the unity of our party like the apple of our eye. We swear to thee, Comrade Lenin, that this obligation too, we will fulfill with honor![56]

The seminarian was clearly in a better position than the cosmopolitan to create a national religion of Leninism. He felt no sense of embarrassment as Lenin's embalmed body was laid out for public veneration with hands folded in the manner of the saints in the monastery of the caves of Kiev. The incongruous mausoleum in Red Square, which paid tribute to Lenin and the new order by exemplifying the purely proletarian "constructivist" style of architecture, was forced to pay a deeper tribute to an older order represented by the crypt beneath and the Kremlin walls above it. Stalin transformed the simple building into a shrine for pilgrims and the site of his own periodic epiphanies on festal days. He chose the traditional, theological way of immortalizing Lenin in contrast to the Promethean effort by the Revolutionary intellectuals to discover after Lenin's death the material forces behind his genius through "cyto-architectonic" research (involving imported German scientists, innumerable microphotographs of his brain, and the projected comparative study of minute cranial slices from other leading thinkers).[57]

For the rest of his life Stalin claimed to be nothing more than the rock on which Lenin had built his church. His theoretical writings were always presented as updated thoughts on "problems of Leninism." In the name of Lenin's theory of the past Stalin felt free to contradict both Lenin and himself and, of course, to suppress Lenin's final uncomplimentary assessment of Stalin.

Along with the forms of theological discourse went the new content of Great Russian patriotism. Stalin rehabilitated a whole host of Russian national heroes in the thirties and introduced ever sharper differentiations in pay and privilege to goad on production. The ingeniously Marxist and almost nameless sociological histories of Pokrovsky, which had dominated Soviet historical writing until his death in 1932, were "unmasked" two years later as a deviation from "true Marxism," which henceforth glorified such unproletarian figures as Peter the Great and General Suvorov. The fiercely proletarian novels of the period of the first five-year plan, such as *Cement* and *How the Steel Was Tempered,* were replaced by a new wave of chauvinistic novels and films glorifying Russian warriors of the past.

By the late thirties, Stalin had produced a curious new mass culture that could be described by inverting his classic phrase "nationalist in form, socialist in content." The *forms* of Russian life were now clearly socialist: all agriculture had been collectivized and all of Russia's expanding means of production brought under State ownership and central planning. But socialization throughout the Stalin era brought few material benefits to the consumer, or spiritual benefits to those concerned with greater equality or increased freedom. The *content* of the new ersatz culture was retrogressively nationalistic. Under a patina of constitutions and legal procedures lay the dead hand of Nicholas I's official nationalism and some of the macabre touches of Ivan the Terrible. Stalin's proudly announced "wave of the future" looks, on closer analysis, more like backwash from the past: ghostly voices suddenly returning like the legendary chimes from the submerged city of Kitezh on Midsummer Eve—only to jangle on uncontrolled and out of tune.

Even the most servile of Bolshevik poets, Efim Pridvorov ("the courtier"), who wrote under the name Bedny ("the poor"), was thrown out of court in 1936 for his *Bogatyrs,* which made the "vulgar Marxist" error of burlesquing these popular heroes of the early Russian epics. The following year saw a host of purely patriotic festivals: a Pushkin centenary, a 125th anniversary of the Battle of Borodino, and a revival of Glinka's *Life for the Tsar* (under the alternate title of *Ivan Susanin*). The growing fear first of Japan and then of Germany accelerated Stalin's tendency to rely on nationalistic rather than socialistic appeals. The general staff and many traditional army titles were reintroduced in the late thirties; the League of the Militant Godless was abolished shortly before the German invasion of Russia in 1941, and a limited concordat with the Patriarch of Moscow agreed upon shortly after. So traditionalist did Stalin seem to have become that many in the West were prepared to accept at face value the gesture of their wartime ally in abolishing the Communist International in 1943.

Yet for all these links with Russian tradition, the age of Stalin introduced industrial development and social changes that should not be compared lightly with anything that preceded it. His effort to destroy the free creative culture of Russia was more sweeping than that of his authoritarian ancestors, and was launched against a culture that had attained unprecedented variety, sophistication, and popular support. He enlisted in his campaign all the cynical manipulative techniques of modern mass advertising, lacquering over his atrocities with a veneer of misleading statistics and insincere constitutional guarantees.

Behind it all lay untold human suffering and degradation. The peasants' hopes—rekindled during the era of the New Economic Policy—for a better life and greater freedom from their traditional urban exploiters were dashed by Stalin's determination to collectivize. The burning of grain and slaughter of livestock by the protesting peasantry at the beginning of the thirties launched a chain reaction of unnatural death in the human realm. Peasants perished as *kulak* "class enemies," repopulated forced laborers, or victims of artificial starvation from bad planning or forcible grain collections. The "leftist" activists who perpetrated this horror in the countryside were the next to perish in the purges of the mid-thirties; and, then the executors were themselves executed to placate the masses and insure the safety of the supreme assassin.

Deaths were recorded not individually or by the thousands but by the millions. More than ten million cattle were slaughtered in the early stages of collectivization, perhaps five million peasants in the social upheaval of the thirties. Membership in the Party elite provided no refuge, for 55 out of its 71 Central Committee members and 60 of 68 alternate members disappeared between the Seventeenth Congress of the party in 1934 and its Eighteenth Congress in 1939. Indeed, all but a very few of those who had made the Revolution and launched the Soviet state were purged in the thirties. Then came Hitler and the terrible suffering of the war, in which twelve million Russians perished.

Always and unremittingly, Stalin suspected those flights of the imagination and experiments with form and idea which lay at the heart of creative culture. None was more suspect in Eastern Europe than the large Jewish community, with its intellectual traditions and international perspectives. Jewish Bolsheviks were deprived of their revolutionary names and sent to the anonymous death that was shortly to become the fate of the Jewish masses under the more systematic and distinctively racist totalitarianism of Nazi Germany. The final reprise on the totalitarian age was Stalin's effort to cut out "the ulcer of cosmopolitanism" by obliterating the survivals of Yiddish culture and the new interest in Western Europe that appeared in Russia in the wake of World War II.

Stalin's most important contribution to world culture lay in his perfection of a new technique of governing through systematic alternation between terror and relaxation. This "artificial dialectic" required the building of a manipulable and "cast-iron" apparatus totally dependent on the dictator, and the determination to make "permanent purge" a calculated instrument of statecraft.[58] The true *homo sovieticus* was the disciplined and secretive professional officer of the dictator's sprawling police and intelligence apparatus.[59] Just as technicians in the infamous Special Section of the Ministry of the Interior found that one of the simplest ways to "break" a reluctant prisoner was by a blinking alternation of total light and total darkness, so the servants of Stalin sought to disorient and subdue the outside world with an incessant and bewildering alternation between smiles and scowls, amity and threat.

In the remote apex of this society stood the solitary dictator, regulating the ebb and flow of mood, ingeniously playing on the masochistic and xenophobic impulses of a populace long accustomed to collective suffering and feelings of inferiority. Whenever rewards were in order or respites to be granted, the Caligula of collectivism suddenly emerged smiling from inside the Kremlin. When terror was loose, even the victims tended to speak of it as the creation of an underling: *Yezhovshchina* in the thirties, *Zhdanovshchina* in the forties.

In his last years, Stalin kept about him such shadowy figures as Beria, a fellow Georgian and Yezhov's successor as head of the ever-growing police empire; Poskrebyshev, his private secretary; and Michael Suslov, a lean and ascetic former Old Believer who bore the name of the founder of the flagellant sect.

On Christmas eve of 1952, Suslov sounded the first note in a fresh campaign of denunciation that was both a throwback to the witch-hunting at the court of Ivan III and the apparent harbinger of a vast new purge. Suslov's denunciation of editors for insufficiently rigorous self-criticism over long-forgotten issues of economic development was followed by an announcement in *Pravda* that nine doctors had been charged with assassinating through mistreatment and poisoning a variety of leading Soviet figures, including Zhdanov. This campaign against the predominately Jewish "doctor-poisoners" who had allegedly infiltrated the Kremlin was apparently directed against Beria, as head of state security, and his close associate, Georgy Malenkov. As the most intelligent and powerful of Stalin's lieutenants, they were the logical candidates for victimization; and their careers were saved (though only temporarily) by the convenient death of Stalin himself on March 5, 1953. The last time he was seen alive by a non-Communist observer, Stalin was doodling wolves in red ink; and the last officially announced medical treatment administered to him before death was bleeding with leeches.[60]

For nearly ten years, a mummified and faintly smiling Stalin lay alongside Lenin in the Red Square mausoleum. It was an awesome reminder of the carefully cultivated myth of infallibility—the idea that, however absurd Soviet policy may have seemed to those on the front lines, there was always an omniscient leader at the command post: a "magic citadel" within the Kremlin inviolable to assault from ordinary experience and common-sense doubts. As one student of the Stalin formula wrote:

> The strength of communism and its originality come from the disinterested militants and sympathizers. . . . Their sympathy and faith will not become untenable while the remote inner citadel remains intact—that magic citadel within which evil is transformed to good, fact into myth, history into legend, and the steppes of Russia into paradise.[61]

Giant, omnipresent statues of Stalin had provided Russia with a new image of omnipotence: a macabre parody of the Byzantine *Pantokrator*. This divine image had stared down from the central domes of the original cathedrals of the holy wisdom to provide sanctifying power and some mystical foretaste of the splendors of heaven to those who gathered on feast days in these original centers of Russian civilization. So Stalin smiled down his assurances of holy wisdom and sanctifying authority to those who gathered on the new feast days for the pathetic foretaste of heaven on earth provided by a "park of culture and rest." This quasi-religious myth of Stalin with its many psychologically satisfying features could not be easily dispelled. When his body was finally removed from the mausoleum in Red Square late in 1961, an ancient woman who had known Lenin and spent seventeen years in prison under Stalin issued the call rather in the manner of a sectarian prophetess:

> The only reason I survived is that Il'ich was in my heart, and I sought his advice, as it were. (Applause) Yesterday I asked Il'ich for advice, and it was as if he stood before me alive and said: "I do not like being next to Stalin, who inflicted so much harm on the Party." (Stormy prolonged applause.)[62]

The scene of ritual reburial is reminiscent of late Muscovite politics, with Khrushchev calling forth his sanctifying approval of the woman's recommendation from the podium of the Twenty-second Party Congress as it bellowed forth its antiphonal responses of "Stormy, prolonged applause." One Soviet intellectual of the post-Stalin era has written:

Ah, if only we had been more intelligent; if only we had surrounded his
death with miracles! We should have given it out on the radio that he was
not dead but had gone up into heaven, whence he was still looking at us
silently, over his mystical moustache. His relics would have cured para-
lytics and people possessed with devils. And children, before going to bed,
would have been praying by their windows, with their eyes turned toward
the bright stars of the celestial Kremlin.[63]

Perhaps the best synoptic view of Russian culture under Stalin is
provided by the development of the cinema, an art medium with little
history prior to the Soviet period. The innumerable movie theaters large
and small that sprang up all over the USSR in the twenties and thirties were
the new regime's equivalent to the churches of an earlier age. Within the
theaters, the prescribed rituals of the new order—its chronicles of success
and promises of bliss—were systematically and regularly presented to the
silent masses, whose main image of a world beyond that of immediate
physical necessity was now derived from a screen of moving pictures rather
than a screen of stationary icons. Like Soviet industry, the cinema produced
in the age of Stalin a great quantity of films, including some of real quality.
Yet despite the many new techniques and skilled artists involved, the
Stalinist cinema represents a regressive chapter in the history of Russian
culture. At best, it offered little more than a pretentious extension of the
most chauvinistic aspects of pre-Revolutionary culture; at worst it was a
technological monstrosity seeking to cannibalize one of the world's most
promising theatrical traditions.

Hopes were high when idealistic young revolutionaries first wandered
into the deserted studios of the infant Russian film industry during the
Revolutionary period. Here was an art medium closely linked to the liberating force of technology, uniquely suitable for spreading the good news of
a new social order to all people. Here also was a relatively untouched world
of artistic possibility: a cultural *tabula rasa*. For, since the first public movie
theater had appeared in 1903, the Russian film industry had assumed no
very distinctive character. It was an imitative, commercially oriented medium largely involved in producing never-never land sentimentality and
melodramatic happy endings.

Placed under the commissariat of education by a Leninist decree of
August, 1919, and faced with the emigration of almost all its artists and
technicians, the Soviet film industry became a major center for on-the-job
training in the arts and an arena for florid experimentation.

During the relatively relaxed period of the early twenties a variety of
new styles appeared, and a vigorous discussion ensued about the nature of
cinematic art and its relation to the new social order. The remarkable

"movie eye" (*kinoko*) group flourished briefly, with its fanatical dedication to documentary accuracy and precise chronology; a former architect and sculptor, Leo Kuleshov, pioneered in the use of open-air scenes, untrained actors, and monumental compositions; and scattered efforts were made to break down the flow of pictures into expressionistic or abstract forms.

But as in all fields of Soviet culture, the rise of Stalin to absolute power in the late twenties led to the adoption of a propagandistic official style that brought an end to creative experiment. The new style was perhaps the best example of that blend of Revolutionary message and realistic form that came to be called socialist realism. At the same time, the subject matter of the cinema in the thirties and forties illustrates the increasing drift toward chauvinistic traditionalism in Stalinist Russia.

There were many influences behind the new Soviet film style. In a sense it was a return to the old tradition of the illustrated chronicle (*litsevaia letopis'*) with which the heroic history of the Church Victorious had been popularized in the late Muscovy. It was also a continuation and vulgarization of the traditions of heroic historical painting and mammoth exhibitions that had been developed in the nineteenth century. To these traditions was added the dream of a new type of revolutionary mystery play originated during the exciting days of War Communism. Open-air mass theatrical pageants were improvised as thousands took part in a cycle which attempted to re-enact seven major popular revolutions in Russian history; eighty thousand took part in Maiakovsky's *Mystery-Bouffe,* and more than one hundred thousand in the ritual re-enactment of the storming of the Winter Palace. Michelet said that the French Revolution really began not with the storming of the Bastille on July 14, 1789, but with the symbolic re-enactment of the event a year later. In like manner, one could say that the Russian Revolution—as a symbol of liberation—was born not in the turbulent events of November, 1917, but in these subsequent scenes of pictorial pageantry and mythic re-creation.

The key cinematic task of Lenin's heir was the transposition to the screen of this monumental myth. As the "movie trains" of Revolutionary days with their itinerant pictorial propaganda were replaced by stationary theaters, it became essential to have a codified version of the Revolutionary myth. This was provided by three major films, which were all produced in honor of the tenth anniversary of the Bolshevik coup and comprise a kind of heroic trilogy: Pudovkin's *Last Days of Petersburg,* Eisenstein's *Ten Days That Shook the World,* and Barnet's *Moscow in October.* Together with the panoramic and equally fanciful picture of the Civil War provided by Alexis Tolstoy's *Road to Calvary* (which became a trilogy in the film version), these films dramatized for the Russian masses the mystery of the new incarnation in which the hopes and fears of all the years suddenly found fulfillment in Russia.

Of the cinematic iconographers of the Revolution, Pudovkin and Eisenstein are deservedly the best remembered. They were both creatures of the experimental twenties and pupils of Kuleshov. Each scored his greatest triumph in 1926—Eisenstein with *Battleship Potemkin* and Pudovkin with the film version of Gorky's *Mother*. Each had a long subsequent career of film-making that came to an end only when they died late in the Stalin era —Eisenstein in 1948, Pudovkin in 1953.

Pudovkin was the more thoroughly Stalinist and—as a result—the less memorable of the two. A rugged and athletic child of the Volga region, he was, from the beginning, anxious to expend his energies in the service of the new order. His theoretical writings emphasized the use of technological innovation for practical purposes of indoctrination. He favored the Stanislavsky method of acting realism over more experimental styles and exalted the semi-dictatorial function of the film editor and director.

Though capable of projecting simple and powerful emotions, he increasingly followed Stalin in turning toward monumental subjects. Traditional Russian patriotic themes replaced Revolutionary ones in his most important later works: *Suvorov, Minin and Pozharsky,* and *Admiral Nakhimov*. At the same time, he demonstrated in his theoretical writings the passion for statistical self-congratulation in pseudo-Marxist terms which was so characteristic of the Stalin mentality.

> On the stage an actor plays before hundreds of persons, in the film actually before millions. Here is a dialectical instance of quantity increasing over the boundary into quality to give rise to a new kind of excitement.[64]

He expressed a kind of *nouveau riche* contempt for the older traditions of the theater with his bluff confidence that "socialist realism is just as immortal, as eternally young and inexhaustible as the people itself."[65]

Eisenstein was a far more complex and interesting figure. Born in Riga and educated as an architect, he was more deeply immersed in the experimental tendencies of the twenties and more broadly versed in twentieth-century European culture than Pudovkin. He was influenced by Kandinsky and others to believe that the basic ingredients of line and color could of their own accord bring spiritual qualities into visual art. He drew directly from mystical precursors of Scriabin like Castel and Eckartshausen the belief that true art must affect a "synchronization of senses."[66] He became active in the constructivist theater of Proletkult and worked as an artistic designer in Meierhold productions before his epoch-making filming of *Potemkin*.

The film used an enormous cast to depict with poetic license and cinematic skill the brief revolt of the crew of the battleship *Potemkin* in Odessa during the Revolution of 1905. Based on a scenario written especially for the movie in honor of the twentieth anniversary of that Revolution, *Potemkin* drew heavily on the old tradition of the open-air mass theater to produce a near-perfect parable of Revolutionary heroism. The battleship itself—rather than any individual—was the hero. Its crew was a triumphant, spontaneous chorus of Revolutionary joy struggling against both the vermin gnawing at their paltry ration of meat, and the priests and officials gnawing at their souls. Just as John the Baptist, "the precursor," was placed next to Christ Enthroned on the iconostasis, so this Revolutionary precursor of October acquired a venerated place in the iconography of the Revolution. Few scenes up to that time had so brilliantly engaged the capabilities of the infant cinema industry for political purposes as the famous sequence of a baby carriage coming loose from its mother's grasp and gathering momentum as it rolled down the steps pursued by a mechanically advancing phalanx of dehumanized Tsarist soldiers.

Unlike Pudovkin, Eisenstein experimented with non-realistic forms of cinematic art and incurred official rebukes for several of his efforts in the late twenties and early thirties. But like Pudovkin, he eventually followed the trend toward more conventional patriotic themes in the thirties. His *Alexander Nevsky* was a milestone in this genre, glorifying the famous monk-warrior so admired by Peter the Great. But whereas the famous cinematic eulogy of Peter the Great produced at the same time merely transposed onto the screen the pictorial images of nineteenth-century painters, Eisenstein's depiction of Peter's patron saint incorporated elements of grotesque hyperbole that suggested continued borrowings from the expressionistic theater.

If Peter the Great, the builder of St. Petersburg and lover of technological innovation, was a natural hero for the early Stalin era, the dark figure of Ivan IV was in many ways a suitable hero for the later years of Stalin, with their macabre reversions to Muscovite ways. Thus, in the late thirties, Eisenstein turned to producing a large-scale life of Ivan the Terrible, assembling an extraordinary array of talent: the music of Prokof'ev, the acting of Cherkasov, the finest black-and-white and color photographers, and even the services of Pudovkin for a minor acting role.

Yet for all its promise, this work became yet another of those unfinished trilogies in which Russian cultural history abounds. The first part was filmed during the war, in the distant haven of Alma Ata, and was hailed with a variety of accolades, including the Stalin Prize First Class shortly after its release in January, 1945. The second part was, however, denounced by the Central Committee in September, 1946. The eerie sounds and shadows of the first part became caricatures in the second, which alternated between black-and-white and color scenes in its depiction of boyar conspiracies. The atmosphere of hovering intrigue and impending assassination was all too close to real life, and the hypersensitive Stalin appears to have seen in the frank depiction of cruelty by Ivan and his *oprichnina* implied criticism of himself and his secret police. Thus, the second part of the trilogy was not publicly released until 1958—ten years after Eisenstein's death and five years after Stalin's. The third part was not completed; and Eisenstein died in the same condition of semi-disgrace that had been his lot in the early thirties.

The cinema in the early post-war years was devoted mainly to stereotyped ideological romances between collective farmers and party activists or to the attempt to hypnotize audiences with the omniscience of Stalin's leadership and the omnipotence of Soviet armed force in films like *The Battle of Stalingrad* and *The Fall of Berlin*. In this age of systematic photographic falsification, Soviet movies disintegrated literally as well as figuratively because of the repeated editorial splicing of films by the Soviet propaganda agencies that controlled their distribution. Small wonder that Eisenstein in his last years was contemplating shifting his efforts from the ill-fated *Ivan IV* to a proposed study of the life of Nero.[67] There seemed no honorable calling left for the human spirit that did not risk martyrdom at the hands of the new Nero. Even Nicholas Virta, who had written the script for *The Battle of Stalingrad,* may have been hinting that calamity was at hand in his play of the late Stalin era that was published only in 1954, *The Fall of Pompeii.*

With Stalin as with Ivan, there was method in the madness. Like Ivan, Stalin vastly increased the power of the Russian state, and his authority over it.[68] Whether by luck or by careful planning, Stalin in a quarter of a century lifted Russia from a position of being one of the least of the world's great powers to being one of its only two super-powers: from fifth or sixth to second place in industrial production. These were the criteria by which Stalin—and many others in the twentieth century—measured success; and in these terms Stalin was successful. Out of the raw strength and complex psychology of the Russian people, he fashioned an impressive political machine, which he handled with great skill and more flexibility than is sometimes remembered.[69] Even in the area of culture he could point to such superficially imposing accomplishments as the virtual disappearance of illiteracy and gigantic editions of all kinds of literary classics.

The only official socialist realism likely to endure beyond the memory of the Stalin era is that of Michael Sholokhov's novels, which captured some of the flavor of its epic transformations and violent inhumanity. The Leninist and Stalinist revolutions are retold in credible if somewhat two-dimensional terms in his *And Quiet Flows the Don* and his *Virgin Soil Upturned,* respectively. But even this scrupulously loyal (and fundamentally anti-Western and anti-intellectual) writer was harassed and delayed in his effort to tell the second of these stories. In the high Stalin era, he withdrew increasingly to the countryside of his native Ukraine, summoning up the image and authority of an enduring nature in titles and descriptive passages, publishing the full version of *Virgin Soil* only after Khrushchev had denigrated Stalin, and becoming after Khrushchev's fall the third Russian writer to be awarded a Nobel Prize.[70]

For the historian of Russian thought, the Stalin era has an importance quite apart from the personality of the dictator. For it was a period in which many long silent forces suddenly came to play an important role in Russian cultural life. Like forms of growth incubating in the frozen subsoil, masochistic and chauvinistic impulses suddenly shot forth as Stalin's mechanized plows dug below the surface and brought them closer to the light.

At the same time, the soil overturned by this "second revolution" proved hospitable to new crops that sprang up from fresh seeds of literacy and learning. Though Stalin liked to fancy himself as having infinite power to control the vegetable as well as the human world (as his deification of Lysenko's environmentalism reveals), he was faced with some unexpected crops on the steppelands that he had so systematically harrowed and burned out. If the political and economic historian must deal largely with Lenin's seeding and Stalin's weeding, the cultural historian must look at the deeper problems of the soil, and—however tentatively—at the relation of present harvests to those of the past and the future.

3 . Fresh Ferment

THE GENERAL NATURE of Russian accomplishments under Bolshevism have long been evident. Urbanization and industrialization have accelerated; the sinews of military strength have dramatically increased; and centralized control has combined with a scientific ideology to achieve greater internal discipline than had previously been attained by Russian rulers. The resourceful, if brutal, leaders of the USSR have perfected—out of their own revolutionary experience—effective means of frustrating any political challenge to their authority, whether through agitation from within or subversion from without. Finally—largely because they were in power during World War II and have registered important material accomplishments since—the Communist leadership has sold itself to the long-suffering Russian people as something more than a passing phenomenon in their long historical experience.

But the plans and accomplishments of the ruling oligarchy have always been only a part of the complex record of Russian history. Just as the Russian heritage influenced in many ways the official culture developed under Stalin, so also the problems that came to perplex him seem strangely familiar. The historian can, of course, never know precisely how the past relates to the present, particularly when surrounded by the unprecedented problems of the atomic age. Nor can he know precisely how the inherited forms of art and thought affect the world of power politics and economic necessity. But it is his duty to point out those themes which sound like echoes from the past, and there was a hauntingly large number in the late Stalin era.

To begin with, there was the stimulus of war: a recurrent theme of modern Russian history. The sense of exhilaration, self-sacrifice, and increased social mobility had traditionally combined with new Western contacts to stimulate reformist sentiment in modern Russia. Indeed, radical agitation had almost invariably followed important wars and enlisted the services of returning veterans: the Decembrists following the Napoleonic wars; the "new men" of the sixties, the Crimean War; the revolutionary populists, the Turkish War; the Revolution of 1905, the war with Japan; and the Revolutions of 1917, World War I. It was not unreasonable to suppose that the dislocations and exposure to the West during World War II would lead to similar reformist pressures—coming in the wake of the suffering and deception of the 1930's. Many Russians did, indeed, defect to the Germans; and Stalin went to extremes to limit contacts with his wartime Western allies. The purges and violent anti-Westernism of the early post-war period were, in large measure, attempts to prevent what might otherwise have been an irresistible drift toward some form of political liberalization and accommodation to long-suppressed consumer needs.

The fact that the key purges of 1948–9 are referred to in Soviet literature as "the Leningrad case" points to a second traditional feature of recent Soviet history: the recurrence of the old tension between Moscow and Leningrad. The revenge of Muscovy had perforce to be directed against its ancient rival for pre-eminence in the Russian Empire. Leningrad was still a "window to the West," and, within the Communist Party, the Leningrad organization had traditionally represented revolutionary idealism and broad international culture from the time of Trotsky and Zinov'ev. These figures had been among the earliest victims of Stalin's intrigues; and he began the purges of the thirties with the murder of their successor as head of the Leningrad Party, Serge Kirov. His successor, Andrei Zhdanov, perished in turn with mysterious suddenness in the midst of the post-war decimation of the Leningrad Party. Having suffered nearly three years of blockade during the war, Leningrad had emerged with certain credentials of heroism that commanded respect in the post-war USSR. It had become the center not only of artistic and intellectual ferment but also of a relative emphasis on light industry in future economic development. Leningrad was still, as it had been in the days of tsarist St. Petersburg, the center and symbol of patterns of development closer to those of the West than those favored in Moscow.

Another recurrent theme is the dilemma of despotic reformism confronted by Stalin's successors. Following, as had Catherine II, Alexander I, and Alexander II, on the heels of a repressive and authoritarian predecessor, Stalin's heirs sought to rekindle popular enthusiasm by sweeping initial amnesties and vague promises of reform. The line first sounded by Malenkov with his amnesties from forced labor camps and promises of a "new course" was taken over and given a new theatrical quality by Khrushchev. But the new ruler soon confronted the classic problem which had so perplexed Catherine and the two Alexanders. How can one introduce reforms without jeopardizing the despotic basis of control? How can one revive initiative without stimulating insubordination? In the wake of his denunciation of Stalin in February, 1956, Khrushchev met in Hungary, Poland, and his own country the equivalent of the shock administered to Catherine by Pugachev and the French Revolution, to Alexander I by the Semenovsky uprising and the European revolutions of the early 1820's, and to Alexander II by the ideological tumult and assassination attempts of the 1860's. Faced with a revolution of rising expectations that he had helped to call forth, he was forced to reassert the authoritarian essence of his position. As so often in the past, reformist rhetoric gave way to renewed repression.

Pressures for retrenchment on reform in the late fifties and early sixties were, however, to some extent countered by yet another recurrence of an old Russian theme: the conflict of two generations. Khrushchev appeared to have sensed the wisdom of attempting to befriend the articulate young generation, whose outlook differed profoundly from that of the shell-shocked survivors and bureaucratic beneficiaries of the Stalin era. For the new generation the material accomplishments of the second, Stalinist revolution seemed as remote as the utopian dreams of the first Leninist revolution had been to their Stalinist parents. The new generation was brought up, rather, amidst the high hopes that had accompanied the wartime effort. It was a better-educated generation, conscious of the disparity between its own technical competence and the bureaucratic sloth and psychotic excesses of Stalin's post-war rule. It had been a silent generation; but it rapidly found things to say, when Khrushchev in his own political insecurity gave it the opportunity in 1956. Even more important, the new generation kept on talking after the inevitable reaction in late 1956 and 1957. Voices began to be heard from creative periods of the Russian past; less timid they seemed, or at least less intimidated. By the early sixties some were speaking of an even more radical generation composed of those in their early twenties and known by the historically venerable term "men of the sixties."

The age of Stalin was at last coming to an end: a quarter of a century dominated by the idea of *zagovor,* or "conspiracy." A conspiratorial code of revolutionary expediency had been transposed into a system of government, and Stalin's own intrigues camouflaged with tales of conspiracy by Trotskyite wreckers, capitalist encirclers, Titoist vampires, or simply "certain circles." All these forces were united in "a conspiracy of the condemned" against the USSR (to cite the title of Virta's violently anti-American drama of 1948). Within the USSR, Stalin's subordinates might be forming a "conspiracy of boyars" (the subtitle of the second part of Eisenstein's *Ivan the Terrible*). Even inside the Kremlin, the possibility existed that conspiratorial doctor-poisoners were secretly at work.

From the populace in general, Stalin was aided by what came to be called "the conspiracy of silence" (a phrase used first in the 1820's by a disillusioned Westernizer, Prince Viazemsky, to describe the political passivity of Russians before the tyrannical methods of Nicholas I).[1] Bruno Jasieński, a Polish Communist who moved to France and then to suicide in Russia during the purges, used the even more telling phrase "conspiracy of the indifferent" (the title of his important unfinished work of the thirties, which was published only after the denigration of Stalin in 1956).[2]

After the death of Stalin, the all-important question was: What could provide an antidote to conspiratorial government supported by conspiracies of silence and indifference? A prophetic hint was provided by yet another concept of conspiracy that had been put forth on the eve of Stalin's second revolution by the last of the short-blooming crop of humorists from Odessa, Yury Olesha. In his tale of 1927, *Envy*, Olesha gathered together a few Old World intellectuals into a "conspiracy of feelings"[3] (which became the title of the dramatic form of the novel). Supremely superfluous people, envious of the brave new world being built about them, Olesha's "conspirators" are implausible egg-head cavaliers (one of them is named Kavalerov) among the revolutionary roundheads: vacillating, yet still princely Hamlets in an age when this symbol of the old intelligentsia was about to be abolished from the stage.

In Olesha's novel the strong arm of Soviet power is represented by two figures, one a soccer player and the other a sausage maker, bent on building a kind of giant supermarket system for the new society. They are clearly the wave of the future, and to sustain their conspiracy Olesha's errant cavaliers flee to the world of fantasy, where they build a machine to destroy all machines and name it "Ophelia." But this missing Madonna for the conspiracy of feelings will not permit herself to be used. It was Hamlet's coldness that killed Ophelia; and now, brought back to life by the Hamlets of the old intelligentsia, Ophelia proves a vengeful lady—turning on them rather than the machines.

The net effect of the story, however, is to arouse sympathy for the "conspiracy" and leave one with the impression that its apolitical opposition to the new order will somehow continue. The activity of the decade since Stalin can be viewed as a posthumous vindication of some of the feelings which Olesha's cavaliers had been unable to defend.

After a quarter of a century of Stalin's "conspiracy of equals" (the title of Ehrenburg's laudatory novel of 1928 about Babeuf's organization of that name[4]), the time had come for "the thaw" (to cite the title of the novel he published in 1954). The killing frost had stricken Russian culture in full blossom, and no one could be sure what would emerge after such a

winter. But one old branch survived unbent, and many new shoots did
appear. Thus, one must turn to the *envoi* left by a "survival of the past,"
Boris Pasternak, and to the fresh voices raised by Soviet youth in the
decade since Stalin.

The Reprise of Pasternak

WHATEVER his historical impact on Russian culture may prove to be,
Pasternak set forth in the last writings before his death in 1960 a remarkable human testament and a moving reprise on the culture of Old Russia
that is deserving of study in its own right.

It was perhaps to be expected that this reprise should be that of a poet.
Man's power to sing spontaneously and implausibly may well provide his
only path to dignity and self-respect in an age of calculation, deception, and
spiritual isolation. Boris Pasternak, one of the purest and most musical
poets of the century, had that power. It put him in communion with the
world of unheard melodies and higher harmony which has always been
suspect to proponents of a closed and authoritarian society. Plato would
have banished the poets from his *Republic,* and Lenin the sounds of the
"Appassionata" from his memory.

But, for Pasternak, poetry was everything: not just a form of consolation for the adversity of contemporary political and economic life, but
rather a way of cutting through all artificiality to the real world—the
throbbing and sensuous world of persons, places, and things. Pasternak
seeks to defend that world against the less real world of abstract slogans,
creeds, and statistics. Individual poetry is the language of the former; corporate prose, the medium of the latter. In a land bent on producing quantities of the most artificial prose in a pretentiously bureaucratic century,
Pasternak remained an uncompromisingly lyric poet. His commitment was
not to ideas but to life itself—from the verses he wrote in the revolutionary
year of 1917 entitled *My Sister Life* to the last poems of *Doctor Zhivago,*
whose name means "living."

Why was the poet of life permitted to survive? He was too well known
to have been overlooked; yet, despite long periods of silence and diversion
into translating, Pasternak never renounced his poetic course nor com-
promised himself by writing servile odes to Stalin and hymns to collectivization. Stalin himself must have willed or agreed to his survival. Perhaps
he was in some way moved by the uncorrupted quality of this pure poetic
offshoot of Old Russia. Or perhaps Stalin sensed a certain occult power

in the one who defined the poet as "brother to a dervish."[5] Certainly Pasternak had a singular record of nonconformity to the artistic mores of Stalinist Russia, beginning with his letter to Stalin at the time of the mysterious death of Stalin's first wife in November, 1932. Refusing to sign the stereotyped letter of consolation offered by other leading writers, Pasternak published a letter of his own to Stalin:

> I align myself with the feelings of my comrades. On the eve I was thinking deeply and tenaciously about Stalin; for the first time as an artist. In the morning I read the news. I was shocked exactly as if I had been alongside, had lived and seen.[6]

Whatever the reasons, Pasternak survived and stayed on in Russia. With the coming of the first "thaw" after Stalin's death, Pasternak published in April, 1954, ten poems described as "poems from the novel in prose, *Dr. Zhivago.*" There was a good deal even in this first announcement. The statement that the poet had nearly finished his first and only novel created considerable anticipation, for it meant that he had for some time been occupied with a new kind of work. He had accepted the prosaic world of contemporary Russia, and decided to communicate at length with it apparently in the language it could understand. The description "a novel in prose" indicated that he intended to replay with variations older literary themes, since Pushkin had characterized his *Eugene Onegin* as a "novel in verse." The idea that the novel would deal with Soviet reality and at the same time recapitulate some of the older Russian cultural heritage was quietly set forth in the author's explanatory note that *Zhivago* was to "cover the period from 1903 to 1929," and deal with "a thinking man in search of truth, with a creative and artistic bent."[7]

There are many ways of looking at this work, which was published abroad three years later despite strenuous Soviet objections, and then awarded a Nobel Prize which its author was forced to decline. Stalinists in Russia and sensationalists abroad have referred to it as a kind of anti-Revolutionary diatribe; literary specialists have demonstrated their critical *sang-froid* by calling it inferior to his poetry and assigning to it a kind of B+ to A— rating on their literary scorecards; students of the occult have looked at the work as a kind of buried treasure chest of symbols and allusions.[8] Behind this critical din stand the massive shadows of two less articulate groups: the millions with no knowledge of Russia who have read and been moved by it; and the millions within Russia who have not been allowed to see it.

If Stalin would not permit Pasternak to be done away with altogether, neither would Stalin's successors permit him to publish freely. Pasternak's

last years were spent in forced isolation, surrounded by petty harassments
and veiled threats. Indeed, no figure within the USSR was treated to a more
shrill and vulgar chorus of official denunciation during "de-Stalinization"
than this mild poet. To the all-powerful Communist bureaucrats of
Khrushchev's Russia he was the bearer of a "putrid infection," the producer
of "decadent refuse," and generally "worse than a pig," because "a pig will
never befoul the place where it eats and sleeps."[9]

There were good reasons why the campaign against Pasternak had to
be pursued vigorously despite awkwardness and embarrassment. For Pasternak's *Zhivago* posed in effect a challenge to the moral basis of the
regime. Rather than follow the approved path of criticizing the particular
cheers which writers had previously rendered to Stalin, Pasternak was
challenging the entire conception of writer-as-cheerleader. He presented in
Zhivago a challenge to the moral superiority of the imitative activist who
has externalized and materialized life, who accepts the constant rationalization that the individual self must be sacrificed for "the good of the social
collective."[10] By creating an essentially passive sufferer and giving him a
credible, even appealing, inner life, Pasternak offered an alternative to the
two-dimensional "new Soviet man."

The editors who rejected his novel for publication in the USSR seemed
particularly peeved that Zhivago did not take sides in the Civil War, so
that the familiar label of counter-revolutionary could be applied to him.
He was, perhaps, a counter-revolutionary, but only in the deeper sense of
advocating "not a contrary revolution, but the contrary of a revolution."
Pasternak was the real alternative to social revolution: one which Stalinist
activists could not understand because it could be neither labeled nor
bought off. Even in humiliation, Pasternak preserved dignity and integrity
in the eyes of his countrymen. He refused to flee abroad as he was urged
to do by his primitive tormentors, who accused him of seeking nothing
more than the "delights of your capitalist paradise." In his letter retracting
acceptance of the Nobel Prize Pasternak insisted that "with my hand on
my heart, I can say that I have done something for Soviet literature."[11] It
was obvious that his tormentors could neither place their hands over their
hearts nor say that they had done anything for Russian literature. No Soviet
writer of the first rank signed the official denunciation that accompanied
the campaign of defamation.

Both his Soviet critics and his Western admirers agree that the book
is in some sense a throwback to pre-Revolutionary Russia, a voice that has
come "as from a lost culture."[12] There is indeed a deliberate assertion of
long silent themes at variance with official Soviet culture. Yet at the same
time the book deals basically with the origins and development of the Soviet

period, and Pasternak clearly viewed the work as a kind of testament to his native land. In his last autobiographical sketch, written after the novel was completed, he pointedly described it as "my chief and most important work, the only one of which I am not ashamed and for which I take full responsibility."[13]

The greatness of the book lies not in the affair that grew around it, still less in the plot of the novel itself, but rather in the alchemy with which he combines three main ingredients: recapitulation of the pre-Revolutionary literary tradition; rediscovery of the deeper religious and naturalistic symbolism in the Russian subconscious; and a new view of the Russian Revolution and the Russian future.

The attempt to recapitulate the Russian literary tradition is evident at every turn. The work is first described in a manner reminiscent of *Eugene Onegin,* and is structured like Tolstoy's *War and Peace*—telling the interrelated tales of a great national epic and a lonely search for truth, complete with two epilogues. Zhivago himself is a combination and fulfillment of two key types in nineteenth-century Russian literature: the *obyvatel'*, or "oppressed little man" who passively observes the misfortunes that fate has sent him, and the *lishny chelovek,* or "superfluous aristocrat" incapable of effective action and alienated from both family and society. Symbols from the Russian literary past are played back slightly out of tune: the troika from *Dead Souls,* the train that crushes Anna Karenina. Long sections of Dostoevskian and Chekhovian dialogue are inserted, often at the expense of the narrative. The old opposition between the rich, uncomplicated world of nature and the artificial world of the machine is played antiphonally throughout the novel. Zhivago dies trying to let fresh air into a crowded trolley car.

Above all stands the idea that increasingly obsessed the literary imagination of the late imperial period: the belief that a woman, some strange and mysterious feminine force, could alone show the anguished intellectuals the way to salvation. This was the missing Madonna of Russian romanticism: the "beautiful lady" of Blok's early poetry, the "sophia" of Solov'ev's theosophy, the "Ophelia" of Olesha's fantasy. As often in Dostoevsky, women are given a special clairvoyance. Pasternak's mysterious lady of salvation has been defiled, yet she offers a mixture of sensual and spiritual quality. Lara is many things: Russia, life, poetry, a tree, unaffected simplicity. The wandering Zhivago seeks her throughout the great events of the revolutionary period. He achieves physical union with her in the snow-covered countryside; and then, beyond death, there is a moving last vignette where she weeps over Zhivago and makes the sign of the cross over his dead body. What might seem trite in another context suddenly becomes transformed into a powerful scene containing elements both of a *Pietà*, wherein the Mother of God weeps over the broken body of her son, and of a *Liebestod*, wherein swelling music finds harmonic release only as Isolde joins her lover in death.

Lara has the same combination of beauty, integrity, and ambiguous depth which lay behind the greatest achievements of Russian literary culture. In the brave new world of twentieth-century Russia, Lara must bear the fate of that culture: disappearance and anonymous death. For Pasternak as for the theologians of the Eastern Church, all of nature participates in the suffering and martyrdom of sacred history. Through one of his innumerable images Pasternak points out that this culture suffers martyrdom at the hands not of evil men but of pharisees with their "retouching" and "varnishing over" (*lakirovka*) of truth. Even the coming of spring is affected by the Civil War.

> Here and there a birch stretched forth itself like a martyr pierced by the barbs and arrows of its opening shoots, and you knew its smell by just looking at it, the smell of its glistening resin, which is used for making varnish.

Yet suffering and deception do not have the last word; for the over-all frame of the book is religious. The work is saturated with images from Orthodox Christianity; and one senses that they will in some way be recovered like the old images on the icons whose purity was only rediscovered through layers of varnish during the years of Pasternak's youth. The name Zhivago is taken from the Easter Liturgy and the communion prayer of John Chrysostom; events are repeatedly related to the Orthodox calendar, and Zhivago's tour with the partisans and experience of atrocities occurs during Lent. The old sectarian idea that people actually re-experience the passion and suffering of Christ is often hinted at, and the idea suggested that the period of revolutionary torment in Russian history is related in some way to that terrifying interlude between Christ's crucifixion and His resurrection.

As with Dostoevsky and so many others, the basic Christian message is placed on the lips of a seeming fool: "God and work." There is really nothing else that matters. Yet these are the very things that have been missing from the lives of the secular intelligentsia. "It has always been assumed that the most important things in the Gospels are the ethical teaching and commandments," Pasternak writes in criticism of the abstract ethical fanaticism of modern Russian thought. "But for me the most important thing is the fact that Christ speaks in parables taken from daily life, that he explains the truth in terms of everyday reality." The natural universality of the central New Testament miracle, the birth of a child, is contrasted with the nationalistic melodrama of the central Old Testament miracle, the passage through the Red Sea. Throughout the work, Pasternak's religious feeling is portrayed in images rather than abstract ideas; and as such his work represents a return to the old Muscovite culture of sounds, sights, and smells rather than the St. Petersburg culture of words and ideas. Pasternak used the old word for "icons" (*obraza*) to describe poetic images, which he defined as "miracles in words"[14] rather as one used to speak of the miraculous paintings "not made by hands." Moscow and the deep interior rather than St. Petersburg and the West provide the *mis-en-scène* for *Zhivago*. For Pasternak Moscow of the silver age "far surpassed Petersburg," and he spent almost all his life in its environs. "Moscow of 1600 belfries" had become the Moscow of Scriabin, who was perhaps the greatest of all formative influences on Pasternak.[15]

Like Scriabin, Pasternak sought to affect a kind of fusion of the arts in which music played a special role. Pasternak's description of Scriabin's artistic quest applies to his own: an effort to find "an inner correspondence in musical terms to the surrounding world to the way people thought, felt, lived, dressed and travelled in those days."[16] To Pasternak Scriabin's work was not just music, but "a feast, a celebration in the history of Russian culture."[17] His own work is an attempt to carry on that interrupted feast. It is not accidental that Lara's faith is described as "inner music," that the prose part of Zhivago ends with "the unheard music of happiness" swelling up out "of this holy city and of the whole world." Thereafter, the novel turns to song, and ends with the posthumous poems of Yury Zhivago, some of Pasternak's most hauntingly musical verse. If his father was a painter and he a student of philosophy, it is the sound of music first heard, perhaps, from his pianist-mother that lends a special magic to both image and idea in Pasternak. It seems fitting that his death and burial should be accompanied, not by the prosaic speeches and editorials of the official Soviet press, but rather by the pure music of Russia's greatest pianist and interpreter of Scriabin, Sviatoslav Richter, playing until drenched with perspiration at a small upright piano in Pasternak's cottage, near the dead body of the poet.

If Pasternak's novel does not reach as high as those of Tolstoy and Dostoevsky, it moves in the same direction. Like them, Pasternak was driven by religious concerns that he was unable to resolve in any conventional way. In his last years, he described himself as "almost an atheist"[18] and denied that he had any philosophy of life whatsoever, admitting only to "certain experiences or tendencies." He confessed a special tendency to see art as an act of "consecrated abnegation in a far and humble likeness with the Lord's Supper,"[19] and to believe that out of voluntary suffering in imitation of Christ would come the miracle of resurrection.

Resurrection is the real theme of the novel—a fact which links him once again with Tolstoy, Dostoevsky, and the submerged culture of Orthodoxy. "Why seek ye the living [*zhivago*] among the dead?"[20] Christ's followers were asked when they came to His tomb on the first Easter. Henceforth, all who would "rightly praise" his name should cry forth "Christ is risen! . . . In truth risen." Dostoevsky's last testament to new life out of death, *The Brothers Karamazov,* begins with the legend: "Except a grain of wheat fall in the ground and die . . ." Tolstoy's last novel bore the title *Resurrection;* and the original illustrations of this work by his father were on the walls of Pasternak's *dacha* at Peredelkino when he was writing *Zhivago.*

Pasternak's novel begins with a funeral and ends with the resurrection on the third day of a man to whom the centuries are moving "out of darkness to judgment." Pasternak suggests, moreover, that God may be bringing a new kind of life out of death on Russian soil; that a cultural resurrection may lie at the end of the revolutionary Calvary even for those like himself and Zhivago: the confused observers and superfluous figures of Old Russia. Nothing which they did earned salvation. But, for all their faults, they had been touched in some mysterious way by the warm forgiving natural world, and by the image of Christ Himself. These two supernatural forces converge on the lonely, dead body of Zhivago. There was to be no formal church funeral; and Lara had already bid him farewell.

> Only the flowers compensated for the absence of the ritual and chant. They did more than blossom and smell sweet. Perhaps hastening the return to dust, they poured forth their scent as in a choir, and steeping everything in their exhalation seemed to take over the function of the Office of the Dead.
>
> The vegetable kingdom can easily be thought of as the nearest neighbour of the kingdom of death. Perhaps the mysteries of evolution and the riddles of life that so puzzle us are contained in the green of the earth, among the trees and flowers of graveyards. Mary Magdalene did not recognize Jesus risen from the grave, "supposing him to be the gardener."

Russia's resurrection is hinted at in a no less powerful manner. Indeed, for the historian of culture, Pasternak's view of the Russian Revolution and of the Russian future is perhaps even more important than his views on personal fulfillment and salvation. It is significant that, despite Zhivago's intimate relationship with Lara, she chose to marry his spiritual opposite, Strelnikov, the "shooter," the revolutionary activist. For the spiritual culture of Old Russia did, to a considerable extent, wed itself to the Revolution in the initial period of purity and new vision.

The story of Strelnikov offers a marvelously distilled account of the drift into revolution. It all began, in Pasternak's view, when the young man named Antipov ceased responding as an individual to the real world and began repeating the abstract slogans dinned about him: in this case the war cries of 1914. He goes off to war under the new name of Pasha, disappears from view under a cloud of shell smoke, and is next seen under the name of Strelnikov in a new capacity as revolutionary leader. Thus, with economy and graphic power Pasternak relates revolution to war, and war to man's flight from the individual and the concrete. Strelnikov becomes the epitome of revolution: intensely devoted to abstract ideas and completely pure personally. He marries Lara, and Pasternak assures us in the last dialogue between Strelnikov and Zhivago that her choice—and thus Russia's attachment to revolution—was not a mistake. The revolution which Strelnikov personified offered men the purity of self-denial in the name of a fresh start in human affairs. This impulse was destroyed in Russia not by counter-revolution but by the destructive logic of revolution itself. Thus Strelnikov dies a suicide even before the Civil War has ended; and the last image of him is that of his sacrificial blood, which Pasternak links with that of Christ by way of the naturalistic images of Russian folklore. Pasternak depicts the dead Strelnikov through the blood from his wound congealed on the snow "like the frozen berries of the rowan tree"—thus calling to mind the popular folk song recited earlier, in which the rowan tree voluntarily threw its red berries to the wind rather than give them over to the ravens.

If the ravens took over in the wake of the Revolution and feasted on the remains of the spiritual culture of Old Russia, Pasternak insists that their day is passing. In the first epilogue one learns that Zhivago and Lara have been survived by a daughter living somewhere in the interior of Russia "where the language is still pure" and that "portents of freedom filled the air throughout the post-war period and they alone defined its historical significance." Pasternak sounded the same theme in characteristic natural imagery during an interview with a Western journalist as *Zhivago* was being readied for publication:

> The proclamations, the tumult, the excitement, are over. Now something else is growing, something new. It is growing imperceptibly and quietly, as the grass grows. It is growing as fruit does, and it is growing in the young. The essential thing in this epoch is that a new freedom is being born.[21]

But Pasternak's "message" is ultimately found in his poetry rather than his prose; and it is appropriate that the final epilogue of his novel takes the form of verse. Whereas Tolstoy's second epilogue had been a statement of his philosophy of history, a retreat from magnificent fiction into polemic prose, Pasternak's second epilogue marks an advance from fine fiction into magnificent poetry. The two epilogues are as different as was Tolstoy's "Kreutzer Sonata" from Beethoven's; and Pasternak, as always, is on the side of music.

There are twenty-five poems in all—the number of songs frequently used in *Akathistoi,* the hymn cycles popularly used in the Eastern Church to honor the Virgin. Pasternak's poems can be looked on as the *Akathistoi* of an *intelligent* feeling his way back to God.

At the beginning of the cycle stands Hamlet, the symbol of indecision about life itself that had so long fascinated the Russian imagination. Pasternak does not resolve the "Hamlet question," but rather changes the Hamlet image. As a translator of Shakespeare he had lived closely with this play, and had suggested years before *Zhivago* that Hamlet was a figure not of weakness but of nobility:

> Hamlet is not the drama of a weak-willed character, but of duty and self-abnegation. . . . Hamlet is chosen as the judge of his own time and the servant of a more distant time.[22]

In the opening poem of the second epilogue, Pasternak identifies himself not with Hamlet himself but with an actor who is forced to play the role before an unfeeling new audience. Then, suddenly, the actor acquires a new dimension as he acknowledges his despair and suddenly repeats the words of Christ: "Father, if it be Thy will, take this cup from me."[23] The agony of Gethsemane, the subject of the last poem, is thus introduced in the very first:

> I am alone, all are drowned in Phariseeism.
> To live out life is not to cross a field.

The cycle continues through a world of progressing seasons and natural images into which are woven poeticized passages from scripture and other religious allusions. At the end, there are several poems on the birth and early days of Christ, two on Mary Magdalen, who mistook Christ for a gardener, and a final poem, "The Garden of Gethsemane." His final affirmation of faith comes only after the Christ of his poem has bid Peter put up the sword and has reconciled Himself to drinking His cup to the full. Thus, Pasternak, in his last three stanzas, writes of coming suffering with the prayerful resignation of a monastic chronicler:

> The book of life has come unto a page
> That is more precious than all holy things.
> Now that which has been written must take place.
> So be it then. Amen.

There is meaning in all of this. Man's only mistake has been that of all the heretics from the early Judaizers to the Bolsheviks: presuming to unravel the secrets and determine the path of history. The ancient flame symbol is summoned up to suggest the impulsive and unpredictable quality of providential history: and the Christian message of voluntarily taking up the cross is suggested:

> Thou see'st the passing of the years is like a parable
> And could burst into flame along the way.
> In the name of its awful majesty
> I go in voluntary suffering to the grave.

In the final verse men move from the world in which they see through a glass darkly toward their final destination and place of judgment. He reverts to the classical image of a ship at sea. It had served him as a symbol of sensual deliverance in his poem of 1917, "Oars at Rest," where a boat lies motionless and the poet and his lover within it are blended into a kind of liquid union with one another and with their natural surroundings.[94] In the last lines of *Zhivago*, however, Pasternak returns the image to its older religious framework. He seems to be saying that beyond the private fate of the poet united briefly with Lara at Varykino, there is another destination; that all the barges so long hauled up the Volga by the sweating multitudes are in truth storied vessels which will yet lead Russia out of its landlocked insularity to worlds beyond.

> I descend into the grave, and on the third day
>   rise again
> And, like barks weaving down a river
> The centuries shall come like a caravan of barges
> Out of the darkness, unto me.

They are the last lines in an extended chronicle, the last image in a long series of icons. The message which Pasternak left to a Russia in turmoil and conflict in the twentieth century is very much like that which a revered metropolitan of Siberia left to his flock amidst the troubles and schism of the seventeenth century—and which the official journal of the Moscow patriarch quietly reprinted in mid-1965:

> Christians! even in darkest days a sunflower completes its circular course, following the sun by unchangeable love and natural inclination toward it. Our sun, which brightens our life's path, is the will of God; it illuminates for us, not always without shadows, the path of life; dark days are often mixed with clear ones; rain, winds, storms arise. . . . But may our

love to our sun, the will of God, be strong enough to draw us inseparably to
it in days of misfortune and sorrow, even as the sunflower in dark days
continues without faltering—navigating through the living waters, with the
"barometer" and "compass" of God's will leading us into the safe harbor
of eternity.[25]

Out of some such deeper vision was it possible for the land of "scientific atheism" ironically to produce through Pasternak some of the most
magnificent religious poetry of the twentieth century. Perhaps his *Zhivago*
is only another poignant Chekhovian farewell, the last afterglow on a solitary peak of a sun that has already set. Yet it may also represent the
beginning of some new magnetic field: a kind of unexpected homing point
for the spinning compasses of the space age. We turn now to that age and
to the aspirations of the young generation in which Pasternak placed such
high hopes.

New Voices

THE CRUCIAL QUESTION for the future of the creative life in Russia
deals not with internal émigrés from late imperial culture but with the purely
Soviet young generation: not with Pasternak but with his judgment that
"something new is growing . . . and it is growing in the young."

It is, of course, extremely difficult to characterize an entire generation
of a sprawling and complex modern nation. Large numbers of competent
and often gifted people obviously enjoy profitable careers as faithful
servants of the state and party. Many more—perhaps even a majority of the
young generation—feel genuine pride in the accomplishments of Soviet
science and technology and a measure of gratitude for the opportunities that
have opened up under the new order.

Yet, there has also been at work within the USSR an unmistakable
and extraordinary ferment, which is popularly identified with those under
thirty-five even though many older people participate in it and many younger
ones do not. The crucial question for the historian is to determine the nature
and significance of this process: to say how present ferment in the USSR
relates to the Russian past, and how it might bear on the future. For all its
confusing and often contradictory qualities, youthful ferment in the USSR
can be divided into four essential aspects or levels.

The first and least elevating is the impulse toward purely negative protest. This restlessness has expressed itself in a variety of ways: the violent
delinquency of "hooligans" (*khuligany*), the flamboyant innovations in style

and dress of the "style boys" (*stiliagi*), and the compulsive opposition to all dogma of the *nibonicho* (an ingenious contraction for the Russian words "neither God nor the devil").

The antagonistic official press has referred bitterly to "nihilists in short pants,"[26] and the most radical of Russia's restless youth have adopted the term "men of the sixties." Thus, both extremes of opinion in the USSR point to a resemblance with the original nihilists and "men of the sixties" who appeared after the repressive reign of Nicholas I just a century before. The opportunity for communal social experiments and revolutionary organization that had given *élan* to the young nihilists under Alexander II was, of course, absent a century later. But the sense of persecution and a need for new answers was, if anything, even more intense.

Certainly, the Communist regime was both distressed and profoundly perplexed by the antagonism of so many young people to official culture. The leaders of the mammoth Communist Youth League are now nearly a decade older than in Lenin's time, and veteran Bolsheviks petulantly acknowledge their inability to understand the indifference of youth to the paths that they have prepared for them to follow. Speaking at a congress of the Young Communist League in March, 1957, Voroshilov complained almost pathetically of "young people among you, in our midst, who are maneuvering. They are dreaming about something—but certainly not what they should be dreaming about." His only prescription for "these bugs and beetles" was to "say 'they shall not exist' and take all steps in this respect."[27]

But the "bugs and beetles" continued to exist and even proliferate. At the next congress of the Communist Youth League in March, 1962, the attitude of the Communist leadership was equally despairing. Khrushchev, having set up new boarding schools to help condition a new Communist elite and a compulsory work period between high school and higher education to help young people "overcome their separation from life," was vehement in his denunciation of the continued nihilism and "parasitism" of the young.[28]

This continuing indifference to official ideals and seemingly pointless search for novelty in clothes, sex, and crime is, of course, part of a more universal antagonism toward the depersonalized and urbanized modern world. This first level of protest is not simply a Soviet phenomenon but rather a particularly unrefined expression of the widespread desire in advanced civilizations to penetrate beyond the monotony of daily routine to more authentic kinds of individual experience.

A second, more positive aspect to the youthful ferment is the rebirth of Russian humor. Genuine comedy had all but vanished from the Russian scene in the Stalin era. All that remained were the crude vulgarities of the dictator himself, compounded largely of lavatorial allusions and heavy-handed insults to national minorities. The rich traditions of literary satire and peasant humor which had flourished under all but the most extreme periods of tsarist repression were severely crippled by Stalin's psychotic sensitivity to all forms of implied criticism in his declining years. Denied the opportunity for public laughter at their system, the Russian people turned increasingly to private bitterness. This damming up of the humorous stream that had traditionally been a free-flowing part of the "broad Russian nature" had dangerous consequences which even Stalin's long-delayed last Party Congress recognized, with its call in 1952 for new Gogols and Saltykovs.[29] The rehabilitation of Russian humor was further aided by the rise to power of Khrushchev, who had a better sense of humor than any preceding leader of Russian Communism and made a jocular style part of his new political technique.

The humor that arose in the post-Stalin era acquired, however, a sharper bite than even reformist Communist leaders could readily accept. Pointed fables and colorful plays on words revealed subtlety, lightness, and irreverence for pretense—attitudes which contrasted sharply with official Soviet culture and provided fresh resources for the fast-evaporating stock of human satire.

Beneath the satirical posture of Soviet youth usually lay, however, the positive conviction that there is still work worth doing in one's private life and professional calling. If one cannot change the political and administrative system overnight, one can at least gain dignity through honorable work, free of either bureaucratic cant or political interference. Thus, humor allied itself, not only with the passion for reform that has always been feared by pretentious authority, but also with the "creeping pragmatism" of a new generation, increasingly confident that expanding islands of creative integrity can yet be dredged out of the sea of official deceit and sloth.

A typical joke of the early sixties told how a collective farmer was brought to Moscow to keep a lookout with a telescope atop Lenin Hills for the coming of the classless society. One day, en route to his sinecure, the peasant met an American, who offered to triple his salary if he would transfer to New York to watch from the Statue of Liberty for the coming of the next crisis in the capitalist system. "The terms are attractive," replies the peasant, "but I can't afford to give up a permanent job for a temporary one."

The simple hero of this tale has a rich ancestry in the popular fables and satirical literature of Great Russia; but he also has ancestors in Yiddish humor, with its idealized Peter Schlemihl and his life-affirming laughter at human foibles and pretense. This joke is, in fact, a variant of an age-old

Jewish joke about waiting for the Messiah—pointing up, perhaps, a subtle way in which the indigenous Yiddish culture of Russia seeks hidden revenge on its latest persecutor. Forced both to assimilate into the atomized society of the USSR and to endure the continuing indignities of anti-Semitism, the Jewish community continues to assert itself anonymously by providing fresh satirical resources to Russian culture as a whole.

The comic contribution of the emigrating Jewish community to the American melting pot in the late nineteenth and the early twentieth century is thus being in some ways duplicated by this inner emigration and assimilation of Yiddish humor in the USSR of the mid-twentieth century. The satirical playwright who has become the posthumous idol of the young generation, Eugene Schwarz, and the man that championed the production of his works, Akimov, are both Jews. The philo-Semitism of the young generation is a mark of gratitude for the Jewish contribution to the new cultural ferment as well as an expression of new-found identity with the long-endured persecutions of Jewry. It is entirely fitting that, of all the half-heretical literary works of the post-Stalin era, Eugene Evtushenko's simple poetic tribute to Jewish suffering, "Babi Yar," should become probably the most important single symbol of fresh feeling and aspiration among the younger generation.[30]

The revival of Russian humor has also benefited from the increasing assimilation of other minority groups, such as the Armenians, who, like the Jews, have an age-old Near Eastern civilization, with folklore accumulated from long centuries of persecution, wandering, and commercial adventure. An imaginary "radio Armenia" is frequently cited by bemused Russians as the source of humorous comment on internal Soviet affairs. Georgians and Armenians played leading roles in developing the art of humorous and satirical folk singing in the early 1960's.

Many of the deeper, positive ideals of the new generation are expressed in the third aspect of ferment: the revival of Russian literature. In the late imperial period literature was, after all, the main medium for developing new ideas about man and society. The revival in the decade since Stalin of this search for ideas in literature is a phenomenon of great importance for Russian development (though not necessarily for world literature).[31]

In part, the new literature seems impressive because of the extreme sterility of that which preceded it. One is repeatedly reminded that there are no Tolstoys or Dostoevskies even *in potentia*. Indeed, the closest present approximation to the epic style of the former and to the psychological religious preoccupations of the latter among Soviet writers of today can be found in the novels of Michael Sholokhov and Leonid Leonov respectively:

two elderly and idiosyncratic figures with little apparent influence on the rising generation. Yet this new literary production has a freshness and vitality of its own. Ever since the publication just after Stalin's death of Pomerantsev's much-discussed essay, "On Sincerity in Literature," which, among other things, contrasted the honesty and resourcefulness of a Siberian peasant woman with the mechanical falsehoods of authority, there had been a rising tide of what might be called neo-populist literature. Stories like Yashin's "Levers" and Nagibin's "Light in the Window" emphasized the contrast between corrupt officialdom and the uncorrupted people.[32] Sometimes an idealistic scientific worker is substituted for a simple *muzhik* as the contrasting force to Communist bureaucracy, as in Granin's "My Own Opinion" or Dudintsev's much-discussed novel, *Not by Bread Alone.* Sometimes the editorial point is made quite bluntly, as in the poem "Careful People," whose title is an ironic comment on the omnipresent "Careful Pigeons" signs which Stalin scattered through Russia at the very heights of his Neronian bloodbaths.[33]

The literature of protest in 1956 proved to be only the harbinger of still more blunt and pointed social criticism which came late in 1962, with the publication of Alexander Solzhenitsyn's portrayal of a Soviet concentration camp in *One Day in the Life of Ivan Denisovich* and Fedor Abramov's scathing depiction of collective farm life in *One Day in the "New Life."*

All in all, a remarkable amount of stylistically conventional but ideologically exciting fiction has been produced in the USSR since the death of Stalin. At the same time, traces have begun to appear of that even more daring literature which is written "for the drawer" or "for the soul" and circulates in manuscript or typewritten copies within the USSR (along with innumerable bootlegged copies of proscribed Western publications and private translations thereof). Some of this literature appears in the leaflet-sized papers that are illegally produced and distributed in the USSR, and some of it has found its way to publication in the West.

Even more important than the novels and short stories of the new generation is the extraordinary revival of two of the most public and yet most personal of all literary forms: poetry readings and the theater. These media—in which Soviet men and women communicate directly with fellow Russians about problems of common concern—have done much to create such sense of communal purpose and aspiration as has come to animate the young generation.

The poetry readings have attracted considerable public attention because of the magnetic appeal of Evtushenko and the *causes célèbres* that have grown up around his name—the first in 1960 following the publication of "Babi-Yar," and the second in 1963, following the publication while abroad of autobiographical sketches and reflections.

It is doubtful if anything written by Evtushenko will find its way into the anthologies of the world's great poetry. Yet well before he was thirty, he was assured an important niche in Russian cultural history, as the recognized spokesman of his generation. His direct and easily understood poems of protest and self-affirmation, his handsome appearance, his simple love of travel and of love itself—all made him a kind of romantic idol. His exploits in forcing open previously closed doors and weaving his way in and out of official favor were followed vicariously by thousands; and he, in turn, shared with the thousands who flocked to his poetry readings verses, comments, and innuendos that he did not dare commit to print.

"Each man has his secret personal world," he wrote in the first poem of a Soviet edition of his printed works;[34] and Evtushenko appeared as the defender of that colorful, uninhibited world against the drab and stereotyped world of "Stalin's heirs." His poem "The Nihilist" tells how someone derisively labeled a nihilist in official circles was capable of more noble human actions than his more conformist contemporaries. His ode "To Humor" praises this quality for its power to scourge tyranny.

The appeal of Evtushenko was, however, based on more than youthful exuberance and a general spirit of protest. For Evtushenko played—even if crudely and perhaps unconsciously—some chords with sympathetic resonance in earlier Russian tradition. For the decade after Stalin he represented a reincarnation—however pale—of Belinsky, the "furious" moral hero of the original "remarkable decade." Evtushenko seems close to Belinsky not only in his effect on contemporaries, but in his refusal to accept rationalizations for human suffering. In "Babi-Yar," particularly when recited by Evtushenko, the emotional climax comes with the mention of Anne Frank and the image of innocent suffering childhood, after which he moves on to naturalistic imagery and a moralistic conclusion. His sense of outrage began—according to his officially criticized autobiography—when he saw a helpless ten-year-old girl crushed to death at the funeral of Stalin simply because no one had the proper authorization to prevent the thoughtless mob from surging forth.[35] At this point Evtushenko returned the ticket of admission to the Stalinist establishment, which a man of his talents could so easily have gained. The motivation is that of Belinsky in rejecting Hegel's ideal world order, and of Belinsky's echo, Ivan Karamazov, in rejecting his ticket of admission to heaven because of the innocent suffering of children. It may be that the most enduring legacy of the Old Russian intelligentsia lies not in any of its utopian dreams, but in this passionate desire "that no child shall weep." The page containing these lines, which Dostoevsky under-lined heavily in his notebook, was long kept on public exhibition in the Dostoevsky museum in Moscow; and it comes close to stating Evtushenko's inner ideal.

But Evtushenko is also, of course, a poet—self-consciously so. His pose as the patriotic voice of liberation in his generation is somewhat reminiscent of the nineteenth-century Eastern European tradition whereby Mickiewicz in Poland, Petöfi in Hungary, and Runeberg in Finland were able to crystallize in verse the inarticulate aspirations of their people. But his true poetic ancestors are Russian, the four poets of the early twentieth century whom he has acknowledged as his models: Maiakovsky, Blok, Esenin, and Pasternak.[36]

Evtushenko described the goal of his poetry as poeticizing the Russian language: continuing the work of Blok and Pasternak in turning language into a thing of beauty and even a means of redemption in human life.[37]

For a time his work seemed in the Maiakovsky tradition of driving and didactic "slaps in the face of public taste." However, he is probably closer in spirit to Esenin, the peasant poet, the least intellectual of the four. Evtushenko's first poem was on the subject of sport, and he was in fact a professional soccer player before turning to verse. He comes from the Siberian hinterland: a simple, almost childlike extrovert, exuberantly self-confident. Perhaps for that reason his vanity and "court poems" for the regime do not seem so reprehensible, and the possibility of a tragic end always seems close at hand. The message that he has to convey is the old contrast between the perversions of power in Moscow and the purity still lying in the deep interior of Russia, personified for him by "Winter Station," the small Siberian town where he was raised and the title of his first important poem. His approach is that of a country boy, a would-be poet of life in all its exuberance, but his final lines, the farewell "advice" of the town to its departing son, seem more like the message of the Old Russian intelligentsia distilled to its inner essence:

> Do not grieve that you have not yet answered
> The question put to you by life.
> Abandon not the search, seek night and day;
> And if you do not find, still go on seeking;
> Truth is good, but happiness is better—so they say,
> but without truth there is no happiness![38]

Andrew Voznesensky, the second of the "fiery chargers" on the poetic front, filled in the color and detail for Evtushenko's bold sketches. Vozne-sensky soon proved to be the better poet. Although born in the same year as

Evtushenko, he began serious publishing five years later. The suddenness with which his name came to be paired with that of Evtushenko in the early sixties is a tribute both to the growing sophistication of the younger generation and to its increasing responsiveness to traditional themes and emphases of the Russian intellectual tradition.

There is something strangely fitting about the fact that his first collection of verse, published in 1960, bore the title *Mosaic*, and was published in Vladimir, the original center of Orthodoxy in Great Russia. Voznesensky's poetry combines a mosaic of visual images with a flow of musical sound. He recaptures something of the genius of old Orthodox culture with his use of sensual suggestion for super-sensual ideas. He is the truest renewal of the poetic tradition of the silver age: a confessed disciple of Pasternak, who has succeeded in incorporating many contemporary ideas into his poetic idiom.

His favorite poem, "Parabolic Ballad," is also one of the favorite subjects of official attack. It is a defense of the "Aesopian language" that the true poet must use to make his point. He must speak not in direct statement but symbolically and indirectly. Gauguin reached the Louvre not by moving down from Montmartre but by going to the south seas.

> ... he sped away like a roaring rocket
> ... and he entered the Louvre, not through stately
>   portals,
> But like a wrathful parabola
>   piercing the roof . . .[39]

Voznesensky's own poetic "Parabola" (the title of his second collection of poetry, published in Moscow in 1961) was more than much of the Soviet bureaucracy could tolerate. Accused of "formalism" by official critics, he uses the magic of language to damn them for smelling of formalin and incense (*formalizm . . . formalin . . . fimiam*). There is the hint of fiery apocalypse in his clipped poetic judgment on Stalinist architecture:

> Farewell architecture!
> Blaze freely on,
> Cow sheds with cupids,
> Rococo savings banks . . .
> To live is to burn.[40]

To Voznesensky, the function of the poet is prophetic, and the reaction of audiences is "an almost sensual expression of feeling" which leaves their souls "wide open like a woman who has just been kissed."[41]

Nothing could be more different from the puritanical didacticism of official Soviet culture. The personalized poetry readings of the early sixties were the scene for original thoughts punctuated by spontaneous applause and boisterous commentary. The rhetorical rallies of the state were, by contrast, characterized by ritual rhythmic applause in response to lengthening stretches of increasingly unoriginal prose. There could be little doubt as to where authentic vitality lay, even though the latter forces retained the power periodically to silence the former, as they did by severe denunciations during the first half of 1963. The work of Evtushenko and Voznesensky seemed to decline during the following two years. But whether these particular figures flourished or faded, the younger generation had built up an oral folklore of its own[42] to preserve the memory of good words and courageous action just as an older oral folklore had kept alive the memory of heroic deeds during the long literary silence of the Mongol occupation.

Hardly less striking is the contrast between the new theater that has arisen since Stalin's death and the stereotyped staging of Soviet success stories in the Stalin era. It was, indeed, on the stage that the first sweeping break with Stalinist literary forms took place late in 1953 with the staging of Leonid Zorin's play *Guests*. If Ehrenburg's novel *The Thaw* provided the key metaphor for the post-Stalin literary revival, and Pomerantsev's "On Sincerity in Literature" provided its combat slogan, Zorin's play dramatized what the conflict was all about. Based on the infamous "doctors' plot," *Guests* portrays the villainy of the secret police in a manner suggesting that it was a natural outgrowth of the entire Soviet system. The drama was severely criticized by the official press and forced to close down after two performances.[43] Criticism of secret police excesses gained official approval only after Alexander Korneichuk's *Wings* rendered the dragon of Beria into almost a caricature in order to render the slaying by Khrushchev even more heroic and melodramatic. Khrushchev put the official stamp of approval on this formula with his attendance and ostentatious applauding at a performance of *Wings* early in 1955; but the question raised by Zorin's more realistic portrayal had not been forgotten merely because it could no longer be directly posed in public.

Almost as important as Zorin's play in opening up fresh perspectives to the Soviet theater was the extraordinarily popular revival of Maiakovsky's *Bedbug* in 1954. Renewed exposure to the blunt, direct speech of Maiakovsky (and to that of Hemingway—perhaps the most popular of all foreign writers with the young generation) provided Russians with a model for simpler forms of discourse. At the same time, the fresh look at the long-prohibited staging of Meierhold reminded a new generation of the expressive possibilities of non-realistic stagings. The rather sterile and pompous schematization of the Stanislavsky method that had become the accepted way of projecting socialist realism on the stage now had a challenger. Insofar as the public was given a chance to choose, it elected to see new productions with a decisiveness clearly embarrassing to vested interests within the party.

More modern methods of staging were evidenced in 1955 in a new production of *Hamlet* by Okhlopkov. He seemed to be reviving the techniques of his teacher Meierhold in order to realize the latter's dream of doing a totally new *Hamlet*. The impresario who broke most completely with the theater of the Stalin era was Nicholas Akimov, who had fallen afoul of Stalin in the early thirties for his "formalist" staging of *Hamlet*.[44]

Unlike the theatrical bureaucrats of the Stalin era, Akimov is both a modern artist and an independent philosopher. Central to his concept of the new theater is the importance of distinguishing between the theater and the cinema, which tended to be two sides of the same dull coin in the Stalin era. The former has a unique role to play in cultural development for two key reasons. First, plays have what he calls "materiality" (*material'nost'*), a sense of material immediacy that can only be conveyed by real people, things, and colors. The failure to develop this sense of immediacy comes largely from conservative adherence to the conventions of the "mechanical" stage of the eighteenth century, and unwillingness to experiment boldly with an "electric" stage for modern man.

A second and even more important factor in distinguishing films from plays is the fact of audience participation. A play is necessarily "a dialogue between audience and actor in which neither can remain silent. The only dialogue in a movie occurs with the mechanic in case of failure."[45] Another outstanding and experimental impresario of the Leningrad stage, Georgy Tovstonogov, has pointed to the significance of the dialogue between living performers and a living audience by speaking of the unique possibility of creating "a charged atmosphere on the stage and an electric silence among the audience."[46]

It is precisely such effects that Akimov was able to produce in his memorable production of Schwarz's *The Shadow*. Based on the fable of Hans Christian Andersen about the man who lost his shadow, Schwarz's play as staged by Akimov is a production with color, lightness, laughter, and fantasy: the antithesis of the Soviet theater under Stalin. At the center of the drama stands a lonely idealist identified in the dramatis personae as "the scholar," but known in the play as Christian Theodore. Traditional realism is challenged at the very outset when he loses his eyeglasses and observes that he sees better without them. A number of stage tricks leave the audience uncertain as to what is real, as Christian loses his shadow, which goes on to become ruler of the kingdom of fantasy in which most of

Schwarz's dramas take place. In the climactic trial scene, the new spectral ruler brings to trial the visionary idealist whose shadow he once was; and at the dramatic moment when a doctor, who was Christian's best and last remaining friend, joins the general chorus of denunciation and betrayal, "electric silence in the audience" is movingly achieved. The context is semi-comical, but the effect is more than that of sudden tears in the midst of laughter; it is a kind of catharsis, a sense of shared involvement in the tragedy, and of unspoken resolve that it shall not happen again. The characters in Schwarz's fable are far more realistic than the wooden puppets of the socialist realist theater. The motives and rationalizations for their evil behavior are psychologically credible: they are skillfully woven out of the venality and compromise of everyday Soviet life. The doctor does not denounce Christian directly in the trial scene but (like those who listen to the Christ-like preachings of Dostoevsky's Idiot) simply pronounces him out of his mind. Here, as elsewhere, the moral is not heavy-handed but only implied. One is made to feel that the message must become a living force in the life of the audience just as it has been a living and dynamic force in the production—if the vital dialogue between performer and spectator is to continue. Akimov has come closest to a short paraphrase of the message:

> The contemporary epoch proceeds under the sign of the struggle of the creative principle with the parasitic; the creative with the decaying; the living with the dead; or, as Schwarz says in his language, of man with his shadow.[47]

Two other recently produced Schwarz plays carry even more pointed political messages: *The Naked King,* in which the Andersen fable about the Emperor's new suit of clothes is turned into a witty satire on the conspiracy of silence that prevailed during the Stalin era; and *The Dragon,* in which the slayer of a tyrannical dragon (that is, the Khrushchevian debunkers of Stalin) proves to be only another tyrant rather than the idealized St. George of Russian hagiography.[48]

These remarkable allegories, for all their popularity among the younger generations, are still primarily the work of older men. In the Stalin era fables and legends had the value of providing remote locations and a new "Aesopian" language with which to talk about vital questions. Others of the older generation used children's tales or "Eastern fables" as media in which serious ideas could be discussed with relative safety. Sergius Mikhalkov, an established writer of children's stories and author of an allegorical satire written in 1952, *The Crayfish,* which was daring for its time, composed an extraordinarily pointed poetic fable about the legendary Khan Akhmet. This cruel, one-armed ruler wanted his portrait painted, but killed the man who portrayed him with only one arm for insulting the state, and killed a second who represented him with two arms for "lacquering over" reality. A third painter found the key to survival in this eminently Stalinesque situation by painting the terrible khan in profile.[49]

Schwarz, the master of dramatic fables, wrote almost all his plays during the Stalin era, though he was understandably not widely produced till after the dictator's death. Schwarz kept himself alive largely by writing for the movie and puppet theaters—the latter providing for him another outlet for Aesopian commentary on Soviet society. His fabulous world combines elements from Russian folklore and the Yiddish theater with the tales of his beloved Andersen in an effort to keep alive "the spirit of music" that had animated the culture of early-twentieth-century Russia. His first book, *The Tale of an Old Balalaika,* published in 1925, told of a balalaika in search of words for its music. His entire dramatic career can be seen as an attempt to provide those words for the fading but still unextinguished music of a rich culture.

The distinctive new feature of the post-Stalin stage was the increasing success of problem dramas on contemporary themes in pushing out older Russian classics and propagandistic melodramas from theatrical repertoires. In the late Stalin era, for instance, Ostrovsky and Gorky tended to be the most frequently performed dramatists. By the early sixties, however, their works received less than one tenth the number of performances in Moscow that they had been given in the last year of Stalin's life.[50]

The harsh official criticism of Zorin's *Guests* just after Stalin's death encouraged aspiring dramatists to be more oblique but at the same time more many-sided in their critiques of Soviet society.[51] The popular and gifted young playwright Volodin ridicules a Young Communist League organizer in his *Factory Girl,* and tells in intimate, unheroic terms of an old love broken up by long years of absence (presumably in a forced labor camp) in his *Five Evenings.* A virtual catalogue of new thematic material is introduced into the play *Everything Depends on People,* which includes a suicide of despair, and a sustained on-stage dialogue between a scientist and a priest in which the latter scores more than a few telling debating points.

Zorin's new play of 1962, *By Moscow Time,* presents the now-characteristic juxtaposition of an old-style party official with a young reformer anxious to press de-Stalinization to the limit. The latter decides that the old man must go because "he is not a town, you can't just rename him." Another play of the same year, *More Dangerous than an Enemy,* works this juxtaposition of the good worker and the bad bureaucrat into a farcical, almost Gogolesque plot. Staged appropriately enough by Akimov, the play depicts the battle of wits between evil party leaders and the good scientific workers in a provincial institute dedicated to the study of yoghurt. When the managers hear a rumor (ultimately proved false) that Moscow is about to launch a new campaign to rid the USSR of fools, they make great efforts to arrange to pin this label on their subordinates—only to be outfooled by the scientific workers after a series of episodes faintly reminiscent of a Damon Runyan story. Aksenov's *Always on Sale* of 1965 is both more inventively fantastic and more bitingly contemporary in vernacular language and satirical thrust than these earlier plays, and may be the harbinger of more interesting drama yet to come.

The new dramas on contemporary themes clearly provide both the best entertainment available in the USSR and some of its most effective social criticism. The old dream of Schiller and so many others of restoring to the theater the quality it once possessed as an educational and moral force in society seems, indeed, closer to realization in these new Soviet plays than in the avant-garde theater of the West. However, in view of the struggle still required to gain official consent for any theatrical production in the USSR, the day is probably still far away when the stage can serve—as Tovstonogov put it—as "a great exponent of public thinking . . . a huge operating table where the actor, the surgeon, can sense the throb of the human heart and brain."[52]

New movies, like new plays and poems, illustrate the "interrupted renewal" of Russian culture. Not only has the recent Soviet cinema recaptured some of the creative vitality of its precocious infancy in the 1920's, it has added as well new dimensions of disinterested humanism and psychological introspection.

Many of the outstanding films of this cinematic renaissance have dealt with the event that has the deepest meaning for the younger generation: the Great Fatherland War (as World War II is known in the USSR). Whereas the many war movies of the late Stalin era emphasized the glory of Soviet victory and the wisdom of the dictator's leadership, the new war movies focus on the impact of this most destructive of all wars on ordinary Russian people. Beginning with Michael Kalatasov's *The Cranes are Flying* of 1957, Russian films began to portray war as devoid of all constructive purpose. The war became an unwelcome intruder into the world of personal and family relationships, which suddenly seemed somehow more real and appealing than the public world of the "new Soviet man." "The fate of a man" is made to seem as important as ultimate victory or defeat in the cinematic version made in 1959 of Sholokhov's short story of that name. The following year appeared *Ballad of a Soldier*, the first of the great films of Gregory Chukhrai, which portrays with photographic skill, heartbreaking simplicity, and a complete absence of propaganda the accidental heroism, brief leave, and return to death of a childlike young Russian soldier. Chukhrai's *Clear Skies,* which provided the occasion for an emotional demonstration of approval at its first performance in Moscow in 1961, contrasts the honor and suffering of Soviet prisoners of war with the brutality of the system which suspected and humiliated them in the post-war period. The picture which makes the most daring technical innovations and at the same time the most moving indictment of war is *My Name Is Ivan,* which appeared in 1962, introducing dream sequences along with documentary excerpts into its tragic tale of a young orphan.

This new cinematic emphasis on the integrity of the individual rather than the nature of his cause has also altered the traditional method of representing the Civil War. Just as Hollywood has introduced "good Indians" into its melodramatic Westerns—partly out of a need to break the monotony and partly out of a belated sense of justice—so Soviet films have begun to find traces of humanity and even nobility in the White opposition. Indeed, audience sympathy is ultimately on the side of an individual White guardsman in two widely admired recent films of the Civil War: Chukhrai's *Forty-First* of 1956 and Vladimir Fetin's *The Foal* of 1960.

Finally, it is interesting to note the return of film makers to those classics which especially fascinated the Russian intelligentsia in the nineteenth century. Thus, Gregory Kozintsev has moved on from his sensitive *Don Quixote* of 1956 to his film version of *Hamlet* in 1964. In contrast to Turgenev's "Hamlet and Don Quixote" of almost exactly a century before, Kozintsev depicted Quixote as a psychologically disturbed and tragic figure, and gave to Hamlet a certain quiet nobility. Like Pasternak (whose translation of the play was used for the script), Kozintsev seemed to be vindicating Hamlet from the symbolic opprobrium heaped on him by Turgenev (and the lesser critics of the Stalin era). The message that the new Soviet drama as a whole is conveying to its interested if often perplexed audiences is essentially that which Hamlet conveyed to the loyal but two-dimensional Horatio: "There are more things in heaven and earth than are dreamed of in your philosophy."[53]

At the same time, it is only fair to note a less flattering resemblance between the present generation and the "Hamletism" of the old intelligentsia: its confusion and uncertainty of objectives. The younger generation is far surer of what it opposes than of what it accepts, and much of its work is not technically impressive by the increasingly refined standards of literary criticism. Yet the authenticity of aspiration and popularity of the quest cannot be denied. Their art has, as Tertz maintains, "hypotheses instead of a goal"; and the testing ground for such hypotheses lies not in the hothouse of literary criticism but in the broad arena of life. The response elicited in the lives of the audience—that indispensable second participant in Akimov's unending dialogue of creative culture—is a truer measure of significance than the reviews of critics. Increasingly, new productions in the USSR are animated by lively and often turbulent "exchange of opinion" sessions in which artists discuss with the audience the nature and significance of a play immediately after the final curtain.[54]

New literary "hypotheses" often seem to draw less inspiration from literature than from other art media. But, whereas the hidden source of inspiration for the new literature of the silver age was music, the controlling medium now tends to be the visual arts. Akimov is a gifted painter; and Voznesensky, who was trained as an architect, has stated:

> I do not think that closeness to his literary predecessors is very good for a writer. "Incest" leads to degeneracy. I have got more from Rublev, Joan Miró, and the later Corbusier than from Byron.[55]

The importance of painting lies not so much in the large numbers and occasional virtuosity of the experimental canvases that are unofficially painted in the USSR, but rather in the fact that visual art tries to do what the most gifted new writers are also trying to accomplish: depict objectively the real world. The Promethean visionaries of the late imperial period sought to leave the material world altogether, and fled into the world of music, the most immaterial of all the arts and the only guide man could hope to find in his quest for a new language of outer space. In the post-Stalin era, however, when the philistine "metal eaters"[56] have thrust their wares out into space, the creative imagination has moved back to earth and sought to grasp once more Russian reality. Thus, young Russians turn to the visual arts for guidance, but they instinctively look beyond the conventional realists to the "more real" art of ancient Russia and the modern West. Hence Voznesensky's juxtaposition of Rublev with Miró and Corbusier, and his powerful anti-war poem that begins "I am Goya" and describes his paintings by means of plays on his name.[57] This disturbed and often grotesque Spanish prophet of artistic modernism also appears in the small list of those whom Tertz commends as guides toward the new "phantasmagorical art which . . . would best respond to the spirit of our epoch."[58]

> May the unearthly imaginations of Hoffmann and Dostoevsky, of Goya and Chagall, of Maiakovsky (the most socialist realist of all), as well as those of many other realists and non-realists—may these teach us how to express truth with the aid of the absurd and fantastic![59]

Akimov speaks of the influence upon his theatrical conceptions of pictorial images from Russian icons, Daumier, Van Gogh, and the post-war Italian cinema.[60] Yutkevich speaks of the ideal Soviet movie of the future as a "synthesis of the style of Watteau and Goya."[61]

One of the most remarkable of recent Soviet short stories, "Adam and Eve" by Yury Kazakov, tells of a young painter and a girl going to a deserted island. It is a kind of return to Eden in search of artistic truth. Yet the painter is as restless as the Soviet youth he personifies. He sees himself as "a prophet without an idea." In a deserted church, however, he has a kind of vision of rediscovering "the genuine life of the earth, the water, and the people." He climbs the belfry, and looks down from the sky above to "another sky . . . the whole immeasurable mass of surrounding waters luminous with reflected light."[62] In the last scene, he departs over those waters amidst the strange, unearthly whiteness of the northern lights.

One is left again with the image of a ship at sea and no fixed destination. But one feels certain that the destination is not to be found on the approved itineraries of the state travel agency. One can almost imagine a middle-aged Communist official rebuking him with the words addressed by a *Pravda* editorial five years earlier "to all Soviet workers in literature and the arts":

> He who tries to reject the method of socialist realism imitates the irresponsible captain who throws the ship's compass overboard on the high seas so that he may guide his ship "freely."[63]

The title and imagery of Kazakov's story are but one illustration of the fourth, and most surprising, aspect of the cultural revival: the renewed interest in religion.

There is, to be sure, no dramatic religious revival in progress; and regular churchgoing continues to be primarily an activity of women and elderly people. But there is a continuing fervor in the liturgical worship of the Orthodox Church which attracts a steady stream of brief appearances for baptism and Easter services.[64] The growing appeal of church marriages has forced the regime to set up its own grotesque "marriage palaces" designed to provide all the material accouterments of a church (music, flowers, and solemn decor) for the approved civil ceremonies of the atheistic state. The number of those seeking training for the priesthood in the post-Stalin era increased to the point where a correspondence course was even introduced to accommodate those who might otherwise have been barred by distance, poverty, or bureaucratic obstruction. A program of sharply increased persecution built around the requirement that all would-be seminarians submit to a preliminary interrogation and discussion with specially chosen committees of the Young Communist League has enabled Soviet authorities to report with grim satisfaction that the numbers in seminaries have sharply declined since 1959 as a result of "extensive individual work with the students."[65]

But there still appears to be some validity to the old comparison reputedly made between religion and a nail by Lunacharsky in the early days of atheistic propaganda: "The harder you hit it, the deeper you drive it into the wood." Some of the continuing excesses of atheistic evangelism—the noisy interruption of church services, the offering of rewards for unearthing secret prayer meetings, and the official glorification of those who break with religion and publish lurid exposés—all serve to arouse a certain sense of sympathy even among the atheists and agnostics who still predominate within the younger generation.

In an ironic inversion of the classical conflict between fathers and sons, the younger generation now often picks up religious interests as a means of shocking their atheistically conformist parents. Young Russians seem particularly fond of ridiculing and embarrassing the stereotyped party lectures on scientific atheism, which were increased in number some threefold in 1958. A favorite cartoon in the Soviet humor journal *Krokodil* shows believers praying for the return of another anti-religious lecturer to their region.[66]

On a deeper level, the story is frequently told among the younger generation of the old peasant woman whose stubborn religious convictions were impairing the ideological training of the young. A leading party propagandist was brought all the way from Moscow to give her a highly technical illustrated lecture on the material origins and evolutionary laws of creation. The old woman listens intently to this brilliant performance designed to demonstrate once and for all the irrefutable wisdom of scientific atheism; and at the end she nods her head and says: "Yes, comrade, great indeed—greater than I had supposed—are the works of the Lord."

The new interest in religion is more than casual curiosity. It arises in the first place out of the re-examination of the Russian past that has been quietly going on among the young in the wake of the denigration of Stalin. The high price now placed on religious art, the staging of Dostoevsky's novels, Melnikov-Pechersky's tales of Old Believer life, and Rimsky-Korsakov's long-proscribed *Invisible City of Kitezh*—all respond to the extraordinary interest of the young in rediscovering these "survivals of the past." A new community of interest began to develop in the fifties between the very young and the very old at the expense of the middle-aged "heirs of Stalin."

Solzhenitsyn's use of the vernacular in *One Day in the Life of Ivan Denisovich* gave an evocative power to that pioneering revelation of suffering under Stalinism not unlike that which Avvakum's use of an earlier vernacular had imparted to his harrowing autobiography. Solzhenitsyn subsequently turned more calmly but no less passionately than the archpriest to the forms of the Old Russian Church for such consolation as he was able to find.

> When you travel the byroads of Central Russia you begin to understand the secret of the pacifying Russian countryside.
> It is in the churches . . . they lift their bell towers—graceful, shapely, all different—high over mundane timber and thatch . . . from villages that are cut off and invisible to each other they soar to the same heaven. . . .
> People were always selfish and often unkind. But the evening chimes used to ring out, floating over the villages, fields, and woods. Reminding men that they must abandon trivial concerns of this world, and give time and thought to eternity. These chimes, which only one old tune keeps alive for us, raised people up and prevented them from sinking down on all fours.[67]

At the very least, religious ideas have opened up new areas of the imagination to a substantial number of young people seeking release from boredom inside the contemporary USSR. The literature of the post-Stalin era contains an increasing number of themes and images borrowed from the Orthodox heritage. Biblical titles are often used, as in Dudintsev's novel, *Not by Bread Alone*. Names often have a symbolic value, as in *The Shadow*, where the idealistic hero who struggles with his shadow is named Christian Theodore, and the maiden who alone stays by him is called Annuntsiata. In the original version of *Everything Depends on People* (which was entitled *The Torch*) the Orthodox priest is represented not as a caricatured reactionary but as an ideal Soviet man—a mathematician and war hero—who converted to Christianity in order to serve humanity. Even after such details were stricken by the censor, the priest in the revised version still manages to explain his beliefs with some dignity. He does not attempt to refute the traditional anti-religious arguments of the atheistic scientist but rather counterattacks at a deeper level, insisting that "our young people are asking questions for which you have no answers."[68]

This very phenomenon makes the revival of interest in religion profoundly disturbing to the regime, whatever the extent of actual religious conviction. In calling "for more atheist books, good ones and varied!"[69] Communist officials rightly complain that much of the literature ostensibly designed to expose religious sects in the USSR is dispassionately objective if not even sympathetic to the object of study. The bizarre life and beliefs of the sects is more in keeping with the phantasmagorical and hypothetical world of the Soviet youth than the colorless world of bureaucratic atheism. Thus sectarian religion seems to have even greater appeal to the young than Orthodoxy or the ultra-Orthodoxy of the schismatics. Communist journals continually complain of fervid but elusive sects, such as Jehovah's Witnesses and Seventh-Day Adventists. These sects are similar in many respects to earlier forms of apocalyptical sectarianism, which also grafted new Western religious forms into a long-standing native tradition.[70]

Far more important because of their impact in large cities and among educated youth are the Baptists, into whose ranks some of the more pietistic and less apocalyptical native sectarians (such as the "milk drinkers") have tended to merge. Communist journals have repeatedly told of young people resigning from the Young Communist League to join the Baptist youth group, popularly known as the "Baptomol."[71] At the congress of the Komsomol in 1962, the head of this heavily subsidized, mammoth organization publicly beseeched his followers to emulate the enthusiasm and dedication of the harassed and indigent Baptist youth.

The biblical simplicity and fervid piety of the Baptists have had an impact on many more than their 600,000 active adult members. A Baptist appears as a leading positive character in N. Dubov's story "A Difficult Test," and as an admirable minor figure in *One Day in the Life of Ivan Denisovich*. Conversions to some such simplified form of Christianity have taken place among a number of educated people. Even the leading Soviet pedagogical journal published an eloquent *profession de foi* of a university-educated teacher (together with a long refutation and an ominous notation that she lost her job in 1959):

> I have recently read in the papers how various people have broken with religion. . . . Why may I not write and publish in a journal about how I came to Christianity, in what way and for what motives I have come to believe in God? . . .
> I felt the need for answers to these questions: Whence came human suffering? Why does man live? and What does true happiness consist of? . . . I thoroughly worked through Indian philosophy, the gospels, etc. And as a result of all of this, I came to the conclusion that only religion, faith in Christ, gives meaning to human life, gives warmth and light to the human soul. Science then should be subordinate to religion, because when unchecked by religion as now, it works towards destruction. . . .[72]

It is impossible to tell from these fragmentary printed excerpts from her letter what, if any, church or sect she has joined, just as it was difficult to determine the exact doctrinal allegiance of the thirty-two Russian Christians who asked in vain for asylum in the American embassy early in 1963.

What is clear is that there are still many anonymous Christians in Russia, and that genuinely pious families often face one of the cruelest of all forms of persecution: the forcible removal of children from the home.

The ferment of the Khrushchev era may have represented only the passing unrest of peripheral intellectuals: foredoomed, if not ultimately meaningless. Certainly the young *révoltés* were more certain of what they were against than of what they favored. They were, moreover, not revolutionaries in any meaningful political sense. The ability of the regime to sustain one-party rule and to anatomize opposition lent an air of unreality to any consideration of alternative forms of political and social organization. In any case, the younger generation in the USSR—in contrast to those of other Communist states, such as Hungary and Poland—did not generally relate communism with foreign domination but saw it as an irreversible part of their history. Communism has been made to appear less odious by the fact that Russia has emerged under its banner to a position of power unprecedented in Russian history. Since there was every material inducement for gifted youth to join the managerial structure of a state able to use and reward the talented, cultural unrest seemed to some observers little more than the passing malaise of a bohemian fringe on the periphery of a growing industrial society.

To the Soviet leadership, however, intellectual ferment was a subject of the most profound concern. The extraordinary amount of time and energy spent on artistic and intellectual affairs by Khrushchev—an earthy figure, who clearly had no personal interest in such matters—must be explained at least partly in terms of the omnipresent concern of insecure autocrats for the realities of power. The Soviet leaders have vivid memories of the extraordinary role played by the intelligentsia in the genesis of their own aging revolutionary movement. They also realize that Leninist governments—no matter how "liberalized" or "de-Stalinized"—are ultimately based on an ideology. Political power in a totalitarian state is not based either on the periodic popular elections of a democracy or on the religiously sanctified hereditary succession of more traditional forms of authoritarian rule. The stated rationale for Communist rule in the USSR has remained the metaphysical pretensions of that party to represent the vanguard of the historical process on the verge of moving "from the realm of necessity to the realm of freedom." Although the USSR could shed its ideological pretensions and become simply another powerful state with a permissive, pluralistic culture, there is no reason to assume (as the history of Nazi Germany demonstrates) that such developments must necessarily result from growing education and prosperity.

There are, nevertheless, at least four reasons for believing that the ferment of the post-Stalin era may represent the beginnings of something new rather than a finished or passing episode. First is the sheer number of people involved in the ferment. Previous ideological unrest in Russian history was invariably confined to a small minority which discussed issues in relative isolation from the populace as a whole. Many more people read Katkov's chauvinistic *Russian Herald* than Mikhailovsky's *Annals of the Fatherland,* the sensationalist illustrated *Niva* than the *World of Art.* In the USSR of the sixties, however, ideological controversy was waged in the most widely circulated journals—and among a populace which has acquired elementary literacy and some schooling in ideological terminology. The monopoly of the Communist party on the organs of communication seemed of decreasing importance in a time when the exact line on many questions remained either unclear or unenforced.

Khrushchev's denigration of Stalin in 1956 opened a Pandora's box of critical questions about where and how things went wrong. The petulant explanation *ad hominem* that the trouble began with Stalin's "cult of personality" in the mid-thirties and his institution of purges against the party did not answer the question or even provide the kind of "profound Marxist analysis" that loyal Leninists were seeking. Some apparently view forced collectivization as the fatal departure; others blame the entire Leninist conception of a totalitarian party and compression of the two revolutions into one. The "Aesopian" tradition of discussing unmentionable political questions in terms of past history has been revived; and the great increase in the late fifties and early sixties in the number of students studying history in effect bespeaks a more lively interest in public affairs among the younger generation.

The party devoted a special Central Committee meeting early in the summer of 1963 solely to ideological and cultural matters. Indications of unrest (even including occasional strikes) in the industrial and agricultural sector point to the fact that the vague desires and rising expectations of the young intellectuals probably correspond more closely to the grass roots attitudes of workers and farmers than in any previous period of intellectual ferment inside Russia.

Even more important than the numbers of people involved is the fact that this ferment is the product of something necessary for Soviet construction itself: expanded contact with the West and increased education. Though the *intention* of the Communist leadership is clearly to use travel and education as subordinate weapons in the development of Soviet strength, the *effects* of its policies may prove more far-reaching. Vasily Kliuchevsky, the great historian of the late imperial period, put the case well in his classic study of the effects produced on Russian culture by increased Western contact in the seventeenth century:

> We may consider that the technical fruits of a foreign culture may not and should not relate to the spiritual bases and roots of the foreign culture, but can people be kept from the desire to acquaint themselves with the roots of a foreign culture when borrowing its fruits?[73]

For the USSR of today the answer is clearly, no. The curiosity about all things Western—art, music, sports, and manner of life—is animated and inescapable.

The scientific and technological emphases that the Soviet leaders have built into their educational system and cultural exchange proposals have led some Western observers to fear for a "new illiteracy,"[74] whereby people are successfully taught to read and even to perform difficult technical tasks without ever learning to think critically. It is difficult, however, to keep technology and ideology in hermetically sealed compartments, particularly in such fields as architecture. Garish and costly monumentalism had become a symbol of the Stalin era, which his successors were anxious to eliminate. By sending delegations to the West to study cheaper and cleaner methods of construction, the regime inadvertently stimulated curiosity about the possibility of integrating architecture with local surroundings and family needs and removing questions of aesthetic judgment from the hands of bureaucrats.[75]

The first important denunciations of "degenerate excesses" in the anti-Stalin campaign after the Twentieth Party Congress in February, 1956, took place in a scientific laboratory.[76] There is receptivity among scientifically trained young Russians to the proposition that Marxism, although a logical outgrowth of nineteenth-century scientific thinking, is inadequate for the more complex and sophisticated thought world of twentieth-century science. Voznesensky, the most technically sophisticated and ideologically heretical of all the young poets, reports that his largest following lies precisely among scientists. Those who work most intimately with the complexities and subtleties of natural phenomena are, he reports, sympathetic to these same qualities in art.[77] Evtushenko makes a similar point by insisting that an art of the "oxcart" age is incompatible with life in the space age.[78]

Increasingly, the literary heroes of the new generation are lonely scientific workers, misunderstood for the most part by their contemporaries and harassed if not persecuted by the Soviet system. Increasingly, the message they seem to be conveying is that of the lonely inventor in Dudintsev's

Not by Bread Alone: "Once a man has started to think, he cannot be denied his freedom."

If, as seems probable, scientifically trained and practically oriented figures are to play an increasingly important role in pressing for change inside the USSR, some of the self-defeating utopianism of past intellectual agitation may well disappear. Creeping pragmatism may not seem an exciting phenomenon to the distant observer. But to those who have seen great expectations so often give way to renewed tyranny and despair this new no-nonsense approach may well provide fortification against disillusionment in the quest for meaningful reform.

A third and even deeper reason for taking the youthful ferment seriously is the psychological need for Russians to make some sense out of the enormous suffering they have undergone in this century. Perhaps forty million people have been killed by artificial means in the last half century —in revolution, civil war, forced repopulation, purges, and two world wars. The myth of Communist infallibility in terms of which all of this suffering was justified is now dead. The papacy of world Communism has been destroyed by Khrushchevian sacrilege—or perhaps moved to Peking. In any event, Russians no longer regard their leadership with the awe and passivity that so long prevailed.

The ordinary man still seeks a credible account of recent Russian history to replace the mythic one of the Stalin era. Thus, the quest for explanation goes on. It feeds on a belief rooted in the chronicles and secularized by Hegel, Marx, and Lenin that there is an intelligible pattern and meaning to history. Behind the quest lies the desire to feel that suffering has not been in vain, that beyond statistical consolations and ideological opiates something better is really coming into being—on earth as it is in space. Many continue to call themselves Communists, because that is the banner under which Russians have worked and suffered in recent years. But Evtushenko is typical in his highly un-Leninist definition of communism as "the decency of the revolutionary idea," deserving of respect because it has become "the essence of the Russian people," entitled to authority only in "a state in which truth is president."[79]

Decency and truth demand an owning up to some of the darker pages of Russian history. Just as the younger generation has embraced a kind of philo-Semitism as a means of atoning for the anti-Semitism of past Russian history, so has it adopted a sympathetic attitude toward the small Baltic states, whose periodic despoliation and repopulation by Russian conquerors from Ivan III to Stalin has long bothered sensitive Russians. The term "Balts" was used as a synonym for Siberian prisoners in the High Stalin era; and recent Soviet literature has tended to praise and indeed idealize this beleaguered region. There is special respect for the Esthonians, whose integrity and fidelity to democratic forms during their brief period of independence between the two world wars won them an admiration comparable to that earned by their cultural kin and northern neighbors, the Finns. The hero of *One Day in the Life of Ivan Denisovich* devotes a special paragraph to the subject:

> Well, it's said that nationality doesn't mean anything and that every nation has its bad eggs. But among all the Esthonians Shukhov had known he'd never met a bad one.[80]

The rebellion of four youths in V. Aksenov's Salinger-like *Ticket to the Stars* is told in terms of their plan to flee to Tallinn, the capital of Esthonia and traditional center of Westward-looking gaiety in the eastern Baltic.[81]

The growing respect for decency and truth can also be measured by the increasing inability of party functionaries to gain support for their periodic campaigns of denunciation. Younger writers seem unlikely to be either fully bought off by the material inducements or fully intimidated by the partial punishments which the regime alternately employs. Sensitive weathervanes of ideological change, such as Ilya Ehrenburg, have unreservedly thrown in their lot with the younger generation. The term "fighter of the first rank" (along with second and third ranks) has been introduced as a kind of informal patent of moral nobility; and Evtushenko has noted that "people someday will marvel at our time when simple honesty was called courage."[82] Even Khrushchev felt obliged to sell himself as the benefactor of youthful expectations against "Stalin's heirs," who were blasted with his approval in *Pravda* by Evtushenko's poem of that name. Khrushchev's successors were, initially at least, deferential if not defensive toward dissident young intellectuals, assuring them that the arbitrary interference of the Khrushchev era would cease and attempting to present themselves as the true friends of "genuine intellectuality" (*intelligentnost'*). This term became late in 1965 the latest in the long line of normative terms derived from *intelligentsia,* but when officially proclaimed to be "in no way opposed to *narodnost'* or *partiinost',*"[83] seemed more likely to remind Russians of the three "ism's" comprising the confining "official nationality" of the nineteenth century than to guide them toward the new world they seek in the late twentieth century.

A fourth and related reason for insisting on the future implications of the current intellectual ferment is the fact that it has roots in Russian tradition as well as Soviet reality. The more one looks at the younger generation and its search for positive ideals, the more one senses that they are not just opposed to their Stalinist parents (often referred to now as "the ancestors"),[84] but are in many ways seeking renewed links with their grand-parents. They are, in short, rediscovering some of the culture which was just reaching new richness in both the political and artistic spheres at the time of the Stalinist blight.

In a short poem written in a Soviet youth magazine in the old folklore form a young Soviet poet seeks to rehabilitate the symbol of Westernization desecrated by Stalin, to free it even of its Leninist name and revolutionary symbols:

> Tell us something of St. Petersburg,
> For as yet we have not seen it.
> Long ago we implored the producers
> Please, do not bring us all those miscellaneous films
> About lovely, deserted ladies,
> But bring us St. Isaac's in a movie
> The Bronze Horseman, the old fortress
> And all about the vast St. Petersburg.[85]

Of course, it is impossible fully to appraise—and would be dangerous to underestimate—the crippling effects of a generation of terror and the continuation of tight censorship and control. "Moral convalescence"[86] may be a long process. The "silence of Soviet culture" is most insidious in the self-imposed censorship that it subtly encouraged. As the Soviet novelist Daniel Granin wrote in a short story in 1956 significantly entitled "My Own Opinion" (and severely criticized by the party bureaucracy):

> Silence is the most convenient form of lying. It knows how to keep peace with the conscience; it craftily preserves your right to withhold your personal opinion on the grounds that someday you will have a chance to express it.[87]

Yet there can also be a positive side to silence: a depth and purity that sometimes comes to those who have suffered in silence. This quality is often hard to discover in the uninhibited and talkative West, but may be more familiar to those who for so long gave special authority to monastic elders trained by long periods of silence and withdrawal from the world.

"Speech, after long silence; it is right," wrote Yeats.[88] Perhaps those who have been so long forced to live with silence may have rediscovered the joy of simple speech or penetrated the mysteries of authentic human communication more fully than many seemingly sophisticated and articulate writers outside. "Music is born in silence," reverently writes one of the best of contemporary Soviet movie directors,[89] and one of the best of the young poets has written vividly:

> I know that men consist of words which
>   have embraced them.
> The word moves. Earth is on fire.
> Deep feelings rest on silence.
> Suffering is mute and so is music.[90]

The respect of so many of the young artists for Pasternak is based on his faithfulness in guarding the integrity of his words, and his faith that a new birth would come out of those regions "where the language is still pure."

The most intense and dedicated of young writers seem to have recaptured some of the old monastic sense of writing as a sacred act, the recording of words so that they may be sung aloud with joyful exaltation. Some of them even seem to be suggesting that the Word of the evangelist may offer an antidote to the "words, words, words" of the old intelligentsia and the endless slogans of the new. One poet has written in honor of the great monastic iconographer:

> Rublev knew how to fall on his knees before the word.
> That is to say
> The One that was in the beginning.[91]

He goes on to point out that Rublev was redeemed and inspired "not by a swineherd symbolizing labor, but quite simply by the Savior."

There is, of course, no way of knowing how deep and lasting the ferment of the Khrushchev era may prove to be, or of evaluating how much and in what ways the young generation will continue to press for reform when tempted by lucrative careers in the official establishment and increasing material prosperity. One recent Soviet story tells how a watchman suddenly discovers on the outskirts of a collective farm Christ in bast shoes saying to the Mother of God: "We have tested men in many ways—by war and hunger. . . . We must try them now with a good harvest."[92] Perhaps with a few good harvests unrest will vanish and the unfulfilled aspirations of Russian culture will linger on only as a kind of wistful memory. All things pass, and the impossibility of knowing what may prove important to the generations ahead is the final fascination and ultimate mystery of history. Perhaps all that the non-prophetic historian can do is make a few last reflections on the historical process itself, and on that part of it which he has examined in search of some final clues to the chapters that lie ahead.

4. The Irony of Russian History

IN LOOKING FOR some way of understanding the perplexities of history, the concept of irony has a certain appeal. A sense of the ironic leads man somewhere between the total explanations of nineteenth-century historicism and the total absurdity of much present-day thought. In his *Irony of American History,* Reinhold Niebuhr has defined irony as "apparently fortuitous incongruities in life which are shown upon closer examination to be not merely fortuitous."[1] Irony differs from pathos in that man bears some responsibility for the incongruities; it differs from comedy in that there are hidden relations in the incongruities; and it differs from tragedy in that there is no inexorable web of fate woven into the incongruities.

Irony is a hopeful, though not a reassuring, concept. Man is not a helpless creature in a totally absurd world. He can do something about ironic situations, but only if he becomes aware of their ironic nature and avoids the temptation to conceal incongruities with total explanations. The ironic view contends that history laughs at human pretensions without being hostile to human aspirations. It is capable of giving man hope without illusion.[2]

Applied to history, irony suggests that there is rational meaning to the historical process, yet that man—as a participant—is never fully able to grasp it. Seeming absurdities are part of what Hegel called "the cunning of reason." History does make sense, though our understanding of it tends to come too late. "The owl of Minerva spreads his wings only at the gathering of the dusk."[3] Ironically, yet not senselessly, the flow of history always seems to be just one turn ahead of man's capacity to understand it. Today's equilibration of forces is said to be an equilibrium or even a permanent solution by those who confidently project current trends forward into the future without considering those deeper forces which account for discontinuous (or "dialectical") changes in human history. Yet such changes do occur—often with great suddenness in ways not foreseen except by isolated thinkers far removed from the rational consensus of their day. Recent Russian history is full of such discontinuous change: both revolutions of 1917, the sudden turn to the NEP, Stalin's second revolution, the Nazi-Soviet pact, the post-war psychosis of high Stalinism, and the sudden thaw after the tyrant's death.

Looking over the sweep of modern Russian history, one's sense of the ironic is compounded. In the Muscovite period the most extreme statements of the exclusive nature and destiny of Russia came in precisely those periods when Westernization was proceeding most rapidly—under Ivan the Terrible and Alexis Mikhailovich. Indeed, the ideologists responsible for insisting on Russia's special destiny were often Western-educated figures: Maxim the Greek and Ivan Peresvetov under Ivan and Simeon Polotsky and Innokenty Gizel under Alexis. The Muscovite rulers concealed from themselves the incongruity of increasing at one and the same time both their borrowings from and their antagonisms toward the West. The pretense inherent in the historical theology of Old Russia was intensified rather than dispelled by initial contacts with the West. The manic xenophobia of Ivan the Terrible and the Old Believers had an enduring popular appeal, and provided the basis for a modern mass culture that was gilded with scientific sanction by zoological nationalists in the late nineteenth century and by dialectical materialists in the twentieth century.

Against such a background, the tsar-reformers of Imperial Russia found their careers beset with ironies. Theoretically freer than other European sovereigns to rule solely by "their own strength" (the literal meaning of the Greek *autokratēs* and the Russian *samoderzhavie)*, they repeatedly found themselves in bondage to the superstitions of their nominally bonded subjects. Grants of freedom and toleration often had the effect of calling forth ungrateful if not despotic responses. "Never did the *raskol* enjoy such freedom as in the first year of Peter's reign, but . . . never was it to prove more fanatical."[4] Catherine, who did far more than any of her predecessors to gratify the aristocratic intellectuals, was the first to experience their ideological enmity. She, who launched the unending discussion in Russia about the liberation of mankind, probably did more than any of her autocratic predecessors to militarize society and freeze the peasantry in bondage. In the nineteenth century the popularity of tsar-reformers tended to vary in inverse proportion with their actual accomplishment. Alexander I, who accomplished surprisingly little and instituted in his late years a far more repressive and reactionary rule than prevailed even under Nicholas I, was universally loved; whereas Alexander II, who accomplished an extraordinary amount in the first decade of his reign, was rewarded by an attempt on his life at the end of the decade—the first of many, one of which eventually proved successful. Among the many ironies of the revolutionary tradition stands the repeated participation of aristocratic intellectuals, who stood to

lose rather than gain privilege. "I can understand the French bourgeois
bringing about the Revolution to get rights, but how am I to comprehend
the Russian nobleman making a revolution to lose them?" asked a reactionary former governor of Moscow when learning on his deathbed of the
Decembrist revolt.[5]

The victorious revolution brought with it a new tissue of ironies. It is
ironic that a revolution begun by pure spontaneity in March, 1917, and
defended by a wide coalition of democratic forces should be canceled out
by a coup engineered by the smallest and most totalitarian of the opposition
forces, and one which played almost no role in bringing tsardom to an
end. It is ironic that communism came to power in the peasant East rather
than the industrial West—and, above all, in the Russia which Marx and
Engels particularly disliked and distrusted; and that the ideology which
spoke so emphatically of economic determinism should be so completely
dependent on visionary appeals and on the individual leadership of Lenin.
It is ironic that the revolution in power should devour its own creators;
and that many of the very first elements to lend genuine grass roots support to the Bolshevik coup in St. Petersburg (the proletarian leaders of the
"Workers Opposition" and the sailors of Kronstadt) were among the first
to be brutally repudiated by the new regime for urging in 1920–1 substan-
tially the same reforms which the Bolsheviks had encouraged them to
demand four years before.

It is ironic that one of the most complete repudiations of democracy
occurred at the very time when Russia was formally adopting the seemingly
exemplary democratic constitution of 1936; ironic that the Stalinist war
on the creative arts should occur at precisely the time when Russia was at
the forefront of creative modernism; ironic that those organs of oppression
that the people were least capable of influencing should be given the label
"people's."

It is ironic that the USSR should succeed where most thought it would
fail: in defeating the Germans and conquering outer space. It is perhaps
most ironic of all that the Soviet leaders should fail in the area where almost
everyone thought they would automatically succeed: in the indoctrination
of their own youth. It is high irony that the post-war generation of Russians
—the most privileged and indoctrinated of all Soviet generations, which was
not even given the passing exposure to the outside world of those who
fought in the war—should prove the most alienated of all from the official
ethos of Communist society. There is the further irony of the Communist
leaders' referring to youthful ferment as a "survival of the past," and the
more familiar irony of partial reforms leading not to grateful quiescence but
to increased agitation.

This remarkable situation is not without ironic meaning for the Western observer. Despite his formal, rhetorical belief in man's inherent longing for truth and freedom, Western man has been strangely reluctant to predict (and slow to admit) that such ideals would have any compelling appeal in the USSR. The tendency during the late years of the Khrushchev era to assume that evolutionary modification of despotism would continue without basic change represented the projection into the future of the trends of the immediate past. There was often also an implicit belief that the USSR (and perhaps also the United States) was evolving naturally toward a position somewhere between Stalinist totalitarianism and Western democracy.[6] Such a balanced conclusion may, of course, be vindicated; but it would take all the cunning away from reason and represent an astonishing victory for the Aristotelian golden mean in a society that has never assimilated classical ideas of moderation and rationality.

A cultural history cannot offer a net prediction; but it must insist on the importance of the national heritage and the vitality of the ferment now at work. This ferment is not like a factor in a mathematical equation that can be resolved on the computers of Eastern political manipulators or Western political scientists. The ferment in the USSR today is more like indeterminate plants appearing on a burned-out field. One cannot tell whether they stem from old roots or fresh seeds blown in from elsewhere. Only time will tell if the landscape will be fundamentally changed. Yet the very appearance of the plants indicates that the soil is fertile; and even if they were to die, their leaves might yet provide humus for a stronger, future growth.

The critical condition for growth in the years ahead will be the continuance of the relatively mild international climate of the post-Stalin era. Sustained storm clouds from East or West could have a chilling effect. Gusts of fresh vitality from neighboring countries could greatly stimulate growth in a culture that has always responded to fertilization from outside and in a world that is increasingly interdependent. Already the assimilation into the Russian orbit of such traditional foes on its Western borders as Poland and Hungary has had not the intended effect of silencing these nations but the ironic one of bringing added Westward-looking ferment into the Soviet sphere. There is no telling how important for future Soviet development increasing contact with the West or a renaissance of ideological *élan* within the West might prove to be.

One cannot wishfully expect automatic evolution toward democracy in the USSR now any more than one should have expected revolution for democracy under Stalin. Forces within one culture do not exist to serve the purposes of another; and the familiar institutional forms of liberal, parliamentary democracy are still incomprehensible to many Russians. But

Russia may well develop new social and artistic forms presently unforeseen by either East or West which will answer the restive demand of its people for human freedom and spiritual renewal. If the West has anything authentic to communicate and has any direct and unpatronizing ways of doing it, it could almost certainly play a key role in this process. For nowhere is curiosity about the West—and particularly America—greater than among the youth of the USSR. Nowhere is the disappointment at the lack of spiritual vitality in the West more keenly felt than among the restless youth of the USSR eagerly looking for some guidance in their unsatisfied search for positive goals and new approaches. It would be a terrifying double irony if American philistinism should lead some Russian youth reluctantly to go along with a Communist ideology which both Russian tradition and contemporary Soviet reality encourage them to reject.

"He is an honest-searching man," says one character in quiet tribute to another in *Everything Depends on People;* and this might well serve as a characterization of the young generation in the USSR. The search is still incomplete; the hopes are unfulfilled; and the entire cultural revival seems at times a kind of evanescent mirage. But, since everything in history is ultimately incomplete, it may be well to introduce a final ironic perspective on the question of reality itself.

At the very height of Stalinist pretense, in the semi-official portrayal of the Revolution in Alexis Tolstoy's *Road to Calvary,* an idiot dreams that the great city of St. Petersburg—artificially wrenched out of the sufferings of thousands—was itself only a mirage that had suddenly vanished. That the phantasmagoria of Soviet construction seems to us the most real thing about Soviet history may be only a reflection of our own essentially materialist conception of reality. The Russians, on the other hand, have always been a visionary and ideological people, uniquely appreciative of the ironic perspectives on reality offered in such works as Calderón's *Life Is a Dream* and Shakespeare's *Tempest.* It may be that only those who have lived through the tempest of Stalinism will be able, like Prospero, to look on it as "the baseless fabric of a vision"; to see in "the cloud-capped towers, the gorgeous palaces, the solemn temples" only an "insubstantial pageant faded," and to find fresh meaning in Prospero's final affirmation that man is, indeed, "such stuff as dreams are made on."

Tertz has spoken of the young generation's "enthusiasm before the metamorphoses of God . . . before the monstrous peristaltic upheaval of his entrails and his cerebral circumvolutions."[7] It would be ironic, indeed, if God were in exile somewhere in the "atheistic" East; and if the culture produced amidst its silence and suffering were to prove more remarkable than that of the talkative and well-fed West. But this, perhaps, is the irony of freedom, which tends to be treasured by those who do not have it and profaned by those who do. Here, too, is the enduring irony of creative culture, which comes into being through the painful self-denial of an individual opening himself up to larger worlds. True creativity in the USSR today involves voluntary suffering, or as Pasternak put it, "an offer of consecrated abnegation in a far and humble likeness with the Lord's Supper."

Such a role seems close to the monastic conception of the dedicated artist; and insofar as this burden of dedication continues to be taken up inside the USSR, it is likely to be sustained, if not by the faith of the Church, at least by its central belief in the Resurrection. *Resurrection* was the title of Tolstoy's last novel, the theme of Dostoevsky's and Pasternak's. It is only in resurrection that there is any final, ironic sense either in the comic incongruity of God disguised as man or in the tragic incongruity of human rebellion against divine authority. It is only in resurrection, some unforeseeable "metamorphoses of God," that sense could ultimately be made out of the implausible aspirations of Russian thought and the repeated rejection of higher ideals in Russian reality.

None can say that rebirth will occur, none can be sure even that there is any sense to be found in the history of a culture in which aspiration has so often outreached accomplishment and anguish impaired achievement. There may be nothing for the historian of culture to do except provide accompanying notes for the great novels, luminous icons, and lovely music and architecture that can be salvaged from an otherwise blighted inventory.

Repeatedly, Russians have sought to acquire the end products of other civilizations without the intervening process of slow growth and inner understanding. Russia took the Byzantine heritage en bloc without absorbing its traditions of orderly philosophic discourse. The aristocracy adopted the language and style of French culture without its critical spirit, and variously sought to find solidarity with idealized sectarian or peasant communities without ever sharing in either the work or the faith of these nonaristocratic elements. The radical intelligentsia deified nineteenth-century Western science without recreating the atmosphere of free criticism that had made scientific advances possible. The exploration of "cursed questions" took place not in academies or even market places but in occult circles and "Aesopian" journals. Even Gogol and Ivanov in fleeing to the sun-drenched centers of Mediterranean classicism could not escape the nocturnal world of German romanticism, of forests and lakes, and of the dark northern winters.

High Stalinism provided a kind of retribution. Russia suddenly found itself ruled by Byzantine ritualism without Byzantine reverence or beauty, and by Western scientism without Western freedom of inquiry. One is tempted to see in the terrible climax, the "cleansing" (*chistka*) of the purge period, either total absurdity or some new and unprecedented form of totalitarian logic. But to the cultural historian, the horrors of High Stalinism may appear neither as an accidental intrusion upon, nor an inevitable by-product of, the Russian heritage. If he adopts the ironic perspective, he might even conclude that the cleansing did lead to a kind of purification far deeper than that which was intended—that innocent suffering created the possibility for fresh accomplishment.

Stalin may have cured Russian thinkers of their passion for abstract speculation and their thirst for earthly utopias. The desire for the concrete and practical so characteristic of the post-Stalin generation may help Russia produce a less spectacular but more solid culture. The harvest may be long delayed in political institutions and artistic expression. But the roots of creativity are deep in Russia, and the soil rich. Whatever plants appear in the future should be more enduring than the ephemeral blossoms and artificial transplants of earlier ages. In an age of pretension, the cunning of reason may require a deceptively quiet rebirth. But Western observers should not be patronizing about a nation which has produced Tolstoy and Dostoevsky and undergone so much suffering in recent times. Impatient onlookers who have come to expect immediate delivery of packaged products may have to rediscover the processes of "ripening as fruit ripens, growing as grass grows." The path of new discovery may well be parabolic, like that of Voznesensky's Columbus:

> Instinctively
>   head for the shore . . .
> Look for
>   India—
> You'll find
>   America![8]

Life out of death, freedom out of tyranny—irony, paradox, perhaps too much to hope for. One must return to the reality of plants not yet mature, of a ship still very much at sea. The last of the tempests may not have passed. We may still be in Miranda's "brave new world," and the perspectives of Prospero may not yet be in sight. This generation may only be, as Evtushenko has put it, "like the men in Napoleon's cavalry who threw themselves into the river to form a bridge over which others might cross to the other bank."[9]

Yet even here there is the image of that other bank. The melodramatic suggestion of a Napoleonic army somehow fades. One feels left rather in the midst of one of those long rivers in the Russian interior. There is no bridge across, no clear chart for the would-be navigator. The natives still move along the river in zigzag patterns which often seem senseless to those looking on from afar. But the closer one gets, the more one notes a certain inner strength: "the good-humored serenity characteristic of people who see life as movement along the winding bed of a river, between hidden sandbanks and rocks."[10] One senses that deeper currents may be slowly pulling those on this river away from bends and banks into more open seas. One feels that neither the "stormy passage"[11] of recent times nor the deceptive reefs that no doubt lie ahead will prevent them from reaching their long-sought and still undiscovered destination: "the other shore."

BIBLIOGRAPHY

Abbreviations

In order to keep the specific gravity of scholarly substance as high as possible in these references, a number of technical economies have been made. Full references are given only on the first usage; all titles are given only in the original language; only the first initial of an author is generally given; and there are no internal cross references. Place of publication is not listed for any French-language work published in Paris or German-language work published in Berlin; P indicates St. Petersburg and Petrograd; L, Leningrad; M, Moscow; NY, New York. All months are abbreviated to the first three letters; p indicates paperback; and mt indicates that I have modified the translation cited. In addition, the following abbreviations are used for periodicals and basic reference works of more than one word:

AAE	Akty sobrannye . . . arkheograficheskoi ekspeditsii
AB	Analecta Bollandiana (Brussels)
AESC	Annales Economies-Sociétés-Civilizations
AHR	American Historical Review
AHRF	Annales historiques de la révolution française
AI	Akty Istoricheskie
AIOS	Annuaire de l'institut de philologie et d'histoire orientales et slaves (Brussels)
AK	Archiv für Kulturgeschichte (Berlin-Leipzig)
AMH	Annals of Medical History
AQC	Ars Quatuor Coronatorum (London)
AR	Archiv für Reformationsgeschichte (Leipzig)
ASR	American Slavic and East European Review (re-titled Slavic Review, 1963)
BE	Brockhaus-Efron, Entsiklopedichesky Slovar', I. Andreevsky, K. Arsen'ev, V. Sheviakov, eds., 43v in 86, 1890–1907
BL	Bibliograficheskaia letopis'
BNYL	Bulletin of the New York Public Library
BRP	Bibliothèque russe et polonaise

BS	Byzantinoslavica (Prague)
BSE (1)	Bol'shaia Sovetskaia Entsiklopedia, 1st ed., O., Shmidt, ed., 66v, 1926–47
BSE (2)	Bol'shaia Sovetskaia Entsiklopedia, 2d ed., S. Vavilov, ed., 51v, 1950–8
BV	Bogoslovsky Vestnik
BZ	Bibliograficheskie Zapiski
CA	Communist Affairs (Los Angeles)
CDSP	Current Digest of the Soviet Press
CH	Church History
ChC	Christian Century
Cht	Chteniia obshchestva istorii i drevnostei Moskovskogo universiteta
CMR	Cahiers du monde russe et soviétique
CS	Le Contrat social
CSP	Canadian Slavonic Papers (Toronto)
CSS	California Slavic Studies
DAN	Doklady Akademii Nauk
DNR	Drevniaia i Novaia Rossiia
DOP	Dumbarton Oaks Papers
DR	Deutsche Rundschau
DRV	Drevniaia rossiiskaia vivliofika
ECQ	Eastern Churches Quarterly (Ramsgate)
EHR	English Historical Review
EII	Ezhegodnik instituta istorii iskusstv
ER	Eastern Review (Klagenfurt)
ESR	Études slaves et roumaines (Budapest)
ESS	Encyclopedia of the Social Sciences, E. Seligman, ed., 15v, 1930–5
FA	Foreign Affairs
FOG	Forschungen zur osteuropäischen Geschichte
GBA	Gazette des beaux-arts
Gr	Entsiklopedichesky Slovar', Granat, 7th ed., V. Zheleznov, ed., 34v, 1910–38
HJ	Historisches Jahrbuch (Munich), Goerres-gesellschaft zur Pflege der Wissenschaft im katholischen Deutschland (Bonn)
HSS	Harvard Slavic Studies
HT	Historisk Tidskrift (Stockholm)
IA	Istorichesky Arkhiv
IaL	Iazyk i Literatura
IAN (G)	Izvestiia Akademii Nauk SSSR, otdelenie gumanitarnykh nauk
IAN (I)	Izvestiia Akademii Nauk SSSR, seriia istorii i filologii
IAN (L)	Izvestiia Akademii Nauk SSSR, otdelenie literatury i iazyka
IAN (O)	Izvestiia Akademii Nauk SSSR, otdelenie obshchestvennykh nauk
IIaS	Izvestiia Akademii Nauk SSSR, otdelenie russkogo iazyka i slovesnosti
IJSL	International Journal of Slavic Linguistics and Poetics (The Hague)
IL	Istoricheskaia Letopis'
IM	Istorik-Marksist
IS	Istorichesky Sbornik
ISR	Istoriia SSSR
IV	Istorichesky Vestnik
IZ	Istoricheskie Zapiski
IZh	Istorichesky Zhurnal
JAH	Journal of American Society of Architectural History
JGO	Jahrbücher für Geschichte Osteuropas (Breslau/Wroclaw, Munich)
JHI	Journal of the History of Ideas
JHR	Journal de l'histoire des religions
JKGS	Jahrbücher für Kultur und

Geschichte der Slaven
JMH   Journal of Modern History
JWI   Journal of the Warburg and Courtauld Institute
KH   Kwartalnik Historyczny (Warsaw)
Kh Cht Khristianskoe Chtenie
KP   Komsomol'skaia Pravda
KR   Kenyon Review
KS   Kievskaia Starina
KUI   Kievskie universitetskie izvestiia
KZ   Krasnaia Zvezda
KZ(Y) Kraevedcheskie Zapiski (Yaroslavl)
LA   Literaturny Arkhiv
LE   Literaturnaia Entsiklopediia, 1st ed., V. Friche, ed., 10v, 1929–39
LG   Literaturnaia Gazeta
LZAK   Letopis' zaniatii arkheograficheskoi komissii
MAV   Mémoires de l'académie de Vaucluse (Avignon)
MB   Mir Bozhii
MF   Mercure de France
MGH   Monumenta Germaniae Historica
MK   Molodoi Kommunist
ML   Music and Letters
MO   Missionernoe Obozrenie
MQ   Musical Quarterly
MS   Missionersky Sbornik
NG   National Geographic
NIS   Novgorodsky Istorichesky Sbornik
NK   Novye Knigi
NL   New Leader
NM   Novy Mir
NS   New Statesman and Nation
NYT   New York Times
NZh   Novy Zhurnal (NY)
NZK   Naukovi zapiski pratsi naukovo-doslikchoï katedri istorii evropeis'koi kul'turi (Kharkov)

OC   Orientalia Christiana Analecta (Rome)
Och   Ocherki istorii SSSR
       (1) Pervobytno-obshchiny stroi i drevneishie gosudarstva na territorii SSSR, P. Tret'iakov, ed., 1956;
       (2) Krizis rabovladel'cheskoi sistemy i zarozhdenie feodalizma na territorii SSSR III–IX vv, B. Rybakov, ed., 1958;
       (3,4) Period feodalizma IX–XV vv v dvukh chastiakh
           I. B. Grekov, ed., 1953; II. B. Grekov, ed., 1953;
       (5) Period feodalizma, konets XV v–nachalo XVII v, A. Nasonov, ed., 1955;
       (6) Period feodalizma, XVII v, A. Khovosel'sky, ed., 1955;
       (7) Period feodalizma, Rossiia v pervoi chetverti XVIII v, B. Kafengauz, ed., 1954;
       (8) Period feodalizma, Rossiia vo vtoroi chetverti XVIII v, A. Baranovich, ed., 1957;
       (9) Period feodalizma, Rossiia vo vtoroi polovine XVIII v, A. Baranovich, ed., 1956;
       (10) Konets XVIII–pervaia chetvert' XIX v, S. Okun', ed., 1956.
OCP   Orientalia Christiana Periodica (Rome)
OSP   Oxford Slavonic Papers
PDL   Pamiatniki drevnerusskoi literatury

PDP	Pamiatniki drevnei pis'-mennosti
PDPI	Pamiatniki drevnei pis'-mennosti i iskusstva
PMLA	Publications of the Modern Language Association of America
PO	Pravoslavnoe Obozrenie
PP	Past and Present
PR	Partisan Review
PRP	Pamiatniki Russkogo Prava
PS	Pravoslavny sobesednik
PSRL	Polnoe sobranie russkikh letopisei
PSS	Polnoe sobranie sochinenii (of the author cited)
PSZ	Polnoe sobranie zakonov
PZM	Pod znamenem marksizma
RA	Russky Arkhiv
RB	Russkoe Bogatstvo
RBPh	Revue belge de philologie et d'histoire
RBS	Russky Biografichesky Slovar', 25v, 1896–1918
RDM	Revue des deux mondes
RES	Revue des études slaves
REW	Russisches etymologisches Wörterbuch, M. Vasmer, ed., 3v, Heidelberg, 1953–8
RF	Russky fol'klor: materialy i issledovaniia
RFe	Rossiisky featr
RH	Revue historique
RHL	Revue d'histoire littéraire de la France
RHMC	Revue d'histoire moderne et contemporaine
RHR	Revue de l'histoire des religions
RiS	Ricerche Slavistiche (Rome)
RL	Radians'ke literaturo-znavstvo (Kiev)
RLC	Revue de littérature comparée
RM	Russkaia Mysl'
RMG	Russkaia muzykal'naia gazeta
ROJ	Russian Orthodox Journal
RoS	Romanoslavica (Bucharest)
RP	Review of Politics (South Bend, Indiana)
RPSR	Research program on the USSR (Mimeographed series, NY)
RR	Russian Review
RRe	Russkaia Rech'
RS	Russkaia Starina
RSH	Revue de synthèse historique
RSMP	Revue des travaux de l'académie des sciences, morales et politiques
RU	Radians'ka Ukraina (Kharkov)
RV	Russky Vestnik
SA	Sovetskaia Arkheologiia
SAP	St. Anthony's Papers
ScS	Scandoslavica (Copenhagen)
SEEJ	Slavic and East European Journal (Indiana)
SEER	Slavonic and East European Review (London)
SEES	Slavic and East European Studies (Montreal)
SIaS	Sbornik otdeleniia russkogo iazyka i slovesnosti, Akademiia nauk
SII	Soobshcheniia instituta istorii iskusstv, Akademiia nauk
SK	Sovetskaia Kul'tura
SKhO	Sbornik Khar'kovskogo istoriko-filologicheskogo obshchestva
SKP	Annales et comptes rendus, Seminarium Kondakovianum (Prague)
SkS	Skandinavsky Sbornik (Tallinn)
SKST	Suomen Kirkkohistorialli-

sen Seuran Toimituksia (Helsinki)
SL   Sovetskaia Literatura
SM   Sovetskaia Muzyka
SMAE   Sbornik muzeia antropologii i etnografii
SN   Starina i Novizna
SO   Slavia Orientalis (Warsaw)
SR   Soviet Review
SRIO   Sbornik russkogo istoricheskogo obshchestva
SRIP   Sbornik russkogo instituta v Prage
SS   Sobranie sochinenii (of the author cited)
SSRIa   Slovar' sovremennogo russkogo literaturnogo iazyka, V. Chernyshev, ed., 7v, 1950–8
SSt   Soviet Studies (Oxford)
Su   Soviet Survey (retitled Survey 1961)
SUN   Skriffter utgitt av det Norske Videnskaps-Akademi (II Hist.-filos. Klasse, Oslo)
SVQ   St. Vladimir's Seminary Quarterly
SW   Selected Works (of the author cited)
SZ   Sovremennye Zapiski (Paris)
TC   The XXth Century (Shanghai)
TGIM   Trudy gosudarstvennogo istoricheskogo muzeia
TH   The Third Hour (NY)
TIAI   Trudy istoriko-arkhivnogo instituta
TIIE   Trudy instituta istorii estestvoznaniia i tekhniki
TKF   Trudy Karel'skogo filiala Akademii nauk SSSR (Petrozavodsk)
TKIZ   Trudy komissii po istorii znaniia

TODL   Trudy Otdela drevnerusskoi literatury
TRHS   Transactions of the Royal Historical Society (London)
TSRIa   Tolkovy slovar' russkogo iazyka, D. Ushakov, ed., 4v, 1934–40
TVO   Trudy vostochnago otdeleniia russkago arkheologicheskago obshchestva
UG   Uchitel'skaia Gazeta
UZAON   Uchenye Zapiski Akademii obshchestvennykh nauk pri tsentralnom komitete VKP (b)
UZIAN   Uchenye Zapiski vtorogo otdeleniia Imperatorskoi akademii nauk
UZIuU   Uchenye Zapiski Imperatorskago Iur'evskago universiteta
UZKU   Uchenye Zapiski Kazanskogo universiteta
UZLGU   Uchenye Zapiski Leningradskogo gosudarstvennogo universiteta
UZMGU   Uchenye Zapiski Moskovskogo gosudarstvennogo universiteta
UZRANION   Uchenye Zapiski: rossiiskaia assotsiatsia nauchno-issledovatel'skikh institutov obshchestvennykh nauk. Institut istorii
VAN   Vestnik Akademii nauk
VDL   Vremennik Demidovskogo iuridicheskogo litseia (Yaroslavl)
VE   Vestnik Evropy
VF   Voprosy filosofii
VFPs   Voprosy filosofii i psikhologii
VI   Voprosy istorii
VIMK   Vestnik istorii mirovoi kul'tury
VL   Voprosy literatury

VR   Vera i Razum (Kharkov)

VSP   Veröffentlichungen der slavistischen Arbeitsgemeinschaft an der Deutschen Universität in Prag

VsV   Vsemirny vestnik

VV   Vizantiisky vremennik

WMR   World Marxist Review

WP   World Politics

WSJ   Wiener Slawistisches Jahrbuch

ZFS   Zeitschrift für Slawistik

ZhChO   Zhurnal Imperatorskogo chelovekoliubivogo obshchestva

ZhMNP   Zhurnal Ministerstva narodnogo prosveshcheniia

ZhS   Zhivaia Starina

ZIAN   Zapiski Imperatorskoi akademii nauk

ZOG   Zeitschrift für osteuropäische Geschichte

ZOR   Zapiski otdela rukopisei Vsesoiuznoi biblioteki imeni V. I. Lenina

ZPU   Zapiski istoriko-filologicheskago fakul'teta Imperatorskago S-Peterburgskago universiteta

ZRIOP   Zapiski Russkogo istoricheskogo obshchestva v Prage

ZRNIB   Zapiski Russkogo nauchnogo instituta v Belgrade

ZRVI   Zbornik radova vizantoloshkog instituta (Belgrad)

ZSPh   Zeitschrift für slavische Philologie (Leipzig)

This introductory bibliography lists basic works of special stimulative or scholarly value and that pertain to more than one particular section of the text. Works of more narrowly defined interest are mentioned in the footnotes of the appropriate section. The index can be used to find the full bibliographical references for each author cited.

The bibliography does not pretend to be comprehensive, and the number of entries under each subject is not necessarily commensurate with the intrinsic importance of the subject. It attempts rather to refer the reader to other reference lists when these are easily available and sufficiently comprehensive.

1. GENERAL HISTORIES OF CULTURE AND THOUGHT

P. Miliukov, *Ocherki po istorii russkoi kul'tury*, Paris, 1930–7, corr. ed., 3v, is inclusive and well-referenced, with a chronological treatment of religion, literature, and the arts, each in one volume. The second part of the first volume ("From Prehistory to History") of this never-completed work has recently been published for the first time from the manuscript which Miliukov completed shortly before his death in an edition by N. Andreev, 's Gravenhage, 1964. An abridged, non-annotated English edition is *Outlines of Russian Culture*, NY, 1962, 3v, p. V. Riazanovsky, *Obzor russkoi kul'tury*, NY, 1947–8, 3 parts in 2v, is less full than Miliukov, but better in interrelating different fields of culture. G. Vernadsky, *Zven'ia russkoi kul'tury*, Ann Arbor, 1962 (repr. of 1938 ed.) considers a broader range of phenomena under culture than Miliukov, but only to the mid-fifteenth century. R. Ivanov-Razumnik, *Istoriia russkoi obshchestvennoi mysli*, P, 1918, 5th augmented and rev. ed., 8v; D. Ovsianiko-Kulikovsky, *Istoriia russkoi intelligentsii*, M, 1907; N. Berdiaev, *The Russian Idea*, NY, 1948, (also p); and *The Origin of Russian Communism*, Ann Arbor, 1960, p; and T. Masaryk, *The Spirit of Russia*, NY, 1955, 2v, rev. ed.—all deal sympathetically with Russian social and philosophic thought, mainly as reflected in nineteenth-century literature and polemics. W. Weidlé, *Russia: Absent and Present*, NY, 1961, p, is a provocative, impressionistic discussion often drawing from the visual arts; S. Volkonsky, *Pictures of Russian History and Russian Literature*, Boston-NY, 1898, is a readable, if superficial discussion, good on the early periods and in its use of German materials; the best Marxist treatment of modern Russian social thought is G. Plekhanov's *Istoriia russkoi obshchestvennoi mysli* (in *Sochineniia*, M-L, 1925, 2d ed., XX-XXII).

This represents only three of the projected seven volumes, and carries the story only to Radishchev. Particularly valuable is the long bibliographical essay and treatment of pre-Petrine Russia in XX, which is altogether left out of the mimeographed English translation of some sections dealing with the first two thirds of the eighteenth century: Plekhanov, *History of Russian Social Thought*, NY, 1938. See also Plekhanov's critical essays on nineteenth-century subjects: *Ocherki po istorii russkoi obshchestvennoi mysli XIX veka*, P, 1923; also material in *Sochineniia*, M-L, 1926, XXIII. Another interesting early Soviet interpretation that reflects more a Christian socialist than a Marxist perspective is V. Sipovsky, *Etapy russkoi mysli*, P, 1924. A one-volume *Istoriia russkoi kul'tury*, covering up to 1917 and under the general editorship of Sh. Levin, will provide an up-to-date Soviet text when it appears early in 1966. A crude, early Marxist interpretation, written largely to refute Miliukov, is M. Pokrovsky, *Ocherki istorii russkoi kul'tury*, M, 1914–8, 2 parts. G. Vasetsky, *et al.*, *Ocherki po istorii filosofskoi i obshchestvenno-politicheskoi mysli narodov SSSR*, M, 1955–6, 2v, is of value mostly for its discussion of modern thought in the lesser known, non-Russian parts of the USSR.

G. Florovsky, *Puti russkogo bogosloviia*, Paris, 1937 (photo reprint, 1963), relates religious thought to broader social and cultural developments and has a rich bibliography, including many rare periodical references. V. Zenkovsky, *A History of Russian Philosophy*, NY, 1953, 2v, is an Orthodox treatment superior to N. Lossky's similarly titled work (NY, 1951), though lacking the full documentation of Zenkovsky's original Russian version, *Istoriia russkoi filosofii*, Paris, 1948–50, 2v.

On early Russian thought and culture see A. Shchapov, "Obshchy vzgliad na istoriiu intellektual'nago razvitiia v Rossii," and "Istoricheskiia usloviia intellektual'nago razvitiia v Rossii," both in his *Sochineniia*, P, 1906, II; also D. Likhachev, *Kul'tura russkogo naroda X–XVII vv*, M-L, 1961; and A. Sakharov and A. Murav'ev, *Ocherki russkoi kul'tury IX–XVII vv*, M, 1962.

E. Bobrov's compendium of materials, *Filosofiia v Rossii*, Kazan, 1899–1901, 6v, and G. Shpet's more interpretive *Ocherk razvitiia russkoi filosofii* (P, 1922) deal mainly with the late eighteenth and the early nineteenth century. A. Vvedensky's "Sud'by filosofii v Rossii," *VFPs*, 1898, Mar–Apr, is a valuable treatment of the travails encountered by the formal study of philosophy in Russia (reprinted separately, M, 1898, and in his *Filosofskie ocherki*, Prague, 1924). Also useful are M. Filippov, *Sud'by russkoi filosofii*, P, 1904; and D. Chizhevsky, *Narisi z istorii filosofii na Ukraini*, Prague, 1931. E. Radlov, *Ocherk istorii russkoi filosofii,* P, 1920, 2d corr. ed., is a valuable concise study with a critical bibliography of works on the history of Russian philosophy. See also the new Soviet *Filosofskaia Entsiklopediia,* the first three volumes of which appeared M, 1960–4, with many articles on Russian as well as general philosophy. O. Lourié, *La Philosophie russe contemporaine,* 1902, is a useful coverage that includes many now-forgotten trends. A Koyré, *Études sur l'histoire de la pensée philosophique en Russie,* 1950, is an invaluable collection of essays. P. Pascal, "Les grands courants de la pensée russe contemporaine," *CMR,* 1962, Jan-Mar, 5–89, is a succinct yet comprehensive coverage of the last hundred years.

N. Arsen'ev, *Iz russkoi kul'turnoi i tvorcheskoi traditsii,* Frankfurt/M., 1959, is a series of essays stressing the importance of familial ties and communal traditions in Russian history. A. Jensen, *Rysk Kulturhistoria,* Stockholm, 1908, 3v; and L. Schinitzky, *El pensamiento ruso en la filosofia y en la literatura,* Buenos Aires, 1946, deserve attention outside the narrower audience to which their respective languages limit them. The Germano-Latvian sociologist, W. Schubart, *Russia and Western Man,* NY, 1950, has written one of the best in the large literature of attempts to characterize the Russian national character. Also valuable in this genre is the less speculative study by W. Miller, *Russians As People,* NY, 1961, p; and N. Vakar, *The Taproot of Soviet Society,* NY, 1962, which examines the impact of peasant institutions and modes of thought on modern, and particularly Soviet, Russian culture.

2. THE CHURCH

A. Kartashev, *Ocherki po istorii russkoi tserkvi,* Paris, 1959, 2v, is an Orthodox treatment with full bibliography. M. Bulgakov, the former Metropolitan Macarius of Moscow, has written the most detailed and comprehensive history through the mid-nineteenth century, *Istoriia russkoi tserkvi,* Ann Arbor, 1963, 12v, photo repr. from 2d ed. But it should be supplemented for the early period by E. Golubinsky, *Istoriia russkoi tserkvi,* M, 1880–1916, 2d rev. & exp. ed., 2v, two parts in each; and, for the later period, by A. Dobroklonsky, *Rukovodstvo po istorii russkoi tserkvi,* Riazan-Moscow, 1883–93, 4v; and by the rich first volume of I. Smolitsch, *Geschichte der russischen Kirche, 1700–1917,* Leiden-Cologne, 1964. P. Znamensky, *Rukovodstvo k russkoi tserkovnoi istorii,* Kazan, 1886, is an excellent short history, and provides in many ways the best introduction to the subject. See also G. Fedotov, "Religious Backgrounds of Russian Culture," *CH,* 1943, Mar, 35–51.

Among Roman Catholic appraisals A. Ammann, *Abriss der ostslawischen Kirchengeschichte,* Vienna, 1950 (original in Italian, Turin, 1948) is the most scholarly treatment; J. Danzas, *The Russian Church*, London, 1936, is stimulating, particularly on the role of the sects; and N. Brian-Chaninov, *The Russian Church*, NY, 1930, contains good sections, particularly on Catholic-Orthodox relations by a Russian convert to Catholicism. Also still valuable is A. Palmieri, *La chiesa russa*, Florence, 1908, and the lengthy study by H. Gomez, *La iglesia rusa. Su historia y su dogmatica*, Madrid, 1948. Among Protestant histories see E. Benz, *The Eastern Orthodox Church: Its Thought and Life*, NY, 1963, p; and R. French, *The Eastern Orthodox Church*, London, 1951, for sympathetic treatments by a Lutheran and Anglican scholar respectively. See also A. Oakley, *The Orthodox Liturgy*, London-NY, 1958. General surveys by Orthodox scholars are P. Evdokimov, *L'Orthodoxie* (Neuchâtel-Paris, 1959); S. Bulgakov, *L'Orthodoxie*, 1932; and T. Ware, *The Orthodox Church*, Baltimore, 1963, p. V. Nikol'sky, *Istoriia russkoi tserkvi*, M, 1930, is the only serious effort to write a Marxist history. A. Pawłowski, *Idea Kościoła w ujęciu Rosyjskiej Teologji i Historjozofji*, Warsaw, 1935, is a well-referenced study of the history of the idea of the Church in Russia.

The fullest study of Russian sectarianism is K. Grass, *Die russischen Sekten*, Leipzig, 1907, 2v; but S. Margaritov, *Istoriia russkikh misticheskikh i ratsionalisticheskikh sekt*, Simferopol, 1914, 4th corr. ed. is more succinct and analytical. See also T. Butkevich, *Obzor russkikh sekt i ikh tolkov*, P, 1915, 2d ed. (like Margaritov, a study designed largely to refute the sectarians, but containing valuable material and references, including some not available to Grass). F. Conybeare, *Russian Dissenters*, NY, 1962, p, is detailed, but somewhat unhistorical and out of date. S. Bolshakoff, *Russian nonconformity*, Philadelphia, 1950, is a useful English introduction. There is no comprehensive history of the schismatic or Old Believer tradition, though one is in preparation by S. Zenkovsky. The fullest available treatment (with good bibliography) is that of P. Smirnov, *Istoriia russkogo staroobriadchestva*, P, 1895, 2d corr. ed. For a brief introduction, see K. Plotnikov, *Istoriia russkogo raskola staroobriadchestva*, P, 1914; for the best analysis of the early history of the schism see P. Smirnov, *Vnutrennie voprosy v raskole v XVII veke*, P, 1898, and *Spory i razdeleniia v russkom raskole v pervoi chetverti XVIII v*, P, 1905; also the other monographs and articles by Smirnov, and other materials (much of it mimeographed or published clandestinely by the schismatics themselves) in the catalogue based on the V. Druzhinin collection, covering up to 1917: *Raskol i sektantstvo*, P, 1932. More of the vast material on this subject is referenced in F. Sakharov, *Literatura istorii i oblicheniia russkogo raskola*, Tambov, 1887, P, 1892–1900, 3v. The impact of the Old Believer tradition on Russian culture is assessed (particularly for nineteenth-century literature) in V. Pleyer, *Das russische Altgläubigentum*: *Geschichte, Darstellung in der Literatur*, Munich, 1961; and for Russian religious thought generally, by V. Riabushinsky, *Staroobriadchestvo i russkoe religioznoe chuvstvo*, Joinville le Pont, 1936, (mimeographed without notes). See also G. Strel'bitsky's Orthodox history: *Istoriia russkogo raskola*, Odessa, 1898, 3d ed.

The interaction of Russian and Western religious life is stressed in L. Boissard, *L'Église de Russie*, 1867, 2v; relations with early Protestantism (and with Europe generally) exhaustively treated in D. Tsvetaev, *Protestantstvo i Protestanty v Rossii do epokhi preobrazovanii*, M, 1890; I. Sokolov, *Otnoshenie Protestantizma k Rossii v XVI i XVII vekakh*, M, 1880; and with Catholicism in the monumental work by the Jesuit scholar P. Pierling, *La Russie et le Saint-Siège*, 1901–12, 5v; and the learned but unbalanced work of the East German scholar, E. Winter, *Russland und das Papsttum*, 1960–1, 2v. On the Church in West Russia see I. Chistovich, *Ocherk istorii zapadno-russkoi tserkvi*, P, 1882–4, 2v; on the Church in the Ukraine and its general impact on the Russian Church see K. Kharlampovich's large and rich *Malorossiiskoe vliianie na velikorusskuiu tserkovnuiu zhizn'*, Kazan, 1914.

On Russian monasticism see the old but still basic histories of P. Kazansky, *Istoriia pravoslavnago monashestva na vostoke*, M, 1854–6, 2 parts, and *Istoriia pravoslavnago russkago monashestva*, M, 1855 (covering only up till the founding of the monastery of St. Sergius); also I. Smolitsch, *Russisches Mönchtum*, Würzburg, 1953, with valuable bibliography, and his *Leben und Lehre der Starzen*, Cologne, 1952; Rouët de Journel, *Monachisme et monastères russes*, 1952; and the general inventory and descriptions in L. Denisov, *Pravoslavnye monastyri Rossiiskoi imperii*, P, 1910.

On sainthood see N. Barsukov, *Istochniki russkoi agiografii*, P, 1892; V. Vasil'ev, "Istoriia kanonizatsii russkikh sviatykh," *Cht*, 1893, Kn 3, ch 3, 1–256; E. Golubinsky, *Istoriia kanonizatsii sviatykh v russkoi tserkvi*, M, 1903; V. Kliuchevsky, *Drevnerusskiia zhitiia sviatykh kak istorichesky istochnik*, M, 1871; P. Peeters, "La Canonisation des Saints dans l'Eglise russe," *AB*, XXXIII, 1914, 380–420; G. Fedotov, *Sviatye drevnei Rusi*, Paris, 1931; I. von Kologrivov, *Essai sur la sainteté en Russie*, Bruges, 1953; E. Behr-Sigel, *Prière et sainteté dans l'église russe, suivi d'un essai sur le role du monachisme dans la vie spirituelle du peuple russe*, 1950.

In English there is a valuable anthology of Russian spiritual writings by G. Fedotov, *A Treasury of Russian Spirituality*, NY, 1948; a popular study by Constantin de Grunwald, *Saints of Russia*, London, 1960; and N. Gorodetzky, *The Humiliated Christ in Modern Russian Literature*, London, 1938. Robert Payne, *The Holy Fire: The Story of the Eastern Church*, London, 1958, offers a good popular introduction (with English-language bibliography) to the early Eastern fathers who played a key role in the development of Russian Orthodox thought. N. Zernov, *Eastern Christendom*, London, 1961, fits Russian Christendom into its broader context and supplies a good English-language bibliography. An invaluable study of the Byzantine background is provided by H. Beck, *Kirche und theologische Literatur im Byzantinischen Reich*, Munich, 1959.

On Church law see G. Rozenkampf, *Obozrenie kormchei knigi v istoricheskom vide*, P, 1839, 2d corr. ed.; N. Kalachov, *O znachenii kormchei v sisteme drevnego russkago prava*, M, 1850; N. Nikol'sky, "K voprosu o zapadnom vliianii na drevnerusskoe tserkovnoe pravo," *BL*, III, 1917; M. Krasnozhen, *Kratky ocherk tserkovnago prava*, Tartu, 1900, with valuable bibliography, and *Inovertsy na Rusi*, Tartu, 1903, 3d corr. ed., for the status and role of non-Orthodox. See also the doctoral thesis of the recently deceased Metropolitan Nicholas of Moscow, N. Yarushevich, *Tserkovny sud v Rossii do izdaniia Sobornogo Ulozheniia Alekseia Mikhailovicha*, P, 1917.

For a well-organized doctrinal study see F. Gavin, *Some Aspects of Contemporary Greek Orthodox Thought*, Milwaukee-London, 1923. More recent research is incorporated in Iōannēs Karmirēs, *Ta Dogmatika kai Symvolika Mnēmeia tēs orthodoxou katholikēs ekklēsias*, Athens, 1952–3, 2v, (2d ed. 1960). The catechistic and doctrinal works of the Russian Church do not have the status of infallible dogmatic pronouncement, and often reflect the peculiar concerns and features of an age. Concise and reasonably up-to-date treatments are D. Sokolov, *Kratkoe uchenie o bogosluzhenii pravoslavnoi tserkvi*, P, 1915, 37th ed.; and I. Zhilov, *Pravoslavno-khristianskoe katekhizicheskoe uchenie*, Tartu, 1919, 3d corr. ed. For an English text of the longer and shorter catechisms together with other basic documents see R. Blackmore, *The Doctrine of the Russian Church*, London, 1845. See also S. Salaville, *An Introduction to the Study of Eastern Liturgies*, London, 1938; and the official publication of the Moscow Patriarchate, *The Russian Orthodox Church Organization, Situation, Activity*, M, 1958. For a critical examination of Russian mysticism see V. Yankelevich, "Les Thèmes mystiques dans la pensée russe contemporaine," in *Mélanges Paul Boyer*, 1925.

3. THE DEVELOPMENT OF POLITICAL IDEAS

M. Kovalevsky, *Russian Political Institutions*, Chicago, 1902, provides a valuable synoptic treatment, which is not, however, always reliable in detail. Another brief introduction is S. Utechin, *Russian Political Thought*, NY, 1963, p. M. Cherniavsky, *Tsar and People*, New Haven, Conn., 1961, is a stimulating and learned, if somewhat historically blurred treatment of the image of tsardom through the ages. Also interesting is the work of the revolutionary-turned-reactionary, Leo Tikhomirov, *Russia, Political and Social*, London, 1888, 2v.

Valuable collections of essays on predominately political questions may be found in E. Simmons, ed., *Continuity and Change in Russian and Soviet Social Thought*, Cambridge, Mass., 1955; and C. Black, ed., *The Transformation of Russian Society*, Cambridge, Mass., 1960; the issue ed. by R. Pipes on "The Russian Intelligentsia" of *Daedalus*, 1960, summer; J. Curtiss, ed., *Essays in Russian and Soviet History* in honor of Gerold Tanquury Robinson, NY, 1963; the edition of *HSS*, IV, 1957, printed in honor of M. Karpovich. See also V. Al'tman, ed., *Iz istorii sotsial'no-politicheskikh idei*, M, 1955; R. Tucker, *The Soviet Political Mind*, NY, 1963, p; and P. Mosely, ed., *The Soviet Union 1922–1962*, NY, 1963, p (articles reprinted from *FA*).

On the earlier period see M. Shakhmatov, *Opyty po istorii drevnerusskikh politicheskikh idei*, Prague, 1927; V. Val'denberg, *Drevnerusskie ucheniia o predelakh tsarskoi vlasti. Ocherki russkoi politicheskoi literatury ot Vladimira Sviatogo do kontsa XVII veka*, P, 1916; and books and articles by M. Priselkov, L. Goetz, and M. D'iakanov—particularly and respectively their *Ocherki po tserkovno-politicheskoi istorii Kievskoi Rusi X–XII vv*, P, 1913; *Staat und Kirche in Altrussland, 988–1240*, 1908; and *Ocherki obshchestva i gosudarstvennogo stroia drevnei Rusi*, P, 1912, 4th ed. (also available in German). For an eccentric interpretation see V. Alekseev, *Narodovlastie v drevnei Rusi*, Rostov/Don, 1904. For valuable legal documents see G. Vernadsky, ed., *Medieval Russian Laws*, New Haven, Conn., 1947. For an erudite, if at times overextended, effort to read later traditions of "publicistic" controversy into the literature of the Kievan and Muscovite periods respectively see I. Budovnits, *Obshchestvenno-politicheskaia mysl' drevnei Rusi*, M, 1960, and *Russkaia publitsistika XVI veka*, M-L, 1947. For a stimulating, if at times fanciful, "Eurasian" attempt to prove that the conception of politics in pre-Petrine Russia was "broader" and more humane in Russia than in the West, see M. Shakhmatov, "Opyt istorii gosudarstvennykh idealov v Rossii," *Evraziisky Vremennik*, Paris, III, 55–80, and IV, 268–304. For the structure of pre-Petrine government see V. Stroev, *Ocherki gosudarstva moskovskago pered reformami*, Rostov/Don, 1903; also S. Veselovsky's short *Prikazny stroi upravleniia Moskovskogo Gosudarstva*, Kiev, 1912; A. Lappo-Danilevsky, "L'Idée de l'état et son évolution en Russie depuis les troubles du XVIIe siècle jusqu'aux réformes du XVIIIe," in P. Vinogradoff, ed., *Essays in Legal Theory*, Oxford, 1913, 356–83. G. De Vollan, *Istoriia obshchestvennykh i revoliutsionnykh dvizhenii v sviazi s kul'turnym razvitiem russkago gosudarstva*, M-P, 1913–6, covers to the mid-eighteenth century.

For the imperial period, see S. Zezas, *Études historiques sur la legislation russe, ancienne et moderne*, 1862; A. Blok's excellent *Politicheskaia literatura v Rossii i o Rossii*, Warsaw, 1884; and S. Svatikov, *Obshchestvennoe dvizhenie v Rossii 1700–1895*, Ann Arbor, 1963, repr. The increasing development and rationalization of Russian law is discussed in I. Ditiatin, *Stat'i po istorii russkogo prava*, P, 1895 (particularly rich on the eighteenth century); V. Sergeevich, *Lektsii i issledovaniia po drevnei istorii russkogo prava*, P, 1910; A. Filippov, *Uchebnik istorii russkogo prava*, Tartu, 1912, 4th corr. ed.; L. Schultz, *Russische Rechtsgeschichte von den Anfängen bis zur Gegenwart*, Lahr, 1951; and V. Leontovich, *Geschichte des Liberalismus in Russland*, Frankfurt/M., 1957 (stressing the *Rechtsstaat* tradition). H. Dorosh, *Russian Constitutionalism*, NY, 1944, is a useful brief survey from the early *veche* tradition to the Revolution of 1905. See also S. Kucherow, *Courts, Lawyers, and Trials under the Last Three Tsars*, NY, 1953; and M. Szeftel, "The Form of Government of the Russian Empire Prior to the Constitutional Reforms of 1905–06," in Curtiss, *Essays*, 105–10.

4. Secular Enlightenment

A valuable general introduction is A. Lappo-Danilevsky, "The Development of Science and Learning in Russia," in J. Duff, ed., *Russian Realities and Problems*, Cambridge, 1917, 153–229. For the history of education see W. Johnson, *Russia's Educational Heritage*, Pittsburgh, 1950; N. Hans, *Russian Educational Policy, 1701–1917*, London, 1931; V. Simkhovich, "History of the School in Russia," *Educational Review*, 1907, Mar; and (for pedagogic theory from Catherine the Great to Stalin) L. Forese, *Ideengeschichtliche Triebkräfte der russischen und sowjetischen Pädagogik*, Heidelberg, 1956. Also P. Kapterev, *Istoriia russkoi pedagogii*, P, 1915, 2d corr. and exp. ed. S. Rozhdestvensky,

Ocherki po istorii sistem narodnogo prosveshcheniia v Rossii v XVIII– XIX vekakh, P, 1912, I, is the most detailed of a number of studies of Russian educational history written or edited by Rozhdestvensky.

There are valuable histories of almost every important higher educational institution, society, and seminary in Russia. Especially useful for general thought and culture are P. Pekarsky, *Istoriia Imperatorskoi Akademii nauk*, P, 1870–3, 2v; M. Sukhomlinov, *Istoriia Rossiiskoi Akademii*, P, 1874–88, 8v; V. Grigor'ev, *Imperatorsky S. Peterburgsky universitet v techenie pervykh piatidesiati let ego sushchestvovaniia*, P, 1870; S. Shevyrev, *Istoriia Imperatorskogo Moskovskogo universiteta, 1755–1855*, M, 1855; N. Kulakko-Koretsky, *Aperçu historique des travaux de la société impériale libre économique, 1765–1897*, P, 1897; S. Rozhdestvensky, *Istorichesky obzor deiatel'nosti Ministerstva narodnogo prosveshcheniia, 1802–1902*, P, 1902; A. Yakhontov, *Istorichesky ocherk Imperatorskogo Aleksandrovskogo Litseia*, Paris, 1936; N. Zagoskin, *Istoriia Imperatorskogo Kazanskogo universiteta za pervyia sto let ego sushchestvovaniia, 1804–1904*, Kazan, 1902–6, 4v; E. Petukhov, *Imperatorsky Iur'evsky, byvshy derptsky, universitet za sto let ego sushchestvovaniia (1802–1902)*, Tartu, 1902; and K. Ostrovitianov, *Istoriia Akademii nauk SSSR*, M, 1958–64, 2v, covering to 1917.

For the broader cultural role of the universities see V. Ikonnikov, "Russkie universitety v sviazi s khodom obshchestvennogo obrazovaniia," *VE*, 1876, Sep, 161–206, Oct, 492–550; Nov, 73–132; and for the Marxist view, M. Tikhomirov, ed., *Istoriia Moskovskogo universiteta*, M, 1955, 2v.

Valuable Russian works covering less investigated aspects of educational development are (for elementary and secondary schools) N. Konstantinov and V. Struminsky, *Ocherki po istorii nachal'nogo obrazovaniia v Rossii*, M, 1953, 2d ed.; (for the education of women) E. Likhacheva, *Materialy dlia istorii zhenskago obrazovaniia v Rossii (1086– 1856)*, P, 1899; and (for pre-Petrine literacy and education) F. Uspensky, *Ocherki po istorii vizantiiskoi obrazovannosti na Rusi*, P, 1892; A. Sobolevsky, *Obrazovannost' moskovskoi Rusi XV–XVII vv*, P, 1892; and A. Arkhangel'sky, *Obrazovanie i literatura v moskovskom gosudarstve kontsa XV–XVII vv*, Kazan, 1898–1901, 3v. The more secular views of human nature contained in the forbidden books of pre-nineteenth-century Russia are discussed in detail in M. Sokolov, *Ocherki istorii psikhologicheskikh vozzrenii v Rossii v XI–XVIII vekakh*, M, 1963.

A richly documented, sociologically oriented history of the slow growth of the scientific attitude in Russia is provided by A. Vucinich, *Science in Russian Culture. A History to 1860*, Stanford, 1963. Also useful is N. Figurovsky *et al.*, eds., *Istoriia estestvoznaniia v Rossii*, M, 1957–62, I (3v in 4); B. Kuznetsov's more elementary treatment, *Ocherki istorii russkoi nauki*, M-L, 1940; and the valuable history of technology by V. Danilevsky, *Russkaia tekhnika*, M, 1948, 2d corr. ed. T. Rainov, *Nauka v Rossii XI–XVII vekov*, M-L, 1940, is a classic treatment of the early period. See also A. Petrunkevich, "Russia's Contribution to Science," *Transactions of the Connecticut Academy of Sciences*, XXIII, 1920, 611–41; and A. Zvorikin, "Inventions and Scientific Ideas in Russia: Eighteenth-Nineteenth Centuries," in G. Métraux and F. Crouzet, eds., *The Nineteenth-Century World*, NY, 1963, p, 254–79.

On other aspects of secular thought in the pre-Soviet period see J. Hecker, *Russian Sociology*, NY, 1915; J. Normano, *The Spirit of Russian Economics*, NY, 1944; V. Sviatlovsky, *Istoriia ekonomicheskikh idei v Rossii*, P, 1923, I (no other volumes published), covering principally the impact of the physiocrats and classical school; and *Istoriia russkoi ekonomicheskoi mysli*, M (vol. I, two parts, 1955–8, ed. A. Pashkov, covering to 1861; vol. II, two parts, 1959–60, eds. A. Pashkov, N. Tsagolov, covering through the 1890's). J. Letiche, ed., *A History of Russian Economic Thought*, Berkeley-Los Angeles, 1964 (a frequently inadequate translation of the first part of the first volume of the Pashkov work, covering from the ninth through the eighteenth century).

A general synoptic view of journalism and other informal media of popular enlightenment through the ages may be gained by reading, successively, A. Poppé, "Dans la Russie mediévale, X^e–XVIIe siècles: écriture et culture," *AESC*, 1961, Jan-Feb, 12–35; A. Karpov, *Azbukovniki ili alfavity inostrannykh rechei po spiskam solovetskoi biblioteki*, Kazan, 1877; N. Lisovsky, *Periodicheskaia pechat' v Rossii, 1703–1903*, P, 1903; E. Kluge, *Die russische revolutionäre Presse*, Zurich, 1948; V. Rozenberg, *Iz istorii russkoi pechati*, Prague, 1924; N. Engel'gardt, *Ocherk istorii russkoi tsenzury v sviazi s razvitiem pechati (1703–1903)*, P, 1904; the collaborative work under the general editorship of V. Evgen'ev-Maksimov *et al.*, *Ocherki po istorii russkoi zhurnalistiki i kritiki*, L, 1950, only the first vol. covering the eighteenth and the early nineteenth century, has appeared; also the more elementary work edited by A. Zapadov, *Istoriia russkoi zhurnalistiki XVIII–XIX vekov*, M, 1963.

On historiography see D. Likhachev, *Russkie letopisi i ikh kul'turno-istoricheskoe znachenie*, M-L, 1947; L. Cherepnin, *Russkaia istoriografiia do XIX veka kurs lektsii*, M, 1957; S. Peshtich, *Russkaia istoriografiia XVIII veka*, L, 1961–5, 2v (making use of several unpublished essays by Russian historians); V. Astakhov, *Kurs lektsii po russkoi istoriografii*, Kharkov, 1959–62, 2v (particularly valuable for the second volume, which covers the late nineteenth and the early twentieth century); P. Miliukov, *Glavnyia techeniia russkoi istoricheskoi mysli*, P, 1913, 3d ed.; the work by a professor in the St. Petersburg Theological Academy: M. Koialovich, *Istoriia russkogo samosoznaniia po istoricheskim pamiatnikam i nauchnym sochineniiam*, P, 1901, 3d ed; and the study of nineteenth-century views by N. Kareev, *Filosofiia istorii v russkoi literature*, P, 1912.

See also V. Ikonnikov's vast compilation, *Opyt russkoi istoriografii*, Kiev, 1891–1908, 2v in 4; N. Rubinstein's comprehensive treatment, *Russkaia istoriografiia*, M, 1941 (severely criticized in the High Stalin era); A. Mazour, *Modern Russian Historiography*, Princeton, 1958, 2d rev. ed. (useful discussions of lesser-known eighteenth-century figures and non-Great Russian nineteenth-century historians); I. Gapanovich, *Russian Historiography Outside of Russia*, Peiping, 1935; and M. Tikhomirov, ed., *Ocherki istorii istoricheskoi nauki v SSSR*, M, 1955–63, 3v, which goes only as far as the 1917 revolution. The first volume, edited by M. Tikhomirov, is better than the second and third, edited by M. Nechkina; C. Black, ed., *Rewriting Russian History*, NY, 1962, p. includes a translation of the Soviet critique of the first edition of this collection of articles criticizing Soviet historians. A useful and surprisingly readable guide to source materials for Russian history is *Istochnikovedenie istorii SSSR*, M, 1940, 2v (I, ed. M. Tikhomirov, covers to the end of the eighteenth century; II, ed. S. S. Nikitin, continues to the 1890's).

5. LITERARY CULTURE

A good synoptic view of Russian literature can be gained from reading successively N. Gudzy, *History of Early Russian Literature*, NY, 1949, or D. Chizhevsky, *History of Russian Literature, from the Eleventh Century to the End of the Baroque,* 's Gravenhage, 1960; or R. Picchio, *Storia della letteratura russa antica*, Milan, 1959; D. Mirsky, *A History of Russian Literature*, NY, 1958, p (to 1881), and *Contemporary Russian Literature, 1881–1925*, NY, 1926; and V. Alexandrova, *A History of Soviet Literature, 1917–1962, or from Gorky to Evtushenko*, NY, 1963, p. Also on the Soviet period see G. Struve, *Soviet Russian Literature, 1917–1950*, Norman, Oklahoma, 1951, and L. Labedz and M. Hayward, eds., *Literature and Revolution in Soviet Russia, 1917–1962*, Oxford, 1963. See also N. Nilsson, *Sovjetrysk litteratur 1917–47*, Stockholm, 1948. Comprehensive interpretations are given by A. Stender-Petersen, *Den russiske litteraturs historie*, Copenhagen, 1952, 3v (also in German, Munich, 1957, 2v); and E. Lo Gatto, *Storia della letteratura russa*, Florence, 1950, 4th ed. and *L'estetica e la poetica in Russia*, Florence, 1947. Brief though unreferenced treatment of major figures and topics may be found in W. Harkins, *Dictionary of Russian Literature*, Paterson, N. J., 1959, p.

Various aspects of the modern period are treated uniquely well in L. Maikov, *Ocherki iz istorii russkoi literatury XVII i XVIII vv*, P, 1896; D. Blagoy, *Istoriia russkoi literatury XVIII veka*, M, 1945 (there is also a rev. 4th ed., 1960). D. Ovsianiko-Kulikovsky, *Istoriia russkoi literatury XIX veka*, M, 1908–1911, 5v, repr., Ann Arbor, 1948, is a rich anthology of articles; A. Skabichevsky, *Istoriia noveishei russkoi literatury 1848– 1892*, P, 1897, 3d corr. ed., is an imaginative history of letters during the golden age of the Russian novel by a populist critic; P. Kropotkin, *Ideals and Realities in Russian Literature*, NY, 1916. P. Berkov, *Vvedenie v izuchenie istorii russkoi literatury XVIII veka*, L, 1964, is a uniquely valuable example of literary historiography, offering a fascinating picture of changing critical judgments down to the early 1960's.

G. Struve, *Russkaia literatura v izgnanii: opyt istoricheskogo obzora zarubezhnoi literatury*, NY, 1956, deals with the literature of the emigration. See also N. Brian-Chaninov, *La Tragédie des lettres russes*, 1938; the recent Soviet *Istoriia russkoi literatury*, M-L 1941–56, 10v in 13. B. Gorodetsky, ed., *Istoriia russkoi kritiki*, L, 1958, 2v, is less interesting than the earlier work edited by V. Poliansky and A. Lunacharsky, *Ocherki po istorii russkoi kritiki*, M, 1929–31, 3v; or I. Ivanov, *Istoriia russkoi kritiki*, P, 1898–1900, 4 parts in 2v.

For material on irregularly appearing almanacs and collections see the richly illustrated study by N. Smirnov-Sokol'sky, *Russkie literaturnye al'manakhi i sborniki XVIII–XIX vv*, M, 1964; much material on and bibliographical references to the history of publishing are also included in the illustrated collection *400 let russkogo knigopechataniia*, M, 1964, 2v. The first volume covers the pre-Soviet and the second the Soviet period.

In addition to standard reference works and encyclopedias, much valuable bibliographical material on modern literary figures may be found in S. Vengerov, *Kritiko-biograficheskhy slovar' russkikh pisatelei i uchenykh*, P, 1889–1904, 6v (2d ed. in 2v, P, 1915–16), good only for early letters of the alphabet; N. Rubakin, *Sredi knig*, M, 1911–15, 3v, is rich in discussion and references, arranged by subjects; and A. Mez'er, *Slovarny ukazatel' po knigovedeniiu*, M-L, 1931–3, 2v, for information on periodicals. See also N. Zdobnov, *Istoriia russkoi bibliografii do nachala XX veka*, M, 1955, 3d ed.

Of the many books dealing with the history of the Russian

language see particularly L. Cherepnin, *Russkaia paleografiia*, M, 1956, with ample references; V. Vinogradov's ranging *Ocherki po istorii russkogo literaturnogo iazyka XVII–XIX v*, Leiden, 1949; H. Durnovo, *Ocherki istorii russkogo iazyka*, 's Gravenhage, 1959 (repr. of M, 1924); and G. Vinokur, *Izbrannye raboty po russkomu iazyku*, M, 1959.

On oral traditions and folklore see Yu. Sokolov, *Russian Folklore*, NY, 1950; A. Afanas'ev, *Narodnyia russkiia skazki i legendy*, Berlin, 1922, 2v; W. Ralston, *Russian Folk-Tales*, London, 1873; L. Magnus, *Russian Folk-Tales*, London, 1915; and *Russian Fairy Tales* (commentary by R. Jakobson), NY, 1945: V. Dal, *Poslovitsy russkogo naroda*, M, 1957; I. Illiustrov, *Zhizn' russkogo naroda v ego poslovitsakh i pogovorkakh*, M, 1915, 3d ed. (esp. bibliography 10–39); B. Putilov, ed., *Poslovitsy pogovorki zagadki v rukopisnykh sbornikakh XVIII–XX vekov*, M-L, 1961; D. Sadovnikov, *Zagadki russkogo naroda*, M, 1959 (originally P, 1876) with intr. by V. Anikin, who has also edited *Russkie narodnye poslovitsy, pogovorki, zagadki i detsky fol'klor*, M, 1957. For a selection in English with analysis see A. Guershoon, *Russian Proverbs*, London, 1941. See also M. Speransky, *Russkaia ustnaia slovesnost'*, M, 1917, with valuable bibliography; also his *Istoriia drevnei russkoi literatury*, M, 1914, 2d rev. ed.; A. Pypin, *Istoriia russkoi etnografii*, P, 1890–2, 4v; also his *Istoriia russkoi literatury*, P, 1898–9, 4v; and, for the general impact of folklore on Russian culture of the eighteenth and nineteenth centuries, M. Azadovsky, *Istoriia russkoi fol'kloristiki*, M, 1958, fully documented. See also the collaborative work under the general editorship of V. Adrianova-Peretts *et al.*, *Russkoe narodnoe poeticheskoe tvorchestvo*, M, 1953–6, 2v in 3, covering from the tenth to the early twentieth century. See also D. Zelenin, *Russische (Ostslavische) Volkskunde*, Berlin-Leipzig, 1927; and his rich *Bibliografichesky ukazatel' russkoi etnograficheskoi literatury o vneshnem byte narodov Rossii 1700–1910 gg*, P, 1913. See also M. Poltoratskaia, *Russky fol'klor*, NY, 1964.

6. THE ARTS

On the plastic arts G. Hamilton, *The Art and Architecture of Russia*, London, 1954, is a well illustrated and annotated treatment of the prerevolutionary period. See also T. Rice, *A Concise History of Russian Art*, NY, 1963, p. There are three important illustrated Russian histories of art—all bearing the title *Istoriia russkogo iskusstva:* the old but still valuable work edited by I. Grabar, M, 1910–5, 6v; the more popular two-volume work edited by N. Mashkovtsev, M, 1957–60, has an excellent bibliography; and the more detailed collaborative work under the editorial committee of I. Grabar, V. Kemenov, and V. Lazarev, of which nine volumes have appeared, M, 1953–63, I–VIII (through the first third of the nineteenth century), and XI–XII (1917–41). Two other valuable surveys are E. Lo Gatto, *Gli artisti in Russia*, Rome, 1934–43, 3v; and L. Réau, *L'Art russe*, 1921–2, 2v, with valuable glossary of terms.

On painting, basic works, all illustrated, are N. Kondakov, *Russkaia ikona*, Prague, 1928–33, 4v, condensed as *The Russian Icon*, Oxford, 1927; K. Onasch, *Ikonen*, Gütersloh, 1961, a valuable, frequently almost devotional historical study by an East German scholar with many illustrations not otherwise available; and V. Antonova and N. Mneva, *Katalog drevnerusskoi zhivopisi*, M, 1963, 2v, an exhaustively referenced and illustrated work on the historical and artistic classification of icons. The origins of modern Russian portraiture are traced in E. Ovchinnikova, *Portret v russkom iskusstve XVII veka*, M, 1955; and E. Gollerbakh, *Portretnaia zhivopis' v Rossii XVIII veka*, M-P, 1923. A. Benois, *The Russian School of Painting*, NY, 1916, is a stimulating if impressionistic essay; G. Lukomsky, *History of Modern Russian Painting (1840–1940)*, London, 1945, emphasizing the realist tradition; and V. Fiala, *Die russische realistische malerei des 19. jahrhunderts*, Prague, 1953. For popular engravings see D. Rovinsky's monumental *Russkiia narodnyia kartinki*, P, 1881, 5v (2d ed. P, 1900). On architecture see A. Voyce, *Russian Architecture: Trends in Nationalism and Modernism*, NY, 1948; N. Brunov et al., *Istoriia russkoi arkhitektury*, M, 1956, 2d rev. and exp. ed. For the decorative and peasant crafts respectively see G. Lukomsky, *L'Art décoratif russe*, 1928; and A. Nekrasov, *Russkoe narodnoe iskusstvo*, M, 1924. See also E. Gollerbakh, *Istoriia graviury i litografii v Rossii*, M-P, 1923; A. Sidorov, *Drevnerusskaia knizhnaia graviura*, M, 1951; A. Nekrasov, *Drevnerusskoe izobrazitel'noe iskusstvo*, M, 1937; and G. Sternin, *Ocherki russkoi satiricheskoi grafiki*, M, 1964, covering from early wood prints to the eve of the Bolshevik Revolution. On recent archeology see A. Mongait, *Archeology in the USSR*, M, 1959 (also condensed, NY, 1961, p). On the history of heraldic seals and symbols see E. Kamentseva and N. Ustiugov, *Russkaia sfragistika i geral'dika*, M, 1963. See also, for general cultural impact of art, M. Alpatov, *Russian Impact on Art*, NY, 1950; and O. Wulff, *Die neurussische Kunst im Rahmen der Kulturentwicklung Russlands von Peter dem Grossen bis zur Revolution*, Augsburg, 1932.

On Russian music, an introduction is provided by R. Leonard, *A History of Russian Music*, NY, 1957, which should be supplemented for the earlier period by N. Findeizen, *Ocherki po istorii muzyki v Rossii s drevneishikh vremen do kontsa XVIII veka*, M-L, 1928–9, 2v; and for the modern period by R. Mooser, *Annales de la musique et des musiciens en Russie au XVIII*e *siècle*, Geneva, 1948–51, 3v; G. Abraham and M. Calvocoressi, *Masters of Russian Music*, NY, 1944; G. Abraham, *On Russian Music: Critical and Historical Studies*, NY, 1939; and B. Asaf'ev, *Russian Music from the Beginning of the Nineteenth Century*, Ann Arbor, 1953. See also the history of pre-revolutionary music published by the Moscow Academy of Arts, *Istoriia russkoi muzyki*, M, 1957–60, 3v, with rich bibliography; and the useful general study edited by T. Livanova, M. Pekelis, and T. Popova, *Istoriia russkoi muzyki*, M-L, 1940, 2v.

For the musical stage see V. Cheshikhin, *Istoriia russkoi opery*, Ann Arbor, 1953 (repr. from P, 1905, 2d rev. and exp. ed.) and A. Gozenpud, *Muzykal'ny teatr v Rossii; ot istokov do Glinki*, L, 1959; and R. Hofmann, *Un siècle d'opéra russe (de Glinka à Stravinsky)*, 1946. On the ballet see S. Lifar, *A History of Russian Ballet from its origins to the present day*, London, 1954 (unfortunately without documentation); A. Pleshcheev, *Nash balet, 1673–1896*, P, 1896; and Yu. Bakhrushin, *Istoriia russkogo baleta*, M, 1964 (announced *NK* 1964, no. 9, 44).

For the theater see R. Fülöp-Miller and J. Gregor, *The Russian Theatre, Its Character and History*, Philadelphia, 1930; B. Varneke, *History of the Russian Theatre, Seventeenth through Nineteenth Century*, NY, 1951; M. Slonim, *Russian Theater from the Empire to the Soviets*, Riverside, N. J., 1961. Probably the best single treatment—rich in illustrations and bibliographical references—is E. Lo Gatto, *Storia del teatro russo*, Florence, 1952, 2v. N. Evreinov, *Histoire de la théâtre russe*, 1947, is a valuable short treatment by a twentieth-century Russian playwright. See also V. Vsevolodsky, *Istoriia russkogo teatra*, M-L, 1929, 2v; and the collaborative work under the editorship of G. Berdnikov *et al.*, *Russkie Dramaturgi XVIII–XIX vv*, M-L, 1959–62, 3v. P. Berkov, *Russkaia narodnaia drama, XVII–XX vekov*, M, 1953, provides invaluable texts and commentaries on the popular theater. N. Smirnova, *Sovetsky teatr kukol, 1918–1932*, M, 1963, provides a history and bibliography of the early, as well as the Soviet, puppet theater, 41 ff. and esp. note 68 on 42. More interesting is V. Peretts, *Kukol'ny teatr na rusi*, P, 1895.

7. LINKS WITH EUROPE

Among the works that are of broad interest and go deeper than the usual level of impressionism on this familiar topic are G. Alexinsky, *La Russie et l'Europe*, 1917; D. Groh, *Russland und das Selbstverständnis Europas*, Neuwied, 1961, with an excellent bibliography; also the anthology edited by Groh and D. Chizhevsky, *Europa und Russland*,

Darmstadt, 1959; A. von Schelting, *Russland und Europa im russischen Geschichtsdenken*, Bern, 1948; R. Pletnev, *Entretiens sur la littérature russe des XVIIIe et XIXe siècles*, Montreal, 1964 (containing both Russian and French texts); V. Zenkovsky, *Russian Thinkers and Europe*, Ann Arbor, 1953; H. Roberts, "Russia and the West: A Comparison and Contrast," *ASR*, 1964, Mar, 1–13, also commenting articles by M. Raeff and M. Szeftel; E. Shmurlo, "Vostok i zapad v russkoi istorii," *UZIuU*, 1895, no. 3, 1–37; and E. H. Carr, " 'Russia and Europe' as a theme of Russian history," in R. Pares and A. Taylor, eds., *Essays presented to Sir Lewis Namier*, NY, 1956. Keller's *East Minus West=Zero*, NY, 1962, includes a good deal of information on Western influence in Russia and some interesting cultural maps (66, 181, 219), but is not always accurate and is marred by an excessive desire to minimize native Russian achievement and by a lack of precise documentation. L. Karsavin, *Vostok, Zapad i russkaia ideia*, P, 1922, is a good statement of the opposite "Eurasian" position, which emphasizes the anti-European nature of Russian culture. There is a good deal of fresh material in S. Pushkarev, "Russia and the West: Ideological and Personal Contacts Before 1917," *RR*, 1965, Apr, 138–64. Also, V. Bartold, "Vostok i russkaia nauka," *RM*, VIII, 1915.

Critical guides to the rich literature on Russia compiled by pre-Petrine Western travelers are F. Adelung, *Kritisch-literärische Übersicht der Reisenden in Russland bis 1700*, P, 1846, 2v; V. Kliuchevsky, *Skazaniia inostrantsev o moskovskom gosudarstve*, P, 1918; V. Kordt, *Chuzhozemni podorozhni po skhidnii Evropi do 1700 r*, Kiev, 1926; and T. Arne, *Europa upptäcker Ryssland*, Stockholm, 1944; I. Lubimenko, "Le rôle comparatif des différents peuples dans la découverte et la description de la Russie," *RSH*, 1929, Dec, 37–56; and L. Rushchinsky, *Religiozny byt russkikh po svedeniiam inostrannykh pisatelei XVI i XVII vekov*, *Cht*, 1871, Kn III, ch I, 1–338 (and M, 1871). Particularly useful among the thousands of post-Petrine travelers' accounts is the anthology of impressions compiled by P. Putnam, *Seven Britons in Imperial Russia (1698–1812)*, Princeton, 1952.

Good monographs dealing broadly with the impact of individual countries on Russian development include L. Pingaud, *Les Français en Russie et les Russes en France*, 1896, principally military and court contacts of the late eighteenth and the early nineteenth century; V. Kordt, *Doneseniia poslannikov respubliki soedinennykh Niderlandov pri russkom dvore*, P, 1902, especially the introduction on Russo-Dutch links up to 1631; J. Scheltema, *Rusland en de Nederlanden, beschouwd in derzelver wederkeerige betrekkingen*, Amsterdam, 1817–9; A. Florovsky, *Chekhi i vostochnye slaviane: ocherki po istorii cheshsko-russkikh otnoshenii (X–*

XVIII vv), Prague, 1935–47, 2v with rich references; A. Steuart, *Scottish Influences in Russian History*, Glasgow, 1913, from the end of the sixteenth to the beginning of the nineteenth century; M. Anderson, *Britain's Discovery of Russia, 1553–1815*, NY, 1958; M. Radovsky, *Iz istorii anglo-russkikh nauchnykh sviazei*, M, 1961, from Lomonosov to Mendeleev; M. Laserson, *The American Impact on Russia: Diplomatic and Ideological, 1784–1917*, NY, 1950; D. Hecht, *Russian Radicals Look to America, 1825–94*, Cambridge, Mass., 1947; and A. Babey, *Americans in Russia, 1776–1917*, NY, 1938, with valuable bibliography; A. Cronia, "The Italian Contribution to Slav Cultural Life," *ER*, 1948, Oct-Nov, 3–21; and *La conoscenza del mondo slavo in Italia: bilancio storico-bibliografico di un millennio*, Padua, 1958; M. J. Fucilla and J. Carrière, *Italian Criticism of Russian Literature*, Columbus, Ohio, 1938 (a bibliography including many short studies not referenced elsewhere); M. Tikhomirov, "Istoricheskie sviazi russkogo naroda s iuzhnymi slavianami s drevneishikh vremen do poloviny XVII veka," in *Slaviansky sbornik*, M, 1947, 125–201; K. Grigor'ian, "Iz istorii russko armianskikh kul'-turnykh sviazei, X–XVII vekov," *TODL*, IX, 1953, 323–36; and A. Shepeleva, "K istorii sviazei Gruzii s Rossiei v X–XVII vekakh," *TODL*, IX, 1953, 297–322; to be supplemented for later periods by Z. Avalov, *Prisoedinenie Gruzii k Rossii*, P, 1902; K. Forstreuter, *Preussen und Russland von den Anfängen des deutschen Ordens bis zu Peter dem Grossen*, Göttingen-Berlin-Frankfurt/M., 1955. J. Badalić, ed., *Hrvatska Svjedočanstvo o Rusiji*, Zagreb, 1945.

Noteworthy studies relating literary influences to the entire development of culture are T. Potanin, *Vostochnye motivy v srednevekovom evropeiskom epose*, M, 1899; A. Veselovsky's rich and stimulating *Zapadnoe vliianie v novoi russkoi literature*, M, 1916, 5th exp. ed.; A. Rogalski covers literary links with Poland, France, England, and Germany and provides a good bibliography in *Rosja-Europa*, Warsaw, 1960; E. Haumant, *La Culture française en Russie 1700–1900*, 1910 (2d corr. ed., 1913); E. Simmons, *English Literature and Culture in Russia (1553–1840)*, Cambridge, Mass., 1935; V. Kiparsky, *Norden i den ryska skönlitteraturen*, Helsinki, 1947; D. Chizhevsky, *Aus zwei Welten: Beiträge zur Geschichte der slavischwestlichen literarischen Beziehungen*, 's-Gravenhage, 1956; M. Alekseev, *Ocherki iz istorii anglo-russkikh literaturnykh otnoshenii (XI–XVII vv)*, L, 1937; and his *Ocherki istorii ispano-russkikh literaturnykh otnoshenii XVI–XIX vv*, L, 1963. A broad range of foreign influences on Russian painting is examined, albeit rather cursorily, in A. Grishchenko, *O sviaziakh russkoi zhivopisi s Vizantiei i zapadom XIII–XX vv*, M, 1913. For Western influence on Russian poetry see I. Sozonovich, *K voprosu o zapadnom vliianii na slavianskuiu i russ-kuiu poeziiu*, Warsaw, 1878. V. Koroliuk, ed., *Slaviano-germanskie otno-sheniia*, M, 1964, is a collection of articles with rich bibliography. This is one of a series of recent studies written or edited by Koroliuk on Russian links with its Slavic and Germanic neighbors to the West.

Important general studies of pre-Petrine Western influence are S. Platonov, *Moskva i zapad v XVI i XVII vekakh*, Berlin, 1926; V. Kliu-chevsky, "Zapadnoe vliianie i tserkovny raskol v Rossii XVII v. (istoriko-psikhologichesky ocherk)," in *VFPs*, 1897, Jan-Feb (also *Ocherki i rechi*, P, 1918, 373–453); A. Brückner, *Die Europäisierung Russlands*, Gotha, 1888; A. Zimin, V. Pashuto, eds., *Mezhdunarodnye sviazi Rossii do XVII v, sbornik statei*, M, 1961; P. Berkov, "Ostslavische Studenten an deut-schen Hochschulen in der vorpetrinischen Zeit," *ZSPh*, XXX, 2, 1962, 351–74; and G. Stökl, "Russland und Europa vor Peter dem Grossen," *HZ*, 1957, Dec, 531–54.

8. General Histories and Anthologies

Among general histories, still the richest in detail (up to its terminal point of 1780) is S. Solov'ev's twenty-nine-volume *Istoriia Rossii s drev-neishikh vremen*, the first volume of which appeared in 1851; the first com-plete edition appeared in 1893–5; and it is now being reprinted with added commentary under the editorship of L. Cherepnin in a fifteen-volume edition, of which the first twenty-four parts (in 12 volumes) have appeared, M, 1959–64. V. Kliuchevsky, "Kurs russkoi istorii" in *Sochi-neniia*, M, 1956–8, I–V (with valuable notes and a better version of V than appeared in earlier Russian editions) goes deeper in social analysis than Solov'ev, and continues to the reign of Alexander II. The English transla-tion, *A History of Russia*, NY, 1911–31, 5v, is unreliable. S. Platonov, *Histoire de la Russie des origines à 1918*, 1929, is probably the best one-volume history, though it follows a somewhat traditional and narrative framework. (His English-language *History of Russia*, NY, 1929, is a dif-ferent, more elementary treatment.) N. Riasanovsky, *A History of Russia*, Oxford, 1963, is perhaps the fullest on cultural matters of the many com-prehensive one-volume histories in English. B. Sumner, *Survey of Russian History*, London, 1947, 2d rev. ed., contains the most information and richest documentation. See also M. Florinsky, *Russia: A History and an In-terpretation*, NY, 1953, 2v; D. Mirsky's stimulating *Russia, a Social His-tory*, London, 1931; J. Mavor, *An Economic History of Russia*, NY, 1925, 2v, 2d ed. Invaluable for social history is J. Blum, *Lord and Peasant in Russia from the Ninth to the Nineteenth Century*, Princeton, 1961 (NY,

1964, p), with full documentation. Great importance is attached to the river routes in R. Kerner, *The Urge to the Sea: The Course of Russian History*, Berkeley-Los Angeles, 1942. M. Pokrovsky, *History of Russia from the Earliest Times to the Rise of Commercial Capitalism*, NY, 1931; and E. Stählin, *La Russie des origines à la naissance de Pierre le Grand*, 1946, offer contrasting one-volume treatments of the same subject from an extreme Marxist and a conventional conservative point of view respectively. (Both are condensations of longer works, originally in Russian and German respectively). For the later period, the two may again be contrasted in Stählin's *Geschichte Russlands von den Anfängen bis zur Gegenwart*, Berlin, 1923–39, particularly the last three of the four volumes; and Pokrovsky's *Brief History of Russia*, NY, 1933, 2v. Concise and critical (though unfortunately without documentation) is P. Kovalevsky, *Manuel d'histoire russe*, 1948.

Also valuable are these: for the early period see the four volumes that have so far appeared of G. Vernadsky and M. Karpovich, *A History of Russia*, all written by Vernadsky, with full documentation, and published in New Haven: I. *Ancient Russia*, 1943; II. *Kievan Russia*, 1948; III. *The Mongols and Russia*, 1953; and IV. *Russia at the Dawn of the Modern Age*, 1959; for internal developments of the imperial period see the composite émigré history edited by P. Miliukov, C. Seignobos, and L. Eisenmann, *Histoire de la Russie*, 1932–3, 3v; A. Leroy-Beaulieu, *The Empire of the Tsars and the Russians*, NY, 1898, 3v; and A. Kornilov, *Modern Russian History*, 1916–7, 2v. Valuable information, with indexes and supplementary maps, is mixed in with uneven and generally unimaginative texts in the volumes that have thus far appeared in the Soviet historical series *Och*.

Valuable on the subject of cultural and ideological developments is E. Shmurlo, *Istoriia Rossii*, Munich, 1922; also his *Kurs russkoi istorii*, Prague, 1931–5, 3v; W. Walsh, *Russia and the Soviet Union*, Ann Arbor, 1958; and, for the modern period, S. Pushkarev, *The Emergence of Modern Russia 1801–1917*, NY, 1963 (with a rich bibliography).

Valuable historical maps can be found in *Atlas istorii SSSR*, M, 1955, two parts (designed for use in secondary schools); and a host of invaluable illustrations are in M. Dovnar-Zapol'sky, ed., *Istoriko-kul'turny atlas po russkoi istorii*, Kiev, 1913–4, 3v, 2d ed. (with explanatory texts by N. Polonskaia). See also the illustrated *Atlas historique et culturel de la Russie et du Monde Slave*, Brussels, 1961 (German edition, Munich, 1964). M. Florinsky, *Encyclopedia of Russia and the Soviet Union*, NY, 1961, is the most comprehensive and up-to-date English-language reference work.

Basic histories of important related areas are A. Vasiliev, *History of the Byzantine Empire*, Madison, Wis., 1958, 2v, p, with excellent bibliography; G. Ostrogorsky, *History of the Byzantine State*, New Brunswick, N. J., 1957; W. Reddaway *et al.*, eds., *Cambridge History of Poland*, Cambridge, 1941, 2v; M. Liubavsky, *Istoriia Litvy*, M, 1911; W. Allen, *The Ukraine: A History*, Cambridge, 1941; and from a more nationalistic viewpoint, M. Hrushevsky, *A History of the Ukraine*, New Haven, 1941 (tr. of 1911 ed.); S. Dubnov, *History of the Jews in Russia and Poland, from the Earliest Times until the Present Day*, Philadelphia, 1916-20, 3v, can be usefully supplemented on cultural matters by Yu. Gessen, *Istoriia evreiskogo naroda v Rossii*, L, 1925-7, 2d ed., 2v. (The first volume should be consulted in the first edition, P, 1914, which has a good bibliography, and fuller treatment of the earlier period.)

A comprehensive direct exposure to Russian thought and letters can be gained from such English-language anthologies as S. Zenkovsky's valuable *Medieval Russia's Epics, Chronicles and Tales*, NY, 1963, p, with good introduction; L. Wiener, *Anthology of Russian Literature from the Earliest Period to the Present Time*, NY-London, 1902–3, 2v; H. Kohn, *The Mind of Modern Russia*, NY, 1962, p; B. Guerney, *The Portable Russian Reader*, NY, 1961, p; J. Cournos, *A Treasury of Russian Humor*, NY, 1943; G. Noyes, *Masterpieces of the Russian Drama*, NY, 1933; A. Yarmolinsky, *A Treasury of Great Russian Short Stories, Pushkin to Gorky*, NY, 1944; also his *A Treasury of Russian Verse*, NY, 1949; F. Reeve, *An Anthology of Russian Plays*, NY, 1961, 2v, p, (I covers 1790–1890, with a good introduction, 1963, and II goes up to the present.) T. Anderson, *Masters of Russian Marxism*, NY, 1963, p, presents both approved and condemned figures. N. von Bubnoff, *Russische Religionsphilosophen: Dokumente*, Heidelberg, 1956, contains interesting and often inaccessible philosophic writings of the nineteenth and twentieth centuries, as does the collection of speculative theological ideas by A. Schmemann, *Ultimate Questions: An Anthology of Modern Russian Religious Thought*, NY, 1965. A comprehensive anthology of Russian philosophical thought since the late eighteenth century is the three-volume work edited by J. Edie, J. Scanlan, and M. Zeldin with the collaboration of G. Kline, *Russian Philosophy*, Chicago, 1965. For earlier philosophy, which was primarily West Russian in origin, see the valuable anthology with bibliography and commentary covering the sixteenth through early ninteenth centuries: V. Serbent, ed., *Iz istorii filosofskoi i obshchestvenno-politicheskoi mysli Belorussii*, Minsk, 1962.

Among books of readings which mix primary and secondary materials, I. Spector and M. Spector, *Readings in Russian History and Cul-*

ture, Boston, 1965; M. Blinoff, *Life and Thought in Old Russia,* University Park, Pa., 1961; S. Harcave, *Readings in Russian History,* NY, 1962, 2v, p; W. Walsh, *Readings in Russian History,* Syracuse, NY, 1950; and most comprehensive of all, T. Riha, *Readings in Russian Civilization,* Chicago, 1964, 3v, p; on the "cursed questions" see S. Zhaba, *Russkie mysliteli o Rossii i chelovechestve,* Paris, 1954.

Particular use has been made in this study of five Russian-language anthologies: N. Gudzy, *Khrestomatiia po drevnei russkoi literature XI–XVII vekov,* M, 1955; A. Alferov and A. Gruzinsky, *Russkaia literatura XVIII veka, Khrestomatiia,* M, 1908, 2d rev. and exp. ed.; N. Ashukin and M. Ashukina, *Krylatie Slova,* M, 1960, 2d exp. ed., a useful anthology of familiar Russian phrases, complete with short essays on their derivations; A. Stender-Petersen, *Anthology of old Russian Literature,* NY, 1954; and the collection of songs by I. Rozanov, *Russkie pesni,* M, 1952.

REFERENCES

PREFACE

1. *Webster's Second New International Dictionary*, unabridged (Springfield, Mass., 1959), 643: a somewhat more succinct definition than that given in the third edition, but not at variance with it, or with the use of the term by Malinovsky (*ESS*, IV, 621-46) or its definition by Ushakov (*TSRIa*, I, 1546) and by current Soviet lexicography as "the complex of accomplishments of a human society in its productive, social and mental life." (*SSRIa*, V, 1827).

2. These three usages are to be found, respectively, in Oswald Spengler's *Decline of the West;* in widespread popular usage in both the West and the USSR; and in Pitirim Sorokin, *Social Philosophies in an Age of Crisis*, Boston, 1950, 187 ff.

3. *Webster's Third New International Dictionary*, unabridged (Springfield, Mass., 1961), 552. This is the first edition to include a definition of "cultural history."

4. V. Belinsky, *Izbrannye filosofskie sochineniia*, M, 1941, 163.

5. N. Berdiaev, *Idea*, 2.

6. Berdiaev, *Idea*, 196-7 ff.

7. V. Rozanov, cited in Weidlé, *Russia*, 149.

I. BACKGROUND

1. KIEV

1. V. Adrianova-Peretts, ed., *Povest' vremennykh let*, M, 1950, ch I, 20; N. Voronin, *Drevnerusskie goroda*, M, 1945, 15. See also M. Tikhomirov, *The Towns of Ancient Rus*, M, 1959.

Important works dealing exclusively with the Kievan period are G. Fedotov, *The Russian Religious Mind*, NY, 1960, p (a second volume, to be published posthumously by the Harvard University Press, will cover the early Muscovite period.); M. Karger and N. Voronin, *Istoriia kul'tury drevnei Rusi, domongol'sky period*, M-L, 1948–51 (I deals with material culture, II with social and spiritual culture. Together they represent the first part of a projected history of Russian culture never continued beyond this point); and B. Grekov, *The Culture of Kiev Rus*, M, 1947.

Among more comprehensive Soviet treatments—all stressing national continuity and downgrading Byzantine and Western influences—see particularly V. Mavrodin, *Obrazovanie edinogo russkogo gosudarstva*, L, 1951, which is relatively full in its treatment of the diverse strands in early Russia; and D.

Likhachev, *Kul'tura Rusi epokhi obrazovaniia russkogo natsional'nogo gosudarstva*, L, 1946, which is more clearly focused on cultural matters.

2. Dal, *Poslovitsy*, 329.

3. The eighth century appears to be the earliest sure date (see M. Karger, "Drevny Kiev," in *Po sledam drevnikh kul'tur: drevniaia Rus'*, M, 1953, 44–6), though there were earlier settlements of some kind on the site; and a case can be made for the existence in the region of a continuing civilization based on urban commercial centers in pre-Slavonic as well as pre-Christian times. See M. Rostovtsev, "The Origin of the Russian State on the Dnieper," *Annual Report of the American Historical Association for the Year 1920*, Washington, D.C., 1925, 165–71. The first Russian dynasty and its retinue were almost certainly Scandinavians, but their cultural influence was slight. See N. Riasanovsky, *History*, 25–30, on this much-labored "Normanist" controversy.

4. Documented in N. von Baumgarten, "Généalogies et mariages occidentaux des Rurikides russes du Xᵉ au XIIIᵉ siècle," *OC*, IX, 1927, May, 1–96; the oldest links of all with the West are examined and analyzed by Th. Ediger, *Russlands älteste Beziehungen zu Deutschland, Frankreich und der römischen Kurie*, Halle, 1911. The mission of the Western church to Kiev in the tenth century just prior to the formal acceptance of Eastern Christianity is discussed by M. Daras, "Les Deux Premiers Évêques de Russie," *Irénikon*, III, 1927, 274–7. A fresh examination of the provenance of Kiev, emphasizing the pre-Christian, pre-Slavic settlements appears in M. Braichevsky, *Kodga i kak voznik Kiev*, Kiev, 1964. See also F. Dvornik, "The Kiev State and Its Relations with Western Europe," *TRHS*, XXIX,

1947, 27–46; and B. Lieb, *Rome, Kiev et Byzance à la fin du XIᵉ siècle*, 1924. V. Potin, *Drevniaia Rus' i evropeiskie gosudarstva X–XII vv*, L, 1964, shows trade links on the basis of recent archeological discoveries, including coin deposits. S. Cross, "Medieval Russian Contacts with the West," *Speculum*, 1935, Apr, esp. 143–4, sees Western influence in Novgorod from the time of the building of its first cathedral, and the influence of romanesque architecture extending well into the Russian interior.

For the "material culture" of the early Slavs, balance B. Rybakov's rich but nationalistic *Remeslo drevnei Rusi*, M, 1948, with H. Preidel's characterization of generally similar conditions among the Western Slavs and in central Europe generally: *Slawische Altertumskunde des östlichen Mitteleuropas im 9. und 10. Jahrhundert*, Munich, 1961, part I. For a bibliographically rich historiographical discussion of periodical and geographical divisions within "Eastern Europe," see J. Macůrek, *Dějepisectví evropského východu*, Prague, 1946. For a comprehensive early history of the Slavs that stresses Russia's common patterns of development and links with the West, see F. Dvornik, *The Slavs: Their Early History and Civilization*, Boston, 1956; also his subsequent work which in effect continues the story from the thirteenth to the early eighteenth century, *The Slavs in European History and Civilization*, New Brunswick, N.J., 1962, with full bibliography. See also V. Koroliuk, *Zapadnye slaviane i Kievskaia Rus'*, M, 1964.

5. *La Chanson de Roland*, v. 3225 (ed. J. Geddes, Jr, London, 1914, 222); *Das Nibelungenlied*, v. 1339–40 (ed. K. Bartsch, H. De Boor, Wiesbaden, 1956, 216). More than sixty references—largely favorable to the Russians—

have been counted in the early *chansons de geste,* as against only four to Poland. See the use made of E. Langlois' study by G. Lozinsky, "La Russie dans la littérature française du moyen âge," *RES,* IX, 1929, 71, note 2; additional examples and references are discussed 71–88, 253–69.

6. L. Cherepnin (*Paleografiia,* 83–111) summarizes the still inconclusive controversies generated by the sudden appearance of two alphabets within a short space of time, and concludes that Glagolitic probably appeared earlier—a conclusion that is presented as the "almost unanimous" view of specialists by F. Dvornik in "The Missions of Cyril and Methodius," *ASR,* 1964, Jun, 197, note 9. I. Shevchenko discusses sceptically the recently advanced idea that this sudden literary effloresence must indicate a pre-Cyrillo-Methodian stage of literary activity in Glagolitic. "Three Paradoxes of the Cyrillo-Methodian Mission," *ASR,* Jun, 235–6, and notes. The discussion in this entire section on the mission (195–236, also includes H. Lunt's "The Beginning of Written Slavic" and a short final statement by F. Dvornik) provides a valuable commentary and rich documentation of the extensive recent scholarship on the mission. Dvornik points out (here, 210–1, and in "Les Bénédictins et la christianisation de la Russie," *L'Église et les églises,* Chevetogne, 1954, 323–49) that in Catholic Bohemia prior to the dominance of centralizing tendencies in Rome, particularly under the pontificate of Gregory VII in the late eleventh century, the Slavonic liturgy existed side by side with the Latin, and that Benedictines made many of the copies of Slavonic texts, which were then transposed and uniquely preserved in Russian manuscripts.

7. Voronin, *Goroda,* 16–7. The pioneering study of Byzantine influence in Russia by V. Ikonnikov, *Opyt issledovaniia o kul'turnom znachenii Vizantii v russkoi istorii,* Kiev, 1869, overstated the case, considering Russia virtually part of the Eastern Empire until its collapse. Many subsequent Russian historians (and almost all in the Soviet period) have leaned far in the other direction to minimize the impact of Byzantium. They went so far in the High Stalin era as to contend that the Santa Sophia in Kiev was shaped after pre-Christian burial mounds, that the thickness of its pillars, pilasters, and apses gave expression to popular Russian feelings for the "materiality" and "bodily character" of buildings. N. Brunov, "Kievskaia Sofiia—drevneishy pamiatnik russkoi kamennoi arkhitektury," *VV,* III, 1950, esp. 184, 186.

A balanced appraisal of Byzantine influence can be found in the works of Byzantinists of Slavic extraction. The problem posed by A. Vasiliev in "Was Old Russia a Vassal State of Byzantium?" *Speculum,* 1932, Jul, 350–60, is somewhat more fully dealt with in G. Ostrogorsky, "Die Byzantinische Staatenhierarchie," *SKP,* VII, 1936, 41–61. For more general impact see D. Obolensky, "Russia's Byzantine Heritage," *OSP,* I, 1950, 37–63 and "Byzantium, Kiev and Moscow: a Study in Ecclesiastical Relations," *DOP,* XI, 1957, 23–78; and F. Dvornik, "Byzantium and the North," and "Byzantine Influence in Russia," in M. Huxley, ed., *The Root of Europe,* London, 1952, 85–106; and "Byzantine Political Ideas in Kievan Russia," *DOP,* IX–X, 1956, 73–121. For comparative purposes see G. Ostrogorsky, "Byzantium and the South Slavs," *SEER,* 1963, Dec, 1–14. For a well-documented, synoptic treatment that likens the relations of the Slavs with Byzantium to that of the Germanic tribes with the Western

Roman Empire, see the excellent *Vorspiel* of a larger work by the Bulgarian scholar I. Duichev, *Les Slaves et Byzance,* Sofia, 1960.

For a critical analysis of Soviet attitudes on Byzantine influences see I. Shevchenko, "Byzantine Cultural Influences," in Black, ed., *Rewriting,* 143–97; also A. Florovsky, "K izucheniiu istorii russko-vizantiiskikh otnoshenii," *BS,* XIII, 2, 1952–3, 301–11. Somewhat more balance is attained in such works of the post-Stalin period as M. Levchenko, *Ocherki po istorii russko-vizantiiskikh otnoshenii,* M, 1956, with intr. by M. Tikhomirov; also D. Likhachev, *Kul'tura russkogo naroda X–XVII vv,* M-L, 1961, in contrast to some of his earlier works.

8. Chizhevsky, *History,* 33.

9. G. Florovsky, "The Problem of Old Russian Culture, "*ASR,* 1962, Mar, 14.

10. S. Zenkovsky, *Epics,* 67–8. See also Fedotov, *Mind,* 373, for the importance attached by Andrew Bogoliubsky to the beauty of Orthodox worship in impressing and evangelizing the Russian north.

11. A. Grabar, "Cathédrales multiples et groupements d'églises en Russie," *RES,* XX, 1942, 91–120; Znamensky, *Rukovodstvo,* 78–9; I. Likhnitsky, *Osviashchenny sobor v Moskve v XVI–XVII vekakh,* P, 1906.

12. Voronin, *Goroda,* 15. For other comments by Thietmar, Bishop of Merseburg, see his chronicle in *MGH,* IX, 1935, 488, 528–32. His statement that there were "more than 400 churches" in Kiev in 1018 (530) probably qualifies him as the first in the long line of Western reporters to produce exaggerated statistics of Russian accomplishments; and it does not strengthen the otherwise credible contention of H. Paszkiewicz (*The Making of the Russian Nation,* London, 1963, 94) that the Christianization of Russia was taking place from a variety of sources and that Christian churches were actually built in Kiev before Vladimir's conversion. Concrete evidence of the minor influence of Western Christianity may be found in Vladimir's institution of tithing (in a manner not completely identical with the West, but quite unknown in Byzantium). See A. Presniakov, *Lektsii po russkoi istorii I. Kievskaia Rus',* M, 1938, 114–5 and other referenced material note 1.

13. Gudzy, *Khrestomatiia,* 60.

14. Fedotov, *Mind,* 263.

15. N. Volkov, "Statisticheskiia svedeniia o sokhranivshikhsia drevnerusskikh knigakh XI-XIV vekov i ikh ukazatel'," *PDP,* CXXIII, 1897, 24. This figure is incorrectly reproduced and inadequately referenced in Cherepnin, *Paleografiia,* 130.

16. See citations and discussion in Shchapov, *Sochineniia,* II, 586–7.

17. See discussion and references in Gudzy, *History,* 96–113, 225. For writings see S. Zenkovsky, *Epics,* 87–102. The valuable discussion of Theodosius, Boris, and Gleb in Fedotov, *Mind,* 94–157, considers them as seminal figures in a distinctively Russian form of "kenotic" spirituality, emphasizing a life of service and self-emptying love in imitation of Christ and in full expectation of persecution and suffering as against more traditional forms of Eastern asceticism.

Efforts to read Soviet virtues retroactively into figures of the past sometimes become almost ludicrous. Boris and Gleb become patriots and fighters for peace "warding off by ideological means, the perils threatening the government." (Budovnits, *Mysl',* 20, 162–3). Russian icons of St. George are said to be less conceited and warlike and "without that unrestrained boldness . . . [and] provocative fervor" of the picture as painted by other nations. M. Alpatov, "Obraz Georgii-voina v iskusstve Vizantii i drevnei Rusi," *TODL*, XII, 1956, 310. (There is *some* truth in this.)

18. Epiphanius the Wise in Shchapov, *Sochineniia*, II, 584–5.

19. N. Trubetskoy, "Introduction to the History of Old Russian Literature," *HSS*, II, 1954, 93. This is one of the best short introductions to Old Russian culture, 91–103.

20. V. Zenkovsky, *History*, I, 37.

21. Fedotov, *Mind*, 382.

22. The study which unravels most systematically and successfully the veiled propaganda and polemics contained in the chronicles is M. Priselkov, *Istoriia russkogo letopisaniia XI–XV vv*, L, 1940. See also Tikhomirov, ed., *Ocherki istorii istoricheskikh nauk*, 49 ff. and a forthcoming study of the chronicles by J. Fennell.

On Schlözer and his fascination with Russian chronicles in the late eighteenth century, see E. Winter, *August Ludwig von Schlözer und Russland*, 1961, esp. 45 ff.; also *BE*, LXXVIII, 698–701; and H. Butterfield, *Man on His Past*, Cambridge, 1955, 32–61, esp. 56–9, where Schlözer's edition of the Nestor chronicle is seen as a decisive landmark in the development of modern historical study. For favorable comparison of Russian to Western chronicles see S. Volkonsky, *Pictures*, 43–4.

23. For analysis and references on this popular early-twelfth-century account by Hegumen Daniel of his pilgrimage to the Holy Land see Yu. Glushakova, "O puteshestvii igumena Daniila v Palestinu," in *Problemy obshchestvenno-politicheskoi istorii Rossii i slavianskikh stran: sbornik statei k 70-letiiu akademika M. N. Tikhomirova*, M, 1963, 79–87, esp. 85–6. Also Gudzy, *History*, 114–17.

On the controversial stairwell frescoes see A. Grabar, "Les Fresques des escaliers à Sainte-Sophie de Kiev et l'iconographie impériale byzantine," *SKP*, VII, 1935, 103–17.

24. For secular literature included in holy writings see Tikhomirov, *Towns*, 291–300; and, in the *Lay*, V. Rzhiga, "Slovo o polku Igoreve i russkoe iazychestvo," *Slavia*, XIII, 1933–4, 422–33.

There has been a return recently in some scholarly circles to the position that has been periodically advanced for more than a century that the *Lay* is in fact an eighteenth-century forgery. Whereas a few years ago most seemed to acquiesce in the insistence on authenticity of Soviet scholars (see, for instance, Gudzy's belligerent summary of the controversy, *History*, 149–58), and of G. Vernadsky, R. Jakobson, M. Szeftel, and H. Grégoire (*La Geste du Prince Igor*, *AIOS*, VIII, 1945–7, 217–360), doubts have recently been voiced by the émigré Bulgarian Slavicist V. Nikolaev; H. Paszkiewicz, *The Origins of Russia*, London, 1954, 336–53; and H. Taszycki, *RES*, XXXVI, 1959, 23–8. The most sustained new argument for eighteenth-century authorship was advanced by the distinguished Soviet medievalist A. Zimin, who defended his position in a lively session of the Academy of Sciences on Jun 23–24, 1964. The printed account of the proceedings (*VI*, 1964, no. 9, 119–40) does not present Zimin's arguments in a favorable light; and his principal opponent, D. Likhachev, has inveighed further against his thesis in "Kogda bylo napisano 'Slovo o polku Igoreve'?" *VL*, 1964, no. 8, 132–60.

Until all the evidence and argumentation of Zimin and others is made public and subjected to disinterested examination, the historian is bound to harbor lingering doubts about the authenticity of a medieval epic which was found during a time of national self-consciousness and antiquarian passion in a single manuscript copy, and then lost during the Moscow fire of 1812. Likhachev, however, seems on strong ground with the argument that the particular quality and style of this work would make it an even more unique and anomalous accomplishment for the eighteenth century than for the thirteenth.

Whatever its origin, this relatively short and readable epic is now available in a twentieth-century English version, V. Nabokov, *Song of Igor's Campaign*, NY, 1960, p.

25. D. Likhachev, *Letopisi*, 8.

26. According to the ingenious argument put forth by N. Rozov on the basis of a newly found text of the sermon (of which more than forty separate early manuscript copies have been preserved): "Sinodal'ny spisok sochinenii Ilariona-russkago pisatel'ia XI v," *Slavia*, XXXII, 1963, esp. 141, 147–8.

27. Gudzy, *Khrestomatiia*, 32. S. Zenkovsky, *Epics*, 78–83.

28. Abraham was much influenced by the fourth-century apocalyptical writer Ephrem the Syrian. See S. Rozanov, ed., "Zhitiia prepodobnago Avraamiia Smolenskago i sluzhby emu," *PDL*, vyp I, 1912, 4. Ephrem was to enjoy a continuing influence in Russia, and his example of withdrawing from the world to a cave was one of the models for this form of monastic asceticism in Russia. The tradition of ascetic extremism and an almost masochistic acceptance of filth and self-mortification in Russia is more reminiscent of the Syrian tradition within early Byzantine Christendom and of the primitive monastic tradition of that frequently heretical center of early Christendom.

Our astonishment at this aspect of Syrian (and Russian) asceticism may well reflect the fact that "organized Christianity preferred to forget the beginnings of monasticism and later preferred to paint over them with an ecclesiastical brush." (A. Vööbus, *History of Asceticism in the Syrian Orient*, Louvain, 1958, 169.) Whether or not some form of neo-Manichean dualism was as influential on Russian asceticism as original Manicheanism was on Syria (Vööbus, 109–69 and 152 ff. on Ephrem) remains a question that has never been systematically studied.

It is somewhat surprising that the influence of the Macedonian and Bulgarian Bogomils, the progenitors of many of the dualistic and prophetic heresies of the medieval West, was not greater in early Russia than has yet been demonstrated, because the Eastern Slavs were indebted in many other respects to the region. However, Fedotov minimizes the probability of Bogomil influence (*Mind*, 353–7), viewing Abraham as an idiosyncratic figure 158–75), and E. Anichkov sees almost all of neo-Manichean influence flowing in a westerly direction ("Les Survivances manichéennes en pays slavs et en occident," *RES*, VIII, 1928, 203–25). A Ukrainian student of early Slavic folklore, M. Dragomanov also minimizes Bogomil influence on Russian dualistic thinking and stresses the probability of parallel ideas developing independently in a variety of areas on the basis of older Manichean apocrypha from the East. *Notes on the Slavic Religio-Ethical Legends: The Dualistic Creation of the World*, Bloomington, Ind, 1963, 1–20, and esp. 94–140. This richly annotated study is translated by E. Count from the original Bulgarian manuscript written sometime prior to 1895.

29. Paszkiewicz, *Making*, 281 ff. Despite awkward exposition and considerable a priori antagonism for Great Russian historiography, Paszkiewicz argues persuasively that there was even less national unity in Kievan Russia than in

early Poland and Czechoslovakia, that the only real cohesion was provided by the Orthodox faith, and that the Russo-Soviet idea of a "gathering in" of three different Russian nations "Great," "White," and "Little" reflects late-seventeenth-century Russian imperial propaganda rather than historical reality. See 307, 311–22; also the rich bibliography.

30. See the valuable illustrated study (with French résumé) by V. Lazarev, *Freski staroi Ladogi*, M, 1960.

31. S. Zenkovsky, *Epics*, 122–9, for text; also Gudzy, *History*, 46–50. For a special study of the legend see N. Bokadorov, *Izbornik Kievsky*, Kiev, 1904, 39–94; and for popular engravings illustrating the Virgin's descent see D. Rovinsky, *Kartinki*, P, 1881, IV, 546–9.

32. F. Dvornik, *The Idea of Apostolicity in Byzantium and the Legend of the Apostle Andrew*, Cambridge, Mass., 1958; A. Pogodin, "Povest' o khozhdenii Apostola Andreia v Rusi," *BS*, VII, 1937–8, 128–48; L. Goetz, *Das Kiever Höhlenkloster als Kulturzentrum des vormongolischen Russlands*, Passau, 1904; R. Stupperich, "Kiev–das zweite Jerusalem," *ESPh*, XII, 1935, Dec, 332–54; and A. Sipiagin, "Aux Sources de la piété russe," *Irénikon*, II, 1927, 1–30.

The Andrew legend was, of course, not an ancient one even in Byzantium, first appearing there probably in the eleventh century and, in Russia, in the late twelfth. The discussion by Pogodin suggests that legends of the Christians in the Caucasus may have played a key role in the development of this idea in Russia.

33. For Mongol influences supplement Vernadsky, *Mongols*, 333–90; with M. Cherniavsky, "Khan or Basileus," *JHI*, 1959, Oct–Dec, 459–76; and N. Veselovsky, *Tatarskoe vliianie na posol'sky tseremonial v moskovsky period russkoi istorii*, P, 1911. See also A. Sakharov, "Les Mongols et la civilization russe," in *Contributions à l'histoire russe (Cahiers d'histoire mondiale)*, Neuchâtel, 1958, 77–97. Prostration was, of course, also used in Byzantine ritual.

34. Karl Wittfogel considers prostration "the great symbol of total submission" of Oriental despotism. (*Oriental Despotism: a comparative study of total power*, New Haven, 1957, 152–4). But other characteristics of this type (control of water supply, and so on) do not really seem applicable to Russia, and the whole concept (which includes Byzantium as well as Russia) does not seem rigorous enough to be of much help in explaining Russian peculiarities, let alone in concluding that Mongol influence was as all-pervasive in Russia as the somewhat romantic "Eurasian" school has contended. See the symposium led by Wittfogel on "Russia and the East" in *ASR*, 1963, Dec, 627–62, esp. the rejoinder by N. Riasanovsky, " 'Oriental Despotism' and Russia" and B. Spuler, "Russia and Islam." For earlier links with Islam (from the mid-seventh to late tenth century) see A. Harkavy *Skazaniia musul'manskikh pisatelei o slavianakh i russkikh*, P, 1870; and *dopolneniia*, P, 1871.

35. O. Spengler, *Decline of the West*, NY, 1928, II, 435, mt.

36. *Ibid*.

37. Zenkovsky, *History*, I, 23.

2. THE FOREST

1. G. Florovsky in *ASR*, 1962, Mar, 35. This article and that of D. Likhachev ("Further Remarks on the Problem of Old Russian Culture," *ASR*, 1963, Mar, esp. 115–7) stress the continuities between the

Kievan and Muscovite periods (in contrast to my stress on discontinuity, "Images of Muscovy," *ASR*, 1962, Mar, esp. 24–7). Although the changes are clearly evolutionary rather than mutational (in contrast to the situation in the West depicted in E. Panofsky, *Renaissance and Renascences in Western Art*, Stockholm, 1960, I, 162), there is a real need to modify the relatively rigid mold of integral continuity superimposed by Great Russian historians (partly overreacting to the claims of Polish and Ukrainian nationalist scholars that ancient Kiev really belongs to their national tradition) on a very fragmentary historical record. Professor Florovsky's distinction between changing societies and a relatively unchanging culture implies that the two can be separated more clearly than I would feel to be the case. Architecture—a medium in which the evidence is plentiful and the changes from Kiev–Vladimir to Moscow striking—clearly belongs to both "culture" and "society." Professor Likhachev's contention that historical continuity is proved ˙by the fact that later generations "turned to their own national past" in times of trouble actually weakens his argument. Nostalgic efforts to stress (and artificially create) links with the past are often the best sign that living historical continuity has been broken (see, for instance, E. Panofsky, "Renaissances and Renascences," *KR*, 1944, Spring, esp. 227–9). A continuing sense of history is not the same thing as historical continuity.

2. Lozinsky, "La Russie," 269.

3. V. Mavrodin, *Proiskhozhdenie nazvanii "Rus'," "Russky," "Rossiia,"* L, 1958, 17–19. Note that the references to "Rus'" in the broader sense of the word" occur mainly in the epic literature, and are not prominent in the chronicles.

This broader usage of Rus' expressed a religious rather than a political identity. See Paszkiewicz, *Making*, 313–14, and esp. note 322.

4. Tikhomirov, ed., *Ocherki istoricheskikh nauk*, 59, 65.

5. For recent discussions, see N. Andreev, "Pagan and Christian Elements in Old Russia," *ASR*, 1962, Mar, 16–23, and works referenced 18, note 8; and L. Sadnik, "Ancient Slav Religion in the light of recent research," *ER*, 1948, Apr, 36–43. Also of great value (precisely because it is largely a collection of material rather than an attempt to sustain a theory about pagan influences) is the work of D. Zelenin, "Tabu slov u narodov vostochnoi Evropy i severnoi Azii," *SMAE*, VIII, 1929, part I; and IX, 1930, part II. See also his *Le Culte des idoles en Siberie*, 1952; and Znamensky, *Rukovodstvo*, 11–13.

6. Tikhon Zadonsky, cited in N. Gorodetzky, *Tikhon Zadonsky*, London, 1952, 163. Also, on the importance of Easter, Trubetskoy, "Introduction," 95–6.

7. *Rodina, narod—rod; otechestvo* or *otchizna, otchina* or *votchina—otets*. For various uses of "startsy" (elders) see Brian-Chaninov, *Church*, 102, note 1. It is possible that the verb "to try" *(starat'sia)* comes from this root *(REW*, III, 4).

The patronymic also served as the basis for many family names, which, on the whole, came late to Russia. See B. Unbegaun, "Family Names of the Russian Clergy," *RES*, XXX, 1942, 41–62, and materials noted in his *A Bibliographical Guide to the Russian Language*, Oxford, 1953, 68–72, as well as V. Chichagov, *Iz istorii russkikh imen otechestv i familii*, M, 1959, esp. 109–25.

8. A. Gezen (Heesen), *Istoriia slavianskogo perevoda simvoly very*, P, 1884, 90–102; also Brian-Chaninov, 147–8.

The Slavophil A. Khomiakov first insisted on the importance of the distinction in the course of his polemic controversy with Russian converts to catholicism. See his 1860 "Pis'mo k redaktoru 'l'Union chrétienne' o znachenii slov: 'kafolichesky' i 'soborny,' " in his *PSS*, M, 1900–1907, II, 3d exp. ed., 307–14. Writers like N. Berdiaev (*Russian Idea*, 156–6) saw in *sobornost'* an underlying principle of Russian life in which familial spiritual consensus replaces formal legalisms of all sorts. Despite the vague, romantic usage of the word in both thinkers, the change in the creed combined with the multiple and idiosyncratic early uses of *sobor* above implies some early importance for the concept.

W. Weidlé (*Russia*, 130–4), influenced by such works as S. Aksakov's *Family Chronicle* and L. Tolstoy's *Anna Karenina* and *Family Happiness*, elevates family feeling into a basic Russian characteristic. V. Varshavsky (*Nezamechennoe pokolenie*, NY, 1956, 384) accuses Weidlé of exaggeration, suggesting that his view is more appropriate for China than Russia. N. Arsen'ev, *Iz . . . traditsii*, 15–65, makes a more convincing case for the importance of the family.

9. In the one case where romance is at the center of a Russian epic, *The Life of Peter and Fevronia* (Zenkovsky, *Epics*, 236–47) the emphasis is on the healing and sanctifying loyalty of the wife.

10. See I. Zabelin, *Domashny byt russkikh tsarits v XVI i XVII st*, M, 1869, 299–300; the important study by P. Smirnov, "Znachenie zhenshchiny v istorii vozniknoveniia raskola," *MS*, 1891, Nov-Dec, 330–65; and Claire Claus, *Die Stellung der russischen Frau von der Einführung des Christentums bei den Russen bis zu den Reformen Peter des Grossen*, Munich, 1959.

11. See, for instance, V. Dunham, "The Strong Woman Motif," in C. Black, ed., *Transformation*, esp. 467–75; and the powerful war poem of Boris Slutsky, "Everyone grew weaker. But the women did not weaken . . ." "Schast'e," *NM*, 1956, no. 10, 160.

12. Fedotov, *Mind*, 13 v. On popular terminology for "Tsar" and "Russia" see Cherniavsky, *Tsar*, 93–4, 101 ff. For the *mat'-syra* cult (echoed in the character of Maria Lebiadkin in Dostoevsky's *Possessed*) see in addition to Fedotov, 11–15, V. Komarovich, "Kul't roda i zemli v kniazheskoi srede XI–XIII vv," *TODL*, XVI, 1960, esp. 97–104, and works referenced therein. Note also the special importance of the Mother of God in the earliest religious charms and medallions of Christian Russia. E. de Savitsch, "Religious Amulets of Early Russian Christendom," *GBA*, 1943, Feb, 111–16.

For the presence of similar cults in other primitive civilizations see A. Dieterich, *Mutter Erde. Ein Versuch über Volksreligion*, Leipzig-Berlin, 1925, 3d exp. ed Following through on Dieterich's comparative method, M. Alekseev suggests that the cult in Russia was derived not from indigenous pagan mythology but from Indian and Greek dualistic cosmologies. See his " 'Prenie zemli i moria' v drevnerusskoi pis'mennosti," in *Problemy . . . Tikhomirova*, esp. 32 ff.

On the idea of "universal motherhood" in Russian reverence for Mary and the blending of older fertility rites into the cult of the Virgin see D. Strotmann, "Quelques aperçus historiques sur le culte marial en Russie," *Irénikon*, XXXII, 1959, esp. 184–7; also S. Chetverikov, *"Piété orthodoxe. De l'esprit religieux russe et de la dévotion du peuple russe pour la Mère de*

Dieu," *Irénikon*, III, 1927, 385–90, 459–67.

13. On the folksong (transcribed in 1619 by the Englishman Richard James) see K. Kuznetsov, "Iz muzykal'nogo proshlogo Moskvy," *SM*, 1947, no. 5, 39. "Volga, Volga, Mat' rodnaia, Volga Russkaia reka" begins the last verse of the nineteenth-century harmonization of an earlier folk song.

14. M. Tikhomirov, *Towns*, 415, note 1 and ff. The importance of the forest for the formation of Russian culture is stressed by Sumner, *Survey*, Chapter 1; and (with a somewhat stronger suggestion of environmental determinism borrowed in part from Buckle's *History of Civilization in England*) in Solov'ev's epic *Istoriia*. Both of these authorities relate the long history of Russian political and military conflict to the geographical division between the forest and the steppe. New interest has recently been shown by W. Benesch, "The Use of Wood as a Building Material in Pre-Modern Russia: Its Extent and Potential Cultural Implications," *Cahiers d'histoire mondiale*, 1964, part 1, 160–7 (an interesting but uninterpretive collection of testimony); and M. Devèze, "Contributions à l'histoire de la forêt russe," *CMR*, 1964, Jul-Sep, Oct-Dec.

15. S. Maksimov, *SS*, P, 1909, XII, 39 and ff; see also his "Lesnaia glush' kartiny narodnago byta," which appears as vols. XIII and XIV, P, 1909. Even today, the Russian language has special words for groups of trees just as other languages have for animals: *sosnovy bor* (pine), *berezovaia roshcha* (birch), etc.

16. M. Tikhomirov, *Towns*, 272. F. Locatelli, one of the first in a long line of urbane French visitors to be ill-impressed with Russia, pointed out (*Lettres moscovites*, Königsberg, 1736, 287) that Russia was, psychologically speaking, not so much

a land of cold as a land of fire—because its people spent three fourths of the year locked up in insufferably overheated houses and huts.

17. The primary chronicle depicts St. Andrew noticing sauna-type baths in Novgorod, and Oleg insisting on provisions for baths "in any volume needed" during his negotiations with the Greeks. See S. Cross and O. Sherbowitz-Wetzor, *The Russian Primary Chronicle*, Cambridge, Mass., 1953, 54, 65; also 79–80. Dragomanov (*Notes*, 96) relates the old Slavic legend that God made man from a towel after taking a bath. Finnish folklore often portrays the birth of Christ as taking place in a sauna.

18. D. Zelenin, "Tabu slov," I, 99–103; V. Dal, *PSS*, M-P, 1898, X, 402 ff; also N. Voronin's richly documented "Medvezhy kul't v Verkhnem Povolzh'e v XI veke," *KZY*, IV, 1960, 25–93, with seals illustrated on 70; also in Kamentseva, *Sfragistika*, 129–30. On early woodcarving and animal figures thereon see V. Vasilenko, *Russkaia narodnaia rez'ba i rospis' po derevu XVIII–XIX vv*, M, 1960, 24–33, 47–51.

19. The secretly admired "qualities of dogged persistence and patient diligence" that H. Zinsser attributes to the louse (*Rats, Lice and History*, Boston, 1935, 227) are, interestingly enough, rather close to the qualities of long-suffering perseverance most admired by the monastic writers. Russian monks were occasionally accused—only partly in jest—by foreigners of having some hidden admiration for lice in view of their reluctance to rid themselves of the creatures. For a useful if impressionistic "natural history of the louse" see *ibid.*, 166–88; however, Zinsser's conclusion that typhus did not appear in Europe until the fifteenth century (218) probably needs to be modified in view of the

mention of infections similar in description to typhus in the Russian chronicles.

20. As in the case of typhus, there has been no serious attempt to trace the early epidemiology of Russia from the fragmentary but repeated references to epidemic diseases in the chronicles. Careful studies of the statistical and psychological affects of plague and famine in the seventeenth century, however, give some idea of the astonishing impact of this phenomenon. See (on the "Time of Troubles" at the beginning of the century) N. Firsov, *Istoricheskie kharakteristiki i eskizy,* Kazan, 1922, I, 5–17; and (on the plague of the 1650's) A. Brückner, *Beiträge zur Kulturgeschichte Russlands im XVII Jahrhundert,* Leipzig, 1887, 33–57.

21. N. Nikitina, "K voprosu o russkikh koldunakh," *SMAE,* VII, 1928, 321.

22. This warning, says the Earl of Carlisle, "put some of us on a sudden desire to know if the Rats were so big at Mosco." Charles Howard, First Earl of Carlisle, *A relation of three embassies from his Sacred Majestie Charles II to the Great Duke of Muscovie, the King of Sweden, and the King of Denmark. Performed by the . . . Earle of Carlisle in the years 1663 & 1664,* London, 1669, 140.

23. V. Kravchinsky (Stepniak), *The Russian Peasantry,* NY, 1888, 128.

24. See R. Matlaw, "Recurrent Imagery in Dostoevsky," *HSS,* III, 201–25, who follows Chizhevsky in attributing this interest in insects to the influence of Schiller rather than to older Russian folk tradition.

25. See particularly *Sot,* 1930 (Eng. trans. *Soviet River,* NY, 1933), *Skutarevsky,* 1932 (translated excerpt in G. Reavey and M. Slonim, *Soviet Literature: An Anthology,* NY, 1934, 195–203); and R. Hingley, "Leonid Leonov," *Su,* 1958, Jul-Sep, 69–74.

26. Zelenin, "Tabu," II, 62; Golubinsky, *Istoriia,* I, 619. See also the large section on fire and furnaces in Sadovnikov, *Zagadki,* 41–50. Note the elaborate, rather ghoulish immolation rites of the pre-Christian Russians on the Volga reported by a tenth-century Arab traveler (Spector, *Readings,* 16–19); and the Russian rebuke to the Arabs for leaving a man's "remains to be eaten by insects and worms" rather than "burn him in the twinkling of an eye so that he immediately enters into paradise" (19).

27. *The Celestial Hierarchy,* book XV, cited in Payne, *Fire,* 241. For the Greek text with French translation and a full analysis of the derivation and history of the image of sacred fire see Denys l'Aréopagite, *La Hiérarchie Céleste,* 1958, 166–71, notes by M. de Gandillac.

28. Luke 12:49; Acts 2:3.

29. S. Collins, *The Present State of Russia,* London, 1671, 25, also 8–9.

30. *pozhar.* N. Gudzy, ed., *Zhitie protopopa Avvakuma im samim napisannoe i drugie ego sochineniia,* M, 1959, 313, 448, 464. The designation was used well into the seventeenth century.

31. See the official publication of the Moscow patriarchate, *The Russian Orthodox Church,* 47.

32. Simeon the new theologian, cited in I. Uspensky and V. Lossky, *The Meaning of Icons,* Boston, 1952, 36. The metaphor originates with Origen (see G. Prestige, *Fathers and Heretics,* London, 1940, 221–2).

33. Cited in Payne, *Fire,* 241–4.

34. *Soviet River,* 347.

35. "Slavonic Cities IV, Moscow," *SEER,* 1947, Apr, 336–55; Voronin, *Goroda,* 8.

36. Carlisle, *Relation,* 301; for similar testimony by earlier Western visitors, see Hamilton, *Art,* 106–7.

37. On the *peshchnoe deistvo,* see M. Velimirovich, "Liturgical Drama in Byzantium and Russia," *DOP, XVI,* 1962, 351–85, esp. 365, for differences between the Byzantine and

Russian versions. In addition to extensive materials cited therein A. Famintsyn, *Skomorokhi na Rusi*, P, 1889, 100–5 and references for the way in which the wanderings of the three saved from the furnace often turned into general merrymaking lasting throughout the twelve days of Christmas. Note also the insistence of the Russians on having furnaces in the churches they were permitted to build in Baltic cities under Hanseatic control. N. Kazakova, "Ganzeiskaia politika russkogo pravitel'stva v poslednie gody XV v," in *Problemy . . . Tikhomirova*, 153.

38. Luke 3:16. P. Pascal, *Avvakum et les débuts du raskol: la crise religieuse au XVIIᵉ siècle en Russie*, 1938, 9–12.

39. A. Pokrovsky, "K biografii Antoniia Podol'skogo," *Cht*, 1912, II, ch 3, 33–8.

40. The institution of "self-immolation" has been analyzed and discussed with full documentation by D. Sapozhnikov, *Samosozhenie v russkom raskole*, M, 1891; and even more in I. Syrtsov, *Samozhigatel'stvo sibirskikh staroobriadtsev v XVII i XVIII stoletii*, Tobol'sk, 1888. Self-destruction was, however, opposed by many Old Believers. See the 1691 tract by a certain Evfrosin, *Otrazitel'noe pisanie o novoizobretennom puti samoubiistvennykh smertei*, repr. with valuable intr. and bibliography by Kh. Loparev in *PDP*, CVIII, 1895.

41. E. H. Carr, *Michael Bakunin*, NY, 1961, p, 187–8; R. Wagner, *My Life*, NY, 1911, I, 465–99, 527–32. On the contact between the two, which is strangely overlooked by most Wagnerian scholars, see Carr, 195–203.

42. Viacheslav Ivanov in "A Correspondence Between Two Corners," between him and M. Gershenzon, *PR*, 1948, Sep, 955. Also his reference to the need for "fiery death in the spirit," 1045.

43. N. Gumilev, *Ognenny stolp*, P, 1921. On him, see S. Makovsky's invaluable, posthumously published, "Nicolas Gumilev (1886–1921). Un Témoignage sur l'homme et sur le poète," *CMR*, 1962, Apr-Jun, 176–224, which places the origin of the title in his earlier lines "henceforth I am ablaze with the flame which reaches up to heaven out of hell." (209)

44. Cited by B. Rybakov, *Remeslo drevnei Rusi*, M, 1948, 183. Technically there was a distinction between the working axe (sekira) and the weapon (topor), but the latter term became generally used for all axes. Nor was the term supplanted in popular usage by the term for ceremonial axe (*protazan*) taken over along with its shape from the Polish *partyzana*, introduced by the courtiers of the False Dmitry and placed on the famous seal of Yaroslavl, showing the bear carrying an axe. *BE*, L, 505; Kamentseva, *Sfragistika*, 128–9.

45. "S toporom ves' svet proidesh'," *Russkie narodnye poslovitsy i pogovorki*, M, 1958, 236. "Topor-vsemu delu golova," V. Vasilenko, *Russkaia narodnaia rez'ba i rospis' po derevu XVIII–XX vv*, M, 1960, 25. Sadovnikov begins his famous collection of Russian riddles with a section on the axe (not including the one cited by Vasilenko) *Zagadki*, 31 and 263 notes.

46. Shchapov, II, 508. See also 486 for additional testimony to the psychological importance of the axe, drawn from Shchapov's unique reading of the archives of the Solovetsk Monastery.

47. Saws were considered a "foreign" or "German" implement and were not accepted for general use until the late seventeenth century. See N. Voronin, *Ocherki po istorii russkogo zodchestva XVI–XVII vv*, M-L, 1934, 101–3. Even in the late eighteenth century, the axe was still used exclusively for all woodwork

in many parts of the country. See Putnam, *Britons,* 256-7. On Perun's axehead, see *BE,* LXVI, 532-4.

48. Mashkovtsev, ed., *Istoriia,* I, 56 and table 28g.

49. For a detailed study of this remarkable institution (and of much else about pre-Petrine society) see A. Yakovlev, *Zasechnaia cherta Moskovskogo gosudarstva v XVII veke,* M, 1916.

50. "Chai pit'—ne drova rubit' "; "Chto napisano perom, to ne vyrubish' toporom." *Russkie . . . poslovitsy,* 259, 158.

51. B. Chicherin to A. Herzen in 1858, in the latter's *PSS i pisem* (ed. Lemke), IX, 418-20.

52. F. Venturi, *Roots of Revolution,* NY, 1960, 295-6, also 169; and Carr, *Bakunin,* 398 and 390-409.

53. L. Leonov, "Concerning Large Chips of Wood," *LG,* Mar 30, 1965, in *CDSP,* Jun 9, 1965, 13. Khrushchev's remarks (addressed directly to Leonov) cited in *CDSP,* May 24, 1961, 6. Speech first given Jul 17, 1960, and reprinted in *Kommunist.* For a more negative appraisal of Leonov's *Russky les,* M, 1954, see A. Gerschenkron, "Reflections on Soviet Novels," *WP,* 1960, Jan, esp. 165-76. For earlier important literary efforts to use the forest as a symbol of old Russian values see Ostrovsky's play, *Les* (P, 1871) and P. Mel'nikov (Pechersky)'s long novel, *V lesakh* (M, 1868-74) recently reprinted and adapted for the stage in the USSR. For details on the cult of the forest in popular folklore and an appreciation of similarities and differences with other parts of Europe, see D. Zelenin, *Totemy-Derev'ia v skazaniiakh i obriadakh evropeiskikh narodov,* M-L, 1937; also his "Totemichesky kul't derev'ev u russkikh i u belorussov," *IAN (O),* 1933, no. 6, 591-629.

54. The basic account of E. Kitzinger, "The Cult of Images in the Age before Iconoclasm," *DOP,* VIII, 1954, 83-150, can be enriched by the recent finding in the Monastery of St. Catherine on Mt. Sinai of a substantial number of these early icons. The provisional account given by K. Weitzmann, "Mount Sinai's Holy Treasures," *NG,* 1964, Jan, 104-27, is based on the first findings from the unprecedented collection of some 2,000 icons from various periods which will provide the material for a six-volume history of icon painting to be published by the Princeton University Press. The fullest collection of illustrations from Sinai yet published is G. Soteriou, *Eikones tēs Monēs Sina,* Athens, 1956-8, 2v.

55. J. Tixeront, *Les Origines de l'église d'Edesse et la légende d'Abgar,* 1888; P. Perdrizet, "De la Véronique et de Sainte Véronique," and J. Myslivec, "Skazanie o perepiske Khrista s Avgarom na russkoi ikone XVII veka," *SKP,* V, 1932, 185-90; and other materials referenced Hamilton, *History,* 273, note 7.

56. Uspensky and Lossky, *Meaning,* 46. In addition to this excellent semidevotional analysis see E. Trubetskoy, *Umozrenie v kraskakh,* M, 1916; B. Meshchersky, *Russian Icons,* NY, 1941; P. Muratov, *Les Icones russes,* 1929, *Trente-cinq primitifs russes,* 1937; and *L'ancienne peinture russe,* Rome, 1925; H. Gernard (pseud. of H. Skrobucha), *Welt der Ikonen,* Recklinghausen, 1957; J. Myslivec, *Ikona,* Prague, 1947; and K. Onasch, *Ikonen,* Gütersloh, 1961, which contains many new illustrations and is scheduled to appear in English translation. In addition to the already cited general works of Kondakov (still the outstanding authority), see his *Ikonografiia Isusa Khrista,* P, 1905, and *Ocherki i zametki po istorii srednevekovogo iskusstva i kul'tury,* Prague, 1929 (this last work having benefited from the new riches of color and

technique revealed by the massive cleaning and restoration of Russian icons on the eve of the Revolution).

57. V. Lazarev, *Andrei Rublev*, M, 1960, 19. Among other recent Soviet studies see M. Alpatov, *Andrei Rublev*, M, 1959; and, for a spiritual interpretation of Rublev's "Old Testament Trinity," Evdokimov, *Orthodoxie*, 233–8. For a vivid illustration of Rublev's accomplishment contrast his famed Old Testament Trinity with the sixteenth-century Rumanian icon on the same theme in D. Wild, *Les Icones*, Lausanne, nd, plate XVIII. Perhaps the best characterization of the differing schools and their historical interrelationships is in P. Schweinfurth, *Geschichte der russischen Malerei im Mittelalter*, The Hague, 1930, 198–353. See also T. Rice, *Icons*, London, 1961; Hamilton, *Art*, chapters 10–13; Uspensky and Lossky, *Meaning*, 47, note 3; and V. Lazarev, *Russian Icons*, NY, 1962, p.

58. This is evident from the evidence presented (though somewhat obscured in the discussion) by A. Romm, *Russkie monumental'nye rel'efy*, M, 1953, 16–22, and appears to have been one of the important consequences of the transfer of power from Vladimir-Suzdal to Moscow. On the imaginative, epic themes of sculptured reliefs in Vladimir-Suzdal, see G. Vagner, *Skul'ptura Vladimiro-Suzdal'skoi Rusi*, M, 1964; and (more generally and with an accompanying French text) his *Dekorativnoe iskusstvo v arkhitekture Rusi X–XIII vekov*, M, 1964.

59. The correlation between these two phenomena is particularly stressed by Russian students of the still inadequately researched iconoclastic movement (in addition to references and discussion in Vasiliev, *History*, I, 251–65, see A. Schmemann, "Byzantine Iconoclasm and the Monks," *SVQ*, 1959, fall, 8–34.), and may reflect an awareness that, however true of Byzantium, such a correlation did in fact come to exist in Russia. The posthumously published valedictory on this subject by K. Uspensky ("Ocherki po istorii ikonoborcheskogo dvizheniia v vizantiiskoi imperii v VII–IX v.: Feofan i ego khronografiia," *VV*, III, 1950, 393–48 and IV, 1951, 211–62) includes references to recent work on iconoclasm (notes 393–4) and a plea for investigating a wide range of phenomenon not usually related to the controversy (261–2). A. Grabar, *L'Iconoclasme Byzantin—dossier archéologique*, 1957, is a ranging illustrated study and far more than a mere archeological dossier.

60. This last clause is a paraphrase of G. Every, *The Byzantine Patriarchate 451–1204*, London, 1947. 111. The insistence of Eastern iconography on stressing the Chalcedonian formulation on the dual nature of Christ was a principal theme of K. Weitzmann's lecture "Icons from Mt. Sinai," Apr 15, 1964, Princeton, N.J.

61. See the excellent and succinct illustrated study by A. Anisimov, *Our Lady of Vladimir*, Prague, 1928; also V. Antonova's illustrated "K voprosu o pervonachal'noi kompozitsii ikony vladimirskoi bogomateri," *VV*, XVIII, 1961, 198–205. Contrast the devotional approach of *Skazanie o chudotvornoi ikone bogomateri imenuemoi vladimirskoiu*, M, 1849, with the sociological-historical approach to the legends in V. Kliuchevsky, *Skazanie o chudesakh vladimirskoi ikony bozhiei materi*, P, 1879. For a general study of the iconography of the Virgin, N. Kondakov, *Ikonografiia bogomateri*, P, 1914–5, 2v.

62. Uspensky and Lossky, *Meaning*, 94, note 3; Platonov, *Histoire*, 163; D.

Uspensky, "Videniia smutnogo vremeni," *VE*, 1914, May, 134–71.

63. According to the section on old Russian art of the Tret'iakov Gallery, Jan 1965; N. Scheffer ("Historic Battles on Russian Icons," *GBA*, XXIX, 1946, 194) counts more than 200. One cannot, of course, attach any great precision to such computations, because it is often unclear what is a separate type and what merely a variation.

64. J. Ştefănescu, *L'illustration des liturgies dans l'art de Byzance et de l'Orient*, Brussels, 1936, 22 ff.

65. V. Georgievsky, *Freski Ferapontova monastyria*, P, 1911, 98 ff.

66. *Ibid.;* the subject was apparently taken over from Mt. Athos—see Ştefănescu, 177–9. See also Myslivec, "Ikonografiia: akatistu panny Marie," *SKP*, V, 1932, 97–130; N. Scheffer, "Akathistos of the Holy Virgin in Russian Art," *GBA*, XXIX, 1946, 5–16; and, on the general translation of hymns into icons in Russia, her "Religious Chants and the Russian Icon," *GBA*, XXVII, 1945, 129–42.

The Akathistos hymns were originally designed for the fifth Saturday of Lent, but came to be sung on other occasions as well—always standing (*akathistos* meaning "not sitting").

67. See Scheffer, "Battles." This aspect of Russian icons has never been systematically studied, though there has been an effort to extract the extra-theological historical source material from miniatures in A. Artsikhovsky, *Drevnerusskie miniatiury kak istorichesky istochnik*, M, 1944.

68. For early illustrations of icons panneled onto beams see Soteriou, *Eikones*, figures 95, 107, 111; for a thirteenth-century Russian carved beam, which already includes many more panels than was customary on a contiguous beam in Byzantine practice see Romm, *Rel'efy*, figure

21. Romm insists (18) that this *tiablo* form is in no way related to the earlier traditions of bas relief craftsmanship.

69. Mashkovtsev, *Istoriia*, I, 83–91; Uspensky and Lossky, 59, 68. The development of the iconostasis has been generally neglected in Soviet scholarship, and its importance underestimated. G. Filimonov (*Vopros o pervonachal'noi forme ikonostasov v russkikh tserkvakh*, M, 1889) refutes the pioneering work of E. Golubinsky ("Istoriia ikonostasa," *PO*, 1872, Nov), which played down Russian originality and dated the appearance of the continuous (*sploshnoi*) iconostasis in the seventeenth century. Filimonov's findings are generally upheld and usefully amplified in the general history by D. Trenev, "Kratkaia istoriia ikonostasa s drevneishikh vremen," in his *Ikonostas smolenskago sobora*, M, 1902, 1–50. The importance of the iconostasis for the subsequent development of Russian art is discussed in Muratov, *Peinture*, 77–107. Much the best study of the entire subject is N. Sperovsky's "Starinnye russkie ikonostasy," which contends that the first iconostasis appeared in the late thirteenth or early fourteenth century; *Kh Cht*, 1891, Nov–Dec, 347–8. See also continuations of this article in *Kh Cht*, 1892, Jan–Feb, 1–23; Mar–Apr, 162–76; May–Jun, 321–34; Jul–Aug, 3–17; Nov–Dec, 522–37.

70. Uspensky and Lossky, 59.

71. *Ibid.*, 39.

72. An admiring study of the Russian Church by R. Korper is entitled *The Candlelight Kingdom*, NY, 1955.

73. Mark 9:2–8; Matthew 17:1–9; Acts 2:1–4.

74. Matthew 11:28. Sperovsky, "Ikonostasy," 1892, Jul–Aug, 17; Nov–Dec, 537.

75. For the biblical and patristic authorities and the apologetic theology for

Orthodox icon veneration (carefully distinguished from worship, which is addressed only to God), and the contrast with the West, see Evdokimov, *Orthodoxie*, 216–33. In actual practice, however, the popular attitude was often so idolatrous that even intelligent foreign visitors in the seventeenth century could write that "monks are not even permitted to pray except in front of icons." A. Mayerberg, *Relation d'un voyage en Moscovie*, Amsterdam, 1707, 89.

76. Fedotov, *Mind*, 208.

77. On the concept of *chin* see, in addition to material and references in my "Images of Muscovy," 31–2, esp. note 22, the partial English translation of Alexis' *chin* for falcons (with highly inaccurate commentary) in *SEER*, 1924, Jun, 63–4.

78. Belinsky, letter to Gogol of 1847, in *Selected Philosophical Works*, M, 1948, 507.

79. Paintings discussed in *The Idiot* and *A Raw Youth* respectively. The print of the Sistine Madonna is still over his desk in the Dostoevsky Museum in Moscow. Dostoevsky's view of the Holbein painting is discussed at length in Z. Malenko and J. Gebhard, "The Artistic Use of Portraits in Dostoevsky's *Idiot*," *SEEJ*, 1961, Fall, 243–54; the Lorraine picture is also discussed with the same meaning in "Stavrogin's Confession," the suppressed chapter of Dostoevsky's *Possessed*.

80. V. Bonch-Bruevich, cited in M. Gorlin's excellent article, "The Interrelation of Painting and Literature in Russia," *SEER*, 1945, Nov, 140: See also *TODL*, XXII, 1966.

81. Tsvetaev, *Protestantstvo*, 596–7. Note also the way in which icon painters began to double as military map makers in the Muscovite era. Voronin, *Ocherki*, 63–4, 73–4.

82. V. Riabushinsky, "Russian Icons and Spirituality," *TH*, V, 1951, 48.

83. According to a Dutch visitor at the time of Boris Godunov, cited in N. Oslovianishnikov, *Istoriia kolokolov i kolokoliteinoe iskusstvo*, M, 1912, 40–1. In this invaluable and richly documented study of bells in Russia, see esp. 41–55 for the various early methods of bell ringing.

Paul of Aleppo tells how ringing bells on the eve of feasts would "rouse the whole city" and continue "in the common churches, from midnight till morning," *The Travels of Macarius*, London, 1836, II, 31.

84. Oslovianishnikov, *Istoriia*, 40. N. Fal'kovsky, *Moskva v istorii tekhniki*, M, 1950, 243–53.

85. R. Fry, "Russian Icon Painting from the Western-European Point of View," in M. Farbman, ed., *Masterpieces of Russian Painting*, London, [1930], 58, 38.

86. N. Kompaneisky, "O sviazi russkago tserkovnago pesnopeniia s vizantiiskim," *RMG*, 1903, 825; also 661–3, 733–41, for suggestion of deep discontinuity between the Byzantine *kondakarnoe penie* that prevailed from the eleventh through the fourteenth century in Russia and the *znamennoe penie* that was dominant thereafter.

Early Russian church music has not been as intensively studied as that of Byzantium in recent years, and the relationship between the two remains a largely unexamined question. Among the still basic studies of V. Metallov on the Russian "signed chant" see *Osmoglasie znamennogo raspeva*, M, 1900. See also the useful collection of articles edited by the leading Soviet authority M. Brazhnikov, *Puti razvitiia i zadachi rasshifrovki znamennogo rospeva XII–XVIII vekov*, M-L, 1949. For an English-language introduction see A. Swan, "The Znamenny Chant of the Russian Church," *MQ*, XXVI, 1940, 232–43, 365–80, 529–45; also, for secular music, see the discussion and references in his "The Nature of the Russian Folk-Song," *MQ,* XXIX, 1943, 498–516.

87. A valuable English-language course of instruction in the signed chant together with illustrations of these and other of the *kriuki,* or "hooked" notes, used therein is provided in the mimeographed study of the Rev. V. Smolakov, leader of an Old Believer community in Erie, Pa.

88. Archimandrite Leonid, *Pis'ma sviatogortsa k druz'iam svoim,* P, 1850, 11, 78–80. On the institution of the icon procession (*obraznoe khozhdenie*) see Yarushevich, *Sud,* 450, also Oslovianishnikov, *Istoriia,* 17–18.

89. J. Smits van Waesberghe, *Cymbala (Bells in the Middle Ages),* Rome, 1951, 17–20; also 13–17 for the history of the metal bell in the West already being cast by the seventh century); and A. Bigelow, *Carillon,* Princeton, 1948, 25–57, for the subsequent refinement of the bell and incorporation into ordered carillons in the West, principally in the Low Countries. Like so many works in other fields, these outstanding volumes pay no attention to concurrent developments in Eastern Europe, but B. Unbegaun has suggested that the term *mallnovy zvon* "mauve ringing" is derived from "Malines" in Belgium, thus indicating the probability of close borrowing from the West.

90. Voronin, *Goroda,* 84–5. For the advanced state of forging in Westward-looking Tver, whence Boris apparently came, see Rybakov, *Remeslo,* 603.

91. Oslovianishnikov, *Istoriia,* 38, 41; 103–4, 164–7; A. Voyce, *Moscow and the Roots of Russian Culture,* Norman, Oklahoma, 1964, 106–8. The contemporary Swedish description of stoning is in the valuable unpublished dissertation of H. Ellersieck, *Russia under Aleksei Mikhailovich and Fedor Alekseevich, 1645–1682: The Scandinavian Sources,* UCLA, 1955, 355, note 17.

92. Syrtsov, *Samozhigatel'stvo,* 6–15.

93. V. Odoevsky, as cited in A Koyré, *La Philosophie et le problème national en Russie au début du XIX⁰ siècle,* 1929, 31.

94. "Zvuchal kak kolokol na bashne vechevoi/ Vo dni torzhestv i bed narodnykh." Lermontov, "Poet" (1839) in *PSS,* M, 1947, I, 34. Lines also in widespread Soviet usage. See *Krylatye Slova,* 228.

95. *Kolokol,* Jul 1, 1857, 1.

96. *Nabat* first appeared in 1875; and like *Kolokol* was published abroad. On the meaning and development of the bell itself see D. Uspensky, "Nabatny Kolokol," *RS,* 1907, v. 129, 614–20.

97. M. Creighton, "The Imperial Coronation at Moscow," in *Historical Essays and Reviews,* London, 1902, 321. Oslovianishnikov reports (*Istoriia,* 51–2) that the coronation of Fedor was the first at which the characteristic ringing of bells was incorporated into the ceremony. Paralleling Chaikovsky's insistence on using real cannon was Stanislavsky's insistence on using real cathedral bells onstage for the Moscow Art Theater production of A. Tolstoy's *Tsar Fedor.*

98. Stalin, "Groznoe oruzhie krasnoi armii," *KZ,* Nov 19, 1944, 2. Stalin also referred to artillery as "the God of War." See Major General I. Prochko, "Artilleriia—Bog voiny," *Bol'shevik,* 1943, no. 18, 19–32.

See also R. Garthoff, *Soviet Military Doctrine,* Glencoe, Ill., 1953, esp. 301–7; L. Hart, *The Red Army,* NY, 1956, 344–66; and, on the early history of artillery in Russia, A. Chernov, *Vooruzhennye sily russkogo gosudarstva v XV–XVII vv,* M, 1954, 13, 35–46; V. Danilevsky, *Tekhnika,* 123–5; and *BSE* (2), III, 132–46. Vernadsky points out (*Mongols,* 365–6) that, whereas hand-firing weapons came from the East, artillery came from the West, presumably via the Czechs.

99. Margaritov, *Istoriia sekt,* 142–6, and

references, esp. those in *MO*, 1906, nos. 10, 11, discuss Il'in's sect, which was variously called "The Tidings of Zion," "The Jehovahites," and the "Brotherhood of the Right Hand." See also V. Bonch-Bruevich,

Izmirasektantov, M. 1922, 192–203.

100. See Fedorov's posthumous *Filosofiia obshchego dela*, I, Verny (Alma Ata), 1906, 656–76; II, M, 1913, 248–53; Florovsky, *Puti*, 322–31; *SSt*, 1958, Oct, 129–31.

II. The Confrontation

1. The Muscovite Ideology

1. Northern origins of the tent roof seem implied in the analysis of J. Strzygowski, *Early Church Art in Northern Europe*, NY-London, 1928 (suggesting similarities of appearance despite different construction methods in a text that unfortunately does not consider Great Russia); and in the analysis of Finno-Karelian wooden architecture by L. Pettersson, *Die kirchliche Holzbaukunst auf der Halbinsel Zaonež'e in Russisch-Karelien*, Helsinki, 1950. The possibilities of Caucasian and Mongol derivation are sugested in materials referenced Hamilton, *Art*, 277, notes 21 and 22 respectively—the somewhat more plausible Mongol theory being supported by the apparently Tatar derivation of the Russian word for "tent roof," *shater*.

W. Born doubts both the Iranian derivation of the onion dome suggested by Strzygowski (*Die altslawische Kunst*, Augsburg, 1929) and the widely held theory of Mongol derivation, suggesting that the form had emerged indigenously in Russia by the thirteenth century at the very latest. See Born's "The Origin and the Distribution of the Bulbous Dome," *JAH*, 1943, no. 4, esp. 39–45, and illustrations opposite 32; see also his "The Introduction of the Bulbous Dome into Gothic Architecture and Its Subsequent Development," *Speculum*, 1944, Apr, 208–21.

For the peculiarities of Muscovite architectural development see I. Evdokimov, *Sever v istorii russkogo iskusstva*, Vologda, 1921, esp. 30–5; also A. Voyce, "National Elements in Russian Architecture," *JAH*, 1957, May, esp. 11 ff; *Moscow and the Roots of Russian Culture*, Norman Okla., 1964, 95–121; M. Krasovsky, *Ocherki istorii moskovskago perioda drevne-tserkovnago zodchestva*, M, 1911; and the excellent, illustrated study of wooden architecture by S. Zabello et al., *Russkoe dereviannoe zodchestvo*, M, 1942.

2. Cited from E. Trubetskoy, *Umozrenie* in Evdokimov, *Sever*, 31.

3. Population estimate by M. Tikhomirov, *Rossiia v XVI stoletii*, M, 1962, 66. Paul of Aleppo estimated in the mid-seventeenth century that Moscow had "more than 4,000 churches and 10,000 chapels or sacristies where mass was celebrated," *Travels*, 11, 31.

4. P. Struve, "Nazvanie 'krest'ianin'," *SRIP*, 1929. I; also Vernadsky, *Mongols*, 375. Evidence for the continued interchangeability of the two terms (questioned by some authorities) is provided by the use of the term *khristiianin* for peasant in the first Russian military manual of 1647. See the analysis of C. Stang in *SUN*, 1952, 86.

5. Likhachev, *Kul'tura*, 24.

6. For an invaluable study of hesychasm by an Athonite monk, see Basil Krivoshein, "The Ascetic and Theological Teaching of Gregory Palamas," *ECQ*, III, 1938–9, 26–

33, 71–84, 138–56, 193–214; see
also J. Meyendorff, *St. Grégoire
Palamas et la mystique orthodoxe*,
1959; and the more historically
oriented account by I. Smolitsch,
Leben und Lehre der Starzen,
Cologne-Olten, 1952, 23–63, with
critical bibliography 234–9 and additional material referenced in his
Mönchtum, 107–8. Other important studies with critical documentation are A. Ammann, *Die Got-
tesschau im palamitischen Hesy-
chasmus*, Würzburg, 1938; I. Haus-
herr, *La Méthode de l'oraison
hésychaste*, OC, XXXVI, 1927; G.
Ostrogorsky, "Afonskie isikhasty
i ikh protivniki," *ZRNIB*, V, 1931;
F. Uspensky, "Filosofskoe i bogo-
slovskoe dvizhenie v XIV veke,"
ZhMNP, 1892, Feb.

7. "Tam ved' es'-to, skazhut, stoit
tser'kva sobornaia,/Tam sobornaia
tser'kva vse Priobrazhen'skaia," S.
Shambinago, *Pesni-pamflety XVI
veka*, M, 1913, 262.

8. See plate in Chizhevsky, *History*,
opposite 190. See also material discussed in Voronin, "Kul't," 46,
note 5.

9. Sumner (*Survey*, 182) gives this
figure for 1340–1440. J. Řezáč
("De monachismo secundum re
centiorem legislationem Russi-
cam," *OC*, CXXXVIII, 1952, 6)
gives the figure 180 for the fourteenth century alone. Journel
(*Monachisme*, 39, 43) estimates
that from the beginning of the
fourteenth through the mid-
fifteenth century there were 180
new monasteries and that in the
fifteenth and sixteenth centuries as
a whole 300 were added. Smolitsch
follows Kliuchevsky in suggesting
a smaller over-all total of 104
large monasteries and 150 small
ones (*pustyn'*) for the fourteenth
through sixteenth centuries inclusive, with the total numbers for
each century almost identical and
the principal change being the
great increase in the relative num-

ber of smaller cloisters between
the fourteenth and fifteenth centuries. (*Mönchtum*, 81–2 note 2).

10. On Stephen, see L. Leger, *La Russie intellectuelle*, 1914, 36–50; M.
Dane, "Epiphanius' Image of St.
Stefan," *CSP*, V, 1961, 77–86; and
text in Zenkovsky, *Epics*, 206–8.

11. E. Golubinsky, *Prepodobny Sergei
Radonezhsky i sozdannaia im Tro-
itskaia Lavra*, Sergiev Posad, 1892;
A. Gorsky, *Istoricheskoe opisanie
Sviato-Troitskoi Sergievoi Lavry*,
M, 1890, 2v; P. Kovalevsky, *Saint
Serge et la spiritualité russe*, 1958,
p (fitting Sergius into the general
context of early Russian religious
development); N. Zernov, *St. Sergius—Builder of Russia*, London,
1938; and text in Zenkovsky,
Epics, 208–36.

12. Volkov, "Svedeniia," 24–5.

13. On the *pletenie sloves* see S. Zenkovsky, *Epics*, 205; on the less
generally discussed *pletenie remnei*
in fourteenth-century ornamentation (which like the "weaving of
words" seems largely derived
from Southern Slav models) see
A. Nekrasov, "Ocherki iz istorii
slavianskago ornamenta," in *PDP*,
CLXXXIII, 1913, 10.

14. Kondakov, *Icon*, 92. For an interpretation of Russian literary development that puts greater stress
on discontinuities between Kievan
and Great Russian literature than
is customary among most historians of Russian literature see I.
Nekrasov, *Zarozhdenie natsional'-
noi literatury v severnoi Rusi*,
Odessa, 1870.

15. D. Likhachev has traced this migration of anti-Catholicism through
Cyril in his "Galitskaia literaturnaia traditsiia v zhitii Aleksandra
Nevskogo," *TODL*, V, 1947, 49–
53. The story of the Latin sack of
Constantinople also found its way
into early Russian literature see
N. Meshchersky, "Drevnerusskaia
povest' o vziatii tsar'grada Fria-
gami v 1204 godu," *TODL*, X,

1954, 120–35; for other early anti-Roman tracts see A. Popov, *Istoriko-literaturny obzor drevne-russkikh polemicheskikh sochinenii protiv latinian (XI–XV vv),* M, 1875.

16. Mashkovtsev, ed., *Istoriia,* I, 84–5, table 39; Chizhevsky, *History,* 191–201; Gudzy, *History,* 244–57.

17. This contrast becomes particularly striking if one views *The Lay of Igor's Raid,* which bears many similarities to the *Zadonshchina,* as an authentic work of the Kievan period. See the new edition relating it closely to *The Lay* by R. Jakobson and D. Worth, *Sofonija's Tale of the Russian-Tatar Battle on the Kulikovo Field,* 's Gravenhage, 1963. Tikhomirov insists that the *Zadonshchina* was a product of Moscow, not Riazan as is often contended, *Moskva v XIV–XV vekakh,* M, 1957, 256–60.

18. Tikhomirov, ed., *Ocherki istorii istoricheskikh nauk,* 63 ff. and esp. 68–9. A good recent Soviet student of historical songs and genealogical-political oral folklore contends that the introduction of epics alongside (and in amplification of) the chronicles must be dated from the fourteenth and fifteenth centuries rather than the sixteenth, as had been previously contended by Sokolov and others. See M. Skripil, "Voprosy nauchnoi periodizatsii russkogo narodnogo poeticheskogo tvorchestva (X–XVII vekov)," I, 1956, 33–4. For an analysis distinguishing the historical song from the byliny see C. Stief, *Studies in the Russian Historical Song,* Copenhagen, 1953.

19. See references in D. Stremooukhoff, "Moscow the Third Rome: Sources of the Doctrine," *Speculum,* 1953, Jan, 85, and 84–6; also Val'denberg, *Ucheniia,* 287; and W. Hammer, "The Concept of the New or Second Rome in the Middle Ages," *Speculum,* 1944, Jan, esp. 52–5 on Constantinople. The idea was also applied to Western cities, particularly Treves (Trier), *ibid.,* 57 ff.

20. A contrast between Augustine and the "Christian progressivists" of the East is made by T. Mommsen, "St. Augustine and the Christian Idea of Progress," *JHI,* 1951, Jun, 346–74. On Origen's prophetic and allegorical philosophy of history see R. Milburn, *Early Christian Interpretations of History,* London, 1954, 38–53.

    The discussion of the early Russian understanding of heaven by A. Sedel'nikov suggests a greater belief in the final attainability of heaven on earth than was present in the medieval West: "Motiv o rae v russkom srednevekovom prenii," *BS,* VII, 1936, 164–73.

21. Golubinsky, *Istoriia,* II, ch. 1, 297–356, on Cyprian and other key ecclesiastical figures; *PSRL,* XII, for Cyprian's *Life of Peter,* the first metropolitan of Moscow.

    On the Balkan principalities see Vasiliev, *History,* II, 301–19; and added material in Smolitsch, *Mönchtum,* 86, note 1; Stremooukhoff, "Rome," 85, note 8. On Serbia see G. Soulis, "Tsar Stephen Dushan and Mount Athos," *HSS,* II, 125–39. For the Byzantine-Bulgar derivation of the Russian sense of destiny see H. Schaeder, *Moskau das Dritte Rom,* Darmstadt, 1957, 2d ed., 1–12; and R. Wolff, "The Three Romes: The Migration of an Ideology and the Making of an Autocrat," *Daedalus,* 1959, spring, 291–311. See also K. Radchenko's generally neglected *Religioznoe i literaturnoe dvizhenie v Bolgarii v epokhu pered turetskim zavoevaniem,* Kiev, 1898.

    The basic work on the "second South Slav influx" into Russia is still A. Sobolevsky, *Iuzhno-slavianskoe viliianie na russkuiu pis'mennost' v XIV–XV vekakh,* P, 1894; and *Perevodnaia literatura moskovskoi Rusi XIV–*

XVII vekov, P, 1903, 1–14. More recent surveys are M. Tikhomirov, *"Sviazi,"* in *Slaviansky Sbornik;* and V. Moshin, "O periodizatsii russko-iuzhno-slavianskikh literaturnykh sviazei X–XV vv," *TODL,* XIX, 1963, 28–106.

For linguistic influence see G. Vinokur, *Izbrannye raboty po russkomu iazyku,* M, 1959, 59–62; religious influence, S. Smirnov, "Serbskie sviatye v russkikh rukopisiakh," *Iubileisky sbornik russkogo arkheologicheskogo obshchestva v Iugoslavii,* Belgrade, 1936, 252–64; artistic influences, V. Lazarev, *Feofan Grek i ego shkola,* M, 1961.

There were also, of course, Byzantine influences transmitted without other Slavic intermediaries from the so-called Paleologian renaissance. See D. Likhachev, *Die Kultur Russlands während der Osteuropäischen Frührenaissance,* Dresden, 1962, 31–41; I. Duichev, "Tsentri vizantiisko-slavianskogo obshcheniia i sotrudnichestva," *TODL,* XIX, 1963, 107–29. Tikhomirov contends that there was a Greek monastery in Moscow and other centers of Greek learning at the Monastery of St. Sergius and elsewhere inside Russia. "Rossiia i Vizantiia v XIV–XV stoletiiakh," *ZRVI,* VII, 1961, 36.

22. Text and notes on this legend by Pachomius Logothetes in Stender-Petersen, *Anthology,* 252–8; see also xiv–xv.

23. Golubinsky, *Istoriia,* II, ch. 1, 414–91; also G. Alef, "Muscovy and the Council of Florence," *ASR,* 1961, Oct, 389–401, and works referenced therein, esp. M. Cherniavsky, "The Reception of the Council of Florence in Moscow," *CH,* XXIV, 1955, 347–59.

24. Tikhomirov, "Rossiia i Vizantiia," 33–4. The author rightly points out (38) that Russo-Byzantine relations during the period of Byzantine collapse have been very inadequately studied. Evidence that the Russian church was tending to exalt the Muscovite princes and derogate the Byzantine emperor during the fourteenth century is set forth in Wolff, "Migration," 297–8, and references.

25. *PSRL,* VI, 232. Tikhomirov, "Rossiia i Vizantiia," 38, proposes Serbian authorship.

26. V. Malinin, *Starets Eleazarova monastyria Filofei i ego poslaniia,* Kiev, 1901, appendix, 50, 54–5.

27. See G. Vernadsky, *Russia at the Dawn,* 166–7 and references. Ivan III's increasing use of the title of Tsar provides an indication, but not conclusive proof, that he viewed himself as a kind of successor to the Byzantine emperor. The term "Tsar" had a complex earlier usage (summarized in Miliukov, *Outlines,* I, 18–9 note 4) and —until used in the full coronation service by Ivan IV in 1547—no necessarily imperial significance. For the best discussion of the complex links between Byzantine precedent and Russian practice see V. Savva, *Moskovskie tsari i vizantiiskie vasilevsy. K voprosu o vliianii Vizantii na obrazovanie idei tsarskoi vlasti moskovskikh gosudarei,* Kharkov, 1901.

G. Alef suggests (in an unpublished manuscript, "The Adoption of the Muscovite Two-Headed Eagle: a discordant view") that the seal may have been adopted by Ivan III in the 1490's as a result of establishing relations with the Hapsburg emperors (who also used this Byzantine emblem), and not simply as an automatic consequence of his marriage to the niece of the last Byzantine emperor.

28. Joseph Sanin of Volokolamsk as cited in J. Fennell, "The Attitude of the Josephians and the trans-Volga Elders to the Heresy of the Judaizers," *SEER,* 1951, Jun, 492 and note 26. For the prophetic

writings at the end of the church calendar which encouraged chiliastic expectations see Smolitsch, *Mönchtum*, 131–2 and V. Zhmakin, "Mitropolit Daniil," *Cht*, 1881, II, 361–7; also I, 1–226.

29. Letter of Archbishop Gennadius of Novgorod to Archbishop Ioasaf of Rostov and Yaroslavl, 1489, Feb, in *Cht*, 1847, no. 8, separate pagination at the end, 3.

30. Chizhevsky, *History*, 161; Stremooukhoff, "Third Rome," 96. Chizhevsky cautions (229) against transposing the "eschatological psychosis" of later periods back into the fifteenth century, but the prophetic words at the end of the church calendar indicate that this psychosis was already well developed. In addition to Zhmakin, "Daniil," see V. Sakharov, *Eskhatologicheskie sochineniia i skazaniia v drevne-russkoi pis'mennosti i vliianie ikh na narodnye dukhovnye stikhi*, Tula, 1879.

N. Ul'ianov's argument ("Kompleks Filofeia," *NZh*, XLV, 1956, 249–73) that the "Third Rome" idea is more a retroactive projection of nineteenth-century romantic nationalism than a real force in Old Russian thought (at least prior to usage by the Old Believers) requires some modification in view of the use of the term in the basic *Kormchaia Kniga*.

31. Budovnits, *Publitsistika*, 172; and Revelation xvii: 10–1, cited in *PSRL*, IV, 282, and interpreted in Vernadsky, *Dawn*, 146.

32. I. Kovalevsky, *Iurodstvo o Khriste i Khrista radi iurodivye vostochnoi i russkoi tserkvi*, M, 1900, 136, note, and 132–50. See also A. Kuznetsov, *Iurodstvo i stolpnichestvo*, P, 1913.

G. Fedotov, *Sviatye drevnei Rusi*, Paris, 1931, 205, counts six holy fools in the entire history of the Byzantine Church; Hieromoine Lev ("Une Forme d'ascèse russe. La folie pour le Christ," *Irénikon*,

III, 1927, 15) counts "four or five" in Byzantium from the second to the tenth century.

33. G. Fedotov ("The Holy Fools," *SVQ*, 1959, fall, 2–4) counts four holy fools in Russia of the fourteenth century, eleven in the fifteenth, fourteen in the sixteenth, and seven in the seventeenth (during which prohibitions on canonizing this form of sanctity were introduced).

This useful study emphasizes the qualitative as well as the quantitative distinctions between Russian and Byzantine "holy fools." The texts cited in support of holy folly are all Pauline: I Corinthians 1:18–27; 4:9–13; and Colossians 2:8.

34. Ya. Shchapov, " 'Pokhvala Gluposti' Erazma roterdamskogo v russkikh perevodakh," *ZOR*, XX, 1958, 102–17, documents the large number of French and Russian editions and digests that began to appear in Russia beginning in the eighteenth century. For the tradition of "praising folly" by the early fathers and references to Tertullian see the section "The Primacy of Faith," in E. Gilson, *Reason and Revelation in the Middle Ages*, NY, nd, p, 3–33.

35. Dostoevsky in speech on Pushkin in 1880, just before his death, (F. Dostoevsky, *The Diary of a Writer*, NY, 1954, 967–80); Musorgsky in *Boris Godunov;* and Berdiaev in *The Russian Idea*, 196–200, 225. See also the romanticized but valuable (and influential) study by S. Maksimov, "Brodiachaia Rus'— Khrista radi," which appear as vols. V, VI of his *SS*.

36. On Nil, see Smolitsch, *Mönchtum*, 101–18, and *Leben*, 64–80; Chizhevsky, *History*, 216–22; and selection in Fedotov, *Treasury*. Also, A. Arkhangel'sky, *Nil Sorsky i Vassian Patrikeev, ikh literaturnye trudy i idei v drevnei Rusi*, P, 1882; and for his code of the

monastic life, *Nil Sorskago pre-danie i ustav*, PDPI, CLXXIX, 1912, with introductory article by M. Borovkova-Maikova. For his links with Hesychasm see A. Orlov, "Iisusova Molitva na Rusi v XVI veke," *PDPI*, CLXXV, 1914, 29–92; also F. von Lilienfeld, *Nil Sorskij und seine Schriften*, 1961.

37. On Dionysius and the Spaso-Kamenny cloisters, Smolitsch, *Mönchtum*, 97–9 and table 534. See also Smolitsch, *Leben*, 57–63; B. Grechev, "Zavolzhskie startsy," *BV*, 1907, Jul-Aug.

38. See G. Florovsky, "Empire and Desert: Antinomies of Christian History," *The Greek Catholic Theological Review*, 1957, winter; G. Ostrogorsky, "Otnosheniia tserkvi i gosudarstva v Vizantii," *SKP*, IV, 1931, 121–32. T. Parker says that "to speak of church-state relations in the East is really a glaring anachronism." *Christianity and the State in the Light of History*, NY, 1954, 78, and section 54–80.

39. The first use of *prikaz* to mean an established institution rather than an order apparently occurs under Vasily III in 1512 (see documentation for *Russkaia povest' XVII veka*, M, 1954, 450). General use of this term for institutions is usually traced to the reign of Ivan IV (see *Gr*. XXXIII, 460–2.) The research of V. Savva (*O posol'skom prikaze v XVI v*, Kharkov, 1917) makes it clear, however, that this *prikaz* at least was a full-time chancery from the late fifteenth century despite his hesitation about generalizing (iii–iv and note iv, note 1) and the uncompleted nature of his research. The treasury (*Kazenny dvor*) must also have been operating on a continuing basis.

40. Fedotov, *Mind*, 208. Fedotov's suggestion that the Orthodox conception of tsardom as a "social extension of the dogma of icon-veneration" fits in with the trend already well marked in Byzantine iconography to depict emperors with the divinized attitudes of Old Testament kings and even of Christ Himself. See A. Grabar, *L'Empereur dans l'art byzantin*, 1936, 93–122. Myslivec, *Ikona*, 47, sees in the icon "an everlasting memorial . . . of the victory of Platonic idealism" in the East.

41. Shchapov, *Sochineniia*, II, 593–4, for full discussion and usages of *pamiat'*. The emphasis on epics rather than romances in early Russian literature also betrays a preference for tradition rather than innovation. As Max Remppis has said, in another context, "the epic searches out the old, the romance aspires towards the modern." *Die Vorstellungen von Deutschland in altfranzösischen Heldenepos und Roman und ihre Quellen*, Halle, 1911, 146, also 168.

42. Chizhevsky, *History*, 161–2.

43. Legends about the transfer of the true seal of empire from Babylonia to Byzantium lent added pedigree to the imperial line. See Gudzy, *History*, 257–69; and, in addition to material referenced 269 note 14, see articles by M. Speransky and M. Skripil in *TODL*, X, 1954, 136–84, on Russian writings about the fall of Constantinople; and (particularly for the Russian borrowings of South Slav and even Rumanian writings on this subject) I. Duichev, "La conquête turque et la prise de Constantinople dans la littérature slave contemporaine," *BS*, XIV, 1953, 14–54; XVI, 1955, 318–29; and XVII, 1956, 276–340, esp. 316 ff.

44. V. Zenkovsky, *History*, I, 37.

45. The religious and devotional nature of Joseph's teaching is stressed by G. Florovsky, who likens (*Puti*, 18) the compulsion to give up one's riches to that of the renunciation of wealth and privilege in the 1870's. For a sympathetic Roman Catholic appraisal

see Th. Špidlík, "Joseph de Volokolamsk. Un chapitre de la spiritualité russe," *OC*, CXLVI, 1956;
for a concise summary of the controversy with Nil, see J. Meyendorff, "Partisans et ennemis des
biens ecclésiastiques au sein du
monachisme russe aux XVᵉ et
XVIᵉ siècles," *Irénikon*, XXIX,
1956, 28–46, 151–64. Joseph's
principal polemic work is *Prosvetitel', ili oblichenie eresi zhidovstvuiushchikh*, Kazan, 1904; see also
A. Zimin and Ya. Lur'e, *Poslaniia
Iosifa Volotskogo*, M–L, 1959, esp.
the essay by Lur'e, "Iosif Volotsky
kak publitsist i obshchestvenny deiatel'." His political views are characterized by M. Shakhmatov, *Poli-
tická ideologie Josefa Volokolams-
kého, sborník věd právních a
státních*, Prague, 1928; and in
Zhmakin, "Daniil."

The general role of the clergy
in developing imperial ideology is
discussed in V. Sokolovsky, *Uchastie russkogo dukhovenstva i monashestva v razvitii edinoderzhaviia i
samoderzhaviia v Moskovskom
gosudarstve v kontse XV i pervoi
polovine XVI vv*, Kiev, 1902.

46. N. Andreev suggests that fear of
confiscation of church lands was a
principal motivation behind Philotheus' appealing so powerfully to
the Tsar. This could be true, even
though his supporting suggestion
that Philotheus may have first propounded the theory in an earlier
correspondence with Ivan III
("Filofey and His Epistle to Ivan
Vasilyevich," SEER, 1959, Dec,
1–31) seems untenable in the light
of the careful argument advanced
by N. Maslennikova for believing
that this correspondence (and indeed Philotheus' fullest exposition
of his views) was in fact with Ivan
IV. See the referenced work and
amplification of the argument in
Ya. Lur'e's *Ideologicheskaia bor'ba
v russkoi publitsistike kontsa XV–
nachala XVI veka*, M-L, 1960,
346–57, 482–97.

47. Malinin, *Filofei*, appendix, 50.

48. In discussing the Josephite use of
this passage from the sixth-century
Byzantine work, *Agapetus*, I. Shevchenko remarks that "though autocracy was a native creation, the
garb it donned was of foreign making." "A Neglected Byzantine
Source of Muscovite Political Ideology," *HSS*, II, 1954, 172. On the
obligation to inform under the
tradition of "slova i dela gosuda-
reva," *BE*, LIX, 413–14, discusses
its development in the eighteenth
century; N. Evreinov, *Istoriia
telesnykh nakazanii v rossii* [M,
1913?], 23, traces its origins to the
sixteenth century.

Lur'e argues convincingly that
Joseph was not himself a "Josephite" in the sense of advocating
autocratic centralization until late
in life. See his *Ideologicheskaia
bor'ba;* also discussion by Szeftel
in *JGO*, 1965, Apr, 19–29.

49. Budovnits, *Publitsistika*, 199–201,
for Philotheus and Silvester on
sodomy; for the exhortations on
this subject in the church decrees
of 1551, see L. Duchesne, ed., *Le
Stoglav ou les cent chapitres*, 1920,
92–3; for typical foreign observations, M. Anderson, *Discovery*,
26–7.

50. For more details see N. Krasnosel'-
tsev, *K istorii pravoslavnogo bogosluzheniia*, Kazan, 1889; N. Odin-
tsov, *Poriadok obshchestvennago i
chastnago bogosluzheniia v drevnei
Rossii do XVI veka*, P, 1881; and
Smolitsch, *Mönchtum*, esp. 266 ff.

51. Tradition said to be typical of
Russia by G. Fedotov. See his
Mind, 94–131; introduction to (and
selections for) his *Treasury;* and
N. Gorodetzky, *The Humiliated
Christ*.

V. Rozanov ("Vozle 'Russkoi
Idei'," *Izbrannoe*, NY, 1956, 144–
50) contends that Russia cherished

a love of pure, but always humiliated and usually despoiled femininity as opposed to the strident masculinity of Western Europe. He cites the sense of identity Russians felt with Cordelia in *King Lear,* and with the characters of Dickens ("almost a Russian writer"), whose humiliations set them off from the typical English ideal of a beefeater. In French literature, Rozanov contends that Russians much prefer the suffering underworld characters of Eugène Sue's novels to "the kings and ministers of Racine, Corneille, Victor Hugo and Dumas."

52. The modern word "ascetic" is derived from the Greek word for athlete (*askētēs*), for which *podvizhnik* is the Russian equivalent. The *podvig,* or disciplined holy deed, is represented as the cornerstone of Russian spirituality by S. Graham, *The Way of Martha and the Way of Mary,* NY, 1916, iii ff; and of early Russian political life by M. Shakhmatov, who sees the ruling prince as an idealized *podvizhnik vlasti* (title of the first part of his "opyt"). See also Sipiagin, "Sources," 18; Behr-Sigel, *Prière,* 30; Arsen'ev, *Iz . . . traditsii,* 81

53. Interpretations of Ivan IV are complicated by the fact that most of the crucial documents and almost everything written in his own hand were lost amidst the fire and fighting of his last years and those of his ill-fated successors. For critical introductions to the immense literature on his reign see articles by G. Bolsover (*TRHS,* series 5, VII, 1957, 71–89) and L. Yaresh (on the *oprichnina* in C. Black, ed., *Rewriting,* 224–41).

The historiographical guide provided by I. Budovnits in the Stalin era ("Ivan Grozny v russkoi istoricheskoi literature," *IZ,* XXI, 1947, 271–330) has been superseded by the valuable first chapter

of A. Zimin, *Reformy Ivana Groznogo,* M, 1960, 7–62. See also the convenient summary in S. Veselovsky, *Issledovaniia po istorii oprichniny,* M, 1963, 11–37.

54. On Peresvetov, see W. Philipp, *Ivan Peresvetov und seine Schriften zur Erneuerung des Moskauer Reiches,* 1935; A. Zimin, *I. S. Peresvetov i ego sovremenniki,* M, 1958; and the review by Ya. Lur'e in *IAN(L),* XVIII, no. 5, 1959, 450–3.

On the more general problem of Turkish influences see G. Vernadsky, "On some parallel trends in Russian and Turkish history," *Transactions of the Connecticut Academy of Arts and Sciences,* XXXVI, 1945, 25–36.

55. Gudzy, *History,* 269–75.

56. From the unpublished report of an admiring Venetian visitor to Moscow of about 1565, "Relatione del Gran Regno di Moscovia," MS, 963, Venicia, Biblioteca Nationale, Madrid. I am indebted to Professor Hamm of Vienna for this reference.

57. Oath cited in P. Sadikov, *Ocherki po istorii oprichniny,* M L, 1950, 23. This is a relatively early use of the term "government" in official Russian documents.

58. Kliuchevsky, *Skazaniia,* 85–6. See also Veselovsky, *Issledovaniia,* 38–53.

59. Kovalevsky, *Iurodstvo,* 143 and note 2, 144; also 137–42 on the *iurodivy* Nicholas Salos, whose prophetic reprimands of Ivan IV were popularly credited with saving Pskov from the same destruction that Ivan visited on Novgorod in 1470. Although these tales of "holy fools" were adorned with apocryphal detail in popular folklore and romanticized à la Walter Scott by Karamzin, the activities of these fools were also noted by sober foreign visitors, such as Giles Fletcher, and their historical im-

portance in the late sixteenth century is beyond doubt. M. Tikhomirov speaks of the "blessed hooliganism" of Vasily in *Rossiia v XVI stoletii*, M, 1962, 78.

60. E. Maksimovich ("Tserkovny Zemsky Sobor 1549," *ZRNIB*, 1933, IX) argues that the *sobor* of 1550, which approved the law code (*Sudebnik*) of 1550, was in fact a direct outgrowth of the previous church council and retained its essentially ecclesiastical character.

61. Budovnits, *Publitsistika*, 188–207, for details and references on these compendia. On the officially sponsored gathering in of literature from the appanages to Moscow under Ivan see P. Pascal, "Le Métropolite Macaire et ses grandes entreprises littéraires," *Russie et Chrétienté*, 1949, no. 1–2, 7–16.

62. Ya. Lur'e, "O putiakh razvitiia svetskoi literatury v Rossii i u zapadnykh slavian v XV–XVI vv," *TODL*, XIX, 1963, 282–3. The discussion and documentation, 262–88, illustrate the extent of earlier and later links.

63. Ya. Lur'e and N. Kazakova, *Antifeodal'nye ereticheskie dvizheniia na Rusi XIV-nachala XVI veka*, M-L, 1954, 109–10; also Fennell, "Attitude," 498; Budovnits, *Publitsistika*, 52.

64. *AAE*, I, 1836, 479, cited in E. Denisoff, "Aux Origines de l'église russe autocéphale," *RES*, XXIII, 1947, 81; and see the entire discussion 66–88. For a Russian version of the reply and discussion thereof, see A. Sedel'nikov, "Rasskaz 1490 ob inkvizitsii," *Trudy Komissii po drevne-russkoi literature Akademii Nauk*, I, 1932, 33–57. Early Russian contact with Spain was more extensive than might seem likely. See, for instance, the flurry of diplomatic contact in the 1520's documented in A. Lopéz de Meneses, "Las primeras ambajadas rusas en España," *Cuadernos de historia de España*, Buenos Aires, V, 1946, 111–28. Much the best discussion of the entire Russo-Spanish contact is in Alekseev, *Ocherki . . . ispano-russkikh . . . otnoshenii*.

65. The term "purge" (*purgieren, purgiren*) was also used by German visitors to Muscovy. See K. Schreinert, *Hans Moritz Ayrmanns Reisen durch Livland und Russland in den Jahren 1666–1670*, Tartu, 1937, 56.

66. Denisoff, "Origines," 88.

67. D. Davydov, *Opyt teorii partizanskogo deistviia*, M, 1822, 2d ed., 22–38; also V. Lamansky, "O slavianakh v Maloi azii, v Afrike i v Ispanii," *UZIAN*, V, 1859, 365–8, and references therein. For material published in Russia about the Spanish resistance movement see *Ocherki po istorii zhurnalistiki*, I, 200.

Davydov was not only an important, neglected theorist of partisan warfare (with his basic idea being to combine Asian primitiveness with a European command system on the model of the Cossacks, *Opyt*, 42), but also a poet. See V. Zherve, *Partizan-poet D. V. Davydov*, P, 1913.

Actually, Alexander I had sent troops to fight with Napoleon against the Spanish partisans, and later sent frigates to repress the democratic revolutions in Spanish America. Napoleon sensed a similarity between Spain and Russia even before his defeat in Russia. When he rebuked a Russian general en route to Moscow in July, 1812, that the excess of churches in Moscow was a sign of backwardness "in an age when no one is even Christian!" he was told by the general "the Russians and the Spaniards still are." Finding "insolence" in the suggested comparison of his forthcoming adversary with his troublesome preceding one, Napoleon noted in his diary ". . . he is wrong. The Russians will never be Christians. The Spanish never have been." J. Lo Duca, ed., *Journal secret de Napoléon Bonaparte*, 1962, 125.

68. P. Shchegolov, "Katekhizis Sergeia Murav'eva-Apostola," *MG*, 1908, no. 11, 63–7; S. Volk, *Istoricheskie vzgliady dekabristov*, M-L, 1958, 270–2; and M. Nechkina, "Revoliutsiia napodobie ispanskoi," *K i S*, 1931, no. 10, 3–40; and M. Alekseev, *Ocherki*, 116 ff. In the early nineteenth century, Nadezhdin compared the role Russia was about to play in spiritually awakening Europe to that which Spain had played in bringing Europe out of the Middle Ages. See N. Koz'min, *Nikolai Ivanovich Nadezhdin*, P, 1912, 184–5. See also V. Botkin, *Pis'ma ob Ispanii*, P, 1847.

69. J. Ortega y Gasset, *Invertebrate Spain*, NY, 1937, 71 mt; see also 155. One also detects in such critiques of "indolent and stupidly fatalistic" Russia as that of F. Araujo, "Nitchevo," *La España moderna*, 1904, Dec, 177–80, a certain understanding born of similarity.

Spanish fascination with Russia was probably originally stimulated by close Spanish links with Catholic Poland, and produced a flurry of books and pamphlets on Russia in the early seventeenth century (see Lamansky, "O slavianakh," esp. 352). Russian figures appear in Spanish literature of the later seventeenth century (the Duke of Muscovy, for instance, in Calderón's *Life Is a Dream*); and another great Spanish writer, Lope de Vega, wrote the first in a long line of Western dramatic elaborations of the story of the false Dmitry: *El Gran Duque de Moscovia y Emperador Perseguido* in 1607 just a few months after Dmitry's death, though it was not published until 1612 and has (for good artistic reasons) never become popular.

There was renewed Spanish interest in Russian literature in the late nineteenth century. See G. Portnoff, *La literatura rusa en España*, NY, 1932.

70. F. Dostoevsky, *PSS*, P, 1895, X, 114; also "the most magnificent and saddest of books ever created by the genius of man." (XI, 306.) See L. Turkevich, *Cervantes in Russia*, Princeton, 1950, for the extraordinary impact of the work on nineteenth-century Russian literature and criticism; and N. Evreinov, *The Theater in Life*, NY, 1927, 83–97, for an ecstatic, early-twentieth-century paean to "Don Quixotism." See also G. Schanzer, "Lazarillo de Tormes in Eighteenth-Century Russia," *Symposium*, 1962, spring, 55–62.

71. See "La literatura española en Russia," *La España moderna*, 1900, Oct, 186. A convert to Orthodoxy of Spanish extraction has emphasized the concomitant antipathy of Spanish Christendom to Rome: Archimandrite P. de Ballester, "The Subconscious Orthodoxy of the Spanish Race," *ROJ*, 1960, Dec, 4–7. The Muscovite attitude that the twin agents of the Antichrist were the Turkish Sultan and the Roman Pope was concurrently widespread in Spain (and present in both countries prior to the Reformation). See P. Alphandery, "Antichrist dans le moyen âge latin," in *Mélanges Hartwig Derenbourg*, 1909, 274–7.

72. E. Lehrman, ed., *Turgenev's Letters*, NY, 1961, 21–2.

73. "La causa es, que de mi pecho/ tan grande es el corazon,/ que teme, no sin razon,/ que el mundo le viene estrecho." Cited in G. Brenan, *The Literature of the Spanish People*, Cambridge, 1953, 277, in the midst of a good gen-

eral discussion of "Calderón and the Late Drama," 275–314.

74. Lamansky, "Istoricheskiia zamechaniia k sochineniiu 'O slavianakh . . .'," *UZIAN*, V, 1859, second series of pages, 100–11.

75. An *opera seria* by Francesco Araja, *La forza dell'amore e dell odio*. See Findeizen, *Ocherki*, II, 12–13; M. Cooper, *Russian Opera*, London, 1951, 10 ff. Part of the musical fascination with Spanish themes may come from the fact that many musicians and composers imported with the first professional companies in the eighteenth century were Spaniards.

   In the world of poetry, Lermontov wrote a youthful melodrama, "The Spaniards," and originally set his masterpiece "The Demon" in Spain. D. Chizhevsky sees a parallel between the dream of absolute freedom in Calderón and the utopian expectations of Maiakovsky, the poetic troubador of Bolshevism, in "Majakovskij und Calderon," *Aus zwei Welten*, 308–18.

   The Russian sense of identification with the grotesque art of Goya, which was to become particularly strong during the Soviet period, was already anticipated in Constantine Balmont's essay on Goya ("Poeziia uzhasa," *Mir Iskusstva*, 1899, nos. 1–12, 175–85) which called the Spaniard the prophet of an altogether new world that puts "in place of the divine harmony of the spheres the irresistible poetry of horror" (176).

76. Cherepnin, *Paleografiia*, 107; Introduction by P. Blake to "New Voices in Russian Writing," *Encounter*, 1963, April, 32–5.

77. Malinin, *Filofei*, appendix, 63.

78. See the neglected study by N. Efimov, *"Rus'-Novy Izrail' "*: *Teokraticheskaia ideologiia svoezemnogo pravoslaviia v do-petrovskoi pis'mennosti*, Kazan, 1912. See also I. Zabelin, *Russkoe Iskusstvo*.

Cherti samobytnosti v drevnerusskom zodchestve, M, 1900, 16–17.

79. See, for instance, "Skazanie o mamaevom poboishche," in *Russkie povesti XV–XVI vekov*, M-L, 1958, 17.

80. The dating of the New Year from September was a later, sixteenth-century innovation, which was apparently related to the growing importance of celebrating the "Farewell to Summer" (*letoprovodstvo*) on September 1 (on which see B. Unbegaun, "Remarques sur l'ancien calendrier russe," in *Mélanges Georges Smets*, Brussels, 1952, 641–7). There is no evidence of a Jewish derivation; but September 1 (Feast of St. Simeon) would not seem to be either intrinsically or ecclesiastically a good time to celebrate the coming of the New Year. Nor should one automatically assume Byzantine derivation. V. Moshin has concluded (*TODL*, XIX, 1963, 46) that the previous Russian system of dating the new year from March 25 (the Feast of the Annunciation of the Virgin) was taken from Western Europe rather than Byzantium. The adoption of this new system occurred long after the fall of Byzantium and the initial flight of monks to Muscovy. The only other apparent example of New Year's Day being celebrated on September 1 was in pre-Christian Greece. See A. Giry, *Manuel de diplomatique*, 1925, 108. The proclamation of the New Year on September 1 in Old Russia was associated with the scriptural passage (Luke 4:18) in which Christ entered the synagogue and read the passage from Isaiah proclaiming "the year of the Lord's favor"; and was accompanied by an elaborate procession into a cathedral, symbolically re-enacting the divine entry into the synagogue.

81. S. Zenkovsky, *Epics*, 81.

82. A. Poppé, "Russie," 28–30; E.

Bickermann, "Sur la Version vieux-russe de Flavius Josèphe," *AIOS,* VI, 1936, 53–84; N. Meshchersky, *"Istoriia Iudeiskoi voiny," Iosifa Flaviia v drevnerusskom perevode,* M-L, 1958.

83. A. Harkavy, *Hadashim gam Ye-chanim,* P, 1885, cited in N. Slouschz, "Les Origines du Juda-ïsme dans l'Europe Orientale," in *Mélanges Derenbourg,* 79.

84. On the puzzling matter of the Khazar decline and legacy see D. Dunlop, *A History of the Jewish Khazars,* Princeton, 1954, 222–63; also S. Szyszman ("Les Khazars: problèmes et controverses," *RHR,* CLII, 1957, 174–221), who berates the lack of attention paid to the Khazar legacy (220–1); also the bibliography in *BNYL,* 1938, Sep, 696–710.

Present-day differences in assessing the role of the Khazars in the development of Russian civilization seem to reflect a kind of historiographical sparring between Muscovite chauvinism and Leningrad cosmopolitanism. For the former, B. Rybakov speaks of Khazaria as "parasitical" and devoid of cultural significance (*SA,* XVIII, 1953, 147), for the latter, V. Mavrodin gave, even in the Stalin era, a more positive appraisal, demonstrating their influence on subsequent place names (*Obrazovanie,* 184–5). M. Artamanov has taken vigorous issue with Rybakov and much of Stalinist scholarship on the subject in his important *Istoriia khazar,* L, 1962, but feels that Khazar influence on Russian culture was largely short-lived and superficial, 365–495, esp. 458–9. See also 366, note 5, for Russian use of the Khazar title in the first half of the ninth century; and the section from Artamanov translated in Spector, *Readings,* 3–13.

For Jewish literary influences in the Kievan period, the sketchy

discussions in Gudzy, *History,* 183, and Chizhevsky, *History,* 161–2, should be supplemented by the long if somewhat rambling and inconclusive study of Kievan texts by G. Baratts, *Sobranie trudov po voprosu o evreiskom elemente v pamiatnikakh drevne-russkoi pis'-mennosti,* Berlin-Paris, 1924–7, three parts in 2v. See also the neglected study by I. Malyshevsky, "Evrei v iuzhnoi Rusi i Kieve v X-XII vv," *TKDA,* 1879, Sep. Some reciprocal early Russian influence on Jewish letters is suggested by A. Harkavy, *Ob iazyke Evreev zhivshikh v drevnee vremia na Rusi i o slavianskikh slovakh vstrecha-emykh u evreiskikh pisatelei,* P, 1865. N. Meshchersky sees substantial evidence of Khazar influence, "Vizantiisko-slavianskie lite-raturnye sviazi," *VV,* XVII, 1960, esp. 67–8.

85. On this 174-word glossary of 1282 appended to a Novgorod copy of the church canon see A. Karpov, *Azbukovniki ili alfavity inostran-nykh rechei po spiskam solovetskoi vivlioteki,* Kazan, 1877, 12, also 43-4.

86. V. Deliuev, "Kastalsky and his Russian Folk Polyphony," *ML,* 1929, Oct, 387–90.

Among the similarities between Jewish and Russian folk music are the repeated reliance on augmented seconds and the setting of songs of joy and humor in a minor key rather than a major; but the interrelationship between the two musical traditions has never been systematically studied.

87. N. Kompaneisky suggests that the decline of the authority of the Greek (*kondakarnoe*) chant in the fourteenth century may be related to the fact that Russia had a pre-Byzantine musical culture derived from the Jewish chant; and that the Greek system of notation was never able to superimpose itself

completely on this tradition. ("O sviazi," 733–8, 820–7).

Some links between Jewish and Eastern Slavic cantillation are apparently hinted at for the seventeenth century by Rabbi S. Margolis, *Chibbure Likkutim,* Venice, 1715. Some other similarities are noted by E. Werner in E. Wellesz, ed., *Ancient and Oriental Music,* Oxford, 1957, esp. 317, 329–32; and A. Idelsohn, in *Acta Musicologica,* IV, 1932, 17–23; and in *MQ,* 1932, Oct, 634–45. The question seems never to have been seriously studied from the Slavic side.

88. On their influence see Vernadsky, *Dawn,* 216–9 and references.

89. Dubnov, *History,* I, 93. A Latin derivation is possible for *arrendare* and a Turkish one for *kabala,* though the latter term also has the meaning "secret contract" as well as "secret teaching" in Hebrew. See the early use in the sense of "service contract" in I. Sreznevsky, *Materialy dlia slovaria drevne-russkogo iazyka,* P, 1893, I, 1169–70; see also *REW,* I, 494.

On the influx from the West and the coming of Yiddish culture from Poland into West Russia see Y. Hertz, *Die Yiden in Ookruyne,* NY, 1949; Slouschz, "Origines," 70–81; L. Wiener, "Evreisko-nemetskie slova v russkikh narechiiakh," *ZhS,* V, 1895, 57–70.

90. An excellent (though unhistorical) picture of small-town Yiddish culture in Eastern Europe is presented by M. Zborowski and E. Herzog, *Life Is with People. The Culture of the Shtetl,* NY, 1962, p. See J. Raisin, "The Jewish Contribution to the Progress of Russia," *The Jewish Forum,* 1919, Feb,

129–38; Apr, 870–80; May, 939–51, for many little-known illustrations from the modern period. A hostile but sometimes revealing Orthodox treatment is N. Gradovsky, *Otnosheniia k evreiam v drevnei i sovremennoi Rusi,* P, 1891.

91. Compare the chronicle account in *PSRL,* XX, 354–5, with that in W. Leonhard, *The Kremlin Since Stalin,* NY, 1962, p, 45–9.

92. Margaritov, *Istoriia,* esp. 128–33.

93. A. Castro, *The Structure of Spanish History,* Princeton, 1954, 529; and 524–44 for a classic characterization of the Jewish impact on Spain.

94. See L. Shapiro, "The Role of the Jews in the Russian Revolutionary Movement," *SEER,* 1962, Jun, 148–67.

95. H. von Eckhardt, *Ivan the Terrible,* NY, 1949, 49.

96. J. Fennell, ed., *The Correspondence between Prince A. M. Kurbsky and Tsar Ivan IV of Russia, 1564–1579,* Cambridge, 1955, 46.

97. *Ibid.,* 35; see also 33, 47–9.

98. *Ibid.,* 21–3.

99. *Ibid.,* 2–3.

100. *Ibid.,* 207–9, referring to I Samuel 27.

101. Shevchenko, "Source," 172–3.

102. See the new interpretation advanced by G. Mozheeva, *Valaamskaia Beseda, pamiatnik russkoi publitsistiki serediny XVI veka,* M-L, 1958, 89–93, 98–105; for another discussion of this puzzling document, see Val'denberg, *Ucheniia,* 299–307.

103. Shevchenko, "Source," 173.

104. Citations from Rzhiga edition of Peresvetov's works in *Cht,* 1908, I, otd II, "Skazanie o tsare o Konstantine," 70–1; "Skazanie o magmete-saltane," 72.

2. THE COMING OF THE WEST

1. Noting these influences, Nekrasov insists (*Izobrazitel'noe iskusstvo,* 113 ff.) that the major idiosyncra-

cies of the art of Vladimir-Suzdal are explicable either from Eastern influences or from the primitive, semi-animistic predilections of the native Finnish and Slavic population of the northern region. See also M. Alpatov, "K voprosu o zapadnom vliianii v drevnerusskom iskusstve," *Slavia*, III, 1924–5, 96–7. This is an invaluable survey.

2. Nekrasov, *Iskusstvo*, 222 ff.; Likhachev, *Die Kultur*, 31 ff.; also the seminal new study of I. Golenishchev-Kutuzov, *Ital'ianskoe Vozrozhdenie i slavianskaia literatura XV–XVI vekov*, M, 1963, which points out how Western ignorance of Eastern Europe has limited Western scholarly understanding of the Renaissance period.

3. Dal, *Poslovitsy*, 329.

4. Kovalevsky, *Manuel*, 90–1 and ff. for a succinct discussion of the integration of Novgorod into Muscovy. There was a German-Scandinavian merchant quarter in Novgorod by the early eleventh century and at least one Western church by the twelfth. See A. Stender-Petersen, *Varangica*, Aarhus, 1953, 255–8.

5. N. Porfiridov, *Drevny Novgorod. Ocherki iz istorii russkoi kul'tury XI–XV vv*, M-L, 1947, 14, 226–7.

6. *BE*, XLI, 248. The studies of M Lesnikov (referenced *Uch (5)*, 88, note 1) cast doubt on the assumption of many Great Russian historians that the Hanseatic link was an unequal one of—in effect—colonial dependency. The studies of N. Kazakova (referenced *ibid.*, 88, notes 2 and 3) trace the series of actions taken by Ivan III and Vasily III to break the link. See older studies of the connection by M. Berezhkov, *O torgovle Rusi s Ganzoi do kontsa XV veka*, P, 1879; and L. Goetz, *Deutsch-russische Handelsgeschichte des Mittelalters*, Lübeck, 1922.

One interesting illustration of the links is the Slavonic inscriptions on a processional cross of the North German town of Hildes-heim, revealing an apparently twelfth-century gift to the town by the Archbishop of Novgorod. See *BLDP*, I, 1914, 36–40. For more illustrations M. Alpatov, "K voprosu," 97 ff. For early German literary influences see E. Petukhov, "Sledi neposredstvennogo vliianiia nemetskoi literatury na drevnerusskuiu," *ZhMNP*, 1897, no. 7, 145–58. Novgorod's link with the East also left traces on its folklore and architecture. See, for instance, A. Nikitsky, "Sledy vostoka v Novgorode," *Trudy Vgo Arkheologicheskago S'ezda v Tiflise 1881*, M, 1887, 262–3.

7. Compare the account in Poppé, "Russie," 22–7, with the estimate here cited from Likhachev, *Die Kultur*, 24. The latter purports to hold true for the Russian north generally, but because the evidence is drawn almost exclusively from the extensive recent excavations in Novgorod, it would seem more reasonable to limit its application there.

8. Artsikhovsky views the extensive excavations at Novgorod (which he has headed) as confirming the existence of a mixed government prior to the fourteenth century, and of a pure republic by the end of the fifteenth. XI Congrès International des Sciences Historiques. *Résumés des communications*, Uppsala, 1960, 93–4. D. Obolensky *(ibid.*, 92) emphasizes the concurrent hugeness of the ecclesiastical establishment.

9. *PSRL*, III, 83. See also A. Nikitsky, "Ocherk vnutrennei istorii tserkvi v Velikom Novgorode," *ZhMNP*, 1879, Jul, 39–41. Nikitsky's discussion, 34–86, remains a solid and subtle reading of the complex political-ideological tensions of the period. Also valuable is Zhmakin, "Daniil," 38 ff. On the archbishop who defended the faith and his ideas see A. Sedel'nikov, "Vasily Kalika: l'histoire et la

légende," *RES*, VII, 1927, 224–40.

It seems fairer to speak of a "Muscovite fifth column" than of Russian and Lithuanian factions within Novgorod (as Great Russian historians generally do), because Moscow was the aggressive party. Expanding ties with Lithuania was in the traditional Novgorodian pattern, and the real pressure for change in Novgorod came from the Muscovite party and its allies

10. Budovnits, *Publitsistika*, 75–7 and references; also D. Stremooukhoff, "La Tiare de Saint Sylvestre et le klobuk blanc," *RES*, XXXIV, 1957, 123–8; Gudzy, *History*, 278–95.

11. Nikitsky, "Ocherk," 41 ff. for discussion and references.

12. See *Cht*, 1847, no. 8, 1–6 (separate pagination at the end), especially Gennadius' allegation that (2) "Novgorod is not one in Orthodoxy with Moscow." See also his call to the Metropolitan of Moscow to make his prince worthy of the Old Testament kings (*AAE*, I, 480) "for the sake of his eternal salvation" and "our pastorship" (482). Also later letters of Gennadius to Metropolitan Simon of Moscow in *AI*, I, 104, 147.

G. Vernadsky stresses the considerable sympathy Ivan felt for the heretics because of their congruent opposition to ecclesiastical wealth ("The Heresy of the Judaizers and Ivan III," *Speculum*, 1933, Oct, 436–54).

13. Fedotov, "Fools," 9–10.

14. Tver also served, however, as an intermediary, like Novgorod and Pskov, for the "third Rome" doctrine. See Stremooukhoff, "Third Rome," 88, note 25; Gudzy, *History*, 302–5, esp. note 4.

15. Zhmakin, "Daniil," 1–2 note 2, 23.

16. Cited in Nikitsky, "Ocherk," 60.

17. B. Parain, "La Logique dite des Judaïsants," *RES*, XIX, 1939, 315–29; A. Sobolevsky, *Logika zhidovstvuiushchikh i "taina tainykh,"* *PDPI*, CXXXIII, 1897.

There is still no comprehensive analysis of the Judaizers, and their history (like that of the far more numerous Albigensians in the West) may never be properly written, because many of their own writings have not been preserved. For a recent study which presents some new material but tends to minimize Western influence by largely neglecting the problem of origins see Lur'e and Kazakova, *Antifeodal'nye dvizheniia*, esp. 87, 109–224. For a general survey of recent Soviet work see A. Klibanov, "Les Mouvements hérétiques en Russie du XIIIᵉ au XVIᵉ siècles," *CMR*, 1962, Oct-Dec, 673–84. For bibliography of earlier works and still valuable discussion of basic sources, see L. Bedrozhitsky, "Literaturnaia deiatel'nost' zhidovstvuiushchikh," *ZhMNP*, 1912, Mar, 106–22.

18. The population of Novgorod has been estimated for the mid-sixteenth century to have been somewhat in excess of 20,000 by N. Chechulin (*Goroda Moskovskago gosudarstva v XVI veke*, P, 1889, 50–2), which is considerably less than the total of 72,000 said to have been deported from Novgorod to Moscow by V. Zhmakin ("Daniil," 48 note 1, following Kostomarov). Although this latter figure is almost certainly inflated, it seems probable that early deportations exceeded the numbers left behind.

19. M. Tikhomirov, *Srednevekovaia Moskva v XIV–XV vekakh*, M, 1957, esp. 125–31, 147–53, for discussion and references on the Italians and their agents (collectively known as *surozhane*, from *Surozh* or *Sudak*, one of the two principal Crimean-Italian ports). Tikhomirov's otherwise valuable section on urban culture of the period (238–

71) offers no speculation on, or investigation of, possible cultural influences of this foreign community. On the use of paper with Italian (and subsequently other foreign) watermarks see N. Likhachev, *Bumagi i drevneishiia bumazhnyia mel'nitsy v moskovskom gosudarstve*, P, 1891, esp. 93; and his restated conclusions in *Diplomatika*, P, 1901, esp. 174–5, 181–3, 191.

For further details on the Genoese links with Muscovy see G. Brătianu, *Recherches sur le commerce de Gênes dans la second moitié du XIII⁰ siècle*, 1929; Levchenko, *Ocherki*, 522 ff.; and Kovalevsky, *Manuel*, 97–102 and references. On fourteenth-century Genoese charting of Russia see Lubimenko, "Role," 41. F. Skrzhinskaia points out ("Petrarka o genueztsakh na levante," *VV*, II, 1949, esp. 246–7) that Genoa was in effect trying to counter Venetian dominance of the Adriatic by gaining dominance over the Eastern sea approach to Slavdom: the Black Sea. M. Tikhomirov ("Rossiia i Vizantiia," 32–3) points out that because of the developing Genoese alliance with the Mongols, Russia increasingly cultivated the Venetian side in this dispute.

20. For the discussion of this little-known church at Volotovo, just south of Novgorod, which was built in 1352, restored and studied just before World War II, and apparently destroyed during it, see N. Porfiridov, "Zhivopis' Volotova," *NIS*, VII, 1940, 55–65. The outward appearance seems to have been that of a conventional small church of the Kievan period (*ibid.*, 48–54).

21. Veselovsky, *Vliianie*, 14; and his "Italianische Mysterium in einem russischen Reisebericht des XV Jahrhunderts," *Russische Revue*, X, 1877, 425–41; and A. Popov, 100–6. On the Russian participa-

tion in the Council of Florence see (in addition to previously referenced works) (from the Catholic point of view), G. Hofmann, "S. I. Kardinal Isidor von Kiev," *OC*, XXVII, 1926; and O. Halecki, *From Florence to Brest 1439–1596*, Rome, 1958, which has made fresh use of Vatican archival materials; and (from the Orthodox) Kartashev, *Ocherki*, I, 349–62, 517–29. The first translation from Latin to Russian was apparently made in connection with the Council. See A. Sobolevsky, *Perevodnaia literatura*, 39, note 1.

22. V. Snegirev, *Aristotel Fioravanti i perestroika moskovskogo kremlia*, M, 1935. There is also believed to have been some indigenous sculpturing in Moscow in the 1460's, prior to Sophia's arrival, probably of Italian inspiration. See "Iz istorii russkoi skul'ptury," *IL*, 1914, no. 7, 874–5; also Tikhomirov, *Moskva*, 211–14. New material on Russo-Italian contacts during the High Renaissance is discussed and referenced in M. Gukovsky, "Soobshchenie o Rossii moskovskogo posla v Milan (1486 g)," in S. Valk, ed., *Voprosy istoriografii i istochnikovedeniia istorii SSSR*, M-L, 1963, 648–55.

For the Italian and Roman Catholic impact on Russia during this early period the basic works of P. Pierling, *La Russie*, I, II, should be read in the light of the detailed review essay based on Pierling's earlier work on this subject by F. Uspensky, "Snosheniia Rima s Moskvoi," *ZhMNP*, 1884, Aug, 368–411, Oct, 316–39. See also the archival materials, excerpts, and references assembled for the Academy of Sciences under the editorship of E. Shmurlo, *Rossiia i Italiia*, P, 1907–15, 3v, each in two parts. Except for the second part of the third volume (which deals with Spanish relations with

Russia in the late sixteenth century), almost all of these materials pertain to Russo-Italian relations prior to the seventeenth century, many of them from libraries unused by Pierling. For the contact and struggle with Latin and Italian influences in Pskov see Kliuchevsky, *Otzyvy i izsledovaniia*, M, (nd), 71–87.

23. See the discussion of Sophia's influence in Vernadsky, *Dawn*, 18–26, 122–33; also referenced works of V. Savva and K. Bazilevich.

24. The translation of the Bible by Skorina (published in Prague, 1517–9, and Vilnius, 1525) was into a kind of embellished White Russian which was not intended to be the vernacular tongue of anyone and could be read only with difficulty in Great Russia. A number of partial, vernacular translations subsequently appeared; but the fullest and best was the Ostrog Bible of 1580, which was based on the translation of Gennadius. See basic discussion and references in *BE*, VI, 690–6; also I. Evseev, *Gennadievskaia bibliia 1499*, M, 1914.

The importance of Latin influences on the Novgorod hierarchy is stressed by Denisoff, "Origines," 77–88; and (in addition to works cited therein) by A. Sedel'nikov, "Ocherki katolicheskogo vliianiia v Novgorode v kontse XV-nachale XVI v," *DAN*, L, 1929, 16–19. On the Croatian Dominican Benjamin see Budovnits, *Publitsistika*, 102, esp. note 1, suggesting that he was the author of the influential *Slovo kratko*, defending church landholding (text in *Cht*, 1902, Kn. II, otd. ii, 1–60).

25. The fact that the *Donation* came into general Russian usage a century after Lorenzo Valla's exposure had discredited it in the West is a good illustration of the

extent to which the Eastern Slavs were out of touch with contemporary Western intellectual life. For the extensive sixteenth-century Russian use of the *Donation* see Val'denberg, *Ucheniia*, 212, note 4, 270, 284–9. It was officially incorporated into the "Hundred Chapters" by the church assembly of 1551; see Duchesne, *Stoglav*, 171–3.

26. Letter of October 1490 to Metropolitan Zosima of Moscow, *AAE*, I, 480.

27. I. Bloch, *Der Ursprung der Syphilis*, Jena, 1901, 280–1; and V. Ikonnikov, "Blizhny Boiarin Afanasy Ordyn-Nashchokin," *RS*, 1883, Nov, 289, note 1. M. Kuznetsov, *Prostitutsiia i sifilis v Rossii*, P, 1871, 68, points out that syphilis arrived in Cracow shortly before Russia.

28. The term used was *friaz* rather than *latinian;* but the former was used in Muscovy with a meaning closer to "Latin" than to "Frankish," from which it is technically derived. *Friaz* was generally used for secular Latin elements in Moscow; *latinian;* to designate the more distinctively ecclesiastical West. Volpe was renamed *Friazin* in Muscovy; and Gennadius spoke admiringly of how the *Friazove* kept their faith firm in the face of heresy (*AAE*, I, 482).

29. According to G. Uspensky (*Opyt povestvovaniia o drevnostiakh russkikh*, Kharkov, 1818, 2d corr, ed., 77–8) the distillation of vodka was perfected on the island of Majorca, and transmitted to the Genoese by Raymond Lully, the alchemist-philosopher and bitter foe of Dominican rationalism.

The early history of alcoholic beverages has never been adequately written. A process of distillation sounding very much like that used for aqua vitae is described by Bernard of Gordon,

Tractatus de gradibus in 1303, and was almost certainly known even earlier to Arnold of Villanova. If knowledge of aqua vitae in the West probably predates Lully, the transmission of the knowledge to Russia may well have occurred later than the late fourteenth or early fifteenth century—particularly in the absence of references to it in the sources of the period. Nevertheless, the substantial early Italian links with Moscow, the Russian interest in Lully, and Uspensky's own stature as an eminent professor of history and geography at Kharkov (see the appraisal by I. Zil'berman, *Kniga G. F. Uspenskogo "Opyt povestvovaniia o drevnostiakh russkikh" 1818 g. i eia chitateli,* Kharkov, 1916) give an air of authority to his derivation. He mentions (83) the prohibitionary regulations introduced by the khans in the late fourteenth century after their conversion to Islam; and this could be one of the reasons for the relative paucity of information on alcoholic drinks in the documents of the time. There are ample references to vodka and other drinks beginning in the late sixteenth century. But the first clear listing of the term "vodka" in a dictionary is in Polikarpov's *Leksikon* of 1704 (*SSRIa,* II, 507). Whether or not vodka was actually introduced through alchemistic channels, it did acquire a kind of magical aura for the Russian national mentality, as the pseudonymous Soviet writer A. Tertz recently affirmed in characterizing drunkenness as "our *idée fixe.* The Russian people drink not from need and not from grief, but from an age-old requirement for the miraculous and extraordinary—drink, if you will mystically, striving to transport the soul beyond earth's gravity and return it to its sacred noncorporeal

state. Vodka is the Russian *muzhik's* White Magic; he decidedly prefers it to Black Magic—the female." "Thought Unaware," *NL,* 1965, 19 Jul, 19.

On early drinking in Russia see E. Bartenev *et al., Tekhnologiia likero-vodochnogo proizvodstva,* M, 1955, 3; Tsvetaev, *Protestantstvo,* 717; and I. Pryzhov, *Istoriia kabakov v Rossii,* Kazan, 1914, 2d ed., 5–24. Wine arrived late in Russia (the first native production dating from the mid-seventeenth century) and was regarded as a foreign drink down to modern times. See B. Raikov, *Ocherki po istorii geliotsentricheskogo mirovozreniia v Rossii,* M-L, 1947, 2d ed., 53–65, for the influence of Lully.

30. M. Alekseev, "Zapadnoevropeiskie slovarnye materialy v drevnerusskikh azbukovnikakh XVI-XVII vekov," in *Akademiku Vinogradovu,* 41. Danckaert, *Beschrijvinge van Moscovien ofte Rusland,* Amsterdam, 1615, 63; cited in J. Locher, *Gezicht op Moskou,* Leiden, 1959, 22.

31. D. Tsvetaev, *Mediki v moskovskoi Rossii i pervy russky doktor,* Warsaw, 1896, 11–12; see also works referenced in the full bibliography, 3–6, esp. the studies by Richter and Novombergsky.

32. Rainov, *Nauka,* 264–5; Raikov, *Ocherki,* 78.

33. Veselovsky, *Vliianie,* 91, note 2; Kliuchevsky, "Vliianie," 144, 151–2.

34. Raikov, *Ocherki,* 55–7. Vucinich's useful survey (*Science,* 3), which pays less attention to pre-Petrine science, errs in saying that "Russia was noted for the absence of persons engaged in [alchemy]."

35. Nikitsky, "Ocherk," 72, note 3.

36. See Budovnits, *Publitsistika,* 139–40, note 1, for full references and a short biography; also 59, 172, 183.

37. *Ibid.,* 183.

38. A Cambridge mathematician, Dee was well known as a spiritist throughout Eastern Europe, having spent most of the 1580's in Poland and Bohemia. A study of Dee by the Russo-German student of occult lore, Carl Kiesewetter, is inadequately referenced in Veselovsky, *Vliianie*, 20, and I have been unable to locate it in book form in any major library in the United States, Western Europe, or the USSR.

39. Most of these practices were of Byzantine and Eastern origin, and many were specifically outlawed by the "hundred chapters" and again by the Ulozhenie of 1649 (ch. 21, g. 15). See Raikov, *Ocherki*, 72–4; and V. Peretts, "Materialy k istorii apokrifa i legendy. I. K istorii gromnika," *ZPU*, ch. LIX, vyp. 1, 1899, which stresses Jewish as well as Greco-Byzantine sources.

40. This quasi-religious attitude toward science in early Russia is discussed in my "Science in Russian Culture," *American Scientist*, 1964, Jun, 274–80.

41. Cited in V. Zhmakin, "Daniil," ch. II, 376; and Val'denberg, *Ucheniia*, 302, note 1. See also discussion by Zhmakin (366–77) of the long campaign of the church against astrology dating from at least the early fifteenth century. Val'denberg suggests (228, note 1) that Daniel was less versed in Byzantine history than Joseph, and raises the implication that this influential metropolitan may have been even more influenced by Roman Catholic doctrines.

42. Val'denberg, 302.

43. Vucinich, *Science*, 7. For a scientific analysis of "The Six Wings" (*Shestokryl*), which was apparently translated directly from the Hebrew of Immanuel ben-Jacob, and for signs that the group had links with Crimean Jews as well as Novgorodian circles see D. Sviatsky, "Astronomicheskaia kniga 'Shestokryl' na Rusi XV veka," *Mirovedenie*, 1927, May, 63–78; and Rainov, *Nauka*, 265 ff.; Raikov, *Ocherki*, 65, 88.

Some idea of the considerable extent of the Jewish mediation of classical, Arab, and even Persian scientific knowledge with Russia between the fifteenth and seventeenth centuries is provided in I. Gurliand, "Kratkoe opisanie matematicheskikh, astronomicheskikh, i astrologicheskikh evreiskikh rukopisei iz kollektsii firkovichei," *TVO*, XIV, 1869, 163–222.

44. On church opposition to systematic measurement, yet willingness to make extensive practical uses of mathematics, see the introduction to the sixteenth-century mathematical manuscript *Schetnaia mudrost'* in *PRPI*, XLIII, 1879, esp. 11–13. Also A. Kol'man. "Zachatki matematicheskogo myshleniia i vyrazheniia v dopetrovskoi Rusi," *Slavia*, XVIII, 1947–8, 306–15, who points out (308) that even in the early period Russia acquired mathematical knowledge from the West rather than Byzantium.

45. Veselovsky (*Vliianie*, 16) also includes the Pskovian correspondent of Philotheus, the d'iak Misiur-Munekhin, among the freethinkers. The re-examination of I. Viskovaty's career by N. Andreev ("Interpolation in the 16th century Muscovite Chronicles," *SEER*, 1956, Dec, 95–115, esp. 102 ff.) suggests that Viskovaty was an Orthodox Josephite, but does not deal with the reasons for the forced penance imposed on him in 1553–4 or his sudden execution by Ivan in 1570. Since these were both times in which Ivan was systematically purging Westward-looking ideological dissent from his realm, it would seem reasonable (though, of course, far from certain) to assume

that Ivan at least identified him to some extent with that point of view.

Perhaps the best study of Russian humanism is I. Golenishchev-Kutuzov, *Gumanizm u vostochnykh slavian*, M-L, 1963; but the richness of its picture depends largely on the inclusion of Ukrainian and White Russian cultural activity, which he agrees bore little connection with Great Russian culture until the late seventeenth and the eighteenth century.

46. V. Adrianova-Peretts, *Khozhenie za tri moria Afanasiia Nikitina*, M-L, 1948; discussion in A. Klibanov, *Reformatsionnye dvizheniia v Rossii v XIV-pervoi polovine XVI vv*, M, 1960, 367–83.

47. Klibanov, *Dvizheniia*, 291–4.

48. Quoted by A. Klibanov, "Istochniki russkoi gumanisticheskoi mysli," *VIMK*, 1958, Mar-Apr, 60; also 45–61 for summary of heretical ideas in fifteenth- and sixteenth-century Russia. See also R. Lapshin, "Feodosy Kosoi—ideolog krest'ianstva XVI v," *TODL*, IX, 1953, 235–50.

49. *Paradoxa* 4 and 6, in Fennell, *Correspondence*, 218–27. See also I. Yasinsky, "Sochineniia Kurbskago, kak istorichesky istochnik," *KUI*, 1888, no. 10–1; *Skazaniia Kurbskago*, P, 1868, 3d ed., 93–4; Veselovsky, *Vliianie*, 16–7; and references in Vernadsky, *Dawn*, 282–3, note 36.

50. Budovnits, *Publitsistika*, 183, and note, for the use of "Homeric" as a term of praise in Muscovy.

51. Chizhevsky, *History*, 271–5; Budovnits, 182–6; and V. Rzhiga, "Boiarin-zapadnik XVI veka (Fedor Ivanovich Karpov)," *UZ RANION*, IV, 1929.

52. Cited without reference in Budovnits, 185; for text see *LZAK*, XXI, 106–13. *Muchitel'stvo* was the standard Russian rendering of the Greek *tyrannis*, but also carried some of its present meaning of torture.

53. Budovnits, 221–9. For text of Erazm's *Blagokhotiashchim tsarem pravitel'nitsa i zemlemerie* see appendix to V. Rzhiga, "Literaturnaia deiatel'nost' Ermolaia Erazma," in *LZAK*, XXXIII, esp. 184–97. Erazm used the term *rataeve* for peasant. For a more detailed study superseding Budovnits' see T. Kolesnikov, "Obshchestvenno-politicheskie vzgliady Ermolaia Erazma," *TODL*, IX, 1953, 251–65. The theme of a utopian heaven on earth appears to have been first sounded on Russian soil by the heretical *strigol'niki* (shorn-heads) in fourteenth-century Novgorod. See the discussion of the *Poslanie Episkopa Fedora o zemnom rae* in Lur'e and Kazakova, *Dvizheniia*, 30 ff.

54. *Cht*, 1880, Kn. IV, 63–7; discussion in Klibanov, *Dvizheniia*, 288–9.

55. For the Russian side of Maxim's activities see V. Ikonnikov, *Maksim Grek i ego vremia*, Kiev, 1915, 2d ed. For the Western side see N. Gudzy, "Maksim Grek i ego otnoshenie k epokhe ital'ianskogo vozrozhdeniia," *KUI*, 1911, no. 7; K. Viskovaty, "K voprosu o literaturnom vliianii Savonaroly na Maksima Greka," *Slavia*, XVII, 1939–40, 128–33; and E. Denisoff, *Maxime le Grec et l'Occident*, 1943. See also the documented discussions of his polemic activities in Russia by D. Tsvetaev (*Literaturnaia bor'ba s protestantstvom v Moskovskom gosudarstve*, M, 1887, 8–21), V. Rzhiga ("Opyt po istorii publitsistiki XVI veka. Maksim Grek kak publitsist," *TODL*, I, 1934, 5–120), and Budovnits, *Publitsistika*, 136–66.

It remains unclear how much of the Russian version of Maxim's writings was done by him (or even subject to his review), because his

basic literary language was Greek
(a form far closer to the elegant
language of the humanists than to
contemporary, vernacular Greek).
See the analysis by Kh. Loparev in
BLDP, 1917, III, 50–70. For a
synoptic discussion of recent Greek
and Soviet writings on Maxim see
R. Klostermann, "Legende und
Wirklichkeit im Lebenswerk von
Maxim Grek," *OCP*, 1958, no. 3–
4, 353–70.

56. The first detailed information on
the discovery of America did not
reach Russia, however, until the
first translation (in 1584) from the
original Polish of Marcin Bielski's
Kronika Polska. See the introduction to the N. Charykov edition of
Kosmografiia 1670, P, 1878–81, 69.

57. Raikov, *Ocherki*, 88–96.

58. *Sochineniia prepodobnago Maksima Greka v russkom perevode*,
Sergiev Posad, 1910, ch. I, 100.

59. Budovnits, 137, note 1; M. Speransky, *Istoriia drevnei russkoi literatury*, M, 1914, 2d ed., 474–7 and
notes. Denisoff contends (*Maxime*,
245 ff.) that Maxim was in fact a
Dominican during his stay in
Italy.

60. *Sochineniia Maksima*, ch. I, 114.

61. *Ibid.*, ch. III, 51.

62. *Ibid.*, ch. I, 110.

63. *Cht*, 1847, no. 7, 10. Zhmakin,
"Daniil," ch. I, 151 ff. for the conflict between Maksim and Daniel.

64. *Sochineniia Maksima*, ch. I, 72.

65. *Ibid.*, 101.

66. *Ibid.*, 117.

67. *Ibid.*, 224.

68. B. Dunaev (*Pr. Maksim Grek i
grecheskaia ideia na Rusi v XVI v*,
M, 1916), contends that Maxim
continued to be preoccupied with
freeing the Greek church from
Turkish bondage, and relates his
difficulties in Russia less to ideology than to changes in Russian
policy toward Turkey (unconvincing to me and to the critical reviewer in *BLDP*, 1917, III, 13–15).

69. *Sochineniia Maksima*, ch. I, 108.

70. *Ibid.*, 213; text 203–14; derivation
from Savonarola discussed in K.
Viskovaty, "K voprosu."

71. A. Solov'ev, *Holy Russia: The
History of a Religious-Social Idea*,
The Hague, 1959.

72. M. Cherniavsky, "'Holy Russia':
A Study in the History of an Idea,"
AHR, 1958, Apr; and his review
of Solov'ev in *AHR*, 1961, Jul,
1121–2.

73. *Sochineniia Maksima*, 214.

74. E. Denisoff, "Une Biographie de
Maxime le Grec par Kourbski,"
OCP, XX, 1954, 44–84; and
"Maxime et ses vicissitudes au sein
de l'église russe," *RES*, XXXI,
1954.

75. Veselovsky, *Vliianie*, 13.

76. T. Livanova, *Ocherki i materialy
po istorii russkoi muzykal'noi kul'-
tury*, M, 1938, 55–7; and A. Swan,
"Chant," XXVI, 1940, 539–42.
Among other things, the codifica-
tion by Shaidurov introduced the
red diacritical marks over the
black hook notes as a guide to
pitch, the so-called *Shaidurovskie
pometki*.

77. For an interpretation of Fedorov's
historical role different from
others published in the USSR in
connection with the recent four
hundredth anniversary of the first
published volume in Muscovy
(his *Acts of the Apostles*) see N.
Ivanov's consideration in terms of
the development of religious
knowledge in *Zhurnal Moskovskoi
patriarkhii*, 1964, no. 4, 69–75; no.
5, 75–8; no. 6, 68–77. See also R.
Jakobson, *Ivan Fedorov's Primer*,
Cambridge, Mass., 1955.

78. Cited in Denisoff, *Maxime*, 244–5.

79. Zhmakin, "Daniil," I, 254 note 5.

80. B. Unbegaun, *La Langue russe au
XVIᵉ siècle (1500–1550)*, 1935,
20–8. The Latinized German of
the Imperial Ambassador was
called the "Caesarish language"
(*tsezarsky iazyk*).

81. Deemed probable by M. Tikhomirov, *Srednevekovaia Moskva*, 212.

82. Discussion and text in P. Berkov, "Odna iz stareishikh zapisei 'Tsaria Maksimiliani' i 'Shaiki razboinikov,' (1885)," *RF*, IV, 1959, 331–74. The first emperor with whom formal diplomatic arrangements were established was Maximilian's father, Frederick III; but Maximilian became the symbol of Latin emperor for the Russian imagination.

The play is usually thought to have originated in the seventeenth or early eighteenth century (Lo Gatto, *Teatro*, I 120–1), but may be even older. It is variously connected with Peter the Great, Alexis Mikhailovich, and Ivan IV (Evreinov, *Histoire*, 133–5); and was also presented in variant forms under the title *Tsar-Herod*. See the illustrated study by I. Eremin, "Drama igra 'Tsar Irod,' " *TODL*, IV, 1940, 223–40.

83. Tsvetaev, *Protestantstvo*, 369–72. Of the many histories of the Russian Church, L. Boissard's otherwise outdated *L'Église* is particularly perceptive in relating Russian Church history to that of the Western European religious wars (see esp. II, 56–129). A similar approach at a much higher level of scholarship was projected by N. Chaev, but was never brought to fruition because of his death during the siege of Leningrad. See, however, his posthumously published "Moskva-Trety Rim v politicheskoi praktike moskovskago pravitel'stva XVI veka," *IZ*, 1946, esp. 3, 17–8, for indications of his approach.

84. Harkavy, "Ob iazyke," 119–20; Popov, *Obzor*, 111, for use in the early twelfth. On the German suburb see Tsvetaev, *Protestantstvo*, 30–1; see also, for the sixteenth-century confrontation with Protestantism in the Baltic region, W. Kahle, *Die Begegnung des baltischen Protestantismus mit der russisch-orthodoxen Kirche*, Leiden-Cologne 1959; L. Arbusow, *Die Einführung der Reformation in Liv-, Est-, und Kurland*, Leipzig, 1921; and the extensive material—much of it never used, even by Tsvetaev—in H. Dalton, *Beiträge zur Geschichte der evangelischen Kirche in Russland*, Gotha, 1887–1905, 4v.

85. Tsvetaev, *Protestantstvo*, 122, 584, also 6, 25–31, 41–8, 115–23; Dalton, *Beiträge*, I, 16, note. Russians distinguished between different "Germans" by affixing the adjective English, Dutch, Hamburgish, and so on, before *nemtsy*. (See, for instance, the petition for the closing of the "German suburb" in 1646; *AAE*, IV, 14–23.) The term is usually derived from *nemoi:* "mute" or "not speaking Russian." The term "Saxon" was a common synonym for "German" in Northeast Europe—*saksa* even today being the Finnish word for German.

86. Tsvetaev, *Protestantstvo*, 212–13; Yu. Tolstoy, "Pervye snosheniia Anglii s Rossieiu," *RV*, 1873, no. 6; and works by I. Gamel' and I. Lubimenko referenced in *Bibliografiia po istorii narodov SSSR*, M-L, 1932, ch II, 35.

87. See S. Polčin, "La Mission religieuse de P. Antoine Possevin S.J. en Moscovie (1581–1582)," *OC*, CL, 1957. In keeping with the shifting opportunities of the era Possevino, who eventually ended up as an ideological ally of Poland, had previously played an important role in the diplomatic-ecclesiastical effort to win Scandinavia back for Catholicism. See O. Garstein, *Rome and the Counter-Reformation in Scandinavia*, Bergen, 1963, I (up to 1583).

For the introduction of ideological overtones into the Livonian War see V. Vasil'evsky, "Pol'skaia i nemetskaia pechat' o voine Batoriia s Ioannom Groznym," *ZhMNP*, 1889, Jan, 127–67; Feb, 350–90; and P. Pierling, *Bathory et Posse-*

vino, 1887 for documents, and *Le Saint-Siège, la Pologne et Moscou, 1582–1587*, 1888, for careful analysis. Of the numerous studies of Ivan, the work of the Latvian scholar, R. Vipper, *Ivan Grozny*, M, 1947 (3d ed. in English trans.) is particularly full on the Livonian Wars. See also Florovsky, *Chekhi*, 367–98.

88. Jan Rokyta as cited in Lur'e "O putiakh," 279–80.

89. S. Avaliani, *Zemskie sobory*, Odessa, 1910, ch. II, 38–42, 127, sees a parallel between the *chiny* of this *sobor* and the *états, Stände,* and *ordines* of the West. His careful study shows (11) that one fifth of the representatives were moneyed tradesmen and that (38) at least one seventh (and probably considerably more) were from provincial cities including those traditionally subservient to Lithuania.

For an historiographical guide to the controversies surrounding the thinly documented history of the zemsky sobors see I. A. Strationov's survey in *UZKU*, 1906, Mar, 1–32; and Avaliani, 1–134. It has long been believed that the "council of reconciliation" in 1550 was the first *zemsky sobor* (see E. Maksimovich in *ZRIB*, 1933, vyp. 9, esp. 14–15), and S. Shmidt has recently shown its representation to have included military figures belonging to the lower estates (*PRP*, IV, 1956, 261–3). However, the nature of this council was falsified by later forgers for political purposes (see the analysis by P. Vasenko and S. Platonov in *ZhMNP*, 1903, Apr, 386–400), and it appears to have been closer in spirit to the old ecclesiastical councils (on which see I. Likhnitsky, *Osviashchenny sobor*), of which there were some twenty-eight between 1105 and 1550 (according to V. Latkin, *Zemskie sobory drevnei Rusi*, P, 1885, 23, note 1).

The term *zemsky sobor* was not actually used at the time, but does usefully suggest the blending of the older ecclesiastical *osviashchenny sobor* into a council "of all the land" (*vseia zemlia*) assembled on any of a variety of representative principles to approve of important decisions of law or tax assessment. The only full-length Western study of the *sobors* is F. de Rocca's posthumously published and now-outdated *Les Zemskie Sobors*, 1899. See also J. Keep's study of the seventeenth-century *sobors* (and comparison therein to parliamentary bodies in the West): "Decline of the Zemsky Sobors," *SEER*, 1957, Dec, 100–22.

90. Avaliani, *Sobory*, 65–87. Kliuchevsky suggests that Dmitry summoned two councils in 1605 (*Opyty*, 549–51); and Rocca (*Sobors*, 25, 57–8) contends that the council confirming Fedor's succession to the throne in 1584 also passed on broader financial questions. Neither of these views is generally accepted; but Kliuchevsky demonstrates that representation was more widespread in terms of both regions and social classes in 1598 than in 1566 (*Opyty*, 476–500).

91. For the constitutional background of the new Polish republic and the contribution thereto of Lithuanian conciliar bodies the general account in Vernadsky, *Russia at the Dawn*, 171–89, 220–49, should be supplemented by M. Liubavsky, *Litovsko-russky seim*, M, 1901, 509–850.

The balance between conscious borrowing from the West and parallel independent improvisation has never been systematically assessed and may never be determined in view of the fragmentary documents available. The only hint of any link with previous Russian political traditions lies in the requirement in the imperial charter of 1616 that delegates to a new *sobor* be "self-supporting" (*postoiatel'ny*): the stipulation previously attached to participation in the Novgorodian *veche*. See A. Kabanov, "Organizatsiia vyborov na zemskikh soborakh XVII v." *ZhMNP*, 1910, no. 9, 107–8. Avaliani suggests, however, that conciliar ideas may have been more prevalent in sixteenth-century Russia than is generally assumed. *Sobory*, 3–17.

92. This sum was far in excess of anything comparable in the sixteenth century. Vasily III had given only 60 rubles in memory of his father, Ivan III; Ivan IV gave 100 for his son Vasily in 1563, and 1,000 for his wife Anastasia; and Ivan's successor, Fedor, despite his own compulsive piety and some debasement of the currency, gave a total of only 2,833 for his father. S. Veselovsky, *Izsledovaniia*, 330, note 11. Ivan also gave large sums to Sinai, Athos, and Jerusalem, *ibid.*, 339.

93. On the facts of the Tsarevich's death and Ivan IV's subsequent contrition see Veselovsky, 337–40; on the echoes in folklore, B. Putilov, "Pesnia o gneve Ivana Groznogo na syna," *RF*, IV, 1959, 5–32.

94. "U vsenarodnykh chelovek," N. Ustrialov, ed., *Skazaniia kniazia Kurbskago*, P, 1842, 39; "vsenarodnago mnozhestva," text of the official *opredelenie* of the sobor of 1598 in Yu. Got'e, *Akty otnosiashchiesia k istorii zemskikh soborov*, M, 1909, 13.

95. For the best study of this sad if colorful exodus see N. Golitsyn, "Nauchno-obrazovatel'nyia snosheniia Rossii s Zapadom v nachale XVII v," *Cht*, 1898, IV, ch. III, 1–34 and supplements 1–2. See also Sokolov, *Otnoshenie*, ch. 10; and on German admiration for Boris see I. Lubimenko, "Un Pré-

curseur de Pierre le Grand: Boris Godunov," *La Revue du mois*, 1909, Feb, esp. 210–12.

96. Particularly by Arnold Toynbee. See the abridgment by D. Somervell, *A Study of History*, NY-London, 1947, 12 and chart 561.

97. M. Roberts, *The Military Revolution, 1560–1660*, Belfast, nd, 32. Roberts, like the generally complementary work by G. Clark (*War and Society in the 17th Century*, Cambridge, 1958) and by J. Nef (*War and Human Progress*, Cambridge, Mass., 1950, esp. 3–370), excludes Eastern Europe almost completely. Roberts' argument can be extended east on the basis of the account of military changes in Russia provided in Bobrovsky, *Perekhod*, together with such basic accounts as A. Grishinsky and V. Nikol'sky (*Istoriia russkoi armii i flota*, M, 1911, I, 44–79) and W. Hupert (*Historju wojenna porozbiorowa*, Lwow 1921, I, 150–248) and A. Chernov in *TIAI*, 1948, no. 4, 115–57.

98. On this recently discovered document see the unpublished Radcliffe Doctoral dissertation of V. Tumins, *Polemics of Tsar Ivan IV against the Czech Brother Jan Rokyta*. For the text of Ivan's reply to Rokyta see "Drevnerusskiia polemicheskiia sochineniia protiv protestantov," *Cht*, 1878, II, esp. 2–20; see also discussion and references in A. Yarmolinsky, "Ivan the Terrible contra Martin Luther," *BNYL*, 1940, Jun, 455–60.

99. For the growing correspondence and sense of identity between Counter-Reformation Spain and Poland see Don Guillén de San Clemente, *Correspondencia inédita sobre la intervención de España en los sucesos de Polonia y Hungria 1581–1608*, Zaragoza, 1892, esp. xiv ff. in the introduction; correspondence and other materials in *Cht*, 1848, IV, ch. III, 1–14; and

1915, IV, ch. I; as well as the text of the Polish-Hapsburg treaty of 1613 together with commentary by F. Barwinski, *Przewodnik naukowy i literacki*, XXIII, 1895, 984–1003. For the basic documents showing the rise of Protestant-Catholic conflict in the Baltic see G. Forsten, *Baltiisky vopros v XVI i XVII stoletiiakh*, P, 1894, 2v; and his *Akty i pis'ma k istorii baltiiskago voprosa*, P, 1889, 2v (esp. I, 245–56, 275–83 for Spanish-Polish royal correspondence of the 1620's).

100. See A. Berga, *Les Sermons politiques du P. Skarga, S.J.*, 1916, for French translation of, and sober commentary on, the sermons of 1597. See also a series of articles by two different authors, "Politicheskaia deiatel'nost' Petra Skargi," *KUI*, 1902, no. 9; 1903, no. 2–3; 1905, nos. 7, 10; 1906, nos. 5, 11, 12; 1907, no. 3–4.

101. See Pierling, *La Russie*, III, 36–310; and "Barezzo Barezzi ou Possevino?" *RS*, 1900, Oct, 193–200. See also A. Florovsky, *Čeští Jesuité na Rusi*, Prague, 1941, esp. 97, note 5 (as well as much general material on Jesuit activities 3–103); and *Chekhi*, 402–3, notes.

102. S. Grochowski, *Rzym nowy szczęśliwszy nad stary*, Cracow, 1610, as quoted in the valuable article by Ambroise Jobert, "Les Polonais et le rayonnement intellectuel de Rome au temps de la Renaissance et de la Contre-Réforme," *RES*, XXVII, 1951, 183, also 168–83.

103. Letter of January, 1612, reprinted in *Cht*, 1915, IV, ch. I, 121–2. For the ambitious and conspiratorial Polish plan to establish hegemony in the late stages of the interregnum see the text of Sigismund's secret dispatch to his military leader Hetman Żółkiewski, together with commentary by A. Romanovich in *IM*, 1936, 92–6.

104. This process is chronicled in three well-documented articles by L.

Lewitter, "Poland, the Ukraine, and the 17th century," *SEER*, 1948, Dec, 157–71; 1949, May, 414–29; and "Peter the Great, Poland and the Westernization of Russia," *JHI*, 1958, Oct, 493–506.

105. On the complex problem of origins (which have sometimes also been traced to the more general influence of late medieval guilds) see E. Medynsky, *Bratskie shkoly Ukrainy i Belorussii v XVI–XVII vv i ikh rol' v vossoedinenii Ukrainy s Rossiei*, M, 1954, 26–9. This book makes the familiar error of using modern concepts to describe medieval institutions, labeling the brotherhood schools a "national" and "anti-Polish" movement rather than a religious movement with tinges of concern for local rights and traditions, as is made clear in K. Kharlampovich's excellent *Zapadno-russkie pravoslavnye shkoly v XVI i nachale XVII veka*, Kazan, 1898, and *Zapadno-russkie tserkovnye bratstva i ikh prosvetitel'naia deiatel'nost' v kontse XVI i v nachale XVII vv*, P, 1899. For other valuable materials on the brotherhoods see articles referenced in Veselovsky, *Vliianie*, 17–18; and *Bibliografiia po istorii*, ch. II, 161–3. For an exposition that seeks to dissociate their history from that of Great Russia altogether see Hrushevsky, *History*, 188–276. For the general struggle between Catholic and Orthodox in Russia see A. Arkhangel'sky, *Ocherki iz istorii zapadno-russkoi literatury*, M, 1888, 2v.

106. See M. Koialovich, "O snosheniiakh zapadno-russkikh pravoslavnykh k litovsko-pol'skim protestantam vo vremia unii," *Kh Cht*, 1860, Sep, esp. 225–38. See also the massive study of P. Zhukovich, *Seimovaia bor'ba pravoslavnago zapadno-russkago dvorianstva s tserkovnoi uniei*, P (till 1609, 3v, 1901; from 1609 to 1632, 6v,

1903–12). He paints on the whole a less diabolic picture of Sigismund than most Russian historians, indicating that 1611 was really the turning point in Sigismund's reign; and that his program of joint persecution of Protestant and Orthodox elements in the East was in large measure an attempt to compensate himself for Polish Catholic losses and persecutions in the West. (See second series, I, 54–115 and esp. 78–89). For more recent analyses of Protestant-Orthodox attempts at common action and mutual support see B. Lel'avsky, "Popytka unii evangelikov s pravoslavnymi v Pol'she," *Voskresnoe Chtenie*, Warsaw (Year 11, no. 32); and D. Oljančyn, "Zur Frage der Generalkonföderation zwischen Protestanten und Orthodoxen in Wilna 1599," *Kyrios*, 1936, no. 1, 29–46; and the important document on this meeting with Oljančyn's notes in *Kyrios*, 1936, no. 2, 198–205. See also S. Kot, "La Réforme dans le Grand-Duché de Lithuanie. Facteur d'occidentalisation culturelle," *AIOS*, XII, 1952, 201–61, with maps of Protestant churches and lists of converts and students in Western universities.

107. Medynsky, 22–4.

108. B. Unbegaun, "Russian Grammars before Lomonosov," *OSP*, VIII, 1958, 98; Medynsky, 52.

109. Based on Gennadius' earlier work in Novgorod, A. Arkhangel'sky, *Ocherki*, I, 345.

110. For the origins and spread of the anti-papal and anti-Catholic use of the Antichrist symbol see H. Preuss, *Die Vorstellungen vom Antichrist im späteren Mittelalter, bei Luther und in der konfessionellen Polemik*, Leipzig, 1906. For text of Zizanius' *Kirillova Kniga* see *Pamiatki polemichnogo pis'menstva kintsia XVI i poch XVII v*, Lwow, 1906, I, 31–20; for discussion A. Balanovsky, *Stefan*

Zizany, Pochaev, 1887; Tsvetaev, *Protestantstvo*, 611–46; and *Literaturnaia bor'ba*, 104–9.

The author of the second Slavic grammar, Miletius Smotritsky, moved in the opposite direction, accepting union after writing in 1610 his famous *Lament of the Eastern Church against Rome*. He became Bishop of Polotsk and a foe of Cyril Lukaris. See E. Shmurlo, "Milety Smotritsky v ego snosheniiakh s Rimom," *Trudy Vgo s'ezda russkikh akademicheskikh organizatsii za granitsei*, Sofia, 1932, 501–28.

111. According to the balanced appraisal of his career by Germanos Strenopoulos (the Orthodox Exarch of Western and Central Europe), *Kyrillos Loukaris 1572–1638*, London, 1951, 91. For Lukaris' links with England, *Journal of Religion*, XVI, 1936, 10–29; for his links with Russia, O. Vainshtein, *Rossiia i tridsatiletniaia voina*, L, 1947, 110 ff.; and for his correspondence and other basic materials, E. Legrand, *Bibliographie hellenique du XVII⁰ siècle*, 1896, IV, 161–521.

112. Letter of Rudolf Schmid reprinted in E. von Hurmazaki, *Fragmente zur Geschichte der Rumänen*, Bucharest, 1884, III, 106.

113. Florovsky, *Chekhi*, 408–10.

114. Medynsky, *Shkoly*, 76–86.

115. An event celebrated in the famous Finnish novel *Juho Vesainen* by Santeri Ivalo (*Valitut Teokset*, Porvoo, 1953), which had considerable impact on Finnish national self-consciousness after its first appearance in 1894.

116. Swedish documents in G. Forsten, "Politika Shvetsii v smutnom vremeni," *ZhMNP*, 1889, Feb, 333.

117. Fronsperger's *Kriegsbuch*. P. Bobrovsky, *Perekhod Rossii k reguliarnoi armii*, P, 1885, 131–7; *Och (6)*, M, 1955, 572–3. By the time Wallhausen's more elaborate treatises appeared a few years later in

Germany, they were almost immediately translated into Russian.

118. Appeals of Jun 15 and Sep 24, 1608, and Jun 3, 1609, in Forsten, "Politika," 339–41.

119. See the important posthumously published study of G. Bibikov, "Opyt voennoi reformy 1609–1610 gg," *IZ*, XIX, 1946, 3–16. Skopin-Shuisky was the hero of the most authentic folk ballads and tales of military heroism of the period (see Gudzy, *History*, 369–72; I. Eremin, ed., *Russkaia povest' XVII veka*, L, 1954, 28–38 for text of the tale of his death and 344–9 for commentary), and was probably not replaced in popular favor until the rise in acclaim of Minin, Pozharsky, and the campaign of 1612–13 in the nineteenth century.

120. See G. Zamiatin, *K voprosu ob izbranii Karla Filippa na moskovsky prestol*, Tartu, 1913, with historiographical discussion 1–7. See also V. Bochkarev, *Shvedo-russkie otnosheniia v smutnoe vremia i osada Pskova 1615 g*, Pskov, 1916; and for valuable additional details from the Swedish side see H. Almquist, *Sverige och Ryssland, 1595–1611*, Uppsala, 1907; "Die Zarenwahl des Jahres 1613," *ZOG*, 1913, III, 161–202; from the Russian side, P. Liubomirov, *Ocherk istorii nizhegorodskogo opolcheniia 1611–1613 gg*, M, 1939.

121. I. Lubimenko, "A Project for the Acquisition of Russia by James I," *EHR*, XXIX, 1914, 246–56.

122. Florovsky, *Chekhi*, 355–6 on the *kuranty* (from *courante* and also meaning in Russian "peal of bells"). A. Shlosberg, "Nachalo periodicheskoi pechati v Rossii," *ZhMNP*, 1911, Sep, 75–6, implies that the *kuranty* were in circulation even earlier. For reproduced texts and analysis see Shlosberg, 78–118, and *Cht*, 1880, II, 37–46. On the Anglo-Dutch rivalry see I. Lubimenko, "The Struggle of the Dutch with the English for the Russian Market in the Seventeenth Century," *TRHS*, VII, 1924, esp. 38–50; and other articles by her in *RH*, 1922, Sep-Oct, 1–22; and *RES*, IV, 1924; also articles by Lappo-Danilevsky in *ZhMNP*, 1885, Sep, and S. Arkhangel'sky in *IS*, 1936, no. 5. English investment never reached even one third the level of Dutch investment in the early seventeenth century; and English involvement declined precipitously during the English Civil War. By 1631 even the Vatican was relying on a Dutchman, the Catholic Nicholas Jansen, for information from Moscow. See E. Shmurlo, *Kurie a Pravoslavný východ v letech 1609–1654*, Prague, 1928, 316–17, part 2, 78–83.

123. For these and other attempted Western marriages see D. Tsvetaev, "Iz istorii brachnykh del v tsarskom sem'e moskovskogo perioda," *RV*, 1884, no. 7, 8.

124. For the program of Lutheran education in Livonia see Dalton, *Beiträge*, I, 50–132. On Skytte and the specifically Swedish role in Livonia see R. Liljedahl, *Svensk förvaltning i Livland 1617–1634*, Uppsala, 1933, esp. 273–80; 487–540.

The Swedish-Russian confessional warfare in the 1630's and 1640's has been analyzed for Ingermanland (the region in which St. Petersburg was later built) by C. Öhlander, *Om den Svenska Kyrkoreformationen uti Ingermanland (1617–1704)*, Uppsala, 1900, esp. 9–15, 29–121; and A. Soom, "Ivangorod als selbständige Stadt 1617–1649," *Öpetatud Eesti seltsi Aastaraamat*, Tartu, 1937, esp. 242–64.

On the essentially defensive Orthodox activities in the region see I. Chistovich, *Istoriia pravoslavnoi tserkvi v Finliandii i Estliandii*, P, 1856; also J. Salenius,

Kreikanusko Suomessa, Porvoo, 1873; E. Bäckman, "Den Kalvinska kyrkans trosbekännelse och katekis," *Suomen Kirkkohistoriallisen Seuran Vuosikirja,* 1938, 30–2; and the historical section (1–178) of N. Berg, *Exercitatio historico—theologica de statu ecclesiae et religionis Moscoviticae,* Stockholm, 1704 (Lübeck, 1709). Written by the head of the theological academy at Uppsala, this work is the first thorough study written anywhere of the Russian Church, and is still an invaluable source. See Rushchinsky, *Byt,* 33–4.

125. All were apparently built after the destruction by the Polish occupation of all suspected Protestant places of worship. Tsvetaev, *Protestantstvo,* 49–66. Olearius (*Voyages,* Amsterdam, 1727, 382–3) identifies two Lutheran, two Dutch reformed, and one English church in Moscow of the 1630's, and estimates the Protestant population of the city to be in excess of a thousand households. See also A. Fechner, *Chronik der Evangelischen Gemeinden in Moskau,* M, 1876. I, 20–369, and map, opposite vii.

126. B. Silfversvan ("Erüs põhittinen haavellija 1600-luvulla," *Historiallinen Aikakauskirja,* Helsinki, 1934, 161–83) believes the catechism to have been prepared for the Tsar's entourage by the adventurer-diplomat, Jacob Roussel, who had a French Huguenot background and was an intriguing adventurer who played a leading role in bringing Russia into the anti-Catholic coalition of the early 1630's. This conclusion is questioned by E. Bäckman ("Den trosbekännelse"), who views it as a late-seventeenth-century work, but whose investigations reveal other interesting evidence of Protestant proselyting on Orthodox Russian soil. (See esp. material cited 30–2.)

Unreferenced, added arguments for Roussel's authorship are given by I. Mikkola, "Un Zélateur du Calvinisme auprès du Tsar Mikhail Fedorovich," *Mélanges Jules Legras,* 1939, 215–19. The catechism (in the Finnish National Library at Helsinki) is bound with a number of materials pertaining to Holland in the late seventeenth century and was apparently from the library of the Matveev family, but this is no reason to rule out the calligraphic and stylistic reasons for assuming that the early seventeenth century was the time of original composition—with one of the many Dutchmen in the Muscovite service probably the translator. There was a 1577 edition of Calvin's Institutes in the library of the Valaam monastery prior to World War I ("Redkosti valaamskoi monastyrskoi biblioteki," *IL,* 1914, no. 2, 242–3; no longer in the library now at Kuopio, Finland, when consulted in Feb, 1961).

127. Muliukin, *Priezd,* 111–5; Tsvetaev, *Protestantstvo,* 4, 173–8.

128. For the attempts to expand Catholic influence in West Russia and the Ukraine after the Time of Troubles see the materials and analysis in E. Shmurlo, *Kurie;* also I. Chistovich, *Ocherk istorii,* 98 ff. For concurrent efforts in Orthodox Moldavia see R. Ortiz, *Per la Storia della cultura Italiana in Rumania,* Bucharest, 1916, 67 ff. For the complex Swedish diplomacy which subsidized and recruited mercenaries to help bring Russia into the Thirty Years' War as, in effect, an Eastern ally in 1632, the basic work is now D. Norrman, *Gustav Adolfs politik mot Ryssland och Polen under tyska kriget (1630-32),* Uppsala, 1943, which is supplemented from Russian and Hungarian materials by Vainshtein, *Rossiia,* esp. 102–62. See also materials in numerous articles by

B. Porshnev on this subject, esp. *IAN(I)*, 1945, no. 5, 319–40; *IZh*, 1945, no. 3; and *SKS*, 1956, I. Porshnev's rather myopic view that the main interest of everyone concerned was persecuting Russia (made explicit in *UZAON*, 1948, 110) is partly countered by A. Arzymatov's article in *SkS*, 1956, I, esp. 77–93, and, implicitly, by Vainshtein's far more sophisticated analysis. The general neglect of the religious factor, common to all Soviet treatments, can be redressed by consulting the articles by A. Szełagowski (*KH*, 1899, IV, 685–700) dealing with Swedish links with Polish Protestants and G. von Rauch dealing with the Protestant-Orthodox conflict (*AR*, 1952, II, 187–98).

Muliukin's detailed study of personnel, and Platonov's invaluable *Moskva i Zapad,* make the extent of the Northern European Protestant influx into Russia in the early seventeenth century abundantly clear. Additional material stressing Swedish economic contacts and influence (always less appreciated than those of the Dutch, English, Danes, and Holsteiners, who were more likely to write books about their impressions) are K. Yakubov, "Rossiia i Shvetsiia v pervoi polovine XVII veka," *Cht,* 1897, III; A. Soom, *Die Politik Schwedens bezüglich des russischen Transithandels über die estnischen Städte in den Jahren 1636–1656,* Tartu, 1940; and the important documents from the Novgorod and Pskov region published in *Russko-shvedskie ekonomicheskie otnosheniia v XVII veke,* M-L, 1960. For much documentary material on the Scottish impact see A. Francis Steuart, *Scottish Influences;* and *Papers Relating to the Scots in Poland,* Edinburgh, 1915. On the structure of the foreign settlements in Moscow

see the analysis by E. Zviagintsev in *IZh*, 1944, no. 2–3.

129. Olearius, *Voyages,* 352–4.

130. See articles by A. Chernov (*IZ*, XXXVIII, 1951, 281–90) and A. Zimin (*IZ*, LV, 1956, 344–59). N. Shpakovsky points out (*ZhMNP*, 1898, Sep, 146) that there were foreigners as well as Russians in the *streltsy* from the beginning.

131. My estimate from the figures in *Och (6)*, 441.

132. Bibikov, 7–15; Rainov, *Nauka,* 380–4. Military map making had apparently begun in Eastern Europe under Stephen Báthory. Roberts, *Revolution,* 27.

133. These figures, which Kliuchevsky (*Skazaniia,* 96) suggests for the general increase from a peacetime to a wartime army, seem applicable to this period, because the estimates on which the 300,000 figure is based are drawn from the period of the 1654–67 war with Poland. This figure is actually lower than overall figures suggested for maximum wartime strength by E. Stashevsky (*Smeta voennykh sil Moskovskogo gosudarstva v 1663 godu,* Kiev, 1910, 13–16) and R. Boussingault (*BRP,* V, 1859, 3–4, 28). P. Miliukov (*Gosudarstvennoe khoziaistvo Rossii v pervoi chetverti XVIII stoletiia i reforma Petra Velikago,* P, 1905, 52–3) puts the strength of the army in 1681 at 260,000.

Bobrovsky (*Perekhod,* 75–6) estimates the size by 1676 to be 255,000; *Och (6)* (450) estimates "more than 200,000" after the absorption of the Left Bank Ukraine in 1667. Even if one is mindful of the tendency to exaggerate military strength in early periods (see Nef, *War,* 91–2) and insists on the core figure of 215,000, which Stashevsky establishes from a document of 1663 (*Smeta,* 13, but considers it unrepresentatively small), there is no real increase in *size* of the army between this date and that of the next firm estimate made by V. Kabuzan ("Materialy revizii kak istochnik po istorii naseleniia Rossii XVIII-pervoi poloviny XIX v," *ISR*, 1959, no. 5, 136 and table), which is 219,000 for 1719. Thus, the Petrine reform emerges as essentially one of administrative restructuring rather than of massive population changes and social rearrangement such as occurred under Alexis. Of course, Peter's reform provided a firmer basis for further expansion, which led to the doubling of the size of the army by the time of Catherine's accession (Kabuzan, 13).

134. Stashevsky (*Smeta*, 12–14) counts 60,000 out of an army of 215,000, exclusive of Cossacks, in 1663. The Austrian emissary Mayerberg in 1662—without making any systematic computation of foreigners — counted four generals, more than one hundred colonels, and innumerable lesser officers (Kliuchevsky, *Skazaniia*, 96). V. Picheta (*Istoriia moskovskago gosudarstva*, M, 1917, 71) estimates that the percentage of mercenaries rose from 6 per cent of the relatively small army of 1632 to 27 per cent of the much larger army of 1663. E. Trifil'ev (*Novyia kul'turnyia techeniia v moskovskom gosudarstve v XVII veke*, Odessa, 1913, 10) estimates that the foreign contingent numbered 90,000 by 1681.

135. See M. Yablochkov, *Istoriia dvorianskago sosloviia v Rossii*, P, 1876, 216–17; and bibliographical article by V. Beneshevich in *RBS*, XXII, 214–15 (which estimates him to have been the richest man in Muscovy) and, for his father, 195–6. For itemization of some of the gifts given him (and Sheremetev, who enjoyed a parallel and equally spectacular rise) see Savva, Archbishop of Tver, *Sacristie patriarcale dite synodale de Moscou*, M, 1865, (2d ed. with plates), 24–30; also *Och (6)*, 157.

136. I. Gurliand, *Prikaz sysknykh del*, Kiev, 1903, esp. 8–9, 15–19, for the functioning of this "bureau for investigative affairs" (whose leaders were known as "strong-men," *sil'nye*) and Cherkasky's control thereof; also A. Chernov, "K istorii pomestnogo prikaza," *TIAI*, IX, 1957, 227, for indications of another *prikaz* that Cherkasky controlled on the basis of more recent investigation.

137. From a letter of consolation to the governor of Livonia on the occasion of the death of Gustavus Adolphus, in N. Golitsyn, "K istorii russko-shvedskikh otnoshenii," *Cht*, 1903, IV, 6–7; see also Vainshtein, *Rossiia*, 134–5.

138. He communicated directly with the Tsar in a secret alphabet created by Patriarch Philaret "for our governmental and secret ambassadorial affairs." See A. Popov, *Russkoe Posol'stvo v Pol'she v 1673–1677 godakh*, P, 1854, 268, 271.

139. On the *Uchenie i khitrost' ratnogo stroeniia pekhotnykh liudei* see A. Sidorov, *Drevnerusskaia knizhnaia graviura*, M, 1951, 252–5; illustration from it in *Och (6)*, 455. For an appraisal of its influence see the study by P. Epifanov in *UZMGU*, CLXVII, 1954, 77–98. See analysis of the language (and illustrations of the borrowings of Dutch military terms) by C. Stang in *SUN*, 1952, 1–86; the text was republished in P, 1904, ed. Myshlaevsky. It is a Wallhausen translation.

140. See A. Yakovlev, *Cherta*, 5–14 and detailed maps in the back of the book, as well as *Och (6)*, 467–77. On the continued menace from the Tatars, Nogai, and other steppe invaders in the early seventeenth century see A. Novosel'sky, *Bor'ba moskovskogo gosudarstva s tatarami v pervoi polovine XVII v.* M-L, 1948, 222–7.

141. See the valuable study by E. Kvashnin-Samarin, *Morskaia ideia*

v *russkoi zemle, istoriia dopetrovs-koi Rusi s voenno-morskoi tochki zreniia.* P, 1912, for full discussion of Russia's largely forgotten pre-Petrine naval interests; and for the role played therein by Holland (and to a lesser extent England and Denmark) see esp. the summary

147. For further details of the efforts under Michael see the article by V. Druzhinin in *Zh-MNP,* 1917, Feb, esp. 234–9; under Alexis that of N. Popov in *Russkaia Beseda,* 1858, IV, 2–5.

142. *Nauka, nauk,* see Stang, *SUN,* 1952, 84.

III. THE CENTURY OF SCHISM

1. Letter to Oxenstierna of Apr 1, 1628, cited in Vainshtein, *Rossiia,* 110. It was characteristic of Swedish diplomacy to speak of the war in the singular, Roussel referring in a letter to the Tsar a few years later of "the great civil war which God has sown in all corners of Christendom." Cited by B. Porshnev, *SkS,* I, 1956, 65, and note 144. In Germany also, the war was viewed as a single, sustained holocaust, though the term "Thirty Years' War" is an artificial, Germano-centric designation. (See F. Carsten, "A Note on the Term 'Thirty Years' War,'" *History,* 1958, Oct, esp. 190–1).

Many of the best general histories of seventeenth-century Europe make little or no mention of Northern and Eastern Europe (see, for instance, G. Clark, *The Seventeenth Century,* Oxford, 1947, 2d ed.; C. V. Wedgwood, *The Thirty Years' War,* London, 1957, p; C. Friedrich, *The Age of the Baroque, 1610 to 1660,* NY, 1952, p; and even the deliberately comparative work of R. Merriman, *Six Contemporaneous Revolutions,* Glasgow, 1937). Works which make some effort to include the region are D. Ogg, *Europe in the Seventeenth Century,* London, 1925; W. Reddaway, *A History of Europe from 1610 to 1715,* London, 1948; and particularly W. Platzhoff, *Geschichte des europäischen Staatensystems, 1559–*

1660, Munich-Berlin, 1928. See the recent discussion of a "general crisis of the seventeenth century" which "reached its most acute phase between 1640 and 1670's," E. Hobsbawm, "The General Crisis of the European Economy in the 17th Century," *PP,* 1954, May, 38; also the second part of this important and richly documented article, *PP,* 1954, Nov, 44–65; the article of the Czech historian J. Polišenský, "The Thirty Years' War," *PP,* 1954, Nov, 31–43; and the monographic and documentary work of Vainshtein, Porshnev, and others in the USSR, which make possible a much richer picture of interrelationships than has yet been drawn in the general historical literature of any European country.

2. Estimates vary widely on all casualty counts of this era; but the Khmelnitsky massacre probably killed about 200,000, or more than one third of the Jewish population of Eastern Europe. See various estimates in N. Hanover, *The Abyss of Despair* (from Yeven Metzulah: literally "deep mire"), 122, note 1; also Dubnov, *History,* I, 66, 153–8; H. Graetz, *History of the Jews,* Philadelphia, 1895, V, 15; *Mélanges Derenbourg,* 76.

3. As cited opposite the preface in Merriman, *Revolutions.*

4. For some idea of the distinctive Swedish contribution to modern war and statecraft, see M. Roberts,

Revolution, and O. Ribbing, "Nordic Characteristics of War," *Revue internationale d'histoire militaire,* 1955, no. 15, 231–2.

For this innovation in the European conduct of war see the volume by G. Zeller in P. Renouvin, ed., *Histoire des relations internationales,* 1955, II, 207–8. For an excellent, continent-wide treatment of the pivotal and much-neglected First Northern War as a kind of extension and amplification of the brutal stages of the Thirty Years' War see E. Haumant, *La Guerre du nord et la paix d'Oliva,* 1893. For the horror of this war in Russia see Bobrovsky, *Perekhod,* 113–24.

5. Pierling, *La Russie,* III, 36–310, 445–8; *Rome et Démétrius,* 1878, 145–6; Tsvetaev, "Snosheniia s Abissiniei XVII v," *RA,* 1888, kn. I, 205–10. Yury Krizhanich, the Croatian Catholic, prepared a memorandum in 1641, long before his first visit to Russia, placing Russia in a strategic context that included the Balkans, Ethiopia, and India. See S. Belokurov, *Iz dukhovnoi zhizni moskovskago obshchestva XVII v,* M, 1902, 88–106, also *JGO,* 1964, Oct, 331–49.

6. See Hanover, *Abyss;* another contemporary Jewish account entitled "Time of Troubles" (Meir of Szczebrzeszyn, *Tzok Ha-itin,* Cracow, 1650); the article on the Polish and Ukrainian "deluge" *(potop)* by D. Maggid in *Zbirnik prats' zhidivs'koi istorichno-arkheografichnoi komisii,* Kiev, 1929, II, 247–71; and the tale of how Polish Protestants were also made scapegoats during this period by J. Tazbir, "Bracia Polscy w latach 'potopu,'" in L. Chmaj, *Studia nad arianizmem,* Warsaw, 1959, 451–90.

7. S. Hoszowski, "L'Europe centrale devant la révolution des prix XVI⁰ et XVII⁰ siècles," *AESC,* 1961, May-Jun, esp. 455–6.

8. For a sober, documentary study of the sweeping population changes in the relatively insulated central region of Moscow see Yu. Got'e, *Zamoskovny krai v XVII veke,* M, 1937.

9. F. Prinzing has shown *(Epidemics Resulting from Wars,* Oxford, 1916, esp. 76) that the plague killed even more people in Germany during the Thirty Years' War than battles.

Precise statistics are not available prior to the eighteenth century, and estimates must be made with caution. V. Koretsky estimates *(VI,* 1959, no. 3, 121–2) that one third of the population died of famine alone at the onset of the Time of Troubles. A foreign visitor at the time, J. Margeret *(Estat de l'empire de Russie et grand duché de Moscovie,* 1860, 72), estimated that there were 120,000 public burials in Moscow alone. N. Firsov *(Golod pred smutnym vremenem v moskovskom gosudarstve,* Kazan, 1892, 6–7) says that there were 500,000 deaths. Even if one takes the lowest figure, assumes that it suffices for all of Great Russia and also includes plague and war casualties, one would still seem to have a total of at least one third of Got'e's population estimate of 600,000–700,000 for the Moscow region *(Krai,* 167).

Statistics are more fragmentary but even more appalling for the early plague-ridden years of the 1654–67 war. Apparently 80 per cent of the tax-paying population of the foreign quarters of Moscow were felled (L. Abtsedarsky, *Belorusy v Moskve XVII v,* M, 1957, 20); and Brückner's statistics *(Beiträge,* 48–52) on monasteries and other traceable blocs of the population indicate that fatalities were rarely below 45 per cent. Only nineteen of 362 servants of the boyar Boris Morozov survived

—suggesting that the mortality rate was even higher among the poor, for whom statistics are hardest to find. Collins *(Present State,* 45) estimates total casualties at no less than 700,000–800,000; and Medovikov *(Istoricheskoe znachenie tsarstvovaniia Alekseia Mikhailovicha,* M, 1854, 76, note 2) estimates 700,000. This would be about one tenth of the empire as newly expanded at that time. For a general account of the plague of 1654–6, see E. Volkova, *Morovoe Povetrie,* P, 1916.

10. Collins, *Present State,* 45; Berkh, *Tsarstvovanie,* 129.

11. Evreinov, *Istoriia nakazanii,* 34. See also the various prescriptions for cutting off limbs, 25–32, and the intensification of legal cruelties in the late seventeenth and particularly the early eighteenth century discussed 48–72.

12. Olearius, *Voyages,* 204–5.

13. *Passages from the Diary of General Patrick Gordon,* Aberdeen, 1859, 53.

14. Florovsky, *Chekhi,* 405, note 1.

I. THE SPLIT WITHIN

1. V. Riazanovsky, *Obzor,* I, 147–8; D. Tsvetaev, *Obrusenie zapadnoevropeitsev v moskovskom gosudarstve,* Warsaw, 1903. For usage of the term already at the beginning of the sixteenth century against Nicholas of Lübeck, see Budovnits, *Publitsistika,* 139. For a typical plea to save "rossiiskie blagochestiia ot prelesti antikhristovoi khitrosti" see the eighteenth-century Old Believer tract "O poslednem vremeni i o pastyriakh tserkovnykh," Manuscript section of the Lenin Library, rukopisi T. F. Bolshakova, no. 78.

For a general account of the schism which tends to relate it to the process of Westernization see Kliuchevsky, *Sochineniia,* III, 256–318; also S. Zenkovsky, "The Rus-sian Church Schism," *RR,* 1957, Oct, 37–58; Kharlampovich, "K voprosu o sushchnosti russkogo raskola staroobriadchestva," *UZKU,* LXVII, 1900, no. 12, 133–52; V. Belolikov, *Istoriko-kritichesky razbor sushchestvuiushchikh mnenii o proiskhozhdenii, sushchnosti i znachenii russkogo raskola staroobriadchestva,* Kiev, 1913; and N. Chaev and N. Ustiugov, "Russkaia tserkov' v XVII v," in N. Ustiugov, *et al.,* eds., *Russkoe gosudarstvo v XVII veke,* M, 1961, 295–329.

2. Got'e, *Akty,* 14. Monastic translators of sacred texts during the *Smuta* also pledged to work "bez vsiakie khitrosti," *Kh Cht,* 1890, Sep–Oct, 440.

3. Avvakum, as cited in N. Subbotin,

Even among the generally sober and well-informed Dutch, Adrian van Nispen groups an account of Muscovy together with that of Iceland, Greenland, and Siam *(Verscheyde Voyagien,* Dordrecht, 1652). It was widely believed that the Ob River led to China. See Lubimenko, "Role," 50 and ff., for other misconceptions of the pre-Petrine period.

15. Theses of J. Bothvidus (praes.) A. Prutz (resp.), *Theses de Quaestione utrum Muschowitae sint Christiani?,* Stockholm, 1620 (repr. Lübeck, 1705). See A. Galkin, *Akademiia v Moskve v XVII stoletii,* M, 1913, 9, note 3. This thesis is not as primitive as Rushchinsky, Miliukov, and others imply. As late as 1665, the treatise by a former Lutheran pastor at Reval/Tallinn, Esthonia, asks the same question: J. Gerhard (praes.) J. Schwabe (resp.), *Tsurkov' Moskovsky sive dissertatio theologica de religione Ritibusque Ecclesiasticis Moscovitarum,* Jena, 1665.

Materialy dlia istorii raskola za pervoe vremia ego sushchestvovaniia, V, 298–9. The ten volumes of this documentary collection (M, 1875–87) are still the basic source material for study of the early schismatics.

4. See Ashukin, *Krylatye Slova*, 641; and the often-reprinted popular story *Khitraia Mekhanika. pravdivy rasskaz, otkuda i kuda idut den'gi*, Zurich, 1874.

5. V. Goncharov, "Ia nenavizhu," in *Den' Poezii*, M, 1956.

6. Malinin, *Starets*, 50, 54; Fennell, *Correspondence*, 20, 14. See also 22, where Ivan praises Kurbsky's martyred messenger for preserving *blagochestie* even in an erring cause.

7. See Yu. Arsen'ev, *Oruzheiny prikaz pri Tsare Mikhaile Fedoroviche*, P, 1903; Rainov, *Nauka*, 380–4; Raikov, *Ocherk*, 113, on weathervanes; and articles by Lappo-Danilevsky, *ZhMNP*, 1885, Sep; and I. Lubimenko, *RES*, IV, 1924. Clocks with bells had arrived in Moscow as early as 1404, but became fixtures on the Kremlin walls only after the Time of Troubles. See V. Danilevsky, *Tekhniku*, 128.

8. I Cherepnin, ed., *Skazanie Avraamila Palitsyna*, M-L, 1955, 253.

9. Cited in S. Platonov, *Skazaniia o smute kak istorichesky istochnik*, P, 1913, 206.

10. For concise summary discussion of this work, commissioned by Philaret in 1630, see Cherepnin, *Istoriografiia*, 123–8; for the weakness of the case against Boris see G. Vernadsky, "The Death of the Tsarevich Dmitry," *OSP*, V, 1954, 1–19.

11. Pascal, *Avvakum et les débuts du raskol*, 1938, 20.

12. S. Platonov, *Moskva i Zapad*, 72.

13. On these "church people" (tserkovnye liudi) who clustered about the churches see Yarushevich, *Sud*, 146–9; for the degradation of the concept of tsardom during the *smuta* see E. Shmurlo, *Istoriia*, 260–2; for the religious revival thereafter, Pascal, *Avvakum*, 1–73.

14. *Povest' XVII veka*, 82–115, for texts; Zenkovsky, *Epics*, 374–97, 409–22. N. Baklanova's erudite arguments for eighteenth-century authorship of these tales are too permeated with a priori antagonism toward (and ignorance of) the seventeenth century to merit credence in the absence of a more objective investigation (see *TODL*, IX, 1953, 443–59; XIII, 1957, 511–18.)

15. A. Burtsev, *Materialy dlia istorii russkago raskola* [no place, no date; copy in Shoumatoff collection, Princeton], second set of pages, second illustration after 24; Rovinsky, *Kartinki*, I, 30.

16. *Cht*, 1893, III, 13–16.

17. At least forty of these lavish creations were built between 1620 and 1690 according to Hamilton, *Art*, 135–7. V. Shkvarikov counts forty for the second half of the seventeenth century and twenty-nine churches destroyed in the fire of 1658. *Ocherk istorii planirovki i zastroiki russkikh gorodov*, M, 1954, 182.

18. See J. Keep, "The Regime of Filaret (1619–1633)," *SEER*, 1960, Jun, 334–60; also Yarushevich, *Sud*, 147–8, 334–5; and P. Nikolaevsky, *Patriarshaia oblast' i russkiia eparkhii v XVII veke*, P, 1888; S. Chernyshev, "Tsar Mikhail Fedorovich i Patriarkh Filaret Nikitich Romanovy v ikh vzaimnykh otnosheniiakh," *TKDA*, 1913, nos. 7–8; A. Shpakov, *Gosudarstvo i tserkov' v ikh vzaimootnosheniiakh v Moskovskom gosudarstve*, Odessa, 1904–12, 2v.

19. *BE*, XLVI, 484.

20. The Latin original of Mogila's Confession is reprinted with commentary in *OC*, X, 1927, Oct-Dec; see also Karmirēs, *Dogmatika*, II, 989–97 and particularly 575–92.

P. Panaitescu, "L'Influence de l'oeuvre de Pierre Mogila," *Mélanges école roumaine en France,* I, 1926; also the long biography S. Golubev, *Kievsky mitropolit Petr Mogila i ego spodvizhniki,* Kiev, 1883–98, 2v; subsequent material and information in Legrand, *Bibliographie hellenique,* IV, 104–59; and the short account by Hugh Graham, "Peter Mogila—Metropolitan of Kiev," *RR,* 1955, Oct.

21. On this lesser known work of Mogila see A. Amfiteatrov, *Russky pop XVII veka,* Belgrade, 1930, 69; also 53–4, 56 ff., and 7–14 for the "duality of belief" and irrationalism in the seventeenth-century Russian church.

22. Sobolevsky, *Obrazovannost',* 14–8.

23. Tsvetaev, *Literaturnaia bor'ba,* 89–99, 109–25.

24. A. Galkin *(Akademiia v Moskve v XVII stoletii,* M, 1913, 12) and K. Kharlampovich *(Vliianie,* I, 115–17, 128–38) both conclude on the basis of independent analysis that Rtishchev's "academy" was founded in 1645, though Kharlampovich effectively argues that there were no Ukrainian monks prior to 1649. Lewitter ("Poland," *SEER,* 1949, May, 422–9) seems to doubt that it was a very serious institution.

N.A.A.'s biography of the patriarchs indicates *(Cht,* 1847, IV, 123, III, 35–6) that Philaret established a monastic study center modeled on that of Mogila even earlier at the Chudov Monastery, though Galkin (11) is doubtful and S. Belokurov *(Adam Oleary o Grekolatinskoi shkole Arseniia Greka v Moskve v XVII v,* M, 1888, 43) flatly denies its existence prior to 1653.

The accelerating influx of Ukrainian clergy into Muscovy during the "deluge" of the First Northern War is treated by V. Eingorn, *Cht,* 1893, II, ch. 4, 98–

210; as well as Kharlampovich. For the apologetic life of Rtishchev see *DRV,* ch. V, T. III, 18–34; also *RBS,* XVII, 334–42, 357–66.

25. From the text of a long contemporary description of the events of July 5, 1648, in Kursk, in the useful anthology (ed. S. Piontkovsky, intr. by K. Bazilevich) *Gorodskie vosstaniia v moskovskom gosudarstve XVII v,* M-L, 1936, 113. Also on these events see P. Smirnov, *Pravitel'stvo B.I. Morozova i vosstanie v Moskve 1648 g,* Tashkent, 1929; and M. Tikhomirov, *Pskovskoe vosstanie 1650 g: iz istorii klassovoi bor'by v russkom gorode 1650 goda,* M-L, 1935. A. Speransky's review of the latter in *IM,* 1934, no. 40, 24–36, reveals the problems of applying Marxist categories to the complex social tensions of old Russian cities. M. Shakhmatov, ed., *Chelobitnaia "Mira" moskovskago tsariu Alekseiu Mikhailovichu 10 iunia 1648 g,* Prague, 1934, gives a more positive and purposeful image of the rebels' program (based on a copy of their program found in Tartu) than do most other Russian accounts based on other versions of their petition. M. Tikhomirov, "Dokumenty zemskogo sobora 1650," *IA,* 1958, no. 4, 141–3, vigorously challenges the official *Och (6)* for depicting the *sobors* as "some kind of inert mass only answering yes or no in response to a government proposal." For annotated text of the *Ulozhenie* edited by Sofronenko, see *PRP,* VI. For the relation of the *Ulozhenie* to the *zemsky sobor* and the urban riots see the analysis by P. Smirnov in *ZhMNP,* 1913, no. 9–10, 36–66; also A. Zertsalov, *Novyia dannyia o zemskom sobore 1648–1649 gg,* M, 1887.

26. Pierre Chevalier, *Histoire de la guerre des cossaques contre la Pologne,* (1663), repr. *BRP,* 1859, VII, 121.

27. V. Berkh, *Tsarstvovanie tsaria Alekseia Mikhailovicha*, P, 1831, 52–60. Alexis knew about Ankudinov by 1648, and perhaps about some of the list of thirteen others of the early seventeenth century cited on 55.

28. P. Struve, *Istoriko-sotsiologicheskie nabliudeniia nad razvitiem russkago pis'mennago iazyka*, Sofia, 1940, 8, also 4–5; Vinogradov, *Ocherki*, 6.

    H. Ludolph—in the preface to the first systematic printed grammar of the Russian language in 1696—considered the *Ulozhenie* the only printed book in vernacular Russian. (*Grammatica Russica*, Oxford, 1959, second and third unnumbered pages of the preface). For a detailed study of the language of the *Ulozhenie* see Chernykh, *Iazyk Ulozhenia 1649 goda*, M, 1953, esp. 732, emphasizing its importance.

    Crimes against the faith were included for the first time within a civil code in part I, and the rights of the sovereign set forth in essentially secular terms in part II. See *PRP*, VI, 22–36.

29. Cited in S. Mel'gunov's stimulating *Religiozno-obshchestvennye dvizheniia XVI–XVIII vv v Rossii*, M, 1922, 12. See also N. Korenevsky, *Tserkovnye voprosy v Moskovskom gosudarstve v polovine XVII veka i deiatel'nost' patriarkha Nikona*, Kiev, 1912, 20 and ff; for more details, N. Kapterev, *Kharakter otnoshenii Rossii k pravoslavnomu vostoku v XVI i XVII st*, Sergiev Posad, 1914, 2d ed. For Paissius' meetings with and recognition of Nikon see S. Belokurov, *Arseny Sukhanov*, M, 1891, ch. I, 181–2.

30. Bartenev, *Sobranie pisem*, 210; M. Khmyrov, "Tsar Aleksei Mikhailovich i ego vremia," *DNR*, 1875, no. 10, 105.

31. Bartenev, *Sobranie*, 191–2, note 24.

32. Pascal, *Avvakum*, 151; and the discussion and references, 148–98.

33. Kapterev, *Kharakter*, 363–4; O. Ogloblin, *Moskovs'ka teoria III Rimu XVI–XVII stoletii*, Munich, 1951, 39–41; Belokurov, *Sukhanov*, 23 ff.; 165 ff. Whether or not the later idea of a Russian conquest of Constantinople actually motivated Russian policy at this time is not clear; but the idea was frequently expressed by panegyrists in the Tsar's entourage, and the secretary to the Queen of Poland wrote as early as January, 1657, that Alexis himself "has a grand design in mind to liberate Greece from oppression." P. des Noyers, *Lettres*, Berlin, 1889, 291.

34. For concise categorization see Shmurlo, *Istoriia*, 244–60.

35. Pascal, *Avvakum*, 194.

36. Both the pledge which Nikon extracted from the Tsar and his major arguments for patriarchal authority were taken from the ninth-century Byzantine treatise of Patriarch Photius, the Epanagoge, which was an extreme statement even within Byzantium. Kapterev, *Patriarkh Nikon i Tsar Aleksei Mikhailovich*, Sergiev Posad, 1909–12, 2v. M. Zyzykin (in his erudite but inadequately documented *Patriarkh Nikon, ego gosudarstvennyia i kanonicheskiia idei*, Warsaw, 1931–8, 3v) defends the canonical validity of Nikon's position on the basis of its conformity with the Epanagoge rather than with Byzantine tradition as a whole. See also the general article on the Epanagoge in Russia by G. Vernadsky, *Byzantinisch-Neugriechische Jahrbücher*, 1928, no. 6, esp. 129–42. For a brief survey see M. Spinka, "Patriarch Nikon and the Subjection of the Russian Church to the State," *CH*, 1941, Dec, 347–66; and for a critical bibliography by R. Stupperich, *ZOG*, IX, 1935, 173–80.

    Nikon studied the Epanagoge from a translation made by Slavinetsky from a sixteenth-century German compendium of Byzantine texts, *Jus Graeco-Romanum*, and other Byzantine texts from Venetian digests and translations. Little use seems to have been made of the 500–700 manuscripts brought back by Sukhanov or of Nikon's own library—though the entire problem has never been systematically and objectively studied. See Belokurov, *Sukhanov*, 331 ff.; M. Tikhomirov, ed., *Sokrovishcha drevnei pis'mennosti i staroi pechati*, M, 1958, 26–30.

37. Zyzykin, *Patriarkh*, II, esp. 315–18.

38. Rainov, *Nauka*, 454 ff.

39. For a concise summary of the controversies over Nikon's fall see Platonov, *Histoire*, 443–8. Many documents of and on Nikon—particularly those dealing with his long ordeal prior to the council—are printed with admiring commentary in W. Palmer, *The Patriarch and the Tsar*, London, 1871–6, 6v. The basic collection is still N. Gibbenet, *Istoricheskoe izsledovanie dela patriarkha Nikona*, P, 1882–4, 2v, which (like Platonov) specifically seeks to balance the incomplete and generally antagonistic picture presented by Solov'ev, *Istoriia*, Kn. VI, 192–281. A good summary of Nikon's reforms is in N. Korenevsky, *Tserkovnye voprosy;* and the troubled, early history of book-correction in Muscovy is admirably set forth in P. Nikolaevsky's "Moskovsky pechatny dvor pri patriarkhe Nikone," *Kh Cht*, 1890, Jan–Feb, 114–41; Sep–Oct, 434–67; 1891, Jan–Feb, 147–86; Jul–Aug, 151–86.

On Nikon's actual reforms (the extra-ecclesiastical extent of which are often not fully appreciated) see, in addition to works already cited, details about his rituals for processions in *Kh Cht*, 1882, II, 287–320; his building program in *Cht*, 1874, III, ch. I, 1–26; his opposition to tent roofs in *Trudy V-go arkheologicheskago s'ezda v Tiflise 1881*, M, 1887, 233; his architectural program and its impact in *Istoriia russkogo iskusstva*, M, 1959, IV, 162–78; and his opposition to the *Ulozhenie* in *RA*, 1866, II, 53–66.

On the opposition to the Nikonian reforms in Solovetsk see I. Syrtsov, *Vozmushchenie solovetskikh monakhov-staroobriadtsev v XVII veke*, Kostroma, 1888, 47–56; also 11–19 for indications that the antipathy to Solovetsk had origins in his earlier experiences in the north. See also N. Barsukov, *Solovetskoe vosstanie 1668–1676*, Petrozavodsk, 1954.

40. Kapterev, *Patriarkh*, I, 81–105; A. Preobrazhensky, "Vopros o edinoglasnom penii v russkoi tserkvi XVII v," *PDP*, CLV, 1904, 7–43. For a neglected characterization of Avvakum, see S. Mel'gunov, *Veliky podvizhnik protopop Avvakum*, M, 1917.

41. Mooser, *Annales*, I, 21. On hops (thought by some to have caused the plague) see Rainov, *Nauka*, 454–60; also the study of V. Bakhtin and D. Moldavsky, *TODL*, XIV, 1958, 421–2; Gudzy, *History*, 469. For similar superstitions about tea, coffee, and even potatoes see *PS*, 1867, no. 5, 67 ff.; no. 6, 167 ff.

Tobacco was admired by Ivan IV, subjected to increasing though generally ineffective prohibitions in the seventeenth century (Michael outlawed it in 1634, and Alexis considered applying the death penalty for smoking), and came into widespread use in the early eighteenth century. See V. Picheta, *Istoriia moskovskago gosudarstva*, M, 1917, 68; E. Ragozin, *Istoriia tabaka i sistemy naloga na nego v Evropy i Amerike*, P, 1871, 19–20.

42. *RIB*, XXXIX, 1927, 282; see also Avvakum, *Life*, 23–4; discussion in Hamilton, *Art*, 151–61.

43. N. Andreev, "Nikon and Avvakum on Icon-Painting," *RES*, XXXVIII, 1961, 37–44.
44. See E. Ovchinnikova's analysis of the frescoes in the Moscow church of the Georgian Mother of God in *TGIM*, XIII, 1941, 147–66; and N. Romanov on the painting of Nikon by Daniel Vukhters in *Pamiatniki iskusstva razrushennye nemetskimi zakhvatchikami v SSSR*, M-L, 1948, 200–16. See also Ovchinnikova, *Portret v russkom iskusstve XVII veka*, M, 1955.
45. Pascal, *Avvakum*, 62–4, 341–2.
46. P. Znamensky, "Ioann Neronov," *PS*, 1869, I, 238, 266–7, 271–4.
47. P. Smirnov, "Znachenie"; Subbotin, *Materialy*, V, 176 (on Avvakum), and VIII, 137–53 (on Morozova *et al.*); Tikhonravov, "Boiarynia Morozova," *Sochineneiia*, II, 12–51; A. Mazunin, "Ob odnoi pere rabotke Zhitiia boiaryni Morozovoi," *TODL*, XVII, 429–34. For a popular account see S. Howe, *Some Russian Heroes, Saints and Sinners*, London, 1916, 322–59; and the magnificently detailed and illustrated study of the transposition of history and myth into the Surikov painting by V. Kemenov, *Istoricheskaia zhivopis' Surikova*, M, 1963, 275–445.
48. Amfiteatrov, *Pop*, 171–4. Objections were repeatedly raised against printing holy scripture because of the need to change the physical appearance of the letters. Glaring inaccuracies did occur in early Russian printing. See F. Otto, *History of Russian Literature*, Oxford, 1839, 33–4.
49. Shchapov, *Sochineniia*, II, 596.
50. *Ibid.*, 593.
51. Pascal, *Avvakum*, 64.
52. Syrtsov, *Vozmushchenie*, 110–11; P. Smirnov, *Istoriia raskola*, 91. See also "Iz istorii russkago raskola: D'iakon Fedor," *PS*, 1859, Jul, 314–46; Aug, 447–70.
53. Cited by I. Khromovin in his prefatory article (*Staroobriadcheskaia*

Mysl', 1912, 10, 971) to the edition of *Kniga o vere edinoi istinnoi pravoslavnoi*, M, 1912, published as a special supplement to this Old Believer periodical. On this work, apparently compiled by Nathaniel of Kiev, a former Uniat, and sponsored in Moscow by Stephen Vonifatiev, see Subbotin, *Materialy*, IV, 143; Mel'gunov, *Dvizheniia*, 18.
54. Cited by S. Solov'ev in *BZ*, 1858, no. 9, 276. For a concise and documented treatment of Vyshensky see Chizhevsky, *Aus zwei Welten*, 129–41. Solov'ev's version (and dating) of this work is here used, however, because it is referenced and seems drawn from the manuscript.
55. Selections from Vyshensky's dialogue of 1614 between the Devil and the pilgrim, in Chizhevsky, 138–9.
56. Cited in A. Florovsky's valuable *Le Conflit de deux traditions—la latine et la byzantine—dans la vie intellectuelle de l'Europe orientale aux XVI–XVIIe siècles*, Prague, 1937, 16, 6.
57. Avvakum, *Life*, 134; Florovsky, *Le Conflit*, 12, note 22; N. Kapterev, *Patriarkh Nikon i ego protivniki v dele ispravleniia tserkovnykh obriadov*, M, 1887, 94–7, note 1.
58. Cited in Florovsky, *Le conflit*, 9.
59. For the influence of Ephrem on Russian eschatological teaching see F. Sakharov, *Eskhatologicheskie sochineniia*, esp. 141–91; also Avvakum, *Zhitie*, 110, 133; Subbotin, *Materialy*, VIII, 361.
60. Belokurov, *Arseny*, 220–3; and 218–27, for his debates of 1650 with the Greek clergy of Wallachia (*Preniia s Grekami o vere*), which were widely circulated among Old Believers, and his report to Nikon on Orthodox practices from Egypt to Georgia (*Proskinitariia*); Sukhanov is the only contemporary figure cited in the early account of the coming of the Antichrist in

Subbotin, *Materialy*, VII, 1885, 234–51. See also Archimandrite Leonid's account of Russian pilgrimages to Jerusalem during the fourteenth to seventeenth centuries in *Cht*, 1871, I, ch. 2, 79–122.

61. On the older Tikhvin legend see K. Plotnikov, *Istoriia*, 14; the Georgian icon, first brought from the Georgian monastery on Athos in 1648, was credited with having miraculous powers, particularly against the plague. Two of the great monuments of the period (the Moscow Temple of the Georgian Mother of God and the Iversky Monastery just outside Moscow) were dedicated to this icon. See Kondakov, *Icon*, 149, 179; S. Loch, *Athos: The Holy Mountain*, NY [1954?], 169–70.

With the first printing of the *Kormchaia Kniga* during this period the concept of Moscow as the "third Rome" received increased popular attention. The original words of Philotheus' letter to Ivan were reproduced as the statement of Patriarch Jeremiah of Constantinople to Tsar Fedor at the time of the establishment of the Moscow Patriarchate. See N. Levitsky, "Uchenie raskola ob antikhriste i poslednikh dniakh mira," *Strannik*, 1880, Aug, 529 ff.

The passage "From Zion . . ." is from the eschatologically oriented section of Michah 4:2.

62. "sviatoe tsarstvo," Gibbenet, *Izsledovaniia*, I, 48 and 46–9. See Archimandrite Leonid, *Istoricheskoe opisanie stavropigial'nogo Voskresenskogo, Novy Ierusalim imenuemogo, monastyria*, M, 1876. Boris Godunov had intended to build a church in imitation of that at the Holy Sepulchre in Jerusalem inside the Moscow Kremlin, and the building of the bell tower of Ivan the Great was apparently related to this more grandiose project. (*Istoriia russ-*

kogo iskusstva, III, 480–1). The idea of building a similarly modeled "New Jerusalem" had occurred in the West at the time of the crusades (see V. Tapié, *La Russie de 1659 à 1689*, 1957, 200), but never received as much attention as in Russia. The theme of liberating Jerusalem gained favor in popular art during the Time of Troubles (see Rovinsky, *Kartinki*, II, 479–80), and encouraged a popular identification of the liberated city of Moscow with the New Jerusalem.

63. P. Pascal, "Un Pauvre Homme, grand fondateur: Ephrem Potemkin," in *Mélanges Jules Legras*, 221–9; P. Smirnov, *Istoriia*, 66–9. See Daniel 9:20–7.

64. Zakharius Kopystensky, archimandrite of the Monastery of the Caves, in his *Palinogodiia*, *RIB*, IV, 1878, 315–6.

65. P. Smirnov, *Vnutrennie voprosy*, xciii–xciv. For other examples of the computation among the fundamentalists see Subbotin, *Materialy*, IV, 1881, 14 ff.; 155–7; 282–4; and in White Russia, *Pamiatki polemichnogo*, IX, 200.

66. Revelations 13:17–8. See H. Guy, *The New Testament Doctrine of the "Last Things,"* Oxford, 1948, 146–9; also W. Bousset, *The Antichrist Legend*, London, 1896; and the fascinating if fantastic *The Computation of 666*, London, 1891, by "Two Servants of Christ."

67. V. Farmakovsky, "O protivogosudarstvennom elemente v raskole," *OZ*, CLXIX, kn. 24, 1866, 633. F. Livanov, *Raskol'niki i ostrozhniki: ocherki i razskazy*, P, 1872, 4th corr. ed., I, 394. In addition to this rich if somewhat unscholarly and romanticized collection see, for the Old Believer conception of Antichrist, two anonymous publications: *Kniga ob antikhriste*, Pskov, 1876 (a book of sermons) and *Veshchaniia svia-*

tago ob antikhriste i poslednei sud'be sego mira, M, 1888. There are other valuable studies of this concept among the early Old Believers, by F. Sakharov, *Tambovskiia Eparkhial'niia Vedomosti*, 1878, nos. 20, 21, 23, 24; N. Levitsky, *Kh Cht*, 1890, Nov–Dec, 695–738; and I. Nil'sky, *Kh Cht*, 1889, Jan, 693–719. Levitsky discusses the computation of 666 made from the word for "emperor" in "Uchenie," 556. For the computations of 666 on Napoleon see E. Benz, *Die abendländische Sendung der östlich-orthodoxen Kirche*, Mainz, 1950, 29; H. Schaeder, *Die dritte Koalition und die Heilige Allianz*, Königsberg-Berlin, 1934, 59, note 109.

For the impact of the concept of Antichrist on Russian culture generally see the detailed and perceptive article of the early Soviet period by B. Kisin in *LE*, I, 169–81; also N. Nikol'sky's article "Apokalipticheskaia literatura," *ibid.*, 183–91.

68. Syrtsov, *Vozmushchenie*, 99–108; P. Smirnov, *Istoriia*, 54–5; *Voprosy*, lxxxi–lxxxvi. In the latter work, Smirnov concludes that the work was not written by Theoktist, who died in 1666, but by someone else writing between his death in 1666 and Alexis' in 1676.

69. V. Peretts, "Slukhi i tolki o patriarkhe Nikone v literaturnoi obrabotke pisatelei XVII–XVIII vv.," *IAN (L)*, V, 1900, 140–3; P. Smirnov, *Istoriia*, 90; Subbotin, *Materialy*, VII, 421; Levitsky, *Kh Cht*, 1890, Nov–Dec, 704–5.

70. P. Nikolaevsky, *Patriarshaia oblast'*, 29–31.

71. Subbotin, *Materialy*, VI, 233–4.

72. *Ibid.*, 229. The literal accuracy of these quotes is subject to considerable question, because they occur only in polemic Old Believer literature. Nevertheless, the fact that they were widely accepted as correct gave them the force of truth; and the quotes do seem to reflect the attitudes adopted by much of the post-Nikonian church.

73. On the treaty of Andrusovo as a turning point in the history of Eastern Europe see Z. Wójcik, *Traktat andruszowski 1667 roku i jego geneza*, Warsaw, 1959 (with lengthy English summary). On the new trade statute, which in many ways marked the beginnings of protectionist mercantilism in Russia, A. Andreev, "Novotorgovy ustav 1667 g," *IZ*, XIII, 1942, 303–7.

74. V. Ikonnikov, "Blizhny boiarin A. L. Ordyn-Nashchokin, odin iz predshestvennikov petrovskoi reformy," *RS*, 1883, Oct, 17–66; Nov, 273–308. A good general study of the growth of diplomatic sophistication and of centralized bureaucratic power in this period. See also G. von Rauch, "Moskau und die europäischen Mächte des 17 Jahrunderts," *HZ*, 1954, Aug, 29–40; and the Swedish designation of Ordyn-Nashchokin as "the Russian Richelieu," 36, note 2.

75. Belokurov, *Arseny*, 215–18; L. Lavrovsky, "Neskol'ko svedenii dlia biografii Paisiia Ligarida Mitropolita Gazskago," *Kh Cht*, 1889, no. 11–12, 672–736; E. Shmurlo, "Paissy Ligarides v Rime i na grecheskom vostoke," *Trudy V-go S'ezda russkikh akademicheskikh organizatsii za granitsei*, Sofia, 1932, ch. 1, esp. 538–87; "Russkaia kandidatura na pol'sky prestol v 1667–1669," in *Sbornik statei posviashchenykh P. N. Miliukovu*, Prague, 1929, esp. 280; documents in Legrand, *Bibliographie hellenique*, IV, 8–61; and *Mélanges russes*, P, 1849–51, I, 152–9; 611–13.

76. "Da pobeditel' budesh' vsego mira/I da ispolnit mir toboiu vera," I. Eremin, "Deklamatsiia Simeona Polotskogo," *TODL*,

1951, VIII, 359–60. This declamation of 1660 on the recapture of Polotsk is according to Eremin (354–6) the first use of stylized syllabic verse in Russian. The *Orel rossiisky* is reprinted with an introduction by N. Smirnov as *PDP*, CXXXIII, 1915, vii, 65–78. See also the flowery verse on the occasion of the birth of Peter the Great with references to the deliverance of Constantinople in Gudzy, *History*, 505–6; bibliography 510, note 14; and, in addition, I. Tatarsky, *Simeon Polotsky, ego zhizn' i deiatel'nost'*, M, 1886; I. Eremin, ed., *Simeon Polotsky: Izbrannye sochineniia*, M-L, 1953.

A. Beletsky postulates a substantial previous literary career for Polotsky in Polish and Latin as well as White Russian (*Sbornik statei v chest' A. I. Sobolevskogo*, L, 1928, 264–7). A. Pozdneev relates Polotsky to the traditions of musical versification and part-singing of the Polish baroque in "La Poésie des chansons russes aux XVIIᵉ et XVIIIᵉ siècles," *RES*, 1959, 29–40. The best general study of Polotsky's work is L. Maikov, *Ocherki iz istorii russkoi literatury XVII i XVIII vv*, P, 1896, 1–162. For a good, critical study of Polotsky's polemics with the Old Believers (showing him to be more interested in matters of dogma than of ritual, generally ignorant of the Eastern fathers, but devoid of any general plan or ulterior motives) see D. Yagodkin, "Simeon Polotsky kak polemist protiv raskola," *Strannik*, 1880, Sep–Oct, 73–110; Nov, 316–82; Dec, 542–56.

77. Cited in the excellent article by I. Eremin, "K istorii obshchestvennoi mysli na Ukraine vtoroi poloviny XVII v," *TODL*, X, 1954, 217, 219. The *Sinopsis* first appeared in 1674 and underwent many editions, remaining the most widely known history of Russia for most of the eighteenth century.

78. L. Maikov, *Simeon Polotsky, O russkom ikonopisanii*, P, 1889; Imperial charter of 1669 in *AAE*, IV, 224–6.

79. Picture in the manuscript entitled *Dukhovnoe lekarstvo*. See A. Uspensky, *Tsarskie ikonopistsy i zhivopistsy XVII veka*, M, 1910, II, 314–16. Uspensky calculates (II, 24) that there were sixty foreign artists in the armory alone by 1662; Ovchinnikova (*Portret*, 25–6) notes the presence of another Dutch painter in Russia in the forties even before Vukhters but challenges Vukhters' authorship of the painting of Nikon, believing it to have been done later and thus exonerating Nikon from a violation of Muscovite attitudes toward art. V. Nikol'sky (*Istoriia russkago iskusstva*, M, 1915, I, 143) discusses changes in style and themes.

Numerous portraits of Russian diplomats were painted abroad by foreign masters under Alexis (*Istoriia russkogo iskusstva*, IV, 452–3). By 1670 there were fifty German prints on the walls of the room of Alexis' son in the Kremlin (Zabelin, *Domashny byt*, I, 169–70). The large number of manuscript books produced during this period in the *posol'sky prikaz* combine the essentially rationalistic philosophy of Spafary with the realistic portraiture of Bogdan Saltanov. See I. Mikhailovsky, *Vazhneishie trudy Nikolaia Spafariia (1672–1677)*, Kiev, 1897; and I. Kudriavtsev, "Izdatel'skaia deiatel'nost' posol'skogo prikaza," in *Kniga: Issledovaniia in materialy, VIII*, 1963, 179–244.

80. Livanova, *Ocherki i materialy po istorii russkoi muzykal'noi kul'tury*, M, 1938, 189. The text of Pastor Gregory's *Act of Artaxerxes*, long presumed to have been lost, has been discovered in

two different copies: one apparently belonging to the Saxon doctor in Moscow, Rinhuber, was found in Lyon and published in Paris in 1954 under the editorship of A. Mazon and F. Cocron; the other, apparently belonging to the Russian statesman A. Matveev, was published in M-L, 1957, under the editorship of I. Kudriavtsev. For a general discussion of Gregory's repertoire see the article by A. Mazon in *TODL*, XIV, 1957; and, particularly for documents dealing with the organization of the theater in Moscow, S. Bogoiavlensky, *Moskovsky teatr pri tsariakh Aleksee i Petre*, M, 1914. For the musical involvement (in addition to the catalogue of these plays and ballets set forth in Gudzy, *History*, 517) see Gozenpud, *Muzykal'ny teatr*, 13.

On Polotsky and the "school dramas" see Gudzy, *History*, 522–7; Livanova, *Ocherki*, 179–85; A. Beletsky, *Starinny teatr v Rossii*, Ann Arbor, 1964 (repr. of M, 1923).

81. Collins, *Present State*, 33.
82. Cited from instructions to Ivan Gebden in J. Patouillet, *Le Théâtre de moeurs russes, des origines à Ostrovski*, 1912, 23. On music at the Tsar's second wedding, Findeizen, *Ocherki*, I, vyp. iii, 311–13.
83. Carlisle, *Relations*, 142.
84. Tikhonravov (as cited in J. Patouillet, *Théâtre*, 24), referring to van Staden's mission abroad to recruit players for the new theater.
85. One ambassador was sent to Northern Europe, a second to Rome and Central Europe, a third to Western Europe (including Spain); and in the following year a fourth ambassador was sent as the first permanent Russian ambassador to Poland. See von Rauch, "Moskau," 38–42; N. Charykov, *Posol'stvo v Rim i sluzhba v Moskve Pavla Meneziia*

(1637–1694), P, 1906; A. Popov, *Russkoe posol'stvo*, 1–27; D. Likhachev, *Puteshestviia russkikh poslov XVI–XVII vv*, M-L, 1954, 426–41.

86. On this *Tituliarnik* or *Koren' velikikh gosudarei* of 1672 (second edition 1673–7) see Ovchinnikova, *Portret*, 65–70.

Under Tsar Michael, Russians sometimes used the title "emperor," particularly in dealings with the West. See the usage on May 1, 1633, in the proclamation of the recruiter of Tsarist mercenaries in Scotland (A. Steuart, *Scottish Influences*, 34). The *Respublica Moscoviae et Urbes*, Leiden, 1630, indicates that the title "Magnus Dominus, Imperator" was used even in 1613. The French referred to Alexis as "empereur" in 1654 (Berkh, *Tsarstvovanie*, I, 85), but attached the title to the name Alexander, which hardly bespeaks intimate familiarity with Russian reality. Cromwell and Charles II both addressed him as "emperor" (Ikonnikov, "Ordyn-Nashchokin," 283, note 1).

87. A. Vel'tman, *Le Trésor de Moscou (oruejynaia palata)*, M, 1861, 2d rev. ed., 45.
88. Savva, Archbishop of Tver, *Sacristie patriarcale dit synodale de Moscow*, M, 1865, 2d ill. ed., 9–10; Sidorov, *Graviura*, 218–19, print facing 216; also 203–4.
89. " . . . wie soll ich gnug preisen/ den unverglichen tzar, den Gross-Herzog der Reussen?/ der unser teutsches Volk mehr als die Reussen liebt,/ und ihnen Kirch und Siz, Sold, Ehr und Schatze giebt./ o hochst-gepriessner tzar, Gott wolle dich belohnen,/ wer wolte doch nicht gern in diesem Lande wohnen?" cited by N. Likhachev (*Inostranets-dobrozhelatel' Rossii v XVII stoletii*, P, 1898, 6) from the manuscript given by Gregory in October, 1667, to Johann Allgeyer,

a native of Stuttgart who had previously traveled with Olearius to Russia.

90. Postal service had been farmed out as a concession to foreigners and was notoriously insecure as a means of diplomatic communication. See Shlosberg, "O nachale," 75–7 and bibliography 77, note 5; also I. Kozlovsky, *Pervaia pochta i pervye pochtmeistery v Moskovskom gosudarstve*, Warsaw, 1913, 2v. After 1668 it came under the *posol'sky prikaz;* but security remained poor on both of the two routes west: through Smolensk and Riga.

91. Rainov, *Nauka*, 434–7. Copernicus and Brahe were both Eastern Europeans, and Danzig had the largest astronomical observatory in the world after Brahe's Copenhagen observatory burned. Thus, the influx of astronomical materials during this period is not surprising—though the admixture of astrology was considerable and little practical use was made of the knowledge Russia did possess (*ibid.*, 439–54).

92. D. Ursul, *Filosofskie i obshchestvenno-politicheskie vzgliady N. G. Milesku Spafariia*, Kishinev, 1955, 83–5; text of report in Church Slavonic of this remarkable Moldavian-born emissary published with intr. by A. Yatsimirsky, *Kitaiskoe gosudarstvo*, Kazan, 1910. See also P. Yakovleva, *Pervy russko-kitaisky dogovor 1689 goda*, M, 1958, 101–9. Formal relations were established in 1675; the Tsar had previously sent a less formal delegate in 1653 (*ibid.*, 90–2). Alexis' reign was an important period in expanding diplomatic links with central Asia also. See V. Ulianitsky, *Snosheniia Rossii s Sredneiu azieiu i Indieiu v XVI–XVII vv*, M, 1889, esp. 18, 38–43.

93. *Istoriia russkogo iskusstva*, IV, 358 ff. on the armory, which was directed from 1654 until his death in 1680 by one of Nikon's principal court persecutors, Khitrovo. Artamon Matveev became in the 1670's after the passing of Nikon and the eclipse of Ordyn-Nashchokin, the leading friend and counselor of Alexis. See A. Suvorin, *Boyarin Artamon Sergeevich Matveev*, P, 1900, 32 ff., esp. 48 on clocks; Tsvetaev dates the introduction of mirrors—which, together with the simultaneous introduction of realistic portraiture and naturalistic iconography, helped increase consciousness of the human body and its appearance—from 1665 (*Protestantstvo*, 737).

94. S. Polotsky, *Sochineniia*, 71, 10–1, 233; Polotsky, *Vertograd mnogotsvetny* (1678), S. Denisov, *Vinograd rossiisky* (1720's).

95. V. Kruglikov, *Izmailovo*, M, 1948, esp. 8–19. For reconstructions of the ornate decor and concentrically circular format of the gardens see S. Palantreer, "Sady XVII veka v Izmailove," *SII*, VII, 1956, 80–104.

96. *Istoriia russkogo iskusstva*, IV, 308–10, 406–8; Polotsky, *Sochineniia*, 104–5; A. Korsakov, *Selo Kolomenskoe*, M, 1870; and descriptions in Z. Schakovskoy, *La Vie quotidienne à Moscou au XVIIe siècle*, 1962, 257–60; N. Likhachev; A. Ershov, *Selo kolomenskoe*, M, 1913; and the exhaustive reconstruction and analysis contained in the unpublished kandidat thesis of I. Makovetsky, *Kolomenskoe: issledovanie istoricheskogo razvitiia planirovki arkhitekturnogo ansamblia*, M, 1951.

97. V. Snow, "The Concept of Revolution in Seventeenth Century England," *The Historical Journal*, V, 2, 162, 164–74. This essentially astronomical conception of revolution apparently began to be replaced only late in the seventeenth century by the modern concept of

a more cataclysmic and irrevocable change.

98. Deacon Fedor in Subbotin, *Materialy*, VI, 49–50, 219; and in *PS*, 1859, Aug, 456–8.

99. Innokenty Gizel, *Mir s Bogom chelovek*, Kiev, 1666 (repr. M, 1669, 1671) discussed in N. Sumtsov, "Innokenty Gizel'," *KS*, 1884, Oct, 207–17.

100. Lazar Baranovich, *Mech dukhovny*, Kiev, 1666. Note the elaborate military crusading symbolism of the first three pages, the fifteen pages of dedication to the Tsar, and the preface to the reader beginning with Christ's instruction to his disciples in Luke 22:36 to sell one's mantle and buy a sword. See also I. Goliatovsky, *Nebo novoe z novymy zvezdami sotvorennoe*, Lwow, 1665, the very title of which purports to speak of the new heaven described in the Book of Revelation. See also the apocalyptical symbolism in Simeon Polotsky, *Zhezl pravlenia*, M, 1763, ch. 1, 14, ch. 2, 122 (originally written in 1666 and officially endorsed by the council of 1666–7). See also the note on the origin of the work by I. Nil'sky in *Kh Cht*, 1860, Nov, 482–500.

101. Uspensky, *Ikonopistsy*, I, 55.

102. This book consisting of ninety-seven chapters and two additions was written for Queen Christina of Sweden (who was later a convert to Catholicism) by Simon Igumnov, who was born in Viazma, then moved to Smolensk and Moscow before settling in Swedish-controlled Kexholm. No copy of it is known to survive; and the only description of it is the Swedish one by Anders Wallwick (secretary to the governor general of Esthonia in Riksarkivet, Stockholm, collection of manuscripts, Nr. 69): in the appendix to his letter of June, 1662, to Mattias Björnklou. The letter itself indicates that a serious, if somewhat patronizing study of religion in Russia was being undertaken by the Swedes *(Riksarkivet,* Bjornklou collection, Nr. 6, E 3259). This illustration reinforces Tsvetaev's insistence on the basis of other evidence *(Protestantstvo,* 513 esp.) that Solov'ev and others have erred in assuming that foreigners were not interested in Russian religious matters. Indeed, Swedish Lutheran propaganda could have helped steer the Russian Orthodox into apocalypticism and anti-Catholicism. The first professor of rhetoric and leading figure in the 1650's at the newly founded Swedish Theological Academy at Turku (Åbo) in Finland (center of the Lutheran educational program in Finland and Karelia) was Eskil Petraeus, whose principal work was *De Antichristo magno, qui est Romanus pontifex,* Uppsala, 1653. See I. Salomies, *Suomen Kirkon historia*, Helsinki, 1949, II, 334–49. On the eschatological bent of Swedish religious thought during the struggle between Reformation and Counter-Reformation, see H. Sandblad, *De Eskatologiska föreställningarna i Sverige,* Uppsala, 1942.

103. Population estimated in P. Smirnov, *Voprosy*, 093; churches in Krasnozhen, *Inovertsy*, I, 88.

104. Avvakum, for instance (Subbotin, *Materialy*, I, 25).

105. The late writings of Comenius (esp. *Lux e Tenebris*, 1665) were a principal weapon of reinforcement for radical, apocalyptical elements in the Reformation. This distinction between a "radical Reformation" and a "magisterial Reformation" (that is supported by local political authorities whether princely or cantonal) has been made by G. H. Williams (see his introduction to *Spiritual and Anabaptist Writers*, Philadelphia, 1957, 18–25), and extended as far east as Poland and Lithuania in his "Anabaptism and Spiritualism in

the Kingdom of Poland and the Grand Duchy of Lithuania: An Obscure Phase of the Pre-history of Socinianism," in *Studia nad arianizmem*, 215–62. The Calvinism in Lithuania and White Russia is discussed by W. Ryzy-Ryski, *The Reformation in Byelorussia*, Princeton Theological Seminary, unpublished, revised Th. M. thesis.

106. This comparison was frequently made by early Western students of Russian religious life. See, for instance, J. Bellermann, *Kurzer Abriss der russischen Kirche*, Erfurt, 1788, 240–3.

For the pacifism of Neronov and Avvakum see S. Zenkovsky, "The Ideological World of the Denisov Brothers," *HSS*, III, 1957, 61–2 note 45; Subbotin, *Materialy*, I, 38; Pascal, *Avvakum*, 48–9. The Old Believer term for "church," "temple of prayer" *(molitvenny khram)*, was widely used during the time of Alexis. Recent Old Believer literature claims that some of the temples built even before the schism were theirs. Indeed, the Old Believer calendar for 1960 celebrates the three hundredth anniversary of their first, allegedly built near Dünaburg. See *Staroobriadchesky tserkovny kalendar' na 1960 god* (Preobrazhenskaia Staroobriadcheskaia Obshchina), 58.

107. This elder, Joseph, also began his preaching activities in 1660 at distant Eniseisk, well before the formalization of the schism. See A. Pallady, *Obozrenie permskago raskola*, P, 1863, 1–2; and I. Syrtsov, *Samozhigatel'stvo*, 6–9, 12–3. The increasing absorption of Armenian merchants into the Russian Orthodox fold (see Krasnozhen, *Inovertsy*, 91) may point to another source of Old Believer strength, because they were particularly strong among merchant classes. Nikon, however, was also accused of initiating Armenian rites; see Polotsky, *Zhezl*, ch. 2, 73.

108. This is the clear implication of the excellent pseudononymous discussion of a new edition of I. Goliatovsky, *Kliuch razumeniia* (Kiev, 1672), entitled "Iuzhnorusskoe dukhovenstvo i evrei v XVII veke," *Voskhod*, 1887, Apr, esp. 4–6. Goliatovsky's work and the campaign in Russia against Sabbataian ideas is also dealt with, albeit less satisfactorily, in Gradovsky, *Otnosheniia*, 338–56; and related to his general fear of heresy by I. Ogienko, "Propoved' Ioannikiia Galiatovskago," *SKhO*, XIX, 1913, esp. 423–6. See also the catalogues of heresies in Goliatovsky's *Nebo novoe*, 51–64, 68–74.

109. G. Scholem, "Le Mouvement sabbataiste en Pologne," *JHR*, XLIII, 1953, 30–90, 209–32, and XLIV, 1953, 42–77, documents the enormous impact inside Poland of Sabbataian messianism and indicates its substantial legacy to Polish thought, principally through Frankist sectarianism. Some hints and indications of Sabbataian influence in Russia are contained in Scholem's *Schabbetai Zvi*, Tel Aviv, 1957, I, 1–74, II, 493 ff.

On the influx of Jews into Muscovy in the late seventeenth century see material listed in the special supplement to the Russian Jewish periodical *Voskhod: Sistematichesky ukazatel' literatury ob evreiakh na russkom iazyke (1708–1889)*, P, 1892, 53–5, esp. P. Liakud, "K istorii evreev v Rossii," *Voskhod*, 1888, May–Jun, 198–208, which stresses the lack of special restrictions against Jews during the reign of Alexis. See also E. Mel'nikov, *Uchastie iudeev i inovertsev v delakh tserkvi*, M, 1911, esp. 11–13, for official accusations of direct Jewish (and Armenian) influence among Old Believers and 65–6 on the subsequent need of Old Believers to make common cause with Jews and other minority groups in order to survive under conditions of persecution. Yu. Gessen, "Evrei v Moskovskom Gosudarstve XV–XVII v," *Evreiskaia Starina*, 1915, no. 1, 1–19; and esp. no. 2, 153–72, documents other cases of Jews in high places. Jews were particularly used for translating (see K. Wickhart, *Moscowittische Reiss-Beschreibung*, Vienna, 1675, 43–4.)

There are some hints of a Jewish presence or influence even within the most notoriously anti-Jewish (the term "anti-Semitic" is inaccurate for this period) groups: the Cossacks (see the study by S. Borovoy in *IS*, I, 1934, 141–9; and Slouschz, "Les Origines," 80) and the Old Believers (Smirnov, *Voprosy*, 093–4, 096–100). For Jews in Moscow in the late seventeenth century see *Evreiskaia Starina*, 1913, no. 1, 96–8. As with the Judaizing heresy, the precise role of the Jews in the Russian religious ferment of the late seventeenth century has never been precisely determined; but in contrast to the situation in the fifteenth century, the seventeenth-century problem has never been systematically investigated.

110. De Rodes cited by V. Nikol'sky, "Sibirskaia ssylka protopopa Avvakuma," *UZ RANION*, II, 1927, 154.

111. Dispatch of A. Alegretti and J. Lorbach of Jan 18, 1656, in Haus, Hof und Staatsarchiv, Vienna, 8 Russland I Russica, VI, 27.

112. Paul of Aleppo, *Travels*, I, 410; also I, 386–95, II, 74–9.

113. See article 53 of the *Kormchaia* of 1653 (which has never been fully reprinted or analytically compared with the pre-Nikonian edition of 1651. A substantial section is in W. Palmer, *The Patriarch*, I, 617–65). On Nikon's use of the Donation, see *ibid.*, I, 207–16, and Zyzykin, *Nikon*, II, 161–4 (where it is contended that Nikon was un-

aware that it was a forgery, and free of any intent to establish papal claims for himself). The fifteen-page supplement on church history (consulted in the copy of the 1653 *Kormchaia* in the Harvard Law School Library) gives much detail on the apostolicity of the Russian church; presents the founding of the Russian patriarchate as a kind of divine compensation for the apostacy of the Roman Church; and accuses Rome of having seduced the English Church away from alleged prior fealty to Orthodoxy and "the Greek Tsar." The most sustained effort to trace papal inclinations to Nikon (largely on the basis of other argumentation than is here advanced) is I. Andreev, *Papskiia tendentsii patriarkha Nikona*, P, 1908.

114. Belokurov, *Materialy*, 101–2. An even more apocalyptical dream taken from a letter of December, 1661, in Gibbenet, *Izsledovanie*, II, 48 ff., depicts the Uspensky Sobor in flames and the great church leaders of the past rising from their graves in holy procession towards the altar, while Metropolitan Peter tells Nikon of his despair over the Tsar, and fire slowly mounts toward the Tsar himself. For another vision of Peter during the Advent fast of 1664, see *ibid.*, II, 112–13.

115. Gibbenet, *Izsledovanie*, I, 63; also 122.

116. Gibbenet, II, 47. On regulation about rebaptism see Krasnozhen, *Inovertsy*, 33–4, 100 ff.

117. Zyzykin, *Nikon*, II, 46. The Patriarch of Constantinople was also convinced that "second Lutherans" were at work in Russia, Subbotin, *Materialy*, VI, 198. Odoevsky was both head of the newly created *prikaz* of monastic affairs and government interrogator of Nikon.

118. Ligarides' letter to Nikon of Jul 12, 1662, in Gibbenet, *Izsledovanie*, I,

113. See also Zyzykin, *Nikon*, III, 72–4.
119. *Zhitie* 110 (mt of *Life*, 134).
120. *Life*, 66.
121. *Ibid.*, 134, 34.
122. *Ibid.*, 131.
123. *Ibid.*, 34 ("pravoverny," *Zhitie*, 55). See E. Hoffer, *The True Believer*, NY, 1951.
124. Subbotin, *Materialy*, V, 204.
125. Avvakum, *Life*, 22.
126. Subbotin, *Materialy*, VIII, 224 ff.
127. I. Shusherin, "Izvestie o rozhdenii i o vospitanii i o zhitii sviateishago Nikona, patriarkha Moskovskago i vseia Rossii," *RA*, 1909, no. 9, 1–110, particularly valuable for the early years of Nikon.

   On the genre of spiritual autobiography, its development in the seventeenth century, and the texts and interrelationships of the *zhitie* of Avvakum and of Epiphanius see A. Robinson, *Zhizneopisaniia Avvakuma i Epifaniia*, M, 1963.
128. A. Kluyver, "Over het Verblijf van Nicolaas Witsen te Moskou (1664–65)," *Verslagen en Mededeelingen der Koninklijke Akademie van Wetenschappen*, Amsterdam, 1894, 5–38, esp. 19–22.
129. Text of Witsen's report, folio pages 136a–137b, consulted while on temporary deposit in the University of Leiden Library, 1961, May.
130. Belokurov, *Materialy*, 84–100; Zyzykin, *Nikon*, I, 25; also III, 47–52, where Nikon likens his fate to that of the Hebrew prophets. For alleged early miracles on the Old Believer side see Subbotin, *Materialy*, I, 204–5; VII, 35–40.
131. Gibbenet, *Izsledovaniia*, II, 77, 47.
132. Reprinted in Ya. Barskov, *Pamiatniki pervykh let russkago staroobriadchestva*, P, 1912, 1–5 and comment 265–75. Also, for Nikon's use of the Antichrist symbol (much less known generally than that of the Old Believers), see *Strannik*, 1880, Aug, 526–67.
133. *Och* (6), 300–2; *Opisanie doku-*
mentov i bumag khraniashchikhsia v moskovskom arkhive Ministerstva iustitsii*, M, 1912, XVI, 18, note 2. See also V. Lebedev and A. Novosel'sky, eds., *Krest'ianskaia voina pod predvoditel'stvom Stepana Razina: sbornik dokumentov* M, 1954, I, 277 for Stenka Razin's unsuccessful negotiation with Nikon.
134. P. Verkhovskoy's monumental study of the church reforms of Peter (*Uchrezhdenie dukhovnoi kollegii i dukhovny reglament*, Rostov/ Don, 1916, 2v) considers the humiliation of Nikon and the *sobor* of 1666–7 the decisive stage in the secularization of the church and its subordination to the state (I, 44–5, 684). Another excellent and neglected study (I. Kozlovsky, "Znachenie XVII veka v russkoi istorii," in *Sbornik istoriko-filologicheskago obshchestva*, Nezhin, VI, 1908) considers the *sobor* of 1666–7 in effect the first synod of the state church; a contemporary study by the Saxon Pastor at Vilnius (Herbinius, *Religiosae*, 150) also refers to the gathering of 1666–7 as a Lutheran type of synod (in the midst of an interesting analysis of the church schism largely in terms of Western parallels, 144–70, see also 72–9).
135. Mel'nikov, *Uchastie*, 12–13, 86–7; Gessen, "Evrei," 161, note 1; Gibbenet, *Izsledovanie* I, 122; Simeon Polotsky, *Zhezl*, ch. I, 17; Paul of Aleppo, *Travels*, I, 276; Collins, *Present State*, 113–21.
136. Krachkovsky, *Ocherki*, 62.
137. The act of 1839 formally abolishing the Uniat Church inside Russia links it to the "khitraia politika byvshei pol'skoi respubliki." Cited in S. Mel'gunov, *Iz istorii religiozno-obshchestvennykh dvizhenii v Rossii XIX v*, M, 1919, 73.
138. Smirnov, *Istoriia*, 91–5, 121; *Voprosy*, 61–7.
139. S. Bezsonov, *Rostov veliky*, M, 1945, 9–10, 14–23

140. Pascal, *Avvakum,* 371–2.
141. All of these are to be found in the frescoes of the Church of Ilya Prorok in Yaroslavl, which was built in 1647–50 but adorned with its present frescoes only in 1680–1. A new study of the composition of these frescoes and their celebrated borrowings from the Piscator Bible is M. Nekrasova, "Novoe v sinteze zhivopisi i arkhitektury XVII veka," in V. Lazarev, *et al.,* *Drevnerusskoe iskusstvo: XVII vek,* M, 1964, 89–109.
142. Contrast, for instance, the uneasy figure and cluttered composition of the late-seventeenth-century Yaroslavl icon of Christ enthroned in Bunt, *Russian Art,* 108, with the earlier Novgorodian composition on the same theme on 87.

   The increasing representation of scenes of suffering on seventeenth-century icon screens is discussed by Sperovsky ("Ikonostasy,"

Kh Cht, 1892, Jan–Feb, 10–16), who points out (15) that the same trend was also evident in the iconography of the apostles; and (12) that the Church Council of 1667 markedly accelerated the trend by requiring a representation of the cross on each icon screen so that "the holy church, by looking upon the crucifixion and passion of our savior Jesus Christ, may be cured of gnawing penetration by the invisible serpent-devil."
143. There is no thorough, scholarly study either of Sysoevich or of Rostov; and my account of its treasures (and to a considerable extent, those of Yaroslavl) is largely drawn on observations and impressions during visits there in Mar, 1961, and Jan, 1965.

   For an article on the still-magnificent bells of Rostov, largely cast under Sysoevich, see *Soviet Life,* 1965, Dec, 44.

2. THE WESTWARD TURN

1. On Medvedev, see the edition of his works edited by A. Prozorovsky in *Cht,* 1896, II, iv, 1–148; III, iv, 149–378; IV, iii, 379–604; also S. Belokurov, *Sil'vester Medvedev. Izvestie istinnoe pravoslavnym,* M, 1886 (also in *Cht,* 1885, IV): I. Kozlovsky, *Sil'vester Medvedev. Ocherk iz istorii russkago prosveshcheniia i obshchestvennoi zhizni v kontse XVII v,* Kiev, 1896; I. Shliapkin, *Dmitry Rostovsky i ego vremia,* P, 1891, 144–76, 208 ff.; and for the influx of Latin terms and scholastic concepts into the Russian language during this time see Vinogradov, *Ocherki,* 18–33.

   On the prodigious literary and theological activies of the Likhudies see M. Smentsovsky, *Brat'ia Likhudy,* P, 1899, and supplementary volume of materials *Tserkovno-istoricheskiia materialy,* P, 1899; also *BE,* XVII, 857–8. For the battle of the Grecophiles and Latiniz

ers see K. Kharlampovich, *Bor'ba shkolnykh vliianii v dopetrovskoi Rusi,* Kiev, 1902; A. Galkin, *Akademiia, 27*–59; and the discussion of C. O'Brien, *Russia under Two Tsars 1682–1689. The Regency of Sophia Alekseevna,* Berkeley–Los Angeles, 1952, 43–61.
2. The proliferating Western theses and treatises are listed and critically discussed in Rushchinsky, "Religiozny byt." Saxon links are discussed by J. Herbinius, *Religiosae,* 4, 34–46; Swedish links by N. Berg, *Exercitatio.* See also H. Bendel, *Johannes Herbinius, Ein Gelehrtenleben a.d. XVII Jahrhunderts,* Leipzig, 1924; and two articles by I. Pokrovsky on the curriculum and cultural impact of the theological seminaries, indicating frequent borrowings from the West: *Strannik* 1869, Jul, 24–55; Aug, 109–38.
3. Karmirēs, *Ta Dogmatika,* II, 687–773.

4. Zyzykin, *Nikon*, II, 164.
5. See *Catholic Encyclopedia*, V, 572–90.
6. Gavin, *Aspects*, 335; also the general discussion 324–53.
7. See G. Markovich, *O vremeni presushchestvleniia sviatykh darov: spor, byvshy v Moskve vo vtoroi polovine XVII v*, Vilnius, 1886, for this controversy and A. Gavrilov, "Literaturnye trudy patriarkha Ioakima,"*Strannik*, 1872, Feb, 89–112, for the preoccupation of the official church with schismatics, which permitted the Latin position to come into widespread usage.

   The continued Russian insistence on viewing the manner and timing of transubstantiation as unknowable mysteries (see Sokolov, *Kratkoe uchenie*, 41–2; I. Zhilov, *Katekhizicheskoe uchenie*, 99) is similar to the attitudes of the Jansenists a century later, who were anathemized by Pius VI (in the bull, *Uctorem fidei* of 1794).
8. On Medvedev's conflict with the radical Lithuanian Protestant Jan Belobodsky see A. Gavrilov, "Propovedniki 'nemetskoi very' v Moskve i otnoshenie k nim patriarkha Ioakima," *Strannik*, 1873, Mar, 126–37. On the Likhudies (who also wrote against Protestants and Old Believers) see Smentsovsky, *Brat'ia*, 33–4.
9. On Krizhanich's early career see S. Belokurov, "Yury Krizhanich v Rossii," in *Iz dukhovnoi zhizni moskovskago obshchestva XVII v*, M, 1902, esp. 152/13–159; and for his polemic activities 168–88.

   For a good discussion and basic bibliography see the article by M. Petrovich in *ASR*, 1947, Dec, 75–92; for an excellent analysis of his political ideas see V. Val'denberg, *Gosudarstvennye idei Krizhanicha*, P, 1912. The spirited article by L. Pushkarev (*VI*, 1957, no. 1, 77–86) and vigorous supporting comments of other academicians (*VI*, 1957, no. 2, 202–6) seem to have restored Krizhanich from the Stalinist anathema as a reactionary plotter for the Vatican (and a Yugoslav at that). A new and complete edition is being prepared of Krizhanich's major work (previously published in a confusing and somewhat abridged version by P. Bezsonov as *Russkoe gosudarstvo v polovine XVII veka*, M, 1859–60, 2v) principally by A. Gol'dberg, whose articles on Krizhanich (*UZLGU*, CXVII, 1947; *TODL*, XIV, 1958; *ISR*, 1960, no. 6; *Slavia*, 1965, no. 1) contain valuable new information. Krizhanich's polemic pro-Catholic and anti-German writings inside Russia are partly contained in M. Sokolov, *Sobranie sochinenii Krizhanicha*, M, 1891, supplemented by recent manuscript discoveries in *IA*, 1958, no. 1, 154–89.
10. M. Murko, *Die Bedeutung der Reformation und Gegenreformation für das geistige Leben der Südslaven*, Prague-Heidelberg, 1927, 24–59 and esp. 38, 46, note 4, and 48, note 2, for the Croatian emissaries to Moscow in the 1590's and 1620's.
11. Pesaro, 1601. Vandals, Goths, and Avars are included among the "Slavs" and the role of the Southern Slavs is stressed by the Croatian Benedictine in this remarkable work, which was translated into Russian by Prokopovich (P, 1722). See E. Shmurlo, "From Krizhanich to the Slavophils, An Historical Survey," *SEER*, 1927, Dec, 321–7; and *BE*, XLII, 91.
12. Shmurlo, "Ligarides"; and *Kurie*.
13. *Russkoe gosudarstvo*, I, 92–8.
14. *IA*, 1958, no. 1, 170; see also Val'denberg, *Idei*, 155–8.
15. On Kuhlmann see particularly his collection of mystical and prophetic poems *Der Kühlpsalter*, London, 1679, and second expanded edition, Amsterdam, 1685–6, two parts, of which the first fourteen pages of part two are full of interesting prophecy. See also his prophetic appeal "wherein the reformation

from Popery is fundamentally asserted and the Union of Protestants convincingly urged," *To the Wiclef-Waldenses, Hussites, Zwinglians, Lutherans, and Calvinists*, London, 1679 (and in Latin, Rotterdam, 1679); and his appeal to the Tsar, *Drei und Zwanzigstes Kühl-Jubel ausz dem ersten Buch des Kühl-Salomons an Ihre Czarischen Majestäten*, Amsterdam, 1687.

For the best basic discussion see R. Beare, "Quirinus Kuhlmann: The Religious Apprenticeship," *PMLA*, 1953, Sep, 828–62; also his bibliography in *La Nouvelle Clio*, VI, 1954, 164–82; and, for his Russian activities, Tikhonravov, *Sochineniia*, II, 305–75; and Chizhevsky, *Aus zwei Welten*, 231–52. There is a valuable analysis of his spiritual poetry by Claus Bock (*Quirinus Kuhlmann als Dichter*, Bern, 1957), showing among other things striking resemblances in his imagery and versification to John of the Cross (89–95).

Adam Olearius, the merchant from Holstein who wrote the most widely read foreign account of Russia in the seventeenth century, was, like Kuhlmann, a member of the Fruchtbringende Gesellschaft. See B. Unbegaun, "Un Ouvrage retrouvé de Quirin Kuhlmann," *La Nouvelle Clio*, 1951, May–Jun, 257.

16. Quoted in Beare, "Apprenticeship," 854.

17. Theophilus Varmund, *La Religion ancienne et moderne des Moscovites*, Cologne, 1698, 25–7 (the account first published in Latin in 1694 by a German who visited Russia just after the death of Kuhlmann).

18. Tikhonravov, *Sochineniia*, II, 306, 346; see also Chizhevsky, *Aus zwei Welten*, 197–203; Gavrilov, "Propovedniki," 139–43.

19. Tikhonravov, *Sochineniia*, II, 373–5. "It is known from the history of this Kuhlmann that some of the boyars closest to the Tsar strongly

interceded with the Patriarch for Kuhlmann." A. Labzin in the introduction to his translation of Boehme's *Christophia (Put' ko Khristu*, P, 1815). xxiii–xxiv; cited in *BZ*, 1858, I, 131.

20. Compare the patronizing tone of the general Russian reaction as reported by the Dutchman Keller in a letter of Jun 7, 1689 (unpublished letter in Archives of the Estates General, Leiden) with the patronizing treatment of apocalyptical prophets that was concurrently becoming fashionable in England. Whereas Sir Henry Vane had still been taken with deadly seriousness for his prophecy that the Second Coming would occur in 1666, similar prophecies twenty-five years later were looked at in the modern manner, as the ravings of madmen. See Christopher Hill, "John Mason and the End of the World," *History Today*, 1957, no. 11, 776–80. By the 1680's earlier eschatological expectations had generally been replaced by a tone of weary resignation to the reign of Antichrist (Antoinette Bourgignon, *L'Antéchrist découvert*, Amsterdam, 1681) or by scholarly and quasi-mathematical analyses (Jacques Massard, *Harmonie des prophesies anciennes avec les modernes, sur la durée de l'Antéchrist et des souffrances de l'Église*, Cologne, 1687).

21. Paul Hazard, *La Crise de la conscience européenne* (trans. *The European Mind 1685–1715*, London, 1953) traces the sudden move in these years "from Bossuet to Voltaire"—a change which did not occur in Russia until late (basically under Catherine) but took place earlier in England. See S. Bethell, *The Cultural Revolution of the Seventeenth Century*, Boston, 1957.

22. The *khlysty* were alleged to have originated in Kuhlmann's teachings by R. Reutsky (*Liudi bozhii i skoptsy. Istoricheskoe izsledovanie*, M, 1872, esp. 1–22). This hypothe-

sis is rejected by most scholars (including J. Sévérac, *La Secte russe des Hommes-de-Dieu*, 1906, who summarizes the controversy 96–8, and suggests a derivation of *khlyst* from *Khrist*, 7, note 1). The inconclusive discussion of origins by Grass, *Sekten*, I, 588–648, considers a variety of possible links with Western Protestant extremists. A major, neglected work that relates all the major sects to Protestant influences is that of I. Sokolov, "Vliianie protestantstva na obrazovanie khlystovskoi, dukhoborskoi i molokanskoi sekt," *Strannik*, 1880, no. 1, 96–112; no. 2, 237–60.

23. Sévérac, *Secte*, 106.

24. *Signatura Rerum* and *Mysterium Magnum* were the popular titles of Boehme's two most important works: his treatise on cosmology and his "spiritual commentary" on the book of Genesis. In addition to Boehme (on whom see Z. David, "The Influence of Jacob Boehme on Russian Religious Thought," *ASR*, 1962, Mar, 43–64) considerable influence was exercised on Kuhlmann (and on Russian esoteric and sectarian thought) by Lully, partly through the intermediacy of the heretical seventeenth-century Jesuit Athanasius Kirchner. See Tikhonravov, *Sochineniia*, II, 312 ff. For indications of his influence on the Old Believers see Archimandrite Nikanor, " 'Velikaia Nauka' Raimunda Liulliia v sokrashchenii Andreia Denisova," *IIaS*, XVIII, kn. 2, 1913, 10–36.

25. Gavrilov, "Propovedniki," 131.

26. Margaritov, *Istoriia*, 84. The figure, Tveritinov, was a doctor—illustrating the continued appeal of occult, anti-Orthodox thought to this small educated and isolated intellectual elite.

27. T. Butkevich, *Obzor*, 18–20; G. Protopov, "Istorichesky vid misticheskikh sekt v Rossii," *TKDA*, 1867, Oct, 93–4; *BSE (1)*, LIX, 811–2. Grass analyzes the legends about Daniel and Suslov, *Sekten*, I, 78–95; also Sévérac, *Secte*, 82–109. P. Mel'nikov (*RV*, 1868, May, 5–70) suggests Bogomil origins; the anonymous author of the valuable article on Suslov in *RBS*, XIX, 182, notes a similarity with the Hindu idea of reincarnation; Shchapov (*Delo*, 1867, no. 11, 160–4) sees Tatar origins and Cossack intermediacy in transmitting the sect; and Sévérac (*Secte*, 154–70) tends to suggest some link with Moslem dervishes. Pre-Christian or Finnopagan origins are also postulated particularly by Shchapov; and P. Smirnov (*Voprosy*, 093–100) hints at a partly Jewish derivation by relating the flagellants to the ascetic traditions of Kapiton.

There are many interesting parallels between Russian sectarianism and more recent sectarian movements in outlying regions just entering the throes of modernization. V. Lanternari (*The Religions of the Oppressed; a Study of Modern Messianic Cults*, NY, 1965, p) sees these new sects as indigenous protest movements fusing local paganism with eschatological religious ideas taken over from the resented Western intruders in order to protest against the secular and technological eschatology imposed upon them from the West.

28. Suslov was said to have died on Jan 1, 1700,—presumably as a kind of protest against the new century and the change of New Year's Day from September to January. Actually, Suslov died a natural death in 1716 (Margaritov, *Istoriia*, 21–5). The tendency to blend anti-innovationist ideas and prophetic wandering into the sectarian tradition reflects in part a grafting of schismatic ideas onto the flagellant tradition—also evidenced in the tendency to transform the Boyarinia Morozova into a kind of Mary Magdalen figure for their original martyred "Christs." See *RBS*, XIX,

180–4; *BE*, LXIII, 123–4; Sévérac, *Secte*, 128–31, 146–8, 217.

29. On Prokopy Lupkin, who proclaimed himself Christ in 1732, and on the trials and scandals that followed see Sokolov, "Vliianie," 244–5; Margaritov, *Istoriia*, 18 ff.

30. *BE*, LXXIII, 407, and the entire article, 402–9; Margaritov, *Istoriia*, 14.

31. Margaritov, *Istoriia*, 88 ff.

32. *Ibid.*, 106 ff.; 125–8 for the links between *Dukhobory* and *Molokane;* 128–33 for Judaizing influences. The distinction is often made between these eighteenth-century "rationalistic" sects and the so-called "mystical" sects that appeared earlier (the flagellants, and so on). However, the theoretical basis for the distinction is not very clear; and, in practice, there is little agreement on the category to which many sects (for example, the Dukhobors) properly belong. The close links of the later sects with Protestantism are frequently and more convincingly asserted. See, for instance, S. Bolshakoff, "Russian 'Protestant' Sects," in *Nonconformity*, 97 ff.; N. Sokolov, *Ob ideiakh i idealakh russkoi intelligentsii*, P, 1904, 307 ff.

33. Cited in *RBS*, IX, 546.

34. Butkevich, *Obzor*, 84–5. F. Livanov points to the relative newness of Tambov (formally a city only in 1636 and seat of a bishopric in 1662) and the large number of foreigners in the city—implying that these factors contributed to its rather unstable fascination with extremism. *Raskol'niki*, I, 285 ff.

35. *VF*, 1960, no. 1, 143–8.

36. Cited in Mel'gunov, *Dvizheniia*, 104.

37. *Ibid.*, 117, 129. Grigory Talitsky's proclamation of Peter as Antichrist was taken so seriously that the highest ecclesiastical authority, Stepan Yavorsky, wrote a reply in 1703: *Znameniia prishestviia antikhristova i konchiny veka*. See the discussion and Old Believer response

in N. S-n [Subbotin?], *Katalog ili biblioteka starovercheskoi tserkvi sobranny tshchaniem Pavla Liubopytnago*, M, 1861, 27.

38. Francesco Algarotti, in 1739, after visiting the city. See L. Réau, *Saint-Pétersbourg*, Paris, 1913, 16; and S. Graciotti, "I 'Viaggi di Russia' di Francesco Algarotti," *RiS*, IX, 1961, 129–50.

For an exhaustive account of the early construction of the city, S. Luppov, *Istoriia stroitel'stva Peterburga v pervoi chetverti XVIII veka*, M-L, 1957; for a detailed but undocumented English account of the cultural life of St. Petersburg through the reign of Elizabeth see C. Marsden, *Palmyra of the North*, London, 1942.

There are three excellent attempts to deal with the city as a cultural symbol: H. Hjärne, *Från Moskva till Petersburg. Rysslands omdaning. Kulturhistoriska skildringar*, Uppsala, 1888–9, 2v; E. Lo Gatto, *Il mito di Pietroburgo. Storia, leggenda, poesia*, Milan, 1960 (esp. 152–75, contrasting Moscow and St. Petersburg); and N. Antsiferov, *Byl' i mif Peterburga*, P, 1924. See also G. Florovsky's valuable review of two other books by Antsiferov on St. Petersburg, *SEER*, V, 1926–7, 193–8.

39. On Dutch terminology see W. Christiani, *Über das Eindringen von Fremdworten in die russische Schriftsprache des 17 und 18 Jahrhunderts*, 1906, 37–43. On the short-lived early German schools in Moscow (which had as many as ten well-paid teachers and seventy-seven students working twelve hours a day, largely on languages) see S. Belokurov, *O nemetskikh shkolakh v Moskve v pervoi chetverti XVIII v, 1701–1715*, M, 1907. Pastor Glück, whose servant became the second wife of Peter the Great, had previously set up a school in 1684 to convert Russian schismatics to Lutheranism in Livonia under the

patronage of the king of Sweden before setting up his school in the Naryshkin home in Moscow (*ibid.*, iii–viii). On the education of Russians abroad see M. Nikol'sky, "Russkie vykhodtsy iz zagranichnykh shkol v XVIII stoletii," *PO,* 1863, III. On the founding of the Academy of Sciences see L. Richter, *Leibniz und sein Russlandbild,* 1946, 107–42. On the early, unhappy history of Petrozavodsk see V. Shkvarikov, *Planirovka gorodov v Rossii XVIII-nachala XIX veka,* M, 1939, 52–4.

40. L. Lewitter, "Peter and Westernization," *JHI,* 1958, Oct, 496.

41. V. Danilevsky, *Russkaia tekhnicheskaia literatura pervoi chetverti XVIII veka,* M–L, 1954, 239–62; V. Pogorelov, *Materialy i originaly Vedomostei, 1702–1727,* M, 1903. The extent to which scientific development in eighteenth-century Russia grew in response to military needs has been skillfully spelled out in the case of the navy by T. Rainov, "O roli russkogo flota v razvitii estestvoznaniia XVIII v," *TIIE,* I, 1947, 169–218. The degree to which foreigners continued to dominate the Academy of Sciences throughout the eighteenth century (comprising more than two thirds the total membership for the century) is brought out by I. Yanzhul, "Natsional'nost' i prodolzhitel'nost' zhizni nashikh akademikov," *IAN,* 1913, no. 6, 284; and this entire useful article 279–98.

42. In addition to examples already discussed see the use of "science" by theologians such as Ioanniky Goliatovsky, rector of the brotherhood school at Kiev, particularly the chapter dealing with the technique of preaching, "Nauka albo sposob zlozheniia," in *Kliuch razumeniia,* Kiev, 1659, 241, 125–33. Mogila, the founder of the school, seems to have used *nauka* in the sense of theoretical knowledge (*BE,* XLVI, 484–5), probably translating from

Latin (rather than drawing on the earlier uses of *nauk, nauka,* documented in Sreznevsky, *Materialy,* II, 344, but long out of use in the Muscovite period).

Magnitsky's arithmetic was in the genre of such unprinted seventeenth-century texts as the anonymous "Practical Geometry" (*Geometriia praktika*) and the useful guide to arithmetic published in Amsterdam in 1689 by I. Kopievsky, *Kratkoe i poleznoe rukovenie v arifmetiku.* See Kol'man, "Zachatki," 312, 315. See also the insistence (309–10) that the first general understanding of theoretical mathematics came through the mystics. A good example of the continued emphasis on practical "science" under Peter is in the title of Tatishchev's tract of 1730, *Razgovor dvukh priiatelei o pol'ze nauk i uchilishch* (ed. N. Popov, M, 1888), in which only the "useful" skills of medicine, economics, law, and philosophy are recommended for study.

43. The basic armory of abstract words ending in tsiia was derived from Polish ending *cja;* and a mass of Latin and general European terms dealing with manners, politics, architecture, music, and so on, were adopted in the distinctive forms they acquired in Poland, particularly in the late years of the reign of Alexis (who spoke Polish). See Christiani, *Eindringen,* esp. 10–33, 42–54. For other aspects of the influence see Lewitter, "Peter and Westernization," 493–505; and Vinogradov, *Ocherki,* 17–34, for the role of Ukrainians and White Russians as transmitters of the Polish linguistic legacy to Great Russia under Alexis as well as Peter. For the fullest over-all picture of Western borrowings under Peter see N. Smirnov, "Zapadnoe vliianie na russky iazyk v petrovskuiu epokhu," *SlaS,* LXXXVIII, no. 2, 1910, 1–360; and 361–86 for an appendix with several early eighteenth-century

handbook guides to the Russian equivalents of the transliterated foreign words.

44. P. Pierling, *La Sorbonne et la Russie (1717–47)*, 1882, esp. 22–38; A. Adariukov, "Ofort v Rossii," *Iskusstvo*, 1923, no. 1, 284.

45. B. Sumner, *Peter the Great and the Emergence of Russia*, London, 1956, P, 132. For the growing influence of Grotius and Swedish practice even before Peter and the intellectual origins of Peter's *Polizeistaat* see Lappo-Danilevsky, "L'Idée," 369–83; Verkhovskoy, *Uchrezhdenie*, I, iii–xv.

46. Yu. Serech, "Feofan Prokopovich as writer and preacher in his Kievan period," *HSS*, II, 1954, 223. See Prokopovich, *Pravda voli monarshei*, P, 1726 (many subsequent editions); and other of his works in *Sochineniia*, ed. I. Eremin, M-L, 1961. Lappo-Danilevsky, "L'Idée," 374 and note 1 for the influence of Buddeus and Grotius in addition to that of Hobbes. See also R. Stupperich, "Feofan Prokopovič und Johann Franz Buddeus," *ZOG*, IX, 1935, 341 ff.; G. Bissonnette, *Pufendorf and the Church Reforms of Peter the Great*, Columbia University Ph.D., 1961; Brian-Chaninov, *Church*, 128–33; and E. Temnikovsky, "Odin iz istochnikov dukhovnago reglamenta," *SKhO*, XVIII, 1909, 524–34.

For his opponent Yavorsky's final struggle against the subordination of church to state under Peter see Tikhonravov, *Sochineniia*, II, 156–304; and for the largely Roman Catholic derivation of his arguments see I. Morev, *"Kamen' Very" Mitropolita Stefana Yavorskago*, P, 1904, esp. 1–50, 187–247. Also Yu. Serech, "Stefan Yavorsky and the Conflict of Ideologies in the Age of Peter the Great," *SEER*, XXX, 1951, 40–62.

On Prokopovich himself I. Chistovich, *Feofan Prokopovich i ego vremia*, P, 1868, is still valuable.

The discussion therein of Western influences (366–84) is expanded in G. Gurvich, *"Pravda voli monarshei" Feofana Prokopovicha i ee zapadno-evropeiskie istochniki*, Tartu, 1915.

Neither East nor West seems overly anxious to claim Prokopovich. The Orthodox G. Florovsky declares flatly that he "was not just under the influence of Protestantism, he simply was a Protestant," ("Westliche Einflüsse in der russischen Theologie," *Kyrios*, II, 1937, 11); whereas the German Catholic R. Stupperich insists that Prokopovich was always Orthodox ("Feofan Prokopovičs theologische Bestrebungen," *Kyrios*, I, 1936, 350–62).

47. F. Prokopovich, *Slova i rechi*, P, 1760, I, 24; II, 74–6. Cited in V. Kiparsky, "Finland and Sweden in Russian Literature," *SEER*, 1947, Nov, 175. S. Zenkovsky, "Schism," 49, claims that Prokopovich "created" as well as popularized the word *rossianin;* but it appears to have been already in use during the Time of Troubles. See S. Platonov, *Sotsial'ny krizis smutnogo vremeni*, L, 1924, 67.

48. Christiani, *Eindrügen*, 18, 23.

49. "Vol'nokhishchna Amerika/ Liud'mi, v nravakh, v tsarstakh dika . . ./ Ne znav Boga, khuda duma/ Nikto zhe bo chto uspeet,/ Gde glupost' skvern' i grekh deet." Karion Istomin, in P. Berkov, ed., *Virshi: sillabicheskaia poeziia XVII–XVIII vekov*, L, 1935, 151. It also was popular in eighteenth-century sectarian literature to blame America for tobacco, "this American plague" which has "taken away the spiritual peace of man." (. . . Amerikanskaia chuma/ lishila mir dukhovnago uma") F. Livanov, *Raskol'niki*, I, 237 (and entire poem, 234–52).

50. As by G. Florovsky in the chapter heading on Peter in *Puti*. See also the typical Slavophile usage by I. Aksakov, *RA*, 1873, kn. 2, 2511.

51. "Geometria iavisia,/ Zemlemerie vsem mnisia./ Bez mery nest' chto na zemli." Karion Istomin in Berkov, ed., *Virshi*, 150.

52. L. Lewitter, "Peter the Great and the Polish Dissenters," *SEER*, XXIII, 1954–5, 75–101; R. Wittram, "Peters des Grossen Verhältnisse zur Religion und den Kirchen," *HZ*, 1952, no. 2, 261–96.

53. P. Pierling, *La Sorbonne*, esp. 22–38; and Richter, *Leibniz*, esp. 11–37 for Leibniz's view of Russia as a bridge between Europe and China and a means of helping restore unity to Christendom.

The interest in enlisting Orthodox collaboration for a fresh approach to church unity was principally championed by the Jansenists and Pietists within the Catholic and Protestant communions respectively. The Pietist interest was, culturally, much more important—because it related the search for lost Christian unity to the quest for the original "natural" language that had presumably existed prior to the fall of Adam and the confusion of tongues (on which see the important forthcoming book by H. Aarsleff, *Language, Man and Knowledge in the Sixteenth and Seventeenth Century*).

Heinrich Ludolph, who published the first systematic printed grammar of the Russian language (*Grammatica Russica*, Oxford, 1696 repr. B. Unbegaun, ed., Oxford, 1959) originally went to Russia in search of new opportunities for the reunification of Christendom. Like the Swede J. Sparwenfeld (on whom see C. Jacobowsky, *J. G. Sparwenfeld: bidrag till en biografi*, Stockholm, 1932, esp. 50–79) his friend and the only other important seventeenth-century Western student of the Russian language, Ludolph turned to the study of language for largely religious reasons (see D. Chizhevsky, "Der Kreis A. H. Frankes in Halle und seine slavis-

tischen Studien," *ZSPh*, XVI, 1939, 16–68). The education of Ludolph was largely supervised by his uncle, Hiob Ludolph, the famed Oriental linguist and author of the first grammar of Abyssinian. This background probably helps explain the transmission via his friend, the Saxon doctor at the Tsar's court, Laurent Rinhuber, of the already mentioned project for an anti-Moslem alliance between Muscovy and Abyssinia. See J. Tetzner *H. W. Ludolph und Russland*, 1955, 10–31, 44–93; and, on Rinhuber, P. Pierling, *Saxe et Moscou: un Médecin diplomate*, 1893. See also materials cited in A. Florovsky, "Pervy russky pechatny bukvar' dlia inostrantsev 1690 g," *TODL*, XVII, 1961, 482–94.

54. N. Klepinin, *Sviatoi i blagoverny veliky kniaz' Aleksandr Nevsky*, Paris, 1928, 183.

55. On the ideas, intrigues, and downfalls of Tveritinov see Tikhonravov, *Sochineniia*, II, 156–304, and note 392 on supplementary pages 53–8; also Chizhevsky, *Aus zwei Welten*, 252–68.

56. See A. Brückner, *Iwan Possoschkow: Ideen und Zustände in Russland zur Zeit Peters des Grossen*, Leipzig, 1878; and V. Kafengauz, *I. T. Pososhkov: zhizn' i deiatel'nost'*, M, 1951, 2d ed., and the same author's critical edition of *Kniga o skudosti i bogatstve i drugie sochineniia*, M. 1951. K. Papmehl, "Pososhkov as a Thinker," *SEES*, 1961, Spring-Summer, 80–7, stresses the religious and conservative basis of Pososhkov's thought.

57. A new edition of Tatishchev's *Istoriia rossiiskaia*, M, 1962, 2 vols. and more to follow, is now being published in the USSR with scholarly notes. For an excellent rehabilitation of Tatishchev from previous scornful Soviet treatment and general scholarly neglect see M. Tikhomirov, "Vasily Nikitich Tatishchev," *IM*, 1940, no. 6, 43–56 and

bibliography 57–62; for more detailed discussion of Tatishchev's *History* see Peshtich, *Istoriografiia*, 222–62 and notes. See also C. Grau, *Der Wirtschaftsorganisator, Staatsmann und Wissenchaftler Vasilij N. Tatiščev (1686–1750)*, 1963. For consideration of Tatishchev in the context of his collaboration with the "learned guard" (a term used by Prokopovich) see Plekhanov, *History of Social Thought*, 83–118; and (particularly for their popularization of scientific ideas) P. Epifanov, " 'Uchenaia druzhina' i prosvetitel'-stvo XVIII veka," *VI*, 1963, no. 3, 37–53.

58. For a detailed contemporary description by a leading physicist at the Academy of Sciences see the brochure by Krafft, *Wahrhaffte und Umständliche Beschreibung und Abbildung des in Monath Januarius, 1740, in St. Petersburg aufgerichteten merkwürdigen Hauses von Eiss*, P, 1741; and the Russian version, *Podlinnoe i obstoiatel'noe opisanie ledianogo doma*, Myshkin, 1887, with a preface by K. Griaznov. See also V. Guillon, *Un Épisode peu connu de l'histoire de Russie*, Toulouse, 1873; Veselovsky, *Vliianie*, 57, note 1; and Marsden, *Palmyra*, 96 ff., including pictures opposite 98.

In the same bizarre category stands the tradition of placing dwarfs inside giant pies and having them burst forth at some prescribed time to provide "table entertainment." Peter, for instance, at a fete for his son, had two cakes brought forth containing naked dwarfs (one of each sex), who proceeded to "address each other." See "Zapiski Vebera," *RA*, 1872, no. 7–8, 1370.

59. On Golitsyn's political ideas see A. Lappo-Danilevsky, "L'Idée," 372–81; and, in addition to materials referenced in 377, note 2, D. Korsakov, *Iz zhizni russkikh deiatelei XVIII veka*, Kazan, 219–82. Tatishchev was also deeply interested in natural law theory (Lappo-Danilevsky, 377, 381–2), as was Simeon Polotsky, who approached it more from the position of a medieval schoolman and whose use of the term *zakon estestva* in 1680 is the earliest I have been able to find (Berkov, *Virshi*, 108).

60. H. Hjärne, "Ryska konstitutionsprojekt år 1730 efter svenska förebilder," *HT*, 1884, no. 4, 189–272; Lappo-Danilevsky, is less sure of Swedish derivation and gives the references for other theories in "L'Idée," 380, note 1.

61. In 1733, 237 students were studying German, 51 French, and only 18 Russian in the school. See M. Viatkin, *Ocherki istorii Leningrada*, M-L, 1955, I, 213; and, for more details of early elementary education, Konstantinov and Struminsky, *Ocherki*, 39 ff.

62. B. Unbegaun, "Le 'Crime' et le 'criminel' dans la terminologie juridique russe," *RES*, XXXVI, 1959, 56, also entire discussion 47–58. On the other terms see *REW*, II, 343; Christiani, *Eindringen*, 24–31 (esp. 28–9, note 10), 45, 52–3.

63. The use of terms like "baroque" and "rococo" is even more imprecise in the artistic history of Russia than in that of early modern Europe generally. F. Shmit (" 'Barokko' kak istoricheskaia kategoriia," in *Russkoe iskusstvo XVII veka*, L, 1929, 7–26) provides probably the best and most ranging short discussion in his review of the collection edited by A. Nekrasov, *Barokko v Rossii*, M, 1926. Also valuable for relating Russian developments to the baroque among the Western Slavs is A. Angyal, *Die slawische Barockwelt*, Leipzig, 1961.

The distinguished French student of the Baroque, V. Tapié, ends his inconclusive discussion of the Russian baroque (*La Russie*, 203, and 194–204) by speaking generally of a "Russian baroque" prior to Peter, and of "the baroque in Russia" thereafter—thus stressing (1) the impossibility of clearly differentiating different architectural styles in the second half of the seventeenth century and (2) the transition to an essentially foreign style imposed from above under Peter (called "cosmopolitan" by Angyal, 265–6). A distinction can be made, however, in the late seventeenth century between the more original "Muscovite" or "Naryshkin" baroque (see M. Il'in, "Problemy Moskovskogo barokka," *EII, 1956,* M, 1957, 324–39) and the more typically Central European "Kievan" baroque (the importance of which is often minimized by Great Russian historians). See M. Tsapenko, *Ukrainskaia arkhitektura perioda natsional'nogo pod'ema v XVII–XVIII vv,* M, 1963—covering from the 1670's to the 1770's. The term "Elizabethan rococo," (used, for instance, by Hamilton, *Art,* 177–83) is useful in suggesting an increased interest in the interior and decorative arts, but misleading if taken to suggest any sharp break with the precedent baroque or sudden passion for systematic imitation of a clearly recognized new Western style.

64. A. Pozdneev, "Knizhnye pesni-akrostikhi 1720-kh godov," *ScS,* V, 1959, 165–79.

65. B. Menshutkin, *Russia's Lomonosov,* ©1952 by Princeton Univ. Press, 174–5.

66. V. Garshin, "Attalea Princeps," in *Sochineniia,* M-L, 1960, 89–96.

67. Description of G. Kennan, *Russia Leaves the War,* Princeton, 1956, 3–4.

68. *Ibid.*

69. The parallel here is with the interpretation put forth in Max Weber, *The Protestant Ethic and the Spirit of Capitalism.* Of course, many who were or became Old Believers fled to Siberia simply to escape serfdom; and ideological motivation in colonization may have been less widespread (though perhaps more intense) in Siberia than in North America.

70. For the spread of schismatic ideas in the north see P. Vladimirov, "Ocherki iz istorii literaturnago dvizheniia na severe Rossii vo vtoroi polovine XVIII veka," *ZhMNP,* 1879, no. 10; for the building of the Solovetsk legend, K. Chistovich, "Nekotorye momenty istorii Karelii v russkikh istoricheskikh pesniakh," *TKF,* X, 1958, 68–78.

71. S. Zenkovsky, "Denisov Brothers," 49–66; also *BE,* XIX, 391–2.

In 1724, the *prikaz* of church affairs recorded 14,043 Old Believers (A. Sinaisky, *Otnoshenie russkoi tserkovnoi vlasti k raskolu staroobriadchestva,* P, 1895, 165. An excellent study by a scholarly priest even though confined to the years 1721–5). This figure is one of the few solid ones in the entire history of the Old Believer movement, but is almost certainly incomplete. The statistics compiled by the ministry of the interior in 1863 indicated that eight million, or about one sixth of the Orthodox population were Old Believers—with three million of them priestless. There were also estimated to be 110,000 *Molokane* and *Dukhobory* and the same number of *khlysty* and *skoptsy.* See A. Prugavin, *Raskol-Sektantstvo,* M, 1887, 80 (and a bibliography on the controversial statistical question, 77–81).

72. *BE,* XIV, 486–7; Ya. Abramov, "Vygovskie pionery," *OZ,* 1884, nos. 3, 4; V. Druzhinin, *Slovesnyia nauki v Vygovskoi pomorskoi pustyni,* P, 1911, 2d ed.; and V. Malyshev, "The *Confession* of Ivan Filippov, 1744," *OSP,* XI, 1964, 17–27, and works referenced therein. For new details of Old Beliver activity on the lower Pechora in Central Siberia based on recent expeditions see V. Malyshev, *Ust-tsilemskie rukopisnye sborniki XVI-XX vv,* Syktyvkar, 1960.

73. Cited in the valuable detailed study

of N. Sokolov, *Raskol v Saratovskom krae*, Saratov, 1888, 23, 22.

74. *Ibid.*, 18 and ff. for similar illustrations.

75. See A. Prugavin, "Raskol i Biurokratiia," *VE*, 1909, Oct, 650–78; Nov, 162–83. The vital division for the schismatics was not the split between "churches" (theirs and the new Orthodoxy), but the schism between their religious society and the irreligious society of the new state. For the beginning of the process by which the old merchant class was destroyed and the cities repopulated with elements more dependent on the central power see P. Smirnov's monumental *Posadskie liudi i ikh klassovaia bor'ba v pervoi polovine XVII veka*, M, 1947–8, 2v—a work which unfortunately gives no real consideration to the broader consequences and ideological implications of the changes it describes.

76. The so-called *tarabarsky iazyk* (a kind of vagabond patois) and the *ofensky iazyk* (virtually a separate language), as well as numerous codes based on straight word and letter substitutions (probably growing out of the long-established Southern Slav and Russian tradition of secret writing, *tainopis'*). See Farmakovsky, "Raskol," 638–40; *PS*, 1859, Jul, 320 ff. Little serious study has been made of these and other examples of *vorovskoi iazyk*. See *BE*, XIII, 202–3.

77. Mel'gunov, *Dvizheniia*, 157–62. These two communes survive even to the present day, and are the centers of the two major branches of contemporary Old Believers: the *Preobrazhenskoe kladbishche* of "priestless" Theodosians and the "priested" *Rogozhskoe kladbishche*. The unparalleled collection of some eight hundred old icons still to be found in the cathedral and library of the latter community gives eloquent testimony to the wealth and fidelity to early artistic models of the Old Believers. See the limited edition put out by the community, *Drevnie ikony staroobriadcheskogo kafedral'nogo Pokrovskogo sobora pri Rogozhskom kladbishche v Moskve*, M, 1956. The use of terms like "cemetery," "commune," and "house of prayer" are necessitated by the Old Believer conviction that since the schism there can be no more validly consecrated "churches" or "cathedrals."

78. The Bulavin uprising has been more neglected than the Razin and Pugachev uprisings, but was in fact the first to be deeply based in the peasantry. See the valuable analytical and bibliographical discussion by A. Zimin and A. Preobrazhensky, "Izuchenie v sovetskoi istoricheskoi nauke klassovoi bor'by perioda feodalizma v rossii," *VI*, 1957, no. 12, esp. 149 ff. See also the general interpretations of the phenomena of peasant wars offered by Sumner, *Survey*, 161–70; and by V. Mavrodin, I. Kadson, N. Sergeeva, and T. Rzhanikova, *VI*, 1956, no. 2, esp. 69–70; as well as by V. Mavrodin in *Soviet Studies in History*, 1962, fall, 43–63. The direct role of religious dissenters in the uprisings does not appear to have been great until the Pugachev rising.

79. Yu. Got'e, *Smutnoe vremia*, M, 1921, 30–1. The Cossacks concurrently developed a tradition in the late sixteenth century of supporting pretenders to the Moldavian throne (see N. Kostomarov, *Geroi smutnago vremeni*, Berlin, 1922, 62–3). For the basic study of this tradition see D. Mordovtsev, *Samozvantsy i ponizovaia vol'nitsa*, P, 1867, 2v; and S. Solov'ev, "Zametki o samozvantsakh v Rossii," *RA*, 1868, 265–81. For a romanticized, populist account see I. Pryzhov, *Dvadtsat' shest' moskovskikh lzhe-prorokov*, M, 1864.

80. For new material on this uprising see *Vosstanie Bolotnikova: Dokumenty i materialy*, M, 1959. Various interpretive studies of the movement by I. Smirnov are less perceptive

than the pre-Soviet work of Got'e, and Kostomarov.

81. G. Aleksandrov, "Pechat' antikhrista," (with illustration) *RA*, 1873, T.2, 2068–72, 02296; Sinaisky, *Otnoshenie*, 299; Mel'gunov, *Dvizheniia*, 118; Farmakovsky, "Raskol," 632–4; E. Shmurlo, *Petr veliky v otsenke sovremennikov i potomstva*, P, 1912, I, 19–26; and N. Sakharov, "Starorusskaia partiia i raskol pri imperatorom Petre I," *Strannik*, 1882, no. 1, 32–55; no. 2, 213–31; no. 3, 355–71.

82. Figures in Mel'gunov, *Dvizheniia*, 51; and K. Sivkov, "Samozvanchestvo v Rossii v poslednei treti XVIII v," *IZ*, XXXI, 1950, 89. On lesser-known nineteenth-century echoes see two articles by the famous writer V. Korolenko, "Sovremennaia samozvanshchina," *RB*, 1896, no. 5, 2d pagination, 172–93; no. 8, 2d pagination, 119–54.

83. "Khleb ne roditsia potomu, chto zhensky pol tsarstvom vladeet." N. Firsov, *Pugachevshchina: opyt sotsiologo-psikhologicheskoi kharakteristiki*, P-M, nd, 9. See also his equally valuable and succinct, *Razinovshchina kak sotsiologicheskoe i psikhologicheskoe iavlenie narodnoi zhizni*, P-M, 1914. The attempts by scholars of the late imperial period to analyze all these phenomena in psychological terms are, on the whole, far more convincing than Soviet efforts to relate these movements to economic factors (let alone economic classes). See, for instance, L. Sheinis, "Epidemicheskiia samoubiistva," *Vestnik vospitanii*, 1909, Jan, 137 ff.; and numerous articles in S. Mel'gunov's *Iz istorii religiozno-obshchestvennykh dvizhenii v Rossii XIX v*, M, 1919, esp. his "Sektanstvo i psikhiatriia," 157–202, which treats a wide spectrum of dissenting movements and deals extensively with pre-nineteenth-century developments.

84. Firsov, *Pugachevshchina*, 151–3, 53–7.

85. Palmieri, *Chiesa*, 107–8; Brian-Chaninov, *Church*, 99, note 1, 97–100.

86. M. Semevsky, "Samuil Vymorkov, prorok ucheniia ob antikhriste v 1722–1725," *OZ*, 1866, Aug, kn. 1, 449–74, kn. 2, 680–708.

87. Palmieri, *Chiesa*, 108–9, for statistics on this increase.

88. First published in 1207 folio pages in Venice in 1782, the *Philokalia* was abridged by Velichkovsky (*Dobrotoliubie v perevode* Paiisiia, M, 1793). A much fuller, and more vernacular version appeared in 1877. Velichkovsky's version was carried and drawn on by the anonymous nineteenth-century author of *The Way of a Pilgrim*, London, 1941. The longer, later version is drawn on in two useful English language anthologies by E. Kadloubovsky and G. Palmer, *Writings from the Philokalia on Prayer of the Heart*, London, 1951; *Early Fathers from the Philokalia*, London, 1954.

On Paissius' life see *Zhitie i pisaniia startsa P. Velichkovskago*, Odessa, 1887, and, for the best study of his general impact and the tradition of elders, S. Chetverikov, *Moldavsky starets Paissy Velichkovsky*, Petseri (Esthonia), 1938, 2v. (This is an abridged translation stripped of valuable references from an almost totally unavailable earlier Rumanian-language version of this work.) His ancestor, the poet Ivan Velichkovsky, is discussed in D. Chizhevsky, *Aus zwei Welten*, 172–8.

89. See N. Gorodetzky, *Saint Tikhon Zadonsky: Inspirer of Dostoevsky*, London, 1951.

90. Fedotov, *Treasury*, 259; selections from Tikhon and Seraphim. For an excellent discussion of Seraphim's impact, Behr-Sigel, *Prière*, 104–20.

91. Fedotov, *Treasury*, 257.

92. Gorodetzky, *Tikhon*, 180–8. See also the 1912 thesis of the Moscow Theological Academy by V. Troit-

sky, "Vliianie Optynoi pustyni na russkuiu intelligentsiiu i literaturu," *BV*, 1913, no. 4, appendix.

93. See E. Temnikovsky's critical review of Golubinsky's *Istoriia kanonizatsii sviatykh v russkoi tserkvi*, M, 1903, in *VDI*, LXXXVIII, 1904, second series of pages, 1–77, esp. 1–3, 31–40.

94. Saying of Tikhon, placed at the be-

ginning of his "Sokrovishche dukhovnoe ot mira sobrannoe" in *Sochineniia preosviashchennago Tikhona Episkopa Voronezhskago i Eletskago*, M, 1837, X, 1.

95. Brian-Chaninov, 103, note 1.

96. Letter of the executive committee of the "People's Will" to Alexander III on Mar 10, 1881, in *Literatura narodnoi voli*, 1905, 903–8.

IV. THE ARISTOCRATIC CENTURY

1. Tatishchev's "Honorable Mirror of Youth," cited from the 4th ed. in Alferov *et al.*, *Literatura*, 6.

   Recent studies of the eighteenth-century aristocracy (all with copious references) include M. Raeff, "L'État, le gouvernement et la tradition politique en Russie impériale avant 1861," *RHMC*, 1962, Oct–Dec, 295–307; and "Home, School and Service in the Life of the 18th century Russian Nobleman," *SEER*, 1962, Jun, 295–307; K. Ruffmann, "Russischer

Adel als Sondertypus der europäischen Adelswelt," *JGO*, 1961, Sep; and J. Blum, *Lord*, 345 ff., and materials referenced in the bibliography.

A valuable older study is V. Zommer, "Krepostnoe pravo i dvorianskaia kul'tura v Rossii XVIII veka," in *Itogi XVIII veka v Rossii*, M, 1910, 257–412. For the derivation of the terms *shliakhetstvo* and *dvorianstvo* see A. Liutsk, "Russky absoliutizm XVIII veka," in *Itogi*, 228; and Blum, 347.

1. THE TROUBLED ENLIGHTENMENT

1. See P. Berkov, ed., *Problemy russkogo prosveshcheniia v literature XVIII veka*, M-L, 1961, 10–11.

   Soviet scholars of the Enlightenment era are placed in a difficult position, because Lenin said little about the eighteenth century to serve as a guideline for later interpretation—indeed his only reference to "enlighteners" was to the radicals of the 1860's. In apparent deference to this fact, some Soviet scholars now distinguish enlightenment as a process (*prosvetitel'stvo*) from enlightenment as a non-revolutionary but progressive ideology (*prosveshchenie*), and claim that the former extends from the mid-seventeenth to the mid-eighteenth century, and the latter primarily from the 1760's through the 1780's in Russia. See Berkov's introduction to *ibid.*, 5–27.

2. The significance of this figure, as cited by Vucinich, *Science*, 51, is somewhat lost by coupling it with Shchapov's highly negative appraisal of the quality of Ukrainian education. For a more positive discussion and references see F. Ya. Sholom, "Prosvetitel'skie idei v ukrainskoi literature serediny XVIII veka," in Berkov, ed., *Problemy*, 45–62, esp. 46–7.

3. E. Winter, *Halle als Ausgangspunkt der deutschen Russlandkunde im 18 Jahrhundert*, 1953; W. Stieda, *Die Anfänge der Kaiserlichen Akademie der Wissenschaften in St. Petersburg*, *JKGS*, 1926, Bd. II, Heft 2.

   P. Pekarsky's basic study (*Nauka i literatura v Rossii pri Petre Velikom*, P. 1862, 2v) tended to minimize the immediate effects of Peter's reforms on Russian thought, while recognizing their long-term implications. Soviet scholars now tend to emphasize their importance and, by implication, downgrade those of Catherine. See, in addition to D. Blagoy, *Istoriia*, V. Desnitsky, "Reforma Petra I i russkaia literatura XVIII v," in his *Izbrannye stat'i po russkoi literature XVIII-XIX vv*, M-L, 1958, 5–37; and A. Pozdneev, "Prosvetitel'stvo i knizhnaia poeziia," in Berkov, ed., *Problemy*, esp. 107, 109.

4. Figures cited by V. Zommer in *Itogi*, 389.

5. The increase from 328 to 2,315 computed by V. Sipovsky and cited in M. Strange, "Rousseau et ses contemporaines Russes," *AHRF*, 1962, Oct-Dec, 524.

6. Both were monthlies: *Uedinenny poshekhonets* (later *Ezhemesiachnoe sochinenie*), Yaroslavl, 1786–7; and *Irtysh, prevrashchaiushchiisia v Ippokrenu*, Tobol'sk, 1789–91—a somewhat more radical journal. See *Ocherki (7)*, 531–2; on the theater, see M. Liubomudrov, *Tvorchesky put' yaroslavskogo dramaticheskogo teatra imeni F. G. Volkova*, M, 1964.

7. G. Vinsky. On his defense of Voltaire see Veselovsky, *Vliianie*, 63, note 1; and "Zapiski G. S. Vinskago," *RA*, 1877, kn. 1, 76–123, 180–97, esp. 87, 102–4.

8. Vucinich, *Science*, 145–54; P. Pekarsky, "Ekaterina II i Eiler," *ZIAN*, VI, 1865, 59–92; and a number of the articles on Russo-German cultural contacts in E. Winter, ed., *Die deutsch-russische Begegnung und Leonhard Euler*, 1958, esp. 13 ff. on Euler, and 158–63 on his son.

9. To appreciate the full range of his activities, the standard biography by the chemist B. Menshutkin, *Lomonosov*, should be supplemented by P. Berkov, *Lomonosov i literaturnaia polemika ego vremeni*, M-L, 1936, and "Lomonosov ob ora-

torskom iskusstve," in *Akademiku Viktoru Vladimirovichu Vinogradovu, k ego shestidesiatiletiiu*, M, 1956, 71–81; L. Maistrov, "Lomonosov, Father of Russian Mathematics," *SR*, 1962, Mar, 3–18; M. Radovsky, *M. V. Lomonosov i Peterburgskaia akademiia nauk*, L, 1961; and (for his exchange of ideas with Schlözer on history) E. Winter, *August Ludwig v. Schlözer und Russland*, 1961, esp. 45–76.

10. Haumant, *La Culture*, 108–9, 155; F. Kogan-Bernshtein, "Vliianie idei Montesk'e v Rossii v XVIII veke," *VI*, 1955, no. 5, 101, note 13; K. Shafranovsky, " 'Razgovory o mnozhestve mirov' Fontenellia v Rossii," *VAN*, 1945, no. 5–6, 223–5. See also A. Lortholary, *Le Mirage russe en France au XVIII° siècle*, 1951, 18–25; and (in addition to the copious materials in Lortholary's notes) the official and ecclesiastical contacts discussed in Pierling, *La Sorbonne*.

Kantemir, who translated Fontenelle's *Discourse*, (see M. Ehrhard, *Un Ambassadeur de Russie à la cour de Louis XV, le prince Cantemir à Paris*, 1938) also helped introduce Newton's ideas into Russia during the early years of the Academy of Sciences (see M. Radovsky, *Antiokh Kantemir i Peterburgskaia Akademiia nauk*, M-L, 1959; and "Niuton i Rossiia," *VIMK*, 1957, no. 6, 96–106, esp. 104. For a full bibliography on the extraordinary activities of Kantemir see P. Berkov, ed., *Problemy russkogo prosveshcheniia v literature XVIII veka*, M-L, 1961, 190–270. On Tred'iakovsky, R. Burgi, *A History of the Russian Hexameter*, Hamden, Conn., 1954, esp. 40–60; also M. Widnäs, "Fremdsprachliches bei Wassilij Tredjakowskij" *Neuphilologische Mitteilungen* (Helsinki), LXI, 1960, 97–129.

11. Likhacheva, *Materialy*, 100–2; also H. Grasshoff. "Kantemir und Féne-

lon," *ZfS*, 1958, Bd III, Heft 2–4, 369–83; and A. Rambaud, "Catherine II et ses correspondants français," *RDM*, 1877, 15 Jan, 278–309; 15 Feb, 570–604.

12. Veselovsky, *Vliianie*, 83–5; L. Réau, "Les Relations artistiques entre la France et la Russie," in *Mélanges Boyer*, 118–20; *REW*, III, 218.

13. For the *skazka* of Tsarevich Khlor (which was only a variant of a popular stage piece of the day) see *Sochineniia imperatritsy Ekateriny II*, P, 1893, III, 94–103, translated in Wiener, *Anthology*, I, 276–87. For the most elaborate stage version see *RFe*, XXIV, 1788, 195–232.

On Catherine's cultural activities see L. Réau, *Catherine la Grande Insptratrice d'Art et Mécène*, 1930; and articles by L. Leger in his *La Russie intellectuelle*, 76–105; R. Vipper in *MB*, 1896, no. 12; V. Sipovsky in *ZhMNP*, 1905, no. 5; and Sukhomlinov in *ZhMNP*, 1865, no. 10. More generally on Catherine see G. Gooch, *Catherine the Great and Other Studies*, London, 1959; V. Bil'basov, *Istoriia Ekateriny Vtoroi*, Berlin, nd, covering only to 1764 (also in German, Berlin, 1891, 2v); and the serviceable introduction by G. Thomson, *Catherine and the Expansion of Russia*, London, 1947. The most complete edition of her works is the twelve-volume edition of A Pypin and Ya. Barskov, 1901–8. The best biography (none is entirely satisfactory) is probably still A. Brückner, *Katherine die Zweite*, 1893. Soviet work on Catherine's period, which has been meager and disappointing, is summarized in L. Yaresh, "The Age of Catherine II," *RSPR*, LXXVI, 1955, 30–42 and notes, 57–9.

14. W. Reddaway, *Documents of Catherine the Great*, Cambridge, 1931, includes a full English version of the final draft, together with much of Catherine's correspondence with Voltaire in French.

For analysis of the drafts of the *Nakaz* and their connection with court intrigue see. Georg Sacke, "Die Gesetzgebende Kommission Katherinas II," *JGO*, 1940, Beiheft 2; also his article on the commission in *AK*, XXI, 1931, no. 2; on Catherine's succession to the throne in *AK*, XXIII, 1932, no. 2; and on the aristocracy and bourgeoisie under Catherine in *RBPh*, XVIII, 1938. The *Nakaz* acquired a formal title only in the printed version of the final draft: "Instruction *(Nakaz)* . . . given to the commission for composing a new law code." The best edition is that of N. Chechulin, P, 1907. For analysis see F. Taranovsky, *Politicheskaia Doktrina v nakaze Imperatritsy Ekateriny II*, Kiev, 1903; G. Fel'dshtein, *Ugolovnopravovye idei nakaza Ekaterinoi II i ikh istochniki*, Yaroslavl, 1909; and Ditiatin, "Verkhovnaia Vlast' v Rossii XVIII v," *Stat'i*, 591–631.

15. The figures on the composition of the commission cited in *Ocherki* (7), 276–80, largely by extrapolation from A. Florovsky, are refined by M. Beliavsky, "Predstavitel'stvo krest'ian v ulozhennoi komissii 1767–1768 gg," *Sbornik . . . Tikhomirovu*, 322–9. His conclusion (329) that only 12 to 15 per cent of the peasantry had any delegated representatives still makes it appear a remarkably representative body for its time. Beliavsky's forthcoming work *Razvitie anti-feodal'noi ideologii nakanune krest'ianskoi voiny* (scheduled to appear M, 1965) promises to give a panoramic view of the opposition to Catherine in the sixties and early seventies.

16. See Vucinich, *Science*, 187; Normano, *Spirit*, 14–5.

17. Reddaway, *Documents*, xxiii-xxiv, 255, 217-9, 220.

18. Carlo Gastone della Torre di Rezzonico, *Ragionamento sulla filosofia del secolo XVIII*, 1778.

19. Chechulin, *Nakaz*, CXXXII-III. T. Cizova, "Beccaria in Russia," *SEER*, 1962, Jun, 384-408; Veselovsky, *Vliianie*, 76 notes.

20. Letter of Aug 3, 1756, in *Correspondance de Catherine Alexeievna, grand-duchesse de Russie et de Sir Charles H. Williams, ambassadeur d'Angleterre 1756 et 1757*, M, 1909, 3.

21. Figure from Casanova cited in Haumant, *La Culture*, 110. On the short-lived journal, *Le Caméléon Littéraire* see M. N. Popova, "Teodor Genri Chudi i osnovanny im v 1755 g. zhurnal," *IAN(G)*, 1929, no. 1, 17-47.

22. Veselovsky, *Vliianie*, 71, note 1, and 58 ff.; D. Yazykov, "Vol'ter v russkoi literature," in the Festschrift for Nicholas Storozhenko, *Pod znamenem nauki*, M, 1902, 696-714; S. Artamanov, *Vol'ter, kritiko-biografichesky ocherk*, M, 1954, 127-59; "Rossiia i Frantsiia," *LN*, XXIX-XXX, 1937, 7-200; and M. Strange, *La Révolution française et la société russe*, M, 1960, 45-9 (with further references) and, for the later influence of Voltaire, A. Rammelmeyer, "Dostojevskij und Voltaire," *ZSPh*, XXVI, 2, 1958, 252-78 and notes. On the "Voltaire chair" see *SSRIa*, II, 640.

23. From letters in *SRIO*, XLIV, 1885, 3-5.

24. Cited in Gooch, *Catherine*, 61, 69.

25. This dedication, though actually added by the publisher (the work being printed only after Helvétius' death in 1771), appears to have been fully in accord with Helvétius' wishes (see preface, xv to *Oeuvres complètes de M. Helvétius*, Liège, 1774, III; also M. Tourneux, *Diderot et Catherine*

II, 1899, 67). Helvétius, during much of his long ideological exile from France was in touch with Dmitry Golitsyn, Catherine's ambassador to the Hague and principal intermediary with the encyclopedists. Golitsyn tried to get Catherine to publish the work in Russia. For this and the later impact of Helvétius see A. Rachinsky, "Russkie tseniteli Gel'vetsiia v XVIII veke," *RV*, 1876, May 285-302.

Helvétius' concept of Asiatic despotism is not discussed in the valuable article on the concept of inherent Eastern despotism by F. Venturi, "Oriental Despotism," *JHI*, 1963, Jan-Mar, 133-42, nor in the doctoral dissertation at Uppsala on the subject by J. Hultin, *De fundamentis despotismi asiatici*, 1773.

26. See the special emphasis put on the impact of Montesquieu's work by Daniel Mornet at the beginning of his section "La Guerre ouverte" in *Les Origines intellectuelles de la révolution française (1715-1787)*, 1954, 71-3. For his influence in Russia see A. Pypin, "Ekaterina II i Montesk'e," *VE*, 1903, May, 272-300; Kogan-Bernshtein, "Vliianie," 99-110.

27. Field Marshal B. von Münnich, cited by V. Zommer in *Itogi*, 391.

28. Letter of 1765 to d'Alembert in *SRIO*, X, 1872, 31. See also Taranovsky, *Doktrina*, 40; Tourneux, *Diderot*, 139-40.

29. Chechulin (intr. to *Nakaz*, CXXIX-CXXX), counted 294 out of 526. There was a total of 655 articles in the *Nakaz*, including the two supplements of 1768 printed in Reddaway.

30. Lortholary, *Mirage*, 88-99, 198-242.

31. See Tourneux, *Diderot*, 63; Lortholary, *Mirage*, 179-86.

32. N. Kulakko-Koretsky, *Aperçu historique des travaux de la société impériale libre économique 1765-*

1897, P, 1897 5–6; Veselovsky, *Vliianie*, 68–9. See also M. Confino, "Les Enquêtes économiques de la 'société libre d'économie de Saint-Petersbourg' 1765–1820," *RH*, 1962, Jan–Mar, 155–80; and V. Semevsky's discussion of the replies in the first part of his *Krest'iansky vopros v Rossii v XVIII i pervoi polovine XIX veka*, P. 1888. For the remarkably early attention to Adam Smith see M. Alekseev, "Adam Smith and His Russian Admirers in the Eighteenth Century," in W. Scott, *Adam Smith as Student and Professor*, Glasgow, 1937.

33. See the excellent treatment of the fate of encyclopedias in Russia in *BSE (I)*, LXIV, esp. 487–90; also the more detailed discussion of nineteenth- and twentieth-century encyclopedias by I. Kaufman, *Russkie entsiklopedii*, M, 1960.

34. C. de Larivière, *Catherine II et la révolution française*, 1895, 24, 187, n. 1.

35. J. Herder, "Journal meiner Reise im Jahre 1769," in *Sämtliche Werke* (ed. B. Suphan), 1878, IV, 402.

The importance of Herder's formative years in Riga and the influence of his ideas inside Russia have been insufficiently appreciated in both East and West despite considerable available material. See L. Keller, *Johann Gottfried Herder und die Kultgesellschaften des Humanismus*, 1904, 1–30; F. McEachran, *The Life and Philosophy of Johann Gottfried Herder*, Oxford, 1939, 27–9; A. Pypin, "Gerder," *VE*, 1890, no. 3, 277–321; 1891, no. 4, 625–72; A. Gulyga, *Gerder*, M, 1963, 186–92; A. Wegener, *Herder und das lettische Volkslied*, Langensalza, 1928; K. Bittner, "Herders Geschichtsphilosophie und die Slawen," *VSP*, 1929, Reihe 1, Heft 6, (esp. 104–5 for a valuable list of largely forgotten eighteenth-century German books on Russia), and "J. G. Herder und V. A. Zhukovsky," *ZSPh*, 1959, no. 1, 1–44.

36. Lortholary, *Mirage*, 174–9 on Bernardin.

37. H. Halm, "Österreich und Neurussland," *JGO*, 1941, Heft 1, 275–87.

38. "Nachal'noe upravlenie Olega, podrazhanie Shakespiru bez sokhraneniia featral'nykh obyknovennykh pravil" of 1786 in *Sochineniia Imperatritsy Ekateriny II*, P, 1893, II, 109–39.

Oleg's last line delivered to the Byzantine Emperor is: "Pri otshestvii moem, Ya shchit Igorev na pamiat' ostavliaiu zdes'. Pust' pozdneishie potomki uzriat ego tut." 139. For a description of the play, which celebrated victory over the Turks, see C. Masson, *Mémoires secrets sur la Russie*, 1804, I, 94–6. The full musical score (written by Giuseppe Sarti and several collaborators) is available in the New York Public Library, P, 1791.

For the general growth of national consciousness under Catherine, see H. Rogger, *National Consciousness in Eighteenth-Century Russia*, Cambridge, Mass., 1960; also A. Lipski, "Boltin's Defense of Truth and Fatherland," *CSS*, II, 1963, 39–52.

39. On Bentham's early visits to Russia see A. Pypin, *Ocherki literatury i obshchestvennosti pri Aleksandre I*, P, 1917, 6–22. For later contacts see 23–109; also W. Kirchner, "Samuel Bentham and Siberia," *SEER*, 1958, Jun.

40. On the silhouette as cultural symbol see E. Friedell, *A Cultural History of the Modern Age*, NY, 1930, II, 283–4; on Catherine's theatrical tastes, see R. A. Mooser, *Opéras, intermezzos, ballets, cantates, oratorios joués en Russie durant le XVIIIᵉ siècle*, Geneva-Monaco, 1955, esp. I, 111–12; also his

L'Opéra-comique français en Russie au XVIIIe siècle, Geneva-Monaco, 1954, rev. and exp. ed; and Kliuchevsky, *Ocherki*, 319.

The legend of the Potemkin villages is one of a number of apocryphal tales about Potemkin's misdoings by the Saxon diplomat Helbig. The phrase *Potemkinsche Dörfer* has subsequently enjoyed considerable vernacular usage in German. See G. Soloveytchik, *Potemkin*, London, 1948, 181–2. There was, however, a deeper truth behind the legend, symbolized by the so-called continuous façade *(sploshnoy fasad)*. See *Arkhitektura SSSR*, 354, which was prescribed for the new cities, giving them an unreal impression of imperial elegance.

41. F. Lacroix, *Les Mystères de la Russie*, 1845, 201, note. (He also counts additional feast days for the family.) See also W. Bishop, "Thomas Dimsdale, MD, FRS, and the Inoculation of Catherine the Great," *AMH*, 1932, Jul, 331–8.

42. C. Dany, *Les Idées politiques et l'esprit public en Pologne à la fin du XVIIIe siècle. La constitution du 3 Mai 1791*, 1901; U. Lehtonen, *Die polnischen Provinzen Russlands unter Katharina II*, Sortavala (Finland), 1906; and a valuable new collection of articles on the Polish Enlightenment edited by P. Francastel, *Utopie et institutions au XVIIIe siècle*, 's Gravenhage, 1963.

43. Cited in Hans Blumenfeld, "Russian City Planning of the 18th and early 19th Centuries," *JAH*, 1944, Jan, 26. In addition to this valuable article (with illustrations of the plans opposite p. 22), see V. Shkvarikov, *Ocherk*, esp. 134–202, for the principles of central city planning in the late eighteenth century (also 21–62 for a good discussion of pre-eighteenth-century city planning; and, for more detail,

L. Tverskoy, *Russkoe gradostroitel'stvo do kontsa XVII veka; planirovka; zastroika russkikh gorodov*, L, 1953).

See also the earlier work of Shkvarikov, *Planirovka*, which seeks to relate Soviet city planning of the thirties (in which he was an active leader) to older Russian traditions of planned city construction; and I. Ditiatin, *Ustroistvo i upravlenie gorodov Rossii*, P, 1875, I, covering the eighteenth century. For provincial participation in the new architectural activities see I. Grabar, "U istokov klassitsizma," *EII*, 1956; and for other illustrations and plans see *Arkhitektura SSSR*, 82–9, 418–23, 428, 438.

44. Raeff, "L'État," 296. Veselovsky, *Vliianie*, 58; G. von Rauch, *Die Universität Dorpat und das Eindringen der frühen Aufklärung in Livland, 1690–1710*, Essen, 1943; Likhacheva, *Materialy*, 100–2. Herder, *Sämtliche Werke*, 1878, IV, 343–461; G. Teplov, *Znaniia, voobshche do filosofii kasaiushchiiasia*, P, 1751; *RBS*, XX, esp. 475–6.

45. This surprising fact is stressed in A. Timiriazev, *Ocherki po istorii fiziki v Rossii*, M, 1949, 81, 85–6. For the influence of Locke see Veselovsky, *Vliianie*, 77; P. Maikov, *Ivan Ivanovich Betskoy*, P, 1904, prilozhenie, 49; Likhacheva, *Materialy*, 97; and Betskoy, *Système*, I, 4; II, 171, 305–8.

On Catherine's educational projects, the useful section in W. Johnson, *Heritage*, should be supplemented by N. Hans, "Dumaresque, Brown and Some Early Educational Projects of Catherine II," *SEER*, 1961, Dec, 229–35; and S. Rozhdestvensky, "Proekty uchebnykh reform pri Ekaterine," *ZhMNP*, 1907, Dec; 1908, Feb, Mar.

46. On Pnin and Repnin, see V. Orlov, *Russkie prosvetiteli 1790–1800-kh godov*, M, 1953, 2d ed., 95 ff.;

and (for analysis of Pnin's *Opyt o prosveshchenii otnositel'no k Rossii*), 158 ff.

Betskoy has been strangely neglected by historians despite an admirable, prize-winning monograph on his life and works by Maikov, which includes the text of many of his proposals. See also I. I. *Betskoy drug chelovechestva*, P, 1904; and discussion and references in *RBS*, III, 5–12; *BE*, VI, 649–50, XIII, 276–7.

Misinformation on him (and on much else) abound in the memoir literature of the period, where he is generally referred to by the French version of his name, Betzky. (Even Bil'basov assigns him incorrect dates.) Relatively valuable is Chevalier de Corberon, *Un Diplomate français à la cour de Catherine II*, Paris, 1901, 2v. See also Strange, "Rousseau," 518–19; Tourneux, *Diderot*, 2–5.

Most of his proposals are printed in his *Sobranie uchrezhdenii i predpisanii kasatel'no vospitaniia v Rossii oboego pola blagorodnago i meshchanskago iunoshestva*, P, 1789–91, three parts; also in his *Système complet d'éducation publique, physique et morale*, Neuchâtel, 1777, 2v.

47. Strange, "Rousseau," should be supplemented by D. Kobeko, "Ekaterina II i Zh. Zh. Russo," IV, 1883, Jun, 603–17; and Maikov, *Betskoy*, 47–60. Rousseau was, of course, particularly admired by the Poles, and also by Ukrainian reformers such as Ya. P. Kozel'sky (on whom see Yu. Kogan, *Prosvetitel' XVIII veka Ya. P. Kozel'sky*, M, 1958). Kozel'sky's *Filosoficheskiia predlozheniia* (P, 1768) has been called "the first system of philosophy to come from the pen of a Russian author" (*BE*, XXX, 596). See particularly Kozel'sky's Rousseauian *Razsuzhdenie dvukh indiitsev, Kalana i Ibragima, ochelovecheskom poznanii*, P, 1788.

For the influence on Russian literature of Rousseau's ideal of the anti-social noble savage (beginning with P. Bogdanovich's *Diky chelovek*, P, 1781, and continuing through Radishchev to the anonymous *Dikaia evropeanka*, P, 1804), see the study by Yu. Lotman in Berkov, ed., *Problemy*, 89–97.

48. Maikov, *Betskoy*, prilozhenie, 7; also 157; and 101 ff. for an excellent history of the institution of the foundling home in the eighteenth century.

49. *Sochineniia Derzhavina*, P, 1895, I, 192–3; see also 234, note 56.

50. Cited by Kobeko, "Ekaterina," 612.

51. Raeff, "L'Etat"; "Home, School and Service"; also, on the failure to develop a civic spirit, Blok, *Politicheskaia literatura*, 90–1, and more generally, 59–79.

52. Maikov, *Betskoy*, 343–55. See also E. Falconet, *Correspondance de Falconet avec Catherine II, 1767–1778*, with intr. by L. Réau, 1921; and D. Arkin, *Medny vsadnik, Pamiatnik Petru I v Leningrade*, L, 1958.

53. Betskoy, *General'noe uchrezhdenie o vospitanii oboego pola iunoshestva*, P, 1766, 3–10. See also A. Lappo-Danilevsky, *Ivan Ivanovich Betskoy i ego sistema vospitaniia*, P, 1904. Shchapov (*Sochineniia*, II, 537) suggests that Betskoy's concept of a third class of educated people may have originated with the Zotov family at the time of Peter the Great.

54. Haumant, *La Culture*, 128; and 119–29.

55. Cited in M. Popova, "Chudi," 26.

56. "Skol'kob liudi ni khitrili,/ skol'-kob razum ni ostrili,/ Pravda liudiam govorit':/ Vas liubov perekhitrit'." From *Opekun professor ili liubov' khitree krasnorechiia*, in *RFe*, 1788, no. 24, 61–2; Kliuchevsky, *Ocherki*, 319; "Kak khotite, tak zhiviti/ my ne budem vam meshat'," from *Novoe Se-*

meistvo, in *RFe*, 1788, no. 24, 279.
57. *Russkie dramaturgi*, II, 81; for Sumarokov's definition of comedy, *BE*, LXIII, 58.
58. Varneke, *History*, 63.
59. Maikov, *Betskoy*, 354; D. Stremooukhoff, "Autour du 'Nedorosl' de Fonvisin," *RES*, XXXVIII, 1961, 185; and text of La Harpe's memoir of 1784 in *Le Gouverneur d'un Prince*, Lausanne, 1902, 253; see also 134–5.

For the general influence of Stoicism on the European Enlightenment see P. Hazard, *La pensée européenne au XVIIIème siècle de Montesquieu à Lessing*, 1946, II, 103–5; and the more recent study by M. Rombout, *La Conception stoïcienne du bonheur chez Montesquieu et chez quelques-uns de ses contemporains*, 1958.

60. Sumarokov, *Izbrannye proizvedeniia*, L, 1957, 104.
61. A. Mel'gunov, *Seneki khristianstvuiushchago nravstennyia lekarstva*, M, 1783, dedicated to Metropolitan Platon of Moscow and Kaluga, an admirer of the Stoics.
62. V. Tukalevsky, "Iz istorii filosofskikh techenii Russkogo obshchestva XVIII v," *ZhMNP*, 1911, May, 4–5; partial text in Alferov, etc., *Literatura*, 7, 11.
63. V. Hehn, *De moribus Ruthenorum*, Stuttgart, 1892, 71.
64. *Sochineniia D. I. Fonvizina*, P, 1893, 113. Cited without attribution in D. Blagoy, *Istoriia russkoi literatury XVIII veka*, M, 1945, 241; see also Blagoy, 236–7, and discussion and references 214–43 on Fonvizin, and the older study by Tikhonravov, *Sochineniia*, III, 90–129.

On the Viennese production of 1787 see G. Wytrzens, "Eine Ünbekannte Wiener Fonvizin Ubersetzung aus dem Jahre 1787," *WSJ*, 1959, VII, 118–28.

On general European ignorance of Russian literature even in the late eighteenth century see P. Berkov, "Izuchenie russkoi literatury inostrantsami v XVIII veke," *IaL*, V, 1930; and Lortholary, *Mirage*, 269–74.

For an English translation see Noyes, *Masterpieces*, 27–28. The title used therein, *The Young Hopeful*, and the more frequently used title, *The Minor*, are (like the title adopted here) all inadequate for the Russian *Nedorosl'*, which has a more distinctively negative meaning of "not full grown" and unable to perform governmental (and by implication any useful) service.

65. Skovoroda, *Sochineniia*, ed. Bonch-Bruevich, P, 1912, 406. For the best discussion of Skovoroda's ideas in English see V. Zenkovsky, *History*, I, 53–69. For widely divergent interpretations see D. Chizhevsky, *Filosofija H.S. Skovorody*, Warsaw, 1934; B. Skitsky, *Sotsial'naia filosofiia G. Skovorody*, Vladikavkaz, 1930; V. Ern, *Grigory Savvich Skovoroda*, M, 1912; and T. Bilych, *Svitogliad G. S. Skovorody*, Kiev, 1957. For supplementary material see also *Istoriia ukrainskoi literatury*, Kiev, 1955, I, 113–24; N. Maslov, "Perevody G. S. Skovorody," *NZK*, III, 1929, 29–34; and T. Ionescu-Nisçov, "Grigory Skovoroda i filosofskie raboty Aleksandra Khidzheu," *RoS*, II, 1958, 149–62.

In addition to the one-volume Bonch-Bruevich edition of his works see also the original one-volume *Sochineniia*, ed. Bagalei, Kharkov, 1894; and the two-volume edition published by the Ukrainian Academy of Sciences under the editorship of Bilecki, *et al.*, in Kiev, 1961. See also his *Kharkivs'ki baiki*, ed. Tichini, Kiev, 1946, and the list and basic discussion of his works in *BE*, LIX, 217–19; also Edie, *Philosophy* I, 11–62.

66. Zenkovsky, *History*, I, 56.
67. *Istoriia ukrainskoi literatury*, I, 120.
68. T. Kudrinsky, "Filosof bez sistemy," *KS*, IX, 1898, 43. Mel'gunov, *Dvizheniia*, 190–1.
69. Ern, *Skovoroda*, 31.
70. Cited in *ibid.*, 136.
71. "Skazhi mne imia ty, skazhi svoe sama;/ Ved' vsiaka bez tebe durna u nas duma./ U grekov zvalas' ia sofiia v drevny vek,/ A mudrost'iu zovet vsiak russky chelovek./ No rimlianin mene mineivolu nazval,/ A khristianin dobr khristom mne imia dal." Skovoroda, *Sochineniia* (ed. Bagalei), 293.
72. Radishchev, *Puteshchestvie*, M, 1944, 9–10, 59–60. There is an English translation by L. Wiener, edited by R. Thaler, Harvard, 1958; and a biography and bibliography on Radishchev by D. Lang, *The First Russian Radical*, London, 1959. Lang includes additional references and a critical discussion of Soviet scholarship on Radishchev in his "Radishchev and Catherine II," in Curtiss, ed., *Essays*, 20–33. See also A. McConnell, *A Russian philosopher: Alexander Radishchev, 1749–1802*, The Hague, 1964.
73. "Ia tot zhe chto i byl/ i budet ves moi vek/ Ne skot, ne derevo, ne rab,/ no chelovek." Cited in V. Yakushkin, "K biografii A. N. Radishcheva," *RS*, 1882, Sep, 519.
74. Lang, *Radical*, 217–23. This idea was apparently derived from Herder's *Ideen zur Geschichte der Menschheit*. See K. Bittner, "I. G. Herder und A. N. Radishchev," *ZSPh*, XXV, 1956, 8–53; also V. Sipovsky, "Iz istorii russkoi mysli XVIII–XIX vv. Russkoe Vol'terianstvo," *GM*, 1914, Jan, 108.
75. According to a letter of Bonch-Bruevich (who had been Lenin's personal secretary) to A. M. Nizhenets, written in 1955 shortly before Bonch-Bruevich's death, discussed in Nizhenets, "V. D.

Bonch-Bruevich pro G. S. Skovorodu," *RL*, 1958, no. 3; and (more briefly) by F. Sholom in Berkov, ed., *Problemy*, 61–2.
76. A. Afanas'ev, "Nikolai Ivanovich Novikov," *BZ*, 1858, no. 6, 166–7. See also L. Fridberg, "Knigoizdatel'skaia deiatel'nost' N. I. Novikova v Moskve," *VI*, 1948, Aug, 23–40.
    There is no adequate account of Novikov's extraordinary career in a Western language, and no fully satisfactory account in Russian. The valuable standard work by V. Bogoliubov (*N. I. Novikov i ego vremia*, M, 1916) has neither full references nor a bibliography, for which one should consult G. Vernadsky, *Nikolai Ivanovich Novikov*, P, 1918, 143–63. The philosophic and occult interests of Novikov are minimized and at times even suppressed in Soviet treatments, such as that of G. Makogonenko, *Nikolai Novikov i russkoe prosveshchenie XVIII veka*, M-L, 1951. More balanced is the recent anthology of articles and documents edited by I. Malyshev, *N. I. Novikov i ego sovremenniki*, M, 1961, which chides the efforts to exclude this aspect of Novikov's work by Makogonenko and Berkov (502). For Novikov's later years and religio-philosophic interests, all of the above should be supplemented by M. Longinov, *Novikov i Moskovskie Martinisty*, M, 1867; and his neglected later correspondence in B. Modzalevsky, *K biografii Novikova*, P, 1913. Fresh archival materials (particularly from the Shliakhetsky Korpus) have been used by M. Strange to show the considerable student interest that developed in the writings of Radishchev and Novikov. See his *Formirovanie raznochinnoi intelligentsii XVIIIogo veka* (forthcoming, M, 1965).
77. See A. Lipski, "Boltin's Defense," 39–52. The first collection of Rus-

sian songs, published by G. Teplov in 1759, may have been preceded by others. See M. Azadovsky, *Istoriia*, 149. However, real interest in Russian folk music began only with Chulkov's publications of fable and song: *Kratky mifologichesky leksikon* (1767); *Peresmeshnik ili slavianskiia skazki* (1766–8), four parts; *Russkie skazki* (1780–3), published in ten parts by Novikov on the university press; and *Sobranie raznykh pesen'*, some of which was published in the early or mid-seventies, but which has survived only in the expanded second edition published in collaboration with Novikov in 1790–1 and known as the "Novikov songbook." See *BE*, LXXVII, 32–3. P. Struve considered the publication of this latter work the "most influential and important development of the eighteenth century," in the formation of modern Russian literature (*Nabliudeniia*, 9).

78. Sumarokov, preface to the tragedy "Dmitry Samozvanets," text in Alferov, *Literatura*, 138. On Falconet's travels, see Réau, "Relations," in *Mélanges Boyer*, 127–8.

79. For this estimate and other details on the wealth and indolence of Moscow see Zommer, in *Itogi*, 391–5. See also Putnam, *Seven Britons*, 334–6; M. Anderson, "Some British Influences on Russian Internal Life and Society in the 18th Century," *SEER*, 1960, Dec, esp. 154 ff.; and P. Berkov, "English Plays in St. Petersburg in the 1760's and 1770's," *OSP*, VIII, 1958.

Many aristocrats of the late eighteenth century enjoyed a totally apolitical life of leisure modeled to a large extent on that of the English landed aristocracy. There was a sudden interest in gardening, yachting, hunting, and dancing, and a rash of "English clubs" in major cities. See *BE*, XXIX, 426–8; also A. Afanas'ev, "Cherty russ-

kikh nravov XVIII stoletiia," *RV*, 1857, Sep, 248–82.

80. "Chto novogo pokazhet mne Moskva?/ Segodnia bal' i zavtra budet dva." A. Griboedov, "Goria ot uma," in *Sochineniia*, M, 1953 (ed. Orlov), 19. For an excellent description of Moscow in Griboedov's time as reflected in his plays see M. Gershenzon, *Griboedovskaia Moskva*, M, 1916, 2d corr. ed.

81. The vast literature available on Masonry contains relatively little dispassionate analysis, and has been relatively untouched by intellectual historians. The best work has been done on French Masonry: A. Lantoine, *Histoire de la franc-maçonnerie française*, 1925; G. Martin, *La Franc-maçonnerie française et la préparation de la révolution*, 1926; and D. Mornet, *Origines intellectuelles*, 357–87, with excellent bibliography 523–5. The latter conclusively demonstrates that "the majority of masons" were "not revolutionaries, not even reformers, nor even discontent." (375) Unfortunately, Mornet makes no real effort to say what they in fact were, and betrays little awareness of the international importance of Masonry—a failure common to almost all French studies of the subject.

For some appreciation of the extraordinary, Europe-wide impact of the movement see the good introduction by G. Huard, *L'Art royal. Essai sur l'histoire de la franc-maçonnerie*, 1930; the excellent bibliography of masonic works published between 1723 and 1814 in C. Thory, *Acta Latomorum ou chronologie de l'histoire de la franche maçonnerie*, 1815, II, 349–400; the detailed study of A. Wolfstieg, *Werden und Wesen der Freimaurerei*, 1923, 2v; and the vast bibliography compiled by Wolfstieg, *Bibliographie der frei-*

maurerischen Literatur, Leipzig, 1923–6, 4v.

For the impact of the movement in individual countries see F. Schneider, *Die Freimaurerei und ihr Einfluss auf die geistige Kultur in Deutschland am Ende des 18 Jahrhunderts*, Prague, 1909; Ernst Friederichs, *Geschichte der einstigen Maurerei in Russland*, 1904; and *Die Freimaurerei in Russland und Polen*, 1907; and V. Viljanen's less comprehensive, *Vapaamuurariludesta Suomessa ja Venäjällä*, Jyväskyllä, 1923.

Masonry is analyzed as a religious movement by L. Keller, *Die geistigen Grundlagen der Freimaurerei*, Berlin, 1922 (2d ed.); and (more critically) by C. Lyttle, "The Religion of Early Freemasonry," in J. McNeill *et al.*, *Environmental Factors in Christian History*, Chicago, 1939, 304–23.

Among the many studies of Russian Masonry, two are particularly good in relating Russian developments to those in Europe as a whole: I. Findel's pioneering study, *Istoriia Frank-Masonstva*, P, 1872–4 (which is a Russian translation and elaboration of a revised German edition); and the richly illustrated collaborative work edited by S. Mel'gunov and N. Sidorov, *Masonstvo v ego proshlom i nastoiashchem*, M, 1914–15.

The most stimulating and sophisticated studies are those by Tira Sokolovskaia, published largely as short articles in *RS* during the first fifteen years of the twentieth century. See also her invaluable monograph based almost entirely on primary materials: *Russkoe masonstvo i ego znachenie v istorii obshchestvennago dvizheniia*, P, nd; and her *Katalog Masonskoi Kollektsii D. G. Burylina*, P, 1912; "Ionnov Den'—Masonsky Prazdnik," *More*, 1906, 23–4; and

especially "Masonstvo kak polozhitel'noe dvizhenie russkoi mysli v nachale XIX veka," *VsV*, 1904, May, 20–36. See also the well-documented older studies by M. Longinov, A. Pypin, and S. Eshevsky referenced in the notes to Longinov, *Sochineniia*, M, 1915, I; G. Vernadsky, *Russkoe Masonstvo v tsarstvovanie Ekateriny II*, P, 1917 (particularly for membership statistics, 85–90); and Ya. Barskov, *Perepiska moskovskikh masonov XVIII-go veka*, P, 1915; and *Russkoe masonstvo i ego znachenie v istorii obshchestvennago dvizheniia (XVIII i pervaia chetvert' XIX stoletiia)*, P, nd.

More tendentious but useful for detail are the English account by a Russian Masonic émigré, B. Telepnev, "Freemasonry in Russia," *AQC*, XXXV, 1922, 261–92; the Nazi-sponsored research of H. Riegelmann, *Die Europäischen Dynastien in ihrem Verhältnis zur Freimaurerei*, 1943 (esp. 295–314 for information suggesting close links between the Romanov dynasty and European Masonry); and V. Ivanov's impressionistic *O Petra Pervago do nashikh dnei, Russkaia intelligentsiia i Masonstvo*, Harbin, 1934. For another literary portrayal besides the famous caricature in Tolstoy's *War and Peace*, see A. Pisemsky, *Masony*, P, 1880, a novel of nearly 1,000 pages.

Of all the Bolshevik leaders, the only one who appears to have made any study of Masonry was Trotsky, who confessed (most uncharacteristically) his total inability to assess its historical significance. See *My Life*, NY, 1930, 120. The renewed influence of Masonry in the early twentieth century (particularly among the non-Bolshevik reformers and within the Provisional Government of 1917) is stressed by G. Aronson,

"Masony v russkoi politike," *Rossiia nakanune revoliutsii*, NY, 1962, 109–43.

82. Detailed, if fragmentary and far from conclusive, evidence for deriving Freemasonry from the medieval guild of stone masons is presented by D. Knoop and G. Jones, *An Introduction to Freemasonry*, Manchester, 1937.

83. Eshevsky, *Sochineniia*, M, 1870, III, 445; also Telepnev, "Freemasonry," 261–2.

84. Telepnev, 263.

85. Cited in Tukalevsky, "Iz istorii," 12.

86. Listed in Telepnev, "Freemasonry," 264–9.

87. Cited in Bogoliubov, *Novikov*, 258.

88. The term "higher order Masonry" is used here for all the various lodges that preached the necessity of attaining grades beyond the original three of Masonry. This includes the Scottish rite, the primarily German lodges of "strict observance," most Swedish orders, and others—generally known as "red" or "purple" Masonry as distinct from the "blue" Masonry of the lower orders; and, in Russia, orders of Andrew as distinct from John.

The term "higher order Masonry" is also used to include societies that were technically separate from the Masonic structure but were largely outgrowths of Masonry, seeking to answer the same demand for occult knowledge and stricter moral discipline (that is, Rosicrucians, *élus cohens*, and so on). The term as used here does *not* include those outgrowths of Masonry that were interested primarily in radical social and political reform such as the "illuminists" of Bavaria (who sought to extend the reforms of Joseph II, referring to Vienna as the "new Rome") and some of the Polish lodges that were interested in radical reform rather than inner regeneration. These rationalistic and reformist societies have been inaccurately bracketed with the far more numerous conservative and mystical "higher orders" by anti-Masonic pamphleteers.

For the best analysis of the origins of the higher orders and the tangled conflicts that developed among them see R. Le Forestier, *L'Occultisme et la franc-maçonnerie écossaise*, 1928, *La Franc-maçonnerie occultiste au dix-huitième siècle et l'ordre des Élus Coëns*, 1928; and *Les Plus Secrets Mystères des hauts grades de la maçonnerie dévoilés*, 1914. See also the well-documented iconoclastic study by P. Arnold, *Histoire des rose-croix et les origines de la franc-maçonnerie*, 1955.

89. T. Tschudi, *L'Étoile flamboyante ou la société des francs-maçons considerée sous tous ses rapports*, Frankfurt-Paris, 1766, 2v. See esp. I, 4–5, 160; and 41–7 for his speech to a lodge in St. Petersburg; also II, 179–232 for his catechism. Tschudi was the original Franco-Swiss spelling of his name, under which works published in the West appeared. For his Masonic activities see J. Bésuchet, *Précis historique de l'ordre de la franc-maçonnerie*, 1829, I, 42–3, 47; II, 275–9.

The passion for new catechisms was particularly marked in Germany. See J. Schmitt, *Der Kampf um den Katechismus in der Aufklärungsperiode Deutschlands*, Munich, 1935.

90. Bogoliubov, *Novikov*, 285.

91. Tukalevsky, "Iz istorii," 29–31, 18–20.

92. Findel, *Istoriia*, I, 273; also 253–73, 306–18. See also Zdenek David, "Influence of Boehme," 49 ff.; and D. Chizhevsky, "Swedenborg in Russland," *Aus zwei Welten*. The only work known to me which views the struggle between French and German ideas as a major theme for understanding

Russian thought of the era is M. Kovalevsky, "Bor'ba nemetskago vliianiia s frantsuzskim v kontse XVIII i v pervoi polovine XIX stoletiia," *VE*, 1915, 123–63.

93. Paul was almost certainly a practicing Mason. See T. Sokolovskaia, "Dva portreta imperatora Pavla I s Masonskimi emblami," *RS*, 1908, Oct, for pictures of Paul in Masonic garb 82–3; text 85–95; also *Masonstvo*, 11–12, and *AQC*, VIII, 1895, 31; Riegelmann, *Dynastien*, 298–301; and, particularly for the impact of higher order Masonry on his ideological education and later policies, G. Vernadsky, "Le Césarévitch Paul et les francs-maçons de Moscou," *RES*, VIII, 1925, 268–85.

94. *BE*, XXXVI, 511–12. Tukalevsky, "Iz istorii," 33 ff. On Schwarz, see Tikhonravov, *Sochineniia*, III, 60–81; M. Longinov, "Novikov i Shvarts," *RV*, 1857, Oct, 539–85; comments on this article by S. Eshevsky, *RV*, 1857, Nov, 174–201; *RBS*, XI, 621–8; and the sophisticated discussion together with documents and references in Barskov, *Perepiska*.

   "Sons of the university" or "alumni" are probably more accurate modern equivalents than "foster children" for the term *pitomtsy* as used in Schwarz's group.

95. *RBS*, XXII, 625; Tukalevsky, 27; also "Materialy dlia istorii druzheskogo uchenogo obshchestva," *RA*, 1863, vyp, 3, 203–17; A. Afanas'ev, "Nikolai Ivanovich Nokikov," *BZ*, 1858, no. 6, 161–81.

96. See F. Valjavec, "Das Woellnersche Religionsedikt und seine geschichtliche Bedeutung," *HJ*, 72, 1953, 386–400; Tukalevsky, 41–2; *RBS*, XXII, 623–4.

97. Cited in Tukalevsky, 29.

98. From text in Malyshev, ed., *Novikov*, 216.

99. *Ibid.*, 217.

100. Tukalevsky, "Iz istorii," 31–8. See also A. Viatte, *Les Sources occultes du romantisme*, 1928, I, 33–41, 120, on triadic ideas in the occult tradition; and C. Bila, *La Croyance à la magie au XVIIIe siècle en France*, 1925, for ample signs that the occult tradition was far more widespread even in "enlightened" French circles than is often appreciated.

101. Cited in Tukalevsky, "Iz istorii," 51, note 3. The manuscript which was located in Jan, 1965, under the number referenced by the usually reliable Tukalevsky (Q III, 175, of the manuscript collection of the Saltykov-Shchedrin Library in Leningrad) does not include this quotation, but many similar ones, asking "Chto takoe sut' idei?" referring to Christ as "ideia vsekh idei" (5b) and his true followers as "smysliashchie/ intelligentes" (55b). Tukalevsky's quotation may, thus, be only a paraphrase. However, since his page reference of 107 seems completely inappropriate to this document in any case, it may be that reference numbers have been changed, or that he was citing some other document in this rich collection of occult literature. The extensive translation of German and Latin philosophical terminology into Russian by Schwarz and his followers has never been systematically studied; but it seems probable that the term "intelligentsia" was derived not directly from Latin as is generally assumed, but indirectly through the adoption of Latin terms in German occult literature. The usage of "intelligentsia" cited by Tukalevsky is close to the concept of pure spirits, or *Intelligenzen*, in German occultism (see C. Kiesewetter, *Geschichte des neueren Occultismus*, Leipzig, 1891, 259). Ivan Aksakov, who apparently was the first to introduce the term "intelligentsia" into more

general usage in the 1860's (see A. Pollard, "The Russian Intelligentsia: The Mind of Russia," *CSS*, III, 1964, 7, note 19), derived (like Schwarz) his philosophic training and terminology from the German. The transposition of the Latin *t* into the Russian *ts* suggests the possible intermediacy of the German *z* or perhaps the Polish *cja*.

This later Russian idea that the intelligentsia bears a message of liberation for all mankind recalls the original chiliastic idea of Joachim of Flora that a new "third realm" of the spirit was coming in which men would be ruled no more by coercion, but by *intelligentia spiritualis*. See R. Kestenberg-Gladstein, "The 'Third Reich,'" *JWI*, XVIII, 1955, 245, 270.

102. Findel, *Istoriia*, II (published in Jan, 1874).

103. From his diary of Baron Schroeder, the new grand master, on his arrival in 1784 at the age of twenty-eight, in Barskov, *Perepiska*, 215. Schroeder referred to the Rosicrucians as "Protestant Jesuits" (225), but felt that there was a natural affinity between Protestantism and Orthodoxy, Prussia and Russia.

104. M. de Vissac, "Dom Pernety et les iluminés d'Avignon," *MAV*, XV, 1906, 219–38; A. Pypin, "Materialy dlia istorii masonskikh lozhov," *VE*, 1872, Jan, esp. 204–6; Viatte, *Sources*, I, 89–92; and Vernadsky, "Césarévitch."

105. *RA*, 1908, no. 6, 178. Note that even after the French Revolution (in the preceding document of 1790 on the same page), while accusing the Masons of preaching an "equality not existing in nature," she categorizes it as a "mystical heresy" and not a political movement.

Her opposition to Masonry began as early as 1759, according to Longinov, "Novikov i Shvarts,"

584. Catherine's anti-Masonic plays are reprinted in her *Sochineniia*, P, 1893, I, 138–209; and her general attitude toward Masonry examined in depth by A. Semeka, "Russkie rozenkreitsery i sochineniia Ekateriny II protiv masonstva," *ZhMNP*, 1902, no. 2, 343–400.

106. Cited in Mel'gunov, *Dvizheniia*, 181; and see entire excellent discussion of the sociopolitical ideas of dissenters under Catherine, 179–95.

107. V. Flerovsky, *Tri politicheskiia sistemy* London, 1897, 46–7, note.

108. On Alexis Elensky and the bozhestvennaia kantseliariia see A. Prugavin, *Raskol vverkhu, ocherki religioznykh iskanii v privilegirovannoi srede*, P, 1909, 76–83. For a fantastic example of latter-day efforts to attribute conspiratorial political genius to the *skoptsy* see E. Josephson, *The Unheeded Teachings of Jesus, or Christ Rejected*, NY, 1959, which contends, among other things, that the USSR was at that time ruled by a secret coterie of *skoptsy* operating within the Communist system.

109. Mel'gunov, *Dvizheniia*, 180.

110. Citations in Longinov, "Novikov," 563–4. Lopukhin, in fact, used the schismatic image of the Antichrist in his treatise on the "inner Church": Bogoliubov, *Novikov*, 209. Like almost all subsequent movements within the Westernized educated classes, Masonry was rigorously rejected by the schismatics. See Riabushinsky, *Staroobriadchestvo*, 48–9.

111. Longinov, "Novikov," 572, and 565 ff.

112. See Saint-Martin's *Mon Portrait historique et philosophique (1789–1803)*, 1961, ed. R. Amadou; also P. Arnold, *Histoire*, esp. 259–63, as well as M. Matter, *Saint-Martin, le philosophe inconnu*, 1862, esp. 134–45 for Russian contacts in London in the mid-1700's. Infor-

mation on his Masonic activities and influence in Russia is provided by H. C. de la Fontaine, "The Unknown Philosopher," *AQC*, XXXVII, part 3, 1924, 262–90 (including comments). For his central influence on two of the greatest nineteenth-century European writers, Balzac and Mickiewicz, P. Bernheim, *Balzac und Swedenborg: Einfluss der Mystik Swedenborgs und Saint-Martins auf die Romandichtung Balzacs*, 1914. W. Weintraub, *Literature as Prophecy, Scholarship and Martinist Poetics in Mickiewicz's Parisian Lectures*, 's Gravenhage, 1959.

Some authorities derive the term "Martinist" from Martinez rather than Saint-Martin. See, for instance, M. Kovalevsky, "Masonstvo vo vremia Ekateriny," *VE*, 1915, Sep, 108 note 1.

113. *Mon Portrait*, 56.
114. On the treatise *Réintégration des êtres*, by Martinez de Pasqually, the shadowy teacher of Saint-Martin, De Maistre, and others, see De Maistre, *Franc-maçonnerie*, 15–16.
115. A. Herzen, *PSS i pisem*, ed. Lemke, XI, 11.
116. Cited in Veselovsky, *Vliianie*, 95, note 2.
117. N. Mikhailovsky, *Sochineniia*, P, 1896, I, v.

On some of Lavater's links with Russia see Viatte, *Sources*, II, 72–3; Lavater, *Correspondance inédite avec l'Impératice Marie de Russie sur l'avenir de l'âme*, 1863; "Perepiska Karamzina s Lafaterom," German and Russian facing texts published as an appendix to *ZIAN*, LXXIII, 1893.
118. Merzliakov, cited in V. Istrin, "Druzheskoe Literaturnoe Obshchestvo," *ZhMNP*, 1910, Aug, 291–2.
119. N. Drizen, "Ocherki teatral'noi tsenzury v Rossii v XVIII v," *RS*, 1897, Jun, esp. 555–62; and for the general atmosphere of the time

and ample references see M. Strange, *La Révolution;* C. de Larivière, *Catherine II*, 139–40; also 357–75 for her *mémoire* of 1792 on the subject of revolution.
120. *Ocherki po istorii russkoi zhurnalistiki i kritiki*, L, 1950, I, 82.
121. E. Al'bovsky, "Imperator Pavel I i Mitropolit Sestrentsevich-Bokush," *RS*, 1897, May, 279–82; Pierling, *La Russie*, V, esp, 183–97.
122. Cited by V. Istrin, "Russkie studenty v Gettingene v 1802–1804 gg," *ZhMNP*, 1910, no. 7, 125. For some of the later terms of adulation for Alexander, particularly during the Napoleonic wars, see Cherniavsky, *Tsar*, 128 ff. For the continuing impact of Göttingen on Russian intellectual life, see E. Tarasov, "Russkie 'gettingentsy' pervoi chetverti XIX v. i vliianie ikh na razvitie liberalizma v Rossii," *GM*, 1914, no. 7, 195–210.
123. Cited in Lang, *Radical*, 254. For the ideas of La Harpe and their impact on Alexander see several articles by L. Mogeon in *Revue Historique Vaudoise*, particularly "L'influence de La Harpe sur Alexandre," 1938, May–Jun.
124. See G. Vernadsky, "Reforms under Czar Alexander I: French and American Influences," *RP*, 1947, Jan, 47–64; M. Raeff, "The Political Philosophy of Speransky," *ASR*, 1953, Feb, 3–18; "The Philosophical Views of Count M. M. Speransky," *ASR*, 1953, Jun, and *Michael Speransky: Statesman of Imperial Russia 1772–1839*, The Hague, 1957, esp. 204–27.
125. Raeff, *Speransky*, 1–118; see also A. Pypin, *Ocherki*, esp. 42–8, on the influence of Bentham and his followers on Speransky.
126. Raeff, *Speransky*, 23, note 2.
127. See A. Yakhontov, *Istorichesky Ocherk Imperatorskago Litseia*, Paris, 1936.
128. Raeff, *Speransky*, 119–69.
129. Letter of Alexander to La Harpe

of Mar 12, 1811, in *SRIO*, V, 1870, 41.

130. "Svoboda—tam gde est' ustavy,/ Svoboda mudraia sviata,/ No ravenstvo—mechta." Cited in *Ocherki . . . zhurnalistiki*, 147.

131. See discussion in N. Bulich, *Ocherki po istorii russkoi literatury i prosveshcheniia s nachala XIX veka*, P, 1902, I, 273–303; also *Ocherki . . . zhurnalistiki*, 132–52 for Karamzin's impact on journalism and letters; and R. Pipes, *Karamzin's Memoir on Old and New Russia*, Cambridge, Mass., 1959; an analysis together with translation of the text; also Pipes' "Karamzin's Conception of the Monarchy," *HSS*, IV; W. Mitter, "Die Entwicklung der politischen Anschauungen Karamzins," *FOG*, Bd. 2, 1955, 165–285, and H. Rothe, "Karamzinstudien II," *ZSPh*, Bd. XXX, Heft 2, 1962, 272–306.

132. See account of the story and citations in Bulich, *Ocherki*, I, 82; also Karamzin, *Istoriia gosudarstva rossiiskago*, P, 1819, 2d ed., VI, 130–2.

133. Cited in Bulich, *Ocherki*, I, 82.

134. See especially K. Ryleev, "Otryvki Dumy 'Marfa Posadnitsa'," and notes thereto in *LN*, LIX, 1954, 23–4.

135. See the extraordinary forty-six points put forward by Count Mamonov for his would-be society of "Russian knights" in the valuable anthology edited by A. Borozdin, *Iz pisem i pokazanii dekabristov. Kritika sovremennago sostoianiia Rossii i plany budushchago ustroistva*, P, 1906, 145–8. The secret "society of the united Slavs," one of the last to form (and most radical) of the groups participating in the Decembrist movement, used as their emblem four anchors signifying the White, Black, Baltic, and Mediterranean seas, which they envisaged as the natural boundaries of a united Slavic federation that would require a navy and a great port on each sea. See M. Nechkina, *Obshchestvo soedinennykh slavian*, M-L, 1927, 91–2, 104–6, and symbolic signs of the society in the fold-out appendix.

For a valuable but undocumented account of the movement Zetlin, *The Decembrists*, NY, 1958. For more detail and documentation, see M. Nechkina, *Dvizhenie dekabristov*, M, 1955, 2v; also the bibliography of Soviet writings on the movement between 1928 and 1959 edited by Nechkina and bearing the same title *Dvizhenie dekabristov*, M, 1960; for discussion of their ideas, V. Semevsky, *Politicheskie i obshchestvennye idei dekabristov*, P, 1909; and H. Lemberg, *Die nationale Gedankenwelt der Dekabristen*, Cologne, 1963. For new materials on the neglected figure of Mamonov see articles by Lotman referenced in the bibliography *Dvizhenie*, 79, 199.

136. For the range of these early journalistic activities see *Ocherki . . . zhurnalistiki*, 194–235.

137. M. Lunin, *Sochineniia i pis'ma*, P, 1923, 82.

138. For exhaustive discussion of the Decembrists' idealization of Novgorod see Volk, *Vzgliadi*, 321–47.

139. See P. Ol'shansky, *Dekabristy i pol'skoe natsional'no-osvoboditel'noe dvizhenie*, M, 1959, including 165–213 on links with Lithuania, particularly the Philomat society at Vilnius University, which was actually one of the earliest of the radical student secret societies to appear in the Russian Empire. Fear of Polish connections and of repercussions in Poland of any slackening of authority inside Russia was almost an obsession with the official interrogators of the Decembrists prior to their trial. See, for instance, the examination

of Pestel in Borozdin, ed, *Iz pisem*, 99–108.

140. On his speech to the sejm of Mar 15/27, 1818, see Semevsky, *Idei*, 265–74, also 281. Semevsky finds the revolutionary events in Western Europe and the Americas more important influences on the Decembrists than any writings. *Ibid.*, 234–57.

141. Materials discussed in G. Naan, ed., *Istoriia Estonskoi SSR*, Tallinn, 1958, 208–10. See also Mickiewicz's *Pan Tadeusz*. Küchelbecker also popularized Russian reformist ideas in the West glorifying Novgorod in his lectures of 1821 at the Athenée Royal in Paris. See his *Dnevnik*, L, 1929; and Yu. Lotman, *Uusi materjale dekabristide võitlusest baltl aadli vastu*, Tartu, 1955; also Mel'gunov, *Dela*, 265–7.

142. F. Glinka, "Zinovy Bogdan Khmel'nitsky," cited in *Ocherki ... zhurnalistiki*, 216.

143. Text of the project in V. Yakushkin, *Gosudarstvennaia vlast' i proekty gosudarstvennoi reformy v Rossii*, P, 1909, appendix. This belief in the federal distribution of power within the Russian empire aroused opposition of Great Russian chauvinists and, curiously enough, of the Polish Patriotic Association founded in Warsaw in 1819 and sympathetic to the idea of greater Poland. Note that most Decembrists tended to admire the American and even the Dutch revolution and the federal systems that emerged from them over the French Revolution and the forms of rule that issued from it. See Volk, *Vzgliady*, 237–81, and more briefly, 443–4.

144. For documents and discussion on Pestel, see M. Nechkina, ed., *"Russkaia Pravda" P. I. Pestelia i sochineniia, ei predshestvuiushchie* (*Vosstanie dekabristov: dokumenty, VII*), M, 1958. See also A. Adams, "The Character of Pestel's Thought," *ASR*, 1955, Apr; J. Schwarz-Sochor, "P. I. Pestel: The Beginning of Jacobin Thought in Russia," *International Review of Social History*, III, part 1, 1958, 71–96, and M. Kovalevsky, *"Russkaia Pravda* Pestelia," *MG*, 1958, no. 1, 1–19. Volk shows (*Vzgliady*, 263) that Pestel was not alone in his advocacy of a temporary, interim dictatorship; Nechkina shows (*Obshchestvo*) that the Society of the United Slavs also favored abolition of the monarchy and an end to most forms of aristocratic privilege. See also P. Miliukov, "La Place du Décabrisme dans l'evolution de l'intelligencija russe," and B. Mirkine-Guétzévitch, "Les Idées politiques des Décabristes et l'influence française," *Le Monde slav*, 1925, Dec, 333–49; 380–3.

145. The connection between Masonic and revolutionary groups appears to be tenuous if not mythic outside of certain extremely conservative Catholic milieux (parts of Bavaria, Austria, and Spain). Although a large number of Decembrists were former Masons, their association was largely with the lower order forms of philanthropic Masonry, and was for the most part much less sustained and intimate than was the association of imperial officials and counter-revolutionaries with higher order Masonry. See V. Semevsky, "Dekabristy Masony," *MG*, 1908, Feb, 1–50; Mar, 127–70; also *Idei*, 286–377. Semevsky's evidence does not sustain the belief in a close connection which led him to begin the study and may have prevented him from drawing as clear a conclusion as seems warranted.

The membership of Pestel (*Idei*, 289) does not itself appear to have been a determining influence (see T. Sokolovskaia, "Lozha trekh dobrodetelei i eia chleny dekabristy," *RA*, 1908, no. 20, 321–2); and his later interest in adopting Masonic forms appears to have been largely opportunistic (though quite extensive). See N.

2. THE ANTI-ENLIGHTENMENT

1. *Soirées de St. Pétersbourg,* in *Oeuvres complètes,* Lyon, 1884, IV, 170.
2. *Oeuvres,* I, xiv-xv.
3. *Oeuvres,* IV, 106.
4. See M. J. Rouët de Journel, *Un Collège de Jesuites à Saint-Pétersbourg, 1800–1816,* 1922; A. Boudou, *Le Saint-Siège et la Russie, 1814–1847,* 1922, I, 13–28. There were at least 400 Jesuits in Russia by 1812 (V. Nadler, *Imperator Aleksandr I i ideia sviashchennago soiuza,* Riga, 1886, I, 66). The Jesuits were valued not only as a bulwark against revolution but as a source of skilled personnel for everything from education (for which purpose Catherine had welcomed them) to the making of confections (for which Paul particularly valued the general of the order, *ibid.,* I, 57 ff.).
5. *Essai sur le principe générateur des constitutions politiques et des autres institutions humaines,* P, 1814, 100 (written in May, 1809, as a memorandum to Alexander I and published in an English version as *On God and Society,* Chicago, 1959, p).
6. *Oeuvres,* IV, 282.
7. *Oeuvres,* XIII, 290–1.
8. *Oeuvres,* XIII, 204.
9. De Maistre, *La Franc-maçonnerie. Mémoire inédit au Duc de Brunswick* (1782), 1925, esp. 22–3. Cf. F. Vermale, "L'Activité maçonnique de J. de Maistre," *RHL,* 1935, Jan, 72–6; G. Goyau, "La Pensée religieuse de J. de Maistre," *RDM,* LXII, 1921, 137–63; 585–624.
10. *Oeuvres,* V, 190.

Druzhinin, "Masonskie znaki P. I. Pestelia," in *Muzei revoliutsii SSSR, vtoroi sbornik statei,* M, 1929, 12–49.

11. *Oeuvres,* IV, 271–2.
12. *Oeuvres,* V, 23 and ff. for the famous apotheosis of war; also V, 93, where he argues against Berkeley's contention that symmetry in the rational world proves the existence of God. Would it have helped lead men to God, he asks, if Nero had burned human beings in a more orderly and symmetrical manner? See also his praise of sacrifices V, 283–360.

Soviet ideologists have cited De Maistre's view that war is divinely ordained (rather than the product of specific social and economic forces, as they contend) as a model rationalization for the alleged subconscious assumption of the West that war with the USSR is inevitable. See V. Gantman *et al.,* "Mirovye voiny XX veka i dialektika istorii," *Mirovaia Ekonomika i Mezhdunarodnye Otnosheniia,* 1964, no. 8, 3–4.
13. *Oeuvres,* V, 125–6.
14. *Principe générateur,* 6.
15. Cited in Goyau, "Pensée," 598.
16. *Oeuvres,* IV, 107.
17. *Oeuvres,* I, xli.
18. *Oeuvres,* IV, 2–3; V, 281–2.
19. M. Stepanova, "Zhosef de Mestr v Rossii," *LN,* XXIX–XXX, 1937, 587.
20. *Ibid.,* 588.
21. *Ibid.,* 584; and the entire section 577–726.
22. Goyau, "Pensée," 611–12; *Oeuvres,* I, xxi–xxxvi.
23. *Oeuvres,* VIII, 163–232.
24. *Oeuvres,* VIII, 279–360.
25. *Oeuvres,* VIII, 265; and 233–65. He is commenting on Fesler's plan of study.

26. *Oeuvres,* XIII, 290; V, 228–57; and for a more direct attack on Alexander see his later (1819) work, *Sur l'Etat du christianisme en Europe,* in *Oeuvres,* VIII, 485–519.

27. *Oeuvres,* V, 247, 242; XIII, 290–2, 282; *LN,* XXIX–XXX, 613–21. De Maistre originally saw this mysterious process of unification of humanity as *le grand oeuvre* which would reunify but transcend Christianity and fulfill the longing for the lost light of the ancient East, so central to higher order Masonry. See *Mémoire inédit,* 35–6, 100–20.

28. *Oeuvres,* III, 287–401; English edition, *Letters to a Russian Gentleman on the Spanish Inquisition,* London, 1851.

29. P. Pierling, *L'Empereur Alexandre Ier, est-il mort catholique?,* 1913, esp. 12–44; and commentary in Mel'gunov, *Dela i liudi Aleksandrovskogo vremeni,* I, Berlin, 1923, 105–9; A. Boudou, *Le Saint-Siège,* I, 126–39.

30. For full discussion and references on the pietist influx see E. Winter, *Halle,* esp. 227–54 on Todorsky. Perhaps out of necessary deference to his Communist publishers, Winter tends to underplay the religious and evangelical aspects of the pietistic influx, which are more fully brought out in studies not used in Winter's work, such as E. Benz, "August Herman Francke und die deutschen evangelischen Gemeinden in Russland," *Auslanddeutschtum und evangelische Kirche,* 1936, 143–92; and E. Seeberg, *Gottfried Arnold, Die Wissenschaft und Mystik seiner Zeit,* Meerane, 1923. The standard history of Pietism is still A. Ritschl, *Geschichte des Pietismus,* Bonn, 1880–6, 3v. The broader cultural impact of Pietism is measured in another context by K. Pinson, *Pietism as a Factor in the Rise of German Nationalism,* NY, 1934.

31. Winter, *Halle,* 290–338.

32. On the organization of the Herrnhut Community and its missionary activities in the East see E. Langton, *History of the Moravian Church. The Story of the First International Protestant Church,* London, 1956; E. Winter, *Die tschechische und slowakische Emigration in Deutschland im 17 und 18 Jahrhundert,* 1955; O. Uttendörfer, *Wirtschaftsgeist und Wirtschaftsorganisation Herrnhuts und der Brüdergemeinde,* Herrnhut, 1926 (an exhaustive study from 1743 to the end of the eighteenth century); H. Grönroos, *Suomen yhteyksistä herrnhutilaisuuteen 1700-luvulla, SKST,* XII, 1938, with bibliography, 268–72, for all Baltic languages; and the invaluable study by A Klaus, "Sektatory-kolonisty v Rossii," *VE,* 1868, Jan, 256–300; Mar, 277–326; Jun, 665–722; Jul, 713–66; also Klaus' "Dukhovenstvo i shkoly v nashikh nemetskikh koloniiakh," *VE,* 1869, Jan, 138–74; May, 235–74. For the hostility of their reception in Russia prior to Catherine see *RA,* 1868, Sep, 1391–5.

33. A. Khodnev, "Kratky obzor stoletnei deiatel'nosti Imperatorskago vol'nago ekonomicheskago obshchestva s 1765 do 1865," *Trudy vol'nago ekonomicheskago obshchestva,* 1865, Nov, 268–9. An important role in publicizing Sarepta was played by Ivan Boltin's description, *Khorografiiia sareptskikh tselitel'nykh vod,* P, 1782.

34. *O Istinnom Khristianstve,* in *Sochineniia,* M, 1836, vols IV–IX. N. Gorodetzky (*Tikhon,* 95) and G. Florovsky (*ASR,* 1964, Sep, 577–8) doubt, however, that there was much influence of J. Arndt on Tikhon. On the transmission of Arndt's work into Russian, see Chizhevsky, *Aus zwei Welten,* 220–30.

35. See Viatte, *Sources,* I, 32–7; V.

Černý, "Les 'Frères moraves' de Mme. de Stael," *RLC*, 1960, Jan–Mar, 37–51; P. Kireevsky, *Sochineniia*, M, 1861, II, 303, note; and *RA*, 1868, Sep, 1352–8.

36. On this extraordinary witch hunt see R. Le Forestier, *Les Illuminés de Bavière et la franc-maçonnerie allemande*, 1914; also J. Droz, "La Légende du complot illuministe en Allemagne," *RH*, 1961, Oct–Dec, 313–38.

37. J. Bodemann, *Johan Caspar Lavater*, Gotha, 1856, 367, also 396 ff.

38. "Perepiska s Lafaterom," 3, 5–6; see also Karamzin, *Letters of a Russian Traveller, 1789–1790*, NY, 1957.

39. Cited in Droz, "Légende," 329.

40. De Maistre, *Oeuvres*, V, 258–60.

41. Quoted from the Russian edition, *Oblako nad sviatilishchem*, P, 1804, 149, 152, 154. The original, *Die Wolke über dem Heiligtum*, Munich, 1802. See also Viatte, *Sources*, II, 44–51.

42. P. Znamensky, *Chteniia iz istorii russkoi tserkvi za vremia tsarstvovaniia imperatora Aleksandra I*, Kazan, 1885, 157, counts twenty-five different works of Eckartshausen rendered into Russian during the decade 1813–23.

43. Lopukhin, *Nekotoryia cherty o vnutrennei tserkvi, o edinom puti istiny i o razlichnykh putiakh zabluzhdeniia i gibeli*, P, 1798. See Ya. Barskov's detailed and fully annotated account of this neglected figure in *RBS*, X, 650–82; also Bulich, *Ocherki*, I, 316–59, who contends (329) that Lopukhin's work was finished in 1791. See also V. Sadovnik, *Masonskie trudy I. V. Lopukhina*, M, 1913.

44. Cited in Bogoliubov, *Novikov*, 209.

45. Klaus, "Sektatory," *VE*, 1868, Mar, 305; also *BE*, IX, 50–1.

46. N. Popov, "Ignaty-Aurely Fesler," *VE*, 1879, Dec, 586–643; I. Chistovich, *Istoriia St-Petersburgskoi Dukhovnoi Akademii*, P, 1857, 182–266. Fesler's ecumenical views are contained in his *Ansichten von Religion und Kirchentum*, 1805; and are discussed in V. Ternovsky, "Materialy dlia istorii mistitsizma v Rossii," *TKDA*, Mar, 164–5. For his Masonic activities, Thory, *Acta*, I, 198, 313; for his previous contact with secret societies in Germany prior to his arrival in Russia, J. Droz, *L'Allemagne et la révolution française*, 1949, 96–7.

47. For a vivid account of Alexander's movement away from rationalism to pietism during this period see "Rasskazy kniazia Golitsyna," *RA*, 1886, kn. 2, 87, and entire account 65–108.

48. The classical interpretation of the stabilizing force of Methodism is put forward by E. Halevy (*History of the English People*, NY, 1961, I, part iii, p, 387–485). G. Clark (*The Making of Victorian England*, London, 1962, 36–7) doubts that the capacity for revolution in England was very great in any case—a doubt that might apply equally well (if for different reasons) to Russia.

English non-conformism was perhaps the most important of the many spiritual influences on the formation of Alexander's vague religious views. His original religious instruction was by Andrew Samborsky, a Pole who had married an Englishwoman and spent most of his life in England (Nadler, *Imperator*, I, 9–12); and his entire concept of renovation through popular moral and religious education was decisively influenced not only by the Methodist Bible Society, but also by Quaker ideals of free public education through daily readings propounded by Joseph Lancaster (see Pypin, *Dvizheniia*, 1–293, on the former; and 397–418 on the latter). He had important subsequent contacts with English Quakers, particularly Stephen Grillet, with whom Alexander worshipped in London in 1815, and had further close contacts in St. Petersburg in 1818–9. See R. S. "Aus dem Restaurationszeitalter, der Quäker Grillet in St. Petersburg," *DR*, XLVII, 1886, 49–69, unfortunately without documentation.

49. In addition to Pypin see N. Stelletsky, *Kniaz' A. N. Golitsyn i ego tserkovno-gosudarstvennaia deiatel'nost*, Kiev, 1901; S. Sol'sky, "Uchastie Aleksandra I v izdanii Biblii," *TKDA*, 1879, Jan, 172–96.

50. Cited from 1818 communication with Bishop Eiler in Znamensky, *Rukovodstvo*, 433. G. Florovsky (*Puti*, 130) shows that Alexander's religious turn preceded the fire.

51. A. von Tobien "Herrnhut i Livland," in *Die livlandische Ritterschaft*, 1930, 116–39, esp. 128–9; and H. Plitt, *Die Brüdergemeinde und die lutherische Kirche in Livland*, Gotha, 1861, 168–81; Nadler, *Imperator*, I, 298–309; E. Knapton, *The Lady of the Holy Alliance*, NY, 1939, esp. 125–91; C. de Grunwald, "Les Russes à Paris en 1814," *RSMP*, 1954, 1st semester, I–14.

52. *Arkhiv brat'ev Turgenevykh*, P, 1913, III, 251.

53. *RBS*, X, 674; "Lettres de Mme. de Stael à Alexandre I, 1814–7," *La Revue de Paris*, 1897, Jan–Feb, 16–7; Grunwald, "Les Russes," 5–6.

54. W. Baur, *Religious Life in Germany*, London, 1872, 317–38; *Autobiography of Heinrich Jung-Stilling*, NY, 1848; E. Benz, *Sendung*, 15–32, for some of the prophetic utterances and compilations of the time.

55. The valuable study of E. Knapton, *Lady*, 125–66, tends on the whole to play down the role of this "lady of the Holy Alliance."

56. F. Baader, *Über das durch die französische Revolution herbeigeführte Bedürfniss einer neuern und innigern Verbindung der Religion mit der Politik*, completed early in the summer of 1814 and dedicated to Prince Golitsyn; first published Nürnberg, 1815. Baader first sent copies of his proposal (which was influenced by the theocratic ideas of Novalis and Saint-Martin (F. Büchler, *Die geistigen Wurzeln der Heiligen Allianz*, Freiburg, 1929, 53–60) in apparently rough form to the monarchs of Austria, Prussia, and Russia in the spring of 1814. For the varied West European influences on the idea of a Holy Alliance see Büchler and H. Schaeder, *Die dritte Koalition*, 1934.

57. Text in W. Phillips, *The Confederation of Europe*, London, 1920, 301–2. See also Knapton, *Lady*, 165–6; Sukhomlinov, *Izsledovaniia*, I, 174–5. Nadler's six-volume investigation of the problem concludes that Alexander was the author of the text and the originator of the idea of a "Holy Alliance," (see esp. vol. V); but his analysis suggests the importance of German émigrés in St. Petersburg—particularly the conservative Baltic German nationalist Ernst Arndt and the later Prussian reform leader Baron Stein—in conditioning elite opinion in the Russian capital for the idea of some such alliance.

58. Klaus, "Dukhovenstvo," 147; also 138 ff.; Benz, *Sendung;* E. Susini, *Lettres inédites de Franz von Baader*, 1942, esp. 293–4.

59. *ZhChO*, 1817, Jul, 18. This was the lead article in the first number of the society's official periodical.

60. T. Sokolovskaia, "Masonstvo kak polozhitel'noe dvizhenie," 20–36.

61. Between 1817 and 1821 over-all Masonic membership appears to have increased by more than half, while the increase in St. Petersburg was only 10 per cent: *RS*, 1908, Oct, 87–8; and, for the general history of this last period of Masonry, Pypin, *Istoricheskie*

*ocherki: Obshchestvennoe dvizh-
enie v Rossii pri Aleksandre I*, P,
1900, 296–333; also B. Telepnev,
"Some Aspects of Russian Freemasonry during the Reign of
Emperor Alexander I," *AQC*,
XXXVIII, 1925, 15–31.

62. *Put' ko Khristu*, P, 1815, xxiii-
xxiv, cited in *BZ*, 1858, no. 5, 131;
see also 136. Bulich, *Ocherki*, I,
340–3.

63. I. Katetov, *Graf M. M. Speransky
kak religiozny myslitel'*, Kazan,
1889, 39–40 notes, 42 ff.; Znamensky, *Chteniia*, 149–63.

64. Listed in *Toska po otchizne*, M,
1818, V, 307–8. "Homesickness"
does not fully convey the overtones of metaphysical longing in
the German *Heimweh* or the Russian *toska po otchizne*.

65. Katetov, *Speransky*, 65–77. Saint-
Martin, *Oeuvres posthumes*, Tours,
1807, II, 245–68.

66. P. Shelley, "Adonais," LII, lines
1–4.

67. Znamensky, *Rukovodstvo*, 433.

68. Znamensky, *Chteniia*, 156–7, and
entire discussion 111–63.

69. This can only be inferred. See F.
Hoffmann, *Franz von Baaders
Biographie und Briefwechsel*, Leip-
zig, 1857, 79.

70. N. Popov, "Fesler," 639–40; Pypin,
Dvizheniia, 132–5, 200–4.

71. *RS*, 1907, Apr, 213; *RA*, 1868,
no. 9, 1358–90; Pypin, *Dvizheniia*,
197–200; and Bulich, *Ocherki*, II,
289–320, for the fall of Golitsyn.

72. Pypin, *Dvizheniia*, 200.

73. *RS*, 1896, Aug, 426.

74. "Raskolnicisme," Susini, *Lettres*,
364; also to Golitsyn, 368–9. Benz,
Sendung, discusses later contacts
with Russia, but deals mainly with
questions of church unification and
should be supplemented by Benz's
*Franz von Baader und Kotzebue.
Das Russlandbild der Restaura-
tionszeit*, Mainz, 1957.

75. De Maistre, *Oeuvres*, VIII, 328;
on De Maistre's friend Paulucci,

see Semevsky, "Dekabristy," 27–
33.

76. V. Zhmakin, "Eres' Esaula Kotel'-
nikova," *Kh Cht*, 1882, no. 11–
12, 739–95; Pypin, *Dvizheniia*,
419–58.

77. E. Bakhtalovsky, "Opisanie dukhovnykh podvigov i vsekh sluchaev
zhizni sviashchennika Feodosiia
Levitskago," *RS*, 1880, Sep, 129–
68. For Levitsky's writings, see L.
Brodsky, ed., *Sviashchennik Feodosy Levitsky i ego sochinenie*, P,
1911.

78. F. von Baader, *Les Enseignements
secrets de Martinès de Pasqualis*,
1900, 4.

79. See, for instance, "Iz istorii
masonstva," *RS*, 1907, no. 3, 539–
49; T. Sokolovskaia, *Katalog masonskoi kollektsii D. G. Burynina*,
P, 1912, 22–3.

80. On the history of this sect, which
is even more shrouded in mystery
than most, see A. Scheikevitch,
"Alexandre Ier et l'hérésie sab-
batiste," *RHM*, III, 1956, 223–35.

The Jewish equivalent of mystical pietism, Hassidism, may also
have played some obscure role in
developing the idea of a supra-
confessional "inner church." At
any rate, the parallelism between
Hassidism and Pietism is as striking as that between Old Believer
chiliasm and that of the Sabbataians a century earlier.

On Hassidism in Eastern
Europe during this period see G.
Scholem, *Major Trends in Jewish
Mysticism*, NY, 1954, 3d ed., esp.
301–50; and for the general im-
pact of Jewish Kabbalistic mysti-
cism on Christian thought in the
West during the early modern
period see E. Benz, *Die Christliche
Kabbala*, Zurich, 1958.

81. Zhmakin, "Kotel'nikov," 753–4,
note 2; also 745–64.

82. Cited in S. Sol'sky, "Uchastie,"
195; see also 172–96.

83. Matter, *Saint-Martin*, 315–28,

354–410; Pypin, *Dvizheniia*, 318–21; Jung-Stilling, *Theorie der Geisterkunde*, 1808; Eckartshausen, *Bog vo ploti ili Khristos mezhdu chelovekami*, P, 1818, I; also his *Oblako nad sviatilishchem*, P, 1804, 7, 149–54; and Lopukhin's inscription to *Dukh Ekkartsgauzena ili sushchnost' ucheniia sego znamenitago pisatelia*, M, 1810. For the influence of Jung-Stilling on the later "Tidings of Zion" sect, see E. Molostova, *Iegovisty*, P, 1914, esp. 17–34.

84. R. Labry, *Alexandre Ivanovič Herzen 1812–1870*, 1928, 177–8 note 2; Popov, "Fesler," 640–1. G. Florovsky pointedly entitles the excellent chapter on this period in his *Puti* "The Struggle for Theology."

85. I. Pokrovsky, "O sposobakh soderzhaniia dukhovnykh uchilishch v Rossii ot osnovaniia ikh, v 1721 g, do preobrazovaniia v nachale nastoiashchago stoletiia," *Strannik*, 1860, Aug, 111–13; also 109–38; and Jul, 24–55 for further discussion of this often neglected element in the Russian educational picture.

86. Letter of Jul 31/Aug 12, 1815, to Mme Svechin (later one of De Maistre's converts to Catholicism and an émigré patron of Russian Catholics in Paris) in De Maistre, *Oeuvres*, XIII, 125. The basic works of the French-speaking Platon are listed in *BE*, 46, 851–2; his ideas and activities discussed in A. Barsov, *Ocherk zhizni Mitropolita Platona*, M, 1891.

87. *Considerations sur la doctrine et l'esprit de l'église orthodoxe*, Stuttgart, 1816; and reviews in *ZhChO*, 1817, Aug, 181–98, and Sep, 239–51. *Mémoire sur l'état actuel de l'Allemagne*, 1818. On Sturdza, see *RBS*, XIII, 602–6; Sukhomlinov, *Izsledovaniia*, I, 219; Benz, "Baader und Kotzebue," 88–99. Carl Brinckmann suggests that Sturdza may actually have been the principal author of the Holy Alliance, and shows the close tie-in between the German and Russian reaction in "Die Entstehung von Sturdza's 'Etat actuel de l'Allemagne'," *HZ*, CXX, 1919, 80–102.

Sturdza's sister, Roxanne, the Countess Edling, was also an important influence in the turn toward reaction and mysticism (see A. Shidlovsky, "Grafinia R. S. Edling v pis'makh k V. G. Tepliakovu," *RS*, Aug, 404–43). Indeed, her beauty and magnetism considered together with that of Baroness Krüdener, Mme Tatarinova, Zinaida Volkonsky, and Countess Orlova-Chesmenskaia (the real power behind Photius and the key foe of Golitsyn, see "Arkhimandrit Foty i Grafinia A. A. Orlova-Chesmenskaia," *IL*, 1914, Feb, 195–204) tempts one to suggest that the influence of attractive women in mobilizing men against Westernizing innovation was as great on the reactionaries around Alexander I as it had been among the conservative boyars around Alexis Mikhailovich. At another level the heroic role of women came to be stressed in the legends that developed about resistance to Napoleon. See A. Svobodin, "Vasilissa Kozhina," *Soviet Woman*, 1961, no. 3, 24–5.

88. The lodge under attack was that of Prince Barataev, son of a former governor of Simbirsk and a leading theorist of syncretic and cosmopolitan Masonry. See T. Sokolovskaia, "K masonskoi deiatel'nosti Kn. Barataeva," *RS*, 1908, Feb, 424–35.

89. Sukhomlinov, *Izsledovaniia*, I, 224, and 511, note 277.

90. E. Feoktistov, "Magnitsky. Materialy dlia istorii prosveshcheniia v Rossii," *RV*, 1864, Jun, 484; and, for basic materials on Magnitsky,

Jun, 464–98; Jul, 5–55; and Aug, 407–49.

91. *Ibid.,* Jun, 484–5.

92. *Ibid.,* Jul, 11, (the term used is *blagochestie),* and 5–22.

93. Bulich, *Ocherki,* II, 269–71, corrects Feoktistov's account in some respects.

94. Feoktistov, "Magnitsky," Jul, 23–6.

95. *Ibid.,* Aug, 409, also 408; and for the general purge of universities, Jun, 467–73, Jul, 11–18.

96. From texts of his memoranda in *RA,* 1864, no. 3, 324–5.

97. Cited from the *Zhurnal uchenoi kommissii,* 1820, in Sukhomlinov, *Izsledovaniia,* I, 185.

98. Argument of Kruzenshtern in *ibid.,* 186.

99. Feoktistov, Aug, 426–7.

100. *Ibid.,* 426, citing A. Perovsky (Pogorel'sky), an educational overseer of the Kharkov district.

101. From the famous memorandum to Shishkov, "Zapiski o kramolakh vragov Rossii," probably the work of Prince Peter Meshcherskin, published with introduction and analysis by N. Moroshkin in *RA,* 1868, no. 9, 1384.

102. Feoktistov, Jun, 473, and text of memorandum 469–73.

103. Feoktistov, Jul, 47.

104. J. Laurens, *Vocabulaire,* 66–7.

105. *RBS,* X, 670.

106. Feoktistov, Jul, 42–3. For discussion of Uvarov's ideas, their roots in German romantic ideas about the East, and their contrast with the harsher imperialist views that Pogodin developed a few years later see N. Riasanovsky, "Russia and Asia—Two Nineteenth-Century Russian Views," *CSS,* I, 1960, 170–81; of correspondence of De Maistre and Uvarov, *LN,* XXIX/XXX, 1937, 682–712. On Senkovsky, N. Riasanovsky, *Nicholas I and Official Nationality in Russia, 1825–1855,* Berkeley–Los Angeles, 1959, 65–72; and P. Pletnev, "O narodnosti v literature,"

ZhMNP, 1834, no. 1, ch. 2, 1–30.

107. N. Shil'der, "Dva donosa v 1831 godu," *RS,* 1898, 517–38; 1899, Jan, 67–87; and particularly Feb, 289–314; and Mar, 607–31; also Feoktistov, Aug, 437–49.

108. Sakulin, *Russkaia literatura i sotsializm,* I, 400–1, note 2.

109. For her earlier and later careers respectively see *LN,* IV–VI, 1932, 477–86; and N. Gorodetzky, "Zinaida Volkonsky as Catholic," *SEER,* 1960, Dec, 31–43.

110. M. J. Rouët de Journel, *Madame Swetchine,* 1929.

111. Augustin Golitsyn, *Un Missionaire russe en Amérique,* 1856; P. Lemcke, *Life and Work of Prince Demetrius Augustine Gallitzin,* London–NY, 1940; Bolshakoff, *Nonconformity,* 144–7; Boudou, *Le Saint-Siège,* 328–556.

112. Zhmakin, "Kotel'nikov," 772–95; and "Materialy dlia istorii mistitsizma v Rossii. Zapiski Iakova Zolotareva," *Strannik,* 1879, May; Margaritov, *Istoriia,* 109–12.

113. For the influence of De Maistre on Solov'ev see Radlov, *Ocherk,* 14, note 1. On Solov'ev's vision of reunited Christendom, which explicitly included Jews, see S. Frank, ed., *A Solovyov Anthology,* London, 1950, 75–126; for his Catholic sympathies see *ibid.,* 249–52, and the first part of his *La Russie et l'église universelle,* Paris, 1889. His last apocalyptical vision of a reunited Christendom (*Anthology,* 229–48) was influenced by Jung-Stilling's prophetic writings of the Alexandrian age; and the leader of the Orthodox component in the new reunited church is a mysterious elder who is rumored to be Fedor Kuzmich (*Anthology,* 237).

114. E. Simmons, *Leo Tolstoy,* Boston, 1946, 20–2; T. Sokolovskaia, "Obriadnost' prezhniago russkago masonstva," *RS,* 1907, Dec, 709–10.

115. Noted and deplored by Turgenev, Simmons, *Tolstoy,* 342.

116. J. Bienstock, *Tolstoy et les Doukh-obors,* 1902.

117. Tolstoy was the model for the superhuman Antichrist of Solov'-ev's last work, "Three Conversations," in *Anthology,* 229–48.

118. See I. Berlin, *The Hedgehog and the Fox,* NY, 1957, p, 75–124.

119. The general assumption that Alexander I died in 1825, that Kuzmich had no connection whatsoever with the Tsar, and that the legend is pure fantasy (see, for instance, S. Mel'gunov, *Dela i liudi,* 109–111) still needs critical re-examination in line with the questions posed by L. Liubimov's balanced study, *Taina Imperatora Aleksandra I,* Paris, 1938.

120. Cited in Liubimov, *Taina,* 78.

121. Pushkinsky Dom, L, Arkhiv "Russkoi Stariny," XVI, 1875–8, to *Russkaia Starina,* 1878, no. 1, esp. 122–6. Accounts differ about his last movements, but this one also mentions his visiting "a village inhabitant to see a religious ceremony," which may suggest sectarian contacts as well.

122. The words of Michael Viel'gorsky, leader of the last important "higher order" lodge to be founded in Russia prior to the prohibition by Alexander. "Iz aforizmov masona grafa M. Yu. Viel'gorskago o masonstve," *RS,* 1908, Nov, 391.

123. For the difficulties that faced the sculpting even of religious subjects as late as the 1750's, see "Iz istorii russkoi skulptury," *IL,* 1914, Jul, 874–7.

124. Bulich, *Ocherki,* I, 343; Veselovsky, *Vliianie,* 93.

125. Florovsky, *Puti,* 538.

126. "Nikolai Bestuzhev i ego zhivopisnoe nasledie," *LN,* LX, 1956, 20, 37–8, and picture 39. See also the discussion of his cultural activities during his long Siberian exile in *Studies in Romanticism,* 1965, summer, 185–205.

127. See Labry, *Herzen,* 143. Palingenesis occurs frequently in the titles of Masonic books. See A. Lantoine, *Histoire,* 231–2.

128. Katetov, *Speransky,* 61–2. See also T. Sokolovskaia, "Obriadnost' vol'-nykh kamenshchikov," in Mel'gunov, *et al., Masonstvo,* II, 80–112, for the most lucid general exposition of masonic symbols; also her "Obriadnost'," *RS,* 1907, Nov, 349–59; and Dec, 707–17.

129. Telepnev, "Freemasonry," 276.

130. *Kurzer Katechismus für teutsche Soldaten* was published in five editions under different titles between 1812–15, and was part of a joint Prussian-Russian ideological crusade against French ideas. The work was addressed to the people and soldiers rather than to the princes of Germany. See Nadler, *Imperator,* III, 91–139; esp. 106–7; 168, and 184–222.

131. M. Strange, *La Révolution,* 47 ff. Despite his own dedication to toleration, Voltaire feared that "dans l'Europe enfin l'heureux tolérantisme/ De tout esprit bien fait devient le catéchisme"—a conception which influenced Dostoevsky in his concept of the Grand Inquisitor. See Rammelmeyer, "Dostojevskij und Voltaire," 267 ff., and citation from Voltaire (*Oeuvres,* X, 402), 278.

132. From text in A. Borozdin, *Iz pisem i pokazanii dekabristov,* P, 1906, 87; see also *Ocherki . . . zhurnalistiki,* 200; Haumant, *La Culture,* 330–1.

133. M. Shcherbatov, *Puteshestvie v zemliu ofirskuiu G-na S. shvedskago dvorianina,* is included in *Sochineniia,* P, 1896–8, 2v. Shcherbatov is often remembered primarily for his glorification of pre-Petrine Russia in *O povrezhdenii nravov v Rossii* (written 1786–9, first published in 1858 by Herzen) and for his fifteen-volume history, which reached Shuisky by the time of his death in 1790. But he was a vigorous political theorist, beginning with his first French-

language work *Reflexions sur le gouvernement* (1759–60) and continuing through his activity on Catherine's legislative commission. His political theory is not identical with that of the *Puteshestvie*, his only novel. See the discussion and analysis by V. Fursenko in *RBS*, XXIV, 104–24; also M. Raeff, "State and Nobility in the Ideology of M. M. Shcherbatov," *ASR*, 1960, 363–79. Another neglected "utopian" romance of this period is the *Noveishie puteshestviia* of Vasily Levshin, which apparently portrays the "natural" harmony of dwellers on the moon, free from written laws, formal government, or ecclesiastical establishment. See Sipovsky, *Etapy*, 40–2.

134. Cited in Riasanovsky, *Nicholas*, 1.

135. *Ibid.*, 13. Even here, the role of Alexander in preparing the way for Nicholas' methods must be acknowledged. Alexander's creation of centralized ministries freed of any effective restraints led immediately in the view of some authorities to a "ministerial despotism" in which a semi-militarized command structure was imposed on the conduct of all civil affairs, thus denying any sense of creative participation in the business of government even to the nominally privileged classes. See E. Shumigorsky, "Nachalo biurokratii v Rossii," *RS*, 1908, Jan, 71–6.

136. M. Zagoskin, " 'Moskva i Moskvichi' zapiski Bogdana Il'icha Bel'-skago," *SS*, M, 1902, III, ch. ii, 1. Alexander had revived the idea of Moscow as Jerusalem (Nadler, *Imperator*, II, 133; III, 39–40); and the national school of music led by Balakirev and Musorgsky regularly referred to Moscow as "Jericho." J. Leyda and S. Bertensson, *The Musorgsky Reader*, NY, 1947, 7, 17.

137. The collection was edited in two parts by N. Nekrasov, the editor and poet, *Fiziologiia Peterburga*,

sostavlennaia iz trudov russkikh literatorov, P, 1844–5. For the impact of phrenology see P. Sakulin, *Iz istorii russkago idealizma: Kniaz' V. F. Odoevsky*, M, 1913, I, 488 ff.; for discussion of Nekrasov's collection and other brooding considerations of St. Petersburg during this period see the chapter "Physiology of Petersburg" in Lo Gatto, *Mito*, 176–205. See also the criticism of this collection (and of the naturalism associated with St. Petersburg) by Moscow-based journalists, who tended to agree with Bulgarin that "nature is good only when washed and combed." K. Harper, "Criticism of the Natural School in the 1840's," *ASR*, 1956, Oct, 403 note 3 and 400–14.

The controversy between the two cities in the 1840's even extended to matters of musical style and taste. See, for instance, A. Grigor'ev, "Moskva i Peterburg," *Moskovsky gorodskoi listok*, 1847, no. 43.

138. S. Shevyrev, *Istoriia Imperatorskago moskovskago universiteta*, M, 1855, 20. Moscow was chosen as the university site because of its greater population and central location (10). Shevyrev's readable centennial volume is useful in reflecting at times the romantic imagination of its author as well as reciting the often prosaic facts of university history.

139. From A. Khomiakov, *Dmitry Samozvanets* (1832), cited in A. Gratieux, *A. S. Khomiakov et le mouvement slavophile*, 1939, I, 23.

140. His project predated that of Magnitsky and attracted the admiration of Goethe (G. Schmid, ed., *Goethe und Uwarow und ihr Briefwechsel*, P, 1888) and the scorn of De Maistre *(LN, XXIX/XXX, 1937). The text of Uvarov's project is in *Études de philologie et de critique*, 1845, 1–48; his political ideas are best sketched in *Esquisses politiques et littéraires*,

1848. See also the bibliography in *RA*, 1871, 2106-7; and biography in *BE*, LXVII, 419-20.

"Archeology of General Metaphysics" is cited from N. Riasanovsky, "Russia and Asia," 174.

141. *Esquisses*, 187.
142. Cited in Sakulin, *Iz istorii*, I, 336.
143. *Eniseisky Al'manakh*, Krasnoiarsk, 1828, esp. 114-20. Fesler may have provided the model for these Mongolian novels with his *Attila, König der Hunnen*, Breslau, 1794. See Zotov's *Tsyn-Kiu-Tong, ili tri dobryia dela dukha t'my*, M, 1844; and *Posledny potomok Chingiskhana*, published posthumously, P, 1881. Zotov wrote and translated some 117 plays and novels, almost all on historical themes. See *BE*, XXIV, 688; *RBS*, XXIII,

484-94. *Yunost' Ioanna III, ili nashestvie Tamerlana na Rossiiu*, P, 1823.

There was already in eighteenth-century Russia an occasional tendency to see the Orient as the true source of wisdom and the secrets of happiness. See, for example, the work *Kitaisky mudrets, ili nauka zhit' blagopoluchno*, referenced in V. Malyshev, *Drevnerusskie rukopisi Pushkinskogo doma. Putevoditel'*, M-L, 1965, 94.

144. *Esquisses*, 64.
145. *Ibid.*, 42.
146. *Ibid.*, 42.
147. Suggested in Riasanovsky, *Nicholas*, 70-2.
148. *Esquisses*, 13.

3. THE "CURSED QUESTIONS"

1. This famous incident occurred under Alexander I, and is recounted along with other similar illustrations by I. Golovin, *La Russie sous Nicholas I[er]*, 1845, 131. For one of the best contemporary (or indeed subsequent) analyses of the links between the Russians and the Germans as they developed during the aristocratic century, climaxing under Nicholas, see S.-R. Taillandier, "Les Allemands en Russie et les Russes en Allemagne," *RDM*, 1854, VII, 633-91. See also F. Weigel, *La Russie envahie par les Allemands*, Paris–Leipzig, 1844.

Even the Russian national anthem, which was written at the Tsar's request by Alexis L'vov in 1833, was apparently plagiarized from a Prussian march of the early 1820's. See "Kto kompozitor nashego nyneshniago narodnago gimna," *RMG*, 1903, no. 52, 1313-14.
2. Golovin, *Russie*, 130.
3. This bon mot is cited in the Harvard Doctoral dissertation of S. Monas, the published version of which, *The Third Section: Police*

and Society in Russia under Nicholas I, Cambridge, Mass., 1961, provides a valuable picture of police controls at work under Nicholas. The most celebrated of all the shocked accounts by foreign visitors is the deservedly famous one by Marquis de Custine, *Russia*, London, 1854. See also the parallel development in an even more famous French conservative, Balzac, from high initial hopes to disillusionment with Nicholaevan Russia, *LN*, XXIX–XXX, 1937, 149-372. A reconstruction of the official thinking of the age giving rational balance to the picture is in N. Riasanovsky, *Nicholas I*.
4. Riasanovsky, *Nicholas*, 105-15.
5. A. Vasil'ev, *Lobachevsky*, P, 1914; I. Kuznetsov, *Liudi russkoi nauki*, M, 1961, 76-93; and A. Vucinich, "Nikolai Ivanovich Lobachevskii," *Isis*, LIII, 1962, 465-81. Vasil'ev's sketch in *RBS*, X, esp. 539-40, seems to indicate that Lobachevsky's relations with Magnitsky were not as hostile as Soviet authorities insist.

6. *Ibid.*, 94–103; *BE*, XL, 587–9; F. W. Struve, *Études d'astronomie stellaire*, P, 1847; and the almanac, *Kometa Bely*, P, 1833, esp. M. Pogodin, "Galeeva Kometa," 1–23.

  If Russian interests fled into outer space, they also burrowed deep into the earth. Russia acquired a sophisticated understanding of stratigraphy and conducted an important series of excavations in search of prehistoric animals (all through the St. Petersburg Mining Institute). See A. Borisiak, "Kratky ocherk istorii russkoi paleozoologii," *TIIE*, I, 1947, esp. 6–8. For an excellent description of the Pulkovo observatory under Struve by a contemporary Scottish astronomer, see C. Smyth, *Three Cities in Russia*, London, 1862, I, 73–186.

7. "Pervy sbornik pamiati Karla Maksimovicha Bera," *TKIZ*, 1927, no. 2, 56–7.

8. Krizhanich: "Russi inquam non verbis sed rebus sunt filosofi," *Dialogus de Calumnis, IA*, 1958, no. 1, 162.

9. Liubopytny, cited in A. Sinaisky, *Otnoshenie*, 300.

10. For the early travails of formal philosophy in Russia see Koyré, *La Philosophie*, 46–87; Radlov, *Ocherk*, 1–17; Vvedensky, "Sud'ba."

11. An important intermediate source of the doctrine of Sophia was the work of the German syncretic mystic and historian of heresy, Gottfried Arnold, *Das Geheimnis der göttlichen Sophia* (1700). See the new edition with intr. by W. Nigg, Stuttgart, 1963.

12. Quoted from his essay of 1798, "On the Pythagorean Quadrant in Nature," by E. Susini, *Franz von Baader et le romantisme mystique*, 1942, I, 256–7; also 235–79.

13. *Sofiia to est' Blagopriiatnaia vechnaia deva Bozhestvennoi premudrosti*, see P. Sakulin, *Iz istorii*, I, 424 note 2. Sakulin's work is the best general study of the transmission of the Boehmist tradition through Saint-Martin into Russia.

14. See Labzin's translation of Jung-Stilling, *Oblako*, title page and 7.

15. For the discussion of *Izbrannoe chtenie dlia liubitelei istinnoi filosofii, O pokaianii. Kratkoe ukazanie na kliuch razumeniia tainstv bozhikh, kakim obrazom dusha mozhet dostignut' sozertsaniia bozheskago v sebe*, P, 1819–20, and other such works, see S. P-v, "Perevodchiki," *BZ*, 1858, I, 134 ff.

16. Telepnev, "Some Aspects," 23. This was, of course, the greeting "Remember death" *(memento mori)*, of the Capuchin order.

17. Koyré, *Philosophie*, 37, note 3. The slogan, which is not traced in any Russian materials, is from Horaces *Epistles* (Liber I, Epistula II, line 40), though it had extensive intermediate usage in both German philosophy and Masonic literature.

18. V. Koshelev, *Zapiski*, 1883, 19; and the excellent account in Koyré, *Philosophie*, 33–45.

19. Particularly L. Oken, *Lehrbuch der Naturphilosophie*, Jena, 1809, 3v, which defines Naturphilosophie as "die Lehre von der ewigen Neuwandlung Gottes in die Welt." Koyré, 139, note 4; and 137–52, for the influence of Schelling.

20. Professor M. Pavlov, as described in A. Herzen, *Selected Philosophical Works*, M, 1956, 515.

21. Koyré, *La Philosophie*, 91, note 1; and, for the thought of Kireevsky, 164–93; and his *Études*, 1–17, where the conjoint influence of Schleiermacher is also brought out.

22. Ionescu-Nişkov, "Skovoroda," 157.

23. Nikitenko on Nadezhdin in 1834, quoted in N. Koz'min, *Nikolai Ivanovich Nadezhdin*, P, 1912, 260–1.

24. B. Koz'min, "Dva slova o slove 'Nigilist,'" *IAN(L)*, 1951, no. 4, 378–85. The method of transmission from early German uses in figures like Jacobi to Nadezhdin's

usage is a problem not seriously discussed in the materials on this subject (referenced in my "Intelligentsia," 810–11, note 9). One possibility is Baader, who refers in 1824 to the disintegration of Protestantism into two parts: a "destructive, scientific nihilism" and an "unscientific separatistic Pietism." *Sämtliche Werke*, Leipzig, 1851, I, 74.

25. Sakulin, *Iz istorii*, I, 462, 465, note 1, also 474–90.

26. V. Odoevsky, "Russkie nochi," in *Sochineniia*, P, 1844, I, 15. Besides Koyré's account of the influence of Schelling see M. Filippov, *Sud'by*, part I, and E. Bobrov, *Filosofiia*, esp. III and IV; and W. Setschkareff, *Schellings Einfluss in der russischen Literatur der 20er und 30er Jahre des XIX Jahrhunderts*, 1939. Note that the principal initial popularizer of Schelling's world view was (as so often in the past with heretical cosmologies) a doctor: D. Vellansky, professor at the medical-surgical academy of St. Petersburg. The influence of Schelling paralleled and occasionally merged with that of Baader. See discussion and references on both figures in Riasanovsky, *Nicholas*, 173–7.

27. Baron A. Haxthausen's famous study of the Russian peasantry (*Studien über die innern Zustände, das Volksleben und insbesondere die ländlichen Einrichtungen Russlands*, Hanover-Berlin, 1847–52, 3v) profoundly influenced the Slavophiles; while Hilferding was in turn influenced by them to undertake extensive investigations during his forty-two-year life not only of the *byliny* of the Onega region, but of the interconnections of all Slavic popular literature and their connections with earlier languages and cultures. See his *Sochineniia*, P, 1868–74, 4v.

28. Riasanovsky, *Nicholas*, 102 ff.

29. See articles by E. Gavrilova, *Is-*

kusstvo, 1959, no. 7, 72–4; and E. Atsarkina, *Iskusstvo*, 1952, no. 3, 73–80.

30. See D. Mirsky's review of V. Zhirmunsky, *Bairon i Pushkin*, L, 1924, in *SEER*, 1924, Jun, 209–11.

31. V. Koshelev, cited in Koyré, *Philosophie*, 148.

32. Schelling's comment to P. Kireevsky, cited in Sakulin, *Iz istorii*, I, 349, note 2.

33. Herzen, *PSS i pisem*, P, XLII, 243 ff. See the basic discussions by C. Quénet (*Tchaadaev et les lettres philosophiques*, 1931) and A. Koyré (*Études*, 20–102). R. McNally is preparing a newer and fuller translation than has yet appeared; M. Malia, a new French edition.

34. Letter to A. Turgenev of 1837 in M. Gershenzon, ed., *Sochineniia i pis'ma P. Ya. Chaadaeva*, M, 1913, I, 214. Cf. his references between 1833–5 to Russia's "universal mission" (I, 188) to solve "all the questions which Europe is debating" (I, 181) and "to pronounce one day the answer to the human enigma." (I, 182).

35. In 1834, cited in Koyré, *Études*, 70, note 1.

36. Cited in Koz'min *Nadezhdin*, 231; also 82–5.

37. Cited in Sakulin, *Iz istorii*, I, 574.

38. H. Desmettre, *A. Towianski et le messianisme polonais*, Lille, 1947, 2v; Weintraub, *Literature as Prophecy;* and "Adam Mickiewicz the Mystic-Politician," *HSS*, I, 1953, 137–78; and on the Society of Cyril and Methodius, P. Sakulin, *Literatura*, ch. 1, 288–312. See also, among many relevant studies by W. Lednicki, his ranging "Christ et révolution dans la poésie russe et polonaise," in *Mélanges Legras*, 99–121.

39. Cited in Koyré, *La Philosophie*, 160, note 1. The expression was italicized in Pogodin's text.

40. Cited in P. Struve, "S. P. Shevyrev i zapadnyia vnusheniia i istochniki

teorii-aforizma o 'gnilom' ili 'gni-iushchem' zapade," *ZNIB*, XVII, 1940, 263, note 10. See also M. Kovalevsky, "Filosofskoe ponimanie sudeb russkago proshlago mysliteliami i pisateliami 30-kh i 40-kh godov," *VE*, 1915, Dec, 163–201.

41. Cited from *RDM*, 1840, Nov, 363–4, in Struve, "Shevyrev," 229–30.

42. *RDM*, 1840, Nov, 364, cited in Struve, "Shevyrev," 230. Struve sees, as a key influence on both Chasles and Chaadaev, the Danish Catholic Baron d'Eckstein (233–6).

43. Odoevsky, *Sochineniia*, I, 309–12.

44. Cited in Sakulin, *Iz istorii*, I, 593.

45. Odoevsky, *Sochineniia*, I, 100–11.

46. Odoevsky, *Povesti i rasskazy*, M, 1959, 422; story reprinted 416–48. See the discussion of various drafts 490–3; and P. Sakulin, "Russkaia ikariia," *Sovremennik*, 1912, kn. 12, 193–206; *Iz istorii*, I, ch. ii, esp. 178–84, for other utopias of the period; and the perceptive critical comments of Belinsky (one of the few to take it seriously) even before publication; *OZ*, 1839, Dec, 3–15.

47. "Umom Rossiiu ne poniat',/ Arshinom obshchim ne izmerit':/ U nei osobennaia stat' — / V Rossiiu mozhno tol'ko verit'." F. Tiutchev, *PSS*, P, 1913, 202. See also the introductory essay to this volume by V. Briusov, and D. Stremooukhoff, *La Poésie*, 1937, esp. 45–54.

48. Gratieux, *Khomiakov*, II, 50–78. Text and notes were published in his *PSS*, M, 1878, III; 1882, IV.

49. N. Riasanovsky makes this comparison in detail, *Russia and the West*, 215–18. Actually, Khomiakov's two contending camps are considerably closer theologically to the eighteenth-century Dukhobors' "Sons of Cain" (Slaves to the Flesh) and "Sons of Abel" (Fighters for the Spirit), *BSE(1)*, XXIII, 651–3, though Khomiakov

was temperamentally far closer to the tolerant and pietistic romantics than to the fanatical and authoritarian sectarians. Important new works on the Slavophiles are P. Christoff, *An Introduction to Nineteenth-Century Russian Slavophilism: A Study in Ideas*, Vol. 1: *A. S. Xomjakov*, The Hague, 1961; also A. Walicki, *W Kręgu konserwatywnej utopii*, Warsaw, 1964; and "Personality and Society in the Ideology of Russian Slavophiles," *CSS*, II, 1963, 1–20.

The discussion by E. H. Carr (" 'Russia and Europe' as a Theme . . .") suggests a somewhat more inclusive definition by pointing out (368 note 2) that the term "Slavophile" was actually first used in the beginning of the nineteenth century in derisive reference to Shishkov (a reactionary opponent of linguistic modernization who is solemnly excluded from the "Slavophile" ranks by all authorities); and by designating some of the chauvinistic expansionists of the post-Crimean War period (who were also often called Slavophiles in their time, but who are now generally set apart as Pan-Slavs) the "second wave of Slavophilism."

50. Gratieux, *Khomiakov*, I, 19–24.

51. Letter of Jun 2, 1821, in De Maistre, *Lettres et opuscules*, 1851, I, 584–5.

52. Cited in Sakulin, *Iz istorii*, I, 348, note 2; and 343–7 for the influence of Lamennais; also Sakulin, *Literatura*, 14–9, for the influence of Lamennais and another less-known early Christian socialist, A. de Villeneuve-Bargement, esp. his *Economie politique chrétienne*, 1834. For Lamennais' later influence on the *Petrashevtsy*, see V. Semevsky, *Iz istorii obshchestvennykh idei v Rossii v kontse 1840-kh godov*, Rostov/Don, 1905, 27–9.

Chaadaev was influenced by Lamennais as well as De Maistre in his search for a new spiritual answer for the human condition; but was repelled by Lamennais' deification of the people and wrote a cutting critique of Christian socialism: "How can one search for reason in a mob? Where has a crowd ever been rational? *Was hat das Volk mit der Vernunft zu schaffen? . . ."* (*Sochineniia,* I, 300–1).

53. N. Rusanov, "Vliianie zapadnoevropeiskago sotsializma na russky," *MG,* 1908, May-Jun, 14.

54. As related by Hippolyte-Nicolas-Just Auger, "Iz zapisok Ippolita Ozhe," *RA, 1877,* kn. 2, 61; also, on Auger, *RA,* 1877, kn. 1, 519.

55. "Iz zapisok," 65–6.

56. See my "Intelligentsia," 807–8 and notes.

57. M. Saltykov, "Za rubezhom," *Izbrannye sochineniia,* M-L, 1940, 30.

58. Cited in Sakulin, *Iz istorii,* I, 346–7.

59. A. Herzen, *PSS i pisem,* P, I, 71, 117, and esp. 126.

60. Billington, *Mikhailovsky,* 32–40; "Intelligentsia," 812–5.

61. N. Polevoy, *Istoriia russkago naroda,* 1829–33, 6v; V. Belinsky, *N. A. Polevoy,* P, 1846, in *PSS,* IX, 671–96. In the same spirit, the Slavophile journalist and editor N. Giliarov-Platonov criticized Macarius' massive history of the Russian Church for dealing with the institution and particularly the hierarchy of the church rather than the history of popular spirituality: "the life of the Russian people as a society of believing people." Cited in V. Senatov, *Filosofiia istorii staroobriadchestva,* M, 1908, vyp. I, 22. (This review when it first appeared in the 1850's was severely censored and delayed for several years in publication — as were many of the writings of Aksakov and the more radical Slavophiles.)

62. Cited in F. Nelidov, *Zapadniki 40kh godov,* M, 1910, xxxiv. For Stankevich's translation of a French vulgarization of Hegel see N. Stankevich, *Stikhotvoreniia, tragediia, proza,* M, 1890, 183–238. For his thanks for having "the chains taken from my soul" by Hegel see Stankevich, *Perepiska,* M, 1914, 450. For succinct discussion and critical review of the literature on Hegel's influence in Russia see Koyré, *Études,* 103–70; see also M. Kovalevsky, "Shellingianstvo i gegel'ianstvo v Rossii," *VE,* 1915, Nov, 133–70; and D. Chizhevsky, *Gegel' v Rossii,* Paris, 1939. For the role of Hegel in Poland and throughout the Slavic world see Chizhevsky, ed., *Hegel bei den Slaven,* Bad Homburg, 1961. Hegel (like Schelling, though not so emphatically or frequently) had predicted a great future for Russia. See B-P. Hepner, *Bakounine et le panslavisme révolutionnaire,* 1950, 93, note 21.

63. Letter to Bakunin of Sep 10, 1838, in Belinsky, *PSS,* M, 1956, XI, 296.

64. *Ibid.,* 293–4.

65. Letter of Feb 4, 1837, in A. Kornilov, *Molodye gody Mikhaila Bakunina, iz istorii russkago romantizma,* M, 1915, I, 376.

66. I. Kireevsky, *PSS,* M, 1861, II, 296; also 318–25. The older generation of Russian romantics looked eagerly to Schelling to uproot the "fatalistic logic" of Hegel after the German government moved him into the chair in Berlin University that Hegel had once held. Chaadaev wrote to Schelling in 1842 that he was providing leadership in the "intellectual crisis which will probably decide the future of our civilization." (*Zven'ia,* V, 1935, 219; also 225, and 219–32); and Russians also looked on Baader as providing an underpinning for Slavophile ideology, a means of restoring the Christian faith from alleged onslaughts of Hegel. See Baader's *Revision der Philosopheme der*

Hegel'schen Schule bezüglich auf das Christenthum, nebst zehn Thesen aus einer religiösen Philosophie, Stuttgart, 1835; Struve, "Shevyrev," esp. 210 ff.

67. M. Bakunin, *God and the State,* NY, 1916; *L'Empire Knouto-Germanique et la Révolution Sociale* (1871), reprinted as *La Révolution sociale ou la dictature militaire,* 1946. On Herzen's Hegelianism, see *PSS i pisem,* II, 242, and passage on the movement of humanity toward self-consciousness in III, 137.

68. Belinsky, *PSS,* XII, 22–3.

69. *Ibid.,* 70–1.

70. P. Lavrov, *Istoricheskie pis'ma,* P, 1906, 358.

71. Koyré, *Études,* 161.

72. Hepner, *Bakounine,* esp. 236–84; Herzen, "The Russian People and Socialism," (letter to Jules Michelet) in I. Berlin, intr., *From the Other Shore,* London, 1956, 165–208. Also comparison of two figures (partial to Herzen) by Berlin; and image of the commune by Herzen as compatible with (if not a guarantor of) individual liberties by M. Malia, "Herzen and the Peasant Commune," in E. Simmons, *Continuity,* 197–217. For this entire period and these contesting figures see I. Berlin, "The Marvelous Decade," *Encounter,* 1955, Jun, 27–39; Nov, 21–9; Dec, 22–43 (on Belinsky); 1956, May, 20–34 (on Herzen); and two excellent panoramic sets of memoirs: Herzen, *My Past and Thoughts,* NY, 1924–8, 6v, and P. Annenkov, *Literaturnye vospominaniia,* M, 1960 (the term "remarkable decade" having been coined by the latter). A. Walicki stresses the impact of Feuerbach on Belinsky and Herzen in his "Hegel, Feuerbach and the Russian 'Philosophical Left,' 1836–1848," in *Annali dell'Instituto Giangiacomo Feltrinelli,* Milan, 1963, 105–36.

The development of the tradi-tion of salons and circles throughout the first half of the nineteenth century is admirably and vividly traced in the anthology introduced and edited by N. Brodsky, *Literaturnye salony i kruzhki,* M-L, 1930.

73. Letter to his son prefatory to *From the Other Shore,* 3.

74. *Selected Philosophic Essays,* 576–95.

75. Khomiakov, *PSS,* M, 1878, 2d ed., I, 695.

76. Matter, *Saint-Martin,* 354–68; Weintraub, *Literature,* 13–17.

77. "Uchit' narod dobru—obiazannost' poeta!/ On istinny gerol'd, uchitel' grozny sveta,/ Ego udel porok razit' i oblichat',/ Liudei na pravy put' nastavit', nauchat'./ Poet khristianin est' organ istin vechnykh." Cited in Koz'min, *Nadezhdin,* 12. On Schelling's impact on Russian literature and aesthetics see Setschkareff, *Schellings Einfluss,* esp. 6–29 on the Schellingian professors. For the influence of Swedenborg on occult romanticism see E. Benz, "Swedenborg und Lavater. Über die religiösen Grundlagen der Physiognomik," in *Zeitschrift für Kirchengeschichte,* LVII, 1938, 153–216; also F. Horn, *Schelling und Swedenborg,* Zurich, 1954.

Venevitinov echoed the definition in Schelling's *Bruno:* "die Philosophie sei die höchste poesie," in Setschkareff, *Einfluss,* 53; Bobrov, *Filosofiia,* II, 8. Cf. Nadezhdin "Poeziia i filosofiia—vot dusha sushchago/ eto zhizn', liubov'; vne ikh vse mertvo." Cited in Nelidov, *Zapadniki,* 49.

78. As cited in Koyré, *Études,* 155.

79. Ya. Polonsky as cited in Billington, *Mikhailovsky,* 93; Odoevsky, as cited in Sakulin, *Iz istorii,* I, 502.

80. V. Timofeeva, cited in Billington, *Mikhailovsky,* 63.

81. Quoted in Sakulin, *Iz istorii,* 413–14, note 3; Koyré, *La Philosophie,* 139–45. On Venevitinov and the

poetry of the 1820's see G. Wytrzens, *Dmitrij Vladimirovič Venevitinov als Dichter der russischen Romantik,* Cologne, 1962. Venevitinov's "Sculpture, painting and music," *Severnaia Lira,* 1827, 315–23; *Sochineniia,* 127–30. See also Gogol, "Skul'ptura, zhivopis' i muzyka," *PSS,* L, 1952, VIII, 9–13.

82. N. Stankevich, *Stikhotvoreniia,* 174–5. See also 176–82, "The Relationship of Philosophy to Literature."

83. N. Beliavsky, "Lermontov-khudozhnik," *Iskusstvo,* 1939, no. 5, 5–20.

84. Nadezhdin cited in M. Filippov, *Sud'ba filosofii,* 184.

85. D. Mirsky, *Pushkin,* London, 1926, 150.

For a perceptive critical discussion of some of the vast literature on Pushkin see M. Gorlin, *Études littéraires et historiques,* 1957, 2d ed., 119–37. Writing in 1937, Gorlin bemoans the lack of clear general presentations and philosophical analyses of Pushkin's work. For a succinct, recent general characterization stressing the classical and aristocratic sides of Pushkin see M. Dowia, "Pushkin," *OSP,* I, 1950, 1–15; also E. Wilson, *The Triple Thinkers,* NY, 1963, corr. ed., p, 31–59 (including a translation of *The Bronze Horseman*). The particularly valuable essay in Frank's collection, "Pushkin kak politichesky myslitel'," should be consulted in the separate edition, Belgrade, 1937, which also includes a good general introduction by P. Struve. For articles covering a wide variety of subjects in Pushkin's thought see S. Cross and E. Simmons, eds., *Centennial Essays for Pushkin,* Cambridge, Mass., 1937.

86. V. Yakovlev, *Pushkin i muzyka,* M-L, 1949; M. Zagorsky, *Pushkin i teatr,* M, 1940.

87. Lifar, *History of Ballet,* 65–6.

88. Frank, *Etiudy,* 28.

89. "Zautra kazn', privychny pir narodu;/ No lira iunogo pevtsa/ O chem poet? Poet ona svobodu:/ Ne izmenilas' do kontsa!/ . . . No ty, sviashchennaia svoboda,/ Bogini chistaia, net,—ne vinovna ty." A. Pushkin, *Sochineniia,* M, 1955, I, 199; and Mirsky, *Pushkin,* 57–60, for the influence of Chenier on Pushkin.

90. Frank, *Etiudy,* 56.

91. Cited together with other similar expressions of Pushkin's underlying pessimism in Frank, *Etiudy,* 112.

92. "E. I. Guber," *Kosmopolis,* 1898, Apr, 34–59; May, 162–9; see the vast study of Goethe's influence in Russia in *LN,* IV–VI, 1932, esp. 961–993, on Russian translations, and bibliography 996–1007. There were forty nine different Russian translations of all or part of *Faust* (989).

93. Stremooukhoff, *La Poésie,* esp. 90–101, stresses the influence of Goethe on Tiutchev.

94. M. Baring's translation cited in Mirsky, *Pushkin,* 98, is used here despite the slight modulation in meaning from "Otverzlis' veshchie zenitsy,/ kak u ispugannoi orlitsy." *Sochineniia,* I, 223.

95. M. Gorlin, "The Interrelationship of Painting and Literature in Russia," *SEER,* 1946, Nov, 134–48.

96. Stankevich, *Stikhotvoreniia,* 31–2.

97. Cited in G. Semin, *Sevastopol: istorichesky ocherk,* M, 1955, 24.

98. I. Murav'ev-Apostol, *Puteshestvie po Tavride v 1820 gode,* P, 1823; and the discussion of this book as well as Pushkin and Mickiewicz in S. Karlinsky, "The Amber Beads of Crimea," *CSS,* II, 1963, 108–20. In addition to works there cited, the writings of the mystical patriot and poetic admirer of the Russian navy Semen Bobrov played a role in developing this romantic cult. See his *Tavrida,* Nikolaev, 1798, retitled *Khersonida* in the second edition, P, 1804.

The increased nineteenth-century Russian interest in Dante is discussed in *Italia che Scrive*, 1921, Apr, 69–70; May, 94.

99. On Zinaida Volkonsky see Gorodetzky, "Zinaida"; and *LN*, IV–VI, 1932, 478 ff.; on Gogol's love of Rome and occasional signs of sympathy for Catholicism see D. Borghese, *Gogol a Roma*, Florence, 1957.

100. V. Rozanov, cited in D. Magarshack, *Gogol. A Life*, London, 1957, 16.

101. On Narezhny, see *LE*, VII, 589–91 with bibliography; A. Fadeev, "Peredovaia russkaia intelligentssia i tsarsky kolonializm v doreformenny period," in *Problemy . . . Tikhomirova*, 398–9. Parts 4–6 of Narezhny's *Rossiisky Zhil' Blaz, ili pokhozhdeniia kniazia Gavrily Simonovicha Chistiakova* were confiscated and destroyed because of various irreverent comments on Russian life and institutions in the first three parts (1814). *Cherny god, ili gorskie kniaz'ia* was written earlier, but not published until four years after Narezhny's death. His works were published posthumously in ten parts, P, 1835–6, and widely discussed during the period in which Gogol was writing *Dead Souls*. The germinal idea for *Dead Souls* probably came, however, from Pushkin via Vladimir Dal, the great student of folklore and linguistics. See E. Bobrov, "Iz istorii russkoi literatury XVIII i XIX st," *IIaS*, 1910, 67–74.

102. Cited in Magarshack, *Gogol*, 250–1. For Gogol's ideas see D. Chizhevsky, "The Unknown Gogol," *SEER*, XXX, 1952, Jun, 476–93; V. Zenkovsky, "Gogol als Denker," *ZSPh*, IX, 1932, 104–30; and "Die ästhetische Utopie Gogols," *ZSPh*, XII, 1936, 1–34. The latter is a particularly interesting analysis of Gogol's frenzied and eventually despairing effort to believe that beauty alone can lead to the good.

See also V. Gippius, *Gogol*, P, 1924.

103. Here as in the case of Pushkin's *Bronze Horseman*, I have echoed in somewhat modified form a judgment of Prince Mirsky. See his *History*, 160.

104. Though Zhivago and other oppressed figures in Soviet literature are in part direct descendants of the hero of Gogol's tale, the authoritarian overseers of culture in the USSR are still anxious to claim this story as their own. A. Gerasimov, president of the Soviet Academy of Arts and high priest of uncompromising "socialist realism," has insisted that "Russian literature passed through its entire course in Gogol's 'Greatcoat' . . . in that greatcoat it should still be clothed today." Cited by S. Gerasimov in *XXII s'ezd KPSS i voprosy ideologicheskoi raboty*, M, 1962, 102.

105. Cited from an article of 1834 in N. Mashkovtsev, "N. V. Gogol' i izobrazitel'noe iskusstvo," *Iskusstvo*, 1959, no. 12, 46 (see 46–51 for other of Gogol's theoretical pronouncements on the visual arts).

106. Cited in Gorlin, "Interrelation," 137. For the relationship between Gogol and Ivanov (also between Gogol and other painters) see N. Mashkovtsev, *Gogol' v krugu khudozhnikov: ocherki*, M, 1955.

There is a curious parallel between Gogol's admiring attitude to Ivanov and that of John Keats's somewhat earlier toward his "everlasting friend" Benjamin Haydon. The latter painted a great canvas ("Christ's Entry into Jerusalem") on a theme similar to Ivanov's, and like Ivanov incorporated the faces of his literary friends into the work. See Hyder Rollins, *The Keats Circle*, Cambridge, Mass., 1948, I, xc–xciii.

107. Cited by L. Réau, "Un Peintre romantique russe: Alexandre Ivanov," *RES*, XXVII, 1951, 229. See also his *Art Russe*, II, 141–54.

A full recent study of the painter is provided by M. Alpatov, *Aleksandr Andreevich Ivanov: zhizn' i tvorchestvo*, M, 1956, 2v; but older studies (particularly M. Botkin, *Aleksandr Andreevich Ivanov: ego zhizn' i perepiska 1806–58*, P, 1880) often penetrate more deeply into the peculiar ideological anguish of Ivanov.

108. V. Zummer, "Eskhatologiia Aleksandra Ivanova," *NZK*, vyp III, 1929, 387 (also the entire invaluable article with many citations from otherwise unpublished materials, 387–409). More materials on the "project of the golden age of Russian artists" are referenced by A. Askariants and N. Mashkovtsev in "Arkhiv A. A. i S. A. Ivanovykh," *ZOR*, XX, 1958, 27–8.

109. Cited in Zummer, 388.

110. Botkin, *Ivanov*, 411–12; also 423. See also G. Pavlutsky, "Istochniki khudozhestvennago tvorchestva A. A. Ivanova," *Iskusstvo*, 1914, 1–9.

111. Cited in A. Andreev, "Eskizy A.A. Ivanova iz bibleiskoi istorii," *Mir Iskusstva*, 1901, no. 10, 239 note. Particularly important in instilling a sense of mission in Ivanov (and in stimulating popular interest in his work) was the work of the neglected Slavophile-industrialist Fedor Chizhov, *Pis'ma o rabotakh russkikh khudozhnikov v Rime*, M, 1845. He cited Ivanov as proof that Russian *"narodnost'* had a content peculiar to itself" (14); that "we dwellers of the north" can recapture our essential "brotherhood with the artist" (6), who in turn can help re-create "the golden age" when paintings "often became the source of faith" (4).

112. Cited in Zummer, "Eskhatologiia," 403; see also 409.

113. *Ibid.*, 401, also 403, 405–6; and Zummer, "O vere i khrame Aleksandra Ivanova," *Khristianskaia Mysl'*, 1917, nos. 9–10, 50, 57.

114. Zummer, "Eskhatologiia," 395. The proposed over-all iconography represented a curious blend of the tradition of ecclesiastical fresco painting into the Masonic concept of a supra-confessional pantheon of heroes. Mythological gods and great men were to be depicted along with Christian saints and martyrs, and the temple was to be a consecrated building, though not a church. See Zummer, "Sistema bibleiskikh kompozitsii A. A. Ivanova," *Iskusstvo*, 1914, i–xxi.

There are some curious similarities between Ivanov's proposed frescoes and the great painting that Ingres was undertaking in the 1840's in an attempt to redecorate a castle with symbols of "the golden age." Like Ivanov, Ingres spent much of his life in Rome. Moreover, he later attracted the attention of Napoleon III in rather the way that Ivanov attracted that of Nicholas I. However, Ingres' project was more secular in subject matter. See N. Schlenoff, *Ingres: ses sources littéraires*, 1956, 246–70.

115. Zummer, "O vere," 60–1.

116. A. Ivanov, *Izobrazheniia iz sviashchennoi istorii*, Berlin–St. Petersburg, 1879–84, plates 21 and 60. See also, for illustration of other points, 81–2, 88–9, 111–15. This is a rare but invaluable collection of large reproductions.

117. Cited by D. Filosofov in his "Ivanov i Vaznetsov v otsenke Aleksandra Benua," *Mir Iskusstva*, 1901, no. 10, 226. See also Botkin, *Ivanov*, 409–10. This quote alone should be enough to prove the inaccuracy of the comparison frequently made between the late work of Ivanov and that of the pre-Raphaelites.

118. Cited in Botkin, *Ivanov*, 287.

119. Koyré, *Études*, 38, note 1. Chaadaev revealed that he conceived of his self-assigned role of "precursor" not in traditional Christian but in occult Masonic terms—by changing the title of

Kant's book to "An Apologia for the Reason of Adam" (*Apologie der adamitischen Vernunft*). The importance of the festival on June 24 of John the Baptist was apparently related to the coincidence of the day of greatest sunlight with that of "the precursor"; and the ceremony was already the central one in eighteenth-century Russian Masonry. See, for instance, the correspondence of A. Petrov with Karamzin, *RA*, 1863, vyp. 5–6, 476 note.

120. G. Huard, *L'Art royal.*

121. *LN*, "Gersten i Ogarev I," M, 1953, 167.

122. Cited in V. Semevsky, *Iz istorii*, 1904, 29, note 1.

123. Khomiakov, *PSS*, M, 1878, 2d ed., I, 695. M. Kovalevsky contends (in the guide to the pre-revolutionary Ivanov exhibit, *Otdelenie iziashchnykh iskusstv, Imperatorsky Rumiantsovsky Muzei*, M, 1915, 103–46, note 109) that because of repeated illnesses, Ivanov was able to work actively on the painting for only twelve years of his long exile.

124. Some of the ensembles of the early nineteenth century (such as the university buildings at Kazan) were constructed over a period of time even longer than that taken to build St. Isaac's. See N. Evsina, "Zdaniia Kazanskogo universiteta," *Pamiatniki Kul'tury, IV*, 1963, 107–27. For the cult of the Renaissance, see Veselovsky, *Vliianie*, 135.

125. V. Pecherin cited in M. Gershenzon, *Zhizn' V. S. Pecherina*, M, 1910, 54.

126. "Akh, ne s nami obitaet/ Genii chistoi krasoty:/ Lish' poroi on naveshchaet/ Nas s nebesnoi vysoty." Cited with other Russian tributes to the painting by M. Alpatov, "Sistinskaia madonna Rafaelia," *Iskusstvo*, 1959, no. 3, 66–8. See also Lermontov, *PSS*, M, 1947, I, 100–1. This fascination dates back at least to Novalis, who likened his own romantic philosophy to "a fragment of some ruined picture of Raphael" (*Henry of Ofterdingen*, Cambridge, Mass., 1842, 228), and Hegel, who placed Raphael at the zenith of his aesthetics. The fascination continues even among uncultured Russians of the Soviet period. See Marshal Konev's description of his awe upon discovering the Sistine Madonna in its hiding place outside Dresden at the end of World War II: *NYT*, Aug 23, 1965, 33.

127. A. Nikitenko, "Rafaeleva sistinskaia madonna," *RV*, 1857, Oct, kn. I, 586.

128. Lunin, *Sochineniia*, 15.

129. Belinsky, letter to Botkin from Dresden on July 7/19, 1847, in *PSS*, XII, 384.

130. Alpatov, "Madonna"; Uvarov, *Esquisses*, 180–1.

131. Gogol, *PSS*, L, 1952, VIII, 146, and 143–7. Magarshack, *Gogol*, 78–80. For the feminine models used for both Christ and John the Baptist in Ivanov's "Appearance," see A. Novitsky, *Al'bom etiudov kartin i risunkov k opytu polnoi biografii A. A. Ivanova*, M, 1895, xl.

The important if elusive interrelationship of sexual and ideological attachments in the Nicholaevan period has been examined in L. Leger's study of Zhukovsky (*La Russie intellectuelle*, 130–48; H. McLean, "Gogol's Retreat from Love: Toward an Interpretation of *Mirgorod*," *American Contributions to the Fourth International Congress of Slavicists*, 's Gravenhage, 1958, 225–43; and A. Malinin, *Kompleks Edipa i sud'ba Bakunina, k voprosu o psikhologii bunta*, Belgrade, 1943. Prince Viazemsky said of the poet Yazykov's mystical patriotism of this period that he was simply and literally "in love with Russia." V. Smirnov, *Zhizn' i poeziia A.M. Yazykova*, Perm, 1900, 212. Some idea of the dimensions of this problem can be gained by reading, successively, I. Zamotin, *Romantizm dvadtsatykh godov XIX stoletiia v russkoi literature*, P-M, 1911, 2v; P. Miliukov, "Liubov' idealistov tridtsatykh godov," in *Iz istorii russkoi intelligentsii*, P, 1903; and E. H. Carr, *The Romantic Exiles*, NY, 1933.

Still awaiting biographical study is the remarkable figure of Elena Gan (Hahn), a kind of Russian George Sand, whose active career as a novelistic advocate of women's rights and dignity was brought to a premature end with her death in 1842 at the age of twenty-eight. See material in *IIaS*, 1914, XIX, kn. 2, 211–63; and *RM*, 1911, no. 12, 54–73. She was the sister of the future Pan-Slav Rostislav Fadeev and mother of the future founder of the Theosophical Society, Helena Blavatsky.

For psychologically oriented studies of key radical figures that do not emphasize distinctively sexual problems so much as the general problems of personal alienation and search for identity, see P. Sakulin, "Psikhologiia Belinskago," *GM*, 1914, no. 3, 85–121; and M. Malia's detailed study of the young Herzen, *Alexander Herzen and the Birth of Russian Socialism, 1812–1855*, Cambridge, Mass., 1961.

132. See M. Malia, "Schiller and the Early Russian Left," *HSS*, IV, 1959, 169–200; and, in addition to materials cited therein, Yu. Veselovsky's study in *RM*, 1906, no. 2; and the anthology of Russian commentary on Schiller edited by W. Düwel, *Tribun der Menschheit*, 1957. See also E. Kostka, *Schiller in Russian Literature*, Philadelphia, 1965.

133. Ivanov, *Izobrazheniia*, plate 28.

134. S. Bulgakov, cited in V. Riabushinsky, "Icons," 47. For the powerful initial impact of Raphael's painting on Bulgakov, see his "Dve vstrechi," in *Avtobiograficheskiia zametki*, Paris, 1946, 103–13.

135. Belinsky, *Izbrannye filosofskie sochineniia*, M, 1941, 143.

136. For Sand's influence, see Veselovsky, *Vliianie*, 224–31, 246–7. M. Gorlin deals almost entirely with this period in his "Hoffmann en Russie," *Études littéraires et historiques*, 1957, 189–205.

137. N. Nilsson, *Gogol et Pétersbourg*, Stockholm, 1954, deals largely with Jouy's influence on Gogol's portrayal of St. Petersburg.

138. *Ibid.*, 156–7; also W. Schamschula, *Der russische historische Roman vom Klassizismus bis zur Romantik*, Meisenheim/Glan, 1961, 152 and 85–7. Note also the self-confessed influence of Scott on one of the assassins of Alexander II. P. Shchegolev, "K biografii N. I. Kibalchicha," *KiS*, 1930, no. 11, 47. The importance of Scott is stressed in G. Lukacs, *The Historical Novel*, Boston, 1963, p. 30 ff. See also P. Struve, "Walter Scott and Russia," *SEER*, 1933, Jan, 397–410.

139. McEachran, *Herder*, 5.

140. On his version of *Hamlet* see G. Makogonenko, ed., *Russkie dramaturgi XVIII–XIX vv*, M-L, 1959, esp. 9, 17, 104–6; for the date, however, see A. Sumarokov, *Izbrannye sochineniia*, L, 1957, 35, note 1. The play was first performed in Russia in 1750—nineteen years before its first French production. See the generally complimentary study by D. Lang, "Sumarokov's 'Hamlet,'" *Modern Languages Review*, 1948, Jan, 67–72.

141. Zetlin, *Decembrists*, 25; Evreinov, *Histoire*, 133–4.

142. Veselovsky, *Vliianie*, 80, note 3. For the tradition of treating the monologues as "loud tirades" to be rewritten by the actor and interrupted with applause by the audience see Timofeev, *Vliianie*,

90. For the suggestion that the reading of the "To be" monologue may have been derived from Voltaire's contention that it is an anti-Christian speech see I. Aksenov, *Gamlet i drugie opyty*, M, 1930, 134–5.

143. "Perepiska Karamzina s Lafaterom," 26; see also 44–51.

144. Karamzin, *Briefe eines russischen Reisenden*, 1959, 193–207, 528–9.

145. Sukhomlinov, *Izsledovaniia*, I, 424–5; M. Strange, *La Révolution*, 144–6; and N. Kotliarevsky, *Mirovaia skorb' v kontse XVIII i v nachale XIX veka*, P, 1914, 3d cd. For the general European background of the concern see L. Crocker, "The Discussion of Suicide in the Eighteenth Century," *JHI*, 1952, Jan, 47–72.

146. Belinsky, *PSS*, IX, 674. For Ivanov, the "final question" of all his anguished reflection on art was "Is painting to be or not to be?," Zummer, "O vere," 47.

147. Hegel, *Sämtliche Werke*, Stuttgart, 1928, XIII, 195–207. "ohne kräftiges Lebensgefühl . . . Bildungslosigkeit." 204–5.

148. Belinsky, " 'Gamlet' Drama Shekspira. Mochalov v roli Gamleta," *PSS*, M, 1953, II, 253–345. For Hegel's many uses of *individuum* see *Sämtliche Werke*, XXIX, 1112–16.

149. R. Jakobson, "Marginalia to Vasmer's *Russian Etymological Dictionary (R-Ya)*," *International Journal of Slavic Linguistics and Poetics*, 1959, I–II, 274.

150. Nelidov, *Zapadniki*, 29, and note 1. For a summary of the impact of Mochalov and controversy about him see D. Tal'nikov, "Mochalovskaia 'zagadka'," *Teatr*, 1948, Mar, 26–33. See also Stankevich, *Perepiska*, 509–10.

The romantic tendency to see in the performances of a brilliant, enigmatic actor hidden sources of inspired prophecy was intensified by the extraordinary impact of the French actor Talma during the Revolutionary and Napoleonic era. Napoleon referred to Alexander I as "the Talma of the North," just as later generations were to refer to him as "Hamlet on the Russian throne." A. Predtechensky, *Ocherki obshchestvenno-politicheskoi istorii Rossii v pervoi chetverti XIX veka*, M-L, 1957, 5.

151. Gershenzon, *Zhizn'*, 102, and selections from the text in 93–104.

152. Gershenzon, *Zhizn'*, 134–5. For discussions of Pecherin, relating him to the Revolutionary tradition see P. Scheibert, *Von Bakunin zu Lenin: Geschichte der russischen revolutionären Ideologien, 1840–1895*, Leiden, 1956, I, 21–35; and Sakulin, *Literatura*, 92–106.

One is tempted to say of Pecherin's unfinished work what Karl Barth has said of one of the first of these great unfinished romantic fantasies, Novalis' *Henry of Ofterdingen*: "The conclusion to this manuscript is missing. It is missing in every respect. And in so far as we all, as children of the age which began with Novalis, have something of . . . the pure Romantic, in our blood, the same might well be said of us too." *Protestant Thought from Rousseau to Ritschl*, London, 1959, 267. Pecherin provided a kind of epitaph for both himself and the intelligentsia of his age in a verse of the seventies: "Za nebesnye mechtan'ia/ Ia zemnuiu zhizn' otdal/ I tiazhely krest izgnan'ia/ Dobrovol'no ia pod'ial." Cited in Sakulin, *Literatura*, 106.

153. *PSS*, XII, 383.

154. For a description of this production of 1932 (apparently the last major production of the play during the Stalin era, and the work of N. Akimov, who was to do far better things in the post-Stalin era) see J. Macleod, *The New Soviet Theatre*, London, 1943, 158–63.

155. I. Aksenov, *Gamlet*, 118–21. See the partial anticipation of this view in Herzen, *Other Shore*, 79.

V. On to New Shores

1. D. Sokolov, *Kratkoe uchenie*, 7. The term "nave" is, of course, derived from the same root as "naval"; and Russian churches are explicitly said to be built "in an elongated fashion like a boat" (Sokolov, 7). According to J. Strzygowski *(Early Art,* esp. 154–60), the keel of a boat was the model for the pointed horseshoe arch of early Scandinavian architecture; and, if one accepts a strong degree of Scandinavian influence at least through Novgorod, this may well account for the introduction of this shape and perhaps even the onion dome into Russian wooden architecture.

   The rich early history of the symbols of sea and ship in both Eastern and Western Christendom is admirably outlined in H. Rahner, *Symbole der Kirche*, Salzburg, 1964, esp. 239 ff. The development of these symbols in Kievan times is well covered in V. Adrianova-Peretts, *Ocherk poeticheskogo stilia drevnei Rusi*, M-L, 1947, 45–50.

2. See the discussion and account of a pilgrimage by V. Nemirovich-Danchenko, *Solovki*, P, 1904, 11–20, 72–5. This is the work of Vasily, brother of the famed director and co-founder of the Moscow Art Theater, Vladimir Nemirovich-Danchenko.

3. N. Arsen'ev, "Studies in Russian Religious Life," *Irénikon*, 1959, winter, 21–2.

4. Avvakum, *Life*, 44–5; Sévérac, *La Secte*, 236.

5. "Voda-devitsa/ Reka-kormilitsa!/ . . . Vot tebe podarok:/ Beloparusny korablik!" Cited in the section on "the Birth of a Ship" in B. Shergin, *Pomorshchina-Korabel'shchina*, M, 1947, 106. See also 6 and the epic poem *Bratanna*, 32–3.

6. Lo Gatto, *Storia*, I, 21–3; P. Berkov, in *RF*, IV, 1959, 332–3 and references therein.

7. Magnitsky as cited in Sukhomlinov, *Izsledovaniia*, I, 219. In the late seventeenth century, the Likhudy brothers saw Latin influences cutting the Russian church adrift on the high seas. See V. Vinogradov, *Ocherki*, 10. For concurrent use of the same metaphor in early Old Believer writings see Ya. Barskov, *Pamiatniki pervykh let russkago staroobriadchestva*, P, 1912, 265.

8. Cited in Semevsky, "Dekabristy," *MG*, 1908, May-June, 425.

9. Quoted in Lang, *Radical*, 250–1.

10. Lunin, *Sochineniia i pis'ma*, 17. He proposed "the ship of the catholic church" as the only salvation from the sea of doubt which man unaided "can never calm."

11. From the beginning of Turgenev's "Literary and Artistic Reminiscences," quoted in R. Freeborn, *Turgenev*, Oxford, 1960, 5. Compare also Belinsky, *PSS*, XI, 293, for his longing to sink into the "ocean" of simplicity.

12. Georges Florovsky, "The Historical Premonitions of Tiutchev," *SEER*, 1924, Dec, esp. 340. For other prophetic reflections by Tiutchev on the revolution of 1848, see Kohn, *Mind*, 94–103; and his correspondence in *SN*, XXII, 1917, 278–83.

13. A. Herzen, *From the Other Shore*, London, 1956 (tr. Budberg), 3. The sense of being in transit on ship between different worlds—so central to this work of Herzen—is also present in the similarly titled work of another gifted and literate Russian émigré a century later: Vladimir Nabokov's *Drugie berega*, NY, 1954 (memoirs, the English title of which is *Conclusive Evidence*).

14. ". . . à l'Église militante doit succéder au dernier jour une Église triomphante, et le système des contradictions sociales m'apparaît comme un pont magique jeté sur le fleuve de l'oubli." The last lines

of Proudhon's *Système des contradictions économiques, ou philosophie de la misère* in *Oeuvres complètes,* 1923, II, 413.

15. From letters to Stasov of 1872 and
1875, cited in O. von Rieseman,
Moussorgsky, New York, 1929, 105,
248.

16. "Oi, rebiata, plokho delo!/ Nasha
barka na mel' sela./ Tsar nash bely
kormshchik p'iany!/ On zavel nas
na mel' priamo . . ./ Podbavim
barke khodu,/ pokidaem gospod v
vodu." Verse by the populist-
agitator Ivanchin-Pisarev, reproduced by B. Itenberg in "Nachalo
massovogo 'khozhdeniia v narod',"
IZ, LXIX, 1961, 160 and note 88.

17. *Purgatorio,* Canto I, 1–3. "Per
correr miglior acqua alza le vele/
omai la navicella del mio ingegno,/
che lascia retro a sè mar sì crudele."

18. *Paradiso,* Canto II, 1, 4–7. "O, voi
che siete in piccioletta barca,/ . . .
tornate a riveder li vostri liti:/ Non
vi mettete in pelago; chè forse,/
perdendo me, rimarreste smarriti./
L'acqua ch' io prendo, giammai non
si corse."

19. On V. Vonliarliarsky, a typical popularizer of this genre, see A. Skabichevsky, *Istoriia noveishei russkoi
literatury 1848–1908,* P, 1909, 7th
corr. ed., 15–16. On the exploration
and opening of the seas in the early
nineteenth century see A. Berg,
"Ocherk istorii russkoi geograficches-
koi nauki," *TKIZ,* 1929, no. 4, 44–
7.

20. Lines used by Lermontov as the
English heading for a poem *(PSS,*
M-L, 1947, II, 401); Pushkin's "I
hail thee, free ocean" is used as the
heading for a valuable study by N.
Barsamov, *More v russkoi zhivopisi,* Simferopol, 1959, which discusses in full with many illustrations
the vogue of seascapes in nineteenth-century Russia.

    Both of these symbolic mean-
ings of the sea can also be found in
Old Russian literature: the "blue
sea" carrying overtones of romance

in the early epics; the sea as "sister
to the sun" being a source of purification in popular tales. The latter
meaning is particularly dramatic in
the early cosmological dialogues
between the land and the sea, in
which the holy church issues forth
from the sea. See M. Alekseev,
" 'Prenie zemli i moria' v drevne-
russkoi pis'mennosti," in *Problemy
. . . Tikhomirova,* 31–43; esp. 42,
"Posredi moria okeanskogo/ Vykh-
odila tserkov' sobornaia,/ . . . Iz-
toi tserkvi iz sobornoi,/ . . . Vykh-
odila tsaritsa nebesnaia, . . ."

21. From Herzen's preface of 1858 to
*Memoirs of the Empress Catherine
II,* NY, 1859, 14.

22. V. Stasov, *Izbrannye sochineniia,*
M, 1937, I, 193.

23. Mikhailovsky, *Sochineniia,* P, 1896,
III, 707. Note, however, Mikhailovsky's atypical determination to
"preserve that spark of truth and
ideal which I succeeded in acquiring
for the sake of that same people."
See my characterization of "critical
populism" in *Mikhailovsky,* 94–8.

24. ". . . Erinnrung schmilzt in kühler
Schattenflut." Novalis, *Schriften,*
Stuttgart, 1960, 2d corr. ed., by
Kluckhohn and Samuel, I, 142.

    The importance of water im-
ages for depicting death in Novalis
is stressed by Bruce Haywood, *Novalis: The Veil of Imagery,* Cambridge, Mass., 1959, 62–4, and is
equally noticeable in Tieck, Bren-
tano, Heine, and so on. Their influence in Russia has never been
fully assessed, but is most evident
in the poetic work of Tiutchev,
with his hymns to the night and his
occult cosmology, and of Yazykov.
See D. Stremooukhoff, *La Poésie,*
47–60; D. Chizhevsky, "Tjutčev und
die deutsche Romantik," *ZSPh,*
1927, IV, 299–322; and, best of all,
S. Frank, "Das kosmische Gefühl
in Tjutčev's Dichtung," *ZSPh,* III,
1926, 20–58.

25. For the permeating influence of
Schopenhauer on Turgenev see A.

Walicki, *Osobowość a Historia,* Warsaw, 1959, 278–354.

26. I. Turgenev, *On the Eve,* London, 1950, p (tr. G. Gardner), 223–4. The dream occurs in Venice following a splendid description of the city in spring and a symbolic performance of *Traviata.*

   Wagner claims to have been partly inspired for *Tristan* by the sounds of this city, in which he was working during the very months of 1859 when Turgenev was writing *On the Eve* (Wagner, *My Life,* NY, 1911, II, esp. 697–9). Venice, of course, subsequently became a kind of symbol of beauty fading into decay and death for the literary imagination, not only in Mann's *Death in Venice,* but in Proust, James, Eliot, and others.

   Another curious parallel between these seemingly different figures lies in the traumatic effect of virtually simultaneous stormy voyages west from the eastern Baltic in the late 1830's. Turgenev first contemplated suicide during a fire aboard a ship *(Literary Reminiscences,* 304), just as Wagner was deeply moved during a storm to write *The Flying Dutchman* and to begin his descent into brooding Schopenhauerian pessimism *(My Life,* I, 198–202).

27. *"Vull morir en pèlag d'amor."* Cited by M. Schmidt, "Thomas Aquinas and Raymundus Lullus," *CH,* 1960, Jun, 126.

28. "è la sua volontate è nostra pace;/ ella è quel mare, al qual tutto si move," *Paradiso,* Canto III, 85–6. See also Novalis' *Henry of Ofterdingen,* 220–1, for a typical romantic echo of this theme. Among the land-locked Mongols the word for "supreme" and "universal" *(dalai)* also meant "ocean." Russian occultists of the late eighteenth century advocated channeling all human thought into "the divine ocean of Christ," *O Chetyrekh rekakh raia,* Manuscript section of Saltykov-Shchedrin Library in Leningrad, Q III, 175, 7.

29. Chekhov, *Love and Other Stories,* London, 1922 (tr. Garnett), 67, 46–7.

30. John Frazer's lengthy discussion of the appearance of this belief throughout the world covers almost every area except Russia. See "The Great Flood" in his *Folklore in The Old Testament,* London, 1918, I, 104–361. See also Mel'gunov, *Dvizhenie,* 119.

31. See George Posener, "La Légende egyptienne de la mer insatiable," *AIOS,* XIII, 1955, 461–78; and A. Pallady, *Obozrenie permskago raskola,* P, 1863, 128–9, 132–3.

32. Cited by Barsamov, *More v russkoi zhivopisi,* 70. See also the discussion on Aivazovsky (52–73) and the illustrations of his most famous paintings (frontispiece and the sixth and seventh of the unnumbered reproductions at the back of the book). For more detailed treatment and additional reproductions see Barsamov, *Ivan Konstantinovich Aivazovsky,* M, 1963. For discussion and illustration of the morbid romantic fascination with catastrophe at sea, see T. Bonac, "Shipwrecks in English Romantic Painting," *JWI,* XXI, 1958, 332–46.

33. Particularly by means of the cinema. Eisenstein devoted one of his finest feature films to the romanticized exploits of the *Potemkin;* and the heroic portrayals of the Revolution by both him and Pudovkin allot a prominent place to the activities of the *Aurora,* which is now permanently moored in Leningrad as a kind of Revolutionary landmark. For valuable background information on the early history of Russian warships and their impact on Russian thinking see E. Kvashin-Samarin, *Morskaia ideia v russkoi zemle,* P, 1912. There is, unfortunately, no comparable work for the more important post-Petrine period. B. Zverev, *Stranitsy russkoi*

morskoi letopisi, M, 1960, is a competent recent summary of naval history up till the Crimean War.

For an interesting account of early Russian naval activity on the sea prior to the thirteenth century see V. Mavrodin, *Nachalo morekhodstva na Rusi,* L, 1949, who suggests (130 ff.) that the Greek word for "ship," *karabos,* derives from the Russian *korabl'.* A. Meillet considers this "one of the oldest borrowings from Slavonic into Greek," "De quelques mots relatifs à la navigation," *RES,* VII, 1927, 7.

For a stimulating general interpretation of Russian history that represents landlocked Moscow as in effect a "port of five seas," and the

overland expansion across Siberia as only another aspect of Russia's expansive impulse across and down rivers toward the sea, see R. Kerner, *Urge to the Sea.* Stanisław Rożniecki seems to err in the opposite direction, making the Russian epic tradition a virtual adaptation of the Scandinavian sagas with their fixations on the sea. See his *Varøgiske minder,* and the restatement and partial refutation of his position by A. Stender-Petersen, *Varangica,* 233 and 217–40.

34. O. Mandel'shtam, "O sobesednike," *SS,* NY, 1955, 322. On this important figure see C. Brown, ed. and intr., *The Prose of Osip Mandelstam,* Princeton, N.J., 1965.

1. THE TURN TO SOCIAL THOUGHT

1. Letter to Stankevich of Oct 2, 1839, *PSS,* XI, 387.
2. A. Pypin, a cousin of Chernyshevsky and one of the first to attempt to chronicle the history of Russian social thought, saw Bentham's influence as a major symbol of an earlier, more practical form of reformist thought, and his "fall" with the advent of the Holy Alliance and Alexander's more mystical cast of mind as a fateful turning point toward a new and more visionary type of social thinking, with which Pypin was less sympathetic. See *Ocherki,* 1–109, 418.

The invaluable basic study of the period from the 1840's to the 1880's by F. Venturi *(Roots of Revolution,* NY, 1960) provides ample information and rich documentation on the social and economic ideas and revolutionary organizations of the period; and on radical figures like Chernyshevsky who are not treated in detail here. See also the valuable introduction by Isaiah Berlin, and my review of the work in *RR,* 1961, Jul, 254–8.

Recent works (not included in

the references to my *Mikhailovsky* or Venturi, *Roots)* providing new details on the pervasive effect of the populist movement include R. Filipov, *Pervy etap "Khozhdeniia v narod,"* Petrozavodsk, 1960; B. Itenberg, "Khozhdenie"; on literary echoes, see J. Lothe, *Gleb Ivanovič Uspenskij et le populisme russe,* Leiden, 1963; K. Sanine, *Les Annales de la patrie et la diffusion de la pensée française en Russie, 1868–1884,* 1955; the same author's *Saltykov-Chtchédrine: sa vie et ses oeuvres,* 1955; and M. Teplinsky, "O Narodnichestve 'Otechestvennykh Zapisok' (1868–1884)," *RL,* 1964, no. 2, 55–70. See also, on revolutionary populism, the posthumously published collection of essays by B. Koz'min, *Iz istorii revoliutsionnoi mysli v Rossii,* M, 1961; the historiographical review thereof by A. Gleason, *Kritika,* 1964–5, winter, 25–40; the somewhat glorified picture presented in the kandidat thesis of V. Tvardovskaia (daughter of the Soviet poet A. Tvardovsky), *Vozniknovenie revoliutsionnoi organizatsii "Narodnaia*

Volia" (1879–1881 gg.), M, 1960;
and the more exhaustive and critical
doctoral thesis presented by S. Volk
on the same subject in 1965 (consulted in manuscripts, Leningrad,
Jan 1965).

There is little agreement among
scholars on the nature of the
populist movement. Some writers,
like Venturi, include virtually every
radical movement from the late
forties to the early eighties. Others
have attempted to define the term
far more narrowly. For recent
studies of the complex usages of the
terms *narodnik* and *narodnichestvo*
see B. Koz'min, " 'Narodnik' i
'narodnichestvo,' " *VL,* 1957, no. 9,
116–35; and R. Pipes, *"Narodnichestvo: A Semantic Inquiry,"
ASR,* 1964, Sep, 441–58. These
terms were first given fixed usage
in the second half of the seventies
by the activists who formed the
second *zemlia i volia* organization
to characterize a new attitude of
confidence in the strength and ideals
of the oppressed masses themselves.
However, faith in the transforming
power of the people and in the
sanctifying nature of all manner of
narodny labels had already been
present for some time. The slogans
zemlia i volia, v narod—even the
terms *narodniki* and *narodnichestvo*
according to a leading Soviet student of the movement, Sh. Levin
(*Obshchestvennoe dvizhenie v Rossii
v 60–70e gody XIX veka,* M, 1958,
386–7, note 4)—were in use in the
sixties. The term used for the mass
movement of the early seventies,
khozhdenie v narod, literally means
"procession" or "pilgrimage" to the
people; and when the later revolutionaries speak of "going over to
the *narodniks"* they have in mind
the adoption for their own ends of
an attitude that was already in
being.

A reading of the legal press
along with the pamphlets of revolutionaries has led me to conclude
that, by the late sixties, a reasonably coherent tradition of radical
protest had come into being inside
Russia, which can legitimately
(though it need not necessarily) be
called populist. It was an anti-
authoritarian movement dedicated
to a radical transformation of Russian society. It was led principally
by students fanning out from St.
Petersburg, and was animated by a
common moral idealism and sense
of solidarity in the face of official
repression. The introduction in the
late sixties of the term "intelligentsia" and the rapid simultaneous
spread of an optimistic new (essentially Comtean) philosophy of history and a more activistic (essentially Proudhonist) desire for direct
identification with the demands and
the hidden power of "the people"—
all converged to create a movement
which—for all its inner, Proudhon-
like contradictions and lack of organization—maintained at least to
the end of the nineteenth century an
ideological identity on the left that
was distinct both from revolutionary
Jacobinism and democratic reformism (whether liberal or social democratic). The fact that the meaning
of the term *narodnichestvo* was subject to intense debate in the 1880's
and was narrowed and distorted by
the Marxists in the 1890's into an
anti-Westernizing economic creed
indicates that there was a very real
—if somewhat confused—tradition
that had to be either annexed
through definition or discredited
through caricature by any serious
aspirant to radical leadership in late
Imperial Russia.

3. ". . . mezhdu nami dolzhna byt'
priamota, bez vsiakoi politiki." A
visiting Serb to Chizhov while in
the garden of P. J. Šafařík, the
Slovak philologist who was in many
ways the spiritual father of Pan-
Slavism, cited in I. Koz'menko,

"Dnevnik F. V. Chizhova 'puteshe-stvie po slavianskim zemliam' kak istochnik," in *Slaviansky arkhiv*, M, 1958, 211.

4. N. Turgenev, *La Russie et les russes*, 1847, II, 376; and 368–77; I, 174, 520–38; III, 49–50, 115–24. I. Golovin's "Catechism of the Russian People," which appeared in 1849 in Paris in 1,000 copies, is also more a voice from the past, with its catechistic format and idealization of Novgorod. However, it is also a document in the development of populist thinking, with its attempt to distinguish between *Tsarsky* and *Narodny* Russia. See "Pervaia revoliutsionnaia broshiura russkoi emigratsii," *Zven'ia*, 1932, I, 195–217; Venturi, *Roots*, 727–8, note 120. On the *Sekta obshchykh*, see Margaritov, *Istoriia*, 138.

5. "toska o normal'nosti": letter to Stankevich of Oct 2, 1839, *PSS*, XI, 387.

6. See I. Franko, "Taras Shevchenko," *SEER*, 1924, Jun, 110–16.

7. K. Pazhitnov, *Razvitie sotsialisticheskikh idei v Rossii ot Pestelia do gruppy "Osvobozhdenie Truda"*, P, 1924, I, 71–6.

8. Cited by Vengerov, *BE*, XXXV, 374. See also Maikov, *SS*, Kiev, 1903, 2v, and biographical studies by his brother Leonid Maikov (as the introduction to Valerian's revealing *Kriticheskie Opyty*, P, 1901, 2v). An apparant attempt to "promote" Maikov to the level of Belinsky and Herzen by A. Levitov ("Peredovaia ekonomicheskaia mysl' Rossii 40-kh godov XIX veka i ee znachenie v ekonomicheskoi nauke," *Uchenye Zapiski Rostovskogo n/D finansovo-ekonomicheskogo instituta*, II, Rostov/Don, 1948, 25) is beaten down in *Istoriia russkoi ekonomicheskoi mysli*, I, ch. 2, 263.

9. Semevsky, *Iz istorii*, 27–35; Scheibert, *Von Bakunin*, 281–314; Sakulin, *Literatura*, 288–312.

10. Semevsky, *Iz istorii*, 59–67.

11. A. Dolinin, "Dostoevsky sredi Petrashevtsev," *Zven'ia*, VI, 512 ff. V. Semevsky, "Petrashevtsy Durov, Pal'm, Dostoevsky i Pleshcheev," *GM*, 1915, nos. 11, 12.

12. Under the entry *orakul* in the pocket dictionary, cited and discussed by Pazhitnov, *Razvitie*, 57; also 55–70. The outlook of the Cyril and Methodius society, one of the few subjects not covered by Venturi, is characterized as Christian federalism by J. Sydoruk, "Ideology of Cyrillo-Methodius and Its Origin," *Slavistica*, 1954, no. 19, 168–83.

13. Cited in Pazhitnov, 66. The assumed difference between "liberal" constitutions and "democratic" assemblies is underscored in the jingle of the *Petrashevtsy*: "konstitutsiiu mogut dat',/ no zemskuiu dumu nado vziat' " *Zven'ia*, II, 449.

14. Belinsky, *PSS*, XII, 66.

15. "A socialism which tried to dispense with political liberty, with equality of rights, would quickly degenerate into authoritarian communism." Herzen (1868), *PSS i pisem* P, 1923, XX, 132. "Communism is . . . primarily negative, a storm-cloud charged with thunderbolts, which, like the judgment of God, will destroy our absurd social system unless men repent." *PSS i pisem*, III, 319 (mt of citation amidst useful discussion in Venturi, *Roots*, 17).

16. N. Kirillov, ed. *Karmanny slovar' inostrannykh slov voshedshikh v sostave russkago iazyka*, P, 1846, 52; see also 133–4. This second volume of the never-completed dictionary was largely the work of Petrashevsky; the first (P, 1845), of V. Maikov and R. Shtrandman.

17. Cited in Pazhitnov, *Razvitie*, 107, note 1.

18. A. Nifontov, *1848 god v Rossii*, M-L, 1931, 64–8, 76. For a less statistical but more penetrating study see I. Berlin, "Russia and 1848," *SEER*, 1948, Apr.

19. Belinsky, *PSS*, XI, 216. On the term

"Europeanism" see Sakulin, *Litera-tura*, 222, note 1; and the use by Kireevsky in 1837 discussed in Kovalevsky, "Ponimanie," 168.

20. Nifontov, *1848*, 68.

21. On the author Ivan Turchaninov, who later emigrated to America, fought in the Civil War under the name of Turchin, and acquired a reputation for cruelty in Alabama, see "Gertsen i Ogarev I," *LN*, 1953, II, 591–2; also I, 704–5, for the influence of J. Fenimore Cooper. On Bakunin's various schemes for federation sce Hepner, *Bakounine*, 201 ff. For the general impact of American thought on Russian radicalism see Hecht, *Russian Radicals*.

22. Herzen, "Amerika i Rossiia," *Kolokol*, no. 228, Oct 1, 1866, 1861–2. This idea was also developed by Bakunin; see Yu. Semyonov, *Siberia*, Baltimore, 1954, 281–2.

N. Yadrintsev, a veteran of revolutionary agitation in St. Petersburg in the sixties, moved to Siberia, where he became the champion of a radical regional federation, which led him to propose—among other things—the separation of Siberia from Russia and the development of it as a federal republic similar to the United States. See his article "Istoriia odnogo stranstviia," *OZ*, 1871, no. 12, esp. 215–6. For other aspects of his largely journalistic activites see Venturi, *Roots*, 318 ff.; M. Lemke, *Nikolai Mikhailovich Yadrintsev*, P, 1904, esp. 96 ff. Novikov apparently entertained the idea much earlier of setting up a small republic in or near Siberia as a political base for the renovation of Russia, See *RS*, 1877, Apr, 658.

23. Saltykov, "Brusin," as cited in Venturi, *Roots*, 79–80.

24. Cited by G. Florovsky, "Premonitions," 340 and ff.

25. M. Pogodin, cited in Riasanovsky, *Nicholas*, 166.

26. See F. Chizhov, *Parovyia mashiny, istoriia, opisanie i prilozhenie ikh*, P, 1838; *BE*, LXXVI, 821–2;

RBS, XXII, 376–81; and especially A. Liberman's biographical sketch in *Sbornik v pamiat' stoletiia so dnia rozhdeniia Fedora Vasil'evicha Chizhova*, Kostroma, 1911, 49 ff.

In his later years, Chizhov became a close friend of another railroad-builder, S. Mamontov, who also became a patron of the arts and perpetuated into the twentieth century the ideal of a distinctively Russian national art. Chizhov entrusted to Mamontov an enormous nineteen-volume diary apparently containing a prophetic testament to his native land with the specific instruction that it "not be printed or read until forty years after the day of the author's death." *Otchet moskovskago publichnago i rumiantsevskago muzeev za 1876–1878 g*, M, 1879, 98. Much interest was sustained in this work up until the fateful anniversary in the revolutionary year 1917. Plans for publication announced in *Knizhny ugol*, P, 1918, no. 2, 33, were, however, frustrated by the forced closing of that remarkable journal by Soviet authorities, and I was unable to find any trace of the document or information about it in Leningrad or Moscow in 1961 or 1965.

27. M. Dreksler, rector of the Riga Theological Seminary, in *Strannik*, 1872, Dec, 98–9. Similar misgivings were expressed by an anonymous peasant writer in 1835 even before the building of the first railroad. See M. Kovalensky, *Khrestomatiia po russkoi istorii*, M-P, 1923, IV, 77–8.

28. P. Viazemsky, *PSS*, P, 1879, II, 353. Belinsky, *PSS*, XI, 325. For similar literary fears elsewhere see M. Brightfield, "The Coming of the Railroad to Early Victorian England as Viewed by the Novels of the Period," *Technology and Culture*, 1962, winter, 45–72; O. Handlin, "Man and Magic: Encounters with the Machine," *The American Scholar*, 1964, summer,

408–19; and L. Marx, *The Machine in the Garden: Technology and the Pastoral Ideal in America,* Oxford, 1964.

Some discussion of the railroad as both a literary symbol and a revolutionary force in Russian society is contained in M. Al'tman, "Zheleznaia doroga v tvorchestve L. N. Tol'stogo," *Slavia,* XXXIV, 2, 1962, 251–9.

29. E. Barrault, "La Russie et ses chemins de fer," *RDM,* 1857, May 1, 179, 176, 208. See also G. Weill, *L'École Saint-Simonienne,* 1896, 245; and Keller, *East,* 162–4.

30. Cited in P. Shchegolev, "K biografii," 57. For an account of the plight of the peasant passenger, see the widely read "Chronicle of Progress" in the satirical journal *Iskra,* May 26, 1861, 281–2.

31. Cited in Venturi, *Roots,* 157, mt.

32. Pisarev, *Izbrannye sochineniia,* M, 1934, I, 228. The generally hostile critic N. Strakhov also recognized the importance of what he called the "aerial revolution" *(vozdushnaia revoliutsiia)* of the years 1858–63: *Bor'ba s zapadom v nashei literature,* P, 1882, I, 48.

To the general picture of unrest provided in Venturi and other studies of individual agitators, there remains a need to stress the depth and passion of the reaction to youthful iconoclasm (see C. Moser, *Antinihilism in the Russian novel of the 1860's,* The Hague, 1964) and the extent to which the activities of the young radicals were in fact anticipated by the *Petrashevtsy.* Their insufficiently appreciated interest in Feuerbach anticipates the turn by the "men of the sixties" to a cruder later generation of German materialists. Pisarev's ideal of a radical renovation of society through scientific education is in many ways merely an extension of Petrashevsky's program for public enlightenment. The two-plus-two image of

Bazarov was used in an equally dogmatic and axiomatic sense by the *Petrashevtsy (Delo Petrashevtsev,* M-L, 1951, III, 441–2); the distinctive "censorship of the left" introduced by Chernyshevsky and his associates was clearly envisaged in the plans of the earlier group *(Delo Petrashevtsev,* M-L, 1941, II, 185–6). The *Petrashevtsy* will be analyzed in detail in a forthcoming Princeton Doctoral dissertation of F. Bartholomew.

33. Cited in Venturi, *Roots,* 159, mt. Chernyshevsky's authorship of this pseudonymous "Letter from the Provinces" to Herzen's *Kolokol* is far from certain; and it may have been the work of Dobroliubov or another associate. See *ibid.,* 744–5, notes 94, 95; also I. Novich, *Zhizn' Chernyshevskogo,* M, 1939, 207–8.

34. The development of this school from Sechenov to Nobel laureate Ivan Pavlov (as well as its vulgarized integration into Soviet ideology) is briefly outlined by W. Gantt, "Russian Physiology and Pathology," in R. Christman, ed., *Soviet Science,* Washington, D.C., 1952, 11 ff. See also B. Babkin, "Sechenov and Pavlov," *RR,* 1946, spring, 24–35.

The debate between Sechenov and the positivist historian Kavelin in the 1870's was both the culmination of a long series of exchanges between materialists and idealists (that had begun with that of Chernyshevsky and P. Yurkevich in the early sixties), and, at the same time, an anticipation of the aggressive Leninist opposition to critical positivism as well as traditional idealism. The Soviet accounts of these debates are partial even to the point of suppressing minor concessions on the part of the materialists, and may be balanced by reading the vigorously anti-materialist accounts presented in Florovsky, *Puti;* V. Zenkovsky, *History;* and particularly A.

Volynsky (Fleksner), *Russkie kritiki*, P, 1896.

35. Cited in *BSE* (I), XXVIII, 609: I was unable to locate this un-referenced citation in Pisarev's works ("Intelligentsia," 812, note 12); nor was A. Pollard consulting another edition. In his "The Russian Intelligentsia," Pollard has traced the later use of the word and cast grave doubt on the contention that the term was first used in Boborykin's novels—a derivation that is repeated uncritically in almost every Soviet reference work. I have found the apparent basis for the attribution to Boborykin in his explicit claim (in a lecture November 5, 1904) of having introduced not only the term *intelligentsia*, but also *intelligent* and *intelligentny* "about 40 years ago, in 1866, in one of my critical studies." *RM*, 1904, no. 12, second set of pages, 80–1. I have been unable to find any such original usage; but even if it should exist, the date he suggests is five years later than that of Aksakov's usage of the term *intelligentsia* at least. On *intellektual'ny*, see *Karmanny slovar'*, 83.

36. *Kolokol*, no. 187, Jul 15, 1864, 1534.

37. N Shelgunov, *Sochineniia*, P, 1904, I, 19. Shelgunov explains in his memoirs (written in 1883) that his "Proclamation to the Young Generation," was written during the winter of 1861–2 under the direct inspiration of Saint-Simon's famous passage in his *Parabola* of 1809) saying how little the world would suffer if all its princes and land-owners and generals were taken away, but how disastrous it would be if someone were suddenly to take away "littérateurs, scientists . . . the intelligentsia of the country" (*Vospominaniia*, M-P, 1923, 33). Shelgunov conceived of his procla-mation (repr. *ibid.*, 287–302) as a bid to the young generation to re-nounce wealth and privilege in order to provide that consecrated elite leadership characteristic of the followers of Saint-Simon and of his disciple Comte.

For the influence of Comte, see, in addition to works cited in my "Intelligentsia," 813–15 and notes, M. Kovalevsky, "Stranitsa iz istorii nashego obshcheniia s zapadnoi filosofiei," *VE*, 1915, no. 6, 157–68.

38. Shelgunov, 1868, Aug, in *Sochin-eniia*, I, 279–80.

39. *Kolokol*, no. 110, Nov 1, 1861; cited in Pazhitnov, *Razvitie*, 116.

40. Ya. Abramov, *Nashi voskresnyia shkoly: ikh proshloe i nastoiashchee*, P, 1900, esp. 6–24; also *JMH*, 1965, Jun.

41. Shelgunov, *Vospominaniia*, 292.

42. T. Polner, "N. V. Chaikovsky i bo-gochelovechestvo," in *Nikolai Vasil-evich Chaikovsky: religioznyia i ob-shchestvennyia iskaniia*, Paris, 1929, 97–166.

43. A. Yarmolinsky, *Road to Revolu-tion*, NY, 1959, 247–9.

44. Cited in Engel'gardt, *Ocherk*, 279. Chizhov had long ago declared to Mickiewicz in a similar vein: "*Je n'ai qu'un titre des titres—Je suis russe.*" *Sbornik Chizhova*, 24. The messianic nationalism which the Polish poet developed (partly in re-action to such chauvinism among his erstwhile Russian friends) is curiously similar to that developed by Chizhov's friend, the national-istic poet A. Yazykov. See V. Smir-nov, *Zhizn' i poeziia A. M. Yazy-kova*, Perm, 1900.

45. L'udovít Štúr, *Das Slawenthum und die Welt der Zukunft*, discussed in M. Petrovich, "L'udovít Štúr and Russian Panslavism," *Journal of Central European Affairs*, 1952, Apr, 1–19; also Petrovich, *The Emergence of Russian Panslavism, 1856–1870*, NY, 1956, 241–54, esp. 248.

The importance of the dream of Constantinople is stressed by

F. Fadner, *Seventy Years of Pan-Slavism in Russia: Karazin to Danilevsky, 1800–1870,* Washington, D.C., 1962; and (with particular reference to Leont'ev and Dostoevsky) by L. Kozlovsky, "Mechty o Tsar'grade," *GM,* 1915, no. 2, 88–116; no. 11, 44–74.

46. For increased recent attention to Ogarev see Scheibert, *Von Bakunin,* 222–31; and S. Utechin, "Who Taught Lenin?" *Twentieth Century,* 1960, Jul, 8–16. M. Karpovich also portrays Lavrov as more of a revo-lutionary in the 1870's than is generally thought, stressing the impact of the Paris Commune. "P. L. Lavrov and Russian Socialism," *CSS,* II, 1963, 21–38.

47. The principal passages of the *Catechism* are printed in Venturi, *Roots,* 365–7; see 733, note 24 for further references.

48. Cited in B. Koz'min, *Tkachev i revoliutsionnoe dvizhenie 1860kh godov,* M, 1922, 156.

49. *Delo pervogo marta 1881,* P, 1906 (intr. L. Deutsch), 6–7.

2. THE AGONY OF POPULIST ART

1. Garshin, *Sochineniia,* 209.
2. *Ibid.,* 71–88. See also his essays on painting, 305–54, and discussion thereof in Gorlin, "Interrelation." Garshin was popularly likened to John the Baptist in another Dresden painting. See P. Zabolotsky, "V. M. Garshin i ego literaturnaia deiatel'nost'," *TKDA,* 1908, Jul, 491–2. For the best critical study see G. Bialy, *V. M. Garshin i literaturnaia bor'ba vos'midesiatykh godov,* M-L, 1937. Also L. Stenborg, "V. M. Garšin och den historisk-politiska bakgrunden till hans författarskap," in *Studia Slavica Gunnaro Gunnarsson Sexagenario Dedicata,* Uppsala, 1960, 107–18.
   For the English edition of Tarsis' work, see *Ward 7; an autobiographical novel,* NY, 1965.
3. Garshin, *Sochineniia,* 357–8.
4. O. von Riesemann, *Moussorgsky,* 99. See also M. Calvocoressi, *Modest Mussorgsky, His Life and Works,* London, 1956 (also his much shorter *Mussorgsky,* London, 1946, repr. NY, 1962 p); Leyda and Bertensson, *Musorgsky Reader;* and the valuable collection of articles edited by Yu. Keldysh and V. Yakovlev, *M. P. Musorgsky: k piatidesiatiletiiu so dnia smerti,* M, 1932. New material is promised for the forthcoming study by G. Khubova, *M. P. Musorgsky, zhizn' i tvorchestvo.* E. Evtushenko has hailed "Musorgsky, who held the whole stage in his embrace." "Prologue," *Saturday Evening Post,* Aug 10–17, 1963, 62.
   For excellent introductions to each of the "handful" see Calvocoressi and Abraham, *Masters;* for the technical importance of the somewhat older composer, Dargomyzhsky (particularly his aria-free, anti-melodic opera, *The Stone Guest,* first performed posthumously in 1872), in preparing the way for a new, realistic opera growing out of the natural cadences of the spoken word, see Cheshikhin, *Istoriia,* 219–20. For an unusual analysis of Russian national music that includes fresh insights on Musorgsky and stresses a general Russian preoccupation with minor chords, see I. Lapshin, *Khudozhestvennoe tvorchestvo,* P, 1922, esp. 86, 191, 218, and computations 207–8.
5. Cited in von Riesemann, 105, 9.
6. Calvocoressi, *Mussorgsky,* 1946, 147.
7. Cited in von Riesemann, 9.
8. Ostrovsky did, however, extend the bounds of theatrical realism by becoming the first to make suitable dramatic material out of the Moscow merchant classes and the provincial *glush'* generally—just as Pisemsky, a lesser playwright, simultaneously helped mold suitable ma-

terial out of peasant life. See S. Timofeev, *Vliianie Shekspira*, 98 ff. Ostrovsky also created a new literary type, the stubborn, capricious tyrant—coining and popularizing the term *samodur*.

9. A. Benois, *The Russian School of Painting*, NY, 1916, 131.

10. Cited in Calvocoressi and Abraham, *Masters*, 183.

11. Cited in Calvocoressi, *Mussorgsky*, 1956, 160. In the original version of the opera this lament is placed at the end of the scene before St. Basil's prior to Boris' death. Of all the components of the Kromy scene, only that of the fool is lifted from the St. Basil's scene, which was left out of the second version, but is usually partly or totally reinserted in modern productions. The addition of everything else in the Kromy forest scene and the decision to end the opera with it places a different context on the opera, and gives the fool the quality of returning prophet. See Victor Beliaev, *Musorgsky's "Boris Godunov" and Its New Version*, Oxford, 1928, 49–59. For the comparison with the original by Pushkin see G. Abraham, "Mussorgsky's 'Boris' and Pushkin's," *ML*, 1945, Jan, 31–8.

12. ". . . slezy gor'kie,/ Plach', plach', dusha pravoslavnaia!/ Skoro vrag pridet i nastanet t'ma,/ Temen' temnaia, neprogliadnaia./ Gore, gore Rusi!/ Plach', plach', russky liud,/ Golodny liud!" M. Musorgsky, *Boris Godunov*, M, 1958, 102.

13. von Riesemann, 9.

14. Venturi, *Roots*, 350–1.

15. V. Pereverzev as cited in V. Alexandrova, "Dostoevsky Returns," *NL*, 1956, Feb 27, 19–20.

16. Cited from Ehrenburg's *Out of Chaos* (also *The Second Day*) by Alexandrova, 19–20. See also discussion of this novel in R. Jackson, *Dostoevsky's Underground Man in Russian Literature*, 's Gravenhage, 1958, 192–200; and for the fluctua-

tions in critical judgment see V. Seduro, *Dostoyevski in Russian Literary Criticism 1846–1956*, NY, 1957. Also V. Shklovsky, *Za i protiv: Zametki o Dostoevskom*, M, 1957.

17. Letter of Dec 11/23, 1868 to Apollon Maikov in *Letters of Fyodor Michailovitch Dostoevsky to his Family and Friends* (trans. E. Mayne), NY, 1915, 158.

18. Phrase of Viacheslav Ivanov in his stimulating *Freedom and the Tragic Life: A Study in Dostoevsky*, NY, 1952 (also p), 49–50.

The number of books on Dostoevsky is enormous and somewhat repetitive. Good basic studies are E. Simmons, *Dostoevsky, the Making of a Novelist*, NY, 1940; E. H. Carr, *Dostoevsky, 1821–1881*, NY, 1931; and R. Payne, *Dostoevsky: A Human Portrait*, NY, 1961. See also N. Berdiaev, *Dostoevsky*, NY, 1957, and the valuable collection of essays edited by R. Wellek, *Dostoevsky*, Englewood Cliffs, N.J., 1962, p. D. Merezhkovsky, *Tolstoy as Man and Artist with an Essay on Dostoievsky*, NY, 1902, and G. Steiner, *Tolstoy or Dostoevsky*, NY, 1959 (also p), are stimulating comparisons of the two great figures, the former emphasizing their contrasting religious views, the latter their relations to the divergent European literary traditions of the epic and the drama respectively. See also L. Grossman, *Poetika Dostoevskogo*, M, 1925, which emphasizes the influence of Balzac and the Gothic novels on Dostoevsky; and D. Fanger, *Dostoevsky and Romantic Realism: A Study of Dostoevsky in Relation to Balzac, Dickens, and Gogol*, Cambridge, Mass., 1965.

An introduction to the large memoir material and a valuable discussion and bibliography is contained in K. Mochulsky, *Dostoevsky: zhizn' i tvorchestvo*, Paris, 1947 (also in French, 1963). An invaluable collection by A. Dolinin of memoir material on Dostoevsky is *F. M. Dostoevsky v vospominaniiakh sovremennikov*, M, 1964, 2v; a systematic catalogue of his ideas is contained in *Slovar' k tvoreniiam Dostoevskago*, edited by Metropolitan Anthony of Kiev and Galich, Sofia, 1921. A dictionary of names in Dostoevsky is contained in *O Dostoevskom: sbornik pod redaktsiei A. L. Bema*, Prague, 1933, II. An analysis of Dostoevsky's views on the "cursed questions," concentrating on his early years with a good discussion of recent critical writings, is R. Przybylski, *Dostojewski i "Przeklęte Problemy,"* Warsaw, 1964.

19. Cited in Zenkovsky, *History*, I, 402. See the valuable discussion of the *pochvenniki* 400–32. The citation is not precisely referenced even in the more richly documented original Russian version of Zenkovsky's work.

The imagery of shared roots in a common soil was juxtaposed to the European idea of separate classes and interests based on artificial divisions and abstract considerations by Dostoevsky in his writings of 1861. Criticism of this position by both contemporary radicals and Soviet writers is set forth in U. Gural'nik, " 'Sovremennik' v bor'be s zhurnalami Dostoevskogo," *IAN (L)*, IX, 1950, 265–85. See also G. Gibian, "Dostoevsky's Use of Russian Folklore," in .A. Lord, ed., *Slavic Folklore, a Symposium*, Philadelphia, 1956, 41–55.

An eloquent defender of the *pochvennik* position was the critic and poet Apollon Grigor'ev, who was close to Dostoevsky in the early sixties and who viewed the plays of Ostrovsky as the best example of a new living art rooted in Russian reality. For the recollections of his unhappy life see R. Matlaw, ed., *My Literary and Moral Wanderings*, NY, 1962, p.

20. Carr, *Dostoevsky*, 43–4, from an unreferenced letter to his brother. The claim is excessive, because the type is at least as old as Hoffmann.

21. "Zapiski iz podpol'ia," in *SS*, M, 1956, IV, 136.

22. *Letters*, 158, and 157–71.

23. *Ibid.*, 158.

24. *Ibid.*, 214. This characterization (by Strakhov) particularly pleased Dostoevsky.

25. E. Konshina, *Zapisnye tetradi Dostoevskogo*, M, 1935, 61, also 244. For the real-life equivalents of the characters in the novel see, in addition to this work, the notes to the new Soviet edition of Dostoevsky's works: *SS*, M, 1957, VII, 707–57.

On *The Possessed* see R. Blackmur, "In the Birdcage," *HR*, 1948, spring, 7–28; P. Rahv, "Dostoevsky and Politics," *PR*, 1938, Jul, 25–36; and the translation of *Stavrogin's Confession* by Virginia Woolf and S. Koteliansky, with particularly valuable articles by Freud and Komarovich, NY, 1947.

Subsequent citations from *The Possessed* and other of Dostoevsky's works are taken from the Constance Garnett translations, with occasional minor modifications.

26. The prophetic quality of this scene is missed in the otherwise useful discussion of Dostoevsky's depiction of the strike in the Stieglitz paper factory in St. Petersburg, *SS*, VII, 750–1.

27. Cited in Carr, *Dostoevsky*, 281–2.

28. De Maistre, *Considérations sur la France*, in *Oeuvres*, I, 157.

29. The influence of Schiller on the young Dostoevsky is traced in M. Alekseev, "O dramaticheskikh opytakh Dostoevskogo," in L. Grossman, ed., *Tvorchestvo Dostoevskogo*, Odessa, 1921, 41–62, esp. 43–6; and R. Przybylski, "F. M. Dostojewskiego Młodzieńcze Opowiadania o Marzeniu," *SO*, VIII, 1959, esp 3–17. (A school friend introduced Dostoevsky to the playwright, reading *Don Carlos* and other plays

to him). The influence of Schiller on *The Brothers Karamazov* is traced in textual detail by D. Chizhevsky, "Schiller und die Brüder Karamazov," *ZSPh*, VI, 1929, 1–42.

On *The Brothers* see also V. Komarovich, *Die Urgestalt der Brüder Karamasoff*, Munich, 1928; R. Matlaw, *The Brothers Karamazov: Novelistic Technique*, 's Gravenhage, 1957. For an interesting Catholic critique of the image of Christ presented in the "Legend" see R. Guardini, *Religiöse Gestalten in Dostojewskijs Werk*, Munich, 1947, 113–62. For another critical perspective, see K. Onasch, *Dostojewski als Verführer*, Zurich, 1961.

30. *The Aesthetic Letters, Essays and the Philosophical Letters of Schiller*, Boston, 1845, 366.

31. Dostoevsky, *SS*, IV, 160–1. See also his novella *The Gambler* (*Igrok*), in *ibid.*, 283–432, and commentary 603–7.

32. à Kempis, *Of the Imitation of Christ*, NY, 1957, 78. Dostoevsky had a copy of this work in his library and may have been influenced directly by it. See M. Al'tman, "Gogolevskie traditsii v tvorchestve Dostoevskogo," *Slavia*, XXX, 1961, 459.

33. Carr, *Dostoevsky*, 157.

34. "Ode to Joy," in *The Poems and Ballads of Schiller*, London–Edinburgh, 1844, I, 169.

3. NEW PERSPECTIVES OF THE WANING CENTURY

1. N. Mashkovtsev, *Vasily Surikov, His Life and Work*, M [1960?], 33. Note also the extraordinary impact of Ivanov's religio-artistic quest on Surikov and the entire effort to produce a distinctively Russian art (*ibid.*, 15–18).

Detailed references for this section will not generally be repeated for material already used in my *Mikhailovsky*. For an invaluable new history of revolutionary movements and events, which begins where Venturi's *Roots* ended in 1881 and ends on the eve of the Revolution of 1905, see V. Zilli, *La rivoluzione russa del 1905. I la formazione dei partiti politici*, Naples, 1963 (a projected second volume will deal with the revolution itself). Also valuable is the new translation of T. Dan's *The Origins of Bolshevism*, NY, 1964.

2. From Igor's monologue in Act II, see particularly the lines "Ty odna golubka, lada . . ./ V teremu tvoem vysokom,/ V teremu tvoem vysokom,/ v dal' glaza ty progliadela," and "O, daite, daite mne svobodu."
For brief introductions to the musical and the chemical-medical sides respectively of Borodin's career see Calvocoressi and Abraham, *Masters*, 155–77, and F. Sunderman, "Alexander Porfirovich Borodin," *AMH*, 1938, Sep, 445–53.

3. See the excellent short study by the writer C. Paustovsky, *Isaak Levitan*, M-L, 1961.

4. Cited in E. Simmons, *Leo Tolstoy*, Boston, 1946, 337; and N. Gusev, *Letopis' zhizni i tvorchestva L'va Nikolaevicha Tolstogo, 1828–90*, M, 1958, 537.

5. " 'Moia literaturnaia sud'ba: avtobiografiia Konstantina Leont'eva," *LN*, XXII–XXIV, 1935, 465–6.

6. Cited by N. Berdiaev, *The Bourgeois Mind*, NY, 1934, 12; see also Berdiaev, *Constantin Leontieff* (undated French translation by H. Iswolsky of one of Berdiaev's better studies, with bibliography 343–50); also brief studies by R. Hare, *Pioneers of Russian Social Thought*, NY, 1964, p, 323–57; and G. Ivask, "Konstantin Leont'ev's Fiction," *ASR*, 1961, Dec, 622–9.

7. *Avtobiografiia*, 436.

8. C. Pobedonostsev, *Reflections of a*

Russian Statesman, London, 1898, 5.

9. *Ibid., 29.* For interpretation see R. Byrnes, "Pobedonostsev's Conception of the Good Society: An Analysis of his Thought after 1880," *RP,* 1951, Apr, 169–90; "Dostoevsky and Pobedonostsev," in Curtiss, ed., *Essays,* 85–102; and J. de Proyart, "Le Haut-procureur du Saint-Synode Constantin Pobedonoscev et 'le coup d'état' du 29 avril 1881," *CMR* 1962, Jul–Sep, 408–58.

10. Merezhkovsky, *Tolstoy;* G. Steiner, *Tolstoy or Dostoevsky.* A more vulgar Soviet version of this classic juxtaposition contrasts Tolstoy's world of "deeds" with Dostoevsky's world of "words." B. Bursov, "Tolstoy i Dostoevsky," *VL,* 1964, Jul, 66–92.

11. V. Dokuchaev, *K ucheniiu o zonakh prirody. Gorizontal'nye i vertikal'nye pochvennye zony,* P, 1899, 5.

12. *Ibid.* For valuable material on Dokuchaev and his intellectual influence see the proceedings of a memorial session on Mar 30, 1924, in *Trudy pochvennogo institute imeni V. V. Dokuchaeva,* II, L, 1927, 289–347, esp. 318–20 for indications of his links with *Naturphilosophie.* There is a Soviet edition of his works, *Izbrannye sochineniia. Russky chernozem,* M, 1948, 3v. There is a brief discussion of Dokuchaev's influence in J. Joffe, "Russian Contributions to Soil Science," in R. Christman, ed., *Soviet Science,* Washington, D.C., 1952.

13. *Trudy . . . Dokuchaeva,* 318 ff. "Phyto-sociology" is best expounded in G. Morozov, *Uchenie o lese,* P, 1912; and was influential in the journal of forestry of late Imperial Russia, *Lesnoi zhurnal.*

14. For Tolstoy's links with Russian sectarians see J. Bienstock, *Tolstoy et les Doukhobors,* 1902; N. Reinhardt, *Neobyknovennaia lichnost',* Kazan, 1889; L. Nikiforov, "Siutaev i Tolstoy," *GM,* 1914, no. 1, 142–58; and O. Lourié, *La Philosophie de Tolstoï,* 1899, esp. 56–61. For Tolstoy's substantial interest in Western Protestants see F. Philipp, *Tolstoj und der Protestantismus,* Giessen, 1960. Tolstoy's ideas enjoyed more of a vogue in Protestant Finland than in perhaps any other section of the Russian Empire. (See A. Nokkala, "Tolstoilaisuus Suomessa," *SKST,* LIX, 1958, 78–176.) For the development of his philosophy see N. Weisbein, *L'Evolution religieuse de Tolstoi,* 1960. Among the many general studies, see the lengthy recent work of V. Shklovsky, *Lev Tolstoy,* M, 1963.

15. A. Kaplan, *Gandhi et Tolstoi (Les sources d'une filiation spirituelle),* 1948; K. Nag, *Tolstoy and Gandhi,* Patna, 1950. See also D. Bodde, *Tolstoy and China,* Princeton, 1950; P. Biryukov, *Tolstoi und der Orient,* Zurich, 1925.

Tolstoy also had Japanese admirers and visitors, though the most important early literary influence in Japan was Goncharov's *Oblomov* (particularly on Futabatei Shimei's *The Drifting Cloud* of 1887–9). The tone of gloom in Russian literature permitted it to become probably the most influential of all European literatures in modern Japan. See S. Shigeki, "The Influence of Russian Literature in Japan," *Japan Quarterly,* 1960, Jul–Sep, 343–9.

16. N. Gusev, *Letopis' zhizni i tvorchestva L'va Nikolaevicha Tolstogo, 1891–1910,* M, 1960, 836.

17. *Ibid.,* 255–6.

18. When asked "Is there not a difference between the killing that a revolutionist does and that which a policeman does?" Tolstoy answered: "There is as much difference between cat-shit and dog-shit. But I don't like the smell of either one or the other." Simmons, *Tolstoy,* 651.

19. Last letter to his wife of Oct 31, 1910, in Gusev, *Letopis',* 826.

20. Zummer, "Sistema," 408.

21. More sophisticated recent Soviet analyses have begun to fill in some

of the gaps created by excessive deference to traditional Marxist class analysis. L. Erman, "Sostav intelligentsii v Rossii v kontse XIX i nachale XX v," *ISR*, 1963, no. 1, 161–77, shows that the extent of education was uneven but surprisingly high among some sections of the working class at the turn of the century, leading to the widespread use of the category "semi-intelligent." This term (which is used by Lenin, and has been reintroduced—apparently independently of the original usage—by modern Western scholars, such as Hugh Seton-Watson) may derive from Yiddish usage.

22. Berdiaev in particular derived his picture of bourgeois individualism as a kind of moral cannibalism from Ibsen. See J. Sheldon, "Berdyaev and Ibsen," *SEER*, 1959, Dec, 32–58; also N. Nilsson, *Ibsen in Russland*, Stockholm, 1958.

23. On Witte's reign as a decisive stage in Russian modernization see T. von Laue, *Sergei Witte and the Industrialization of Russia*, NY, 1963. The Russian economic spurt of the nineties—in many ways the most spectacular in Russian history—is discussed in A. Gerschenkron, "Problems and Patterns of Russian Economic Development," in C. Black, *Transformation*, 47–55. Gerschenkron goes on to point out, however, that "the Westernization of Russian industrialization" (credit banks, end of the tyranny of commerce, decline in dependence on the government, and so on) occurred only later, between 1906 and 1914 (55–7). In addition to this essay, an interesting treatment of "Economic Development in Russian Intellectual History of the Nineteenth Century" is reprinted in Gerschenkron, *Economic Backwardness in Historical Perspective*, Cambridge, Mass., 1962, 152–87.

The importance of the 1890's as a turning point in the development of a broadly based constitutional liberal movement in Russia is stressed by George Fischer, *Russian Liberalism*, Cambridge, Mass., 1958, in whose text and references can be found greater detail on the various components of the liberal movement here discussed.

24. V. Bezobrazov, *Gosudarstvo i obshchestvo: upravlenie, samoupravlenie i sudebnaia vlast'*, P, 1882, xxii, 231 and ff.; 487 and ff., esp. 496, 543–5. Also *RA*, 1889, no. 12, 502.

25. On Granovsky, his *Sochineniia*, M, 1866, 2v, should be supplemented by the discussion and materials referenced in I. Ivashin, "Rukopis' publichnykh lektsii T. N. Granovskogo," *IZh*, 1945, no. 1–2, 81–4. Granovsky's importance in developing critical, comparative thinking about history is stressed in the valuable article by V. Buzeskul, "Vseobshchaia istoriia i ee predstaviteli v Rossii v XIX i nachale XX veka," *TKIZ*, L, 1928, no. 7, esp. 43–58. For his impact on moderate reformers of the late imperial period see Miliukov's *Iz istorii russkoi intelligentsii*, P, 1902/1903, 2d ed., (repr. 1963 Ann Arbor), 325–6; K. Kavelin's excellent long article "Istoricheskoe mirosozertsanie Granovskogo," *SS*, P, 1912, II, 1–66; also P. Vinogradoff, "T. N. Granovsky," *RM*, 1893, no. 4. Granovsky (like Kavelin and Vinogradoff, liberal professors who can properly be considered his ideological heirs) is not mentioned in Fischer's book; nor are any of their works included in his otherwise very full bibliography.

26. For a comprehensive history of this tradition in Russia, which includes a large number of moderate constitutional reformers who are not normally considered liberals, see Leontovich, *Geschichte*. For the ideas of Kavelin and Chicherin at the beginning of the reform period see V. Rozental, "Pervoe otkrytoe vystuplenie russkikh liberalov v

1855–6," *ISR*, 1958, no. 2, 113–30; these and other lesser known figures including many in the government are discussed in N. Sladkevich, *Ocherki istorii obshchestvennoi mysli Rossii v kontse 50-kh i nachale 60-kh godov XIX veka*, L, 1962, 87 ff. A perceptive critique by Kavelin of his radical opponents in 1866 is reprinted in *IA*, V, 1950, 326–41.

27. T. Riha, "Miliukov and the Progressive Bloc in 1915. A Study in Last-Chance Politics," *JMH*, 1960, Jan, 16–24. Miliukov wrote valuable characterizations of Russian liberalism in English just before and just after the Revolution of 1905. "Present tendencies of Russian Liberalism," *Atlantic Monthly*, 1905, Mar, 404–14; and "The Case of the Second Duma," *The Contemporary Review*, 1907, Oct, 457–67. His "The influence of English Political Thought in Russia," *SEER*, 1926, Dec, 258–70, deals in good measure with the impact of Mill.

For an excellent characterization of the perennial conflict between radical and moderate liberalism see M. Karpovich, "Two Concepts of Liberalism: Miliukov and Maklakov," in Simmons, *Continuity*, 129–43. See also J. Walkin, *The Rise of Democracy in Pre-Revolutionary Russia: Political and Social Institutions under the Last Three Tsars*, NY, 1962.

See also M. Kovalevsky's introduction to Woodrow Wilson, *Gosudarstvo: proshloe i nastoiashchee konstitutsionnykh uchrezhdenii,* M, 1905.

28. "Vzgliad na iuridichesky byt drevnei Rossii," *Sochineniia*, M, 1859, I, 378.

29. E. Markov, "Talmudizm v zhurnalistike," *RRe*, 1879, Jan, 259. See also the analysis of Russian socialism as a "symptom of distress" within the intelligentsia rather than a genuine social or political movement, by A. Gradovsky, "Sotsializm na zapade Evropy i v Rossii," *RRe*,

1879, Feb, 140–59; and esp. Mar, 76–116.

30. Markov, "Talmudizm," 261.

31. Markov, "Knizhka i zhizn'," *RRe*, 1879, Mar, 216. "Moskovskaia shkola v literature," *RRe*, 1880, Apr, esp. 326–30.

32. Markov, "Knizhka," 225.

33. Markov, "Literaturnaia khandra," *RRe*, 1879, Feb, 247; also 235, 246, 247–9.

34. *Ibid.*, 257.

35. *Ibid.*, 260.

36. Markov, "U Golgofy," *RRe*, 1881, Apr, 191.

37. On Kropotkin, see the enthusiastic biography by George Woodcock and Ivan Avakumovich, *The Anarchist Prince*, London–NY, 1950, with bibliography 445–8; also for the use of scientific concepts in his ideology see the unpublished Doctoral dissertation of James Rogers, Harvard, 1956.

Anarchism was Russia's most —perhaps its only—original contribution to nineteenth-century European political thought. For the derivation of Kropotkin's ideas from Proudhon and the general early development of anarchism during this period see Max Nettlau, *Der Anarchismus von Proudhon zu Kropotkin: Seine historische Entwicklung in den Jahren 1859–1880*, Berlin, 1927. See also his *Bibliographie de l'anarchie*, Brussels, 1897; M. Nomad, *Aspects of Revolt*, NY, 1961, p; and J. Joll, *The Anarchists*, Boston, 1965.

On Bakunin's more militant anarchism see (besides the biographical treatments already cited) Alexander Brorovoy, ed., *Mikhailu Bakuninu 1876–1926, Ocherki istorii anarkhicheskogo dvizheniia v Rossii*, M, 1926; G. Maximoff, ed., *The Political Philosophy of Bakunin: Scientific Anarchism*, Glencoe, Ill., 1953; E. Pyziur, *The Doctrine of Anarchism of Michael A. Bakunin*, Milwaukee, Wisc., 1955. The integrity of Tolstoy's religious anarchism is gaining a measure of acknowledgment even among necessarily hostile Soviet critics. See V. Asmus, "Mirovozzrenie Tolstogo," *LN*, LXIX, 1961, 58–76.

38. On Sokolov and the influence of Proudhon on populism see my *Mikhailovsky*, esp. 129–32, 188, note 3; also Venturi, *Roots*, 328–9. R. Labry, *Herzen et Proudhon*, 1928. The influence of Christian ideas on Proudhon is stressed in the perceptive study of his controversy with Marx by the French Jesuit H. de Lubac, *The Un-Marxian Socialist*, NY, 1948.

39. Marx's letter to V. Zasulich of Mar 8, 1881, in *Narodnaia Volia v dokumentakh i vospominaniiakh*, M, 1935, 240–1.

40. Engels' letter to V. Zasulich of Apr 3, 1890, in *Proletarskaia revoliutsiia*, 1929, no. 2, 53.

41. All the phrases are italicized in the preface to his "Socialism and the Political Struggle," in G. Plekhanov, *Selected Philosophical Works*, M, 1960, I, 57–8.

42. *Ibid.*, 65.

43. Plekhanov, *Sochineniia*, M-P, 1923, 2d ed., IV, 248. There is a French tr., Ghent, 1917; and an English one, Minneapolis, nd. This work (like his important *Role of the Individual in History*, NY, 1940, p) is not discussed in S. Baron's biography, *Plekhanov the Father of Russian Marxism*, Stanford, Cal., 1963, which is generally focused on the development of his political-economic views and Revolutionary controversies, and pays only passing notice to his numerous writings on more purely ideological and cultural matters.

44. *In Defense of Materialism*, London, 1947, 73.

45. *Ibid.*, 220.

46. *Works*, 396–8, mt.

47. "Programme of the Social-Democratic Emancipation of Labour Group," (1884) in *Works*, I, 400–1. Note also the emphasis—characteristic of German Social Democracy of the era—on the immediate need to work for "a completely *democratic* state" in order to lift the cultural level and political consciousness of the workers to a point where it can properly assume full authority.

48. The impact of List and German economic thought in late-nineteenth-century Russia is discussed in Normano, *Spirit*, 64–81, and bibliography 158–60.

49. See O. Pisarzhevsky, *D. I. Mendeleev*, M, 1954, p. The many-sided economic and pedagogic activities of this practical-minded and generally conservative nationalist are treated in the forthcoming Doctoral dissertation at Brown University by Mrs. Beverley Almgren.

50. For an analysis and bibliography on the debates in the radical camp over economic development in the 1880's and 1890's see A. Mendel, *Dilemmas of Progress in Tsarist Russia. Legal Marxism and Legal Populism*, Cambridge, Mass., 1961. On the "legal Marxists" see R. Kindersley, *The First Russian Revisionists: A Study of "Legal Marxism" in Russia*, Oxford 1962; and on the Social Democratic movement see R. Pipes, *Social Democracy and the St. Petersburg Labor Movement, 1885–1897*, Cambridge, Mass., 1963; and J. Keep, *The Rise of Social Democracy in Russia 1898–1907*, Oxford, 1963; as well as L. Haimson, *The Russian Marxists and the Origins of Bolshevism*, Cambridge, Mass., 1955.

51. For a French translation of the original German text together with a critical introduction by Pipes (who is preparing an extended biography of Struve) see *Cahiers de l'institut de science économique appliquée*, 1962, Sep, 105–56. Kindersley's *Revisionists* also deals extensively with Struve.

52. Struve, "Intelligentsiia i revoliutsiia," *Vekhi*, M, 1910, 5th ed., 156–74.

Some idea of the range of Struve's interests can be gained from two general collections of his writings: *Na raznye temy*, P, 1902 (from 1893) and *Patriotica*, P, 1911 (from 1905). He continued to write on a variety of themes in the emigration; and set forth a retrospective view of his contacts with the liberal Rodichev in *SEER*, 1934, Jan, 347–67; and with Lenin, in *SEER*, 1934, Apr, 373–95, and Jul, 66–84.

53. See account in Baron, *Plekhanov*, 341–54; and, in addition to materials referenced therein, the useful short study of Plekhanov in E. H. Carr, *Studies in Revolution*, London, 1950, 105–19.

54. *A Solovyov Anthology*, arranged and introduced by S. Frank, London, 1950, 10. This excellent anthology has a bibliography of English editions of Solov'ev's works. Biographies of Solov'ev with expositions of his religious thought include K. Mochulsky, *Vladimir Solov'ev: zhizn' i uchenie*, Paris, 1936; and D. Stremooukhouf, *Vladimir Soloviev et son oeuvre messianique*, Strasbourg, 1935. His social ideas are brought out more fully and related to his philosophic conceptions in two unpublished Doctoral dissertations by W. Chrzanowski (Fribourg, 1911) and Z. David (Harvard, 1960). His influence on early-twentieth-century thought and culture is discussed by Berdiaev, *Dream and Reality*, London, 1950, and N. Lossky, "The Successors of Vladimir Solovyev," *SEER*, 1924, Jun, 92–105.

55. *Anthology*, 10.

56. *Ibid.*, 35.

57. *Ibid.*, 38.

58. *Ibid.*, 14.

59. For the influence of Comte on Solov'ev see works referred in my "Intelligentsia," 814, note 22; also his speech of 1898 on the centenary of Comte's birth in *Anthology*, 51–9.

60. *Anthology*, 104.

61. *Ibid.*, 122–3. A variety of attitudes toward the Jews within the intelligentsia are perceptively discussed by P. Berline, "Russian Religious Philosophers and the Jews," *Jewish Social Studies* 1947, Oct, 271–318. Faced with pogroms in the 1880's and new restrictions against settling in rural areas even within the pale of settlement, the Jewish community was drawn increasingly into the main arena of a more complex urban culture. On the one hand there was considerable interest in Zionism (indeed the *kibbutzim* of present-day Israel are largely the product of Russian Jews imbued with populist notions about the *obshchina);* and in the development of vernacular Yiddish culture, which flourished as never before in the period between the founding in 1878 of the first Yiddish theater in Moscow and the almost simultaneous deaths just prior to the Bolshevik takeover of the three recognized giants of Yiddish literature: Mendele, Peretts, and Sholom Aleichem.

On the other hand, many Jews tended to assimilate their energies into the general creative life and reformatorial agitation of the Russian Empire. There were twelve Jewish members of the first Duma, and wealthy Jews were important backers of the liberal movement. A Jewish railroad financier, Ivan Bliokh, painted a grim picture of the horrors of any future war in his *Budushchaia Voina* of 1898 (English edition: *The Future of War, in Its Technical, Economic and Political Relations*, Boston, 1914), and helped persuade Nicholas II to play a leading role in establishing the Court of International Justice at the Hague. Another attempt at internationalism launched by Russian Jews was Esperanto, the most successful of all attempts at a synthetic universal language, perfected by Lazarus Zamenhof between 1878 and 1887, after a prior effort to adopt a form of Yiddish as the base for such a language. See J. Raisin, "Jewish Contribution," esp. May, 939–51.

The Jewish Workers' Bund, organized in 1897, was one of the leading organizing forces in the formation of the Russian Social Democratic Party. Its leaders opposed both Zionism and the centralizing Social Democrats who denied autonomy to parties of the various nationalities (see K. Pinson, "Arkady Kremer, Vladimir Medem, and the Ideology of the Jewish 'Bund,'" *Jewish Social Studies*, 1945, Jul, 233–64; also the forthcoming Princeton Doctoral dissertation of A. Pollack). For a survey and references on the extensive Jewish participation in the Bolshevik—and even more the Menshevik—wing of subsequent Social Democratic activity (and to a lesser extent in the populist–Socialist Revolutionary tradition) see L. Shapiro, "The Role of the Jews."

62. On the growth of Pan-Asianism at the turn of the century see E. Sarkisyanz, "Russian Attitudes toward Asia," *RR*, 1954, Oct, 245–54; also N. Setnitsky, *Russkie Mysliteli o Kitae*, Harbin, 1926.

63. *Anthology*, 236.

64. *Ibid.*, 247–8. E. Benz has shown that much of Solov'ev's apocalyptical thinking was influenced by Jung-Stilling; G. Florovsky suggests that Dante had a considerable influence on the formation of Solov'ev's more positive ecumenical vision. See his "Vladimir Soloviev and Dante: The Problem of Christian Empire," in *For Roman Jakobson: Essays on the Occasion of His Sixtieth Birthday*, The Hague, 1956, 152–60.

VI. The Uncertain Colossus

1. Crescendo

1. N. Evreinov, *Theatre*, 14. The complaint of the S.R. leader V. Chernov about "electric charges" is contained in his *The Great Russian Revolution*, New Haven, 1936, 445, in his generally stimulating final chapter, "The Spirit of the Russian Revolution." The first use of "Soviet power plus electrification" appears to have been made by Lenin in his report to the Council of People's Commissars on Dec 22, 1920. See *Sochineniia*, L, 1950, 4th ed., XXXI, 484. The definition is repeated in the official Soviet ideological handbook, O. Kuusinen, ed., *Fundamentals of Marxism-Leninism*, M, 1961, 799.

2. A. Blok, *The Spirit of Music*, London, 1946, 5.

3. W. Grohmann, *Wassily Kandinsky Life and Work*, London, 1959, 87.

N. Vorob'ev, *M. K. Čiurlionis: der Litauische Maler und Musiker*, Kaunas-Leipzig, 1938, 32 ff. The influence within Russia of Chiurlionis (*ibid.*, 65 ff.) and of another Lithuanian, the symbolist poet and translator Jurgis Baltrushaitis, testifies to the increasing cosmopolitanism of Russian culture, now able to bring into its orbit leading figures from this most westerly and German-oriented of its Baltic provinces.

4. Cited by R. Poggioli, *The Poets of Russia .1890–1930*, Cambridge, Mass., 1960, 262. On Khlebnikov and the originality of Russian futurism see V. Markov, *The Longer Poems of Velimir Khlebnikov*, Berkeley-Los Angeles, 1962.

5. On Bely's musical style and the four "symphonies" written between 1902 and 1909 see O. Maslenikov,

The Frenzied Poets: Andrey Biely and the Russian Symbolists, Berkeley, 1952, 70 ff. On Burliuk, C. Gray, *Experiment,* 94–107, 195.

6. Meierhold, "The Booth," *The Drama,* 1917, Aug, 447. Rimsky-Korsakov's *Coq d'Or,* the last opera to come from the pen of the original "Big Five," or "mighty handful" (written in 1906-7, and produced only after his death in 1908), was staged with the singers immobile on the side and the acting done solely by dancers. See A. Bakshy, *The Path of the Modern Russian Stage,* London, 1916, 85–8. The chromatic nature of the music also represents a distinct departure from the relatively conventional harmonies of his earlier work.

   For some interesting ideas on Diaghilev as the "John the Baptist of the classico-mathematical Renaissance," who helped prepare the way for Einstein by projecting into European culture the insight of the modern dance that "motion not language is truthful," see F. Kermode, "Poet and Dancer before Diaghilev," *PR,* 1961, Jan-Feb, 48–65.

7. A. Bogdanov, *O proletarskoi kul'ture,* M, 1921. For the tortured and humorless criticism of these ideas of Bogdanov advanced during the High Stalin era see A. Shcheglov, *Bor'ba Lenina protiv Bogdanovskoi revizii Marksizma,* M, 1937, 203–6.

8. M. Gorky, *Days with Lenin,* NY, 1932, 52.

9. Cited in E. Friedell, *Cultural History,* II, 381.

10. Phrases used by Friedell, *ibid.,* 380, 382.

11. I. Stravinsky, *The Poetics of Music in the Form of Six Lessons,* NY, 1956, p, 109.

12. D. Mirsky, "The Eurasian Movement," *SEER,* 1927, Dec, 312; and citations from L. Karsavin, 316–17. There is a similarity of Kar-

savin's position to the early idealistic conception of fascist corporatism—involving both a fascination with Bolshevism and an aesthetic-physiological fondness for organic images of society—the Eurasian movement being influenced by Dokuchaevan ideas about the inner continuities between human and natural phenomena on the Eurasian plain and also by much of the same philological mysticism that possessed Nazism in its early "runic" stage.

   A more elevated use of the symphonic metaphor by "Eurasian" sympathizers is in E. Trubetskoy's insistence that "our present world contains numberless indications of the symphony of light and sound in the world to come." Cited by N. Lossky in *SEER,* 1924, Jun, 95. See also B. Ishboldin, "The Eurasian Movement," *RR,* 1946, Spring, 64–73.

13. See Gray, *Experiment,* 308.

14. Cited and discussed in Makovsky, "Gumilev," 190 ff.

15. Cited in Stravinsky, *Poetics,* 121.

16. Title of an analysis of the accomplishments and possibilities of Soviet culture by I. Berlin in *FA,* 1957, Oct, 1–24.

17. Stravinsky, *Poetics,* 111. See also J. Sullivan, *Beethoven,* NY, 1949, 77. On the importance of the Prometheus myth, see M. Gorky, *Literary Portraits,* M, nd [1959?], 217; also *LE,* IX, 314–20. The most recent popular life of Marx in the USSR is a romanticized trilogy entitled *Prometheus:* G. Serebriakova, *Prometei,* 1963, M, 3v (described in *NK,* 1963, no. 25, entry 239). Note also the ideological importance attached to Aeschylus' *Prometheus Bound* when issued in a tirage of 150,000: *Prometei prikovanny,* M, 1956.

18. Article of 1906, reprinted in *Sub Specie Aeternitatis,* P, 1907, 397.

19. *Smysl' tvorchestva,* M, 1916, 220, also 7. Berdiaev considered this

his "most inspired" work *(Samopoznanie,* Paris, 1949, 229–37), and subtitled it "an attempt at the justification of man." These two works have been translated respectively as *The Meaning of the Creative Act,* London, 1955, p; and *Dream and Reality,* London, 1950 —the latter autobiographical work being of particular value for the period under discussion, though the English version often distorts the meaning of the original Russian.

20. Gray, *Experiment,* 93–4; R. Clough, *Futurism: The Story of a Modern Art Movement,* NY, 1961; G. Lehrmann, *De Marinetti à Maiakovski,* Zurich, 1942; and N. Khardzhiev, "Maiakovsky i zhivopis'," in *Maiakovsky: Materialy i issledovaniia,* M, 1940.

21. Cited in Gorlin, "Interrelation," 146–7.

22. Cited in *ibid.*

23. "Ne slyshno shumu gorodskogo, /Za Nevskoi bashnei tishina,/ I na shtyke u chasovogo/ Gorit polnochnaia luna." *Russkie pesni* (coll. Rozanov), 347. The song is based on a poem by F. Glinka; for another, slightly variant version, see the notes to Blok, *Sochineniia,* M, 1955, I, 774.

24. "I bol'she net gorodovogo-/ Guliai, rebiata, bez vina!" Blok, *Sochineniia,* I, 531. Blok also changes the preposition to *nad* in the previous sentence.

25. Cited in M. Cooper, "Scriabin's Mystical Beliefs," *ML,* XVI, 1935, 111. For the extraordinary vogue of seances and spiritism beginning in the 1880's and affecting even scientists like the chemist Butlerov and the biologist Wagner, the basic account in *BE,* LXI, 224–6, should be supplemented by M. Petrovo-Solovovo-Perovsky, *Ocherki iz istorii spiriticheskago dvizheniia v Rossii,* P, 1905 (first printed as an appendix to the Russian translation of the works of the English spiritist Frank Podmore).

26. Cited in Cooper, "Beliefs," 110.

27. Cited in *ibid.,* 112.

28. Stravinsky, *Poetics,* 107.

29. Calvocoressi, *Masters,* 472–3.

30. B. Asaf'ev, *Skriabin,* Petersburg-Berlin, 1923, 44–8. For the influence of Wagner on Scriabin, L. Sabaneev, *Skriabin,* P, 1923, 189 ff.

On the popularity of Wagner during the silver age see F. Reeve, *Aleksandr Blok,* NY, 1962, 33; Blok, *Spirit of Music,* 58–70; V. Ivanov, "Vagner i Dionisovo deistvo," *Vesy,* 1905, no. 2, 13–6; and N. Findeizen, "Vagner v Rossii," *RMG,* 1903, no. 35, 755–69. The music of *Lohengrin* helped impress on Kandinsky the possibility of color in music (Grohmann, *Kandinsky,* 31); The magic fire music of *Walküre* helped inspire Eisenstein to work out methods of integrating the music and colors of his movies (E. Nazaikinsky and Yury Rap, "Music in Color," *USSR,* 1963, Feb, 47).

31. Cited in M. Bill, *Wassily Kandinsky,* Boston, 1951, 163–4.

32. Kandinsky, *On the Spiritual in Art,* NY, 1946, 43.

33. *Ibid.,* 39–70, see also W. Grohmann, *Kandinsky,* 78, 87.

34. For general description A. Swan, *Scriabin,* London, 1923, 97–111; also *A. N. Skriabin: Sbornik k 25-letiiu so dnia smerti,* M-L, 1940; B. Schlözer, *Aleksandr Skriabin,* Berlin, 1923; Gerald Abraham, "Alexander Scriabin," in Abraham and Calvocoressi, *Masters,* 450–98; and, for a negative reading of Scriabin as a "consistent paranoiac," who was the first "to reduce musical insanity to a peculiar sort of scheme, even to a theory," see Sabaneev, *Skriabin,* 46.

Scales equilibrating color and sound as well as sound and taste were discussed in the eighteenth century (see D. Schier, *Louis Bertrand Castel, Anti-Newtonian Scientist,* Cedar Rapids, Iowa,

1941, 133–96). An octave of smells was later devised by a Parisian perfume manufacturer in 1865 (S. Piesse, *Des Odeurs*, 1865); and some other pioneering works of modern music had a color accompaniment scored throughout (Arnold Schönberg, *Die glückliche Hand* of 1913). Nevertheless, Scriabin's system stands as the most fully developed, ideologically pretentious effort. His system has never been fully studied, but important investigations of more recent times include P. Dickenmann, *Die Entwicklung der Harmonik bei A. Skrjabin*, Bern, 1935; V. Berkov, "Nekotorye voprosy garmonii Skriabina," *SM*, 1959, Jun, 90–6. For the interest of Eisenstein and signs of recent Soviet interest in the problem see Nazaikinsky and Rap, "Music in Color," 46–7.

35. Cited in Grohmann, *Kandinsky*, 86, 98.

36. S. G. Lazutin's *Russkaia chastushka: voprosy proiskhozhdeniia i formirovaniia zhanra*, Voronezh, 1960, demonstrates convincingly that the chastushka form developed only in the final third of the nineteenth century. See especially 249–52.

37. For the leadership of the Mamontov circle in establishing a distinctive new tradition of Russian art in the late imperial period see Gray, *Experiment*, 9–34. For Mamontov's links with the musical world see A. Solovtsov, *Zhizn' i tvorchestvo N. A. Rimskogo-Korsakova*, M-L, 1963.

38. Cited in the introduction by C. Gray to the program of the London exhibition of Malevich paintings, held in Oct–Nov 1959, *Kasimir Malevich*, London, 1959, 7.

39. Manifestoes using these terms cited in *ibid.*, 12, 14–15. On Malevich see also, Gray, *Experiment*, 128 ff.; and in addition to works

referenced therein see David Sylvester, "Kasimir Malevich," *Encounter*, 1960, May, 48–52; and, for further illustrations of his work, E. Penkala, "Malewitsch's Oeuvre geborgen," *Das Kunstwerk*, 1958, Apr, 3–16; P. Bucarelli, intr., *Casimir Malevic*, Rome, 1959; and Malevich, *The Non-objective World*, Chicago, 1959.

40. Gray, *Malevich*, 12.

41. N. Punin, cited in Gray, *Malevich*, 7.

42. Cited from *Bog ne skinut. Iskusstvo, Tserkov', Fabrika*, Vitebsk, 1920–2, in Gray, *Malevich*, 15.

43. A. Kosmodemiansky, *Konstantin Tsiolkovsky*, M, 1956, 95; and for the earlier history of rocketry (dating back to the Russo-Turkish War of 1877–8) *ibid.*, 49 ff.; also see Z. Kopal, "Soviet Astronomy," *Su*, 1961, Jan-Mar, 65–9. For the direct influence of Nicholas Fedorov on Tsiolkovsky's youthful development, see V. Shklovsky, "Zhili-byli," *Znamia*, 1963, Feb, 177–8.

44. On Tatlin see Gray, *Experiment*, 40–8, 250; on *planity* see plates T, V, and X in Gray, *Malevich*.

45. Shestov, *All Things Are Possible*, NY, 1920, 241. The translated title *Apofeoz bezpochvennosti*, P, 1905, which was published under his original name, L. I. Schwarzmann. On the early years of this generally neglected figure see B. Schlözer, "Un Penseur russe: Léon Chestov," *MF* (159), 1922, 82–115; and D. Strotmann, "Le Credo de Léon Chestov," *Irénikon*, XVI, 1937, 22–37.

46. Illustrated Gray, *Experiment*, plates 223–4.

47. There is considerable ambiguity about whether the long, pseudo-scientific asides in the work are serious attempts at elaboration of the problem (they were widely discussed as such at the time) or subtle satirical jabs at the scientism of the age. For Mechnikov's

ideas on the subject see his *Essais optimistes,* 1907.

A sect called the "deathless ones" *(Bessmertniki)* attracted a number of intellectuals, including Berdiaev, during this period; (Berdiaev, *Dream and Reality,* 196 ff.), and this interest in prolonging life has remained a major subject of inquiry in the USSR. See for the Stalin era Olga Lepeshinskaia, "On the Road to Longevity" *(Izvestiia,* Dec 2, 1953, 3; in *CDSP,* Jan 10, 1953, 24–5), with her objections to the "statistical, metaphysical approach" of the West to the problem of old age. She argued well for her own approach by living to ninety two on her soda and bath prescriptions. (See her obituary, *NYT,* Oct 4, 1963.) See also, more recently, L. Leont'ev, *Starost' otstupaet,* Alma Ata, 1963.

For other materials and a general discussion of this theme in pre- and post-Revolutionary Russia (and in the emigration) see P. Wiles, "On Physical Immortality," *Su,* 1965, Jul, 125–43; Oct, 142–61. The meeting between Mechnikov and Tolstoy in May, 1909, just before the latter's death, to discuss the question of death and immortality was widely regarded as a kind of cosmic council of war against the power of death between "the two monarchs of universal literature and science, Leo I and Elie I . . . Yasnaya Polyana, and not the *Standart,* the imperial yacht on which the Kaiser and the Tsar [were meeting simultaneously] held the center of the stage in Russia." H. Bernstein, cited in Wiles, 145.

48. P. Uspensky's ideas were propagated after his exile in London through a community known as the Gurdjieff Institute, and from the time of the bombing of London until his death in 1947, in New York. See his *Tertium Organum, A Key to the Enigmas of the World,* NY, 1934; *A New Model of the Universe,* NY, 1943; and his posthumously published *The Fourth Way,* NY, 1957, which contains some of his most important talks and answers to questions during the period 1921–47.

49. *The Fourth Way,* 97–104.

50. See especially the attack on the "neo-Christianity" of the "God-seekers" by V. Bazarov (pseud. of V. Rudnev), "Lichnost' i liubov' v svete novago religioznago soznaniia," *Literaturny Raspad,* P, 1908, Kn. 1, 213–30; "Khristiane tret'iego zaveta i stroiteli bashni vavilonskoi," *Literaturny Raspad,* P, 1909, Kn. 2, 5–38.

51. Gorky, *Ispoved',* Berlin, 1908, 196. There is an English translation from the German by W. Harvey, *A Confession,* London, 1910. See also V. Botsianovsky, *Bogoiskateli,* P, 1911, and the valuable article "Bogoiskatel'stvo i Bogostroitel'stvo," in *LE,* I, 538; N. Minsky (pseud. of N. Vilenkin), *Religiia budushchego: filosofskie razgovory,* P, 1905; Lunacharsky, *Religiia i sotsializm,* P, 1908–11, 2v; and his *Three Plays,* London, 1923; Gorky, "Razrushenie lichnosti," in the important collection *Ocherki filosofii kollektivizma,* P, 1909, and published in an abridged translation in his *Literature and Life,* London, 1946, 112–25. The term "God-seeker" was taken from the work of the popular Austrian novelist Peter Rosegger, *Der Gottsucher* (originally published 1883), which portrayed an ascetic Promethean hero excommunicated by the Church for murdering a tyrannical pastor, seeking in the solitude of the mountains and eventually finding an altogether new religion for a "godless" community there. See H. Sorg, *Rosegger's Religion,* Washington, D. C., 1938, 53 ff.

52. Baronov cited in Blok, *Spirit,* 34.

53. *Ispoved',* 196.

54. *O proletarskoi etike,* M, 1918, 38 (first published 1906 and republished again Kharkov, 1923.) This and the following reference taken from material used in a seminar by George Kline at the Harvard Russian Research Center on Nov 18, 1958, with his translations.

55. "Pered litsom roka: k filosofii tragedii," in *Obrazovanie,* P, XII, 1903, 58.

56. *Three Plays,* 132.

57. *Ibid.,* 134.

58. *Ibid.,* 399. See also the revealing short introduction by Lunacharsky, xi–xiii.

59. On Bogdanov see articles in *LE,* I, 526–30; and *BSE* (I), VI 574–82; and his own major works, *Osnovnye elementy istoricheskago vzgliada na prirodu,* 1899; *Poznanie s istoricheskoi tochki zreniia,* 1901; *Iz psikhologii obshchestva: sbornik,* 1904; *Vseobshchaia organizatsionnaia nauka (tektologiia),* three parts, 1913, 1917, 1922 (the last part was published in Berlin and included all three parts); and *Filosofiia zhivago opyta,* 1928. For a critical discussion of Bogdanov's views see N. Karev, "Tektologiia ili dialektika," *PZM,* 1926, nos. 1, 2, 3. For the philosophy of Proletkult see A. Lunacharsky, *Self-education of the Workers: The Cultural Task of the Struggling Proletariat,* London, 1919.

60. *Krasnaia zvezda,* P, 1908; and *Inzhener Menni,* M, 1923.

61. Discussed in Max Nomad, *Aspects of Revolt,* NY, 1961, p. 116–17. See also S. Utechin, "Philosophy and Society: Alexander Bogdanov," in L. Labedz, ed., *Revisionism,* NY, 1962, p, 117–25.

62. A. Kraisky, *Ulybki solntsa,* P, 1919; and article on him in *LE,* V, 538.

63. Citations from the Blacksmith poets V. Kirillov and M. Gerasimov respectively in the article on Cosmism in *LE,* V, 501–2.

64. See the valuable discussion of Machajski's views and relation of them to other European thinkers in Nomad, *Aspects,* 96–117, also the introduction by Edmund Wilson, the selection from his *Intellectual Worker* in V. Calverton, ed., *The Making of Society,* NY, 1931, 427–36, and the early Soviet characterization *(BSE (1)* XIII, 64–6) of his views as a kind of Siberian theory that never penetrated the center of Russia. For the other thinkers see in addition to Nomad, H. Stuart Hughes, *Consciousness and Society,* NY, 1958 (and p); Georges Sorel, *Reflections on Violence,* NY, 1961, p, with valuable introduction by E. A. Shil.

65. Trotsky, *Literature and Revolution,* NY, 1957, 256. For Trotsky's views on culture during this period see the excellent section "Not by Politics Alone . . ." in I. Deutscher, *The Prophet Unarmed,* London, 1959, 164–200.

66. "Sinie okovy," in Khlebnikov, *Sobranie proizvedenii,* L, 1930, I, 286–7, discussed by V. Markov, *Poems,* 194–8.

67. On Kubin see Grohmann, *Kandinsky,* 62–7, 87.

68. Dostoevsky, *SS,* IV, 165.

69. M. Kuzmin, *Kryl'ia: povest',* M, 1907. His popularity was augmented by official efforts to confiscate his work; V. Ivanov, "Veneris Figurae, stikhi," *Vesy,* 1907, Jan, 16.

70. *Sanine,* NY, 1931 (tr. P. Pinkerton). *The Petty Demon,* NY, 1962, (tr. A. Field, intr. E. Simmons).

71. For citations from Schopenhauer and indications of his influence on Turgenev see A. Walicki, "Turgenev and Schopenhauer," *OSP,* X, 1962, 12. T. Seltzer, "Michael Artzybashev," *The Drama,* 1916, Feb, 1–12, points (12) to the influence of Max Stirner on Artsybashev.

72. The influence of Quixote on Sologub is stressed in Zamiatin's ex-

cellent essay in *Litsa,* NY, 1955, 31–37; and is even more evident in Sologub's play, *The Triumph of Death,* translated by John Cournos in *The Drama,* 1916, Aug, 346–84, and preceded by a valuable essay by Cournos, "Feodor Sologub as Dramatist," *ibid.,* 329–45. For an excellent review of the *Demon* by Sidney Hyman, see *NL,* 1962, Sep 3, 19–20.

73. Sologub, *SS,* P, 1913, XVIII, 3. See the synopsis and discussion of the Legend by A. Field in *SEEJ,* 1961, winter, 341–9; and the more detailed textual analysis by J. Holthusen, *Fedor Sologubs Roman-Trilogie,* 's Gravenhage, 1960.

74. F. Sologub, *The Sweet-Scented Name and Other Fairy Tales, Fables and Stories,* London, 1915, 155.

75. *Ibid.,* 156.

76. *Ibid.,* 134.

77. Cited in Poggioli, *The Phoenix,* 173. Poggioli's essay, which contains a good basic bibliography on Rozanov, is also reprinted separately as *Rozanov,* NY, 1962.

78. V. Rozanov, *Legenda o velikom inkvizitore F. M. Dostoevskago,* P, 1906, (3d ed.), 81–3.

79. Term used by Poggioli, *The Phoenix,* 162.

80. Cited in Maslenikov, *Poets,* 202.

81. *Vesy,* 1904, no. 5, 17–30; *Novy Put',* 1904, nos. 1–3, 5, 8, 9; *Voprosy zhizni,* 1905, nos. 6–7; and *Dionis i pradionisiistvo,* Baku, 1923. See also L. Shestov, "Viacheslav Velikolepny," *RM,* 1916, no. 10, 80–111.

82. Rozanov, *Izbrannoe,* 95–108.

83. L. Shestov, *Dostoevsky i Nittsshe: Filosofiia tragedii,* P, 1903 (also German edition, Cologne, 1924). There were a number of other works published in 1903 comparing these two figures. See, for instance, M. Kheisin, "Dostoevsky i Nittsshe," *MB,* 1903, Jun, 119–41; and the antagonistic study by the priest A. N. Smirnov, *Dostoevsky i Nittsshe,* Kazan, 1903. The influence of Nietzsche was critical on A. Blok, who took over particularly from Nietzsche's *Birth of Tragedy* the idea that culture was essentially musical and the world little more than "music made concrete." See R. Labry, "Alexandre Blok et Nietzsche," *RES,* XXVII, 1951, esp. 204–5. Also *LE,* VIII, 105–8; and a series of articles by Bely on Nietzsche: *Vesy,* 1908, nos. 7, 8, 10.

84. *Dobro v uchenii gr. Tolstogo i F. Nittsshe,* Berlin, 1923. Shestov later became, during his exile in Paris, the major Russian popularizer and translator of Kierkegaard. See his *Kirgegard i ekzistentsial'naia filosofiia (glas vopiiushchago v pustyne),* Paris, 1939.

85. A. Z. Shteinberg, *Sistema svobody F. M. Dostoevskogo,* Berlin, 1923.

86. Gray, *Experiment,* 90 ff. and plates 73–4.

87. *Ibid.,* 121 ff.

88. Stravinsky, *An Autobiography,* NY, 1936, 47.

89. Gray, *Experiment,* 308, for hitherto unpublished description of this production; also *ibid.,* 99 and plate 75 on "Drama in Cabaret, No. 13"; Poggioli, *Poets,* 238–49. Also A. Ripellino, *Majakovskij e il teatro russo d'avanguardia,* Turin, 1959. Sologub proposes in his "Liturgy of Me" a kind of ego-sensualism at the same time as the "ego-futurists" were flourishing. See Sipovsky, *Etapy,* 109.

90. See, for instance, N. Evreinov, *The Theatre of the Soul: a Monodrama in One Act,* London, 1915, tr. M. Potapenko and C. St. John.

91. Cited in Gray, *Experiment,* 193.

92. I. Babel', "Mama, Rimma i Alla. Ilya Isaakovich i Margarita Prokof'evna," *Letopis',* 1916, Nov, 32–44.

93. René Fülöp-Miller, *Rasputin: The Holy Devil,* NY, 1928, 345 and the entire section 321–68.

94. Blok, *Dnevnik,* L, 1928, II, 72;

Maslenikov, *Poets*, 164–5; Revelation, xii, 1–6.

95. M. Dudkin, as cited in J. Catteau, "A Propos de la littérature fantastique: André Belyj, héritier de Gogol et de Dostoïevski," *CMR*, 1962, Jul–Sep, 372. Lilac was the "Promethean" color in Scriabin's scheme, and generally a favorite for aesthetes of the Silver Age.

96. Pil'niak, *Ivan-da-mar'ia*, 1921, cited in Mirsky, *Contemporary Russian Literature*, 309.

97. Zamiatin, "Iks," in *Nechestivye rasskazy*, 1926, cited in A. M. van der Eng-Liedmeir, *Soviet Literary Characters*, 's Gravenhage, 1959, 76.

98. 2 × 2 = 5, M, 1920; *Razvratnichaiu s vdokhnoveniem*, M, 1921. The movement apparently viewed itself as developing out of the English Imagism of Ezra Pound and Wyndham Lewis. See *LE*, IV, 461–4.

99. Cited from *Estradnaia arkhitektonika*, M, 1920, in V. Zavalishin, *Early Soviet Writers*, NY, 1958, 135.

100. For a brief discussion of Kollontai's views, including selections from and a listing of some of her numerous works published in English and other Western languages, see T. Anderson, *Masters*, 163–89. The articles alluded to in the present discussion are *Novaia moral' i rabochy klass*, M, 1918; "Liubov' pchel trudovykh" from *Revoliutsiia chuvstv i revoliutsiia nravov*, M-L, 1923 (and also in *Svobodnaia liubov'*, Riga, 1925); and "Doroga krylatomu Erosu," in *Molodaia gvardiia*, 1923, no. 3. See also the critical literature referenced in *LE*, V, 384–5, esp. Budnev Finogen, "Polovaia revoliutsiia," *Na postu*, 1924, no. 1.

101. This famous theory is expanded by the daughter in the short story "The Love of Three Generations," in *Liubov' pchel trudovykh* referenced above, also in her *A Great Love*, NY, 1929. For the controversy generated by the story see L. Luke, "Marxian Woman: Soviet Variants," in E. Simmons, ed., *Through the Glass of Soviet Literature*, NY, 1961, p, 34 ff.

102. Max Jakobson, *The Diplomacy of the Winter War*, Cambridge, Mass., 1961, 203–17, 272.

103. Cited in O. Sayler, *Inside the Moscow Art Theatre*, NY, 1925, 112. See the discussion and illustration of this production in the section "Spanish Passion—and Russian," 106–24.

104. Mochulsky, *Solov'ev*, 247 ff.

105. *LE*, III, 321–2; Maslenikov, *Poets*, 25 ff.

106. Remizov, *Ognennaia Rossiia*, Reval/Tallinn, 1921, esp. 71. There is a concise discussion of Remizov in Harkins, *Dictionary*, 332–4; fuller discussion and references in *LE*, IX, 606–9. Vorob'ev, *Čiurlionis*, 82 ff. L. Andreev, *Satan's Diary*, NY, 1920, with a useful preface by H. Bernstein. The work was completed just a few days prior to Andreev's death in Finland in 1919. Just as the early Bolsheviks looked for inspiration to America as the model for a modern industrial society, so conservatives like Andreev tended to view America as the principal bearer of the virus of materialism. In the same vein see I. Bunin (the Nobel Prize-winning émigré writer —like Andreev essentially a craftsman of realistic prose) *The Gentleman from San Francisco*, and perhaps also Nabokov's *Lolita*. See also recent discussions of Andreev's ideas by J. Woodward (*CSP*, VI, 1964, 59–79) and H. Peltier-Zamoyska (*CMR*, 1963, Jul-Sep, 205–29).

107. S. Yaremich, *Vrubel', Mikhail Aleksandrovich: Ego zhizn' i tvorchestvo*, M, 1911; *Vrubel'*, L-M, 1963 (a collection including

correspondence, memoirs, etc.); and C. Gray, *Experiment*, 18–21.

108. Critical opinion of Ivanov's painting had also changed dramatically. Contrast the worshipful attitude of the wanderers toward Ivanov's work (N. Mashkovtsev, *Surikov*, 15–18) with the critical anti-populist attitude of Rozanov ("Aleksandr Aleksandrovich Ivanov," *Zolotoe Runo*, 1906, Nov-Dec, 3–6), who suggests (among other things) that the painter's "Appearance of Christ to the People," be re-entitled "The Eclipse of Christ by the People."

109. Cited in A. Haskell, *Diaghileff: His Artistic and Private Life*, NY, 1935, 137. See also S. Lifar, *Serge Diaghilev*, NY, 1940, 111–17.

110. For citations and discussions see V. Erlich, "The Dead Hand of the Future: The Predicament of Vladimir Mayakovsky," *ASR*, 1962, Sep, 433–40. Note also the title of F. Sologub's collection, *Soborny blagovest*, P, 1921.

111. See paintings in Grohmann, *Kandinsky*, 404–5. Judaic influences also contributed to the apocalypticism of late imperial culture: the emotionally disturbing effect of breaking loose from the pale of settlement, the classical Jewish opposition to portraiture, etc. See E. Szittya, *Soutine et son temps*, 1955, 13–22.

112. Within the trilogy (all available in English translation) see particularly the epilogue to *Peter and Alexis;* see also C. H. Bedford, "Dmitry Merezhkovsky, the Intelligentsia, and the Revolution of 1905," *CSP*, III, 1959.

The crisis of the revolutionary camp was also represented as a kind of apocalypse in the work of the S.R. Boris Savinkov. *The Pale Horse*, of 1905, published under the pseudonym of Vsevolod Ropshin (English ed., Dublin, 1917), is 444–61. Savinkov's other celebrated tale of revolution *The Tale of What Was Not* (English ed. *What Never Happened*, NY, 1917) prompted a fresh discussion of the "Hamlet question." See E. Koltonovskaia, "Byt' ili ne byt'?," *RM*, 1913, no. 6, 24–40.

113. On Bely see in addition to Maslenikov, *Poets;* K. Mochulsky, *Andrei Bely*, Paris, 1955; and *LE*, I, 422–9.

114. "Griadushchie gunny," in Briusov, *Stikhotvoreniia i poemy*, L, 1961, 278–9. Also in an apocalyptical vein is his play of 1904, *Zemlia* (analyzed by R. Poggioli "Qualis Artifex Pereo! or Barbarism and Decadence," in *Harvard Library Bulletin*, XIII, 1959, winter, 135–59), which depicts the total destruction of humanity; and his *Republic of the Southern Cross*, London, 1918, which tells of the end that eventually came to the utopian city of the future.

115. See Bely, *Petersburg*, NY, 1959. See also his early work, "Apokalipsis v russkoi poezii," *Vesy*, 1905, no. 4, 11–28.

116. Bely, "Khristos voskres," *Stikhotvoreniia*, Berlin, 1923, 347–71.

117. "Pevuchy zov," in the collection *Sergei Esenin*, M, 1958, 107–9. See the discussion by P. Pascal, "Esenine, poète de la campagne russe," *OSP*, II, 1951, 55–71.

118. All works included in N. Kliuev, *PSS*, NY, 1954, 2v; "Pesn' solntsenostsa," I, 381–3; "Chetverty Rim," II, 85–90; and "Lenin," I, 414–23.

119. See, for instance, the last two books published by Berdiaev in Russia before his emigration abroad: *Konets renesansa*, P, 1922; and *Osvald Shpengler i zakat Evropy*, M, 1922.

120. Reeve, *Blok*, 102–4; Blok, *Sochineniia*, I, 102–3.

121. L. Andreev, "Prokliatie Zveria," *PSS*, P, 1913, VIII, 144, 114.

122. Esenin, "Sorokoust," of 1920 in *Esenin*, 154–6.

123. Subtitle of Kliuev's *Pesn' solntse-nostsa*, Berlin, 1920.

124. S. Klychkov, *Posledny Lel'*, Kharkov, 1927, as cited in *LE*, V, 323; V. Khlebnikov, "Zhuravl'," as cited in Markov, *Khlebnikov*, 63.

125. "Gorod, gorod, pod toboi i zemlia ne pokhozha na zemliu . . . Ubil, utramboval ee satana chugunnym kopytom, ukatal zheleznoi spinoi, kataias' po nei, kak kataetsia loshad' po lugu v myle . . ." Klychkov, *Lel'* as cited in *LE*, V, 323.

126. "Videli li vy,/ Kak bezhit po stepiam,/ V tumanakh ozernykh kroias',/ Zheleznoi nozdrei khrapia,/ Na lapakh chugunnykh poezd?/ A za nim/ Po bol'shoi trave,/ Kak na prazdnike otchaiannykh gonok,/ Tonkie nogi zakidyvaia k golove,/ Skachet krasnogrivy zherebenok?" "Sorokoust," of 1920, in *Esenin*, 155.

127. V. Ivanov, *Bronepoezd No. 14–69*, M, 1922 (*Armoured Train 14–69*, London, 1933); B. Pil'niak, *Goly god*, M-P, 1923 (2d rev. ed., first in 1920); *The Naked Year*, NY, 1928, esp. chapter five "Deaths," 233 and ff.; and N. Nikitin, "Noch'," in the almanac *Krug*, M-P, 1923.

128. Cited from Poggioli, *Phoenix*, 173.

129. V. Rozanov, *Okolo tserkovnykh sten*, P, 1906, 2v.

130. Cited from the slightly abridged version of Rozanov's apocalypse, translated by V. Pozner and B. Schlözer, with a valuable introduction by the latter, *L'Apocalypse de notre temps précédé de Esseulement*, 1930, 277; 173–281.

131. Khlebnikov's play *Mirskontsa*, discussed in V. Markov, *Poems*, 27; the poem *Igra v adu* (successive editions 1912 and 1913, coauthored by Khlebnikov and A. Kruchonykh) is discussed at greater length in Markov, 83–6.

132. Zamiatin, *My*, NY, 1952, 197; also available as *We* (trans. G. Zilbourg), NY, 1959, p. See also M. Hayward, "Pilnyak and Zamyatin: Tragedies of the Twenties," *Su*, 1961, Apr-Jun, 85–91; and D. Richards, *Zamyatin—A Soviet Heretic*, NY, 1962.

133. Zamiatin, "Peshchera," in G. Struve, *Russian Stories*, NY, 1961, p, 292 (there is a facing English translation of the Russian text and useful explanatory notes).

Pil'niak, "Mashiny i volki," (1923–4) *SS*, M-L, 1930, II; "Mat' syra-zemlia," (1927) *SS*, 1929, III, 17–75; P. Wilson, "Boris Pilnyak," *Su*, 1963, Jan, 134–42. Leonov, "Konets melkogo cheloveka," (written in 1922 and printed in an apparently revised version M, 1924) in *SS*, M, 1960, I, 197–273. Pil'niak's interest in Old Russia dominated his early writings; and, judging from the discussion of Leonov's early period in V. Kovalev, *Tvorchestvo Leonida Leonova*, M-L, 1962, 38–42, there are important unpublished works of Leonov from this period, including one with selections from Avvakum, a figure in whom Leonov has had an abiding personal interest.

If Zamiatin's *We* anticipates Huxley's *Brave New World*, so also does his "Cave" anticipate in some respects *Ape and Essence*.

134. E. Zamiatin, *Litsa*, 249. The article is reprinted 247–56; and is now available in an English translation by W. Vickery, *PR*, 1961, no. 3–4, 372–8.

135. On *Attila*, a major part of which was completed in verse in 1928 but never published, see the obituary on Zamiatin by A. Remizov, "Stoiat'—negasimuiu svechu," *SZ*, LXIV, 1937, esp 429; *Navodnenie*, L, 1930. See also W. Edgerton, "The Serapion Brothers: An Early Soviet Controversy," *ASR*, 1949, Feb, 47–64; and Zamiatin's letter to Stalin of June, 1931, in *Litsa*, 280.

Other literary works of the immediate post-Revolutionary period showing the apocalypticism that was prevalent even among those not at all interested in Marxism-Leninism (as Zamiatin was, to a considerable extent), see Pil'niak's story of 1919 *Tysiacha let* (*SS*, 7–14) and S. Grigor'ev, *Proroki i predtechi poslednego zaveta: imazhinisty Esenin, Kusikov, Mariengof*, M, 1921.

136. *Litsa*, 8, cited from the famous article "Ia boius'," in *Dom iskusstv*, 1920, no. I.

137. *Litsa*, 251–2.

138. The *Liebestod* in Wagner's *Tristan and Isolde* was designated by Wagner as a *Verklärung* (Transfiguration); and *Tod und Verklärung* became the title and theme of one of Richard Strauss's most iridescent tone poems.

139. See, for instance, Blok's "Kometa" discussed in Reeve, *Blok*, 162–3; D. Sviatsky, *Strashny sud kak astral'naia allegoriia (istoriko-astronomichesky ekskurs v oblast' khristianskoi ikonografii)*, P, 1911, 47–8.

140. Reeve, *Blok*, 42–4. See also A. Kuprin "Hamlet" in *A Slav Soul*, London, 1916, 72–93.

141. For description and illustration of these productions see Sayler, *Inside*, 165–72. Laertes and the Queen were, apparently, portrayed as vacillating between the two camps. For Chekhov's philosophy of acting, in which one was to immerse oneself emotionally in the entire personality of the part being played, see *To the Actor: On the Technique of Acting*, NY, 1953; and also, *To the Director and Playwright* (compiled and edited by C. Leonard), NY, 1963.

142. Gorky, *Ispoved'*, Berlin, 1908, 196. C. Balmont, *Budem kak solntse*, 1903; A. Remizov, *Posolon'*, 1907.

143. "Beri svoi cheln, plyvi na dal'ny polius/ V stenakh iz l'da . . ./ I k vzdragivan'iam medlennogo khlada/ ustaluiu ty dushu priuchi,/ Chtob' bylo *zdes'* ei nichego ne nado,/ Kogda *ottuda* rinutsia luchi." Blok, *SS*, M-L, 1960, III, 189.

144. ". . . vspoem/ u mira v serom khlame./ Ia budu solntse lit' svoe,/ A ty-svoe stikhami/ . . . Svetit' vsegda,/ svetit' vezde,/ do dnei poslednikh dontsa, svetit'—/ i nikakikh gvozdei!" Maiákovsky, *The Bedbug, and Selected Poetry*, NY, 1960, 142–3 (on the basis of the facing Russian text).

145. "A nad nami solntse, solntse, i solntse./ . . . Solntse—nashe solntse!/ Dovol'no! . . ./ Igru novuiu igraite! V krug!/ Solntsem igraite. Solntse kataite. Igraite v solntse!" Maiákovsky, *PSS*, M, 1956, II, 240. This hymn is absent from the second, more blatantly propagandistic version of *Mystery Bouffe*, written in 1920–1 and presented before a meeting of the Third International. However, the Communist leadership is referred to therein as "worshippers of the sun in the temple of the world" (Solntsepoklonniki u mira v khrame, *ibid.*, 354). For an English translation of the second version of the *Bouffe* see the translation of G. Noyes and A. Kaun in Noyes, ed., *Masterpieces*, 801–81. See also Khlebnikov's determination to "wake up the sun," in *Sobranie proizvedenii*, I, 285–6; and the ecstatic suggestion of nirvana-like annihilation in space at the end of "Chains of Blue": "Zeleny plesk i pereplesk—/ I v siny blesk ves' mir ischez." *Ibid.*, 303.

146. Meierhold, "The Booth," *The Drama*, 1917, May, 205.

147. Cited in Markov, *Poems*, 16.

148. Roger Fry, "Russian Icon Painting from the Western-European Point of View," in Farbman, ed., *Masterpieces*, 58, 38. See also the excellent section by G. Mathew, "The Harmony of Colors" (in *Byzantine Aesthetics*, London, 1963, 142–61), which often seems strikingly similar to Kandinsky's concept of "the spiritual" in art.

149. Maiakovsky, *The Bedbug*, 142–3.
150. Characterization of the program for forced industrialization by the Menshevik Abramovich, as paraphrased by B. Souvarine, *Stalin*, NY, 1939, 259–60.

2. THE SOVIET ERA

1. For the profusion of literary schools in the early Soviet period see the relevant pages in G. Struve, *Soviet Literature;* Zavalishin, *Early Soviet Writers;* and H. Ermolaev, *Soviet Literary Theories 1917–1934*, Berkeley–Los Angeles, 1963; also two pre-Stalinist Soviet studies: P. Kogan, *Literatura velikogo desiatiletiia*, M-L, 1927; and V. Polonsky (pseud. of V. Gusin), *Ocherki literaturnogo dvizheniia revoliutsionnoi epokhi*, M-L, 1929 (2d ed.). See also the synoptic treatment by M. Hayward, "Soviet Literature 1917–1961," *PR*, 1961, May–Jun, 333–62.

2. "Golubye goroda" (1925) in A. Tolstoy, *PSS*, M, 1947, V.

3. N. Gourfinkel, "Habima et le kamerny juif," in the valuable collection *Le Théâtre Juif dans le monde*, 1931, 70–1. See also her *Le Théâtre russe contemporain*, 1931, for further discussion of the cultural milieu of the twenties; also her *Naissance d'un monde*, 1953, particularly the evocative description of Odessa, 9–25.

Among Ehrenburg's early works, see his tale of a wandering Jew loose in a Europe in upheaval, *The Stormy Life of Lasik Roitschwantz*, NY, 1960 (written in Paris, 1927–8). For the last flowering of Yiddish culture in Eastern Europe and its legacy to Soviet literature as a whole, see E. Schulman, "Die Sovietishe-Yiddishe Literatur, 1918–48," in *The Jewish Book Annual*, IX, 1950–1; also C. Szmeruk, "Soviet Jewish Literature: the last phase," *Su*, 1961, Apr–Jun, 71–7; and (for a flurry of Yiddish cultural activity since that "last phase"), *NL*, 1963, Feb 4, 6–7.

4. Gourfinkel, "Habima," 71. Founded in White Russia in 1909–10, the Habima was re-established in 1916 in Moscow, where it played steadily for a decade, leaving Russia in 1926, eventually to settle down permanently in Israel.

5. V. von Wiren, "Zoshchenko in Retrospect," *RR*, 1962, Oct, 348–61, esp. 353. See also Zoshchenko, *Stat'i i materialy*, L, 1928 (an invaluable Academia collection of his early period); also H. McLean, ed. and intr., *Nervous People, and Other Satires*, NY, 1963. On Ilf and Petrov see their *Twelve Chairs*, NY, 1961, p, with intr. by M. Friedberg.

6. See W. Kolarz, *Religion*, 287–91; also Bonch-Bruevich, *Iz mira sektantov*, M, 1922. A full bibliography of this remarkable and neglected figure is supplied with an introduction by G. Petrovsky, *Vladimir Dmitrievich Bonch-Bruevich*, M, 1958.

7. E. Brown, "Voronsky and Pereval," *Su*, 1961, Apr–Jun, 92–8; R. Ahlberg, "Forgotten Philosopher: The work of Abram Deborin," *Su*, 1961, Jul–Sep, 79–89.

8. For some of the early radical plans for educational reform see *Narodny kommissariat prosveshcheniia 1917–1920. Kratky otchet*, M, 1920.

9. Figures from A. I. Nazarov, *Ocherki istorii sovetskogo knigoizdatel'stva*, M, 1962, cited in M. Hayward, "Potentialities for Freedom," paper delivered at St. Anthony's College, Oxford, in July, 1957, conference on "Changes in Soviet Society," page 2, note 2. For the importance of the mid-twenties as an ideological turning point see the valuable analysis of the period and the critical loss of ground by Bukharin and the "right wing" Bolshevik faction (which also included

such surprising bedfellows as Dzerzhinsky) N. Valentinov, *CS*, 1962, Nov-Dec, 1963, Jan-Feb, and Mar-Apr. See also Souvarine, *Stalin;* and R. Daniels, *The Conscience of the Revolution: Communist Opposition in Soviet Russia,* Cambridge, Mass., 1960.

10. The importance of the founding of this journal, and of the early debates over the role it should play is stressed in P. Sorlin, "La Crise du Parti communiste bolchevik et les *débuts* du 'Bol'ševik' (Avril 1924-Avril 1925)," *RHM*, 1962, Apr-Jun, 81–110.

11. Stalin's report to the Sixteenth Congress of the Communist Party of the USSR, Jun 27, 1930, in *Works*, M, 1955, XII, 314. See also note 36 on 394. For a classic necrology on the passing of the poets of the twenties see R. Jakobson, "O pokolenii rastrativshem svoikh poetov," in *Smert' Vladimira Maiakovskogo,* Berlin, 1931.

12. Cited in *Revoliutsiia prava,* 1925, no. 3, in G. Kline, " 'Socialist Legality' and Communist Ethics," *NLF*, VIII, 1963, 24. See also works referenced 23, note 6; and selections from Soviet legal writers in J. Hazard, ed., *Soviet Legal Philosophy,* Cambridge, Mass., 1961. For the purges of statisticians and scientists that also began 1929–30 see L. Labedz, "How Free Is Soviet Science," *Commentary,* 1958, Jun.

13. Stalin, *Works*, XII, 380–1, mt.

14. A. Zalkind, *Ocherki kul'tury revoliutsionnogo vremeni,* M, 1924, 59; as cited in R. Bauer, *The New Man in Soviet Psychology,* Cambridge, Mass., 1959, 73.

Zalkind was one of the leading Communist theorists of education active in the Agitation and Propaganda bureau of the Communist Party and in organizing the congresses and journals of the science of pedology, which flourished in the 1920's in the USSR (Bauer, 85). The reaction against Freud in the 1930's marked a return to vogue of the determinist school of I. Pavlov, who had won a Nobel Prize in 1904, and lived on to 1936. See, in addition to Bauer, J. Wortis, *Soviet Psychiatry,* Baltimore, 1950, 72–81; B. Simon, ed., *Psychology in the Soviet Union,* Stanford, 1957; and Kh. Koshtoiants, *Ocherki po istorii fiziologii v Rossii,* M-L, 1946; and *Russkaia fiziologicheskaia shkola i ee rol' v razvitii mirovoi nauki,* M, 1948. For indications that Pavlov himself was, ironically, moving beyond his earlier physiological determinism at the very time it was becoming official Soviet doctrine, see N. Nizhal'sky, "Evoliutsiia Pavlova," *NZh,* LXV, 1961, 248–54.

15. Citation also from Zalkind in Bauer, *New Man,* 99. Zalkind's efforts to bend with the new line appear to have been unsuccessful, because he vanished in the mid-1930's: an apparent victim of the purges.

16. Stalin, *Works*, XII, 197–205. Speech of Mar 2, 1930. For the dominance of Pokrovsky and L. Averbakh in their respective intellectual domains during this period see, respectively, P. Aron, "M. N. Pokrovskii and the Impact of the First Five-Year Plan on Soviet Historiography," in Curtiss, ed., *Essays,* 283–302; and E. Brown, *The Proletarian Episode in Russian Literature, 1928–32,* NY, 1953.

17. Stalin, *Works*, XIII, 67–75. The actual phrase "new Soviet intelligentsia" came into use later, but the idea is clearly contained here. Contrast the attitude of selective deference toward all technologically trained intellectuals with the anti-intellectual attitude in a report to the Sixteenth Party Congress, *Works*, XII, 311.

18. Stalin, *Leninism,* London, 1940, 490. Speech of May 4, 1935.

19. For his tender relationship with the multi-lingual French radical feminist Inessa Armand, which somewhat mitigates the picture of total emo-

tional discipline and puritanical preoccupation with mission that has dominated Soviet hagiography on Lenin, see L. Fischer, *The Life of Lenin,* NY, 1964; S. Possony, *Lenin: The Compulsive Revolutionary,* Chicago, 1964, 118 ff.; B. Wolfe, "Lenin and Inessa Armand," *ASR,* 1963, Mar, 96–114. For the life of Inessa herself see the laudatory account by the French Communist, J. Fréville, *Inessa Armand: une grande figure de la révolution russe,* 1957. Some other indications of the emotional side of Lenin's life may be found in N. Valentinov, *Vstrechi s Leninym,* NY, 1953.

20. The possibility that redirected sexual drives played an important role in Lenin's inner development, with suppressed homosexuality contributing to the aggressive masculinity of Bolshevism, is suggested by N. Leites and succinctly discussed by D. Bell in his "Ten Theories in Search of Reality," *The End of Ideology,* NY, 1962, 2d rev. ed., 326–37.

21. Lenin, "What the 'Friends of the People' Are and How They Fight the Social Democrats," (1894) *SW,* London, 1939, XI, 635.

22. *Ibid.,* 606.

23. S. Utechin, "The 'Preparatory Trend' in the Russian Revolutionary Movement in the 1880's," *SAP,* 12, 1962, 7–22, for this "Volga Marxism" and Lenin's early contact with it. On the extra-Marxist Jacobin ancestry of Leninism, S. Utechin, "Who Taught Lenin?" *The Twentieth century,* 1960, Jul, 8–16, points to curious and neglected anticipations in Ogarev; M. Karpovich, "A Forerunner of Lenin: P. N. Tkachev," *RP,* 6, 1944, 346–50, points to Tkachev; V. Varlamov, "Bakunin and the Russian Jacobins and Blanquists As Evaluated by Soviet Historiography," *RPSR,* 79, 1955, shows how Soviet historians after much confusion eventually set-

tled on their present line denying any links between Leninism and the earlier Jacobins.

24. *Nakanune,* 1901, Feb. See also Chernov's masterful short political obituary of Lenin in Mosely, ed., *Soviet Union,* 26–32.

25. From the last section, entitled "Dictatorship over the Proletariat," in L. Trotsky, *Nashi politicheskie zadachi,* Geneva, 1904, 54; cited in I. Deutscher, *The Prophet Armed,* NY, 1954, 90.

26. Principally in his *State and Revolution,* written on the eve of the coup in 1917 (the key passages dealing with "withering away" are in Lenin, *SW,* 1951, Part I, 213–20, 284–92). For recent discussion of the concept see three articles under "The Withering Away of the State" in *Su,* 1961, Oct, 63–9; also the notes and discussion in Lenin, *Sochineniia,* M, 1962, 5th ed., XXXIII.

   The concept of the dictatorship of the proletariat was elaborated by Marx in his "Critique of the Gotha Program" in 1876 and redefined by Lenin in an article of 1905 entitled "The Revolutionary Democratic Dictatorship of the Proletariat and Peasantry" (Lenin, *Sochineniia,* M, 1962, 5th ed., X, 20–31). Lenin's usage of the term prior to 1917 is overlooked in the otherwise useful discussion of the concept by R. Carew-Hunt, *A Guide to Communist Jargon,* NY, 1957, 62–5.

27. Lenin, *The Proletarian Revolution and the Renegade Kautsky* (1918), in *SW,* London, 1937, VII, 123. Lenin is referring here to "dictatorship" in general, but the characterization is clearly meant to apply even to the sanctified form that he is advocating.

28. Lenin's resurrection of this term—widely used in the mid-nineteenth century, but out of fashion and virtually forgotten in the late nine-

teenth and the early twentieth century—apparently dates from his publication in 1915, together with Bukharin of the short-lived journal *Kommunist*. The formal adoption of the new name in March, 1918, was a means of dramatizing the irrevocability of Lenin's split with the "reformist" social democratic tradition; and all parties affiliating with the Comintern were required (by its second congress in 1920) formally to adopt the name "Communist" as a condition of membership—a visible demonstration of their repudiation of the traditions of the Second International.

29. Lenin, *What Is To Be Done?* (1902) NY, nd, p, 131. See also the fresh translation, with valuable intr. by S. Utechin, Oxford, 1963.

30. From a critique of Struve in Lenin, *Sochineniia*, M, 1935, 3d ed., I, 276.

31. *What Is To Be Done?* 105–6. The term used is *stirat'sia:* literally, "wiped out." The importance of providing leadership from the intelligentsia for the workers was fully recognized by Lenin (see discussion in E. H. Carr, *The Bolshevik Revolution,* London, I, 16–17), though the point is somewhat blunted by subsequent Soviet glosses and even by shadings in the official Soviet translation of *What Is To Be Done?* which refers to the revolutionary intellectuals' ideas as developing "quite independently of the spontaneous growth of the worker's movement" *SW*, II, 53—"quite" being a weak word for *sovershenno,* "completely."

32. *What Is To Be Done?* 101.

33. *Two Tactics of Social Democracy in the Democratic Revolution* (1905) in *SW*, III, 293–302, a work as violent in opposing "tailendism" as was *What Is To Be Done?* in opposing "spontaneity" in the development of social revolution.

What Is To Be Done? was the title not only of the famous works here discussed, but also of many less famous tracts. See, for instance, V. Bazanov, "Aleksandr Livanov i ego traktat 'Chto Delat'?'," *RL*, 1963, no. 3, 109–38.

34. The theory of the growing-over of one revolution into another seems to have originated in the pessimism of the Odessa-born German Social Democrat Alexander Helfand (Parvus) about the capacity of the bourgeoisie to provide genuine revolutionary leadership in Eastern Europe; acquired critical elaboration in Trotsky's writings during the revolutionary crisis of 1904–5; and gained Lenin's belated but enthusiastic approval during the early months of 1917.

Lenin's analysis (*Imperialism, the Highest Stage of Capitalism,* 1916, in *SW*, V, 3 122) of the development of imperialism through the growth of monopolistic finance capitalism was largely derived from Western economists (Hilferding, Hobson); his quasi-apocalyptical conception of capitalist leaders as "ravening beasts" leading the masses to war by merely "clipping coupons" but unconsciously preparing the world for a revolutionary deliverance, in which the oppressed colonial peoples will play a revolutionary role along with the Western proletariat, was largely derived from Rosa Luxembourg, and was incorporated into the theses on the national and colonial question adopted by the second congress of the Comintern in 1920.

35. Title of *Pravda* article of April, 1917, in Lenin, *Sochineniia*, M, 1962, 5th ed., XXXI, 304.

36. P. Tkachev, *Offener Brief an Herrn Fr. Engels*, Zurich, 1874; as cited in G. Plekhanov, "Our Differences" (1884) in *Works*, 179 (mt—"intelligentnaia" being rendered as "intelligentsia-dominated" rather than "of the intelligentsia"). One of the

sources of Lenin's falling-out with Plekhanov was the posture of almost unmitigated opposition which Plekhanov assumed toward Tkachev in this and subsequent works.

37. Lenin, *SW*, VII, 3–112 (especially 43–54, and 78–94).

38. From the dream of Versilov in Dostoevsky, *Raw Youth* (repeated in variant form in Stavrogin's confession in *The Possessed*, inspired in both cases by Claude Lorraine's "Acis and Galatea," in the Dresden art gallery).

39. See Billington "Intelligentsia," 818–9; and "The Bolshevik Debt to Russian Populism," *Occidente*, 1956, Jul-Aug, 319–28.

40. Just as official publications of the "People's Will" had used the term "enemy of the people" nearly four decades before it came into general use in the USSR, so the official records of the second congress of the Social Democratic Party in 1903 contain the term "people's democracy" more than forty years before it came into use in the Soviet empire. Bonch-Bruevich, later Lenin's personal secretary, used the term in a remarkable and neglected speech, "The Schism and Sectarianism in Russia," advocating common action with the persecuted religious dissenters of the Russian empire. The Bolsheviks no less than the populists fancied that these dissenters could be won over as allies, and empowered Bonch-Bruevich to set up a special Social Democratic journal, *The Dawn,* to aid in this campaign. Bonch-Bruevich characterized them as "popular democratic elements" interested in breaking with "bourgeois democracy," and argued that Social Democrats could aid in "the growth of political consciousness of the millions who comprise the people's democracy." (From the text of his report to the Congress in *Razsvet,* Geneva, 1905, no. 6–7, 173.) Only a few numbers of the journal appeared, but there

were some optimistic reports on the campaign (no. 3, 72–8).

Bonch-Bruevich lived in Finland for a long period (offering Lenin shelter there during 1917) and knew Otto Kuusinen, the Comintern ideologist and long-time émigré leader of Finnish communism, who introduced the term "people's democracy" into general usage as an approved alternative to "dictatorship of the proletariat" in the Finnish Communist party program of 1944. This usage (like that of Bonch-Bruevich) is overlooked in otherwise valuable studies of the postwar concept of "people's democracy," such as M. H. Fabry, *Théorie des democraties populaires,* 1950, 11 (where he explicitly declares that the term "appeared only in 1945"); Z. Brzezinski, *The Soviet Bloc: Unity and Conflict,* NY, 1961, rev. ed., 25 (who traces it more tentatively to Yugoslavian usage in 1945); and G. Skilling, "People's Democracy and the Socialist Revolution: A Case Study in Communist Scholarship," *SSt,* 1951, Jul, Oct.

41. While Communist ideologists generally continue to deny that the intelligentsia is a separate class or a group above class interest, the intelligentsia has become in practice a third category of "progressive humanity" along with workers and peasants. This can be seen from posters showing a man with a book alongside one with a hammer and a second with a sickle. The definition of the Soviet Communist Party adopted at its Nineteenth Party Congress in 1952, was "a voluntary, militant union of like-minded Communists, consisting of people from the working class, the working peasants and the working intelligentsia." (*For a Lasting Peace! For a People's Democracy!* Aug 23, 1952, 3). During his reign, Khrushchev used the trilogy of "workers, peasants and intelligent-

sia" without the modifying adjective "working" (see, for instance, his speech at the Grivita Rosie plant in Rumania of Jun 19, 1962). The term "people's intelligentsia" is also sometimes invoked (as by V. Platkovsky, *Kommunist*, 1962, no. 15, 28–9).

42. Note that Lenin's favorite Russian novelist was Turgenev, who had provided a relatively realistic portrayal of revolutionary figures in the sixties and seventies, the golden age of Russian social thought, rather than Dostoevsky or Tolstoy, who filled their works of the same period with broader religious and philosophical concerns. See L. Fischer, *Lenin*, esp. 499–500. Lenin read Turgenev continuously as a student, and used a German translation of his work to learn that language (*ibid.*, 19, 34).

43. See Lenin's turgid broadside, *Materialism and Empiriocriticism*, first published in 1908 during a period of general disillusionment among revolutionaries and reprinted in *SW*, London, 1939, XI, 89–409.

44. "Partiinaia organizatsiia i partiinaia literatura," in *Sochineniia*, 5th ed., XII, 100–1. There is considerable controversy over whether or not Lenin conceived of anything but "party literature" once the party seized power. M. Hayward ("Potentialities," 2) and R. Hankin (in Simmons, ed., *Continuity*, 445–6) seem to think Lenin would not have been displeased to see this conception of "party literature" expanded to include all literature—as was generally done in the USSR under Stalin; while E. Simmons ("The Origins of Literary Control," *Su*, 1961, Apr–Jun, 78–82) implies that Lenin never intended this doctrine to apply to belles lettres.

It is sometimes argued that the achievement of the revolutionary goal provides an external criteria by which the Leninist party's actions can be judged. However, this goal was never clearly enough defined to be invulnerable to constant reinterpretation by the party itself, and thus could hardly provide any effective external check on party actions. A more substantial defense of Lenin lies in the contention that the person who sacrifices means for ends under Communism may be no more relativistic morally than the man who perennially sacrifices ends for means under some other system.

45. Text in B. Wolfe, *Khrushchev and Stalin's Ghost*, NY, 1957, 261–3.

46. *Works*, M, 1953, VI, 47, 59, 58.

47. Cited by V. Bonch-Bruevich, *Pereezd sovetskogo pravitel'stva iz Petrograda v Moskvu*, M, 1926, 19. Bonch-Bruevich's account of this transfer is filled with foreboding about the end of the "Petersburg period" and the beginning of the "Moscow period." See also his *V. I. Lenin v Petrograde i v Moskve, 1917–1920*, M, 1956, 19–21, which tells of Lenin's banning of the sword from the new hammer-and-sickle emblem early in 1918.

48. Ivan Gronsky, who was by this time editor of *Izvestiia* and a leading party organizer. See Herman Ermolaev, "The Emergence and the Early Evolution of Socialist Realism (1932–1934)," *CSS*, 2, 1963, 141 ff.

49. Title of the valuable study by a former German Communist, Wolfgang Leonhard, *Die Revolution entläst ihre Kinder*, Cologne, 1950 (translated by C. Woodhouse as *Child of the Revolution*, London, 1957).

50. Andrew Zhdanov, *Lectures on Literature, Philosophy and Music*, NY, 1950.

51. "Stil empir vo vremia chumy." The phrase suggests "feast amidst famine" because of its resemblance to Pushkin's "Pir vo vremia chumy," "Feast in the time of the plague." *Sovnovrok* is the label of G. Kline. The final adoption of full stylistic control over architecture occurred in October 1934, and brought to an

end a tradition of experimentation that was more impressive (in plans, if not in actual accomplishment) than is often realized. See the richly illustrated discussion by V. De Feo, *URSS Architettura 1917–1936*, Rome, 1963, esp. 72 ff.

52. See V. G. Geiman, "Proekt Volgo-belomorskogo kanala v XVII v," *IS*, 1934, no. 1, 253–68.

53. From the historical sketch of the monastery by A. Priklonskoy, in *Solovetskie ostrova* (III, no. 2–3), 1926, Feb-Mar, 121. See also *Solovetskie ostrova*, 1926, May-Jun, chronicle of April, 1926, for other activities; and Priklonskoy's historical study in *Solovetskoe obshchestvo kraevedeniia*, Solovki, 1927, 44, for his description of the small prison cell in which political prisoners took part in holy services.

For the fascinating history of the learned societies and activities in Solovetsk in the early 1920's, all of which were run by those "in one way or another linked with the camp," see *Otchet Solovetskogo otdeleniia Arkhangel'skogo obshchestva kraevedeniia za 1924–26 gody*, Solovetsk, 1927 (a lithographed publication of the OGPU).

54. *Istoriko-arkheologicheskie pamiatniki solovetskogo arkhipelaga (I, registratsionnoe obsledovanie)*, 1934, 2; and *(II, opisanie zdanii)*, 1935, especially the portions in the back, which provide hints for the reasons that the work was abandoned, by referring to "pressing questions on the utilization of natural productive resources." On Solovetsk and the development of the Stalinist prison empire see D. Dallin and B. Nikolaevsky, *Forced Labor in Soviet Russia*, New Haven, Conn., 1947.

55. See S. Afanasiev, "Cultural Movement of the Masses," *Soviet Culture Bulletin*, 1931, Jul, 11–14, for an enthusiastic account of the *kul'turnaia estafeta*.

56. Stalin, *Works*, M, 1953, VI, 47, 48 mt; and the entire address delivered at Second All-Union Congress of Soviets, Jan 26, 1924; *ibid.*, 47–53. He also invoked (51) the traditional ecclesiastical-conservative image of the rock of faith surrounded by an ocean of disbelief.

57. For this extraordinary episode, which involved the founding of a special institute to study Lenin's brain and the taking of some 31,000 slices therefrom, see the section ". . . and Transfiguration" in Possony, *Lenin*, 362–75.

58. See the analysis of O. Utis (Isaiah Berlin), "Generalissimo Stalin and the Art of Government," *FA*, 1952.

Z. Brzezinski, *The Permanent Purge: Politics in Soviet Totalitarianism*, Cambridge, Mass., 1956, sees recurrent purge as an inevitable support mechanism for totalitarian rule, which he has analyzed as a basically new type of rule together with C. Friedrich in *Totalitarian Dictatorship and Autocracy*, Cambridge, Mass., 1956: a systematic study which elaborates the inner identity suggested by H. Arendt (*Origins of Totalitarianism*, NY, 1951) between Nazi and Soviet rule in comparison with precedent autocratic forms.

For a study that suggests greater idiosyncrasy in the Stalinist era, and offers the more general and inclusive analytical model of "the revolutionary mass-movement regime under single-party auspices," see R. Tucker, *The Soviet Political Mind*, NY, 1963, esp. 3–19. For a range of possible explanations of the purges (the majority of which tend to de-emphasize the element of totalitarian calculation) see F. Beck and W. Godin [both pseud.], *Russian Purge and the Extraction of Confession*, NY, 1951; also A. Orlov, *The Secret History of Stalin's Crimes*, NY, 1953.

59. See the characterization of the Soviet intelligence officer in A. Dulles, *The Craft of Intelligence*, NY, 1963, 95. For some indication

of the extent to which the Bolsheviks were at times building on secret police practices of the imperial government in its later years see the personal memoir of one of the leading police figures, General P. Kurlov: *Das Ende des russischen Kaisertums*, (posthumously published in Berlin), 1920, esp. 154 ff.

60. W. Leonhard, *The Kremlin Since Stalin*, NY, 1962, p, 43–53; also H. Salisbury, *American in Moscow*, NY, 1955, 154. Dec 24 was not, of course, Christmas eve by the Orthodox calendar.

Leeches were used at least twice. See texts of official medical bulletins in *NYT*, Mar 5, 1953, 2; and Mar 6, 1953, 10.

61. J. Monnerot, *The Sociology of Communism*, London, 1953, 254.

62. Cited from proceedings of the congress in L. Gruliow, ed., *Current Soviet Policies*, IV, NY, 1962, 215–6.

63. A. Tertz (pseudonym of an unidentified Soviet author), "Socialist Realism," *Su*, 1959, Jul-Sep, 13.

64. V. Pudovkin, *Film Technique and Film Acting*, NY, 1960, p, 293.

65. Cited by H. Hoffmann, "Revival of the Cinema," *Su*, 1963, Jan, 102. For an excellent account of the early, experimental days of the Russian cinema see V. Shklovsky, "Zhili-byli," *Znamia*, 1962, no. 12, 171–86, and his more philosophical essay in P. Blake and M. Hayward, eds., *Dissonant Voices in Soviet Literature*, NY, 1962, 20–8. See also D. Macdonald, *The Soviet Cinema*, London, 1938; and R. Sobolev, *Liudi i fil'my russkogo dorevoliutsionnogo kino*, M, 1961.

66. S. Eisenstein, *The Film Sense*, NY, 1942, esp. the section "Synchronization of Senses," 69–109; also "Color and Meaning," 115–53, references 88, and his "One Path to Colour; An Autobiographical Fragment," *Sight and Sound*, 1961, spring, 84–6, 102.

67. Z. ben Shlomo, "The Soviet Cinema," *Su*, 1959, Jul-Sep, 70. See also Eisenstein's recantation, reprinted in *NL*, Dec 7, 1946; and M. Seton, *Sergei M. Eisenstein, A Biography*, NY, 1952; S. Eisenstein, *Film Form and the Film Scene*, NY, 1957, p. The full scenario of Eisenstein's *Ivan* has now been published, together with a host of photographs and drawings: S. Eisenstein, *Ivan the Terrible*, London, 1963.

The *Battle of Stalingrad* is a rare combination of photographic realism (the list of photographers killed filming it was run off at the beginning along with the list of actors) and a kind of iconographic glorification of Stalinist leadership. Parts of the script (which is the only reminder left after the film was withdrawn from circulation during the period of de-Stalinization) are written in the style of the chronicles. See N. Virta, *Stalingradskaia bitva*, M, 1947, particularly 5 ff.

The propagandistic art of the post-war Stalin era represented almost a pure throwback to early church art. See the perversion of the central triptych of the iconostasis (showing God enthroned with the Virgin on one side and John "the precursor" on the other) in a "triptych" "Enemies of Peace," *Iskusstvo*, 1952, Mar-Apr, 31–3.

The mosaics added to the Komsomolskaia subway station in Moscow represented Soviet victories in a stylized iconographic manner that posed numerous problems for the rewriting of history in the post-Stalin era. A Soviet official explained in 1958 that the figure of Stalin had not been removed from the center of the mosaic of Soviet leaders reviewing Russian troops before the Kremlin after the victory over Nazi Germany because no one was yet sure that anyone else deserved this virtually God-like central position; and because it would look absurd to have a picture seen by thousands every day showing no one reviewing the troops (Beria, Malenkov, and

Molotov already having been removed from the center of the reviewing line). In Jan 1965 this mosaic was completely boarded up and was soon replaced by a large mosaic of Lenin.

68. On Stalin's sense of identification with Ivan IV see Tucker, *Mind*, 37–8; 44–5; and, in addition to works referenced therein and in the earlier discussions of Ivan IV in this volume, the seminal article by S. Bakhrushin, "Ivan Grozny," rehabilitating Ivan in the theoretical journal of the Party, *Bol'shevik*, 1943, no. 13, 48–61. The move back into history also resulted in an identification of Stalin's elaborately rationalized policy of "active defense," with the Scythian policy of luring the enemy into the interior of a land mass that is then scorched and used as a vast arena for harassment. See A. Mishulin, "O voennom iskusstve skifov," *IZh*, 1943, no. 8–9, 64–9; also K. Mehnert, "Stalin the Historian," *TC*, 1944, Oct, 173–88.

For more recent Soviet views

of Ivan IV see E. Delimars, "Déstalinisation d'Ivan le terrible," *CS*, 1965, Jan-Feb, 9–20. See also, more generally, S. Roberts, *Soviet Historical Drama, Its Role in the Development of a National Mythology*, Leiden, 1965.

69. For a discussion which illustrates the often-forgotten subtlety of his post-war foreign policy see M. Shulman, *Stalin's Foreign Policy Reappraised*, Cambridge, Mass., 1963.

70. Sholokhov's *Tikhy Don* (English: *And Quiet Flows the Don, The Don Flows Home to the Sea*) was published in four parts, 1928–40; *Podniataia tselina* (English: *Seeds of Tomorrow, Harvest on the Don*) was published in two volumes, 1932 and serially 1955–60. A useful Soviet study of his work is I. Lezhnev, *Put' Sholokhova*, M, 1958; but the complex textual evolution of Sholokhov's works and the pressures and changes involved in the long delay of the second volume of *Podniataia tselina* remain to be traced.

3. FRESH FERMENT

1. P. Viazemsky,. *PSS*, P, 1878, I, xlv, on the "zagovor molchaniia."
2. B. Jasieński, "Zagovor ravnodushnykh," in his *Izbrannye proizvedeniia*, M, 1957, I (also *NM*, 1956, Nos. 5, 6, 7).
3. The story is reprinted in Olesha, *Izbrannye sochineniia*, M, 1956; also see the intr. by V. Pertsov.
4. I. Ehrenburg, *Zagovor ravnykh*, Berlin, 1928. The entire concept of an egalitarian social revolution beyond the original political revolution of 1789 dates to some extent from Babeuf's "conspiracy of equals." See J. Talmon, *Origins of Totalitarian Democracy*, NY, 1960, p.
5. A characterization taken from Pushkin and cited by M. Koriakov, "Termometr Rossii u Pasternaka," *NZh*, LV, 1958, 141.

6. Texts and discussion of the two letters from *LG*, Nov 17, 1932, in Koriakov, "Termometr," 139–41. For other information on Pasternak in the Stalin era see R. Payne, *The Three Worlds of Boris Pasternak*, NY, 1961, 146–67; also R. Conquest, *Courage of Genius—The Pasternak Affair*, London, 1961. The letter allegedly written in September, 1956, by the editors of *NM* explaining their refusal to publish *Zhivago* was published in *LG*, Oct 25, 1958, and translated in *CDSP*, Dec 3, 1958, 6–11, 32.
7. *Znamia*, 1954, Apr, 92.
8. See E. Wilson's perceptive appreciation of the novel and linguistic lifesmanship about the translation in "Doctor Life and His Guardian Angel," *The New Yorker*, Nov 15, 1958, 213–38; also his quarrying of

symbols in "Legend and Symbol in *Doctor Zhivago,*" in *Encounter,* 1959, Jun, 5–16; and A. Gerschenkron's sympathetic analysis and amusing rebuke to the "egg hunt" for symbols in "Notes on *Doctor Zhivago,*" in *Backwardness,* 341–52.

9. Cited from *LG,* Oct 26, 1958; *Pravda,* Oct 29, 1958; and V. Semichastny's nationwide television speech of Oct 29, 1958 (given in his official capacity as secretary of the Communist Youth League on the occasion of its fortieth anniversary).

10. The co-translator of *Zhivago,* Max Hayward, relates the character of Zhivago to the tradition of passive "observers" (*obyvately*) in Russian literature that dates from the figure of the oppressed clerk in Gogol's "Greatcoat"; *Encounter,* 1958, May, 38–48.

11. Text of his letter to Khrushchev in *Pravda* and *Izvestiia,* Nov 2, 1958; and second letter to the editor of *Pravda* in the issue of Nov 6, 1958.

12. Subtitle of a critical appreciation of the novel by S. Hampshire, in *Encounter,* 1958, Nov, 3–5.

13. Pasternak, *Essay in Autobiography,* London, 1959, 119. Citations taken (with occasional minor modifications) from *Doctor Zhivago,* NY, © 1958 by Pantheon Books, tr. by M. Hayward and M. Harari. The work is also available p and in the Russian original, Ann Arbor, 1959.

14. Pasternak, *Povest',* L, 1934, 83.

15. *Essay,* 39–51.

16. *Ibid.,* 50.

17. *Ibid.,* 51.

18. Quoted by G. Ruge, "A Visit to Pasternak," *Encounter,* 1958, Mar, 22–5. For details on his funeral see P. Johnson, "Death of a Writer," *Harper's,* 1961, May, 140–6.

19. Ideas contained in an unpublished letter from Pasternak in English early in 1959:

"The chief spirit of my experiences or tendencies (philosophy I have none) is the understanding of art, of creative embodiment and inspiration as an offer of concentrated abnegation in a far and humble likeness with the Lord's Supper and the Eucharist, that the pictorial side of our culture, the figures and images of the European history have a certain relation or are in a certain sense a kind of Imitation de Jesus-Christ, that the Gospels are the foundation of what is called in the realm of writings, realism. . . ."

20. Luke 24:5.

21. Ruge, "Visit," 24; *cf.* N. Nilsson, "We Are the Guests of Existence," *Reporter,* Nov 27, 1958, for other valuable citations from Pasternak.

22. Pasternak, "Some Remarks by a Translator of Shakespeare," *Soviet Literature,* 1946, Sep, 51–6.

23. Luke 22:42. The link between Christ in Gethsemane and Hamlet had previously been made by Pasternak in his "Some Remarks . . .," 52.

24. This poem, "Slozha vesla," is reprinted in the new Soviet edition of Pasternak's works, *Stikhotvoreniia i poemy,* M, 1961, 55, and well analyzed (along with "Hamlet" of *Zhivago*) by N. Nilsson, in *ScS,* V, 1959, 180–98. For another analysis see D. Obolensky, "The Poems of Doctor Zhivago," *SEER,* 1961, Dec, 123–35.

25. Cited in the commemorative article by A. Prosvirnin, "Sviat. Ioann, mitropolit tobol'sky i vseia Sibiri (k 250-letiiu so dnia konchiny)," *Zhurnal Moskovskoi patriarkhii,* 1965, no. 6, 74.

26. *KP,* Jul 21, 1961. The term "nihilist" was defended as a proud radical designation by A. Turkov at an apparently turbulent meeting of the Moscow branch of the Soviet Writers' Union in March, 1957 (account in *LG,* Mar 19, 1957, 1, 3). Subsequent use of this and other terms is discussed with profuse illustration from the Soviet press in the symposium *Youth in Ferment* published by the Institute for the Study of the USSR in Munich, 1962, Jul. The term *nibonicho,*

which has been most notably used by Lev Kassil, finds an anticipation though probably not its origin in V. Briusov's poem of 1901 "Nekolebimoi istine/ Ne veriu ia davno/ . . . I Gospoda, i D'iavola/ Khochu proslavit' ia." *Stikhotvoreniia i poemy*, L, 1961, 229.

On the concept of generation, see the distinction between an historical and a genealogical generation in Ortega y Gasset, *Man and Crisis*, NY, 1962, 30–84. The belief that youth was already in ferment in the late wartime period was advanced by K. Mehnert in "Stalin's Grandchildren," *TC*, 1944, Jul, 1–18. Among the many articles dealing with the problem of generation in post-Stalinist Russia see particularly L. Haimson, "Three Generations of the Soviet Intelligentsia," *FA*, 1959, Jan, 235–46; and M. Fainsod, "Soviet Youth and the Problem of the Generations," *Proceedings of the American Philosophical Society*, 1964, Oct, 429–36, and works referenced therein.

Soviet leaders at the all-union conference on ideological work in late December, 1961, expressed alarm and indignation at "the efforts appearing now to prove the existence of a so-called 'fourth generation,' which is distinct from, and even opposed to, those which stormed the Winter Palace, built the Komsomol on the Amur, and routed Fascism." S. Pavlov in *XXII s'ezd KPSS i voprosy ideologicheskoi raboty*, M, 1962, 145.

27. References to this, and the League decree itself, *CDSP*, Apr 17, 1957, 16–18. See also R. Fisher, *Pattern for Soviet Youth: A Study of the Congresses of the Komsomol, 1918–1954*, NY, 1959; A. Kassof, *The Soviet Youth Program: Regimentation and Rebellion*, Cambridge, Mass., 1965.

28. *CDSP*, May 16, 1962, 12–15. S. Pavlov, First Secretary of the League, referred on Aug 29, 1965, to the danger of *kul'turnichestvo* [apolitical cultural activity]. *CDSP*, Sep 22, 1965, 14.

29. *CDSP*, Nov 8, 1952, 44–5.

30. First published *LG*, Sep 19, 1961; translated by G. Reavey, *Evergreen Review*, 1962, Jan–Feb, 57–9.

31. See V. Erlich, "Post-Stalin Trends in Russian Literature," and the accompanying pieces by G. Gibian, M. Hayward, together with Erlich's reply in *ASR*, 1964, Sep, 405–40.

32. These stories appeared in the rich and bitterly criticized collection *Literaturnaia Moskva*, M, 1956, II, 502–13; 396–403; and are translated in the anthology edited and introduced by H. McLean and W. Vickery, *The Year of Protest 1956*, NY, 1961, p, 193–208; 224–33.

33. Ya. Akim's "Careful People" is in *Den' poezii*, 1956. Granin's "Opinion" (*NM*, 1956, Aug) appears in McLean and Vickery, *Year*, 255–69; also P. Johnson, *Khrushchev and the Arts: the Politics of Soviet Culture 1962–1964*, Cambridge, Mass., 1965 (including both documents and analysis); and the vivid firsthand report of a perceptive Yugoslav, M. Mihajlov, "Moscow Summer 1964," *NL*, 1965, Mar 29, June 7.

Other well-presented English-language collections of short and ideologically interesting literary works published in the USSR since the death of Stalin include T. Whitney, *The New Writing in Russia*, Ann Arbor, 1964; *Odyssey*, 1962, Dec, 9–182; *Encounter*, 1963, Apr, 27–90; and M. Hayward and P. Blake, eds., *Dissonant Voices* (a work largely dominated by earlier Soviet heretics, however). Also of great interest (partly because it is one of the rare examples of a provincial collection becoming both widely discussed and generally available) is *Tarusskie stranitsy: literaturno-khudozhestvenny illiustrirovanny sbornik*, Kaluga, 1961 (English: A. Field, ed., *Pages from Tarussa*, Boston, 1963). More recent

Soviet writings are in P. Blake and M. Hayward, eds., *Half-way to the Moon*, NY, 1965, p.

Among many discussions and analyses of recent Soviet literature see those in *Su*, 1963, Jan; *Harper's*, 1961, May; *Atlantic Monthly*, 1960, June; and *Problems of Communism*, 1961, May–Jun, 1–31. See also the fascinating if pessimistic appraisal by a well-known Soviet writer using the pseudonym of N. Gavrilov, "Letter from a Soviet Writer," *NL*, Dec 9, 1963, 14–8; also the edition of Khrushchev's speech on culture of Mar 8, 1963, with rich commentary and annotation *Khrushchev on Culture*, London, 1963 (*Encounter* Pamphlet No. 9). See both the translations and articles in the special issue "Creativity in the Soviet Union," of the Northwestern University publication *Tri-Quarterly*, 1965, spring.

A lengthy firsthand report of the oscillations of Soviet policy in this field by R. Blum ("Freeze and Thaw: the Artists in Russia," *The New Yorker*, 1965, Aug 28, Sep 4, and Sep 11) deals with the visual as well as the literary arts, and suggests a somewhat less hopeful prospect than many others.

34. "U kazhdoi vse osoboe, svoe,/ . . . U kazhdogo—svoi tainy lichny mir." Evtushenko, *Nezhnost'*, M, 1962, 5.

35. Evtushenko, "Precocious Autobiography," *Saturday Evening Post*, Aug 10–Aug 17, 1963, 62, 64. A translation of "To Humor" by G. Reavey is in *Encounter*, 1963, Apr, 89–90.

36. *Su*, 1963, Jan, 29.

37. In an interview with the present writer in Moscow in September, 1958, setting up a line of thought that has not been repudiated—though it has not been much developed during his subsequent travels and press conferences, or evident in his poetry.

38. Cited mt from lengthy excerpts in McLean and Vickery, *Year*, 131. Originally written 1953–6, printed in *Oktiabr'*, 1956, Oct.

39. As cited by P. Forgues in his analysis, "The Young Poets," *Su*, 1963, Jan, 37. For a translation by W. H. Auden of the "Parabolic Ballad," see *Encounter*, 1963, Apr, 52.

40. Voznesensky, "Evening on the Building Site," in *ibid.*, 70 (discussed by P. Blake, 31); "Fire in the Architectural Institute," as cited by Forgues, "Poets," 40 (full translation in *Encounter*, 1963, Apr, 54).

41. Cited by P. Blake in *Encounter*, 1963, Apr, 32.

42. A conclusion of decline emerges from the discussion by P. Forgues, "Russian Poetry 1963–1965," *Su*, 1965, Jul, 54–70; and from a reading of Evtushenko's "Bratskaia Ges," *Yunost'*, 1965, Apr, 26–67, as well as personal attendance in Jan 1965 at a performance of a melodramatic revolutionary ballad "Kazn' Stepana Razina," in which Shostakovich set to music a selection from the lengthy Evtushenko work. A humorous example of oral folklore is the popular and widely circulated (in 1965) "Skazka o Tsare tol'ko ne Saltane," which provides an unofficial version of recent Soviet political history through satirical couplets easily remembered for oral transmission because it is a reworked Pushkin poem.

43. For the denunciation by the ministry of culture, see *SK*, Jun 5, 1954; for the text of the play, *Teatr*, 1954, Feb.

44. On Okhlopkov's Hamlet see B. Malnick, "The Soviet Theatre," *SSt*, 1958, Jan, 251–2; on Akimov's *Hamlet*, J. Macleod, *The New Soviet Theatre*, London, 1943, 160–3. Akimov even had the temerity to label the Moscow Art Theater, the bastion of realism, a "kindergarten for mental defectives," (*ibid.*, 158).

45. N. Akimov, *O teatre*, M-L, 1962, 178.

46. "New Solutions for the Theatre," *SR*, 1962, Mar, 47.

47. Akimov, *O teatre*, 242. This discussion of *The Shadow* by Akimov was written in 1940 at the time of the play's first brief appearance. On the movie made of the play in 1953 see *ibid.*, 271–2; for the text of *The Shadow* and nine other of his 25 major dramatic works see the edition published as *E. Schwarz*, L, 1960, with introduction by S. Tsimbal. For an English translation by F. Reeve see his *Plays*, II, 381–458. Observations about the Akimov production of *The Shadow* and about other contemporary Soviet productions are based on three weeks of theatergoing in the USSR early in 1961.

48. For a surprisingly favorable Soviet review of *The Dragon* see *Literatura i zhizn'*, Jul 1, 1962.

49. Mikhalkov, "Tri portreta," *Literaturnaia Moskva*, II, 528–9; translated in McLean and Vickery, *Year*, 120–1.

   Mikhalkov was co-author of the new Soviet national anthem and wrote several xenophobic plays of the High Stalin era; see François de Liencourt, "The Repertoire of the Fifties," *Su*, 1963, Jan, 60.

   For one of the most ingenious of children's stories see Lev Kassil, "The Tale of the Three Master Craftsmen," Hayward and Blake, *Voices*, 137–55. The legendary framework is sometimes so Aesopian as to be virtually incomprehensible. See, for instance, V. Dudintsev, "New Year's Fable," *Encounter*, 1960, Jul, 6–19.

50. De Liencourt, "Repertory," 61 ff.

51. The programmatic demands of the new theater are well stated in *LG*, Oct 15, 1953; and A. Kron, "A Writer's Notes" (from *Literaturnaia Moskva*, II), in McLean and Vickery, *Year*, 164–90, with notes. For general discussions of the new Soviet theater, see in addition to de Liencourt, "Repertory," A. Campbell, "Plays and Playwrights," and M. Frankland, "The Current Season," all in *Su*, 1963, Jan.

52. *SR*, 1962, Mar, 47. For more recent ideas of Tovstonogov see E. de Mauny, "Current Trends in the Soviet Theatre," *Su*, 1965, Oct, 73–80. This article and mine in *University* (Princeton, N.J.), 1965, Dec, discuss productions of the 1964–5 season.

53. A recent article on Soviet space achievements pointedly begins with this quotation: A. Chizhevsky, "Effekt Tsiolkovskogo," *NM*, 1963, no. 3, 201–7. In the same spirit of inquiry stands the brief work of V. Mass and M. Chervinsky in *Den' poezii*, 1956, 197, which juxtaposes to Bazarov's $2 + 2 = 4$ and Dostoevsky's $2 + 2 = 5$, its own title: "$2 + 2 = ?$"

   Most of the films discussed have been widely seen and reviewed in the West. For a good synoptic discussion which also considers the cinema in other Eastern European nations see H. Hoffmann, "Revival," 102–11. Chukhrai discusses his extraordinarily comprehensive philosophy of art in *Izvestia*, Jul 9, 1961. Kozintsev's exalted conception of the character of Hamlet is set forth in A. Anikst and A. Shtein, eds., *Shekspirovsky sbornik*, M, 1961, 134–61. Most of this collection (which includes extremely short and often inaccurate English summaries of each article) is devoted to discussions of *Hamlet*. Particularly interesting is the discussion by a leading present-day Hamlet, M. Astangov, of the traditions of playing the role in the Russian theater (162–5), and D. Urnov's psychological analysis of the monologues (173–84).

54. The author witnessed such a session after a performance of *Everything Depends on People* in Mar, 1961, in Leningrad, at which the first speaker, who attempted to criticize the play for its lack of respect to

Soviet ideology, was literally shouted to his seat with derision.

55. *Su*, 1963, Jan, 28. For a balanced appraisal with illustrations see A. Besançon, "Soviet Painting: Tradition and Experiment," *Su*, 1963, Jan, 83–93. For a spirited though far from optimistic review of the famous Moscow exhibition of abstract art in December, 1962, see R. Etiemble, "Pictures from an Exhibition," *Su*, 1963, Jul, 5–18. For Khrushchev's famous blast at such experimentalism during his visit to an exhibit of modern art at Moscow in December, 1962, see *Encounter*, 1963, Apr, 102–3.

56. This term derives from Khrushchev's criticism in Jan, 1961, of the disproportionate emphasis on heavy industry by neo-Stalinists who have "developed an appetite for giving the country as much metal as possible." Cited in S. Ploss, *Conflict and Decision Making in Soviet Russia*, Princeton, 1965, 212.

57. Discussed in *Encounter*, 1963, Apr, 31.

58. *Su*, 1959, Jul-Sep, 13.

59. *Ibid.*

60. Akimov, *O teatre*, 341. Chukhrai is even more lavish in his praise of Italian films (see his "Art and the Individual," *WMR*, 1963, Jan, 38–44). The awarding of first prize in the Moscow Film Festival of 1963 to Fellini's *8½* further underscored this attachment.

Perhaps the most successful transposition of the Italian style (particularly the dialogue of Antonioni) into Soviet movies is the work of the veteran producer Michael Romm. His *Nine Days of the Year* (original title *I Journey into the Unknown*), which won the Grand Prix at Karlsbad in 1962, represented by his own testimony "a fresh start—from scratch" after a long career as an exponent of Stalinist realism. (See Hoffmann, "Revival," 102–3). Romm also made an important plea for greater cultural freedom and an end to anti-Semitism at a public meeting of cinema and theater workers late in 1962 (widely circulated in typescript inside the USSR and printed in *Commentary*, 1963, Dec, 433–7; along with Evtushenko's celebrated exchange with Khrushchev at the latter's meeting with intellectuals on Dec 17, 1962).

61. S. Yutkevich, *Kontrapunkt rezhissera*, M, 1960, 29.

62. Yu. Kazakov, "Adam and Eve," *Encounter*, 1963, Apr, 46, 49.

63. *Pravda* (also *Izvestiia*) Jan 8, 1957; cited in *CDSP*, Feb 13, 1957, 32.

64. The range of informed opinion on the condition and vitality of the Orthodox Church moves from very optimistic if somewhat long-range readings by a Dutch Catholic expert on Eastern Church history, P. Hendrix, "Ecclesia triumphans," *de Waagschaal*, Amsterdam, Mar 4, 1961, and the Scandinavian Protestant, A. Gustafson, *Die Katakombenkirche*, Stuttgart, 1957; through more guardedly optimistic appraisals by two long-term American students of Russian religious life, D. Lowrie, "Every Child an Atheist," *ChC*, Jun 12, 1963, 776–7, and P. Anderson, "The Orthodox Church in Soviet Russia," *FA*, 1961, Jan, 299–311; to more pessimistic readings by J. Lawrence ("The USSR: The Weight of the Past," *ChC*, Jun 6, 1962) and P. Blake, "Russian Orthodoxy: A Captive Splendor," *Life*, Sep 14, 1959, 102–13, with accompanying photography by C. Capa and also his "Alliance with the Unholy," *ibid.*, 114, 121–6.

For the history of church-state relations in the USSR see J. Curtiss, *The Russian Church and the Soviet State 1917–1950*, Boston, 1953. On the overall problem of religious vitality see the valuable survey of all major religions, including schismatic and sectarian Christians, by W. Kolarz, *Religion in the Soviet Union*, London, 1961.

Two sensitive and sympathetic appraisals are by M. Bach, *God and the Soviets*, NY, 1958; and H. Berman, "The Russian Orthodox Church," *Harvard Alumni Bulletin*, Nov 26, 1962. For a survey of official attitudes toward religion which differs from that of Kolarz (71–2) see "Khrushchev on Religion in the USSR," *CA*, 1962, Dec, 5–6. For the difficulties of the regime in dealing with the problem see K. Alexandrov, "The Struggle for the Minds of the Young," in *Youth in Ferment*, 57–67. For invaluable testimonials from Soviet citizens and perceptive analysis see the proceedings of a meeting of protest organized in Paris in March, 1964, by the journal *Esprit: Situation des chrétiens en Union Soviétique.*

65. An official euphemism invoked in the Communist publication *SR*, 1961, Jul, 49–50. Comparing the figures of the church for 1959 with those given by the state in 1962, the number of functioning churches, priests, and monasteries appear to have been cut about in half during this brief period, *Situation*, 13, 16.

66. Cover of *Krokodil*, Feb 29, 1960 (reproduced Kolarz, *Religion*, facing 20). See also the cartoon showing grateful believers saying "The Lord God has sent us this lecturer and not the society for the propagation of knowledge," *Krokodil*, May 20, 1963, and the unintentionally humorous account of how students in Voronezh confounded such a lecturer by citing the religious preoccupations of earlier Russian writers: *KP*, May 10, 1957. Mihajlov, who generally stresses the continuing importance of the Christian tradition for both the present ferment and the future development of the USSR, points out that the crude insertion of an atheist museum inside the monastery of St. Sergius "provokes not merely revulsion but the desire to cross oneself publicly in front of it, even

if for the first time in one's life." *NL*, 1965, Jun 7, 5. See also Kolarz, *Religion*, 16; *Esprit: Situation*, II, 1965.

67. A. Solzhenitsyn, "Along the Oka," *Encounter*, 1965, Mar, 8–9. This and the other short sketches printed in this issue had not been published in the USSR. A less traditional, but more earthy and prophetic testament to the continued inspiration of Christian tradition on Russian writers is evidenced in another series of short fragments unpublished in the USSR, A. Tertz's "Thought Unaware," *NL*, 1965, Jul 19, 16–26, with introductory discussion of the work of Tertz by A. Field, 9–15.

68. See the criticism of the play in *SK*, Mar 10, 1959. Written by S. Aleshin, it has not to my knowledge ever been published; and my observations are based on a performance I attended at Leningrad in March, 1961, and a revealing exchange of opinions which followed between the cast and a primarily student audience. Another of Aleshin's controversial plays, *The Ward*, apparently tells of eleven days spent by four patients in a ward dominated by a Stalinist bully. See *NYT*, Nov 29, 1962; London *Times*, Apr 19, 1963.

69. See article under this title by S. Khudiakov in *MK*, 1957, Mar, 118–21.

70. Excellent treatment of this entire world of Protestant-cum-Sectarian Christianity in the USSR is provided in Kolarz, 245–371. For additional testimony to the vitality of the sects, particularly in outlying regions of the USSR, see numerous articles in the publication of the special commission set up by the Siberian Academy of Sciences, *Voprosy teorii i praktiki nauchnogo ateizma* (vyp. 2), Novosibirsk, 1961; and the front page editorial in *RU*, Apr 11, 1959. See also E. and S. Dunn, "Religion as an Instrument

of Cultural Change: The Problem of the Sects in the Soviet Union," *ASR*, 1964, Sep, 459–78.

71. See Khudiakov; Maurice Hindus, *House Without a Roof*, NY, 1961, 130; and entire section "Triumph of the Baptists," 119–36.

72. *UG*, Mar 17, 1960, 2.

73. Kliuchevsky, "Vliianie," 145.

74. A phrase coined—as far as I can tell —by the late R. Blackmur.

75. For the continuing cultural lag in changing architectural style, however, see Richard West, "Moscow Skyline," *NS*, Jun 28, 1963.

76. See lead editorial in *Pravda*, Apr 5, 1956.

77. Cited in *Encounter*, 1963, Apr, 28.

78. "Rockets and Carts," cited in *Su*, 1963, Jan, 42.

79. Evtushenko's answer to the writers' questionnaire in *Su*, 1963, Jan, 29.

80. A. Solzhenitsyn, *One Day in the Life of Ivan Denisovich*, NY, 1963 (tr. Hayward and Hingley), p. 56.

81. V. Aksenov, "Bilet zvezdami," *Yunost'*, 1961, Aug.

82. mt of lines from Evtushenko, "Talk," translated and discussed by M. Kalb in *NL*, 1963, May 27, 21. Ehrenburg's memoirs, written since the Stalin era, provide a rich cultural history set in a broad European context. See *People and Life, 1891–1921*, NY, 1962; *Memoirs, 1921–1941*, Cleveland, 1963; *The War: 1941–1945*, Cleveland, 1965; also his *Chekhov, Stendhal, and Other Essays*, NY, 1963.

83. From the editorial "Our People's Intelligentsia," *Pravda*, Sep 19, 1965, 31. See also A. Rumiantsev, "The Party Spirit of the Creative Labor of the Soviet Intelligentsia," *Pravda*, Sep 9, 1965, in *CDSP*, Sep 29, 1965, 3–6. "Stalin's Heirs" was published in *Pravda*, Oct 21, 1962; translation by G. Reavey in *Saturday Evening Post*, Aug 10–17, 1963, 60.

84. *Izvestiia*, Nov 11, 1960. V. Aksenov makes it clear that the struggle between the young generation and the Stalinist generation involves a sense of identification with the older "revolutionary" generation, in an interesting interview conducted in Poland together with A. Voznesensky, by A. Perlowski, "Pokolenie XX zjazdu," *Polityka*, Mar 2, 1963.

85. Verse by E. Kuchinsky in *Yunost'*, 1960, no. 8.

86. Phrase from Herzen used by N. Gubko in his review of Solzhenitsyn's *One Day:* "Chelovek pobezhdaet," *Zvezda*, 1963, no. 3, 213–15.

87. From *NM*, 1956, Aug, as translated in McLean and Vickery, *Year*, 265.

88. *The Collected Poems of W. B. Yeats*, NY, 1940, 304.

89. Yutkevich, *Kontrapunkt*, 13.

90. Cited from the work of E. Vinokurov in *Su*, 1963, Jan, 45. It is at this level of spiritual depth that Evtushenko recedes from view as a figure of real significance. There is little honor done to either the idea or the sounds of music in verses like "Muzyka revoliutsii/kak muzyka okeana/ muzyka/ vse mozhet. Muzyka—/ eto muzhestvo,/ i vdokhnovenny kak Motsart./ Kastro/ na grebne muzyki." *Nezhnost'*, 185.

91. B. Slutsky, "K diskussii ob Andree Rubleve," *Yunost'*, 1962, no. 2, 41. Compare this with the praise of Rublev by B. Pil'niak, *SS*, I, 97–103.

A. Siniavsky, the distinguished critic and author of a long introduction to the 1964 Soviet edition of Pasternak's collected poems, has cited approvingly the concept of the poet which Gorky set forth in 1894, praising vigorous satirical writing over coldly pure art or dreamy sentimental lyricism. Gorky's call to action as repeated by Siniavsky seems both an echo of old Muscovy (with its talk of bells and "heroic deeds") and a new bid for courageous voices in Siniavsky's own time: "Nuzhny podvigi, podvigi! Nuzhny takie slova, kotorye by zvuchali, kak kolokol nabata, trevozhili vse i, sotriasaia, tolkali vpered." A. Siniavsky, "Gor'ky-satirik," in B. Mikhailovsky and E. Tager, eds., *O khudozhestvennom masterstve M. Gor'kogo, sbornik statei*, M, 1960, 133. (From Gorky, "Ob odnom poete," *SS*, M, 1949, I, 335.) See also in this collection Mikhailovsky's leading article "Iz etiudov o romantizme rannego Gor'kogo: iumor i ego sviaz' s literaturnoi traditsiei"; and the article on Siniavsky by A. Field published, together with translated samples of his critical writings, in *NL*, Nov 8, 1965, 10–17 (after Siniavsky had been arrested in the USSR and accused of being the author of the works published in the West under the pseudonym A. Tertz).

92. The story was related orally to me in 1961 by a Soviet citizen, who indicated that it was derived from a printed story of T. Zhuravlev, which I have not been able to locate.

4. THE IRONY OF RUSSIAN HISTORY

1. R. Niebuhr, *The Irony of American History*, London, 1952, x, and ix–xi.
2. See, in addition to Niebuhr, C. V. Woodward on the need to "penetrate the legend without destroying the ideal," in "The Irony of Southern History," *Journal of Southern History*, 1953, Feb, 19. On irony as "true liberty" for Proudhon and the highest basis for an ethic of "love and simplicity" see V. Jankélévitch, *L'Ironie ou la bonne conscience*, 1940, 2d corr. and exp. ed., esp. 167–8. On the "radical irony" of modern literature, see R. P. Warren, "The Veins of Irony," *Princeton Alumni Weekly*, 1963, Sep 24, 18–20. Those who have made history often come more readily to the ironic perspective than those who write about it. See, for instance, the magnificent, ironic characterization that Napoleon made of his own career in his *Journal secret*, 202.

On the ironic view of the Bolshevik Revolution see my forthcoming historiographical article in *WP*, 1966, Apr.
3. This famous phrase of Hegel is from the end of the introduction to his *Philosophy of Right, Sämtliche Werke*, Stuttgart, 1928, VII, 37.
4. N. Sakharov, "Starorusskaia partiia," *Strannik*, 1882, Jan, 33.
5. Count F. Rostopchin as cited by Tikhomirov, *Russia*, II, 15. There are other versions of this famous remark, such as "Hitherto revolutions have been made by peasants seeking to become gentlemen; now gentlemen have attempted a revolution to become cobblers." Cited in A. Kizevetter, *Istoricheskie otkliki*, M, 1915, 100.
6. The likelihood of convergence has been forcefully challenged by two political scientists, Z. Brzezinski and S. Huntington (*Political Power: USA/USSR*, NY, 1964), who contend that evolutionary change will not necessarily bring the two systems together.
7. Tertz, "Realism," *Su*, 1959, Sep, 2–13.
8. From "Introduction" to Voznesenky's "Three-Cornered Pear," *Znamia*, 1962, Apr, published in Russian, with facing translation by N. Bienstock, in *Odyssey*, 1962, Dec, 140–9.
9. Interview with Evtushenko in *Le Monde*, Feb 14, 1963. As is often the case with Evtushenko, the scene is a romanticized if not altogether imaginary one.
10. Gorky (characterizing the writer Korolenko), *Literary Portraits*, 188.
11. The title and prevailing metaphor of the personal account of twentieth-century Russia written by an economist who was hounded, in turn, by Imperial Russia, the Soviet Union, and Nazi Germany: W. Woytinsky, *Stormy Passage*, NY, 1961.

INDEX

General cultural categories (*Art, Music*) are listed here only to indicate broad, general discussions of the medium. There are separate listings for individual authors and composers, with specific works subsumed under the category of the author and separately sublisted only in the case of a major figure.

Agglomerate categories (*Economics, Military*) have been made for certain topics that fall outside the main concern of the book. In addition, all modern revolutions are sublisted under *Revolutions;* all wars under *Wars;* all cathedrals and churches under *Churches.*

Page references from the bibliography and footnotes are italicized. All authors cited in the footnotes are included in the index, but not names listed in titles or non-substantive references to topics and figures in the footnotes.

There are individual listings for all cities and for those regional place names (*Scotland, Prussia, Ukraine, Pennsylvania*) that are discussed separately in the text from the nation of which they are now a part.

James H. Billington was born in Bryn Mawr, Pennsylvania, in 1929. He received his B.A. (*summa cum laude* in European history) from Princeton University and a D.Phil. in modern European history from Balliol College, Oxford, where he was a Rhodes Scholar. From 1957 to 1960 he taught Russian history at Harvard, and since 1961 has been at Princeton, where he is now a full professor. He was a guest lecturer on Russian history at the University of Leningrad in 1961 and an exchange research professor at the University of Moscow in 1964. His book *Mikhailovsky and Russian Populism* was published in 1958, and he is a frequent contributor to scholarly journals and reviews.

A free catalogue of VINTAGE BOOKS *will be sent at your request. Write to* Vintage Books, 457 Madison Avenue, New York, New York 10022.

VINTAGE POLITICAL SCIENCE
AND SOCIAL CRITICISM

ii

A free catalogue of VINTAGE BOOKS *will be sent at your request. Write to* Vintage Books, 457 Madison Avenue, New York, New York 10022.

VINTAGE HISTORY AND CRITICISM OF
LITERATURE, MUSIC, AND ART

A free catalogue of VINTAGE BOOKS *will be sent at your request. Write to* Vintage Books, 457 Madison Avenue, New York, New York 10022.

A free catalogue of VINTAGE BOOKS *will be sent at your request. Write to* Vintage Books, 457 Madison Avenue, New York, New York 10022.